THE WESTERN EXPERIENCE

Since 1600

Third Edition

PHYSIOGRAPHY OF EUROPE

ART ESSAYS BY THE LATE H. W. JANSON

ADVISORY EDITOR: EUGENE RICE, Columbia University

Third Edition

THE WESTERN EXPERIENCE

Since 1600

Mortimer Chambers
University of California, Los Angeles

Raymond Grew
University of Michigan

David Herlihy
Harvard University

Theodore K. Rabb
Princeton University

Isser Woloch
Columbia University

 Alfred A. Knopf · New York

THIS IS A BORZOI BOOK
PUBLISHED BY ALFRED A. KNOPF, INC.

Third Edition
98765432
Copyright © 1974, 1979, 1983 by Alfred A. Knopf, Inc.

All rights reserved under International and Pan-American Copyright Conventions. No part of this book may be reproduced in any form or by any means, electronic or mechanical, including photocopying, without permission in writing from the publisher. All inquiries should be addressed to Alfred A. Knopf, Inc., 201 East 50th Street, New York, N.Y. 10022. Published in the United States by Alfred A. Knopf, Inc., New York, and simultaneously in Canada by Random House of Canada Limited, Toronto. Distributed by Random House, Inc., New York.

Library of Congress Cataloging in Publication Data

Main entry under title:
The Western Experience.
   Authors: Mortimer Chambers, et al.
   Includes index.
   Contents: [1] To 1715—[2] Since 1600.
   1. Civilization—History. 2. Civilization, Occidental—History. I. Chambers, Mortimer.
CB59.W38   1982c   909   82-17097

ISBN 0-394-33096-X (pbk. : v. 2)

Cover illustration: Pieter Brueghel, "Flemish Proverbs." SCALA/EPA, Inc.

Maps were executed by Jean Tremblay.
Map consultant: D. W. Meinig

Manufactured in the United States of America

Introduction

Everyone uses history, and we use it in many ways. We use it to define who we are, to connect our personal experience to the history of the groups, region, nation, and culture to which we belong. Both individually and collectively we use the past to explain and justify our hopes and ambitions, our fears and conflicts. The Charter of the United Nations, like the American Declaration of Independence, is based on a view of history. When workers strike or armies march, they cite the lessons of their history. Because history is so important to us psychologically and intellectually, historical understanding is always shifting and often controversial. Indeed, the process of historical understanding is in itself circular: We are shaped by values, interests, and customs that like our churches, universities, and political parties have been formed by past experience. At the same time, the way we look at the past and what we see there—the questions we ask and the problems we pose—arise out of current concerns. Today we are likely to ask what industrialization did to the environment; in the 1950s scholars more often asked about the conditions that led to economic growth; a generation earlier the central question was how workers had gained a larger share of industrial wealth. Conservatives were more likely to study industrialization's effects on community and values, liberals to explore its relation to political freedom and education. Similarly, whether the undying interest in ancient Rome focused on civic virtue in the Republic, on Roman law, on the strength of the Roman Empire, or on its decline, the interest usually reflected the pressing issues of the historian's own era.

This circularity in which we, who have been formed by the past, ask of history the questions of our own time in order to learn more about both past and present helps to keep the study of history alive, stimulating new interest and fresh research. Some questions must be asked repeatedly, some issues arise again and again; but much of this knowledge is cumulative, for while asking new questions, historians integrate the answers learned from previous ones, and historical knowledge grows. History is not merely a subjective exercise in which all opinions are equally valid either. No matter what motivated a particular historical question, the answer to it stands until overturned by better evidence. We now know more about the past than ever before. Often we have information that was not available to the historical characters we study. Unlike them, we know how their history came out; we can apply methods they did not have, and sometimes we have evidence they never saw. This knowledge and the ways of interpreting it are the collective achievement of thousands of historians.

We also use history for pleasure—as a cultivated entertainment. The biographies of great figures, dramatic accounts of important events, colorful tales of earlier times can be fascinating in themselves; and in enjoying them we share a pleasure felt by thousands of our ancestors and our contemporaries, thereby rooting ourselves more deeply in our common culture. In general the deeper our understanding of an historical era the richer our response to its art and thought is likely to be. That is not the least of the reasons for studying history, and those who do so are like a privileged tourist, who can turn from the inspiration of a great cathedral to the exciting bustle of a simple village market and is able to see and appreciate more because of all that has been seen and understood before.

We also use history to discover the range and the limits of social behavior. In what kind of God or gods did people believe? What customs and institutions were invented to sustain those beliefs? How did people obtain food and protect human life? What tasks in each society were assigned to men and to women, to young and old, rich and poor? Did formal beliefs, economic activities, established institutions, and social classes sustain each other or did they conflict? Can we estimate for any particular moment the countervailing pressures for change and for continuity? These types of questions concern all the social sciences, and all of them make use of historical examples in seeking answers. Historians, however, tend to emphasize how in a specific place and time the various aspects of social life are interrelated.

Readers of *The Western Experience,* third edition, will find themselves using this book in all these ways: to learn history as a subject in itself, to enrich their culture, and to test their ideas of social behavior; but they will also want to bear in mind how the authors selected what history to include. The very concept of a Western civilization is itself the result of history. The Greeks gave the names east and west to the points on the horizon where the sun rises and sets. Because the Persian Empire and India lay to their east, the Greeks were the first "westerners," their continent, Europe, the west and Asia the east. The distinction between Western civilization and others, ethnocentric, often arbitrary, and frequently exaggerated, continued even as that civilization changed and expanded with the Roman Empire, Christianity, and the European conquest of the New World. The view that this is one civilization with America tied more closely to ancient Greece than Greece to Egypt or Spain to Islam is easily challenged in every respect save the conscious tradition that has shaped our culture.

The Western Experience, then, honors that tradition and gives primary attention to a small part of the world. That focus provides the opportunity to observe the processes of change and continuity over a long period of time. It includes important examples of city and rural life; of empires and monarchies and republics; of life before and after industrialization; of societies in which labor was organized through markets, serfdom, and slavery; of cultures little concerned with science and of ones that used changing scientific knowledge; of non-Christian religions and of all the major forms of Christianity in action. All these types can be found in many other civilizations, but in a single civilization they can be seen evolving, influencing, and borrowing from each other.

Far more is known about Western history than can be put into a single book. Each paragraph is therefore, in some sense, a synthesis of scores (and sometimes more) of valuable books that have treated these same topics in greater depth. One aspect of the Western tradition is the view that certain great thinkers and artists, certain leaders, certain movements and events have been particularly important, for the trends they epitomize, the changes they brought, the influence they have exercised or the inspiration they provide. That tradition, too, is generally recognized here. For a long time historians emphasized politics as the activity that summarized a whole society and determined its course, a view reinforced by emphasis on the development of the national state; and that familiar perspective as well as the familiar chronological framework is generally employed in the text also.

But this book also reflects the influence of a distinctive kind of historical writing, commonly called "social history," which has greatly affected historical understanding in the past twenty years or so. Neither the name nor the impulse behind it is really new. As early as the eighteenth century many historians (of whom Voltaire was one) called for a history that was more than chronology, more than an account of kings and battles. In the nineteenth century even while historical studies paid dominant attention to past politics, diplomacy, and war (taking its evidence primarily from official documents found in state archives), there were important and systematic efforts to encompass the history of intellectual and cultural trends, of law and constitutions, of religion, and of the economy.

Social history, as a field of study, emerged at this same time. For some it was primarily the history of the working class, often narrowed to be the history of labor movements. For others it was the history of daily life—daily life in ancient Rome or Renaissance Florence or old New York as reflected in styles of dress, housing, diet, and so on. This "pots and pans history" was the sort of history featured in historical museums and popular magazines. Social history is an approach to history that pays attention to society in all its aspects (including institutions, culture, all social groups, economic ties, daily life, demography, and climate).

The writing of this sort of history is distinguished by a certain point of view, particular methods and unusual sources, and a characteristic style. The point of view seeks to compensate for the fact that most historical writing has been about the tiny minority of the powerful, rich, and educated (who, after all, left behind the fullest and most accessible records of their activities). The new social history aims to be as mindful of popular culture as it is of formal or official culture, as interested in the family as it is in the state, in living conditions as it is in political theory. Social history tries to recover as much as it can of the experience of ordinary people, to look at the society from the bottom up as well as from the top down.

In method the new social history borrows theories, terminologies, and techniques from the social sciences—especially anthropology, sociology, economics, and political science. Thus social historians use models of "development," "modernization," and "cultural diffusion"; and they employ typologies of social stratification and family structure. They make sophisticated use of techniques developed by statisticians, demographers, behavioral scientists (especially survey researchers), and economists. Characteristically, such methods include a great deal of quantification, and social historians tend to be eager to count and ready to use computers whenever sufficient data can be uncovered. Careful sampling, statistical techniques, and computer analysis when combined with hard work and a new awareness have recently made it possible to discover information previously thought unobtainable about every period of the past. New interests and new techniques have in fact greatly expanded the range of useful historical sources, for important information can be gleaned from anything that records the pulse of human life: coins; pots and lamps; fiscal records and price lists; parish records of births, deaths, and marriages; weather reports and crop records; travel accounts and private letters; minutes of meetings and petitions; police and journalists' reports; and personal diaries.

The social history written with these concerns, sources, and formal methods tends to be analytical rather than narrative in structure. And those mainstays of historical organization, clear chronology and periodization, have been made more complex. The periodization of history based on the rise and fall of dynasties and states and on wars and revolutions usually does not fit the periodization most appropriate for changes in culture and ideas, economic production, or science and technology. Historical surveys are, therefore, frequently organized topically as well as chronologically, with special chapters on economic or intellectual developments. But the history of ordinary life, especially in the period before industrialization, moves on a still different scale. As a history of social processes that tend to move at a glacial pace, it often lacks sharp chronology. A history of structures more than events, it tends to be organized around problems rather than the biographies of individuals or the story of a nation.

In *The Western Experience* an effort has been made to combine the approaches and needs just discussed. The chapters are essentially chronological in sequence, sometimes using groups of chapters to cover a particular period of Western history. At the same time each chapter is presented as an interpretative essay, introducing a set of historical problems important to the understanding of the period treated. The "facts" that follow include the events and figures that all interpretations must take into account—the famous names and dates that are an important part of our historical lore—but the "facts" also include basic information about social organization, modes of production and of exchange, and cultural activity that are crucial to understanding the way of life of a particular society. All this information—much of it narrative after all, some of it good stories and accounts of dramatic events—is used to explore the problems on which a particular chapter focuses. Often it is important to note the kind of evidence on which these interpretations rest and the controversies that accompany them.

The readers of this text, then, can use the book as an introduction to historical method and will find within it a framework to which they can attach whatever else they know about Western society, a framework on which in the future they can build a richer appreciation of Western culture. History is essentially an integrative enterprise in which long-term trends and specific moments, social structure and the actions of particular individuals can all be brought together in the understanding of a given society. Readers should find some of their preconceptions—about the past, about how societies are organized, and about how people behave—severely challenged. Some will want to compare the response to historical problems in different societies and across time (for history is essentially a comparative mode of thought). Others will want to compare other civilizations as they ask themselves what qualities have characterized the Western world.

A college course is not the only way to build a personal culture. Nor is history the only path to integrated knowledge. Western history is not the only history one should know, or an introductory survey necessarily the best way to learn it. Still, as readers consider and then challenge interpretations offered in this text, they will exercise critical and analytical skills. They can begin to erode parochialism that views only the present as important, acknowledge the greatness of their Western heritage, and recognize the injustice, cruelty, and failures it includes. To be able to do these things is to experience the study of history as one of the vital intellectual activities by which we come to know who and where we are.

Contents

Introduction vii

15 · A CENTURY OF WAR AND REVOLT 1560–1660   473
    I. Warfare   *475*
   II. Revolts   *490*

16 · CULTURE AND SOCIETY IN THE AGE OF THE SCIENTIFIC REVOLUTION 1540–1660   519
    I. The Scientific Revolution   *521*
   II. Literature and the Arts   *537*
  III. Social Patterns and Popular Culture   *548*

17 · THE TRIUMPH OF ARISTOCRATS AND KINGS 1660–1715   561
    I. The Absolute Monarchies   *563*
   II. The Anti-Absolutists   *580*
  III. The Culture of the Age   *588*

18 · ABSOLUTISM AND EMPIRE 1715–1770s   601
    I. The State System   *603*
   II. Absolutism in Central Europe   *609*
  III. The Maritime Powers   *615*
  IV. The Midcentury Conflagration   *624*

19 · THE AGE OF ENLIGHTENMENT 1715–1770s   631
    I. The Enlightenment   *632*
   II. Eighteenth-Century Cultures   *640*
  III. The Enlightenment and the State   *651*

20 · REVOLUTIONS OF THE EIGHTEENTH CENTURY 661

    I. The Industrial System 663
    II. Economics and Demography 669
    III. Agriculture 673
    IV. The New Shape of Industry 676
    V. Constitutional Conflicts 682
    VI. The French Revolution 688

21 · THE TERROR AND NAPOLEON 1792–1814 702

    I. The Second Revolution 704
    II. From Robespierre to Bonaparte 718
    III. The Napoleonic Imperium 726

22 · THE POLITICS OF RESTORATION AND REFORM 1815–1850 741

    I. The Conservative Order 743
    II. The Spread of Liberal Government 757
    III. The Revolutions of 1848 767

23 · INDUSTRIALIZATION AND SOCIAL CHANGE 1800–1860 777

    I. Progress of Industrialization 779
    II. The Structure of Society 786
    III. Theories of Change 809

24 · THE NATIONAL STATE AND THE MIDDLE CLASS 1850–1880 819

    I. A Middle-Class Culture 821
    II. The Politics of Nationalism 826
    III. Reshaping Established States 846

25 · THE AGE OF PROGRESS 1860–1914 861

    I. Economics and Population 863
    II. The Culture of Industrial Society 872

III. Attacks on Liberal Civilization *880*
IV. Domestic Politics *889*

26 · IMPERIALISM AND THE GREAT WAR 1870–1920   903
I. European Imperialism *905*
II. The Coming of World War *917*
III. The Course of the War *925*
IV. The Russian Revolution *938*
V. The Peace *945*

27 · DEMOCRACY AND DEPRESSION 1920–1932   957
I. The Postwar Political Order *959*
II. The Culture of Uncertainty *977*
III. The Great Depression *986*

28 · TOTALITARIANISM TRIUMPHANT AND WORLD WAR II 1924–1941   993
I. The Retreat from Democracy *995*
II. Totalitarianism *1000*
III. The Democracies' Response *1020*
IV. World War II: 1939–1941 *1034*

29 · WORLD WAR II AND THE SURVIVAL OF EUROPE 1941–1958   1043
I. The End of World War II *1045*
II. The Circumstances of Peace *1058*
III. European Recovery *1070*

30 · THE PRESENT IN HISTORICAL PERSPECTIVE   1083
I. The Nature of Advanced Societies *1085*
II. Europe's Place in the World *1093*
III. The Politics of Prosperity *1100*
IV. A New Era *1117*

Index follows page *1136*
Color Illustration Sources follows Index

xiv   Contents

ART ESSAYS

The Image of Man in 17th- and 18th-Century Art   follows page *660*
The Image of Man in Modern Art   follows page *880*

MAPS

Physiography of Europe   *ii–iii*
The Netherlands 1579–1609   *481*
Areas of Fighting 1618–1660   *486*
Territorial Change 1648–1661   *489*
Centers of Music 1500–1800   *546*
Cities of Europe in 1700   *552*
Speed of News Traveling to Venice   *557*
The Wars of Louis XIV   *567*
The Austrian Empire 1657–1718   *573*
Conflict in the Baltic Area 1660–1721   *579*
The Expansion of Russia and the Partition of Poland   *605*
Prussia 1721–1772 and the Hapsburg Empire   *612*
Overseas Possessions 1713   *620*
Anglo-French Rivalry in North America and the Caribbean 1754–1763   *627*
France: Provinces and Regions Before 1789   *696*
France: Revolutionary Departments After 1789   *697*
The Revolutionary Republics 1792–1799   *723*
Europe 1810   *734*
Europe 1815   *746*
The Unification of Italy 1859–1920   *835*
The Unification of Germany   *840*
The Decline of the Ottoman Empire 1683–1914   *858*
Africa 1885   *911*
Africa 1914   *913*
Imperialism in Asia   *915*
The Western Front   *926*
World War I   *927*
Territorial Settlements 1919–1926   *949*
Europe 1935–1939   *1032*
The Height of Axis Power 1942   *1035*
The Allied Victory in World War II   *1046*
World War II in the Pacific   *1048*
The Cold War of the 1950s   *1069*
Europe Since World War II   *1099*
Contemporary Europe   *follows Color Illustration Sources*

THE WESTERN EXPERIENCE
Since 1600

Third Edition

LAND AND SOCIETY THROUGH THE AGES
A Cartographic Essay

MICHAEL P. CONZEN
University of Chicago

To accompany *The Western Experience, Third Edition,* by Mortimer Chambers, Raymond Grew, David Herlihy, Theodore K. Rabb, and Isser Woloch.

Maps were executed by David Lindroth.

INTRODUCTION

The history of Western civilization—indeed of any civilization—can be thought of as a kind of dialogue between society and nature. In this dialogue, men and women make a complicated series of choices within the limits imposed by nature. The results of these decisions, the way a society actually *looks* in its habitat, is called its cultural landscape. In a way, then, the history of European civilization is a rich succession of layers of cultural landscape, each showing the ways human beings have tried to occupy and use space during different historical periods. This essay highlights some of the main patterns of cultural landscape that have characterized the Western experience.

Maps that show the spatial distribution of characteristic human activities can communicate much about the relationship between social organization and environmental space. A careful reading of the following maps can lead to a deeper understanding of this complex and ever-changing relationship.

THE CLASSICAL WORLD: THE CITY-STATE

A singular achievement of Greek civilization was the city-state. This institution had a firm geographical basis as well as a political and philosophical significance. The topography of the Greek peninsula was clearly influential in the emergence of this form of government. Essentially, the city-state represented a rational effort to organize populations scattered among coastal and river basins of uncertain fertility and separated by rocky mountain ridges.

Geographic Origins of the City-State

Between Minoan and Mycenaean times, the "polis" developed from a castle stronghold, situated on a hilltop and presiding over a territory of dispersed rural villages, into a more recognizably urban settlement with civilian housing and public spaces. Mycenae illustrates this growth well (Map A-1). Early but elaborate burials testify to the site's central importance for the surrounding region (see text pp. 37–

MAP A–1

MAP A–2

MAP A–4

POLIS DIFFUSION THROUGHOUT THE MEDITERRANEAN WORLD, 250 B.C.–A.D. 400

- To 250 BC
- To AD 1
- To AD 200
- To AD 400

MAP A–3

required direct citizen participation in politics. The area shown in the Boeotia map (A-3) is no larger than that of metropolitan Chicago.

Urbanization in the Roman Empire

Greek overseas settlement spread the concept of the polis throughout the Mediterranean, as later the idea of a city with a politically related territory penetrated every part of the Roman Empire (Map A-4). In practice this form of settlement had to be adjusted to local environments, and many areas of Europe were too sparsely populated to justify such Roman "coloniae." But the seed of an urbanized civilization, the polis, was nevertheless implanted throughout Europe.

The City and Agriculture in the Roman Empire

In addition to establishing the continental road system (Map 4.3, p. 113), town networks, and frontier defense lines, the Romans expanded local economies

41). The hilltop between the two rivers acquired stout defenses, a palace complex, temples, and housing. Hill terraces, evidence of Greek efforts to grow food for the town, indicate the close relationship between the town, its food supply, and the surrounding district. Gradually this fortified hilltop settlement, or "acropolis," became physically more complex as Mycenaean political power and trade grew; a lower town developed adjacent to the fortress site, also surrounded by a military defense wall.

Such a "town," however, was merely the functional center of a territory that might include hundreds of square miles. For instance, Sparta in its early stages of development occupied a small but strategic portion of the Eurotas Valley over which it had primary control (Map A-2). This territory included much of the available cultivated land in the region. Consequently, villages beyond the borders of the polis territory were tied to Sparta by special economic and political bonds (see pp. 52–53).

The Network of City-States

City-states formed a loose regional network, usually without strong domination by any one state. The polis might expand or contract, or change its shape as a result of political alliances (such as the Boeotian Federation) and the fortunes of war. But the natural environment itself had much to do with the way the polis developed. In fact, the marginal fertility of the habitat meant that the polis had to be small. This, in turn, made possible Greek "democracy," which

MAP A–5

MAP A-6

MAP A-7

MAP A–8

through agricultural colonization. Whether reorganizing native farming or clearing tracts of wilderness, they surveyed large areas of arable land into a grid system of fields (a process called centuriation). Traces of this grid system are occasionally visible in present-day landscapes. The Roman sense of order is well illustrated in the grid pattern around the French town of Avignon (Map A-5). Even so, because of environmental and administrative needs the overall grid pattern was irregular.

At regional levels, Roman economic organization was strongly affected by both nature and the demands of imperial defense. In what is now central Germany, agricultural villas worked the lighter alluvial soils found in or near river valleys. Where necessary, roads were cut through dense forests to link vital frontier outposts with mining centers and the cities, such as Augsburg and Trier (Map A-6), that served as administrative centers. Not only did these imperial frontier regions define the edge of the civilized world for the Romans, but, with their natural resources, they contributed directly to the might of Rome.

The Urban Culture of the Roman Empire: The Metropolis

Rome, begun as a union of several villages situated on neighboring hills, grew into a sprawling metropolis as it became the center of an empire (Map A-7). Repeated urban renewal cleared ground for vast ceremonial complexes of temples, public squares, market buildings, theaters, and circuses. Outside these complexes were neighborhoods of crowded buildings and irregular streets, a vibrant mixture of residences and craft shops. Aqueducts brought a vast water supply to the congested city, symbolizing Rome's dependence on outside resources for its survival and growth.

Provincial Towns of the Roman Empire

In its provincial towns Rome built theaters, libraries, and public baths in an attempt to spread a higher culture throughout the Empire (Map A-8). Here, again, the Greek legacy is apparent. For instance, because of a long tradition of intellectual attainment there were many more libraries in Greece than anywhere else in the Empire.

THE ECONOMY OF THE MIDDLE AGES

Economic Life and the Monasteries

The Church played a major role in the political, economic, and social life of Europe after the decline of the Roman Empire. By the height of the Middle Ages monastic orders had proliferated throughout Europe, establishing centers of learning, extending charity, and undertaking agrarian colonization without regard for political boundaries. The Cistercians, a Benedictine reform order devoted to simple living, emerged in northeast France in the twelfth century and quickly grew as the early monasteries expanded their activities by founding daughter houses (Map A-9). Through these daughter houses, the Cistercians spread a common tradition of land colonization in agriculturally marginal areas. At many sites sacred relics drew pilgrims from far and wide. Other religious activities, however, were more regional and centralized. One site, the abbey at Einsiedeln, Switzerland, not surprisingly attracted more visitors from northern regions than from the more mountainous south. Yet the overall pattern of pilgrimage coincided reasonably well with what was later to become the broad transcontinental trade corridor between northern Italy and the North Sea.

Rural Settlement

During the Middle Ages differences in local environments and cultural traditions produced a wide variety of rural settlement forms. Common to many regions was the open-field village shown in the Swedish example (Map A-10). The irregular area of cultivable land was divided into narrow strip plots, and most farmers had fragmented holdings. The pasturelands and woodland of the village, however, were not divided and were used by all farmers.

Clearing the Land

Rural settlement expanded greatly in medieval times as large forest tracts between major river valleys were cleared and villages, like Otterstorpaby (see Map A-10), grew up. Occasionally the reverse happened as populations were decimated by war, famine, or disease. Many cleared areas near the Weser, for example, were lost to readvancing forests between 1290 and 1430, in the aftermath of the Black Death (Map A-11).

The Growth of Towns

Relative political stability and a consolidating agrarian base provided the groundwork for improved trade and growth of towns (see Map A-11). This

MAP A-9

THE NORTHWEST EUROPEAN TRADE NEXUS
In the 14th Century

- ●—·—·— Hansa cities and trade routes
- ○ Other commercial centers
- ▲ Champagne fairs
- ↟ Origins of travelers to the Champagne fairs
- •• Cloth towns

MAP A–13

MAP A–14

ZÄHRINGER TOWN FOUNDATIONS

- ● Berchtold III (AD 1122)
- ● Konrad (1152)
- ● Berchtold IV (1150-1186)
- ● Berchtold V (1185-1218)
- ○ Towns founded in the Zähringer conception (distinguished by major emphasis on the market facilities and little on fortifications)

MAP A–15

Example: Thun, Switzerland

- Oldest settlement
- Zähringer town, AD 1200
- Kiburger extension, c.1260
- Kiburger extension, c.1300

1. Castle
2. Town church
3. Guildhall
4. Town Hall
5. Town granary

MAP A–16

was a slow process, as shown in the case of Vienna (Map A-12), which grew from about 12,000 to 20,000 between A.D. 1200 and 1300. On the site of an earlier Roman fortress at this important Danube River crossing point, a castle was built and a traders' district (Wik) sprang up, surrounded by a town wall (subsequently obliterated by later development). Jewish merchants gathered here, but were forced to live in a settlement outside the city walls, thus being denied the rights of municipal citizenship. Later, other merchant quarters (not necessarily Jewish) and craft districts were established outside the old walls, joined by several newly founded monasteries. There was enough room to lay out "planned" streets to the south of the old town, and a new, enlarged wall was built to enclose the whole settlement, which by then included a new and larger castle. During this period of growth and change, three of the four gates of the Roman fortress were still used as part of the medieval street system.

Trade Routes

The prosperity of towns such as Vienna was made possible through a combination of local and long-distance trade. The axis of trade between the Mediterranean and the Low Countries was anchored at one end around the North Sea, the site of Europe's major clothmaking region (Map A-13). Lying between the Rhine and Seine rivers, this area was supported in part by wool supplies from England and from the Ardennes Hills just south of Liège and Aachen. The robustness of medieval trade was reflected in the great international trade fairs of the Champagne district, where individual merchants gathered from all over Europe. Conversely, competition, uncertain markets, and security problems in the North Sea and Baltic regions produced closed trade associations such as the Hanseatic League of north German cities, which sought to monopolize the northern market (see p. 358).

Colonization

Some regions of Europe were comparatively late in being drawn into international trade or even in acquiring towns of local significance. One example of commercial town founding was the colonization of Eastern Europe by German subjects (see Map 8.1, p. 242); another example, on a smaller scale, is pro-

MAP A–17

THE DIFFUSION OF LUTHER'S IDEAS Through Preaching and Print in Southwest Germany

KNOWN MIGRATION OF IDEAS (generalized)
- ← 1518–1524
- ← 1525–1530s

- ⬤ Large city
- ◉ Medium city
- ● Large town
- · Small town
- · Selected villages

Cities/places labeled: Nuremberg, Augsburg, Nördlingen, Rothenburg, Memmingen, Würzburg, Hall, Gmünd, Ulm, Esslingen, Heilbronn, Stuttgart, Constance, Heidelberg, Rottweil, Zurich, Worms, Speyer, Freiburg, Strassburg, Basel

Rivers: Main River, Rhine River, Danube River

(from northern Germany)
Luther's Address in Heidelberg

0 — 40 miles

MAP A–19

FINANCING TRADE: The Fuggers and Medici Banks

MEDICI BANK (1429–1494)
- ■ Main headquarters
- ■ Branch headquarters
- ● Wholesale depots and manufactories
- ⚒ Mines
- — Medici trade routes

FUGGER BANK (1485–1525)
- ▣ Main headquarters
- ● Major wholesaling centers
- · Minor wholesaling centers
- ⚒ Mines
- △ Metal foundries
- — Fugger trade routes
- --- Other major trade routes

Places labeled: Scotland, Ireland, England, Sweden, Denmark, Poland, France, Burgundy, Holy Roman Empire, Hungary, Ottoman Empire, Portugal, Spain, Venice, London, Bruges, Antwerp, Danzig, Leipzig, Cologne, Frankfurt, Breslau, Cracow, Nuremburg, Augsburg, Hall, Salzburg, Innsbruck, Lyon, Geneva, Milan, Venice, Avignon, Marseilles, Florence, Rome, Naples, Lisbon, Seville, Madrid

0 — 300 miles

vided by the mosaic fiefdom of the counts of Zähringen, knit together from sparsely settled political territories in the Upper Rhine region and central Switzerland (Map A-14).

New Towns

Often new castles, built to control particular areas, stimulated local market and craft activities that gave rise to a new set of towns. Thun was one of these towns (Map A-15). Until 1200 it consisted of a single street tucked between the castle and the river, a pattern typical of European villages, still common even today in Austria and Romania. In the next fifty years Thun extended to the northwest, where the street pattern could branch out and there was room for a marketplace. Further expansion spilled onto the island in the river as the next most logical defensive location.

The Spread of Urban Forms

Founding new towns involved more than choosing a site. Laws for local government had to be worked out. Since one attraction of towns was their departure from feudal ties, their founders often adopted the municipal laws and codification of rights of existing towns, either because the same overlord ruled both the new and the old towns or because settlers from the older town had helped establish the new. This pattern of town law diffusion, characteristic of towns in southwest Germany, illustrates how urban legal "families" evolved (Map A-16).

THE EARLY MODERN ERA

Reformation: Preaching

The fifteenth and sixteenth centuries witnessed major changes both in the climate of ideas and in the means of communicating them across long distances. It was, in fact, during these centuries that explorers boldly extended European knowledge of the world (Map 13.1, p. 416). Of equal significance was Luther's challenge to Church orthodoxy, which rapidly transformed the religious map of northern Europe. Luther's public appearances and the subsequent movements inspired by his example disseminated the new doctrines among the generally larger towns of southwest Germany (Map A-17). In printed form, Luther's ideas swept over Germany without regard for town size. Ideas spread as readily from small towns to large towns as from large to small, although many large towns became the centers from which new ideas radiated.

MAP A–18

THE SPREAD OF PRINTING and Traditional Language Areas, 1455-1500

- To 1470
- 1471-1480
- 1481-1490
- 1491-1500

Color areas distinguish traditional language areas

0　　200 miles

MAP A–20

MAP A–21

Reformation: Printing Networks

Religious transformation was clearly furthered in southern Germany by an unusually well-developed network of towns with printing establishments (Map A-18). From a beginning in Mainz around 1455, printing with movable type spread rapidly throughout southern Germany and, by 1470, to such key distant centers as Cologne, Venice, Paris, and Utrecht. During the next thirty years the further adoption of movable type created dense printing networks in northern Italy, Germany, and the Low Countries—areas long accustomed to outside influences through their mercantile traditions (see pp. 379–381).

The Spread of Renaissance Ideas: Mercantile Ties

Traditions of trade were being modified by new capitalist developments. The wealthiest merchants became bankers to monarchs and supervised vast trading systems. The Fugger family of Augsburg (see p. 422) and the Medici Bank in Italy (see p. 361) created wholesale trading empires, complete with their own warehouses, mines, foundries, trading posts, and fleets that stretched from Danzig to Lisbon (Map A-19).

The Spread of Renaissance Ideas: Style

The cultural dynamism of Italy continued long after the Renaissance. Baroque art, architecture, and town planning in the seventeenth century originated from the same centers and spread across the continent along similar paths, reflecting the influences of trading ties, dynastic connections, and the tastes of rulers (Map A-20). In this case Rome's preeminence first influenced southern Germany and Paris, and later Spain and Stockholm. Paris in turn influenced the cultural climate of London and Stockholm, as London then spread the prevailing ideas of the time to Edinburgh.

The Spread of Renaissance Ideas: The Town

The principles of town planning had meanwhile been revolutionized by the invention of firearms, and town fortifications grew to gigantic proportions. Vast earthworks of mounds, ditches, and berms (flat, grassy open spaces) were constructed outside the town walls so that the town itself was beyond the range of any attacker's cannon. Palma Nova, near Venice, provides a splendid example of new-town construction in which modern concepts of street geometry were combined with defense requirements (Map A-21). As with medieval town extensions or new foundations, walls were built to enclose areas large enough to allow for later building. But by the seventeenth century urban growth had so far outdistanced the provisions of an earlier time that many farmers were displaced as towns expanded into the countryside. In many large towns later expansion occurred completely beyond the earthworks.

THE INDUSTRIAL ERA

Enclosure and Demographic Changes

The greatest transformation of the cultural landscape in modern times, perhaps most conspicuous in the massive shifts of populations from countryside to city, has been associated with the new industrialism. But forces were at work in the preindustrial countryside that paved the way for these demographic changes. An agricultural revolution that was well advanced by the eighteenth century modernized many farming practices and considerably altered the look of the land (see pp. 674–676). A key element of this revolution was the enclosure of traditional open-field village lands to form large fenced fields owned by individuals. This process had taken hold

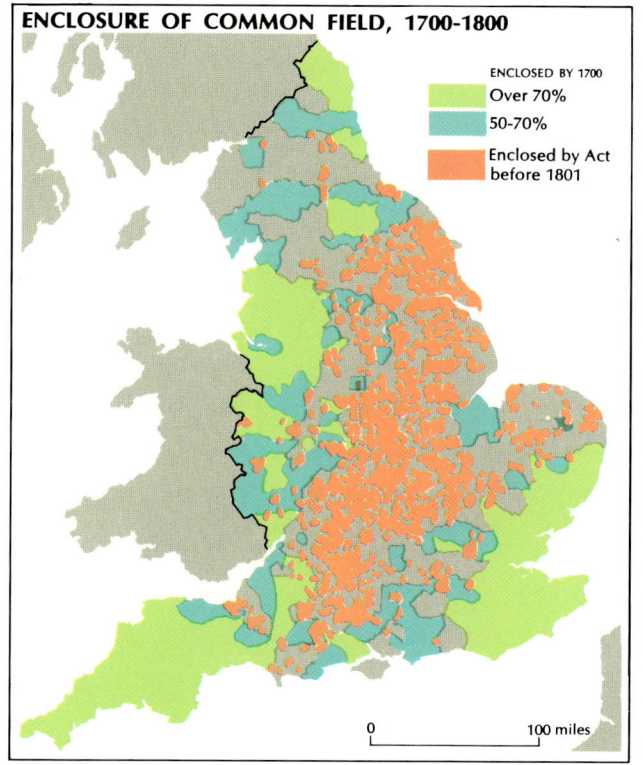

MAP A-22
ENCLOSURE OF COMMON FIELD, 1700-1800

MAP A-24
OPEN AND CLOSED VILLAGES IN NOTTINGHAMSHIRE, 1848

MAP A-23
PARLIAMENTARY ENCLOSURE IN ENGLAND
Wold Newton before and after enclosure

MAP A-25

EARLY INDUSTRIALIZATION IN EUROPE
18th and 19th Centuries

- Free peasantry
- Early emancipation through commutation
- Complete emancipation before the French Revolution
- Emancipation incomplete by the French Revolution
- Emancipation through revolution
- Personal freedom by Napoleon's time without land tenure change
- Emancipation in process, except for small farmers
- Emancipation begun
- Peasantry still bonded

- Industrial zones
- ✹ Coal mining
- ▲ Metal manufacture
- ○ Textile production

MAP A-26

THE COAL INDUSTRY ON TYNESIDE

1799
- Grand Allies working mine
- Other working mine
- Grand Allies wagonway
- Other wagonway

1864
- Coal mines
- Private coal railroads
- Parliamentary district railroads
- Major through railroads

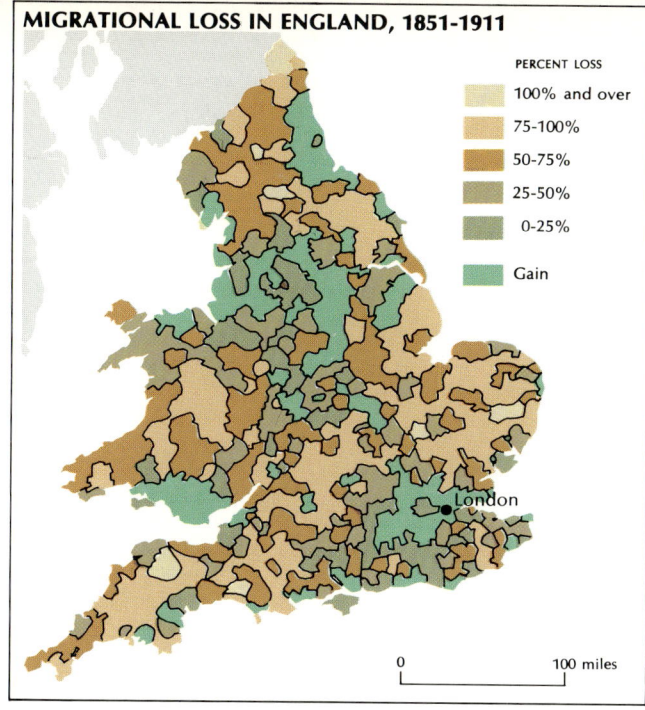

MAP A–27

in England by 1700, and parliamentary action enforced it in the following century. Very few areas were left untouched (Map A-22). The example of Wold Newton illustrates the change on a local scale as two large open fields, which in 1772 contained scores of narrow strip plots (compare with Map A-10), were consolidated into a handful of individual holdings consisting of a few large fields (Map A-23).

Village Work

Change was not smooth, however, and one consequence of the piecemeal reorganization of land tenure in England was that labor opportunities varied from one farming community to another. In "closed" villages, where and ownership was concentrated in only a few hands, farm labor became inflexible. Village laborers that could not be absorbed locally thus had to commute to nearby "open" villages, where diverse ownership created a more fluid labor market (Map A-24). Since farm laborers journeyed to work on foot, most commuted to neighboring villages. In Nottinghamshire, by the middle of the nineteenth century, more than half the villages could be classified as "closed"; two-thirds of these exported some labor to at least one neighboring settlement and in many cases to several villages at a time. Such intervillage migration was a symptom of broader problems of rural employment in a world of tenurial reorganization, farm mechanization, and the increasing lure of industrial job opportunities.

Free Labor

England was the first European country to industrialize intensively, but the agrarian groundwork for this was being laid in many parts of the continent. Emancipation of the peasantry (see pp. 792–794) has long been regarded as a necessary prelude to industrialization, and the progress made toward this goal as early as 1812 clearly indicated which countries would follow Britain's lead (Map A-25).

Coal and Iron

By the nineteenth century industrial regions had emerged primarily where coal and iron ore could be brought together cheaply. When such locations had been major centers of trade since medieval times, old cities, such as those in Belgium and southern Germany and Newcastle or Bristol in England, flourished again. In other cases, coalfield industrialism and the rapid spread of railroads combined to bring entirely new settlement complexes into existence, as happened in the Ruhr valley and the British west midlands (see p. 783).

A region that gained major new impetus from the steam era was Tyneside in northeast England. Newcastle had exported coal to London for domestic use since Roman times. By 1799 the general demand for coal had produced a dense network of wagonways for delivering coal down the valley to the Tyne River (Map A-26). Typical of some early industrial concerns, one-third of the mines were owned by an oligopoly known as the "Grand Allies." Mines multiplied as the demand for coal to fuel steam engines increased. Railroad lines proliferated. Many railroads were simply laid along the former wagon roads, but a clear distinction developed about which railroads handled coal, which handled other freight, and which carried passengers. By the twentieth century, many mines had been exhausted or had become uneconomical to operate and were closed, leaving many railroad lines abandoned in this compact coalfield.

The Move to Cities

The growth of old and new industrial centers was made possible by a heavy immigration of people from rural areas and traditional small towns. Since industrialization was not ubiquitous, the patterns of population movement were geographically biased (see p. 794). Census statistics for the years between 1851 and 1911, the period when Britain's industrial growth reached maturity, show the attraction of port cities and urban job opportunities (Map A-27). With few exceptions the areas that showed gains in population through migration were on or near coalfields. Greater London, continuing its historic role as Brit-

MAP A-28

ain's capital city, provided the chief exception. Areas of poor farming in Wales and northern England suffered drastic population losses. The result was a cultural landscape in which some regions were densely populated and others were almost deserted.

Migration

During the nineteenth and twentieth centuries, expanding worldwide markets spurred industrial production, particularly in the oldest and most successful industrial countries. As a result, larger numbers of people have moved across greater distances more frequently than ever before. The drain of population from rural regions, with restricted opportunities, to urban areas, with their myriad attractions, has been a constant, but the *scale* of movement has changed. Industrial growth has outstripped the locally available labor supply and has led to the phenomenon of temporary "guest workers," from less industrialized countries such as Turkey, Yugoslavia, and Greece, to industrial nations (Map A-28). The social and political consequences of these migrations have posed serious planning problems, particularly within the European Economic Community, and will strongly influence the diversity and cohesion of European society.

15

A CENTURY OF WAR AND REVOLT
1560–1660

In the wake of the rapid and bewildering changes of the early sixteenth century—the dislocations caused by the activities of the new monarchs, the rises in population and prices, the overseas discoveries, and the Reformation—Europe entered a period of fierce upheaval. It was difficult to come to terms with such radical alterations in so many elements of society: the increasing interference in local affairs by bureaucrats from distant capitals, the sudden soaring of food costs, or the questioning of hallowed authorities like the pope. Many people, often led by nobles who saw their power dwindling, revolted against their monarchs. The poor launched hopeless rebellions against their social superiors. And the two religious camps struggled relentlessly to destroy each other. From Scotland to Russia, the events of the century following the Reformation, from about 1560 to 1660, were dominated by warfare.

The pivot of the conflict was the Hapsburg family, which ruled most of southern and central Europe. Until the 1590s its chief representative was Philip II, King of Spain, whose ambitions and world-wide commitments lay at the center of forty years of international disputes. Then, after a short respite, the Thirty Years' War began and involved large areas of Europe in the bloodiest fighting the Continent had ever seen. Domestic tensions, peasant revolts, and civil wars added to the perpetual upheaval. The constant military activity had widespread effects on politics, economy, society, and thought. The fighting was in fact a crucial element in the long and painful process whereby Europeans came to terms with the revolutions that had begun about 1500. Almost imperceptibly, fundamental economic, political, social, and religious changes took root, and troubled Europeans managed to come to terms with their altered circumstances. At last, in the mid-seventeenth century, the long struggle seemed to ease as conflict shifted to different issues. But by the time the long adjustment finally ended, countless lives had been sacrificed and endless suffering had been caused. Few, if any, centuries of European history have been so powerfully shaped by warfare until our own. The military revolution of the period, the international conflicts through which that revolution was worked out, and the domestic upheavals that followed—these were the dominant themes of a violent and complex age.

I. WARFARE

Western Europe was the scene of almost constant fighting during the late sixteenth century and the succeeding era of the Thirty Years' War. Warfare was so widespread between 1600 and 1650 that no country was immune to the effects of the mounting brutality.

The Military Revolution

Dramatic changes took place in the way battles were fought and armies were organized between the early 1500s and the middle of the seventeenth century. Gunpowder, which had been used occasionally and to little effect since the fourteenth century, now came to occupy a central place in warfare. The result was not only the creation of a new type of industry, cannon and gun manufacture, but also a transformation of tactics. Individual castles could no longer be defended against explosives; even towns had to build heavy and elaborate fortifications if they were to resist the new fire power. Sieges became complicated, expensive operations, whose purpose was to bring explosives right up to a town wall so that it could be

(top) A view of the siege of Magdeburg during the Thirty Years' War. Cannon are pouring fire into the city. Star-shaped bastions are visible in the lower right and at the far left.
(Photo: New York Public Library/Picture Collection)

(left) A typical system of trenches approaching a bastion.
(Photo: The Granger Collection)

blown up. This required an intricate system of trenches, because walls were built in star shapes so as to multiply angles of fire and make any approach dangerous (see illustration, p. 475). Although both attack and defense thus became increasingly costly, sieges remained essential to the strategy of warfare until the eighteenth century.

In open battles, the effects of gunpowder were equally expensive. The new tactics that appeared around 1500, perfected by the Spaniards, relied on massed ranks of infantry, organized in huge squares, that made the traditional cavalry charge obsolete. Around the edge of the square were soldiers carrying pikes. They fended off horses or opposing infantry while the men with guns—in the center of the square—tried to mow the enemy down. The squares with the best discipline usually won, and for over a century after the reign of Ferdinand of Aragon, the Spaniards had the best army in Europe. Each square had about 3,000 troops, and to maintain enough squares at full strength to fight all of Spain's battles required an army numbering approximately 40,000. The cost of keeping that many men clothed, fed, and housed, let alone equipped and paid, was enormous. But worse was to come: new tactics emerged in the early seventeenth century that required even more soldiers.

Since nobody could outdo the Spaniards at their own methods, a different approach was developed by their rivals. The first advance was made by Maurice of Nassau, who led the Dutch revolt against Spain from the 1580s. He relied not on sheer weight and power, but on flexibility and mobility. Then one of the geniuses of the history of warfare, Gustavus Adolphus, king of Sweden, found a way to achieve mobility without losing power. His main invention was the salvo—instead of having his musketeers fire one row at a time, like the Spaniards, he had them all fire at once. What he lost in continuity of shot he gained in a fearsome blast that, if properly timed, could shatter enemy ranks. Huge, slow-moving squares were simply no match for smaller, faster units that riddled them with well-coordinated salvos. To add to his fire power, Gustavus had his engineers devise a light, movable cannon that could be brought into action wherever it was most needed on a battlefield.

These changes brought about a further increase in the size of armies because the more units, the better they could be placed on the battlefield. Although the Spanish army hardly grew between 1590 and 1600, remaining at 40,000 to 60,000 men, the Swedes had 175,000 men by 1632; and at the end of the century, Louis XIV considered a force of 400,000 essential to maintain his dominant position in Europe.[1]

This growth had far-reaching consequences. Rulers knew the risks of relying on mercenary troops, who might change sides for a raise in pay, and Gustavus introduced conscription in the late 1620s so that his army, consisting largely of his own subjects, would be easier to control. Because it also made sense not to disband such huge forces each autumn, when the campaigning season ended, the armies were kept permanently ready.

The need to maintain so many soldiers the year round caused a rapid expansion of supporting administrative personnel. Taxation mushroomed. All levels of society felt the impact but especially the lower classes, who paid the bulk of the taxes and provided most of the recruits. To encourage enlistment rulers made military service as attractive as possible—not a difficult task at a time when regular meals, clothing, housing, and wages were not always easy to come by. Social distinctions were reduced; an able young man could rise high in the officer corps, though the top ranks were

---
[1] An excellent analysis of the military revolution and its implications can be found in Michael Roberts' "Gustav Adolf and the Art of War" and "The Military Revolution, 1560–1660," in his *Essays in Swedish History* (1967), pp. 58–81 and 195–225.

Gustavus Adolphus, the Swedish monarch whose domestic and military policies gained his country a position of considerable power in the early seventeenth century, is here shown landing in Germany with his men and immediately thanking God for his success thus far.
(Photo: Nationalmuseum, Stockholm)

still reserved for nobles. Even the lower echelons were given important responsibilities because the new system of small, flexible units required that junior officers, who were sometimes in command of only fifty men, be given considerable initiative. The decline of the cavalry, which had always been an aristocratic preserve, similarly reduced social differentiations.

Life in the army also changed. Maneuverability demanded tighter discipline, which was achieved by the introduction of drilling and combat training. The order of command was clarified, and many ranks familiar today—major, colonel, and the various levels of general—appeared in the seventeenth century. The distinctions were reinforced by uniforms, which became standard equipment. These developments created a sense of corporate spirit among military officers, an international phenomenon that was to occupy an important place in European society for three centuries.

As Gustavus himself put it, war nourishes itself. With ever-larger armies, stimulated by national ambitions and governments in search of wider powers, it was inevitable that the devastations of warfare would proliferate. Gustavus himself enunciated the strategy of devastation—an opponent can be brought to his knees, he said, only if his strength is totally destroyed. Such conclusions clearly reflected the appalling slaughter of the era that has come to be known as the age of religious warfare.

The Wars of Religion

Although many other issues were involved in the wars that plagued Europe from the 1560s to the 1650s, religion was the burning motivation, the one that inspired fanatical devotion and the most vicious hatred. A deep conviction that heresy was dangerous to man and hateful to God made Protestants and Catholics treat one another callously and cruelly. Even the dead were not spared; corpses were sometimes mutilated to emphasize how dreadful their sins had been in their lifetimes. This was the bitter emotion that blended in with political and other ambitions to give Europe a century of almost ceaseless war.

Spain's Catholic Crusade

During the second half of the sixteenth century, the conflict was ignited by the leader of the Catholics, Philip II of Spain (1556–1598), the most powerful monarch in Europe. He ruled the Iberian peninsula, much of Italy, the Netherlands, and a huge overseas empire, but his main obsessions were the two enemies of his church, the Muslims and the Protestants.

Against the Muslims in the Mediterranean, Philip's successful campaigns seemed to justify the financial strains they caused. In particular, his naval victory at Lepanto, off the coast of Greece, in 1571 made him a Christian hero at the same time as it rid the western Mediterranean of Muslim interference. But elsewhere he found little but frustration. He tried to prevent a Protestant, Henry IV, from succeeding to the French crown, and after he failed he continued to back the losing side in France's civil wars even though Henry converted to Catholicism.

Philip's policy toward England was similarly ineffective. After the Protestant Queen Elizabeth I came to the throne in 1558, he remained uneasily cordial toward her for about ten years. But relations deteriorated as England's sailors and explorers tried to take some of the wealth of Philip's New World possessions for themselves. The last straw came in 1585 when Elizabeth began to help the Protestant Dutch in their rebellion against Spain.

Philip decided to end all these troubles with one mighty blow: in 1588 he sent a mammoth fleet—the Armada—to the Low Countries to pick up a Spanish army, invade England, and crush his Protestant enemies. By this time, however, English seamen were among the best in the world; and their ships, which had greater maneuverability and fire power than the Spaniards', made up in tactical superiority what they lacked in size. After several skirmishes with the Armada, they set fire to a few vessels with loaded cannon aboard and sent them drifting toward the Spanish ships, anchored off Calais. The Spaniards panicked, and some of the fleet was lost. The next day the remaining ships retreated up the North Sea. The only way home was around Scotland and Ireland, and wind, storms, and the pursuing English ensured that no more than a few stragglers reached Spain safely. This shattering reversal was comparable in scale and unexpectedness only to Xerxes' disaster at Salamis more than 2,000 years earlier.

The defeat spelled the doom of Philip's foreign policies. Though he improved the defense of the Spanish Empire, English raids multiplied in a tremendous wave of privateering in the 1590s, and his possessions were under almost constant attack thereafter. Enemies to the bitter end, both Elizabeth and Philip died before peace came in 1604.

This engraving was published to arouse horror at Spanish atrocities during the Dutch revolt. As the caption indicates, after the Spanish troops (on the right) captured the city of Haarlem, there was a great bloodbath ("ein gross bliut batt"). Blessed by priests, the Haarlemites are decapitated or hung, and then tossed in a river so that the city is cleansed of them. The caption states that even women and children were not spared.
(Photo: New York Public Library/Picture Collection)

The Dutch Revolt

Philip's most serious reversal was the revolt of the provinces he had inherited from his father in the Netherlands. Here his single-mindedness provoked a determined reaction that grew into a successful struggle for independence, the first major effort in Western Europe to resist the new authority of a monarchy.

The original focus of opposition was Philip's reorganization of the ecclesiastical structure so as to gain control over the country's Catholic Church, a change which deprived the aristocracy of important patronage. The billeting of troops meanwhile aroused the resentment of ordinary citizens. Using this situation, the nobles, led by William of Orange, threatened mass disorder, but Philip kept up the pressure: he put the Inquisition to work against heretics, and summoned the Jesuits to combat religious unorthodoxy. These moves

This detail from Brueghel's *Massacre of the Innocents* shows the brutality of Spanish soldiers toward the local population. The darkest figure, at the center of the detachment of cavalry, has been identified as the duke of Alva.
(Photo: Kunsthistorisches Museum, Vienna)

had a disastrous effect because they further undermined local autonomy and threatened the Protestants of the country.

Philip's interference in religion provoked violence in 1566: Protestant mobs swept through cities, sacking Catholic churches as they went. He therefore tightened the pressure, appointing as governor the ruthless duke of Alva, whose Spanish troops were used to suppress heresy and treason. Protestants were hanged in public, small rebel bands were mercilessly decimated, and two nobles who had been guilty of nothing worse than demanding that Philip change his policy were executed.

The reaction of one observer, the great painter Pieter Brueghel, was a searing indictment of the persecution. (For Brueghel's more general critique of human folly, see Plate 32.) When he painted a famous biblical subject, the *Massacre of the Innocents,* he set the scene in a village in the Netherlands during the harshest season, winter. His own countrymen were the victims, and the murderers were Spanish soldiers, watched over by the sinister figure of the duke of Alva.

Organized revolt broke out in 1572, when a small group of Dutch seamen flying the flag of William of Orange seized the fishing village of Brill, on the North Sea. The success of these "sea beggars," as the Spaniards called them, stimulated uprisings in towns throughout the Low Countries. The banner of William of Orange became the symbol of resistance, and under his leadership full-scale rebellion gathered momentum.

After the sea beggars' capture of Brill, the Spaniards advanced into the province of Holland, but they were stopped in 1574 by the opening of the dikes when they were only twenty-five miles from Amsterdam.[2] Following two more years of fighting, Philip's troops mutinied and rioted in Antwerp. In reaction, sixteen out of seventeen provinces united behind William to drive out the Spaniards. The next year, however, the ten southern provinces

MAP 15.1: THE NETHERLANDS 1579–1609

The seventeen provinces making up the Netherlands, or the Low Countries, were detached from the Holy Roman Empire when Charles V abdicated in 1556. As the map indicates, their subsequent division into two states was determined not by the linguistic difference between French-speaking people of the south and Dutch-speaking people of the north, but rather by geography. The great river systems at the mouth of the Rhine eventually proved to be the barrier beyond which the Spaniards could not penetrate.

again gave their allegiance to Philip in return for a number of compromises, especially with their nobility.

In 1579 the remaining seven formed the United Provinces (Map 15.1). Despite the as-

---

[2] Most areas of the provinces of Holland and Zeeland lay below sea level and were protected by dikes. Defenders could flood them at very short notice by opening sluices in the sea walls. The forewarned population would take to boats, and the enemy soldiers, caught unawares, would have to beat a hasty retreat.

sassination of William in 1584, they managed to hang on, for various reasons: they could always open up the dikes; Philip was often diverted by other wars, and in any case never placed total confidence in his commanders; and the Calvinists, though still a minority, became the heart of the resistance with their determination to establish freedom for their religion as well as their country. William was succeeded by Maurice of Nassau, his son, a brilliant military commander who won a series of victories in the 1590s. The Spaniards could make no progress and agreed to a twelve-year truce in 1609, but final recognition of the independence of the United Provinces did not come until the Peace of Westphalia, in 1648, after twenty-seven more years of fighting. The new state, bound together by religious, economic, and military ties, demonstrated the occasional positive effects of warfare in this period: it could unite a people and give them the means to achieve dignity and full autonomy.

Civil War in France

The warfare that religion inspired had no such redeeming effects in France. By the 1550s Calvinism was widespread among the peasants and poorer middle classes in the southern and southwestern section of the country, and its leaders had virtually created a small, semi-independent state within France. To meet this threat, a great noble family, the Guises, assumed the leadership of a Catholic party, and in response the Bourbons, another noble family, championed the Calvinists. The ensuing war split France apart.

It was ominous that in 1559, the year that Henry II, France's last strong king for a generation, died, the Protestant Huguenots organized their first national synod, an indication of impressive strength. During the next thirty years, a period when factional disputes among the nobles and religious passions overwhelmed the country, the throne was occupied by Henry's three ineffectual sons. The power behind the crown was Henry's widow, Catherine de Medici (see the accompanying genealogical table), who tried desperately to preserve royal authority. But she was often helpless because the religious conflict intensified the factional struggle for power between the Catholic Guises and the Protestant Bourbons, both of whom were closely related to the monarchy and hoped eventually to inherit the throne.

The fighting started in 1562, and lasted for thirty-six years, interrupted only by short-lived peace agreements. Catherine first turned to the Catholics for help but later switched to the Calvinists. When they became too powerful at court, she changed sides again, and she probably gave tacit approval to a massacre in Paris on St. Bartholomew's Day, August 24, 1572, which destroyed the Calvinist leadership. Henry of Navarre, a Bourbon, was the only major figure who escaped. When Catherine switched again and made peace with the Calvinists in 1576, the Guises, in desperation, formed the Catholic League, which for several years virtually ran the government. In 1584 the league made an alliance with Philip II to destroy heresy in France and deny the Bourbon Henry's legal right to inherit the throne.

The defeat of the Armada proved to be the turning point in France's civil war. The duke of Guise lost his principal support, Spain; and Henry III, who had been a pawn of the league, ordered Guise's assassination and threw in his lot with the Bourbons. Within a few months he in turn was assassinated, and Henry of Navarre inherited the throne.

Henry IV (1589–1610) had few advantages as he began the reassertion of royal authority. The Calvinists and Catholics had formed almost independent governments, controlling large sections of France. The Catholic League was in command of the east, including the capital, Paris; the Calvinists dominated the south and southwest, remote from the central government. In addition the royal administration

THE KINGS OF FRANCE IN THE SIXTEENTH CENTURY

was in a sorry state, for power had returned to the crown's oldest rivals, the great nobles, who were now unchallenged in their domains.

Yet largely because of the assassination of the duke of Guise, Henry IV survived and recovered. The duke had been a forceful leader, a serious contender for the throne. He was succeeded by his brother, who had agreed to support a Spanish candidate for the crown. The prospect of a foreign ruler, the loss of a charismatic leader, and war weariness destroyed much of the support for the Catholic League, which finally collapsed as a result of revolts in eastern France against the Guises in the 1590s. The uprisings, founded on a demand for peace, increased in frequency and intensity after Henry IV renounced Protestantism in 1593 to win acceptance by his Catholic subjects. The following year Henry had himself officially crowned, and all of France declared its allegiance to the monarchy so as to join in the effort of repelling the Spanish invader.

When Spain finally withdrew and signed a peace in 1598, the fighting came to an end. To complete the reconciliation, Henry issued (also in 1598) the Edict of Nantes, which granted toleration to the Huguenots. Although it did not create complete religious liberty, the edict made Calvinism legal, protected the rights of the minority, and opened public office to Protestants.

But the effects of decades of strife could not be brushed aside. A basic change in political thought, for example, was an inevitable response to the civil wars, because a number of theorists felt obliged to reassess the relationship between a king and his subjects.

The Huguenots were the first to justify resistance to a monarch. Seizing on a vague passage in Calvin's writings about the sanctity of conscience and ignoring his endorsement of obedience to authority, they asserted that when a king goes against God's wishes and disturbs the faith, he breaks his contract with his people, thus making revolt permissible. Catholics took up a similar argument when they were fighting the king. The Jesuits developed the idea of a contract between ruler and ruled and found excellent biblical support for the overthrow of a tyrant (for example pharaoh) who turned against true religion.

These extreme positions soon lost appeal when order was restored, however, and a group whose views had previously gone unheeded gained the ascendancy: the politiques. Although most were Catholics their main premise was that peace, security, and national unity were far more important than the claims of rival churches. Representing the forces of nationalism and central authority, the politiques were the heralds of a more stable future.

Their most famous representative, Jean Bodin, made his case by examining the basic structure of the state, and his analysis influ-

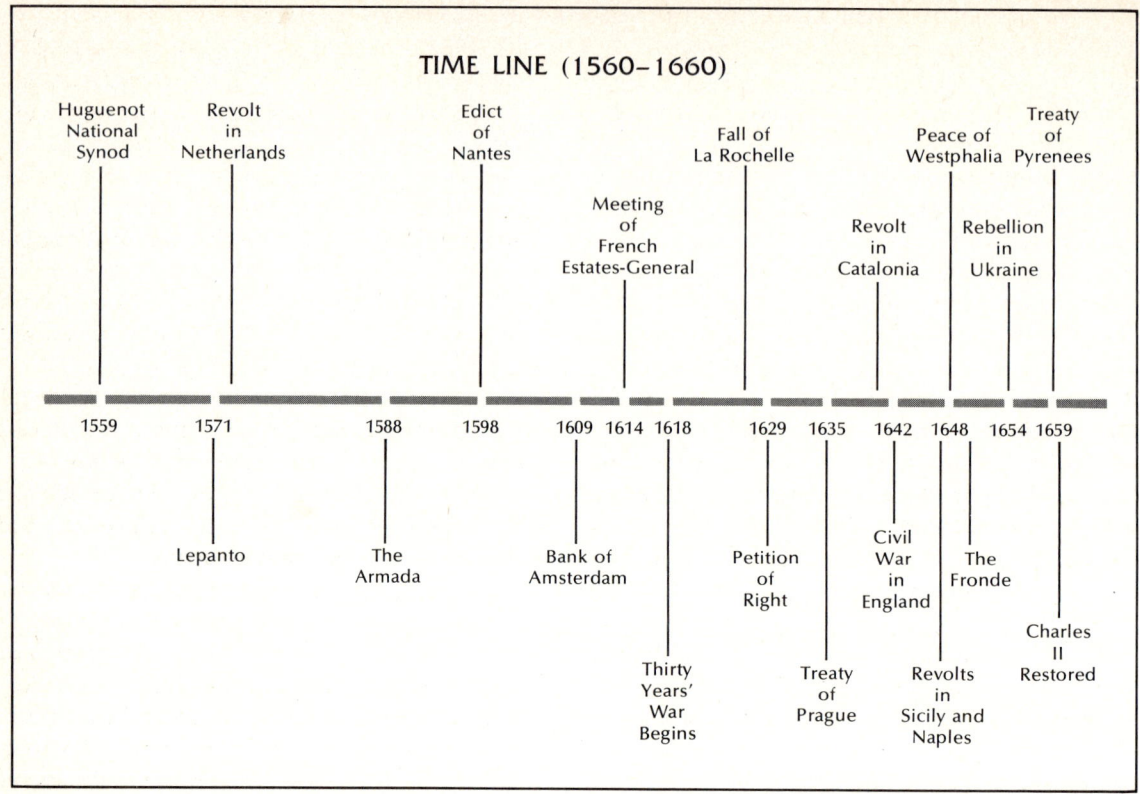

enced political theorists for centuries. His principal work is *The Six Books of the Republic* (1576), in which he tried to define the nature and the limits of authority. By aiming for a balance between power and restraint, Bodin was seeking a principle for restoring stability in an age of shattering upheaval. But in the process he also exposed the paradox that has been the primary focus of political theory ever since: control versus freedom, the need for authority and yet the equal need for individual rights.

The Thirty Years' War

In the Holy Roman Empire fierce religious antagonisms were particularly dangerous because the empire lacked a central authority and unifying institutions. Small-scale fighting broke out repeatedly after the 1550s, always inspired by religion. And though in most of Western Europe the first two decades of the seventeenth century were a time of relative peace, which seemed to signal a decline of confessional conflict, in the empire the stage was being set for the bloodiest of all the wars fired by religion.

Known as the Thirty Years' War, this ferocious series of encounters began in the Kingdom of Bohemia in 1618 and continued until 1648. The principal battleground, the empire, was ravaged by the fighting, and eventually every major ruler of Europe became involved in the struggle. Political ambitions soon began to replace religious motives as the prime concern of the combatants, but the devastation continued to spread until international relations seemed to be sinking into total chaos. The chief victims were of course the Germans, who, like the Italians in the sixteenth century, found themselves at the mercy of well-organized states that used another country as the arena for settling their quarrels.

The immediate problem was typical of the situation in the empire. In 1609 Emperor Rudolf II promised toleration for Protestants in Bohemia, one of his own domains. When his cousin Ferdinand, a pious Catholic, succeeded to the Bohemian throne in 1617, he refused to honor Rudolf's promise, and the Bohemians rebelled. Since the crown was technically elective, they declared Ferdinand deposed, replacing him with the leading Calvinist of the empire, Frederick II of the Palatinate. Frederick accepted the crown, an act of defiance whose only possible outcome was war between the two religious camps.

For more than a decade, little went wrong for the Hapsburgs. Ferdinand became emperor (1619–1637), and the powerful Catholic Maximilian of Bavaria put his army at the emperor's disposal. Within a year the imperial troops won a shattering victory over the Bohemians at the Battle of the White Mountain. Leading rebels were executed or exiled, and Ferdinand II confiscated all of Frederick's lands. Half was given to Maximilian as a reward for his army, and the remainder was offered to the Spaniards, who occupied it as a valuable base for their struggle with the Dutch. It seemed as though the Catholic and imperial cause had triumphed. But in 1621 the truce between the Spaniards and the Dutch expired, hostilities reopened in the Netherlands, and religious warfare resumed in Germany (see Map 15.2).

Until 1630, however, the Protestants could do little in the face of the armies of the Hapsburgs and Bavaria. In 1622 the Spaniards occupied the Valtellina, a Swiss valley that was the best route for their troops traveling to the Netherlands. And in the empire all attempts by Protestants to help Frederick were beaten back. By 1630 Hapsburg power, bolstered by the creation of a new army, had reached its height.

The man who put together the new imperial army was Albrecht von Wallenstein, a minor Bohemian nobleman and a remarkable opportunist who had become one of the richest men in the empire. In 1624 Wallenstein, realizing that the emperor's great weakness was that he lacked his own army, offered to raise a force if he could billet it and raise its supplies among the population in whatever area it happened to be stationed. Ferdinand agreed, and by 1627 his army had begun to conquer the northern region of the empire, the last major center of Protestant strength. To emphasize his supremacy, Ferdinand issued the Edict of Restitution in 1629, ordering the restoration to Catholics of all the territories they had lost to Protestants—mainly in the northern empire—since 1552.

But these successes were more apparent than real because it was only the extreme disorganization of the empire that permitted a mercenary captain like Wallenstein to achieve such immense power. Once the princes realized their danger, they united against the Hapsburgs; and the forced contributions exacted by Wallenstein's army strengthened their determination to curb this growing menace to their independence. At an electoral diet in 1630, they made Ferdinand dismiss his general by threatening to keep his son from the imperial succession. The emperor's submission proved fatal to his cause, for Sweden and France were now preparing to unleash new aggressions against the Hapsburgs, and Wallenstein was the one man who might have been able to beat back the onslaught.

The year 1630 marked the beginning of a change in fortune and also a drift toward the more political aims that now came to dominate the war. Although France was a Catholic country, she was now ready to ally with Protestants and attack other Catholics because of her fear of Hapsburg power on her eastern border. In the spring France attacked the duke of Savoy, a Hapsburg ally, and occupied his lands. Then early in 1631 Gustavus Adolphus of Protestant Sweden, fearing that Swedish territories around the Baltic Sea might be threatened, and alarmed at Ferdinand's treatment of Protestants, signed alliances with France and the elector of Saxony. In July he crossed the Baltic, and at the head of a Swedish-Saxon army destroyed the imperial

MAP 15.2: AREAS OF FIGHTING 1618–1660

force at Breitenfeld in one of the few decisive battles of the war.

Ferdinand hastily recalled Wallenstein, whose troops finally met the Swedes in battle at Lützen in 1632. Although Gustavus' soldiers won the day, he himself was killed, and his death saved the Hapsburg dynasty from total destruction. Nothing, however, could restore Ferdinand's former position. The emperor was forced to turn against Wallenstein once more; a few months later he had him assassinated. The removal of the great general marked the end of an era, for he was the last man in more than two centuries capable of establishing unified authority, throughout what is now Germany.

Encouraged by Gustavus's success, the empire's princes began to raise new armies, and by 1635 Ferdinand had to make peace with them at the Treaty of Prague. In return for their promise of assistance in driving out the Swedes, Ferdinand agreed to suspend the Edict of Restitution and to grant amnesty to all but Frederick of the Palatinate and a few Bohemian rebels. Ferdinand was renouncing most of his ambitions, and it seemed that peace might return to the battle-scarred land.

But the French could not let matters rest. In 1635 they finally declared war on Ferdinand and occupied the Valtellina. For the next thirteen years, the French and Swedes rained unmitigated disaster on Germany. Peace negotiations began in 1641, but not until 1648 did the combatants agree to lay down arms and sign the treaties of Westphalia. Even thereafter the war between France and Spain, pursued mainly in the Spanish Netherlands, continued for another eleven years; and hostilities around the Baltic among Sweden, Denmark, Poland, and Russia, which had started in 1611, did not end until 1661.

The wars killed off more than a third of Germany's population. They caused serious economic dislocations, because a number of princes—already in serious financial straits—sharply debased their coinage. Their action worsened the continent-wide trade depression that had begun around 1620 and had brought the great sixteenth-century boom to an end, causing the first drop in prices since 1500. Few contemporaries perceived the connection between war and economic troubles, but nobody could ignore the interminable drain on men and resources or the widespread effects of the conflict on the life of the time.

The Peace of Westphalia

By the 1630s it was already becoming apparent that the fighting was getting out of hand, and that it would not be easy to bring the conflicts to an end. There had never been such widespread or devastating warfare; in the view of many diplomats, the settlement had to be far more decisive and of far greater scope than any negotiated before. And they were right. When at last the treaties were signed, after seven years of negotiation in the German province of Westphalia, a landmark in international relations was passed—remarkable not only because an anarchic situation was brought under control, but because a new system for dealing with wars was created.

The most important innovation was the

Map 15.2 reveals both the extent and the fluctuations of fighting in Europe from the outbreak of the Thirty Years' War to the end of the Civil War in England. The principal battles are listed to give a more precise indication of the timing and location of major encounters. A look at the route followed by Spain's troops as they marched to the Netherlands, always staying close to friendly Catholic territories, will pinpoint the vital importance of the Valtellina, a vulnerable pass through the Alps that they had to cross.

gathering at the peace conference of all the participants in the Thirty Years' War, rather than the usual practice of bringing only two or three belligerents together. The presence of ambassadors from Bavaria, Brandenburg, Denmark, France, the Holy Roman Empire, Saxony, Spain, Sweden, Switzerland, and the United Provinces made possible, for the first time in European history, a series of all-embracing treaties that dealt with nearly every major international issue at one stroke. Although the Franco-Spanish and the Baltic wars continued for more than ten years, the Peace of Westphalia in 1648 became the first comprehensive rearrangement of the map of Europe in modern history (Map 15.3).

The principal beneficiaries were France and Sweden, the chief aggressors during the last decade of the war. France made important gains on her northeastern frontier, notably the provinces of Alsace and Lorraine; and Sweden obtained extensive territories in the Holy Roman Empire, among them Western Pomerania, Bremen, and Verden. The main loser was the House of Hapsburg, since both the United Provinces and the Swiss Confederation were recognized as independent states and the German princes, who agreed not to join an alliance against the emperor, were otherwise given almost complete independence.

However, the princes' autonomy was not officially established until 1657, when they elected as emperor Leopold I, the head of the House of Hapsburg, in return for two promises. First, Leopold would give no help to his cousins, the rulers of Spain; and second, the empire would be a *Fürstenstaat,* a prince's state, in which each ruler would be completely free from imperial interference. This freedom permitted the rise of Brandenburg-Prussia and the growth of absolutism within the major principalities. In addition the Hapsburgs' capitulation prepared the way for their reorientation toward the east along the Danube River—the beginnings of the Austro-Hungarian Empire (see pp. 572–577).

For more than a century the settlement reached at Westphalia was regarded as the basis for all international negotiations. The Treaty of the Pyrenees in 1659, ending the war between France and Spain, and the treaties of Copenhagen and Oliva in 1660 and Kardis in 1661, ending the Baltic struggles, were considered only to have rounded out the agreements made at Westphalia. Even major new accords, such as the one that ended yet another series of wars in 1713, were viewed primarily as adjustments of the decisions of 1648.

In practice of course multinational conferences were no more effective than brief, limited negotiations as means of reducing international tensions. Wars continued to break out with monotonous frequency, and armies grew in size and skill. But diplomats did believe that the total situation was under better control and that the anarchy of the Thirty Years' War had been replaced by something more stable and more clearly defined.

Confidence was reinforced as it became clear after 1648 that armies were trying to improve discipline and avoid the excesses of the previous thirty years. The treatment of civilians became more orderly, and on the battlefield the casualty rate went from as high as one death per three soldiers in the 1630s down to one death in seven at worst, or one in twenty at best, during the early 1700s. As religious passions declined, combat became less vicious, and the aims of warfare changed significantly.

The most obvious differences after the Peace of Westphalia were that France replaced Spain as the Continent's dominant power, and that northern countries—especially England and the Netherlands—took over economic leadership from the Mediterranean, where it had been centered for 2,000 years. But behind this outward shift a more fundamental transformation was taking place. What had become

A Century of War and Revolt 1560-1660 489

MAP 15.3: TERRITORIAL CHANGE 1648–1661

This map shows the territorial changes that took place after the Thirty Years' War. The treaties of Westphalia (1648) and the Pyrenees (1659) arranged the principal transfers, but the settlements in the Baltic were not confirmed until the treaties of Copenhagen, Oliva (both 1660), and Kardis (1661). The arrows indicate the direction of conquests and the date at which they were accomplished.

apparent in the later stages of the Thirty Years' War was that Europe's states were interested in fighting only for economic, territorial, or political advantages. Dynastic aims were still important—and were to remain so for centuries—but supranational goals like religious advancement could no longer determine foreign policies.

The Thirty Years' War was the last major conflict in which two religious camps organized their forces as blocs. After 1648 such connections gave way to more purely national interests. Despite the universal wish for peace, Pope Innocent X, furious at the Catholics' compromises, denounced the treaties of Westphalia, but his voice went unheard. The declining influence of ideology meant that men would henceforth pursue the glory of their nation or ruler—not the advantage of their faith. This shift marked the final stage of a process that had long been under way: the emergence of the state as the basic unit and object of loyalty in Western civilization.

If the new aims of foreign policies, such as economic advantage, could not yet arouse the same passions as religion, they nevertheless revealed that commitment to one's country, and an interest in the way it was run, was becoming important throughout Europe. Indeed, at the very time that tensions were lessening in international affairs, they reached a new height in the internal affairs of a number of countries. Just as the mid-seventeenth century witnessed the most intense phase and also the settlement of the difficulties among states, so too did it mark the climax and the resolution of an era of upheaval and revolt within states.

II. REVOLTS

The warfare of the century from the 1560s to the 1660s affected the relations between rulers and their subjects no less than relations between countries. The additional taxes and bureaucrats required by the military created burdens that provoked the resistance to governments that was a major feature of the century. By the time the conflicts died away, after a particularly acute outburst in the mid-seventeenth century, they had helped create the national political structures that endured until the age of the French Revolution.

England

The one attempt at a radical transformation of politics and society—a revolution—occurred in England. Compared to her neighbors, England seemed relatively calm during the second half of the sixteenth century and the early years of the seventeenth. But tensions were rising that were to produce the most far-reaching upheaval of the age.

Elizabeth I

The tranquillity of the period from the 1560s to the 1630s had several causes. With only occasional fighting to support, and that largely at sea, England was far less affected by war than the Continental states. Furthermore the people were already united by such common bonds as a national reformation and the institution of Parliament, so the crown did not experience the severe challenges that plagued royal authority in contemporary Spain and France. And the monarch also happened to be extraordinarily clever at the task of calming discontent.

Elizabeth I (1558–1603) has been an appealing figure to every generation because she combined shrewd hard-headedness and a sense of the possible with a charming appearance of frailty. Her qualities are easily appreciated: her dedication to the task of government; her astute choice of advisers—with the one exception of the handsome young earl of Essex, for whom she developed a disastrous infatuation near the

Elizabeth I was strongly aware of the power of propaganda, and she made great efforts to put forward the best possible public image. Legends about her arose in literature. And in art she had herself portrayed in the most elaborate finery imaginable. Here, she is every inch the queen, with her magnificent dress and pet ermine—a pose of strict formality.
(Photo: Courtauld Institute of Art)

end of her life; her careful and usually successful handling of political problems; and her ability to feel the mood of her people, to catch their spirit, to inspire their unquestioning enthusiasm.

Her concern for loyalty made Elizabeth reluctant to break openly with those who opposed her, but this also led to an indecisiveness that had unfortunate consequences, notably where the succession was concerned. Her refusal to marry caused serious uncertainties, and it was only because of the astute planning of Elizabeth's chief minister, Robert Cecil, that a crisis was avoided when she died in 1603 without naming a successor. Thanks to Cecil's diplomacy, the king of Scotland, James Stuart, succeeded without incident. Similar dangers arose from Elizabeth's reluctance to act firmly against England's remaining Catholics. Although most were loyal, a few plotted against her, hoping that if she died, Mary Queen of Scots, a Catholic, would come to the throne. Mary had been driven out of Scotland by the country's Catholic nobles and was a prisoner in England. Not until Elizabeth grudgingly agreed to execute her (in 1587), and to deal more severely with Catholic plots, did this threat subside.

The advisers Elizabeth appointed to the Privy Council, the chief government body, were essential to her success. They distilled the flow of administrative business and worked closely with the queen, but they also represented different views. Some advocated caution, inaction, and discretion in international affairs, whereas others favored an aggressive foreign policy. Elizabeth had great skill in balancing the contrasting viewpoints and her clever maneuvering assured her of her ministers' loyalty at all times.

Even more important than her approval of a policy was the patronage that accompanied her pleasure. Because the government's powers and hence its need for officials had grown rapidly since the 1530s, dozens of new posts were being created for the crown to bestow. Whoever was the queen's favorite therefore had the best chance of nominating a successful candidate for a vacancy in the bureaucracy. But as a result of the patronage system, a swarm of parasites descended on London, hopeful of advancement. Many Englishmen viewed this development with distaste, and after Elizabeth's death it became the cause of serious cleavage between crown and subjects.

Economic and Social Change

Another force with dangerous implications for the future was the result of rapidly shifting patterns in English society. With new methods of warfare, nobles no longer had a vital military role to play. Moreover they were losing their preeminence in government; nearly all the chief ministers were new men in national life, and the House of Commons was becoming at least the equal of the House of Lords in Parliament. The nobles were also not benefiting as much from England's rising prosperity as were other sections of society. Thus they were losing their hold over the power, wealth, and government of the country.

The gentry, the new group that joined them at the head of society, ranged from people considered great men in a parish or other small locality to courtiers considered great men throughout the land. There were never more than sixty nobles during Elizabeth's reign, but the gentry may have numbered close to 20,000 by the time she died.

The majority of the gentry were doing well economically, primarily from the purchase of land that the crown had confiscated when the monasteries were dissolved, in the 1530s. They also benefited from spiraling food prices and rising rents. Many profited too from crown offices; a number became involved in industrial activity; and hundreds invested in new overseas trading and colonial ventures. The gentry's participation in commerce made them unique among the landed classes of Europe, whose members were traditionally contemptuous of business affairs, and it testified to the enterprise and vigor of these Englishmen. Long important in local administration, they wanted their views respected by government, and they flocked to the House of Commons, for they regarded Parliament as the place to express their views. Their ambitions were to pose a serious threat to the monarchy, especially when linked with the effects of rapid economic change.

In the 1550s, stimulated by the general boom in trade and by the help of leading courtiers who recognized the importance of opening new markets, England's merchants began to transform her economic situation. During the next half-century, they started commerce with Russia, the Baltic and Mediterranean lands, the Levant, and East Asia. Although cloth remained the dominant export until the middle of the seventeenth century, it was joined by a growing trade in the reexport of overseas goods, such as Newfoundland fish, which were distributed throughout Europe.

Early attempts at colonization were not successful, with the exception of those in Ireland; but vital experience was gained, and the financial rewards were sometimes considerable. Within England, moreover, there was significant industrial development. The mining and manufacture of a whole variety of commodities, from alum to wire, grew at a rapid pace, and shipbuilding became a major industry. The production of coal alone increased fourteenfold between 1540 and 1680, creating many new fortunes and an expertise in industrial and commercial techniques that took England far ahead of her neighbors.

The most revealing evidence of England's new position was the founding of nearly fifty companies devoted to overseas exploration, commerce, or colonization between 1600 and 1630. The more successful ones laid the foundations for the British Empire. In India, the Caribbean islands, Bermuda, Virginia, Maryland, New England, and Canada, colonies were started that within a century were to become the most populous offshoots of any European nation.

The economic vigor and growth that ensued, apparent also in industrial and agricultural advances, gave the classes that benefited the most—the gentry and the merchants—a cohesion and a sense of purpose that made it dangerous to oppose them when they felt their rights infringed. They increasingly regarded themselves as the leaders of the nation, second only to the nobility, whose importance was diminishing. They wanted respect for their wishes, and they bitterly resented the economic interference and political high-handedness of Elizabeth's successors.

What made the situation particularly dangerous was that many of the gentry were sympathetic to the Puritans. These religious reformers believed that the Protestant Anglican Church established by Elizabeth was still too close to Roman Catholicism, and they wanted further changes. Elizabeth had refused, and although she had tried to avoid a confrontation, in the last years of her reign she had had to silence the most outspoken of her critics. As a result, the Puritans had become a disgruntled minority, ready to add their demands to those of the gentry (some of whom were themselves Puritans). By the 1630s, when the government tried to repress such religious dissent more vigorously, there were many Englishmen who felt that the monarchy was leading the country astray and was ignoring the wishes of its subjects. Leading parliamentarians in particular soon came to believe that only major changes could restore justice to England.

Parliament and the Law

The place where the gentry made their views known to the government was Parliament, the nation's supreme legislative body. Three-quarters of the lower chamber, the House of Commons, consisted of members of the gentry. These men were better educated than before; at the end of the sixteenth century, more than half of them had attended a university, and slightly less than half had legal training. Through the House of Commons, they were beginning to make a bid to influence the government, and since the Commons had to approve all taxation, these members had no compunction about using the power of the purse to promote their demands.

The monarchy was still the dominant force in the country when Elizabeth died in 1603, but Parliament's challenge to that supremacy was beginning to gather momentum. Although the queen had been known for her care with money, in the last twenty years of her reign, her resources had been overtaxed by the war with Spain and an economic depression. Consequently she bequeathed to her successor, James I, a huge debt—£400,000, the equal of a year's royal revenue—and the struggle to pay it off gave the Commons the leverage to expand their powers.

Trouble began to mount in 1604, at the first meeting of Parliament in the reign of James I (1603–1625). Puritans who still hoped to change the Anglican Church by legislation and gentry who wanted to extend their influence led the opposition to the king. They began to dominate proceedings, and through 1629 (after which there was no session for eleven years) they engaged in a running battle with the monarchy. They blocked the union of England with

Scotland that James sought. They drew up an "Apology" explaining his mistakes and his ignorance, as a Scotsman, of English traditions. And they wrung repeated concessions from him until in 1624 they gained the unprecedented right to discuss foreign policy.

The parliamentarians used the law as justification for their resistance to royal power. The basic legal system of the country was the common law—justice administered on the basis of precedents and parliamentary statutes, decided with the assistance of juries. This system stood in contrast to Roman law, prevalent on the Continent, where royal edicts could make law, and decisions were reached by judges without juries. Such practices existed in England only in a few royal courts of law, such as Star Chamber. Proceedings here were popular, because they were quicker, and powerful men could not influence the decisions of the judges who were usually prominent men themselves. But a court like Star Chamber, directly under crown influence, could easily come to be seen as an instrument of repression.

Common lawyers, whose leaders were also prominent in the House of Commons, resented the growth of this rival system, and they attacked royal courts in Parliament. Both James and his successor were accused of putting pressure on the judges to gain their ends—particularly after they won a series of famous cases involving a subject's right to criticize the monarch. Thus the crown could be portrayed as disregarding not only the desires of the people but the law itself. Technically the king had extensive rights, but when he exercised them without regard to Parliament's wishes, his actions began to take on the appearance of tyranny.

Rising Antagonisms

The confrontation in Parliament grew worse during the 1620s. In 1621 the House of Commons forced the king's lord chancellor, Francis Bacon, out of office for accepting bribes, and in reaction to their attacks, James had some of the members sent to prison. Under his son Charles I (1625–1649), the hostilities intensified. At the Parliament of 1628–1629, the crown faced an open challenge, whose climax was the Petition of Right, an appeal that has become a landmark in constitutional history. The petition demanded an end to imprisonment without cause shown, to taxation without the consent of Parliament, to martial law in peacetime, and to the billeting of troops among civilians. Charles agreed, in the hope of gaining much-needed subsidies, but then broke his word.

The issue was now clearly whether Parliament, as the representative of the nation, would hold an essential position in the government alongside the king. To stop further confrontation Charles ordered Parliament dissolved, but in a move of great daring, two members denied the king even this hallowed right by holding the speaker of the House in his chair while they passed a final angry resolution.

Resentful subjects were clearly on the brink of open defiance of their sovereign. Puritans, common lawyers, and disenchanted country gentry had captured the House of Commons, and Charles could avoid further trouble only by refusing to call another session of Parliament. This he managed to do for eleven years, all the while increasing the repression of Puritanism and resorting to extraordinary measures to raise revenues.

But the smooth sailing could not last long. The leaders of the Puritan and parliamentary opposition kept in touch after 1630, and they finally had the opportunity in 1639 to extract from the king the concessions they sought when the Calvinist Scots took up arms rather than accept the Anglican prayer book. Religious persecution had once again sparked military combat: the Scots invaded England, and Charles had to raise an army. To obtain the necessary funds, he turned to Parliament, which demanded that he first redress its grievances. When he resisted, civil war followed.

The English Civil War

The Parliament that met in 1640 was dominated by John Pym, a Puritan and a prominent critic of the monarch for nearly twenty years, who opened the session with a two-hour speech outlining the long-standing grievances against both church and government. Charles refused to change his policies and the Commons refused to grant a subsidy, and so the king angrily dissolved the session. But there was no way to pay for an army without taxes. By the summer of 1640, the Scots occupied most of northern England, and Charles had no alternative but to summon a new Parliament. This one sat for thirteen years, earning the appropriate name of the Long Parliament.

Pym was in complete control of Parliament for the first year. The House of Commons passed legislation abolishing the royal courts, such as Star Chamber, and establishing the writ of habeas corpus (which prevented imprisonment without cause shown) as mandatory; it declared taxation without parliamentary consent illegal; and it ruled that Parliament had to meet at least once every three years, with the additional proviso that the current assembly could not be dissolved without its consent. Meanwhile, the Puritans were preparing to reform the church. Oliver Cromwell, one of the leading members of the House, demanded abolition of the Anglican Book of Common Prayer and strongly attacked the institution of episcopacy. The climactic vote came the next year, when the Commons passed their Grand Remonstrance, outlining for the king all the legislation they had put through and asking that bishops be deprived of their votes in the House of Lords.

This was the prelude to a more revolutionary assault on the structure of the church, but significantly the Grand Remonstrance passed by only 11 votes. A moderate party was detaching itself from Pym, and the beginning of a royalist party was appearing. The nation's chief grievances had been redressed, and there was no longer a uniform desire for change. Still Charles misjudged the situation and tried to arrest five leaders of the opposition, including Pym, ostensibly for plotting treason with the Scots. But Parliament refused to order their arrest, and the citizens of London, now openly hostile to Charles, sheltered the five.

In June 1642 the king received the Commons' final demands: complete parliamentary control over the church, the appointment of ministers and judges, and the army. This would have meant the abdication of all effective royal authority, and Charles refused. Gradually England began to split in two. By the late summer both sides had assembled armies, and the Civil War was under way.

The fascination of this great revolution that sought to transform English government and society has been endless. Much attention has been given to religion and politics, to the motives of Puritans and parliamentarians; it is now clear that simple differentiations cannot be made. Half the parliamentarians joined the king; the Puritans were split; and many members of the gentry, not noticeably committed to either of these opposition groups, fought against Charles.

What made so many people overcome their habitual loyalty to the monarchy? One interesting distinction is that the royalists in Parliament were considerably younger than their opponents; this suggests that it was long experience with the Stuarts and nostalgia for Elizabethan times that created dedicated revolutionaries. Another clear division was regional. The south and east of England were primarily antiroyalist while the north and west were mostly royalist. What this implied was that the more cosmopolitan areas, which were closer to the Continent and also the principal centers of Puritanism, were largely on Parliament's side. Frequently the decision was very much a personal matter: a great man would take his locality to one side because his old rival, the great man a few miles away, had chosen the other. Those who opposed the Church of England were unequivocally antiroyalist, but they were a minority in the country and hardly even a majority in the House of Commons. Like all revolutions, this one was animated by a small group of radicals (in this case Puritans) who alone kept the momentum going.

The Stuarts' long alienation of their subjects can account for the situation in 1640, when Charles could find no support anywhere, but by the end of 1641 many felt that the necessary remedies had been obtained. Thus apart from Puritanism—or to put it more generally, apart from opposition to the Church of England—the historian can point only to the influence of local circumstances to explain how two sides came into being in the summer of 1642.

The Course of Conflict

The first round of fighting was indecisive—a year of small successes on both sides. Then in 1643 the antiroyalists, supported by the Scottish army, gained the first military advantage. The alliance with the Scots was Pym's last accomplishment, because shortly thereafter he died, and the first major split in the antiroyalist ranks occurred.

Increasingly during the last months of Pym's life, a group known as the Independents urged that the Anglican Church be replaced by the congregational system, in which each local congregation, free of all central authority, would decide its own form of worship. The most important representative of the Independents in Parliament was Oliver Cromwell (1599–1658). Opposed to them were the Presbyterians, who wanted to establish a strictly organized Calvinist system, much like the one that had been created in Scotland, in which local congregations were subject to centralized authority, although laymen did participate in church government. Since both the Scots, whose alliance was vital in the war, and a majority of the members of the Commons were Presbyterians,[3] Cromwell agreed to give way, but only for the moment. In addition to the religious issue, there was also a quarrel over the goals of the war because the antiroyalists were unsure whether they ought to attempt to defeat Charles completely. This dispute crossed religious lines, though on the whole the Independents were more determined to force him into total submission, and in the end they had their way.

Meanwhile the fighting continued. Hoping to create a more potent fighting force, Cromwell persuaded the House of Commons early in 1645 to create a completely reorganized army, the New Model Army, to bring the war to an end. Whipped to fervor by sermons, prayers, and the singing of psalms, the New Model Army became a formidable force. At the Battle of Naseby in June, it won a major victory over the royalists and a year later Charles surrendered.

The next two years were chaotic. The Presbyterians and Independents quarreled over what to do with the king, and finally the Civil War resumed. This time the Presbyterians and Scots backed Charles against the Independents. But even with this alliance the royalist forces were no match for the New Model Army; Cromwell soon defeated his opponents and captured the king.

At the same time, in 1647, the Independents abolished the House of Lords and removed all Presbyterians from the House of Commons, leaving behind a "rump" of less than 100 men, about a fifth of the original membership of the Long Parliament. The Rump Parliament tried

---
[3] This was a majority of a depleted House, however, because a few dozen royalists had departed from the Commons during 1641, especially after the Grand Remonstrance, and they never returned.

This contemporary Dutch engraving of the execution of Charles I shows the scaffold in front of the Banqueting House in Whitehall—a building that still can be seen in London. On the far right of the scaffold, the executioner displays the severed head for the crowd.
(Photo: The Granger Collection)

to negotiate with Charles but discovered that he continued to plot a return to power. With Cromwell's approval the Commons decided that their monarch, untrustworthy and a troublemaker, would have to die. A trial without legality was held, and though many of the participants refused to sign the death warrant, the "holy, anointed" king was executed by his subjects in January 1649, to the horror of all Europe and most of England.

England Under Cromwell: The Interregnum

Oliver Cromwell, the hero of the New Model Army, was now master of England. The republic established after Charles' execution was officially ruled by the Rump Parliament, but a Council of State led by Cromwell controlled policy, with the backing of the army. Military activity was far from over because first an Irish rebellion had to be crushed—and it was, brutally—and then the Scots revolted in support of Charles II, the executed monarch's son. This last threat was not suppressed until late in 1651.

At home Cromwell had to contend with a ferment of political and social ideas. One group, known as the Levellers, demanded the vote for nearly all adult males and parliamentary elections every other year. The men of property among the Puritans, notably Cromwell himself, were disturbed by the political egalitarianism implied by these proposals and insisted that only men with an "interest" in England—that is, land—should be qualified to vote.[4]

Even more radical were the Diggers, a communistic sect that sought to implement the spirit of primitive Christianity by abolishing personal property; the Society of Friends, which stressed personal inspiration as the source of faith and all action; and the Fifth Monarchists, a messianic group who believed that the "saints"—themselves—should rule because the Day of Judgment was at hand. Men of great ability contributed to the fantastic flood of pamphlets and suggestions that poured forth in these years—the poet John Milton, Cromwell's secretary, was one of the most prominent pamphleteers—and their ideas inspired many future revolutionaries. But at the time they merely put Cromwell on the defensive, forcing him to maintain control at all costs.

Cromwell himself—as an Independent among the Puritans, a staunch parliamentarian, and a country gentleman—fought for two overriding causes: religious freedom (except for Anglicanism and Catholicism) and constitutional government. But neither came within his grasp, and he grew increasingly unhappy at the Rump's refusal to enact reforms. When the assembly tried to perpetuate itself, he dissolved it in 1653 (the final end of the Long Parliament).

During the remaining five years of his life, Cromwell tried desperately to lay down a new constitutional structure for his government. He always hoped that Parliament itself would establish the perfect political system for England. In fact, though, the three Parliaments he called during these five years seemed to have no inclination to undertake such reforms. Cromwell refused on principle to influence proceedings—except to dismiss the assembly when he felt a selfish faction was seeking its own ends—but in so acting he ignored the realities of politics and left his ideals unfulfilled.

Cromwell was driven by noble aspirations, but he adhered to them so intensely that he could make few compromises. Finally, when he felt he had no other recourse since nobody else was as high-minded as he was, he created a blatant military dictatorship, because the alternatives seemed worse. From 1653 on he was called lord protector and ruled through eleven major generals, each responsible for a different district of England and supported by a tax on royalist estates. To quell dissent he banned newspapers, and to prevent disorder he took such measures as enlisting innkeepers as government spies.

Cromwell always remained a reluctant revolutionary; he hated power and sought only limited ends. Some revolutionaries, like Lenin, have a good idea of where they would like to be carried by events; others, like Cromwell, move painfully, hesitantly, and uncertainly to the extremes they finally reach. It was because he sought England's benefit so urgently and because he considered the nation too precious to abandon to irreligion or tyranny that he remained determinedly in command to the end of his life.

Those final years, however, were filled with plots led by Levellers, royalists, and other dissidents of every shade of belief. The court that gathered around the young Stuart heir, Charles II, who had been in exile on the Continent since 1648, was a breeding ground of conspiracy. Only a superb counterespionage system, organized by the head of Cromwell's postal services (who simply read the mails), enabled him to quench all the plots.

Gradually more traditional forms reappeared. The Parliament of 1656 offered Cromwell the crown, and though he refused, he took the title of "His Highness" and ensured that the

---

[4] It should be recalled that voting rights were still tightly restricted; parliamentary elections by no means assured every Englishman a voice in government. In a town only the freemen (a small group, rarely more than about 20 percent of the population) and in the country only owners of land worth at least 40 shillings in rent a year (considerably less than 10 percent of all landowners) were entitled to vote.

succession would go to his son. Cromwell was monarch in all but name; only he assured stability. After he died his quiet, retiring son Richard proved no match for the scheming generals of the army. To bring an end to the chaos, General George Monck, the commander of a well-disciplined force in Scotland, marched south, assumed control, invited Charles II home from exile, and thus in May of 1660 brought the interregnum to an end.

The Results of the Revolution

Cromwell's chief success had been in foreign policy: he had strengthened the navy, captured Jamaica, gained Dunkirk, and in general reasserted England's importance in international affairs. But at home only the actions taken during the first months of the Long Parliament, in 1640 and 1641—the abolition of leading royal courts, the prohibition of taxation without parliamentary consent, and the establishment of the writ of habeas corpus—persisted beyond the interregnum. Otherwise everything was much the same as before: bishops and lords were reinstated; the repression of religious dissent was resumed; Parliament was called and dissolved by the monarch; and though many old feudal rights were annulled, the king got a set annual income in their place. Inertia and tradition reasserted themselves in the end.

The obvious long-term political and social changes were so minor that one might well question whether this had indeed been a revolution. By comparison with the French and Russian revolutions, its legacy was slim at best. And yet in one fundamental way it had altered the structure of government and society. Henceforth the gentry could no longer be denied a decisive voice in politics. In essence this had been their revolution, and they had succeeded. When in the 1680s a king again tried to impose his wishes on the country without reference to Parliament, there was no need for another major upheaval. A quiet, bloodless coup reaffirmed the new role of the gentry and Parliament (see p. 583).

Thus a new settlement was reached after a long period of growing unease and open conflict. The English could now enjoy untroubled a system of rule that with only gradual modification was to remain in force for some two centuries.

France

Before 1789, the civil wars of the sixteenth century were the closest France came to a revolutionary situation, but the tensions did not disappear when Henry IV brought the fighting to an end. Although the monarchy managed to extend its powers over the next fifty years, resistance continued until a final violent confrontation between the central government and its opponents in the 1640s and 1650s ended in victory for the crown.

Henry IV

Henry IV began the process of strengthening royal power as soon as the civil wars were over. During the remaining years of his reign, from 1598 to 1610, opposition was muted, and he was able to establish his authority in a variety of ways. He mollified the traditional landed aristocracy, known as the nobility of the sword, by giving its leaders places on the chief executive body, the Council of Affairs, and then, when he felt strong enough, by shunting them off to their country estates with large financial settlements that were little better than bribes.

The principal bureaucrats, known as the nobility of the robe, required more careful treatment. They were a formidable group, in control of the country's administration, and led by great officeholding dynasties that were highly suspicious of newcomers. Henry did not try to undermine their position, but he made sure to turn their interests to his benefit. Since all crown offices had to be bought, he used the system both to raise revenues and to confirm the bureaucrats in their loyalty to the king. His tactics involved not only an acceleration in the sales of offices, but also the invention of a new device, an annual fee known as the *paulette*. Regular payments of the *paulette* ensured that an officeholder's job would remain in his family when he died. This not only increased royal profits (by the end of Henry's reign, receipts from the sales accounted for one-twelfth of crown revenues), but also reduced the flow of newcomers and thus strengthened the commitment of existing officeholders to the status quo, that is, to the crown.

By 1610 Henry had succeeded in imposing his will throughout France to a degree that would have been unimaginable in 1598. His treasury was solvent, neither great nobles nor Huguenots gave him trouble, and he was secure enough to plan an invasion of the Holy Roman Empire to extend his power even further. He was assassinated as he was about to leave Paris to join his army, but he had already brought about a quite extraordinary revival of royal authority.

Economic Affairs

In economic affairs the religious wars had taken a toll that was not so quickly remedied. In the 1550s a most fruitful alliance in trading ventures had developed between merchants and nobles. Significant advances had been made overseas, where the French had begun to encroach on the Portuguese monopoly of slaves, gold, and ivory in West Africa. Great ports such as Bordeaux and Marseilles and trade centers such as Lyons had enjoyed unprecedented prosperity. France possessed more fertile agricultural land than any other country of Europe, and her manufactured goods, notably clothes, had been sought throughout the Continent.

The civil war had changed this rosy situation. Trade had suffered heavily, particularly in the once-bustling coastal areas along the Channel. The overseas effort had come to a halt, and the French had soon been replaced by the Dutch and the English as the principal challengers to the Spanish and Portuguese empires. Taxes had mounted, and a large part of the burden had fallen on the merchants in the form of heavy customs dues. Naturally men had abandoned commerce as soon as they could afford to enter the nobility and gain a tax exemption by buying a royal office. The result was that capital had been diverted from trade to unproductive expenditures, and by the end of the century the nobility had developed a lofty contempt for commerce. French trade did not recover its vitality for more than a hundred years. Agriculture had suffered less, but uprisings of peasants, the main victims of the tax system, occurred almost annually in some part of France from the 1590s until the 1670s.

Although the restoration of political stability ended the worst economic disruptions, Henry could do little about the fundamental problems that faced the merchants and the peasants. Nevertheless, once the process of centralization started, the assumption developed that the government was also responsible for the health of economic affairs. This view was justified by a theory known as mercantilism that became an essential ingredient of absolutism, the belief that the king had absolute power in his realm.

Mercantilism was more a set of attitudes than a systematic economic theory. Its basic premise—an erroneous one—was that the world contained a fixed amount of wealth and that each nation could enrich itself only at the expense of others. To some thinkers this meant hoarding as much bullion (gold and silver) as possible; to others it required a favorable balance of trade—more exports than imports. All mercantilists, however, agreed that state regulation was necessary for the welfare of a country. A strong, centralized government was the only power that could encourage native industries, control production, set quality standards, allocate resources, establish tariffs, and take other measures to promote prosperity and improve trade. Thus mercantilism was as much a political as an economic viewpoint and fitted in perfectly with Henry's restoration of royal power.

Mercantilism's principal advocate was Henry's friend and chief minister, the duke of Sully. Sully was concerned that France be self-sufficient agriculturally, in food and drink. But above all he felt that only a strong monarchy could guide the country to prosperity and order. What is significant is that the mercantilists also approved of war. They were men of their times in believing that successful aggression was essential to a country's growth. The linkage of warfare with strong government and even economics reflected the assumptions of the age—shared by Henry himself, who was about to launch a war when he was assassinated in 1610.

The Regency and Richelieu

Unrest reappeared when Henry's death left the throne to his nine-year-old son, Louis XIII (1610–1643). The widowed queen, Marie de Medici, serving as regent, dismissed her husband's ministers, and changed his aggressive foreign policy into friendship with the Hapsburgs. The Calvinists feared for their safety, and their stronghold, the southwest, came close to open revolt. The nobles too began to reassert themselves, infuriated because Marie, an Italian, took advice from her fellow countrymen and not from the aristocrats of the kingdom. Led by the prince of Condé, a cousin of Henry IV's, they demanded an investigation of the Council of Regency and particularly of its financial dealings. In the face of these mounting troubles, Marie summoned the Estates General in 1614.

This was the last meeting of the Estates General for 175 years, until the eve of the French Revolution, and its failings demonstrated that the monarchy was the only institution around which the nation could be united. The session revealed only the impotence of those who wished to oppose the throne, and Marie put the issue beyond doubt by declaring her son to be of age and the regency dissolved. There was now nothing left to investigate, for the Estates General could only offer advice to a king; it had no legislative powers. The remaining aristocratic dissidents were silenced by large bribes, which consumed the entire treasure left by Henry IV, and the Calvinists were partially appeased by guarantees that their status would not be changed.

For a decade after the crisis, the court lacked the energetic direction that was needed to continue the consolidation of power begun by Henry IV. But in 1624 one of Marie's favorites, Armand du Plessis de Richelieu, a churchman who rose to the cardinalate through her favor, took control of the government. For the next eighteen years, there was once more an ambitious and determined head of the central administration.

Many forces pressed on the monarchy as it concentrated its power, and it was Richelieu's great achievement that he kept them in balance. The strongest group was the bureaucracy, whose ranks had been swollen by the sale of office. Richelieu was a classic example of the great ministers of the seventeenth century in that he always paid close attention to the wishes of the bureaucrats and could then face the monarchy as the head of a vast army of indispensable royal servants. He achieved a similar balance with the nobles, whom he integrated into the regime by giving them posts as diplomats, soldiers, officials, and administrators of local regions. With prominent positions in government, the nobility was as eager as the monarch for domestic security.

But the Huguenots still stirred uneasily. Since the death of Henry IV, they had feared

For all his considerable power, his aspirations to grandeur, and his shrewd political ambitions, Cardinal Richelieu always saw himself as a churchman. In his portraits, therefore, he could never appear in the rich clothes of a king or an aristocrat. Yet in some ways his simple church robes, adorned only by a cross, make him appear even more grand and potent.
(Photo: New York Public Library/Picture Collection)

new repressions and had engaged in sporadic fighting with the monarchy. The conflict reached a new intensity in the mid-1620s, and the royal army embarked on a systematic destruction of their military power in their stronghold, the southwest, capturing their chief bastion, the port of La Rochelle, in 1628. Richelieu then imposed strict terms. All the guarantees established by the Edict of Nantes were abolished, and though the Huguenots were allowed freedom of worship, they no longer were permitted local independence, which might threaten the unity of the state.

Richelieu also hoped to reduce administrative expenses, but when money was needed for aggression abroad, the good intentions disappeared. The sale of office was allowed to break all bounds: by 1633 it accounted for approximately one-half of royal revenues. Ten years later more than three-quarters of the crown's direct taxation was needed to pay the salaries of the officeholders. It was a vicious circle, and the only solution was to increase ordinary taxes, which fell most heavily on the lower classes.

As the burden of taxation mounted, Richelieu had to improve the government's control over the realm to obtain the revenue he needed. He increased the power of the *intendants,* the government's chief agents in the localities, and established them as the principal representatives of the monarchy in each province of France—

a counterpoise to the traditionally dominant nobility. The *intendants* recruited for the army, arranged billeting, supervised the raising of taxes, and enforced the king's decrees. They soon came to be hated figures because the rising taxes were creating constant unrest.

In almost every year of the seventeenth century but with greatest intensity from the 1620s to the 1670s, there was a peasant uprising in some area of France, and the main grievance was taxation. But there were other issues too, notably a dislike for the growth of the central government. The peasants were frequently led by local notables who resented the widening powers of the monarchy because the increase in taxes and the rise of the *intendants* threatened their own jurisdiction.

Thus, when Richelieu decided to ignore domestic problems and concentrate on foreign ambitions, he took a major gamble, which almost failed in 1636: troops sent to quell a peasant uprising left a serious gap in France's eastern defenses, allowing Spanish troops to invade to within 100 miles of Paris. But disaster was avoided, the French went on to increasing military success, and when Richelieu died in 1642, it appeared that the twin ambitions of absolutism at home and preeminence abroad were close to realization.

Yet it was clear that the costs of France's foreign policy during the early seventeenth century intensified her domestic problems. Those who resented the growing power of the central government were only waiting for the right moment to reassert themselves. But the centralization was so successful that when the moment came, in a series of revolts known as the Fronde, there was no major effort to reshape the social order or to reorganize the state into a new political system. The Fronde was certainly a strident clash between opposing forces, but it took place within the traditional political and social forms. The principal expressions of discontent came from the upper levels of society: the nobles, townsmen, and members of Parlements. Only occasionally were these groups joined by peasants, who had bitter grievances against taxation and royal officials, and only for a brief while in the city of Bordeaux was there a foretaste of the sweeping revolution that was eventually to overtake France in 1789.

The Fronde

The death of Louis XIII, in 1643, followed by a regency because Louis XIV was only five years old, provided the opportunity for those who wanted to hold back the rise of absolutism. The immediate issues strikingly resembled those of Louis XIII's own minority, under the regency of Marie de Medici. Louis XIII's widow, Anne of Austria, took over the government and placed all the power in the hands of the Italian-born Cardinal Giulio Mazarin, a protégé of Richelieu's who symbolized the influence of foreigners and the Catholic Church that both nobles and parlementaires disliked. Moreover, Mazarin used his position to amass a huge fortune. He was therefore a perfect target for the expression of a deep-seated resentment: anger at the encroachment of central government on local authority.

Early in 1648 Mazarin sought to gain a respite from the monarch's perennial financial trouble by withholding payment of the salaries of some royal officials for four years. In response the members of various administrative and legal institutions in Paris, including the Parlement, drew up a charter of demands. They wanted the office of *intendant* abolished, no new offices created, power of approval over the raising of taxes, and enactment of a habeas corpus law. The last two demands reflected what the English Parliament was seeking at this very time, but the first two were long-standing French grievances, intensified by the officers' fear for their class identity and authority in the face of royal power, and by general opposition to newly created officials and taxes.

Mazarin reacted by arresting the Paris Parlement's leaders, thus sparking a popular rebellion in the city that forced him and the royal family to flee from the capital—an experience the young Louis XIV never forgot. In the spring of 1649, Mazarin promised to redress the parlementaires' grievances, and he was allowed to return to Paris. But the trouble was far from over; during that summer uprisings spread throughout France, particularly among peasants and in the old Huguenot stronghold, the southwest.

The most turbulent developments took place in the city of Bordeaux, where the parlementaires lost control and minor artisans and lawyers, furious at the taxes imposed by the crown and eager to revenge themselves on the less-burdened upper orders of society, took over the municipal government. Peasants and street mobs roamed the city, directing their hostility as much at the rich and powerful as at the representatives of the king.

From Mazarin's point of view, however, a more direct threat was posed by two generals who had turned against the government: Henri de Turenne and Louis II of Bourbon, prince of Condé, who had won a series of brilliant military victories in the 1640s and paved the way for France's gains at Westphalia in 1648. Condé was particularly dangerous because he was the head of the greatest noble family in France, and many aristocrats followed his lead. Their aims had not changed much since the days of the Guises eighty years before: they wanted Mazarin removed, their local powers restored, and a more influential position at court. Some nobles made brief alliances with the regional parlementaires, but each group wanted power for itself, and thus they soon drew apart.

Capitalizing on the disillusionment that soon resulted from the perpetual unrest, Mazarin began to reassert the position of the monarchy. Turenne was simply bought over; military force and the threat to use it subdued Paris and most of the rural rebels; Condé, losing support, fled to Spain; and the vulnerable regency was brought to an end by the declaration that Louis was of age in 1652. When Bordeaux finally fell to royal troops the next year, the Fronde was virtually over. Although peasants continued their occasional regional uprisings for many years to come, no other element in French society seriously challenged the crown as the basis for order in the realm.

Mazarin's remaining years in power, until his death in 1661, were relatively free of trouble. In foreign affairs he brought the war with Spain to a triumphant conclusion at the Treaty of the Pyrenees in 1659. At home the nobles had now been weakened as never before; the royal administration, centered on the *intendants*, faced no significant resistance; and the parlements subsided into quiescence, their demands all rejected when Louis was declared of age. This outcome was very different from the situation across the Channel in 1661, but just as surely as England, France had found a stable solution for long-standing conflicts.

Spain

For Spain the upheavals of the mid-seventeenth century were little short of disastrous. Until they erupted, she was the most powerful state in Europe; when they were over, she had lost her preeminence and was on her way to becoming a second-class power. Yet the seeds of her difficulties—primarily administrative and financial—were already visible in the sixteenth century.

Stresses in the Reign of Philip II

Philip's chief problem was the lack of unity in his diverse domains. From his father he inherited the Low Countries, Naples, Sardinia, Sicily, and Spain and her New World territories. In 1580 Portugal and her possessions also came under his control.

To hold this sprawling empire together, Philip developed an elaborate bureaucracy. But he was an obsessively suspicious man, and he therefore determined to maintain close control over the administrative structure by keeping in touch with every decision. As a result proceedings were agonizingly slow and inefficient in both important and trivial matters. The effect on military affairs was crippling; commanders in the field were often paralyzed, waiting for orders from home before taking action. Moreover the bureaucracy was run by Castilian nobles, who were resented as outsiders in other regions of the empire.

The standing army also caused the king problems. Although the military gave the throne potent support, it was the regime's single largest expense. The cost was readily undertaken since the logistic and administrative needs of the army stimulated the growth of bureaucracy and government authority. But the populace was less appreciative of these outlays, particularly when, to meet some of the expense and to emphasize the might of the crown, soldiers were lodged in the homes of ordinary citizens without recompense. This aroused bitter resentment, especially in the Low Countries, where the Spanish troops were regarded as foreigners (see pp. 481–482).

Within the Iberian peninsula, however, Philip was able to overcome the resentment by using religious belief to arouse his subjects' loyalty. Spaniards regarded their country as the bastion of Catholicism, and Philip's devoutness reflected their mood perfectly. He eradicated any sign of heresy, and his enmity toward unorthodoxy affected even the great flowering of Spanish mysticism, led by St. Teresa of Avila. Neither the king nor the ecclesiastical hierarchy could feel comfortable about the mystics because such extremes of personal faith seemed to weaken the position of the Catholic Church. Nonetheless Philip's emphasis on the nation's faith powerfully stimulated Spain's political cohesion, which was promoted rather than hindered by the military activity in behalf of the Church.

Economic Problems

In other areas, notably the economy, there was little Philip could do to relieve the strains of constant warfare. Spain was a rich country in Philip's reign, but the most profitable activities were monopolized by limited groups, often foreigners. Because royal policy valued administrative convenience above social benefit, the city of Seville was arbitrarily given control over commerce with the New World so as to simplify supervision of this enormous source of income. Other lucrative pursuits, such as wool and wine production, were dominated by a small coterie of insiders who made large profits but needed little manpower. And the pasturage rights throughout Castile that the crown granted sheep breeders removed vast areas of land from use by growers of foodstuffs. The only important economic activity whose income spread beyond a restricted circle was the prosperous Mediterranean trade. This commerce, centered in Barcelona, brought wealth to much of Aragon.

The profits made by non-Spaniards were the most obvious example of the limited domestic benefit of Spain's vast wealth. Most of the American treasure was sent abroad to repay German and Italian bankers whose loans kept Philip's troops in the field. Apart from Seville the cities that gained most from the new wealth were Genoa and Antwerp. And the Genoese mercantile community, with long experience in international finance, dominated Seville's economic life and played a crucial role in financing Philip's campaigns. Antwerp, always important as the meeting place for traders from the Mediterranean and the North, now gained prominence as the focus of Spanish activity in the Low Countries.

Thus even though the influx of silver into Spain continued to rise (it quadrupled between the 1550s and 1590s), the money was not profitably invested within the country. Drastically overextended in foreign commitments, the king declared himself bankrupt three times during his reign. His misguided policies, especially his continuing military involvements, were causing a slow economic deterioration.

IMPORTS OF TREASURE TO SPAIN
FROM THE NEW WORLD, 1601–1660

Decade	Total Value*
1601–1610	66,970,000
1611–1620	65,568,000
1621–1630	62,358,000
1631–1640	40,110,000
1641–1650	30,641,000
1651–1660	12,785,000

*In ducats

Adapted from J. H. Elliott, *Imperial Spain 1469–1716*, New York, 1964, p. 175.

Spain's futile struggles with the Dutch and later with the French proved to be the final blows in a succession of multiplying difficulties—economic, political, and military. For a while it seemed that the problems might be overcome because the second half of Philip III's reign (1598–1621), following the truce signed with the Dutch in 1609, was a time of peace. But in fact Philip's government was incompetent and corrupt, capable neither of dealing with the serious consequences of generations of excessive war spending nor of broadening the country's limited list of exports beyond wool and wine. Moreover, when the flow of treasure from the New World began to dwindle after 1600, the crown was deprived of a major source of income that it was unable to replace (see accompanying table). The decline was caused partly by a growing use of precious metals in the New World colonies but more importantly by a demographic disaster that overtook the Indians who worked as laborers and miners. Disease, overwork, and a drastic fall in the birth rate reduced their numbers with incredible speed. In Mexico and northern Guatemala alone, there had been approximately 25 million natives when the Spaniards first arrived in 1519. By the 1650s there were only 1.5 million.

In the meantime tax returns at home were shrinking, and at best they never covered expenses. The most significant factor in this decrease was a drop in the population of Castile and Aragon from 10 million in 1600 to 6 million in 1700. No other country in Europe suffered a demographic reversal of this proportion during the seventeenth century. In addition, though the wine and wool industries continued to prosper, their spectacular growth had come to a halt by the early seventeenth century, and no other important industries took their place. Worse still, Spain had to rely increasingly on the importation of expensive foodstuffs to feed her people.

It was under these conditions that Spain resumed large-scale fighting under Philip IV (1621–1665), first reopening hostilities against the Dutch in 1621 and then starting an escalating involvement in the Thirty Years' War. With her dwindling resources the burdens now became too much to bear. Through the 1620s a brilliant general, Ambrogio di Spinola, maintained the Spaniards' tradition of military victory, but his death, in 1630, removed their last able commander. The effort to continue the government's commitment to war during the subsequent decades in defiance of totally inadequate financial means was finally to bring the greatest state in Europe to its knees.

Revolt and Secession

The final crisis was brought about by the policies of Philip IV's chief minister, the Count of Olivares. His aim was to unite the kingdom, to "Castilianize" Spain. He wanted all the territories to bear equally the burden of maintaining their country's dominant position in the world. Laws would be uniform, expenses would be apportioned equitably among the provinces, and each province would receive its fair share of the nation's gains. Although Castile would no longer dominate, she would also not have to provide the bulk of the taxes and army.

Olivares' program was called the Union of Arms, and though it seemed eminently reasonable, its implementation caused a series of revolts in the 1640s that split Spain apart. The reason was quite simple. For more than a century, Castile had controlled the other provinces, which had felt increasingly that local independence was being undermined by a centralized regime. The Union of Arms was regarded as the last straw because it added new substance to this long-standing grievance. Moreover Olivares undertook his plan at a time when Spain's military and economic fortunes were noticeably in decline. France had declared war on the Hapsburgs in 1635, and thereafter Spain's position had deteriorated. The funds to support an army were becoming harder to raise, and in desperation Olivares pressed more vigorously for the Union of Arms. But all he accomplished was to provoke crippling revolts against the Castilians in Catalonia, Portugal, Naples, and Sicily.

The precipitant was France's invasion of Catalonia in 1639. Thinking that the Catalans would not refuse to share some of the effort of repelling the invaders from their own territory, Olivares ordered the troops fighting the French to be billeted in Catalonia. But instead of strengthening the government, the order provided the people with the issue that finally goaded them into open defiance in 1640.

Olivares tried to meet the revolt by asking the Portuguese to help subdue the Catalans, but this attempt to bind together the components of the Spanish Empire only aroused further defiance. By the next year both Catalonia and Portugal declared themselves independent republics and placed themselves under French protection. Plots began to appear against Olivares, and Philip dismissed the one minister who had understood Spain's problems but who, in trying to solve them, had made them worse.

The Catalonian rebellion continued for another eleven years, and it was thwarted in the end only because the peasants and town mobs transformed the resistance to the central government into an attack on the privileged and wealthy classes in the province. At this point the Catalan nobility abandoned the cause and joined the government side. About the same time the Fronde forced the withdrawal of French troops. Thus when the last major holdout, Barcelona, fell to a royal army in 1652, the Catalan nobles returned with their rights and privileges guaranteed, and the revolt was over.

The Portuguese, on the other hand, though not officially granted independence from Spain until 1668, were fully capable of defending their autonomy and even invaded Castile in the 1640s. Their revolt against the central government never became tinged with the social unrest that undermined the Catalans' unity. Portugal's nobles maintained their authority throughout the struggle and dominated the government thereafter.

The revolts in Sicily and Naples, aimed at the Castilians who ruled and taxed both provinces, took place in 1647. In Naples the unrest soon developed into a tremendous mob uprising, led by a local fisherman. The poor turned against all the representatives of government and wealth they could find, and chaos ensued until their leader was killed. The violence in Sicily by contrast was more exclusively the result of soaring taxes and was directed almost entirely against government representatives. Severe countermeasures were taken in both Naples and Sicily, and within a few months the government regained control.

Spain had experienced a period of great cultural brilliance during Philip IV's reign, but even this died away as grim times descended on the country. Overextension in foreign war, financial and economic shortcomings at home, and the excessive reliance on Castile had all helped sap the nation's strength. The revolts during the 1640s were the result of decades of growing resentment at the monarch's inability to solve these basic, pressing problems; but the domestic unrest finally brought Spain's international ambitions and thus the worst of her difficulties to an end. Like England and France, she found a new way of life in the 1660s. She was to be a stable, second-level state, heavily agricultural, and run by her nobility.

The United Provinces

Although the United Provinces remained locked in a struggle for survival against Spain until 1648, and in various ways became a unique state, the Dutch did not escape the domestic tensions of the seventeenth century. Despite the remarkable fluidity of their society, they too went through a period of confrontation in the mid-seventeenth century that determined the structure of their government for over a century.

The Structure of the United Provinces

The United Provinces became a unique state for a number of reasons. Other republics existed in Europe, but they were controlled by small oligarchies; the Dutch, who had a long tradition of a strong representative assembly, the estates, created a nation in which many citizens participated in their own government through elected delegates. Although powerful merchants and a few aristocrats close to the House of Orange did create a small elite, the ordinary citizenry, participating in politics and united by a common cause, reduced the social differentiation prevalent elsewhere in Europe. The resultant openness and homogeneity colored the two most remarkable features of the United Provinces: economic mastery and cultural brilliance.

The most striking accomplishment of the Dutch was their rise to supremacy in the world of commerce. Amsterdam displaced Antwerp (and Genoa) as the Continent's financial capital and gained control of the trade of the world's richest markets. And in 1609 the Bank of Amsterdam was established, the first semiofficial financial institution of its kind in modern history; it made a vital contribution to the country's economy by offering the lowest interest rates in Europe. This encouraged native industries, such as shipbuilding, as well as overseas ventures, such as the East India Company, which needed substantial investments. In addition, the Dutch rapidly emerged as the cheapest shippers in international trade. As a result, by the middle of the seventeenth century they had become the chief carriers of European trade.

The openness of Dutch society permitted the freest exchange of ideas of the time. An official church, the Reformed Church, was established, but no religious groups were forbidden as long as they worshiped in private. The new state therefore gave refuge to dissenters of all kinds, whether extreme Protestant radicals or Catholics who wore their faith lightly, and the city of Amsterdam became the center of a brilliant Jewish community. This freedom attracted some of the greatest minds in Europe, and fostered remarkable artistic creativity. Patrons were easy to find among the wealthy merchants, and Dutch painting in the seventeenth century is one of the glories of Western culture (see pp. 545–548 and Plates 39–41). Yet it was not the result of the taste or sensibility of a few patrons and geniuses but an outpouring from many directions; and it was not the climax of a long tradition but a sudden outburst whose greatest expressions appeared in the first generation. The energy that produced the

The Dutch became the best shipbuilders in Europe in the seventeenth century; the efficiency of their ships, which could be manned by fewer sailors than those of other countries, was a major reason for their successes in trade and commerce.
(Photo: The Granger Collection)

wealth and creativity reflected the pride of a tiny nation that was winning its independence.

Domestic Tensions

From the earliest days of the revolt against Spain, there had been a basic split within the United Provinces. The two provinces of Holland and Zeeland dominated the Estates General because they supplied a majority of its taxes. Their representatives formed a mercantile party, which advocated peace abroad so that their trade could flourish unhampered, government by the Estates General so that they could make their power felt, and religious toleration. In opposition to the mercantile interest was a party centered on the House of Orange, which sought to boost that family's leadership of the Dutch. This party stood for war to strengthen a popular national leader, centralized power for the House of Orange, and (after William died) strict religious orthodoxy.

The differences between the two factions came to a head in 1618, when Maurice of Nassau used the religious issue as a pretext for executing his chief opponent, Jan van Oldenbarneveldt, the principal representative of the province of Holland. Oldenbarneveldt opposed the resumption of war with Spain when the truce of 1609 expired in 1621, and his removal left Maurice in full control of the country. The mercantile party had been defeated, and war could resume in 1621.

For more than twenty years, the House of Orange remained in command, unassailable because it led the army in time of war. Not until 1648, when the family was headed by a new leader, William II, could its opponents reassert themselves and sign the treaty of Westphalia that officially recognized the independence of the United Provinces. It then seemed that the mercantile party had gained the upper hand. But the outcome remained in the balance (there was even the threat of a siege of Amsterdam by troops loyal to the House of Orange) until William II suddenly died in 1650, leaving as his successor a posthumously born son, William III.

With serious opposition removed, the mercantile interest could now assume full power, and Jan De Witt, the representative of the province of Holland, took over the running of the government in 1653. De Witt's aims were to leave as much authority as possible in the hands of the provinces, particularly Holland; to weaken the executive in this way and prevent a revival of the fortunes of the House of Orange; to pursue trading advantage; and to maintain peace so that the economic supremacy of the Dutch would not be endangered. For more than a decade, he guided the country in its golden age. But in 1672 French armies overran the southern provinces, and De Witt, with his mercantile inclinations, lacked the military instinct to fight a dangerous enemy. The Dutch at once turned to the family that had led them to independence; a mob murdered De Witt; and the House of Orange, under William III, resumed the centralization that henceforth was to characterize the political structure of the United Provinces. The country had not experienced a mid-century upheaval as severe as those of its neighbors, but it had nevertheless been forced to endure unrest and violence before the form of its government was securely established.

Sweden

The Swedes, too, reached basic decisions in the mid-seventeenth century about political relations in the administration of the state. Violence was avoided, but tensions had to be resolved nonetheless.

The Achievement of Gustavus Adolphus

In the early 1600s Sweden, a Lutheran country of a million people which had gained its independence from Denmark less than a century earlier, was one of the backwaters of Europe. A feudal nobility dominated the countryside and sought to control the government, a barter economy made money almost unknown, and both trade and towns were virtually nonexistent. Moreover the Swedes found themselves in a running battle with the Danes, whose well-organized, well-armed, and prosperous monarchy dominated the Baltic Sea. Sweden, by contrast, lacked a capital, central institutions, and government machinery. The task of ruling was thus entirely dependent on the king and a few courtiers; officials were appointed only to deal with specific problems as they arose.

Gustavus Adolphus (1611–1632) transformed this situation. At the start of his reign, he faced a war that was to involve all the states in the area—his own, Denmark, Poland, and Russia—in a struggle to control the lands around the Baltic. Without his nobles' help, however, Gustavus could not raise an army. He therefore arranged an alliance with the nobles and gave them dominant positions in a newly organized bureaucracy. By winning their support he not only staffed an administrative machine but organized an army, thus equipping himself both to govern and to fight.

During the two decades of his reign, Gustavus engaged in a remarkable series of conquests abroad. By 1629 he controlled the coastline of the eastern Baltic, making Sweden the most powerful state in the area. He then entered the Thirty Years' War, advancing victoriously through the Holy Roman Empire until his death, in 1632, during the showdown battle with Wallenstein (see pp. 485–487). Although without their general the Swedes could do little more than hang on to the gains they had made, they remained for a century a force to be reckoned with in international affairs.

The system of government that Gustavus and his chief adviser, Axel Oxenstierna, established in 1611 was to be the envy of other countries until the twentieth century. At the heart of the system were five administrative departments,[5] each led by a nobleman, with the most important—the Chancellery—run by Oxenstierna, who supervised diplomacy and internal affairs. Gradually an administrative center emerged in Stockholm where, under Oxenstierna's capable leadership, the bureaucracy proved that it could run the nation, supply the army, and implement policy even during the last twelve years of Gustavus' reign, when the king himself was almost always abroad. During his absence Oxenstierna took charge, though executive power was officially vested in the Rad, an assembly of nobles.

Another major institution, the Riksdag, consisted of representatives of four estates: the nobility, the clergy, the townsmen, and (unique in Europe) the peasants. Although officially it was the highest legislative authority in the land, real power was retained by the nobles and the crown. For centuries the Riksdag functioned as no more than a sounding board that gave the appearance of popular approval to royal and aristocratic rule, which by the 1630s was already operating with an efficiency unparalleled on the Continent.

A major cause of Sweden's amazing rise was the development of the domestic economy. Early in Gustavus' reign new discoveries made possible the mining of huge deposits of copper, an important metal for cannon and coin manufacture. With the only other major source of copper being Japan, a Continental monopoly was assured. The crown maximized its profits by taking over the mining itself. To avoid dependence on one commodity, the government also encouraged iron mining. Foreign experts were brought in, and the discovery of a new smelting process made Swedish iron highly prized. At the same time, the country's traditional tar and timber exports were stepped up, and a fleet was built. By 1700 Stockholm had become an important trading and financial center, growing in the course of the century from fewer than 5,000 to more than 50,000 inhabitants—a phenomenal rise and further evidence of the general northward shift of European economic activity.

The Role of the Nobles

The one source of tension amidst this remarkable progress was the position of the aristocracy. They had been Gustavus' partners and after he died they tightened their control over the government and society.

Between 1611 and 1652 nobles more than doubled the proportion of land they owned in Sweden, and increased sixfold their holdings in Finland, which Sweden ruled. Much of this growth was at the expense of the crown, which granted away or sold its lands to help its war efforts abroad. Both peasants and townspeople viewed these developments with alarm. Peasants always fared much worse under nobles than as direct tenants of the king because the

---

[5] They were the Chancellery, the Ministry of Justice, the Treasury, the Department of War, and the Department of the Navy.

great landowners sought the maximum possible return from their possessions. And the towns felt that their place in national affairs was being destroyed by an excessively powerful aristocracy. Both groups were frightened when the Danish nobles took advantage of the death of their country's strong king, in 1648, to gain control of government.[6] Two years later the showdown came in Sweden.

The ruler of Sweden was Gustavus' daughter Christina, an able but erratic young queen who usually allowed Oxenstierna to run the government. In the late 1640s she was becoming increasingly hopeful that she could abdicate her throne, become a Catholic, and leave Sweden—an ambition she fulfilled in 1654. She wanted her cousin Charles recognized as her successor, but the aristocracy threatened to create a nobles' republic if she abdicated. The queen therefore summoned the Riksdag, Sweden's representative assembly, in 1650, and taking advantage of the grievances of townspeople and peasants, she encouraged the three lower estates to mount a campaign against the aristocracy. Believing that they might now gain a new importance in national affairs, the townspeople and peasants demanded the return of nobles' lands to the crown, freedom of speech, and real power in the Riksdag so that the lower estates could outvote the nobles. Under this pressure the nobility gave way and recognized the future Charles X Gustavus as successor to the throne—a good choice, because Charles was an able soldier who consolidated Gustavus Adolphus' gains and confirmed Sweden's mastery of northern Europe.

But the confrontation of 1650 proved to be short-lived. Once Christina had won the argument over her successor, she removed her support from the Riksdag and rejected the demands of the lower estates. Only gradually did power shift away from the great nobles toward a broader elite of lesser nobles and bureaucrats (see pp. 586–587).

Eastern Europe

The major powers of eastern Europe, the Ottoman Empire, Poland, and Russia, were as affected by warfare as their western neighbors. And in Poland and Russia there were also upheavals in the mid-seventeenth century that helped determine these states' future political development.

The Ottoman Empire

In the Ottoman Empire central control was highly effective by the early 1500s. The first signs of a decline of strength at the center began to appear after the death of Suleiman, in 1566. Harem intrigues, corruption at court, and the loosening of military discipline became increasingly serious from the late sixteenth century onward. Yet the Ottomans remained an object of fear and hostility throughout the West—their constant wars with the Hapsburgs devastated Hungary, where most of the fighting took place, and in the eastern Mediterranean they remained a formidable force, though the English and Dutch were coming to play a dominant role in the area after 1600.

The Turkish rulers had unparalleled powers. A crack army of more than 25,000 men stood ready to serve the sultan at all times, and within his domains his supremacy was unquestioned. He was both spiritual and temporal head of his empire, completely free to appoint all officers, issue laws, and raise taxes. But these powers, geared to military conquest and extending over enormous territories, never became a focus of cohesion among the disparate races of the Balkans and the Middle East who were ruled from Constantinople, because the sultan left authority in the hands of local nobles

---

[6] In 1660 the Danish king engineered a countercoup that firmly established absolutism in that country. Denmark was thus yet another state whose political structure was settled for a long time to come during this period.

and princes as long as his ultimate sovereignty was recognized. Whenever questions of loyalty arose (as they did sporadically in the Balkans), they revealed that the authority of the central government rested on its military might. That was more than enough, though, to prevent any serious challenges to the power of the Ottomans until they began to lose ground to the Hapsburgs in the eighteenth century.

Poland

The largest kingdom in Europe, Poland, was as disorganized as the Holy Roman Empire. The king could exercise control over his personal lands but elsewhere the country was entirely in the hands of powerful nobles, who from 1572 onward confirmed their independence by ensuring that the monarchy would be strictly elective. The Diet, an assembly of nobles, was required to meet at least once every two years, and without the approval of this body no policy could be enforced.

In Poland as elsewhere, religion was a major issue during the second half of the sixteenth century. Sigismund III (1587–1632), with the help of some members of the aristocracy and the Jesuits, crushed Protestantism. But not all the nobles favored Roman Catholicism; some belonged to the Greek Orthodox Church. Attempts were made to unite the Roman Catholics with the Greek Orthodox, and one group, known as the Uniate Church, agreed to acknowledge papal supremacy while retaining traditional Greek rites. When the Jesuits tried to increase their influence, however, the adherents of the Orthodox and Uniate churches formed a coalition for common defense that split the country into two religious camps.

Although Poland was constantly at war, Sigismund and his successors were never able to use the military situation to overcome the fragmentation of political authority and create a strong central government. Instead, the religious divisions and the power of local nobles became increasingly serious problems until, in the mid-seventeenth century, the Poles, like so many Europeans, faced a major internal clash.

The crisis arose in the Ukraine, the borderland in the southeast of Poland that had long been occupied by the soldier-farmers known as Cossacks. Like their Russian counterparts, these Cossacks were allowed considerable independence because of their importance in protecting the countryside against turbulent neighbors to the south and east. Firm adherents of the Greek Orthodox Church, they became increasingly annoyed at the government for encouraging Catholicism. Finally in 1648 they rebelled, took control of the eastern Ukraine, and in 1654 offered their allegiance to the Greek Orthodox tsar of Russia.

The Polish monarchy was much too weak to combat the revolt, and the nobility had little wish to undertake a long assault on this frontier region. Thus the Ukraine was lost—yet another casualty of the upheavals of the age—though internally Poland continued much as before, a country dominated by a small yet powerful aristocracy. Once again, the storms that swept political life had been succeeded by a sense of settlement.

Russia

The power of the central authority in Russia was already apparent in the reign of Ivan IV (1547–1584)—called the Terrible—who used his considerable military strength both at home and in conquests that extended Muscovite rule along the length of the Volga River to the southeast.

Ivan's autocracy was hampered by fewer limitations than any other ruler in Europe. Russia was still feudal; her peasants were serfs, and her great lords, known as boyars, controlled local areas but had little say in national affairs. Jealous of their regional powers, Ivan launched a vicious campaign against the boyars and enormously increased the areas of Russia under his

The most violent and feared of the tsars until his death, Ivan IV was even nicknamed "The Terrible." Yet his portrait gives little hint of his reputation. Instead, it draws on the great tradition of the Russian icon—a flat, formal, and idealized depiction—to create an impression of solemn piety.
(Photo: Nationalmuseum, Copenhagen)

direct control. He enlarged his bureaucracy to meet the new administrative tasks created by his conquests, but the authority of the central government was now a divisive rather than a unifying force, discredited and hated because it had grown by military might.

The reaction came after Ivan's death, when the country entered a thirty-year period that would later be called the Time of Troubles. Ivan's son Feodor, the last of the Rurik dynasty, which had ruled since the ninth century, lacked his father's vigor and could not prevent the boyars from reasserting their power. From 1591 onward he virtually handed over control of the government to his brother-in-law, Boris Godunov, whom the boyars regarded as an upstart. When Feodor died in 1598 Boris became tsar and major revolts soon broke out.

For fifteen years the country was in chaos as peasants, townsmen, and petty nobles joined in various coalitions against the government and the boyars. The final confrontation took place when the leading boyars supported a Polish claimant to the throne, and a popular army, led by townsmen and lesser nobles who had been excluded from political prominence by the higher nobility, drove the Polish claimant from Moscow. In his place a national assembly, consisting of nobles and townsmen, elected as tsar a grandnephew of Ivan the Terrible, Mikhail Feodorovich (1613–1645), founder of the Romanov dynasty.

The central government emerged from these disruptions with its powers essentially unimpaired. The boyars had been unable to weaken the tsar's ability to take firm military measures against his opponents, and under Mikhail they returned to docile inaction. They now depended on the throne for their control over local areas, and many had to serve the tsar in order to retain their estates. During the half-century after the Time of Troubles, the monarchy organized its administration systematically, codified Russia's laws, and continued the extension of its authority by the use or threat of armed force.

But the potential for domestic upheaval was not entirely removed, and indeed it was during this half-century that the groundwork was laid for new turmoil as the boyars gradually closed the last loopholes in the system of serfdom. Previously an escaped serf who remained uncaptured for a certain number of years was automatically liberated, but in 1646 the boyars persuaded Tsar Alexis (1645–1676) to abolish the limit. Now a serf remained in his status for life—a hopeless fugitive even if he did escape his master.

The result was constant agrarian unrest, met by harsh repression, which inspired even more violent uprisings. The disturbances were fed by increasing financial demands on both serfs and townspeople from the central government and local lords, and in 1648 the boiling point was reached. A major riot broke out in Moscow, the tsar was forced to hand over to the rebels a number of his financial administrators, and by the end of the year almost every large city in Russia had experienced serious disorders, quelled only by the intervention of royal troops. This year of upheaval, as fierce in Russia as in England and France, marked the beginning of a period of more than two decades when the lower classes made a major effort, for the last time in centuries, to restrain the growing power of the central government and the landowners.

The popular discontent intensified in the 1650s and 1660s, and finally in 1668 the major revolt that had long been brewing exploded in the southern provinces of Russia, led by a Cossack, Stenka Razin, who terrorized the area and launched a fleet that caused chaos on the Caspian Sea. In 1670 Razin led two expeditions up the Volga River, capturing a succession of towns and handing them over to mob rule. His very approach incited peasants to violence, for his troops included thousands of escaped serfs who hoped to bring liberty to all their oppressed brethren. There was open advocacy of what amounted to class war: the poor against the rich, the weak against the powerful. Eventually royal troops shattered the poorly equipped army; and though a number of marauding bands continued to harass the inhabitants of central Russia for years, the major threat was ended in 1671, when Razin was executed in Moscow.

Compounding Russia's troubles was serious dissension within the national Greek Orthodox Church. The dispute arose over the decision of the patriarch of Moscow, the head of the Russian Church, to correct the traditional liturgical books of the faith, which contained errors introduced by copyists over the centuries. A group calling itself the Old Believers, refusing to change usages hallowed by custom, objected to the revision and broke away from the established church. The schism was accompanied by violence, which forced the patriarch and his followers to become entirely dependent on the secular power to maintain their authority. This reliance on the state undermined the clergy's spiritual leadership and helped the monarchy on its way to assuming complete control over all facets of Russian society.

Having overcome two potential threats to his authority—peasant unrest in areas far from Moscow and the rivalry within the church—Alexis began to feel strong enough in his last years to pay less heed to the boyars. It was clear that a determined ruler could once again make the tsar the dominant figure in Russian society, and in the late seventeenth century Peter the Great was to be that ruler.

Throughout Europe in the mid-seventeenth century long-standing tensions that had just passed through an especially virulent phase were resolved, and a period of relative stability began that was to last for over a century. In international affairs a vicious circle of brutality was broken as a degree of restraint was imposed on the anarchy of warfare. Within Europe's states, the resistance to central governments, usually the result of regional loyalties, traditional aristocratic independence, or resentment at soaring taxes, was effectively brought to an end. Whatever the outcomes—and they ranged from England's parliamentary system to France's absolutism—each country's political situation now settled into accepted forms, just as warmaking and diplomacy did after Westphalia.

Because the disturbances had been so widespread, historians have called the mid-seventeenth century an age of "general crisis." It is a rather vague term, but it does convey the flavor of a period when upheaval was common, reached crisis proportions, and then subsided into relaxation. To the extent that the crisis was general, however, one would expect it to be reflected not merely in politics but in thought, art, and society. And indeed, the mid-seventeenth century was the time when, for example, the ideas of the scientific revolution became, after much doubt, an essential part of European civilization. One must not push the connections too far, because simple parallels distort the complexities of the period; nevertheless, the progression from turbulence to calm in politics was not without its analogies in the cultural and social developments of the sixteenth and seventeenth centuries.

RECOMMENDED READING

Sources

*Franklin, Julian H. (tr. and ed.). *Constitutionalism and Resistance in the Sixteenth Century: Three Treatises by Hotman, Beza, & Mornay.* 1969. Three of the most radical tracts of the period, each justifying rebellion.

Studies

*Aston, Trevor (ed.). *Crisis in Europe 1560–1660: Essays from Past and Present.* 1965. This is a collection of those essays in which the "general crisis" interpretation was initially put forward and discussed.

Elliott, John H. *The Revolt of the Catalans.* 1963. The standard history of the growing troubles of the Spanish monarchy in the seventeenth century.

*Forster, Robert, and Jack P. Greene (eds.). *Preconditions of Revolution in Early Modern Europe.* 1972. An excellent series of essays on resistance to central governments, and its causes, in a number of European countries.

Hellie, Richard. *Enserfment and Military Change in Muscovy.* 1971. This study shows the links between military affairs and social change in Russia during the early modern period.

Howell, Roger. *Cromwell.* 1977. The clearest and most reliable short biography of the revolutionary leader.

Koenigsberger, H. G. *Estates and Revolutions: Essays in Early Modern European History.* A most useful set of articles, primarily on political history; of particular interest is a fascinating comparison of the revolutionary parties in France and the Netherlands.

*Mattingly, Garrett. *The Armada.* 1959. This beautifully written book, which was a best seller when it first appeared, is a gripping account of a major international crisis.

Moote, A. Lloyd. *The Revolt of the Judges: The Parlement of Paris and the Fronde 1643–1652.* 1971. This is the most detailed account of the causes of the Fronde and its failures.

*Neale, J. E. *Queen Elizabeth I: A Biography.* 1934. A lucid and affectionate account of the reign by its most distinguished twentieth-century historian.

*Pagès, Georges. *The Thirty Years' War: 1618–1648.* 1971. The most straightforward history of a highly complex period.

*Parker, Geoffrey. *Europe in Crisis 1598–1648*. 1979. A good recent survey of the period with an up-to-date bibliography.

*———. *The Dutch Revolt*. 1977. This brief book gives a good introduction to the revolt of the Netherlands and the nature of Dutch society in the seventeenth century.

Pierson, Peter. *Philip II of Spain*. 1975. A clear and lively biography of the dominant figure of the second half of the sixteenth century.

*Rabb, Theodore K. *The Struggle for Stability in Early Modern Europe*. 1975. An assessment of the "crisis" interpretation, including extensive bibliographic references.

Roberts, Michael. *Gustavus Adolphus and the Rise of Sweden*. 1973. This is the best biography of the Swedish king, emphasizing especially his military and administrative achievements.

*Salmon, J. H. M. *The French Wars of Religion: How Important Were Religious Factors?* 1967. A collection of interpretations of the causes and nature of the civil wars.

*Shaw, Howard. *The Levellers*. 1968. This brief introduction to the ideas and activities of the most famous radical group in the English revolution is accompanied by extracts from their writings.

Stone, Lawrence. *The Causes of the English Revolution, 1529–1642*. 1972. A short but comprehensive assessment of the reasons for the outbreak of the seventeenth century's most far-reaching revolution.

Tapié, V. L. *France in the Age of Louis XIII and Richelieu*. D. McN. Lockie (tr. and ed.). 1974. The standard history of the twenty-year period when the basic development of French absolutism took place.

---

* Available in paperback.

16

CULTURE AND SOCIETY IN THE AGE OF THE SCIENTIFIC REVOLUTION 1540–1660

The sense of upheaval and then crisis followed by a settling down that dominated European politics and international relations from the mid-sixteenth to the mid-seventeenth century is also visible in other areas of life. Indeed it is remarkable how well cultural and social patterns reflect the progression from uncertainty to stable resolution. Here, too, the doubts of more than a century, from the days of the Reformation, the discovery of new worlds, and the beginnings of the scientific revolution, were gradually overcome.

Not only the clearest but also the most important development along these lines was the scientific revolution. Starting with tentative and disturbing questions about the theories of ancient authorities, whose views had been accepted for centuries, scientists eventually created a completely new way of looking at nature and a new way of thinking and arguing about physical problems. Their successes were remarkable, and they became very influential, because the certainty and orderliness of their results appealed to a Europe that was seeking relief from uncertainty.

The central event in the confrontation between the old and the new was the trial and condemnation by the Roman Inquisition of one of the greatest of the seventeenth-century scientists, Galileo. But in the next generation the ideas he represented triumphed, as part of a renewed sense of settlement that descended on European society. Stability was visible throughout intellectual life: in literature as well as in art, in painting as well as in poetry. Where the Mannerist painters and the writers of the late sixteenth century emphasized doubts, upheaval, and insecurity, their successors in the Baroque period gave themselves up to enormous ambitions, but the artists after the mid-seventeenth century increasingly stressed calm, restraint, and order. It was the exact equivalent to the resolution of tension one could see elsewhere in society.

Although for ordinary men and women these high intellectual movements had little meaning, their lives were changed in a similar direction as central governments gained considerable control over them, severely reducing the restlessness and rebelliousness that had been prevalent since the early sixteenth century. Even the inhabitants of country villages found that they were no longer as isolated and self-contained as they had once been. One of the most obvious symptoms of their unease, the tremendous outburst of witchcraft during this period, was curbed from above. And when religion no longer caused disruptions throughout Europe, the common people lost a major occasion for self-expression and violence. In general, with the powers of repression growing and their traditional local independence—and their wages—declining, ordinary people took an unavoidable part in the universal quieting down that characterized Western society in the late seventeenth century.

I. THE SCIENTIFIC REVOLUTION

To contemporaries the wars and crises of the sixteenth and seventeenth centuries seemed to dominate their lives. To us it is clear that European civilization was affected no less deeply in this period by the quiet revolution in ideas about nature that was accomplished by a handful of scholars and experimenters, known at the time as natural philosophers, but to us as scientists.

Origins of the Scientific Revolution

The study of nature by Europeans took its point of departure from the ancient Greeks whose interests shaped subsequent work until the sixteenth century—Aristotle in physics, Ptolemy in astronomy, and Galen in medicine. The most dramatic advances during the scientific revolution came in the fields the Greeks had pioneered, and were to some extent caused by increasing evidence that their theories required highly complicated and perplexing adjustments in order to cover all the facts. For instance, Aristotle's belief that all objects in their natural state are at rest created a number of problems, such as explaining why an arrow kept on flying after leaving a bow; while grappling with this question, some fourteenth-century scientists came up with a new explanation, the belief that a moving body possessed impetus, which kept the motion going until it died out. Similarly, observations revealed that Ptolemy's picture of the heavens, in which all motion was circular around a central earth, could not account easily for the peculiar motion of some planets, which at times seemed to be moving backward. Moreover, Galen's theories, often based on mistaken anatomical information, were shown by dissections to be inadequate.

Still, it is not likely philosophers would have abandoned their cherished theories—they far preferred making adjustments than beginning anew—if it had not been for various other influences at work in the fifteenth and sixteenth centuries. First was the humanists' rediscovery of the work of a number of ancient scientists, which showed that Classical writers themselves had not all agreed with the theories of Aristotle or Ptolemy. One particularly important rediscovery was Archimedes, whose studies of dynamics were an important inspiration for new ideas in physics. A second influence was an increasing interest in what we now dismiss as "magic," but which at the time was regarded as a serious intellectual enterprise. There were various sides to magical inquiry. Alchemy was the belief that by mixing substances and using secret formulae the nature of matter could be understood. A related interest was the theory of atomism, the idea that all matter was made up of tiny particles, whose composition could be changed—again a theory newly recovered from ancient writers. One of the most famous sixteenth-century alchemists, Paracelsus, was also a proponent of new medical theories, notably the belief that diseases were separate entities with lives of their own. Another favorite study was astrology, which claimed that natural phenomena became understandable and predictable if planetary movements were properly interpreted. A similar easy key to the mysteries of nature was promised by Hermeticism, a school of thought that asserted that all of knowledge had once been given to man, that it was contained in some obscure writings, and that with the right approach and intelligence, a complete insight into the structure of the universe could be achieved.

What linked all this magic was the conviction that the world could be understood and that the answers to traditional questions consisted of simple, comprehensive keys to nature. The theories of Neoplatonism, which became very influential during the Renaissance, supported this conviction, as did some of the mystical beliefs that attracted attention in the fifteenth and sixteenth centuries. One of the latter, derived from a system of Jewish thought known as cabala, suggested that the key to the universe might consist of magical arrangements of numbers. For all its irrational elements, it was precisely this longing for new, simple solutions to ancient problems that made natural philosophers capable, for the first time, of discarding the honored theories they had inherited from antiquity, trying different ones, paying greater attention to mathematics, and eventually creating an intellectual revolution.

Two other influences deserve mention. The first was Europe's long fascination with technological invention. The architects, navigators, engineers, and weapons experts of the Renaissance were important pioneers of the belief in measurement and careful observation. For example, at the Arsenal in Venice, where huge cannon were moved and devices invented for handling great weights, Galileo got ideas and made experiments that helped his study of dynamics. A related interest was followed by the anatomists at the nearby university of Padua who created a school famous for its work in dissections and its direct investigations of nature; many of the leading figures of the scientific revolution received their training in methods of experiment and observation at Padua. It was not too surprising, therefore, that the period of the scientific revolution was marked by the invention of important new instruments which often made the discoveries possible: the telescope, the thermometer, the barometer, the vacuum pump, and the microscope. These instruments encouraged the development of a scientific approach that was entirely new in the seventeenth century—it did not go back to the ancients, to the practitioners of magic, or to the engineers. It was pioneered by Francis Bacon and consisted of the belief that in order to make Nature reveal her secrets, she had to be made to do things she did not do normally: in Bacon's phrase, one had to "twist the lion's tail."

What this meant was that one did not simply observe phenomena that occurred normally in nature—for instance, the apparent bending of a stick when placed in a glass of water—but created conditions that were *not* normal. With the telescope one could perceive secrets hidden to the naked eye; with the vacuum pump one could begin to understand the properties of air.

The influences that combined to create the scientific revolution varied greatly. Yet there is no doubt that the heart of the change lay in purely intellectual breakthroughs. A small group of brilliant men, grappling with ancient problems of physics, astronomy, and anatomy—motion, heavenly phenomena, and the structure of the body—came up with persuasive discoveries that changed Western thought forever.

The First Breakthroughs

The earliest advances were in astronomy and anatomy. By coincidence, both were contained in books published in 1543, which was also the year when the first printed edition of Archimedes appeared. *The Structure of the Human Body,* by Andreas Vesalius, a member of the Padua faculty, pointed out errors in the work of Galen, the chief medical authority for over a thousand years. Although Vesalius himself did not always follow strictly the findings of dissections—like Galen, he showed the liver as having five lobes, which is true of some animals but not of humans, though in a corner of the picture he also showed a small two-lobed liver, perhaps to indicate that he knew what the human one really looked like—he opened a new era of careful observation and experimentation in studies of the body.

On the Revolutions of the Heavenly Bodies, by Nicolaus Copernicus, a Polish cleric who had studied at Padua, had far greater consequences. A first-rate mathematician, he felt that the calculations of planetary movements under Pto-

An engraving of Copernicus' conception of the universe shows the sun rather than the earth at the center, the spheres to which planets were attached, and the moons of Jupiter discovered by Galileo.
(Photo: British Museum)

lemy's system had grown too complex. In Ptolemaic astronomy, the planets and the sun, attached to transparent, crystalline spheres, revolved around the earth. All motion was circular, and observed irregularities were accounted for by epicycles—movement around small spheres that were attached to the larger spheres and which themselves revolved. Much influenced by Neoplatonic and related ideas, Copernicus believed that a simpler picture would reflect more accurately the true structure of the universe. In good Neoplatonic fashion, he argued that the sun, as the most splendid of celestial bodies, ought rightfully to be at the center of an orderly and harmonious universe.

Copernicus' system was in fact no simpler than Ptolemy's—the spheres and epicycles were just as complex—and he had no way of proving that his theory was correct. But he was such a fine mathematician that his successors had to use his calculations even if they rejected his assumptions. He thus became part of intellectual discussion, drawn upon when Pope Gregory XIII decided to reform the calendar in 1582. The Julian calendar, in use since Roman times, counted century years as leap years, thus adding extra days which caused Easter—whose date is determined by the position of the sun—to drift further and further away from its normal occurrence in late March. The reform produced the Gregorian calendar, which we still use—ten days were simply dropped, and since then three out of every four century years have not been leap years (1900 had no February 29, but 2000 will have one). The need for calendar reform had been one of the motives for Copernicus' studies, which proved useful even though his theories remained controversial.

What developed during the half-century following the publication of his *Revolutions* was a growing sense of uncertainty. The greatest astronomer of the period, Tycho Brahe, made the most remarkable observations of the heavens before the telescope, plotting the paths of the moon and planets every night for decades. But the only theory he could come up with was an uneasy compromise between the Ptolemaic and Copernican systems. It was a disciple of his, the German Johannes Kepler, who

Kepler, surrounded by the instruments of the astrologer and the astronomer, discussing his work with his patron, the emperor Rudolf II.
(Photo: New York Public Library/Picture Collection)

made the first major advance on the work of Copernicus and who helped resolve the uncertainties that had arisen in the field of astronomy.

Kepler

Like Copernicus, Kepler believed that only the language of mathematics could describe the movements of the heavens. He was an open advocate of the latest magical ideas of his day—a famous astrologer, he also speculated about such subjects as the mystical meaning of geometric shapes—and he was convinced instinctively that Copernicus was right. He threw himself into the task of confirming the sun-centered (heliocentric) theory, and as a result of his study of Brahe's observations, he discovered three laws of planetary motion (published in 1609 and 1619) that opened a new era in astronomy.

The first law states that the orbits of the planets are ellipses, with the sun invariably at one focus of the ellipse. This was an enormous break with the past, for the assumption that circular motion is the most perfect and natural motion had been an essential part of the study of nature since Aristotle. Even Galileo was unable to reject this assumption, but Kepler followed wherever his data and his mathematics took him. The second law states that if a hypothetical line is drawn from the sun to the planet, equal areas will be swept by that line in equal times. What this means is that the planet moves faster—that is, it has to cover more of the orbit in a given period—when it is closer to the sun than when it is farther away (see Fig. 16.1).

The third law enters an entirely different area, describing not the motion of an individual planet, as do the first two, but a relationship among the movements of all planets. It states that the square of the ratio of the *time* it takes any two planets to complete their orbits equals the cube of the ratio of these planets' average

KEPLER'S SECOND LAW

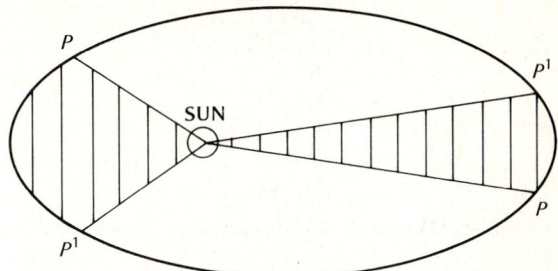

P and P^1 are any two points on the orbit between which the planet passes in equal time. The area described by Sun—P—P^1—Sun is always equal.

distance from the sun. Formulated as an equation, $(T_1/T_2)^2 = (D_1/D_2)^3$, where T_1 and T_2 are the two planets' orbiting times and D_1 and D_2 are their average distances from the sun. This third law was Kepler's most elegant and subtle discovery, a worthy monument to his mathematical skills. However, it had little direct impact on the study of astronomy until Sir Isaac Newton used it late in the century as the foundation for his construction of a new system of the heavens.

Kepler's last major achievement was the publication in 1627 of the *Rudolfine Tables,* named after his patron, Emperor Rudolf II. The tables combined Brahe's observations of planetary positions with Kepler's theories of planetary motion and made it possible to predict celestial movements far more accurately, to the great benefit of navigators as well as astronomers. They demonstrated that Copernicus' and Kepler's discoveries had a practical value, and it became increasingly difficult to ignore or doubt the new findings. Adherents of Ptolemaic cosmology continued to hold firm for decades, but among serious observers of the heavens they were a rapidly dwindling group after the 1620s. A theory that at the beginning

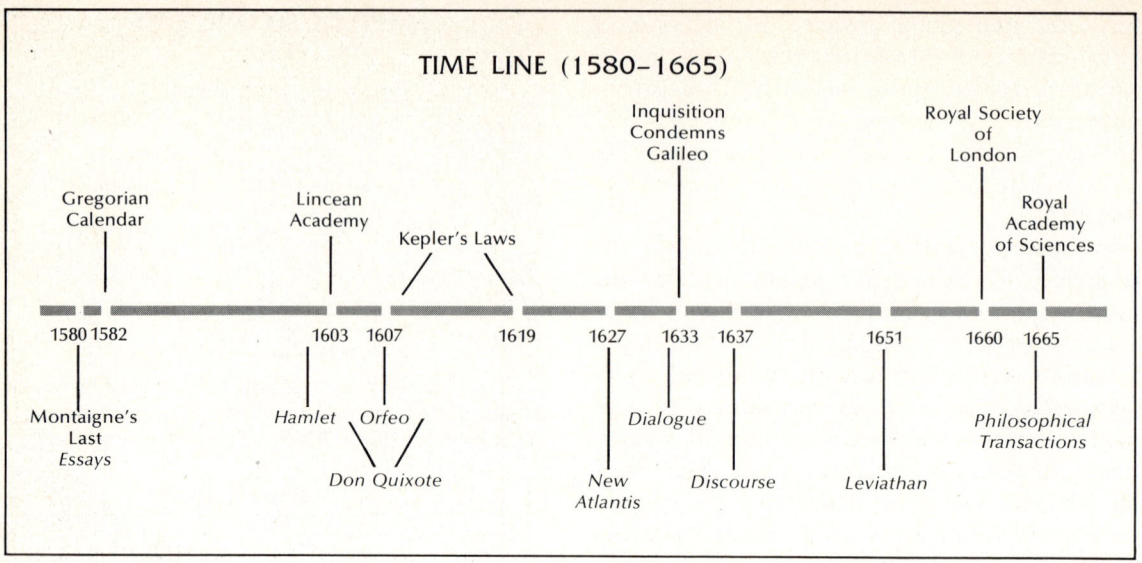

of Kepler's career had been uncertain at best had been transformed by the end of his life into a plausible explanation of planetary motion.

Galileo

A contemporary of Kepler's, the Italian Galileo Galilei, took the breakthrough a stage further when he became the first to perceive the connection between planetary motion and motion on earth, and his studies revealed the importance to astronomy not only of observation and mathematics but also of physics. Moreover he was the first to bring the new understanding of the universe to the attention of a wider public. Galileo's concern with technique, argument, and evidence marks him as one of the first scientists recognizable as such to modern eyes.

The study of motion inspired Galileo's most fundamental scientific contributions. When he began his investigations, the Aristotelian view that a body is naturally at rest and needs to be pushed constantly to keep moving dominated the study of dynamics. Kepler for example believed that some steady force emanating from the sun maintains the planets' motion. Galileo broke with this tradition, developing instead a new type of physical explanation that was perfected by Newton half a century later.

Unlike Kepler, who was concerned with the strictly limited phenomena of planetary movements, Galileo wanted to uncover the principles of all motion. His observations were prolific. At the Arsenal in Venice, he watched the techniques workmen used to lift huge weights; adapting a Dutch lensmaker's invention, he built himself a primitive telescope to study the heavens; and he devised seemingly mundane experiments, employing anything from pendulums to little balls rolling down inclined planes, to test his theories. Moving from observations to abstraction, Galileo arrived at a wholly new way of understanding motion: the principle of inertia.

This breakthrough could not have been made on the basis of observation alone. For the discovery of inertia depended on mathematical imagination, the ability to conceive of a situation that cannot be demonstrated to the senses because it cannot be created experimentally: the motion of a perfectly smooth ball across a perfectly smooth plane, free of any outside forces, such as friction. Galileo's conclusion was that "Any velocity once imparted to a moving body will be rigidly maintained as long as external causes of acceleration and retardation are removed.... If the velocity is uniform, it will not be diminished or slackened, much less destroyed."

This insight completely undermined the Aristotelian view. Physics would never be the same again, because Galileo demonstrated that only mathematical language could describe the underlying principles of nature.

The most immediate impact of Galileo's work was on astronomy. He first became famous when in 1609 he published his discoveries that Jupiter has satellites and the moon has mountains. Both these revelations were further blows to traditional beliefs, which held that the earth is changing and imperfect while the heavens are immutable and unblemished. Now, however, it seemed that other planets had moons, just like the earth, and that these moons might have the same rough surfaces as the earth.

This was startling enough, but Galileo also sought a complete change in the methods of discovery, believing, unlike his predecessors, that the principles he had uncovered in terrestrial physics could also be used to explain phenomena in the heavens. His purposes became apparent when he calculated the height of the mountains on the moon by using the geometric techniques of surveyors, when he described the moon's secondary light—seen while it is a crescent—as a reflection of sunlight from the earth, and when he explained the movement of sunspots by referring to the principles of motion that he had found on earth. In all cases Galileo was treating his own planet simply as one part of a uniform universe. Every physical law, he was saying, is equally applicable on earth and

This sketch of the moon's surface appeared in Galileo's *Starry Messenger* (1610). It shows what he had observed through the telescope and had interpreted as proof that the moon had a rugged surface because the lighted areas within the dark section had to be mountains. These caught the light of the setting sun longer than surrounding lower terrain and revealed, for example, a large cavity in the lower center of the sketch.
(Photo: New York Public Library/Picture Collection)

in the heavens, including the laws of motion. As early as 1597 Galileo had told Kepler that some of his discoveries in physics could be explained only if the earth was moving, and during the next thirty years he became the most famous advocate of Copernicanism in Europe.

Galileo conveyed his arguments with devastating logic. Citing Aristotle's principle that the simplest explanation is the best explanation, Galileo asked how anyone could conceivably accept all the complexities and effort needed to keep the entire universe revolving around the earth when all the motions could be explained by the rotation of only one planet, the earth. When academic and religious critics pointed out that the moon looks smooth, that we would feel the earth moving, or that the Bible says Joshua made the sun stand still, he reacted with scorn to their inability to understand that his observations and proofs carried more weight than their traditional beliefs. And in response to religious objections, he asserted that "in discussions of physical problems we ought to begin not from the authority of scriptural passages, but from sense experience and necessary demonstrations."

For all the brilliance of his arguments, Galileo was now on dangerous ground. Although traditionally the Catholic Church had not concerned itself with the theories used in investigations of nature, in the early seventeenth century the situation was changing. Now deep in the struggle with Protestantism, the church was responding to the increased challenge to its authority by seeking to control any potentially questionable views held by its followers. Moreover Galileo had antagonized Jesuit and Dominican astronomers. These two orders were the chief upholders of orthodoxy in the church in this period, and it was they who referred Galileo's views to the Inquisition and then guided the attack on Copernicanism and its most brilliant proponent.

In 1616 the Inquisition forbade Galileo, within certain limits, to teach the heretical doctrine that the earth moves. When one of his friends was elected pope in 1623, however, Galileo thought he would be safe in writing a major work on astronomy, as long as he remained within the limits set in 1616. The result was Galileo's masterpiece, the *Dialogue on the Two Great World Systems,* published in 1623 (with the approval, probably accidental, of the Inquisition). A marvelously witty, elegant book, the *Dialogue* is one of the few monuments in the history of science that the lay person can find constant pleasure in reading. And so it was intended. Galileo wrote it in Italian, not the Latin that had always been used for scholarly works, because he wanted it to reach the widest possible audience.

In April 1633 he was brought before the Inquisition for having defied the order not to teach Copernicanism. To establish their case, his accusers resorted to a forged document that suggested the 1616 limits were stricter than they really had been. In a trial that has caused controversy ever since, the aged astronomer, under threat of torture, abjured the "errors and heresies" of believing that the earth moved. Legend has it that as he left the hall, he murmured, *"Eppur si muove!"* ("And yet it does move!") and he certainly was not docile for the remainder of his life even though he was under perpetual house arrest and progressively lost his eyesight. He had his principal work on physics, the *Two New Sciences,* published in tolerant Holland in 1638, while many of his letters ridiculed his opponents.

Galileo's condemnation discouraged further scientific activity by his countrymen. Italy had been the leader of the new discipline, but now her supremacy rapidly passed northward, to the English, Dutch, and French. Yet this only showed that the rise of science, once begun, could not be halted for long. By the late 1630s no self-respecting astronomer could deny that Galileo's findings and his *Dialogue,* added to Kepler's laws and the *Rudolfine Tables,* had established the correctness of the Copernican theory beyond reasonable doubt.

In a progression of events remarkably similar to the movement from upheaval to resolution that was taking place in politics at this very time (see Chapter 15), scientists had started out by causing tremendous bewilderment and doubt, but had ended up by creating a new kind of certainty that had far-reaching influence. And this was true not only in physics and astronomy, but also in anatomy. For with Vesalius there had begun a period in the study of the human body when many questions were raised but few answers were found. Finally, though, in 1628, another genius of the scientific revolution, the English doctor William Harvey, provided a new and more certain understanding of anatomy when he identified the function of the heart and proved that the blood circulated.

Scientific Method: A New Epistemology

Both Copernicus and Galileo stressed that their discoveries rested on a way of thinking that had an independent value, and they refused to allow traditional considerations, such as the promptings of common sense or the assumptions of theology, to interfere with their conclusions. What the scientists were moving toward was a new epistemology, a new theory of how to obtain and verify knowledge, based on experience, reason, and doubt, rejecting all unsubstantiated authority. Their methods required a revolutionary definition of what could be accepted as a true description of physical reality.

The process the scientists followed after they formulated a hypothesis consisted, in their view, of three parts: first, observations; second, a generalization induced from the observations; and third, tests of the generalization by experiments whose outcome had to conform with the conclusions deducible from the generalization. A generalization remained valid only as long as it was not contradicted by experiments specifically designed to test it. The scientist used no data except the results of strict observation, and his reasoning was confined to the perception of the laws, principles, or patterns that emerged from the observations. Since measurement was the key to the data, the observations had a numerical, not a subjective, value, and the language of science naturally came to be mathematics.

Perhaps the most famous example of the method was the series of experiments Galileo conducted with inclined planes. His original hypothesis was that all objects fall at the same speed and that the difference we see between the time it takes for a stone and a feather to fall is the result only of friction and air resistance (a hypothesis recently confirmed by astronauts on the moon). He first showed that acceleration is a function of time, a proposition that he proved geometrically and then demonstrated by rolling a ball down a plane, noting the time required to make the descent: "We [then] rolled the ball only one-quarter the length of the [plane]; and having measured the time of its descent, we found it precisely one-half of the former [descent]." He repeated such experiments a hundred times, and always the ratio of the distances was a square of the ratio of the times. From this basic regularity he proceeded to a proof, similarly resting on both geometry and experiment, that regardless of the angle of a descent, the average speed of the descent, and the speed of the body when it reaches the bottom, will always be the same if the vertical height of the descent remains the same.

This was a classic application of the new scientific method. Mathematics, in this case geometry, allowed Galileo to measure and describe natural phenomena. Carefully controlled experiments then verified conclusions that might seem contrary to common sense. And the progression—hypothesis, observation, generalization, and tests, conducted in the language of mathematics—provided him with a logical structure that could be defeated only on its own terms. Nothing was accepted as given. It was a self-contained mode of demonstration whose conclusions could be rejected solely if disproved by identical procedures.

Scientists in fact rarely move through all the steps toward a conclusion in the exact way this idealized scheme suggests. Galileo's perfectly smooth balls and planes, for instance, did not exist, but Galileo understood the relevant physical theory so well that he knew what would have happened if one had rolled across the other, and he used this "experiment" to demonstrate the principle of inertia. In other words, experiments as well as hypotheses can occur in the mind; the essence of scientific method still remains a special way of looking at and understanding nature.

The Wider Influence of Scientific Thought

The principles of scientific inquiry received attention throughout the intellectual community only gradually; it took time for the power of the scientist's method to be recognized. For decades, as Galileo found out, even investigators of nature continued to use what he would have considered irrelevant criteria, such as the teachings of the Bible, in judging scientific work. If acceptance of the new method was to spread, then the literate public would have to be educated in the techniques being employed. This growing understanding was eventually achieved by midcentury as much through the efforts of ardent propagandizers as through the writings of the great innovators themselves.

Francis Bacon

Although not an important scientist himself, Francis Bacon was the greatest of these propagandists, and he inspired an entire generation with his vision of what the discipline could accomplish for mankind. His description of an ideal society in the *New Atlantis,* published in 1627, the year after his death, was the most famous of a series of seventeenth-century descendants of Sir Thomas More's *Utopia,* all of which placed the constant and fruitful advance of science at the center of their schemes. *New Atlantis* is a vision of science as the savior of the human race. It predicts a time when those doing research at the highest levels will be regarded as the most important people in the state and will work on a vast government-supported project to gather all known facts about the physical universe and its properties. By a process of gradual induction, this information will lead to universal laws that in turn will enable people to improve their lot on earth.

Bacon's view of research as a collective enterprise whose aim is the discovery of practical benefits for all made a powerful impact on a number of later scientists, particularly the founders of the English Royal Society. Many cited him as the chief inspiration for their work. Moreover Bacon advocated a total overhaul of the traditional educational curriculum: an end to the study of venerated philosophers and more attention to practical concerns. By the mid-seventeenth century, his ideas had entered the mainstream of European thought, an acceptance that testified to the broadening interest in science and its protagonists.

René Descartes

The French philosopher René Descartes made the first concentrated attempt to apply the new methods of science to theories of knowledge, and in so doing he laid the foundations for modern philosophy. The impulse behind his work was his realization that for all the importance of observation and experiment, people can be deceived by their senses. In order to find some solid truth, therefore, he decided to apply the principle of doubt—the refusal to accept any authority without strict verification—to all knowledge. He began his investigations with the assumption that he could know unquestionably only one thing: he was doubting. This allowed him to proceed to the observation, "I think, therefore I am," because the very act of doubting proved he was thinking, and thinking in turn demonstrated his existence.

The cardinal point of his philosophy was contained in the statement that whatever is clearly and distinctly thought must be true. This was a conclusion drawn from the proof of

The portrait of René Descartes by the Dutch painter Frans Hals shows the austere thinker who fitted well into the sober atmosphere of Amsterdam. Descartes spent a number of years in the United Provinces, where the exchange of ideas was much freer than in his native France.
(Photo: Hubert Joesse/EPI, Inc.)

his own existence, and it enabled him to construct a proof of God's existence. We cannot fail to realize that we are imperfect, he argued, and we must therefore have an idea of perfection against which we may be measured. If we have a clear idea of what perfection is, then it must exist; hence there must be a God.

The proof may not seem entirely convincing to modern readers, particularly since one suspects that a major reason for its prominence was the desire to show that the principle of doubt did not contradict religious belief. Nevertheless the argument is a good illustration of Descartes' assertion that the activity of the mind is the vital element in the search for truth. The title he gave his great work, *Discourse on the Method of Rightly Conducting the Reason and Seeking Truth in the Sciences* (1637), is thus entirely appropriate.[1] Thought is a pure and unmistakable guide, and only by reliance on its operations can people hope to advance their understanding of the world.

Descartes developed this view into a fundamental proposition about the nature of the world and of knowledge—a proposition that philosophers have been wrestling with ever since. He stated that there is an essential dichotomy between thought and extension (tangible objects) or, put another way, between spirit and matter. Various writers, including Bacon and Galileo, had insisted that science, the study of nature, is an undertaking separate from and unaffected by faith or theology, the study of God. But Descartes turned this distinction into a far-reaching principle, dividing not only science from faith but even the reality of the world from our perception of that reality. There is a difference, in other words, between a chair and our understanding of that chair in our minds.

So insistent was he that matter and spirit remain distinct that he undertook a careful examination of human anatomy to discover the seat of the soul. He had to find a part of the body that had no physical function whatsoever, because only there could the soul, a thing of spirit, reside. His candidate was the tiny pineal gland, which did absolutely nothing, according to the medicine of the day; modern investigations still have not discovered the function of the hormone it secretes.

The emphasis Descartes placed on the operations of the mind gave a new direction to epistemological discussions. A hypothesis gained credibility not so much from external proofs as from the logical tightness of the arguments used to support it. The decisive test was how lucid and irrefutable a statement appeared to be to the thinking mind, not whether it could be demonstrated by experiments. Descartes thus applied what he considered to be the methods of science to all knowledge. Not only the phenomena of nature but all truth had to be investigated according to what he regarded as the strict principles of the scientist.

Descartes' own contributions to the research of his day were theoretical rather than experimental. In physics he was the first to perceive the distinction between mass and weight, and in mathematics he was the first to apply algebraic notations and methods to geometry, thus founding analytic geometry. He was, without question, a prime mover of the revolution in Western thought during the seventeenth century. His emphasis on the principle of doubt irrevocably undermined such traditional assumptions as the belief in the hierarchical organization of the universe. Possibly he put too much trust in the powers of the mind, but he did lay down strict logical rules that philosophy—and in fact any speculation about man or his world—had to follow. And the Eu-

---

[1] Like Galileo's *Dialogue,* Descartes' *Discourse* was written in a vernacular language. It thus had a much more popular audience than a Latin book would have received, though after a few years it was translated into Latin so that scholars from all European countries could read it.

ropean intellectual community accepted this approach with enthusiasm. The admiration he inspired indicated how completely the methods he advocated had captured his contemporaries' imagination.

Thomas Hobbes

A notable example of the borrowings inspired by the scientists was the work of Thomas Hobbes, who used their method to make an extraordinarily original contribution to political theory.

A story has it that Hobbes once picked up a copy of Euclid's *Elements* and opened the book in the middle. The theorem on that page seemed totally without foundation, but it rested on a proof in the preceding theorem. Working his way backward, he discovered himself finally having to accept no more than the proposition that the shortest distance between two points is a straight line. He thereupon resolved to use the same approach in analyzing political behavior. The story is probably apocryphal because as a young man Hobbes was secretary to Francis Bacon, who doubtless gave him his first taste of scientific work. Nevertheless it does capture the essence of Hobbes' approach, for he did begin his masterpiece, *Leviathan* (published in 1651), with a few limited premises about human nature from which he rigorously deduced major conclusions about political forms.

Hobbes' premises, drawn from his observation of the strife-ridden Europe of his day, were stark and uncompromising. People, he asserted, are selfish and ambitious; consequently, unless they are restrained, they fight a perpetual war with their fellows. The weak are more cunning and the strong more stupid. Given these unsavory characteristics, the state of nature—which precedes the existence of society—is a state of war, in which life is "nasty, brutish, and short." Hobbes' conclusion was that the only way to restrain this instinctive aggressiveness is to erect an absolute and sovereign power that will maintain peace. Everyone should submit to the sovereign because the alternative is the anarchy of the state of nature. The moment of submission is the moment of the birth of orderly society.

In a startling innovation Hobbes suggested that the transition from nature to society is accomplished by a contract that is implicitly accepted by all who wish to end the chaos. They agree among themselves to submit to the sovereign; thus the sovereign is not a party to the contract and is not limited in any way. A government that is totally free to do whatever it wishes is best equipped to keep the peace. However tyrannous, this solution is always better than the turmoil it has replaced.

Both contemporaries and later writers were strongly influenced by Hobbes, not only because his logic was compelling but also because he seemed so much like a scientist. From his observations of people, he had induced general propositions about human behavior, and from these he had deduced certain political lessons that were verified by European politics. Moreover he had applied a mechanistic view to people more thoroughly than ever before, reducing all that human beings do to simple appetites and aversions.

In doing so he contributed to the popularity of the mechanistic view of the universe, a theory derived in part from the materialistic implications of Descartes' philosophy. In its simplest form mechanism holds that the entire universe, including man himself, can be regarded as a complicated machine and thus subject to strict physical principles. The arm is like a lever, the elbow like a hinge, and so on. Even an emotion is no more than a simple response to a definable stimulus.

But this approach also aroused hostility. Although they were deeply affected by his ideas, most of Hobbes' successors denounced him as godless, immoral, cynical, and unfeeling. These were charges that could be leveled at all practitioners of science, but for a long time they were not raised, largely because the scientists dealt with areas that seemed to have nothing to do with human behavior.

Blaise Pascal

At midcentury only one important voice still protested against the new science. It belonged to a young Frenchman, Blaise Pascal, one of the most brilliant mathematicians and experimenters of the time. Before his death at the age of thirty-nine, in 1662, Pascal's investigations of probability in games of chance led him to the theorem that still bears his name, and his research in conic sections helped lay the foundations for integral calculus. He also explored the properties of the vacuum and invented a versatile calculating machine.

In his late twenties, however, Pascal became increasingly dissatisfied with scientific research, and he began to wonder whether his life was being properly spent. His doubts were reinforced by frequent visits to his sister, a nun at the Abbey of Port-Royal, where he came into contact with a new spiritual movement within Catholicism known as Jansenism.

The movement took its name from Cornelis Jansen, a bishop who had written a book suggesting that the Catholic Church had forgotten the teachings of its greatest father, St. Augustine. Jansen insisted that man was not free to determine his own fate, that salvation was entirely in the hands of an all-powerful God, and that unswerving faith was the only path to salvation. These doctrines sounded ominously like Protestant teachings, and during the years after Jansen's death, the Catholic Church and especially the Jesuits, who placed great emphasis on freedom of will, made various attempts to suppress his beliefs.

Jansenism was not a particularly popular movement at the time, and its adherents consisted of little more than the immediate circle of a prominent family of magistrates, the Arnaulds, one of whom was the head of Port-Royal. But Pascal was profoundly impressed by the piety, asceticism, and spirituality at Port-Royal, and in November of 1654 he had a mystical experience that made him resolve to devote the rest of his life to the salvation of his soul. He wrote a series of devastating critiques of the Jesuits, accusing them of irresponsibility and, as he phrased it, of placing cushions under sinners' elbows.

During the few remaining years of his life, Pascal put on paper a collection of reflections—some only a few words long, some many pages—that were gathered together after his death and published as the *Pensées* (or "reflections"). These writings revealed not only the beliefs of a deeply religious man but also the anxieties of a scientist who feared the growing influence of science. He did not wish to put an end to research; he merely wanted people to realize that the truths uncovered by science were limited and not as important as the truths perceived by faith. In the words of one of his more memorable phrases, "The heart has its reasons that the mind cannot know."

Pascal was warning against the replacement of the traditional understanding of humanity and its destiny, gained through religious faith, with the conclusions reached by the methods of the scientists. The separation between the material and the spiritual would be fatal, he believed, because it would destroy the primacy and even the importance of the spiritual. Pascal's protest was unique, but the fact that it was raised at all indicates how high the status of the scientist and his method had risen by the 1650s. A scant quarter-century earlier, such a dramatic change in fortune would have been hard to predict, but now many intellectuals, seeing an opportunity of ending the uncertainties that had bedeviled their work for decades, eagerly adopted the new epistemology. Turmoil was once again giving way to assurance.

Science Institutionalized

There were many besides Bacon who realized that scientific work should be a common endeavor, pursued cooperatively by all its practitioners, and that information should be exchanged so that researchers might concentrate on different parts of a project instead of wasting time and energy following identical paths. The first major effort to apply this view was undertaken by the Lincean Academy,[2] founded under the patronage of a nobleman in Rome in 1603. Organizations of scientists had existed before, but this was the first assemblage interested in all branches of science and in publishing the findings of its members. After the decline of research in Italy, however, the academy gradually lost its importance.

More fruitful beginnings were made in France, where in the first decades of the seventeenth century a friar named Marin Mersenne became the center of an international network of correspondents interested in scientific work. He increased the dissemination of news by also bringing scientists together for discussions or experiments. The meetings were sporadic, but out of them developed procedures that led to a more permanent organization of scientific activity.

The first important steps toward establishing a permanent body in England were taken at Oxford during the Civil War when the revolutionaries captured the city and replaced many traditionalists at the university. A few of the newcomers formed what they called the Invisible College, a group that met to exchange information and discuss one another's work. What was important was the enterprise, not its results, for the group included only one first-class scientist: the young chemist Robert Boyle. In 1660 twelve members, including Boyle and the architect Sir Christopher Wren, formed an official organization, the Royal Society of London for Improving Natural Knowledge, with headquarters in the capital and a council to supervise its affairs. In 1662 it was granted a charter by Charles II.

The Royal Society's purposes were openly Baconian. Its aim for the first few years—until everyone realized it was impossible—was to gather all knowledge about nature, particularly whatever might be useful. For a long time the members continued to offer their services for the public good, helping in one instance to develop the science of social statistics ("political arithmetic" as it was called) for the government. Soon, however, it became clear that their principal function was to serve as a headquarters and clearing center for research. Their secretaries maintained an enormous correspondence, encouraging foreign scholars to transmit their discoveries to the society. And in 1665 they began the regular publication of *Philosophical Transactions,* the first professional scientific journal.

As a stimulus to new discoveries, the Royal Society was without peer in seventeenth-century Europe. Imitators were soon to follow. In 1666 Louis XIV gave his blessing to the founding of the Royal Academy of Sciences, and similar organizations were established in Naples and Berlin by 1700. Membership in these societies was limited and highly prized, a symptom of the glamour that was beginning to attach itself to the new studies. By the 1660s there could be no doubt that science, secure in royal patronage, had triumphed. Its practitioners were extravagantly admired, and through-

---

[2] The academy was named after Linceus, reputedly the most keen-sighted of the legendary Argonauts of ancient times.

Among the many representations of the public anatomy lessons so popular in seventeenth-century Holland, the most famous is one of Rembrandt's greatest paintings, *The Anatomy Lesson of Dr. Nicolaas Tulp*.
(Photo: A. Dingjan)

out intellectual and high social circles, there was a feverish scramble to apply its methods and its mode of thought to almost every conceivable activity.

Descartes himself had applied the techniques of science to epistemology and more broadly to philosophy in general; Bacon and Hobbes had put them at the service of social and political thought. But the borrowings were not only at these exalted levels. Formal gardens were designed to exhibit the order, harmony, and reason that science had made the most prized qualities of the time. And the arts of fortification and warfare were transformed by the adoption of principles learned from the new investigations, such as accurate measurement.

As the scientists' activities grew in popularity, amateurs known as virtuosos began to proliferate. These were usually aristocrats who spent their time playing at science. Herbariums and small observatories were added to country estates, and parties would feature an evening of star gazing. Some virtuosos took their tasks quite seriously—an early Italian enthusiast, Prince Federigo Cesi, joined in the first investigations with a microscope, a study of bees;

and one English country gentleman inundated the Royal Society with meticulous observations of local sand dunes. But by and large these frivolous scientists are interesting primarily because they reveal the awe and delight aroused by a new discipline that had revolutionized man's understanding of nature.

Science was also beginning to have an impact on the general populace. Among the most eagerly anticipated occasions in seventeenth-century Holland was the public anatomy lesson. The body of a criminal would be brought to an enormous hall, packed with students and a fascinated public. A famous surgeon would dissect the cadaver, announcing and displaying each organ as he removed it.

On the whole, the influence of the scientists on laypeople was not dependent on the technological improvements from their work. And by our standards much of what they did, even at the theoretical level, seems primitive at best. What this suggests is that the reverence for science and its methods developed not from a broad understanding of actual accomplishments or their potential consequences but from the fame of the spectacular discoveries which enabled a few brilliant men to provide startlingly convincing solutions to centuries-old problems in astronomy, physics, and anatomy. Thus the disturbing implications of a Hobbes, like the protests of a Pascal, could be ignored, and the new discipline could be given unblemished admiration. The entire world was coming to be viewed through the scientist's eyes—a striking victory for a recently struggling member of the intellectual community—and the qualities of regularity and harmony that he stood for began to appear in the work of playwrights and poets, artists and architects.

II. LITERATURE AND THE ARTS

Changes in culture were not as clear-cut as in politics or science, but certain parallels are evident. During the second half of the sixteenth century and into the 1610s, the tensions and uncertainties of the age were visible in the paintings of the Mannerists, and in the writings of Montaigne, Cervantes, and Shakespeare. Thereafter, two major styles dominated Europe: the Baroque, which consciously sought to arouse the emotions and achieve dramatic effects, and the Classical, which epitomized discipline, restraint, and sometimes decorum. Very gradually over the course of the seventeenth century, the emphasis moved from the values of the Baroque to those of the Classical. This shift in artistic aims bore a distinct resemblance to the sense of settlement that descended over other areas of European civilization at midcentury.

The Culture of the Late Sixteenth Century

One response to the upheavals of the sixteenth century was the attempt to escape reality, to devise a distorted view of the world. It was especially noticeable in the work of the great painters of the age.

The Mannerists

As early as the 1520s, a reaction had set in against the balance and serenity of the High Renaissance style. The artists involved in this movement, which lasted about eighty years, are generally called Mannerists. No specific characteristics united them, but they all wished to go beyond reality and to develop theatrical and disturbing qualities in their paintings (see Plate 27). They undermined perspective, distorted human figures, and devised unnatural colors and lighting to create startling effects. Even the great figures of the High Renaissance were affected by this orientation. Michelangelo, who lived until 1564, began to create tortured, agonized figures writhing in violent action; Titian, who died in 1576, placed a shrieking Magdalene in his last painting, a subdued *Pietà*.

The movement was embodied, however, in Parmigianino, an Italian, and El Greco, a Greek living in Spain. Parmigianino's *Madonna of the Long Neck* (see Plate 26), named after its most salient feature, typifies his efforts to unsettle the viewer with tricks of perspective, odd postures, and an unbalanced composition. El Greco, a man whose compelling and almost mystic vision symbolized the uneasy age in which he lived, took these devices even farther. His elongated human beings, cool colors, and eerie lighting make him one of the most distinctive painters in the history of art (see Plate 29).

Michel de Montaigne

The man who expressed the most vivid concern about the upheavals and uncertainties of his age was Michel de Montaigne, the greatest humanist and philosopher of the late sixteenth century. Born into the French petty nobility, he suffered a shock at the age of thirty—the death of his closest friend—that changed the course of his life. Obsessed by death, he began one of the most moving explorations in European intellectual history.

Determined to overcome his fears, Montaigne retired to a tower in his country home in order to "essay," or test, his innermost feelings by writing short pieces of prose even about subjects he did not fully comprehend. In the process he created a new literary form, the essay, and shaped the development of the French language. But his chief influence was philosophical: he has inspired the search for self-knowledge since his time, from René Descartes and Blaise Pascal to the Existentialists of the twentieth century.

In the 1570s Montaigne's anxieties led him to Skepticism, which appeared in full flower in his longest essay, "An Apology for Raymond Sebond." Sebond was a Spanish theologian who tried to prove the truth of Christianity by the use of reason. Montaigne firmly rejected Sebond's belief in the power of the mind and emerged from this essay with the total uncertainty of the motto *"Que sais-je?"* ("What do I know?")

In his last years Montaigne struggled toward a more confident solution of his uncertainties, taking as his model the ancient saying, "Know thyself." By looking into one's own person, each human being can find answers and values that hold true at least for the individual: all truths and customs are relative, but by looking inwardly, one can be guided by one's own reflection of all humanity. Montaigne even came close to a morality without theology, because good and self-determination were more important to him than doctrine, and he saw everywhere religious people committing inhuman acts. Man, he argued, can seek his own good and can achieve it by an effort of will. Trying to be an angel is wrong; being a good man is enough.

This process of self-discovery was a radical and totally secular individualism. It required a joyous acceptance of the world that finally gave Montaigne the optimistic answer to his anguish—though it was a unique, personal answer that gave comfort to few other people.

Cervantes and Shakespeare

In Spain the disillusionment that accompanied the decline of Europe's most powerful state was perfectly captured by Miguel de Cervantes (1547–1616). He was heir to a brilliant satirical and descriptive tradition that had already produced a classic literature in the sixteenth century in the writings of Erasmus and Rabelais. Cervantes saw the wide gap between the hopes and the realities of his day—in religion, in social institutions, in human behavior—and made the dichotomy the basis of the scathing social satire in his novel *Don Quixote*.

At one level Cervantes was ridiculing the excessive chivalry of the Spanish nobility in his portrayal of a knight who was ready to tilt at windmills, though he obviously admired the sincerity of his well-meaning hero and sympathized with him as a perennial loser. On another level the author brought to life the Europe of the time—the ordinary people and their hypocrisies and intolerances—with a liveliness rarely matched in literature. His view of that society, however, was far from cheery. "Justice, but not for my house," says Don Quixote as he experiences the foibles of mankind, particularly of those in authority. Cervantes avoided politics, but he was clearly directing many of his sharpest barbs at the brutality and disregard for human values that were characteristic of his fanatical times. What were Spain's repeated crusades accomplishing? Were Quixote's dreams as worthy as Sancho Panza's blunt and sensible pragmatism? These were not easy questions to answer, but they went to the heart of the dilemmas of the age. And in Spain's great enemy, England, another towering figure was grappling with similar problems.

For the English-speaking world, the most brilliant writer of this and all other periods was William Shakespeare, whose characters bring to life almost every conceivable mood—searing grief, airy romance, rousing nationalism, uproarious and farcical humor. Despite modest education he disclosed in his imagery a familiarity with subjects ranging from astronomy to seamanship, from alchemy to warfare. It is not surprising therefore that some have doubted that one man could have produced this amazing body of work.

Shakespeare started writing in the 1590s, when he was in his late twenties, and continued until his death, in 1616. During most of this time, he was also involved with a theatrical company, and he often had to produce plays on very short notice. He thus had the best of all possible tests as he gained mastery of theatrical techniques—audience reaction.

Shakespeare rose far above his setting to timeless statements about human behavior: love, hatred, violence, sin. Of particular interest to the historian, however, is what he tells us about attitudes that belong especially to his own era. For example the conservatism of his characters is quite clear. They believe firmly in the hierarchical structure of society, and throughout the long series of historical plays, events suggest that excessive ambition does not pay. The story begins with Richard II, a legitimate monarch who is overthrown by a usurper, with catastrophic results. Repeated disasters follow as England's history is taken through the War of the Roses to the restoration of order by the Tudors. Again and again legality and stability are shown as fundamental virtues—a natural reaction against turbulent times. Shakespeare's expressions of nationalism are particularly intense; when in *Richard II* the king's uncle, John of Gaunt, lies dying, he pours out his love for his country in words that have moved English people ever since:

> This royal throne of kings, this sceptered isle,
> This earth of majesty, this seat of Mars,
> This other Eden, demi-paradise, . . .
> This happy breed of men, this little world,
> This precious stone set in the silver sea, . . .
> This blessed plot, this earth, this realm, this England.
>   [*Richard II*, act 2, scene 1]

The uncertainties of the day appear in many of the plays. In *Julius Caesar* the optimistic "There is a tide in the affairs of men, which, taken at the flood, leads on to fortune" celebrates vigor and decisiveness but also warns against missing opportunities. More unambiguously, the patriotism expressed by John of Gaunt and Henry V suggests the glory that is England's destiny. Yet Shakespeare's four most famous tragedies, *Hamlet, Lear, Macbeth,* and *Othello,* end in disillusionment: the heroes are ruined by irresoluteness, pride, ambition, or jealousy. He is reflecting the Elizabethans' interest in the fatal flaws that destroy great men and in dramas of revenge, but the plays demonstrate as well his deep understanding of human nature. For all the promise of the future, one cannot forget human weakness, the inevitability of decay, and the constant threat of disaster. The contrast appears with compelling clarity in a speech delivered by Hamlet:

> What a piece of work is man! how noble in reason! how infinite in faculties! in form and moving how express and admirable! in action how like an angel! in apprehension how like a god! the beauty of the world, the paragon of animals! And yet to me what is this quintessence of dust? Man delights not me.
>
> [*Hamlet,* act 2, scene 2]

Despite such pessimism, despite the deep sense of human inadequacy, the total impression Shakespeare gives is of immense vigor, of a restlessness and confidence that recall the many achievements of the sixteenth century. Prospero, the hero of his last play, *The Tempest,* has often been seen as the symbol of the new magician-cum-scientist, and references to the discoveries overseas are abundant. Yet a sense of decay is never far absent. Repeatedly men seem utterly helpless, overtaken by events they cannot control. There is a striking lack of security in the world Shakespeare's people inhabit. Nothing remains constant or dependable, and everything that seems solid and reassuring, be it the love of a daughter or the crown of England, is challenged. In this atmosphere of ceaseless change, where all solid, safe landmarks disappear, Shakespeare forcefully conveys the tensions of his time.

The Baroque and Classicism

From around 1600 onward, new concerns began to gain prominence in the arts and literature. First, in the Baroque there was an attempt to drown uncertainty in a blaze of grandeur and drama. But gradually the aims of Classicism, which emphasized formality, balance, and restraint, came to dominate European culture.

The Baroque: Grandeur and Excitement

The word "Baroque" has been taken to indicate ornateness, grandeur, and excess as well as all the traits, including the Classical, of seventeenth-century art. Historians have applied it to music, literature, politics, and even personality traits. Its usage here will be restricted to its most precise meaning: the characteristics of a style in the visual arts that emanated from Rome in the first half of the seventeenth century. Passion, drama, mystery, and awe are the qualities of the Baroque: the viewer must be involved, aroused, uplifted (see Plates 33 and 34). Insofar as these characteristics are reflected in other kinds of creative work, such as literature and music, it is reasonable to discuss the various examples together; but to regard all manifestations of dramatic splendor or grandiose extravagance as Baroque is to depart from the essentially visual meaning of the term.

The Baroque was closely associated with the Counter Reformation's emphasis on gorgeous display in Catholic ritual. The patronage bestowed by leading church figures and the presence of art treasures accumulated over centuries made Rome a magnet for the major painters of the period. Elsewhere the Baroque flourished primarily at the leading Catholic courts of the seventeenth century, most notably the Hapsburg courts in Madrid, Prague, and

The interior of the St. Andrea della Valle basilica was built in the late seventeenth century. It denotes the elaborate, yet gaudy splendor of the Baroque style, which was the signature of the age of royal absolutism and affluence. Among Roman edifices, the dome of this basilica is second in height only to St. Peter's.
(Photo: Alinari/Scala/EPA, Inc.)

Brussels and the ducal court of Bavaria in Munich, since the style expressed perfectly the pomp of seventeenth-century princes. Few periods have conveyed so strong a sense of grandeur, theatricality, and ornateness.

Peter Paul Rubens (1577–1640) was the principal ornament of the brilliant Hapsburg court at Brussels. His major themes typified the Baroque style: glorification of great rulers (see Plate 37) and exaltation of the ceremony and mystery of Catholicism. His secular paintings convey, by their powerful depiction of human bodies and vivid use of color, the enormous strength of his subjects; his religious works similarly overwhelm the viewer with the majesty and panoply of the church and ex-

The contrasting postures of victory and defeat are masterfully captured by Diego Velézquez in *The Surrender of Breda*. The Dutch soldiers droop their heads and lances, but the victorious Spaniards hardly show triumph, and the gesture of the victorious general, Ambrogio Spinola, is one of consolation and understanding.
(Photo: Prado Museum)

cite the believer's piety by stressing the dramatic mysteries of the faith. Toward the end of his life Rubens' paintings became more lyrical, especially on mythological subjects, but he never lost his ability to generate strong emotions.

Other artists glorified rulers of the time through idealized portraiture. The greatest court painter of the age was Diego Velázquez, some twenty-two years Rubens' junior. His portraits of members of the Spanish court depict rulers and their surroundings in the stately atmosphere appropriate to the theme (see Plate 38). Yet occasionally Velázquez hinted at the weakness of an ineffective monarch in his rendering of the face, even though the basic purpose of his work always remained the exaltation of royal power. And when he painted a celebration of a notable Hapsburg victory, *The Surrender of Breda,* he managed to suggest the sadness and emptiness as much as the glory of war.

Giovanni Lorenzo Bernini was to sculpture and architecture what Rubens was to painting, and like Rubens he was closely associated with the Counter Reformation. Pope Urban VIII commissioned him in 1629 to complete both the inside and the outer setting of St. Peter's, extending and elaborating Michelangelo's original architectural plan. For the interior Bernini designed a splendid papal throne that seems to float on clouds beneath a burst of sunlight, and for the exterior he created an enormous plaza, surrounded by a double colonnade, that is the largest and most imposing square in all Europe.

The glories of Baroque Rome owe much to the work of Bernini. The elaborate fountains he sculpted can be seen throughout the city; his busts of contemporary Roman leaders set the style for portraiture in marble or stone; and his dramatic religious works reflect the desire of the Counter Reformation popes to electrify the faithful. The sensual and overpowering altarpiece dedicated to the Spanish mystic St. Teresa makes a direct appeal to the emotions of the beholder that reveals the excitement of Baroque at its best (see Plate 35). And drama is also immediately apparent in his *David,* which shows the young warrior at his supreme moment, just after he has unleashed his slingshot at Goliath. Bernini emphasized the intense exertion and concentration of this moment as an expression of human vigor, and with a touch that was characteristic of the bravado of the times he gave the figure his own face.

Similar qualities can be seen in the architecture of the age. Ornate churches and palaces were built on a massive scale that paralleled exactly the concerns of painting and sculpture. And it is significant that the three most conspicuous centers of the Counter Reformation—Rome, Munich, and Prague—were also major centers of Baroque architecture (see Map A-20 in the Cartographic Essay).[3]

The seventeenth century was significant, too, as a decisive time in the history of music. New instruments were developed, notably in the keyboard and string families, that enabled composers to create richer effects than had been possible before. Particularly in Italy, which in the sixteenth and seventeenth centuries was the chief center of new ideas in music (see Map 16.1), musicians began to explore the potential of a form that first emerged in these years: the opera. Drawing on the resources of the theater, painting, architecture, music, and the dance, an operatic production could achieve a panoply of splendors beyond the reach of any one of these arts on its own. The form was perfectly attuned to the courtly culture of the age, to the love of display among the princes of Europe, and to the Baroque determination to overwhelm one's audience.

The dominant figure in seventeenth-century

---

[3] A good survey of Baroque architecture can be found in Nikolaus Pevsner, *An Outline of European Architecture* (1943 and later editions), Chap. 6.

music was the Italian Claudio Monteverdi, one of the most innovative composers of all time. He has been called with some justification the creator of both the operatic form and the orchestra. His masterpiece *Orfeo* (1607) was written for his patron, the duke of Mantua, whose court provided Monteverdi with the many skilled professionals needed to mount an opera, from scene painters to singers. The result was a tremendous success, and in the course of the next century, operas gained in richness and complexity, attracting composers, as well as audiences, in ever increasing numbers.

There was a similar extension of the range of instrumental music. The accompaniment to *Orfeo* was still scored primarily for plucked instruments like the lute, which (except for the harp) were soon to disappear from the orchestra, but in his later works Monteverdi began to rely increasingly on bowed strings and woodwinds. He became much freer in his use of extended melodies and readier to introduce unexpected discords, which give his works a flavor decidedly different from the music of earlier composers and reasonably familiar to modern ears.

Classicism: Grandeur and Restraint

Classicism, the second major style of the seventeenth century, attempted to recapture the aesthetic values of ancient Greece and Rome. What this usually meant in practice was an acceptance of the strict forms embodied in the works of antiquity. Like the Baroque, Classicism aimed for grandiose effects, but it achieved them through restraint and discipline,

within the bounds of a formal structure. The gradual rise of the Classical style in the seventeenth century echoed the trend toward stabilization that was taking place in other areas of intellectual life and in politics.

The epitome of disciplined expression and conscious imitation of Classical antiquity is the work of Nicolas Poussin (1594–1665), a French artist who spent much of his career in Italy among the relics of Rome's glory. Poussin was no less interested than his contemporaries in momentous subjects and dramatic scenes, but the atmosphere in his canvases is always more subdued than in those of Velázquez or Rubens. The colors are muted, the figures are restrained, and the settings are serene. Peaceful landscapes, men and women in stately togas, and ruins of Classical buildings are consistent features of his work, even his religious paintings (see Plate 43).

In the United Provinces different forces were at work, but they too led to a style that was much more subdued than the powerful outpourings of Rubens and Velázquez. Two aspects of Dutch society had a particular influence: Protestantism and republicanism. The Reformed Church frowned on religious art and thus reduced the demand, both ceremonial and private, for paintings of biblical scenes. Religious works therefore tended to be expressions of personal faith, not glorifications of the church. The absence of a court meant that the chief patrons were sober merchants, who were far more interested in precise, dignified portraits than in ornate displays (see Plates 39 and 41). The result, notably in the work of the most powerful Dutch master, Rembrandt van Rijn, was an epic and compelling art whose beauty lies in its calmness and restraint.

Rembrandt explored an amazing range of themes, but his greatest paintings are his portraits. He was fascinated by human beings—their personalities, emotions, and self-revelations. Whether children or old people, simple

David by Bernini.
(Photo: Alinari—Art Reference Bureau)

546 Culture and Society in the Age of the Scientific Revolution 1540–1660

MAP 16.1: CENTERS OF MUSIC 1500–1800

This map indicates the shifting centers of new ideas in music from Flanders and Italy in the sixteenth century; to Italy in the seventeenth; and on to Germany, England, and France in the eighteenth.

servant girls or rich burghers, they are presented without elaboration or idealization; always the personality is allowed to speak for itself.

His most remarkable achievement in portraiture—and one of the most moving series of canvases in the history of art—is his depiction of the changes in his own face over his lifetime. The brash youth turns into the confident, successful, middle-aged man, one of the most sought-after painters in Holland. But in his late thirties the sorrows mounted: he lost his beloved wife, and commissions began to fall off. Sadness fills the eyes in these pictures. The last portraits move from despair to a final, quiet resignation as his sight slowly failed (see Plate 40). Taken together, these paintings bear comparison with Montaigne's essays as monuments to man's exploration of his own spirit—a searching appraisal that brings all who see it to a deeper understanding of human nature.

Rembrandt's large-scale, grandiose undertakings, like his smaller works, avoided startling effects. His many religious works, for example, are subdued and reverential in their approach, reflecting his own faith. The atmosphere differs sharply from the swirling passion conveyed by Rubens, who emphasized the drama of an event, whereas Rembrandt entered into the overwhelming emotions of the people present.

One could argue that Rembrandt cannot be fitted into either of the dominant styles of his time. Except for his powerful use of light, his work is far more introspective than most of the Baroque. On the other hand he did not adopt the forms of antiquity, as did Poussin and other Classical painters. Yet like the advocates of Classicism, Rembrandt in his restraint seemed to anticipate the art of the next generation. After his death, in 1669, serenity, calm, and elegance became the watchwords of European painting (see p. 589). An age of repose and grace was succeeding a time of upheaval as surely in the arts as in other spheres of life.

By the middle of the seventeenth century, the formalism of the Classical style was also begin extended to literature, especially drama. This change was most noticeable in France, but it soon moved through Western Europe, as leading critics demanded that new plays conform to the structure laid down by the ancients. In particular they wanted the three Classical unities observed: unity of place, which required that all scenes take place without change of location; unity of time, which demanded that the events in the play occur within a twenty-four hour period; and unity of action, which dictated simplicity and purity of plot.

The work of Pierre Corneille, the dominant figure in the French theater during the mid-century years, reflects the rise of Classicism. His early plays resemble rather complex Shakespearean drama, and even after he came in contact with the Classical tradition, his effervescent genius did not accept its rules easily. His masterpiece *Le Cid* (1636), based on the legends of a medieval Spanish hero, technically observed the three unities but only by compressing an entire tragic love affair, a military campaign, and multitudinous other events into one day. The play won immediate popular success, but the critics, urged on by Richelieu, an advocate of Classical drama, condemned Corneille for imperfect observance of the three unities. Thereafter he adhered to the Classical forms, though he was never entirely at ease with their restraints.

Passion was not absent from the strictly Classical play; the works of Jean Racine, the model Classical dramatist, portrayed some of the most intense emotion ever seen on the stage (see pp. 590–591). But the exuberance of earlier drama, the enjoyment of life and of human nature, was disappearing. Only the figure of Molière was to retain these qualities, and even he respected the formalism of the Classical style (see p. 592). Nobody summed up the values of Classicism better than Racine in his eulogy of Corneille:

> You know in what a condition the stage was when he began to write. . . . All the rules of art, and even those of decency and decorum, broken everywhere. . . . Corneille, after having for some time sought the right path and struggled against the bad taste of his day, inspired by extraordinary genius and helped by the study of the ancients, at last brought reason upon the stage.[4]

This was exactly the progression—from turbulence to calm—that was apparent throughout European culture in this period.

III. SOCIAL PATTERNS AND POPULAR CULTURE

It is difficult to draw analogies between, on the one hand, changes in the way ordinary people lived or in their customs and, on the other hand, the movement of ideas among a small, highly literate group of intellectual and artistic geniuses. There were points of contact and influence, to be sure. The magical interests of astrologers and alchemists were not far removed from the belief in hidden mysteries and spirits that influenced the inhabitants of every European village. In the late seventeenth century the first collections of folk tales were published, put together by writers who assumed that ancient wisdom was revealed in the sayings and stories of peasants. And ordinary men and women could not help but be affected by the attitudes and instructions imposed on them by their rulers. Nevertheless, one must not make the connections too close. Popular culture had roots of its own, determined by social and demographic forces, and if we see certain trends toward restraint and order that parallel what was happening in politics and literate culture, they must not be overdrawn.

Hierarchy and Rank in the Social Order

Seventeenth-century people occupied well-defined places in society. According to a common view, they formed links in the great chain of being, which, ascending by degrees, united all of creation with the angels and God. Man stood in the middle of the chain between animals and angels, and within mankind there were also degrees, rising from the peasant through the well-to-do landowner or professional and the noble to the king. It was considered against the order of nature for someone to move to another level of society.

In fact, though, the people of the seventeenth century divided themselves into multiple groups and strata. Perhaps the clearest way to describe this structure is to liken society to a set of four ladders, each representing a distinct group: those on the land (about four-fifths of the population), those in the clergy, those in commerce (including artisans and shopkeepers), and those in the professions (mainly lawyers, doctors, and teachers). Within each ladder there was a sharply differentiated hierarchy, but most positions on each ladder had rough equivalents on the others. While all four ladders were parallel, the landed ladder was clearly superior in that it rose higher and included the leaders of society, the courtiers and the great magnates.

---

[4] Jean Racine, *Discours Prononcé à l'Académie Française à la Réception de M. de Corneille* (1685), in Paul Mesnard (ed.), *Oeuvres de J. Racine*, IV (1886), p. 366. Translation by Theodore K. Rabb.

Mobility and Privilege

The determinants of status in modern times—wealth, family background, and education—were viewed rather differently in the seventeenth century. Wealth was significant chiefly to merchants, education was important mainly among professionals, and background was vital primarily to the nobility. But in this period the significance of these three social indicators began to shift. Wealth grew increasingly respectable as ever-larger numbers of successful merchants bought their way into the nobility. Education was also becoming more highly prized; throughout Europe attendance at institutions of higher learning soared after 1550 because a smattering of knowledge was now considered to be a mark of gentility.[5] And background was being scrutinized ever more carefully (though to less effect) by old-line nobles, who were dismayed at the multiplication of "new" aristocrats.

The growing social importance of wealth and education indicates that mobility was possible despite the great chain of being. Thanks to the expansion of bureaucracies during the sixteenth and seventeenth centuries, it became easier for men to move to new levels, either by winning favor at court or by buying an office. High status conferred important privileges: great landowners could demand services and taxes from their tenants; city freemen, nobles, and bureaucrats were frequently exempt from taxes; and courtiers controlled portions of the vast patronage that the government disbursed. This period witnessed the rise of some of the most successful self-made men in history, particularly among the ministers who served the kings of England and France.

Somewhat different patterns were emerging in Europe's colonies. From their earliest days, the overseas settlements had reflected their countries of origin. Both the Portuguese and the Dutch for example had concentrated almost exclusively on commerce. They had small populations and were incapable of conquering large areas; instead they established a network of trading posts linked by sea that were marked by some effort to live amicably amid the native populations. The French followed a similar practice for a different reason: because the home country was rich in land and prosperous, few of its inhabitants were willing to emigrate. The Spaniards and the English by contrast flocked to new settlements in search of gold, land, and religious freedom. They remained overseas, occupying vast territories, subduing the natives, and creating extensive political structures that were far more elaborate than the earlier commercial outposts.

The common problem of all the colonies was their vulnerability. They were exposed to attack from the local population and from rival colonizers, and they rarely had the defensive capability to feel completely secure. Under this pressure they often created societies imitative of but even more rigid than those of the countries they had left behind. Representatives of church and king dominated Portugal's settlements, and in her one major colony, Brazil, a few powerful landowners dominated in a way that no noble could in the homeland. Among the Dutch, as might be expected, the merchants took charge completely; and the French were subjected to strict supervision by the government—there was even an *intendant* for Canada. Spain's empire was also focused on the crown, and if its extent and remoteness permitted the emergence of a fairly independent society, great nobles and the church still stood at its head, as at home. And the English created a system in which landed gentry, such as the plantation owners of Virginia, and thriving merchants remained the leading citizens, though independent-minded New England diverged significantly from this pattern, reflecting Puritanism's challenge to the traditional hierarchical view of social structure.

---

[5] See Lawrence Stone, "The Educational Revolution in England, 1560–1640," *Past & Present,* July 1964, pp. 41–80.

All the colonies, however, were distinguished from the mother countries by one institution which was vital to their economies but also degrading to its participants: slavery. The slaves posed yet another military threat to the settlers, thus reinforcing their inclination toward rigid social control.

It is important to realize that, both in Europe and in the colonies, the lower levels of society scarcely participated in the mobility caused by the growth of commerce and bureaucracy. Peasants throughout Europe were in fact entering a time of increasing difficulty at the end of the sixteenth century. Their taxes were rising rapidly, but the prices they could get for the food they grew were stabilizing. Moreover landowners were starting what has been called the "seigneurial reaction"—making additional demands on their tenants, raising rents, and taking as much as they could out of the land. The only escape was to cities or armies, both of which grew rapidly in the seventeenth century. A few lucky people improved their lot by such a move, but for the huge majority a life of poverty in cities caused even more misery and hunger than one on the land. Few were allowed to become apprentices, and day laborers were poorly paid and usually out of work. As for military careers, armies not only destroyed the well-being of the rural areas they passed through but were hardly less dangerous for their own troops. They were carriers of disease, frequently ill fed, and subject to constant hardship. For many, therefore, the only alternative to starvation was crime. In London in the seventeenth century, social events like dinners and outings took place during the daytime, because the streets were unsafe at night.

Demographic Patterns

During the last twenty years, a number of historians have developed a new technique called family reconstitution, which uses analyses of the records of births, marriages, and deaths in parish registers to re-create the patterns of seventeenth-century life.[6] Some of the contrasts they have revealed are startling. For example in France illegitimacy appears to have accounted for only 1 percent of births in the countryside, about 4 or 5 percent in towns, and somewhat more in Paris. In England, however, illegitimacy accounted for 20 percent of births, and the rate reached 40 or 50 percent after 1700. In New England in the same period the proportion evidently rose from 10 to 50 percent. The view that sets the loose French against the proper English or repressed New Englanders is thus the reverse of the truth.

Once the babies were born, no more than 75 percent reached the age of one, only 50 percent survived to be twenty, and less than 10 percent lived to be sixty. This was a society dominated by those in their twenties and thirties, able to rise because their predecessors died earlier than they do in modern times. Because only one child in two reached adulthood, a couple had to produce four children merely to replace themselves.

The likelihood that they would be able to do so was not improved by the practice of marrying relatively late or the fact that women lost the capacity to bear children in their late thirties. The average age of marriage for men was around twenty-seven and for women close to twenty-five. On the average therefore a woman would have some twelve years in which to give birth to four children if the population was to be maintained. Because of lactation the mean interval between births was almost two and a half years, which meant that the average married couple was only just rais-

---

[6] An excellent introduction to the work of the historical demographers is E. A. Wrigley, *Population and History* (1969).

EUROPE'S POPULATION, 1600–1700, BY REGIONS			
Region	1600*	1700	Percentage Change
Spain, Portugal, and Italy	23.6	22.7	−4
France, Switzerland, and Germany	35.0	36.2	+3
British Isles, Low Countries, and Scandinavia	12.0	16.1	+34
Total	70.6	75.0	+6

*All figures are in millions
Source: Jan de Vries, *The Economy of Europe in an Age of Crisis, 1600–1750*, Cambridge, 1976, p. 5.

ing two adults. And in fact population levels were barely being maintained for most of the seventeenth century. There had been an enormous increase before 1600, and a slight rise was sustained thereafter, but the real resumption of growth did not come until the eighteenth century, though cities continued to grow throughout the 1600s (see Map 16.2).

The causes of the high mortality rate were simple but insuperable: famine, poor nutrition, disease, and war. The plague, erupting every few years from the fourteenth century on, swept away mainly the young and the old and it did not disappear until the 1720s. The upper classes, better fed and able to get away from plague centers, had a better chance for survival; but the odds were often equalized by their resort to dangerously incompetent doctors.

How and why the general population trend changed is impossible to know for certain. It is fairly clear that as early as the fifteenth century, the upper levels of society had begun limiting the size of their families in order to preserve their wealth—dowries for a daughter were expensive, and younger sons might not be able to live from family resources. Whether self-limitation was understood, let alone practiced, by other classes is difficult to say, though it is hard to offer an alternate explanation of the fact that the average gap between children sometimes rose to double the usual thirty months, particularly in troubled times. Late marriage for the upper classes was another means of controlling family size. For the lower levels of society, such postponement was a traditional economic defense: children had to work for their families until their parents' death allowed them to strike out for themselves.

Because of late marriages and low life expectancies, two married generations were rarely contemporary. Thus the extended family—more than one nuclear group of mother, father, and children living together—was extremely uncommon. Almost everyone who survived married, so there were few bachelors and spinsters, and usually each family could live on its own (see Plate 42).

These features and consequences of demographic behavior give a sense of the basic patterns of seventeenth-century society, but we still do not know why the population grew so markedly in the sixteenth century, so little in the seventeenth, and then again so rapidly in the eighteenth. One can but suggest that repercussions were felt from the political, economic, and intellectual upheavals of the seventeenth century.

In only one area, the link between war and life expectancy, were the effects obvious. At the simplest level the Thirty Years' War alone caused the death of more than 5 million people. It also helped plunge Western Europe into a debilitating economic depression, which in turn decreased the means of relieving famine. These

MAP 16.2: CITIES OF EUROPE IN 1700

were mighty blows at the delicate balance that maintained population growth, and disasters of such magnitude could not easily be absorbed. The few regions that managed to avoid decline were to become the leaders of Europe's economy (see table on p. 551).

If the seventeenth century was almost everywhere a time of stagnation or decline in population, a period of harsh weather and recurrent famines and plagues, it was so especially for the poorest members of society. The low life expectancy, the frequent deaths of children, and the struggle to survive were constant and desperate pressures. It is small wonder that their culture embraced beliefs in dark forces and rituals of violence and protest. Nor is it surprising that as governments extended their hold over their subjects, they reduced the autonomy of ordinary villagers and limited the extremes of popular self-expression.

Popular Culture

As is natural for people living close to the land and dependent for their livelihood on the kindness of nature—good weather, health, fertility of soil—peasants in sixteenth- and seventeenth-century Europe assumed that outside forces controlled their destinies. Particular beliefs varied from place to place but there was general agreement that a mere human being could do little to assure his or her own well-being. The world was full of spirits and powers, and all one could do was to encourage the good, defend oneself as best one knew how against the evil, and hope that the good would win. Nothing that happened—the death of a calf, lightning striking a house, a toad jumping through a window into a home—was accidental. Everything had a purpose. Any unusual event was an omen, part of a larger plan, or the action of some unseen force.

To strengthen themselves against trouble, people used whatever help they could find. One device was to organize special processions and holidays to celebrate good times (such as harvests), to lament misfortunes, to complain about oppression, or to poke fun at scandalous behavior. These occasions, known as "rough music" in England and "charivari" in France, often used the theme of "the world turned upside down" to make their point. In the set pieces in a procession, a fool might be dressed up as a king, a woman might be shown beating her husband, or a tax collector might appear hanging from a tree. Whether ridiculing a cheating wife or lamenting the lack of bread, the community was expressing its solidarity in the face of difficulty or distasteful behavior through these rituals. It was a way of letting off steam and declaring public opinion.

The potential for violence was always present at such gatherings, especially when religious or social differences became entangled with other resentments. The viciousness of ordinary Protestants and Catholics toward one another—it was not uncommon for one side to mutilate the dead bodies of the other—revealed a frustration and aggressiveness that was not far below the surface. When food was scarce or new impositions had been ordered by their rulers, peasants and townspeople needed little excuse to show their anger openly. In many cases women took the lead, not only because they had first-hand experience of the difficulty of feeding a family but also because troops were more reluctant to attack them. This tradition was still alive in 1789, in the early days of the French Revolution, when a band made up primarily of women marched from Paris to the royal court at Versailles to demand bread.

There was a peasant uprising in one location or another in France every year during the century up to 1675. But ordinary people also had other outlets for their problems. Recognizing their powerlessness in face of outside forces,

they resorted to their version of the magic that the literate were finding so fashionable at this very time. Where the rich patronized astrologers, paying fortunes for horoscopes and advice about how to live their lives, the peasants and the poor consulted popular almanacs or sought out "cunning men" and wise women for secret spells, potions, and similar remedies for their anxieties. Even religious ceremonies were thought of as being related to the rituals of the magical world, in which so-called "white" witches—the friendly kind—gave assistance when a ring was lost, when a new bride could not become pregnant, or when the butter would not form out of the milk.

For most Europeans, such support was all too necessary as they struggled with the unpredictability of nature. Misfortunes, they believed, could never be just plain bad luck; rather, there was intent behind everything that happened. Events were *willed,* and if they turned out badly, they must have been willed by the good witch's opposite, the evil witch. Such beliefs went back to the ancient world and for centuries had been the cause of mass scares and cruel persecutions of innocent victims—usually helpless old women, able to do nothing but mutter curses when taunted by neighbors, and easy targets if someone had to be blamed for unfortunate happenings.

In the sixteenth and seventeenth centuries, the hunt for witches intensified to levels never previously reached. This has been called the era of "the great witch craze," and for good reason. There were outbursts in every part of Europe, and tens of thousands of the accused were executed. The patterns varied—in some areas they were said to dance with the devil, in others to fly on broomsticks, in others to be possessed by evil spirits who could induce dreadful (and possibly psychosomatic) symptoms—but always the punishment was the same: burning at the stake. And the hysteria was infectious. One accusation could trigger dozens more until entire regions were swept with fear and hatred. Political and religious authorities, who often encouraged witch hunts as expressions of piety or as means of stamping out disorder, found themselves unable to stop the flow once it started. It was the perfect symptom of an age of disruption, uncertainty, and upheaval.

By the middle of the seventeenth century, however, the wave was beginning to recede. The rulers of society came to realize how dangerous to authority the witchcraft campaigns could become, especially when accusations were turned against the rich and privileged classes. Increasingly, therefore, cases were not brought to trial, and when they were, lawyers and doctors (who approached the subject from a different point of view than the clergy) cast doubt on the validity of the testimony. Gradually, excesses were restrained and control was reestablished; by 1700 there was only a trickle of new incidents.

The decline reflected not only the more general quieting down of society but also the growing proportion of Europe's population that was living in cities. Here, less reliant on good weather or the luck of fertility, people could feel themselves more in control of their own fates. If there were unexpected fires, there were fire brigades; if a house nevertheless burned down, there might even be insurance—a new idea, just starting in the late seventeenth century. A notable shift in the world view of popular culture was under way, the inevitable result of basic changes in social organization.

This woodcut, by the German artist Grien, shows the popular image of witches in early modern Europe. One carries a potion while flying on a goat. The others, including a ghastly hag, put together the ingredients for a magic potion in a jar inscribed with mystical symbols. The fact that witches were thought to be learned women, in order to understand magic, was another reason they were feared by a Europe that expected women to be uneducated.
(Photo: Private Collection)

Change in the Traditional Village

A number of forces were combining to transform the atmosphere of the traditional village. Over three-quarters of Europe's population still lived in these small communities, but their structure was not what it once had been. In the east peasants were being reduced to serfdom; in the west—our principal concern—familiar relationships and institutions were changing.

The essence of the traditional village had been its isolation. Cut off from frequent contact with the world beyond its immediate region, it had been self-sufficient and closely knit. Everyone knew everyone else, and mutual help was vital. There might be distinctions among villagers—some more prosperous, others less so—but the sense of cohesiveness was powerful. It extended even to the main "outsiders" in the village, the priest and the lord. The priest was often indistinguishable from his parishioners: almost as poor and sometimes hardly more literate. He adapted to local customs and beliefs, frequently taking part in semipagan rituals so as to keep his authority with his flock. The lord could be exploitative and demanding, but he considered the village his livelihood, and he therefore kept in close touch with its affairs and did all he could to ensure its safety, orderliness, and well-being.

The first intrusion onto this scene was economic. As a result of the boom in agricultural prices during the sixteenth century, followed by the economic difficulties of the seventeenth, differences in the wealth of the villagers became more marked. The richer peasants began to set themselves apart from the poorer, and the feeling of unity began to break down. For hundreds of years, most villages had governed themselves through elected councils drawn from every part of the population. Toward the end of the seventeenth century, however, these councils started disappearing as the commitment to common interests declined.

Some of the other outside influences were more direct. In a few areas of Europe, especially in England and the Netherlands, the isolation of the villages was broken down by merchants who were experimenting with new ways of organizing labor. Traditionally, a village would raise sheep, shear them, and sell the wool at market to traders who would have it finished into cloth in towns. Now, aiming at greater efficiency, merchants were organizing production on a larger scale in a new industry that has been called the rural "putting-out" system or "cottage industry." What they were doing was buying up the raw wool in sheep-raising villages, distributing it to other villages that were now geared entirely to weaving and producing cloth, and then taking the finished material to market for sale. Entire areas came to be in the employ of merchants, dependent on them for materials and a livelihood. This created a new set of relationships, based on piecework rather than services, which again helped redirect the traditional patterns of life in the village, reducing independence and the ties of friendship and mutual help.

The isolation was also lessened as cities grew, not only because large urban centers needed ever wider regions to provide them with food and goods, but also because they attracted people who could not make ends meet in the countryside. Long-range communications became more common, especially as localities were linked into national market and trade networks, and immigrants in cities came to know fellow countrymen from distant villages (see Map 16.3).

Noneconomic forces, too, hastened the loss of autonomy. Over the course of the seventeenth century, nobles were looking more and more to central courts and capital cities, rather than to their local holdings, for position and power. Pursuing the seigneurial reaction, they treated the villages they dominated as sources of income and began to distance themselves from the inhabitants. Relations became impersonal where once they had been close. Charity, for example, was no longer thought to be the

Culture and Society in the Age of the Scientific Revolution 1540–1660

MAP 16.3: SPEED OF NEWS TRAVELING TO VENICE

responsibility of neighbors: it was the duty of the church or the government.

The churches were taking on new roles, but these only had the effect of encouraging conformity. In Catholic countries the Counter Reformation produced better-educated priests who were trained to impose official doctrine instead of tolerating local customs. Among Protestants, ministers were similarly well educated and denounced traditional beliefs as idolatrous or superstitious. Regardless of church, the outside world was intruding yet again. Habits did not change overnight, but in the long run the villagers were being forced to accept new values and to abandon their old beliefs.

The final blow was the growing presence of representatives of central government. In 1500 few villagers would have known what a servant of the king was, let alone have seen one. By 1700 they would all have had considerable experience with bureaucrats of one sort or another: tax collectors, recruiting officers, or army suppliers. Villagers no longer lived on their own in a small corner of the land. They were a part of the territorial state, important resources that the national government had to tap if it was to increase its power. Institutions (such as charity) had to be uniform; order had to be maintained. With their autonomy fragmenting and their customs and coherence under assault, the villages had no capacity to resist the integrating forces that were blending them into their nation states and subduing their eccentricities and traditions.

As Europeans entered the last decades of the seventeenth century, they had reason to feel that the upheavals and uncertain times they had gone through for more than one hundred years were behind them. An extraordinarily successful intellectual movement, the scientific revolution, had solved many ancient problems about nature. Artists and writers had developed a new confidence. And throughout society an atmosphere of orderliness was returning after over a century of change, disruption, and excesses like the witch craze. Religion had lost much of its power to arouse hatred and aggression; a calmer time seemed to be dawning, taking as its model the respect for reason that the scientists were encouraging.

The natural beneficiaries of these tendencies were the upper classes throughout Europe. Ordinary villagers may not have felt reconciled to the order being imposed upon them, but they proved unable to resist the forces—economic, political, and cultural—that were pressing them to conform. On the other hand, the sense of order was perfectly suited to the needs of aristocrats. They could now relax, confident that their power was secure. At dazzling princely courts, especially in France, they could enjoy the absence of turmoil and set their stamp on the culture of a new, less troubled age.

RECOMMENDED READING

Sources

*Drake, Stillman (tr. and ed.). *Discoveries and Opinions of Galileo*. 1957. The complete texts of some of Galileo's most important and readable works.
*Hall, Marie Boas (ed.). *Nature and Nature's Laws: Documents of the Scientific Revolution*. 1970. A good collection of documents by and about the pioneers of modern science.

Studies

*Butterfield, Herbert. *The Origins of Modern Science*. 1949. An elegantly written history of the scientific revolution, with a good bibliography.
*Caspar, Max. *Kepler*. C. Doris Hellman (tr.). 1959. A lucid biography of a complicated man, half-scientist, half-magician.
Frame, Donald M. *Montaigne: A Biography*. 1965. The best biography of this influential thinker.
*Geymonat, Ludovico. *Galileo Galilei*. Stillman Drake (tr.). 1965. A straightforward and clear biography.
*Ginzburg, Carlo. *The Cheese and the Worms: The Cosmos of a Sixteenth-Century Miller*. John and Anne Tedeschi (trs.). 1980. A remarkable account, focusing on the beliefs of a man who lived in a small northern Italian town, which brings to life the extraordinary variety of the popular culture of the time.
*Hibbard, Howard. *Bernini*. 1965. A graceful account of the life and work of the artist who was the epitome of the Baroque.
Kamen, Henry. *The Iron Century: Social Change in Europe 1550–1660*. 1971. This thorough, almost encyclopedic overview of the social history of the period also has a good bibliography.
*Kuhn, Thomas S. *The Copernican Revolution: Planetary Astronomy in the Development of Western Thought*. 1957. The most comprehensive account of the revolution in astronomy.
*———. *The Structure of Scientific Revolutions*. 1962. A suggestive interpretation of the reasons the scientific revolution developed and took hold.
*Ladurie, Emmanuel Le Roy. *The Peasants of Languedoc*. John Day (tr.). 1966. A brilliant evocation of peasant life in France in the sixteenth and seventeenth centuries.
Maland, David. *Culture and Society in Seventeenth-Century France*. 1970. This survey of art, drama, and literature contains a good discussion of the rise of Classicism.
Palisca, Claude. *Baroque Music*. The best survey of this period in the history of music.
*Popkin, Richard H. *The History of Scepticism from Erasmus to Descartes*. 1964. Taking one strand in European thought as its subject, this lively study places both Montaigne and Descartes in a new perspective.
*Shearman, John. *Mannerism*. 1968. The best short introduction to a difficult artistic style.
Tapié, V. L. *The Age of Grandeur: Baroque Art and Architecture*. A. R. Williamson (tr.). 1960. Although concentrating primarily on France and Austria, this is the most comprehensive survey of this period in art.
*Thomas, Keith. *Religion and the Decline of Magic*. 1971. The most thorough account of popular culture yet published, this enormous book, while dealing mainly with England, treats at length such subjects as witchcraft, astrology, and ghosts in a most readable style.
White, Christopher. *Rembrandt and his World*. 1964. A brief but wide-ranging introduction to the artist's work and life.
———. *Rubens and his World*. 1968. As good on Rubens as the previous title is on Rembrandt.

---

*Available in paperback.

17

THE TRIUMPH OF ARISTOCRATS AND KINGS
1660–1715

Ever since the time that effective central governments had coalesced in Europe in the Late Middle Ages, nobles and rulers had engaged in a running struggle for power. After the upheavals of the mid-seventeenth century, however, it became clear that central administrations—now highly complex and commanding large bureaucracies—would dominate political life. Yet no ruler could govern without the help of the aristocracy. Of the main orders, or estates, into which society was divided—aristocrats, clergy, townspeople, and peasants—only the aristocrats had the education, experience, and status essential for the running of a state.

The actual control they wielded over policy varied widely. In the absolutist realms they were most powerful in Austria, less so in France and Brandenburg-Prussia, and least in Russia. Moreover influence in the government was usually restricted to a small group; the class as a whole benefited only indirectly. But in England (where the ruling elite had been penetrated by members of the untitled gentry), the United Provinces, Sweden, and Poland, virtually no major decision could be executed without their approval. In effect, the aristocracy had taken possession of the administration of Europe's states and no longer had to compete with towns, representative assemblies, or the ruler himself for the fruits of power.

By the end of the seventeenth century, therefore, Europe's nobility was moving toward a new type of leadership. Historians have called this the domestication of the aristocracy, a process in which great lords who had once drawn their status primarily from the antiquity of their lineage or the extent of their lands gradually came to see service to the throne and royal favor as the best source of power.

To central administrations, eager to restore or confirm orderly government after over a century of disruptions, this alliance was more than welcome, and the rewards they bestowed—whether in patronage, privilege, or perquisites—were enormous. New power structures thus emerged in the age of Louis XIV, though the forms differed from country to country, and the fortunes of the lower classes fluctuated accordingly. Yet throughout Europe the quest for order was the underlying concern, a preoccupation that was already evident in the mid-seventeenth century and that pervaded not only political and social developments, but also thought and taste during the subsequent fifty years.

I. THE ABSOLUTE MONARCHIES

In countries that were ruled by absolutist monarchs—where all power was believed to emanate from the untrammeled person of the king—the center of society was the great court. Here the leaders of government assembled, and around them swirled the most envied social circles of the time. At the court of Louis XIV in particular, an atmosphere of ornate splendor arose that, though primarily intended to exalt the king, inevitably glorified the aristocracy too. No other ruler could match its scale and magnificence, but many tried to imitate its style.

Louis XIV at Versailles

In the view of Louis XIV (1643–1715), absolutism and the building of both the state and the government went hand in hand. But all three had to have a focus, preferably away from the turbulent city of Paris. To this end Louis, at a cost of half a year's royal income, transformed a small château his father had built at Versailles, twelve miles outside of Paris, into the largest building in Europe, surrounded by vast and elaborate formal gardens.

The splendor of the setting was designed to impress the world with the majesty of its principal occupant, and a complex ritual of daily ceremonies centered on the king gradually evolved. The name "Sun King" was another means of self-aggrandizement, symbolized by coins that showed the rays of the sun falling first on Louis and then by reflection onto his subjects, who thus owed life and warmth to their monarch. Versailles also provided an appropriate physical setting for the domestication of the nobility. Each year those who sought Louis' favor had to make an ostentatious appearance at court, and endless factions and plots swirled through the palace as courtiers jockeyed for position, competing for such privileges as handing the king his gloves in the morning. Louis regarded all men as his servants, and they were kept constantly aware of their vulnerable status.

Conditions at Versailles were far from pleasant for these nobles. Crammed into tiny rooms, surrounded by the awful smells of an overcrowded palace without toilet facilities, and so cold that their drinking water froze at dinner parties, they continued to endure the discomforts in order to have access to the power only the court could bestow. In the end, the nobles found it easier to establish their prominence by obtaining offices and positions from the king than by resorting to their traditional unruliness. This domestication gave them a less dangerous route to influence, and it also provided Louis with the talents of able and loyal administrators. Moreover, he justified his supremacy with a new emphasis on an old political concept, the divine right of kings. This theory, which derived from the fact that kings were anointed with holy oil at their coronations, asserted that the monarch was God's representative on earth. He was therefore entitled to absolute power, because treason was also blasphemy. The main theorist at Versailles, Bishop Bossuet, called Louis God's lieutenant and argued that the Bible itself endorsed absolutism. Nothing happened at court that would have given anyone cause to think otherwise.

Government and Foreign Policy

Yet this system was not merely a device to satisfy one man's whim, for Louis was a gifted state builder. In creating or reorganizing government institutions to reflect his own wishes, he strengthened his authority at home and increased his ascendancy over his neighbors. In fact the most durable result of absolutism in seventeenth-century France was the state's winning of final control over three critical activities: the use of armed force, the formulation and execution of laws, and the collection and

expenditure of revenue. These functions in turn depended on a centrally controlled bureaucracy responsive to royal orders and efficient enough to carry them out in distant provinces over the objections of local groups.

In its ideal form an absolute monarch's bureaucracy was insulated from outside pressure by the king's power to remove and transfer appointees. In the case of France, this involved creating new administrative officials—commissioners—to supersede some existing officers or magistrates who claimed their positions by virtue of property or other rights.[1] The process also required training programs, improved administrative methods, and the use of experts wherever possible. This approach was considered desirable both for the central bureaucracy in the capital and for the provincial offices.

At the head of this structure, Louis XIV was able to carry off successfully a responsibility that few monarchs had the talent to pursue: he served as his own first minister, actively and effectively overseeing administrative affairs. He thus filled two roles—as king in council and king in court. Louis the administrator coexisted with Louis the courtier, who cultivated the arts, hunted, and indulged in gargantuan banquets. In his view the two roles went together, and he held them in balance.

Among his numerous imitators, however, this was not always the case. Court life was the pleasanter, easier side of absolutism. It tended to consume an inordinate share of a state's resources and to become an end in itself. The display performed certain useful functions, of course; it stimulated luxury trades, supported cultural endeavors, and thus exercised a civilizing influence on the nobility of Europe. But beyond this it tended to be frivolous and wasteful, lending an undeserved prestige to the leisure pursuits of the upper classes, such as dancing, card playing, and hunting, while sapping the energies of influential figures. Louis was one of the few who avoided sacrificing affairs of state to regal pomp.

Like court life, government policy under Louis XIV was tailored to the aim of state building. As he was to discover, there were limits to his absolutism; the resources and powers at his disposal were not endless. But until the last years of his reign, they served his many purposes extremely well. Moreover Louis had superb support at the highest levels of his administration—men whose viewpoints differed but whose skills were carefully blended by their ruler.

The king's two leading ministers were Jean Baptiste Colbert and the marquis of Louvois. Colbert was a financial wizard who had been raised to prominence by Mazarin and who regarded a mercantilist policy as the key to state building. He believed that the government should give priority to increasing France's wealth. This meant in turn that the chief danger to the country's well-being was the United Provinces, Europe's great trader state, and that royal resources should be poured into the navy, manufacturing, and shipping. By contrast Louvois, the son of a military administrator, consistently emphasized the army as the foundation of France's power. He believed that the country was threatened primarily by land—by the Holy Roman Empire on its flat, vulnerable northeast frontier—and thus that resources should be allocated to the army and to an extensive border fortification program.

Louis shifted back and forth between these considerations, but the basic tendencies of his policy can always be traced. In his early years

---

[1] The *intendants,* who remained the chief provincial administrators, provided the model for the commissioners, because their success derived from dependence on royal approval. It should be noted that all bureaucrats were called officers, but those with judicial functions were known as magistrates.

The Palace of Versailles in 1668.
(Photo: Louvre)

Louis XIV (seated) is shown here in full regal splendor surrounded by three of his heirs. On his right is his eldest son, on his left is his eldest grandson, and, reaching out his hand, his eldest great-grandson, held by his governess. All three of these heirs died before Louis, and thus they never became kings of France.
(Photo: Wallace Collection, London)

he relied heavily on Colbert, who moved gradually toward war with the Dutch when all attempts to undermine their control of French maritime trade failed. But the war, occupying most of the 1670s, was a failure, and so the pendulum swung toward Louvois. Adopting the marquis' aims, in the early 1680s Louis asserted his right to a succession of territories on France's northeast border. No one claim seemed important enough to provoke the em-

MAP 17.1: THE WARS OF LOUIS XIV

pire to military action; moreover its princes were distracted by a growing Turkish threat from the East. Thus France was able to annex large segments of territory, ultimately extending her frontier to Strasbourg, near the Rhine River (see Map 17.1). Finally, however, the defensive League of Augsburg was formed against Louis, and another war broke out in 1688. This one too went badly for him, and when he decided to seek peace, Louvois fell from favor. In a move that surprised all of Europe, Louis then brought back to power a former foreign minister named Simon de Pomponne, who had always stood for peace and careful diplomacy. It was characteristic of the Sun King to use his servants this way—raising and discarding them according to their position on his policy of the moment. But even this balancing process broke down in the last two decades of his reign, when France became involved in a bitter, drawn-out war that brought famine, wretched poverty, and humiliation. Louis was seeking the succession to the Spanish throne for his family, and he was determined to pursue the fighting until he achieved his aim.

This final and ruinous enterprise revealed both the new power of France and her limits. By launching an all-out attempt to establish his own and his country's supremacy, he showed that he felt capable of taking on the whole of Europe; but by then he no longer had the economic and military base at home or the weak opposition abroad to assure success.

The strains had begun to appear in the 1690s, when shattering famines throughout France reduced both tax revenues and manpower at home, while enemies began to unite abroad. Louis had the most formidable army in Europe—400,000 men by the end of his reign—but both William III of the United Provinces and Leopold I of the Holy Roman Empire believed that he could be defeated by a combined assault. They worked persistently to this end, particularly after the Turkish threat to Leopold ended with the failure of the siege of Vienna, in 1683, and William gained the English throne six years later. The League of Augsburg, transformed into the Grand Alliance after William and other rulers joined it, fought a successful holding action against Louis' attempt to intervene across the Rhine, and the final showdown was precipitated when the Hapsburg king of Spain, Charles II, died without an heir.

There were various possible claimants to the throne, and Charles himself had changed his mind a number of times, but at his death his choice was Philip, Louis XIV's grandson (see the accompanying figure). Had Louis been willing to agree not to unite the thrones of France and Spain and to open the Spanish Empire to foreign traders, Charles' wish might well have been respected by the rest of Europe. But Louis refused to compromise, insisting that there were no conditions to Charles' bequest. The rest of Europe disagreed and declared war on France so as to prevent Philip's unrestricted succession and the limitation of trade in the Spanish Empire. Thus Louis found himself fighting virtually the entire Continent in the War of the Spanish Succession, not only at home but also overseas, in India, Canada, and the Caribbean.

Led by brilliant generals, the Englishman John Churchill, duke of Marlborough, and the Austrian Prince Eugène, the allies won a series of smashing victories. France's hardships were increased by a terrible famine in 1709. Yet the Sun King's hold over his subjects was unimpaired. Nobody rose in revolt against him; his policies were not seriously challenged; and despite military disaster he succeeded in keeping his nation's borders intact and the Spanish throne for his grandson (though he had to give up the possibility of union with France and the restrictions on trade in the Spanish Empire) when peace treaties were signed at Utrecht in 1713 and 1714. In sum his great task of state

THE SPANISH SUCCESSION, 1700

NAMES IN CAPITALS = Kings of Spain
Names in italics = Kings of France

*People designated at various times as heirs of Charles II

building, both at home and abroad, had faced and withstood the severest of all tests: defeat on the battlefield.

Domestic Affairs

The assertion of royal supremacy at home was almost complete by the time Louis came to power, but he extended the principle of centralized control to religion and social institutions. Religion was a major area of activity because two groups, the Protestant Huguenots and the Catholic Jansenists, interfered with the spiritual and confessional uniformity that the king considered essential in the absolutist state.

Of the two the Huguenots were the more obviously unintegrated. Government pressures against them mounted after 1668, when their greatest adherent, the famous Marshal Turenne, converted to Catholicism. Finally in 1685 Louis revoked the century-old Edict of Nantes, thus forcing France's 1 million Protestants either to leave the country (four-fifths did) or to convert to Catholicism. This was a political rather than a religious act, taken for the sake of unity despite the economic consequences that followed the departure of a vigorous and productive minority.

Jansenism posed a more elusive problem. It had far fewer followers, though among them were some of the greatest figures in the land, such as the playwright Racine; and it was a movement within Catholicism. But the very fact that it challenged the official church hierarchy and had been condemned by Rome made it a source of unrest and disorder. What was worse, it was beginning to gain support among the magistrate class—the royal officers in the parlements, who had to register all royal edicts before they became law. The Parlement of Paris was the only governmental institution that offered Louis any real resistance during his reign. The issues over which it caused trouble were usually religious, and the link between parlementaire independence and dislike for court frivolity on the one hand, and Jansenism on the other, gave Louis more than enough reason for displeasure. He razed the Jansenists' headquarters, the Abbey of Port-Royal, and then persuaded the pope to issue a bull condemning Jansenism. He was prevented from implementing the bull—over parlementaire opposition—only by his death, in 1715.

The drive toward uniformity that lay behind these actions was reflected in all aspects of domestic policy. Louis rapidly crushed what little parlementaire protest there was; an attempt by peasants in central France to resist the government was ruthlessly suppressed; Parisian publishers came under bureaucratic supervision; and the *intendants*, the government's chief provincial officers, were given increased authority, particularly in connection with the ever-growing needs of the army.

At the outset of his rule, Louis used the government's power to improve France's economy. In this he followed a pattern familiar from earlier monarchs' reigns: an initial burst of reform measures to cure the country's economic ills, which were gradually forgotten because foreign policy demanded instant funds. In the early years, under Colbert's ministry, major efforts were made to stimulate manufacturing, agriculture, and home and foreign trade. Some industries, notably those involving luxuries like the silk production of Lyons, received considerable help and owed their rise to prosperity to royal patronage. Colbert also tried, not entirely effectively, to reduce the crippling effects of France's countless internal tolls. These were usually nobles' perquisites, and they could multiply the cost of goods shipped any distance. The government divided the country into a number of districts, within which shipments were to be toll-free, but the system never removed the worst abuses. And finally, Louis made a concerted attempt to boost foreign trade, at first by financing new overseas trading companies and later by founding new port cities to strengthen maritime forces. He achieved notable success in the West Indies, which became a source of immense wealth.

Louis' overall accomplishments were remarkable, and France became the envy of Europe. Yet ever since the Sun King's reign, historians have recalled the ruination caused by famine and war during his last years and have contrasted his glittering court with the misery of French people at large. Particularly after the famines of the 1690s and 1709, many contemporaries remarked on the dreadful condition of peasants in various regions. Even at Versailles there was disenchantment, expressed not only by a shrewd critic like the duke of Saint-Simon, who looked on the emptiness of court life with disdain, but also by concerned men who had not previously found fault with Louis' policies. A notable example was the great fortifications expert Sébastien le Prestre, marquis of Vauban, who had made a vital contribution to the military successes of the reign (see Map 17.1). Late in life he called on the government to end its obsession with war because taxation was bringing the ordinary French person to a state of hopeless despair.

Such warnings of course went unheeded, but in recent years historians have questioned whether France was in fact so badly off. That there was hardship cannot be denied, but its extent and lasting effect are open to question for two reasons. First, the difficulties caused none of the uprisings that were the normal reaction in the countryside either to excesses on the part of the central government or to severe food shortages. Second, France's quick recovery and unprecedented economic and demographic growth in the years following 1715 could never have taken place if the country had been as shattered as the dramatic tales of catastrophe suggest.

Nonetheless the reign of Louis XIV can be regarded as the end of an era in the life of the lower classes. In the early eighteenth century, the terrible subsistence crisis, with their cycles of famine and plague, came to an end; both manufacturing and agriculture entered a period of great prosperity; and cities enjoyed spectacular new growth. It is likely that the hand of the central government seemed heavier in 1715 than a hundred years before, but the small landowner and urban worker had been struggling with taxes for decades, whether the payee was king or noble. And the Counter Reformation Church, growing in strength since the Council of Trent, provided a measure of blessing, for it began to bring into local parishes better-educated and more dedicated priests who, as part of their new commitment to service, exerted themselves to calm the outbreaks of witchcraft and irrational fear that had swept the countryside for centuries. The fortunes of Jacques Bonhomme, the symbolic French everyman, had probably risen by 1715.

The improvement was also apparent in the mercantile class, which was about to enjoy a level of prosperity that outstripped even the sixteenth-century boom. Discontent at the government's interventions may have been felt by magistrates and parlementaires, who bewailed their lack of power, but these were voices in the wilderness. That there were strains nobody could deny, but on the whole the absolutist structure had achieved its ends—a united, prosperous, and powerful France.

The Hapsburgs at Vienna and Madrid

The pattern set at Versailles was repeated at the court of the Hapsburg Leopold I, the Holy Roman emperor (1658–1705). Heir to a reduced inheritance that gave him effective control over only Bohemia, Austria, and a small portion of Hungary, Leopold nonetheless maintained a magnificent establishment. His plans for a new palace, Schönbrunn, that was to have outshone Versailles were modified only because of a lack of funds. And his promotion of the court as the center of all political and social life turned Vienna into what it had never been before: a city of noble as well as burgher houses.

Nevertheless, Leopold himself did not display the pretensions of the Sun King. He had been a younger son and had inherited his crown only because of the death of his brother. An indecisive, retiring, deeply religious man, he had little fondness for the bravado Louis XIV enjoyed. He was a composer of no small talent, and his patronage laid the foundation for the great musical culture that was to be one of Vienna's chief glories. Whatever his inclinations, however, he found himself the holder of considerable royal authority: for more than a century, except during the Bohemian resistance of 1618 to 1621, the Hapsburg rulers had had few serious challenges to their power in their own domains. This was a tradition that Leopold felt obliged to continue, though unlike Louis XIV he relied on a small group of leading aristocrats to devise policy and run the administration.

The Thirty Years' War had revealed that the elected head of the Holy Roman Empire could no longer control the princes who nominally owed him allegiance (see p. 490), but within his own dominions he could maintain complete control with the cooperation of the aristocracy. The Privy Council, which in effect ran Leopold's domain, was largely filled with members of aristocratic families, and his chief advisers were always prominent nobles. But he did not switch about among representatives of various policies as Louis XIV did. Instead he carefully consulted each of his ministers and then came to decisions with agonizing slowness, even when all of them were agreed.

Unlike the other courts of Europe, Schönbrunn did not favor only native-born aristocrats. The leader of Austria's armies during the Turks' siege of Vienna in 1683 was Charles, duke of Lorraine, a prince whose duchy had long ago been taken over by the French. His predecessor as field marshal had been an Italian, and his successor was to be one of the most brilliant soldiers of the age, Prince Eugène of Savoy. None of these men were members of the Austrian nobility until Leopold gave them titles within his own dominions, but they all fitted easily into the aristocratic circles that controlled the government and the army.

Prince Eugène was a spectacular symbol of the aristocracy's continuing dominance of European politics and society. A member of one of the most distinguished families on the Continent, he had been raised in France but found himself passed over when Louis XIV awarded army commissions, perhaps because he had been intended for the church. Yet he was determined to follow a military career and therefore volunteered to serve the Austrians in their long struggle with the Turks. His talents soon became evident: he was field marshal of Austria's troops by the time he was thirty. For the next forty years, though foreign-born, he was a decisive influence in Hapsburg affairs, the man primarily responsible for the transformation of Vienna's policies from defensive to aggressive.

Until the siege of 1683, Leopold's innate cautiousness kept Austria simply holding the line, both against Louis XIV and against the Turks. In the 1690s, however, he tried a bolder course at Eugène's urging and in the process

MAP 17.2: THE AUSTRIAN EMPIRE 1657–1718

laid the foundations for a new Hapsburg empire along the Danube River: Austria-Hungary (see Map 17.2). He helped create the coalition that defeated Louis in the 1700s, intervened in Italy so that his landlocked domains could gain an outlet to the sea, and began the long process of pushing the Turks out of the Balkans. Leopold did not live to see the advance more than started, but by the time of Eugène's death, the Austrians were within a hundred miles of the Black Sea.

However, the power of the aristocracy blocked the complete centralization of Leopold's dominions. Louis XIV supported his nobles after he had subdued their independent positions in the provinces; Leopold by contrast gave them influence in the government without first establishing genuine control over all his lands. The nobility did not cause him the troubles his predecessors had faced during the Thirty Years' War, but he had to limit his ambitions in territories outside of Austria. Moreover, as Austrians came increasingly to dominate the court, the nobles of Hungary and Bohemia reacted by clinging ever more stubbornly to local traditions and rights. Thus Leopold's was an absolutism under which the aristocracy retained far more autonomous power—and a far firmer base of local support, stimulated by nationalist sentiments—than was the case in France, despite the increased centralization achieved during his reign.

Madrid enjoyed none of the success of its fellow Hapsburg court. Its king, Charles II, was a sickly man, incapable of having children; and the War of the Spanish Succession seriously reduced the inheritance he left. Both the southern Netherlands and most of Italy passed to the Austrian Hapsburgs, and Spain's overseas possessions were already virtually independent territories, paying little notice to the homeland.

The Spanish nobility was even more successful than the Austrian in turning the trappings of absolutism to its advantage. In 1650 the crown had been able to recapture Catalonia's loyalty only by granting the province's aristocracy considerable autonomy, and this pattern recurred throughout Spain's Continental holdings. Parasitic, unproductive nobles controlled the regime almost entirely for their own personal gain. The country had lapsed into economic and cultural stagnation, subservient to a group of powerful families, and reflecting its former glory only in a fairly respectable navy.

The Hohenzollerns at Berlin

The one new power that emerged to prominence during the age of Louis XIV was Brandenburg-Prussia, and here again a close alliance was established between a powerful ruler and his nobles. Frederick William (1640–1688), known as the "great elector," was the ruler of scattered territories that stretched 700 miles from Cleves, on the Rhine, to a part of Prussia on the Baltic. (See Map 17.3.) Taking advantage of the uncertainties and hopes for a new order that followed the chaos of the Thirty Years' War, he made his territories the dominant principality in northern Germany and at the same time strengthened his power over his subjects. His first task was in foreign affairs, because when he took over as elector most of his possessions were devastated by war, with troops swarming over them at will. Frederick William realized that by determination and intelligent planning, even a small prince could emerge from these disasters in a good position *if* he had an army. With some military force at his disposal, he could become a useful ally for the big powers, who could then help him against his neighbors, while at home he would have the strength to crush his opponents.

By 1648 Frederick William had 8,000 troops, and he was backed by both the Dutch and the French at Westphalia as a possible restraint on Sweden in northern Europe. Without having done much to earn new territory, he did very well in the peace settlement, and he then took brilliant advantage of the Baltic wars of the 1650s to confirm his gains by switching sides at crucial moments. In the process his army grew to 22,000 men, and he began to use it to impose his will on his own territories. The fact that the army was essential to all of Frederick William's successes—giving him status in Europe and power within his territories—was to influence much of Prussia's and thus also Germany's subsequent history.

The presence of the military, and its role in establishing the elector's supremacy, was apparent throughout Brandenburg-Prussia's society. In 1653 the Diet of Brandenburg met for the last time, sealing its own fate by giving Frederick William the right to raise taxes on his own authority, though previously he had had to obtain its consent. The War Chest, the office in charge of financing the army, took over the functions of a treasury department and collected government revenue even when the state was at peace. The execution of policy in the localities was placed under the supervision of war commissars, men who were originally responsible for military recruitment, billeting, and supply in each district of Brandenburg-

Prussia, but who now became the principal agents of all government departments.

Apart from the representative assemblies, Frederick William faced substantial resistance only from the cities of his realm, which had long traditions of independence. Yet once again sheer intimidation swept opposition aside. The last determined effort to dispute his authority arose in the rich city of Königsberg, which allied with the Estates General of Prussia to refuse to pay taxes. But this resistance was brought to a swift conclusion in 1662, when Frederick William marched into the city with a few thousand troops. Similar pressure brought the towns of Cleves, along the Rhine, into submission after centuries of proud independence.

The nobles were major beneficiaries of this policy. It was in fact the alliance between the nobility and Frederick William that made it possible for the Diet, the cities, and the representative assemblies to be undermined. The leading families saw their best opportunities for the future in cooperation with the central government, and both within the various representative assemblies and in the localities, they worked for the establishment of absolutist powers—that is, for the removal of all restraints on the elector. The most significant indicator of their success was that by the end of the century, two tax rates had been devised, one for cities and one for the countryside, to the great advantage of the latter.

Not only did the nobles staff the upper levels of the elector's bureaucracy and army; they also won a new prosperity for themselves. Particularly in Prussia they used the reimposition of serfdom and their dominant political position to consolidate their land holdings into vast, highly profitable estates. This was a vital grain-producing area—often called the granary of Europe—and they made the most of its economic potential. To maximize their profits they eliminated the middleman by not only growing but also distributing their produce themselves. Efficiency became their hallmark, and their wealth was soon famous throughout the Holy Roman Empire. Known as Junkers, these Prussian entrepreneurs were probably the most successful group within the European aristocracy in their pursuit of both economic and political power.

Unlike Louis in France, however, Frederick William did not force his nobles to lead a life of social ostentation revolving around his person. The court at Berlin became a glittering focus of society only under his son, Frederick III (1688–1701). The great elector himself was more interested in organizing his administration, increasing tax returns, building up his army, and imposing his authority at home and abroad. He began the development of his capital, Berlin, into a major city and cultural center—he laid out the famous double avenue Unter den Linden, and he founded what was to become one of the finest libraries in the world, the Prussian State Library, in his palace—but this was never among his prime concerns. His son by contrast enjoyed the pomp of his princely status and set about encouraging the arts with enthusiasm.

Frederick III lacked only one attribute of royalty: a crown. He hungered for the distinction, and he gained it when Emperor Leopold I, who still retained the right to confer titles in the empire, needed Brandenburg's troops during the War of the Spanish Succession against Louis XIV. Although none of Frederick's territories had been a kingdom previously, he was allowed to call himself "king in Prussia" (a technicality; the title soon became "king of Prussia"). At a splendid coronation in 1701, Elector Frederick III of Brandenburg was crowned King Frederick I (1701–1713), and thereafter the court, now regal, could feel itself to be on equal terms with the other monarchical settings of Europe.

Frederick undertook a determined cam-

This early eighteenth-century engraving of Berlin shows a skyline marked by the many new churches with which the electors were beautifying their capital. Yet the view also reminds us that, for all their rapid growth, eighteenth-century European cities (with the exception only of the three or four largest, which were surrounded by expanding suburbs) were still very close to the agriculture of the nearby countryside.
(Photo: New York Public Library/Picture Collection)

paign to improve the social and cultural atmosphere in his lands. He founded the noble Order of the Black Eagle to encourage aristocratic ambitions, and he made his palace a center of art and polite society to compete, he hoped, with Versailles. A major construction program in Berlin beautified the city with seven churches and a number of huge public buildings, making it an important center of Baroque architecture. Following English and French models, Frederick also created an Academy of Sciences in Berlin and persuaded the most famous German scientist and philosopher of the day, Gottfried Wilhelm von Leibniz, to become its first president. All these activities obtained generous support from state revenues, as did the universities of Brandenburg and Prussia. By the end of his reign, in 1713, Frederick could take considerable satisfaction from the transformation he had brought about. He had given his realm the prestige of a throne, the reputation derived from important artistic and intellectual activity, and the elegant manners of an aristocracy at the head of both social and political life.

Peter the Great at St. Petersburg

One of the reasons the new absolutist regimes of the late seventeenth and eighteenth centuries seemed so different from their predecessors was that many of them consciously created new settings for themselves. Versailles, Schönbrunn, and Berlin were all either new or totally transformed sites for royal courts. The palaces were far larger and grander and provided a more impressive backdrop than previous seats of government. But only one of the autocrats of the period went so far as to build an entirely new capital: Peter I of Russia, called the Great (1682–1725), who named the city St. Petersburg after his patron saint. Not surprisingly he was also the only man among his contemporaries to declare himself an emperor.

None of the monarchs of the period had Peter's terrifying energy or ruthless resolve. A man of fierce temper, he was determined to impose his will without regard for opposition, though his decisions were often made in anger and then blindly implemented. The supreme example of Peter's callousness was the torture of his own son, a quiet, retiring boy, who was killed by the inhumane treatment he received after trying to escape from his overbearing father.

Peter left no doubt about his intention to exercise absolute control in his realm. Of all the changes brought about in his reign, the most unprecedented was the destruction of ecclesiastical independence. When the patriarch of the Russian Church died in 1700, the tsar simply did not replace him. The government took over the monasteries, using their enormous income for its own purposes, and appointed a procurator (the first one was an army officer) to supervise all religious affairs. The church was in effect made a branch of government.

In the government itself Peter virtually ignored the Duma, the traditional advisory council, and concentrated on strengthening his bureaucracy. He carried out change after change, few of which lasted any length of time, but their cumulative effect was the creation of an administrative complex many times larger than the one he had inherited. Copying Western models, especially the Swedish system, he set up carefully organized executive departments, some with specialized functions, such as finance, and others with responsibility for geographic areas, such as Siberia. The result was an elaborate but unified hierarchy of authority rising from local agents of the government through provincial officials up to the staffs and governors of eleven large administrative units and finally to the leaders of the regime in the capital. Peter's reign marked the beginning of the saturating bureaucratization that was to characterize Russia ever after.

In the process the tsar laid the foundations for a two-class society that persisted until the twentieth century. Previously a number of ranks had existed within both the nobility and the peasantry, and a group in the middle, known as the *odnodvortsy* (roughly, "esquires"), were sometimes considered the lowest nobles and sometimes the highest peasants. Under Peter such mingling disappeared. All peasants were reduced to a uniform level, their equality

In the eighteenth century Peter the Great of Russia outstripped the grandeur of other monarchs of the period by erecting an entirely new city for his capital. St. Petersburg (now Leningrad) was built by forced labor of the peasants under Peter's orders; they are shown here laying the foundations for the city.
(Photo: Tass from Sovfoto)

emphasized by their universal liability to a new poll tax, military conscription, and forced public work, such as the building of St. Petersburg. Below them were the serfs, whose numbers were steadily increased by harsh legislation and who spread throughout the southern and western areas of Peter's dominions where previously they had been relatively unknown. The peasants possessed a few advantages over the serfs, but their living conditions were often equally dreadful.

At the same time Peter created a homogeneous class of nobles by substituting status within the bureaucracy for status within the traditional hierarchy of titles and ranks. In 1722 he issued a table of ranks that gave everyone his place according to the bureaucratic or military office that he held. Differentiations still existed under the new system, but they were no longer unbridgeable, as they had been when antiquity of family was decisive. The result was a more tightly controlled social order and greater uniformity than in France or Brandenburg-Prussia. By definition the Russian aristocracy was the bureaucracy and the bureaucracy the aristocracy.

But this was not a relatively voluntary alliance between nobles and government, such as existed in the West; in return for his support and his total subjection of the peasantry, Peter required the aristocrats to provide manpower for his rapidly expanding bureaucracy and officers for his growing army. When he began the construction of St. Petersburg, he also demanded that the leading families build splendid mansions in his new capital. In effect the tsar

MAP 17.3: CONFLICT IN THE BALTIC AREA 1660–1721

was offering privilege and wealth in exchange for what was virtual conscription into public service. Thus there was hardly any sense of partnership between aristocracy and throne—the tsar often had to use coercion to ensure that his wishes were followed.

On the other hand Peter did a good deal to build up the nobles' fortunes and their ability to control the countryside. As one recent interpreter of the tsar's policy put it, he wanted "the landowning nobility to be rich and powerful; but it must nonetheless be composed of his personal servants who were to use their wealth and power in his services."[2] It has been estimated that by 1710 he had put under the supervision of great landowners more than 40,000 peasant and serf households that had formerly been under the crown. And he was liberal in conferring new titles—some of them, such as count and baron, an imitation of German examples.

In creating an aristocratic society at his court, as in much else that he did, Peter mixed imitations of what he admired in the West with native developments. He forced the nobility to follow the ritual surrounding a Western throne; he founded an Academy of Sciences in 1725; and he encouraged the beginnings of a theater at court. Italian artists were imported, along with Dutch ship builders, German engineers, and Scandinavian colonels, not only to apply their skills, but to teach them to the Russians. St. Petersburg, unquestionably the finest example of a city built in the Classical style of eighteenth-century architecture, is mainly the work of Italians, and the Academy of Sciences long depended on foreigners for whatever stature it had. But gradually the Russians took over their own institutions—military academies produced native officers, for example—and by the end of Peter's reign the nobles had no need of foreign experts to help run the government. Within little more than half a century, the Russian Court would become the elegant, French-speaking gathering so penetratingly described in Tolstoy's *War and Peace*. Peter the Great had laid the foundations for the aristocratic society by which his people were to be ruled for two hundred years.

The purpose of these radical internal changes was not only to consolidate the tsar's power at home but to extend it abroad. He established a huge standing army, more than 300,000 strong by the 1720s, and imported the latest military techniques from the West. One of Peter's most cherished projects, the creation of a navy, had limited success, but there could be no doubt that he transformed Russia's capacity for war and her status among European states. He extended the country's frontier to the south and west, beginning the destruction of Sweden's empire at the battle of Poltava in 1709 and following this triumph by more than a decade of advance into Estonia, Lithuania, and Poland (see Map 17.3). By the time of his death Russia was the dominant power of the Baltic region and a major influence in European affairs.

II. THE ANTI-ABSOLUTISTS

The absolutist regimes provided one model of political and social organization, but an alternative model, in most cases no less committed to uniformity and order, also flourished in the late seventeenth century: governments dominated by aristocrats or merchants. The contrast between the two was perceived by contemporary political theorists, especially opponents of absolutism, who compared France unfavorably with England. And yet the differences were often less sharp than such commentators suggested, primarily because the position of the aristocracy was similar throughout Europe. That there were genuine differences in social structure cannot be denied, but they were subtle and often below the surface.

---

[2] M. S. Anderson, *Peter the Great* (1969), p. 24.

The Triumph of the Gentry in England

To outward appearances Charles II (1660–1685) was restored to a throne not radically changed from the one on which his father had sat before the interregnum. He still summoned and dissolved Parliament, he made all appointments in the bureaucracy, and he signed every law. But the crown's effective power had changed drastically. The royal courts (such as Star Chamber) had been abolished, thus lessening the king's control over judicial matters. He also could not interfere in parliamentary affairs: he could no longer arrest a member of Parliament and he could not create a new seat in the Commons. Even two ancient prerogatives, the king's right to dispense with an act of Parliament (give an exemption to a specific individual or group) and to suspend an act completely, crumbled when Charles tried to exercise them. And he could no longer raise money without parliamentary assent—instead, he was given a fixed annual income, financed by a tax on Englishmen's favorite beverage, beer.

Court life under Charles II of England was similar to that of the absolute monarchs in that formal, elegant, aristocratic gatherings dominated the social scene. The occasion shown here is Charles dancing at The Hague.
(Photo: The Mansell Collection)

The real control of the country's affairs had by this time passed to that large, somewhat amorphous group known as the gentry. Just above the gentry, and giving them some leadership, was a tiny group of aristocrats. In England, only 100 to 200 families held hereditary titles, such as duke or earl, that made them members of the peerage who sat in the House of Lords in Parliament. These nobles were important political figures, but most of the control of the country was in the hands of those just below them on the social scale—the gentry, whose representatives sat in the House of Commons. About 700 members of this class held baronetcies, which were inheritable knighthoods (but not considered peerages); and a few hundred more were knights, which meant that they could call themselves "sir" but could not pass the honor on to their heirs. Beyond these, in a country of some 5 million people, perhaps 15,000 to 20,000 other families were considered gentry, these being people of importance in the various localities throughout England.[3] This proportion, approximately 2 percent, was probably not significantly different from the percentage of the population that belonged to the nobility in most Continental states.

What set the gentry apart from the nobles of other countries was their ability to determine national policy. Whereas in France, Austria, Brandenburg-Prussia, and Russia aristocrats depended on the monarch for their power and were subservient to him, the English gentry regarded themselves as an independent force. Their status was hallowed by custom, upheld by law, and maintained by their representative assembly, the House of Commons, which was both the supreme legislative body in the land and the institution to which the executive government was ultimately responsible.

Not all the gentry took a continuing, active interest in affairs of state, and no more than a few of their number sat in the roughly 500-member House of Commons. Even the Commons did not always exercise a constant influence over the government. All that was necessary was for the ministers of the king to be prominent representatives of the gentry, whether lords or commoners, and that they be able to win the support of a majority of the members of the Commons. Policy was still set by the king and his ministers. But the Commons had to be persuaded that the policies were correct, for without parliamentary approval a minister could not long survive.

Despite occasional conflicts this structure worked relatively smoothly throughout Charles II's reign. Most of the leading elements of society, for example, were united in enacting repressive legislation against dissenters, the descendants of the Puritans who still refused to join the official Anglican Church. But the gentry did have one fear: that Charles' brother, James, next in line for the succession and an open Catholic, might try to restore Catholicism in England. To prevent this they even managed to force Charles to exclude James from the throne for a few years, during a confrontation known as the Exclusion Crisis. But in the end the instinctive respect for legitimacy that was characteristic of the age, combined with some shrewd maneuvering by Charles, ensured that there would be no tampering with the succession.

Very quickly, however, the reign of James II turned into a disaster. Elated by his acceptance as king, James rashly attempted the very encouragement of Catholicism that the English had feared. This was a direct challenge to the gentry's newly won power, and in the fall of 1688, seven of their leaders—including members of some of the oldest families in the

---

[3] These totals are based on the estimates made by an early statistician, Gregory King, in 1696. His calculations were performed with remarkable accuracy, and they produced the oldest figures that historians still accept today.

THE ENGLISH SUCCESSION FROM THE STUARTS TO THE HANOVERIANS

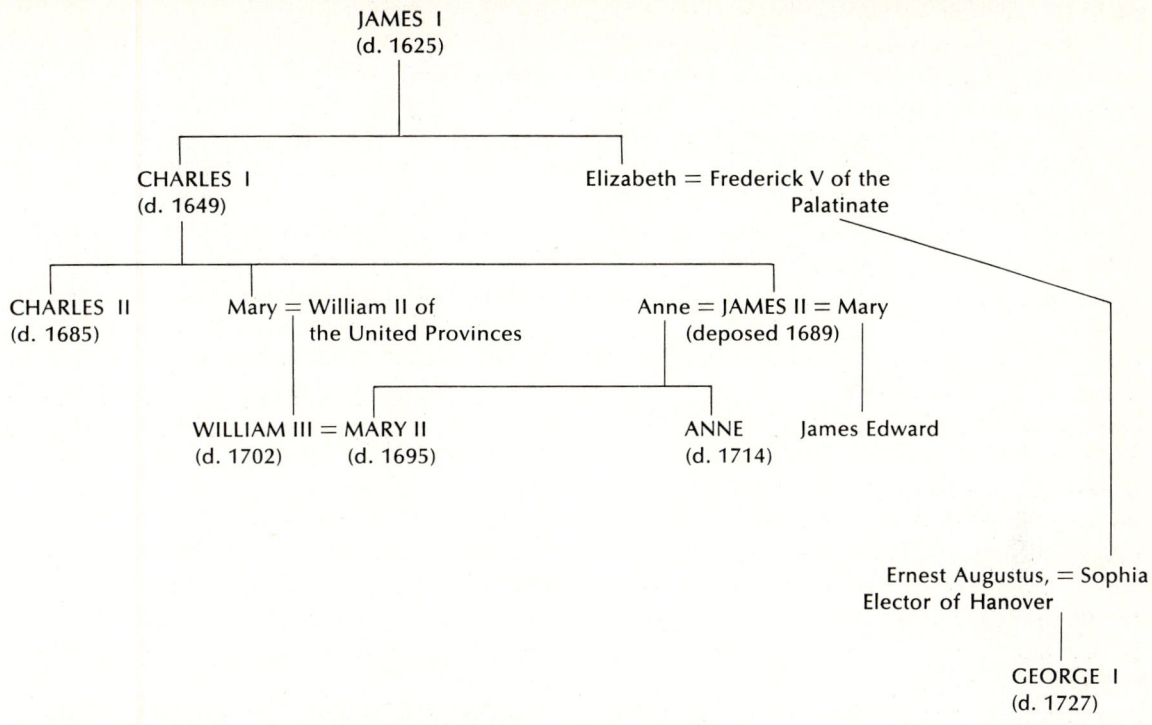

NAMES IN CAPITALS = Monarchs of England

realm—invited the Protestant ruler of the United Provinces, William III, to invade the country and take over the throne. Although William landed with an army half the size of the king's, James, uncertain of his support, decided not to risk battle and fled to exile in France.

The new king gained what little title he had to the crown through his wife, Mary (see the table above), and the couple were therefore proclaimed joint monarchs by Parliament early in 1689. The Dutch ruler had taken the throne primarily to bring England into his relentless struggles against Louis XIV, and he willingly accepted a settlement that confirmed the essential position of Parliament in the government of the country. A Bill of Rights was passed, settling the future succession to the throne, defining Parliament's powers, and establishing the basic civil rights of individuals; an Act of Toleration put an end to all religious persecution, though members of the official Church of England were still the only people allowed to vote, sit in Parliament, hold a government office, or attend a university; and in 1694 a statute laid down that Parliament had to meet and new elections had to be held at least once every three years.

Despite the restrictions on his authority, William exercised strong command. He guided England into a new, aggressive foreign policy, picked the ministers favorable to his aims, and never let Parliament sit when he was out of the country to pursue the war or to attend to Dutch affairs. But unlike James, William recognized his limits. He tried to have the Bill of Rights reversed and a standing army established, but he gave up these attempts when they provoked major opposition. By and large, therefore, the gentry were content to let the king rule as he saw fit. For they had shown by their intervention in 1688 that ultimately they controlled the country.

Politics and Prosperity

The political system in England now reflected the social system: a small elite controlled both the country's policy and its institutions. This group was not monolithically united, however, as was apparent when a party system began to appear in Parliament during Charles II's reign. Its most concrete early manifestation was during the Exclusion Crisis, from 1678 to 1680, when the Whig party emerged in opposition to royal prerogatives and Catholicism. The Whigs were largely responsible for the passage of the exclusion legislation. Their rivals, the Tories, stood for the independence and authority of the crown and favored a ceremonial and traditional Anglicanism.

Because the Whigs were the prime force behind the removal of James II, they controlled the government for most of William III's reign. They naturally supported him in his vendetta against Louis XIV, since France harbored both James and his followers, the romantic but ill-fated Jacobites, who tried for decades to restore James' line to the throne. The Whigs were only too happy to give England what seemed her proper place in the restraining of France's ambitions. But on the whole this was a nonpartisan issue.

Where the sustained rivalry between the Tories and the Whigs was most evident was in their competition for voters. Because the qualification for voting—owning freehold land worth 40 shillings a year in rent—had become less restrictive as a result of inflation and was not to be increased until the late 1700s, this period witnessed the largest electorate in English history before the mid-nineteenth century. It has been estimated that almost 5 percent of the population, or more than 15 percent of the adult males, could vote.[4] Although results were usually determined by the influence of powerful local magnates, as they had been for centuries, fierce politicking took place in many constituencies. And in one election—that of 1700—it brought about a notable reversal: the Tories won by opposing further war, because for the previous three years France seemed to have been contained.

Within two years, however, and despite William's death, England was again at war with Louis XIV, and soon the Whigs were back in power. Not until 1710 did a resurgence of war weariness work in the Tories' favor. Queen Anne made peace with France at Utrecht in 1713, and it was only because the Tories made the mistake of negotiating with the Jacobites after Anne died the next year without heir that the Whigs regained power when the first Hanoverian, George I, came to the throne. They then entrenched themselves, and under the leadership of Robert Walpole, they began almost a century of political control.

The system within which these maneuverings took place remained essentially unchanged until the nineteenth century, though it allowed considerable flexibility. The crown was still the dominant power: the monarch could dismiss ministers and could influence votes in the House of Commons through the patronage at the throne's disposal. But there were strict lim-

---

[4] J. H. Plumb, "The Growth of the Electorate in England from 1600 to 1715," *Past and Present,* November 1969, pp. 90–116.

its to royal power. Despite party struggles the gentry as a whole retained the upper hand. They were quiescent most of the time, but on major issues, such as war or peace, no government could survive without their support.

In this same period England was winning for herself unprecedented prosperity, and the foundations of her world power were being laid. During the reigns of the later Stuarts, the navy was built up and reorganized—largely under the direction of Samuel Pepys, the famous diarist—into the premier force on the sea, the decisive victor over France during the worldwide struggle of the early eighteenth century. In Charles II's time important new colonies were established, particularly along the North American seaboard, where the aristocracy provided the main impetus for the settlement of New Jersey and the Carolinas. The empire expanded rapidly, so that when England and Scotland joined into one kingdom in 1707, the union created a Great Britain ready for its role as a world leader.

This growth was accompanied by a rapid economic advance both at home and in world trade. A notable achievement was the establishment of the Bank of England in 1694. The bank was given permission to raise money from the public and then lend it to the government at 8 percent interest. Within twelve days its founders raised more than a million pounds, demonstrating not only the financial security and stability of England's government but also the commitment of the elite to the country's political structure.

The success of the Bank of England, the rise of the navy, and the overseas expansion were not the only symptoms of England's mounting prosperity. London was becoming the financial capital of the world, and British merchants were gaining control over maritime trade from East Asia to North America. And perhaps most significantly, the benefits of this boom helped the lower levels of society.

There can be little doubt that with the possible exception of the Dutch, the ordinary Englishman was better off than any of his equivalents in Europe. Poverty was admittedly widespread, and London, rapidly approaching half a million in population, contained frightful slums and miserable, crime-ridden sections. Even the terrible fire of London in 1666 did little to wipe out the appalling living conditions because the city was rebuilt much as before, the only notable additions being a series of magnificent churches, including St. Paul's, designed by Christopher Wren. But the grim picture should not be overdrawn.

Compared to the sixteenth century, these years saw little starvation. The system of poor relief may have often been inhumane in forcing the unfortunate to work in horrifying workhouses, but it did provide them with the shelter and food that they had long lacked. After more than a century of crippling inflation the laborer could once again make a decent living, and the craftsman was meeting a growing demand for his work. Higher up in the social scale, more men had a say in the political process than ever before, and more could find opportunities for advancement in the rising economy of the period—in trade overseas, in the bureaucracy, or in the growing market for luxury goods. England had better roads than any other European country, lower taxes, a more impartial judicial system, and a freedom from government interference—especially since there was no standing army—that was unique for the times.

One thing is clear, however: these gains could not compare with those that the gentry had made. In fact many of the improvements, such as fairly administered justice and low taxes, were indirect results of what the upper classes had won for themselves. There is no question that the fruits of the seventeenth century's progress belonged in the first place to the gentry, now more surely than in previous centuries the dominant element in society.

Aristocracy in the United Provinces, Sweden, and Poland

In the Dutch republic the fall of Jan De Witt seemed to signal a move in the direction of absolutism rather than aristocratic control (see p. 510). William III, who took over the government in 1672 and led the successful resistance to Louis XIV in a six-year war, was able to concentrate government in his own hands. Soon, however, the power of the merchant oligarchy and the provincial leadership in the Estates General reasserted itself. William did not want to sign a peace treaty with Louis when it became clear that the French invasion had failed. Like his forebears in the House of Orange, he wanted to take the war into the enemy's camp and reinforce his own authority by keeping the position of commander in chief in a time of war. But the Estates General, led by the province of Holland, brought the war to a conclusion.

A decade later it was only with the approval of the Estates General that William was able to seek the English throne and thus bring the two countries into limited union—limited because the representative assemblies, the effective governing powers of the two countries, remained separate. And when William died without an heir, the Dutch provincial executive offices remained unfilled. His policies were continued by Antonius Heinsius, who now held the position of grand pensionary of Holland that Jan De Witt had once occupied. Heinsius had been a close friend of William's, but to all intents and purposes, policy was determined by the Estates General.

The representative assembly now had to preside over the decline of a great power. In finance and trade the Dutch were gradually overtaken by the English, while in the war against Louis XIV they had to support the crippling burden of maintaining a land force, only to hand command over to England. Within half a century Frederick II of Prussia was to call the republic "a dinghy boat trailing the English man-of-war."

The aristocrats of the United Provinces differed from the usual European pattern. Instead of ancient families and bureaucratic dynasties, they boasted merchants and mayors. The prominent citizens of the leading cities were the backbone of what can be called the Dutch upper classes. Moreover social distinctions were less prominent than in any other country of Europe. The elite was composed of hard-working financiers and traders, richer and more powerful but not essentially more privileged or leisured than those farther down the social ladder. The situation discussed in much eighteenth-century literature and political writing—the special place given to nobles, which sometimes led even to immunity from the law—was far less noticeable in the United Provinces. There was no glittering court with elegant trappings. Although here, as elsewhere, a small group controlled the country, it did so for largely economic ends and with a totally different style.

In Sweden the conditions of court life and political power more closely resembled those of Louis XIV's France, though the reigns of Charles XI and XII, the last half-century in which Sweden was still an imperial power, were marked by a continuing struggle between king and nobility. The nobles eventually established themselves as the dominant force, but not until they had gone through a long and sometimes bitter struggle with the monarch.

The chief issue was the policy of reversions, whereby Charles XI forced great lords to return huge tracts of land they had received as rewards for loyalty during the precarious years of Gustavus Adolphus and Christina (see p. 512). The aristocrats strongly opposed the policy, but the king had the bulk of the population on his side because the crown was always a more lenient landlord for peasant tenants. By clever maneuvering Charles not only had the reversion legislation passed by the Riksdag but also had himself proclaimed virtually an absolute monarch in 1682.

The remainder of his reign was spent consolidating the power of his government at home. He stayed out of war and strengthened both his administration and his finances. The great copper mines of Sweden gave out in the 1680s, and alternatives to this lucrative source of revenue had to be built up—primarily iron and timber products, such as cannon and tar. Tolls and taxes from captured territories helped sustain the empire, but it was clear that Charles' strength depended on his avoiding the strains of war.

His successor, Charles XII, had a different set of priorities. Harking back to the glorious days of Gustavus Adolphus, he wanted to cover Sweden in military glory. His ambitions and those of Peter I of Russia embroiled the Baltic in what came to be known as the Great Northern War. At first the fighting went Sweden's way, mainly because of a brilliant victory over the Russians at Narva in 1700, which immediately established Charles as one of the ablest commanders of his day. But then he decided—the first of a series of generals to do so—that he was capable of conquering Russia. His communications and logistics broke down, and at Poltava in 1709 his invading army was shattered. The dismemberment of the Swedish Empire now began: by the time Charles was killed in battle nine years later, the Danes, Prussians, and Russians had begun to overrun Swedish possessions in Germany, Poland, and around the Gulf of Finland. (Map 17.3.) At a series of treaties signed from 1719 to 1721, the empire was parceled out, and Sweden reverted to roughly the territory she had had a century before.

Naturally the nobles took advantage of Charles XII's frequent absences to reassert their power. They ran Sweden while he was campaigning and forced his successor to accept a constitution that gave the Riksdag effective control over the country. The new structure was consciously modeled on England's political system, and the nobility came to occupy a position analogous to that of the English gentry—as the leaders of society and the controllers of politics. A splendid court arose, and Stockholm became one of the more elegant and cultured aristocratic centers in Europe.

Warsaw fared less well. In fact the strongest contrast to the French political and social model in the late seventeenth century was provided by Poland. No better object lesson can be found to demonstrate what Louis XIV was preventing in France. The sheer chaos and disunity that plagued Poland until she ceased to exist as a state in the late eighteenth century were the direct result of continued dominance by the old landed aristocracy, which blocked all attempts to centralize the government.

There were highly capable kings of Poland in this period—notably John III, who achieved Europe-wide fame by relieving Vienna from the Turkish siege in 1683. These monarchs could quite easily gather an enthusiastic army to fight (and fight well) against Poland's many foes: Germans, Swedes, Russians, and Turks. But once a battle was over, the ruler was rarely in a position to exercise anything more than nominal leadership. Each king was elected by the assembly of nobles and had to agree not to interfere with the independence of the great lords, who were growing rich from serf labor on fertile lands. The crown had neither revenue nor bureaucracy to speak of, and so the country continued to resemble nothing so much as a feudal kingdom, where power remained in the localities.

If Poland seemed a nobleman's paradise, she nonetheless produced no important cultural center like Berlin or Vienna. For that to happen some degree of central authority was necessary, a hub around which national life could revolve.

Two cities in particular—London and Paris—occupied such a position, and therefore at the very beginning of the eighteenth century, they became the heart of Europe's intellectual and artistic activity.

III. THE CULTURE OF THE AGE

The quest for regularity, order, and decorum which was the most notable feature of late-seventeenth-century culture contrasted strongly with the grandiose and dramatic strivings of the preceding age. The change in aesthetics offers striking evidence of the growing sense of settlement and calm in Europe after the crisis of midcentury. And it was paralleled by the emergence of new kinds of cultural institutions—formal, regulated, and controlled from above unlike any that Europe had ever seen before.

The Academy and the Salon

A clear indication that the cultural atmosphere was becoming more ordered and restrained was the rise of academies and salons as mechanisms which organized intellectual life. The most carefully institutionalized setting was the official academy established under royal patronage to supervise cultural affairs. Such bodies were not entirely new—their pedigree went back to the Platonic academy, and there had been more immediate predecessors in sixteenth-century Italy—but their purpose, to set standards for artistic creations, was a departure from tradition.

France led the way in this development. The French Academy, founded by Richelieu in 1635, became the leading upholder of classical drama, while the Royal Academy of Painting and Sculpture, the Royal Academy of Architecture, and the Academy of Inscriptions and Literature, established over the next thirty-five years, performed equivalent functions in other fields. These bodies marked the beginning of a system that in France did not crumble until attacked by such nineteenth-century rebels as the Impressionists.

The cultural institutions that were founded in other countries (mostly in Italy) during this period were less prestigious but no less reflective of cultural trends. The academies were intended to preserve and promote the standards that were considered essential to good art. Just as the Royal Society was regarded as an arbiter of scientific truth, a promoter of proper method, so too in art and literature academies would set the style.

The origins of the salon were diverse and its predecessors many. Artists have frequently united in coteries when they have shared a common outlook, and rich and noble patrons have often given them encouragement. The particular form that developed in seventeenth-century France was a small, intimate gathering that usually met in the drawing room, or salon, of an aristocrat's wife.

These ambitious and often intelligent women tried to attract the most brilliant literary lights of the day. The artists for their part came in search of patronage and reputation, taking advantage of various social forces: the emergence of Paris as the cultural center of France, the clustering of the nobility in the capital as the nearby court grew in size and importance, and the pressures of a fiercely competitive society of women with money to spare. The would-be salon entrant had to make his mark rapidly, and wit, grace, and quick repartee were essential.

The salons stimulated the intimacy and elegance that were now preferred to the heroic ideals of the midcentury. They thus became the natural center and the perfect symbol of contemporary creative expression. An atmosphere of studied gentility was strongly apparent, even to outsiders, and it was well for a writer or painter not to offend the sensibilities of those who were the chief makers and breakers of reputations in the highly competitive world of letters and art.

The intellectual activities of most aristocrats revolved around both cultural centers, the court and the salon. At court they gathered in large, formal affairs to watch a play, a ballet, or an opera; in the salons they gathered in smaller, less formal groups, often including talented nonaristocrats, to discuss the latest gossip or cultural event. Even the enormous halls of a palace, hung with large canvases inherited from the past, contrasted with the frilly drawing rooms that served as salons, adorned with the small paintings that were the new fashion. In some ways the two were rival centers of activity, and a few prominent patronesses consciously sought to outdo a nearby prince.

Yet the contrasts should not be overdrawn. Most leading writers, musicians, and painters were equally at home in the two settings, for they needed the patronage of both; no artist could survive without nobles to commission works or pay salaries, and few were fortunate enough to have all their needs met by a single generous prince. Thus they turned to the multiple sources of support that the aristocracy, better educated than ever before and eager to outdo one another in patronage, were anxious to provide.

There was also a wider audience of course, because salons were urban institutions, and the city offered theaters, opera houses, and publishers. Thus it was occasionally possible for an artist to achieve popular success without gaining aristocratic approval. But this was a hazardous way of making a living, and for this reason the salon, despite its regulation of taste and expression, was a vastly preferable target for most artists. As a result the qualities of harmony and order that were so appealing to the aristocracy came to dominate the aesthetics of the age.

Style and Taste

Discussions of literature and art developed a new emphasis on lightness and grace during the late seventeenth century. The most influential literary critic of the period, Nicolas Boileau, wrote a manual of style, *Poetic Art* (1674), that exalted craftsmanship over feeling. He insisted that the perfectly shaped poem was the ultimate ideal, and he valued obedience to rule as opposed to emotion or an exuberant, disordered vision. Not surprisingly his own literary output consisted of light satires, flawlessly executed but ephemeral.

Boileau's prescriptions gained a large following in France and in other countries as well. The leading English poet of the era, for example, John Dryden, gave his energies to writing hundreds of lines of graceful verse that were often scathing but almost never profound. The sharp end of his wit could sting, as can be seen in the following lines about the duke of Buckingham, a prominent politician known for his inconsistencies and dilettantism:

> A man so various, that he seem'd to be
> Not one, but all mankind's epitome.
> Stiff in opinions, always in the wrong;
> Was everything by starts, and nothing long;
> But, in the course of one revolving moon,
> Was chemist, fiddler, statesman, and buffoon.
> *Absalom and Achitophel,* ll. 545–550

Dryden was greatly admired for writing in this vein because it was a time when the elite prized sardonic aloofness.

Painters reflected these qualities only indirectly, but the change in their concerns was striking nonetheless. Gone were the vast canvases and towering themes of Rubens or Rembrandt. Instead, the leading figures of the decades around 1700 were flattering portraitists, like the Englishman Sir Peter Lely, or delicate genre painters, like the Frenchman Antoine

Jean Racine's plays appealed strongly to the aristocratic sensibilities of his age. He was regarded as the standard by which official taste could be measured and for many years was a major figure at the court of Louis XIV. The title page of *Phèdre*, one of his most enduring contributions to the French theater, is taken from the original 1677 edition.
(Photo: French Cultural Services)

Watteau (see Plate 44). Their canvases were smaller, and their subject matter rarely departed from placid landscapes or melancholic and idealized aristocratic scenes. The art of these exquisite painters epitomizes the new interest in grace, elegance, and repose.

That is not to say that emotion was totally absent from the creative work of the age. Stark passions were expressed in the operas of Henry Purcell and the prose of John Bunyan, both writing in this period. But the characteristic of their work that distinguishes them from the previous generation of artists is precisely their discipline—their anguish pours out of a framework of monumental self-restraint. And thus we are brought back to the theme that runs through the life of the time: the emphasis on order and regularity. It is particularly apparent in the work of the greatest court writer of the epoch, the French playwright Jean Racine.

By its nature Racine's art was not for the multitude. His concern was with tragedy, and he used the Classical drama to create a concentrated and sustained intensity of emotion that had not been achieved since the days of its ancient practitioners, Euripides and Sophocles. Severely disciplined and yet overwhelming passion dominates his plays, which move to agonizing climaxes in superb, controlled language. Racine does not offer the appeal of recognizable human types; his characters are suffering men and women of unattainable nobility racked by impossible dilemmas that revolve around such perennial aristocratic preoccupations as honor and public duty. The heroine of *Phèdre* (1677), for example, falls in love with her stepson and destroys him and herself as she wavers between love and honor. She wrestles with her dilemma in a series of solemn and carefully wrought but tormented speeches that give the play an almost unbearable emotional impact. There is none of the dramatic excitement—the rapid action, changes of pace, and flexible verse forms—of a Shakespearean play; instead, *Phèdre* focuses almost exclusively on the gripping human feelings that it so powerfully conveys.

Racine's appeal to the courtiers at Versailles was enormous. He explored the discipline and aristocratic bearing that, theoretically at least, the more thoughtful among them had adopted. They saw themselves on his stage, highminded characters determined to act as social and political models. Racine thus portrayed an idealized court setting, guided by propriety and restraint, for all the world to see.

The tastes of the middle and lower strata of society are much harder to define, but there were a number of distinct ways in which they entertained themselves. Urban mercantile groups usually aped their superiors, though they were clearly more at home with the bawdiness of Restoration comedy or the scintillating wit of Molière than with Racine. They were also inclined to take part in creative activity themselves. Samuel Pepys for example remarked with satisfaction that his wife's painting efforts were coming along very nicely. And music, at least for the more educated urban dweller, was as much to be played as heard. In this respect the middle classes blended with the lower rather than the upper social levels, for singing was one of the great recreations of the ordinary man. Ballads were a major form of communication, and printers were quick to run off thousands of copies of a new song that was likely to catch on. Churches, moreover, gave congregations an institutionalized setting for creating and hearing music.

Among reading publics the nobility tended to read the Classics and philosophy while the middle class read popular literature such as tales of travel, descriptions of rarities and wonders, and religious writings. The few literate members of the lower classes probably read religious works only; the rest had the Bible or a book like John Bunyan's *Pilgrim's Progress* (1667) read to them. Singing and an occasional troupe of traveling players performing the antics of standard characters like Harlequin and Columbine would have been their main recreation apart from the celebrations they themselves put on—feast day processions, "rough music," and the like (see Chapter 16).

In these interests, however, there was little reflection of the underlying concern for order so noticeable in court circles. Most people looked to music or a play for uplift or for a good time. And nowhere did they find these qualities more brilliantly represented than in the plays of the Frenchman Molière.

Molière (born Jean Baptiste Poquelin) learned his art in the same school that had taught Shakespeare half a century before: the

Molière's plays displayed a trenchant wit that was often aimed at the nobility. For this reason his works had a rather uneasy reception at court but were extremely popular with the Parisian middle class. Shown here is the acting company founded by Molière, La Troupe Royale, which was the prototype for the Comédie Française.
(Photo: French Cultural Services)

---

travelling theatrical company, in which he was actor, manager, and director. After many years of touring the provinces, he came to Paris a master of his profession and founded a company, known as the Comédie Française, which soon became a national institution.

Molière followed the formal Classical style of his day, modeling his verse on that of the ancients and observing the conventions of time and place laid down so strictly by the French Academy. But his objectives could not have been more different from those of a Racine. For he never lost sight of the old tradition of farce and burlesque, which in his youth had still been the chief attraction wherever plays were performed. He used Classical style to create comedies with a serious undertone, a sustained concern with the follies of mankind. He ridiculed such types as the pretentious ladies of the salons, hypochondriacs, and the ignorant but aspiring *nouveaux riches*—these captured forever in *The Bourgeois Gentleman* (1670), whose hero was delighted to discover that all his life he had been speaking prose.

The wit was unmatched, and soon Molière was winning highly favorable attention from Louis XIV himself. But occasionally the barbs came too close. The courtiers were offended when Molière had the nobles in one of his plays speak like ordinary people. And when in *Tartuffe* he ridiculed the hypocrisy that could lie behind ostentatiously displayed religious devotion, he roused powerful enemies in the Catholic Church. The play was banned, and a number of years passed before the playwright returned to the good graces of the monarch. But when *Tartuffe* reappeared in Paris, it was an instant success.

The contrast is revealing. Molière's sparkling dialogue and superb theatrical sense ensured his acceptance at court, but the welcome had its limits, set by standards of taste that the nobility considered unbreachable. In Paris he was always idolized, and for most French people he has remained unrivaled to this day. The difference, slight though it was, gave one of the first hints of the estrangement between court and country that was to build toward the explosion of the revolution over the next century. The aristocrats may have set the style, but they were to become increasingly insulated from the rest of society, which eventually was to find its own cultural models and heroes in the eighteenth century.

Science and Thought

The fascination inspired by the scientist and the widespread efforts to imitate scientific method in other fields were closely connected with the interest in order so characteristic of the age. The second half of the seventeenth century thus became the great age of the virtuosos, the hundreds of noblemen who dabbled in experiments and sought friendships with scientists. But it was less as participants than as eager admirers that the elite embraced science. In the eighteenth century for the first time statues were erected to honor the great discoverers. They were a new kind of hero, and they became the most widely acclaimed men of their age.

The late seventeenth and early eighteenth centuries witnessed in addition a raging controversy known as the Battle of the Books, a long dispute over the relative merits of the so-called Ancients and Moderns. In the end there could

This frontispiece from the 1710 edition of Jonathan Swift's long poem, *The Battle of the Books*, satirizes the controversy that broke out in the late seventeenth century over the relative superiority of ancient and modern writers.

be little doubt that the advocates of the Moderns had won the dispute, largely because of the unprecedented advances in the understanding of nature during the previous century. The achievements in astronomy, physics, mathematics, and anatomy were being seen ever more frequently as a measure of human capabilities. And the qualities that the scientist seemed to represent—order, reason, and logic—corresponded with the aristocrats' aesthetic preferences in this period: balance, uniformity, and decorousness. It was only natural that the supreme scientist of the late seventeenth century, Isaac Newton, should become the idol not only of his own generation but of generations to come.

Isaac Newton

The culmination of the scientific revolution was reached in the work of Isaac Newton, who made decisive contributions in the fields of mathematics, physics, astronomy, and optics and brought to a climax the progress that had been made by Copernicus, Kepler, Galileo, Descartes, and a host of other investigators. He united physics and astronomy in a single system to explain motion throughout the universe; he helped transform mathematics by the development of calculus; and he established some of the basic laws of modern physics.

Part of the explanation of his versatility lies in the workings of the scientific community at the time. Newton was a retiring man who got into fierce arguments with such prominent contemporaries as the English physicist Robert Hooke, who was studying gravity, and the German "universal man," Liebniz, who was working on calculus. Had it not been for his active participation in the Royal Society of London and the effort that was needed to demonstrate his views to the membership, Newton might never have pursued his researches to their conclusion. He disliked the give-and-take but felt forced in self-justification to prepare some of his most important papers for meetings of the society. There could be no better indication of how important it was that science had created its own institutions and competitiveness.

It was to refute another rival, the Cartesian approach to science, which was then much admired, that Newton wrote his masterpiece, *The Mathematical Principles of Natural Philosophy* (1687), usually referred to by the first words of its Latin title, the *Principia*. This was the last widely influential book in European history to be written in Latin, still the international language of scholarship, and useful to Newton because he was determined to have as many experts as possible see his refutation of Descartes' methods. In contrast to the Frenchman, who had placed such emphasis on the powers of the mind, on pure reason, he felt that mere hypotheses, constructions of logic and words, were not the tools of a true scientist. As he put it in a celebrated phrase, *"Hypotheses non fingo"* ("I do not posit hypotheses"), because everything he said was proved by experiment or by mathematics.

The most dramatic of his findings was the solution to the ancient problem of motion. He stated his system in three laws: first, in the absence of force, motion continues in a straight line; second, the rate of change of the motion is determined by the forces acting on it (for example friction); and third, action and reaction between two bodies are equal and opposite. To arrive at these laws, he defined the concepts of mass, inertia, and force in relation to velocity and acceleration as we know them today.

Newton extended these principles to the entire universe by demonstrating that his laws govern the motions of the moon and planets too. Using the concept of gravity, he provided the explanation of the movement of objects in space that is the foundation for current space travel. There is a balance, he said, between the earth's pull on the moon and the forward motion of the satellite, which would continue in a straight line were it not for the earth's gravity. Consequently the moon moves in an elliptical orbit in which neither gravity nor inertia gains control. The same pattern is followed by the planets around the sun. In one of his most elegant insights, Newton described the attraction mathematically in what is known as the inverse square law: gravitational force varies inversely as the square of the distance between the two bodies.[5] The resultant orbit has to be an ellipse, as Kepler had already discovered.

It was largely on the basis of the uniformity and the systematic impersonal forces Newton described that the view of the universe as a vast machine gained ground. According to this theory, all motion is a result of precise, unvarying, and demonstrable forces. There is a celestial mechanics just like the mechanics that operates on earth. It was not far from this view to the belief that God is a great watchmaker who started the marvelous mechanism going but intervenes only when something goes wrong and needs repair. Newton himself considered the creation of the force of gravity, which is not a *necessary* property of a body, as an indication of God's intervention in the assembling of the physical universe.

These general philosophical implications were as important as the specific discoveries in making Newton one of the idols of his own and the next centuries. Aristocrats, concerned with discipline and stability, could easily interpret the idea that a simple structure underlies all of nature as justification for the hierarchical patterns of government and society that were emerging. The educated applauded Newton's achievements, and the gentry made him one of their own—he was the first scientist to receive a knighthood in England. And only a few decades after the appearance of the *Principia,* Alexander Pope summed up the public feeling in a famous couplet:

> Nature and nature's law lay hid in night;
> God said, "Let Newton be!" and all was light.

---

[5] In other words, the attraction increases much more rapidly than the distance closes. Stated as an equation, where G is the gravitational pull and D the distance between the two bodies, the law is $G \propto 1/D^2$.

Although he also devoted a great deal of energy to mystical and numerological investigations (which he kept strictly separate from his science), Newton still managed to find the time to accomplish much else of immense scientific value. He was the main figure in late-seventeenth-century mathematics, particularly in the study of calculus, and his work on dynamics was a milestone in the subject. Another striking achievement, the lunar explanation of tidal action, was almost an aside in his masterpiece. The differences among various tides allowed him to calculate the mass of the moon—again almost in passing. Finally, his second major work, the *Opticks* (1704), presented an analysis that influenced the study of light for more than a century.

But it was the work on motion and the heavens that won Newton his reputation. So overpowering was his stature that in these fields the steady progress of 150 years came to a halt for more than half a century after the publication of the *Principia*. There was a general impression that somehow Newton had done it all, that no important problems remained. In large areas of physics and astronomy, no significant advances were made again until the late eighteenth century. There were other reasons for the slowdown—changing patterns in education, the influence of frivolous virtuosos, an inevitable lessening of momentum—but none was so powerful as the reverence for Newton. The professional was as overawed as the aristocrat in the presence of a man who became the intellectual symbol of his own and succeeding ages.

John Locke

The second idol of the late seventeenth and eighteenth centuries, John Locke, was not himself a scientist, but a major reason for his fame was the belief that he had applied a scientific approach to all of knowledge.

The hero of eighteenth-century thought, John Locke, was almost as familiar from engravings as were warriors and kings. That a man of learning could achieve such fame was an indication of the importance of learning in this society. And the emphasis in the portrait is entirely on Locke's simplicity, intelligence, and straightforwardness—the marks of his work.
(Photo: New York Public Library/Picture Collection)

Locke also wrote to refute Descartes, whose dualism he rejected in favor of his own theory of knowledge. He believed that at birth man's mind is a *tabula rasa,* a clean slate; contrary to Descartes, he asserted that nothing is inborn or preordained. As a human being grows, he observes and experiences the world. Once he has gathered enough data through his senses, his mind begins to work on them. Then, with the help of his reason, he perceives patterns, discovering the order and harmony that permeate the universe. Locke was convinced that this underlying order exists and that every person, regardless of his individual experiences, must reach the same conclusions about its nature and structure.

This epistemology, elaborated in his *Essay Concerning Human Understanding,* published in 1690, was modeled directly on the example of the scientists. The *tabula rasa* is the counterpart of the principle of doubt, experience corresponds with experimentation, and reason plays the role of the process of generalization. Just as in science a single law appears again and again whatever experiments are performed, so in all knowledge any true principle is universal and will become apparent to every person even though individual lives are different.

Locke's thinking thus included a reverence for scientific method, a reliance on material phenomena and empiricism, and a belief in order. In all these respects, his outlook captured the interest of cultivated readers in the late seventeenth and eighteenth centuries, for he provided them with a theoretical model, built on a rejection of emotion and an elevation of reason, that allowed them to regard their mental equipment and functioning as scientific.

When Locke turned his attention to political thought, he caught the feeling of the times even more directly, because he put into systematic form the views of the English gentry and of many aristocrats throughout Europe. The *Second Treatise of Civil Government,* also published in 1690, was deeply influenced by Hobbes. From his great predecessor Locke took the notion of the state of nature as a state of war and the need for a contract among men to end the anarchy that precedes the establishment of human society. But his conclusions were decidedly different.

Employing the principles of the *Essay Concerning Human Understanding,* Locke asserted that the application of reason to the evidence of politics demonstrates the inalienability of the three rights of an individual: life, liberty, and property. Like Hobbes, he believed that there must be a sovereign power, but he argued that it has no power over these three natural rights of its subjects without their consent. Moreover this consent—for levying taxes for example— must come from a representative assembly of men of property, such as the English Parliament.

The affirmation of property as one of the three natural rights (it was changed to "the pursuit of happiness" in the more egalitarian American Declaration of Independence) is significant. Here Locke revealed himself as the spokesman of the gentry. Only people with a tangible stake in their country have any right to control its destiny, and that stake must be protected as surely as their life and liberty. The concept of liberty remained vague, but it was taken to imply the sorts of freedom, such as freedom from arbitrary arrest, that were outlined in the English Bill of Rights. All Hobbes allowed a man to do was protect his life. Locke permitted the overthrow of the sovereign power if it infringed on the subjects' rights—a course the English followed with James II and the Americans with George III.

Locke's intentions were admirable—he had a higher opinion of human nature than Hobbes, he admitted that truth was hard to find, and he tried, as Hobbes had not, to curb the potential for tyranny in sovereign power. His prime concern was to defend the individual against the state, a concern that has remained essential to liberal thought ever since. But it is important to realize that Locke's views served the elite better than the mass of society because of his emphasis on property. With Locke to reassure them, the upper classes imposed their preferences and control on eighteenth-century European civilization.

The situation of Europe's aristocracy in 1715 was a far cry from its position in 1660. Then, in the wake of a series of grave political and intellectual crises, the ancient power of the nobles, based on their local independence, had seemed radically weakened in the face of the bureaucratic state. But as the political structures of the various European countries settled into new and stable forms, it became clear that their cooperation was essential for the running of a state, and they adapted to this new role with remarkable skill. Under the absolute monarchs they became the allies and indispensable agents of government; in other countries they dominated events. In either case they came out of the transition with their power intact and even enhanced.

Thus regardless of the relative levels of order and uniformity the various regimes achieved and regardless of their degrees of absolutism, they were alike in their reliance on aristocrats. No government, however centralized, could function without the participation of the upper classes, and in most states—Peter I's Russia excepted—they took up their transformed role willingly. This new security of aristocratic power, both political and social, showed that the age-old conflict between princes and nobles had been resolved.

Moreover the qualities of order, discipline, and stability that the elite represented and that rulers sought were making themselves felt in culture as well as in society and politics. Changes in taste and even developments in science and philosophy were seen as reinforcing the aristocratic world view. The elaborately mannered life led by this newly invigorated ruling class reflected its confidence. And its remarkable society was to last for a glittering century until its frivolities and arrogance fell before a movement that demanded a better life not merely for the few but for all.

RECOMMENDED READING

Sources

★Locke, John. *An Essay Concerning Human Understanding*. A. D. Woozley (ed.). 1964. This study of the nature of the mind appeared at the same time as Locke's *Two Treatises of Government* and presents the philosophical basis of his political ideas.

Saint-Simon, Louis. *Historical Memoirs*. Lucy Norton (ed. and tr.). 2 vols. 1967 and 1968. Lively memoirs of the court at Versailles.

Studies

Adam, Antoine. *Grandeur and Illusion: French Literature and Society 1600–1715*. Herbert Tint (tr.). 1972. A clear and comprehensive survey of French literature and its social setting during the seventeenth century, with special attention to Classicism.

Baxter, S. B. *William III and the Defense of European Liberty, 1650–1702*. 1966. A solid and straightforward account of the career of the ruler of both England and the Netherlands.

★Carsten, F. L. *The Origins of Prussia*. 1954. The

standard account of the background to the reign of the great elector, Frederick William, and the best short history of his accomplishments and the rise of the Junkers.

Chandler, David. *Marlborough as Military Commander.* 1973. A fluent and energetic narrative of military affairs, centered around the colorful career of a highly intelligent general.

Cranston, Maurice. *John Locke.* 1957. The best basic introduction to the man and his ideas. (See also MacPherson.)

*Goubert, Pierre. *Louis XIV and Twenty Million Frenchmen.* Anne Carter (tr.). 1970. This is not so much a history of the king's reign as a study of the nature of French society and politics during Louis' rule.

Hatton, R. N. *Charles XII of Sweden.* 1968. A thorough and well-written biography that does justice to a dramatic life.

*_____. *Europe in the Age of Louis XIV.* 1969. A beautifully illustrated and vividly interpretive history of the period that Louis dominated.

*Hazard, Paul. *The European Mind, 1680–1715.* J. L. May (tr.). 1963. This stimulating interpretation of the intellectual change that took place around 1700 has become a classic work in the history of thought.

*Koyré, Alexandre. *Newtonian Studies.* 1965. These essays have come to be accepted as the basic introduction to Newton's ideas.

*Lewis, W. H. *The Splendid Century: Life in the France of Louis XIV.* 1953. A colorful account of life at court and in the country during Louis XIV's reign.

Lougee, Carolyn C. *Le Paradis des Femmes: Women, Salons, and Social Stratification in Seventeenth-Century France.* 1976. An interesting study of the place of women and the importance of salons in French high society.

*MacPherson, C. B. *The Political Theory of Possessive Individualism: Hobbes to Locke.* 1962. This provocative, Marxist-inspired study of the importance of property in English political thought views Locke's ideas in largely economic terms.

Manuel, Frank. *A Portrait of Isaac Newton.* 1968. Using psychoanalytic methods, this book shows Newton and the pressures he felt in a very different light from the usual analyses that pay tribute to genius.

*Plumb, J. H. *The Growth of Political Stability in England, 1675–1725.* 1969. A brief, lucid survey of the developments in English politics that helped create Britain's modern parliamentary democracy.

Stoye, John. *The Siege of Vienna.* 1964. An exciting account of the last great threat to Christian Europe from the Turkish empire.

*Sumner, B. H. *Peter the Great and the Emergence of Russia.* 1950. This short but comprehensive book is the best introduction to Russian history in this period.

*Wolf, J. B. *Louis XIV.* 1968. The standard biography, with particularly full discussions of political affairs.

---

* Available in paperback.

18

ABSOLUTISM AND EMPIRE 1715–1770s

The eighteenth century—generally understood as the period between the Peace of Utrecht in 1714 and the beginning of the French Revolution in 1789—is easier to visualize as a whole than the century of extraordinary turmoil that preceded it. It was a century of consolidation and maturation: of absolutism and empire; of demographic growth; of economic prosperity based on agriculture, trade, and traditional industries; of enlightenment and cultural brilliance. These various strands were of course interwoven, but any account must take them in some sequence. The growth of Europe's population—attributable in part to good harvests and the absence of famines—is a subject that historians have recently begun to explore, and it may one day be regarded as the logical starting point of discussion. In the meantime, it is the development of the state, long the focus of historical research, that is at present best understood.

Austria, Britain, France, Prussia, and Russia, the states that would dominate Europe and most of the world until World War I, can trace their emergence to great-power status, as well as their intense rivalry with each other, back to the eighteenth century. Russia and Britain now wielded enough power to play major roles in European affairs, while Prussia's rise to great-power status offers the most spectacular example of successful state building and territorial expansion. On the Atlantic seaboard, the maritime states of France and Britain dueled for trade and colonies in a rivalry that reflected the impact of middle-class commercial interests.

It sometimes seems as if international competition was the foremost preoccupation of eighteenth-century rulers. But in fact competition among states went hand in hand with internal state building—in most cases with efforts to consolidate royal absolutism. Conflict with rival powers compelled rulers to assert their sovereignty as forcefully as possible within their own borders in order to tap the revenues and manpower they required. The issue was power, and the model of absolutism created in Louis XIV's France showed them ways to that power.

With the exception of Britain, countries in which absolutism failed to develop—such as Sweden and the Netherlands—lost influence. Poland, once Russia's mighty rival, could not raise a large standing army or overcome the self-interest of its powerful aristocracy. By the end of the century it stood helpless before the onslaught of Russia, Austria, and Prussia. Three times Poland was partitioned among them, with the final partition in 1794 ending its existence as a sovereign state altogether.

In sum, the eighteenth century saw the maturation and consolidation of the modern state internally, and the testing of each state within the state system. In this process the basic map of modern Europe emerged and the centralized character of the major European states was confirmed.

I. THE STATE SYSTEM

The international rivalry embedded in the eighteenth-century state system was not as chaotic as it sometimes appears to have been. In practice there were limitations on the aggressiveness of states, and a phenomenon that can be called balance of power did exist. It is possible to indicate the sources of the conflicts that erupted and the kinds of appetites that sought satisfaction. Diplomacy and warfare had few ironclad rules, but they did have typical procedures and bounds. In combination these helped provide a context for the development of the European states.

Patterns of International Rivalry

Two terms may be used to describe the broad sweep of international relations, provided their meaning is not exaggerated. On the one hand were the periods of hegemony, or domination by one state; on the other were periods of equilibrium, or balance of power. For reasons that probably derive from Western ethnocentrism, we tend to assume that equilibrium among the several states is natural and that disturbances by overambitious powers are unnatural.[1] Be that as it may, it is true that the great aggressors of modern times, such as Louis XIV, Napoleon, and Hitler, have been resisted and ultimately defeated after stupendous struggles. Their designs on Europe varied considerably, but to their contemporaries they seem to have appeared equally dangerous.

In fact the essential meaning of "balance of power" is this limited or negative one: the situation after a bid for hegemony had been resisted and defeated. It was a genuine goal for Europeans only in the face of some inordinate threat to their accustomed pattern of rivalry. The state system did not have a built-in equilibrium. Apart from the way states concerted to resist the few rulers who sought to dominate the entire Continent, there was little agreement about what would be tolerated. Rarely did Europe's rulers cooperate simply to maintain peace or the status quo. On the contrary they acted in their own interests against the status quo with as much force as they could.

The Peace of Utrecht restored an enormous range of options and opportunities to European states that had been curtailed while Louis XIV seemed to threaten Europe with French domination. When the threat disappeared on Louis' death, in 1715, the more limited appetites and ambitions of Europe's other sovereigns could have freer rein. No country, however, was now necessarily more secure than it had been while Louis lived; nor was the likelihood of peace with justice for all Europe any greater.

---

[1] Thus Leopold von Ranke, the great nineteenth-century German historian, emphasized "the primacy of foreign policy" in the development of Europe. To Ranke the essence of European civilization was a common Christian culture embodied in a diversity of national states whose very competition produced a metaphysical kind of harmony. See T. von Laue, *Leopold Ranke: The Formative Years* (1950), and Ranke's famous essay, "The Great Powers," reproduced as an appendix to that book. For a classic view emphasizing the anarchy of the state system see Albert Sorel, *Europe Under the Old Regime* (tr. 1968).

The series of treaties negotiated at the peace congress at Utrecht in 1713–1714 reaffirmed the balance of power in Europe and provided that the Bourbon thrones of France and Spain would never be united. England gained various colonial and commercial spoils, including Newfoundland and Gibraltar. Spain's overseas empire went to Philip V, while the Spanish Netherlands, Milan, Sardinia, and Naples went to the Austrian Hapsburgs.
(Photo: The Bettmann Archive)

For some eighty years—between Utrecht and Napoleon Bonaparte—no state threatened to dominate Europe. In this sense a balance of power prevailed. During the first twenty or so years, there was almost no war at all because of postwar exhaustion, but this respite came only from depleted resources and special dynastic considerations, not from lessons learned or from a revulsion against war. The ideal of peace had no place in diplomacy and had nothing to do with the eighteenth-century balance of power. For despite the absence of any bid for hegemony, between Utrecht and Napoleon the century saw two international conflicts (the War of the Austrian Succession and the Seven Years' War), the loss of a substantial overseas empire by France, threats of extinction against the Hapsburg Empire and Prussia, and the disappearance of the sovereign state of Poland.

There was thus no absence of aggression and bellicosity in eighteenth-century Europe. But these wars did not mobilize entire societies; the atmosphere of the period can be suggested by such incidents as the English novelist Laurence Sterne's taking his famous *Sentimental Journey to France* while his country was at war with her. Moreover these contests lacked the fanaticism of the religious wars while not yet calling forth the kinds of commitment that came with later wars of revolution, national unification, or ideology. They were wars in which dynastic interests and territorial ambitions interacted with disputes over trade, colonies, and prestige. Eighteenth-century wars had limited, concrete objectives. They were not total wars.

Zones of Conflict

International relations focused on four geographical regions or spheres of interest: the North, Central Europe, Eastern Europe, and the New World across the seas.

The Baltic area in the North was of strategic interest to a number of states. Russia, Sweden, Prussia, and Poland all sought direct territorial control there, which could only be achieved at some other state's expense. Maritime powers like the British and Dutch were concerned both with the trading areas that fronted on the Baltic and the rich prize of naval stores that could be found there.

Most of Central Europe constituted a fragmented power vacuum over which the great powers and their allies vied. The Bourbon-Hapsburg rivalry revolved largely around who

MAP 18.1: THE EXPANSION OF RUSSIA AND THE PARTITION OF POLAND

would have the most influence there. And even lesser dominions like Saxony and Bavaria could be pardoned for dreams of grandeur that were stimulated by the absence of sizable viable states. Moreover Great Britain's dynastic tie through George I with the principality of Hanover involved her in this vortex of Central European instability, which otherwise would have been unimportant to her. Farther south the power vacuum extended into Italy, which was like a colonial area for the satisfaction of dynastic ambitions.

"Eastern Europe" is admittedly an imprecise designation. Yet in regard to the eighteenth century, it conveys a firmer concept of region than the expression "Germany." The eastern boundary of the Holy Roman Empire had lost most of its significance, but it did generally set off the classic area of Europe from the vast reaches of the continent that lay to the east. Here the most important issue was the attempt to push back the Ottomans, a task shared—in a spirit of mutual distrust—by Hapsburgs and Russians (see Map 18.1). As questions of access to the Mediterranean were raised, the maritime powers were drawn in. This is the origin of the so-called "Eastern question" that bedeviled European diplomacy for the next 200 years. However, other complicating issues, such as the ethnic diversity and latent national aspirations of the region, had not yet arisen to complicate the picture.

The fourth theater of activity was the colonized New World. Spain, Great Britain, and France, secure within their own borders, had their most important interests here, though they were not fully aware of this. By 1739 a war had begun between England and Spain that was directly attributable to a dispute in the New World: British smuggling and its repression in the Spanish Empire. Henceforth colonial tensions would severely complicate European diplomatic relations.

There were thus many possible permutations in international affairs. The abler statesmen of the times were the ones who could see past traditional commitments or superficially attractive opportunities to the veritable interests of their states. Ultimately perhaps the most important development in the state system of the eighteenth century was the rise to prominence of Britain and Russia, the two great flanking powers of Europe. Previously both had really stood on the periphery of European power politics. After Utrecht their influence would be second to none.

Diplomacy and Warfare

Diplomacy in the eighteenth century reflected an increasingly complex range of considerations. Traditional dynastic interests were still important: princes and their ministers tried to exclude challenges to the reigning family's succession, to secure client states or new territory by dynastic claims, and to arrange marriages that would bring new titles or alliances.

Dynastic considerations could promote peace in certain circumstances and war in others. When a ruler felt insecure on his throne because of possible internal challenges to his title, he might seek to improve his relations with other states in order to avoid further complications. Coincidentally this was the situation in both France and Britain after Utrecht, and it helps explain the peace that prevailed between those inexorable rivals until 1740. An episode characteristic of the diplomacy of the time involved the Polish succession—the Polish kingship having been an elective office subject to influence by the great powers. Unable to agree over the matter, the powers fought a brief limited war; France's candidate then bowed out but was compensated with the duchy of Lorraine, which would eventually pass directly under French sovereignty by virtue of the new duke's marriage to a French princess.

On the whole, though, dynastic interests gave way to policies based on a more impersonal and abstract conception of the state. Men like Frederick II of Prussia, Count Wenzel Anton von Kaunitz of Austria, and William Pitt of Britain tried to shape their diplomacy to the specific needs of their states as they conceived them. "Reasons of state" centered on security, with the only guarantee of security understood to be the power to assure it by force. The search for defensible borders and the weakening of possible challengers were obvious principles. Eighteenth-century statesmen believed that the end (security and prosperity) justified the means (the maximal use of power). Until a country was completely invulnerable, its leaders felt justified in using the crudest and most amoral tactics in dealing with its neighbors.

Diplomats and armies shared the task of implementing "reasons of state." Emissaries were frequently put to work fabricating or embellishing claims to this province or that princely title. They were understood to be spies or at least snoopers by vocation. They offered the bribes that were a part of foreign policy and negotiated treaties sometimes knowing of their prince's intentions to violate them.

There was another, more conservative side to diplomacy: the eighteenth century marks its growth as a serious profession, parallel to the further rationalization of the state itself. Foreign ministries or foreign offices were started and staffed with corps of experts, clerks, archives, and the like. The heads of the diplomatic machine were the ambassadors, stationed in permanent embassies abroad. This routinized management of foreign relations helped foster a sense of collective identity among the European states despite their interminable struggles. Linguistically and socially the diplomatic corps provided a veneer of sugar coating to international relations. French now reigned supreme as the common language of European diplomats; by 1774 even a treaty between Turks and Russians was drafted in that language. Socially the diplomatic corps was aristocratic and cosmopolitan. Whatever ruler they might be serving, noble ambassadors regarded themselves as members of the same fraternity.

In the wake of the exhaustion that followed the wars of Louis XIV's reign, diplomats began to play a more active role in the affairs of the Continent. Between 1715 and 1725 Europe actually saw a series of international congresses designed to settle differences in advance by means of convenants. This was only a superficial change, however, since the issues decided on were invariably minor.

Moreover the great powers dictated terms, dividing spoils and prestige at the expense of the smaller states. For example the territorial ambitions of Prussia, Austria, and Russia were reconciled at the bargaining table by their series of agreements to partition Poland's outer areas among themselves (Map 18.1). The declaration they issued in 1772, at the time of the first partition, stated boldly that "Whatever the limitations of the respective claims may be, the acquisitions which result must be exactly equal." Rarely was such cynicism perpetrated on so grand a scale, but in its essence it was typical of the European state system. Settling disputes by negotiation could be as brutal and amoral as settling them by war.

Armies

Despite the settlement of many disputes by diplomacy, war was far from an alternative of last resort; it continued to be a commonplace instrument of statecraft. In the major Continental countries, the focus of bureaucratic innovation and monetary expenditure was the standing army, whose growth was enormous. France set the pace for this development. After 1680 the size of her forces never fell below 200,000. The growth of the Prussian army exemplifies what was happening all over Europe: between 1713 and 1786 its manpower increased from 39,000 to 200,000. But the cost, technology, and tactics of these armies served to limit the devastation and horror of eighteenth-century warfare despite the frequency of combat.

Costliness led rulers to husband their armies carefully. Princes were quick to declare war but slow to deploy their armies at full strength or commit them to battle. Observers of eighteenth-century warfare like the English writer Daniel Defoe therefore concluded that there was more money but less blood spent in war.

The techniques of building and besieging fortifications continued to preoccupy military planners. Looking back on those days from the vantage point of the French Revolution, one officer characterized eighteenth-century warfare not even as the art of defending strong places but of "surrendering them honorably after certain conventional formalities." The main body of troops—the infantry—was primarily trained for maneuvering and was taught to fire in carefully controlled line formations. A successful strategy equaled the ability to nudge an opposing army into abandoning its position in the face of superior maneuvering. Improved organization worked to counteract brutality. Better supplied by a system of magazines, more tightly disciplined by constant drilling, troops were less likely to desert or plunder than they had been during the Thirty Years' War.

Rarely was the annihilation of the opposing force the strategic objective of a battle. Some encounters were fought as if they were occurring on a parade ground, while pitched battles in open fields were usually avoided. Moreover important victories were frequently nullified when the winning army retreated toward its home bases to make winter camp. Finally, unconditional surrender was never required from an opponent. The same held true for naval battles. Commanders evinced great caution when engaging in combat and rarely followed up initial contacts by pursuing and destroying the bested squadron.

The officer corps of the military were generally the preserve of the European nobility, though they also served as channels of upward social mobility for wealthy sons of middle-class families who purchased commissions. In either case the officer ranks tended to be sinecures filled by men who lacked the professional outlook and requisite training for effective leadership. Officers were likely to be long on martial spirit and bravery but short on technical skills. The branches of service that showed the most progress were the artillery and the engineers,

This painting of the battle of Fontenoy illustrates the typical battlefield stance adopted by eighteenth-century armies. The infantry was positioned in rigid line formation when firing, which limited its effectiveness.
(Photo: National Army Museum)

in which competent middle-class officers played an unusually large role.

A final element limiting the actual scale of war in the eighteenth century was the inherent weakness of coalitions of belligerents, which formed whenever a general war mushroomed. On paper these alliances looked formidable and seemed to promise vast deeds of destruction against their victims. On the battlefield, however, they were hampered by primitive communications and lack of mobility even at the peak of cooperation. Moreover, the partnerships rarely lasted very long. The anarchy of the state system predictably bred distrust among supposed allies as well as enemies. Sudden abandonment of coalitions and the negotiation of separate peace treaties mark the history of almost every major war fought under this arrangement.

II. ABSOLUTISM IN CENTRAL EUROPE

The relationship between international rivalry and internal modernization is dramatically illustrated in the examples of Prussia and Austria. Already in the mid-eighteenth century these two powers were vying for domination in Central Europe and they instituted reforms better to wage this struggle. Each experienced a period of vigorous state building under their absolute rulers, the essence of which was to increase the size of armies, collect larger revenues to support them, and develop bureaucracies to administer the provinces. It did not seem to matter whether the ruler was a modern-minded deist like Frederick II of Prussia or a pious traditionalist like Maria Theresa of Austria. In their own way each understood their vocation as ruler and the demands of the state system.

The Rise of Prussia

The fate of Brandenburg-Prussia was entirely different from Poland's. As Chapter 17 described, Frederick William the Great Elector had begun the creation of a standing army and bureaucracy in Brandenburg and had bargained the great magnates into yielding much of their political power. These policies had raised Brandenburg from virtual obscurity to a position of second rank in the state system. Frederick I had secured the prestige of a royal throne in Prussia for the Hohenzollern family, but while patronizing new cultural activities in Berlin, he had neglected to forge ahead with the state-building process. His successor, however, more than compensated for this laxness.

Frederick William I

Under the thoroughgoing absolutism of Frederick William I (1713–1740), Prussia began her climb toward great-power status. Strikingly different from his refined father, this spartan ruler approached affairs of state as all business and little pleasure. He disdained court life and considered theaters to be temples of Satan. His standards of frugality were exorbitant: he eliminated three-quarters of the court's expenses, dismissed numerous courtiers, and cut the salaries of those who remained. Uncluttered by royal ceremonies, his days were regulated in timetable fashion as he attempted to supervise everything himself.

It could be said that Frederick William I traded the costume of the courtier for the uniform of the soldier, since his purpose was to organize the state for military power. During his reign the army grew from 38,000 to 83,000, making it the fourth largest in Europe, behind France, Russia, and Austria. While still relying on foreign mercenaries for one-third of his troops, he also instituted a form of conscription known as the canton system. Nobles, bourgeois, and skilled artisans were exempted; the children of peasants were enrolled when very young and called up as needed, serving in peacetime for three months of the year and leaving to work on the land during the harvest period. The soldiers—whether foreign mercenaries, enlistees, or conscripts—were subjected to intensive drilling, wore standardized uniforms, and were maintained by an improved supply system that at least equaled the French.

The king went even farther in the reform of the officer corps. Determined to build an effective cadre of professionals, he forbade his subjects to serve in foreign armies and compelled the sons of nobles to attend cadet schools in which martial skills and attitudes were inculcated.

In this military state Frederick William I was the number one soldier. A colorful commander in chief, he maintained a personal regiment of enormous grenadiers and always wore a uniform, which he declared that he would be buried in.[2] He did not mean that he would die in battle, however. For all his involvement with military life, he studiously refrained from committing his army to battle prematurely or needlessly. Consequently he passed this force on intact to his son, Frederick II.

The process of centralization kept pace with the growth of the army. In 1723 a government superagency was created: called the General Directory of Finance, War, and Domains, it united under one roof the administration of all functions except justice, education, and religion. Its main task was to coordinate the collection of revenue, expenditure (mostly on the army), and local administration. The king mobilized the state's resources in one activity that even French absolutism had not affected: education. Considering it a service to both God and country to give the population some basic instruction, he made education compulsory for all children where schools existed and instructed local communities and parents to set them up where they did not. Teachers held their jobs mainly as sidelines, most coming from the clergy. Uninterested in higher intellectual pursuits, however, the king allowed the universities to decline at the same time. They did not seem to fit in with his design of building state power.

Frederick William I's dour, puritanical attitude left an impact on his reforms that helped give them what would later be considered a peculiarly Prussian flavor. Distrustful of his bureaucrats, he granted them only a minimum of discretionary power, and while insisting on absolute obedience, he held them responsible for inefficiency. This treatment was capped by the operations of a network of inspectors called fiscals, who reported directly and secretly to the king on the behavior of officials. All these policies produced a rigid, rule-book mentality among the bureaucrats that became an oppressive force in Prussia by the end of the nineteenth century.

---

[2] Frederick William I's militarism is the subject of numerous anecdotes but also the graver charge that he inaugurated a style that helped produce Nazism. This view was particularly common during World War II. Thus an excellent study by Robert Ergang of this dynamic ruler, published in 1941, bore the astounding title, *The Potsdam Führer: Frederick William I*.

Frederick the Great

Frederick William I's most notable triumph was perhaps the grooming of his successor. This was no mean task. Frederick II (1740–1786) seemed diametrically opposite in temperament to his father and little inclined to follow in his footsteps. The father was a Teutonic philistine, a God-fearing Protestant, and a self-conscious Hohenzollern. The prince by contrast was a sentimental, artistically inclined youth who composed music and played on the flute, wrote poetry, and fervently admired French culture. Later he would write philosophical treatises and histories and would correspond with Voltaire. Frederick II disdained German culture, had a low estimation of his Hohenzollern relatives, and was a deist.

But the Prussian monarchy was mobilizing all its subjects for the tasks of state building, and the young prince was not exempted. On the contrary he was compelled to work at all levels of the state apparatus so as to experience them directly, from shoveling hay on a royal farm to marching with the troops. Relentlessly the father trained his son for kingship, forcibly reshaping his personality, inculcating him with a sense of duty, and toughening him to the grinding tasks of leadership. Despite Frederick's prolonged resistance, this hard apprenticeship succeeded. In the end, as a modern psychiatrist would put it, the prince identified with the aggressor.

When he assumed the throne, in 1740, Frederick II was prepared to lead Prussia in a ruthless struggle for power and territory. While his intellectual turn of mind caused him to agonize over moral issues and the nature of his role, he never flinched from actually exercising it. He did, however, attempt to justify absolutism at home and encroachment abroad. He claimed undivided power for the ruler not because some divine qualities inhered in the dynasty but because absolute rule was the only kind that could bring results. The monarch, he stated, was the first servant of the state. In the long run, he

MAP 18.2: PRUSSIA 1721–1772 AND THE HAPSBURG EMPIRE

hoped, an enlightened monarch might be in a position to lead his people into a more rational and even moral existence. Certain objectives along this road could be attained immediately; in matters like religious toleration and judicial reform, Frederick was able to implement his ideals and gained a reputation as an "enlightened absolutist."

But these were relatively peripheral matters. The paramount issue was security, and the best justification of absolutism would be its effectiveness in ensuring it. Success for Prussia depended on improving an extremely vulnerable geographic position by acquiring more territory and stronger borders, and ultimately on attaining great enough power to make her truly independent (see Map 18.2). Until such a time Frederick would not undertake social innovations domestically that might disrupt the flow of taxes, conscripts, or officers into the army or provoke the nobility against him. "The fundamental rule of governments," he wrote, "is the principle of extending their territories." This summed up what was in fact his most singular contribution to the rise of Prussia and what earned him his title of Frederick the Great.

Frederick William I had carefully avoided squandering his impressive army in engagements that would not really benefit Prussia. By coincidence the year 1740, which saw Frederick II's accession to the throne, was also the moment when a suitable objective for this army presented itself. Frederick began his reign with a sudden attack on the Hapsburg Empire. His objective was to conquer the province of Silesia. Prussia had no claim to it; it was simply a wealthy and strategically located domain contiguous to Prussia that the Hapsburgs were temporarily unable to defend effectively, for reasons that will be discussed directly. The conquest of Silesia culminated a century of Prussian state building inaugurated by the great elector back in 1648. But this same act would have equal significance for the progress of absolutism in the Hapsburg Empire.

The Hapsburg Empire Under Stress

Even after the Hapsburg dynasty lost control of Spain and its lands overseas, its personal domains remained immense. Its ambitions and its problems were correspondingly large. The Hapsburgs' empire was the antithesis of a unified state; it was rather a dynastic holding company of diverse territories gathered under one crown through marriages, bargains, and conquests: the Archduchy of Austria, the Kingdom of Bohemia (which had included Silesia), the Kingdom of Hungary, and European "colonies" like the Austrian Netherlands, Lombardy, and Tuscany (Map 18.2). The Hapsburgs had hoped to integrate Austria, Bohemia, and Hungary into a centralized, German-speaking, Catholic superstate. But centralization was resisted by the local diets in all provinces, and forced Germanization would be opposed by the Czechs, Magyars, and Slavs. Moreover, the Hapsburgs' Catholicism clashed with the strong Protestant traditions of Bohemia and Hungary.

The War of the Austrian Succession

Under the reign of Charles VI, yet another problem complicated the destinies of his multinational empire. The long history of Hapsburg intermarriage had finally issued in a failure of the male line. Charles' only heir apparent was his daughter, Maria Theresa, an unprecedented situation for the dynasty. In 1713 Charles drafted a document known as the Pragmatic Sanction, declaring that all Hapsburg dominions would pass intact to the eldest heir, male or female. He thereby hoped to prevent a succession crisis and a division of the inheritance, which would dissipate Hapsburg power. Through the labyrinthine interests of the state system, Charles sought for the next twenty-five years to secure recognition and guarantees of the Pragmatic Sanction from the European powers. By making all kinds of concessions and promises, he won this recognition on paper. But when he died, in 1740, his daughter found that such paper commitments were worthless: the succession was challenged by force from several sides. Concentrating on diplomacy alone, Charles had neglected the work of state building, leaving an empty treasury, inadequately trained army, and ineffective bureaucracy. The Pragmatic Sanction was scarcely pragmatic.

In contrast to Austria, Prussia's treasury was full, her army primed, and her ruler self-confident. For Frederick II the moment seemed right to grab off the Hapsburg province of Silesia, with its abundant resources and geographic proximity to Prussia. Without legal claims to it, Prussia's justification was simply her own "reasons of state" combined with the Hapsburgs' faltering fortunes. Frederick struck, assuming that other problems would keep Maria Theresa occupied. This in fact was the case. France's relatively pacific policy was just ending, as a clique of military aristocrats had gained the king's support and persuaded him to resume the traditional battle against the Hapsburgs. France's entering wedge was her ally Bavaria, whose duke, Charles Albert, now put forward a tenuous claim to the disputed Hapsburg succession. Spain entered the lists against Austria also, seeing a chance to walk away with Austria's Italian colonies. Worse yet, Maria Theresa faced a rebellion led by the surviving Czech nobility in Bohemia: in 1741 four hundred of them proclaimed Charles Albert of Bavaria king of Bohemia.

The young archduchess' fate would probably have been hopeless if Hungary's Magyar nobles had followed a similar course. Their grievances, however, were not so sharp, and they listened sympathetically to Maria Theresa's moving pleas for support. In exchange for her promise of autonomy within the Hapsburg Empire, the Magyars offered her loyalty and the troops necessary to resist the invaders.

Austria's principal ally was Great Britain, but Britain was interested only in combating France on the Continent. Therefore the British pressured Maria Theresa to concede Silesia and make peace with Prussia, in order to concentrate on the Franco-Bavarian invasion. With the help of Hungarian troops and British gold, Austria fought these opponents to a stalemate, and Frederick's conquest of Silesia proved to be the only major territorial change produced by this large-scale war. Apart from that, the Treaty of Aix-la-Chapelle in 1748 restored the status quo established by the Utrecht settlement. For England and France, who fought this war in their overseas colonies as well as in Europe, it was a stand-off. For Prussia it was a spectacular gain at Austria's expense. Austria regarded it as merely a temporary setback. The recovery of Silesia and the humiliation of Prussia became the primary objective of Austrian policy. This in turn required a major effort at state building within the Hapsburg domains.

Maria Theresa

The woman whose reign was assured not by her father's negotiations but by force of arms was a marked contrast to her archenemy, Frederick. The Prussian King was practical and irreligious; the archduchess of Austria and Queen of Hungary was moralistic and pious. While Frederick barely tolerated a loveless marriage, the Hapsburg ruler enjoyed an unusually happy domestic life, bearing her husband numerous children and taking great personal interest in their upbringing. Her personality and her ruling style were traditional, but deceptively—under this exterior she was a shrewd innovator in the business of building and reasserting the power of her state.

Unlike Frederick, or for that matter her own son and successor, Joseph II, Maria Theresa still had a strong regard for her dynasty. She did not share the modern conception of the ruler's role as simply first servant of the state; she still believed in the divine mission of the Hapsburgs. Yet utilitarian considerations did increasingly enter into her planning, causing her to think more of her realm and less of the dynasty and the Almighty. Likewise this most pious of Catholic sovereigns—who disdained the permissive idea of religious toleration and who loathed atheists—found herself obliged to undertake stern reforms of the church. Particularly in its monastic wing, she found far too much wastefulness and self-interest; consequently she forbade the establishment of new monasteries or the taking of vows by anyone under twenty-four years of age. Moreover, she abolished the clergy's exemptions from taxes, something her more easygoing French counterpart found impossible to do.

A new bureaucratic apparatus was constructed on the models of French and Prussian absolutism. At the center, in Vienna, reorganized and relatively streamlined central ministries recruited staffs of experts. For the arms and legs of this machine in the provinces, new agents were appointed, largely divorced from feudal and local interests, though in practice some concession had to be made to the enormous vested interests and regional traditions within the Hapsburg realm. The core domains (excluding Hungary and the Italian colonies) were reorganized into ten provinces, each subdivided into districts or circles that were in turn each directed by a royal official. With the help of these trusted agents, the central government could wrest new taxes from the increasingly weakened local diets. Meanwhile, by flattery and consideration, Maria Theresa lured important nobles from all corners of her domains to Vienna to participate in its social and administrative life. It goes without saying that this was matched by military reforms, notably improvements in the training of troops and the establishment of academies to produce a more professional officer corps. By 1756 Austria was ready to face Prussia again.

III. THE MARITIME POWERS

The shift of the economic axis from the Mediterranean to the Atlantic seaboard began in the sixteenth century during the years of Spanish and Portuguese expansion. But it was left to the eighteenth century and to France and Great Britain to consolidate that shift and establish its full significance. Despite their great differences, both countries generated dynamic commercial activity, and both were beyond the state-building stage that other nations were now passing through. For the merchants and governments of France and England, colonial trade was an adjunct of state building—a question not only of profits but of power. In the process an almost global economy was created, whose mainspring was the system of plantation slavery.

The Atlantic Seaboard States

France After Louis XIV

Although France provided a model for absolutism, even under the Sun King centralization of power was never complete. Until the era of revolutions, the French aristocracy remained a strong group in the state that could create trouble for the monarchy.

Louis XIV's death, in 1715, released a great deal of such trouble. French absolutism was too firmly established to be swept away by an aristocratic reaction, but it could not prevent such attempts. For one thing Louis XIV's heir was still a child, and the duke of Orléans, who became regent in this interval, had no interest in the tradition of absolutism. On the contrary, to bolster his own delicate position, he supported key aristocrats in a grab for power. The regent restored the parlements to political power and replaced prominent royal bureaucrats with councils composed of France's most eminent aristocrats. The scheme quickly proved a complete failure since the councils were simply unable to govern effectively. The parlements, however, would never again surrender their power to veto royal legislation. Henceforth they became the rallying point of those who deplored the growth of centralized government and wished to restore the so-called unwritten constitution of France, which was supposed to limit the powers of the king and protect the prerogatives of various groups.

A second major problem facing France was of course her finances. The debt amassed by Louis' wartime expenditures was crushing. Since privileged groups like the nobility and clergy effectively escaped Louis' half-hearted attempts to tax them, other ways of improving the state's credit were sought. The brilliant Scottish financier John Law seemed to have the answer: a government-sponsored central bank that would issue paper notes, expand credit, and encourage investment in a new trading company for the French colonies. By tying the bank to his well-promoted East India Company, a venture promising its subscribers vast profits from the Louisiana territory, Law initiated an investment boom and a tremendous upsurge in available credit. But as was the case in England at the same time, the public's greed and credulity soon led to vast financial overextension as prices for East India Company stock rose to insanely high levels. A bust was inevitable, and when it came, in 1720, the entire scheme of bank notes and credit collapsed with it.

In different forms the same political and financial problems were to plague France through the eighteenth century until the Revolution opened up entirely new options for their solution. Meanwhile the uncertainties of regency government gave way to a long period of stability between 1720 and 1740, when Louis XV conferred almost unlimited authority on his aging tutor and adviser, Cardinal Fleury. Cautious, dedicated to the monarchy, and surrounded by talented subordinates, Cardinal Fleury made the apparatus of absolutism function quietly and with reasonable effectiveness. In these decades France turned the corner out of the low point of misfortunes that marked the end of Louis XIV's reign. Fleury's twenty-year tenure coincided with abundant harvests, slowly rising population, and commercial activity—in short, with recovery.

Moreover, Fleury was able to contain pressures and ambitions within the governing class. When he finally died at the age of ninety, these pressures exploded. War hawks immediately plunged France into the first of several protracted and unsuccessful wars that strained French credit to the breaking point. At home the situation likewise deteriorated. Having no one to replace Fleury as unofficial prime minister, Louis XV put his confidence in a succession of counselors, some capable and some mediocre. But he did not back any of them up when pressure from contending factions at court became uncomfortable. Lacking self-confidence and dedication to his task, the king avoided confrontations and neglected affairs of state, devoting his energy instead to the pleasures of the hunt and a succession of mistresses.

Although Louis XV clearly provided weak leadership for an extended period, France's difficulties must be seen not simply in personal but also in structural terms. The main problems—privilege, political power, and finances—posed intractable and perhaps impossible challenges to policy makers. Taxes have always been unpopular; governments that appear to levy new taxes arbitrarily seem despotic, even if the need for them is clear and the distribution equitable. One of France's soundest taxes was the *vingtième,* or twentieth, which was supposed to tap the income of all elements in French society with some measure of proportionality. The nobility and clergy, however, all but evaded the real brunt of the tax. Naturally the more aggressive royal ministers wished to remedy that situation. In the 1750s for example a plan was advanced for putting teeth into the *vingtième's* bite on the clergy's immense wealth. The plan proved to be the ruination of a capable royal official. With all its corporate might, the clergy attacked the plan; the parlements joined in the attack against the "despotism" of a crown that would arbitrarily tax its subjects. Thus not only did the privileged groups successfully block such useful reforms, but they made the monarch's position more difficult by spreading a spirit of opposition and a fine-sounding rhetoric of liberty. In retrospect we see that the parlements were advancing their own special interests as they fought for a limitation on royal absolutism.

Another of Louis XV's ministers, René Maupeou, recognized that the parlements were an unbreachable obstacle to royal initiative, whether to do good or bad. Hence he prevailed on the king to use force as Louis XIV would have. In 1771 the parlements were dissolved and were replaced by magistrates loyal to the king. But the story could no longer end so simply as it might have a century before. Most of the articulate public now rallied to the parlements' support. The pressure of this elite "public opinion" was so great that it prodded Louis XVI into restoring the parlements and dismissing Maupeou when he succeeded to the throne, wishing to begin his reign (1774–1792) with public confidence and popularity. Predictably the parlements repaid this kindness by persisting in opposing meaningful reform efforts attempted by Louis XVI's ministers, leaving the monarchy in a hopeless impasse by the 1780s: virtually bankrupt, unpopular, and vacillating.

In the face of the structural weaknesses of the state and the special interests of the ruling classes, it is easy to forget the advances made in this most populous and wealthy European nation. Changes in population, rural economy, and the like, which will be discussed in Chapter 20, were clearly among the most important aspects of French history in the eighteenth century. So too was the commercial and maritime activity that went into the building of France's empire and the struggle to maintain it. No one knew at the time that the fate of royal ministers in the 1750s or 1770s foretold a stalemate that would help bring the Old Regime crashing down. The French peasantry at home and empire builders abroad continued to work at their callings, virtually unaffected by these storm signals.

The Growth of Stability in Great Britain

After the Peace of Utrecht, Great Britain too experienced a period of recovery. If the first half of the eighteenth century was an age of aristocratic reaction in France, it was a period of aristocratic dominance in Britain. The gentry and the wealthier freeholders, who elected the members of Parliament, represented a "political nation" of perhaps 100,000 in a population of 5 million in England and Wales in 1700. The distribution of the 558 seats in the House of Commons bore little resemblance to the relative size of the boroughs and shires. In 1793 fifty-one English and Welsh boroughs, counting less than 1,500 voters, elected 100 members of Parliament, nearly a fifth of the Commons. Many of these districts—such as Old Sarum, with an electorate of about six—were safely in the pocket of a prominent local family; little wonder that reformers would later call them "rotten." When a seat was disputed, the campaigns were seldom waged on principle but were competitions in bribery, influence, and intimidation. On a national scale loose party alignments did exist. The Whigs favored a strong Parliament and were somewhat more sensitive to commercial than to agricultural interests. The Tories usually supported the king and the policies that favored large landholders. In truth, however, the realities of politics were based on much smaller factions within these larger groups, and the principal political issue was the control of patronage and office.

But despite the oligarchic character of the social and political system, it is accurate to say that class lines remained considerably more fluid in Britain than on the Continent. The barriers separating the peerage, the gentry, and the commercial (and soon industrial) middle class were frequently pierced by marriage and by business or political associations. Some of the great Whig aristocrats in particular had substantial ties with the mercantile classes of London. Parliament, though scandalously unrepresentative of the population in the eighteenth century, at least was an institution that could be reformed and repaired. France had no similar functioning organism that could conveniently admit a larger part of the nation into participation in government.

A new dynasty, the Hanoverians, assumed the throne in 1714. Neither George I (1714–1727) nor George II (1727–1760) could speak English fluently, and while they showed some interest in their British realm, the language barrier and their concern for their Continental possessions limited royal influence and provided an opportunity for royal ministers and Parliament to grow in authority.

The dominant figure in British political history for the first half of the century was Sir Robert Walpole. He won his reputation for his skillful handling of government finances during

William Pitt is shown here addressing the House of Commons. Pitt had an abiding confidence in England's role as an imperial power, and his oratory, presence, and discerning political intelligence kept him at the forefront of British politics during the midcentury crisis.
(Photo: Radio Times Hulton Picture Library)

a crisis of 1720, the collapse of the "South Sea Bubble." This panic involved shares of the South Seas Trading Company and was similar to the catastrophe that overtook John Law's scheme in France. From 1721 to 1742 Walpole largely controlled the British government and determined its policies. He maintained his power by dispensing patronage liberally and maintaining the friendship of the king. He probably did not pronounce the words attributed to him, "Every man has his price," but the slogan would well describe political life under Walpole. The other phrase that describes his policies at home and abroad is "*Quieta non movere*," "Do not disturb the peace"—or, in the vernacular, "Let sleeping dogs lie."

Although Walpole was responsible for no great new ideas or grand policies, he did contribute both to his country's economic recovery and to the growth of its political institutions. Many historians have called Walpole the first prime minister, though the office still had no official existence and the name itself was first used by his enemies as a kind of insult. He insisted that all the royal ministers follow the same policies, which of course he set himself. He insisted too that the ministers inform and consult with the House of Commons as well as the king. He himself continued to sit in its sessions in order to recruit support for his decisions. Not until the following century would the Commons have the recognized power of forcing ministers it did not approve of to resign, but Walpole took a first step toward rendering the ministers responsible before Parliament. While he was not truly the first prime minister, he certainly helped shape the office.

In Great Britain as in France, the economic expansion from about 1730 on increased the wealth and the social and political weight of the commercial and financial middle class. Walpole's policy of peace pleased the large landlords but angered the merchants and businessmen of London, who viewed the growth of French commerce and colonial settlements with apprehension. They found their champion in William Pitt, later earl of Chatham, himself the grandson of a man who had made a fortune in India. Eloquent, supremely self-confident, infused with a great vision of Britain's imperial destiny, Pitt began his career in Parliament in 1738 by bitterly criticizing the timid policies of the government and demanding that France be driven from the seas. In 1758, when the Seven Years' War was going badly for England, he was called to the ministry, with what results we shall see.

The Decline of the Dutch

The United Provinces, or Dutch Netherlands, emerged from the wars of Louis XIV in an ambiguous position. The country had survived intact, and considering her military vulnerability this was no small accomplishment. On the other hand she suffered from demographic and political ossification. The population of 2.5 million failed to rise during the eighteenth century, thus setting the Dutch apart from their rivals, the French and the British, whose numbers grew rapidly. Likewise a centralized state apparatus failed to develop even during the stress of seventeenth-century warfare. The provinces remained loosely joined in a federation that was barely able to assure the common defense of the state. So self-interested were these seven separate oligarchies that they failed to concert even to repair the ports, which were vital to shipping.

The Dutch were bound to suffer economically when French and English merchants sought to eliminate their role as the middlemen of maritime commerce. Beside this was the failure of Dutch industry to compete effectively with its rivals. Onerous indirect taxes on manufactured goods and the high wages demanded by Dutch artisans forced up the price of Dutch products excessively. Moreover, manufacturers proved unable to modernize their processes and technology. High costs and antiquated organization combined especially to set back the all-important cloth industry. Leiden and Haarlem virtually disappeared from the international market.

What kept the nation from slipping completely out of Europe's economic life was her financial institutions. Shrewdly, Dutch merchants gradually shifted their activity away from the competition of actual trading ventures into the safer, lucrative areas of credit and finance. With their country the first to perfect the uses of paper currency and establish a stock market and a central bank, the Dutch now became financial instead of maritime middlemen. Amsterdam's merchant-bankers loaned great amounts of money to both private enterprises and governments abroad. One estimate places the Dutch holding of the British national debt in 1776 at three-sevenths of the total. Not only did the Dutch underwrite British credit, but Dutch bankers helped funnel British money to Britain's diplomatic allies. When relations between the Dutch and British were strained in the 1770s, Dutch investment easily found new homes in North America and France. The role of the United Provinces in the colonial struggles of the eighteenth century was thus indirect but considerable.

The Eighteenth-Century Empires

After 1715 a new era began in the saga of European colonial development (see Map 18.3).

MAP 18.3: OVERSEAS POSSESSIONS 1713

Three pioneers in overseas expansion had by now assumed a generally passive role, content to defend the domains already acquired. Portugal, whose dominion over Brazil was recognized at the Peace of Utrecht, henceforth retired from active contention. Likewise the Dutch could scarcely compete for new footholds and now protected their interests through cautious policies of neutrality. Although Spain continued her efforts to exclude outsiders from her vast empire, she had to rely increasingly on the power of her kindred dynasty in France for any confrontation with Britain. The stage of active competition was in fact left to these two powers.

Mercantile and Naval Competition

Great Britain, a nation that had barely been able to hold her own in maritime competition against the Dutch in the seventeenth century, now began her rise to domination of the seas. The only serious rival of this island power was France.

Their rivalry was played out in four regions. The West Indies, where France and Britain each colonized several islands profitably, constituted the fulcrum of empire, for reasons that will be discussed shortly. Directly linked to the West Indian economy was the second colonial territory: slave-providing West Africa. The third area was the North American continent, where a significant difference between the two powers developed. Britain's colonies became populous centers of settlement, whereas New France remained primarily a trading area. Finally, both nations sponsored powerful companies for trade with India and other Asian lands. These ventures were supposed to struggle for markets and influence without establishing actual colonies.

There were obvious differences and important similarities between the two royal systems. French absolutism produced a centralized structure, with its colonies being run according to uniform standards. *Intendants* and military governors ruled across the seas as they did in the French provinces. The British North American colonies by contrast were and remained somewhat independent both from each other and from the home government, where crown and Parliament both claimed colonial jurisdiction. Most colonies had a royal governor but also a locally oriented legislature and strong traditions of self-government. Nonetheless the French and British faced similar problems and achieved generally similar results. Most importantly both applied mercantilist principles to the regulation of trade, and both increased naval power to protect it.

Mercantilism was a Europe-wide phenomenon, not limited to the colonial powers. It involved the regulation of economic activity so as to increase the power of the state over that of its neighbors. In this sense Prussia was as mercantilist as Britain, for both regarded the economic activities of individuals as subordinate to government policy.

A key tenet of mercantilism was the need for a favorable balance of trade and an inflow of gold and silver, with the assumption that a nation's share of bullion could increase only at its neighbor's expense. Colonies could promote a favorable balance of trade by producing valuable raw materials or crops for the mother country and providing a market for the latter's manufactured goods. Foreign states had to be excluded from these benefits as much as possible. By discriminatory tariffs, elaborate regulations, bounties, and outright prohibitions, each government sought to channel trade with its colonies in the direction of itself. Mercantilism for the colonies boiled down to an elaborate system of protectionism for this trade.

The colonies were exploited for the benefit of the mother country and not solely for the profit of those who invested or settled in them. But enormous fortunes were made by the West Indies planters as well as by merchants, manufacturers, and ship owners at home. Moreover, illicit trade brought comfortable profits to more than one colonial family. For example, French planters needed North America's beef, fish, and grain and were eager to exchange their own (cheaper) sugar or molasses for it. The Hancocks of Boston among others grew dependent on this kind of smuggling to the French West Indies.

"Empire" was another way of saying "trade," but this trade depended on naval power. Rivals had to be excluded and regulations enforced. Thus there was a reciprocal relationship between the expansion of trade and the deployment of naval forces, which added to the competitive nature of colonial expansion. The merchant traders and the war vessels that supported them needed many stopping places for reprovisioning and refitting. This meant that ports had to be secured for them in strategic locations and denied to rivals whenever possible in Africa, India, and the Caribbean.

The Profits of Empire

Colonial commerce provided new products like sugar and new consumer demand, which in turn created an impetus for manufacturing and capital accumulation at home. This cycle increased the opportunities for the English and French middle classes. It is estimated that French commerce quadrupled during the eighteenth century, the value of its trade being somewhere in the vicinity of 200 million livres in 1716 and reaching more than 1 billion livres in 1787. By the 1770s commerce with their colonies accounted for almost one-third the total volume of both Britain's and France's foreign trade. The West Indies trade (mainly in sugar) bulked largest, and its expansion was spectacular. The value of French imports from the West Indies increased more than tenfold between 1716 and 1788, from 16 million to 185 million livres.

The West Indies seemed to be ideal colonies. By virtue of their tropical climate and the isolation from European society that made slavery possible, they produced abundant crops that were difficult to raise elsewhere: tobacco, cotton, and indigo in addition to sugar, a luxury that European custom turned into a necessity. Moreover, the islands could produce little else. They could not raise an adequate supply of food animals or grain to feed the vast slave population; they could not cut enough lumber for building; and they certainly could not manufacture the luxury goods demanded by the planter class. In other words, the islands yielded up valuable crops and were dependent markets for most other commodities.

Numerous variations of the famous triangular trade therefore revolved around the West Indies. One pattern began with a ship departing from a British port with a cargo of manufactured products—paper, knives, pots, blankets, and the like—destined for the shopkeepers of North America. Landing at Marblehead or Philadelphia, the ship might exchange its goods for New England fish oil, fish, beef, and timber. These would then be transported to Jamaica or Barbados to be traded for sugar that would be turned over to British refineries many months later.

Another variation might see a ship set out from Newport, Rhode Island (the chief slaving port in North America), with a cargo of New England rum. Landing in Africa, it would acquire slaves in exchange for the rum and then sail to the Indies to sell the slaves—for bills of exchange, and for molasses, from which more rum could be distilled.

The final step in the mercantilist colonial process was the reexport of refined and distilled products made of the sugar, indigo, or tobacco provided by the overseas possessions. These were most likely to bring gold into British or French hands since finished goods could command hard cash from customers all over the Western world. For colonial commerce was superimposed on a complex and profitable pattern of European trade in which the Atlantic states carried off the lion's share. The New World's sugar, furs, fish, and tobacco were added to Baltic grain and timber; Italian and Spanish wines, fruits, olives, and silks; and Levantine and Asian spices and fabrics. To all these regions the manufacturing centers of Western Europe continued providing products like nails and pots, glassware and crockery, and shirts and stockings as well as luxuries like carriages and tapestries.

Slavery, the Foundation of Empire

Slavery was the keystone of the eighteenth-century empires. The dynamic qualities of the global trade had slavery as a starting point. Vast, backbreaking labor was necessary to transform a favorable climate and the investment of speculators into harvested crops of staples. As one British merchant put it candidly, colonial trade "increases or diminishes in proportion to the numbers of Negroes imported there, who produce the commodities with which our ships are usually loaded, and enable planters to live well and purchase great quantities of British commodities." About the same time the chamber of commerce of Nantes, France's chief slaving port, publicly argued that without slavery there would be no French colonial commerce to speak of at all.

At the height of the slave traffic, probably about 88,000 Negroes were removed from Africa annually—half in British ships, a quarter in French, and the rest in Dutch, Portuguese, Danish, and American ships. Over 600,000 slaves were imported into Jamaica in the eighteenth century, while the population of Santo Domingo comprised about half a million slaves compared with 35,000 whites of all nationalities and 28,000 mulattoes and free Negroes at the time of the French Revolution.

THE MAGNITUDE OF THE SLAVE TRADE

The following figures represent the best current estimate of the number of persons removed from Africa and transported as slaves to the New World during the entire period of the Atlantic slave trade.

British Caribbean	1,665,000
British North America (to 1790)	275,000
United States (after 1786)	124,000
French Caribbean	1,600,000
Dutch Caribbean	500,000
Brazil	3,646,000
Spanish American	1,552,000

Source: Philip D. Curtin, *The Atlantic Slave Trade: A Census* (1969).

Traffic in slaves was competitive and risky but highly profitable for those who succeeded. The demand for slaves in the Indies, South America, and the Southern colonies in North America kept rising, pushing prices up. In both Britain and France, slaving was originally organized monopolistically, with chartered companies holding exclusive rights in the 1660s. There was no actual colonization or conquest in Africa, but the French and to a lesser extent the British attempted to establish forts, or "factories," on African soil for the coordination and defense of these companies. Gradually the monopolies were challenged by newcomers—groups of merchants and investors who combined to launch single ships on slaving voyages. The West Indian planters, who needed more and cheaper slaves, applauded this additional source. In port cities like Bristol and Liverpool, the independent traders clustered and prospered. By the 1730s the British government was opening membership in its company almost automatically to any subject engaged in the trade. This arrangement was a midway point between the older chartered joint-stock companies and the nineteenth-century pattern of direct government attempts at colonization to promote the interests of British merchants and investors.

Europeans alone did not condemn free blacks to slavery. In this period Europeans scarcely penetrated the interior of the continent; they were confined by the forbidding topography and the resoluteness of the natives to coastal areas. The actual enslavement took place in the interior at the hands of aggressive tribes whose chiefs became the middlemen of this nefarious commerce. These black traders were shrewd and hard bargainers, and prices were set in goods rather than fixed currency. The competition among Europeans for the slaves tended to drive up the prices that the natives could command in hardware, cloth, liquor, and guns. In response some traders sought to open up new areas where the natives would be more eager to come to terms. This combination of competitiveness, increasing demand, and higher prices helped spread the trade and further darken the future of Africa.

Many blacks failed to survive the process of enslavement at all, perishing either on the forced marches from the interior to the coast or on the nightmarish middle passage across the Atlantic, which was comparable to the transit in cattle cars of Nazi prisoners to extermi-

Slave traffic was the basis for empire building in the eighteenth century, and slave ships were a cruel and common sight on international waters. This print shows a method used to quell revolts on board ship and suggests the sheer violence underlying the trade.
(Photo: New York Public Library, Rare Books)

nation camps in World War II. Since the risks of slaving ventures were high and the time lag between investment and return was usually a year and a half or two years, the traders sought to maximize profits by jamming in as many captives as possible. Medium-sized ships carried as many as 500 slaves on a voyage, packed below deck in only enough space for the individual to lie at full length, pressed against neighboring bodies, and enough headroom to crawl, not stand. The food and provisions were likewise held to a minimum. The mortality rate that resulted from these odious conditions was over 10 percent on average. It is no wonder then that agitation against slavery tended to focus initially on the trade rather than the institution itself. After the 1780s participation in slave trafficking diminished considerably both in England and France. A dark chapter in Europe's relations with the outside world dwindled to an end, though the formal suppression of slaving did not come for several more decades.

IV. THE MIDCENTURY CONFLAGRATION

The pressures created by the competition of states, dynasties, and empires in the eighteenth century exploded in midcentury in what was to be the last large-scale war of the prerevolutionary period. For the sake of clarity, it is helpful to consider the conflagration in two parts. One, the Continental phase, known as the Seven Years' War, had at its center Austro-Prussian rivalry and the growing ambitions of Russia. The other revolved around Anglo-French competition for empire in North America, the West Indies, and India. Colonial historians have called it the Great War for Empire, and it was this sector of conflict that had produced the more striking results when the smoke cleared.

The Seven Years' War

At midcentury a reconsideration of alliances began within the European state system under Austria's prodding. Previously the Bourbon-Hapsburg rivalry had been the cornerstone of European diplomacy. But by the 1750s at least two other sets of fundamental antagonisms had superseded it: France's competition with Great Britain in the New World and Austria's vendetta against Prussia over Silesia. For Austria the rivalry with Bourbon France was no longer important. Its position in the Holy Roman Empire depended now on humbling Prussia. France did not yet share a concern over Prussia, but her hostility to Austria had diminished. Austria was therefore free to pursue a turnabout in alliances—a veritable diplomatic revolution—in which an anti-Prussian coalition could be forged. Russia was the key to this coalition. Aside from her personal loathing of the impious Frederick II, Empress Elizabeth perceived Prussia as an obstacle to Russian ambitions in Eastern Europe. Moreover, Prussia's geographical vulnerability made the kingdom an inviting target.

Prussia was understandably active on the diplomatic front in the hope of compensating for that vulnerability. Upset by the initiatives of Austria's brilliant foreign minister Kaunitz, Frederick's panicky countermoves only succeeded in alienating the other powers. Frederick sought to stay out of the Anglo-French rivalry by coming to terms with both these states. Having been France's ally in the past, he sought in addition to negotiate a treaty with England. England—seeking to protect her North German client state of Hanover—willingly signed a neutrality accord with Prussia (the Convention of Westminster) in January 1756. Frederick had no intention of repudiating his friendship with France, but to the French—who had not been informed in advance of these negotiations—the Convention of Westminster appeared as an affront if not an actual betrayal. Such accords with France's mortal enemy England seemed an unscrupulous act by an untrustworthy ally. Hence France overreacted, turned against Prussia, and thus fell into Kaunitz's design. Russia too assumed a more militant anti-Prussian position since it considered the Convention of Westminster a betrayal by *its* supposed ally England. English bribes and diplomacy could no longer keep Russia from actively joining Austria to plan Prussia's dismemberment.

Fearing encirclement, Frederick gambled on launching a preventive war through Saxony in 1756 to break apart the coalition. Although he easily conquered the duchy—the gateway to Hapsburg Bohemia—his plan backfired, for it now activated the coalition that he dreaded. Both Russia and France met their commitments to Austria, and a grand offensive design against Prussia took final shape. Poorly led, France in effect put her army at Austria's disposal for Austrian objectives.

For a time Frederick showed his genius as a general and prevailed over the coalition. His forces achieved a spectacular victory at Rossbach, Saxony, in October 1757 over a much larger combined French-Austrian army. Skillful tactics and daring surprise movements would bring other victories, but strategically the Prussian position was shaky. Frederick had to dash in all directions across his provinces to repel a variety of invading armies whose combined strength far exceeded his own. Each successive year of the war, he faced the prospect of Russian attacks on Brandenburg in the north and Austrian thrusts from the south through Silesia and Saxony. Disaster was avoided mainly because of Russia's policy of evacuating for winter quarters back east regardless of her gains, but even so the Russians occupied Berlin. On the verge of exhaustion, Prussia at best seemed to face a stalemate with a considerable loss of territory; at worst the war would continue and bring about a total Prussian collapse. But then again all the powers were war-weary, and his enemies were extremely distrustful of each other by now.

Frederick was plucked from the jaws of despair by one of those sudden changes of reign that commonly caused dramatic reversals of policy in Europe. In January 1762 his nemesis Empress Elizabeth died and was replaced temporarily by Tsar Peter III, a fanatic admirer of Frederick's. He quickly pulled Russia out of the war and returned Frederick's conquered eastern domains of Prussia and Pomerania. Kaunitz's dream collapsed. At the same time the belligerent British minister Pitt was replaced by the more pacific John Stuart, earl of Bute, clearing the way for an Anglo-French settlement that did not insist on the punishment of Prussia.

The actual terms of the Peace of Hubertusburg (1763), settling the Continental phase of the midcentury conflagration, were therefore surprisingly favorable to Prussia in view of all that had happened. Saxony was returned to its elector, but no compensation was demanded from Prussia for the devastation she had inflicted on the duchy. Silesia was recognized as Prussian by the Austrians. In short the status quo was restored. Frederick could return to Berlin, his dominion preserved. He had marshaled all the state's resources to maintain his army in the field, and this army alone had assured the survival of his state.

Mounting Colonial Conflicts

In the New World, rival French and British colonies had been developing along complementary lines, and both groups were prospering. The thirteen British colonies on the North American continent were experiencing a remarkable growth because of continuous immigration and natural reproduction, reaching a population of about 1.5 million by midcentury. While some pushed the frontier westward and put the soil under cultivation, others clustered around the original settlements, a few of which could by then be called cities.[3] The extension of the frontier and the growth of towns helped impart a particular vitality to the British colonial world in contrast to which New France appeared less dynamic. Since there was little enthusiasm for emigration to Louisiana or Canada, the French remained thinly spread in their substantial territories. Yet their colonies were well organized, profitable, and vigorous in their own way. Indeed French West Indian planters were able to underprice the sugar of their British competitors, and the French trading company in India was initially more effective than its British rival in expanding operations.

While French fishermen and fur traders prospered in Canada, French soldiers established a series of strongholds to support them. These included Fort Louisburg—the greatest bastion of military strength in North America—at the entrance of the Gulf of St. Lawrence and a string of forts near the Great Lakes that served as bridgeheads for French fur traders and as a security buffer for the province of Quebec (see Map 18.4). At the other end of the continent, in Louisiana, New Orleans was established to open the far end of the Mississippi River to trade. During the War of the Austrian Succession, several skirmishes were fought in the New World, but both sides were agreeable to a restitution of captured territories at the peace table, which the Treaty of Aix-la-Chapelle arranged. Obviously this was a truce, not a peace.

On the contrary imperial rivalry intensified and military preparations increased. France reinforced Louisburg, and the British established their first large military base in North America at nearby Halifax, Nova Scotia. The fishing grounds and waterways of the St. Lawrence gulf would be a major scene of contention in any future war. A second area that now loomed into prominence was the unsettled Ohio valley. Pushing south from their Great Lakes trading forts and north from their posts on the Mississippi, the French began to assume control over that wilderness. A new string of forts formed pivots for potential French domination of the whole area between the Appalachian Mountains and the Mississippi—territory claimed and coveted by British subjects in the thirteen colonies. The threat grew that the French could completely cut off the westward expansion of these colonies. Conversely the French feared that British domination in the Ohio valley would lead to encroachments on Canadian territory.

In this jockeying for position, the allegiance of the Indians was vital, and the French gradually gained the upper hand. Being traders only and not settlers, the French did not force the

---

[3] With a population of about 23,000 in 1760, for example, Philadelphia could scarcely be considered a colonial outpost. Commercially and socially (if not culturally) it was a city.

MAP 18.4: ANGLO-FRENCH RIVALRY IN NORTH AMERICA AND THE CARIBBEAN 1754–1763

Indians from their native hunting grounds as the British had done repeatedly. Hence the Indians were willing to cooperate in sealing off the Ohio valley. A large land investment company called the Ohio Company of Virginia was most directly affected by this development, and in 1745 it attempted to break the French and Indian hold by sending an expedition against Fort Duquesne. Led by a young militiaman named George Washington, the expedition failed.

Thus, contrary to the British tradition of letting settled colonies pay for themselves, the home government was compelled to shoulder the burden of defense. An expedition of regulars was sent to do the job that George Washington could not. But it too met defeat in an ambush by experienced French and Indian skirmishers. Limited engagements were now giving way to a full-scale war. Each side began to reinforce its garrisons and naval squadrons. In May 1756, after some two years of unofficial hostilities, war was formally declared between Britain and France. The French and Indian War, as this arc of the Great War for Empire was called in the colonies, originated as a contest to decide the balance of power in the New World, and it remained that throughout.[4]

The Great War for Empire

The midcentury conflagration was to be one of Britain's high moments in history, the stuff of patriotic legends and national self-glorification. The Great War for Empire started, however, in quite another fashion. Jumping to the initiative on several fronts, the better-coordinated French struck the first blows. Calcutta, the Mediterranean island of Minorca, and several key British forts on the Great Lakes all fell, while in Europe the British expeditionary force suffered defeat and humiliation. Yet the French had certain inherent disadvantages that were to show in the long run. Spread so thinly in North America, they would be hard put to follow early success in the French and Indian War with staying power. More important, France was dependent on naval support to reinforce, supply, and move her troops; unfortunately for her, what had been a fairly even match in the 1740s turned into clear British superiority in the 1750s, with British ships of the line outnumbering French almost two to one. When William Pitt became de facto prime minister in 1758, the tide was about to turn.

Pitt brought single-mindedness, clarity of focus, and vigor to his task. Although honoring Britain's commitment to Prussia, he attached highest priority to defeating Bourbon France in the New World. His strategy for achieving this involved an immediate series of offensives and an imaginative use of the British navy. He assigned the largest segment of the British fleet to cover the French home fleet, and he waited.

The French hoped to invade the British Isles as the surest method of bringing the enemy to the peace table, and the French fleet was ordered to prepare the way. In 1759 major battles were joined between French squadrons from Brest and Toulon and the British ships assigned to cover them; the French fleet was decimated and the fate of empires decided. Henceforth the British had an almost free hand at sea. Not only were they now immune from French invasion, but they could prevent France from utilizing her superior military forces in the colonial world. Unable to transport men and supplies, she could no longer reinforce her garrisons. Unable to match the tactical assaults of British ships, she could not repel amphibious landings. In every theater of war, French colonial possessions were now falling thanks to British naval supremacy.

In the French and Indian War, for example,

---

[4] The classic treatment of Anglo-French rivalry in North America was written by the nineteenth-century American romantic historian Francis Parkman. See S. E. Morison (ed.), *The Parkman Reader* (1955), for a convenient selection of his writings.

General James Wolfe defeated General Louis Joseph Montcalm in the battle of Quebec in September 1759. Had the French been able to reinforce Montreal, which they still held, they could have launched a counterattack against Wolfe's overextended lines. Here Pitt's strategy triumphed, since it was now precisely impossible for the French to reinforce overseas garrisons. By September 1760 this last outpost of French power in North America capitulated to the British, who had already ousted the French from the Ohio valley and the Great Lakes area. The same pattern unfolded in Africa and India. And in the West Indies the long duel between the two powers turned into a rout. One by one the French islands were seized, and even Martinique—known as the jewel of the French Empire—had fallen by 1761.

Not all these conquests were preserved at the peace table, however. In exchange for an end to fighting, a war-weary Britain was prepared to return certain colonies in the Treaty of Paris in 1763. France was willing to surrender Canada, and Britain chose to retain the territory—perhaps mistakenly: this removed the threat of French power, which it turned out had been a major factor in the loyalty of the British colonists to the mother country. Since British West Indian planters feared added competition from the possible inclusion of the French islands in the British system, the British government decided to accede to French demands for the return of several of these. In the long run India proved to be Britain's most important colonial territory. Her domination of the subcontinent began with the Treaty of Paris, which excluded French troops from the region, permitting only British influence to have any force.

But there would be momentous repercussions from the Peace of Paris. First, it created a new situation for the thirteen North American colonies, and Britain's triumph turned into disaster twenty years later when they successfully broke away, with French assistance. In addition, though France's ill-fated efforts in the Seven Years' War had strained her finances substantially, she was unable to resist the opportunity to strike back at Britain during the war for independence. Partly for this reason she contracted further debts that could not be absorbed by the monarchy in its existing form. Finally, it is well to remember that supporting the entire state structure were the slaves in the colonies and the peasants in most states, whose labor ultimately produced the revenues that paid for the navies and armies. Their bill would eventually come due in one form or another.

During the eighteenth century the effectiveness of Europe's states in marshaling their power and resources within the state system was increasingly apparent. French and English merchants demonstrated an extraordinary capacity to capitalize on the commercial opportunities afforded by overseas colonies, plantation economy, and slavery. But these traders were backed by their states, especially in the form of naval power. The growth of the British and French empires and with them of the global maritime economy of the eighteenth century was in one sense an aspect of the competitive state system.

In Central Europe direct territorial aggrandizement was the issue. Prussia, Austria, and Russia faced each other directly at war and at the negotiating table. Here helpless lesser states were sacrificed to the "reasons of state" of the great powers; most notable was Poland, whose disappearance from the map in three successive partitions must be accounted as one of the century's most important events.

All these interests clashed in the midcentury conflagration, a classic episode of competition in the European state system. The scale of fighting in the Seven Years' War was enormous. Yet the system was able to contain the massive aggression and survive the convulsion almost intact. Although Prussia had been driven to the brink of extinction, she actually lost little in the peace settlement; in the end Frederick II even retained Silesia. All in all, however, the Continental powers had proved to be well matched. The colonial phase of the hostilities, the great War for Empire, was more decisive, though here too a degree of balance was restored by Britain's concessions to France at the peace table. The significance of these outcomes will be best appreciated when contrasted later with the resulting upheaval of World War I.

RECOMMENDED READING

Sources
Luvvas, J. (ed.). *Frederick the Great on the Art of War.* 1966.
Macartney, C. A. (ed.). *The Evolution of the Habsburg and Hohenzollern Dynasties.* 1969. An excellent collection of documents.

Studies
Anderson, M. S. *Historians and Eighteenth-Century Europe, 1715–1789.* 1979. Past and current viewpoints on a number of fundamental issues.
Barker, Ernest. *The Development of Public Services in Western Europe.* 1966.
Baugh, Daniel (ed.). *Aristocratic Government and Society in Eighteenth-Century England.* 1975. A collection of articles and excerpts designed as an introduction to the subject.
Bernard, Paul. *Joseph II.* 1968. A brief biography.
*Cobban, Alfred. *A History of Modern France: Vol. I, 1715–1799.* 1966.
Corvisier, André. *Armies and Societies in Europe, 1494–1789.* 1979. A comparative study, strongest on the French army.
Craton, Michael. *Sinews of Empire: A Short History of British Slavery.* 1974.
Dakin, Douglas. *Turgot and the Ancien Régime in France.* 1939. A view from the inside of the problems and achievements of enlightened administration in France.
Dorn, Walter. *The Competition for Empire, 1740–63.* 1940. Traditional historiography at its best.
Duffy, Christopher. *The Army of Frederick the Great.* 1974. A view that covers everything from recruitment to military tactics in the field.
Forster, Robert. *The House of Saulx-Tavanes: Versailles and Burgundy, 1700–1830.* 1971. A brilliant portrait of an aristocratic family and the peasant communities that supported its life style.
Goodwin, Albert (ed.). *The European Nobility in the 18th Century.* 1967.
Owen, John B. *The Eighteenth Century, 1714–1815.* 1974. A dry, detailed history of England.
Pares, Richard. *King George III and the Politicians.* 1953. A reliable interpretation of a much-debated subject.
*Parry, J. H. *Trade and Dominion: The European Overseas Empires in the Eighteenth Century.* 1971. A panoramic overview.
Plumb, J. H. *Sir Robert Walpole.* 2 vols. 1956–61. A masterful biography and evocation of the age.
Ritter, Gerhard. *Frederick the Great.* 1968. A sympathetic portrait by a leading pre–World War II German historian.
*Rosenberg, Hans. *Bureaucracy, Aristocracy, and Autocracy: The Prussian Experience, 1660–1815.* 1958. Difficult, highly conceptualized, important history.
Thompson, Gladys. *Catherine the Great and the Expansion of Russia.* 1962.
*Wangermann, Ernst. *The Austrian Achievement, 1700–1800.* 1973. A superb, concise synthesis with a profusion of well-integrated illustrations.
*Woloch, Isser. *Eighteenth-Century Europe: Tradition and Progress, 1715–1789.* 1982. A comprehensive introduction to the period.

* Available in paperback.

19

THE AGE OF
ENLIGHTENMENT
1715–1770s

Sharp breaks in the intellectual and cultural life of Europe have been rare. Nonetheless, taken broadly rather than as literal chronological periods, the seventeenth, eighteenth, and nineteenth centuries represent three distinct phases of Western cultural development. The seventeenth century was the towering age of genius in European thought—a period of great scientific and philosophical innovation. It was also an elitist age in terms of the audience for cultural activity and the system of aristocratic patronage. If we jump ahead to the nineteenth century we encounter a decidedly middle-class intellectual and artistic milieu as well as the beginnings of mass literacy and mass culture toward the end of the century.

Obviously then the eighteenth century is transitional. In the domain of thought it was a time when the impact of science and the growth of religious skepticism matured into a naturalistic world view. Philosophy became less metaphysical and more critically concerned with practical matters, with "enlightenment." The most important eighteenth-century thinkers were not seeking to extirpate Christianity from Western civilization, but they no longer believed in it themselves and wished to counter what they took to be its spirit of complacency and to reduce its influence in temporal affairs drastically. Intellectuals developed a strong sense of their own power to enlighten their society and point it toward change. They were reformers who—contrary to Christian belief and unlike reformers within the Church—believed that there was no reality beyond human society, no afterlife to divert the spirit of man from worldly concerns. In this spirit they provided an arsenal of critical ideas, particularly the notion of social utility as a standard of value, and a preoccupation with the issue of freedom.

While they were thus critics of their society, eighteenth-century intellectuals were very much at home in and proud of European culture. Theirs was an age in which publishing activity increased explosively, in which major new literary and musical genres were developed, and in which a number of cultural trends reflected the presence of an expanding middle class in a still-aristocratic age.

I. THE ENLIGHTENMENT

The eighteenth century reworked and diffused the ideas of the seventeenth. Building on seventeenth-century science, on skepticism in matters of religion, and on a heightened appreciation of Classical antiquity, intellectuals redefined the function of philosophy. They believed that human behavior and institutions could be studied rationally, like Newton's universe, and their faults corrected. They saw themselves as participants in a movement—the

Enlightenment—that was making men and women more understanding, more tolerant, and more virtuous.

The Broadening Reverberations of Science

It is hard to think of two men less revolutionary in temperament than René Descartes and Sir Isaac Newton. Writing for a small, learned audience, each was conservative on matters outside the confines of science, had relatively little concern for social relations or institutions, and was a practicing Christian. Yet their legacy to succeeding generations produced what has been described as "a permanent intellectual insurrection." Their conceptual systems—along with those of John Locke (see pp. 595–597) and the Dutch philosopher Baruch Spinoza—were transformed and propagated in directions and in a spirit undreamed of by their authors.

While eighteenth-century scientists pondered the details of the diverging cosmologies of Descartes and Newton, nonscientists continued the process, begun in the previous century, of applying their basic methodology to all realms of human thought. Experimentation, methodical doubt, and naturalistic explanations of phenomena were fused into a "scientific" or "mathematical spirit," which at bottom meant simply confidence in reason and a skeptical attitude toward accepted dogmas. Its advocates took upon themselves the task of popularizing science, with the aim of transforming the values of Western civilization. As part of this effort men like Bernard de Fontenelle, secretary of the French Academy of Sciences from 1699 to 1741, translated the discoveries of scientists into clear and even amusing general reading. The literary talents of these enthusiasts helped make household words out of Newton and Descartes among the educated laymen of Europe.

A more calculating and ambitious propagandist of the scientific spirit was Voltaire, the Frenchman who is virtually synonymous with the Enlightenment in all its aspects. While his chief talents lay in the realm of literature and criticism, Voltaire also spent several years studying Newton's work, and in 1738 he published a widely read popularization called *Elements of the Philosophy of Newton*. However dry the study of physics, Voltaire argued, it frees the mind from dogma, and its experimental methods provide a model for the liberation of human thought. Moreover, Voltaire situated Newton's achievement in the context of the liberal England that also produced Bacon and Locke, the three of whom Voltaire adopted as his personal Trinity. In his *Philosophical Letters on the English* (1734), a celebration of English toleration and an indirect attack on what he considered French bigotry, censorship, and social snobbery, Voltaire had already noted the popularity and respect enjoyed by British literary figures and scientists. He saw this recognition of talent and distinction as a crucial component of a free society and as necessarily related to the achievements of a man like Newton.

Popularizations of scientific method stimulated public interest in science as well as public and private support for research projects. Mathematicians, cartographers, and astronomers were direct beneficiaries of the support and made notable advances in their fields. But progress was far from linear or automatic. In chemistry for example the traditions of alchemy persisted, and such phenomena as combustion long resisted objective analysis. At the end of the century, however, a major breakthrough occurred when the Englishman Joseph Priestley isolated oxygen and the Frenchman Antoine Laurent Lavoisier analyzed the components of air and water. Lavoisier also came close to explaining the process of combustion.

The more dubious side of the vogue for science could be observed in the great popularity of mesmerism. This pseudoscience of magnetic fields purported to offer its wealthy devotees relief from a variety of ailments by the use of special "electrical" baths and treatments. Although repeatedly condemned by the authoritative studies of the Academy of Sciences in Paris, mesmerism continued to attract both the educated and the credulous.

The scientific enterprise most representative of eighteenth-century attitudes was natural history, the science of the earth's development—a combination of geology, zoology, botany, and historical geography. This field of study was easy for the layman to appreciate, which made its foremost practitioner probably the most widely acclaimed scientist of the century. He was G. L. Buffon, keeper of the French Botanical Gardens—a patronage position that allowed him to produce a multivolume *Natural History of the Earth* between 1749 and 1778. Drawing on a vast knowledge of phenomena such as fossils, Buffon went beyond previous attempts to classify the data of nature, seeking to relate and generalize from them in order to provide both a theory and a description of the earth's development. A nonbeliever himself, Buffon did not explicitly attack religious versions of such events as the Creation. He simply ignored them, an omission whose significance was obvious enough to his many readers. Similarly, while he did not specifically contend that man had evolved from beasts, he implied this, writing for example, "It is possible to descend by almost insensible degrees from the most perfect creature to the most formless matter." Buffon's earth did not derive from a singular act of divine creation that would explain the origins of man. The readers of his *History* or its numerous popularizations in several languages were thus introduced to a demystified universe that had developed through evolution. Buffon's work sharpened the thrusts of science and secularism.

The Rise of Secularism

The erosion of revealed religion as a source of authority is the hallmark of the Enlightenment. The viewpoint it engendered, secularism, derived some of its impetus from seventeenth-century scientists and liberal theologians who were themselves dedicated Christians. They had hoped to accommodate religion to new philosophical standards and scientific formulations and to eliminate the superstitious imagery that could make religion seem ridiculous. They regarded the devil for example as a category of moral evil rather than a specific horned creature with a pictchfork, and they endowed the world of nature with religious significance, perceiving it as a form of revelation in which God's majesty could be discerned. Deemphasizing miracles and focusing on reverence for the Creator and on the moral teachings of the Bible would bolster religion, they hoped. And indeed their modifications retained the adherence of many educated people to Christianity during the eighteenth century. Yet in the final analysis, this kind of thinking served to diminish the force of religion and its authority in society.

A more important source of the secular outlook was the idea of toleration as propounded by the highly respected critic Pierre Bayle. Consciously applying methodical doubt to subjects that Descartes himself had excluded from such treatment, Bayle's *Critical and Historical Dictionary* (1697) put the claims of religion to the test of critical reason. Certain Christian traditions emerged as myth and fairy tale, and historical Christianity was seen as a record of fanaticism and inhumanity. Bayle's chief target was Christianity's sectarianism and attempts (like Louis XIV's revocation of the Edict of Nantes) to impose orthodoxy at any cost. Though himself a devout Calvinist, Bayle argued for complete toleration, which would allow human beings to practice any religion or none at all. A man's moral behavior rather than his creed is what should count. Ethics do not depend on Christian revelation; a Muslim, a Confucian, a Jew, even an atheist can be a moral man.

Christianity had more vehement critics than Bayle. Atheistic and blasphemous attacks were to be found in privately circulated writings rather than published books in the first half of the century. These clandestine tracts treated revealed religion as a form of hysteria that had resulted in centuries of bloodshed. Their titles tell their messages: *Critical Examination of the Apologists of the Christian Religion, Mortal Souls, The Divinity of Jesus Christ Destroyed, Faith Destroyed.* Faith was indeed destroyed here, along with such props as miracles, priests, and divine prophets.

The Enlightenment's most unstinting antireligious polemicist was Voltaire, which was the pen name of François Marie Arouet. This prolific writer was one of the century's most brilliant literary stylists, historians, and poets. Had he been satisfied with merely exploiting these talents, his fame would still have been considerable. But he was also a profoundly sincere antagonist of Christianity who was determined to bring the spirit of the clandestine literature out into the open. For tactical reasons much of his attack against *"l'infâme"* ("the infamous thing"), as he called Christianity, was directed against its more vulnerable practices, such as monasticism. But his ultimate target was Christianity, which, he declared, "every sensible man, every honorable man must hold in horror."

Voltaire's masterpiece was his *Philosophical Dictionary* (1764), a best seller in its day that he was obliged to publish anonymously and that was burned by the authorities in Switzerland, France, and the Netherlands. Modeled after Bayle's dictionary, it was far blunter. In theology, he wrote, "we find man's insanity in all its plenitude." Organized religion is not simply false but pernicious, he argued. Superstition inevitably breeds fanaticism; crimes of organized religion like the St. Bartholomew's Day Massacre are not incidental but are the essence of its irrationality.

Voltaire hoped that educated Europeans would abandon Christianity in favor of deism, a naturalistic belief that accorded God recognition only as the Creator and held that the world, once created, functions according to natural laws that God cannot interfere with. Man is now left to live in an ordered universe essentially on his own, without hope or fear of divine intervention and without the threat of damnation or the expectation of eternal salvation. Religion should be a matter of private contemplation rather than public worship and mythic creeds. Certain figures in the Enlightenment went beyond this to philosophical atheism, but on the whole Voltaire's mild and undemanding deism remained the characteristic view of eighteenth-century nonbelievers. Despite its innocuousness, however, this form of spirituality was wholly secular, and progressive churchmen who could accept many arguments of eighteenth-century science and philosophy could not accept that.

The Philosophes

Science and secularism were the rallying points of a group of French intellectuals known as the philosophes, or philosophers. This term was employed by their traditionalist enemies to mock their pretensions, but they used it themselves with a sense of pride. For they were the avant-garde, the men who raised the Enlightenment to the status of a self-conscious movement.

The leaders of this influential coterie of writers were Voltaire (whom one meets at every turn in eighteenth-century intellectual life) and Denis Diderot (whom we will meet shortly). Its ranks included the mathematicians Jean d'Alembert and the marquis de Condorcet, the jurist baron de Montesquieu, the statesman Jacques Turgot, and the social scientists and philosophers Claude Adrien Helvétius and Baron d'Holbach. Outside of France their kinship extended to a clustering of brilliant Scottish philosophers and thinkers, among them David Hume and Adam Smith; to the German playwright and critic Gotthold Ephraim Lessing and the philosopher Immanuel Kant; to such founders of the American Philosophical Society as Benjamin Franklin and Thomas Jefferson; and to the Italian economist and penal reformer the marquis of Beccaria.

The philosophes and their foreign confreres have been well described by a sympathetic historian as a close family with many distant relatives.[1] The family was troubled by a good deal of internal bickering, but its members always enjoyed a sense of common identity. What they shared above all was a critical spirit, the desire to reexamine the assumptions and institutions of society, to expose them to the tests of reason, experience, and utility. Today this sounds banal, but it was not so at a time when almost everywhere religion still dominated society. To assert the primacy of reason meant to turn away from the essence of religion: faith. It meant a decisive break with the Christian world view, which placed doctrine at the center of intellectual activity. For centuries the intellectual mentors of Western civilization had been urging man to submit to what he could know least—the divine. The philosophes hoped to change this completely. They invoked the paganism of ancient Greece and Rome, where the spirit of rational inquiry prevailed among educated men. They ridiculed the Middle Ages as the "Dark Ages," using the attitudes of that period as a contrast with their own sense of liberation and modernity. In *The Decline and Fall of the Roman Empire* (1776–1788), Edward Gibbon passed the verdict that Christianity had eclipsed a Roman civilization that had sought to live according to reason rather than myths.

The inspiration of antiquity was matched by the stimulus of modern science and philosophy. The philosophes laid claim to Newton, who made the universe intelligible without the aid of revelation, and Locke, who uncovered the workings of the human mind. From Locke

---

[1] Peter Gay, *The Enlightenment: An Interpretation.* (1966).

they argued that human personality is malleable—its nature is not immutably fixed, let alone corrupted by original sin. Men are therefore ultimately responsible to themselves for what they do with their lives. Inherited arrangements are no more nor less sacred than experience has proved them to be. The philosophes acclaimed the role of the enlightened intellectual in society. As the humanists had several centuries before, they placed man at the center of thought. What distinguished them from the humanists was that they placed thought in the service of change. This at any rate was their hope, and in pursuing it the philosophes launched a noisy public movement.

They appeared clamorous to their contemporaries because they had to battle entrenched authority. Intellectual freedom was absolutely essential to them, and in most places they had to fight for it against not only the church and traditionalists but also the state and its apparatus of censorship. They were often obliged to publish their works abroad and anonymously. Sometimes they were pressured into withholding manuscripts from publication altogether or into making humiliating public recantations of controversial books. Even with such cautionary measures, almost all philosophes saw some of their publications confiscated and burned; and a few were forced into exile—Voltaire himself spent several decades across the French border in Switzerland—or sent to jail: Voltaire and Diderot both spent time in the Bastille. True, the very notoriety produced by these repressions often stimulated the sale of their works, but the anxiety outweighed the advantages. Allies of the philosophes in Italy and Spain labored under even greater constraints since the Inquisition still existed in the eighteenth century to suppress heresy with surprising ruthlessness.

By the 1770s, however, the philosophes had survived their running war with the authorities. Some of them lived to see their ideas widely accepted and their works acclaimed. Thus, even if they had contributed little else to the Western experience, their struggle for freedom of expression would merit them a significant place in its history.

But they contributed far more than that. In their scholarly and polemical writings, they investigated a wide range of subjects and pioneered in several new disciplines. Some philosophes—Voltaire for example—were pathbreaking historians. Moving beyond traditional historiography, which chronicled battles and rulers' biographies, they studied culture, social institutions, and government structures in an effort to understand as well as describe the past. Practically inventing social science, they dissected on a theoretical level the basis of social organization (sociology) and the human mind (psychology) and on a more practical level such matters as penology and education. These studies were in turn related to the issues of morality and the study of ethics. Their characteristic approach to ethics was utilitarian. With David Hume they tried to define value judgments about good and evil in more pragmatic terms than was common, and they concluded that social utility should become the standard for public morality. This approach to moral philosophy, however, raised the question of whether any human values were absolute and eternal. Responding to this challenge affirmatively, Kant tried to harmonize the tradition of philosophical idealism with the Enlightenment.

A major branch of Enlightenment social science was the physiocratic school. Its adherents believed that economic progress depended on freeing agriculture and trade from mercantilist restrictions and on reforming the tax structure by levying a uniform and equitable land tax. To stimulate agricultural productivity they advocated allowing the grain trade to operate according to the laws of supply and demand, which, they reasoned, would encourage growers to expand productivity and transport their harvest to where it was most needed. In this way the chronic grain shortages that plagued France could be eliminated.

In Britain Adam Smith made a parallel attack on mercantilist restrictions in *The Wealth of Nations* (1776). Like the physiocrats, Smith believed that economic progress required that each individual be allowed to pursue his own self-interest freely rather than regimented by the state, the guild, or tradition. Smith argued that on all levels of economic activity—from the manufacturing process to the flow of international trade—a natural division of labor should be encouraged. High tariffs, guild restrictions, and the like artificially obstructed this. Both Smith and the French physiocrats were thus early proponents of the economic doctrine of "laissez faire la nature," meaning simply "let nature take its course," which would be taken up by manufacturing interests during the Industrial Revolution.

By contrast other Enlightenment figures, analyzing the origin and role of private property, concluded, on the level of theory at least, that it was a form of primitive usurpation that should be replaced by some collective principle. Men like the French philosopher and historian Gabriel Bonnet de Mably were accordingly the forerunners of a utopian socialism that would be an alternative response to the early Industrial Revolution.

All in all the Enlightenment produced not only a characteristic intellectual spirit but also a wide range of critical writings on many aspects of human society. In addition the philosophes collectively generated a single work that exemplified and fulfilled their notion of how knowledge could be useful: Diderot's *Encyclopedia*.

Diderot and the Encyclopedia

Denis Diderot never achieved the celebrity of his friend Voltaire, but his career was equally central to the concerns and achievements of the philosophes. The son of a provincial cutler, he was educated in Jesuit schools as were many other young Frenchmen but at the first opportunity headed for Paris. Continuing to educate himself while living a bohemian existence, Diderot soon developed an unshakable sense of purpose: to make himself into an independent and successful intellectual.

Within a few short years, he had published a remarkable succession of writings—novels and plays, mathematical treatises, some notable pieces of muckraking (including a devastating attack on inept medical practices), and several works dealing with religion and moral philosophy. The most original aspect of his philosophical writings is his examination of the role of passion in human personality and in any system of values derived from an understanding of human nature. In particular, he affirmed the role of sexuality, arguing against artificial taboos and restrictions. As an advocate of what was sometimes called "the natural man," Diderot belies the charge leveled against the philosophes that they overemphasized reason and neglected emotion. The thread of religious criticism in these works is likewise notable. Starting from a position of mild skepticism, he soon passed to deism but ended beyond that in a position of atheism.

Diderot's unusual boldness in getting his works published brought him a considerable reputation but also some real trouble. Two of his books were condemned by the authorities as contrary to religion, the state, and morals. And in 1749 he spent 100 days in prison, being released only after making a humiliating apology.

At about that time Diderot was approached by a bookseller (roughly, today's publisher) to translate a British encyclopedic reference work into French. After a number of false starts, Diderot persuaded the bookseller to sponsor instead an entirely new work that would be more comprehensive and up-to-date and would reflect the attitudes of the philosophes. The *Encyclopedia, or Classified Dictionary of the Sciences, Arts, and Occupations* would inventory all important fields of knowledge from the most the-way of thinking." Or as Diderot put it in a letter to a friend, they were promoting "a revolution in the minds of men to free them from prejudice." Written in this spirit by an array of talented collaborators, the twenty-eight-volume *Encyclopedia* (1751–1772) fulfilled the fondest hopes of its editors and 4,000 initial subscribers.

In such a work religion could scarcely be ignored; nor could it be attacked frontally. Instead it was treated with artful satire or else relegated to a merely philosophical or historical plane. Demystified and subordinated, it was probed and questioned as was any other subject, much to the discomfort of learned but orthodox men.

If the *Encyclopedia* had a core, it was science. But the editors' preferences ran toward the utilitarian and technological side of science. Great attention was lavished for example on articles and plates illustrating various manufacturing processes and tools, and the roles of the mechanic, engineer, and artisan were elevated in the *Encyclopedia*'s scheme of values. The implication was that theoretical scientists could profit from closer attention to technological problems and closer collaboration with technicians. This suggested that the handicrafts and applied technology constituted a realm of knowledge comparable to pure sciences, such as physics and mathematics. At the same time it emphasized an important social perspective: the social utility of the artisan and the benefits of efficient production, as distinct from the role of the elite classes, in the advance of civilization.

Social science also figured prominently in the *Encyclopedia*. Learned articles summarized many theories about social organization and human nature, and again the emphasis was placed on the notion of social utility. On economic topics the encyclopedists tended to echo the physiocratic crusade against mercantilist restrictions on trade and agriculture. But no articles reflected the preoccupations and opinions of the popular masses on such issues as wages

Diderot's *Encyclopedia* focused much of its attention on technology. Plates illustrating the mechanical process, such as the one shown here for casting sculpture, were provided in separate volumes.
(Photo: The Bettmann Archive)

oretical to the most mundane and would constitute an arsenal of critical concepts. As the preface stated: "Our Encyclopedia is a work that could only be carried out in a philosophic century.... All things must be examined without sparing anyone's sensibilities.... The arts and sciences must regain the freedom that is so precious to them." More important, the ultimate purpose of the encyclopedia, according to the editors, was "to change the general or subsistence policy. While the *Encyclopedia*'s bent was not specifically middle-class, it did echo many aspirations of the bourgeoisie while threatening none of its existing prerogatives, especially in matters of property. And on political issues the *Encyclopedia* did not take a particularly controversial line on the central question of authority and sovereignty. It tended to accept absolute monarchy with equanimity, provided it was reasonably efficient and just. The major concerns of the editors were civil rights, freedom of expression, and the rule of law.

Measured from the perspective of the French Revolution—that is, with hindsight—the *Encyclopedia* thus does not seem revolutionary. Yet in the context of the times, it was. The revolution that Diderot sought was in intellectual orientation: his purpose was to spread the "critical spirit" from the precincts of the philosophes to the educated elites in general. Judging by the reaction of religious and government authorities, he was eminently successful. "Up till now," commented one French bishop, "hell has vomited its venom drop by drop." Now, he continued, it could be found assembled between the *Encyclopedia*'s covers. And the attorney general of France declared in 1758, "There is a project formed, a society organized to propagate materialism, to destroy religion, to inspire a spirit of independence, and to nourish the corruption of morals."

The *Encyclopedia* was accordingly banned, and its bookseller's license to issue the remaining volumes was revoked. Most of the contributors prudently withdrew, but Diderot was too committed. Retreating underground, he continued the herculean task until the subscribers received every promised volume, including eleven magnificent folios of illustrations. By the time these appeared, the persecutions had receded, and indeed the *Encyclopedia* was reprinted in several cheaper editions that sold out rapidly, making a fortune for their publishers. More important, this turn of events ensured the renown of the philosophes' most impressive achievement—a work recognized both in its own time and thereafter as the landmark of an age.

II. EIGHTEENTH-CENTURY CULTURES

The Enlightenment was merely one dimension of Europe's proliferating cultural life. The economic expansion and prosperity, which will be discussed in the next chapter, were matched by a marked increase in literary output serving increasingly diverse audiences. Although the aristocracy still dominated society, people of lesser origins were prominently participating in and supporting culture. Eighteenth-century high culture was distinctly cosmopolitan—that is, spilling across national borders as well as social class lines. Its trends included an increase in travel within Europe, a dramatic expansion of publishing activity, the creation of new literary and scientific academies, and the development of new genres in fields like fiction and music. Popular culture, on the other hand, remained extremely traditional and localized.

High Culture

As the expansive, cosmopolitan aspects of European high culture are described here, it must be remembered that the mass of Europe's population remained entirely parochial and virtually untouched by these developments. Most peasants and urban laborers continued to live within the culturally hermetic boundaries of their parish, their family, their job. But for the educated and wealthy, the numerically small but extremely influential elites, there was a sense of belonging to an international European civilization. It was a civilization dominated by France and by the French language, which had now displaced Latin and Italian as the language of the educated. Even Frederick II of Prussia favored French over German. Whatever deleterious effects such an attitude might have—and the German dramatist Lessing considered it a disastrous prejudice—this meant that ideas and literature circulated without language barriers among Europe's elites.

Travel

Europeans' sense of their common identity was sharpened by a flood of travel literature and by their appetite for visiting foreign parts. Although transportation was slow and uncomfortable, many embarked on a "grand tour" of the Continent and Great Britain. The highlights of such a trip were visits to large cities and to the ruins of antiquity—to the glories, that is, of both the modern and the ancient world.

London, Paris, Rome, and Vienna were already large, bustling, and impressive metropolises. These and smaller cities in Germany, Italy, and the United Provinces were undertaking considerable urban improvement. With generally excellent taste, rulers and municipal authorities were continuing to embellish their cities with large plazas, public gardens, airy boulevards, theaters, and opera houses. Toward the end of the century, amenities such as street lighting and public transportation began to appear in cities, with London leading the way. From the private sector came two notable additions to the urban scene: the coffee shop and the storefront window display. Coffeehouses, where customers could chat or read, and enticing shop windows, which added to the pleasures of city walking (while also stimulating consumer demand), enhanced the rhythms of urban life for tourists and natives alike. Sophisticated Europeans took great pleasure in their cities. When a man is tired of London, Samuel Johnson remarked, he is tired of life.

Travelers on tour invariably passed from the attractions of bustling city life to the monuments of antiquity. The philosophes called attention to pagan philosophers like Cicero; paralleling this, interest heightened in the remnants of Greek and Roman architecture and sculpture. Europeans endorsed the view of the German art historian Johann Winckelmann that Greek sculpture was the most worthy standard of aesthetic beauty. A lasting result of this fascination with antique ruins was Edward Gibbon's decision, on visiting the awesome remains of ancient Rome, to undertake *The Decline and Fall of the Roman Empire*.

The Republic of Letters

Among writers, intellectuals, and scientists, the sense of a cosmopolitan European culture devolved into the concept of a republic of letters. The phrase, introduced by sixteenth-century French humanists, was popularized by Pierre Bayle, a great progenitor of the Enlightenment, who published a critical journal that he called *News of the Republic of Letters*. The obvious import of the rubric is that the realm of culture and ideas is an intellectual homeland that cuts across all political and geographical borders. In one sense it is an exclusive republic, limited to the educated; but it is also an open society in that people may belong regardless of their social origins. For this reason European intellectuals felt that their republic of letters was a model for general social values.

Aside from the medium of the printed word, the republic of letters was organized around two institutions; the salons and the academies. Each advanced the process of social interchange, gathering together people from various countries distinguished by either status or talent. The philosophes themselves exemplified this social mix, for their "family" was composed in almost equal measure of nobles (Montesquieu, Holbach, Condorcet) and commoners (Voltaire, Diderot, d'Alembert). Voltaire insisted that he was as good as any aristocrat but had no intention of trying to topple the aristocracy from its position; rather he sought amalgamation. As d'Alembert put it, talent on the one hand and birth and eminence on the other both deserve recognition and deference.

The salons, conducted mainly by wives of wealthy bourgeois or noble families, sought to bring together important writers with the influential aristocrats they needed for favors and funds. The marquise de Pompadour, Louis XV's mistress, was the most notable personage to run such an assembly. Since a premium was placed on style and elegance in the salons, the intellectual was required to make his ideas lucid and comprehensible to the layman, which in turn increased the likelihood that his thought would have some influence. The salons helped particularly to enlarge the audience and contacts of the philosophes and served to introduce them to a flow of foreign visitors ranging from German princes to Benjamin Franklin. Private newsletters to which interested foreigners subscribed kept them abreast of activities in the Parisian salons when they could not attend personally.

Throughout Europe freemasonry played a similar role of cultural diffusion, promoting interchange across both national and social lines and creating another cosmopolitan dimension to European intellectual life. Operating in an aura of secretiveness and symbolism, the masonic lodges fostered a curious mixture of medieval mysticism and modern rationalism. They had begun really as clubs or fraternities dedicated to humane values; thus they attracted a wide range of enlightened nobles and distinguished commoners. But toward the end of the century, they were rent by sectarian controversies, and their initial sense of universalism eroded.

Far more important for the dissemination of ideas in the eighteenth century were the learned academies. These ranged from the Lunar Society in Birmingham, a forum for the most progressive British industrialists and technologists, to state-sponsored academies in almost every capital of Southern and Central Europe, which served as conduits for advanced scientific and philosophical ideas coming from the West. In France, moreover, academies were established in more than thirty provincial cities. This promoted widespread intellectual activity and created strongholds of advanced thinking in almost every region of that large country.

These provincial academies were founded after the death of Louis XIV, as if in testimony to the liberating effect of his disappearance. They began as literary institutes, concerned with upholding traditional values like purity of style. A few remained conservative adherents to the status quo into midcentury: the motto of the Cherbourg Academy in 1755 was "Religion and Honor." But most of them gradually shifted their interests from conventional literary matters to scientific and utilitarian questions in

A lecture at a learned gathering.
(Photo: Lauros-Giraudon)

such domains as commerce, agriculture, and local administration. They became offshoots so to speak of the *Encyclopedia*. Indeed when a Jesuit read a harangue against the *Encyclopedia* in the Lyons Academy, many members threatened to resign unless he retracted his remarks. By the 1770s and 1780s, the essay contests sponsored by the provincial academies and the papers published by their members had turned to such topics as population growth, capital punishment and penology, education, poverty and welfare, the grain trade, highways, guilds, and the origins of sovereignty.

There was a parallel shift in membership. The local academies began as privileged corporations, dominated by the nobility of the region. Corresponding or associate membership was extended to commoners from the ranks of civil servants, doctors, and professionals. Gradually the distinction between regular and associate participants crumbled. More commoners were admitted to full membership, and a social fusion took place, though it remained fragile and untested until 1789. Nobles and commoners alike were eager to discuss reforms and work for the betterment of local conditions. The scientific spirit had spread to them, making them receptive to the cause of practical reform and utilitarian ideas.

Publishing and Reading

The printed word was of course the chief medium of cultural diffusion. To be sure, the eighteenth century was not an age of mass education or literacy. Rudimentary public schools in Prussia, charity schools for the poor in Britain, and parish schools run by local priests in France did not produce literacy among the majority of the lower classes. Nonetheless the proportions of those who could read were advancing slowly, and population increases caused a substantial overall gain in literacy. Both factors help explain the tremendous rise in publishing activity geared to several different reading publics.

Untapped markets for reading material were opened up by itinerant circulating libraries, which originated in England around 1740; by the end of the century, almost 1,000 had been established. Recognizing a specialized demand among women readers, publishers also began to increase the output of new kinds of fiction and "ladies' magazines." Moreover, they were more receptive to women writers of fiction and poetry, especially the so-called bluestockings of the salons, who were early literary feminists.

The most notable development in publishing during the eighteenth century was the proliferation of journals and newspapers. In England, which pioneered in this domain, the number of periodicals increased from 25 to 158 between 1700 and 1780. There were several kinds. Single-essay periodicals, whose objective was moral and aesthetic uplift and whose model was Joseph Addison and Richard Steele's *Spectator,* continued to be popular. By contrast, the miscellany contained extracts and summaries of books and covered current events and entertainment; one such, the *Gentleman's Magazine,* had the impressive circulation of 15,000 in 1740. More sophisticated periodicals, like the *Monthly Review* and the *Journal des Savants,* specialized in critical book reviews and serious articles on science and philosophy, and they served the important function of extending the republic of letters beyond the scholar's study into the public domain. Most important for the future of reading habits in Europe was the daily newspaper, originated in England. Papers like the *London Chronicle* were originally intended for family reading and entertainment. Gradually they assumed other functions: they took classified advertisements, they began to report news, and finally—after considerable battling—they began to cover politics and report parliamentary debates. Under France's censorship regime, newspapers did not become politically oriented until the French Revolution, at which time a politically aroused France probably surpassed England as the country of extensive newspaper reading.

England broke new ground in publishing by introducing the daily newspaper. The page shown here is from a 1760 issue of "The Public Ledger," a London paper.
(Photo: Radio Times Hulton Picture Library)

In the field of general publishing, booksellers now assumed strategic prominence. They were the intermediary between reader and author—they combined the functions of editor, printer, salesman, and (if need be) smuggler. Their judgment and marketing techniques helped create as well as fill the demand for books since they conceived, commissioned, and financed a variety of works. The system had varying results. We have seen the *Encyclopedia* originate as a bookseller's project. So too did such enduring masterpieces as Samuel Johnson's *Dictionary,* a monumental lexicon that helped purify and standardize English usage. Many respectable popularizations of scientific, historical, and philosophical treaties were likewise brought into print by publishers, who commissioned skillful stylists like Oliver Goldsmith to write them. But there was a demeaning side to this system, for booksellers also employed hack writers to turn out potboilers, romances, and other works that pandered to low tastes, paying them for quantity and speed rather than quality. These drudges led a precarious and struggling existence along with marginal theatrical people in the milieu known as Grub Street. And Grub Street had even lower depths: for the more unscrupulous booksellers and desperate writers, there was money to be made in scurrilous political pamphlets committing character assassination and, of course, in pornography. Sometimes the two were combined in pamphlets dwelling on the alleged perversions of kings and queens.

With the growth of publishing, the vocation of writer was taking on a variety of forms. To be sure, practically all writers aspired to hold some lucrative sinecure or to be supported by important aristocrats. But authors valued their independence as much as patronage and security; the most successful could now live off their own work without patrons. On the other hand, the number of would-be writers increased enormously, and many were decidedly unsuccessful and frustrated. The explosion of the printed word therefore raised troubling questions. Would refinement and moral sensitivity be overwhelmed by vulgarity and commercialism? This is a problem gripping today's media, and it was born in the eighteenth century. On balance it seems reasonable to conclude that the new demand for books and the new economics of publishing created significant opportunity for professional writers to express and fulfill their own talents and for literate citizens to expose themselves to a variety of ideas, new and old. The entertainment and instruction of a middle-class audience became a principal focus of writing.

Popular Culture

While the culture of aristocratic and middle-class elites has been extensively studied, the cultures of artisans, peasants, and the urban poor are only dimly known. In those sectors of society culture primarily meant recreation and was essentially public and collective. Moreover, while there was a written form of popular culture that we shall discuss, it was minor compared to the prevalent oral culture, which has left few traces in the historical record. Nonetheless it is possible to suggest some of the rich variety of cultural materials and recreations of the common people.

Popular Literature

Far removed from the markets for Voltaire and the *Gentleman's Magazine,* there existed a distinct world of popular literature—the reading matter consumed by artisans and peasants, the poor and the almost poor, those who could barely read and even those who could not read at all. From the seventeenth through the early nineteenth century but particularly in eighteenth-century France, a type of literature was specially produced for this audience. It consisted of small booklets and brochures written anonymously, printed on cheap paper, and costing only a few pennies. They were sold by colporteurs—itinerant hawkers—who knew the tastes of these customers and saw to it that they were satisfied. The booklets were often read aloud by those who could read to those who could not; but even the illiterate bought them, apparently somewhat in awe of the printed word and valuing its possession.

There were three major varieties of popular literature. The first was explicitly religious: devotional tracts, saints' lives, catechisms, manuals of penitence, and Bible stories, all written simply and vividly and generously laced with miracles. Preoccupied with fears of death and damnation, the readers sought reassurance here that a virtuous, sensible life would end in salvation. A second kind of popular literature was the almanac, which corresponded with a concern for getting along in this life as well. Almanacs and how-to-live-successfully pamphlets (forerunners of the *Reader's Digest* and Norman Vincent Peale) discussed things like cleanliness, nourishment, and the kinds of potions to take for illnesses. They also featured astrology—how to read the stars and other signs for clues about what the future might bring. The third type was entertainment literature: tales and fables, burlesques and crude satires, mixtures of fiction and history in which miraculous events frequently helped bring the story to a satisfactory conclusion.[2]

---

[2] See Geneviève Bollème, *La Bibliothèque bleue.* (1971).

Although important information may have trickled down through these booklets, most of them were blatantly escapist. The pervasive religiosity and superstition of popular literature marks it off decisively from the growing rationalism and secularism of middle-class and avant-garde culture. Moreover, it could be argued that by ignoring the real problems of famine, taxes, and material insecurity, these writings fostered submissiveness, a fatalistic acceptance of a dismal status quo. Seeing the nature of popular literature helps us understand why Voltaire had no hope of extending his ideas on religion to the masses and indeed even feared to discuss them in front of his servants.

Almanacs and pamphlets were produced for the lower classes by outsiders, printers and writers who were themselves educated. A more common and authentic form of popular culture was oral: folk tales told at the fireside on long winter nights and songs that expressed bawdiness or violence far more directly and meaningfully than the written word. Themes relating to hunger or sex or oppression were more likely to turn up in songs, often sung in local dialects that would have been incomprehensible to an educated Parisian, Londoner, or Viennese.

Groups and Recreations

If the educated had their freemasons' lodges and learned societies, the people also had organized groups. Many journeymen artisans, for example, belonged to secret societies that combined fraternal and trade-union functions. These young artisans usually toured their country, stopping periodically to work with comrades in other towns in order to improve their own skills. But the main emphasis of their associations was on camaraderie and ritual celebration. Rivalries were common between federations of such associations and occasionally degenerated into pitched battles—a far cry from the nineteenth-century ideal of labor solidarity.

Corresponding to the coffee shop and salon of the urban middle classes were the public house or "pub," the cafe in local urban neighborhoods, and the *guinguette* in the suburbs of the common people. These "dives" (as they would doubtless be called today) catered to a large, poor clientele, especially on Sunday and Monday, which working people often took as a day off. The *guinguettes* were located outside the city walls so that the wine they sold would not be subject to urban excise taxes. Wine was just beginning to be consumed by the common people in the eighteenth century. And even then it was something of a luxury except in its cheapest form, which was always adulterated or watered. In England, however, gin was the poor person's drink—cheap and plentiful until a hefty excise tax was levied following the government's realization that too many people were drinking themselves into disability and death.

More commonly, drinking was not done in that morbid fashion but as part of a healthy and vibrant outdoor life. A recent study of popular pastimes in England suggests the outlines of a traditional popular culture that flourished before the Industrial Revolution. It was marked by a full calendar of holidays that provided numerous occasions for group merrymaking, eating, drinking, dressing-up, contests, and games. This was a particularly beneficial setting for boys and girls in their teens and twenties to meet each other. The highlight of a country year usually came either between spring sowing and the summer harvest or in the early autumn after the summer harvest was in, when most villages held a public feast lasting several days. In Catholic countries similar festivities were often linked with church rituals, with the most popular observances including the commemoration of saints and pilgrimages to holy places.

Popular culture involved "relaxation in noise and tumultuous merriment," preferably in public and out in the open. Football matches, for example, were a popular form of recreation in England, both for participants and observers. At times the high spirits generated on these

In this famous "Gin Lane" etching of 1750 by Hogarth, the results of excessive gin drinking by the common people are depicted as death, apathy, and decay. A cheerful and orderly companion piece called "Beer Street," however, made it clear that drinking in moderation was a perfectly acceptable habit.
(Photo: Metropolitan Museum of Art, Harris Brisbane Dick Fund, 1932)

occasions turned into good-natured riots. In August 1765 the *Northampton Mercury* reported: "We hear from West-Hadden, in this county, that on Thursday and Friday a great number of people being assembled there, in order to play a Foot-Ball Match, soon after meeting formed themselves into a tumultuous mob, and pulled up and burnt the fences designed for the inclosure of that field, and did other considerable damage."

Blood sports were another type of popular recreation in the preindustrial era. Bullbaiting, for example, involved setting loose a pack of dogs on a tied-up steer, and was often arranged by the collaboration of a butcher (who provided the steer that would subsequently be slaughtered and dispensed as meat) and a publican (who provided the yard of his inn as the arena and sold refreshments to the spectators). Cockfighting was similar in its gory results and was popular with gentlemen and commoners alike, who enjoyed wagering on the outcome. These so-called sports appear repulsive today, and by the end of the eighteenth century such cruelties to animals were being denounced by reformers and moralists. It is notable, however, that no similar attack was leveled against the gentry's organized bloodletting in the form of fox hunting.

Literature, Music, and Art

Unlike the seventeenth century, sometimes classified as Baroque, the eighteenth can be given no comprehensive stylistic label. Literary styles varied, ranging from Neoclassicism in poetry to major innovation in fiction. The nature of the audience and the sources of a writer's support varied considerably. The same was true for composers. But if any trends may be singled out for attention, they are the rise of the novel and the development of the symphony.

The Novel and Poetry

For all practical purposes the novel may be said to have originated in England, where writers and booksellers were particularly aware of a growing middle-class reading public. The acknowledged pioneer of this new genre was Samuel Richardson, himself a bookseller. Epistolary in form—a series of letters telling the story—*Pamela, or Virtue Rewarded* (1740) was a melodrama of the trials and tribulations of an honest if somewhat hypocritical servant girl whose sexual virtue is repeatedly challenged but never conquered and whose wealthy employer finally agrees to marry her. *Pamela* was an instant success. Breaking away from the standard forms and heroic subjects of most previous narrative fiction, Richardson dealt with the qualities of recognizable types of people. Pamela's earnest hypocrisy, however, prompted a playwright and lawyer named Henry Fielding to pen a short satire called *Shamela,* which he followed with his own novel *Joseph Andrews*. Here comedy and adventure replaced melodrama; indeed Fielding prefaced the book with a remarkable manifesto claiming that the novel was to be a comic epic in prose. Fielding realized the full potential of this bold innovation in *Tom Jones* (1749), a colorful, robust comic panorama of English society featuring a gallery of brilliantly developed characters. Fielding was providing a literary counterpart to the world that William Hogarth was creating in his etchings—vivid exaggerations of the various social milieus, particularly the period's low life.

In general, the novel was emerging as a form of fiction that told its story and treated the development of personality in a realistic social context, and in some ways it mirrored its times better than any other form of fiction. Novelists could use broad comedy, as did Laurence Sterne, or they could be totally serious, as was Johann Wolfgang von Goethe in *The Sorrows of Werther* (1774), a *Bildungsroman* (novel of development) telling the tragic story of the coming of age of a melancholy youth. In either case the writer freed himself from classic aesthetic norms and specified rules of composition. Authors could now experiment endlessly with forms and techniques and could deal with a wide range of social settings. Consequently they drew less and less on the life styles of aristocrats for their social ideals, and much of the century's fiction, in the drama as well as the novel, focused on middle-class family life and its everyday problems of morality, love, and social relations. This reflected actual changes in middle-class values, which were increasingly emphasizing close family relations.[3]

Meanwhile a genre called the philosophical tale was being perfected by writers with more didactic objectives. The chief progenitor of the form was the great Irish satirist Jonathan Swift, notably in his well-known *Gulliver's Travels* (1726). The French philosophes naturally grav-

---

[3] In his *Centuries of Childhood* (1962), Pt. 3, Philippe Ariès points out how parents were becoming much closer to their children in the eighteenth century. Instead of sending them to boarding school, they more frequently placed them in schools near home. Families also now insisted on more privacy for themselves in household architecture.

itated toward this genre of satire since it allowed them to criticize their society covertly and hence to avoid open clashes with the censors. Thus Montesquieu created a range of mythical foreign settings, exotic backgrounds, and travelers from the Levant to ridicule contemporary mores in *The Persian Letters* (1721). Likewise Voltaire achieved great success in his tale *Candide* (1759), a critique of the notion that this was the best of all possible worlds. His wholly fictional characters and incidents disguised an Enlightenment sermon against the idiocy and cruelty that he saw in European society. Voltaire and Fielding met on this ground, for both were concerned with imparting a commonsensical notion of morality and humanity.

During most of the century, the innovation that was occurring in prose fiction contrasted with the traditionalism of poetry, still the most prized form of literary expression. Here unchanged rules on what made "good literature" still prevailed. Each type of poem had its particular essence and rules; diction was supposed to be elegant and sentiments refined and elevated. The raw materials of emotion were to be muted and transformed into language and allusions that only the highly educated could appreciate. Art was viewed in this Neoclassical tradition as imitative of eternal standards of truth and beauty. It was not permissible for the poet to unburden his soul or hold forth on his own experience. The audience for poetry was the narrowest and most elitist segment of the reading public—"the wealthy few," in the phrase of William Wordsworth, who criticized eighteenth-century poets for pandering exclusively to that group.

By the end of the century, the restraints of Neoclassicism finally provoked rebellion in the ranks of English and German poets. Men like Friedrich von Schiller and Wordsworth defiantly raised the celebration of individual feeling and inner passion to the level of a creed, which eventually became known as Romanticism. Hoping to appeal to a much broader audience, these writers decisively changed the nature of poetic composition and made this literary form, like the novel, a far more flexible vehicle of expression.

Music and Art

The rise of the novel in literature was paralleled by the development of the symphony in music. But it must be noted at once that a great deal of eighteenth-century music was routine and undistinguished. For much of the century, composers were still obliged to serve under royal, ecclesiastical, or aristocratic patronage. They were bound by rigid formulas of composition and by a public taste tyrannically insistent on conventions. A pleasant melody in a predictable form was what the listener wanted from his composers. Much instrumental music was commissioned as background fare for dancing or other social occasions. Likewise Italian opera was popular and quantitatively impressive—Alessandro Scarlatti, for example, composed 115 operas. But very few of these repetitive compositions have survived the test of time; their sheer number is an obvious clue to the casual circumstances of their composition and their likely fate.

The heartland of Europe's music tradition was Austria. Here a trio of geniuses transformed the routines of eighteenth-century composition into vibrant, original, and enduring masterpieces. The early symphonies of Franz Joseph Haydn and the prodigy Wolfgang Amadeus Mozart were conventional exercises in Rococo decorativeness. The music was light and as tuneful as its audience could wish, but it had little emotional impact. By the end of their careers. Haydn had written 104 symphonies and Mozart 41. They had stabilized the form into its familiar four movements (fast, slow, minuet, fast); they had each developed extraordinary harmonic virtuosity; but more than these accomplishments, they had infused the form with a lyricism that often crossed the border into the realm of passion. In short, the

The ornate interiors of eighteenth-century opera houses began filling to capacity as music grew in popularity. Italy was a focal point of the musical world, with four opera houses in Rome and three in Naples.
(Photo: Librairie Larousse)

symphony had changed radically from the elegant trifles of earlier years.

The German composer Ludwig van Beethoven consummated this development and assured that the symphony, like the novel, would be adaptable and ever-malleable. In each of his nine symphonies as well as his five piano concertos, he progressively modified the standard formulas. The orchestra was much enlarged, and the movements were made far more intricate and longer. His last symphony burst the bonds of the form. Striving to make a Promethean musical statement, Beethoven introduced a large chorus singing one of Schiller's odes to conclude the composition, making it an explicit celebration in music of freedom and brotherhood. Laden with emotion and programmatic content, the music is yet recognizable as an advanced form of the eighteenth-century symphony. Thus it provides a bridge between the culture of two periods: eighteenth-century Classicism and nineteenth-century Romanticism.

Beethoven also progressed farther than

most of his predecessors in freeing himself from subordination to a powerful single patron. Haydn had pioneered in this direction by signing a lucrative contract with a London music publisher and impresario that underwrote the composition and performance of his last twelve symphonies. Beethoven relied even more on public concerts and specific commissions instead of tying himself to a particular patron.[4]

Unlike fiction and music, painting did not experience notable innovations in the eighteenth century, and with the exception of Jacques Louis David (see Plate 46) eighteenth-century painters were overshadowed by their predecessors as well as by their successors of the Romantic and post-Romantic schools of nineteenth-century art. Neoclassicism was a dominant style in the late eighteenth century, with its themes inspired by antiquity and its timeless conceptions of truth and beauty, similar to those of Neoclassical poetry. There were, however, at least two developments which paralleled the widening social context of the other arts. In the first place, just as composers and musicians began to perform in public concerts, so did painters begin to exhibit regularly in public, especially in the annual salons sponsored by the royal academies of art in London and in Paris. The head of London's Royal Academy, founded by George III in 1768, was Sir Joshua Reynolds. A notable portrait painter, Reynolds—solely by virtue of his talent—rose to a position of wealth and eminence, thus exemplifying the Enlightenment ideal of opportunity. Moreover, his success brought him the independence from a patron that writers, composers, and artists all aspired to.

A second development in the social history of eighteenth-century art lay in the new kinds of subject matter and themes taken up by certain artists, which paralleled what novelists and playwrights were doing. Jean Baptiste Greuze, for example, made a hit in the Parisian exhibitions of the 1770s with his sentimentalized paintings of common people in family settings caught in a dramatic situation, such as the death of a father. William Hogarth was not primarily a painter at all but an engraver working through the medium of prints and book illustrations. His art therefore had a much wider circulation than the work of any painter. And his choice of subjects ranged far and wide through the ranks of society—especially in scenes of low life among the poor and the working classes (see illustration, p. 647). Hogarth's art was not only technically brilliant, it remains a basic source for the study of English social history.

III. THE ENLIGHTENMENT AND THE STATE

On the whole the Enlightenment was not highly critical of existing forms of government, though specific policies of rulers and ministers were often criticized. In Central Europe monarchy was the starting point of most political theory or reform programs. In France the monarchy and the aristocracy were more evenly matched, and the contrasting political views of Montesquieu and Voltaire reflected this fact. With Jean Jacques Rousseau, however, we come to the century's most original political theorist—a man less concerned with actual political arrangements than with the inherent possibilities for individual and political freedom.

German Absolutism and the Problem of Reform

During the late nineteenth centry, German historians invented the concept of "enlightened

---

[4] Johann Sebastian Bach (1685–1750) is considered by many music lovers a genius on a par with Mozart and Beethoven. But in his own day, as the organist and resident composer for a number of obscure German churches, Bach was little known to the outside world. Ironically, whereas today he is admired by "highbrows," in his time he provided what was in effect popular music for the people—organ music, hymns, and cantatas for religious worship.

absolutism" to describe the Prussian and Hapsburg monarchies of the eighteenth century. Apologists for German development and critics of the liberal and revolutionary traditions associated with France, they argued that the strength of an enlightened ruler was the surest basis for progress in early modern Europe. A king who ruled in the interest of his subjects, they implied, precluded violent divisions like those of the French Revolution. Heads of state came to govern in this manner only after a long evolution, for according to these historians, absolutism had evolved through three phases. First came the period of "confessional absolutism," when kings were preoccupied with religious uniformity; it was exemplified by Philip II of Spain and the notion that the prince's religion is the religion of the state. This phase was followed by a more secular and dynastic state, "courtly absolutism," exemplified of course by Louis XIV and his famous epigram, "I am the state." In contrast to Louis' extravagant style and goals, Frederick II of Prussia marked the "enlightened" phase of absolutism, as evidenced by his dictum that the ruler is the first servant of the state.

This three-phase scheme is a distortion of history. Earlier chapters have amply demonstrated that fundamental issues differed little in these supposed stages of absolutism. Absolute monarchs strove at all times to assert their authority over the constituent elements of society and to maximize the power of their state in relation to other realms, principally by means of territorial expansion. Any notion that the Enlightenment caused the monarchs to alter this is erroneous. Still, there were visible modifications of specific practices and style in the way that absolute monarchy conducted its business. And in this the role of culture and ideas was not entirely absent.

Conceptions of "Enlightened" Rule

Some of the modifications observable in eighteenth-century absolutism may well have been prompted by prominent philosophes, with whom sovereigns like Frederick II and Catherine II of Russia (1762–1796) maintained significant contacts. Voltaire, for example, spent a long sojourn at Frederick's palace, while Catherine offered to buy Diderot's library to help him out of financial troubles and delay taking possession of it until his death. At various times monarchs and philosophes lavished saccharine praise on each other. How significant was this mutual admiration? For the monarchs it was probably primarily a question of public relations, of image making. Yet the fact that they should even find it desirable to be supportive of men like Voltaire and Diderot is suggestive. They may have felt the need to justify themselves publicly and even to coopt the prestige of Europe's leading intellectuals.

Catherine the Great played this game to its limit, promising at one point in her reign to begin moving gradually toward representative government and constitutionalism—a policy that was hailed as a historic landmark by philosophe admirers who were too remote from St. Petersburg to see its falsity. In 1767 she convened the Legislative Commission, a quasi-representative body of delegates from various strata of Russian society. They were invited to present grievances, propose reforms, and debate such proposals. In the end nothing came of this except some good publicity for Catherine. She soon dissolved the commission under the pretext of having to turn her attention to a new Turkish war. Some time later she promulgated a Charter of the Nobility, which, instead of limiting the nobility's privileges, strengthened its corporate status and increased its control over the serfs in exchange for a pledge of loyalty to the throne.

No such experiment in representation was even tried in Central Europe, where other conceptions of enlightened rule and reform prevailed. German writers were particularly adept at finding theoretical justifications for the powers of an autocrat. They viewed the state as a machine and the ruler as its necessary mainspring. Progress came from sound administration, whose instrumentalities were an enlightened monarch and well-trained bureaucrats. In keeping with this notion, German universities began to train civil servants, and the rudiments of a merit system of civil service recruitment were introduced in Prussia and other states.

The orders for the bureaucracy were to come from the ruler, who was expected to dedicate himself to the welfare of his subjects in return for their obedience. The vehicle for the command-obedience chain was to be a coherent and explicit body of public law, fairly administered by the above-mentioned bureaucrats. According to its advocates, this system would produce the rule of law, the *Rechtsstaat*. A society thus based on "right" did not require a written constitution or public representation; the monarch and the bureaucrats together, following their sense of public responsibility, ensured the citizen's rights.

Many German intellectuals subscribed to this view and accordingly believed that they were living in a free and progressive society—free from arbitrary injustice, and progressive because rationality was exercised in government. Although many would sympathize with the French Revolution of 1789, they were inclined to regard the turmoil of a revolution as unnecessary for their own situation.

Joseph II and the Limits of Absolutism

The most notable sponsor of reforms from above was Joseph II, Hapsburg ruler from 1765 to 1790. Although he did not identify with the philosophes and maintained his own Catholic faith, he was actually the most "enlightened" of the major monarchs of the eighteenth century—as well as one of the most autocratic personalities. It was a difficult combination.

Joseph believed that the primary right of the people was to be governed well. But for him this entailed far more than the customary administrative and financial modernization necessary for survival in the state system. The emperor began by implementing several reforms long advocated by Enlightenment thinkers: freedom of expression, religious toleration, state control over organized religion, and legal reform. By greatly reducing royal censorship, Joseph opened the way for Vienna to become a major center of literary activity. In an edict of toleration in 1781, he emancipated Protestants and Jews, granting them the right to worship publicly and to hold property and public office; he went so far as to ennoble some Jews. On the other hand he worked to reduce the influence of the Catholic Church by ordering the dissolution of numerous monasteries on the grounds that they were useless and corrupt. Part of their confiscated wealth was used to support the medical school at the University of Vienna. In an attempt to force the church to serve its parishioners better, he eliminated much of Rome's authority and forced the clergy to modernize rituals and services. It should come as no surprise, however, that most

Joseph II visiting Austrian peasants, whom he hoped to convert from serfs to free tenants.
(Photo: Bildarchiv Nationalbibliothek, Austria)

of his Catholic subjects preferred their traditional ways to this nationalized brand of Catholicism.

When Joseph ordered the drafting of a new criminal code, he substantiated the Enlightenment's belief in legal reform as an instrument of social progress. Certain categories of crimes, such as witchcraft, were abolished altogether. The death penalty and various brutal punishments were eliminated for most crimes; the use of torture in criminal proceedings was forbidden; motive was recognized as a factor in determining guilt. Most striking, the code recognized no class difference in the application of criminal law. Noble offenders were subject to the same laws as were commoners and could be sentenced to the same punishments.

These significant departures from the status quo were preliminaries to the most important of Joseph's efforts at social reform: to improve the lot of the peasants. In this respect the emperor was far bolder not only than any other eighteenth-century sovereign but than most philosophes and civil servants. The question of social justice for the rural lower classes was a weak point of "enlightened absolutism" elsewhere. Catherine II not only failed to improve conditions among the serfs but allowed their status to deteriorate even further, to the point where those on royal lands, who could be bought and sold at will, were being treated almost as slaves. Frederick II had better intentions but accomplished little. He attempted to stop corporal punishment of serfs by their masters, but even this modest reform was not forced on the nobles and was carried out only on royal lands. As for the more basic issues, land ownership and labor services, nothing was done to place limits on the lords' prerogatives. While most Prussian peasants could not be sold, they could not move of their own volition or lay claim to the land they tilled, and they spent much of their time performing services directly for their lord.

Faced with a roughly comparable situation in the Hapsburg domains, Joseph attacked all aspects of the problem. He set out to eradicate the system of serfdom and transform the peasant into a free citizen in command of his person and of the land he cultivated. To begin with, Joseph abolished personal servitude and gave peasants the right to move, marry, and enter any trade they wished. He then promulgated various laws to help secure their control over the land they worked. Finally and most dramatically, he made a decisive attempt to ensure the income and limit the obligations of the peasant tenant. All land was to be surveyed and subject to a uniform tax. Twelve percent of its annual yield would go to the state, and beyond this the peasant would be obliged to pay a maximum of 18 percent of his income to the lord in lieu of his former feudal obligations. No longer would he owe the labor service to his lord that sometimes consumed more than 100 days each year.

These reforms were ordered in a purely authoritarian fashion, with no regard for public opinion and no notion of consent from any quarter. They provoked a predictably vigorous opposition from the landowning classes. But they also won scant visible support from the peasant masses, who were deeply distrustful of anything the central government did because of its religious policies. No effort was made to build support among the peasants by explaining the reforms in the hope of offsetting the nobility's reaction. As a sympathetic chronicler of Joseph's reign sadly observed, "He brought in his beneficial measures in an arbitrary manner."

The arbitrariness was not incidental to Joseph's methods. He acknowledged no other way of doing things, no limitation on his own sovereignty. His reaction to the opposition that his reforms aroused illustrates this: he moved to suppress the unexpected dissent in the firmest possible way. Not only did he restore censorship in his last years, but he elevated the police department to the status of an imperial ministry, granting it unprecedented powers. By the time he died, in 1790, he was a disillusioned man. His realm resembled less a *Rechtsstaat* than a police state.

Contrasting the century's two most notable monarchs points up the limits of "enlightened absolutism." On basic social issues like the status of the rural masses, who made up about 90 percent of the population, absolutism displayed little capacity to initiate change regardless of the ruler's intentions. Frederick II resigned himself to the impossibility of improving established practice and attempted to do little in the peasants' behalf. Joseph II tried to do a great deal in their behalf—for them, not with them—only to find that autocracy could not accomplish his objectives without provoking major upheaval.

French Liberal Thought

Like "nature" and "reason," the word "freedom" was central to the Enlightenment. Its most important meaning to the philosophes was the freedom of the human mind to throw off centuries of what they considered ignorance and tyranny. Their foremost practical concerns were freedom of expression and of religion, which they viewed as the necessary preconditions for other kinds of liberty. If human beings were able to confront the world without bowing to the supernatural and subordinating thought to any arbitrary authority, then society's problems could be progressively dealt with. It is to the great credit of eighteenth-century intellectuals that they fought for this cause so relentlessly that freedom of thought has become a hallmark of the Western liberal tradition.

Few philosophes, however, can be considered precursors of egalitarianism. Toward the mass of impoverished peasants and laborers, the educated had two attitudes: pity and fear. Pity took the form of organized, inadequate philanthropy, sponsored by church and state and doled out condescendingly. Fear of the mob—the *canaille* ("rabble"), Voltaire called it—was axiomatic. Even in Great Britain the disfranchisement of the poor and the need for instruments of social control like the poor law were taken for granted. By today's standards, then, the perimeters of controversy in political and social thought were extremely narrow. For most writers the issue of political freedom was relevant to only a small segment of the population—the classes at the top of the social pyramid.

The Balance of Powers Versus the Royal Thesis

In France, still under the shadow of Louis XIV's stifling centralism, many people were intrigued by Britain's political institutions, as idealized in the writings of John Locke. Obvious defects like the Corporation and Test acts, which denied civil rights to dissenters and Catholics, or the corruption in the parliamentary borough system, were either unknown to Frenchmen or overlooked in favor of liberties like the requirement of a writ of habeas corpus. The Continent was particularly impressed by the Glorious Revolution of 1688, and by the House of Commons, which stood up to both crown and Lords.

This inspiration is echoed in *The Spirit of Laws* (1748) by the great French jurist Montesquieu. His book was a pioneering effort in political sociology, the comparative study of governments and societies. Montesquieu was not proposing that Britain serve as a model for other countries, for he was arguing precisely that there is no absolute or universal standard of good government. The subtitle of this long and rambling discourse conveys this: *The Relation that the Laws Should Have to the Constitution of Each Government, the Customs, Climate, Religion, Commerce, etc*. Yet Montesquieu sought to display the virtues of the idealized British system, feeling that all societies could learn from it about liberty.

The sections on liberty won a wide readership in Europe and in America, where the book was influential among the drafters of the United States Constitution. Political liberty, said Montesquieu, is the absence of one dominating power in the state, whatever its kind: the king, the aristocrats, the people. The conservation of liberty depends on the separation and balance of powers, such as the executive, the legislative, and the judicial. If a single leader or group controls all functions, the country lives under despotism.

The only power in most states that can effectively check the possibility of royal despotism without itself degenerating into the despotism of the mob, he felt, is the aristocracy, the upper classes. In effect Montesquieu was arguing that "privilege was the ancestor of liberty," as one historian put it recently. This might seem paradoxical, since privilege appears to be the opposite of liberty. But this was not the view of the eighteenth century, which commonly considered strong privileged groups—noblemen, corporations, chartered towns—the only effective bulwarks against encroachments of royal power. Only such intermediary bodies, independent of both the masses and the crown, could prevent tyranny. To put it another way, the price of a society free from despotism is privilege for some of its members. For Montesquieu the pivotal privileged group in France was the magistrates of the parlements (he himself was a magistrate in Bordeaux), for they were the guardians of the law. Protected by the ownership of their own offices, these men were for Montesquieu the most likely champions of French liberty.

Montesquieu thus hoped to limit the central government's power by balancing it with other power centers. Precisely the opposite argument was put forward by other thinkers: to maximize the central government's strength and thus its capacity to accomplish reforms. The separation of powers could guarantee certain kinds of freedom, but it could also perpetuate inequities and inefficiency. Executive authority could be a source of tyranny, but it could also be a stimulus to social and economic reform. Therefore Voltaire, for one, tended to regard an independent aristocracy not as a bulwark of freedom but on the contrary as an obstacle to change. While Montesquieu justified the power of the parlements to prevent arbitrary decrees, Voltaire argued that they were bastions of special interest that themselves exercised a heavy hand in society and repeatedly prevented necessary reforms.

Men who, like Voltaire, considered the monarchy as the likeliest agent for reform in France—as the best of several weak alternatives—were proponents of what was called the royal thesis. They hoped that a new power elite of enlightened administrators would cluster around the monarchy to replace the age-old power elite of nobles and priests. Voltaire did not advocate any kind of despotism, enlightened or otherwise. He merely felt that for all its dangers a strong monarchy was preferable to a strong corporate nobility.

The royal thesis seemed particularly justified when Louis XVI ascended the throne in 1774 and appointed Jacques Turgot, a contributor to the *Encyclopedia* and one of France's most progressive thinkers and talented administrators, as his finance minister. The philosophes unanimously applauded this appointment and looked forward to a truly reformist administration. The policies that Turgot initiated for tax reform and economic opportunity were relatively modest moves toward a more open society and increased initiative for private citizens. Modest though they were, however, they encroached on a number of special preserves. Turgot was therefore attacked by the entrenched interest groups, including the parlements. Within two years he was dismissed by a king who disliked agitation and controversy. The flaws in the royal thesis were numerous, but the most obvious was the disinclination of the Bourbon king himself to support it vigorously.

Rousseau

Only one major political theorist advanced well beyond the two classic eighteenth-century positions associated with Montesquieu and Voltaire. But to understand the profound originality of his thought, one must first appreciate his unique position in the republic of letters. For Jean Jacques Rousseau provided in his life and writing a critique of the Enlightenment as well as of the status quo. Obsessed with the issue of moral freedom and individual autonomy, he found society far more oppressive than most philosophes allowed.

Young Rousseau won instant fame when he submitted a prize-winning essay in a contest sponsored by a provincial academy on the topic, "Has the restoration of the arts and sciences had a purifying effect upon morals?" Unlike most respondents, Rousseau answered that it had not. He argued that the lustrous cultural and scientific achievements of recent decades were producing pretentiousness, conformity, and useless luxury. Most scientific pursuits, he wrote, "are the effect of idleness which generate idleness in their turn." The system of rewards in the arts produces "a servile and deceptive conformity . . . the dissolution of morals . . . and the corruption of taste." Against the decadence of high culture he advocated a return to "the simplicity which prevailed in earliest times"—manly physical pastimes, self-reliance, citizens instead of courtiers.

These strictures against his own society led commentators to think of Rousseau as a "primitivist," extolling the virtues of the state of nature and the "noble savage." But this was not the case. Rousseau regarded the state of nature as a state of anarchy where force ruled and men were slaves of appetite. Yet this opinion made him no less contemptuous of eighteenth-century salon society, whose artificial rituals prevented the display of genuine emotion, and valued style over substance. Worse yet, he said, the educated and refined elite nurtured a sense of superiority that undermined common sense moral standards.

For Rousseau the basis of morality was conscience, not reason. "Virtue: sublime science of simple minds," he wrote, "are not your principles graven on every heart?" This theme he returned to in his two popular works of didactic fiction, *Julie, or the New Heloise* (1761), and *Emile, or Treatise on Education* (1762). In the novel *Julie* the hero is repeatedly tempted into immoral acts by passions and appetites but triumphs over them in the end. *Emile* recounts the story of a young child raised to be a moral adult by a tutor who emphasizes experience rather than book learning and who considers education as a process of individual self-development. Both books attack the complacent secularism or deism that prevailed among intellectuals of the time, arguing for a more profound, personal religiosity. For these reasons Rousseau's fiction was highly prized by young poets, who were themselves seeking a more personal idiom of expression and who valued the force of the emotions that classical rules of composition discouraged. Thus Rousseau was both a pioneer of progressive education and a precursor of literary romanticism.

Rousseau himself was by no means a saint. On the contrary his struggle against his own passions—illustrated by the illegitimate child whom he fathered and abandoned—doubtless contributed to his preoccupation with morality and conscience. Nonetheless his life as well as his writings influenced the generation of intellectuals coming of age in the 1770s and 1780s. He was a true rebel among his contemporaries, rejecting much of the celebrity that his pen brought him. Not only did he quarrel with the repressive authorities of Church and state—

who repeatedly banned and burned his books—but he attacked the pretensions of his fellow philosophes, whom he considered arrogant and cynical. By the 1770s heroes of the Enlightenment like Voltaire and Diderot had won their battles and had become almost too successful to serve any longer as critics of society. They were masters of the most important academies by then, and in a sense they had themselves become the establishment. For younger writers and thinkers who were critical of the existing distribution of power and patronage, Rousseau remained an inspiration. He was a cultural hero for frustrated intellectuals and reformers, some of whom became revolutionaries in 1789.

What proved to be Rousseau's most famous work, *The Social Contract* (1762), became so only after the French Revolution, which dramatized many of the issues that it raised. The Revolution did more for the book than Rousseau did for the Revolution, which he neither prophesied nor advocated. *The Social Contract* was not meant as a blueprint for revolution but rather as an ideal standard against which the reader might measure his own society. Rousseau did not expect that this standard could be achieved in practice since existing states were too large and complex to allow the kind of participation that was the essence of his vision.

A free society in Rousseau's conception is one in which authority and sovereignty derive from the individual himself. A government that is entirely distinct from the individuals over whom it claims to exercise authority has no validity. In short, Rousseau denied the almost universal idea that some men are meant to govern and others to obey. In the ideal polity, an individual has had a role in making the law to which he submits. By obeying it he is thus obeying himself as well as all his fellow citizens. For this reason he is free.

The foundation for a society of this kind lies in a primal act of sovereignty in which each citizen voluntarily subscribes to a social contract that establishes the society's ground rules. The government that is erected under such a contract is a revocable trust. To the perceptive reader *The Social Contract* suggested a community based on the voluntary participation of its members rather than the chance destiny of history or inheritance. The only legitimate "sovereign," then, is the people. This sovereign in turn creates a government that will carry on the day-to-day business of applying the laws.

Rousseau was not advocating majority rule but rather consensus as to the best interest of all citizens, even if it *appears* contrary to the welfare of some. For in fact the best interest of the community must be their best interest too since they are voluntary members of the community. This concept, which Rousseau called the general will, is paradoxical and difficult to grasp. Acceptance of the general will is an act of moral freedom, a very demanding principle. Freedom for the citizen means doing what one *ought*, not what one *wants*. It derives from conscience, which must do battle within the individual against passion, appetite, and self-interest. Thus, to use Rousseau's most striking phrase, the government must occasionally "force its citizens to be free." Freedom cannot exist in a state of nature or in any arrangement dictated by force. It is a tenuous social arrangement involving consent, participation, and subordination of individual self-interest to the commonweal.

More than any of the philosophes, Rousseau understood that the issue of freedom—one of the Enlightenment's central concerns—cannot be dealt with simply in terms of individual autonomy and well-being. The moral freedom of a man depends on the arrangements governing the collectivity of men.

Shortly after the French Revolution began in 1789, conservatives such as the Irish statesman Edmund Burke charged the philosophes with causing it. Burke thought the philosophes had subverted their society by consciously undermining all authority, particularly that of the monarchy and the church. As if substantiating Burke's claim, but in an opposite spirit, many revolutionaries made a cult of the memory of Voltaire and Rousseau. All this has confused the issue of the actual nature and impact of the Enlightenment.

The philosophes, most of whom had died by the 1770s, were far from being incipient revolutionaries. Members of Europe's cultural elite, they intended only that their society gradually reform itself. Distrustful of the uneducated masses, afraid of sedition and popular anarchy, they had everything to fear from a revolutionary upheaval. They were critics of their society but not its subverters.

Nonetheless the Enlightenment did challenge the traditional values of European society. From Voltaire's early polemics against Christianity through the sober social science of the *Encyclopedia* and the impassioned writings of Rousseau, new ideas and new modes of thought were diffused among important elements of Europe's educated classes. The philosophes did not offer new doctrines such as Socialism for men to implement. Rather they challenged the automatic respect for convention and authority, promoting the habit of independent-minded reflection and the conviction that change was both necessary and possible.

In and of themselves the crusades of the philosophes against religion and against glaring contemporary abuses were by no means revolutionary. But they promoted a climate in which the status quo was gradually put on the defensive and in which revolution—when provoked under other circumstances—was not unthinkable.

RECOMMENDED READING

Sources

Crocker, L. G. (ed.). *The Age of Enlightenment.* 1969.
Gendzier, Stephen J. (ed.). *Denis Diderot: The Encyclopedia: Selections.* 1967.
Rousseau, Jean Jacques. *The Social Contract and Discourses.* 1950.
★Voltaire. *The Portable Voltaire.* 1949, 1977.

Studies

★Behrens, C. B. *The Ancien Régime.* 1967. An interpretive essay, lavishly illustrated.

Bruford, W. H. *Germany in the Eighteenth Century: The Social Background of the Literary Revival.* 1952.

*Cassirer, Ernst. *The Question of Jean-Jacques Rousseau.* 1963. Brief and reliable.

*Cragg, G. R. *The Church and the Age of Reason, 1648–1789.* 1966.

Darton, Robert. *The Business of Enlightenment: A Publishing History of the Encyclopedia.* 1979. The "biography of a book" and of the century's most important publishing venture.

Ford, Franklin. *Robe and Sword: The Regrouping of the French Aristocracy After Louis XIV.* 1953. Should be read in conjunction with Montesquieu's ideas.

Gay, Peter. *Voltaire's Politics: The Poet as Realist.* 1959. A lively and sympathetic portrait.

*Hampson, Norman. *A Cultural History of the Enlightenment.* 1969. Possibly too interpretive to serve as an introduction, it nonetheless presents the subject most interestingly. (For a more advanced study see Peter Gay's two-volume work, *The Enlightenment: An Interpretation,* 1966 & 1969.)

Herr, Richard. *The Eighteenth-Century Revolution in Spain.* 1958. Absolutism and Enlightenment in Spain—a case study not discussed in the present text.

Kors, Alan. *D'Holbach's Coterie: An Enlightenment in Paris.* 1976.

Korshin, P. J. (ed.). *The Widening Circles: Essays on the Circulation of Literature in Eighteenth-Century Europe.* 1976.

*Krieger, Leonard. *Kings and Philosophers, 1689–1789.* 1970. A good introduction to eighteenth-century thought and government.

Link, Edith M. *The Emancipation of the Austrian Peasantry, 1740–1789.* 1949. Traces the efforts and frustrations of agrarian reformers.

Malcolmson, R. W. *Popular Recreations in English Society, 1700–1850.* 1973.

Palmer, Robert R. *Catholics and Unbelievers in Eighteenth-Century France.* 1939. The response of Catholic intellectuals to the century's philosophic and scientific thought.

*Paulson, Ronald. *Hogarth: His Life, Art, and Times* (abridged ed.). 1974.

Payne, Harry. *The Philosophes and the People.* 1976. An analysis of the Enlightenment's liberal elitism.

Schackleton, R. *Montesquieu.* 1961.

Venturi, Franco. *Italy and the Enlightenment.* 1972. Essays on important Italian philosophes by a leading historian.

*Watt, Ian. *The Rise of the Novel: Studies of Defoe, Richardson, and Fielding.* 1957.

Wilson, Arthur. *Diderot.* 1972. An exhaustive, masterful biography.

---

* Available in paperback.

THE IMAGE OF MAN
In 17th and 18th Century Art

The art of the time span that concerns us here—from about 1600 to the French Revolution—is designated by two awkward terms: Baroque and Rococo. They were coined at the end of the eighteenth century by advocates of the "Greek Revival" to mock the style of the previous two hundred years as bombastic, overblown, and artificial. A residue of their original negative flavor still clings to these terms today, and some scholars hesitate to use them on the ground that not all art of the seventeenth century is Baroque nor all of the eighteenth Rococo. We can sympathize with their dilemma; what does Caravaggio (Plate 33) have in common with Rubens (Plate 37), Frans Hals (Plate 39) with Poussin (Plate 43), or Tiepolo (Plate 36) with Watteau (Plate 44)? The contrasts are indeed astonishing. But earlier periods encompass a similar range of styles—compare, for example, Plates 9 and 10 or 21 and 23—yet this does not discourage us from calling them Medieval or Renaissance. The difficulty in the case of Baroque and Rococo is that, unlike Medieval and Renaissance, which refer to entire phases of Western civilization, these terms were invented specifically for art criticism and thus had a much narrower meaning from the start. In present-day use the meaning has broadened a good deal and its negative implication lessened, although we still do not speak of Baroque thought or Baroque society the way we do of Medieval thought or Renaissance society. Such terms, it seems, have a life of their own; once they have won general acceptance they are as difficult to replace as they are to do without. On the other hand, the very fact that we have no satisfactory name for the civilization of the seventeenth and eighteenth centuries tells us something about the character of this period, or at least about our perception of it: we see it, and its art, as no-longer-Renaissance and not-yet-Modern, rather than as a clear-cut entity in its own right.

It is no surprise, therefore, to encounter the same double aspect in the Baroque image of man. For the first time since recorded history began, the human form is no longer taken for granted as every artist's central concern; landscape and still life—where the presence of a person is either incidental or merely implied—emerge as important subjects in painting. Man, if he (or she) happens to be an absolute sovereign claiming rule by divine right, may be glorified more than ever, but only at the risk of drowning in the allegorical apparatus (as does Marie de Medici in Plate 37). Tiepolo (Plate 36) needs all the gods of Olympus to sing the praises of his patron, the Prince-Bishop, yet the ostensible center of all his splendid display is no more than a portrait medallion that has been pushed off to one side to make room for the soaring deities. At the other end of the scale, the image of man now includes the poor of this earth. They may be manifestations of the divine presence, as in Caravaggio (Plate 33), or they may be endowed with a dignity of suffering (as in Louis Le Nain's "Peasant Family," Plate 42) that seems to anticipate the social conscience of the nineteenth century (compare Plate 57). Whatever their station, people more often than not are shown as acted upon rather than acting, subject to forces beyond their control. The figures in Guercino's or Tiepolo's ceiling frescoes (Plates 34 and 36) are carried along by an overpowering stream of movement; Bernini's "St. Teresa" (Plate 35) is borne aloft semiconscious on a cloud as the angel of divine love prepares to pierce her heart. Even David's murdered "Marat" (Plate 46) must be understood as a secular successor of martyred Baroque saints, no less than Goya's Madrileños (Plate 48). Rembrandt, as seen by himself in old age (Plate 40), reflects a lifetime of troubled self-scrutiny. Watteau's "Gilles" (Plate 44) stands very still so that we may sense the pathos of his role as the universal butt of his fellow players' pranks. The fleeting form of Vermeer's "Girl with the Red Hat" (Plate 41) seems forever suspended in a beam of light, as does the assembled company in Velázquez's "Maids of Honor" (Plate 38). The spirited "Bathers" of Fragonard (Plate 45) share the weightlessness of the floating figures in Tiepolo's ceiling (Plate 36); they are buoyed up, and tossed back and forth, by the same irresistible currents we observe in Guercino's "Aurora" and Bernini's "St. Teresa" (Plates 34 and 35) although separated from them by more than a century.

Baroque art, then, in contrast to that of the Early and High Renaissance, no longer accepts the humanists' vision of man as the master of his own fate. Its image of man is contingent on three factors that govern man no less than they do the rest of the natural world—the flow of time, the flow of light, and the flow of motion. We sense them in Caravaggio's "Calling of St. Matthew" (Plate 33), at the very beginning of the period; light here is an active force that permits the artist to seize the most dramatic moment: Christ has just moved out of the shadows into the path of the beam illuminating his face and hand, and Matthew realizes he is being called but does not yet grasp the full meaning of the divine command. Thirty years later, in "The Jolly Toper" of Frans Hals (Plate 39), the subject is caught as he might have been by a modern camera, with the artist's dashing, open brush strokes recording a race against time. Vermeer's "Girl with the Red Hat" (Plate 41) has an equally casual pose, but we are now asked to observe not the movement of the figure but the movement of light, which settles on the surfaces in the picture like a rain of tiny droplets of color so that everything looks slightly "out of focus." Vermeer, fascinated by optical phenomena, may well have observed this effect by viewing his subject through a camera obscura, a device then in use that resembled a present-day camera but projected its images onto a translucent screen rather than a piece of light-sensitive film—one of the by-products of the age that invented the telescope and microscope.

The use of the camera obscura by Vermeer and other painters makes us wonder how the image of man in Baroque art might be related to the scientific thought of the period. This, after all, was the first age to acknowledge that the earth was not the center of the universe but merely a planet revolving around the sun; could so shattering an insight have remained without effect on art? Was it coincidence that the great scientists of these two centuries, from Galileo to Newton, were concerned with problems of time, light, and motion (though surely not in the same way as the artists)? Having noted the parallel, we must confess that so far we are unable to establish any real links. In the Renaissance, an artist could be a humanist and a scientist as well, but now science and philosophy had become too complex, abstract, and systematic for artists to share; gravitation did not kindle their imagination any more than did calculus or Descartes's "I think, therefore I am." Still, artists and scientists (or "natural philosophers" as they were then called) could have expressed the same basic world view without necessarily being aware of each other.

Be that as it may, Baroque art had one thing in common with science: an internationalism that respected neither creeds nor national boundaries. Caravaggio had a greater impact in Catholic Spain and Protestant Holland than he did at home. Tiepolo, the Venetian, produced his largest works in Würzburg and Madrid. Poussin spent almost his entire adult life in Rome, yet his style became the acknowledged ideal of the French Royal Academy of Painting. Rubens worked in Italy for eight years and could have had as successful a career there as he did in Antwerp. Even Rembrandt, who never crossed the Alps, had admirers in Italy and in turn admired Italian art. It had taken the rest of Europe two centuries to absorb the achievements of Italian Renaissance art; the Baroque, in contrast, was an international style almost from the beginning. In this respect, too, it paved the way for the Modern era.

At the end of the sixteenth century Rome once again became the artistic capital of Europe. Now that the Catholic faith had weathered the storm of the Reformation, popes could resume the task their predecessors had set themselves a hundred years earlier: to make Rome the most beautiful city of the Christian world. The ambitious young artists they attracted soon replaced the waning tradition of Mannerism with a dynamic new style, the Baroque.

The greatest of these was Caravaggio, who coined a radically new image of man to fit the new era. In this respect, his *Calling of St. Matthew* is comparable to Michelangelo's *Creation of Adam* (Plate 24). Both are confrontations of Man and God, but the meeting now takes place in a common Roman tavern, and God has descended to man's everyday world. Matthew points questioningly at himself as two figures approach from the right. They are poor people, their bare feet and simple garments contrasting strongly with the colorful costumes of Matthew and his companions. What identifies one of the two as Christ? It is mainly his commanding gesture, borrowed from the Lord in Michelangelo's fresco and made even more emphatic by the strong beam of light that illuminates the Saviour's face and hand, thus carrying his call across to Matthew. Without this light, we would not be aware of the divine presence. Caravaggio here gives moving, direct form to an attitude no less appealing to Protestants than to Catholics—that the mysteries of faith are revealed not by intellectual speculation but spontaneously, through an inward experience open to all men.

Plate 33. Caravaggio
THE CALLING OF ST. MATTHEW
ca. 1597–1598, canvas, height 11'1"
S. Luigi dei Francesi, Rome

Plate 34. Guercino
AURORA (*ceiling*)
1621–1623, wall painting
Villa Ludovisi, Rome

Caravaggio's work, although acclaimed by artists and connoisseurs, never was widely popular in Italy. The simple people resented meeting their likes in his canvases, and the sophisticated objected to them as lacking propriety and reverence. They preferred the style exemplified in Plates 34 and 35: dynamic, illusionistic, rhetorical, spectacular in its appeal to the beholder's emotions. The *Aurora* of Guercino covers the ceiling of the main room in an aristocratic villa, but similar sweeping visions were soon to appear on the ceilings of countless churches. Through a cunning use of perspective, the walls of the room continue upward in the fresco, so that we cannot tell where the real architecture leaves off and the painted illusion begins. They leave an opening for the morning sky; Aurora, the personification of Dawn, rushes across it in her chariot drawn by dappled horses, driving the shadows of night before her. In another context, the scene might be a saint carried to heaven or a triumphant allegory of faith. If Guercino's invention strikes us as theatrical, we must keep in mind that this was the time that created the opera, a new, compound art form, and similar scenes were actually presented on the stage.

Bernini, the greatest Baroque sculptor, was also deeply involved with the world of the theater, both as a designer and a playwright. His *Ecstasy of St. Theresa* is "staged" with consummate skill. Housed in an architectural frame that has the function of a proscenium arch, the group occupies a space that is real but beyond our reach. Theresa of Avila, one of the important saints of the Counter-Reformation, had described how an angel pierced her heart with a flaming golden arrow: "The pain was so great that I screamed aloud, but at the same time I felt such infinite sweetness that I wished the pain to last forever. It was not physical but psychic pain, although it affected the body as well to some degree. It was the sweetest caressing of the soul by God." Bernini has made this visionary experience sensuously real—the angel is indistinguishable from Cupid, and the saint's ecstasy is palpably physical. Yet the two figures on their floating cloud are illuminated (from a hidden window above) in such a way that they seem almost dematerialized in their gleaming whiteness. Their visionary character is further reinforced by the stream of golden rays, which balances the heavenly wind that carries the figures heavenward, causing the turbulence of their drapery. It is hard to imagine a greater contrast than that between Bernini's group and another meeting of saint and angel, Donatello's *Annunciation* (Plate 17) carved two hundred years before, so gently human and the very opposite of theatrical. Yet it was the earlier master who ultimately made Bernini's achievement possible.

Plate 35. Gianlorenzo Bernini
THE ECSTASY OF ST. THERESA
1645–1652, marble, lifesize
Sta. Maria della Vittoria, Rome

Plate 36. Giovanni Battista Tiepolo
THE GODS OF OLYMPUS (*detail of ceiling, Grand Staircase*)
1750–1753, wall painting Residenz, Würzburg

These two paintings, however different they may be in other respects, are linked by a common purpose—the glorification of a sovereign. In the age of absolutism, great kings as well as petty rulers insisted that they embodied the power of the state by the will of God, and their desire to see themselves depicted in this superhuman role provided the artists of the period with many splendid commissions, especially in the Catholic parts of Europe. Such a task fell to Rubens when the great Flemish master, at the height of his career, was asked to produce a cycle of large pictures for the Luxembourg Palace in Paris celebrating the life of Marie de' Medici, the widow of King Henry IV and mother of Louis XIII. Plate 37 shows the artist's oil sketch for one episode, the young queen arriving on French soil after a sea voyage from Italy. Hardly an exciting subject, yet Rubens has turned it into a spectacle of drama and splendor. As Marie walks down the gangplank, Fame flies overhead sounding a triumphant blast on two trumpets, and Neptune rises from the sea with his fish-tailed crew to steady the ship and to rejoice at the queen's safe arrival, while other classical deities welcome her ashore. Everything flows together here in swirling movement: heaven and earth, history and allegory— even drawing and painting, for Rubens used oil sketches such as this one to prepare his compositions, leaving the execution of the final version mostly to his assistants. Unlike earlier artists, he liked to design his pictures in terms of light and color from the very start (most of his drawings are figure studies or portrait sketches). This unified vision was Rubens's most precious legacy to later painters.

A century and a quarter after Rubens, the Venetian painter Tiepolo faced a similar assignment in the newly completed palace of the Prince-Bishop of Würzburg in Central Germany. Here we see the last and most refined stage of illusionistic ceiling decoration represented by its greatest master, whose grace and felicity of touch had made him famous far beyond his homeland. Tiepolo's ceiling fresco in the Grand Staircase is so huge that Plate 36 shows only about a quarter of the total area. Unlike Guercino (compare Plate 34), Tiepolo no longer depends on a foreshortened architectural framework to create the necessary sense of distance between the beholder and the heavenly vision above; his illusion is achieved mainly by contrasts of light and color. Solid clusters of figures along the edges of the ceiling, larger and more strongly modeled, served to make those soaring amid the blue sky and sunlit clouds in the center seem infinitely farther away. Who they all are and how they relate to the Prince-Bishop (who is present only as a portrait medallion, not visible in our plate) is a question we are not likely to ask as we admire this celestial pageant.

Plate 37. Peter Paul Rubens
MARIE DE' MEDICI LANDING IN MARSEILLES
1622–1623, wood panel, height 25"
Alte Pinakothek, Munich

Plate 38. Diego Velázquez
THE MAIDS OF HONOR
ca. 1656, canvas, height 10'5"
Prado Museum, Madrid

Although the bulk of his work consists of portraits—mostly of the Spanish royal family and members of the court—Velázquez began his career as a painter of scenes of everyday life under the strong influence of Caravaggio. He admired the Italian master's sympathy for the common people and his handling of light, but did not share his interest in dramatic action. When, still in his twenties, Velázquez moved from his native Seville to Madrid, he was befriended by Rubens, who may have helped him to see the beauty of the numerous paintings by Titian in the king's collection (compare Plate 25). He also traveled in Italy. All these experiences are reflected in *The Maids of Honor,* painted at the height of his career. A more suitable title might be "The Painter in His Studio," for Velázquez shows himself at work on a huge canvas that juts into the picture on the left; in the center is the little Princess Margarita, who has been posing for him, among her playmates and maids of honor, which include a large dog and a dwarf. This foreground group is caught in the bright light streaming into the room from an unseen window on the right. Two other figures, a bit farther back, are less clearly seen in the shadowy, high-ceilinged gallery; in the rear a courtier, brilliantly illuminated, is framed by an open door. Evidently, something has interrupted the painting session, and most of the figures are turning to look at the beholder: an unobtrusive but commanding presence makes itself felt. What could it be? The solution, it seems, is the bright rectangle above the head of the princess, which must be a mirror rather than a painting: in it, we see two heads, those of the King and Queen.

Have they just stepped into the room, to see the scene exactly as we do? Or does the mirror reflect part of the canvas—presumably a full-length group portrait of the royal family—on which the artist has been working? Be that as it may, the painting reveals Velázquez's fascination with the action of light, which seems infinitely more varied and dramatic than the action of the figures. His rich, fluid brushwork renders the full range of its effects on shape, color, and texture, from the sparkling highlights on the princess's hair and dress to the dimly perceived canvases in the background. For Velázquez, light *creates* the visible world. No wonder that the pioneers of Impressionism two hundred years later considered him the most "modern" of seventeenth-century painters.

Frans Hals, half a generation older than Velázquez, was born in Antwerp but as a young man moved to Haarlem in the newly independent northern part of the Netherlands, where he became a portrait painter as renowned as Velázquez was in Spain. He too divided his attention between portraiture and scenes of everyday life and owed an essential debt to the influence of Caravaggio. *The Jolly Toper* is surely a portrait, but Hals seems far less concerned with the sitter's individual personality than with the effect of the picture as an "action shot"—everything is tilted, from the huge hat that frames the face like a black halo to the wine glass in the sitter's left hand, thus conveying instability and transitory movement. The brushwork itself is open and lightning-quick, each stroke so clearly separate that we are tempted to count the total number. Caravaggio's sense of the "fruitful moment" here becomes a split-second race against time.

Plate 39. Frans Hals
THE JOLLY TOPER
1627, canvas, height 32"
Rijksmuseum, Amsterdam

Plate 40. Rembrandt
SELF-PORTRAIT WITH PALETTE
1660, canvas, height 44½"
Louvre Museum, Paris

Rembrandt, the greatest genius of Dutch art, is one of a small company of artists (Leonardo da Vinci, Michelangelo, and Van Gogh are others) whose popular fame as legendary figures distorts or obscures their true achievement. He has been the subject (or better perhaps, the victim) of many fictionalized biographies that present him as a "glorious failure," deserted in mid-career by a fickle public and plunged into poverty and neglect. Actually Rembrandt's fortunes during his later years declined far less catastrophically than his romantic admirers have claimed. He retained important patrons and received some major public commissions even toward the end of his life. It is true, however, that his work from the mid-1620s to the early 1640s, with its emphasis on dramatic display, differs markedly from that of the 1650s and 1660s, which is gently lyrical and introspective. The change reflects the maturing of a powerful personality. Nowhere is this process of growth recorded more completely than in the artist's numerous self-portraits (he produced more than sixty), culminating in the self-analytical frankness and simple dignity of those he did during his final years. In the example shown in Plate 40, we see him standing at his easel, palette and brushes in hand; he gazes at the beholder (or rather, at himself) with a look, sad and tender at the same time, that seems to convey an entire lifetime's experience of thought and feeling. What makes this revelation of character possible is the magic glow of Rembrandt's light, which filters into the picture space quietly from the upper left, endowing the artist's features with their strange mute eloquence. Unlike Velázquez, Rembrandt here explores the metaphysical and expressive rather than the optical aspects of the element that

Caravaggio had introduced into Western painting as an active force.

Rembrandt was unique among the Dutch painters of his time not only for his depth of human insight but for the wide range of his subjects, which included biblical and mythological themes, landscapes, scenes of daily life, portraiture, and still lifes. Most seventeenth-century painters tended to specialize, and more so in Holland than elsewhere because of the pressure of competition. Dutch artists had to rely on private collectors rather than state or church as their chief source of support. Many of them produced "for the market," and dealing in pictures became an important trade that followed the law of supply and demand. Since the market reflects the dominant, not the most discerning, taste of the time, it could happen that some artists whom we now regard as mediocre were over-priced while others, highly esteemed today, were undervalued. The most astonishing instance of this is Vermeer, whose genius seems to us second only to Rembrandt's but who was almost forgotten until a century ago. His specialty was domestic interiors, with one or two figures, usually women, engaged in quiet everyday tasks; he also did occasional outdoors views and portraits. Some pictures, such as *The Girl with the Red Hat*, leave us in doubt: is it a portrait or a figure study? The same question arises when we look at Hals's *Jolly Toper* (Plate 39). In every other respect, however, the two canvases offer a fascinating contrast. If Vermeer is akin to any other painter of his time, it is neither Hals nor Rembrandt but Velázquez; even more than the great Spaniard, he concentrates on the optical properties of light and color. Yet the jewel-like freshness of his vision suggests that his true progenitor is Jan van Eyck (see Plate 18).

Plate 41. Jan Vermeer
THE GIRL WITH THE RED HAT
ca. 1660, canvas, height 9"
National Gallery of Art
Andrew W. Mellon Collection
Washington, D.C.

Plate 42. Louis Le Nain
PEASANT FAMILY
ca. 1640, canvas, height 44½"
Louvre Museum, Paris

That the two pictures reproduced on these pages should both have been painted by Frenchmen born within a year of each other seems almost incredible. It attests not only the extraordinary diversity of Baroque art within a single country but the intermediate position of France between North and South. Louis Le Nain, although strongly indebted to Caravaggio, is even more closely linked with the Netherlandish tradition of realism stemming from Jan van Eyck and continued by Pieter Bruegel. Poussin, in contrast, is a classicist whose sources of inspiration are Titian (compare Plate 25), the Roman High Renaissance masters, and the world of antiquity. His style was formed in Rome, where he spent almost his entire adult life, yet his patrons and his influence were largely in France. He is the father of what was to become known as the "grand manner" in painting, based on firmly held theoretical ideas about the aim of art which he expounded in his voluminous correspondence. As his starting point he took the ancient dictum that "painting is mute poetry"; like the poet, the painter must strive to elevate the mind of his audience by dealing with noble and serious themes. He will reach his goal only if he suppresses the imperfections of nature-in-the-raw and depicts instead an ideal world of nature perfected. Nor must he give too much importance to color, lest he cater to sensuous pleasure instead of appealing to man's moral impulses. Logic and order, clarity of form and composition, are to be of primary importance. In Poussin's own work such as *The Inspiration of the Epic Poet,* this prescription could yield canvases of extraordinary beauty. Others, who followed in his footsteps and took over his formula ready-made, were less successful. There were to be a great many of them, for Poussin's doctrines became the official program of the French Royal Academy of Painting and Sculpture, founded under Louis XIV to foster a single "approved" style. It, in turn, was the model for countless similar academies in the other countries of Europe, so that "Poussinism" survived until close to the end of the nineteenth century as the ideal of conservative, state-sponsored artists.

Plate 43. Nicolas Poussin
THE INSPIRATION OF THE EPIC POET
ca. 1628, canvas, height 6'
Louvre Museum, Paris

Plate 44. Antoine Watteau
GILLES
ca. 1717, canvas, height 6'
Louvre Museum, Paris

In France, the power of the Royal Academy to enforce "Poussinism" remained unchallenged for almost half a century. During the final years of Louis XIV's long reign, however, there appeared signs of an internal revolt, led by a faction that declared its allegiance to the style of Rubens (exemplified by such pictures as our Plate 37). These "Rubenists" advocated color rather than drawing as being more true to nature and appealing to everyone, while drawing can be appreciated only by the expert few. Their argument had revolutionary implications, for it made the layman the ultimate judge of artistic values ("I don't know anything about art, but I know what I like"). The final triumph of the "Rubenists" came in 1717 with the admission to the Academy of Antoine Watteau, whose pictures violated all official canons; instead of noble and elevating themes, they depicted, in a superbly elegant and sensuous style, scenes of refined society or of comedy actors in parklike settings. Often Watteau interweaves theater and real life so that no clear distinction can be made between the two. In his *Gilles* (Plate 44) the central figure is a stock character of the French comedy stage, a kind of "straight man" who invariably becomes the victim of pranks and comic misfortunes. In his awkward white satin costume, he stands isolated from the gay throng behind him, seemingly impassive yet suffering in silent agony. If Watteau's actors lack the robust vitality of Rubens, they play their roles so well that they touch us as if they were real-life characters.

Plate 45. Jean-Honoré Fragonard
BATHERS
ca. 1765, canvas, height 25"
Louvre Museum, Paris

The victory of the "Rubenists" signaled a shift in French art and French society. After the death of Louis XIV, the power of the absolute monarchy declined and with it the art patronage of the state, so that artists came to depend increasingly on private patrons. That the latter preferred Watteau to the disciples of Poussin is hardly surprising; it was they who sponsored what later was derisively termed the Rococo, an intimate, sensuous style uninhibited by classicistic doctrines. Watteau, who died at the early age of 37, had a great many followers, although none had the emotional depth that distinguishes his art.

The last, and finest, among these is Fragonard, who painted the *Bathers* (Plate 45): his brushwork has a fluid breadth and spontaneity reminiscent of Rubens's oil sketches (compare Plate 37), and his figures move with a floating grace that also links him with Tiepolo (see Plate 36), whose work he had admired in Italy. Fragonard had the misfortune to outlive his era. After the French Revolution, he was reduced to poverty and died forgotten, in the heyday of Napoleon, when classicism, and with it the doctrines of Poussin, had once more become the order of the day.

Plate 46. Jacques Louis David
THE DEATH OF MARAT
1792, canvas, height 65"
Royal Museums of Fine Arts, Brussels

The third quarter of the eighteenth century saw a gradual turning of the tide throughout European art. While Tiepolo and Fragonard were creating the last masterpieces of the Rococo, there was a growing reaction, in the name of Reason and Nature, against Baroque "artificiality." These two concepts had been proclaimed as supreme values by the thinkers of the Enlightenment; in art, they signaled a return to the doctrines of Poussin and a new admiration for the "noble simplicity and calm grandeur" of the Greeks (in the famous phrase of Johann Winckelmann, the influential German archaeologist and critic). Rome was the birthplace of this Neoclassic style, although its leading early protagonists were visitors from the north rather than Italians. It was there that Jacques Louis David, a highly gifted young French painter trained in the Rococo tradition, became a convert to the new style. After his return to Paris, David's artistic conversion became a political one as well: he passionately espoused the revolutionary ideas of the Enlightenment and, in 1789, the Revolution itself. At the height of the struggle, he painted his greatest picture, *The Death of Marat* (Plate 46). David's deep emotion has made a masterpiece from a subject that would have embarrassed any lesser artist; for Marat, one of the political leaders of the Revolution, had been murdered in his bathtub. A painful skin disease caused him to do his paperwork there, with a wooden board serving as his desk. One day a young woman named Charlotte Corday burst in with a petition and plunged a knife into him while he read it. David has composed the scene with awe-inspiring starkness as a public memorial to the martyred hero: it is Neoclassic in the clarity and simplicity of the forms and in the way the principal planes are arranged to parallel the picture surface, but the Neoclassic ideal of Nature Perfected is not in evidence. David must have realized that it could not help him achieve his purpose—to produce a historic account that was also a moving devotional image. For that he had to revert to the Caravaggio tradition of religious art, with its realism and dramatic lighting (compare Plate 33).

A few years later David became an ardent admirer of Napoleon. He was to produce several large pictures glorifying the emperor, but a favorite pupil, Antoine-Jean Gros, eclipsed him as the chief painter of the Napoleonic myth. Gros's first portrait of the great general shows him leading his troops at the battle of Arcole in northern Italy (Plate 47). It conveys Napoleon's magic as an irresistible "man of destiny" with an enthusiasm David could never match. Much as Gros respected his teacher's doctrines, his emotional nature impelled him toward the color and drama of the Baroque: hence the stormy sky, the spiral movement of the flag, the hero's disheveled, streaming hair, the violent turn of his body, the dynamic open brushwork—all of them devices of "visual rhetoric" that carry us back to Rubens (see Plate 37).

Plate 47. Antoine-Jean Gros
NAPOLEON AT ARCOLE
1796, canvas, height 29½"
Louvre Museum, Paris

Plate 48. Francisco Goya
THE THIRD OF MAY, 1808
1814–1815, canvas, height 8'9"
Prado Museum, Madrid

If Gros's *Napoleon at Arcole* may be termed Neo-Baroque, the same is true even more emphatically of Goya's *The Third of May, 1808* (Plate 48). But the great Spanish painter had never been a Neoclassicist. His early works are in a delightful late Rococo vein. During the 1780s he came to sympathize with the Enlightenment and the French Revolution. He now abandoned the Rococo for a Neo-Baroque style based on Velázquez and Rembrandt, the masters of the previous century he admired most. When Napoleon's armies occupied Spain in 1808, Goya and many of his countrymen hoped that the conquerors would bring the liberal reforms so badly needed, but the savage behavior of the French troops crushed these hopes and generated a popular resistance of equal savagery. *The Third of May, 1808,* commemorating the execution of a group of Madrid citizens, reflects this bitter experience. Its blazing color, fluid brushwork, and dramatic nocturnal light endow the picture with all the emotional intensity of religious art, yet these martyrs are dying for Liberty, not the Kingdom of Heaven; and their executioners are not the agents of Satan but of political tyranny—a formation of faceless automatons impervious to their victims' despair and defiance. With the clairvoyance of genius, Goya has created an image that was to be reenacted countless times in modern history.

20

REVOLUTIONS OF THE EIGHTEENTH CENTURY

The eighteenth century forms a bridge in Western history between two fundamentally distinct epochs. Europe in 1700—the Europe of the "old regime"—largely preserved the institutions and the way of life that it had acquired over the long centuries of the past. In 1700 the economy remained based predominantly upon agriculture. People were aided in their labors by animals, wind, and water, but their technology offered them comparatively little help. In social and political life, inequality was the rule. Kings and emperors, who claimed to hold their authority directly from God, presided over realms which were composed of distinct orders or estates, each with its own obligations and privileges.

In contrast, the European society of 1800 was witnessing violent upheavals at every level. Western man had begun a radical transformation of his methods of raising food and producing goods. This Industrial Revolution, which continues in our day, achieved a stunning conquest of the material world, restructured society, changed all aspects of Western life in its early phases, and now offers similar promises and poses similar problems to all the peoples of the earth.

Concurrently with the inauguration of the Industrial Revolution, profound changes were undermining the stability of Western society. As we have seen, the leaders of the Enlightenment broke with traditional religious assumptions; they denied that morality and social order had to be based on divine revelation and supernatural grace. Human reason could replace or was equivalent to the word of God. In a larger context growing numbers of men—not only from the middle classes but from the older privileged orders as well—had come to believe that society was ill-served by traditional institutions, and they agitated powerfully to reform them. The demand for reform bore as its principal fruit the great revolutions that swept across wide areas of both Europe and North America in the late eighteenth century.

The latter 1700s thus initiate the great age of revolutions in the West. Of course all periods of the Western past have experienced change, and all have contributed to the making of our present society. But the economic changes and popular revolts begun toward the end of the century hold a pivotal position in the growth and transformation of Western civilization. Perhaps no other movements have left such visible marks on the character of our modern life—our government, our economy, and our social ideals.

I. THE INDUSTRIAL SYSTEM

Since the eighteenth century, the economy of the Western world has been in nearly continuous transformation. Humankind has achieved spectacular efficiency in raising food, producing goods, amassing wealth, multiplying itself, and changing the face of the earth. While no one can be certain, it is probable that more human beings are alive today than inhabited the earth over all the millennia before 1700. In a series of lectures given in 1880–1881, a young sociologist and economist at Oxford University named Arnold Toynbee chose (though he did not coin) the phrase "Industrial Revolution" to describe this metamorphosis.[1]

Characteristics of an Industrial Economy

With a fund of information unavailable to Toynbee, it is easy to criticize the term that he more than anyone made part of the historical vocabulary. It does not, for example, encompass changes in agriculture or transportation, without which the Industrial Revolution properly speaking would not have occurred. The traditional dates for it in Great Britain, 1760 to 1815 or 1830, are much too confined. If great factories are the mark of an industrial society, Britain and, even more, the Continent would have to be considered still underdeveloped by 1830. The revolution did not end in 1830. Indeed, the great advances based on the spread of the railroads, the application of chemistry to manufacturing, and the development of electrical power and the internal combustion engine did not affect the economy until the middle and late nineteenth century; moreover computers, atomic power, and automation carry the changes forward into our own future.

There are then many industrial revolutions, and they cannot be considered as marked off by precise dates. Nor was the initial transformation confined to manufacturing. But most historians would be reluctant to deny that there was a period beginning in the late eighteenth century, initially in Great Britain, when profound changes occurred in the production of goods and food that eventually equipped a significant part of the Western world with a kind of economy unknown in all prior historical ages. This is the period of what is conventionally called the Industrial Revolution.

What essentially distinguishes an industrial, or modern, economy from the traditional economies of previous epochs? Arnold Toynbee and many later writers equated the Industrial Revolution with the application of steam power to manufacturing, which brought about the factory system. The steam engine, used to drive mills from the 1780s on, replaced the putting-out system of domestic industry, in which artisans worked at home with their own tools on materials delivered to them by merchants or entrepreneurs. The use of steam power required that the workers congregate in great mills or factories, and they thus came to form a new social unit. But the emergence of the factory system does not seem today an adequate explanation of this economic transformation. In agriculture and transportation there were no factories; yet the progress in these economic sectors was an essential component of the Industrial Revolution, as noted before.

Perhaps the most distinctive feature of an industrial economy is its capacity for sustained growth. Its productivity is so great that it is able not only to meet its current consumption needs and replace its worn tools but also to invest in new capital equipment, which expands its means of producing. In short, the wealth produced, the capital equipment, and

---

[1] Arnold Toynbee was the uncle of Arnold J. Toynbee, the distinguished author of *A Study of History*, perhaps the most ambitious effort at developing a philosophy of history to appear in recent years. His own lectures on the Industrial Revolution were compiled and edited by friends after his death in 1883, at the age of thirty.

the economy will not be the same at the end of a given period as they were at the beginning. The essential feature of an industrial economy—we might say of a modern society, in contrast to all societies we have studied so far—is that it never stays the same. Since the eighteenth century, far more than in any other age, continuous, rapid, and all-pervasive change has been the law of Western life.

Of course the whole of European economic history before the Industrial Revolution cannot be described as stable and changeless. It would clearly be misleading to link together the Europe of Charlemagne and the Europe of the sixteenth and seventeenth centuries as if they were equally representative of a preindustrial, or traditional, economy. Preindustrial societies can experience profound changes; witness the agricultural and commercial expansion of the Central Middle Ages and the commercial boom of the sixteenth century. The economy advances, but after a spurt of growth it tends to stabilize, though on a higher plateau of productivity. The reason for this is that changes in the capacity to produce set in motion changes in levels of consumption, which absorb the new output and limit further capital investments. A society that attains some new wealth may elect to spend it on supporting a larger population or on raising the standard of living. A balance is reestablished between production and consumption, and investment is reduced. The economy has not achieved the capacity of self-sustaining growth. It is not industrial or modern.

The Course of Industrialization

How did the Industrial Revolution happen? In analyzing any economic system—traditional or modern, capitalist or socialist—economists distinguish between performance and structure. Performance is measured by output—the total or gross product, and the amount produced per individual in the community. This per capita productivity is in fact the best measure of an economy's performance. Structure refers to all those characteristics of a society that support or affect performance. Economic, legal, and political institutions; fiscal policies; technology; demographic distributions and movements; even culture and ideology—all make up the structure of a society, in the language of economic theory.

The Industrial Revolution was in essence a revolution in technology, which dramatically and continuously raised per capita productivity. In older treatments, historians stressed the numerous inventions that ushered in the factory era (see pp. 676–682). But technology alone does not offer an adequate explanation for the advent of industrialism. It was not an independent, or "exogenous," factor, to use again the language of economic theory. Social structure profoundly influences technological development, in any age. To ask why the revolution occurred is thus to pose two deeper questions: what were the structural obstacles to technological innovation and entrepreneurship in traditional European society? And what were the changes that, from the late eighteenth century, produced a structure that promoted and rewarded innovation?

One major obstacle was the small size of many European markets, cut off one from the other by physical barriers, political frontiers, tariff walls, and different laws, moneys, and measurements. Small markets slowed the growth of specialized manufacture, and they limited the mobility of capital and labor. Then, too, the highly skewed distribution of wealth, characteristic of many European communities, distorted the structure of demand. In many countries, a narrow aristocracy absorbed nearly all the disposable income, and the economy organized itself largely to serve the wealthy few. Catering to the desires of the rich, the economy produced expensive goods, often exquisite in quality and workmanship, but always

Revolutions of the Eighteenth Century 665

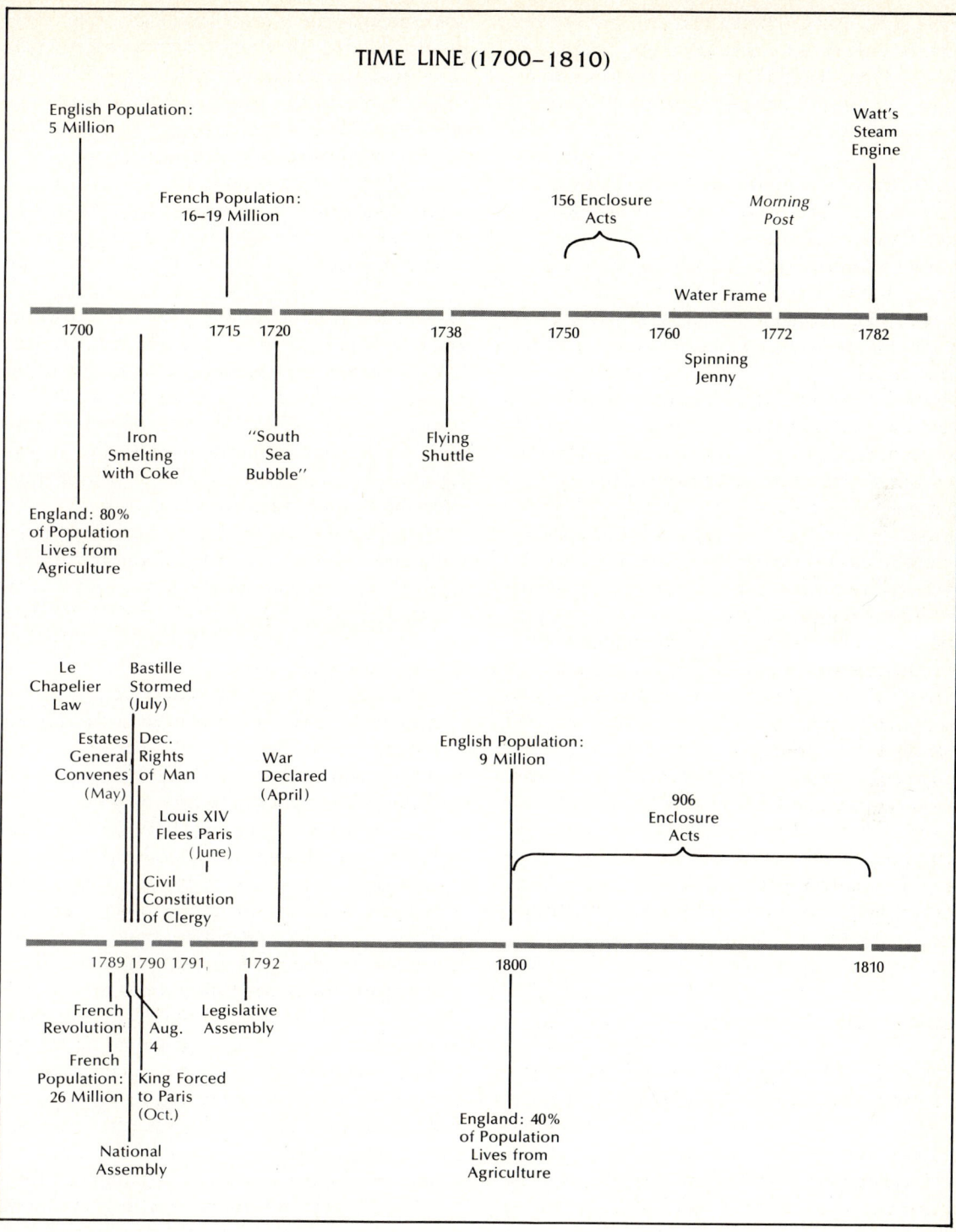

in small quantities. Small markets and skewed demand could not easily support a change in the mode of production, which, at least initially, sacrificed quality of product to quantity of output.

Even when markets were large, organizational faults weakened their power to promote specialization and mobilize labor and capital. Big markets and advancing specialization augmented the number of market transactions and their associated costs. To lower these "transaction costs" (again in the language of the economist) required efficient business and banking institutions.

Crucial to the industrializing process was a set of property rights, which raised the rate of return to technological innovation. Many institutions in traditional Europe (especially bearing on property) did the opposite: they repressed inventiveness and entrepreneurship. Through feudal or seigneurial rents and tolls, lords throughout Europe collected payments for which they rendered no service in return. Increased production was likely to benefit these parasites as much as the entrepreneurs. In the villages of northern Europe, under the open-field system (see pp. 674–675), cultivators had to follow the same routines of working the soil; they were not free to change farming methods without the agreement of neighbors. In the towns, the guilds presented a major obstacle to economic innovation. Guild regulations, which in the eighteenth century were more exactly government regulations enforced by the guilds, prescribed the techniques to be used in production and often dictated the terms and conditions under which goods could be sold, apprentices taken on, or workers hired. In their policies both urban guilds and rural villages tended to favor the poor and inefficient over the rich and entrepreneurial. They also tended to block innovation, freeze technology, and discourage effort.

Governments too helped to sustain these restrictive practices, principally by exploiting them for their own fiscal benefit. For example, governments frequently collected fees from guilds and other privileged institutions and parties. Another governmental policy that obstructed innovation was the licensing of monopoly companies, with exclusive rights to trade in certain regions, such as the East Indies, or to manufacture certain products. With assured markets and profits, these companies were not likely to assume the risks of new ventures, and they blocked others from doing so.

Cultural attitudes may also have discouraged entrepreneurial efforts. Many persons, particularly in the aristocratic classes, still regarded money made in trade or manufacture as somehow tainted. Particularly on the Continent, the highest aspiration of the successful businessman seems often to have been the purchase of a noble title.

Although these institutions and attitudes still marked European life in the eighteenth century, they were subject to ever sharper criticisms. From midcentury on, social thinkers associated with the Enlightenment—the physiocrats in France, Adam Smith and the liberal economists in England—attacked the communal management of land in the countryside, the guild control of industry in the towns, and privilege and monopoly in all forms. In the name of economic rationalism, they denounced both the special advantages held by a favored few and special consideration extended to the poor and the weak. No privilege, no pity: this was the appropriate policy for enlightened society. Their hard but telling logic slowly affected policy. Guilds were already weak in the countryside and in towns of recent growth, like Manchester and Birmingham in England. Also, new industries, such as cotton manufacturing, largely escaped their supervision. The government of revolutionary France, in the Le Chapelier law of 1791, permanently outlawed guilds and trade associations. In the Corporation Act of 1835, the British Parliament similarly abolished the guilds, but they had long since become ineffective in their function of regulating the economy. The government policy of chartering monopolies was gradually abandoned (the English East India Company, for example, lost its exclusive trading rights in India in 1813). Legally and socially, the entrepreneur was winning unprecedented freedom.

England

Of all the nations of Europe, England was the first to develop a social structure strongly supportive of innovation and economic growth. Its advantages were many, some of them deeply rooted in geography and history. This comparatively small realm contained an excellent balance of resources. The plain to the south and east, which contained the traditional centers of English settlement, was fertile and productive. The uplands to the north and west possessed rich deposits of coal and iron, and their streams had given power to mills since the Middle Ages.

The sea too was a major natural asset. No part of the island kingdom was distant from salt water. At a time when water transport offered the sole economic means for moving bulky commodities, the sea brought coal close to iron, raw materials close to factories, and products close to markets. And the sea gave Britain's merchants easy access to the much wider world beyond their shores.

Efficiency of transport was critical in setting the size of markets. From the late eighteenth century, Britain witnessed a considerable expansion of canals and turnpikes. Usually short in this compact land, they were cheap to build and profitable to operate. By 1815 the country possessed some 2,600 miles of canals. In addition, there were few institutional obstructions to the movement of goods. United under a strong monarchy since the Middle Ages, Britain was free of internal tariff barriers. Merchants everywhere counted in the same money, measured their goods by the same standards, and conducted their affairs under the protection of the common law.

Other characteristics of Britain's society favored innovation. The population had a long tradition of skill and could adapt rather easily to the personal and collective discipline required by the factory system. In about 1700, the standard of living of the English masses was probably the highest in Europe. English society was also considerably less stratified than that on the Continent, and the propertied classes tended to be oriented toward innovation. Primogeniture was the rule among both the peers (the titled members of the House of Lords) and the country gentlemen or squires, and the need to provide for their frequently large families encouraged them to increase their estates and revenues. From their ranks came the so-called improving landlords. Their younger sons, left without lands, had to seek careers in other walks of life, many of them in commerce and manufacturing. They frequently recruited capital for their ventures from their landed (and sometimes titled) fathers and elder brothers. Capital, therefore, like people, frequently crossed class lines in England. Another important pool of entrepreneurs was the considerable number of English religious dissenters, chiefly Calvinists and Quakers, who concentrated their energies on business enterprises because they were denied careers in government or the church.

The responsiveness of the propertied elements to investment opportunities was a remarkable feature of English society in the eighteenth century and one of the chief reasons why Britain was the home of the Industrial Revolution. These entrepreneurs and investors had a relatively greater influence on government than comparable groups on the Continent. Since the revolution of 1688, the government had been particularly sensitive to the interests of the propertied classes. They in turn had confidence in the government. The close ties between property and power facilitated the economic growth of the realm and was one important reason for the relative stability of the British regime in this age of revolutions.

Historians are not sure exactly what precipitated the takeoff of the eighteenth-century British economy or even what sectors led others in the industrializing effort. At one time scholars stressed the work of individual leaders, the improving landlords in agriculture or inventors and entrepreneurs in the cotton industry. Today it is generally recognized that agricultural changes came only slowly and that the growth of the cotton industry, however rapid, still accounted for only a small part of England's gross national product. Historians are thus inclined to lay greater emphasis on broad economic stimuli felt in several sectors simultaneously. One recently formulated theory, partially Marxist in inspiration, stresses the economic and political exploitation of overseas colonies as the critical stimulus in early industrialization. Colonies offered a huge market for inexpensive goods, especially cotton fabrics, which the new machines produced most efficiently. They provided cheap raw materials, and the large profits of the colonial trade promoted the formation of industrial capital.

Overseas trade was certainly booming in the eighteenth century, and certainly gave a powerful thrust to industrialization. Still the possession and exploitation of a colonial empire could not of itself assure early industrialization—witness Spain, Portugal, or Holland. Probably no less important was the growth of home population, which assured an enlarged domestic market and an abundance of cheap labor. Cultural changes may also have had an effect in that many men were willing to risk replacing old methods by new, and on other planes people were questioning and transforming traditional ways of thought and behavior. Then too the industrial growth itself, once initiated, seems to have exerted a reciprocal influence on trade, population, and attitudes.

The processes of this first industrialization are thus highly complex and still not entirely understood. What seems certain is that a strong demand for cheap goods was growing at home and abroad in the eighteenth century, and that

THE GROWTH OF ENGLAND'S FOREIGN TRADE IN THE EIGHTEENTH CENTURY

Three-year moving averages of combined imports and exports.
(Adapted from Dean, Phyllis, and Cole, W. A., *British Economic Growth, 1688–1959*, Cambridge, 1964, p. 49.)

---

important segments of the British community perceived this opportunity and responded to it. English law and policy gave them crucial support, by ensuring a high rate of return for innovation and enterprise.

France

Structural obstacles to economic growth were more deeply entrenched in France than in England. The kingdom of France in the early modern period did not form a single national market; rather, it was a federation of regional markets. France was large, and the expense of transportation grew rapidly with distance. Waterways were not conveniently distributed, and roads were miserable even in the age of Louis XIV's minister Colbert. Internal tariffs at provincial borders continued to restrain trade. In 1664 Colbert had created an area of free trade that embraced the older central provinces of the monarchy, but beyond these "five great farms" tariffs, tolls, and seigneurial dues burdened commerce. Merchants in the northeastern provinces of the Franche-Comté and Alsace, for example, found it easier to trade with the imperial cities of the Rhineland than with Paris. Contrasts in legal systems and in weights and measures further complicated and slowed exchange. As Voltaire sarcastically remarked, the traveler in crossing France by coach changed laws as frequently as horses.

Guilds and other forms of monopoly exerted a harmful influence within these regional markets. They paid fees to the central government in return for their privileges. In effect, the government was foregoing freer markets and more efficient economic performance in return for present revenue.

In spite of these obstacles, the French economy was not stagnant during the eighteenth century. After 1715 France enjoyed some seventy-five years nearly free from foreign invasions and internal uprisings; this was the calm before the terrible storms of the Revolution. The period of peace saw a remarkable proliferation of communications arteries. By 1738 the Picardy Canal linked the Somme and Oise rivers in the north. The Central Canal, built between 1783 and 1793, joined the Loire and Saône. Work was begun in 1777 on the Burgundy Canal, which enabled barges to move from the English Channel to the Mediterranean. The improvement of French roads, given major attention by Philibert Orry, a chief financial officer under Louis XV, was perhaps even more impressive. In 1738, he imposed a heavy corvée on the parishes, requiring from them contributions in labor for the construction and maintenance of roads. About a decade later the government founded the École des Ponts et Chaussées ("School of Bridges and Roads"), which soon became probably the best engineering school in Europe and which still functions today. By the late eighteenth century, France had acquired a magnificent system of royal highways that many contemporaries considered unsurpassed in Europe.

Foreign trade expanded too, especially with the West Indies and the Levant, despite the military reversals in North America and India. The number of French ships engaged in foreign commerce increased about fourfold between 1716 and 1789; on the eve of the Revolution, some 1,800 vessels showed the French flag. In the same period exports of manufactured products rose by 221 percent and all other commodities by 298 percent. The great ports of Bordeaux and Marseilles enjoyed a period of prosperity unequaled since the Middle Ages.

Stable coinage aided the financing of enterprises. In 1726 the government fixed the value of the principal gold coin, the louis, and kept it stable for the remaining years of the old regime—a remarkable feat in the light of the monarchy's desperate financial needs. The collapse of John Law's investment scheme in 1720 had a regressive effect on French banking, to be sure. French investors developed a lasting suspicion of banks, paper money, and joint-stock companies. Businessmen tended to rely on resources that they or their close relatives could muster and preferred to deal in hard cash rather than commercial paper. Small size, small capital, and conservative management worked to hold back French business enterprises. But this only dampened, not suppressed, the expansion of the eighteenth century. That expansion in turn created powerful pressures to reform the archaic structure of the French society and government.

II. ECONOMICS AND DEMOGRAPHY

The birth of the new economic system required the development of effective ways of recruiting, managing, and channeling capital into those enterprises with the greatest potential for profit. The commercial capitalism of the previous centuries was thus gradually being transformed into industrial capitalism. Changes in monetary practices affected trade and prices, and price movements had a major impact not only upon the economy but upon government as well. At a still more fundamental level, these economic changes influenced the patterns of marriages, births, and deaths in European so-

Financial Management

Critical to the takeoff of the industrialization process is a high rate of reinvestment, which in turn depends on the skillful management of money by both individuals and public institutions. Here again Great Britain was the most advanced country of Europe. From the sixteenth century on, the demands of overseas trade promoted the formation of joint-stock companies. By the seventeenth century, great concerns controlling trade with India, the South Seas, Africa, and the Levant were dominating England's overseas commerce. The financial panic in 1720 caused by the collapse of the South Sea Bubble prompted Parliament to pass the so-called Bubble Act, which required that all joint-stock ventures secure a royal charter. This limited the formation of stock companies, for a charter was difficult and expensive to obtain. Eventually, however, the joint-stock company was to become as much the child of modern capitalism as the factory.

The early industrial enterprises, chiefly partnerships, could rely on a growing banking system to meet their capital needs. In the seventeenth century the goldsmiths of London had assumed the functions of bankers. They accepted and guarded deposits, extended loans, transferred upon request credits from one account to another, and changed money. In the eighteenth century banking services became available beyond London; country banks, of which there were 300 in 1780, numbered more than 700 in 1810. The English businessman was familiar with bank notes and other forms of commercial papers, and his confidence in paper facilitated the recruitment and flow of capital.

The founding of the Bank of England in 1694 itself marked an epoch in the history of European finance. It enjoyed a phenomenal success in the eighteenth century as it has since. It assumed responsibility for managing the public debt and sold shares in the debt (equivalent to shares in the bank) to the public. It faithfully met the interest payments due to the shareholders, with the help of government revenues it was given to administer, and simultaneously placed at the disposal of the government financial resources unavailable to any Continental state. The bank was so well run that it may have attracted investments away from the private sector of the economy. But stability in government finance also assured stability in the entire money market. Moreover the system also enlisted the tax powers of the government in the cause of industrialization. Taxes and interest payments took money from the mass of the people, who were likely to consume it, and gave it to the wealthy, who were likely to invest it. Some kind of forced savings was probably essential in preserving the high rate of reinvestment essential for industrialization.

Prices

The eighteenth century in Britain and in France and other regions of the West as well was thus an age of increasing wealth, but the economy did not expand steadily. Rather it experienced periods of sharp fluctuation, of rapid growth and severe decline, of boom and bust. French scholars have made particularly rigorous studies of the economic cycles of the period in France as revealed primarily through the history of prices. Their analyses have provided a new and powerful if sometimes controversial tool for investigating social change in eighteenth-century France and for interpreting the French Revolution itself.[2] We are less well in-

---

[2] The French historian E. Labrousse has written the fundamental studies on price movements in eighteenth-century France; see especially his *La crise de l'économie française à la fin de l'Ancien Régime et au début de la Révolution*. 1944.

formed concerning price movements and business cycles in other parts of Europe and in North America, but the available information suggests that the economy in these societies was behaving comparably to France's.

For the first thirty years of the eighteenth century, prices in France and apparently in England too remained stable. The economy similarly remained relatively stagnant, one reason being the exhaustion of the European states during the War of the Spanish Succession and the difficult decade and a half of readjustment following it. The economic eighteenth century, as some French scholars call it, began about 1730 and lasted until about 1817, the time of the peace settlements following the Napoleonic wars. Inflation in prices dominated the era. Since French money was kept stable after 1726, the strong upward movement must be attributed to other causes. The great increase in foreign trade brought a new abundance of precious metals to Europe, especially gold from Brazil. But primarily, as we shall see further, the price rise reflected the pressures of a growing population and a growing demand for food, land, goods, and employment.

The present-day reconstruction of price movements in the eighteenth century distinguishes four periods:

1. Phase A: inflation. After 1730 prices moved slowly upward. The movement accelerated between 1758 and 1770, bringing prosperity to some segments at least of French society and making these years the "splendor of Louis XV."
2. Phase B: depression. Prices leveled off about 1770 and began to move downward after 1778. The next decade was one of hard times, which aggravated the financial difficulties of the government.
3. The Revolution cycle. From 1787 to 1791 a series of bad harvests raised the prices of grain. Striking after a protracted period of hard times, these shocks helped precipitate the social and political crisis that ended France's *"ancien régime,"* the Old Regime.
4. Continuation of phase A. Inflation and prosperity, after 1791.

Over the long term the inflation did not affect all products, all sectors of the economy, and all segments of society equally. Prices in France between 1726 and 1789 increased by an average of about 65 percent. The cost of cereals, the basic food for the poor, rose slightly more than the average and considerably more than other agricultural products, such as wine and meat. Rents rose sharply, suggesting a shortage of available land; in relation to averages for the decade of the 1730s, rents paid in money had grown by 98 percent in the years 1786–1790. Wages on the other hand increased by a meager 22 percent in the same period, which would point to a glut of workers competing for employment.

These differentials had important social and economic effects. High rents in the countryside and low wages in the city took wealth from the poor and delivered it to the landlord and employer. This movement of money particularly benefited the entrepreneurial groups. Inflation helped drive many of the poor from the soil, to the advantage of their better-off neighbors, who were eager to expand their holdings; it was thus a principal cause of acute rural unrest. In the city it enabled the industrial entrepreneur to sell his goods for more and pay his workers less. Burdening the poor, it also worked against the economically inactive members of society—the nobles, for example, who lived from fixed rents or dues set in money. Inflation hurt the government too, for its revenues did not grow so fast as its expenditures. A large portion of French lands, owned by the aristocracy or the clergy, was tax-exempt. The government therefore relied primarily on indirect taxation that weighed on the lower classes, and they controlled less and less of the national wealth. Inflation was thus shrinking the traditional tax base of the French monarchy and paving the way for financial crisis.

These price changes were in turn influenced

by another factor, which also helped make the eighteenth century an age of revolutions—an enormous increase in the numbers of Europeans.

Population

What some French historians now call the demographic eighteenth century began about 1730. Reasonable estimates put the population growth of Europe at between 60 and 80 percent over the following 100 years. Probably never before had Western Europe experienced so rapid and substantial an increase in its people, and never has it since. (In Eastern Europe, especially the lands of the Russian Empire, a comparable population explosion occurred after 1860.) The growth was particularly marked in Great Britain and France. England grew from an estimated 5 million people in 1700 to more than 9 million in 1801, the date of the first British census. Swelled by continuous immigration and a high birth rate, the population of England's North American colonies grew at probably twice the English rate—from an estimated 275,000 in 1700 to 3.93 million in 1790. The French, according to various estimates, numbered 16 to 19 million at the death of Louis XIV, in 1715, and probably 26 million or more in 1789. With an estimated 18 percent of the total population in Europe about 1750, France was by far the most populous nation in the West; the Russian Empire alone surpassed her, and only by a few million. Her proportion of Europe's inhabitants reached its peak in the age of the Revolution and Napoleon, after which it fell continuously until the present generation. The country's military and political dominance of Europe under Napoleon was in no small measure founded on this demographic preponderance.

Spain increased from perhaps 7 to 10 million and the Italian states from 9 to 13 million. Prussia was growing more rapidly, from perhaps 1.7 to 3.1 million. But all these countries remained thinly populated in comparison with France, and they were not to feel the full pressures emanating from population growth until the following century.

Much mystery surrounds the reasons for this population explosion. Historians once spoke with confidence of a "demographic transition." According to this simple and appealing theory, the population in traditional societies reproduces itself at a rate close to the biological maximum, but its growth is impeded by an equivalently high death rate. The immediate impact of industrialization is a reduction of the death rate, principally through improved measures of public health. The yawning gap between the steady birth rate, which continues high, and the dropping death rate results in substantial expansion of total numbers. Eventually, however, in the later stages of industrialization, the birth rate declines, settles to equilibrium with the death rate, and this slows to a halt the further growth of population.

The most recent research in historical demography has questioned and modified, without entirely rejecting, this classical model. The system of reproduction prevailing in traditional European society seems to have been homeostatic or self-adjusting: that is, birth rates rarely attained the biological maximum, but tended to vary in exact correspondence with death rates. This assured a stable population, which lived well within its available resources. The initial break with this homeostatic system involved births rather than deaths. In England, for example, according to rough but reliable estimates, the birth rate rose from 33.6 per thousand population in the first half of the eighteenth century to 39.7 in the latter half, a peak never since attained. Thereafter the English birth rate entered upon a path of slow, irregular but eventually substantial decline.

Why did births initially increase? A likely explanation is that the booming commerce and new industries created jobs. Jobs in turn enaplentiful, and washable cotton garments allowed new levels of personal cleanliness. Soon, cheap iron pipes brought clean water into households and carried sewage away, both moved by the cheap power of steam. Medical advances such as the development of the vaccination helped protect the population. On the other hand, the growth of large cities introduced millions into a biologically unfavorable environment. In many great European cities, death rates did not sink below birth rates until the second half of the nineteenth century. In most great European cities, infant mortality remained stubbornly high for well into the twentieth century.

Still, over the long term, the death rate was declining, and it fell more rapidly than the relative number of births. The theory of a demographic transition retains a certain crude validity. But it is not at all a full description of the behavior of the population in the period of industrialization. As research continues we may hope to learn more concerning this basic change in the terms of human life, one of the great turning points in Western history.

III. AGRICULTURE

The term "Industrial Revolution" misleadingly conveys that the economic changes of the time were confined to the cities, but in fact the countryside too was necessarily affected. In England in 1700, an estimated 80 percent of the population lived directly from agriculture; by about 1800 that portion had fallen to approximately 40 percent. This massive shift of labor and resources from agriculture to industry would have been inconceivable had the countryside not been able to supply a greater abundance of food with a reduced amount of labor. To be sure, change came only slowly to rural areas, especially on the Continent; the peasant cultivators clung tenaciously to traditional ways. But significant improvements were still

---

THE VITAL REVOLUTION IN IRELAND

Year	Millions of Persons	Year	Millions of Persons
1712	2.8	1781	4.0
1718	2.9	1785	4.0
1725	3.0	1788	4.4
1732	3.0	1791	4.8
1754	3.2	1821	6.8
1757	3.5	1831	7.8
1772	3.6	1841	8.2
1777	3.7		

Ireland, thinly settled in the seventeenth century, experienced one of the highest rates of population growth in Western Europe from c. 1700 until 1841. The increase was closely associated with the spread of potato cultivation, but it cannot be determined whether the potato removed previous limits on population size, or whether the population, growing for other reasons, turned more and more to that easily cultivated plant. The figures to 1791 are adopted from K. H. Connell, *The Population of Ireland* (Oxford, 1950), p. 25. The later figures are from official censuses.

---

bled young persons to depart early from the homes in which they grew up, to marry, and to begin families sooner than would otherwise have been possible. Ready employment also favored procreation; children could earn wages at early ages and were more an asset than a burden to their families. Still, this spurt in births may have occurred in advance of significant economic expansion. Did incremented births stimulate the economy, or did a stimulated economy encourage births? Historians can only affirm that the two were intimately connected.

The impact of industrialization upon deaths was slow in appearing and equally complex. In many ways, the industrial system aided people to longer lives. Established trading networks and cheap transport allowed food to be carried efficiently over great distances, and took the edge off most years of famine and dearth. Living standards, fluctuating but slowly improving, led to better care for children and the sick and better nutrition and hygiene for all. Cheap, achieved in agricultural methods, and these in turn enabled the countryside to supply the industrial towns with food, labor, capital, and markets.

The Enclosure Movement in Great Britain

The considerable improvement that Britain experienced in agricultural technology in the eighteenth century contributed greatly to her industrialization. In any agricultural system the central problem is the restoration of fertility to the soil, especially after repeated harvests. Since the Early Middle Ages, farmers in Europe had relied principally on resting their lands periodically under the two- and three-field system of crop rotation (see Chapter 6). This allowed bacteria in the soil to take needed nitrogen from the air. A quicker method, heavy manuring, could not be used widely because the poorly productive farms could not support sufficient animals.

The secret of improving agricultural productivity lay in suppressing the fallow periods. This required that more animals be produced to provide the necessary fertilizer. One of the first of the British landlords to seek a solution was Jethro Tull, an agriculturist and inventor. Much of his work was impeded by false assumptions prevalent in the first half of the eighteenth century—for example that plants actually devour the soil and that animal fertilizer is bad for them. But the zeal with which he conducted his experiments proved infectious. He also designed a horse-drawn hoe and a mechanical seeder, early steps in the mechanization of agriculture.

By the late eighteenth century, Norfolk, in the east of England, had achieved particular prominence for its techniques of "high farming." In the 1730s Tull's contemporary Charles "Turnip" Townshed stressed, as his nickname suggests, the value of using turnips and other field crops in a rotation system of planting instead of letting the land lie fallow. Some five decades later Thomas William Coke wrote extensively on field grasses, new fertilizers such as oil-cake and bone manure, and the principles of efficient estate management. The eighteenth-century high farmers also experimented with the selective breeding of animals. Coke improved the Suffolk breed of pigs, adding to the advances made by Robert Bakewell, a generation his senior, who had developed the Leicestershire breed of sheep and dramatically increased the weight of marketed cattle.

To make use of the new methods, the improving farmers had to be free to manage the land as they saw fit. This was all but impossible under the open-field system, which had dominated the countryside since the Middle Ages. Characteristically even the largest landlords held their property in numerous elongated strips that were open to the land of their neighbors. Owners of contiguous strips had to follow the same routines of cultivation. One could not raise grasses to graze cattle when another was raising wheat. The village as a whole determined what routines should be followed and was thus the effective manager of each holding. The village also decided such matters as how many cattle each member could graze on common meadows and how much wood he could take from the forest. The open-field system froze the technology of cultivation at the levels attained in the Middle Ages. The landlord who wished to form a compact farm and apply new methods could not function within this framework. He needed the freedom to innovate.

He could gain that freedom only by enclosing his property. But both common law and cost considerations ruled out fencing the long, narrow strips. The entire village had to be enclosed, and this required the agreement of all its members, even the poorest. Voluntary enclosures were thus nearly impossible to arrange. There was an alternative, however: an act of Parliament, usually passed in response to a petition, allowing the enclosure of a village even against the opposition of some of its members. The procedure was difficult and expensive. The lands of the village had to be surveyed and redistributed in compact blocks among the members in proportion to their former holdings. Frequently, too, roads had to be constructed to ensure access to the fields. But over the course of the eighteenth century, the high rents and returns to be earned thanks to the new methods were making enclosures very desirable investments.

The first parliamentary act authorizing the enclosure of a village was registered in 1710, but this recourse was not exercised often until after the 1750s. Then the number of acts soared: 156 passed in 1750–1760 but 906 in 1800–1810. This sweeping change all but eradicated the traditional village and the open-field system from the British countryside.

While the enclosure movement was clearly rational from an economic standpoint, it brought much human misery in its wake. The redistribution of the land deprived the poor of their precious rights in the commons and often left them with tiny, unprofitable plots. Frequently they were forced to sell their holdings to their richer neighbors and seek employment as landless laborers or urban workers.

Historians have interpreted the importance of enclosures in English economic and social history variously. They have viewed the system as a counterpart or even a precondition of industrialization in the cities. The peasant cultivator, thrown off the soil, provided the factories with cheap labor; the productive fields yielded the needed food; the prosperous gentry and its tenants purchased the manufactured products and helped provide industrial capital. Today research is showing that enclosures did not perhaps mesh quite so neatly with industrialization. There was no massive rural depopulation in their wake; the industrial labor force seems to have recruited its members as much from artisans already established in the towns as from the dislodged rural poor.

On the other hand, it would be unwise to discount the importance of this movement. It transformed the English countryside even in a physical sense, giving it the appearance it retains today: the large, verdant fields, neatly defined by hedges and walls. It resulted in the near-disappearance of the peasant cultivator, working his own land in the village of his ancestors. If enclosures did not violently push people to the towns, neither did they encourage growth in rural settlements. They were therefore a major factor in the steady shift of population from countryside to city and in the emergence of the first truly urban, truly industrial society in the modern world.

Agriculture on the Continent

Change came more slowly to the countryside in Continental regions. The centers that witnessed the most active development were the Netherlands, the Paris basin and the northeast of France, the Rhineland, and the Po valley—all areas of dense settlement where high prices for food encouraged investments in agricultural improvements. Many great landlords emulated the British in improving methods of cultivation.

Continental farmers also waged a battle for managerial freedom, though it was by no means so sweeping as the English enclosure movement. For example many French villages worked the land under a system similar to the open-field arrangement known as *vaine pâture* ("empty pasture," or fallow). This too required owners to follow the same routines of cultivation as their neighbors, with the village determining the rights of its members on common lands. From the middle of the century on, the representative assemblies of several provinces outlawed obligatory *vaine pâture* and allowed individual owners to enclose their land, and some authorized the division of communal properties. But the French monarchy did not adopt enclosures as national policy, and after 1771 even the provincial governments no longer seem to have authorized or required them. Traces of the medieval village and the medieval countryside thus lasted longer in France and other Continental regions than in England.

There is a further contrast between Great Britain and the Continent that is of considerable interest in social history. Enclosures in Britain led to the domination of rural society by great landlords and prosperous tenant farmers, who usually held the land under long leases. In France on the eve of the Revolution, probably 35 percent of the land was owned by the peasants who worked it. In this regard the French peasants were more favored than those of any other European country, Britain included.

If the soil had been worked efficiently and if the population had remained stable, the distribution of the land would clearly have been socially advantageous. But in fact small peasant proprietors rarely had the resources to adopt new techniques, and their very numbers, apparently growing rapidly, obstructed their efforts. The society of small farmers was therefore vulnerable to population pressures and was easily disturbed by violent movements in prices—two major characteristics of eighteenth-century economic history, as we have seen. Because of poor transportation one region could easily suffer a food shortage or even famine while neighboring areas were enjoying relative plenty. The pattern of land distribution in France and the character of rural society, superficially so favorable to the peasant, was thus also a source of acute unrest in the countryside.

In the regions close to the Mediterranean Sea, difficult geographical and climatic conditions—the often rugged terrain, thin soil, and a dearth of summer rain—did not readily allow the introduction of new techniques. The peasants continued to work their lands much as they had in the Late Middle Ages and for the same poor reward. The eastern regions of the Holy Roman Empire, Poland, and Russia had participated hardly at all in the commercial expansion of the early modern period; capital remained scarce and interest rates high. The political fragmentation of the empire and a paucity of transportation in Poland and Russia limited the size of the markets and the incentives to higher production. Areas close to the Baltic Sea, such as east Prussia, benefited from the growing demand for cereals in Western countries, but on the whole Eastern Europe was not to experience the full force of agricultural change until the next century.

IV. THE NEW SHAPE OF INDUSTRY

In manufacturing, the essential achievement of the Industrial Revolution was an enormous increase in the productivity of labor. This was attributable to two innovations: the development of more efficient tools and machines, and the exploitation of new sources of energy. Economists would call this process "factor substitution," whereby capital, represented by the new tools and machines, was substituted for the skills and energy of men. Initially the new tools were cheap and simple enough to be used by artisans in the home or in small workshops. But the growing complexity of machinery, in particular the application of steam, called into being a new social unit—the factory. The new system of production changed the face of the great European cities and brought in its wake acute new social and political problems.

Coal and Iron

The most successful innovations of the Industrial Revolution were dependent upon efficient utilization of raw materials, particularly cheap metals such as iron, which could be formed into machines, and cheap fuel such as coal. Countries poorly endowed with these resources (as, for example, the Mediterranean lands of Europe) faced formidable obstacles in their industrial growth. England, on the other hand,

Revolutions of the Eighteenth Century 677

In this design of a blast furnace, taken from a French copper engraving of the eighteenth century, the large water wheel powers the bellows, which in turn supply the needed jets of air to raise the temperature of the furnace. The continued importance of water power was a principal reason why many early factories were built in rustic settings.
(Photo: The Granger Collection)

was well supplied, and her deposits of coal were found in convenient proximity to her iron ore.

Since the Late Middle Ages, the English economy was handicapped by a shortage of wood, as the once great forests had been progressively cut down. Consequently England turned in ever greater measures to the use of coal as fuel, to heat homes, brew beer and ale, heat the vats for dyeing cloth, or fire the furnaces for making glass, pottery, or bricks. As miners began taking coal from deeper veins, they often penetrated beneath the water table and faced the critical task of pumping out the water. The need for powerful pumps stimulated experiments to harness steam in the late seventeenth century. A successful solution came with the development of the Savery and Watt engines. In the nineteenth century when steam was used to propel ships and trains, coal could be transported cheaply from mine to furnace. This allowed the price of coal to plummet.

In one process, however, coal was not satisfactory: the smelting of iron. Here the fuel had to be burned in direct contact with the iron ore, and mineral impurities in the coal combined with the iron to make an unsatisfactory product. Ironmasters traditionally used charcoal in the making of high-quality, malleable or wrought iron, but charcoal was expensive and the output of wrought iron consequently limited. In 1709 Alexander Darby succeeded in smelting ore with coke prepared from coal, but his invention had little immediate impact on the industry. Ironmasters used coke for smelting pig iron, which could be cast but not worked or machined. To refine the metal into wrought iron or steel they continued to use charcoal.

But the demand for and price of iron rose after 1760, and this stimulated the development of new techniques. In the early 1780s Henry Cort devised the puddling process, the first commercially feasible effort to purify iron using coke alone. This invention freed ironmaking from dependence on forests. Ironmasters were simultaneously growing more adept at utilizing the metal. Perhaps the most skilled of them was John Wilkinson, a man with boundless faith that iron would become the basic building material of the new age. His improved techniques for boring cylinders made both better steam engines and better cannons possible. He built the first iron bridge in the world over the Severn River in 1779, experimented with iron rails, launched an iron boat, and at his death was buried in an iron coffin.

Lost-cost metal, which could be precisely machined, and low-cost fuel in turn removed the chief obstacles to major and continuing improvements in the techniques of making goods.

Inventions in Textile Production

In Great Britain the industry that led all others in growth and technological improvements was the manufacture of cotton cloth. Its beginnings were modest; wool had been the traditional basis of urban industry everywhere in Europe. Spinners could not produce a sturdy thread from cotton fiber, so that weavers used it principally in combination with other threads, such as linen or wool.

In the early eighteenth century, several factors gave a powerful stimulus to both technological development and investment in cotton manufacturing. Trade with India had brought large quantities of muslin, calico, madras, and other fine cottons to England and built a healthy market. Wool could not be painted or printed, and cotton fabrics with bright designs appealed to the tastes of the age. To limit the competition that Indian cottons offered to domestically produced wool, in 1700 Parliament prohibited the importation of printed calicoes from India, Persia, and China and in 1721 even tried to prohibit the wearing of certain kinds of cotton cloth. By obstructing imports the government unwittingly provided a marvelous opportunity for the domestic entrepreneur. Fortune awaited those who could market cottons comparable in quality and price to those once imported from the East.

The industry thus had a double task: to speed its production processes and to improve the quality of the finished cloth. Spinning could be done by women in conjunction with their daily chores, but weaving was slow and difficult work, almost always done by men. In 1738 John Kay of Lancashire, by profession a clockmaker, invented a flying shuttle, propelled by hammers instead of passed by hand. It accelerated the weaving process, removed restrictions on the width of the cloth, and reduced the number of workers needed on a broadcloth loom.

Now the weavers could work more quickly and efficiently than the spinners. To speed the production of thread and restore equilibrium among the processes of manufacture, James Hargreaves devised his spinning jenny in the mid-1760s. The jenny, like the flying shuttle, required no source of power beyond the worker's muscle, and it could spin between six and eight threads simultaneously; later models could make as many as eighty. About the same time Richard Arkwright produced a spinner called the water frame that drew cotton fibers through rollers and twisted them into thread. Much dispute surrounds Arkwright's claim to this invention; it is likely that he pirated its basic design. But if his originality is questionable, he did possess qualities of imagination, daring, and drive. He was an entrepreneur, one of the first self-made men to lead the Industrial Revolution.

The water frame, as its name suggests, was too large to be driven by human exertion. Arkwright first used horses, but within a few years he built a factory driven by a water mill. In 1785 he adopted the steam engine as his source of power, and the modern factory was born. Technical advances kept apace. A weaver named Samuel Crompton combined the features of the jenny and the water frame into a spinning mule—so called because it was a hybrid—which spun a fine and strong thread, excelling in quality the best Indian product. Once more the equilibrium of the productive processes was disrupted, and the now-slower work of weaving restricted output. In 1784 Edmund Cartwright designed a power loom, though technical difficulties and the violent opposition of weavers limited the use of the loom until after the Napoleonic wars.

Other inventions accelerated other processes in cotton manufacturing during the last two decades of the century. An American, Eli Whitney, produced the cotton gin, which mechanized and enormously accelerated the separation of seed from fiber in the raw cotton. Sir Thomas Bell developed a method for printing the cotton cloth on cylindrical copper presses, and British and Continental inventors improved the chemical processes of bleaching and tinting the cloth.

Cotton production soared. Lancashire, with its great city of Manchester, and the neighboring counties became the great centers of cotton manufacture, soon serving the entire world. These were thinly settled areas before the eighteenth century, with few incorporated towns and no established guild systems to obstruct innovation. Lancashire offered the further advantages of water power, coal, and a good harbor, Liverpool. In 1743 England had imported about 1 million pounds of raw cotton; the figure was over 60 million by the turn of the century. And by the early 1820s cotton exports made up 46 percent of Britain's export trade.

Harnessing Steam

Arkwright's water frame, Crompton's spinning mule, and Cartwright's power loom all required energy beyond the ability of men or horses to provide. Even earlier, as we have seen, the mining industry had developed a critical need for cheap power. Since ancient times men had noticed that steam exerts strong pressure. The third-century Greek scientist Hero of Alexandria had employed a jet of steam to spin a small wheel; the account of his experiments, translated into English in 1575, helped alert scholars to a simple means by which heat could be converted into motion. However, the first experiments with engines powered by fire were based on another principle: the pressure the atmosphere exerts against a vacuum.

In the seventeenth century several scientists—among them Pascal in France and Otto von Guericke in Germany—proved that the atmosphere has weight. Guericke used atmospheric pressure to push a piston through a cylinder, overcoming the efforts of twenty men to restrain it. Sensational experiments like this one led directly to efforts to construct an "atmospheric engine." To create the vacuum some inventors tried gunpowder, but the fuel was too unstable to control. Steam was more manageable, and before the end of the century, atmospheric machines were being designed both in England and on the Continent that utilized the condensation of steam to create the needed vacuum.

The inventor of what must be considered the first commercially successful atmospheric engine was an Englishman, Thomas Savery, who described it to the public in a book published in 1702 and significantly entitled *The Miner's Friend*. Working as a pump, Savery's invention allowed the steam to come into direct contact with the water it was moving; this condensed the steam, dissipated heat, and rendered the pump woefully inefficient. However, Savery's engine at least proved that a fire pump was a practical possibility. A decade later another Englishman, Thomas Newcomen, returned to the piston and cylinder design and completely separated the engine from the pump. Although it still wasted a great deal of power, its reintroduction of the piston made it more efficient than Savery's by a third, and Newcomen engines were soon being used not only in Great Britain but in Hungary, Austria, France, and Denmark.

In the 1760s a young mechanic and instrument maker working at the University of Glasgow, James Watt, was given the task of repairing a small Newcomen engine used in scientific lectures. He recognized its two major inefficiencies: its great weight in relation to its power output and the quantities of fuel it required. Fascinated by the problem, he redesigned the machine and made the fundamental change of providing a separate chamber for the spent steam to condense in. His first engine, patented in 1769, was essentially an improved Newcomen engine, still relying on atmospheric pressure for its principal motive force.

But Watt had also recognized the advantage of using the pressure of expanding steam directly. The implementation of this idea took many years and required new levels of precision in machining cylinders and pistons, new designs for valves, and new knowledge of lubricants and the properties of steam itself. Watt's first practical model incorporating this principle, patented in 1782, was nearly three times more efficient than the Newcomen engine, its distant parent. He also devised a system of gears, called the sun and planet, for converting the reciprocating motion of the piston to the rotary motion needed to drive most machines. A still more important invention was the governor, or flywheel, which smoothed the movements of the engine.

Watt's partner, the industrialist Matthew Boulton, shared the merit of placing the inventions at the service of the economy. The site of Boulton's plant was Birmingham, which became the first great center for the manufacture of these new and powerful machines. From the 1780s on the steam engine was giving power to factories as well as pumps; some 500 were built before 1800.

Even these early machines represented a remarkable improvement over traditional sources of power, ranging as they did between 6 and 20 horsepower. The average man working hard can muster about one-tenth horsepower, or about 75 watts. This would not be enough to drive most of the major appliances in American homes today, such as washers, vacuum cleaners, dryers, even beaters and blenders. The horse itself works continuously at a power output of only one-half horsepower. James Watt himself first defined the unit of horsepower as 33,000 foot-pounds per minute, but this could be achieved only by the strongest horses and only for short periods. So poor in power output are animals—men and horses—that even before the advent of the steam engine they were far surpassed by windmills and water mills.

The largest windmills in the eighteenth century could develop probably as much as 50 horsepower, but perhaps two-thirds of this was lost in friction as the power was transmitted from the rotors to the pump or mill. The best water mills of the period seem to have produced 10 horsepower, but most of them rarely surpassed 5. Still, this would replace 10 or more horses and save the miller the expense of feeding and caring for so many animals. With such advantages the construction of water mills rapidly quickened over the course of the eighteenth century; flowing water rather than steam powered the early phases of the Industrial Revolution. But then too sometimes winds ceased and streams froze, and water and wind power could not be transmitted from where it was harnessed to where it was needed. Steam engines could both produce more power more reliably and be placed where they were needed. To the traditional power-starved economy of Great Britain as of the world, the steam engine offered an enormous increment in its capacity to do work. More than any other invention, its appearance marks the advent of a new era.

Industry on the Continent

Industrial growth was much slower on the Continent than in England. The numerous political divisions, tolls and tariffs, and the difficulties of transport restricted the size of markets. Continental society was more stratified than the English and did not develop effective mechanisms for recruiting the sons of nobles and gentry for business careers. It was also apparently less wealthy and could not initially generate a strong demand for industrial products. Business enterprises tended to be small, largely restricted to members of the same family, and cautious in policy. Cultural attitudes still placed high prestige on the life of the country gentleman, and this blocked the flow of men and capital from agriculture to manufactures.

Yet the Continental countries were experiencing important industrial changes, if not a revolution, in the eighteenth century. In France, cotton industries were taking root in Alsace, Normandy, and the region of Lille on the borders of the Austrian Netherlands. At Rouen, in Normandy, the largest center of cotton manufacture, production grew by 107 percent between 1732 and 1766. John Kay introduced his flying shuttle at Rouen in that period, and toward the end of the century the industry, while still comparatively backward, was adopting English-model mechanical spinners. The silk cloth industry, first promoted by Colbert, enjoyed a comparable boom, benefiting from the growing affluence of eighteenth-century fashionable society. At Lyons, the center of silk manufacture with a population of perhaps 143,000, the silk shops alone came to employ some 30,000 workers.

Coal production was also expanding. At Anzin, in northeastern France, one of the earliest centers of large-scale coal mining, output grew by 681 percent between 1744 and 1789. Iron manufacture at first lagged behind. The first foundry utilizing coke rather than charcoal went into operation only in 1769, and the industry's total output increased by only 72 percent in the half-century preceding 1789. Nonetheless, the iron as well as the coal works furnished France early if still restricted examples of the factory system; they also equipped her with an armaments industry destined to serve her well during the wars of the French Revolution.

Switzerland too was a region of early industrial growth. Her ancient mercantile traditions, abundant resources in water power, and strategic position on the passes linking northern and southern Europe gave her distinct advantages in developing cotton manufactures and other forms of light industry. French Flanders (the southern half of the Austrian Netherlands), the valley of the lower Rhine, Silesia (acquired by Prussia in 1741), and Bohemia-Moravia were other centers of modest but real industrial growth, especially in textiles. In Germany and Central Europe the wars and reforms of the French revolutionary period, while frequently disruptive, also served to eradicate many of the institutional obstacles to trade. Growth still came slowly, and no continental region could challenge the industrial supremacy of England before 1850. But well in advance of that date, these areas were laying the basis for a strong leap forward.

While changing its basic methods of raising food and producing goods, European society was also engaged in reforming its fundamental institutions and principles of government.

V. CONSTITUTIONAL CONFLICTS

The great expansion in population, the growth of the economy, and changes visible in almost every other aspect of eighteenth-century life profoundly disturbed the political structures of European society. Groups within the various states believed, often with good reason, that these transformations were hurting their interests, and that their governments were unresponsive to their needs. They therefore agitated for constitutional reforms, which would ensure them a stronger voice in the determination of policy. The latter half of the century in particular was a period of high political tension, constitutional crises, and spirited debate over the proper functions and organization of government.

The Estates

To understand the nature of the constitutional crises, we must first recall a salient characteristic of government under the old regimes. In virtually all the governments of Europe, a role of major importance was assigned to the corporations of citizens known as estates. By definition an estate was a functional group within society—clerics, who prayed; nobles, who fought and counseled; merchants, who traded; and artisans and peasants, who labored. Birth or appointment gave people admission to the various estates, and membership conferred certain distinctive rights and obligations. Through parliaments or assemblies the estates were also supposed to play a role in making government decisions.

Traditionally the clergy constituted the first estate and the nobles the second, but usually these two groups maintained a common aristocratic viewpoint. The ruler was also an estate, considered a corporation of one in his person—or rather his office; he had, in the political imagery of the day, another body that never died. This is implied in the usual acclamation of subjects at the death of their sovereign: "The king is dead. Long live the king!" Beneath these privileged orders was the estate of the common people, the third estate in France or simply the commons in England. In most European domains this was the most amorphous and the least influential of the constituent bodies of society.

The estates were developing self-awareness and political ambition in the eighteenth century, and most remarkable, in the latter half even the third estate came to exert its latent power. In 1788 a French priest, Emmanuel Joseph Sieyès, posed the question in a pamphlet, "What is the third estate?" He replied simply that it was everything—the entire nation, the people. He noted further that in the past it had been nothing, but now its ambition was to become a force in the state. His assessment of both the past and the future was accurate. The rise to prominence and power of the common people at the expense of the hitherto dominant aristocratic orders make this period, as one historian calls it, the "age of the democratic revolution."[3]

Monarchical Reforms

In the great eighteenth-century struggle over the exercise of power, the ruler was often the first to seek and effect constitutional change. The rights and immunities of the separate estates, primarily the aristocratic orders, reduced his fiscal resources and often deprived him of authority in conducting foreign affairs and pursuing internal reform. The privileges and monopolies enjoyed by provinces, towns, and guilds further restrained trade, hampered economic growth, and militated against the common welfare, of which eighteenth-century heads of state increasingly believed themselves the chief defenders.

The enlightened despots of the period made an attack on obstructive privilege a usual part of their policy, and many of them may be considered crowned constitutional reformers. Sweden offers perhaps the best example. Her estates, meeting in a four-house Diet (or Riksdag), long held the king in trammels, as he could not tax, change the laws, or make war, peace, or alliances without their agreement. The Diet itself offered no effective leadership because it was divided into hostile factions, especially among the nobles, that spent their energies in ceaseless battles for office and patronage and readily sold their support to foreign powers eager to influence Swedish policy, notably France or Russia.

In 1771 a new king trained in France and imbued with liberal ideas, Gustavus III, ascended the throne. The following year, with the aid of the army and French support, he mounted a coup d'état against the Diet. At the point of bayonets, he forced a constitution on the houses—the first comprehensive, written document of its kind adopted by a European state. It gave the king broader if still limited powers: the Diet could assemble only on royal summons and could discuss only what the king proposed, though its agreement was still necessary for new taxes and laws.

Gustavus then proceeded to remake Swedish institutions, almost without the Diet's participation. He changed the laws governing ownership and inheritance of land, opened offices to all classes, reformed the courts, tried to suppress corruption, established freedom of the press and of religion, and lifted restrictions on trade in grain. Stung by the reforms, which often touched their privileges, the nobles grew ever more disgruntled and from 1786 on openly challenged the king's authority. In 1788 they refused to support him in a war he had declared against Russia. In response, through the Act of Union and Security the next year, Gustavus once more altered the constitution, allocating to the king sole authority in foreign affairs and still further diminishing the role of the aristocracy in the Swedish state. Deprived of constitutional means of expressing their dissent, the dissatisfied nobles conspired against the king, who was shot dead at a masquerade in 1792. This dramatic incident later inspired Giuseppe Verdi's opera *The Masked Ball,* first produced in Rome in 1859. To soothe the censors, who looked askance at successful conspiracies, Verdi changed the locale to Boston, Massachusetts; he made Gustavus himself an English governor, who presumably could die on stage without undermining the public order.

If Gustavus' career offers an excellent example of fundamental reforms imposed from above, it also shows the violent opposition such policies could evoke from the aristocracy. In many European states the aristocracy was not content simply to defend its traditional privileges but agitated for a still larger share in the exercise of power.

---

[3] See especially R. R. Palmer, *The Age of the Democratic Revolution.* 1959–1964.

Aristocratic Resurgence

Europe's aristocracies had understandable cause for discontent with the changes occurring in the eighteenth century. The growth of trade, the expansion of capital, and pervasive inflation left many nobles hard-pressed economically, and as a countermeasure many of them tried to reactivate their ancient and half-forgotten feudal prerogatives over the peasants. In the political sphere as well, monarchs were allocating a progressively smaller place to the nobles in the business of government.

Aristocracies all over Europe thus sought to advance their fortunes and consolidate what they took to be their rightful place under their countries' constitutions. Armed with the ideas of Montesquieu, they claimed that nobles had the exclusive right to serve as the chief counselors of the king as well as the obligation of leading the community in the conduct of its important affairs. By the last decades of the century, the aristocracy had in fact secured a near-monopoly over high offices in both the state and the church. In 1781 for example the rank of commissioned officer in the French army was limited almost exclusively to those who could show four generations of nobility. And on the eve of the Revolution, the 18 archbishops, 118 bishops, and 8,000 canons (high ecclesiastics) in the French Church were all of noble extraction; in contrast half this group had come from bourgeois stock in 1730. Simultaneously aristocrats demanded that the assemblies of estates, which they dominated or hoped to dominate, be granted a larger share of political power.

Perhaps the best example of a revolution led by the aristocracy in support of such claims arose in the Austrian Netherlands. The ten provinces were governed under charters granted by the Hapsburgs and other rulers that dated back to the Middle Ages. Representative assemblies, which controlled the government in all the provinces, largely determined the laws and imposed the taxes, apparently the lightest

The Comte de Mirabeau (1749–1791), depicted here in a sketch by the great revolutionary artist J. L. David, was one of the most colorful and capable leaders of the Estates General and the Constituent Assembly. Scarred from childhood by smallpox, he enjoyed unlikely success in pursuing and seducing women. Involved in many scandalous affairs, he was several times imprisoned. His experiences in jail led him to write a tract on prison reform, on which his political reputation was founded. In the heady days of the early Revolution, his sharp intellect and fluid rhetoric won him prominence. "I am a mad dog," he once proclaimed, "from whose bites despotism and privilege must die."
(Photo: Photographie Bulloz, Paris)

in the whole of Europe. Guilds, whose privileges similarly dated from the Middle Ages, were particularly strong in the Flemish towns and tightly regulated the economy.

In the 1780s Holy Roman Emperor Joseph II of Austria as part of a general reform of his realm sought to centralize and modernize Hapsburg administration of the southern Netherlands. He tried to abolish the special privileges enjoyed by the ten provinces, and in the interest of freeing the economy, he also sought to break the guild monopolies. Much to the alarm of the United Provinces and Britain, he tried as well to reopen the port of Antwerp, which had been closed to international trade since 1648. These changes were coupled with other liberal reforms—the abolition of torture, the introduction of religious toleration, the suppression of some few monasteries, and the important social reforms for the rural population that were discussed in Chapter 19. Finally, in 1787 he overhauled the court system, under which the estates had exercised their chief judicial and administrative prerogatives.

The patricians protested these reforms. In late 1788 the representative assemblies of two provinces refused to grant Joseph money, and the emperor retaliated by revoking their ancient charters, with the aim of bringing them under the direct and unlimited powers of the crown. The frightened aristocrats organized secret societies, called Pro Aris et Focis ("For Altars and Hearths"), the name implying an objection to Joseph's treatment of the Catholic Church. The following year, doubtless encouraged by the defiance of the Estates General in France, the provinces declared their independence. In the face of concerted opposition, Austrian rule collapsed. But the revolutionaries now found themselves divided. One party, led by a Brussels lawyer, held that independence from Austria sufficed and no further changes were required. The provinces should be ruled by their assemblies, which meant by their traditional aristocracies. But a second party, led by another lawyer, sought to limit the privileges of the provinces, guilds, and assemblies. These democrats, as they were called, now faced the aristocrats in a struggle over the constitution of the land. In 1790, with the support of the church and most of the peasants, the conservatives prevailed, and the leaders of the democratic faction were forced into exile.

The death of Joseph II the same year and the succession of his brother Leopold II further complicated the picture. Leopold was about as sympathetic to reform as a monarch could be in the eighteenth century, and he energetically sought to make a common front with the democrats against the aristocrats. The coalition was successful, and Austrian rule was restored in the provinces in December. The democrats flocked back, but the coalition between the monarch and the people never had the opportunity to reform the government freely. The increasing radicalism of the Revolution in France made Leopold progressively suspicious of the intentions of his own democratic allies. Finally, in 1792 French revolutionary armies poured into the Austrian Netherlands and ended all possibility of peacefully wrought change.

Popular Movements

In their competition for power, both monarchs and aristocrats were likely to seek an ally in the politically inert but potentially powerful third estate, the people. The small Swiss city of Geneva offers an early example of popular participation in movements for reform. In England too, by the late eighteenth century, popular reform movements were assuming major importance in politics.

Geneva

Socially and juridically, the population of Geneva was divided into three groups. The patricians held the highest offices and dominated the Small Council, the executive body or board of governors of the city. The burghers, representing about a fourth of the population, elected the Great Council, which could approve but not propose legislation and which chose the chief officers from lists prepared by the Small Council. The majority of the population, called natives, had no political rights and were also excluded from certain professions.

In the 1760s the patricians and burghers entered into a protracted argument over the exercise of power in the government. The Small Council for example tried to suppress certain writings of Jean Jacques Rousseau, himself born in Geneva and an honorary citizen; the burghers protested. In addition they claimed the right to initiate legislation and present it to the Small Council. Because they realized that this violated traditional constitutional procedure, the burghers took the step of appealing to theories of popular sovereignty—a fateful decision, for the same theories could be used against their own privileged status. They also cultivated the support of the totally disfranchised natives. In the face of violent agitation, the Small Council accepted a reform edict that enlarged the role of the Great Council in the government and extended certain minor concessions to the natives. The natives, now politically aroused, demanded that they be allowed to participate in political life. Riots broke out in 1770, and the government responded by suppressing the natives' political clubs and even threatening their leaders with death. In 1782, with the support of France, the government rescinded the reform edict. Fear of the people had brought a counterrevolution.

Great Britain

In Great Britain too a tripartite conflict arose involving the king, the aristocracy, and the people in the late eighteenth century. As elsewhere a major role in initiating a popular movement was played by a reforming monarch, George III (1760–1820). Unlike his namesake grandfather and great-grandfather, George had been born in England and knew the land, its language, and its political system well. He was also intent on advancing royal authority. He did not seek to bypass Parliament but rather tried, much as the Whig ministers had before him, to control its members through patronage and influence. The Whigs saw the royal ambitions and the system through which it worked as a threat to their own traditional hegemony. Not only did they oppose the king and his ministers in Parliament, but they enlisted the support of reform elements originating outside of Parliament itself.

One such group, known as the Radical Dissenters, was led by such men as the clergyman Richard Price and the scientist Joseph Priestley. The appearance of daily newspapers (the *Morning Post* was founded in 1772 and the *Times* in 1785) gave them a marvelous means of spreading their views, and they leveled destructive criticism against the defects of the British political system. Characteristically they called for representation proportionate to population, stricter laws against corruption, exclusion from the Commons of royal officeholders, and freedom of the press.

The most notorious of popular agitators was a journalist by the name of John Wilkes. Ambitious, eloquent, and ruthless, Wilkes purchased a seat in Parliament with the aid of an opportune marriage. But success through traditional channels came too slowly, and he assumed the risky but promising role of a popular champion for reform. He viciously attacked in print the king's prime minister, and indirectly the king himself over the terms of the Treaty of Paris in 1763, which he considered unfavorable to Britain's imperial interests. The government arrested him for sedition and libel on a general warrant—that is, with the name of the accused omitted. During his trial crowds in London marched in his support shouting "Wilkes and liberty," and the courts quashed the indictment. The government then accused him of having authored a pornographic poem, called "An Essay on Women," and this time Wilkes fled to France. There he stayed for four years, but in 1768, still under indictment, he returned to stand once more for Parliament. At his second attempt he was elected. Three times the Commons refused to seat him, and three times he was returned. With the ardent support of radicals and to the acclaim of the London crowds, Wilkes finally won his seat.

The agitation for parliamentary reform in Great Britain was soon swept up in the larger issues raised by the outbreak of the French Revolution. The events of 1789 across the Channel naturally frightened certain social groups, but the Revolution's opponents were initially drowned out in a chorus of enthusiasm that swept the literate classes in Britain as on the Continent. It was hard after all to defend what was taken to be the traditional despotism of the French monarchy. But the increasing radicalism of the Revolution generated disenchantment and hostility.

The Wilkes affair, the agitation for parliamentary reform, and the reactions to the uprisings in France characterized the reform movements in a British context; revolutionary action did not. Wilkes and other radicals appealed not only to the London crowds but also to many underprivileged groups—traders, craftsmen, and the like—who did have the franchise and were thus able to express their political dissatisfaction by voting Wilkes and other men displeasing to the government into Parliament. This added to the effectiveness of the reform movement, but it also diluted its revolutionary thrust. Most radicals called only for the reform, not the replacement, of the British political system. They still retained some measure of respect for the nation's political traditions.

Ireland and North America

Great Britain did face revolutionary agitation in her overseas possessions, notably Ireland and North America. In Ireland a largely Protestant gentry was demanding autonomy for the country's Parliament under the British king and reform in the trade laws, which injured the Irish economy. But the religious and cultural gulf that divided the Protestant gentry from the Catholic people prevented an effective alliance between them, and the throne was usually able to purchase the loyalty of the upper classes with relatively minor concessions. In 1782 for example, in response to agitation led by the Protestant patriots Henry Flood and Henry Grattan, Britain gave the Irish Parliament the sought-for autonomy. This assured the loyalty of Irish gentry during the final phase of the American Revolution and the more difficult struggle with revolutionary France.

In her thirteen North American colonies, Britain faced a much different situation. George III and his prime minister, Lord North, attempted to force the colonies to pay the costs, past and present, of their own defense. The policy would have meant a pronounced centralization of authority within the government of the British Empire.

The prominent landlords and merchants of the Eastern seaboard took the leadership in opposing the fiscal measures and the constitutional changes they implied. Like the upper classes in many European lands, they too applied to the third constituent division of society—the people. But the resistance in North America otherwise differed profoundly from comparable movements in Europe. The American social leaders could not appeal to a body of corporate privileges that the actions of the king were allegedly violating. They therefore appealed to the traditional rights enjoyed by all British subjects, regardless of rank, and to theories of popular sovereignty as advanced particularly by John Locke; the Declaration of Independence was to give eloquent expression to these broad concepts. The same lack of a true estate system in colonial American society, the amorphous and fluid margins separating the social strata, further prevented the development of conflicts between patricians and the lower social orders, which so often occurred in Europe.

These differences partially explain the unique character of the American Revolution. Its effects on society were limited. But in the theory that supported it and in the close and continuing alliance between the upper and lower classes, it was perhaps the most democratic of the revolutions of the eighteenth century. It created the first state and government in which the exercise of power was explicitly declared to be based not on divine right or inherited privilege but on the consent of the governed. It also represented the first successful revolution of an overseas colony against a European country. The example and effects of the American Revolution were thus of major importance in the dissolution of Europe's old regimes.

VI. THE FRENCH REVOLUTION

The pivotal event of European history in the eighteenth century—some would say in the modern epoch—was the French Revolution. From its outbreak in 1789, the Revolution touched and transformed social values and political systems, in France, in Europe, and eventually throughout the world. France's revolutionary regime conquered much of Europe with its arms and, slowly and inexorably, all of Europe with its ideals. Those ideals defined essentially the aspirations of modern, liberal society. The Revolution advocated liberty, that is, it rejected all forms of unwilling service—feudal charges laid upon the land, vestiges of personal serfdom, or slavery overseas. It further preached equality, denying the claims of privileged estates, guilds, corporations, and religions to special treatment before the law. A final revolutionary goal was fraternity, which meant that all citizens, regardless of race, status, or religion, should have equal access to every benefit society offered. *Liberté, egalité, fraternité:* this proud revolutionary slogan still represents a social ideal, to which most contemporary Europeans and Americans would continue to subscribe.

Origins

Those who made the Revolution thought they saw clearly the reasons for it. They were rising against tyrannical government, in which the people had no voice; and against inequality, in which taxes were imposed or benefits distributed unfairly. But these reasons, however accurate, cannot alone explain the revolutionary upsurge from 1789. The government of France was not more tyrannical or more unjust, than it had been for centuries. What failed in France's long-standing, long-accepted political system?

An easy answer would be to point to the incompetence of the head of state and his consort, Louis XVI and the queen, Marie Antoinette. Louis was a confused and indecisive man, much preferring to hunt deer and fix clocks than to supervise closely the routines of government. His young queen was frivolous and meddling. Perhaps better leaders might have saved the monarchy; we cannot tell. But even the most capable rulers could not have escaped challenge and crisis in the late eighteenth century. The roots of that crisis, not its mismanagement, claim the principal interest of historians.

In eighteenth-century France, ideological revolt preceded political revolt. The philosophes bombarded with devastating salvos many traditional practices, beliefs, and prejudices of society. They undermined the confidence that the old ways were the best ways. Expressed before the Revolution, these enlightened ideas guided many revolutionary policies. But did they cause the revolution? Probably not. The philosophes themselves never advocated violent change, and most harbored deep suspicions of the restless, ignorant masses. They did not question the fact that elites should rule society; they wished only that the elites should be enlightened.

Did the structure of French society provoke revolution? Karl Marx, and the many historians inspired by him, respond with a resounding

The Faubourg St.-Antoine was one of Paris' working-class quarters. In 1789 a dispute broke out between the workers and the owners of the Reveillon workshop, and the workers sacked both the shop and the owners' house. The French and Swiss Guards dispatched to punish them, were met with stones and pieces of tile rained down from the rooftops. The soldiers fired on their attackers, killing several. The incident, here depicted in a slightly later etching, illustrates the high social tension prevailing at Paris before the convocation of the Estates General.
(Photo: New York Public Library/Picture Collection)

yes. In their view, the Revolution was rooted in class struggle. In the words of a prominent French (and Marxist) historian, Albert Soboul, the upheaval represents "the classical model of a bourgeois revolution." In this view, the French middle classes, gaining in wealth during the eighteenth century, resented the privileges of the nobility and the obstacles that the old regime placed in the path of capitalist development. They fought to change social institutions in their own interest and claimed the seats of power in their own name. The Revolution, in sum, placed a bourgeois regime atop an already bourgeois economy.

This compelling theory has, however, evoked an equally vigorous rebuttal. Its critics question the coherence, some even the existence, of a capitalist bourgeoisie in eighteenth-century France. The barrier between the second and third estates was porous and often overlooked, and the lines of social division were frequently blurred. The gap between the nobles and the upper bourgeoisie was as nothing compared to the gulf that separated these orders, both privileged, from the common people. Moreover, the revolutionary leaders were lawyers and administrators, rarely merchants or industrialists. The leaders of the new economy looked with doubt and fear upon the revolutionary course, supposedly (according to Soboul) flowing in their favor. The bourgeoisie, in this interpretation, did not make the Revolution. Rather, the Revolution made the bourgeoisie, in the sense that the reforms it achieved stimulated decisive growth in the capitalist economy. While the arguments of the Marxists and their critics may appear contradictory, the two sides nevertheless agree that political and economic changes were intimately related in setting the course of revolution.

But class was not the only determinant of structure in French society in the revolutionary epoch. Another factor, which historians have come only recently to recognize, was age. In a period of rapid growth in population, French society needed to accommodate, with jobs and careers, the enlarged numbers of its young. Those who aspired to careers in the professions, as lawyers, doctors, clerics, officers, or administrators, faced exceptionally bitter competition for few openings and encountered frequent frustration. Numerous leaders of the Revolution were young lawyers from small towns whom the Revolution elevated and then devoured. Danton was a lawyer from Troyes in Champagne; at age thirty-three, he organized the first victories of the republican armies. Robespierre, the most charismatic of the revolutionary rulers, a lawyer from Arras, gained power and lost power, and his life as well, before age thirty-six. The Revolution, or a segment of it, was a fronde of the frustrated, an upheaval of the young.

The disruptive pressures playing on French society were many, and hard to rank in importance. They were rooted in a rapidly growing population; bigger numbers of the young, seeking and often failing to attain a stable place in society; new forms of economic organization; acute dissatisfaction with France's traditional constitution and leadership; and new values and ideas. The monarchy struggled, and failed, to contain these forces within the established social and political systems. "Never," wrote Alexis de Tocqueville, a great nineteenth-century historian of the Revolution, "was any such event so inevitable yet so completely unforeseen."

Fiscal Crisis

The spark that ignited this unexpected conflagration was the fiscal troubles of the French government. In 1789 the government was facing bankruptcy. The prospect that the state could not meet its obligations alarmed its creditors, most of whom were drawn from the richest levels of French society; it concerned hardly at all the great mass of the people. But the populace too was distraught, and angry at the government. Harvests had been bad in 1788, and would be bad again in 1789. The threat of famine added fuel to the popular demands for reform. In short, failures in fiscal management and failures in stocking markets for the people combined to make 1789 a year of anger and uprising.

Why was the government facing bankruptcy in 1789? In the 1730s, the French economy had entered upon a period of expansion, and the growing resources it developed should have provided the monarchy with adequate revenues. Despite this the government faced nearly continuous fiscal straits. The chief reason for its poverty in the midst of plenty was the narrow tax base of its finances. The system of privilege largely exempted ecclesiastical and noble lands from a proportionate contribution to fiscal needs.

The last years of the reign of Louis XV witnessed both bad economic times and deepening fiscal distress. In 1771 the chancellor, René Nicolas de Maupeou, tried to force reform decrees through the Parlement of Paris, and when he met with concerted opposition, he dissolved the Parlement and exiled more than 100 aristocrats from the capital. His action almost exactly parallels Gustavus III's attack on the Swedish Diet. Maupeou abolished the sale of offices and created a new system of courts in which the judges held their positions by royal appointment, not by inheritance or purchase. While still not touching tax exemptions, Maupeou's policies seemed a first, bold step in reducing privilege in French government and society.

However, the monarchy was ill-served by the man who guided it. The aging Louis XV gave himself to his pleasures, and the extravagance of the court spread resentment against him. He died in 1774, and the court felt it advisable to carry the king once hailed as the Beloved to his final resting place at night, almost without ceremony, almost in secret. But many people in France still expected great things from the monarchy in the person of his grandson and heir, a young man who showed authentic concern for his people.

Louis XVI and His Finance Ministers

Louis XVI was nineteen years old when he succeeded his grandfather as king of France in 1774. A man of blameless private life, he was nonetheless critically lacking in confidence in himself and was psychologically incapable of either conceiving or pursuing a firm course of action. His still younger queen, Marie Antoinette, daughter of Maria Theresa, was prone to intervening in her husband's decisions, which earned her the resentment of the court and the people.

Louis at once tried to conciliate the nobles, whose position in government had been gravely threatened by Maupeou's reforms. He restored to the parlements their former prerogatives. This was a popular gesture as it seemed to mark a move away from royal absolutism toward a limited and responsible monarchy. But it proved to be a major tactical error, for it gave a voice and a constitutional position to the nobles, the chief defenders of privilege. Louis was better served by his choice of ministers—in particular Jacques Turgot, a former *intendant* and a man of high talents steeped in the thought of the physiocrats, who assumed the office of controller general of finance.

Turgot imposed a policy of austerity to put France's house in order—no new taxes, no new loans, and no new expenses. He sought reform too; in 1774 he removed all restrictions on commerce in grain, and in 1776 he abolished the guilds. As a good physiocrat he contemplated replacing all indirect taxes that hampered trade with a single tax on land—all land—which he called the territorial subsidy and which would have represented the end of all noble privileges. Privately, he favored a system of advisory assemblies to replace the parlements, culminating in a national congress called the Great Municipality of the realm. Turgot in sum desired a constitution for France.

The king refused to support him. His economic policies aggravated the court, his philosophical ideas and support of tolerance offended the clergy, and his schemes for tax reform frightened the nobles. Above all, his austerity and refusal to make certain appointments angered the queen. Louis, worn down by complaints against the minister, dismissed him in 1776. With him went the last hope for reform in France under royal leadership.

The king then turned to a Protestant banker from Geneva with a reputation for financial wizardry, Jacques Necker. A shrewd man with a strong sense of public relations, Necker abolished the last vestiges of serfdom on the royal lands, ended torture in judicial proceedings, and reorganized hospitals and prisons. He thus earned an enormous and largely unmerited popularity. His solution for the financial crisis, which was greatly aggravated when war broke out with England in 1778, was more loans, for was not France after all a rich nation? His policy of borrowing and spending helped several bankers on to fortune and raised his popularity among the financial bourgeoisie. But new loans only delayed and in delaying worsened the eventual reckoning. With bankruptcy ever closer and support decaying around him, Necker adroitly maneuvered the king into asking for his resignation. He left the government in 1781 with his reputation as a financial reformer still intact.

After a further shuffle of ministers, in 1783 Louis turned to another experienced administrator and former *intendant,* Charles Alexandre de Calonne. He first proceeded on the principle that the government's credit was based on confidence and that confidence was best assured by the court's carefree spending. Never had the fêtes at Versailles been so splendid since the days of the Sun King. But fear of bankruptcy steadily mounted. Then in 1786 Calonne reversed his casual policies and proposed a single tax on all lands without exception—Turgot's territorial subsidy. Rather than submitting the reform to the Parlement of Paris, which would be certain to reject it, the king at Calonne's bidding summoned an Assembly of Notables, which met in February 1787. To Calonne's shock the 147 notables refused to accept the decrees, and after several stormy sessions he was dismissed by the king. His successor, Loménie de Brienne, the former archbishop of Toulouse, brought the proposal for a land tax before the Parlement of Paris, which as predicted rejected it. The full dimensions of the king's mistake in restoring rights to the Parlement were now revealed. Louis dissolved it and exiled its members to the small provincial town of Troyes, but they continued to defy the government, asserting that only the Estates General could authorize new taxes.

The government now faced mass defiance by the nobility. The provincial parlements issued declarations of support for their counterparts in Paris. Riots broke out in several cities and provinces. The civil administration seemed on the verge of breakdown, and the loyalty of the army itself was uncertain. Louis was forced to retreat before the uprising of the privileged.

He summoned the Estates General to convene in May 1789 and recalled Necker. The summoning of the national assembly was the critical first step in the Revolution, for it represented the failure of royal absolutism to achieve reform; it meant, too, entry onto the scene of the middle classes and beyond them the people.

The Estates General and the Constituent Assembly

From February to May 1789, a period of growing scarcity of grain, the three traditional orders of France elected their representatives to the Estates General, which had last been convened in 1614. By a special royal concession, the third estate was accorded twice as many delegates as the two higher orders. The delegates also drew up lists of grievances (*cahiers de doléances*). Recent analyses of their content, pursued in France and America, have shown that the great majority were conservative in tone: they refer only to local ills and express confidence that the royal government would recognize and redress them. Only a few delegates from large cities, Paris especially, allude to the general principles of social order and of justice elaborated by the philosophes. It is impossible, in other words, to read in the *cahiers* the future course of the Revolution. Still they promoted widespread reflection on France's failings; their preparation was a stage in the raising of a revolutionary consciousness.

The popular expectation that the monarchy would provide leadership in reform proved to be ill-founded. When the representatives met on May 5, Louis proposed nothing. He even left unsettled the critical question of whether the assembly would vote by order, which would assure control by the privileged, or by head, which would give the dominant voice to the third estate, since many nobles and ecclesiastics sympathized with its cause.

In the absence of royal direction, the third estate seized the initiative and demanded that the privileged orders meet with it to constitute a national assembly. The king, who finally decided to cast his lot with the nobility and clergy, locked the third estate's delegates out of their meeting room until a session could be arranged in which he would state his will. Unable to sit in their usual hall, they retired to a tennis court, and there all but one swore that they would not separate until they had given France a constitution. This "oath of the tennis court," on June 20, 1789, was an act of defiance directed against the monarchy, and a first step toward revolution. But the vacillating king once more retreated, and on June 24 allowed the three estates to form together the National Assembly, called shortly thereafter the Constituent Assembly, empowered to write a constitution.

Meanwhile unrest was growing daily in this year of hunger, and Louis' own ill-considered actions added to the turmoil. He gathered 20,000 soldiers around Paris and on July 11 dismissed the popular Necker. The dismissal provoked open insurrection in Paris. On July 14, in search of arms, the insurgents first attacked the military hospital of the Invalides and then stormed the Bastille, an old fortress used as a prison. When news of its fall reached Versailles, Louis was asleep, exhausted after a day of hunting. It is said that when he was awakened, he asked an aide: "Is this a rebellion?" "No, sire," he was told, "it is a revolution."

Again the king capitulated. He removed the troops around Paris and recalled Necker. On July 17, to please the populace, he donned a cockade bearing the colors of white for the monarchy and blue and red for the city of Paris. This tricolor was to become the flag of the new France.

But these gestures hardly pacified the hungry masses. Rather, unrest reached the provincial towns, which rallied to declare their solidarity with the third estate, and then spread fully into the countryside. The sources of peasant dissatisfaction were many and long standing. Population growth and the parceling of holdings had sown widespread rural impoverishment. It has been estimated that one-tenth of the country population lived solely by begging; still larger proportions were reduced to mendicancy during years of dearth. Feudal dues and the ecclesiastical tithe weighed heavy upon those struggling to survive on the margins of subsistence. Suspicions, too, were rampant that the nobles were hoarding grain and pursuing a policy of fomenting famine in order to block reform. In July, peasants of Normandy, Franche-Comté, Alsace, the Mâconnais, and elsewhere sacked the castles and homes of the nobles and burned the documents that recorded their feudal obligations. From about July 20, this peasant insurgency blended imperceptibly into a popular panic, known as the Great Fear. Rumors flew through the countryside that "brigands" of unknown origin and loyalties—perhaps hirelings of the nobles—were marching on the villages, intent on destroying the new harvest upon which depended all hope of relieving the famine. The fear was baseless, but it prompted a mass recourse to arms in the provincial towns and villages, stirred up hatred and suspicion of the nobles, and destroyed what confidence remained in the traditional social and constitutional order. Peasant insurgency and the Great Fear showed that the royal government faced something far more ominous than bread riots in the capital; it was confronting a national and popular revolution.

Peasant unrest also frightened the delegates of the Constituent Assembly. On the night of August 4, the representatives of the nobility and clergy vied with one another in dramatically renouncing their ancient privileges, and the Assembly solemnly decreed that the feudal regime was forever abolished in France. The delegates showed a high regard for the rights of property, however, in insisting that the nobles be compensated for the feudal rents they were losing. But the peasants seem to have been satisfied with the concessions they attained. Strongly religious, traditionally suspicious of the motives of townspeople, rural France thereafter became a largely conservative presence in the further unfolding of the Revolution.

On August 26 the Assembly drew up the Declaration of the Rights of Man and of the Citizen. In phrases reminiscent of the American Declaration of Independence, the document affirmed the rights of men to practice what religion they chose, to receive quick and fair justice, to assemble, to own property, and to be represented in government. So also all citizens were obligated to assume a fair share of the tax burden.

But still the hunger continued, and social tensions remained high. On October 5 crowds of women demanding bread besieged Versailles and forced the king and the royal family to come to Paris. The Assembly followed within a few days. Versailles, Louis XIV's great palace, symbolized not only royal absolutism but the detachment of the government from the people. The government's return to Paris thus indicated the new power of the popular forces in France.

The Restructuring of France

From 1789 to 1791, the Constituent Assembly labored hard and productively on a constitution for the new France. While recognizing the rights of all French citizens, the constitution effectively transferred power from the privi-

In October 1789, the hungry women of Paris marched to Versailles and forced the king and the royal family to return to Paris with them. With the government now located in the city, the Parisian populace was able to exert a much stronger influence upon it.
(Photo: New York Public Library/Picture Collection)

leged estates to the general body of the rich and the educated, in which the nobility remained as individuals without titles or privileges. In reshaping institutions, the Assembly sought to implement principles of rationality, efficiency, and humanity, much as the philosophes advocated. Especially as they touched local administration, justice, and the courts, the reforms proved remarkably durable; even today, the work of the Assembly is visible in France.

At the center, the constitution created a limited monarchy with a clear separation of powers. The king was to name and dismiss his ministers at will, but he would be required to secure their approval for his major decisions. The legislative branch would consist of a single house, the Legislative Assembly, with members elected for two years by a complex system of indirect voting. The king would exercise a suspensive veto over their enactments, but if the bill was passed by three Assemblies, it would become law even without royal approval. The franchise was to be limited to "active" citizens who paid a certain sum in taxes, and the property qualification would be even higher for those who wished to stand for public office. But some two-thirds of the adult male population attained the right to choose the electors, who in turn would choose the delegates. Although the system favored the rich, it was considerably more liberal than the political structure in, for example, contemporary Britain.

With regard to local government, the Constituent Assembly abolished the parlements and provided a standardized provincial administration in France. The land was divided into eighty-three departments, each allowed considerable autonomy—something not characteristic of later French constitutions. (See Maps 20.1 and 20.2) Offices were no longer to be sold, and torture and unusual punishments in judicial procedures were prohibited. The Assembly called for a new codification of French law, but this desideratum was to be achieved only by Napoleon. In economic affairs the principle of laissez faire inspired the Assembly's decisions. It lifted all internal tariffs and did away with all chartered trading companies and monopolies. The law also forbade the formation of associations of workers since they too were considered hindrances to freedom of trade and contract.

In finance the Constituent Assembly decided to honor the royal debt, which it considered, as it did all forms of commitment involving property, an inviolable obligation. To find new revenue it confiscated all ecclesiastical property in November 1789, placing it "at the disposition of the nation" and simultaneously making the government responsible for the costs of religious services. On the basis of this fund of church lands (to which the property of émigré nobles and the crown would subsequently be added), the Assembly issued paper bills known as assignats, which circulated as money. The secularization of ecclesiastical holdings had one important social result. Those bourgeois and rich peasants who acquired them acquired too a vested interest in the work of the Revolution. They were numerous and strong enough to assure that the achievements of the Constituent Assembly would never be undone.

The following July the Assembly reformed the Catholic Church in France through the Civil Constitution of the Clergy. The law reduced the number of bishops to eighty-three, reshaping diocesan boundaries to conform with those of the departments; required that both bishops and parish priests, like civil officials, be elected by those they served; and when resistance became manifest to these enactments, the Assembly demanded that all clerics swear to uphold the new legislation. The Civil Constitution ignored the traditional canon law and would have suppressed the autonomy of the church or for that matter the authority of the pope in France had it been able.

The Civil Constitution raised a storm of protest among both the clergy and the Catholic

MAP 20.1: FRANCE: PROVINCES AND REGIONS BEFORE 1789
(From Breunig, Charles, *The Age of Revolution and Reaction, 1789–1850*, New York: Norton, 1970, p. 18.)

faithful. All but seven bishops and half the parochial priests refused to take the required oath. These were called the refractory clergy. Reforms in the French Church were a recognized need, and many of the provisions corresponded with the wishes of informed and pious Catholics. But the effort to impose reforms without consideration of traditional procedures in the church was a grave tactical error. The Revolution had hitherto found much sympathy among the lower clergy. But the Civil Constitution linked the cause of reform with anticlericalism and impiety. It made enemies for the Revolution when it desperately needed friends.

MAP 20.2: FRANCE: REVOLUTIONARY DEPARTMENTS AFTER 1789
(From Breunig, Charles, *The Age of Revolution and Reaction, 1789–1850,* New York: Norton, 1970, p. 18.)

Counterrevolution

The Constituent Assembly permanently changed France, but it failed to find broad social support for its reforms. The radical left denounced its deference to the monarchy, its favoring of the rich, and the restricted suffrage granted under the new constitution. The radicals organized themselves into clubs and associations of clubs to discuss, develop, and disseminate their views. One of the most powerful of the clubs was the Jacobin, so called because its members met in the former Dominican convent of St. Jacques in Paris. On the right the nobles resented the fact that the Revolution they had hoped to lead had turned against their interests. The king himself, who might have given stability to the new regime, again hesitated, now favoring and now opposing the reforms.

In June 1791 Louis and his family secretly fled from Paris. He hoped to reach the city of Metz, near the Rhine frontier, where he expected to find a garrison of troops favorable to him and where help from Austria would be close if needed. But he was recognized at the small post station of Varennes near Reims and brought back to Paris. The Assembly, which saw the critical need for royal support, pretended that the flight had been forced on him and reaffirmed his status as king. But the nearly traitorous act lent strength to the radical agitation.

The Constituent Assembly itself adopted a measure that would withdraw power from those most committed to enforcing its reforms: its own members. Still seeking popular support, it decreed that no present delegates could stand for election to the new legislature. This self-denying ordinance assured that the Legislative Assembly would be composed of men younger, less experienced, and probably more daring than their predecessors.

The new national body was elected as provided by the constitution, and it convened for the first time on October 1, 1791. Almost from the first the question of war dominated its mood and work. By an odd coincidence both the right and the left in France saw advantage in a war between France and Austria. The king and the court hoped that military defeat would discredit the new regime and restore full power to the monarchy, and many Jacobins were eager to strike down the foreign supporters of counterrevolutionaries at home and émigrés abroad. When Francis II took the throne of the Hapsburg dominions in March 1792, the other half of the stage was set. Unlike his father, Leopold, who strongly rejected intervention, Francis fell under the influence of vengeful émigrés and shortsighted advisers. He determined to assist the French queen, his aunt, and he hoped to achieve territorial gains for Austria at the expense of France. With both sides geared for battle, France went to war against the Austro-Prussian coalition in April.

Each camp expected rapid victory, but both were deceived. The French offensive was quickly driven back, and soon invading armies were crossing French borders. The Legislative Assembly ordered the exile of refractory clergy and the establishment of a special corps of 20,000 national guardsmen to protect Paris. Louis vetoed both measures and held to his decision in spite of demonstrations in the capital. This was for all practical purposes his last act as king. Meanwhile the Assembly declared the mother country to be in danger and called for volunteers from the provinces to defend the frontiers. As France mobilized for war an officer named Rouget de Lisle composed a marching song for his volunteer battalion—a song eventually known as the *Marseillaise*. Now the national anthem of France, it ranks among history's most stirring summons to patriotic war.

The *Marseillaise* accurately reflected the spirit of resistance that was developing in France. As Prussian forces began a drive toward Paris, their commander, the duke of Brunswick, recklessly demanded that Paris disarm itself and threatened to level the city if it resisted or if it harmed the royal family. This seemed the final proof that Louis was in league with the enemy. Far from intimidating the revolutionaries, the threat drove them into action. Since the Legislative Assembly had refused to act decisively in the face of royal obstructionism, the Parisians organized an insurrection. On August 10, 1792, a crowd of armed Parisians stormed the royal palace at the Tuileries, literally driving the king from the throne. The Assembly then had no choice but to declare him suspended. That night more than half its

This contemporary text and music of the *Marseillaise* carries a sketch of the "sons of the revolution" marching and singing. The anthem's original title was *War Song for the Army of the Rhine*.
(Photo: The Mansell Collection)

members themselves fled Paris, making it clear that the Assembly too had lost its legitimacy. Recognizing this, the representatives who remained prepared to dissolve the Assembly permanently and ordered elections for a new body, the National Convention. The representatives left to the Convention the responsibility of declaring a republic in France and of judging her former king. Even more than the storming of the Bastille in July 1789, the events of August 10, 1792, marked the passing of the old regime in France.

In the eighteenth century major transformations began in all aspects of Western life. The inhabitants of Europe and North America expanded at an extraordinary rate to unprecedented numbers, initiating a population explosion that has continued into modern times and now affects the entire world. The demographic revolution was closely related in both effect and cause to a revolution in manufacturing. The new industrial economy, if still of small size, created a new organization of production based on steam power and high engineering skill, factors that would sustain the economic growth of the following century. And the overall economic system took on a configuration that differed from the patterns of all prior periods in its capacity to transform itself ceaselessly and thus to lend a new dynamic quality to the society living from it.

These profound changes were accompanied by a crisis in social and political institutions. A tripartite struggle developed involving the ruler, the aristocracy, and the people over the proper allocation of power in the state. Several European monarchs sought to impose reform from above. The aristocracies on the other hand bitterly resented encroachments on their privileges, and some were willing to pursue the defense of their interests to the point of revolution. Both rulers and patricians appealed to the third estate, the people, often with unexpected results. The emerging claim to power of the unprivileged classes is the greatest change effected by the revolutions of the eighteenth century. No longer would the political history of the Western world focus exclusively on the elite.

The peoples of the West thus faced the task of building a new economic, social, and political order. What should its character be? How should power be managed, and how should wealth be distributed? What values should now govern human lives? There were the issues destined to occupy the Western nations as they entered the industrial and democratic age.

RECOMMENDED READING

Sources

Aspinall, Arthur, and E. Anthony Smith (eds.). *English Historical Documents, Vol. XI: 1783–1832.* 1959.

*Burke, Edmund. *Reflections on the Revolution in France.* 1969.

Higgins, E. L. (ed.). *The French Revolution as Told by Contemporaries.* 1939.

Horn, D. B., and Mary Ransome. *English Historical Documents, Vol. X: 1714–1783.* 1957.

*Smith, Adam. *Enquiry into the Nature and Causes of the Wealth of Nations.* 1961.

Stewart, John H. (ed.). *A Documentary Survey of the French Revolution.* 1951.

*Young, Arthur. *Travels in France During the Years 1787, 1788, 1789.* 1972.

Studies

*Ashton, T. S. *The Industrial Revolution, 1760–1830.* 1968.

Chambers, J. D., and G. E. Mingay. *The Agricultural Revolution, 1750–1880.* 1966.

*Cobban, A. *The Social Interpretation of the French Revolution.* 1968. Lively critique of the theory that the Revolution was engendered by class conflict.

*Deane, Phyllis. *The First Industrial Revolution.* 1975. Based on lectures, covering the years 1750–1850.

*De Tocqueville, Alexis. *The Old Regime and the French Revolution.* Stuart Gilbert (tr.). 1955.

Doyle, William. *Origins of the French Revolution.* 1980. A distillation of thirty years of historical research and controversy.

Egret, Jean. *The French Pre-Revolution, 1787–88.* 1978. A masterly account of the unraveling of the old regime.

Flandrin, Jean-Louis. *Families in Former Times: Kinship, Household, and Sexuality.* 1979. From demographic history to the history of the family.

Godechot, Jacques. *France and the Atlantic Revolutions of the Eighteenth Century.* 1965. Good comparative study of revolutions, by a French scholar.

*Greenlaw, Ralph (ed.). *The Social Origins of the French Revolution: The Debate on the Role of the Middle Classes.* 1975. Collected essays.

*Hampson, Norman. *A Social History of the French Revolution.* 1963. Institutional rather than social; clearly organized and written.

*Landes, David S. *The Unbound Prometheus: Technological Change and Industrial Development in Western Europe from 1750 to the Present.* 1969. Broad survey, effectively written.

*Lefebvre, Georges. *The Coming of the French Revolution.* R. R. Palmer (tr.). 1957. Short, clear, classical analysis by a prominent French historian.

———. *The Great Fear of 1789.* 1973. A classic account of the peasant revolution of 1789.

*Mantoux, Paul. *The Industrial Revolution in the Eighteenth Century.* 1962. Basic introduction, with stress on inventions and factories.

North, Douglass C. *Structure and Change in Economic History.* 1981. Stresses the importance of supportive legal institutions in the coming of industrialism.

Palmer, Robert R. *The Age of the Democratic Revolution: A Political History of Europe and America, 1760–1800.* 1959–1962.

*Roberts, J. M. *The French Revolution.* 1979.

Rudé, George F. *Paris and London in the Eighteenth Century: Studies in Popular Protest.* 1975.

*Soboul, Albert. *The French Revolution, 1787–1799.* 1975. The Revolution seen as an uprising of the bourgeoisie.

Wrigley, E. A., and R. S. Schofield. *The Population History of England, 1541–1871: Studies in Social and Demographic History.* 1981. Recent and authoritative.

---

*Available in paperback.

21

THE TERROR
AND NAPOLEON
1792–1814

The end of the eighteenth century is often called the age of the dual revolution—the Industrial Revolution beginning in England and the social and political revolution centering in France. But where the former unfolded gradually, the latter exploded. By 1791—just two years after the fall of the Bastille—the foundations of government and society in France had been profoundly altered. The estate structure, dominated by the monarch and the nobles, had been destroyed; middle-class values and leaders were in the ascendant; the peasantry had been freed from many remnants of the seigneurial system; absolutism had been replaced by constitutional monarchy, legislative representation, and local self-government; freedom of religion and expression had been inaugurated.

Yet the Revolution was far from over, and in the short view one might say that it was only just beginning. True, the gains just enumerated ultimately proved to be the most enduring and doubtless the most important. But they had been won at the price of great opposition, and the old order was far from admitting defeat. Priests, émigrés, and royalists in France were seconded by Old Regime monarchs, aristocrats, and armies elsewhere in Europe in their resistance to the Revolution. Moreover, within France itself vast sections of the population were disaffected from the "patriots" of 1789 for a variety of reasons.

Challenged in 1792 by war and counterrevolution, the patriots themselves were divided. Some were alienated by the leaders of the Revolution and ultimately joined its opponents. Others were radicalized and gave their allegiance to the Jacobins. These in turn were seeking allies among the urban popular classes—the sans-culottes. Building on the momentum of August 1792, when Louis XVI had been driven from the throne, the Jacobins forged a coalition with the sans-culottes, who sought to revolutionize the Revolution. The goals of this second revolution were more advanced than those of 1789: a democratic republic based on an ever-widening definition of social equality. Its hallmark was a posture of relentless militancy.

Each increment of revolution produced new opponents at home and abroad, but each increment of opposition stiffened the determination of the Revolution's supporters. An epochal confrontation was in the making that would engulf Europe. It began with a power struggle between revolutionary factions, a conflict of personalities as much as of political orientations; it ended in a coup that led France into a dictatorship under Napoleon Bonaparte.

I. THE SECOND REVOLUTION

The National Convention elected after the fall of the monarchy had a challenging mandate. It was supposed to consolidate the achievements of the first revolution but also establish a democratic republic, in effect moving the Revolution into a second stage. It is impossible to say how this would have proceeded had the times been calm, but of course they were not. France was immediately beset by an emergency situation—a convergence of invasion, civil war, and economic crisis. This situation demanded new initiatives which affected the course of the second revolution. To save and expand freedom, it was argued, force and terrorism were necessary. Thus the ideals of democracy and social equality were confused with problems of national defense and with the brutal dilemma of means versus ends. Although the second revolution lasted for little more than two years (1792–1794), it challenged the very foundations upon which government and society had always been organized.

The National Convention

The insurrection of August 10, 1792, had created a vacuum. Until the National Convention was elected and until it was able to govern effectively, the fabric of authority in France was extremely fragile. A revolutionary city government, or Commune, in Paris organized itself as one power center, but that bastion of radicalism could not control the course of events even within its own domain, as evidenced by the September massacres—perhaps the bloodiest single event of the Revolution. As able-bodied volunteers left for the battlefront, Parisians nervously eyed the capital's jails, filled with political prisoners and common criminals. Seeing these prisoners as a potential counterrevolutionary striking force, and fearing a plot to open the prisons, radical journalists like Jean Paul Marat warned of the threat. A growing sense of alarm finally exploded early in September. For three successive days groups of Parisians invaded the prisons, set up popular tribunals, and executed over 1,000 prisoners. No official dared intervene to stop the slaughter.

The sense of panic soon eased, however, with the belated success of the French armies. Bolstered by units of citizen volunteers, the army halted the invading coalition at the Battle of Valmy in September. Two months later it defeated the forces of the old order at Jemappes in the Austrian Netherlands, which were now occupied by the French. Meanwhile, the National Convention, elected under universal male suffrage, convened at the end of September, promptly declared France a republic, and set about trying to govern the country until a new democratic constitution could be drafted and implemented.

Louis XVI's fate was the Convention's first major business and it proved an extremely divisive issue. While the king was found guilty of treason unanimously, there was a sharp and prolonged debate over his punishment. Some argued for clemency, while others insisted on his execution as a symbolic break with the old order as well as a fitting punishment for his betrayal. Finally, by a vote of 387 to 334, Louis was sentenced to death, and efforts to reprieve this sentence or delay it for a popular referendum were defeated. On January 21, 1793, Louis was beheaded, put to death like an ordinary citizen. The French in general and the Convention in particular had become regicides—king-killers. This decision made compromise with the counterrevolution unlikely and total victory imperative. The Revolution would have to move forward.

France was now a republic, a country in which the influence of kings, priests, and nobles was to be eliminated, in which regionalism was supposed to give way to unity, in which social justice and reform could advance. Yet in a few months everything began to go wrong, and the Revolution faced a new and more serious crisis. By the early spring of 1793 the republic was

Tried and sentenced by the National Convention for treason, Louis Capet (formerly Louis XVI) stoically mounted the guillotine on January 21, 1793. His execution made it clear that the Revolution had taken a sharp turn and that it would deal implacably with its enemies.
(Photo: The Granger Collection)

under siege, internally divided and foundering. At least five problems faced the Convention: factionalism and conflict within its own ranks; a new invasion by a coalition of anti-French states; peasant dissatisfaction and internal civil war; economic dislocation including inflation and scarcity of bread; and growing militancy among Parisian radicals.

From the Convention's opening day two groups of deputies vied for leadership. The bitterness of their rivalry proved to be extremely divisive and threatened to paralyze the republic altogether. Yet this conflict reflected a painful reality: opinion *was* divided by what had already happened, and a consensus or stable majority was extremely difficult to find. The factional conflict originated in 1791–1792 as a quarrel within the Paris Jacobin Club and intensified after the insurrection of August 10. A group of deputies and journalists centering on Jacques Brissot had helped lead the country into war, but had then shrunk back from the vigorous measures necessary to pursue it. (This group later would be labeled the "Girondists" since several of its spokesmen were elected deputies to the Convention from the department of the Gironde.) Advocates of provincial middle-class interests, fiery orators, and ambitious politicians, they gradually fell out of step with the growing radicalization of Paris.

Brissot and his friends were forced out of the Jacobin Club, while the Parisian electors sent a deputation to the Convention that included leading members of the club such as Danton, Robespierre, and Marat. This Parisian deputation became the nucleus of a group called "the Mountain," since it occupied the upper benches of the Convention's hall. The Mountain attracted to its ranks the more democratically oriented provincial deputies, and attacked the Girondists as compromisers, as men unattuned to the new demands of the French people. The Girondists in turn denounced the Mountain as would-be tyrants who were captives of Parisian opinion to the detriment of the provinces and the propertied classes.

Between these two factions stood several hundred deputies in the center (called the Plain, in contrast to the Mountain). Committed to the Revolution, they were uncertain whom to trust and would support those men or policies that promised success in consolidating the Revolution. They disliked and feared popular agitation, but they were reluctant to turn against the popular movement, agreeing with the Mountain that the Revolution depended on it. In the debate on the king the center was split, but a majority finally embraced the Jacobins' demand for execution, whereas a few prominent Girondists had argued for clemency. Military and economic problems were eventually to propel the majority to disavow the Girondists and support the Mountain.

The Revolutionary Crisis

Within a few months the Convention faced a perilous convergence of invasion, civil war, and economic crisis that demanded new policies and imaginative responses. The military victories of 1792 were quickly forgotten when Austria and Prussia mounted a new offensive in 1793, an alliance soon strengthened by the addition of Spain, Piedmont, and England. Between March and September reversals occurred on every front, while the regular army was weakened by the emigration of officers and by poor leadership. In fact the French commander, General Dumouriez, the Revolution's first military hero the year before, sought—unsuccessfully—to bring his army back to Paris in order to topple the Convention.

The Convention's first response to the deteriorating military situation was to introduce a system of conscription. But this in turn touched off a peasant rebellion in western France. Long-simmering resentments by a traditional peasantry, who hated the small patriot middle class in the towns for monopolizing political power and who resented the Revolution's persecution of their priests, finally ignited when the republic tried to conscript them. Peasants and weavers in the Vendée region south of the Loire River soon attacked the government's supporters in the region's isolated towns. Gradually this insurrection was influenced by priests and émigrés who organized the rebels into guerrilla bands and finally into what called itself the Catholic and Royalist Army. Wherever it triumphed, the Bourbons were proclaimed kings again and patriots were massacred. Several major cities were occupied briefly and for a while the rebels threatened the port city of Nantes, which could have been used for a landing of British troops if it fell from the government's control.

The bitter factionalism in the Convention had meanwhile generated conflict elsewhere in the country. Various provincial centers that sympathized with the Girondists hovered on the brink of rebellion against the Convention's leadership and against Parisian radicalism. In Normandy and Brittany forces were raised to threaten Paris, while in the south local Jacobins lost control of Marseilles, Bordeaux, and France's second largest city, Lyons. Like the Vendée rebellion, the Lyons resistance to Paris was eventually taken over by royalists who hoped to ignite the entire south of France against Paris. This was an intolerable challenge to the Convention. Labeling the anti-Jacobins in Lyons and elsewhere "federalists," the Con-

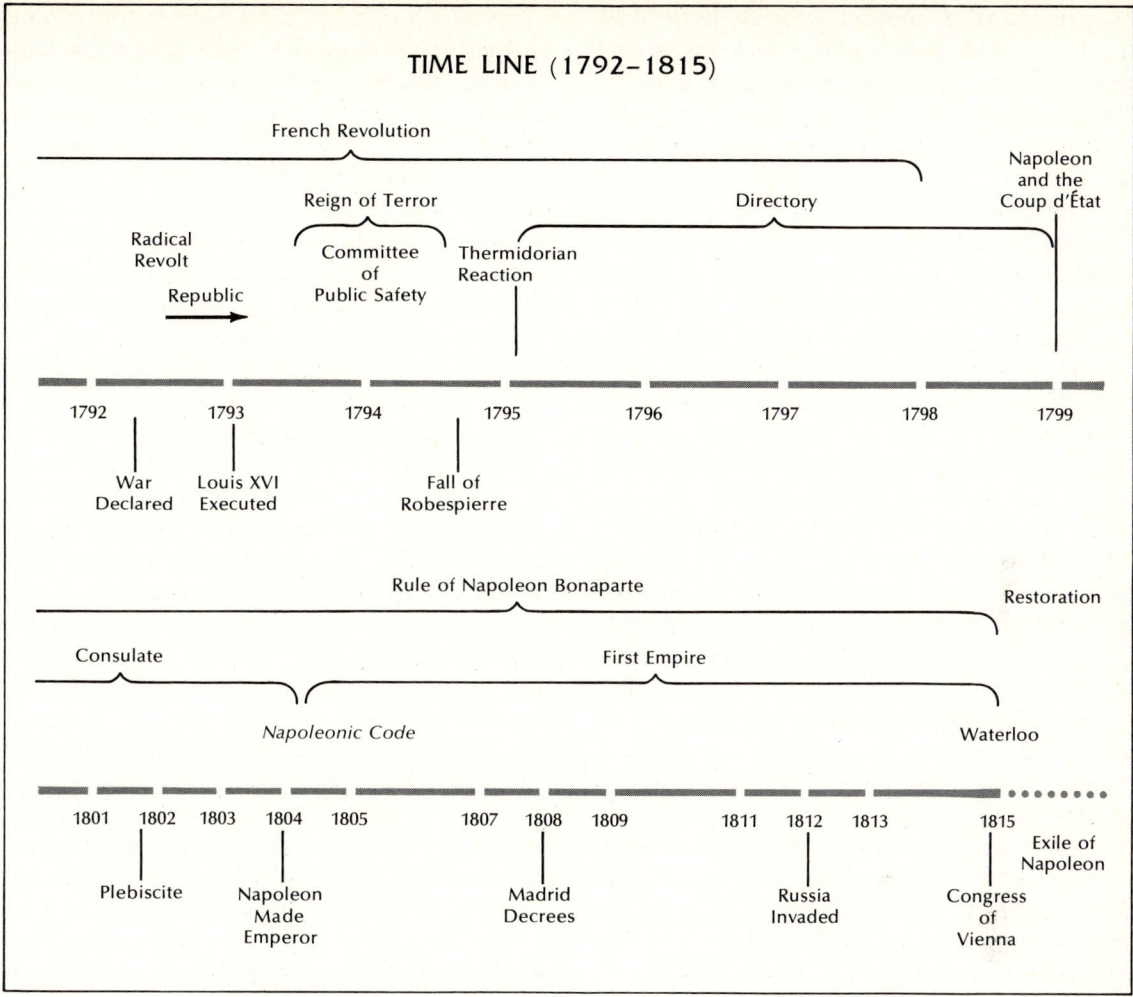

vention sent out armed forces to suppress them. Ironically, in the United States at this time the word "federalist" referred to those who advocated a strong central government. In France it was used in the opposite sense, meaning those who sought to undermine the republic's unity. As such, the federalists were considered counterrevolutionary, for to disavow Paris meant to disavow the Revolution itself.

Parisian radicalism—against which the federalists were reacting—was in large measure provoked by severe economic troubles that were engulfing the infant republic. By February 1793 the Revolution's paper money, the assignats, had declined to 50 percent of its face value in the marketplace, and it continued steadily downward after that, to as low as one-third. This disastrous devaluation was compounded by a poor harvest. Panic over the scarcity of grain and flour swept across France, especially in the cities. Municipal leaders attempted to fix the price of bread so as to make it available to the masses, but they simply could not secure adequate supplies. Likewise the central government could not supply its armies under these conditions. Human greed of course made matters worse; uncivic-minded Frenchmen attempted to profit from the situation by hoarding scarce commodities or by speculating in assignats.

The strongest impetus for taking vigorous measures against all these problems, military, political, and economic, came from the urban populace in Paris and other cities. But the vehemence of certain Parisian militants posed yet another threat to the Convention: the threat of excessive radicalism and anarchy. The ultra-radicals, like their enemies the federalists, were unwilling to defer to the Convention. Spokesmen for the people, or sans-culottes, as they were called, communicated the view that the Convention, the Jacobin Club, and even the Paris city government were not sufficiently responsive to popular demands. They therefore demanded a purge of the Convention to rid it of its moderates; a program of revolutionary public safety; and radical economic intervention to break through the laissez-faire immobility of the government: (1) price control (called a law of the Maximum) for all necessary commodities, (2) severe laws against hoarding and speculation, and (3) forced requisitions on the peasantry, to be carried out with the assistance of an armed force or revolutionary army of the interior.

Behind these demands lay the threat of armed insurrection. Many Parisians were sympathetic to this platform, aimed at revolutionizing the Revolution. For the Jacobins the pressure from the sans-culottes provided aid in their struggle against the Girondists and federalists, but it posed the danger of spilling over into anarchy.

In a sense all elements of the revolutionary crisis hinged on one problem: the lack of a strong, effective government that would not simply respond to popular pressure but organize and channel it into constructive action. The first step in the creation of such a government seemed to be the purge demanded by the radicals. On May 31 the sans-culottes launched a demonstration to force home their demands, and the Plain at this point decided that the Mountain must be supported against the Girondists, who were thundering against sans-culotte "tyranny." On June 2 twenty-three Girondists were expelled by the Convention and placed under house arrest; they would subsequently be tried for treason. A turning point had come, but the future course of the Revolution was still in question.

The Jacobin Dictatorship

The popular movement in Paris had hoisted the Mountain to power in the Convention. The question now was which side of the coalition would dominate. Popular demands swelled for terrorism against counterrevolution and for vigorous provisioning policies. The conviction was spreading among the urban masses that the sovereign people could dictate its will to the Convention by demonstrations and the threat of insurrection. At the same time federalism exploded in the provinces in response to the purge of the Girondists; Lyons and Marseilles were now in full-scale rebellion.

The high point of popular agitation came on September 5, when a massive demonstration placed demands for drastic measures before the Convention. The demonstrators' main slogans were "Food—and to have it, force for the law" and "Let terror be placed on the order of the day." Concretely they won the passage of laws imposing general price control, forbidding hoarding, creating revolutionary armies of the interior, and empowering local revolutionary committees to incarcerate citizens whose loyalty was suspect or who seemed to threaten the public safety—the so-called law of suspects.

The Revolutionary Government
Back in June the triumphant Jacobins had drafted a democratic constitution, one of the

original purposes for which the National Convention had been called. It had been submitted to a referendum and overwhelmingly approved by 3 million voters; thus it provided the cornerstone for a new legitimate government. But the constitution could not be implemented in the throes of such a crisis as now faced the nation, particularly in view of her internal divisions. In October the Convention acknowledged this, formally placed the constitution aside, and proclaimed the government "revolutionary until the peace." Such luxuries of citizenship as the elections, local self-government, and guarantees of individual liberty promised in the constitution would be enjoyed only after the republic was secure from its enemies within and without.

An array of revolutionary laws and institutions now existed; it remained for a group of determined and skillful political leaders to take the reins and make them effective. Such men were to be found on the Committee of Public Safety, appointed by the Convention to supervise military, economic, and political affairs.

The committee's leading personality and tactician was Maximilien Robespierre. An austere bachelor in his mid-thirties and a provincial lawyer before the Revolution, Robespierre had been a prominent spokesman for the left in the Constituent Assembly where he had advocated the rights of women, Jews, and free blacks, and had crusaded for the democratization of the regime. In 1792 he was an official of the Paris city government and a newspaper editor. But his principal political forum was the capital's Jacobin Club, which by 1793 he more or less dominated. Elected to the Convention from Paris, he was selfless and self-righteous in his total dedication to revolutionary causes. He sought to guide the sans-culottes and serve their interests as much as possible, but at all times he placed the survival of the Revolution above their particular grievances. Thus in his leadership he struck a delicate balance between his sense of responsibility and his sympathy for popular aspirations. The two were not always compatible. His main object was to bring the republic through the emergency by creating confidence and efficiency in the revolutionary government, and in this he succeeded. His hope of reconciling class interests in the cause of democracy was ultimately frustrated.

The legislation for creating a centralized revolutionary government was passed in December 1793, at last filling the vacuum left by the fall of the monarchy. Under a law enacted December 4—or 14 Frimaire year II, according to the new French calendar—revolutionary committees in towns and villages were made responsible to the Committee of Public Safety, which could purge them. Local officials were redesignated national agents, their initiative was curbed, and they too were subject to removal by the Committee. Revolutionary tribunals, representatives on mission (deputies sent to the provinces as commissars), and revolutionary armies of the interior were all placed under the Committee's scrutiny and control.

Crucial links in this chain of revolutionary dictatorship were the Jacobin clubs. They too were organized into a centralized network, led by the Paris Jacobin Club. They nominated citizens for posts on revolutionary committees and exercised surveillance over them. The clubs were to be "arsenals of public opinion," to support the war effort in every way possible, and to denounce uncivic behavior among their fellow citizens.

No serious dissent was tolerated under the Jacobin reign. Freedom of expression was limited by the government's sense of the need for unity during the emergency, and the politically outspoken were purged. The first to fall were a group of ultraleftists led by Jacques René Hébert, a radical journalist and Paris official. They were accused of a plot against the republic. In reality they had questioned what they considered the Convention's leniency toward "enemies" of the people. Next came the turn of the so-called indulgents, among them Danton. They had argued—prematurely, in the government's view—for a relaxation of terror-

The Paris Jacobin Club was founded by a group of progressive deputies to the Constituent Assembly of 1789. After August 1792 and the elections to the Convention, it became a forum for democratic deputies and middle-class Parisian radicals, as well as a "mother club" with which popular societies in the provinces affiliated themselves. As such, it was the closest thing the French revolutionaries had to a party apparatus.
(Photo: New York Public Library/Picture Collection)

ism and centralization. They were arrested, indicted on trumped-up charges of treason, and sentenced to death by the revolutionary tribunal. This succession of purges, starting with the Girondists and ultimately ending with Robespierre himself, seemed to suggest, as one contemporary put it, that revolutions devour their own children.

The Reign of Terror

Most of those devoured by the French Revolution, however, were not its own children. They were rather an assortment of armed rebels, counterrevolutionaries, and unfortunate citizens swept into the vortex of war and internal strife. The Reign of Terror developed in response to the multifaceted crisis described on the previous pages. On the level of attitude, the Terror reflected a revolutionary mentality that saw threats and plots all around (some real, some imagined). The laws of the Terror were designed to intimidate a wide range of people perceived as enemies of the Revolution. They included the law of suspects, which led to the incarceration of 400,000 to 500,000 prisoners, and laws against the life and property of refractory priests and émigrés. They included also the price-control regulations and other legislation aimed at preventing the collapse of the Revolution from economic chaos or food shortages.

The Terror was the force behind the law— the determination and techniques to make these laws work. Its purpose was to coerce French people into abiding by the Revolution in some minimal fashion and into accepting certain sacrifices of self-interest to permit the republic and the Revolution to survive. By the same token the emphasis on organizing the Terror, on supervising it from some central point of authority, was designed to prevent anarchic violence like the prison massacres of September 1792 and the infamous *noyades* (drownings) of Nantes, in which hundreds of Vendée rebels and priests were brutally drowned in the Loire River. Wholesale slaughter was disavowed by the Committee of Public Safety, which for example prevented the indiscriminate condemnation of federalists and put a stop to violent de-Christianization. The Terror was meant to impress by the severity of examples, not by the liquidation of whole groups.

Statistical analysis of the death sentences

during the Terror suggests that there was a relationship between executions and clear-and-present danger. A total of 17,000 death sentences were handed down by the various revolutionary tribunals and commissions, and an estimated 10,000 additional armed rebels were executed without trial. Over 70 percent of the sentences were passed in the two zones of intense civil war: 19 percent in the southeast (the Lyons region) and 52 percent in the west (the Vendée region). Moreover 72 percent of these were for armed rebellion. Conversely one-third of the departments had fewer than ten death sentences each and were relatively tranquil. While much of the revolutionary rhetoric and some of its legislation were aimed at the upper classes, the death sentences of the Terror hit hardest at the largest groups in the population: urban and rural common people who actively participated in the rebellions.[1]

Apart from the repression of the Vendée revolt, the Terror's bloodiest episode took place in Lyons. The Convention laid siege to the city until it capitulated in October 1793. Implacable in its hostility, the Convention declared that "Lyons has made war against liberty and thus Lyons no longer exists." The entire population was disarmed, and the houses of many wealthy citizens were burned. On-the-spot courts-martial were held and executions followed immediately. Some were carried out gruesomely, with the encouragement of irresponsible commissars. Almost 2,000 people were put to death, two-thirds of them from the upper classes. The fanaticism of the Parisian sans-culottes sent against Lyons reflected both their class consciousness and their revolutionary fervor during the dark days of crisis.

---

[1] These statistics are drawn from Donald Greer, *The Incidence of the Terror.* 1935.

The Sans-Culottes and the Popular Revolution

After their massive revolt against the old order in 1789, the peasants were generally passive or overtly hostile to the Revolution's further progress. They contributed little as a group to the second revolution. The urban common people, or sans-culottes, however, not only propelled the insurrectionary movements in the cities in 1789, but became ardent proponents of further revolutionizing in the social, political, and economic spheres. Their participation in the second revolution was essential to its success.

The role of the people in the Revolution has always been noted but until recently they have not been studied directly and in their own right. Instead their actions and concerns have been refracted through the eyes of their enemies or their spokesmen, themselves middle or upper class and far removed in their own life style from the common people. Inspired by Georges Lefebvre's classic studies of the peasants, historians have recently been writing about the French Revolution "from below"—about specific groups of common people. These studies convey their social identity, their aspirations, attitudes, and revolutionary activity as they tried to place their collective stamp on what they regarded as their Revolution.

The most dramatic impact made by the sans-culottes on the Revolution came during the famous insurrectionary *journées,* or "days" of crowd actions, demonstrations, and uprisings, that marked most turning points in the Revolution's course (see table). The participants in these crowds and striking forces were not criminals and drifters, as antirevolutionary writers have claimed. They were Parisian workingmen—carpenters, cobblers, wine sellers, clerks, tailors, cafe keepers, stonemasons—mainly small-scale artisans, shopkeepers and journeymen. The sans-culottes were not a class in the Marxist sense, for they varied in their relationship to the means of production: some, such as small workshop proprietors, owned them; others provided only their labor. But all shared the life style of Paris' popular neighborhoods and had a strong sense of community.

Popular Attitudes

The long hours of hard work that characterized the sans-culottes' existence generally yielded a modest livelihood that was painfully reduced by rises in the cost of living. Accordingly they were extremely concerned over the availability and prices of basic commodities like bread, candles, meat, and fuel. As consumers they faced the economic crisis of the revolutionary period with distress and anger. Their most basic demand was for government intervention to assure them the basic necessities of life. This incidentally is one reason that women were prominent among revolutionary activists: they were most directly concerned with putting food on their family's table. This concern was summarized by the call for "Food—and to have it, force for the law." By 1793 the Revolution's leaders were compelled to recognize this, and the right to subsistence was prominently proclaimed in the Jacobin constitution of 1793. Concretely it meant a combination of government price control, requisitioning, and a public works program to provide employment. Most of this violated the middle-class laissez-faire view of how the economy should work.

The sans-culottes, while firm believers in property rights, insisted that they must be limited by considerations of social utility. The right of an individual to a modest amount of property, like one small workshop or one store, was considered inviolate, but the sans-culottes denied that anyone had the right to "misuse" property by hoarding, speculating, or accumulating far more than he needed. Concepts of freedom and equality had a practical economic side in their opinion. As one petition put it, "What is the meaning of freedom, when one class of men can starve another? What is the meaning of equality, when the rich, by their monopolies, can exercise the right of life and death over their equals?"

Under the stress of soaring inflation and economic dislocation, the sans-culotte call for the right to subsistence and the middle-class call for laissez faire clashed dramatically. The willingness of the Mountain and the Jacobin Club to acknowledge the right to subsistence and to regulate the economy, at least during the

---

TURNING POINTS IN THE REVOLUTION

July 14, 1789:	Storming of the Bastille and triumph of the third estate.
August 10, 1792:	Storming of the Tuileries and end of the constitutional monarchy.
September 2–5, 1792:	Paris prison massacres.
May 31–June 2, 1793:	Sans-culotte march on the Convention and purge of the Girondists.
September 5, 1793:	Demonstration before the Convention and enactment of terroristic legislation and economic controls.
9 Thermidor year II (July 27, 1794):	Fall of Robespierre.
1–2 Prairial year III (May 20–21, 1795):	Unsuccessful insurrection by the Parisian sans-culottes for "Bread and the constitution of 1793."
18 Brumaire year VIII (November 9, 1799):	Coup d'état by Napoleon Bonaparte and the revisionists.

war emergency, won them support among the urban people.

Bitterly antiaristocratic, the sans-culottes feared that the middle class might replace the nobility as a new kind of elite. This social attitude was reflected in everyday behavior. Extolling simplicity in dress and manners, they attacked opulence and pretension wherever they found or imagined them to be. Under their disapproving eye, high society and fancy dress generally disappeared from view. There was a revolution too in manners and morals. Vices like prostitution, pornography, and gambling were attributed to aristocrats and were denounced in the virtuous and austere society of the Revolution; drinking was the common man's vice and was tolerated.

The sans-culottes symbolized their break with the past by changing the names of their streets, cities, and public places to eliminate signs of royalism and aristocracy. The Palais Royal became the Palais d'Égalité ("Equality Palace"). Many people underwent debaptizing, exchanging their Christian names for the names of secular heroes like Gracchus, the ancient Roman reformer, or names derived from trees and plants. The Gregorian calendar was replaced with a more geometric revolutionary calendar, computed from September 22, 1792, forward, in which weeks were replaced by units of ten days. Titles like "monsieur" and "madame" were dropped in favor of the simple, uniform designation of "citizen"—just as revolutionaries of a later generation would call each other "comrade."

Ever alert to conspiracies, real or imagined, Hébert's *Père Duchêsne* was a favorite newspaper of the sans-culottes. Lively, slangy, and blasphemous, its targets included moderates, "aristocrats," and clergy. During 1793 and 1794 it was distributed in vast quantities among the Republic's armies.
(Photo: The Research Libraries, The New York Public Library)

Participatory Democracy

The Convention believed in a system of parliamentary or representative democracy, with an active political life at the grass roots but with power delegated to elected officials. And as we saw, during the emergency the Jacobins were willing to impose a virtual dictatorship in the form of the highly centralized revolutionary government. The sans-culottes, on the other hand, favored a popular scheme of participa-

On the Revolutionary Calendar the first day of the year became the date on which the Republic was proclaimed (September 22, 1792). The twelve months (renamed to reflect seasonal conditions) were divided into three *décades* of ten days each. The tenth day, or *décadi*, became the official day of rest in place of Sundays—an obvious source of resentment for devout Catholics.
(Photo: Musée Carnavalet/Photo Bulloz)

tory democracy. They believed that the local voters or in larger cities the local section assembly of citizens was the ultimate sovereign body; it could never permanently delegate its authority, even to the popularly elected Convention. In short they wanted the decision-making power actively lodged with the people rather than their deputies. To Robespierre this ideal of unrestrained direct democracy appeared unworkable and akin to anarchy.

At the beginning of the revolutionary year II (1793–1794), the forty-eight sections in Paris functioned almost as tiny autonomous republics in which the people ran their own affairs directly in the general assembly, a system an

American would call town-meeting democracy. When necessary the sections cooperated with each other to exert collective pressure on the government. On the various *journées* the sans-culottes demonstrated their conviction that the people, if necessary in a state of armed insurrection, ought to be the ultimate arbiter of the republic. Political life in those months, especially but not exclusively in Paris, had a naïve, breathless quality, generating high enthusiasm among thousands of sans-culottes, making them feel that for the first time the power of self-government was theirs.

The Convention looked on with mixed feelings. On the one hand they were uneasy allies, committed to the ideals of democracy and equality. On the other hand they were pragmatists who feared the anarchic force of this popular movement—its unpredictability, its disorder, and its inefficiency. The Mountain attempted to steer a difficult course between encouraging this civic participation and controlling it. The sans-culotte militants did a great deal for the war effort: they rooted out counterrevolutionaries, spread revolutionary usages, recruited soldiers, and formed committees for public relief. Like the Jacobin clubs in the provinces, the Parisian sans-culottes promoted the ideal of self-help.

From the sections, however, there came an endless stream of exhortations, petitions, denunciations, and veiled threats to the government. In the end the Convention decided that politically and administratively the direct democracy of the sections had to be disciplined. In the spring of 1794, it passed a series of measures restricting the meeting times, activities, and rights of the sections that removed most of their effective powers. What the government failed to realize was that once the ardor of the sans-culottes was forcibly cooled off, that group's support of the Convention, and their willingness to sacrifice, would also diminish. The results would leave these leaders vulnerable to reaction.

The Victories of the Year II

Even while the Mountain was curtailing the powers of the sans-culottes, however, it continued to bank on their support for the military defense of the nation. For the Revolution's more far-sighted leaders knew that France's ultimate fate rested in the hands of her armies. Drawing on the citizenry at large, the Convention forged a new armed force that overcame the coalition of hostile states arrayed against France.

Revolutionary Foreign Policy

As initially formulated in 1789, revolutionary ideology had offered no direct threat to the status quo of the European state system. It had perceived its influence as consisting only in the force of example. French power was not to be felt across the country's borders except as persuasion. Indeed, the orators of the National Assembly had argued that the best foreign policy for a progressive and free society was peace, neutrality, and isolation from the diplomatic intrigues of monarchs.

But peace did not imply pacifism. When counterrevolution at home coalesced with threats from abroad, the revolutionaries were eager to resort to war against both. The hostilities that broke out in 1792 were for the most part defensive in origin as far as the French were concerned. But as in all major wars the initial objectives were rapidly forgotten, and as the conflict spilled over large parts of Europe, it disrupted the political organization and boundaries of many Continental states.

The revolutionary wars involved considerations that were perennial in international conflicts as well as certain new and explosive purposes. On the one hand the French adopted traditional objectives such as rounding off and extending their frontiers and exacting agreements from adjoining states aimed at protecting those frontiers. At the same time they pursued revolutionary principles such as the right of a people to self-determination. As early as September 1791, the National Assembly had declared that "the rights of peoples are not determined by the treaties of princes."

As we have seen in the previous chapter, there were people in many areas of Western Europe who were eager to challenge the ancient arrangements—"the treaties of princes"—that determined their political destiny. Particularly in the zone of Europe lying west of the Elbe River, several internal conflicts had already arisen before 1789, and the success of the French could not help but renew liberal and revolutionary sentiment. Patriots in Geneva, the United Provinces, and the Austrian Netherlands had already tasted repression. They were eager for another round in their various struggles and looked to France for assistance.

Refugees from these regions had fled to France and formed pressure groups that lobbied with French leaders and corresponded with rebels back home. Their fondest hopes rested on the chance that in fighting against the coalition, the French might liberate their own lands. If they were contiguous to France (as were the Austrian Netherlands, Savoy, and the Rhineland), France might then annex them to her own republic; elsewhere (in Holland, Lombardy, Ireland, and the Swiss Confederation) she might help set up independent republics by overthrowing the ruling princes or oligarchies. In the wake of war and revolutionary enthusiasm, the foreign patriots induced the Convention to declare in November 1792 that it "accords fraternity and aid to [foreign] people who wish to recover their liberty," though the French had in mind only those whose governments were actively leagued against France.

While there had been some talk of mounting a universal crusade to bring freedom to oppressed peoples, French leaders were in reality committed to a pragmatic policy. As the war spilled over into the Austrian Netherlands and Germany, they had to organize their forces and ensure a base of support abroad. This in turn required that the primary aims of war embody the spirit and stated objectives of the revolutionary society, not the age-old motive of aggrandizement through occupation and domination. Thus in December of 1792 the government proclaimed further that it would establish the freedom of those to whom it had brought or would bring armed assistance. This meant that in each land where the French prevailed, feudal practices, hereditary privileges, and repressive institutions would be abolished. A provisional government would be established to cooperate with the French forces in supervising and paying for the liberation. Full independence was a long-term promise; more immediately the occupied territory would be obliged to underwrite the expenses of French troops.

These intentions were greeted enthusiastically by progressive elements in the middle and noble classes and in some instances by artisans. But most nobles, priests, and peasants and large sections of the middle class were hostile or indifferent to them, resenting the requisitions and special taxes, though they did not necessarily wish a restoration of the old order.

By 1794 France had a permanent foothold in the Austrian Netherlands, which was shortly to be annexed to the Great Nation, as France now called herself. Apart from this, however, Robespierre proved to be relatively isolationist. Arguing that freedom had to be secured at home before it could be exported abroad, the Committee of Public Safety declined to intervene in behalf of a Polish revolutionary movement, refused to invade Holland, and designed a strategy that precluded any involvement in Italy. In short, while occupying the Austrian Netherlands and hoping to annex the left bank of the Rhine, the Convention renounced any drive for the establishment of new "sister republics."

The Revolutionary Armies

The fighting men who carried the Revolution abroad were a very different body from the corps inherited from Louis XVI. The royal army had undergone major reforms since 1789 that opened military service as a decent career to all kinds of Frenchmen. At the same time the organization of militias and national guards, with their elected officers, introduced a new concept of the citizen-soldier as against a professional army apart from civil society.

The army's chief problem came after the war began, when large numbers of royalist officers either deserted altogether or behaved disloyally. At the crucial Battle of Valmy, a remnant of the old army showed that it could fight effectively, but its numbers were too reduced by desertion and neglect to offer continued resistance. A hasty call-up of volunteers proved inadequate both in numbers and effectiveness.

The coalition launched its second major assault in 1793, and the poor performance of the French troops made it clear that drastic innovations were required. The Convention initiated far-reaching conscription and mobilization, the so-called mass levy of August 1973 (levée en masse). All unmarried men between the ages of eighteen and twenty-five were drafted for combat service, while older and married men were assigned convoy and guard duty or similar tasks. All social classes were affected, and in a short time almost half a million French citizens were placed under arms. With elected officers at their head, the citizen-soldiers marched off to the front under banners reading, "The French People, risen against the tyrants."

The Convention had already decided to combine these blue-uniformed recruits with their white-uniformed counterparts from the old professional army in units called demi-brigades. In the future noncommissioned officers would be elected by all troops, but higher ranks would be chosen by superior officers according to merit and seniority. The expectation was that discipline would be taught to the new troops by the professionals, who in turn would absorb a spirit of patriotism from the recruits. Although the actual amalgam took several years to complete, its spirit proved immediately successful.

One reason for this success was the Convention's attitude toward military discipline in a revolutionary society. Civilian control over the military was firmly established, and discipline now applied to officers as well as men. The government insisted that generals show the will to win, confidence in the republic, and talent. A large number of young men were raised quickly through the ranks to command positions. Lazare Hoche, perhaps the most spectacular case, led an entire army at the age of twenty-five and died a military hero at twenty-seven. Other generals were less fortunate. The commander of the ill-fated Rhine army in early 1793 was branded a traitor, tried, and guillotined. The revolutionary slogan "Win or die" was a serious matter.

A dramatically new approach to military life was thus taking shape: citizen-soldiers recruited through conscription, concern for their needs and morale, generous veterans' benefits if they were wounded, quick promotions for loyal and capable men, exemplary discipline for officers who wavered in spirit or on the battlefield. The question still remained of how the new army would be used in the field, and the answer reflected the combination of revolutionary spirit and hardheaded practicality that prevailed in the republic.

The mass of soldiers in the new demi-brigades did not have the necessary training to be deployed according to the traditional tactics of Old Regime armies. Conversely they were infused with a sense of patriotism that it would be well to utilize. Hence strategists perfected the new battle formation of massive columns that could move quickly without much practice in drilling. Mass and mobility characterized the armies of the French Revolution. As General Hoche put it, "No maneuvers, no art; only fire and patriotism," and the Committee of Public Safety advised its commanders, "Act offensively and in masses. Use the bayonet at every opportunity. Fight great battles and pursue the enemy until he is utterly destroyed." In this spirit the Jacobins and sans-culottes sought all-out war, and strategy was shaped to achieve it.

The Jacobins did not neglect the home front, whose contributions to the war effort were obviously crucial for victory. Economic mobilization, directed by the Convention and the Jacobin clubs, produced the necessary material support for the armies. Weapons, ammunition, clothing, and food were all produced or requisitioned in extraordinary quantities by herculean effort. Without them the military reforms would have achieved no purpose.

In late 1793 and early 1794, the armies won a series of decisive battles. They culminated in the Battle of Fleurus in June 1794, when the Austrian Netherlands was once again occupied; the annexation, officially conceded by the Hapsburgs in 1797, would last until 1814. At the Pyrenees and the Rhine, French armies were victorious, forcing their enemies one by one to come to the peace table—first Spain and Prussia, then Piedmont, and finally Austria. An army crippled at the outset by treason and desertion, defeat, lack of training and discipline, and collapsing morale had been forged into a potent force in less than two years. Militarily the second revolution was a brilliant success.

II. FROM ROBESPIERRE TO BONAPARTE

To its most dedicated supporters, the revolutionary government had two major purposes: first, to surmount a crisis and steer the republic to victory; second, to democratize France's social fabric. Only the first objective won the widespread adherence of middle-class republicans. It is not surprising, therefore, that after the victories of the year II, the revolutionary government was overthrown and the second revolution dismantled. Jacobinism and democracy, however, had become a permanent part of the French experience, as had royalism and reaction. The political spectrum of modern Europe had been created. Within this spectrum the men of 1789 attempted to command an elusive centrist or moderate position, but they proved inadequate to the task. During the four unsteady years of the Directory regime, however, revolutionary expansion outside of France proceeded aggressively. It triumphed briefly but soon precipitated a second anti-French coalition. This challenge brought the weaknesses of the Directory regime to a head and opened the way to the ascendancy of Napoleon Bonaparte.

The Thermidorian Reaction (1794–1795)

The National Convention held a polarized nation together, consolidated the republic, and defeated the Revolution's foreign enemies. But in achieving these successes, the ruling Jacobins increasingly isolated themselves, making enemies on every side. Moderates and ultrarevolutionaries alike resented the rule that they imposed. Wealthy peasants and businessmen chafed under the economic regimentation. Moreover the pressure of events and the relentless necessity to make hard and unpopular decisions wore out the Revolution's most prominent leaders.

After the decisive victories of the year II, the Convention's unity disintegrated. As the fifth anniversary of the Bastille's fall approached, Robespierre's enemies were emboldened to rise against him. Long-standing rivalries, differences over policy, and clashes of temperament now exploded. Robespierre girded himself to denounce yet another group of unspecified intriguers, presumably to send them to the fate of Danton and Hébert. But his rivals both left and right formed a hasty coalition and struck back. They denounced Robespierre to the Convention as a tyrant and would-be dictator.

The plotting of these individuals was crucial, but Robespierre's downfall is attributable also to the fact that he was no longer needed by the Convention. Having supported him with reluctance during the emergency, the moderate deputies were now willing to abandon him. The Parisian sans-culottes might have maintained Robespierre in power despite this desertion, but as we have seen, the Jacobins had alienated them by curbing the autonomy of the sections. Many sans-culottes were therefore indifferent to the struggle of personalities that took place in the Convention that July.

On the twenty-seventh—9 Thermidor—Robespierre was declared an outlaw by the Convention. Efforts to rally a popular force in his defense that night proved ineffective, and on the following day he and several loyal associates were seized and guillotined. French people perhaps did not realize it at the time, but 9 Thermidor thus became one of those crucial *journées* on which the Revolution's course was decisively altered.[2]

After Robespierre's fall the Revolution's momentum was broken, and the apparatus of the Terror was dismantled. Soon the anti-Jacobins began to attack the revolutionaries in turn. Their strident calls for retribution against the terrorists eventually produced a terrorism of their own—a "white terror" aimed against Jacobins and sans-culottes that resulted in street fighting, assassinations, and in the south of France massacres.

To survey the unfolding of the Thermidorian reaction is equivalent to viewing a film of the preceding half-decade run backward through the projector. Suspects were released, the revolutionary committees abolished, defendants before the revolutionary tribunals acquitted, and their former accusers indicted in their place. The Paris Jacobin Club was closed, while in the provinces the affiliated clubs gradually withered away under harassment and restrictive legislation. Amnesty was extended to the Girondists and to the Vendée rebels; Mountain deputies were now denounced. Paris underwent "de-sans-culottization"—the section leaders of the year II were driven out of political life and threatened with retribution. At all levels those who had borne the burden of responsibility and action in the year II suddenly found themselves attacked.

Paralleling these political reversals was a marked change in the state of public morals and social behavior. The upper classes now set the tone. For those who sought a life of pleasure and luxury, Thermidor was a reprieve from the austerity and restraint of the year II. Public virtue gave way before indulgence and license. Luxury not only reappeared but by all contemporary accounts was flaunted with scandalous vulgarity. High society, with its balls, salons, and fancy dress, was reestablished. The titles "monsieur" and "madame" replaced the republican designation "citizen." Most important, this high society of the rich showed itself bored by the spectacle of popular misery.

Unfortunately this social reaction occurred at a time of extensive mass suffering. In keeping with free-trade ideology, the Thermidorians abandoned the legislation regulating the economy. The marketplace was again permitted to operate by its "natural laws" of supply and demand, producing a skyrocketing inflation. Worse yet, France experienced a harvest in 1795 more meager than in the crisis years of 1788–1789 and 1793. But despite such ill luck, the Thermidorians declined to intervene to protect small consumers from economic ravages. They refused to try to provide a minimum supply of bread at an affordable price, a relief effort that the revolutionary government and even the Old Regime monarchs had made. In the face of near-famine, every index of social welfare

---

[2] "Thermidor" has become a generic term to denote the phase in a revolution when the pendulum swings back toward moderation or reaction. It has been argued that the drafting of the United States Constitution in 1787 was the Thermidor of the American Revolution and that Stalin's reign was the Thermidor of the Bolshevik Revolution.

now revealed disaster. Suicide and mortality rates rose markedly; police reports spoke of little else besides popular misery, discontent, and destitute people collapsing in the streets from undernourishment.

Since the government would not help, the former militants attempted to spark a political reversal to halt the reaction and force the authorities to act. Their hopes centered on the constitution of 1793, whose prompt and full implementation they now demanded. The slogan of sans-culottes in the sections during the spring of 1795 was simply "Bread and the constitution of 1793." The Thermidorians, however, were moving in precisely the opposite direction. Viewing that constitution as far too democratic, they were looking for an excuse to scrap it altogether.

The militants began demonstrating in April, and the government countered by ordering local authorities to disarm them. The only recourse left was insurrection, and it began on 1 Prairial year III (May 20, 1795). It was a grim, mournful uprising, a rear-guard action against disaster. The sans-culottes took over the Convention briefly in cooperation with a handful of sympathetic deputies. But their hours were numbered, for the Thermidorians had retreated merely to organize their armed forces. In two days of street fighting, the sans-culottes were driven back, cut off, and defeated. Severe repression followed: 36 people were executed, some 1,200 imprisoned, and an additional 1,700 interrogated and disarmed. Probably the majority of these had not even taken part in the insurrection but were being singled out in retribution for the role of the sans-culottes during the Terror.

These *journées* were the end of the popular movement, the last time that the Parisian revolutionary crowd would be mobilized. It was now clear just how much the sans-culottes and the Jacobins had needed each other. Isolated from each other, they had both been defeated. In the process the democratic republic of the year II was lost. Whatever the possibilities had been for achieving some form of social democracy (and the issue remains ambiguous), they were now severely reduced.[3] The Thermidorian reaction seemed to guarantee that the middle class would maintain control of France.

The Directory (1795–1799)

By the end of 1795, the remaining members of the Convention assumed that the Revolution was over. The extremes had been vanquished, and the time for the "peaceable enjoyment of liberty" was at hand. They had drafted a new constitution—the constitution of the year III—and proclaimed a general amnesty, and they were prepared to turn a new page. The revolutionary government, which had replaced the fallen constitutional monarchy, had in turn been replaced by a middle-class constitutional republic. It was known as the Directory, after its five-man executive body.

The Directory's proponents, concerned above all with retaining power, openly declared that the republic would "be governed by the best citizens, who are found among the property-owning class." Accordingly the constitution abandoned the universal suffrage of 1793 and restored the propertied franchise of 1791 and the multilayered system of indirect elections. Its elected two-house legislature was designed to moderate the political process, while it guarded against the rise of a potential dictator by installing the five-man Directory. Equally

---

[3] The Convention's measures to promote social democracy included the abolition of slavery, the final abolition of seigneurial rights without compensation to the lords, and equal division of estates among heirs. Legislation for a system of free public education, a progressive income tax, a war veterans' bonus, and the distribution of the property of convicted suspects to indigent patriots was never implemented.

important, it omitted devices to facilitate active democracy, such as referendums, and said nothing of popular rights, like the right to free education and to subsistence, all of which were specified in the 1793 constitution. The concern with eliminating the popular democracy of the year II was balanced by measures to prevent a royalist resurgence. Fearing that free elections at this point might swing the republic too far to the right, the Convention decided to coopt two-thirds of its membership into the new legislature established by the constitution. A royalist attempt to oppose this with an armed protest was crushed.

The government thus repudiated both the royalist movement and the second revolution. As regicides the directors necessarily opposed royalism; on the other hand they were determined that popular democracy and terrorism would not recur. Apart from these considerations they were inclined to forgive and forget. They attempted to command a position somewhere near the hypothetical center of the political spectrum, a stance that one historian has aptly called the mirage of the moderates.

To maintain themselves in power, the Directory politicians were obliged to remove with one hand freedoms that they had granted with the other. They repeatedly purged locally elected officials; they periodically undermined freedom of the press and of association, ostensibly guaranteed in the new constitution, by suppressing new Jacobin clubs and hostile newspapers. Above all they refused to acknowledge the legitimacy of organized opposition, whether rightist or leftist. This explains the succession of coups and purges that marked the Directory's four years. Although the repressive measures were mild compared with those of the second revolution—deportation was generally the harshest punishment meted out for dissent—their net effect was to make the regime dysfunctional. In the end a significant number of Thermidorians were obliged to abandon their own creation altogether.

The Political Spectrum

For all its dictatorial qualities, however, the Directory regime was free enough to allow most shades of the political spectrum some visibility. Obliterated previously by the Jacobin commonwealth and later by the Napoleonic dictatorship, the full range of opinions and divisions in France was clearly revealed during the years of the Directory and would persist with certain modifications down to the fall of the Third Republic, in 1940.

The most important legacy of all was probably apathy, born of exhaustion or cynicism. Most citizens, especially peasants, were weary of controversy, distrustful of politicians, and hostile to administrators and tax collectors, whatever government they served. As a result participation in the Directory regime's annual elections was extremely low.

Within this context of massive apathy, politically conscious Frenchmen were deeply divided. The ultraroyalists were uncompromising enemies of the Directory, dedicated to overthrowing it. They included émigrés, armed rebels, and refractory priests, along with their peasant followers, and many of them cooperated with the exiled Bourbons and English spies. Shading off from the ultraroyalists were the monarchists, mainly from the middle and peasant classes. They hoped to alter the republic's foundations and to drift gradually back toward royalism without necessarily overthrowing the republic by force. Their goals included allowing the émigrés to return, restoring the position of the refractory clergy, and stamping out entirely the last vestiges of Jacobinism. Since Napoleon largely acquiesced in these changes, they formed a major base of his support.

On the left of the spectrum stood the Jacobins, or democrats. They were committed not only to preserving the Revolution of 1789 and the republic but to identifying positively with the second revolution as well. They did not advocate a return to the Terror, hoping rather, like the constitutional royalists, to work legally within the new institutions of the Directory to regain power. The Jacobin policy was to promote grass-roots activism through local political clubs, petitions, peaceful demonstrations, newspapers, and electoral campaigns. The clubs attracted a small cross section of middle-class revolutionaries and sans-culotte militants, thus keeping alive the egalitarian social ideals of the year II. In addition to calling for the implementation of existing laws against counterrevolutionaries, the Jacobins advocated free public education, a veterans' bonus for soldiers, the right to subsistence, and progressive taxation.

At the far end of the spectrum emerged a tiny group of collectivists whose significance would loom much larger in the nineteenth century than it did in 1796. This was the circle of Gracchus Babeuf. They viewed the year II as simply a stage in the revolutionary process that now had to be followed by a final revolution against the middle-class republic in the name of the masses. Their objectives were a vaguely defined "real equality" and a "community of goods," a distributive type of communism. Believing that the middle-class republic was simply a new form of tyranny, they plotted its overthrow by means of a highly centralized secret conspiracy. When Filippo Buonarroti published a firsthand account of the plot in the 1820s, it became a handbook of revolution, influencing Karl Marx and ultimately Lenin.

The Directory's adherents stood somewhere in the center of this broad spectrum, shifting their ground uncertainly and unsuccessfully to find a solid position. They were hostile to the royalists, but possibly even more antagonistic to the Jacobins. Thus they sometimes collaborated with the reactionaries, as when they used the Babeuf plot as a pretext for repressing the entire left, though most democrats had deplored Babeuf's calls for insurrection and did not take his communism seriously.

This propelled the Directory into a tentative alliance with the right, and the climate of public opinion became increasingly reactionary. However, when the first regular elections held in the year V (1797) produced a royalist victory, the moderates reversed themselves. Backed by General Bonaparte's army of Italy, they purged the legislature of the most notorious royalists, annulled numerous elections, suppressed about forty royalist newspapers, restored the sanctions against priests and émigrés, and allowed the Jacobins to open new clubs.

But after a few months, as the clubs began to revive a democratic spirit, the Directory grew fearful. During the elections of the year VI, democratic and conservative republicans began to campaign against each other in what almost amounted to party rivalry. The Directory again intervened, closing the clubs, manipulating the electoral assemblies, and where this failed, purging the democrats elected. It is revealing to note that almost at the same time the American republic was going through a similar process, but there the rival parties finally agreed to disagree, and organized opposition was accepted as part of the legitimate political system. In France organized opposition was not tolerated, and that crucial decision contributed to the republic's demise.

The Rise of Bonaparte

While France was retreating from her Revolution internally, however, she supported and spread it more forcefully than ever abroad. For the Revolution in Europe, the Directory years marked a high point of success. Under the Directory she gradually turned to a policy of encouraging wars of liberation and the establishment of sister republics (see Map 21.1). This eventually led to the creation of progressive representative governments in the United

MAP 21.1: THE REVOLUTIONARY REPUBLICS 1792–1799

Provinces and the Swiss Confederation, which became known respectively as the Batavian and Helvetic republics. It led also, despite the Directory's attempt to prevent it, to the spread of war and liberation to the entire Italian peninsula. This in turn came about because certain commanders in the field began to create their own diplomacy. Among them was a young brigadier general, Napoleon Bonaparte.

The Making of a Hero

Bonaparte personifies the world-historical figure—the rare person whose life decisively affects the mainstream of human events. Born in 1769 of an impoverished but well-connected family on the French-controlled island of Corsica, he scarcely seemed destined to play such a role. His youthful ambitions were limited to Corsica itself, and most of his adolescent fantasies seem to have involved leading the island to independence from France. He was sent to French military academies, where he proved a diligent student, very adept at mathematics, and an eager reader of history. Aloof from his aristocratic classmates, whose pretensions he resented, young Bonaparte was extraordinarily self-reliant and energetic. Imagination and energy would remain among his chief personality traits, but before the Revolution he lacked any notable objective. Meanwhile he became an expert in artillery.

The Revolution saw him return to Corsica, but his ambitions ran afoul of more conservative elements on the island, and eventually the heat of provincial factionalism drove him and his family off Corsica altogether. At that juncture Napoleon moved onto a far larger stage of action. His rise as a military officer was steady and rapid; it was based in part on the luck of successive opportunities but equally on his ability to make fast, bold decisions and carry them out with remarkable efficiency. On leave in Paris in 1795, he made important contacts among the leaders of the Directory and was assigned to the planning bureau of the war ministry. This put him in a position to advocate a new strategy—the opening of a major front in Italy for a French strike at the Hapsburg forces from the south, pushing northward into Germany while armies on the Rhine drove in from the west. The strategy approved, he was given command of the Army of Italy in 1797.

The total number of opposing Austrians outnumbered the French, but Bonaparte moved his troops rapidly and skillfully to achieve surprise and numerical superiority in specific encounters. The end result was a major victory that brought the French the Hapsburg province of Lombardy with its capital, Milan. Bonaparte's overall plan almost miscarried since the army of the Rhine was unsuccessful in its part of the offensive. But this fact made his own victories all the more important to the Directory. Moreover Napoleon ensured his popularity with the Paris government by making his campaign self-supporting through organized levies on the Italians instead of allowing his troops the customary prerogative of looting.

On the scene in Italy, Bonaparte brought a great new sense of excitement and showmanship to the French occupation. His personal magnetism, his theatrical skill, and his ability to manipulate men and policies all won him tremendous popularity among the Italians. He encouraged them to organize their own revolutionary movement, seeing the liberation of Italy as a means of both solidifying support for his army among them and ultimately enhancing his own reputation. This distressed the Directory since its own objective was to trade off conquests in Italy for security on the Rhine frontier. But in the end the government had to accept the fruits of the young general's victories over Austria and the Treaty of Campo Formio, which he personally negotiated in October 1797. Austria recognized a new and independent state in northern Italy, the Cisalpine Republic, and made peace with France, though leaving the Rhine question to future negotiations.

Patriotic aspiration in France now focused on defeating the last member of the coalition—the hated British enemy. Bonaparte naturally yearned for the glory of accomplishing this, and he was authorized to prepare an invasion force. Previous seaborne landings directed at Ireland had failed, and Napoleon too was finally obliged to abandon the scheme because of insufficient naval capability.

In the spring of 1798 Bonaparte instead turned southward to launch an expedition to Egypt. The objective was to strike at Britain's colonial interests, ultimately including the approaches to India. But British naval superiority, in the form of Admiral Horatio Nelson's fleet, turned the mission into a debacle. At the Battle of the Nile, the French fleet was decimated, and the army was marooned without support in North Africa. In addition Napoleon suffered reversals in engagements with Turkish forces. Only skillful news management prevented the full dimensions of the defeat from being known in France; the expedition's exotic details—including the much-publicized element of scientific exploration—dominated the version of the events that most Frenchpeople learned. Ultimately Napoleon extricated himself from this morass by slipping off through the blockade alone, to all intents and purposes abandoning his army. Since important things were happening in France, he was confident that this would be overlooked.

The Brumaire Coup

While Bonaparte was in Egypt, the Directory was faltering under the political pressures discussed earlier. Charges of tyranny and ineffectiveness accumulated against the executive. Its diplomacy had proved a failure; further expansion in Italy, which had produced several new sister republics on the peninsula, had precipitated a new coalition against France—Great Britain, Russia, Austria, Naples, and Turkey. Facing a new war in the spring of 1799, the government was denounced for tolerating corruption by war contractors and for harassing patriotic generals.

In the elections of that spring, the widespread discontent was manifested in the defeat of many government-sponsored candidates. Shortly thereafter the legislature was able to oust four of the five directors and replace them with an ill-fated consortium of Jacobins and conservatives led by Sieyès. The pretext for toppling the incumbents came from military reversals in June, when ill-supplied French forces were compelled to evacuate most of Italy and were yielding in the Helvetic Republic. Sieyès' supporters were secretly eager to alter the constitution itself. They had lost confidence in the seemingly ineffectual institutions of the Directory regime and the instability that they felt in its annual elections. They were "revisionists," hoping to redesign the republic along more oligarchic lines. Their main enemies were the Jacobins, who wished conversely to democratize the Directory gradually. The moderate or centrist position had virtually disappeared.

The military crisis briefly favored the Jacobins, who responded with a battery of emergency measures to rally the country. Simultaneously they urged legislation to guarantee freedom for newspapers, political clubs, and other forms of organized dissent. The revisionists opposed these proposals, stalled, and ultimately succeeded in having them rejected. Meanwhile the autumn brought success for the French forces in the Helvetic state and in the Batavian Republic, where they repulsed an Anglo-Russian invasion. Most of Italy was lost, but the real threat to France herself had passed. At this point the revisionists began a concerted offensive at home against the democrats, closing down their clubs and newspapers and preparing for a coup d'état against the constitution, whose main supporters were now the powerless Jacobins.

Bonaparte's return to France seemed fortuitous at this time of uncertainty. No dire military threat remained to propel the country into the arms of a general; the revisionists were primarily concerned with scrapping a relatively open-ended regime that might evolve in a democratic direction and establishing a more rigid, oligarchic republic. But they did need a general's cooperation, for generals were the only national heroes in this demoralized period, and a general would come in handy to organize whatever force might be necessary to ensure the success of the coup. Bonaparte was not the revisionists' first choice, but he proved to be the only one available. In addition his trip up from the Mediterranean was greeted with a hero's welcome; the people had only a dim knowledge of the Egyptian fiasco and saw him in his well-earned role of victor in the Italian campaign.

Contrary to the intentions of Sieyès and his coconspirators, Bonaparte proved to be the tail that wagged the dog. As the plans were prepared, he thrust himself into an increasingly prominent position, emerging as the most ambitious and boldest of those involved. It was he who addressed the legislature to denounce a mythical Jacobin plot and to demand emergency powers to set up a new provisional government. These powers were granted, and Bonaparte joined with the two remaining directors to form a new executive, charged with bringing in a new constitutional draft. Soldiers were present to prevent any resistance. The legislature was then purged, with a cooperative rump left to ratify the new arrangements. This was how the *journée* of 18 Brumaire, year VIII (November 9, 1799), unfolded.

The Brumaire coup had not been designed to create a dictatorship, let alone a military dictatorship, but that was precisely its eventual result. In the ensuing maneuvering among the revisionists, Bonaparte's ideas and personality prevailed. The general came out of the coup as the strong man in a triumvirate of consuls, and Sieyès' elaborate plans for a republican oligarchy ended in the wastebasket, he himself accepting a pension and retiring to the country.

In other respects the plotters' plans succeeded. Elections and legislative power were meant to be limited, and they were; the middle-class elite was meant to erect barriers against the advance of democracy, and it did. The social changes propounded in the revolution of the year II were permanently blocked, while those of 1789 were consummated and protected. The price was a surrender of popular sovereignty and parliamentary liberalism.

On one final point the revisionists were to be particularly deceived. With Bonaparte's cooperation they had implicitly held out the promise of obtaining a durable peace through victory. Instead, the new regime promoted expansion and continuous war of unparalleled dimensions.

III. THE NAPOLEONIC IMPERIUM

Bonaparte rapidly became a forceful and skillful dictator. Certain of his institutional and social reforms proved so durable that they survived his downfall by well over a century. At the time, however, it was his success on the battlefield against France's foes that gave him a free hand domestically. And it was again on the battlefield that his enigmatic ambitions began to grow, transforming him from a general of the Revolution to an imperial conqueror of the Continent. Bonaparte's occupation of Italy, Germany, Spain, and other lands set contradictory forces of change in motion, for nationalism, liberalism, and reaction alike were sparked by his presence.

The Napoleonic Settlement in France

Napoleon's prime asset in his rapid takeover of France was the resignation of its citizens. Most Frenchmen were so weary politically that they were inclined to see in Napoleon what they wished to see. The Committee of Public Safety had won grudging submission only through its terroristic policies; Napoleon achieved the same result almost by default. The fact that he was highly eclectic, an effective propagandist for himself, and a man of great personal magnetism helped placate a divided France. Ultraroyalists and dedicated Jacobins were never reconciled to his regime, but most citizens fell between those extremes and were able to find something to cheer about in the general's accomplishments.

Napoleon's attitudes are not easily classified: he was not a reactionary or a Jacobin, not a conservative or a liberal, though his opinions were flavored by a touch of each persuasion. The things he was most concerned with were authority and justification of his actions through results. The men of 1789 could find in him an heir of the Revolution because of his hostility toward the Old Regime. The corporate system, the creaking institutions of absolutism, and the congealed structures of aristocratic hierarchy were all immensely distasteful to him; he considered them unjust and ineffective. Apart from these negative perspectives, Napoleon valued the Revolution's positive commitment to equality of opportunity. This was the major liberal concept of 1789 that he continued to defend. Other rights and liberties he apparently felt could be curtailed or ignored.

Ten years of upheavals had presented a grim paradox: the Revolution had proceeded in the name of freedom, and yet successive forms of repression had been mounted to defend it. Napoleon fitted comfortably into this mold; unlike the Directory, he made no pretense about it. The social gains of the Revolution would be preserved through the exercise of strong control. His field of action was far greater than that of the most powerful eighteenth-century monarch, for no entrenched aristocracy existed to resist him. Benefiting from the clearing operations of the Revolution, he could reconstruct far more than any previous ruler and thus could show more results in justification of his authoritarian measures.

Tragically, however, Napoleon drifted away from his own ideal of rationalization. Increasingly absorbed in his personal power, he began to force domestic and foreign policies on France that were geared to his imperial ambitions. As a result he increasingly directed his government toward raising men and money for the military machine, abandoning the fragile revolutionary legacy in the process.

Political and Religious Settlements

Bonaparte imposed a constitution on France that placed almost unchecked power in the hands of a single man, the first consul, for ten years. It also called for his own appointment to that position. Two later constitutional revisions, which were approved in plebiscites, further increased executive authority while diminishing the legislative branch until it disappeared altogether. The first, in 1802, converted the consulship into a lifetime post; the second, in 1804, did away with the republic by proclaiming Napoleon emperor of the French with hereditary title. The task of drafting legislation was transferred from elected representatives to appointed administrators in the Council of State. This new body was charged with advising the emperor, drafting legislation under his orders, and supervising local authorities and public institutions. This marked the birth of government by experts that remained an alternative to parliamentary government throughout subsequent French history.

The system of local government established in 1800 came ironically close to restoring the centralized bureaucracy of the Old Regime, which had been unanimously condemned in 1789. Under Bonaparte local elections, which the Revolution had emphasized, were virtually eliminated. Each department was now administered by a prefect appointed by Paris. The 400-odd subprefects on the district level as well as the 40,000 mayors of France's communes were likewise chosen in Paris. With minor changes the prefect system survived in France until the socialist victory of 1981, severely limiting local autonomy and self-government.

Police-state methods finished what constitutional change began: the suppression of genuine political activity in French life. Inheriting a large police ministry from the Directory, Napoleon placed it under the control of a former terrorist, Joseph Fouché, directing him to eliminate organized opposition and dissent. Newspapers were reduced in number and drastically censored;[4] the free journalism born in 1789 was replaced by government press releases and news management—the propaganda techniques Napoleon had adopted in Italy and Egypt became standard procedure for the consulate and empire. Clubs were prohibited, certain dissidents deported, and other presumed opponents placed under surveillance by police spies. All this wrested submission from the whole range of political activists—royalist die-hards, sansculotte militants, and liberal intellectuals. Opposition was reduced to clandestine plotting or passive resistance in such forms as desertion from the army.

Napoleon's actions in the religious sphere were designed to promote stability at home and popularity abroad. By 1800 revolutionary policy amounted to half-hearted secularism, with Catholicism tolerated but barred from a voice in public activity. Continuing proscription of the refractory clergy made the free exercise of the religion difficult, and the orthodox Catholic world continued to stigmatize the entire Revolution as antichurch.

Napoleon judged that major concessions to Catholic sentiment were in order, provided they could be carefully controlled by the state. He proceeded to negotiate an agreement with Pope Pius VII, the Concordat of 1801, acknowledging Catholicism as the "preferred" religion of France but explicitly protecting freedom of conscience and worship for other cults.

The church was now permitted to operate in full public view; indeed primary education would be more or less turned over to the clergy, and clerical salaries would be paid by the state. Bishops would again be consecrated by the pope, but they would be nominated by the consul. Most important, the concordat reserved to the state the power to regulate the place of the church within French society. One major revolutionary change was sustained: lands confiscated from the church and sold during the Revolution were to be retained by their purchasers. Another major change was abandoned: the ten-day week was dropped and the Gregorian calendar restored.

The balance of church-state relations was firmly fixed in the state's favor, for it was Napoleon's intention to use the clergy as a major prop of the new regime. With priests now responsible to the government, the pulpit and the primary school became instruments of social control, to be used, as the imperial catechism put it, "to bind the religious conscience of the people to the August person of the Emperor." Napoleon summarized his approach to religion in his statement that the clergy would be his moral prefects. Eventually devout Catholics came to fear that this highly national version of church organization would be detrimental to true Catholicism, and Pius renounced the concordat—to which Napoleon responded by removing the pontiff to France and placing him under house arrest.

The Social System

With Old Regime obstacles to civil equality removed, Napoleon believed that the Revolution was complete. It remained now to erect an orderly, hierarchical society to counteract what he regarded as the excessive individualism of revolutionary social reforms. The foundation stones of social change—the transfer of church lands, the end of the guild system, the abolition of feudalism—would be consolidated. At the same time the authority of state and family

---

[4] Before the Brumaire coup Paris had had seventy-three newspapers; by 1811 it had only four, all hewing to the official government line.

would be reasserted and the social dominance of the middle class reaffirmed.

In the absence of electoral politics, Napoleon used the state's vast appointive powers to confer status on prominent local figures, thus associating them with his regime. These regional dignitaries were chosen from among the prosperous landowners and middle class, while the common people were definitively returned to their supposedly rightful place of deferential passivity. A new source of status was added to enhance the prestige of those who served the regime well: the Order of the Legion of Honor, nine-tenths of whose members were military men. "It is with trinkets that mankind is governed," Napoleon is supposed to have said. Legion of Honor awards and local appointments under the patronage system were precisely such trinkets, and they endured long after their creator was gone.

Napoleon helped consolidate middle-class dominance in more practical ways. A system of compulsory labor "passports" gave employers control over their workers' movements; trade unions and strikes were strictly prohibited. Leading bankers realized their long-standing ambition to have a national bank chartered that they themselves fully controlled and that enjoyed the credit power derived from official ties to the state. In education Napoleon created elite secondary schools, or lycées, designed in part to produce high civil servants and officers. They were joined to a rigidly centralized academic system that survived intact into the twentieth century, dominating the pattern of French education and some would say retarding it. Teachers and professors were certified and assigned by Paris; an enormous bureaucracy regulated educational affairs down to the smallest detail of curriculum and maintenance.

An equally durable legal codification covered social relations and property rights. The Civil Code, renamed the Napoleonic Code in 1807, guaranteed fundamental departures from Old Regime practices, and as such it was a revolutionary document that progressives were pleased to see exported throughout Europe. Feudal aristocracy and the property relations deriving from it were obliterated. Instead all citizens could now exercise unambiguous contractual ownership. The code established the right to choose one's occupation, to receive equal treatment under the law, and to enjoy religious freedom. At the same time it confirmed the Thermidorian and Directory retreat from the social policies of the second revolution. Property rights for example were not matched by anything resembling a right to subsistence.

Revolutionary legislation had emancipated women and children by establishing their civil liberties. Napoleon undid most of this progress by restoring the father's absolute authority in the family. A wife owes obedience to her husband, said the code, which proceeded to deprive her of property and juridical rights that had been granted during the Revolution. The rights of illegitimate children were also eliminated, and the husband's options in disposing of his estate were enlarged, though each son was still guaranteed a portion. Napoleon insisted on relatively liberal provisions for divorce—but only as far as the husband was concerned. Penal codes and criminal procedures also rolled back revolutionary libertarianism. Defendants' rights and the role of juries were both curtailed.

The Napoleonic Code, the concordat, the education system, and the patronage structure all proved extremely durable institutions. They fulfilled Napoleon's desire to create a series of "granite masses" on which French society could be permanently reconstructed. His admirers emphasize that these achievements contributed to social stability despite France's chronic lack of stable governments. One can argue that they were skillful compromises between revolutionary equality and libertarianism on the one hand and a sense of hierarchy and authority on the other. Detractors point out

This etching of the Battle of Austerlitz (December 1805) dramatically captures the two faces of Napoleonic warfare: the glory and the gore. In the background an Austrian flag is being presented to the Emperor—the mark of his brilliant victory in that engagement. But in the foreground the mangled corpses of the casualties are plainly evident. As the years went on, the glory became more and more dubious, while the dead and disabled grew too numerous to contemplate.
(Photo: Culver Pictures, Inc.)

first that they were class-oriented, withdrawing from the mass of Frenchpeople promises held out by the second revolution; and second that they created an overcentralized, rigid institutional structure that sapped French vitality in succeeding generations. Whatever their merits or defects, these institutions did take root. They did not prove ephemeral reflections of the luster of the imperial throne, as did other aspects of Napoleon's reign—notably his attempt to create a hereditary empire and a French-dominated Europe.

Napoleonic Hegemony

Although Bonaparte was not needed to repel an imminent invasion at the time of the Brumaire coup, he was expected to provide strategy and command for a successful conclusion of the war against the second coalition. Accordingly the first consul left France at the earliest opportunity in late 1799 with an army prepared to engage Hapsburg forces in northern Italy. The outcome of this campaign would confirm or destroy the settlement he had imposed on the revisionists. A decisive victory would make him impregnable; a rout would obviously destroy his political future.

Napoleon's strategy called for a repeat of the 1797 campaign: he would strike through Italy while the army of the Rhine pushed eastward against Vienna. This time it worked. Following French victories at Marengo, in Lombardy, and Hohenlinden, in Germany, Austria sued for peace. The Treaty of Lunéville, in February 1801, essentially restored France to the position she had held after Napoleon's triumphs in 1797.

In the British Isles a war-weary government, now standing alone against Napoleon, decided to negotiate a treaty also. The Peace of Amiens, March 1801, ended hostilities and reshuffled territorial holdings outside Europe. But it was a precarious truce because it did not settle the future of French influence and expansion or commercial relations between the two nations. Napoleon soon showed that he was willing to violate the spirit of the treaty while abiding by its letter. The British and Austrians alike were dismayed by the continued expansion of French influence in Italy, the Helvetic Republic, and North America. Most important perhaps, France made it clear that she would exclude British trade rather than restore normal trading relations. Historians generally agree that the Peace of Amiens failed because neither side was strongly interested in making it last. Their century-long struggle for preeminence had yet to be decided.

A third coalition, a replay of its predecessors, formed as the treaties broke down. France's ostensible war aims were still the preservation of the regime at home and the sister republics abroad. The coalition had the ideological and diplomatic objectives of restoring the Batavian Republic and Italy to "independence," dissolving French influence elsewhere, and if possible reducing France to her original borders. But like most alliances of its sort, the third coalition was to be dismembered piecemeal.

Among its other functions, the Napoleonic Empire provided great spoils for the Bonaparte siblings. With Napoleon now an Emperor, it was only fitting that his sisters were married off to princely husbands, and that his brothers were provided with thrones of their own in French-occupied Europe. Here, Prince Jérôme Bonaparte marries Princess Catherine of Württenberg.
(Photo: Bulloz)

French hopes of settling the issue directly by invading England proved unrealizable. At the Battle of Trafalgar, in October 1805, an already outnumbered and outmanned French navy was crushed by Admiral Nelson's fleet. An innovative tactician who broke rule-book procedures on the high seas as French generals had been doing on land, Nelson ensured the security of the British Isles for the remainder of the Napoleonic era.

Napoleon turned now against the Austro-Russian forces. Moving 200,000 French soldiers with unprecedented speed across the Continent, he took his enemies by surprise and won a succession of startling victories. After occupying Vienna he proceeded against the coalition's main army in December. Feigning weakness and retreat at the moment of battle, he drew his now numerically superior opponents into an exposed position, crushed the center of their lines, and inflicted a decisive defeat. The Battle of Austerlitz was Napoleon's most brilliant tactical achievement, and the Hapsburgs were compelled to jump for the peace table. The resulting Treaty of Pressburg was extremely harsh and humiliating for Austria. Not only was a large indemnity imposed on her, but she was required to cede her Venetian provinces.

The Conquest and Reorganization of Europe

By this time Napoleon had far surpassed his role of general of the Revolution and was beginning his imperial march toward the conquest of Europe. The French sphere of influence had increased dramatically to include most of southern Germany, which was organized into the Confederation of the Rhine, a client realm of France. At the moment only Prussia stood outside this sphere. Her neutrality during the war with Austria had been effected by skillful French diplomacy and Prussian miscalculation. Only after Austria had been forced to the peace table did Prussia recognize the threat she had allowed to rise against her interests by missing her chance to combine effectively with her neighbor to the south. Belatedly she mobilized her famous but antiquated army; it was rewarded with stinging defeat by France in a number of encounters culminating in the Battle of Jena in October 1806. With Prussian military power proved a paper tiger and the conqueror ensconced in Berlin, the prestige of the ruling class disintegrated, and the masses docilely accepted the occupation that followed. Napoleon was now master of the northern German lands as well as the south. For a while it appeared that he would obliterate Prussia entirely, but in the end he restored her sovereignty after amputating part of her territory and imposing a crushing indemnity.

The subsequent reorganization of Central Europe brought Napoleon considerable gratification and prestige. He formally proclaimed the end of the moribund Holy Roman Empire in 1806—Francis II had already changed his own title to Emperor Francis I of Austria two years earlier—and proceeded to liquidate numerous small German principalities whose profusion had created such chaos. In their place he erected two new states: the Kingdom of Westphalia, on whose throne he placed his brother Jérôme; and the grand duchy of Berg, to be ruled by Joachim Murat, his brother-in-law. His ally Saxony was proclaimed a full-scale kingdom, while a new duchy of Warsaw was created out of Prussian Poland. This "restoration" of Poland had major propaganda value; it made the emperor appear a champion of Polish national aspirations in view of the fact that the rulers of Prussia, Russia, and Austria had dismembered Poland in a series of partitions ending in 1794. Moreover Napoleon could now enlist a Polish army and use Polish territory as a base of operations against the last Continental member of the coalition, Russia.

In February 1807 Napoleon confronted the colossus of the East in the Battle of Eylau; the resulting carnage was horrifying but inconclusive. When spring came Napoleon was in a desperate position. Only a dramatic victory could preserve his conquests in Central Europe and vindicate the extraordinary decisions of the past two years. Fortunately for the Emperor the Battle of Friedland in June was a French victory that demoralized Tsar Alexander I and persuaded him to negotiate.

Meeting at Tilsit, the two emperors buried their differences and proceeded to create a mighty alliance of two superstates that would dominate Europe, essentially partitioning it into Eastern and Western spheres of influence. Each would support the other's conquests and mediate in behalf of the other's interests. The Treaty of Tilsit of July 7 sanctioned Napoleon's reorganization of Europe as well as the dramatic expansion of French territory eastward. Apart from outright annexations the chief vehicle for Napoleon's rearrangements was the creation of satellite kingdoms. The old sister republics were now induced to evolve into kingdoms just as France herself had. And it happened that Napoleon had a whole family of brothers ready to assume royal crowns.

The distorted shape of Napoleonic Europe at its high point, around 1810, is best appreciated on a map (see Map 21.2). His chief satellites included the Kingdom of Holland, comprising the Batavian Republic, with brother Louis on the throne; the Kingdom of Italy, with Napoleon himself as king and stepson Eugène de Beauharnais as viceroy; the Confederation of the Rhine, including brother Jérôme's Kingdom of Westphalia; the Kingdom of Naples, covering southern Italy, with brother Joseph wearing the crown until he was transferred to Spain and passed it to brother-in-law Murat; and the duchy of Warsaw. The old Austrian Netherlands, the Rhineland, Tuscany, Piedmont, Genoa, the Illyrian provinces, and the Ionian Islands had been directly annexed to France. Switzerland persisted as the Helvetic Republic but under a new constitution dictated by France. In 1810, after yet another war with Austria, imperial policy was consummated by a marriage between the house of Bonaparte and the house of Hapsburg: Napoleon, having divorced Joséphine de Beauharnais, married Marie Louise, daughter of Francis I.

The Continental System

Only Britain remained to be vanquished; meanwhile she stood between Napoleon and his dream of complete hegemony over Europe, not to mention the world beyond. Since Britain was invulnerable to invasion, Napoleon's objective was to destroy her influence by means of economic warfare.

Unable to blockade British ports directly, the emperor sought to close the Continent—to blockade Britain from her markets, stop her exports, and thus ruin her trade and credit. In mercantilist fashion he reasoned that if she had nowhere to sell her manufactured goods, no gold would come into the country, which would eventually bankrupt her. At the same time overproduction would cause unemployment, and the ensuing labor unrest might turn the British people against the government and force it to make peace with France. On the other hand French advantages in Continental markets would naturally increase with the elimination of British competition.

Accordingly Napoleon mounted his so-called Continental system: he would prohibit British trade with all French allies and all commerce by neutrals carrying British products, prevent all ships coming from British ports from landing in Europe, and have any goods coming from or belonging to the British Isles impounded.

The British responded in 1807 with the Orders in Council that in effect reversed the blockade: they *required* all neutral ships to stop at British ports to procure trading licenses and pay tariffs. In other words they intervened in all trade between neutrals and most European

MAP 21.2: EUROPE 1810

ports. Violators became lawful prizes to seize. Napoleon's angry answer to this was the threat simply to commandeer any neutral ship that obeyed the Orders in Council by stopping at British ports.

Thus a total naval war involving neutrals grew out of the Continental system. Indeed there scarcely remained such a thing as neutral immunity since every ship was obliged to violate one system or the other and thus run afoul of naval patrols or privateers. While the British took only about 40 French ships a year after 1807 (for few were left to sail the seas), they seized almost 3,000 neutrals a year, including many American ships.

Britain was hurt by the Continental system. Her gold reserves dwindled, and internal strife did erupt in 1811, a year of widespread unemployment and rioting. France was affected adversely by the counterblockade, which cut her off from the raw materials necessary for industrial production as well as from British finished goods, extremely popular on the Continent. But the satellite states probably suffered the most, becoming economic vassals of France. In Amsterdam for example shipping volume declined from 1,350 ships entering the port in 1806 to 310 in 1809; as a result commercial revenues dropped calamitously. Out of loyalty to the people whom he ruled, King Louis Bonaparte tolerated smuggling. This so infuriated Napoleon that he ousted his brother from the throne and annexed the Kingdom of Holland to France. Smuggling was in fact the weak link in the system, creating holes in Napoleon's dike of economic sanctions that constantly needed plugging. This in turn drove Napoleon to more drastic policies.

Resistance to Napoleon

Having vanquished every major European power on the battlefield except Britain, Napoleon now felt that nothing stood in his way. Since Spain and Russia did not seem responsive enough to his will, the emperor chose to deal with each of them by force, assuming that his plans against Britain could then be pursued to their conclusion. On all counts he was mistaken. Napoleon's confrontations with Britain, Spain, and Russia proved in various ways that his reach had exceeded his grasp.

The Spanish Ulcer

Spain and France had a common interest in weakening British power in Europe and the colonial world. But their alliance after 1795 brought only reversals for Spain, including the loss of her Louisiana Territory and (at the Battle of Trafalgar) most of her fleet. Domestically things were no better. The royal household had been the scene of scandalous and bitter controversy for some time. A lover of Queen Maria Louisa's, Manuel de Godoy, had achieved astonishing ascendancy as prime minister and proved to be a corrupt opportunist who was extremely unpopular with the people. He was despised by Crown Prince Ferdinand, who was equally hostile to Godoy's protectors, the king and queen.

Napoleon looked on the resultant turbulence with extreme irritation. At the zenith of his power, he easily drifted toward the solution of reorganizing Spain himself. As a pretext for military intervention, he put in motion a plan to invade Portugal, supposedly to partition her with Spain. Once the French army was well inside Spain, it could impose the political solution to Spain's instability that Napoleon desired.

The squabbling King Charles IV and his son were tricked, threatened, and bribed into abdicating, one after the other; a group of Spanish notables was gathered to petition Napoleon to provide a new sovereign, preferably his brother Joseph; and Joseph was duly proclaimed king of Spain. With French troops already settled around Madrid, Joseph prepared to assume his new throne, sincerely eager to rule well under a liberal constitution that was drawn up. But as he took up the crown, an unanticipated drama unfolded.

Faced with military occupation, the disappearance of their royal family, and the crowning of a Frenchman, the Spanish people rose in rebellion. It began on May 2, 1808, when an angry crowd rioted against French troops, who responded with brutal reprisals. This bloody incident, known as the Dos de Mayo and captured in Goya's famous paintings (see Plate 48), has been preserved in Spanish legend. The kidnapping of Prince Ferdinand a short time later galvanized the uprising into a sustained offensive against the French and pro-French Spaniards. Local notables created juntas to organize the rebels, mainly peasants, priests, and monks, and coordinate them with regular Spanish troops.

The troops were generally ineffective against the French but did produce one telling victory: two French divisions were forced to surrender at Bailén in July, an episode that broke the aura of Napoleonic invincibility. The main brunt of professional military operations in what had now become the Peninsular War was borne by the British, whose expeditionary force first drove the French out of Portugal and eventually rolled them back across Spain under the inspired command of Arthur Wellesley, later duke of Wellington. All the while as many as 30,000 Spanish guerrilla fighters were providing another dimension to the conflict and contributing to its brutality. Their atrocities and harassment of the French kept the foreign invaders in a constant state of anxiety and led to reprisals that in turn escalated the war's bitterness.

All told the juntas, the guerrillas, and the British held a massive French army of up to 300,000 men pinned down in Spain and made it impossible for Napoleon to mobilize fully elsewhere on the Continent. He referred to the war as the "Spanish ulcer." In addition, though Napoleon had contempt for the rebel monks and peasants, other Europeans were inspired by their example that resistance to the French emperor was possible.

Meanwhile the war proved a disaster for Spanish liberals. Torn between Joseph, who would have been a liberal ruler, and the nationalist rebels, they ended by falling into an unviable position between the two. Those who supported Joseph found that he was never able to rule independently. It was Napoleon who gave the orders in Spain, relying on his generals to carry them out. Those who stood behind the rebels were able to organize a provisional government in 1812 by convening the ancient parliament, the Cortes, in the town of Cádiz. There they drafted a liberal and nationalist constitution, which pleased the British and therefore was tolerated by the local juntas. But in reality the priests, peasants, and nobles who made up the bulk of rebel sympathizers disdained the liberals and were fighting rather for the Catholic Church and the Spanish Bourbons. When in 1814 the French were finally expelled and Ferdinand VII took the throne, the liberals' joy was short-lived. Ferdinand tore up the constitution of 1812, restored the monasteries and the Inquisition, closed down the universities, revived censorship, and arrested the leading liberals. The main beneficiaries of the Spanish rebellion and the Peninsular War were thus Spanish reactionaries and the British expeditionary force.

The Russian Debacle

In 1811 Napoleon did not yet realize how his entanglement in Spain would drain French military power and encourage intellectuals and statesmen in Central Europe to contemplate nationalist uprisings against him. On the contrary never were Napoleon's schemes more grandiose than in that year. Surveying the crumbling state system of Europe, he imagined that it could be replaced with a supranational empire, ruled from Paris and Rome and based on the Napoleonic Code. He believed that the era of the balance of power was over and that nationalist strivings would not stand in his way. On both counts he was mistaken.

The key obstacle to imperial reorganization and French domination was Russia. Wishing to retain her sphere of interest in Eastern Europe and the Baltic region and increasingly discontented with the restrictions of the Continental system, Russia was a restive ally. Alexander was being pressured on the one hand to resist France by British diplomats, French émigrés, anti-Napoleonic exiles such as Baron Stein of Prussia, and nationalist reactionaries. On the other hand Russian court liberals, more concerned with domestic reforms, were eager for him to maintain peace with France; but by 1812 their influence on Alexander had waned. On his side Napoleon wanted to enforce the Continental system and reduce Russia's capacity to interfere with Europe's destiny. As he put it with characteristic bluntness, "Let Alexander defeat the Persians, but don't let him meddle in the affairs of Europe." Once again two major powers were facing each other with progressively less interest in maintaining peace.

Napoleon decided to strike, and he embarked on his most ambitious military campaign. His objective was to annihilate the Russian forces or barring that to conquer Moscow and chase the army to the point of disarray. Almost 600,000 men (many drawn from the satellite states), long supply lines, and repeated forced marches were his principal weapons. The Russian response was to retreat in collected fashion and avoid a fight until a propitious moment. Meanwhile many nobles abandoned their estates and burned their crops to the ground. At Borodino, however, the Russians turned and took a stand. In the enormous battle that ensued, they sustained 45,000 casualties but managed to withdraw in order. The French lost 35,000. At this price they were able to enter Moscow on September 14, 1812, but the Russian army was still intact and far from demoralized.

On the contrary Moscow demoralized the French. They found the city deserted, bereft of badly needed supplies. The next night it was mysteriously set ablaze, causing such extensive damage as to make it unfit for winter quarters. Realistic advisers warned the emperor that his situation was untenable, while others told him what he wished to hear—that Russian resistance was weakening. Napoleon indulged in a reverie of false optimism and indecision. Militarily it was imperative that the French begin to retreat immediately, but that would constitute a political defeat. On October 19 Napoleon finally ordered a retreat, but it was too late.

The delay forced an unrealistic pace on the army that it was in no condition to sustain. Supplies had been outrun, medical care for the thousands of wounded was nonexistent, horses were lacking. The French officers were poorly organized for the march, and the soldiers were growing insubordinate. Food shortages compelled foraging parties to sweep some distance from the main body of troops, but these men fell prey to Russian irregulars, who operated with increasing effectiveness. And there was the weather—just a normal Russian winter in which no commander would wish to find himself on a march of several hundred miles, laden with wounded and loot but without supplies, horses, and food. Napoleon's poor planning, the harsh weather, and the operation of guerrilla bands made the long retreat a nightmare of suffering for the Grand Army. It is estimated that no more than 100,000 troops survived the ordeal. Worse yet, the Prussian contingent took the occasion to desert Napoleon. This opened up the possibility of mass defections from the empire and with them the formation of a new coalition.

German Resistance and the Last Coalition

It is testimony to Napoleon's fortitude—if also to his imperviousness to the horror around him—that he was unshaken by all this. On the lonely sleigh ride back to his main lines, he was already planning how to recoup his losses, raise new armies, and set things aright. Other statesmen were equally determined to capitalize on Napoleon's defeat and destroy the empire once and for all.

Just as Goya's brilliant paintings "The Horrors of War" captured the unique ferocity of the Spanish campaign (see Plate 48), this picture evokes the particular agonies of the Russian debacle. One writer would later call Napoleon "The greatest fabricator of disabled men in modern times."
(Photo: Photo Archives, National bibliotek Austria)

Napoleon's credibility with liberal reformers in Central and Eastern Europe still stood, but it was now challenged by ringing cries for a nationalist revival in the Confederation of the Rhine that would throw off the tyrant's yoke. This type of thinking reinforced the continuing efforts of statesmen like the Prussian Stein and the Austrian Prince Klemens von Metternich to revive the struggle against Napoleon. Less spectacularly, military reformers in Prussia had adopted French methods of conscription and organization, the better to oppose France. On the level of propaganda and the symbolic gesture, German publicists talked of a popular war of liberation—the ultimate tribute to the French Revolution.

Against this background of growing nationalist sentiment and military reform, the diplomats worked and waited. Finally, in March 1813, Frederick William III of Prussia signed a treaty with Russia, forming the nucleus of an offensive coalition against Napoleon. A great struggle for Germany ensued between the Russo-Prussian forces and Napoleon and his allies. Austria continued to claim neutrality and offered to mediate the dispute. At a conference in Prague, Napoleon was invited to restore all conquests made after 1802. Napoleon rejected this, and the allies sighed with relief, since the proposal was merely a stalling tactic until Austria could be persuaded to enter the war.

In August Emperor Francis I finally declared war on his son-in-law, while Napoleon learned of new defeats in Spain. Calling up underage conscripts, Napoleon was able to field one last army, but he found that his major southern German ally, Bavaria, had finally been induced to change sides. At Leipzig a major battle raged for three days in October, at the end of which Napoleon was defeated. His last confederation allies deserted him.

With Napoleon driven back into France, the British reinforced the coalition to assure that it would not disintegrate now that Central Europe had been liberated. Final terms were offered to the emperor: he could retain his throne, but France would be reduced to her "normal frontiers." (The precise meaning of this was purposely left unclear.) Again Napoleon counted on a dramatic reversal and chose to fight. With some reluctance the allies invaded France. Napoleon led the remnants of his army skillfully but to no avail; the French had lost confidence in him, and no civilian spirit of resistance to invasion developed as it had in 1793. Paris fell in March 1814. The price for this last defeat was the demand for unconditional surrender and the emperor's abdication. Napoleon was removed to the island of Elba, between Corsica and Italy, and was granted sovereignty over it. After twenty-two years of exile, the Bourbons returned to France.

The second revolution, guided by the Jacobin dictatorship and propelled by the sans-culottes, lasted little more than two years in 1792–1794. When the crisis had been surmounted and counterrevolution vanquished, France disavowed the Jacobin leaders. The National Convention put an end to the Terror and also to the promise of social democracy. It attempted to install a moderate republican government, in essence by recreating the middle-class regime of 1791 without a king. This proved impossible. While France exported revolution to receptive states in the years of the Directory, the revolution at home foundered.

In supporting a coup whose leadership was taken over by General Bonaparte, conservatives did not foresee that his solution to the problem would be a dictatorship. But France soon succumbed to Bonaparte's one-man rule as his prestige grew thanks to his feats on the battlefield. Before long the republic disappeared, replaced by the Napoleonic Empire.

Under the empire, confrontation of France with Old Regime Europe engulfed the entire Continent. France still embodied the specter of revolution, but by this time it amounted to little more than Napoleon's contempt for the inefficiency and irrationality of the old order. Even so this was a powerful challenge to the status quo. Napoleon believed that the state system was dead, that Europe must be reorganized under French hegemony, and that administrative reform and the Napoleonic Code should be spread to the new realms. His conquests eventually overreached his ability to maintain them except by increasingly tyrannical measures, which in turn provoked a whole range of responses in Europe. Resistance coalesced, the empire came crashing down, and the Bourbons returned to France. But the clock could not really be set back from Europe's experience of revolution and Napoleonic transformation. The era of modern political and social conflicts had begun.

RECOMMENDED READING

See also titles listed for Chapter 20.

Sources
*Beik, Paul H. (ed.). *The French Revolution*. 1971.
De Caulaincourt, Armand. *With Napoleon in Russia*. 1935.
*Herold, J. C. (ed.). *The Mind of Napoleon*. 1961.
Stewart, J. H. *A Documentary Survey of the French Revolution*. 1951.
Thompson, J. M. (ed.). *Napoleon Self-Revealed*. 1934.

Studies
The best general history of this period is a series of volumes by the great French historian Georges Lefebvre: *The French Revolution* (2 vols.) and *Napoleon* (2 vols.), all published in translation by the Columbia University Press, with full bibliographies.
Anderson, Eugene. *Nationalism and the Cultural Crisis in Prusia, 1806–1815*. 1939.
*Bergeron, Louis. *France Under Napoleon*. 1981. A fresh evaluation of the Napoleonic settlement in France, which supersedes most older works.
Chandler, David. *The Campaigns of Napoleon*. 1966. For military history buffs.
*Cobb, R. C. *The Police and the People: French Popular Protest*. 1970. A discussion of peasants and sans-culottes that should be compared to Soboul's.
*Connelly, Owen. *Napoleon's Satellite Kingdoms*. 1965.
Gershoy, Leo. *Bertrand Barère, a Reluctant Terrorist*. 1962. Perhaps the best English-language biography of a revolutionary figure.
Geyl, P. *Napoleon, For and Against*. 1949. Napoleon and the historians—as interpreted by a leading Dutch historian.
Herold, J. C. *The Age of Napoleon*. 1963. A brilliant example of "popular" history.
Kennedy, Michael. *The Jacobin Club of Marseilles*. 1973.
*Lyons, Martyn. *France Under the Directory*. 1975. A brief topical survey of the Revolution's later, unheroic phase.
*Markham, Felix. *Napoleon*. 1966. Perhaps the best biography in English.
*Palmer, Robert R. *Twelve Who Ruled: The Year of the Terror in the French Revolution*. 1941. A modern classic.
*Rudé, George. *The Crowd in the French Revolution*. 1959. Description and analysis of popular participation in the Revolution's crucial turning points.
——. *Robespierre: Portrait of a Revolutionary Democrat*. 1975. An admiring portrait.
Schama, Simon. *Patriots and Liberators: Revolution in the Netherlands 1780–1813*. 1977. An exhaustive but lively account.
*Soboul, Albert. *The Parisian Sans-Culottes and the French Revolution*. 1964. An abridgment of a landmark French thesis; should be compared to Cobb's treatment.
Woloch, Isser. *The French Veteran from the Revolution to the Restoration*. 1979. The cycle of revolutionary and Napoleonic policy as it affected one social group.

---

* Available in paperback.

22

THE POLITICS OF RESTORATION AND REFORM 1815–1850

Peace brought the chance to build again. After a generation of fighting, Europe's nations in alliance had established once more that no one state should dominate the Continent. The first task, then, was to preserve the balance at last established. The wars against France, however, had been about more than territory or balance of power; they were also battles for monarchy and against revolutionary ideas. To the victors, peace and security required that revolution as well as French aggression be prevented in the future. Painfully aware that political order was fragile and that rulers could be toppled from within, the allies sought to restore the social as well as the international equilibrium of prerevolutionary Europe.

To protect their hold on power, the regimes reestablished would need to be more effective than before the Revolution—to maintain large armies and collect more taxes, to support a better-trained bureaucracy, dispense justice more evenly, and provide more services. Governments would affect the lives of their people more directly and thus depend upon popular acquiescence more heavily than in the past. For even the most reactionary rulers, therefore, restoration would always mean some compromise between refurbishment of the old and acceptance of the changes brought by revolution, war, and Napoleonic occupation.

Politics was the vehicle for reestablishing social order and for effecting the required compromises. The organization of the state, it seemed, could shape society as well as maintain order. In the nineteenth century people divided with religious intensity over questions of government, its proper form, powers, and policies. Conservatives and the liberals who fought them shared this focus on politics and made it a hallmark of the era.

But political conflict proved hard to contain either by repression or by reform. Where the revolutions of 1830 brought moderate, reforming governments, they suffered no less dissension than their more conservative predecessors; and France's liberal monarchy was the first to fall in the wave of revolution that swept the Continent in 1848. In their democratic aims and then in their divisions and defeats, the revolutions of 1848 exposed the fact that recent changes in society went even deeper and were more problematical than the changes in political forms.

I. THE CONSERVATIVE ORDER

In setting the terms of peace, allied leaders above all sought stability. Proper political arrangements were expected to accomplish that. International agreements would establish an intricate balance of power as a guarantee of peace. Conservative monarchies, maintaining order in their own lands, would cooperate to stamp out the threat of revolution anywhere in Europe.

The Congress of Vienna

The most pressing issue was the future of France. Some of the allies, including the tsar of Russia, were willing to accept a conservative republic, but most favored some sort of monarchy. The Treaty of Paris, signed in May 1814, recognized Louis XVIII, a brother of Louis XVI, as king and granted France her "ancient limits"—the frontiers she had gained by 1792.

A settlement covering all the territory affected by the Napoleonic wars would take longer. Warily watching each other, the allies agreed to call an international congress where their respective interests could be carefully weighed and balanced.

The congress met in Vienna in September 1814, an occasion for serious deliberations and elaborate pomp. The crowned heads of Austria, Prussia, Russia, and dozens of lesser states, ministers of nearly every government, advocates of special causes, expert advisers, princesses and countesses, dancers and artists, and the ambitious of every rank flocked to the Aus-

The Congress of Vienna. In this watercolor, the fashionable artist J. B. Isabey presents the congress as a kind of elegant salon in which the very clothes the statesmen wore mix the styles of the old regime and the new century.
(Photo: The Granger Collection)

trian capital. Their contrived gaiety made the Congress of Vienna a symbol of aristocratic restoration from the first.

The business of the congress remained the responsibility of the four great powers—Austria, Great Britain, Russia, and Prussia—an inner circle to which France was soon admitted. Prince Klemens von Metternich, who had led the Austrian Empire to this triumph, conducted the affairs of the congress with such skill that its provisions can be seen as largely his work. Handsome, elegant, and arrogant, Metternich was an eighteenth-century aristocrat embattled in a revolutionary age. Fluent in all the major European languages and a dandy who dabbled in science, he was as proud of his success with women as of his dissembling diplomacy. More consistently than any single figure he had understood the extent of Napoleon's ambitions and had welded the international alliance that defeated the French emperor. Named foreign minister of Austria in 1809, he would hold that position for nearly forty years, associating his vision of Europe as an international community built upon order, balance, and restraint with his protection of Austria's vital interests and his personal career.

Metternich was generally supported by the reserved and able Lord Castlereagh, who made his broad view of British interests a major factor throughout the negotiations. Tsar Alexander I, who acted as his own chief diplomat, was more unpredictable. Educated in the ideas of enlightened despotism, but now more given to mysticism and conservative fear, he was attracted to grand visions likely to upset the careful calculations of self-interest by which the congress reached agreement. By contrast, Prince Talleyrand moved more comfortably in these circles. The former bishop who had served the First Republic and then the Directory, who had helped Napoleon to power and been his foreign minister for eight years, Talleyrand was now the indispensable servant of Louis XVIII, using all his famous shrewdness

In the tradition of aristocratic portraits, Prince Metternich is conveyed as a polished courtier; the medals, symbolic of his position and power, are also a reminder of the purpose of his policies.
(Photo: The Mansell Collection)

to regain for Bourbon France her former influence.

The concerns of these men focused on Continental Europe, for only Great Britain among the victors had extensive holdings overseas, and British designs on South Africa, Ceylon, and Malta were modest enough to be accepted with little dispute. Europe was considered the sphere of the great powers; each closely weighed the claims of the others, and all especially watched Russia, with her mammoth armies, undefined ambitions, and quixotic tsar.

Disposing of Polish and Saxon territory proved the thorniest issue. The three partitions of Poland in the eighteenth century suggested one solution: to keep the balance of power in

Eastern Europe by dividing Poland among the three Eastern monarchies. Napoleon's creation, the duchy of Warsaw, suggested another: to set up an independent but greatly reduced Poland. Because the king of Saxony had remained loyal to Napoleon too long, Prussia claimed his realm as compensation for past suffering; Russian armies, however, now held the land in question. For Austria the expansion of Russia and Prussia was an ancient nightmare no more acceptable after Napoleon than before. Her fears drove Austria closer to Great Britain, and the rift among the allies made room for France to play a major part.

In the final settlement, a triumph of diplomacy in eighteenth-century style, everyone got something (see Map 22.1). Russia received most of Poland as a separate kingdom under the tsar. Prussia got about half of Saxony and as compensation for the rest was given greatly enlarged territories in the Rhineland. Thus formidable Prussian armies would stand along the French border. The Austrian Netherlands were absorbed in a new independent Kingdom of the Netherlands, which created another strong buffer against France and met the British desire that no major power control the Low Countries' important river ports. In return for her loss of the southern Netherlands, Austria acquired Venezia, which with Lombardy greatly strengthened her dominance of northern Italy. The other duchies of northern Italy went to dukes with close Austrian ties (in a touch of chivalry, Marie Louise, Napoleon's now throneless Austrian wife, was given Parma to rule).

By these and similar exchanges in less pressing cases, the most extensive European settlement since the agreements at Westphalia in 1648 established the balance of power as an interlocking system.[1] Each of the victors had gained territory, and the areas that France might easily overrun were now held by states—the Kingdom of the Netherlands, Prussia in the Rhineland, and Austria in northern Italy—capable of resisting future French aggression. The final act was signed in June 1815 by the five great powers and by Sweden, Spain, and Portugal, a gracious recognition of their past importance.

The Hundred Days

The deliberations of the Congress were interrupted in March 1815 by the terrifying news of Napoleon's escape. He had tried to make the best of ruling Elba and even showed something of his old flair as he designed uniforms, held receptions, and inquired into the local economy. But the island principality was far too small to contain an emperor's ambition. Landing in the south of France, he made his way to Paris. Important parts of the French army defected, and Louis XVIII, after hoping for support that did not develop, once again climbed into his carriage and headed for the eastern border. Napoleon had become the ruler of France without firing a shot. He then tried to negotiate with the allies, but they declared him an outlaw and quickly assembled their troops. After several minor battles he was defeated for the last time at Waterloo on June 18 and surrendered to the British. They dispatched him to the more distant island of St. Helena, in the South Atlantic.

Napoleon's dashing venture lasted only a hundred days, but its effects were felt far longer. The terms of peace were altered, the possibility of a stable restoration questioned, and the meaning of Bonapartism redefined. France seemed once more a threat, and a new treaty reduced her boundaries to those of 1789 (which entailed the loss of much of the Saar to Prussia) and required her to pay the allies an indemnity. The Bourbons of course returned to the throne of France, but their claims to popularity were embarrassed by the ease with

---

[1] The Kingdom of Sardinia would have liked Lombardy but got Genoa, the last of the ancient Italian republics to fall. Russia took Finland from Sweden, which in turn got Norway from Denmark.

MAP 22.1: EUROPE 1815

which Napoleon had regained power, and they lived with the specter of renewed revolution. During his Hundred Days Napoleon had offered a liberal government that softened the memory of his despotism (he even banned slave traffic in the French colonies), and from St. Helena he continued to propagandize for Bonapartism as the best means of achieving both liberty and order. Allied diplomats, less expert in playing to popular opinion, planned instead for frequent meetings to maintain by international force the settlement so carefully contrived.

The Nature of the Settlement

The Congress of Vienna had not attempted simply to restore the prerevolutionary world. A Bourbon ruled again in France, but he was a king with a constitution. Despite past glories the Republic of Venice was not reestablished. Nor were the Holy Roman Empire and hundreds of its minor German principalities; instead the reorganization effected under Napoleon was kept, with modifications, and thirty-nine German states, including Prussia and Austria, were joined in a loose and ill-defined German Confederation. The aristocrats at Vienna sought advice from teams of experts on matters of history and law, a very modern use of specialists. They laid down rules of diplomatic conduct useful to this day, and in provisions such as those establishing free navigation on international riverways, displayed their enlightened reasonableness. For a century Europe would be free of universal war, and something of that stability was due to the wisdom at Vienna, which left twice-defeated France a respected power and the interests of other states intricately connected.

The congress was less impressive, however, in the realm of ideas. Talleyrand had proposed the concept of legitimacy as a general principle that would dignify the deliberations. The powers, he argued, should favor regimes that had lasted and proved acceptable to their subjects; this would obviate the need to restore every shaky and petty throne. But even so vague a principle proved inconvenient. Tsar Alexander aimed for something grander and proposed a Holy Alliance, based on an agreement that all states would conduct their affairs according to Christian teachings. Three governments refused: the sultan cared too little for Christian teachings and the pope too much, and Britain would not be committed to Continental ties. All the others signed but with public skepticism, and historians have similarly tended to dismiss the Holy Alliance as a meaningless product of Alexander's mysticism. Yet there was something modern and maybe wise in the tsar's awareness of public opinion.

The next generation of Europe's liberals, reformers, and nationalists would remember the Congress of Vienna not as the occasion of realistic compromise but as a brutal shuffling of territory by men indifferent to the claims of nationality or promises of constitutions, where aristocrats danced while foisting reactionary regimes on the people of Europe. For fifty years every revolution and every war in Europe would include among its goals the dismantlement of the arrangements made at Vienna. The plan to hold frequent congresses among the great powers implied that the wartime alliance would be continued. For Castlereagh this would be the means of accommodating inevitable change. But Metternich sought instead a Concert of Europe, under his leadership, to snuff out the flames of revolution wherever they occurred.

The Pillars of the Restoration

The new international order expressed conservative principles and required conservative governments throughout Europe. This major political experiment depended on the guardians of the restoration—Russia, Austria, and Prussia. Only they could shore up the less secure regimes established elsewhere, but to sustain that role they themselves needed effective governments and domestic stability.

Conservative Thought

In every period of European history, there have been leaders in politics and philosophy who

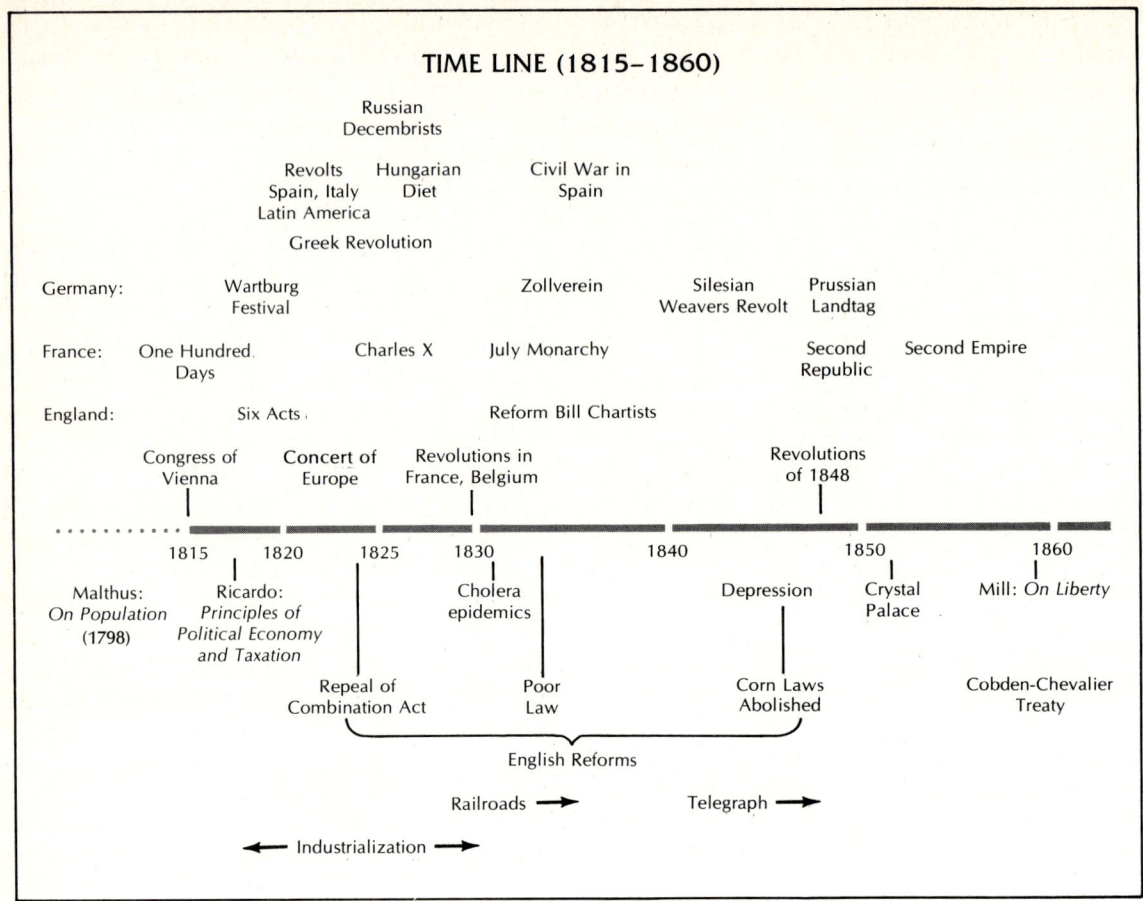

could fairly be labeled conservative. But in the long battle against the French Revolution, conservatism had become what today would be called an ideology, a coherent view of human nature, social organization, political power, and the roots of change that was intended to justify social hierarchies and established institutions. Conservatives might disagree about particular policies, but conservatism had become a broad school of thought that would help shape political discourse throughout the nineteenth century.

The eloquent reasoning of Edmund Burke, whose writings appeared throughout the latter half of the eighteenth century, provided perhaps the most influential formulation of the conservative position. Society, he argued, is a partnership of the living, the dead, and those yet to be born. It depends on continuity. By granting special privileges to certain groups, it adapted to social needs in a way conducive to order, achieving a delicate arrangement in which rank was related to social role and differences of status, having evolved through time, were acceptable to all. This "natural" order is far wiser than the "artificial" plans of radicals, however well-intentioned, who necessarily undo more than they intend and ultimately threaten society itself.

The Burkean view thus allowed for gradual

change, at least in theory, but was clearly suspicious of sudden reform for immediate ends. It became more opposed to change, however, as it underwent the experience of revolution and found support in new intellectual currents. One of these was a distrust of reason, a turning away from the Enlightenment, expressed in the argument that mankind's highest achievements and deepest understanding do not result from cold calculation. This persuasion spread with the Romantic movement which deeply influenced contemporary thought. Primarily literary and artistic rather than political, Romanticism affected radicals as well as conservatives; but in its appreciation of human experience as unique, subjective, and emotional, it made an important contribution to conservatism. Romantics yearned for absolute values and ultimate meanings, and whether they found the source of these in God, historical process, or nature, they agreed that human knowledge is a puny thing compared with the great forces outside it.

Conservatives thus considered that rational plans for a just society are simply beside the point and that nations cannot be ruled by mere man-made constitutions or law. Society was seen as a great interconnecting web, an organic whole not suitable for piecemeal reform, and phrases about individual rights seemed dangerous abstractions hiding selfish interests and encouraging false hopes.

The early nineteenth-century fascination with history and the contemporary interest in Christian philosophy gave further stimulus to conservatives, who found in history a record of how painfully civilization had evolved and how fragile it remained, and they often sought, particularly in recent events, evidence of human error and divine will to give larger meaning to their political battles. They viewed Christianity as the source of Europe's strength and Christian fear as a necessary restraint on man's selfish and prideful nature. Without it, society would dissolve into revolution and anarchy. Conservatives tended therefore to connect religion with their own politics and to attach the Church to aristocracy and monarchy. They regarded political battles as merely part of a far larger and millennial conflict.

Such views gave conservative thought both a militancy and a depth to which German contributions were perhaps the most original and lasting. For Europeans used to receiving radical ideas from France, however, two of the most striking exponents of conservatism in the restoration period were men who wrote in French, Joseph de Maistre and Louis de Bonald. Society's first task, they argued, is self-preservation. Authority alone can check the selfish wills of individuals, and authority requires undivided sovereignty, social hierarchy, and the vigilant suppression of dangerous ideas. Having experienced revolution, they were fascinated by power and demanded its vigorous use by an unfettered monarch. They declared that church and state must be closely linked, and de Maistre held the international authority of the papacy to be a social necessity. Revolution he explained as divine retribution for false ideas.

Conservatism in this form contained little that was humane or tolerant. With its praise of hangmen and censors, it spoke only to those who already shared its fears. It left little space for compromise and lambasted every concession as a dangerous weakening of the dikes restraining revolution. Like liberalism, republicanism, and socialism, nineteenth-century conservatism became an ideology that divided while calling for unity and that emphasized political power while speaking of the social good.

The Russian Empire

By 1820 Tsar Alexander had abandoned an earlier enthusiasm for new ideas to become Metternich's staunchest ally. In his last years censorship was harsher, universities were more restricted, and the constitution granted the newly organized Kingdom of Poland was largely ignored. On Alexander's death, in 1825, a group of young army officers, the Decembrists, attempted a coup in the name of a constitution. Poorly planned, their isolated conspiracy was easily defeated, but they would later be remembered as part of Russia's radical tradition; Nicholas I, Alexander's younger brother who succeeded to the throne, believed that only a loyal army and his own decisiveness had prevented revolution.

Under Nicholas Russia became Europe's strongest pillar of reaction. A diligent administrator, he gave close attention to the army and extended the influence of the police into every aspect of Russian life. The bureaucracy, made more independent of the nobility, became more efficient and centralized but still could barely meet the demands of overseeing a vast land of varied peoples where communications were poor and educated men scarce. Petty corruption, the arrogance of local officials, and fear of change seriously weakened the government's capabilities.

The growth of a European market for Russian grain stimulated the economy, and many large estates became more prosperous and more specialized as they produced for export. Industry, primarily small-scale and domestic, was also growing; but the smaller lord suffered in a money economy, and the growing indebtedness of many a Russian noble became another source of social tension. Most thoughtful men, including the highest officials of the state, agreed that serfdom had become a hindrance, but the commissions ordered to study the matter could propose no solution not likely to increase unrest. Thus information was collected, and hundreds of peasant uprisings were noted with concern and suppressed with force, but the few steps taken to improve the lot of peasants remained thoroughly inadequate.

Sensing the importance of public attitudes, the government attempted to establish a kind of official philosophy based on the teachings of the Orthodox Church and utilized censors and police to enforce these precepts of autocracy. Despite fears that education bred discontent, schools were built (to provide a literate minority). Discussion of Russia's destiny became a compelling theme. Those who expected her to develop along familiar European lines were called Westernizers. Slavophiles, though making use of many Western (especially German) ideas, stressed rather the uniqueness of Russia. Her religion, peasant communes, and traditional culture, they argued, were the source of a unique mission in world civilization. Neither group was entirely consistent or well defined, but within a great culture an urgent questioning had begun about Russia's place in a changing world, giving shape to an intellectual ferment that lasted through the century.

The authority of the Russian state, however, continued to tower over the social tensions and intellectual debates. Despite loquacious exiles, bitter Poles, angry peasants, and its own immobility, the Russian government seemed enormously solid. Nicholas would watch with pride as his empire remained secure while revolution swept over most of the thrones of Europe.

The Hapsburg Monarchy

The German, Italian, and Eastern European lands under Hapsburg rule were administered by a well-organized and centralized bureaucracy. Forged by Maria Theresa and Joseph II, it had enabled Austria to survive the Napoleonic wars without the dramatic reforms that transformed Prussia and become a source of conservatism. Metternich and others recognized the need for more coherent and far-reaching domestic programs, but their projects—for a strong Imperial Council, for more influential diets of local landholders, and for an administration that reflected national differences—came to nothing. It was easier to guarantee order through bureaucratic restrictions, police surveillance, and energetic censorship.

Hungary, with her independent traditions and powerful aristocracy, proved particularly troublesome to the Hapsburgs. Emperor Francis I was forced in 1825 to convene the Hungarian Diet when the counties refused to pay needed taxes, and Hungary's traditional privileges of partial autonomy were grudgingly acknowledged then and again in 1830. Finding it easier to relinquish some authority rather than make the changes that might have assured the empire's prosperity and power, Austria remained locked in a stalemate between a cautious central bureaucracy and a selfish local aristocracy. Both rested on a peasant society that had no direct voice in politics. By the 1840s Magyar had been made the official language of the Hungarian administration and schools, but this was followed in turn by demands for a more representative parliament and a campaign conducted by Lajos Kossuth in newspapers and meetings for the full panoply of liberal and national reforms.

The agitation in Hungary, stimulated by nationalist ferment in Italy, encouraged others under Hapsburg rule to claim their "natural rights." A revolt in Polish Galicia in 1846 was defeated by Austrian arms, aided by the bitter divisions between Polish peasants and their masters, and new signs of restlessness appeared in Croatia and Bohemia.

The confusion of conflicting claims was one of the monarchy's assets, for the national and religious groups opposed to Hapsburg rule were equally hostile to each other. Divided by class, religion, and language, they were not often politically effective. The growing consciousness of nationality was, however, a significant change. These movements, which enabled lawyers and merchants to seek popular support in their cry for governmental reform, reflected economic developments and intellectual currents sweeping Europe. Men who sought merely to strengthen noble privilege or local authority (the Magyars, for example, of Hungary) joined with those who wanted better administration, parliaments, and schools in opposing the authorities in Vienna.

At the center weak Ferdinand I, who had inherited his father's crown in 1835, presided over an aristocratic government that found inaction the safest compromise of internal differences. Metternich saw the need to acknowledge national sentiment within the empire and worried about Prussia's growing dominance in Germany. His chief antagonist among Ferdinand's ministers, Count Kolowrat, stressed the desperate need for fiscal reform. Their insights, like the advantages of the well-structured imperial bureaucracy, were slowly dissipated in an isolated, divided, and frightened court accustomed to relying on the effectiveness of tradition and Metternich's foreign policy.

The German Confederation and Prussia

Germans called their battles against Napoleon the Wars of Liberation; and after that common, national experience, talk of "Germany" meant more than it had before. But the German Confederation, a tacit acknowledgment of the changes Bonaparte had wrought, was one of the Congress of Vienna's more cautious compromises. The rivalry of Austria and Prussia, distaste for reform, and the claims of German princes combined to prohibit a politically strong union. Nearly forty sovereign entities, ranging in size from the Austrian Empire and Prussia to four free cities, were made members of the loose league under the permanent presidency of Austria. Its diet, which was to meet at Frankfurt, was more a council of ambassadors than a representative assembly, and a unanimous vote was required on fundamental questions. Primarily another buffer against France, the confederation was permitted to legislate only on certain matters—restriction of the press was characteristically among them. If such advisory councils seemed unavoidable (each member of the confederation was expected to establish one), they were to be kept limited. In practice the German Confederation was important in German politics largely when Metternich wished to make it so.

He used it for example to suppress student agitation. University fraternities, especially *Burschenschaften,* were generally nationalist and reformist, full of rhetoric about mystic brotherhood. In 1817 they celebrated the tercentenary of Luther's theses with a rally, the Wartburg Festival. Several hundred representatives gathered to drink, listen to speeches, sing songs, and cheer as a corporal's cane and a Prussian military manual were tossed into a bonfire. The symbolism was clear enough. Alarmed, governments in both Berlin and Vienna investigated and concluded that closer censorship and more careful surveillance of universities were needed. After the assassination of a reactionary writer, they called on the confederation to pass the Carlsbad Decrees of 1819, which intensified censorship, proscribed dangerous professors and students, outlawed fraternities and political clubs, and required each state to appoint commissioners to certify the ideological reliability of the universities.

Despite these alarms, there was less agitation in Germany than in most of Europe. Rather, the cultural life of these largely rural lands thrived in complacent university and market towns that seemed to eschew politics on a larger scale. The universities were strongest in philosophy and theology, and German Romanticism, when political at all, tended to become more conservative. In the last days of Beethoven and Schubert, Goethe and Hegel, German politics remained quiescent. The German states most influenced by France did adopt constitutions, but the diet Frederick William III promised for Prussia was never called, and the Council of State established in its place included only the most important military men, officials, and aristocrats. Prussian strength was not associated with representative government.

Prussian influence increased, however, as an efficient state continued to sponsor education and to spur economic growth. A unified tariff established in 1818 included all her territory, east and west; lowered duties (in part to discourage smuggling); and allowed free entry to raw materials. These progressive measures worked so well that within a decade many of the smaller states nearly surrounded by Prussia adopted them; and by 1833 most German governments except Austria had joined Prussia's customs union, the *Zollverein,* whose revenues, collected by Prussian inspectors, were shared and used primarily for better roads. One of the most important steps toward German unification under Prussia had been taken without nationalist intent by the government that knew how to win the benefits of liberal institutions without paying the price of liberal practice.

Germany had few modern factories, but the Zollverein proved a remarkable spur to commerce. Moreover, by 1848 manufacturing and trade would be stimulated by one of the best railroad networks in Europe, built with considerable state support, especially from Prussia. These developments caused serious social dislocations. Some old trades found it difficult to compete with factory production and cheaper goods from other countries. The revolt of Silesian weavers in 1844, bloodily put down by Prussian troops, is only the most famous of many desperate and fruitless protests. Caught between rural immigrants competing for their jobs and the increased competition their products faced in the marketplace, workers looked to local governments for help; but they, too, were caught between their conservative social base and centralizing pressures from state bu-

---

Students, burghers, and plain people were brought together in song and drink to celebrate national feeling (note the German tricolor) in festivals like this one at Wartburg in 1848.
(Photo: The Bettmann Archive)

reaucrats eager to impose efficiency and uniformity.

Constitutional issues depended in part on accidents of dynasty. In Hanover a reactionary king set aside a four-year-old constitution in 1837, but in Prussia the reign of Frederick William IV, which began in 1840, raised prospects of significant constitutional reform. The new king, the least militaristic of Prussian monarchs, had a liberal reputation; and though he was no friend of constitutions, in 1847 he reluctantly called for a United Landtag, to be composed of representatives of the eight provincial diets meeting in two houses. Short of revenue, in part because of its heavy investment in railroads, the government seemed in a situation like France's in 1789.

The Landtag optimistically insisted on regular sessions and some authority over the budget, but the king replied that a Prussia made by the sword would never allow petty legalisms to come between her monarchs and her people. After two months the delegates were sent home, leaving Prussia without a constitution or new taxes. Some serious ferment continued, particularly in Rhineland cities, where meetings and manifestoes demanded representative government, civil liberties, and sometimes—most frightening of all—a graduated income tax and guarantees of the right to work.

Demands for constitutional change gathered force as they combined with nationalist aims. Talk of German unification became so acceptable that both the Hohenzollern and the Hapsburg rulers paid it verbal respect. Western German reformers, and particularly those in exile, like the poet Heinrich Heine, associated their dreams of a German nation with their desire for a liberal government. Despite the difficulty of defining what territory a German nation should include or determining how it could be organized, political programs accompanied the spread of education, railroads, and economic modernization. Dismissing the Landtag did not do much to settle anything.

Order Imposed

While the governments of Russia, Austria, and Prussia dealt with serious domestic challenges, Metternich led the effort to maintain the status quo through international cooperation and force. But even conservative powers had conflicting interests, and the political systems they had restored in Spain, Italy, and France proved dangerously vulnerable.

The Declining Concert of Europe

Uprisings much like the Decembrist revolt in Russia, took place in Italy and Spain in 1820 and 1821, led by young army officers who were influenced by memories of Napoleonic reforms and convinced that personal advancement and efficient government required a constitution. In Italy especially their movements won some brief popular support and measured the weakness of restoration regimes that had to be sustained by outside force.

The availability of that force was Metternich's achievement. When representatives of Great Britain, Prussia, Russia, and France met at Aix-la-Chapelle in 1818 (to acknowledge payment of the French indemnity and to ratify the withdrawal of foreign troops from France), they embodied the concept of Europe the Austrian prince had envisioned at the Congress of Vienna. By the time of their meetings at Troppau and Laibach in 1820 and 1821, however, the tenor had changed. Metternich, determined to guard against the virus of revolution anywhere in Europe, called for action against the revolt in Naples, but Great Britain disapproved of such direct intervention in the domestic affairs of European states, and France, unwilling to antagonize opinion at home, was hesitant. Only Metternich interpreted the Congress of Laibach as a mandate for Austrian troops to march to Naples.

The breach among the powers became more apparent when they met the following year—

without British representation. They approved French intervention in Spain, a royal parade to display the French monarchy's revived prestige. But the subsequent hope of reestablishing European authority in Latin America brought stern warnings from Britain and the proud declaration of the Monroe Doctrine from the United States. The sphere of Metternich's concert was being delimited.

It was hardly evoked at all when the Greeks revolted against Ottoman rule in 1821. Russia was restrained from declaring war on the Ottoman Empire by Metternich's strenuous warnings. But the cries for freedom from the ancient home of democracy excited liberals throughout Europe. By 1827 the sultan seemed at last about to subdue the Greeks; but the British and French fleets intervened, and Russia declared war a few months later. Greece was granted independence in 1829 on terms arranged by the European powers, who carefully stipulated that a king should be chosen from one of the Continent's lesser ruling families. The response to revolution within the Ottoman Empire had been more like the diplomacy of imperialism that would emerge later in the century than the concert's commitment to the status quo. Diplomacy, despite Metternich's skill, proved an uncertain weapon against political change.

The Restoration Regimes in Spain and Italy

In Spain the Bourbon king Ferdinand VII had regained his throne with the expulsion of Napoleon's army. Strong enough to denounce the constitution he had promised, he was too weak to do much more. Ferdinand enjoyed some popularity because of patriotic resentment against French rule, but his government found no solution for its own inefficiency or the nation's poverty. In Spanish America the revolts led by José de San Martín and Simón Bolívar gained strength,[2] and the army that was assembled in Spain to reconquer the colonies mutinied and marched instead on Madrid in 1820.

This revolution forced the king to grant a constitution, and for three years the constitutional regime struggled to cope with Spain's enormous problems, weakened by its own dissension and its uncooperative king. But restrictions on religious orders raised powerful opposition from the church; freedom of the press produced more devastating criticism; and having a constitution was no help with the colonies. When a French army once again crossed into Spain in 1823, this time in the name of order, the Spaniards, who had fought French invasion so heroically just ten years earlier, were strangely acquiescent. With the rebellion defeated, the constitution disappeared again. Yet Ferdinand's repression neither ended the threat of revolution nor satisfied the more reactionary monarchists.

Restoration in Italy meant the return of the aristocracy, the reestablishment of old political boundaries, and the overwhelming dominance of Austria.[3] Yet the years of French rule had struck deep roots in Italy. The new regimes won acceptance with promises of constitutions, enlightened administration, peace, and lower taxes; but the rulers who headed them were frightened and often bitter. Unimaginative, harshly or moderately repressive, and conveniently corrupt, the governments provided the sleepy stability Metternich thought appropriate for Italians.

---

[2] The history of these uprisings and of the impact of European events on Latin America is discussed in Richard Graham, *Independence in Latin America* (1972), a companion volume to *The Western Experience* in the Studies in World Civilization series.

[3] Italy was divided into the Kingdom of the Two Sicilies; the Papal States; the grand duchy of Tuscany; the duchies of Lucca, Modena, and Parma; the Kingdom of Sardinia (Piedmont and Sardinia); Lombardy-Venezia, annexed to Austria; the principality of Monaco; and the republic of San Marino. All the duchies were held by friends or relatives of the Hapsburgs. The disappearance of Venice and Genoa as independent states left tiny San Marino, safe on its mountaintop, the oldest republic in the world.

Such an atmosphere bred some conspiracy and rumors of far more. Across Italy secret groups, known collectively as the Carbonari, began to meet; their name, which means charcoal burners, evoked the image of Christ's poverty. Some talked of tyrannicide, some of equality and justice, and some of mild reform. They had in common the excitement of secret meetings, terrifying oaths, and ornate rituals.

The news of the revolution in Spain in 1820 was enough to prompt revolt. In Naples young army officers led the demand for a constitution, but royal concessions were followed by a more amorphous uprising in Sicily, which the Neapolitan revolutionaries then helped defeat. Their own constitutional regime died with the invasion of an Austrian army less than a year after revolution had broken out.

While the Austrians were marching to Naples, a similar revolt erupted in Piedmont. The king abdicated and the prince regent, Charles Albert, hastily granted a constitution before the new monarch arrived. When he came, the Austrian army was with him; Piedmont's constitution lasted two weeks.

The revolutions of 1821 in Italy left reactionary governments more rigid and Austrian influence more naked. They showed the inadequacies of loose, romantic conspiracies. But they contributed something as well to a radical and patriotic tradition.

The Bourbon Restoration in France

The crucial test of postwar stability, however, was the domestic tranquillity of France. More than elsewhere, restoration there was a complex compromise carefully designed to build from political forms the means to maintain a balance between the old regime and the changes that followed from revolution. The charter that Louis XVIII granted by grace—not as a right—allowed the legislature more authority than Napoleon had permitted but made cabinet ministers directly responsible to the king. The old estates were now ignored, but membership in the Chamber of Peers was hereditary, and the right to vote in elections to the Chamber of Deputies was limited to men of landed wealth. Napoleon's centralized administration was kept and his taxes enthusiastically maintained.

Supporters of the new regime, shaken by how easily Napoleon had displaced it during the Hundred Days, returned to power determined to crush their enemies, and the Chamber elected after Waterloo was too reactionary even for Louis XVIII. In parts of the countryside a violent "white terror" broke out, in which some of those tainted with a revolutionary past were ousted from office or even killed. Yet Louis XVIII resisted as best he could the more extreme demands of the ultraroyalists. Land confiscated from the aristocracy and the church during the Revolution was not returned, and most of those who had benefited since 1789 were allowed quietly to live out their lives. The king and his ministers, moderate and able men, pursued a course of administrative efficiency and political restraint. From 1816 to 1820 they governed well in a relatively peaceful and prosperous country, and Paris became again Europe's most brilliant center of science and the arts.

The Catholic Church, weakened by the loss of property and still more by a scarcity of new priests in the postrevolutionary generation, revived remarkably. Missions of preachers toured the countryside calling for a return to the faith, praising the monarchy, and planting crosses of repentance. The nobles, traditionally rather skeptical, were now more pious; and so too for the first time in more than a century were France's leading writers. To the surprise of many Catholics, however, the Concordat of 1801 remained in effect, another of Napoleon's institutional arrangements to prove a lasting one.

Despite its achievements the regime remained insecure and uncertain, satisfying relatively few, neither all Catholics nor anticlericals, neither ultraroyalists nor liberals. The assassination of the duke of Berry in 1820 reminded everyone of how fragile the monarchy was. The son of Louis' younger brother, the Count of Artois, he was the last Bourbon likely to produce an heir, and the royal line seemed doomed until the widowed duchess gave birth to a son eight months later. Louis XVIII feared the radicalism that appeared to be reviving throughout Europe, and he reacted to his nephew's assassination by naming more conservative ministers, increasing restrictions on the press, and dismissing some leading professors.

The air of reaction grew heavier in 1824 when the Count of Artois succeeded to the throne as Charles X. A leader of the ultraroyalists, he had himself crowned at Reims in medieval splendor, a ceremony redolent with symbols of the divine right of kings and the alliance of throne and altar. The new government, led by a skillful but impolitic ultra, passed measures that gave the Church fuller control of education, declared sacrilege a capital crime, and granted a cash indemnity to those who had lost land in the Revolution.

In fact the law against sacrilege was never enforced, and the indemnity, which helped end one of the most dangerous issues left from the Revolution, was a limited one. France remained freer than most European countries, but Charles' subjects worried about the intentions of a regime that disliked the very compromises on which it rested. Public criticism grew, leading figures passed over to the parliamentary opposition, and secret societies blossomed. Disturbed by liberal gains in the elections of 1827, Charles X dutifully tried a slightly more moderate ministry, but he could not conceal his distaste for the increasingly hostile left nor offer enough concessions to win its support. By 1829 the king could stand no more. While political disputes grew more inflamed, he appointed a cabinet of ultras, but the Chamber of Deputies refused a vote of confidence. He called new elections, but instead of regaining seats the ultras lost still more.

Determined not to make the mistakes of Louis XVI, Charles X reacted with firmness. In 1830 he and his ministers suddenly issued a set of secretly drafted decrees, the July Ordinances, which dissolved the new Chamber even before it met, further restricted suffrage, and muzzled the press. Having shown his fiber, the king went hunting. A shocked Paris slowly responded; crowds began to mill about, some barricades went up, and stones were thrown at the house of the king's premier. Newspapers breached the ordinances to charge that the constitution had been violated, and the government responded with troops enough to raise tempers but too few to enforce order. By the time Charles acknowledged the need to appoint more acceptable ministers, people were being killed (nearly 700 died in the three days of Paris fighting). Many troops began to mingle with the crowds, and liberal leaders started planning for a new regime. Paris was again the scene of a popular uprising, and Charles X, once again victim of what he most detested—revolution—abdicated on August 2.

For fifteen years and for the only time in her history, France had been administered by her aristocracy, who had performed with probity and seriousness. The crown had won the church's enthusiastic support, and the nation had prospered at home and enjoyed some success in foreign affairs. But the monarchy was meant above all to provide political stability, and that the restoration's most important experiment had failed to do.

II. THE SPREAD OF LIBERAL GOVERNMENT

Political Liberalism

The revolution that arose in France in 1830 and the revolt that created Belgium were not reversed by conservative powers, and the differences between the representative monarchies of the West and the autocratic governments of Central and Eastern Europe sharpened. The great age of liberalism began in 1830, with England as its model. Liberal movements in this period would come to seem very moderate by later standards. The movements focused on politics, especially on the Continent, and sought institutional and legal change even at the risk of revolution, while defending private property.

The Revolutions of 1830

After Charles X's speedy abdication, the provisional government, organized largely in newspaper offices, had a faintly republican coloration. But when the Marquis de Lafayette, still a republican and a popular hero, presented Louis Philippe from the balcony of the Hôtel de Ville as the candidate for the throne, the issue had been largely settled in favor of what most men of influence preferred, a liberal monarchy. The new king headed the House of Orléans, a radical branch of the royal line (his father had voted with the Jacobins for the death of Louis XVI). His posters proclaimed him citizen-king, and the flag he chose—the Revolution's tricolor in place of the Bourbon fleurs-de-lis—signified a return to revolutionary traditions. Pressures from the people of Paris had led Louis Philippe to appear more liberal than he was, and the new government hastened to assure Europe's other monarchs that this French revolution would send no militants to sponsor or support revolution elsewhere.

The revolution, brief and largely limited to Paris, was a revolution nevertheless, and any uprising in France was a European event. Minor revolts occurred in central Italy, Spain, Portugal, and some of the German principalities, and revolution broke out in Poland. But Austria, though somewhat inhibited by France, once again extinguished revolt in Italy, and the Russian army crushed Poland's rebels. Closer to France, the Swiss cantons were forced to liberalize their constitutions. And Catholics and liberals of the southern Netherlands took the occasion to rise against Dutch rule. Once assured that France had no territorial designs on the region, Britain led in winning international guarantees for the independence of the southern Netherlands with a mounting show of force that brought Dutch acquiescence. The new state of Belgium was born.

Liberal Thought

Liberalism was not a compact doctrine but rather a set of attitudes closely tied to ideas of social progress, belief in economic development, and values associated with the middle class. It varied considerably by country and changed everywhere over the course of the nineteenth century.

Liberal political values were rooted in the writings of John Locke and the philosophes; and liberals generally honored the French Revolution, despite its excesses, as a great moment in the history of freedom, while accepting those aspects of Romanticism that stressed individual creativity. A leading French liberal during the restoration, Benjamin Constant, put his case unequivocally: "The liberty of the individual is the object of all human association; on it rest public and private morality; on it are based the calculations of industry and commerce, and without it there is neither peace, dignity, nor happiness for men." By this creed freedom itself would be the source of morality, prosperity, and progress. The freedom liberals sought was primarily political and legal (their views on economic rights were frequently far more narrow), and they favored those who fought in any country for a constitution, freedom of the press and of assembly, an extension of the jury system, separation of church and state, public education, and administrative reform. Most liberals were not democrats, feeling that education and leisure were necessary for political wisdom, but nearly all believed that policies beneficial to everyone would follow from allowing ideas a free hearing and propertied voters a free voice.

Liberal Politics in Britain

Britain's withdrawal from Metternich's Concert of Europe in the 1820s and her growing sympathy for Continental reform represented more than insular habit. She was becoming the world's leading example and advocate of liberalism, but that identification with a particular ideology only came after years of acrimony.

The end of war against Napoleon brought a depression to the British Isles as wartime markets collapsed and Europe's most developed economy stumbled before the problems of demobilization. The government's policies clearly favored the rich; it rescinded the wartime income tax and raised the tariff on grains, which increased the price of bread. These measures provoked agitation in town and country, and newspapers, political clubs, and popular meetings echoed with cries of class resentment. In 1816 a crowd demanding parliamentary reform grew violent, and the next year an alarmed government suspended habeas corpus for the first time in English history. A mass meeting

This cartoon of the 1819 Peterloo Massacre captures the sense of class hatred it evoked. The hungry poor, peaceably seeking reform, are wantonly trampled by His Majesty's overfed officials.
(Photo: The Mansell Collection)

for reform at St. Peter's Field, Manchester, in 1819 so terrified the local magistrates that they called out troops. In the ensuing charge hundreds of demonstrators, including women and children, were wounded, and several were killed. With bitter mockery people called it the Peterloo Massacre.

Parliament decided to preserve order by passing the Six Acts of 1819, which restricted public meetings, facilitated the prosecution of radicals, and imposed a stamp tax intended to cripple the radical press. In 1820 the discovery of a clumsy plot to blow up the cabinet at dinner added to the sense of danger. When George IV followed his succession to the throne in 1820 (he had been prince regent since 1811) by instituting divorce proceedings against Queen Caroline on the ground of adultery, the public used the scandal to demonstrate its contempt. Even the Church of England was attacked as a bastion of privilege in a land where Protestant dissenters and Roman Catholics could not hold public office. Gradually agitation focused on the Corn Laws, which set tariffs on grains, of which the most important was wheat; the Combination Acts, which made it illegal for workers to organize; and Parliament itself, criticized as the unrepresentative protector of inefficient administration by a closed ruling caste.

Even an unreformed Parliament could be sensitive to public opinion, however. In 1822 George Canning replaced Castlereagh as foreign secretary and leader of the House of Commons, and he was joined by other Tories who favored temperate reforms that taken together marked a new direction. As president of the Board of Trade, William Huskisson, a member of the commercial community of London and Liverpool and an admirer of liberal economic theories, reduced some tariffs. At the Home Office Sir Robert Peel quietly ceased the prosecution of newspapers and the use of political spies. Uniformed police, instituted in London in 1829, made law and order the responsibility of civil authority, and the list of capital crimes was halved. Radicals even won the repeal of the Combination Acts; and though subsequent violence brought an amendment effectively outlawing strikes, the legality of workingmen's associations was preserved.

Such reasonable reforms were intended to make the government both more efficient and more popular, but they also reflected a widening acceptance of liberal ideas that disturbed many Tories. Increasingly their party came to depend on the unimpeachably conservative duke of Wellington, the prestigious victor over Napoleon at Waterloo, to hold their party together. Expected to resist change, he too found further concessions unavoidable. Agitation over religious freedom and other issues swelled in Ireland, and Wellington pushed through Parliament a measure he himself disliked, allowing Catholics and dissenters to vote and to hold public office. But radicals, workers, merchant reformers, and doctrinaire liberals demanded more—the reform of Parliament itself. Elections in 1830, required by the death of George IV and the accession of William IV, only raised the political temperature, and in the countryside laborers set haystacks afire by night while by day stern magistrates ordered laborers accused of seditious activity transported to Australia.

The Reform Bill of 1832

As public turmoil rose and British leaders watched with concern the course of revolution in France, a new cabinet—the most thoroughly aristocratic of the century—proposed the reform of Parliament. Initially defeated in the House of Commons, the measure passed only after a new election increased the number of reformers and after the king reluctantly threatened to create enough new peers to get the measure through the House of Lords, where it had been defeated several times. Each setback for reform made the public mood uglier, and the king's intervention came amid demonstrations, the burning of the town hall and the bishop's palace in Bristol, and much dark talk about the French example.

The bill, far from radical, offered much less than the more outspoken radicals had wanted, but it marked a fundamental change. Suffrage was increased, especially in the counties, allowing some 800,000 men of substance to vote, well-to-do property-owners in the boroughs, property-owners and some tenants in the counties.[4] More important still, however, was the abolition of local variations, for a uniform national standard could, as many Tories complained, be easily broadened in the future. Before the Reform Bill of 1832, many boroughs that had solemnly been sending representatives to Parliament were barely villages; the most notorious, Old Sarum, was uninhabited. The bustling cities of Birmingham and Manchester had had no representatives at all, while perhaps a third of the members of Parliament had owed their seats to the local influence of some lord. Now such "pocket boroughs" were abolished; twenty-two larger cities were assigned two representatives each and twenty-one smaller ones one apiece. Although landed interests would continue to dominate Parliament, the worst abuses had been corrected, representation was at least crudely related to population, and the voices of commerce and manufacturing were both more numerous and louder.

Restricted suffrage and social tradition (and the open ballot) still assured the dominance of the upper classes. But the political mood was different, and a series of other reform measures followed the 1832 bill. Slavery was abolished in Britain's colonies in 1833, a victory for Protestant reformers and humanitarian radicals. The Factory Act soon followed, limiting children's workweek to forty-eight hours for those six to thirteen and sixty-nine hours for those fourteen to eighteen, and a new Poor Law was passed in 1834 (see Chapter 23). The Municipal Corporations Act the next year established a uniform system for the election of town and city officials and allowed all those who paid taxes in a municipality to vote in its elections—a more direct attack on aristocratic privilege than the Reform Bill of 1832.

Grave political and social problems remained to be faced, but most Britons could now reasonably hope that these might be resolved within Parliament. When the young Victoria ascended the throne in 1837, she commenced a reign of more than six decades that would rival Queen Elizabeth I's as a period of glory and power. Like Louis Philippe, Victoria was well informed and determined to play an active role in affairs of state. Like him too, she had some of the tastes and many of the values of a good bourgeoise. But she was subordinate (often against her wishes) to an increasingly flexible political system.

The 1840s in Britain

Two great popular movements in Britain agitated for change. Chartism was a huge, amorphous movement that grew out of disappointment with the reforms of the 1830s and the frustrations of workers' organizations. Its central aim, spelled out in what was called the People's Charter, was political democracy.[5] Chartists' meetings were watched with suspicion in 1839 and 1840, and their petitions to Parliament were summarily rejected. Their propaganda circulated widely, and riots on be-

---

[4] This was a considerably broader electorate than in France or Belgium, though Belgium, the only country to give her elected representatives a salary, had in many respects Europe's most liberal constitution. About one Frenchman in 160 could vote in 1830, one Briton in 32 after the Reform Bill of 1832, and one Belgian in 95 by 1840 and one in 20 by 1848. Universal male suffrage permits approximately one in 5 to go to the polls.

[5] The six points of the People's Charter were universal manhood suffrage, a written ballot, abolition of property qualifications for members of Parliament, payment of the members, constituencies of equal population, and annual elections. All but the last of these were adopted by 1918.

half of Chartist demands ended in scores of deaths. Yet by 1842 the movement was petering out. It failed despite its size to find a program that could for long mobilize the masses struggling for survival; and it failed, despite its emphasis on political rather than more threatening economic goals, to stir the consciences of those in power. Angry or desperate workers could riot here or there, but in England they were too isolated from each other and from other classes to gain even their political goals.

The other great movement, against the grain tariff, was victorious. The Anti-Corn Law League grew out of urban resentment over the high cost of bread, maintained by a tariff that benefited the landowning classes. From Manchester the movement spread throughout the country, becoming a kind of crusade, an attack on the privileges of aristocracy in the name of the "productive orders" of society, the middle and working classes united. The league propagandized with the new techniques of popular politics: parades and rallies, songs and speeches, pamphlets and cartoons. Its slogans were printed on trinkets for children, ribbons for women, drinking cups for men. Two manufacturers, Richard Cobden and John Bright, effective writers and orators, became among the best-known and most influential men in British life, spreading the gospel of liberalism across the land. To the upper classes such activity seemed in terrible taste; and conservatives argued from conviction that the nation's greatness was rooted in her landed estates. Nevertheless Sir Robert Peel's government twice

The London police, newly organized in the 1830s to deal with the increasing violence of mass demonstrations, are shown here awaiting the arrival of a Chartist procession.
(Photo: The Mansell Collection)

passed measures lowering duties on a wide range of items, including grain. The league demanded more.

Finally, in 1845, Peel announced his support for outright repeal of the Corn Laws. The threat of famine in Ireland had decided the issue for him. Almost simultaneously the Whig leader, Lord John Russell, affirmed his conversion to the principles of free trade. Yet neither man was eager to carry the fight through the houses of Parliament. Only when Russell was unable to form a government did Peel undertake the task, and in 1846 he shepherded the measure through both the Commons and Lords. The grain tariff was reduced to almost nothing, and nearly all duties were abolished or greatly lowered.

As in 1832 the political system had bent when demands for reform gained widespread support among the middle class, but Peel's courage split his party and ended his ministry. He was jeered by angry Tories as a young backbencher, Benjamin Disraeli, rose to decry Peel's treachery to the aristocracy. Britain's adoption of free trade had not come easily, but it signified the growing weight of both public opinion and the liberal creed. In their very triumph, however, liberals broadened the sphere of political attention from questions of suffrage, efficiency, and formal justice to more difficult ones of social well-being.

Liberal Monarchy in France

Louis Philippe's regime, known as the July Monarchy, was another compromise between order and liberty. The new constitution, with stronger guarantees of political freedom, was presented as a contract the king swore to keep, not a gift he granted. Similar to the one it replaced, it lowered property requirements for voters, nearly doubling their number—though suffrage was still safely restricted to some 170,000 men of means—and the hereditary upper house was replaced by lifetime peers. More important, most of the old aristocracy resigned their offices, never to return to public life. Those who replaced them, professional people and bearers of newer (often Napoleonic) titles, differed from their predecessors more in outlook than social origin.

In France the overriding political question of the 1830s was the July Monarchy itself, attacked from left and right. A mass held in Paris in memory of the duke of Berry became a legitimist (pro-Bourbon) demonstration, in turn prompting an anticlerical crowd to sack and loot the archbishop's palace and a nearby church. The duchess of Berry tried to spur an uprising in 1832 on behalf of her son, now the legitimist claimant to the throne; on the other hand, the strike of silk workers in Lyons was considered a republican revolt and suppressed with the bitterness of class hatred by the bourgeois National Guard. Secret republican organizations with provocative names like the Society of the Rights of Man spread nonetheless, and Louis Napoleon, Bonapartist heir after the death of the emperor's son in 1832, attempted to stir a revolt in 1836 and again in 1840.

Yet all these attempts failed; and the July Monarchy, having established itself as a vehicle of monarchist stability, could even appeal to the cult of Napoleon I by bringing the emperor's body back from St. Helena and placing it with patriotic pomp in the marble crypt of the Invalides. A little self-consciously claiming its place in the revolutionary tradition of France, Orléanist rule did not usher in a period of great reforms like those in Britain in the 1830s, but the administrative system developed under the Revolution and Napoleon made such reforms less necessary. The provision for a nationwide system of public education in 1833 was a step English liberals would long envy. Gradually, as the regime benefited from the enthusiasm for railroads and visions of economic growth, its ministries became more confident and stable; the press, under some restriction, grew more tame. And many who had made their reputations under Napoleon or had been moderate republicans rallied to its support.

The 1840s in France

Within government circles political conflict in the 1840s largely involved two factions, led by Adolphe Thiers and François Guizot. Both men were journalists and historians of great talent. With Thiers stood those who considered the revolution of 1830 one step in a process of evolution toward increased suffrage and constitutional reform. Those associated with Guizot, including the king himself, believed the constitution of 1830, having achieved a proper balance between liberty and order, should be preserved intact. Neither party was organized in any modern sense, and the differences between Guizot and Thiers were not very great, being at least as subtle as those between Peel and Russell, but their competition (legitimists and republicans had little voice in parliament) appeared to guarantee free and stable government. Later, it would seem a weakness that the skillful verbal duels of Guizot and Thiers failed to evoke in the nation at large the resounding echoes of English agitation over the Corn Laws.

From 1840 to 1848 the government of France was dominated by Guizot, Louis Philippe's premier during those years. A Protestant in a Catholic country, an intellectual in politics, a man who held broad principles rigidly, Guizot had in excess failings common to many liberals of the nineteenth century. He spoke of liberty, progress, and law in eloquent terms that made his cautious practices seem hypocritical. The policies he pursued were, like Louis Philippe himself, lacking in the idealism that excites or the sense of larger purpose that gives dignity to compromise. When defending himself he thought he was defending liberal government, and he cleaved to his positions to the point where rigidity itself became a principle.

The two freest and most prosperous of Europe's great nations had developed similarly since 1830. In both, liberal governments led by able men sought through reasonable compromise, the rule of law, and parliamentary government to unify their nations and to make "progress" compatible with stability. Discontent and workers' misery, though frightening, were understood in the councils of government primarily as a threat to order. In England there was a powerful aristocracy from whom reform had to be painfully wrung, but they conceded under pressure in part because they felt secure. In France the aristocracy counted for little after 1830, but more radical visions of democracy and social justice, finding little to hope for within the system, flourished outside it more strongly than across the Channel. The July Monarchy, which felt the insecurity of its recent and revolutionary origins, held to its narrow political forms until it, too, fell with the ease of incumbents losing an election. The differences between England and France are too often exaggerated, but they became greater after the revolutions of 1848.

Liberal Victories in Other Countries

The political victories of French and British liberalism seemed part of a general trend, not only because of the prestige and influence of those countries but because of similar developments elsewhere. In Belgium, and Switzerland also, liberal political institutions accompanied notable economic growth. And the strength of liberal movements in Spain and Italy further measured the weakening of that conservative dominance Metternich had sought to assure.

Belgium

The Belgian monarchy established in 1830 was one of the triumphs of liberal constitutionalism.

The next year the new state, which owed its existence to French restraint and British protection, took as its king Leopold I, who had lived long in England (he was an uncle of Queen Victoria's) and who soon married the daughter of Louis Philippe. The constitution went farther than France's in guaranteeing civil rights and the primacy of the Chamber of Deputies, and politics continued to revolve around the coalition—rare in Europe—of Catholics and liberals, aristocrats and members of the upper-middle class who had led the revolt against the Netherlands.

Rapidly becoming the most industrialized nation on the Continent, Belgium was prosperous; and if her lower classes were more miserable and more largely illiterate than those of France, that very fact made the social isolation of her leaders politically less dangerous. Self-confident and satisfied with the new order of things, they built on the administrative traditions left from Austrian and French rule and proved themselves remarkably adept at planning railroads, reforming taxes and schools, and making timely political concessions.

Switzerland

Liberal institutions spread to Switzerland too as part of the international trend and were spurred by the revolutions of 1830. Beginning in 1828, some cantons adopted such measures as representative government and freedom of the press, and ten cantons formed a league in 1832 to agitate for religious freedom and for a stronger, secular central government within the Swiss confederation. These policies were resisted by seven largely Catholic cantons, dominated by their aristocracies; and the conflict, combining religious and political issues, became passionate. In 1845 the seven conservative cantons formed an alliance, the Sonderbund; two years later the leagues were at war. The Sonderbund looked for support from conservative and Catholic states, but none came—the papacy, Austria, and Piedmont had their hands full in Italy—and so the liberal sympathies of Britain and France once again proved decisive. With the Sonderbund's defeat Switzerland adopted a new constitution in 1848 influenced by the example of the United States and providing for universal male suffrage; the old union of cantons was transformed into a federal state.

Spain

In Spain the monarchy itself had turned to liberals to seek support against attacks from the right. King Ferdinand VII, who died in 1833, had carefully arranged for the succession of his three-year-old daughter, Isabella; but his brother, Don Carlos, claimed the throne.[6] Rural, regionalist, and reactionary, Carlism was a loosely organized and badly divided movement that found its support primarily in the more isolated regions of the north—Navarre, the Basque country, and parts of Catalonia and Aragon. The Carlists, who favored autocracy and the traditional claims of Spanish Catholicism, began open fighting on Isabella II's succession that ended only in 1839 with their defeat. But Don Carlos won a place in Spanish legend as a dashing and chivalric hero, the protector of old Spanish virtues, and Carlism would remain a factor in every subsequent Spanish revolution as a conservative rallying cry.

To win liberal support the regency granted a constitution in 1834. Cautiously modeled on the French constitution of 1814, it allowed narrow suffrage and protected the monarch's prerogatives, but it established representative institutions as a lasting feature of Spanish politics.

---

[6] Salic law, dating from Merovingian times, prohibited the accession of women to royal thrones. Generally followed on the Continent, it meant that in 1837 Queen Victoria could not also assume rule over Hanover as her father had, and it passed to the duke of Cumberland. In Spain Ferdinand VII had abolished the Salic law by a pragmatic sanction in 1830 so that Isabella could be his heir.

Even so modest a step was enough to place Spain in the liberal camp, and Isabella's government relied on extensive support from Britain and France. Similar developments in Portugal under young Queen Maria II led to an alliance of the four countries in 1834, a league of constitutional regimes to offset the interventions of young princes sent from Italy and Germany to fight for Don Carlos.

Internal war led army generals to engage in politics and divided the liberals. The moderates supported the constitution of 1834 and admired Guizot's France, while the more anticlerical progressives called for a democratic constitution and the election of local officials. The progressives won a more radical constitution in 1837 and in 1840 led an uprising on behalf of General Baldomero Espartero, who displaced the queen mother as regent and established a dictatorship. Three years later General Ramón María Narváez brought a government of the moderates into power that lasted until 1854. In Spain, too, regimes needing popular support turned to parliamentary forms; in the 1840s Spain seemed to be taking its place among the liberal nations of Europe.

In his portraits, as in much of his private life, Giuseppe Mazzini seemed more a romantic poet than a revolutionary agitator.
(Photo: The Granger Collection)

Italy and the Ideas of Giuseppe Mazzini

Ferment continued in Italy following the events of 1830, though order was restored throughout the peninsula and its governments remained staunchly conservative. Uprisings and demonstrations broke out in town after town, and most of them were related to the work of Giuseppe Mazzini.

A Genoese, Mazzini absorbed something of the republican and radical traditions of his native city. In exile most of his life, mainly in London, he ceaselessly conspired, corresponded with acquaintances all over Europe, and published highly effective propaganda. His intent was revolutionary, and his Young Italy movement was far more democratic and radical than the Carbonari or the discontented officials who led revolts in the 1820s. Italy was his first concern, but his influence was European-wide, for he brought together patriotic visions of national independence, democracy, social reform, and progress.

The French Revolution, Mazzini argued, overemphasized negative and individual rights, leaving "humanity" a weak abstraction. He stressed instead the moral duties of man to man and the role of the nation, which gives individuals a social purpose, humanity a concrete meaning, and liberty to all. While attacking privilege he rejected socialism as materialistic, liberalism as lacking in social values, and conservatism as stiflingly paternalistic. Yet like most leaders of his generation, he put politics first; with the right kind of government, social, cultural, even moral problems would find their solution. All nations should educate men to brotherhood; every nation has its mission. Italy, having given to Europe Roman law, the Roman Catholic Church, and the Renaissance, would now create the first of this new kind of nation.

Mazzini was vague about the sources of political power and imprecise about economic organization. His unquenchable faith in the moral potential of simple people and their readiness to rise spontaneously in a great cause approached delusion. Yet he wrote tellingly about the specific grievances of peasants, artists, professionals, and intellectuals. Most of the revolts he supported ended in tragic failure, but he educated a generation to share at least a part of his dream.

Especially in northern Italy young lawyers, liberal landowners, and some members of the aristocracy began to find national implications in nearly all they did. Annual congresses of Italian scientists became quiet demonstrations; disputes over where railroad lines should be built became means of expressing discontent with Austrian rule. Literary journals and societies for agricultural improvement took up the national theme. Piedmont's efforts to win trade away from Austria by commercial treaties and projected railroads excited Italian patriots and worried the imperial government.

This ferment, more genteel than the revolution Mazzini envisioned, gained new force with the election in 1846 of Pope Pius IX. He was not the Austrian candidate, and he brought to the papacy a reputation for moderation, reformist sympathies, and deep Italian feeling. When he declared amnesty for all political prisoners in the Papal States, there were jubilant demonstrations in nearly every Italian city. Talk of administrative reforms in papal territory spurred demands elsewhere for further liberal measures, including citizen militias and the abolition of censorship in Tuscany and Piedmont. When Austria tried to exercise her traditional influence, new demonstrations broke out. In fact the various Italian governments were embarrassed by their new popularity and were being pushed farther than they had meant to go when they undertook to negotiate a common Italian tariff and allowed their citizens to jeer the Austrians and talk of constitutional union.

Southern Italy had been rather removed from this agitation, but in the fall some of its towns attempted revolt, and in January 1848 well-organized revolution broke out in Palermo. By the end of the month, Neapolitan armies had been swept from Sicily except for units in a few fortresses. The Sicilian revolt, which demanded the honored Spanish constitution of 1812, led to heightened demands in Naples itself. When the Bourbon monarch granted a constitution, the dikes were broken. Early in February Piedmont and then Tuscany gained similar constitutions, all resembling France's of 1830, and the Papal States were expected to follow suit. The demand for liberal institutions, when combined with the cry for a free and independent Italy, seemed invincible.

III. THE REVOLUTIONS OF 1848

Both conservatives and liberals had assumed that political measures of the proper sort could assure domestic order. But in 1848 revolution swept across Europe from France to Hungary. Within a few weeks of each other, very different regimes gave way before rather similar demands. Social and national issues—issues on which political liberals disagreed—now proved even more divisive than constitutional questions. One factor common to most of the uprisings was economic distress, marked by rising food prices after a poor harvest and a recession that struck many new industries after the expansion of the 1840s.

Revolution in France

Economic crisis does not make a revolution; the death from starvation of more than a million Irishpeople in the famine years of 1846–1849 did little more than the Chartists to shake British rule. In France, however, a faltering economy added to political pressure for a more liberal and representative regime while Guizot held firm to the constitution he believed in and Louis Philippe to the minister he trusted.

To protest against the government's intransigence, a series of banquets took place across the country, the most important of which was scheduled for Paris on February 22. When a frightened government banned it, some deputies announced they would attend anyway. Crowds began to gather in the streets, occasionally clashing with police, and workers who could never have afforded banquet tickets started building barricades. Revolution had begun.

The government had careful plans, though perhaps not the right generals, for dealing with insurrection; but when even the respectable citizenry of the National Guard sullenly refused to cheer their king, Louis Philippe, like Charles X before him, abdicated in favor of his grandson and left for England. Once again, however, the Paris crowds had more revolutionary aims, and on February 24 the Second Republic was declared from the Hôtel de Ville.

Political clubs and pressure groups organized quickly, and members of the provisional government, "nominated" in the offices of two rival newspapers, were "confirmed" by cheers from the crowd outside the Hôtel de Ville. The leading figure was Alphonse de Lamartine, a handsome and eloquent poet, converted to Republicanism on the day of revolution. But the cabinet also included a scientist and several journalists; a radical republican, Alexandre Ledru-Rollin; a socialist, Louis Blanc; and even one worker, Albert Martin, always referred to with unconscious condescension by his first name only.

Despite their distrust of each other, moderates and radicals compromised with some skill. The republic adopted universal male suffrage, a degree of democracy allowed in no other large nation; declared the citizen's right to work a principle of government; and erected a commission to hold public hearings on problems of labor. Noting that each French revolution "owed it to the world to establish yet one more philosophic truth," the republic abolished the death penalty.

At the same time pains were taken to demonstrate the new regime's restraint. Foreign war was rejected, Lamartine's eloquence persuaded the crowd to abandon a red flag in favor of the tricolor (with a red cockade), and new taxes were levied to balance the budget. Relations with the Catholic Church were better than those of any French government in the century, and the April elections for a Constituent Assembly took place in good order, though the more radical had wanted elections postponed, with nearly 85 percent of the eligible electorate voting—striking evidence of political awareness. The result was an overwhelming majority for the moderate republicans and a serious setback for the left, which had fewer deputies than the monarchists. The Second Republic seemed solidly established.

The Spread of Revolution

As news of the events in France sped across Europe, a conservative nightmare became a reality. Nearly every capital, it developed, had citizens who found exciting promise in words like "constitution," "rights," "liberty," "free press." In Hungary the Diet cheered Kossuth's call on March 3 for representative government, and revolution broke out at the same time in

The Politics of Restoration and Reform 1815–1850

This contemporary engraving of the fighting in Frankfurt on September 18, 1848 contrasts the fighting styles of troops and the people.
(Photo: The Granger Collection)

the Rhineland and later in Vienna (March 12), then in Berlin (March 15), Milan (March 18), and Venice (March 22).

As spontaneous and loosely organized as the rising in Paris, these revolts followed a similar pattern. The news from France would attract excited crowds; groups of men—especially journalists, lawyers, and students—would meet in cafés to discuss rumors, newspaper accounts, and their own aspirations. Governments, as ready as local radicals to believe that revolution was at hand, would call out troops to maintain order, and with a kind of inevitability, some incident would occur—a shot fired by a soldier insulted once too often or by someone in the crowd with an unfamiliar gun.

Now barricades would rise in the style that came from Paris, constructed of paving stones, a passing coach ceremoniously overturned, nearby trees, and furniture. Barricades became the peoples' voice, threatening but vague, as workers and doctors, women and children labored together through the night. When blood was shed, the crowd had its martyrs. In Paris corpses were carried around on a cart as a spur to revolutionary determination; in Berlin the king supported his fainting queen while bareheaded he paid the homage his subjects demanded to citizens his troops had killed.

When new concessions were won, the atmosphere would grow festive. New flags would fly, often a tricolor, symbolizing national union. In the almost universal dedication to politics, newspapers and pamphlets would appear in floods (100 new newspapers in Vienna, nearly 500 in Paris). Workers burst into the Tuilleries and jovially ate the lunch prepared for a king who had no time to eat it. Republicans met at the police station to read with amusement (and sometimes the shock of betrayal) police reports on their activity. Radicals would seek ever after to recapture the unanimity, the joy, the power of a day of revolution. Others, and not just conservatives, would never quite forget the fearsomeness of the mob, fanatical faces, and ugly threats.

The revolutions had in common the psychology they manifested and many of the liberals goals they demanded. Scarcity of food, depression, and the economic dislocation caused by new industry played some part in all of them; in most cities so did the fact of recent and rapid growth in the numbers of the urban poor. Peasant discontent was critical in Central Europe. Yet the revolutions of 1848 were not a single phenomenon; specific issues, the personalities who expressed them, and the forces that resolved them varied from state to state.

Revolution in Germany and Italy

Frederick William IV had been replying to growing agitation in Prussia with vague assurances, a promise to reconvene the united Landtag, and a strengthening of his troops. With the incredible news of revolt in Vienna and the fall of Metternich, the king softened, relaxing censorship and calling the Landtag. Fighting broke out despite these concessions, and he gave way to demands that the hated troops leave Berlin, using the magic word "Germany" in proclamations to "my dear Berliners" and even wearing the national colors: black, gold, and red. A constituent assembly was elected in May by universal but indirect suffrage, and when it met in Berlin, where a civic guard now kept order, revolution in Prussia seemed to have triumphed.

Events in the rest of Germany confirmed that triumph. In March some 600 delegates had met in Frankfurt in a preparliamentary assembly, and no government dared oppose their call for elections by universal male suffrage to a national assembly. In May the national assembly convened at Frankfurt included 830 delegates, mostly from the smaller states of the more liberal west, more than half of them lawyers and professors. But there were businessmen, members of the liberal gentry, and even nobles suddenly awkward in such society. The great majority favored a monarchical German state with an almost democratic constitution, and the brilliant, difficult, and noisy assembly set about to write a constitution claiming for itself executive authority over a united Germany.

In the Austrian Empire, by mid-March the Hungarian Diet had established a free press and a national guard, abolished feudal obligations (with compensation to be paid the lords), and resolved to require nobles to pay taxes. Everyone noticed the parallel to 1789. The demands that Hungary be allowed to levy her own taxes and direct her own army, briefly resisted in Vienna, were soon granted, and a new cabinet, which included Kossuth, began to govern through established institutions.

A constitutional regime in Hungary alone, however, could hardly be secure; but its example encouraged students in Vienna to demand representative government for Austria and especially in the capital city. The crowds soon clashed with the troops and once fired upon became more militant. In rapid order Metternich resigned, censorship was abolished, a constitution was promised, and arms were passed out to the students. The government attempted again and again to circumscribe these concessions but quickly retreated before renewed outbursts. When students rejected the proposal that the vote be granted everyone but factory workers and servants, universal male suffrage was conceded in mid-May. At the same time Hungarian autonomy brought similar demands from Czechs in Bohemia, Croats in Croatia, and Rumanians in Transylvania (these last two domains under Hungarian rule). The old Austrian Empire had all but collapsed.

In Naples, Tuscany, and Piedmont the measures won through the March Laws in Hungary and the March Days in Berlin had been gained a few days earlier. Then the Papal States were granted a constitution, though it awkwardly preserved a veto for the pope and the College of Cardinals. With revolution in Vienna, open revolt broke out in Milan; and after five days of bitter fighting, the Austrian army retreated from the city. The Five Glorious Days of Milan added their luster to the heroic legends of March. A people aroused, it appeared, could defeat a great army. Soon Venice too rose up to reestablish the Venetian republic.

Shortly nationalist pressure pushed Piedmont to declare war on Austria, and papal troops with papal blessing were sent to join a Neapolitan army in the common battle against Austrian rule in Italy. But a few days later Pius IX declared he could hardly fight against Catholic Austria, and Ferdinand II recalled his army from the front after his Swiss mercenaries defeated the revolutionaries in Naples. Piedmont was left alone to bear the brunt of the national war against Austria. Still, patriotic spirits remained high; and when at the end of May Piedmontese troops won a battle, the prospects for a free and independent Italy seemed good.

The Fatal Dissensions

Political freedom exposed the disagreements among those who had fought for it. In France these divisions were primarily social—between Paris and the countryside, between middle class and workers. The moderate majority of the new assembly were satisfied with what their republic had already achieved and determined that liberty should not be threatened by disorders. Workers on the other hand found conditions little improved by revolution or the new republic and agitated for a social program.

Frightened, the government dissolved the national workshops, which had been established to provide useful work for the unemployed. Only a faint echo of ideas popularized by Louis Blanc, the workshops in fact offered more relief than employment. The good bourgeois saw in them a dangerous principle, outrageous inefficiency, and wasteful expense; but they symbolized the hope of the lower classes, and unemployed men from Paris and the countryside had joined them by the tens of thousands. On news of their dissolution, barricades went up in the workingmen's quarters of Paris, and the poor fought with the ferocity of hopelessness as republican troops under General Louis Eugène Cavaignac systematically crushed the threat to order. The accidental death of the archbishop of Paris, killed while trying to mediate, seemed to prove the inevitability of civil war. After three days of fighting, June 24–26, the government troops triumphed. More than a thousand people died, and thousands more workers would be sent to prison or into exile. Paris had never seen greater bloodshed.

For the young Karl Marx and for socialists ever since, the June Days were the classic example of open class conflict, and radicals never quite recaptured their faith that democracy would lead to social justice. Given almost dictatorial powers, Cavaignac took steps to restrict the press, suppress radical societies, and discipline workers. The creation of a French republic still seemed in itself a radical step, and Cavaignac remained a convinced republican. The assembly continued to write a constitution, which, announced in November, kept universal suffrage and provided for a unicameral parliament (with no conservative upper house) and a president elected directly by popular vote. But while its official acts might have been unexceptionably republican, after June there was something a little hollow about the representativeness of the Second Republic.

In Germany and Austria revolutionary change uncovered latent conflicts among artisans, peasants, and nobles as well as between workers and members of the middle class. Furthermore revolts in these lands had not deposed their rulers, who kept control of loyal armies. Above all, nationalism, which evoked such popular enthusiasm, separated the constitution makers from each other.

Czech patriots had refused representation in the Frankfurt parliament, insisting that Slavs should not be subject to German rule. Instead a pan-Slav congress met at Prague in June. When disorder resulted, the Austrian field marshal Prince Windischgrätz, long disgusted with his emperor's weakness, bombarded Prague, crushed all resistance, and established military rule. The Frankfurt parliament congratulated him on his German victory.

It was no more sympathetic to Italian nationalism. The Austrian general Count Joseph Radetzky had retreated from Milan only as far as the great fortresses that had dominated the Lombard plain since the Middle Ages. In July, disregarding orders to negotiate, he skillfully attacked the Piedmontese and overwhelmingly defeated them. Austrian troops, once more in control of Lombardy, marched back into Milan. Radetzky too won congratulations from Frankfurt.

The German parliament also acquiesced as Prussian troops put down a Polish rising in Posen, and it called on Prussia to fight Denmark in behalf of Germans in Schleswig and Holstein, who opposed the extension of Danish authority in these duchies. In September riots broke out in Frankfurt itself, an expression of both nationalist and economic complaints; and the assembly, without revenue or a military force of its own, invited Austrian and Prussian troops to restore order.

Meanwhile many Croats had been demanding autonomy from Hungary just as Hungary had from Vienna, and General Joseph Jellachich with his emperor's encouragement built on Croat sentiment to weld an effective army that overpowered desperate Hungarian resistance and moved almost to Vienna. Before that threat the city rose again in October, but the armies of Windischgrätz and Jellachich bombarded Vienna into submission. The emperor returned, his authority reestablished in all his empire save Hungary and the Venetian Republic.

Rome too witnessed another revolutionary outburst in November; and like the June Days in Paris, the September riots in Frankfurt, and the October revolt in Vienna, this rising showed a popular fury and frustration that had not been so apparent in February and March. For hungry and desperate people, freedom added political awareness to old suspicions, and turmoil had taught the usefulness of force. The pope had proved of course not to be a nationalist; and within Rome an entrenched and reactionary administration choked each effort at reform. The appointment of Count Pellegrino Rossi, who had been French ambassador to Rome and was a friend of Guizot's, to be prime minister of the Papal States would earlier have justified the wildest hopes; but now the cautious and rigid Rossi merely increased antagonisms. In November he was assassinated, Pius

IX slipped away to the safety of Gaeta in the Neapolitan kingdom, and the eternal city under Mazzini's leadership assumed the ancient title of the Roman Republic.

Venice and France also remained republics, and assemblies were still busy drafting constitutions in Vienna, Berlin, and Frankfurt. There could be no doubt, however, that in general the forces of order were gaining ground at the end of the year. Nationwide elections in December selected a president for the French republic. There were four candidates: Lamartine, the most prominent figure of government from February to June, received the fewest votes; Ledru-Rollin, leader of the republican left, fared somewhat better; Cavaignac, who had held executive powers since wiping out the June uprising, made a respectable showing; and Louis Napoleon Bonaparte won 70 percent of the votes. All campaigned as republicans, but all save Napoleon symbolized disillusionment. The Louis Napoleon who once had fought with the Carbonari in Italy could claim to be the man of revolution. He was clearly also a man of order, and yet he had written more about social questions and workers' needs than any other candidate. He was supported by the Catholic Church and the monarchists, for want of anyone else. Above all he had his name.[7] In December he became the first and only president of the Second Republic.

Austria too found a strong new leader. Prince Felix von Schwarzenberg filled the place Metternich had left vacant, and in December he persuaded Ferdinand I to abdicate in favor of his eighteen-year-old son, Francis Joseph I, who had made no embarrassing commitments during the year. In Prussia the king dissolved the Landtag and promulgated a constitution of his own, very similar to Piedmont's and Belgium's. Ten months of turmoil had led back to the arrangements of February.

The Final Phase

Many of the revolutionary regimes nevertheless proved difficult to subdue. Not until May 1849 did Neapolitan armies reconquer all of Sicily, and the bombardment of Messina earned Ferdinand II the cruel nickname of King Bomba. The Roman Republic maintained better order than the regime it replaced, and for three months it fought with heroic tenacity before bowing to French troops sent by Louis Napoleon to restore the pope. In March Piedmont, pressed by radical demands and Austrian provocation, had again declared war, only to be immediately defeated. Charles Albert abdicated, and for her efforts in the Italian national cause, all the kingdom had was an enormous debt and an unpopular government, a new ruler, a constitution, and the red, white, and green flag of Italian nationalism. Ten years later the constitution and the flag would seem quite a lot; for the time being Austria's position in the Italian peninsula was secure.

Austria invaded Hungary in January, but her forces were pushed back; and when Schwarzenberg rejected its draft constitution, the Hungarian Diet declared a republic. The Hungarians continued to battle against the armies of Austria and against Croats, Slavs, Slovaks, and Rumanians as national animosities reached new heights of fury. In June Russian intervention sealed the fate of the Hungarian republic; the conservative powers were coming to cooperate once again.

By March 1849 the Frankfurt Assembly had completed the constitution so carefully debated and elected Frederick William IV of Prussia German emperor; but after brief hesitation, he announced that the crowns he recognized came

---

[7] On trial for his attempted coup in 1840, Louis Napoleon concluded his defense with these words: "I represent before you a principle, a cause, and a defeat: the principle is sovereignty of the people; the cause, that of the Empire; the defeat, Waterloo. The principle you have recognized; the cause you have served; the defeat you want to avenge."

by grace of God. The Frankfurt constitution, with its universal male suffrage and touching list of old abuses to be abolished, its promises of civil rights and education, would never be tested. The assembly dissolved, and new revolutions broke out in the Rhineland, Saxony, and Bavaria (Baden's third revolution in a year led to a brief republic there), all of them quashed in June and July with the aid of Prussian troops.

The last of the revolutionary regimes to fall was that of the Venetian republic, defeated in August 1849 more by starvation and cholera than by Austrian artillery, though it accomplished the unprecedented feat of lobbing shells three miles from the mainland into the city.

A famous liberal historian has called 1848 "the turning-point at which modern history failed to turn,"[8] and his epigram captures the sense of destiny thwarted that still colors the liberal view of 1848. Historical analyses of that year, concerned with explaining the failure of the revolutions, generally include five broad points. First, liberal constitutions, new economic policies, and increased civil rights failed to pull strong and lasting support from the masses whose more immediate needs were neither met nor understood. Second, the revolutions of February and March were made primarily by the middle classes, strengthened by popular discontent; but when radicals sought more than representative government and legal equality, the middle classes were reminded of their concern for order and private property.

Outside France the middle classes, once isolated from the masses, were too weak to retain power. Third, the leaders of the revolutions were so moved by abstract principles that, inexperienced in practical politics, they mistook arguments for power. Fourth, nationalism divided revolutionaries and prevented the cooperation that was essential for durable success. Fifth, while the military power of Austria and Russia was left intact, no major nation was ready to intervene in behalf of change. Britain was sympathetic, France encouraging, and the United States, whose consulates were centers of republicanism, enthusiastic; but none offered the kind of help Russia gave the Austrian emperor.

From a different perspective, however, the fact of revolution so widespread and tenacious was as significant as its collapse, for 1848 also measured the failures of restoration, displayed again the power of political ideas, and uncovered the effects of a generation of social change. Many of the gains won in that year endured: the peasants of eastern Prussia and the Austrian Empire, emancipated in 1848, remained free of servile obligations; and the new constitutions were kept in Piedmont and Prussia. On all sides important lessons were learned. The monarchs triumphant in 1849 punished revolutionaries with execution, flogging, prison, and exile, but they gave increased attention to winning some popular support. Nationalists and liberals on the other hand would never again depend so optimistically on the spontaneous power of the people, and advocates of social reform became more skeptical of liberal institutions.

---

[8] George Macaulay Trevelyan, *British History in the Nineteenth Century and After* (1937), p. 292.

The period from 1815 to 1849 was an era of political experiments, each claiming to be permanent. For the most conservative regimes the problem was to achieve the administrative efficiency essential to survival while preserving as many of the privileges of inherited social rank as possible. In Western Europe the problem was in a sense reversed. The benefits of regular justice, legal equality, and broader participation in politics came to be widely (although by no means universally) acknowledged; the question was how far in this direction society could go without undermining the differences of wealth and opportunity on which, most educated people believed, civilization itself depended. The extent of suffrage aroused so much fury because it put political rights in social terms, defining by law (and therefore by conscious choice) who should participate, who constituted the political nation. Universal suffrage—few people in this period considered that the term might include both sexes—was radical because it seemed to declare men politically equal whatever their social differences. Constitutions, by making the rules of political life formal and explicit, acknowledged such rules to be man-made and subject to change.

The battles over these issues were often narrowly political, reflecting an almost universal confidence that political systems could make the critical difference in the very nature of society. The course of that conflict established ideologies of conservatism and liberalism, and their competition proved a lasting part of European public life. With time, these positions grew more varied and complex. Conservatives often learned to live with representative government while remaining determined to defend the principles of authority and social order. Liberals, while insisting that the proper political forms and legal procedures could guarantee liberty and thus assure progress, often divided over the social responsibilities of the state. Increasingly, the focus of politics broadened. In part, political leaders, seeking wider support, deliberately took up social issues, aware that peasants and workers were a potential force or at least a threat. But society was changing too, often quite independently of political decisions and in ways for which those in power were ill-prepared. These changes, frightening and promising at the same time, are the subject of Chapter 23.

Neither the political devices of the restoration nor the timid liberalism of the 1830s achieved the stability they sought. If the revolutionary governments of 1848 fared no better, they tested still more directly the political implications of social change. In the next generation political leaders would find themselves greatly extending the authority of the state, as shown in Chapter 24. Politics would be understood less as an autonomous sphere of activity and more in terms of its relations to the changes in social structure, economic organization, and style of life taking place in an age of industrialization.

RECOMMENDED READING

Studies

Anderson, Eugene N., and Pauline R. Anderson. *Political Institutions and Social Change in the Nineteenth Century.* 1967. Comprehensive view of constitutional and legal change.

*Artz, Frederick B. *Reaction and Revolution, 1815–1832.* 1968. First written in 1934, this remains a valuable effort to interpret the period as a whole.

*Briggs, Asa. *The Making of Modern England, 1784–1867.* 1967. A wide-ranging and readable survey of English society and politics.

Carr, Raymond. *Spain, 1808–1939.* 1966. The most balanced and comprehensive account in any language.

De Bertier de Sauvigny, Guillaume. *The Bourbon Restoration.* Lynn M. Case (tr.). 1967. An able and affectionate reappraisal of the Bourbon regime.

*Duveau, Georges. *The Making of a Revolution.* Anne Carter (tr.). 1967. Skillfully pulls together modern research on 1848 in France.

Gash, Norman. *Politics in the Age of Peel, 1830–1850.* 1953. The standard study of the changes in British politics following the reform of 1832.

Greenfield, Kent Roberts. *Economics and Liberalism in the Risorgimento: A Study of Nationalism in Lombardy.* 1966. A classic study of the connection between economic change and nationalism.

*Grew, Raymond (ed.). *Crises of Political Development in Europe and the United States.* 1978. Ten essays on the patterns of political modernization in major countries.

*Hamerow, Theodore S. *Restoration, Revolution, and Reaction: Economics and Politics in Germany, 1815–1871.* 1958. A complex analysis of the relationship of social classes and the state to economic change.

*Hobsbawm, E. J. *The Age of Revolution, Europe 1789 to 1848.* 1970. A stimulating Marxist assessment.

Johnson, Douglas. *Guizot: Aspects of French History, 1787–1874.* 1963. Insightful essays focusing on the dominant figure of the July Monarchy.

Kreiger, Leonard. *The German Idea of Freedom.* 1957. This profound and sometimes difficult study covers a broad period of German political thought.

*Langer, William L. *Political and Social Upheaval, 1832–1852.* 1969. Richly detailed, this study treats all of Europe in all its major aspects.

*Nicolson, Harold. *The Congress of Vienna, A Study in Allied Unity, 1812–1822.* 1946. A lively and balanced account of the process of peacemaking.

Pinkney, David H. *The French Revolution of 1830.* 1972. The study that has transformed our understanding of this revolution.

Salvemini, Gaetano. *Mazzini.* 1957. Still the best introduction to Mazzini's thought.

Seton-Watson, Hugh. *The Russian Empire, 1801–1917.* 1967. A solid, largely political survey.

*Stearns, Peter N. *1848: The Revolutionary Tide in Europe.* 1974. Brings together important recent research.

*Taylor, A. J. P. *The Hapsburg Monarchy, 1809–1918.* 1965. This concise account emphasizes the effects of nationalism on diplomacy and politics.

---

* Available in paperback.

23

INDUSTRIALIZATION AND SOCIAL CHANGE 1800–1860

The political conflict that marked the first half of the nineteenth century was part of a larger process of social change. Social relations, long governed by rank and custom, were increasingly treated as matters of free contract between individuals, a development that made it easier for some to seek new opportunities and left the poor more unprotected. Economic changes were the most obvious of all. Land had always been the primary and surest source of wealth, but technology and the spread of the industrial system were changing that, even though only a fraction of any population was directly engaged in industrial occupations. Economic growth became a continuing process in which inventions, the demand for more capital, factory organization, and more efficient transportation reinforced each other. Economic development in turn was intricately connected with population growth, urbanization, and new social groupings. The concentration of people, wealth, and power in great cities altered culture, social structure, and politics.

These changes that justified optimistic visions of continuing progress also brought grave human distress. Slums, poverty, and unemployment appeared to be inseparable byproducts of economic growth, and increasingly society was perceived as consisting of antagonistic classes. The proper relations between rich and poor, worker and employer, men and women were called into question as established social patterns were undermined.

Despite these changes, which affected so deeply what people believed, where they lived, what they ate, and how they related to those around them, there was also much historical continuity. Traditional ways eroded slowly, and the institutions of government, culture, and religion maintained old forms but served altered purposes, thereby adding to the painful dissonance between professed goals and everyday reality. While the middle class increased in size, self-confidence, and importance, the aristocracy remained socially and politically dominant in most of Europe. Western civilization once again showed its remarkable adaptability, but the strain was great.

The fact of change became the focus of intellectual as well as economic life. Liberals and socialists offered contrasting visions of the sources of change and where it must lead and argued from the study of history as to what the future must bring. In all spheres faith was placed in the rational individual, freed to calculate his own best interest, and in a proper organization of society, one that would encourage flexible adaptation to ever-changing needs. The emphasis on social organization, which showed in the concern for charity and education as well as efficient production and responsive government, underscored the need for some social solution to the misery of the masses.

I. PROGRESS OF INDUSTRIALIZATION

The most obvious economic change was in the way goods were produced. Industrialization, which had begun in the eighteenth century, was then both stimulated and disrupted by the effects of the French Revolution and subsequent years of warfare. In the nineteenth century industrialization became a recognizable process spreading from industry to industry, involving governments as well as capitalists and workers, and spreading from nation to nation.

The Effects of Revolution and War

The preconditions of industrialization discussed in Chapter 20 had continued to develop in much of Europe: the exploitation of resources had become more systematic, population was growing, transportation had generally improved, the means of recruiting capital had expanded, and the number of able political and business leaders concerned with speeding industrial growth had increased. These factors were especially evident in Great Britain, whose lead over Continental countries in goods produced, capital invested, and machinery employed had widened steadily from 1789 to 1815.

On the Continent the French Revolution and the Napoleonic era had in important respects cleared the way for future industrialization. In France, western Germany, northern Italy, and the Low Countries, land tenure was no longer the pressing economic and social issue; rural life was less restricted by traditional rights; and peasant proprietors, now relatively content, had become firm defenders of private property and were ready to be drawn into production for a national market. The abolition of old commercial restrictions and guilds had eliminated some obstacles to the free movement of workers and the establishment of new enterprises. Adopted on much of the Continent, French commercial law and the Napoleonic Code not only favored free contracts and an open marketplace but introduced the advantages of uniform and clear regulations. The French government had exported a common and sensible standard of weights and measures, encouraged the establishment of technical schools (the Polytechnic School in Paris long remained the world's best), and honored inventors and inventions of every sort from improved gunpowder to new techniques for raising sugar beets. Under Napoleon Europe had benefited from improved highways and bridges and a large zone of free trade; the Bank of France, as restructured in 1800, had become the European model of a bank of issue providing a reliable currency.

In the short run, however, the long warfare had slowed and disrupted economic growth. Vast resources in material and men were destroyed or consumed, and the Continental system, which had initially swung production and trade in France's favor, had collapsed with Napoleon's fall, bringing down many of the enterprises that it had artificially sustained. Both instability and renewed British competition discouraged daring investment. Great Britain, which had found compensation in American markets for her exclusion from the Continent and had avoided the shock of invasion, suffered a severe slump in the postwar years when the anticipated Continental demand for her goods failed to materialize and the transition to a peacetime economy proved difficult.

Patterns of Industrialization

By the mid-1820s, however, British trade was reviving, and by 1830 rapid expansion was transforming the whole economy. No single industry was yet fully mechanized, but the pattern of industrialization was clearly recognizable. Cotton was the most important industry, its spinning mechanized, its weaving becoming so. Growth in one economic sector stimulated growth in others. Increased textile production, for example, accelerated the use of chemical dyes; greater iron production required more coal. A few factories in one place encouraged others in the same region where they could take advantage of the available work force and capital, and the concentration of production increased in turn the demand for roads, canals, and later railways (see Map A-26 in the Cartographic Essay). All this required more capital, and on the cycle went. In continuity, range of industries affected, national scope, and rate of increase, Great Britain's industrial growth was the greatest mankind had yet experienced; current estimates are that her gross national product was rising about 3 percent per annum.

With dazzling speed new inventions became whole industries and were integrated into the economy. The steam engine's application to rail travel is a classic case. When the patents expired on the Boulton and Watt steam engine in 1800 some 500 such engines were in use—and a number of British cotton mills had switched to steam power, although the less efficient Newcomen engines invented nearly a century before were also still being built. The first successful steam railway line was not built in England until 1825; a few years later an improved engine impressed spectators by outracing a horse, and in 1830 the first passenger line took its riders the thirty-two miles from Liverpool to Manchester in an hour and a quarter. There were 2,000 miles of such rail lines in Great Britain just over a decade later and 7,000 by 1851. Similarly the telegraph, slowly developed by a generation of scientists in many countries, rapidly progressed from an adjunct of railroading to a military necessity and a conveyor of general news. The most impressive of the early long lines was Samuel F. B. Morse's from Philadelphia to Washington, opened in 1843. Less than a decade later, Britain laid 4,000 miles of telegraph lines, and a cable to the Continent was in operation.

Yet the leap from new invention to industrialization was not necessarily direct or predictable. Often dozens of subsidiary inventions or improvements were necessary to make a new machine competitive. More often on the Continent even than in Britain, old manufacturing techniques and commercial methods persisted alongside the new. Machines themselves were usually made of wood and frequently still driven by wind, water power, or horses. But the water-driven mills, charcoal-fired smelters, and hand-powered looms that dotted the countryside would be gradually but relentlessly displaced as would hundreds of thousands of skilled artisans and rural families working in their homes to produce in the old ways—a transformation that accounted for much of the human suffering occasioned by industrialization.

In 1815 many regions of the Continent, including such traditional commercial centers as Barcelona and Naples, had seemed ready to follow the British example of industrial growth, but by the 1850s the zone of industrialization had narrowed to eastern and northern France, Belgium and the Netherlands, western Germany, and northern Italy. Within this area industrial change was more uneven than in Britain. Most of Germany remained an area of quiet villages in which peddlers and trade fairs were major avenues of commerce, though by midcentury German states were crisscrossed by the Continent's largest railway network. In the 1830s and 1840s, steamboats plied all the navigable rivers of Western Europe.

Belgium, which had prospered from her former connections with Holland, continued to build on technological skills, geographical advantages, and excellent supplies of coal. Extracting more coal than France or Germany and the first country to complete a railway net-

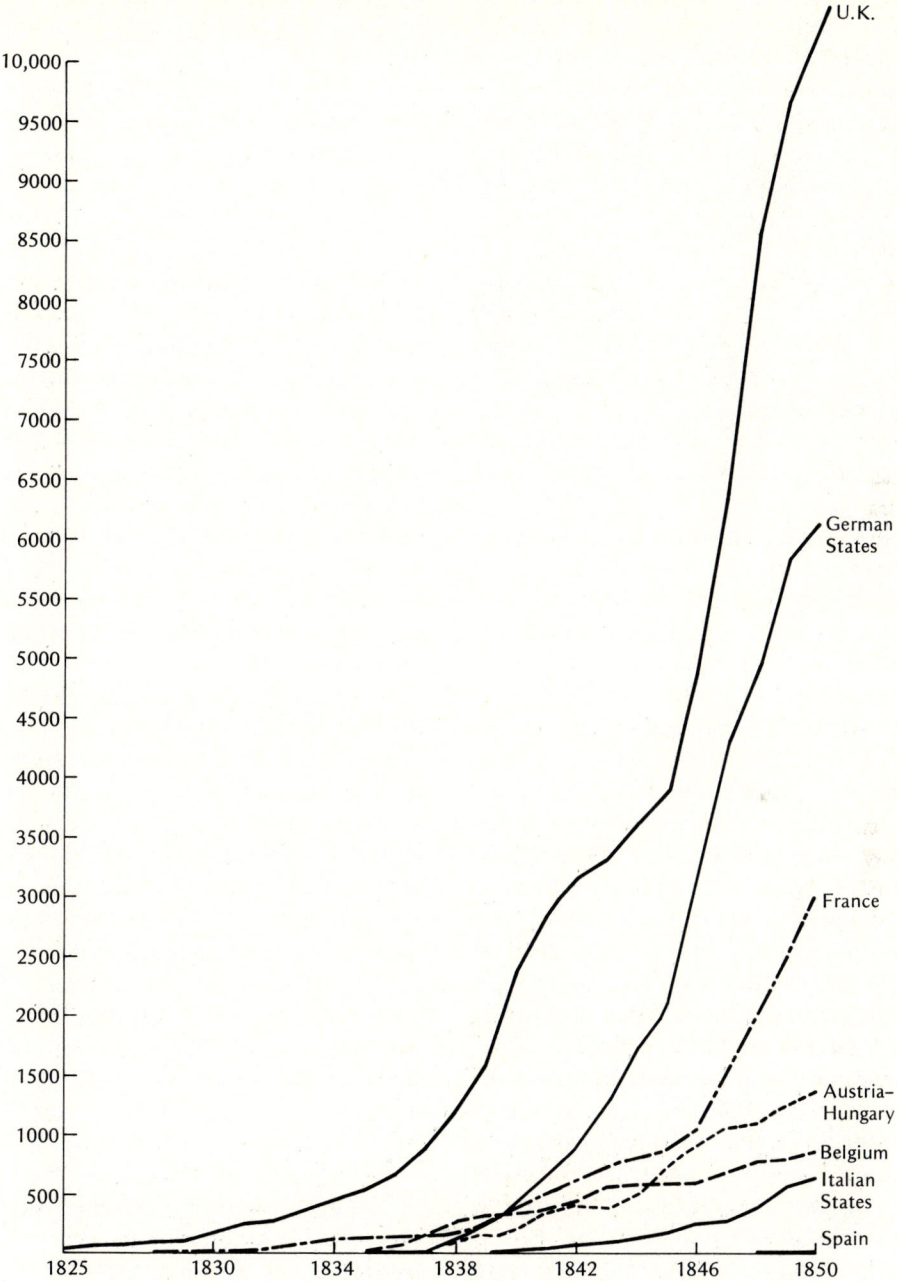

(Source: Mitchell, B. R., *European Historical Statistics, 1750–1970*, 1975, pp. 581–582.)

This train traveled from Paris to Rouen about 1860, but note that the new technology had little effect on the laborers' tools.
(Photo: H. Roger Viollet)

work, Belgium was the mainland's first industrialized state. The French railway system on the other hand was not finished until after the German, for it was slowed by political conflict despite early and ambitious plans. France's canals, considered good in 1815, had trebled by 1848; and her production of iron, coal, and textiles increased severalfold in the same period. A generation earlier this would have been impressive growth, but Britain's expansion in each of these sectors was several times greater. In iron production for example the two countries were about equal in 1800, but Britain's output was six or seven times greater by 1850. She outstripped France still more in textiles and coal, producing half the world total in these as well as iron by midcentury.

Everywhere increased production led to more commerce and closer international ties as capital, techniques, workmen, and managers moved across the Channel and from Belgium and France into the rest of Europe. The Bank of France granted an emergency loan to the Bank of England in 1825, only a decade after Waterloo; and the domestic banking policies of President Andrew Jackson of the United States in response to a financial panic there in 1837 led to a wave of crises in the financial centers of Europe.

The Role of Government

Most observers of the new prosperity believed it followed from natural economic laws that worked their wonders more fully the freer the economy was from governmental intervention. Yet by midcentury the state was centrally involved in the process of economic growth. Railroads required franchises and the power of eminent domain before a spike was pounded. Inevitably routes, rates, and even the gauge of the track became political matters to be settled by parliaments or special commissions. In Belgium and in most of Germany, railroads were owned as well as planned by the state.

Tariffs, the dominant issue in British politics in the 1840s, became a critical question in every country. Britain's abolition of the Corn Laws in 1846 was not only an expression of confidence in her position as the world's greatest producer but a decision that industrial interests had become more important to the nation's welfare than agriculture. The German Zollverein and the unification of Italy in the 1860s created larger areas of free trade; and after the Cobden-Chevalier treaty of 1860 between Britain and France, mutually reducing tariffs, a general international reduction of trade barriers allowed goods to move across borders with unparalleled freedom.

Equally important was the role of governments in banking and currency. Just before the middle of the century, Parliament granted the Bank of England a monopoly on issuing money and as a guarantee to investors required com-

PRODUCTION IN BELGIUM, FRANCE, GERMANY, AND THE UNITED KINGDOM

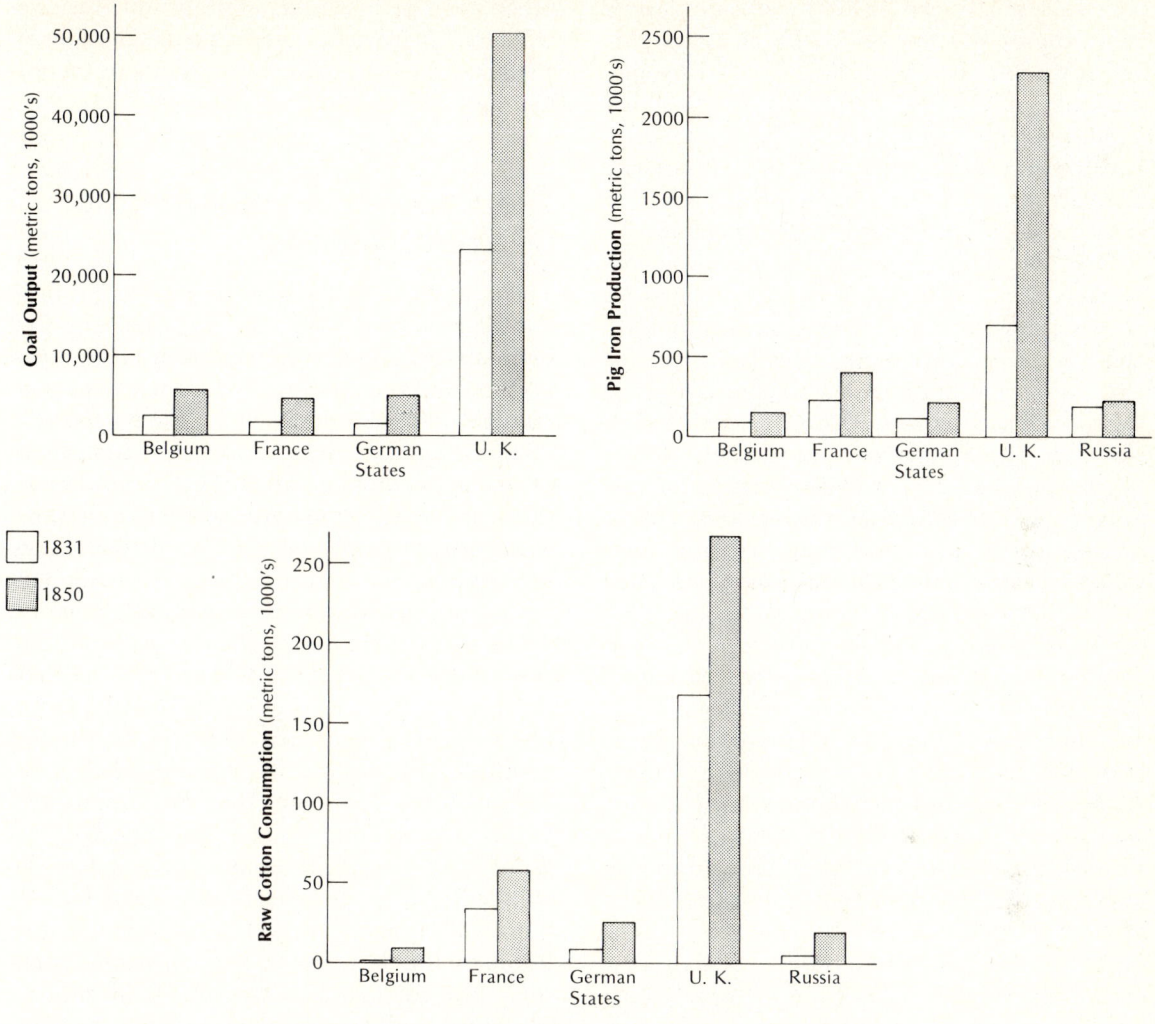

(Source: Mitchell, B. R., *European Historical Statistics, 1750–1970*, 1975.)

panies to register with the government and publish annual budgets. Similar steps were taken across Europe. In 1852 Louis Napoleon established the Crédit Mobilier, a joint-stock bank for starting or assisting important companies, and the Prussian government offered benefits to banks and industrialists. Before industries could effectively tap private wealth, the investor needed assurance that he risked only the money he invested, without being liable as he would be in a partnership for all a firm's debts. That assurance required new legislation establishing limited liability and encouraging the formation of corporations, and every major country passed such measures.

The growth of cities and the benefits of new

technology created social demands involving government. By the 1840s most cities had a public omnibus, some sidewalks, and gas lighting in certain areas. Usually provided by private companies, such services had to be subsidized, regulated, and given legal protection by government, and as their cost and importance increased, so did the state's participation in them, usually extending to full ownership.

The role of government, the economic importance of public facilities, and the possibilities of using new techniques were exemplified by postal service, which most states had provided since the seventeenth and eighteenth centuries. With few exceptions graft-ridden and unreliable, these postal systems became intolerable in the industrial age. In Britain agitation for improvement was led by an inventor and radical who argued in terms of the new economic analysis—reduced rates would make the service pay for itself by increasing volume—and the demands of progress. He also proposed standard envelopes, payment in advance, and an adhesive stamp as means of reducing costs and graft. Denounced as dangerous and impractical, his reforms were nevertheless passed in 1840. Within twenty years the volume of mail in Britain increased sixfold, and money orders, postal savings, and the telegraph were added to postal services. In France mail delivery was extended even to rural areas, and by the 1850s every major government was adopting the new system, including the postage stamp, which quickly became the object of a fashionable middle-class hobby.

Effective government, in short, was now expected to further industrialization—by subsidizing ports, transportation, and new inventions; by registering patents and encouraging education; by encouraging investment and enforcing contracts; by maintaining order and preventing strikes. In the 1840s the leaders of Britain, France, and Belgium busily did these things–in Great Britain the number of government employees increased about fourfold in the first half of the century—and the desire for other states to more fully follow suit was elsewhere an important part of the revolutions of 1848 and the nationalist movements of the following period.

The Relative Development of Different Nations

The British celebrated their position as the masters of industrialization in 1851 with the first international industrial exhibition. Prominent people from the aristocracy, business, and government joined in the planning, and a specially designed pavilion was built in London, a sort of giant greenhouse called the Crystal Palace, that proved to be an architectural milestone. Many governments feared that Britain risked revolution by attracting huge mobs to London, but the admiring crowds proved well behaved.

In fact, the exhibition provided a significant comparison of the relative economic development of the participating countries. Russia displayed primarily raw materials; Austria showed mainly luxury handicrafts. So did the Zollverein and the Italian states, but their appearance as single economic units foretold much. Although unable to fill all the space it had demanded, the United States impressed viewers with collections of fossils, cheap manufactured products for domestic use, mountains of dentifrice and soap, and a series of new inventions, including Colt revolvers, a sewing machine, McCormick's reaper, and a vacuum coffin. French machines, which ranged from a much-admired device for folding envelopes to a little-noticed submarine, were generally considered the most elegant. But British machines surpassed everyone's efforts in terms of quantity, size, and variety. It is, explained the *Morning Chronicle,* "to our wonderful industrial discipline—our consummately arranged organization of toil, and our habit of division of labour—that we owe all the triumph."

London's imposing Crystal Palace was designed to house the first international industrial exhibition, held there in 1851. The building was constructed of cast iron and glass, a significant innovation in architecture.
(Photo: Radio Times Hulton Picture Library)

The wealthiest nation in history by 1850,[1] Great Britain increased her lead over other countries in goods produced during the next twenty years. Important changes were taking place, however. While textiles were still important, they were no longer the leading sector of industrialization, and steel replaced the less processed forms of iron as the metal adapted to the greatest variety of crucial industrial uses.

Economic expansion in France and the German states was now comparable to Britain's a generation earlier. France's rate of growth was greater than Britain's, but it was lower than that of Germany, which was just beginning to take advantage of rich resources (especially coal), a rapidly growing population, and traditions of technical education. During the 1860s Germany out distanced France in the critical indexes of coal, iron, and steel production. A major shift in the locus of European economic and political power was part of the extensive social change that accompanied Europe's industrialization.

---

[1] Although all estimates for this period are uncertain, it seems likely that in 1860 the per capita wealth of Frenchmen was about two-thirds and of Germans about two-fifths that of Britons.

II. THE STRUCTURE OF SOCIETY

Economic growth on such a scale was accompanied and indeed promoted by changes in the fabric of society. Population was rapidly rising, and cities were increasing in size and importance. Society came to be perceived as consisting of a few classes rather than as a social pyramid built on intricate personal responsibilities to those superior or inferior. The expanding middle class became increasingly prominent, while workers became more and more aware of their own distinct needs and interests. Industrialization and specialization affected all of society, from the state to the family, altering women's roles and the standard of living. At the same time, child labor, tyrannical foremen, teeming slums, and unemployment brought new social problems and required new efforts to meet them. The growing prosperity and security of the middle class contrasted all the more sharply with the destitution of the urban poor.

The Growth in Population

Historians nowadays increasingly stress the far-reaching effects of the growth in European population, but its causes remain uncertain. For a long time industrialization itself was thought to have brought it about, the assumption being that prosperity and opportunities for employment, particularly of children, had induced a rising birth rate. That explanation is now doubted. In fact the increase of population often occurred in rural regions, where the social effects of widespread industrialization were not likely to have been so deeply felt. There is, however, a connection between the growth of population and industry, for generally the two phenomena appeared together as they did in Great Britain, Belgium, and western Germany. The most likely factors stimulating the rise in population were a decline in disease-carrying germs, an increase in the food supply, a lowering of the age at which people married, and after 1870 some improvement in public sanitation.

Although the data are spotty at best, the most recent research suggests that the world experienced a decline in some common diseases beginning in the eighteenth century. Microbes have cycles (like those of locusts but less regular), and undoubtedly remissions had occurred many times before. Now, however, better supplies of food could allow the larger numbers surviving the perilous years of infancy to reach adulthood and form families of their own.

The food supply rose because of better transportation, more effective agricultural techniques, and the potato. Everywhere in Western Europe agricultural societies sprang up, experimenting with and advocating improved means of cultivation, better use of fertilizer, and by the 1840s some mechanization of farming. Primarily the work of enlightened aristocrats, these societies were aided by governments and churches in disseminating their doctrines through the countryside. The humble potato may have had particular importance, for it was easy to cultivate in a small space and yielded more calories per acre than any single crop. Not common on the Continent before 1750, it became the staple of the peasant's diet in most of Europe by 1830.[2] While infant mortality remained enormously high by modern standards, even a slight decline in death rates could make a great difference, so close to subsistence did most Europeans live.

The reasons for the trend toward earlier marriage are less clear, but apparently peasants freed from servile obligations tended to set up new households at a younger age. The spread of cottage industry, prior to the development

---

[2] William L. Langer makes an effective case for the potato's importance in the rise of population in "Europe's Initial Population Explosion," *American Historical Review,* 1963, pp. 1–17.

THE WORK FORCE IN INDUSTRIAL NATIONS MID-1850S

*Including transport and communication, domestic servants, and armed forces.

(Source: Bairoch, P., et al., *The Working Population and Its Structure*, Brussels, 1968.)

of great factories, allowed families to add to their income by spinning or weaving at home, and agricultural changes made it somewhat easier for the new family to find a piece of land sufficient for its survival. The greater numbers of people in one generation—only a slight rise in a single decade or province—multiplied in the next generation and led to an enormous increase in the aggregate. As population grew the proportion of young and thus fertile people within it grew still faster, which increased the ratio of births to total population. The net result was that the 188 million Europeans of 1800 had become 266 million by 1850 and 295 million in 1870.

The growth in population had broad ramifications. More people consumed more food and this necessitated more intense cultivation of available soil and the use of much land previously left fallow. More people meant a larger potential work force readier to leave the countryside for industrial jobs, and that movement of population became a social change of immeasurable importance. To a lesser extent an increasing population meant an expanding market for goods other than food, an element of growth that would have stronger impact later in the century. The greater prominence of the young was in itself significant, and there is some indication that they were more restive and that the educated among them were a potential source of radical leaders.[3] There was also a distinction in birth rate by social class, which demographers call differential fertility. On the whole, the higher a man stood on the social scale, the fewer the children in his family. The

---

[3] In 1789 perhaps 40 percent of France's population was between twenty and forty years old and another 36 percent under twenty, the highest proportion of the young France has ever known. Mazzini limited membership in Young Italy to those under forty, and probably most of the leaders of the revolutions of 1848 would have met that standard. The relation of youth to revolution is interestingly discussed in Herbert Moller, "Youth as a Force in the Modern World," *Comparative Studies in Society and History*, April 1968.

distinction became more notable in the course of the century as families became more concerned with providing education and wealth for their heirs. But to contemporaries it often suggested that the lower classes, lacking foresight and moral restraint, were likely to swamp society.

Indeed one of the most influential books in the first half of the century was Thomas R. Malthus' *An Essay on the Principle of Population as It Affects the Future Improvement of Society,* first published in 1798 and reissued in many subsequent revisions. Observing the Britain of his time, Malthus argued that population increases faster than the supply of food unless checked either by death (through war, famine, or pestilence) or by deliberate sexual continence. A clergyman, he advocated continence but remained pessimistic that mankind was capable of such restraint. Malthus was also an economist well versed in contemporary theory, and for much of the century the demographic method and economic arguments in his controversial work deeply influenced social writing. For Malthusianism was the scientific statement of a natural law containing the harsh but convenient corollary that the misery of the poor resulted from their own improvidence. The view that economic progress rested on immutable laws and that those laws allowed little hope for the masses became a central theme of early nineteenth-century liberalism.

Urbanization

No demographic change was more important than the growth of cities. At the turn of the century, greater London was just reaching 1 million in population. No European city since imperial Rome had ever approached that size. Paris grew to that figure a generation later, but the third largest European city in 1800, Naples, had only 350,000 inhabitants. In all of Europe there were then only twenty-two cities with populations over 100,000. By midcentury there were forty-seven. Great Britain was the leader, with six cities over the 100,000 mark; London's population had surpassed 2.5 million by 1856, Liverpool had grown from 80,000 to almost 400,000, and Manchester and Glasgow each had more than 300,000 people. By this time half of Britain's population lived in towns, making her the most urbanized nation since ancient times.

On the Continent the major capitals burgeoned. Paris reached a population of close to 1.5 million by 1850; Berlin nearly trebled, to 500,000; and a growth rate almost as great pushed Brussels to 250,000. St. Petersburg, Vienna, and Budapest all had populations between 400,000 and 500,000. Most of Europe's old cities increased by at least 50 percent in the first half of the century, and many a town became a city.

By the 1860s the English countryside was actually losing people, as were some sections of France; the tide of urbanization was overwhelming, and nearly all the subsequent increase in European population would go to swell the growth of cities, most of whose inhabitants were now immigrants as rural folk moved to nearby villages, villagers to towns, town dwellers to cities. Clearly the tide of urbanization was strongest where industry was great, but the growth of ports and national capitals demonstrated the importance of great commercial, financial, and political centers as well.

Society had neither the experience nor the means to cope with such an expansion. Urban conditions for all but the reasonably prosperous were unspeakable. Narrow alleys were littered with garbage and ordure that gave off an overpowering stench. The water supply in Paris, better than in most large cities, offered access to safe water only at fountains dotting the city (the affluent paid carriers by the bucket), and in London the private companies that provided water allowed it to flow only a few hours a day. In most cities the water supply came from

In this famous engraving of London by Gustave Doré, the rhythmic sameness and cramped efficiency of new housing suggest a machine for living appropriate to the age of the railroad.
(Photo: New York Public Library/Picture Collection)

dangerously polluted rivers. Sewage was an even more serious problem. A third of Manchester's houses used privies in the 1830s, and a decade later the ratio of inside toilets to population was 1 to 212. In London cesspools were a menace to health overshadowed only by still more public means of disposal.

The most dramatic inadequacy, however, was in housing of any sort. A third of Liverpool's citizens lived crowded in dark, cold cellars, and conditions in Lille were similar. In every city the poor of both sexes crowded into filthy, stuffy, unheated rooms; and over the cities, especially manufacturing and mining towns, chemical smog and coal smoke darkened the sky. It is hardly surprising that crime was rampant, that often more than a third of the births were illegitimate, and that the number of prostitutes soared (reaching perhaps 80,000 in London, where 9,000 were officially registered; 3,600 were registered in Paris).

The maintenance of public order changed its meaning. For the restoration governments the police were primarily secret agents whose job was to ferret out real or potential enemies. But the protection of lives and property in great cities, the effective handling of crowds, and the enforcement of local ordinances required something other than spies or the military. London's police force was established by Peel in 1829,[4] and Paris' Municipal Guard was created under Guizot a few years later.

For all their misery cities continued to grow; and the worst conditions were slowly alleviated by housing codes, public sewers, and reliable water supplies. These improvements were made possible in part by industrialization, which provided iron pipes, water closets, gas lighting, better heating, and sounder buildings. Urban life developed a style of its own, increasingly distinct from life in the countryside. Towns clustered around factories and railway stations, and cities teeming with the poor and indigent were also the thriving centers of communication, commerce, politics, and culture.

Social Classes

So many kinds of change necessarily affected social grouping. In the seventeenth and eighteenth centuries, people spoke of the "orders" or "ranks" in society, implying a social pyramid rising from the lowliest peasant to the ruler and assigning each person a position in it. That position in large part defined his relations with those above and below.

By the beginning of the nineteenth century, the expression "middle" or "middling classes" had begun to appear, and by midcentury society was generally conceived in terms of broad strata, called classes. A person's social class was thought to describe the status of his occupation but also something of the values he held, his style of life, and later the political and social

---

[4] The role played by Sir Robert Peel is still honored in the nickname "Bobbies."

interests he was likely to support. Descriptive of an expanding, fluid, national society, the concept of class expressed an important change in outlook and social reality.

The Aristocracy

The class most easily identified was the aristocracy. It included all nobles and their immediate relatives, whether they held noble titles or not; members of the upper gentry, who were large landholders and lived like nobles; and in the ancient commercial cities of the Netherlands, northern Germany, and northern Italy, the established and wealthy patrician families, who dominated the cities though they might not bear titles.

The aristocracy's privileges and influence had been challenged in the eighteenth century by the French Revolution; the class was threatened in the nineteenth century by new industrial wealth, which overshadowed the fortunes of large landholders and gave greater influence to leaders from the middle class. It lost some traditional authority with every increase in urbanization, every victory of constitutionalism or administrative reform. The decline of the aristocracy in the new age was so clear in fact that the continued importance of the class is easily overlooked.

In most countries aristocrats still controlled most of the wealth, were closely allied to an established church, and dominated the upper levels of administration and the military. By training and tone the most international of social classes, aristocrats remained the preeminent diplomats even under bourgeois regimes. They also stimulated some of the most influential critiques of nineteenth-century society, denouncing the middle class for selfishness and materialism, proclaiming urban life morally inferior to rural, and lamenting the loss of gentlemanly honor. The efforts of the aristocracy

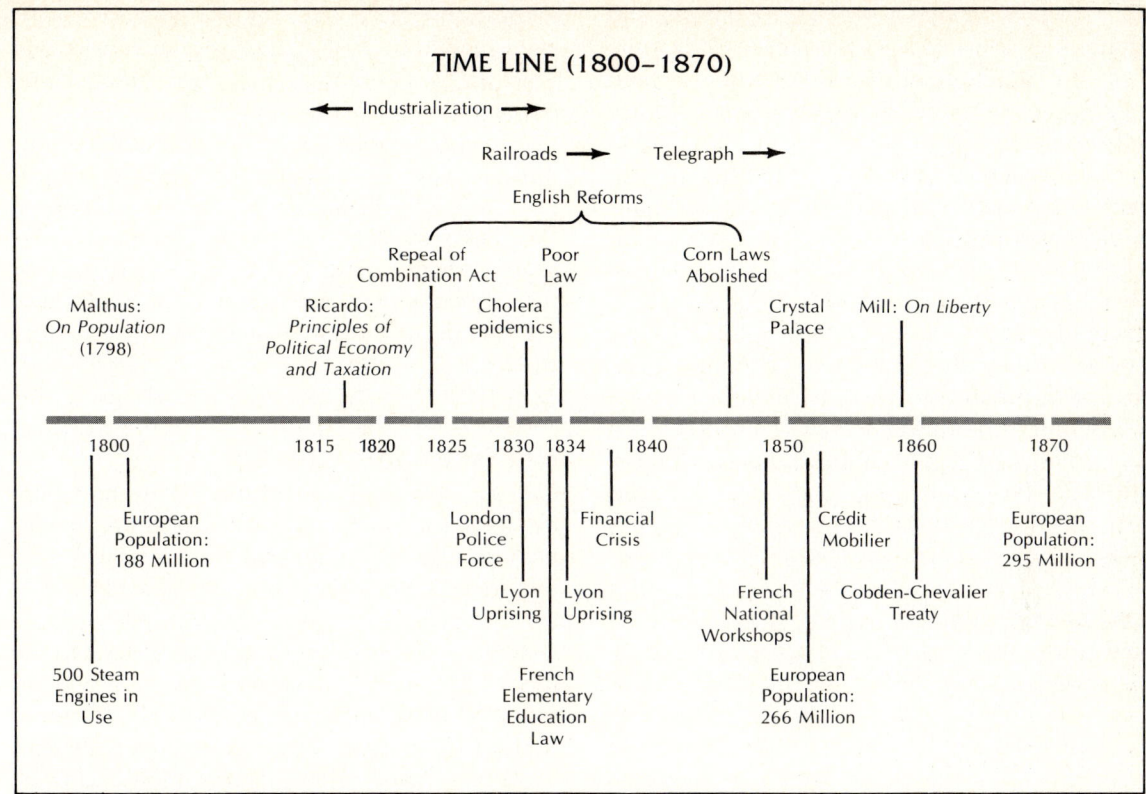

to defend its position, the means used, and the success achieved provide an important measure of social and political development in each country.

In much of Europe, especially the south and east, the aristocracy held on to local power and tremendous wealth, a social pattern exemplified by the Kingdom of Naples and by Russia. In both states the nobility, constituting only about 1 percent of the population, in effect ruled over most of the peasant masses. Three-fifths of the people in southern Italy lived on baronial estates. The Neapolitan aristocracy had lost many of its formal privileges under Napoleon, but with the restoration they reestablished their authority through cooperation with king and Church and by providing the leading profes-

sional men. In Russia just a fraction of the nobility held one-third of the land, and most of the rest was owned by the state and administered by nobles. Russia's aristocrats, tyrants on their estates and dominant over local administration, were the chief pillar of tsarist rule.

Where the nobles made up a higher proportion of the population, the pattern was somewhat different. In Poland, Hungary, and Spain, many of the nobility were extremely poor, and they tended to alternate between desperate allegiance to an empty title and sympathy for radical change, thus becoming another and important source of instability.

In some countries, however, aristocrats sought to strengthen their influence through representative government and decentralization, thereby cooperating with political and economic reformers. The confident Magyars took this position in Hungary, and so, even more generously, did the aristocrats of northern Italy, Belgium, and Great Britain. They were thus prominent during the revolutions of 1848 in Hungary and northern Italy and in the subsequent nationalist movements in those countries. The Belgian aristocracy cooperated with liberals in 1830 and after, accepting an endless string of concessions and reforms. Above all in England the aristocracy proved willing to exchange formal power for general influence. Of the hundred men who served as cabinet ministers in Britain between 1832 and the reform of 1867, sixty-four were sons of nobles; and perhaps four-fifths of the members of Parliament were landholders or their representatives, closely tied to the aristocracy. On the other hand younger sons and lesser aristocrats in England were more closely associated with the upper-middle class, lessening the sharpness of social division.

It was possible of course for an aristocracy to maintain its traditional hold over government even when the state became the instrument of dramatic and rapid change. This occurred in Prussia, where the most influential aristocrats were the Junkers, owners of great estates in east Prussia, some of which included sizable villages. Considered crude and ignorant by most of the aristocracies of Europe, which set great store by polished manners, elegant taste, and excellent French, the Junkers had a proud tradition of service to the state and loyalty to their king. In local government, in the bureaucracy, the army, and the court, their manners and their values—from rectitude to dueling, from arrogance to loyalty—set the tone of Prussian public life.

France is thus the European exception, for there the old aristocracy was reduced to a more minor role in national politics after 1830. Its members retained major influence in the church, army, and foreign service, but those institutions were also on the defensive. Yet even in France aristocrats maintained a strong voice in local affairs and a major influence on manners and the arts. Everywhere, however, they were in danger of being isolated from important sources of political and economic power. It was small compensation to be known for elegance and leisure or a famous name. Lineage was once of such importance that tracing family lines had been a matter of state; now even pride of family was becoming a private matter.

The Peasantry

Closely related to the aristocracy in its dependence on the land and devotion to tradition, the peasant class encompassed the overwhelming majority of all Europeans. Always viewed as at the very bottom of society, peasants too were affected by the changes taking place around them. Agriculture was becoming more commercial, its production increasingly intended for a broad market rather than mere subsistence or local consumption. Profits increased with the cultivation of a single cash crop, the use of machinery, and improved fertilizers, changes primarily available to those with capital and a sizable piece of land. Large farms therefore became relatively more profitable, and landed nobles, bourgeois investors, and the richer peasants sought by every means to expand and consolidate their holdings, a trend encouraged by legislation in much of northern Europe.

The emancipation of peasants from "feudal" obligations—effected by the French Revolution and carried to much of Western Europe by Napoleon, decreed in Prussia as part of the reforms of 1806, and spread to most of Eastern Europe with the revolutions of 1848 (see Map A-25 in the Cartographic Essay)—encouraged their entry into the commercial market, but it also deprived them of such traditional protections against hard times as the use of a common pasture, the right to glean what was left after the first harvest, and the practice of foraging for firewood in the forest. Similarly the decline of the putting-out system and of local industries took away critical income, especially during the winter months. Gradually and with considerable local variation, the peasant was becoming more dependent on the little piece of land to which he had some legal claim or the wages that could be earned from labor. The available land increased as more of it was cultivated, especially in the west, but it was usually of poorer quality and divided into small plots.

Improved communications increased the impact of more distant markets and brought peasants a keener sense of the opportunities and political events in the outside world. In addition, as governments became more efficient, they reached more deeply into peasant society for taxes and conscripts, enforcing regulations that often seemed alien and harsh. And the population of the now disturbed rural world was expanding, adding to economic pressure and restlessness.

Peasants are thus easily seen as passive victims of outside historical forces, but their response was also significant. The despair of reformers who were discouraged by their ignorance and illiteracy, who resented their opposition to change, and who were often defeated by their suspicion of outsiders, peasants tenaciously maintained old loyalties to their region, their priests, their habitual ways. Often they developed elaborate ties of family and patronage that absorbed state-appointed administrators into local social networks. Peasants were frequently shrewd judges of their short-term interests, cooperating with measures immediately beneficial to them and resisting all others with the skepticism of experience.

Their hunger for land, resentment of taxes and military service, and sense of grievance against those above them could also become a major political force. Their involvement made a crucial difference in the early days of the French Revolution and in the Spanish resistance to Napoleon, the wars of German liberation, and the strength of nationalism in Germany and Italy. Rulers were kept on edge by eruptions of peasant violence in southern England in the 1820s; Ireland in the 1830s and 1840s; Wales, Silesia, and Galicia in the 1840s; and on a smaller scale in every country from Spain to Russia. The outbreaks of 1848 almost immediately brought feudal service toppling down in the Austrian Empire and eastern Prussia. At the same time rural indifference to constitutional claims and workers' demands sealed the doom of the urban revolutions.

But the peasantry was far from united. The deepest division was between those who owned land and those forced to sell their labor. Some of the former, especially in the west, grew relatively prosperous and joined the influential notables of their region. More of them lived as little dependent upon cash as possible, vulnerable to the slightest change in weather or market, supplementing their income by whatever odd jobs members of the family could find. In most of Europe tenant-farming was more common, with endless local variations as to who paid for seed or fertilizer and how the final crop was divided. At best such arrangements provided the peasant with significant security, but they tended also to be inflexible, slow to adapt to changes in prices, markets, and technology. Rural laborers were the poorest and most insecure of all, the tinder of violence and the recruits for factory work.

A central problem for nineteenth-century European society was how to integrate the agricultural economy and the masses dependent on it into the developing commercial and industrial economy. By the 1850s the process had gone farthest in France and Great Britain but through opposite means. In Britain the peasantry was largely eliminated as the continuing enclosures of great estates reduced the rural poor to laborers, shifting from place to place and hiring out for the season or by the day (see Maps A-22 to A-23 in the Cartographic Essay).

The concentration of landholding in Great Britain was one of the highest in Europe: some 500 aristocratic families controlled half the land and some 1,300 others most of the rest. In France on the other hand peasants owned approximately one-third of the land, and their share was gradually increasing. Owners of tiny plots outnumbered the landless, and they supported themselves by favoring crops that require intense cultivation, such as grapes and sugar beets, and by maintaining small-scale craft industries.

Elsewhere the patterns lay between these two extremes, though rising populations everywhere made the landless the majority. The tradition of small landholding persisted in western Germany, northern Italy, Switzerland, the Netherlands, Belgium, and Scandinavia alongside a trend toward the consolidation of larger farms that reduced millions to becoming day-laborers. Emancipation in Germany usually required the peasant to pay for his freedom with part (often the best part) of the land he claimed. New historical methods which can compensate for the lack of written records have also established the importance of local variations—the quality of the soil, the favored crop, government policy, and legal custom. The fate of many a national political movement turns out on a closer look to have depended, like the uprisings often misunderstood as simply the violence of the untutored, on peasants' understanding of how in a changing world they could best preserve what little they had.

There was a clear distinction, however, between these Western and Central regions and Eastern Europe, where Russian serfdom was the extreme. In the West the changes that increased agricultural productivity often left the life of peasants more precarious. In the East a heavy social price was paid for preserving the landholder's authority over his peasants and his claims to their labor, which ranged from a month or so a year to several days a week in Russia; and the emancipation of Russian serfs in the 1860s (see Chapter 24) proved unnecessary for economic expansion and minimal military and administrative efficiency. As urbanization and industrialization advanced, many writers waxed nostalgic for the bucolic purity and sturdy independence of peasant life, but the problems of the peasantry were in fact some of the gravest and most intractable of European society.

The Working Classes

Industrial laborers, however, attracted far more attention. In the 1830s and 1840s, serious French analysts wrote of the "dangerous classes" crowding into Paris. By midcentury industrial workers were the examplars of a growing social class, though even in Britain in the 1860s they made up a small fraction of all those who lived by wages paid for physical labor; there were more domestic servants than factory hands. The conception of a working class derived less from what people did for a living or their poor pay than from their dependence on others—for employment, for defining what their job entailed, and for setting the hours and conditions of their work.

The most independent workers were the artisans. Stripped of their tight guilds and formal apprenticeships by the French Revolution, a series of laws passed in Britain up to the 1830s, and a process in Germany completed by the revolutions of 1848, artisans nevertheless continued to ply their crafts in a hierarchy of masters, journeymen, and apprentices working in small shops where conditions varied as much according to the temper of the master as the pressures of the market. Skilled workers, from carpenters and shoemakers to mechanics, moved in a less organized labor market but were distinctly better paid than the masses of the unskilled. Although vulnerable to competition from machines and new products and above all to unemployment during the frequent economic slumps, these men in general were among the beneficiaries of industrialization.

Their real wages tended slowly to increase, and they could expect to earn enough to support their families in one or two bare rooms on a simple diet.

Factory workers on the whole earned too little to sustain a family, and thus the employment of women and children became as necessary to survival as it was advantageous to employers, who appreciated their greater dexterity and the lower wages they would accept. The largest factories were the cotton mills, where commonly half the laborers were women and a quarter children. In coal mines, where women and children were hired to push carts and work in the narrower shafts, they were a smaller proportion of the work force. A class was thereby formed of men, women, and children, clustered about a source of employment, dependent on cash for their subsistence, and subjected to the rigid discipline of the factory. Awakened before dawn by the factory bell, they tramped to work, where the pace of production was relentless and the dangers from machinery and irate foremen was great. Any lapse of attention during a workday of fourteen hours or more, even stopping to help a neighbor, brought a fine and a harsh reprimand. Children were frequently beaten, as men had been before fines proved more effective, and all were spurred by the threats of piece rates and unemployment. Life was still more precarious for the millions of men without regular employment, who simply did such tasks as they could find, hauling or digging for a few pence.

Industrial workers were thus set apart by the conditions of their labor, the slums where they lived, and special restrictions such as the *livret*, or passport, that all French workers were required to present when applying for a job and that recorded the comments of previous employers on their conduct and performance. Understandably the powerful worried about the social volcano on which they lived, and the sensitive feared the effect of the immorality and degradation that accompanied industrial life.

Ignorant and exhausted workers, often strangers to each other, for the most part lacked the means necessary for effective concerted action. Their frequent outbursts of resentment and intermittent strikes usually ended in some bloodshed and sullen defeat. Sometimes the riots, demonstrations, and strikes became local revolutions, spreading across the north of England in 1811 and 1812, breaking out in Lyons in 1831 and 1834, Bristol in 1831, Lancashire in 1841, and Silesia in 1844. Significantly most of these outbursts were led by artisans, who felt most keenly the threat of change and held clearer visions of their rights and dignity. Although the authorities usually blamed the sinister plots of a few agitators for such disturbances, they nevertheless stimulated the vision of a day when laborers of many kinds, both urban and rural, might concertedly demonstrate their power. The June Days in Paris were widely understood, by all sides and perhaps exaggeratedly, as an expression of the new working class.

Trade unions were banned everywhere except in England after 1824, and even there the laws against conspiracy restricted their activity; but various local organizations had developed since the eighteenth century to take the place of the declining or outlawed guilds. By midcentury more than 1.5 million British workers may have belonged to such groups which tended, like the friendly societies, to form around a few of the more skilled workers and to meet in secret, often of necessity but also better to express a sense of brotherhood and trust. Although fond of elaborate rituals and terrifying oaths, their specific purposes were usually modest: burial costs for a member or assistance in times of illness. Equally important was the sense of community they fostered among those having in common their trade and neighborhood. In France workers' groups achieved state recognition as (carefully supervised) mutual aid socities and were given some government subsidies under Louis Napoleon. Above all these organizations were both expressions of and efforts to create a working-class culture with values, interests, and leaders of its own. In this sense the authorities' fear that they would become hotbeds of radicalism had some basis.

There were also workers' political movements, of which Chartism was by far the largest, and cooperatives, which were intended to increase workers' control of their lives. Consumers' cooperatives were numerous by the 1830s in England, and producers' cooperatives, often established with church support in France and Italy, were the model for the French national workshops of 1848. For the most part, however, these expressions of workers' autonomy remained small in scale and local in influence.

The hundreds of strikes that occurred throughout Western Europe in the first half of the century were rarely the result of any lasting organization, but they suggested what unions might accomplish and led to heroic efforts by leaders of the working class, particularly in Great Britain during the 1830s. Without funds, means of communication or common experience, these early efforts at unionizing petered out after a few years or sometimes a few months. Not even the Workingman's Association for Benefiting Politically, Socially, and Morally the Useful Classes, launched with some fanfare in 1836, managed to survive for long or bring off the general strike the more radical dreamed of. Yet these organizations, which gave the more fortunate workers some effective voice and some valuable experience of national political life, did influence Parliament in favor of factory legislation. The meetings, torchlight parades, and special newspapers and tracts all contributed to the growing sense of class. So, above all, did the repression by police and courts that usually followed. By midcentury millions of workers in Britain, somewhat fewer perhaps in France, and smaller numbers elsewhere shared heroes and rituals, believed they faced a common enemy, and accepted organization as the prime means of defending themselves in a hostile world. In Britain the national trades unions of skilled workers formed in the 1830s and 1840s (with only some 100,000 members then) would steadily increase their size and influence, reaching more than a million members a generation later.

The vast majority of the working class, however, remained essentially defenseless, possessing meager skills, dependent upon unstable employment, and living in the isolation of poverty. Ideas of *fraternité* and *egalité,* of the rights of freeborn Englishmen, and of simple patriotism, often expressed in Biblical prose, communicated a common sense of hope and outrage to millions of the men and women who attended rallies, met in dingy cafés, and read the working-class press (or listened as it was read to them)—the newspapers and pamphlets intended for workers became extensive in England after 1815, were less widespread in France in the 1830s and 1840s, and appeared everywhere in 1848. The common themes were man's natural rights, pride of work, and the claims of justice. They burst forth countless times in whole programs for change, phrases proudly tucked into petitions and posters, and anonymous gestures like the direct humor of the British coal miner who left a note to the man whose house he broke into during a strike in 1831:

> I was at yor hoose last neet, and meyd myself very comfortable. Ye hey nee family, and . . . I see ye have a great lot of rooms, and big cellars, and plenty of wine and beer in them, which I got ma share on. Noo I naw some at wor colliery that has three or fower lads and lasses, and they live in won room not half as gude as yor cellar. I don't pretend to naw very much, but I naw there shudn't be that much difference. . . .[5]

---

[5] Cited in Edward P. Thompson, *The Making of the English Working Class* (1966), p. 715.

Outbursts of sabotage, strikes, and riots—most historians now agree—were rarely aimless but had specific targets reflecting immediate needs. Lasting gains, however, normally required some connection between the local crisis and larger, national movements. When that was not the case, and it usually was not, the workers and their families had nevertheless contributed to the creation of a subculture of which their betters knew little.

The Middle Classes

Of all the social classes, the most confident and assertive was the middle class. At the top stood the great bankers, who in London and Paris were often closely connected to the liberal aristocracy and whose political influence after 1830 was considerable. More separate from and a little contemptuous of the traditional elites stood the great industrialists and the wealthiest merchants. At the bottom were the small shopkeepers, office clerks, and schoolteachers, often distinguishable from artisans only by their pretensions. This petite bourgeoisie comprised most of the middle class numerically, but the class was epitomized by those between these groups: most merchants, managers, and upper bureaucrats and nearly all lawyers, doctors, engineers, and professors. That such disparate people could believe they shared common interests and values and therefore a similar position was the result of recent history. They opposed prescriptive privilege and saw themselves as the beneficiaries of social change which allowed the talented to gain security and influence.

They were primarily an urban class and intimately connected with the commerce and politics of city life. In Paris they constituted nearly all of that part of the population, between one-fourth and one-fifth, prosperous enough to pay some taxes, have at least one maid, and leave an estate sufficient to cover the costs of private burial.[6] In other cities their proportion was probably somewhat smaller; among nations they were most numerous in Great Britain, a sizable fraction in France and Belgium, and a smaller minority elsewhere. Belonging to the only class which it was possible to fall out of, middle-class people established their membership by economic self-sufficiency, literacy, and respectability. Their manner, their dress, and their homes were thus symbols of their status and meant to express values of probity, hard work, fortitude, prudence, and self-reliance (see Plate 49). No matter how favored by birth or fortune, they tended to think of themselves as self-made men.

While industrial centers were notoriously drab, the middle-class home became more ornate, packed with furnishings that boasted of elaborate craftsmanship. Women's fashions similarly featured ornamental frills, and shops translated Parisian elegance into forms available to more modest purses. Masculine garb by contrast grew plainer, a point of some pride in a practical age; and clerk and banker tended to dress alike. Those who forged great industries out of daring, foresight, and luck, those who invented or built, those who taught or tended shop or wrote for newspapers came to share a certain pride in each other's achievements as proof that personal drive and social benefit were in harmony and as a harbinger of progress yet to come.

More than any other, the middle class was associated with an ideology; and the triumph of the middle class in this period—so heralded then and by historians since—related as much to constitutionalism and legal equality, individual rights and economic opportunity as it did to any explicit transfer of power. The conquests of the middle class were measured not just by its rise in importance but by a more general adoption of its values. Even being in the mid-

---

[6] Perhaps the most detailed study yet made of the middle class in this period is Adeline Daumard's *La Bourgeoisie parisienne de 1815 à 1848* (1963).

dle, between the extremes of luxury and power and of poverty and ignorance, was seen as an advantage, a kind of inherent moderation. In the nineteenth century, most of Europe's writers, scientists, doctors, lawyers, and businessmen would have felt no need to blush on finding themsevles called by a London paper in 1807 "those persons . . . always counted the most valuable, because the least corrupted, members of society," or on hearing John Stuart Mill speak a generation later of "the class which is universally described as the most wise and the most virtuous part of the community, the middle rank."

Social Conditions

Industrialization and urbanization necessarily affected most aspects of social life. Not only were there new tasks to be performed but traditional ones came to be accomplished in more organized and specialized ways. All of this in turn meant changes in the role of the family and of women, in the standard of living, and in public policies on matters of general welfare. Such changes at first sharpened the differences between social classes and became the subject of anguished debates, and they led to systematic efforts at reform.

Differentiation

Sociologists use the term "differentiation" to describe increased specialization among groups and institutions, and that too was a trend increasingly apparent in the nineteenth century. Its effects were clearest in the division of labor within a large factory and in the tendency to separate production from the home. Thus social differentiation meant in part the increasing separation of family roles from work. It affected institutions too. Banks and markets became more specialized, and the reliance on legal contracts differentiated economic from personal or social relationships. Governments preferred to rely on their officials rather than traditional elites (even when, as frequently happened, local notables were the ones appointed to office), and governmental functions themselves became more specialized. Maintaining the peace, collecting taxes, inspecting factories and schools, and administering welfare fell to separate bureaus. In addition, social tasks once performed by others such as the registering of births and deaths and the providing for education and charity, largely performed by the clergy before the French Revolution, were now increasingly absorbed by the state—another reason for the importance of politics in this period.

Just as each trade and each locality followed its own course of social change, so each nation differed in the pace and manner of institutional differentiation. Britain, more than Continental states, left many public matters to local government and private groups; in France the role of the national government increased, and the German states tended to combine centralizing bureaucracies with considerable local autonomy. Whatever the pattern, the growth of differentiation was a major source of conflict among institutions, between levels of government, and within communities.

The Family and the Role of Women

To a great many nineteenth-century observers, social change appeared to threaten the continued importance of the family, and moralists of every sort warned that the institution most central to civilization was being undermined. Recent research, however, has suggested a different view: heightened concern for the family was not only a response to real stress but an expression of increased belief in the social importance of proper child-rearing; the family proved on the whole an extraordinarily adaptable institution, and the forms of adaptation varied greatly, especially by social class. So did the place of women, and the question of women's proper role joined the long list of social issues on which nineteenth-century society sustained rigid convention yet confessed itself increasingly troubled.

For the aristocracy, family included a wide network of relatives, valuable connections to land, privilege, and power within which women played a critical but subordinate role as carriers of the dowries that joined estates, managers of large domestic staffs, and centers of the social circles in which aristocrats met. The peasant family, on the other hand, varied with local tradition, social structure, and economy. Where plots were large enough, the family unit would be likely to include grandparents or even in-laws, cousins, and nephews. Particularly in Mediterranean regions, such extended families often shared housing in the village but worked in different nearby fields. When they could, however, a young couple generally set up a household of their own. Where peasants owned land, the problem of keeping it intact while giving something to all the children was difficult, a frequent source of dispute whether law and custom required equal division of inheritance as in France, primogeniture (inheritance by the eldest son) as in England, or ultimogeniture (inheritance by the youngest son) as in parts of Germany. The elderly feared dispossession, the children that they would not get their share in time.

An etching of Dean Mills in 1851 shows cotton spinning as contemporaries liked to think of it: women working together with nimble industriousness under the watchful but gentle eye of a sturdy foreman, all in the iron grandeur of an immaculate, orderly, huge new factory.
(Photo: The Mansell Collection)

Yet for peasants the family remained the basic economic unit, pooling income from various sources, dividing labor in customary ways—with the women usually handling household chores and the smaller animals, the men responsible for the heavier work, and everyone working together in critical periods of planting and harvest. Often the women had more access than the men to additional sources of income—piecework from a nearby mill or domestic service for the well-to-do—and they played a central role in marketing. Men, on the other hand, were more likely to travel considerable distances, especially in difficult times, to pick up a bit of work on roads or docks or at some great landlord's harvest. As population increased, the children were more and more pushed out to seek employment in the nearest mills and towns.

For artisans too the family was often the unit of production, although the division of tasks by sex was usually more explicit, and even small workshops had long tended to exclude women, at least from the better-paid tasks. For working-class women and children to labor long hours was thus not the change so many upper-class commentators made it seem. The strain on the family came rather from the lack of housing and the conditions of work. Not only did women and children have to supplement the father's income, but they were less and less likely to work as a family—although many employers in the early nineteenth century did prefer to hire (and fire) entire families. But they rarely worked side by side; if taught a trade, children were less likely to learn it from their parents. Hardened at an early age, adolescents in factory towns were probably more likely to leave home when their pay allowed, and urban conditions made it more difficult for the family to support the aged and the sick. Such factors did weaken family ties as did—at least in the eyes of the upper classes—the common practice for working men and women to live together without the trouble or expense of formal marriage rites. (Indeed many German towns attempted to prohibit the marriage of those without the means to support a household.) Yet among workers, too, the family survived and not only as a nuclear unit; contact was maintained with distant relatives and a mattress was provided for those coming to seek work. The fact that women worked for pay may also have slowly lessened their subordination even if it did not lead very directly to the new and superior stage of family life that Karl Marx thought it might.

In the lower-middle class, especially in France, women were as important as and frequently more visible than men in operating small shops. The life of the middle-class woman, however, contrasted greatly with that of her poorer sisters, and the role allotted wife and mother became one of the most apparent and important indicators of social status. In earlier eras women had played some part in public life, in politics and business as well as high society, and they continued to be the organizers, patrons, critics, and ornaments of many of Europe's most cultivated circles. But the middle class isolated women from the harsh competition of business and politics. As the contemporary French historian Jules Michelet complained, "By a singular set of circumstances—social, economic, religious—man lives separated from woman." In Victorian England gentlemen met in their clubs or withdrew after dinner for their cigars and weighty talk. The nineteenth-century feminine ideal was an idle and pallid creature, encased in corset or bustle, whose most vigorous act of self-expression was fainting.

There are no proven explanations of why

These French illustrations from the 1840s of work in an English coal mine show the classic horrors—naked men, chained women, and straining children—that made industrialization in the English style something to be avoided.
(Photo: New York Public Library/Picture Collection)

Industrialization and Social Change 1800–1860

(Scènes dans les mines de houille, en Angleterre. — Le Trapper.)

(Jeune fille traînant un chariot.)

(Jeune homme employé à l'extraction du charbon.)

such customs should have developed. There was of course a kind of conspicuous consumption in allowing a wife to be idle even if her husband worked hard, a certain partial imitation of aristocratic elegance; but there were signs too of an unconscious effort at maintaining a sort of counterculture. If men must be competitive, hard, and practical, women should be tender, innocent, and gracious, the weak but pure upholders of virtue and aesthetic sensibility. The middle-class woman with no estate to manage and few servants to direct was almost literally placed on a pedestal. Neither her needlework nor her piano playing was viewed as serious, but her role in maintaining the protective calm of the home and as exemplar of the moral virtues was.

Clearly these attitudes were related to the famous prudery of the age and the distrust of sexual passion. Thomas Bowdler produced in 1818 his *Family Shakespeare,* "in which . . . those words and phrases are omitted which cannot with propriety be read in a family," a strange sensitivity after 200 years; and "the anti-English pollution of the waltz . . . the most degenerating that the last or present century can see" was denounced in *The Ladies' Pocket Book of Etiquette* of 1840. The middle classes sought to maintain an orderly world through convention. At a time when prostitution and drunkenness were at new heights, this was more than repression; it was an effort to bend society to the self-discipline on which a thriving commerce, the advancement of knowledge, and personal fulfillment were thought to rest.

The special place of women emphasized the middle-class concern with the family, and the home became a private citadel largely closed to the outside world. In the family the liberal dream of combining individualism and social order came closest to achievement, for the patriarchal father, devoted mother, and carefully trained children were meant to live in disciplined harmony. Childhood itself lasted longer in the middle class, where character, manners, and education required elaborate preparation. The mother made this home; and books, newspapers, magazines, and sermons were filled with accounts of the talents that role required. Motherhood had become an honored occupation, fondly depicted in novels and the new women's magazines founded, like the Parisian *Journal des Femmes* of 1832, to make women "skilled in their duties as companions and mothers."

Before winning fame with their novels, the Brontë sisters professed envy for the working girl, who at least had her own money, but respectable careers were slowly opening to women. The governess was, along with the butler, the chief domestic, and many a bright but poor young woman used that often lonely position to gain some knowledge of the world and establish a career or enhance her prospects for marriage. In England and increasingly on the Continent, most elementary-school teachers were women, and that occupation opened significant opportunities by the 1860s. Florence Nightingale offended her wealthy family by working as a nurse; but she returned from the Crimean War in 1856 a national heroine to become a major influence in public health and in the establishment of her profession, the first woman to win the British Order of Merit. On the Continent George Sand (the masculine pen name says much about the status of women) was one of the most prolific and noted writers of the age, an important figure among the artists of France, who shocked and excited her contemporaries as much by her attacks on marriage and the treatment of women as by her free personal life. In England women writers proved keen and often caustic observers of society, from Jane Austen's deft analysis of genteel life in the countryside to Elizabeth Gaskell's sympathetic picture of industrial workers and the more complex novels of George Eliot (Mary Ann Evans), who was an active participant in the major intellectual and reform movements of the period. By the 1840s, when Flora Tristan traveled across France preaching to workers of the connection between their plight and women's, the emancipation of women had become an important theme in the writings of nearly all the utopian socialists (see the next section), who found in women's role a key to the errors of middle-class society. John Stuart Mill's *Essay on the Subjugation of Women,* published in 1869, and his advocacy of suffrage for them thus stand as a milestone marking the growing strength of the women's movement.

The Standard of Living

There is more agreement among historians about the general pattern of social change in the first half of the nineteenth century than about its specific effects on the standard of living, particularly of the working class. For this period, England is the critical case; and scholars agree that between 1790 and 1840 national wealth about doubled but that the upper classes were the principal beneficiaries. Did workers gain, too? Certainly they were poor, but poverty, even of the bleakest sort, was not new (and a growing desire to correct such destitution was in itself one of the important changes of the period). The poorest peasants of Sicily who lived in caves, like those of Sweden or Ireland who lived in holes dug into the ground, may have been victims of the social system; they were hardly victims of industrialization.

What was new, then, was the terrible crowding and the workers' helpless dependence. The conditions in which workers lived made poverty more miserable, more obvious to all, and more threatening to the general welfare. In part the result of increased population, the crowding followed directly from the sudden growth of factory towns. Even if the hurriedly built housing was drier and cleaner than the peasant hovels that had served for centuries, the squeezing of whole families into a single room and the cramming of hundreds and thousands of people into areas with little light, with a single source of insalubrious water, and with no means for disposing of sewage created problems so different in scale as to be different in kind. Industrialization also added the special hazards of lead and phosphorous poisoning; and the assault of coal mining, cotton spinning, and machine grinding on the lungs made tuberculosis ubiquitous. Everywhere in Europe members of the working class were recognized generally to be thinner, shorter, and paler than other people.

Accompanying this was an often demoralizing dependence. Most new factories employed between 150 and 300 men, women, and children, which would mean many people whose well-being was largely tied to a single employer. A high proportion of these people were new to the area in which they lived, starkly dependent upon cash to pay their rent, purchase rough cotton for clothes, provide the bread that was the staple of their diet, and buy some candles and coal. For millions, employment was never steady; for millions of others unemployment was the norm. It was common for a third of the adult males of a town to be without work, especially in the winter, and pauperism was acknowledged to be the social disease of the century, a state that included some 10 percent of the population in Britain and only slightly less in France. Workers of course suffered most in the periodic depressions that baffled even the most optimistic. The depression of 1846 was nearly universal, and that of 1857 extended from North America to Eastern Europe. Layoffs in the Lancashire cotton industry ran so high as a result of the American Civil War that at one time more than 250,000 workers, better than half the total, lived by what they could get on relief. The recipes for the watery soup handed out by the charitable agencies of every city define the thinness of survival.[7]

---

[7] The French chef of the Reform Club of London was much admired for his "good and nourishing" recipe: ¼ lb. leg of beef, 2 oz. of drippings, 2 onions and other vegetables, ½ lb. flour, ½ lb. barley, 3 oz. salt, ½ oz. brown sugar—and 2 gallons of water! It was by no means the cheapest soup. Cited in Cecil Woodham-Smith, *The Great Hunger* (1964), p. 173.

At the same time there was a countertrend. In some trades and places workers were distinctly better off; in general real wages—wages measured, that is, in terms of what they could buy—may have increased somewhat. Pay rose generally in the mid-1840s and notably again in the 1850s, though these gains meant less in new factory towns, where workers could be forced to buy shoddy goods at high prices in company stores. Alcoholism was so extensive that in many a factory town paydays were staggered in order to reduce the dangerous number of drunks, and this sign of alienation may also reflect an increase in available money. Technology of course brought benefits as well. The spread of the use of soap and cotton underwear was an enormous boon to health, and brick construction and iron pipes had improved housing even for many of the relatively poor by midcentury. Luxuries such as sugar, tea, and meat were becoming available to the lower-middle class and the more prosperous artisans.

The vigorous debate among historians over the standard of living in this period has become in large measure a test of the author's feelings about capitalism. But pessimists and optimists generally agree that whatever improvements occurred reached the masses slowly, that their effects often could not compensate for the added burdens of industrial employment, and that the chasm between the destitute and the regularly employed (who in England were called the deserving poor) became greater than ever before.

For in industrial Europe the urban poor remained a subject of baffled concern. Skilled workers and the middle classes were unquestionably more prosperous than even in the recent past, but that made the contrast with the poverty of those beneath them even more striking. A luxury restaurant in Paris (there were over 3,000 restaurants of every type there by 1830 as contrasted to only fifty or so before the Revolution) might charge twenty-five or thirty times an average worker's daily wage for a single meal; even modest ones charged twice the daily wage to a clientele that ate three or four times a day in contrast to the two meals of many workers. Despite the subtle shadings of status and wealth, the great differences of class were palpable in every aspect of daily life.

Public Welfare

The social questions of pauperism, public health and morals, and class divisions were debated in hundreds of speeches and pamphlets; and the parliamentary and private inquiries in Britain like the elaborate social studies in France expressed a humanitarian attempt to improve the lot of the lower class through the rational techniques that seemed to work brilliantly when applied to issues of profits and politics.

Some employers, especially in Britain and Alsace, built special housing, drab barracks that nonetheless seemed marvels of cleanliness and decency. Middle-class radicals supported the Society for the Diffusion of Useful Knowledge, founded in 1826 to carry enlightenment to the lower classes. They contributed to and gave lectures at night schools for the workingman, such as those run by the Mechanics' Institute (of which there were more than 700 in Great Britain by 1850) and by the Polytechnic Association of France (which had more than 100,000 participants on the eve of the revolution of 1848). Thousands of middle-class people personally carried the lamp of truth to the poor in the form of pious essays, moral stories, and informative descriptions of how machines worked. Bibles by the million added to this

Gustave Doré's engraving of a London slum captures both the sullen hopelessness of the poor and the sense of the dangerous classes continuously breeding children that frightened the upper classes.
(Photo: The Granger Collection)

extraordinary testimony to faith in the power of the printed page and to the spread of literacy. Ambitious members of the lower-middle class were, however, more likely than workers to take advantage of these opportunities.

For the truly poverty-stricken, charities were established at an incredible rate; more than 450 relief organizations were listed in London alone in 1853, and whole encyclopedias were published in France cataloguing these undertakings. A revival of Christian zeal provided powerful impetus to such groups in Britain, and on the Continent new Catholic religious orders, most with specific social missions, were founded by the hundreds. They sponsored lectures, organized wholesome recreation, set up trade apprenticeships, provided expectant mothers with a clean sheet and a pamphlet on child care, opened savings banks that accepted even the tiniest deposit, campaigned for hygiene or temperance, gave away soup and bread, supported homes for abandoned children and fallen women, and ran nurseries, schools, and hostels. These good works were preeminently the province of women. Almost invariably they presented themselves as models of social salvation, which required only that others follow their example. The Society of St. Vincent de Paul, which was organized in Paris in 1835 and soon spread to all of Catholic Europe, required thousands of educated and well-to-do men regularly to visit the poor so they might teach thrift and give hope by their example as well as their charity. Important for some lucky individuals and a significant means of informing the comfortable about the plight of the poor, the heroic efforts of these organizations were never adequate to the social challenge. Most of Europe's urban masses remained largely untouched by charity or religion.

In matters of public health, standards of housing, working conditions, and education, governments were forced to take a more active role. By modern standards the official measures were timid and hesitant, and the motives behind them were as mixed as they were in factory legislation, favored not only by humanitarians but also by landed interests happy to restrain industrialists.

It is not surprising that conditions of health remained appalling. Vaccination, enforced by progressive governments, made smallpox less threatening after the turn of the century, but beyond that any advances in medicine contributed little. The great work of immunization would come later in the century. The most important medical gain of the 1840s was probably the use of anesthesia in surgery, dentistry, and childbirth. Serious epidemics broke out in every decade. Typhus, carried by lice, was a constant threat, accounting for 1 death in 9 in Ireland between 1816 and 1819, and typhoid fever was caused by infected water in city after city. Apparently beginning along the Ganges River in 1826, cholera spread through East Asia, reaching Moscow and St. Petersburg by 1830 (100,000 died of cholera in Russia in two years). From there it spread south and west, to Egypt and North Africa, to Poland, Austria, and into Germany, to be reported in Hamburg in 1831. Despite efforts to put ports in quarantine (a move opposed by shipping interests), the disease reached northern England and later France in the same year, continuing slowly to the south, taking a ninth of Palermo's population in 1836–1837.

The reaction to the epidemic of 1831–1832 in Britain, France, and Germany, however, revealed much about social change. An official day of fasting, prayer, and humiliation in England or the warnings of the archbishop of Paris that the cholera was Divine Retribution expressed widespread distrust of an era of materialism and its belief in progress as well as the strength of traditional faith. But governments were expected to act, and, torn between two inaccurate theories of how the disease spread (contagion on contact and miasmic effluvia; the cholera bacillus was finally identified by Robert Koch in 1883), they did. Inspectors were mobilized to enforce such sanitary regulations as existed (and not infrequently were faced with riots by a populace fearful of medical bodysnatchers). In Paris and Lille tenements were whitewashed by the tens of thousands, food inspected, streets and sewers cleaned on administrative order. Similar steps were taken in the German states and in Britain, where after the inadequacy of local government became apparent, a national Public Health Commission was given extraordinary powers over towns and individuals. Statistics were gathered, and over a period of years doctors and inspectors (with consciences troubled) reported on the terrible conditions they had found among lower-class neighbors whose quarters they had never visited before. There was another such epidemic in the 1840s and lesser ones thereafter, but the shock and uncertainty of what to do was never again so great. Gradually, hospitals too came under more direct state supervision as the cost and complexity of medical treatment increased. By midcentury housing and sanitary codes regulated most of urban construction throughout the West, and inspectors were empowered to enforce these rules. Liberalism showed its other

Photography gained wide acceptance both as a mode of portraiture and as a scientific tool in the nineteenth century. Charles Negre's photograph of "The Doctor's Visit" to the Imperial Asylum at Vincennes in 1860 combines both of these in a stark display of the hospital environment of the era.
(Photo: Philadelphia Museum of Art; Collection of André Jammes)

face in England's handling of the terrible potato famine in Ireland. As the potato blight struck late in 1845, disaster for a population so dependent on a single crop was not hard to predict. For the next several years some of England's ablest officials struggled with bureaucratic earnestness to collect information, organize relief, and maintain order, yet did so in a manner so inhibited by respect for natural economic forces and the rights of property that in practice only meager relief was offered while millions starved.

The 1830s and 1840s witnessed a series of restrictions on child labor, banning employment of those under nine in textile mills in Britain and factories in Prussia, under eight in factories in France, and under ten in mines in Britain. By the end of the 1840s, similar measures had been adopted in Bavaria, Baden, Piedmont, and Russia. Generally the laws held the workday of children under twelve or thirteen to eight or nine hours and of those under sixteen or eighteen to twelve hours. In Britain and France there were additional requirements that the very young be provided with a couple of hours of schooling each day. To be effective such regulations required teams of inspectors, provided for only in Britain, where earnest disciples of Jeremy Bentham (who is discussed in the next section) applied them diligently. This expansion of government authority had been vigorously opposed, but the appalling evidence presented to commissions of inquiry made the need apparent, and the ability to gather such evidence became one of government's most important functions.

The most bitterly controversial welfare measure of the period was Britain's Poor Law of 1834. The old system of relief required counties to supplement local wages up to a subsistence level determined by the price of bread. Expensive and inadequate to changing needs, the system was attacked by liberal economists, who charged that it discouraged workers from migrating to new jobs and cost too much. An extensive campaign led to the Poor Law of 1834, based on the quaint Benthamite notion that unemployment must be made unattractive. Those receiving relief were required to live in workhouses, where the sexes were separated and conditions kept suitably mean. Resented as a cruel act of class conflict, the new law proved unenforceable in much of the nation, though recent studies have suggested that it was less harsh in either practice or intent than its critics charged. On the Continent welfare measures kept more traditional forms while steadily shifting the responsibility for them from local and religious auspices to the state.

Public education also became a matter of national policy. Prussia had made local schooling compulsory in 1716, and a series of reforms culminated in 1807 with the creation of a bureau of education. In the following decades the government, with the cooperation of the Lutheran clergy, established an efficient system of universal education with facilities for training the needed teachers while assuring that the subject matter taught would remain rudimentary and politically safe. The network of secondary schools was also enlarged but kept quite separate, in effect excluding the lower classes. Most of the German states had similar arrangements, establishing nearly universal elementary education. In France the Napoleonic structure provided the framework for public education, in principle although not in practice providing a substitute for the extensive but more informal and largely religious schools of the old regime. The law of 1833 required an elementary school in every commune. Despite many difficulties, the system steadily expanded, the quality of teachers improved, and the power of inspectors over tightfisted local authorities increased. By the revolution of 1848, three-fourths of France's school-age children were receiving some formal instruction. The conflict between the Church of England and the dissenting sects prevented the adoption of a state-controlled system of national education in Britain, a lack welcomed by those conservatives who opposed educating the masses. Nevertheless the subsidy first voted in 1833 to underwrite the construction of private schools proved an opening wedge, and it increased in amount and scope each year. From Spain to Russia elementary schools were favored by every government. Inadequate and impoverished, the public schools of Europe offered little chance of social advancement to those forced to attend them, but few doubted that they could be a major instrument for improving society as well as a force for social peace.

III. THEORIES OF CHANGE

Liberalism

The overwhelming fact of political and social change demanded interpretation; and liberalism not only led to change but explained it. It became an international movement, one led primarily by men of means and education, who watched the successes of their cause throughout Western Europe and encouraged each other in the conviction that history was inevitably advancing toward the fulfillment of their common vision. That confidence rested not only on political victories but on the experience of economic growth. The gains of liberal politics—representative government, free speech, and laws applied equally to all citizens (see Chapter 22)—seemed to accompany the triumph of liberal economic theory and the application of liberal social policies. Liberal politics and liberal economic theory were thus closely related; yet these two aspects of liberalism have proved separable. The advocates of one were not always, and not necessarily, committed to the other, and the question of their relationship is still a matter of controversy, especially in the United States. The model of liberalism was nineteenth-century England.

Economic Liberalism

Adam Smith and the physiocrats had argued that government intervention in the marketplace merely restricted the play of economic forces that if left to themselves would increase productivity and prosperity. This belief, which had become liberal dogma, was expounded systematically by David Ricardo, whose writings represented the keystone of modern economics for generations. Ricardo was one of England's self-made men, a financier who became wealthy during the Napoleonic wars and then retired from business, thereafter contributing enthusiastically to charity, taking part in politics, and developing his economic ideas, which England's leading liberals encouraged him to publish. First issued in 1817, his *Principles of Political Economy and Taxation* presented his theory in flat prose as a science, precise but highly abstract.

The wealth of the community, Ricardo argued, comes from land, capital, and labor; and these three "classes" are compensated by rent, profit, and wages. A product's value results from the labor required to make it—the labor theory of value, which socialists would later use for very different purposes. For Ricardo this theory led to principles of property similar to Locke's and to an emphasis on labor saving as the source of profit foreshadowed by Adam Smith. Rents are determined not by individuals but by the poorest land in cultivation. The most fertile land produces more for the same labor, and that increment constitutes profit, received as rent. As population pressures bring more (and poorer) land into cultivation, rents rise because the difference between the best and worst land increases. Wages are subtracted from profit, but an "iron law of wages" (his phrase is characteristic) decrees that when labor is plentiful the worker would tend to be paid at the subsistence level. Short-term fluctuations in prices are the natural regulator within the system, pushing men to activities for which demand is high. Thus Ricardan economics extended the sphere of inexorable economic laws and riveted them to Malthusian ideas about pressures of population.

Both land and labor are commodities, Ricardo said, their value quite unaffected by sentimental talk about aristocratic values or craftsmanship, and society is a congeries of competing interests. Legislation cannot raise wages or prevent the marketplace from working in its natural way; but if men acknowledge economic laws and act in their own best interest, a natural harmony and progress follow.

Ricardo called his subject political economy, and from it a powerful reform movement developed. Clearly, liberals argued, the landed interest had misused political power to benefit itself, depriving the rest of society. Throughout Europe liberal economic theory added important weight to demands that special privilege be eliminated and that governments be responsive to the people, who would best know their own interests. With the impressive evidence of economic growth before them, it was natural for liberals to add that politicians might well adopt something of the openness, efficiency, and energy of the men of action who were transforming business.

Utilitarianism

A second major stream of liberalism was utilitarianism, a complex and often contradictory philosophy elaborated by Jeremy Bentham. Although English, Bentham was in many respects a philosophe, ready to write a constitution for Russia or codify the laws of Latin American republics. Some of his most important writings before 1789 appeared first in French—the revolutionaries gave him French citizenship—and he combined plans of detailed reform with a theory of psychology in the Enlightenment tradition. At first Bentham stressed reform of the legal system, and he remained all his life an opponent of the precedent-bound, technicality-loving courts of England. In contrast to most philosophes, he rejected the doctrine of natural rights as a meaningless abstraction, and unlike most liberals, he did not hesitate to advocate heavy state intervention in society.

In Bentham's thinking utility replaces natural rights as the test of proper policy, and it is measured by the standard of what provides the greatest good for the greatest number. The good is that which avoids pain and gives pleasure—a calculation that everyone makes for himself anyway and that with education he can learn to make more wisely. (Bentham called this the "felicific calculus," but his verbal pomposity was famous; his after-dinner walks were "postprandial perambulations.") The egocentrism that built great industry could also build a just and happy society. In Bentham's terms the proper estimate of pain and pleasure leads one to behave like a prudent, middle-class Christian; and the task of government is to make sure that pain and pleasure are appropriately distributed for various kinds of behavior.

Bentham's followers, sober intellectuals who called themselves philosophic radicals, became even more influential. They pressed his doctrines in every sphere, and by his death in 1832, they were among the most important reformers of Parliament, law, prisons, education, and welfare. A special group within a larger liberal movement, they shared and contributed to the tendency of liberals everywhere to take pride in pressing for humane reforms on grounds of common sense and natural harmony.

The Broader Liberalism of John Stuart Mill

Thus liberals appraised society primarily in terms of opportunities for individual growth and freedom of individual choice. Such an emphasis gave some ethical dignity to the pain of industrialization and social change. Confident and optimistic, their doctrines seemed universally valid.

Yet liberalism, to the perpetual surprise of its adherents, proved a creed of limited appeal, forever subject to attack and internal division. Enthusiasm for limited constitutional reform, so great in the 1830s, was harder to sustain in 1848. It proved difficult in practice to reconcile liberty with order and equal rights with private property, and the opportunities and freedoms proudly cited by men like Guizot seemed to others the selfishness of the well-to-do. Religious conflict in Catholic Europe, the need first to create national states in Central and Eastern Europe, and the problems of the dispossessed everywhere inhibited the full application of liberal ideas.

Before such problems liberals themselves divided. As maintained by some, liberalism became the narrow and at times mean justification of a social class; for others it expanded until the need for social justice and equal opportunity largely obscured the principles of competitive economics and a noninterfering state that were its original strength. In each country its temper was different, shaped by a national history liberals never wholly dominated.

Its very malleability, however, enabled liberalism to endure as a doctrine and a political force; and its transition to a broader meaning is best exemplified in John Stuart Mill, the most important liberal spokesman of the nineteenth century. Mill's father was a leading Benthamite and he raised his son in the strictest utilitarianism; but the younger Mill gradually came with searching candor to modify received doctrine. Extraordinarily learned, a philosopher, economist, and publicist, Mill's greatest influence has been through his political writings. Fearful of the intolerance and oppression of which any class or even the public at large was capable, he made freedom of thought a first principle, and he advocated universal suffrage as a necessary check on the elite and proportional representation as a means of protecting minorities. Influenced by Auguste Comte (see Chapter 25) and others, he acknowledged the

This photograph of John Stuart Mill shows a solid bourgeois (compare Ingres' portrait of Louis Bertin, color plate 49) who is also a sensitive intellectual.
(Photo: The Granger Collection)

critical role of institutions in social organization and admitted that those institutions, even liberal ones, best suited to one stage of development might not be appropriate for another.

Mill hoped for a beneficial influence from a more open bureaucracy, from organized interest groups, and from cooperatives. Moved by the problems of the industrial poor, he tried to distinguish between production (to which liberal economics could still apply) and distribution (in which the state might intervene in behalf of justice), and he came to see that collective action by the workers could enhance freedom rather than restrict it. He sought a place for aesthetic values within the colder doctrine he inherited and in later years courageously advocated causes, such as the emancipation of women and the confiscation of excess profit, that seemed fearfully radical to most contemporaries. His liberalism, thus modified and extended, remained firm; and his essay, *On Liberty,* published in 1859, stands as one of the important works of European political theory, a careful but heartfelt, balanced but unyielding declaration that society can have no higher interest than the freedom of each of its members.

Early Socialists

Some men, however, envisioned a better society based on quite different principles. Among scores of socialist schemes, the ideas of Saint-Simon, Fourier, and Owen won an important place in the history of socialism by their comprehensiveness, their particular insights, and the intensity with which they were promulgated.

All three men lived through the French Revolution, had some personal experience of burgeoning capitalism, and began to develop systems for remaking the world in the early stages of industrialization, even before Napoleon's final defeat. Turning from political solutions to social problems, they developed economic and moral critiques of the contemporary world. Competition, they argued, is wasteful and cruel, induces hard-hearted indifference to suffering, misuses wealth, and leads to frequent economic crises. Differently organized, society can instead be harmonious and orderly, providing enough for all.

As a young French officer, Claude Henri de Rouvroy, comte de Saint-Simon, fought with George Washington at Yorktown. During the French Revolution he abandoned his title and built a fortune, which he quickly lost, through speculation in land, and under the empire he settled down to the difficult career of a seer. For a society divided between the propertied and the propertyless, Saint-Simon proposed to substitute the direction of experts standing above the conflict: scientists, men of affairs (*industriels*), priests, and artists. These specialists, chosen for their ability, would design plans for the benefit of all, increasing productivity and therefore prosperity. The new society would recapture the integrated, organic quality of ancient Greece and the Middle Ages but with scientists and managers holding the authority once granted priests and soldiers. In a world so structured, the state would have little independent importance; for skilled men would work together, planning and directing, as in an efficient business. The artists and priests of the new order could then lead mankind to self-fulfillment and love.

Saint-Simon's theories won little hearing among the powerful of his day, but they earned a significant following especially among the bright students of the École Polytechnique. An entire cult, the New Christianity, developed among his disciples after Saint-Simon's death in 1827, only to be dissipated by internal division and public ridicule by the 1840s. Nevertheless an extraordinary number of France's leading engineers and entrepreneurs in the next generation fondly recalled the Saint-Simonian enthusiasms of their youth, and in their penchant for planning, grand economic organization, and social reform, they carried elements of his teaching into the world of affairs and respectable politics. There were important Saint-Simonian movements in every country, and later socialists would maintain his conviction that proper planning would make an economy both more just and richer.

François Marie Charles Fourier had been a traveling salesman before dedicating himself, at the same time as Saint-Simon, to a theory which he firmly believed would rank among the greatest discoveries ever made. His cantankerous and shrewd writings on contemporary society were so copious that his manuscripts have still not all been printed despite the devotion of generations of admirers. Largely self-taught, he committed to paper his fantasies of strange beasts and incredible inventions that would abound in a future age, which made him an easy target for critics.

His central concept, however, was an ideal community, the phalanstery (from "phalanx"). Once even one was created, the happiness and well-being of its members would inspire the establishment of others until all of society was converted. A phalanstery should contain some 1,600 men and women, representatives of all the types of personality identified in Fourier's elaborate psychology. He listed a dozen passions that move human beings and proposed to organize the phalanstery in such a way that individuals would accomplish the tasks necessary to society by doing what they wanted. Everyone would perform a variety of tasks, engaging in no one for too long; pleasure and work would flow together. Members of the phalanstery would be paid according to a formula that recognized the capital, labor, and talent each contributed. Largely self-sufficient, a phalanstery would produce some goods for export according to its particular resources, and these would be traded with similar communities.

No phalanstery was ever established exactly as Fourier planned (he even offered designs for the architecture), but communities were founded on Fourierist principles from the United States to Rumania; and if few of them survived for long, the vision did of a society in which cooperation replaces compulsion and joy transforms drudgery.

Robert Owen was one of the success stories of industrial capitalism: a self-made man, he rose from selling cloth to be the manager and part owner of a large textile mill in New Lanark, Scotland. Owen's rule transformed the town, and by the end of the Napoleonic wars, distinguished visitors were traveling from all over Europe to see the miracle he had wrought. The workday was shortened from seventeen to ten hours; new housing was constructed, eventually allowing an employee's family several rooms; inspection committees maintained cleanliness; gardens were planted and sewers installed. In nursery schools with airy, pleasant rooms, children were given exercise, encouraged to sing and dance, taught without corporal punishment from books and projects designed to be attractive, and trained in the useful arts. Most impressive of all, the subjects in this paternalistic kingdom developed a pride in their community; productivity rose and profits increased.

Owen had, he felt, disproved Ricardo's dismal laws, and he turned to projects for establishing ideal communities throughout the nation. Like Fourier's, they would be placed in a rural setting and would supply most of their own needs. Members would take meals and enjoy entertainment in common, and children would be raised communally. Educated to the age of eight, the young would then engage in productive labor until they were twenty-six; after five years in distributive or managerial jobs, adults would assume the tasks of government, cultivating the sciences and the arts in their increasing leisure. The controlled environment would assure good character among community members, and the division of tasks would provide them with varied and rich lives. Standardized production would offer more goods at lower cost (luxuries appealed to a snobbery that would disappear), and higher wages would increase the local market.

Even after losing most of his wealth with the failure of the community of New Harmony in Indiana, Owen continued to be the single most important figure in the labor movement and the workers' cooperatives that spread through England in the 1830s and 1840s. But by the time of his death, in 1858, Owen, who had converted to spiritualism, was largely ignored by the world he had sought to remake.

These early socialists imagined a society of cooperation and love, one enriched by new inventions and new means of production but

A French engraving of Robert Owen's textile mill shows a model of order and calm in which everyone appears to have taken to heart the rules carefully posted along the wall.
(Photo: The Granger Collection)

based on new forms of social organization. Advocates of change, they were transitional figures seeking to combine the best of the old and new eras. Their indictment of capitalism and their insights into the nature of productivity, exchange, social planning, and education had an impact far beyond their relatively small circles of believers. A large number of Europe's best minds were touched by their theories, and the mystique of cooperation so strong in their writings remained part of the socialist and anarchist call to brotherhood and found an echo in nationalists from Mazzini on. Yet nearly everyone ultimately rejected their ideas as impractical and too radical. Bucolic isolation and artisanal production became increasingly unrealistic, and these theories were incredibly vague about problems of politics and power. The charge of radicalism, however, requires some further comment.

The criticisms of liberal society mounted by Saint-Simon, Fourier, and Owen were not so different overall from the conservative attack, and none of them was a thoroughgoing democrat. With some restrictions—Saint-Simon for example insisted on the abolition of inheritance—they even allowed private property. What most shocked contemporaries were their views on the status of women, sexual mores, and Christianity. All rejected the place allotted women in bourgeois society, and Owen not only specified that they should share in governing but believed their emancipation required a smaller role for them in the family. All wrote of sensual pleasure as good and its repression as a characteristic European error. The Saint-Simonians publicly advocated free love, and Fourier carefully provided that neither young nor old should be deprived of the pleasures of the flesh. Owen was only slightly less outspoken in his contempt for Christian marriage. Yet all three stressed religion as the source of community feeling, brotherhood, and human ethics. Their efforts to replace what they had eliminated therefore led to imitations of Christian ritual and foggy mysticism that not only contrasted with their concern for rational planning but invited easy ridicule from a society with many reasons for rejecting their utopias. By the end of the nineteenth century socialist thought would center instead on the more hard-headed and systematic theories of Karl Marx (see Chapter 25).

The Sense of History

Liberals and socialists, like conservatives, argued in terms of history, and its systematic study became the most honored of the human sciences. In England, France, and Germany, national projects were launched for publishing historical documents and for training scholars to interpret them. Some historians were as widely read as novelists, and the most popular dramas were given a historical setting. The Glorious Revolution of 1688, the French Revolution, and the rise of Prussia were favorite themes in their respective countries, and everywhere the search was intense for national roots in the Middle Ages and for patterns of meaning applicable to the present. And in contemporary political battles, historical studies often figured prominently, their writers calling on the past to prove the need for reform or teach the dangers of revolution while patriotically stressing the virtues of their own people.

This preoccupation with history, which affected all intellectual life, received its most powerful expression in the philosophy of Georg Wilhelm Friedrich Hegel. A Rhinelander who had felt the impact of French culture and watched Napoleon's career with fascination, thoroughly trained in philosophy and Lutheran theology, Hegel set out to establish a philosophy as comprehensive as that of Thomas Aquinas or Aristotle. He was determined to reconcile the contradictions between science and faith, Christianity and the state, the ideal and the real, the eternal and the temporal that plagued modern thought.

He sought to do so by establishing an undying purpose at the heart of history and by discovering the process of historical change. That process he described not as the simple increase of reason or wealth so often called progress, but something far more complex and subtle—the dialectic of thesis, antithesis, and synthesis. All the actions, the values, and social structures of a given society constitute a thesis, an implicit statement about life. The thesis, however, is never adequate to every need, and its incompleteness generates contrary views, institutions, and practices—the antithesis. Thus every society gives birth to conflict between thesis and antithesis until finally out of their battle a new synthesis is molded. The synthesis is a new thesis that generates another round of conflict. History moves by this dialectic in a steady unfolding of the World Spirit. Its meaning is the fulfillment of human freedom and self-awareness. In the ancient East only one man was free; in Greece and Rome some were free; in the Germanic Christian kingdoms after the Reformation, all were free. Since the French Revolution men have consciously acted on history, knowing what they want and fulfilling the World Spirit at the same time. Thus cosmic and human reason work together; the meaning of history is essentially religious.

Hegel's complex and abstract philosophy was—as he would have said it to be—an important expression of his age, and it has proved a lasting influence. Like most nineteenth-century thinkers, he was preoccupied with change,

THE SAME TOWN IN 1840

1. St Michael's Tower, rebuilt in 1750. 2. New Parsonage House & Pleasure Grounds. 3. The New Jail. 4. Gas Works. 5. Lunatic Asylum. 6. Iron Works & Ruins of St Maries Abbey. 7. Mr Evans Chapel. 8. Baptist Chapel. 9. Unitarian Chapel. 10. New Church. 11. New Town Hall & Concert Room. 12. Wesleyan Centenary Chapel. 13. New Christian Society. 14. Quakers Meeting. 15. Socialist Hall of Science.

Catholic town in 1440.

1. St Michaels on the Hill. 2. Queens Cross. 3. St Thomas's Chapel. 4. St Maries Abbey. 5. All Saints. 6. St Johns. 7. St Peters. 8. St Alkmunds. 9. St Maries. 10. St Edmunds. 11. Grey Friars. 12. St Cuthberts. 13. Guild hall. 14. Trinities. 15. St Olaves. 16. St Botolphs.

A convert to Catholicism and a leading student of Gothic architecture, Augustus Pugin was one of the architects of the Houses of Parliament. These illustrations, part of a book of *Contrasts* comparing Catholic and Protestant society, sum up the romantic and conservative critique of modern society. (The new prison in the foreground is Jeremy Bentham's Panopticon, designed so that a single guard can see down all the cellblocks.)
(Photo: New York Public Library/Picture Collection)

determined to find an eternal meaning at the core of history, and convinced that his own nation was its highest articulation. After Hegel, philosophy and literary criticism tended to become increasingly historical, and historians sought more systematically for relationships among all aspects of a culture. And within a generation of his death in 1831, just after a wave of the revolutions he abhorred, some of his followers claimed to find in the Prussian state at war man's highest ethical expression, while others, led by Karl Marx, the most famous of the Hegelians, predicted the state's withering away. By then it was an intellectual habit to view society in process and to search in history for the meaning of change.

European society changed in many ways during the two generations following the Napoleonic wars. Factory organization and labor-saving machinery in 1815 showed their economic promise primarily in Britain, but by the 1850s an industrial revolution without apparent end was transforming much of Western Europe, where the population was increasing, cities expanding, and the way of life changing.

The effort to understand these changes dominated intellectual life, and the interpretations of contemporary trends and of history all promised a better future. Except for conservatives, few doubted that the path of progress was marked by liberalism: freedom of speech and representative government protecting the rights of the individual, the laws of competition and self-interest working their magic. These bustling, expanding societies produced a vigorous and varied culture which expressed both the confidence and the concerns of a tumultuous era. Individualism and values associated with the middle class—rationality, probity, thrift, hard work, and a close two-generation family—were the dominant ideals.

In such an atmosphere the misery and subjugation of the lower classes seemed an intolerable contrast with the increasing wealth of society as a whole. Poverty, urban misery, and ignorance appeared no longer as natural conditions but as problems to be solved. More effective charities, better regulations, new institutions for education and welfare, or radical communities—the solutions proposed by the ideologies of change, whether piecemeal or sweeping, concentrated on improved social organization. In a civilization that expected so much of politics, this necessarily pointed to a more extensive and active role for the state.

RECOMMENDED READING

Studies

*Ashton, Thomas S. *The Industrial Revolution: 1760–1830.* 1964. A balanced "optimistic" account of the process of industrialization in Britain.

*Briggs, Asa. *Victorian Cities.* 1970. Studies of the industrial cities and their impact on British life.

The Cambridge Economic History of Europe. Vol. VI, *The Industrial Revolution and After,* 2 parts. 1965. The essay in these volumes by David S. Landes, which emphasizes the role of technology, has been revised and published separately as *Unbound Prometheus: Technological Change and Development in Western Europe from 1750 to the Present.* 1969.

Chevalier, Louis. *Laboring Classes and Dangerous Classes in Paris During the First Half of the Nineteenth Century.* 1973. This study of the Parisian poor also says much about the reactions of those better off.

*Clapham, John H. *The Economic Development of France and Germany, 1815–1914.* 1935. A sober, standard study full of useful information.

Cole, G. D. H. *A History of Socialist Thought.* 5 vols. 1953–1956. Pleasantly written compendium including each of the important movements and schools of thought.

De Ruggiero, Guido. *The History of European Liberalism.* R. G. Collingwood (tr.). 1959. A classic comparison of liberal theory in major European nations.

*Gideon, Siegfried. *Mechanization Takes Command.* 1948. Provocative analysis of the social and aesthetic implications of the machine age.

*Heilbroner, Robert L. *The Worldly Philosophers.* 1967. A good introduction to the ideas of the economic liberals.

*Henderson, W. O. *The Industrialization of Europe: 1780–1914.* 1969. General study contrasting developments in England and on the Continent.

Himmelfarb, Gertrude. *On Liberty and Liberalism: The Case of John Stuart Mill.* 1974. Penetrating and controversial analysis of the still controversial philosopher of liberalism.

*Lichtheim, George. *A Short History of Socialism.* 1970. Well-constructed treatment of the evolution of socialist ideas in their historical context.

*Manuel, Frank E. *The Prophets of Paris.* 1965. An excellent discussion of French utopian thinkers.

Perkin, Harold. *The Origins of Modern English Society, 1780–1880.* 1969. A serious effort to interweave all aspects of social change.

*Rudé, George. *The Crowd in History, 1730–1884.* 1964. Argues that there was a fundamental change in the social composition and demands of crowds after industrialization.

*Thompson, Edward P. *The Making of the English Working Class.* 1964. A remarkable work of sympathetic insight and exhaustive research.

Tilly, Charles, Louise Tilly, and Richard Tilly. *The Rebellious Century, 1830–1930.* 1975. Three studies of patterns of collective action in France, Germany, and Italy.

Walker, Mack. *German Home Towns: Community, State, and General Estate, 1648–1871.* 1971. Sensitive and original treatment of the response of small-town life to political and social change.

---

*Available in paperback.

24

THE NATIONAL STATE AND THE MIDDLE CLASS 1850–1880

In the period following the revolutions of 1848, the national state became more clearly than ever before the dominant institution of political life and the basic unit of economic and social life. The revolutions themselves had demonstrated the importance of public opinion, and had shown that social issues could be explosive. After 1850, governments, especially those that kept some form of representative institutions, used nationalism to enhance their popularity and increased the range of their activities as a means to ensure stability.

Improved communications and nationwide markets also seemed to require national governments, which were in turn expected to foster industry by granting aid to railroads and banks, undertaking public works, and establishing protective tariffs. Nationalist movements promised these benefits while sustaining liberal ideas of the proper relationship between a government and its people. The national state also provided a larger field of action for the middle class who spurred its economy, ran its institutions, and sustained its cultural life. All but the most reactionary could see the benefits of having an articulate middle class that favored expansion and reform, but those in power also knew that such changes could threaten established interests.

The government most willing to experiment with new combinations of public support, innovative programs, and central control was that of Louis Napoleon in France, but the most dramatic political changes of the period were the unifications of Italy and Germany. The governments of Britain, Spain, the Austrian Empire, and Russia faced similar demands as well as an immediate need for increased military power and administrative efficiency. Throughout Europe statesmen sought modes of reform that would strengthen the state without diminishing their own power and that would convert public opinion from a threat into useful support.

The domestic political equilibrium thus achieved differed from nation to nation, but it was everywhere related to momentous shifts in international power. The Crimean War in 1853–1856 marked the breakdown of the old Concert of Europe maintained by the conservative powers after the Congress of Vienna, a change that opened the way for the wars that welded the Italian and German nations. Moreover, the Continental hegemony of France in the 1850s and 1860s ended with the unification of Germany and was followed by the precarious relations manipulated by Otto von Bismarck. In a period of strong and daring statesmen, Europe's great nations found themselves charged with the direction of unprecedented accumulations of economic, military, and political power.

I. A MIDDLE-CLASS CULTURE

Cultural Institutions

The European high culture of the nineteenth century can fairly be called a culture of the middle class—one not marked by any single style; a culture that was national and urban rather than centered in courts, salons, or villages ("provincial" had become a pejorative term); and one that was remarkable for quantity as well as quality, for there were more writers, artists, musicians, and scholars than ever before. For all its deliberate variety, this culture remained distinctive in its institutionalization, the forms of its expression, the themes it emphasized, and the shifting styles it favored.

Before the nineteenth century most paintings were done for a specific commission and often for a particular room; most music was composed for a special (often religious) occasion and designed to fit the talents of performers available in one palace; most books were written for a particular audience whom the author could feel he knew intimately. In the new century this had largely changed. Music moved from palaces, churches, and private salons to public concert halls; artists sold their paintings to any purchaser and, by midcentury, in galleries created for that purpose; and writers found themselves engaged in commerce.

If the artist felt insecure in his dependence on an audience of unknown character and unproved cultivation, he had a larger public than ever before. That public was for the most part the same people active in politics, the professions, and business—or rather such people and their wives. They bought tickets for concerts just as they frequented restaurants with famous chefs, enjoying in both cases pleasures once part of private society and now open to all who had the inclination and money.

Theaters, institutions accustomed to commercial operations, flourished in every city, and they ranged from the new music halls to the great stages and opera houses built (usually by the state) to rank with parliament buildings as monuments of civic pride. Most major cities supported choirs, bands, and symphony orchestras, which grew larger and technically more proficient (the "Mannheim crescendo" was a new marvel of instrumental synchronization and discipline that Beethoven required of every orchestra). Conservatories and museums became national public institutions, maintaining established taste against a sea of change and considerably increasing Europe's stock of skilled artists and musicians. Some of the greatest of these institutions—the British Museum in London, the Bibliothèque Nationale in Paris, the Hermitage in St. Petersburg, the Alte Pinakothek in Munich—opened to the public in the 1840s usually in imposing new structures. The Louvre became the model museum of art, granting access to everyone and arranging its holdings by country and in chronological order. Lending libraries, charging a few pence per volume, were common even in smaller cities.

Those who sought self-improvement also flocked to public lectures on the sober implications of political economy or the wonders of science, among which photography ranked high. Daguerre announced his photographic process to the French Academy in 1839, and it persuaded the French government to purchase all rights so the new technique could be given to the world unencumbered by royalties. Important advances followed rapidly, and photography was enthusiastically applied to the needs of science and exploration, widely used for portraits, and recognized as the newest of the arts.

But no cultural institution was more important than the press. Before 1800 the newspaper, of little importance outside of France and Britain, had been more like a newsletter, gossip column, or political pamphlet. By 1830 there were more than 2,000 European newspapers, despite the censorship, special taxes, and police measures with which governments sought to restrict so awesome a social force. Where these

Increasing numbers of the public (note the middle-class families) flocked to the British Museum in the 1840s to view its exhibits on art and literature as well as natural history.
(Photo: British Museum)

---

restraints were eased, which was a central liberal demand in all countries, sales soared. By midcentury *The Times* of London increased its 1815 circulation of 5,000 to 50,000, and two of the most popular French papers, the *Presse* and *Siècle,* both founded in 1836, had topped 70,000. In attaining such distribution, newspapers changed. The *Presse* and *Siècle* succeeded in halving their subscription rates (which remained substantial) by drawing their revenue primarily from advertising. Articles discussed commerce, the arts, and science as well as politics, and the papers competed for readers with serial novels by Honoré de Balzac and the elder Alexandre Dumas. The *London Illustrated News* created the picture magazine in 1842, which was copied immediately in every large country, and satirical magazines (*Punch* was founded in 1840, a few years after the *Caricature* and *Chiarivari* in Paris) made the cartoon a powerful political weapon. Honoré Daumier's biting pictures of fat bankers and complacent bourgeois raised social criticism to art.

Technology contributed to these developments. The *Times* installed a steam press in 1814, and a flood of technical improvements increased the speed and quality of typesetting and printing. Press services such as the Agence Havas and Reuters switched from carrier pigeons to the telegraph to bring bulletins to a public increasingly eager for the latest news. And paper-making machines reduced the cost and increased the volume of printing in every form.

The Cultural Professions

Newspaper work became a full-time occupation and gradually a profession—the terms "journalism" and "journalist" date from this period—and so did performing, painting, and writing. The virtuoso actor or musician could make an honored career. The violinist Niccolò Paganini, who transformed violin technique, commanded huge fees and enormous crowds wherever he played; Jenny Lind, "the Swedish Nightingale," was the rage of Europe, and Franz Liszt shaped international musical taste and standards of performance. The distinction between the amateur and professional musician became firm. Many a young man announced that he was a painter and proudly starved, in Paris if possible, out of loyalty to his career (there were 354 registered artists in Paris in 1789 but 2,159 in 1838); a few, among them England's great landscape painter J. M. W. Turner, became wealthy. The most popular writers—Balzac, Sir Walter Scott, Victor Hugo, Charles Dickens—were able to live by their pen alone, honored among the famous men of their age. Many responded to their new opportunities with appropriate industry. Scott wrote twenty-eight novels in eighteen years, and Balzac was equally prolific. Few went so far as Dumas, who employed scores of assistants to help crank out his profitable product. The artist making his way in his profession might hope for a prize or fellowship from one of the leading cultural institutions, but ultimately his fate depended on the opinion of his fellow artists and of an often untutored public not sure of its own taste.

That problem of judgment led to still another profession: the critic. The best critics won places for themselves as literary figures in their own right. But their essential role was to extend the canons of taste to a public faced with kaleidoscopic variety, just as the popular books on etiquette and gastronomy taught manners to the man of new means and prepared his bourgeois palate for *haute cuisine*.

Cultural Forms and Styles

Although cultural life in the nineteenth century was full of uncertainties—about the role of the artist, the relationship of art to society, and the values art should express—middle-class culture remained essentially a formal one, proudly removed from the merely popular or customary. In music the forms of the symphony, concerto, quartet, and sonata, established in the eighteenth century, had been enlarged and enriched, especially by Ludwig van Beethoven, whose creative amalgam of formal structure and personal expression became the dominant model for nineteenth-century composers. His music, in whatever form, had the quality of a philosophic yet poetic essay, conceived and presented as high art to be heard in concert, studied and savored for itself and not as part of some larger entertainment or social occasion. This seriousness, intellectual and emotional, and this separation of art from any single context fit well with the changing circumstances in which music was performed by professional musicians before a paying audience. Beethoven's successors maintained that sense of music as an autonomous art and created works of such vitality that to this day most of the concert repertoire consists of music composed between 1800 and World War I.

The novel, which had also achieved its identity in the eighteenth century when it was often written in an epistolary style as if from one acquaintance to another, became the most

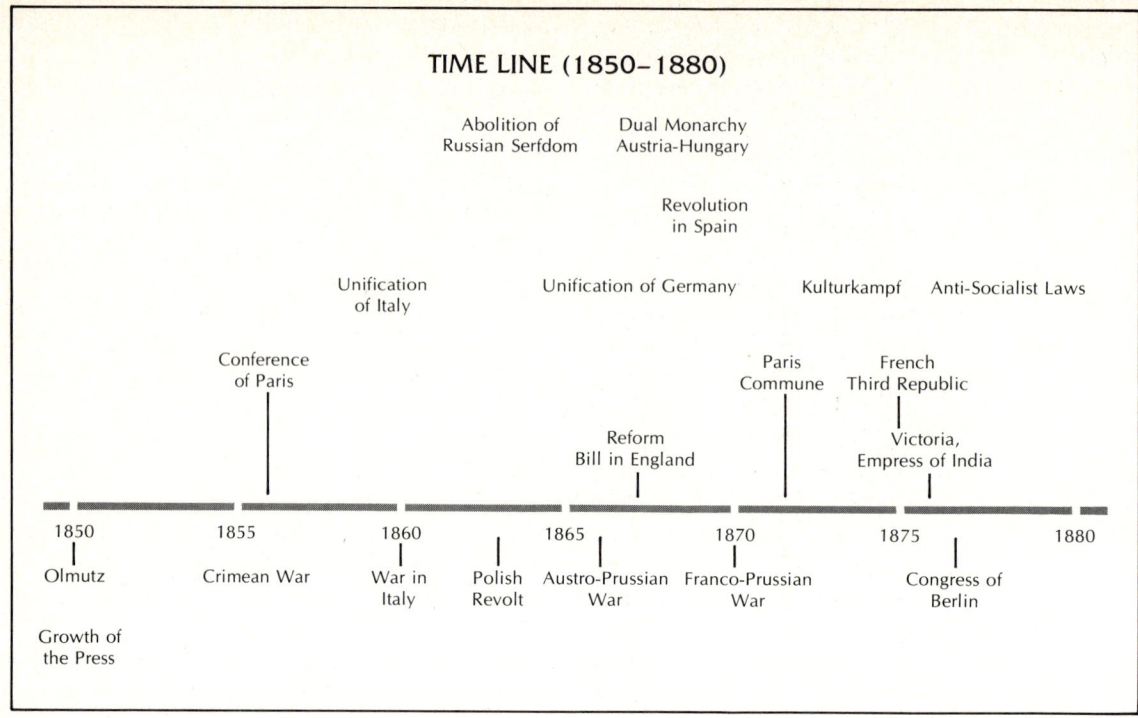

widely enjoyed of the arts in the nineteenth century. Most often presented through an omniscient but anonymous narrator, its most common theme was the conflict between individual feeling (especially romantic love) and the roles and conventions demanded by society. Balzac attempted in his novels to encompass all the "human comedy" (the phrase contrasted with Dante's divine concerns), showing the wealthy, the ambitious, and the poor, soldiers, bankers, politicians, and writers. The novelist analyzed society and individual psychology through concrete types, and sometimes, as with Dickens, challenged the public conscience more effectively than any preacher or politician. Scott's swashbuckling stories of romance and chivalry in an earlier age probed the connection between personal character and social tension in a way that influenced writers throughout Europe. Hugo, Alexander Pushkin, and Alessandro Manzoni promulgated patriotism as they taught their readers of national brotherhood and the need to battle for liberty. Fiction presented the problems of poverty and family and city life, while deftly dissecting the frivolous aristocrat and the self-righteous middle-class merchant. A high proportion of the writer's public was women, and the issues of their lot, of love, dependence, or boredom, were more penetratingly presented in novels—Flaubert's *Madame Bovary* is the outstanding example—than anywhere else. Middle-class culture also had an intimate side, reflected in the popularity of poetry, the lithograph and watercolor, and in the demand for piano music (industrial techniques made the piano, with its iron frame, economical enough to be a common sight in middle-class parlors)—all to be enjoyed in the home and with private emotion.

Romanticism

The themes that run through the artistic work of the period, however, convey a tension. Romanticism's concern with the individual hero or genius—found in the paintings of Delacroix, the plays of Hugo, the poetry of Keats and Shelley—also stressed the artist's personal vision and the capture of a momentary feeling to be set like a precious stone in a carefully wrought piece of music, or poem, or painting (see Plates 51–53). A logically easy step led to the cry of art for art's sake, that the merit of a work lay in its purity, independent of purpose or message. At the same time artists in the nineteenth century were fascinated by society and historical change, seeking the nature of "modernity," in the words of Charles Baudelaire, by extracting "from fashion whatever element it may contain of poetry within history." Behind this lay the desire for an integrated vision encompassing all of life, a coherent understanding that would connect culture to society, economics, and politics. There was a wish as well to integrate the arts themselves; and Baudelaire, a leading poet and critic, writing on the death of Delacroix in 1863, proclaimed it "the spiritual condition of our age that the arts aspire . . . to lend one another new powers."[1]

This reciprocity was part of the vitality of lyric opera, another of the arts to reach its height in the nineteenth century. Opera was first of all theater, combining popular appeal with aristocratic elegance, and performances were important civic events. Elaborate plots, often in historical settings, and flowery poetic texts were taken as seriously as the varied, tuneful, and complex music, the whole further enriched by ballet, colorful sets, and special effects. The two leading operatic composers were Giuseppe Verdi and his exact contemporary Richard Wagner. Verdi was an Italian national hero, whose compelling and often patriotic music, with its paeans to human virtue and its portrayal of every human emotion, remains a staple of opera houses everywhere. Wagner, however, created a kind of revolution in music by carrying the search for an artistic synthesis still further, for he wrote his own texts, often building with patriotic intent on Germanic myths, and identified his major ideas and characters with specific musical themes to create a whole in which voices, instruments, words, and visual experience were inseparable. In every form serious art intended to uplift its audience, morally and intellectually and aesthetically.

Such varied goals and ambitions, diverse audiences, and numerous professional artists led to a further characteristic of nineteenth-century culture, its frequently shifting styles. Romanticism, which emphasized the beauty of nature and the drama of human feeling, gradually gave way by midcentury to a realism that dealt more matter-of-factly with everyday life (see Plates 54–57); and these approaches combined and divided into scores of schools and styles, creating a highly self-conscious art in music, painting, and writing. Innovation was in itself often taken for a sign of genius, and the belief that artists must be in an avant-garde, ahead of their duller public, became a cliché. If society honored the arts, they in turn conveyed more confidence in the future or nostalgia for the preindustrial past than respect for the present. Yet in their universal criticism of the shallowness and materialism of the middle class on which they rested, the artists of the nineteenth century were spokesmen for the inner doubts that were an inherent part of middle-class culture.

Religion

Both the confidence and insecurity of this culture showed in attitudes toward religion. Most thoughtful men appear to have suffered religious shocks, felt both the loss of faith and

---

[1] The comment on Delacroix's death is cited by Morse Peckham, *Beyond the Tragic Vision* (1962), p. 215; the reference to the artist's search for modernity is from an essay on the painter Constantin Guys in Charles Baudelaire, *The Painter of Modern Life and Other Essays,* Jonathan Mayne, tr. and ed. (1965), p. 12.

some religious experience. On the Continent many of the middle class became bitter anticlericals, seeing in the church the barrier to progress. The Abbé Lamennais, one of the most admired of Catholic leaders, broke in the 1830s from a church that would not accept his program for associating the tenets of his faith with democracy. The Protestant David Strauss created a sensation across Europe with his *Life of Jesus,* which appeared in 1835, for it cast erudite doubt on the accuracy of the Gospel, frightening many with the apparent need to choose between historical scholarship and Christ. More typically, especially in England, stern morality and propriety were substituted for theology. Yet men worried terribly that society would lose its direction and individuals their moral purpose without religion. Protestant and Catholic missions combated ignorance and indifference with an intensity not seen since the seventeenth century. The pious became more militant and turned to social action, preaching temperance, teaching reading, and establishing charities. In religion as in the arts, new organization was carrying contemporary confidence and internal conflicts more and more widely.

II. THE POLITICS OF NATIONALISM

Nationalism

Nationalism, looser and more varied than the other ideologies of the nineteenth century, became the most widespread movement, was adopted by the most diverse interests and groups, and proved politically to be the most powerful of all. Why this should be so, why nationalism has assumed such importance remains one of the important questions of modern history. Nationalism's deepest roots, of course, are the shared sense of a common regional and cultural identity, especially as those roots are expressed in custom, language, and religion. Such feelings, which antedate the modern period, may nevertheless have been further stimulated by the advent of increased communication and mobility. Through nationalism they were attached to the modern state, whose power and importance had increased since the state building of the seventeenth century. But it was the experience of the French Revolution and Napoleon that established nationalism as a political force capable of mobilizing popular enthusiasm, of reforming society, of creating seemingly irresistible political movements, and eventually of concentrating unprecedented power in a national state. Nationalism was also a movement of self-conscious modernization, embraced by French people eager to equal the industrial wealth of England and attracting those in other countries who aspired to achieve the prosperity and independence of Britain and France.

Nineteenth-century nationalism was thus a response to social and economic change as well as a political effort to bring middle class and masses together in order to capture established states for new programs and to build new national states where none existed. Like socialists, nationalists stressed the values of community; in most other respects they were, in the first half of the century, usually admirers of liberalism. Although they varied in content and tactics, nationalist movements not only used the latest political devices to hold out promises of freedom, economic growth, and progress but incorporated many of the major cultural trends of the period. In this, Romanticism, with its rejection of the rationalism and universalism of the Enlightenment and the French Revolution, was central. During and after the Revolution, the German intellectuals Johann Gottfried von Herder and Johann Gottlieb Fichte among others urged their countrymen to put aside the values imported from France in favor of a uniquely Germanic culture. And German Romanticism continued to be especially influential in leading Europeans everywhere to value their own traditions and dialects as the expression of national values.

The exploration of ethnic origins took many forms. A group of German scholars made philology a science, and by the 1830s and 1840s an extraordinary revival of national languages occurred across Europe. Gaelic was hailed as the mother tongue of Ireland; in Finland the first public lecture in Finnish marked a break from the dominant Swedish culture; intellectuals in Bohemia began abandoning their customary German to write in Czech. More remarkable still were the number of languages consciously contrived out of local dialects and invented vocabularies. Norwegian became distinct from Danish, Serbian from other Slavic languages, and Slovak from Czech—all literary languages by the 1840s, each the work of but a handful of scholars for whom widespread illiteracy eased the task of establishing a national language.

This fascination with folk culture and a national past fostered the discovery of a special national mission. French historians wrote eloquently of France's call to carry reason and freedom across Europe, and Mazzini proclaimed the destiny of the Third Rome. The poet Adam Mickiewicz, lecturing in Paris, inspired nationalists of many countries with his descriptions of how Poland's history paralleled the life of Christ and had yet to achieve Resurrection. Francis Palacky's pioneering work stressed the role of the Czechs as leaders of the Slavs. Such visions were repeated in poetry and drama, which now blossomed in the native tongue, and justified resistance to alien rule. Cultural nationalism thus served as a weapon of middle-class self-assertion whereby men who felt cramped by social hierarchy, an unsympathetic bureaucracy, and a stagnant economy could win broader support for their own dreams of progress.

In places subject to foreign rule such as Hungary or much of Italy, movements for agricultural improvement, promoted by the liberal aristocracy, became centers of nationalism, and a national tariff, which would enlarge the area of free trade internally and protect native industry, became a nationalist battle cry. Friedrich List, a leading liberal economist, argued from the American example that only behind tariff barriers could a united Germany develop the industry and the vigorous middle class necessary for competitive strength and independence. Everywhere nationalist groups generally demanded public education, more political freedom, and efficient government. Strengthened by its promises of economic growth and its respect for native traditions, nationalism generated political movements of broad appeal, capable of mobilizing popular enthusiasm. Daniel O'Connell's inflammatory speeches won thousands to Young Ireland and its demands for the end of union with Great Britain; by the 1830s he commanded the largest movement of political protest Europe had yet seen. Politically moderate in the 1840s, nationalist movements became more militant and more radical as they benefited from social unrest—a tendency that frightened moderates during the revolutions of 1848. Those revolutions also ran afoul of conflicting national claims, especially in Central Europe. Although most nationalist movements were then defeated, nationalism was not; for its proponents learned greater respect for a strong state and military power, while governments found in nationalist policies a welcome source of popular support. In the following years nationalism would show itself to be a central force in European politics.

The France of Louis Napoleon

In much of Europe the men who held power in 1850 were victors over revolution, and the waves of government repression that followed were hardly surprising. Yet Prussia, where reaction was harsh and the Junkers reasserted

Even official portraits sought to preserve a certain enigma about Napoleon III, both emperor and popular leader.
(Photo: Photographie Bulloz)

their influence, retained the constitution of 1850; and in the Austrian Empire, where the emperor scrapped the constitution, peasants kept their new freedom. But the most daring experiment in combining reform, popular participation, and unchallenged authority was the reign of Louis Napoleon in France. That striking venture in a new political style proved a disturbing influence as an example to others and as a factor in international relations, which became increasingly sensitive to the demands of national prestige and public opinion.

In 1850, with monarchists a majority in the Chamber of Deputies and Louis Napoleon the nation's president, the Second Republic was ruled by its enemies. Napoleon, often at odds with the deputies, continued the appeal to public opinion that had won him the election. When, in the third year of his four-year term, the Chamber rejected a constitutional amendment that would have permitted him a second term, he decided to mount a coup d'état.

He struck on the eve of December 2, 1851—the anniversary of the first Napoleon's coronation as emperor in 1804 and his victory at Austerlitz in 1805. Potential opponents, including 200 deputies, were quickly taken into custody; troops occupied the streets and overran the barricades that rose. At the same time, Napoleon restored universal manhood suffrage, which the conservative Chamber had restricted with a residence requirement aimed at excluding "unstable" workers, and promised a revised constitution. Hundreds were killed, and all told between 20,000 and 30,000 were arrested with nearly 10,000 transported to Algeria. The resistance ended quickly.

Yet Louis Napoleon presented himself as the voice of the people; and three weeks after the coup his actions were ratified by more than 90 percent of the voters in a national plebiscite. The new constitution established a representative assembly, the Corps Législatif, that could debate and vote on but not initiate or amend legislation and a Senate appointed by the president, who was assured a ten-year term and almost full powers. Tired of disorder, Frenchmen were willing to settle for the façade of democracy. Exactly one year after the coup d'état, the Second Republic was transformed into the Second Empire under Emperor Napoleon III, a change even more overwhelmingly supported in another direct vote. Neither plebiscite allowed the citizen to do more than vote yes or no—accepting changes already effected or risking a rejection that might bring any number of unspecified perils in its wake.

The Second Empire found favor with most businessmen and the Catholic Church. It wooed monarchists, local notables, and peasants and played to popular opinion. The regime skillfully used the prefects who headed each *département* to strengthen its authority, and it managed to keep the press in line without official censorship. Throughout Europe people watched with surprise that a government which claimed a democratic mandate could so tightly hold the reins of power, could promise both peace and national glory, and could sponsor programs for social welfare as well as economic growth.

Varied and innovative, the Second Empire has been seen by some historians as a kind of early New Deal and by others as a precursor of Fascism, but all consider it a significant effort to cope with the political implications of a mass industrial society. Napoleon III was influenced by Saint-Simonian socialism, attracted by liberal nationalism, and obsessed by his belief in his own destiny, his Napoleonic star. Alternately decisive and weak, farsighted and misled by vague dreams of glory, he was Napoleon the Little to his opponents, Napoleon the well-meaning to his hard-headed critics, the Emperor to most French.

The decade of the 1850s witnessed an economic boom stimulated at least in part by the policies of the regime, which sought more systematically to foster economic growth than any other government of the period. Tax incentives and laws facilitating the formation of companies with limited liability encouraged investment. The state in addition created special investment funds (of which the Crédit Mobilier was the most famous), paid entrepreneurs a respect they had rarely enjoyed in France, and launched grand public works projects.

One of these was the elaborate rebuilding of Paris, ranging from a vast new sewer and water system to the city's great boulevards and parks, most of which date from this period. A pioneering venture in city planning, these undertakings typified the imperial style. The plans were reviewed by Napoleon III himself, who favored ostentatious and regular structures, and were carried out by his extraordinarily able prefect Georges Haussmann. Slums were cleared, often with painful dislocation for their residents; boulevards, planned for their aesthetic effect and as an aid to traffic, were also expected to make uprisings more difficult; façades often received more attention than the buildings behind them. And the whole project gave rise to rumors of political spoils and speculation. Yet the result was a city healthier and more convenient, envied and imitated throughout the world. The court of Napoleon and Empress Eugénie was brilliant, and French prestige in the arts and sciences (Louis Pasteur achieved his first fame in this period) was never higher. In the Napoleonic tradition the government awarded talent with honors and promotions. The emperor, indefatigable patron and sponsor of educational and social reform, took credit for all this—more in fact than was his due.

Foreign policy, similarly meant to be popular, was marked more by public enthusiasm than by tangible gains. The Crimean War ended with a conference in Paris in 1856, and France's intervention in Italy's war against Austria in 1859 appeared to end in victory. While maintaining good relations with Great Britain, the empire proudly showed its radical roots by supporting the national aspirations not only of Italians but of the Poles who, ever restive, rose against Russian rule in 1863.

By the 1860s, however, the empire's fortunes were changing. Support of Italy had antagonized French Catholics; the annexation of Nice and Savoy, France's reward for that support, had aroused British suspicions; and the French public was troubled by the cost of military glory. Eager to strengthen his domestic support, Napoleon welcomed the chance to intervene in Mexico as an inexpensive venture that would earn Catholic gratitude, but that imperial scheme ended in disaster. England, Spain, and France had sent troops there in 1861 to force payment of foreign debts; and the French remained when the others withdrew, defeating the liberal Mexican government and imposing the Archduke Maximilian of Austria as Emperor of Mexico in 1864. Unexpected Mexican resistance and opposition from the United States forced the French to abandon Maximilian, who was defeated and executed in 1867. Napoleon's vague hope to benefit from the decline of the Ottoman Empire or the expansion of Prussia fared no better when confronted with the clearer and more consistent policies of Bismarck.

The regime was also losing support at home. The church, resentful of the state's energetic intrusion into its traditional spheres of charity and public welfare, was angered by the government's close supervision of its affairs, and Catholics became more militant in their criticism of Napoleon's domestic and foreign policies. A far-reaching tariff agreement with Great Britain in 1860, followed by similar treaties with other countries, was a step toward free trade that appealed to liberal economists but upset many businessmen, particularly those dependent for survival on France's traditionally high tariffs. Laborers wanted more than public works and the government's support for mutual-aid societies. Restrictions of political freedom were increasingly resented, and ideological clashes became more intense.

Aware of these dissatisfied voices, Napoleon III sought new support by gradually making his government more responsive. In 1860 the Corps Législatif was granted permission to present resolutions and to reply to the emperor's annual address. By 1868 freedom of the press and the right of assembly had been reestablished, and the legislature was being allowed to interrogate ministers. The regime established public secondary schools for girls, encouraged the formation of workers' organizations, and acknowledged the right to strike. This liberalism, however, alienated some old supporters without mollifying the empire's critics. In each election the opposition, much of it republican, gained seats until it held nearly half the lower house in 1869. On the first of the year in 1870, a full-fledged parliamentary system was adopted, with ministers responsible to the bicameral assembly and a republican, Émile Ollivier, as prime minister. Eager for public favor, the new administration took a nationalist stand against Prussia in a dispute discussed below, which helped bring about the Franco-Prussian War of 1870 and the end of the Second Empire. The promise of progressive rule and social order, once enough to win middle-class support, was not enough to keep it.

International Relations in the 1850s

Louis Napoleon was not the only ruler to recognize the political rewards of a daring foreign policy. Shortly after the Austrian Empire regained its authority with the defeat of the Hungarian revolution in 1849, Schwarzenberg sought to reassert Austria's influence over the other German states. His chance came when King Frederick William IV of Prussia, moved by the nationalist vision of leading a united Germany, called a meeting of German rulers. Many were reluctant to attend, and Schwarzenberg shrewdly reconvoked the diet of the old German confederation. This put the German states in the dangerous position of choosing between Austrian and Prussian leadership. Austria, with the clear support of Russia, then threatened Prussia with war, citing a number of issues at conflict. Before so grave a challenge, Prussia backed down, and in a conference at Olmütz in 1850, promised to abandon the scheme for a German union under her command. Hapsburg hegemony over Germany seemed assured, reestablished by a fearless minister.

The British foreign secretary also exploited

the advantages of an assertive policy. Henry John Temple, Viscount Palmerston, was a flamboyant aristocrat, frequently at odds with his cabinet colleagues who disapproved of his outspoken sympathy for liberal regimes on the Continent. Often indifferent to procedural niceties, he was shrewdly alert to public opinion. Thus Palmerston saw a national issue in the claims made by one Don Pacifico against the Greek government. An Athenian mob had burned his house because he was a Portuguese Jew, but Pacifico, who was born in Gibraltar, held British citizenship. Palmerston vigorously supported his demands for compensation, sending notes, threats, and finally the British fleet to Greece until an indemnity was paid.

Responsible statesmen in Great Britain were outraged, but Palmerston defended himself in one of the great speeches in the history of the House of Commons. Dramatically he recalled the pride of ancient Romans, who could say, *"Civis Romanus sum,"* "I am a Roman citizen," and know themselves secure throughout their empire. A British subject, Palmerston declared, "in whatever land he may be, shall feel confident that the watchful eye and strong arm of England will protect him against injustice and wrong." To the public at least, Palmerston was vindicated. Like Napoleon III, he recognized the appeal of nationalism.

The Crimean War

The restless ambitions and search for prestige that had come to characterize international relations were a direct cause of the war of France and Great Britain against Russia in 1854–1856. Nothing less would have made so serious a conflict out of the opposing claims to Jerusalem's holy places put forth by Roman Catholic and Greek Orthodox monks in 1851.

France, citing traditions ranging from the Crusades to Richelieu, supported the Latin monks and pressed the Ottoman sultan, whose empire included Jerusalem, to grant them specific privileges. For Louis Napoleon the issue provided a further chance to win Catholic support at home and to upset the balance of power established at the Congress of Vienna. Russia, rising to the defense of the Orthodox faith and anticipating the collapse of the Ottoman Empire, reacted strongly. She demanded a protectorate over Orthodox churches within the empire and in 1853 increased her pressure by occupying the Danubian principalities of Wallachia and Moldavia, lands under Ottoman suzerainty which had last been occupied by Russia in 1848 to put down revolution there. That move increased the involvement of Britain, ever inclined to see a threat to her empire in any Russian expansion. The British encouraged the sultan to resist Russia's demands.

Diplomatic activity reached fever pitch, and Britain and France sent their fleets into the Aegean Sea. Repeatedly negotiations broke down, and in October 1853 the sultan exuberantly declared war on Russia. After Russian forces destroyed an Ottoman fleet, Britain and France declared war on Russia in March 1854, a step greeted with patriotic enthusiasm in London and Paris. Austria, suspicious of a French emperor who supported nationalism in Poland and Italy and unwilling to bear the brunt of a Russian attack, remained neutral. But when Russia withdrew from the Danubian principalities in August 1854, Austria occupied them in turn, leaving the contending powers without a battlefield.

Six months after war was declared, British and French forces landed in the Crimea to continue the fighting against Russia in battles conducted with remarkable incompetence on both sides. Russia could not mobilize or effectively deploy the large armies that made her so feared, and Britain's supply system proved incapable of sustaining hostilities from such a distance. In 1855 the allies welcomed the aid of little Piedmont.

A full year after invading the Crimea, the allied forces finally took Sevastopol. That defeat, threats that Austria and Sweden might enter the war, and the accession of Alexander

The press did much to popularize the Crimean War. This illustration shows Florence Nightingale rushing to the front.
(Photo: The Granger Collection)

II led Russia to sue for peace in December. The final terms were to be set at a European congress in Paris, attended by the belligerents and by Austria and Prussia.

The foreign ministers who met in Paris in 1856 dealt amiably and easily with the specific issues arising from the war. Beyond establishing the status quo ante, the treaty admitted the Ottoman Empire into the European concert, guaranteed her integrity, and greatly reduced Russian influence. Russia ceded some territory at the mouth of the Danube River, surrendered her claims to any protectorate over Christians, and accepted the demilitarization of the Black Sea. Only this last point really rankled.

Napoleon III was unable, however, to launch the full assault on the treaties of 1815 he wished for; Austria and Great Britain distrusted his interest in reshaping Europe. Although the emperor wanted to include it, the question of Polish independence never got on the agenda. The Italian question on the other hand was discussed—the only concession Piedmont won, but even that was enough to produce patriotic outbursts in Italy and terror in Austria. The issue of the Danubian principalities with its implications of Balkan nationalism also frightened Austria. The possibility that the two provinces might be joined was too divisive to be settled then, but by 1858 they were in effect united, the basis for a Rumanian national state.

In many respects the congress had behaved liked its predecessors, but it marked an important change in the prominence of nationalism, even when formally ignored, and in the demise of that alliance of Austria, Prussia, and Russia that had preserved European peace and conservatism for so long. Russia and Austria had cooperated in opposing nationalism and revolution through the crises of 1848, but competition between them for influence in the Balkans now became one of the facts of European politics. Indeed, Russia now counted for less in purely European matters and found herself turning with gratitude to signs of sympathy from Napoleon III. The fact that the congress met in Paris rather than Vienna indicated the altered prestige of the European states. The old balance of power, the old concert of conservative nations, the old diplomacy of European aristocrats who largely ignored public sentiment—all this had been shaken.

Almost 500,000 soldiers died in the Crimean War, the highest toll of any European conflict between the Napoleonic Wars and World War I. Two-thirds of the casualties were Russian, and two-thirds of all losses resulted from sickness and bad care. Yet the outbreak of war produced a surge of enthusiasm no government could ignore. The diplomacy that led to it and the way it was conducted were shaped by concern for national prestige, and the parades of magnificently uniformed soldiers, like the heroic stories reported by an aggressive journalism for an eager public, underscored the political importance of the war. In those terms France, Piedmont, and Great Britain all gained from it; the Ottoman Empire, under Western pressure, began to adopt the modernizing institutions of the West; and Russia, sobered by defeat, launched an era of fundamental reform unequaled since the days of Peter the Great. In Italy and Germany the way was opening for still more drastic changes.

The Unification of Italy

Since the French Revolution the sense of common nationality had grown stronger among Germans and among Italians, supported by common experience and economic change. That nationalism, exemplified by Mazzini, was fostered by numerous organizations, defined in propaganda that ranged from clandestine pamphlets to major literature, and expressed in many a local uprising. Especially among the middle class, nationalist feeling became intense, the core of campaigns for representative government, efficient administration, a dependable system of justice, and a national economy. And the regrouping of domestic forces after 1848, which gave greater prominence to the middle class, as well as the altered international situation following the Crimean War provided new opportunities for the nationalist movements of Central Europe.

In Italy the revolutions of 1848 established that nationalism was a powerful political force. Their failure made it equally clear that separate revolts were not enough to overcome the arms of Austria, the main opponent of Italian unification. The Mazzinian program was thus cast in doubt, but so were old dreams of papal leadership in the national cause. Of the several Italian states, only Piedmont, despite having been twice defeated by the Austrians, maintained an independent foreign policy, still flew the tricolor of Italian nationalism, and kept her constitution.

Piedmont had other strengths. Her aristocracy, narrow in outlook, Catholic, and conservative, was dedicated to the service of the state; and her monarch, Victor Emmanuel II, though no liberal, ruled with a parliament and longed for a patriotic war against Austria. Although a small state, the kingdom had a tradition of military strength and bureaucratic rectitude. More recently her government had encouraged commerce and the building of railroads and had limited the privileges of the Catholic Church, setting Piedmont on the liberal course established earlier in Great Britain, France, and Belgium.

These policies acquired firmer purpose in 1852, when Count Camillo Cavour became prime minister. A member of the Piedmontese aristocracy, well traveled in France and England, Cavour was a gentleman-farmer who believed in economic and scientific progress, representative government with limited suffrage, the rule of law, and religious tolerance. Nationalism he understood primarily as an avenue to modernization, and he found in free trade, sound finances, and railroads a power that could remake Piedmont.

Cavour pursued his liberal goals with tactical brilliance, skillfully using newspapers and parliamentary debate to mold public opinion. With some disloyalty to the cabinet of which he was a member, he suddenly formed a new parliamentary coalition of the left center and right center, a base of power from which he dominated both king and parliament from 1852 until his death in 1861. In that brief time he established himself as one of the outstanding statesmen of the century.

Piedmont's internal strength was Cavour's first concern, but he also sought to make his state the center of Italy's resurgence, the Risorgimento.[2] He welcomed exiles from other parts of the peninsula, encouraged the nationalist press, and sought every opportunity for symbolic gestures of patriotism. He was aided in this by the Italian National Society, one of whose founders was Daniele Manin, the president of the short-lived Venetian republic in 1848. The National Society propagandized for Italian unity under Piedmont's king and established secret committees in most of the cities of Italy. Its members were predominantly liberal aristocrats, local lawyers, and professors. In calling for Italian unity, they freely borrowed and effectively used the ideas of Mazzini, but this idealism was combined with hard-headed insistence on the need for international alliances and military force to defeat Austria. Economic liberalism largely replaced more generous and vaguer social theories, and talk of revolution did not lessen the commitment to a national state that would protect private property, persecute no one, and maintain social order.

Most of all Cavour depended on astute foreign policy. He had pushed for Piedmont's participation in the Crimean War and was rewarded with the discussion of the Italian question at the Congress of Paris. Using his state's enhanced international position, British sympathy, and Napoleon III's ambition, he hoped to gather the forces to defeat Austria.

This hope turned on Louis Napoleon, whose Italian connections, nationalist leanings, and restless search for prestige Cavour assiduously played upon. He was aided by liberal sympathy throughout Western Europe and even by Italian revolutionaries, whose activities helped convince many that an Italy unliberated would remain a dangerous source of European instability.

At last, in July 1858, Cavour and Napoleon III met secretly at the little spa of Plombières in eastern France to plot war against Austria. They agreed that Piedmont would acquire all of nothern Italy and that the grand duchy of Tuscany would be enlarged and become the Kingdom of Central Italy. These two large states and the Kingdom of the Two Sicilies would then form a confederation under the pope. France would receive Nice and Savoy, thus strengthening her border, and Napoleon's cousin Prince Jérôme would marry Victor Emmanuel's reluctant fifteen-year-old daughter. In his desire to tie his throne to the legitimate monarchs of Europe, Napoleon III shared the old-fashioned concerns of Louis Philippe and Napoleon I, but he also hoped to satisfy nationalism while using monarchy as a bulwark against radicalism. The arrangement contrived at Plombières would provide multiple openings for Bonapartist influence while preventing the formation of a unified Italian state that could become a threat to France. The plan, too delicately balanced to be practical, sought cautious ends through cynical daring.

---

[2] Risorgimento, now the historian's label for the whole period of Italian unification, was a term meaning "resurgence" often used by nationalists and made the title of a liberal newspaper that Cavour helped to found and edit.

MAP 24.1: THE UNIFICATION OF ITALY 1859–1920

After Plombières Cavour encouraged the nationalist demonstrations spreading throughout Italy but tried to prevent the kind of outbreak that might cause Napoleon to change his mind. While Cavour hunted for an excuse for war, Great Britain pressured for peace and France hesitated. But Austria, watching young Lombards and Venetians escape conscription by streaming to Piedmont as volunteers, determined to end the nationalist threat once and for all. She sent Piedmont an ultimatum so strong that Cavour needed only to reply with cautious dignity in order to have his war. On April 29, 1859, Austria invaded Piedmont, and France went to the rescue of a small state attacked by her giant neighbor.

The rapid movement of large French armies was impressive, but thereafter the war was fought with little tactical brilliance on either side. In June the Austrians were seriously defeated at Magenta, in Lombardy; but the Battle of Solferino, three weeks later, was as indecisive as it was bloody. As the Austrians retreated to the fortresses controlling the Lombard plain, Napoleon lost his taste for war; and rather than face further losses, a long siege, the danger that Prussia would come to Austria's aid, and discontent at home, he unilaterally agreed to a truce. The emperors of France and Austria met at Villafranca in July to establish the terms of peace, which included ceding Lombardy but not Venezia to Piedmont and maintaining the other Italian states as before (see Map 24.1).

The Formation of the Italian Kingdom

Those states, however, had not survived the excitement of a national war. Gentle revolutions accompanied the march of Piedmontese troops throughout northern Italy. When local patriots gathered in the streets, the dukes of Modena, Parma, and Tuscany simply fled. In these areas and in part of the Papal States (the Romagna), supporters of Cavour—usually members of the National Society—assumed dictatorial powers in provisional governments that adopted Piedmontese laws and currency and called for elections to representative assemblies. Thus the terms of the Villafranca truce could not be carried out. The provisional regimes cautiously went their way, carefully maintaining order, and after a few months arranged plebiscites—a device Napoleon could hardly reject—on the question of annexation to Piedmont. Italians trooped to the polls with bands playing and flags waving, peasants behind their lord and workers with their guilds. The result was as overwhelming as the plebiscites of France; and Victor Emmanuel quietly accepted the request to rule from the Alps to Rimini, on the Adriatic. The province of Savoy and the city of Nice were turned over to France.

The extension of the Piedmontese state was a triumph of moderate liberals with which more democratic nationalists were not altogether content, and sputtering revolts in Sicily gave them a chance to lead a different sort of Risorgimento. Former Mazzinians gathered guns in Genoa and laid plans for an expedition which Cavour dared neither support nor oppose. The leader of this daring venture was Giuseppe Garibaldi. Exiled for his Mazzinian activity in the 1830s, Garibaldi had spent ten years fighting for democratic causes in South America, returning to Italy in time to take part in the wars of 1848. He had directed the heroic defense of the Roman Republic in 1849 and led the most effective corps of volunteers fighting for Piedmont in 1859. One of the most popular figures in Italy, he set sail for Sicily one night early in May 1860 with a thousand men, mainly middle-class youths from Lombardy, Venezia, and the Romagna.

No event in the nineteenth century so captured the popular imagination everywhere as that daring venture. The Expedition of the Thousand was like some ancient epic come to life in an industrial age: untrained men, wearing the red shirts Garibaldi had adopted in South

America, fought with bravery and discipline, enthusiastically supported in the countryside. Garibaldi's tactics confused and defeated the Bourbon generals, despite their far larger and better-equipped forces. In two weeks the Red Shirts occupied Palermo and within two months all of Sicily except Messina. Volunteers flocked from all over Italy, and money was collected for them in the streets, at theaters, and at special meetings from New York to Stockholm.

Garibaldi proclaimed his loyalty to Victor Emmanuel, but he was equally open about his distrust of Cavour, who in turn feared the undiplomatic brashness as well as the republican and radical sentiments of the Garibaldians. When in August Garibaldi sailed across the strait and landed on the Italian mainland, declaring Rome and not just Naples to be his goal, Cavour determined to recapture control.

He encouraged uprisings in the Papal States and then sent Piedmontese troops into the region in the name of order. Carefully skirting the area around Rome, they moved south to meet Garibaldi. On September 18, between lines of suspicious men, Giuseppe Garibaldi and Victor Emmanuel rode out to shake hands. Piedmontese appointees quickly replaced the officials named by Garibaldi, who added to his legend by disdaining all proffered honors and quietly sailing with a bag of seed for his island retreat on Caprera. Plebiscites in the newly

---

The handshake of Victor Emmanuel and Garibaldi, which sealed the unification of Italy as their armies met in 1860, became a favorite subject for illustrations of the Risorgimento. This engraving is English.
(Photo: Culver Pictures)

conquered provinces produced an almost unanimous vote for union, and in March 1861 the Kingdom of Italy was proclaimed before the first Italian parliament. The moderate liberalism of Cavour had triumphed.

Political and Economic Problems 1860–1876

Cavour's death shortly afterward was the first of many setbacks the new kingdom suffered, though the problems Italy now faced were in any case less susceptible to political solutions. The great differences among the regions of Italy seemed to argue for a decentralized federal system, but wartime conditions and fear of separatism prompted the government simply to extend Piedmontese administration and law. Too often, especially in the south, officials with an alien accent applying strange laws seemed almost foreign occupiers. Southern poverty and traditions of local patronage and corruption hobbled the new regime. Outbursts of brigandage in the south, occasionally supported by exiled Bourbons, the papacy, and Spanish Carlists, were an inchoate social protest which the new government met with military suppression, expending more lives than in all the wars of the Risorgimento.

Thrilled to have accomplished so much, Italian patriots could not accept the exclusion of Rome and Venice from united Italy, but both were international problems. Catholics throughout the world, convinced that papal independence required territorial sovereignty, opposed the annexation of Rome, which Napoleon III was pledged to protect; and Austrian troops, massed in Venezia, threatened the new Italian state. Within Italy the constant agitation over Rome, sometimes led by Garibaldi, weakened and divided the government.

The new nation acquired Venezia as a by-product of the Austro-Prussian war of 1866 when both powers offered Venezia to Italy—Prussia as the reward for an alliance and Austria, at the last minute, in return for Italian neutrality. Italy honored her prior pledge to Prussia and went to war, suffering defeats on land and at sea off the Adriatic island of Lissa in the first naval engagement in Europe between ironclads. Prussia's quick victory ended the war, however, and the province of Venezia (without the Tyrol, though Garibaldi had won some of the few Italian victories there) was added to Italy. Rome, all that was left of papal territory, was annexed when French troops withdrew during the Franco-Prussian War of 1870. Italy had gained her capital.

These were impressive achievements, even if they were less glorious than patriots had hoped, but they brought other difficulties to the fore. Italy passed a Law of Guarantees, assuring the full independence of the Vatican and providing an annual indemnity, but it was rejected by Pius IX, who declared himself a prisoner, refused to recognize the Italian state, and forbade Catholics to take part in national elections. Conflict with the church was a source of dangerous division, and Italy's governing class remained seriously isolated from the country at large. Because of the high property qualifications in Piedmont's constitution, now extended to all Italy, only 500,000 Italians out of a population of more than 25 million were able to vote; and this exclusion of the lower classes coupled with the abstention of Catholics made the subtleties of parliamentary conflict seem unreal.

Italy was poor, overwhelmingly agricultural, and the heir to generations of retrogressive policies; she had no coal or iron, and three-quarters of her population was illiterate. With liberal conviction the Italian government assumed the debts of the annexed states, accepted enormous military costs, and sought to balance the annual budget. Despite taxes among the highest in Europe, Italy necessarily continued to lag in schools, railways, and roads. The extension of Piedmontese law brought with it the confiscation of lands held by thousands of monasteries; but they commanded low prices because they were sold quickly, and they went to the wealthy rather than the peasants, who were supposed to benefit. Free trade within the nation and the lower Piedmontese tariffs brought many long-term benefits but instant distress to hundreds of small producers. For millions of artisans and peasants suffering the dislocations of war and social change, few tangible benefits followed from replacing reactionary dukes with a liberal national state.

Steadfastly Italy's leaders tried to foster the process of modernization. When the old Cavourians lost office to men of the left center in 1876, the change so dramatic to politicians was barely discernible to most Italians. A new generation of equally isolated middle-class leaders took charge in a country that was full of disappointments. But Italy was nonetheless free and reasonably stable, her national income rising. Her parliamentary institutions would be more severely tested later.

The Unification of Germany

The unification of Germany was completed a decade after Italy's, the work of Prussia, noted since the eighteenth century for efficient institutions that enabled her to wring impressive military strength from limited resources (see Map 24.2). Like Piedmont, Prussia began the 1850s with a new constitution at home but forced to accept Austrian terms abroad. Prussia was, however, a major European power with a long-recognized claim to economic and political leadership among the German states.

After Olmütz Austria appeared to dominate German affairs. But by 1853 all German states except those directly tied to Austria had joined the Zollverein; and Prussia's position had clearly changed by 1859, with Austria defeated in Italy and Napoleon III agreeing to a sudden truce in part at least out of fear of Prussia. Thus the Hohenzollern monarchy was the focus of nationalist opposition to Napoleon that spread through the German states. The German National Society, founded in the Rhineland in 1859 in direct imitation of the Italian National Society, propagandized vigorously for a Germany united under Prussia, citing her military power, the rapid industrialization underway in both the Rhineland and Prussia, and the liberal possibilities in Prussia's constitution.

Within Prussia the rule of William I, which began in 1858, was also a turning point.[3] After a long period of reaction in which the press had been muzzled, public meetings repressed, many political leaders imprisoned, and the upper house of the legislature dominated by officials and landowners, William permitted such restrictions to be eased and turned his attention to improving the army.

The new era opened with a constitutional crisis. General Albrecht von Roon was appointed minister of war, and Helmuth von Moltke, his chief of staff, proposed a major military reorganization that would double the army's size and provide it with extensive new equipment. The plan won William's support, but the lower house of the legislature, in which liberals had gained an unexpected majority, rejected it. Although the constitution of 1850 allowed universal male suffrage, it avoided democracy by dividing voters into three classes according to the taxes they paid, giving the two wealthier classes as many representatives as the third class, to which the overwhelming majority of the electorate belonged. In addition, the king had the right to veto any legislation and to appoint the ministers he chose. Designed to assure conservative dominance, the three-class system had the unexpected effect of magnifying the voice of new industrial wealth, and the majority of the Landtag was now prepared to challenge the monarch head on.

---

[3] William I (1796–1888) became regent in 1858, when his brother Frederick William was adjudged insane, and king on his brother's death in 1861.

MAP 24.2: THE UNIFICATION OF GERMANY

Liberals distrusted Prussian militarism and the Junkers who dominated the army, preferring a citizen militia; they also opposed increased expenditures. To William and his advisers, royal authority in the form of control of the army and the budget was at stake. As the conflict dragged on, they went ahead with the reorganization despite promises not to, paying for it out of general funds. Elections in 1862, however, only strengthened the opposition, which firmly insisted that the Prussian government be responsible to the legislature. William, calling on God and conscience, threatened abdication and then hesitantly named Otto von Bismarck his chief minister.

Bismarck was a Junker, better educated than

many, whose pride of caste and reactionary views were resented by liberals and whose intensity and imagination made him seem as erratic and dangerous as Napoleon III to most conservatives. For thirty years all of them would have to live with his stinging sarcasm, bruising contempt, and brilliance. Like Cavour, he saw more clearly than his king that nationalism could be used against revolution and made foreign policy the central concern as well as the justification of his program.

In the conflict with the Landtag, Bismarck gave the king firm support. He lectured the deputies on Prussia's national role and the chances too often missed in the past. If Germans looked to Prussia, it was because of her powerful army, not because of any liberal institutions; and he added, in the most famous statement he ever uttered, that "the great questions of the day will not be settled by speeches and majority decisions—that was the mistake of 1848 and 1849—but by blood and iron." He dissolved parliament and applied heavy government pressure in the subsequent elections. But despite conservative gains, the opposition increased still more. Bismarck then shifted tactics. He encouraged whatever divisions within parliament he could find, convoked it as little as possible, and ignored it whenever he could. He bribed the press with money and access to news, and he badgered and closed opposing papers. He made promotions in the civil service and judiciary dependent upon unquestionable loyalty to the government. Then, confident of the army and bureaucracy, Bismarck proceeded to spend funds and collect taxes without parliamentary authorization.

He sought to justify this defiance of Prussia's elected representatives through his foreign policy. He blocked Austria's continuing effort to reorganize the German Confederation, and his threat that perhaps the German Diet could be elected by universal suffrage stunned conservatives with its radicalism and liberals with its cynicism. While underscoring the limitations of Austria as a leader of any German national venture, he sought to win Russian friendship away from the Hapsburgs. When Russia repressed a Polish uprising in 1863 with such severity that Austria, France, and Britain joined in protest, Prussia supported the tsar. Renewed conflict over Schleswig and Holstein in the same year provided further opportunities for Prussian gains. The Danish king outraged German nationalists by attempting to annex Schleswig and to extend his authority over Holstein. But Prussia thwarted any independent policy by the German Diet and persuaded Austria to join in war against Denmark in January 1864. Bismarck then foiled efforts at an international conference until the Danes were defeated and then pressed for a plan whereby Schleswig was placed under Prussian administration and Holstein, surrounded by Prussian troops, under Austrian. The awkward arrangement, a potent source of contention between Austria and Prussia, was clearly impermanent.

Friction with Austria increased almost daily, and Bismarck prepared for war. He dangled visions of territorial gains along the Rhine before Napoleon III, won Italy's support by promising her Venezia, and gained Russia's assurance of neutrality. Both Austria and Prussia were already mobilizing when Austria convened the Holstein diet to discuss the duchy's unclear future. Bismarck denounced the move as a violation of their understandings, and Prussian troops marched into Holstein in June 1866.

Austria won the support of most of the German Confederation, but Prussia forced Hanover to surrender within two weeks. Three Prussian armies swept into Bohemia, and at the Battle of Sadowa, Austria suffered overwhelming defeat. The Austro-Prussian War lasted just seven weeks. Expert opinion had predicted a long fight, but Prussia, well equipped and ready, applied the lessons of the American Civil War, using railroads and telegraph to move with a speed for which Austria was unprepared.

Many Prussian conservatives had been

shocked at Bismarck's belligerent treatment of Austria, but now they were eager to avenge Olmütz and to make heavy territorial demands on Austria. Yet against the wishes of his king and generals, Bismarck insisted that the Hapsburg monarchy be treated leniently; Austria surrendered no territory. But Prussia's gains elsewhere changed the face of Europe; she annexed Hanover, Nassau, Electoral Hesse, and Frankfurt, all of which had sided with Austria in the quarrel, and then established a confederation of North German states under her leadership. Austria was excluded from the new union, and the South German states agreed to a military alliance with Prussia on being told of Napoleon's hope (which Bismarck had encouraged) of some territorial compensation to balance Prussia's gains.

The North German Confederation

The constitution of the North German Confederation was in itself a triumph of Bismarckian policy. The basis for a new national state, it left member states free to regulate their local affairs, but joined together through a bicameral federal parliament. Its upper house, the Bundesrat, was composed of forty-three delegates sent in varying numbers from the separate states, with Prussia's seventeen more than the one-third necessary for a veto. The lower house, the Reichstag, was elected by universal male suffrage. A political structure that seemed to protect local interests while tending toward democracy assured, in practice, the dominance of Prussia and the subordination of parliament. The confederation's hereditary chief executive was the king of Prussia, and he appointed the chancellor, who, responsible to no one else, shared with him full authority over foreign and military affairs. The armies of the separate states were combined under Prussian leadership.

In Prussia herself elections held during the war had strengthened the conservatives in the Landtag. The liberals still maintained a majority, but they could hardly reject Bismarck's amazing achievements. After Prussia's victories, the Landtag voted a bill of indemnity, retroactively legalizing the taxes and expenditures Bismarck had imposed. Unwilling to appeal to the masses, the liberals were as soundly defeated as Austria. Encouraged that the new Reichstag would after all be elected by universal male suffrage, impressed that many conservatives were indignant that Bismarck would accept any parliament at all, and grateful to have a strong national state, most of them joined a new (more pro-Bismarckian) party, the National Liberals. Conservatives unwilling to accept the chancellor's gestures toward constitutionalism countered by banding together as the Free Conservatives. Prussian politics focused on Bismarck; and Germany was set on Bismarck's course, directed by men determined to strengthen the state and to maintain its autonomy.

The North German Confederation represented an enormous expansion of Prussian power and a great step toward unification. While the South German states preserved their separate status, no German nationalist could think Bismarck's federation a satisfactory or permanent solution. Instead, it seemed that the unification of Germany, like that of Italy, was to be achieved in stages, in part through diplomacy. There were other reasons, too, for stopping half-way. North Germany, Protestant and more industrial than the south, offered a sound base for the kind of Germany Bismarck envisioned, as different from the largely agricultural and Catholic south as Naples was from northern Italy. With their own rich cultural traditions and ancient dynasties (which still viewed the Hohenzollerns of Prussia as upstarts), Germany's southern states looked more to Vienna and Paris than to Berlin and remained suspicious of Prussia's militarism and cold efficiency.

Overcoming these differences was a central task of the North German Confederation, and

Bismarck found the threat from France his strongest weapon. Napoleon wished to acquire Luxembourg (all parties appeared willing), and Bismarck manipulated the emperor's designs into a crisis that produced protests against cession to France of an "ancient German land" and brought France a serious diplomatic defeat. But neither such maneuvers nor the benefits of the Zollverein overcame southern resistance. A majority of the southern delegates elected to the Zollverein, led by Bavaria and Württemberg, opposed any extension of its influence, any further "Prussianization" of Germany. Something more than elections and trade were necessary if Germany was to be quickly united.

The Franco-Prussian War

That something more was war with France. Historians once hotly disputed who was to blame for that war and whether it was "necessary." New research and changing perspectives have lessened the controversy; the war was wanted by Bismarck but first declared by France, the result of nationalism in both nations more than long-range calculation. Spain's provisional government, seeking a replacement for Queen Isabella II, forced to abdicate in 1868, settled on Leopold, prince of Hohenzollern-Sigmaringen, who under heavy French pressure finally declined. Eager to win public favor and at last score a point against Bismarck, the French government pressed on. In a famous interview at the western German spa of Ems, where William I was taking the baths, the French ambassador demanded that the Prussian king give public guarantees that the Hohenzollern candidacy would never be brought forward again. The king refused and later telegraphed a report to Bismarck of the difficult though formally correct interview. Bismarck carefully edited the Ems dispatch to make French demands seem even more imperious and the king's refusal even more abrupt, and released it to the press. Bismarck, Roon, and Moltke correctly assumed that war would follow. The French government, which could hardly afford further humiliations, responded to the patriotic fury it had helped ignite and declared war on July 19, 1870.

France hoped for support from Italy and Austria but had failed to establish any formal agreement with either, and they remained neutral. The French army, more formidable than Austria's had been, possessed modern equipment in some respects superior to the German, but the forces of the confederation were more carefully prepared and far more decisively led. By August the Germans had pushed through Alsace and encircled a French army at Metz. With heavy losses on both sides, another French army, attempting to relieve Metz, was severely defeated at Sedan in September, and there Napoleon III surrendered and was taken prisoner. Major fighting was over, but French resistance continued. Paris, quickly surrounded by German troops, held out under a long siege, and a provisional French government continued efforts to maintain a French army in the field. For the rest of the year, German troops were subjected to a kind of guerrilla harassment, and an armistice came only at the end of January, when Paris capitulated.

The brief war had profound effects. A German national state was created. The Second Empire fell; and after bitter internal conflict, the Third Republic was established in France. Even more than defeat itself, the harsh terms of peace—France was required to pay an indemnity of 5 billion francs and to cede Alsace and Lorraine—assured that the enmity between France and Germany would be a central fact of international relations.

The Second Reich 1871–1879

The decision to annex Alsace-Lorraine was primarily a military one, intended to provide Germany with the strongest possible fortifications

The halls of Versailles ring as Prussian soldiers hail the proclamation making King William emperor of Germany.
(Photo: The Granger Collection)

in case of future conflicts with France. But it also responded to a popular demand of German nationalists, and Bismarck still needed their support. His major concern was to complete the unification of Germany, and well before the final French surrender, he began intricate and difficult negotiations with each of the South German states. They had joined in fighting France with a mixture of enthusiasm and fear, but it took concessions, secret funds, threats, and all his skill before Bismarck got the German states, Prussia's generals, and the king to accept his terms for permanent union. When they did, William I was crowned German kaiser (emperor) in the Hall of Mirrors at Versailles on January 18, 1871, his seventy-fourth birthday.

With modifications the constitution of the North German Confederation was extended to all the new nation. The upper house of parliament, the Bundesrat, received increased powers, including the right to declare war, but many domestic affairs were reserved to the twenty-five states that made up the Reich and special privileges were granted Baden, Bavaria, and Württemberg. There was no question, however, that the great new nation created by the popular will, Bismarck's ability, and Prussian arms would be dominated by Prussia.

The Second Reich was from its inception a powerful nation.[4] Germany in 1871 was already

---

[4] The old Holy Roman Empire was patriotically honored as the first Reich.

more populous than France, and her rate of demographic growth was the fastest Europe had ever known. Less than half the population was engaged in agriculture after the first decade of unification, and Germany's industrial production increased at an astounding rate. Because she had developed later than Great Britain and more rapidly than France, her industrial equipment was more modern. The French indemnity added to the available capital, and the government aided industrial efficiency by making heavy investments in railroads, granting tax privileges, establishing tariffs, and encouraging the formation of large combines, the famous German cartels. German universities became the leading ones of Europe in the application of scientific method to every discipline.

Such rapid growth was disruptive in Germany, as elsewhere. Her nationalists stressed the traditional values of the *Volk,* the people, and nowhere were materialistic, commercial, and urban values more intensely attacked than in industrial Germany. This conflict could stimulate achievements as lasting as the work of Richard Wagner, who combined daring musical innovations with old Teutonic myth, and individual genius with mere prejudice; but it increased the dangerous tensions among powerful conservative circles, a growing but defensive middle class, and workers increasingly aware of their distinct interests. The great achievements of the German state rested on its ability to satisfy industrialists and appeal to traditional nationalists by operating democratic institutions through autocratic means.

Bismarck, who wanted not to offend local interests and who left the army essentially autonomous, worried very much about the internal dangers to the new nation. He therefore sought to establish the supremacy of the state by moving against two apparently vulnerable groups likely to oppose Prussian policies: first the Catholic Church and then the socialist party.

Rather grandiosely named the Kulturkampf ("Battle of the Civilizations"), the conflict with the Catholic Church centered on new laws requiring state approval of church appointments, state supervision of Catholic education even in seminaries, and the abolition of religious orders. Many of these measures were part of the secularization common throughout Europe, but others were an effort at "germanization" (Poland and Alsace were heavily Catholic) intended to weaken anti-Prussian sentiment. Passed in the period from 1871 to 1875, they came at a time when the church appeared intransigently opposed to modern society, and they won the support of National Liberals, many conservative Lutherans, and much of the left.

Yet the Kulturkampf was not a great success. The severity of the laws and the harshness with which they were carried out made martyrs of many a priest and nun. A majority of bishops lost their sees, and many went into exile. Catholics rallied to their church, and many others began to fear so intrusive a state; the Catholic Center party steadily gained votes in Reichstag elections. Thus when the more flexible Leo XIII became pope, in 1878, Bismarck sought an understanding with the Vatican. Many of the laws most offensive to Catholics were allowed to lapse, and the battle of the civilizations subsided as the state turned toward the repression of other enemies.

Socialism did not offend Bismarck either in its attacks on laissez faire or in its emphasis upon the social role of the state, and he had gotten on well with the leading German socialist of the 1860s, Ferdinand Lassalle. But as socialists sought to win a mass following, founding the Social Democratic party in 1875, their attacks on autocracy, the military, and nationalism seemed more dangerous. In 1878 two attempts to assassinate the kaiser (neither by a socialist) gave Bismarck his chance, and he called for laws repressing socialism. The Reichstag refused, and the election of 1878 was fought largely on that issue, with conservatives and the Center party gaining some seats. As a result the Reichstag banned most socialist publications, prohibited socialist meetings except under police supervision, and forbade public collections for socialist causes. The Social Democrats were in effect forced underground, and another important element of society learned to hate and fear the German state. Within the Reichstag, however, socialists remained free to speak, and their party gained support with every election.

The abandonment of the Kulturkampf and the offensive against socialism were part of a larger realignment in German politics. Having preserved their strength, the conservatives and Catholics who had resisted the new Germany came to accept her, while liberals, torn between Bismarck's accomplishments and their old principles, grew weaker. Economic troubles, the effect of both the nation's rapid growth and a European agricultural depression, also helped forge a pro-Bismarck coalition more durable than any based on persecution. In 1879 demands for a higher tariff led the chancellor to propose and the Reichstag to grant strong protective tariffs on both manufactured and agricultural goods. The majority supporting that measure included Junker landlords, Rhineland industrialists, and the more nationalist liberals, split once again from their doctrinaire comrades. Bismarck was finding a formula to draw together the most powerful interest groups in German society in support of a conservative state under his strong leadership.

III. RESHAPING ESTABLISHED STATES

The benefits of a strong state, sought through unification in Italy and Germany, were expected in established nations as well. For these countries too military efficiency was an ultimate test, and the defeats of Russia in 1856 and Austria in 1859 and 1866 were interpreted as proof of the need for drastic governmental change. But making the state stronger and more efficient in less developed countries required measures that often threatened the very groups then in power. That dilemma tailored the pattern of reform in each country, leading to durable compromises that took different form in Russia, Austria, and Spain. In Great Britain and France, on the other hand, neither national unity nor effective institutions were at issue; but in those countries, where the middle class had achieved dominance, conflict centered rather on who else should participate in and benefit from the policies of the state—questions that brought civil war and a republic to France, further reform and modern political parties to Britain.

Russia 1855–1881

Immediately after the Crimean War and only a year after assuming the throne, Tsar Alexander II issued a manifesto promising improvements in justice, education, and employment. Goals once envisaged only by liberals were adopted in defeat by the Russian autocrat. The critical reform was the abolition of serfdom. Discreetly but firmly the nobles were told to bring the institution to an end from above rather than wait for its destruction from below.

Months passed in silence while secret committees drafted proposals and most nobles dragged their feet. Intellectuals had argued against serfdom for generations, and peasants spoke through more frequent uprisings. Economic developments—a money economy, foreign trade, new industry—had further weakened the old system. Yet landowners could always argue against taking revolutionary risks just yet. Only in 1861 was serfdom abolished—by the tsar's decree.

The law of 1861 gave legal rights to more than 22 million serfs, providing in general that peasant farmers should gain title to the land they worked or its equivalent. They could either contract a long-term debt to the state, which would in turn compensate the owner, or accept one-quarter of that land free and clear. During an interim of two years, they would continue to owe all former obligations to their masters.

In practice the lord usually kept the best land for himself and through inflated land prices received additional payment for the loss of his serf labor. On the whole former serfs found themselves with less land than they needed to support their families and to make their payments; and provisions for pasture, forest, and water rights were rarely satisfactory. Thus agricultural labor, usually for the former master, remained a necessity for subsistence.

The law of 1861 also gave important responsibilities to the *mir*, or village commune, whose elected officials assigned plots, determined the crops to be planted, and paid taxes to the state for which each plot of land was assessed by the *mir*. The former serf could not leave the commune or sell his land without permission; and even after leaving, he remained liable for taxes. In this way the state made sure that the debts owed to it would be met and that the new peasant society would maintain structures with which the state could deal. Indeed the commune, which came to be considered a characteristic Slavic institution, tended to resist change in favor of traditional ways; similarly few lords really became modern farmers. But this conservatism to some degree eased the adaptation to a social change immense in itself.

A few years later the government liberated all state peasants—nearly 25 million—on more favorable terms, granting on the average more land at a lower price than that available to former serfs. Still sharply segregated from more privileged members of society, with special laws and punishments, including flogging, applicable only to them, peasants remained a caste distinguishable in dress, speech, and customs.

Although the emancipation of the serfs, who constituted about 47 million of Russia's

In this 1861 photograph a Russian official is reading to peasants on a Moscow estate the "Regulations Concerning the Peasantry," the decree that abolished serfdom.
(Photo: Novosti Press Agency)

74 million people, did not establish a laissez-faire economy, it provided the basis for institutions allowing some popular participation in public life. Within each district communes supported their own courts, selected their own judges, and administered the regulations on taxes and conscription. In 1864 district and provincial councils—the zemstvos, elected through a three-class system like Prussia's—were made responsible for primary schools, local roads, and measures of local welfare. Generally cautious, the zemstvos gave important political experience and a sense of political responsibility to many professional men and other members

of the middle class. Cities too were granted increased autonomy and allowed to elect representative bodies.

The number of primary schools, though always inadequate, increased dramatically. In addition the government encouraged secondary and university education, relaxed censorship, and adopted a number of military reforms. The system of requiring twenty-five years of service from selected serfs was altered until by 1874 universal service, with generous exemptions and only six years of active duty, approached the concept of a citizen army.[5]

As each reform uncovered more that needed to be done, the government became more cautious. Concessions to Poland had prompted demands that culminated in the revolution of 1863. Harshly quelled by 1865, it lost Poland her separate status and strengthened conservatism in Russia. The repression extended into Russia, where the police remained independent of local controls. By 1875 the zemstvos had been forbidden to discuss general political issues, and restrictions on what could be taught or printed had been tightened.

As a consequence the movements of radical opposition flourished. The famous division of the generations, expressed in Ivan Turgenev's *Fathers and Sons,* showed in the rejection of leaders like Alexander Herzen, who from exile in London had once inspired reform but whose views belonged to the era of Mazzini and the utopian socialists. New spokesmen, called nihilists by their enemies, rejected compromise within the system and accepted the utility of violence advocated in the anarchism of Mikhail Bakunin (discussed in Chapter 25). Populists talked of going to the people, educating the peasants to a more revolutionary view. Social-ism too was spreading in the 1870s. All these doctrines were affected by pan-Slavist views, which stressed Russia's peculiar destiny and disdained the liberal parliamentarianism of the West. The intelligentsia of Russian society remained isolated and, increasingly disenchanted with a tsar liberator, moved further left. In an atmosphere of conspiracy, terrorists attempted assassination as a way to shake an oppressive regime. Usually they missed their target, but in 1881 a bomb killed Alexander II. Alexander III, his son, took the reigns of power smoothly. However inadequate, the reforms of Alexander II assured that imperial Russia could survive an assassination.

The Hapsburg Empire 1859–1875

Following the revolutions of 1848, the Hapsburg monarchy had sought to meet its political and economic problems by creating a modern, unitary state. Under the young Francis Joseph I, the emphasis on administrative efficiency was renewed, and for the first time in its history, the entire empire was subjected to uniform laws and taxes applied by a single administration. The emperor and the aristocracy, however, were never comfortable with their earnest bureaucrats, and the innovation of centralization was not accompanied by the zeal for reform the policy required. Mounting debts and defeat in Italy were accepted as proof that it had not worked, and in 1860 Francis Joseph's October Diploma announced a new federal constitution giving considerable authority to regional diets.

Intended to reduce resentment against high-handed government, the constitution was a failure from the start. It prompted dangerous arguments among the various nationalities over what the "historic" provinces really were and won the determined opposition of liberals and bureaucrats alike. The emperor therefore reversed himself the next year in the February

---

[5] Most soldiers were of course recruited from the peasantry. A provision reflecting the social importance of education stipulated that those who completed primary school were liable for only four years of duty, those who finished secondary school for two years, and those with university education for just six months.

Patent, which established an imperial bicameral parliament. Having stirred his people to visions of local self-government and autonomous nationalities, he was now again asking for their subordination to rule from Vienna. Furthermore representatives to the lower house were to be elected by a four-class system that assured the dominance of the German-speaking middle class.

In Hungary the liberal nationalist Ferencz Deák led a campaign to reject these arrangements and reestablish instead the constitution of 1848, a far more liberal instrument. The imperial government tried the traditional tactic of recruiting support from the empire's other nationalities against the Magyars, but the response was unenthusiastic. Although not strong enough to force her will, Hungary was able to prevent the new constitution from having its intended effect. Deák then worked for a compromise, which became acceptable after the empire's defeat in the Austro-Prussian War.

In 1867 Francis Joseph was crowned king of Hungary, an autonomous state joined to Austria only in the person of the emperor and by common policies of defense and diplomacy. Thus he preserved his authority in the matters of foreign policy he cared about most by conceding to one nationality what he denied to others. Thereafter two critical issues of Hungary's domestic politics were the divergent economic interests of Austrian industry and Hungary's great landholders (a conflict that centered on the tariff) and the treatment of the non-Magyar majority of her population. On both questions the Magyar landowning aristocracy generally had its way, and after 1875 the dominant Liberal party, led by Kálmán Tisza, made Magyar the language of school and government while protecting Magyar economic interests.

In the Austrian parliament the emperor turned for support first to the German liberals, who offended him by their anticlericalism, and then to Czechs and Poles, who disturbed him with their nationalist demands. Each group won some concessions, but fundamental, lasting reforms were difficult, and government depended increasingly on a reliable, conservative bureaucracy dominated by Germans more than on parliamentary politics. Still, the Hapsburg monarch presided after 1867 over responsible ministers in both halves of his empire, who enjoyed a determining voice in public affairs.

An awkward compromise, the Dual Monarchy gave power to wealthy landlords and merchants and rested on the dominance of Magyars (over Rumanians, Croats, and Serbs) and of Germans in cooperation with Czechs and Poles (over Slovenes, Slovaks, and Ruthenians). It lasted for fifty years as one of Europe's great powers, an empire of diversified peoples and cultures, threatened by nationalism, changing even while resisting change, but with more freedom in practice than in principle, and sustained at its center by the graceful civilization of Vienna.

Spain 1854–1876

In Spain the army, the Church, big business, and regionalist interests could demand a price for their support so high as to assure the government's weakness. For nine years government under General Leopoldo O'Dónnell, the leader of the liberal coalition that displaced General Narváez in 1854, provided political stability by giving more attention to economic matters. Spain experienced on a smaller scale the waves of speculation, railroad building, economic growth, and ostentation associated with the Second Empire in France. A coalition of the political center, the government fell in 1863 before changing demands it could not meet and palace intrigue it could not stop. Its conservative replacement then sought security through repression and electoral manipulation, which ended in revolution in 1868 and the unpopular Queen Isabella II's flight to France.

The disaffection of the military in 1868 was crucial, but the revolution also won support from workers, radicals, liberals, professional groups, and businessmen. The new regime, led by General Juan Prim, sought to combine the liberal appeal of universal manhood suffrage, trial by jury, and freedom of religion and the press with the moderation implied by constitutional monarchy. It proved easier to adopt a new constitution, however, than to find a new king, as each candidate decided against entanglement in Spanish politics and the sort of international complications that precipitated the Franco-Prussian War.

The son of Victor Emmanuel II of Italy who finally agreed to accept the throne in December 1870 ruled for just two years as King Amadeus I. Associated with the Risorgimento's attacks on papal territory, the Italian royal house was anathema to Catholics, and the king was treated as an upstart and foreigner by grandees and courtiers. Finding it impossible to be either a good constitutional monarch or a strong leader, Amadeus abdicated in 1873 as republican agitation and Carlist uprisings became more serious, rather like a prime minister who had lost a vote of confidence.

The majority of the Cortes then declared Spain's first republic, which lasted a year. Republicans, divided between centralists and federalists, were further weakened by Carlist revolts and Catholic distrust. The government alienated much of its following by repressing constitutional liberties in its quest for order, and the military stepped forward to place Isabella's son, who had just come of age, on the throne as Alfonso XII.

He began his reign in 1875 under a new constitution that was closer to the one in effect from 1845 to 1869 than the more democratic one that had then replaced it. The court never again meddled in politics as Isabella had done, and the ringing freedoms proclaimed during the republic were honored at least in theory. Spain thus found stability in a government responsible to a Cortes whose majority was largely determined by manipulated elections and limited suffrage. The Conservative and Liberal parties, as they came to be called, alternated in power with little change in policy. Both provided sensible and mildly corrupt governments that offered something to most influential groups and for a generation masked the bitter divisions between regionalists and centralists, Catholics and anticlericals, the poor and the propertied.

France 1870–1878

With Napoleon's capture at Sedan and the rout of French troops, the Second Empire lost its reason for existence. For the third time in France's history, a republic was announced to cheering crowds. Calling themselves the Government of National Defense, republican leaders tried valiantly to turn 1870 into another 1792, when a republic had mobilized the nation against the monarchical armies of Europe. But German forces had already broken the back of France's army, and they surrounded Paris on September 19, less than three weeks after Sedan. The new government sent some of its members to Tours to organize resistance from there, but even the urgency of war barely covered the divisions between moderate and radical republicans, who were determined to continue the fight at all costs. Their leader, the fiery orator Léon Gambetta, daringly escaped from Paris in a balloon to accomplish remarkable feats of organization from Tours. Enthusiastic national guards and peasant boys were recruited and somehow equipped; Garibaldi arrived to help, and the French seriously harassed German troops, even recapturing Orléans, but by December the overmatched French forces were pushed back. The government retreated to Bordeaux while Paris held out against a German siege. During a winter as severe as any on record, Parisians cut the trees of their boule-

In this cartoon from the siege of Paris in 1870, a butcher prepares to deal with the hungry Parisians waiting in the rain for a bit of horsemeat.
(Photo: New York Public Library/Picture Collection)

vards for fuel, slaughtered pets, and emptied the zoo as a starving city continued to resist. But heroism and patriotic fervor could not defeat a modern army, and at the end of January Paris capitulated. German troops marched down Haussmann's boulevards into a denuded and quiet city.

Although Gambetta wanted to continue the fighting, few others did; the armistice called for elections to establish a government that could ratify the terms of peace. In the absence of political parties or extended campaigning, the successful candidate was usually someone already well known, a local leader committed to ending the war, and thus two-thirds of those elected to the National Assembly that met in February 1871 were monarchists. Some were legitimists, who longed for a Bourbon restoration and were already calling the count de Chambord King Henry V; more were Orléanists. But there were also some republicans, mostly moderate, and a handful of Bonapartists.

Despite the moving speeches of delegates from Alsace and Lorraine, peace on German terms was accepted, and approval was quickly given for an interim government under Adolphe Thiers. The eloquent critic of Guizot, in exile during the 1850s and the empire's public opponent in the 1860s, Thiers gained at seventy-three the power he had long coveted. By naming him chief of the Executive Power, the Assembly avoided declaring whether France's permanent government would be a monarchy or a republic. It then agreed to meet next at tranquil Versailles rather than radical Paris, and adjourned.

Determined to consolidate his position, Thiers recognized Paris as the greatest threat to the sort of compromise between Orléanists and moderate republicans he represented, and one of his first acts was to disarm the city's National Guard. At the end of the German siege, many of the well-to-do had left Paris, but the poor and the radical remained, hardened by months of fighting. When troops arrived to take the city's cannons, they were met by an angry crowd; shots were fired, and by day's end two generals lay dead and most of the soldiers had joined the side of their urban brothers. Faced with insurrection, Thiers followed the advice he had given Louis Philippe in 1848: he withdrew the army to let Paris tastes its revolution so he could first isolate and then crush it.

The municipal council of Paris declared a commune, once again evoking the great Revolution, and called on other cities to do the same. The Paris Commune included moderate and radical republicans, some followers of Pierre Joseph Proudhon and Jérome Adolphe Blanqui, socialists who though more militant were in the tradition of Saint-Simon and Fourier, as well as a few members of the Marxist First International. Its program, favoring democracy and federalism, was not very specific on other matters; and it had little time to experiment with egalitarian and anticlerical measures. Its efforts to make peace with the government at Versailles were rejected, and the Assembly replied to the threat of a radical government in Paris and the Parisian "mob" by suddenly ending the moratorium on debt payment (including rents) that had been in effect during the siege and by ceasing to pay the National Guard, the only income for many. While German armies watched, troops from Versailles began their assault on Paris.

The civil war between the democrats of Paris and the Assembly at Versailles fed on the distrust and despair that accompanied the French war effort, the siege of Paris, and defeat. The city's isolation during that year of anguish, when rumors of treachery were heard at every hand, had amplified other divisions: between industrial and rural France, between urban democrats and middle-class moderates. The two sides fought out of fury for competing

The communards of Paris pulled down the statue of Napoleon I, which stood atop a column in Place Vendôme, and planted a red flag on the empty pedestal; none of the symbolism of that moment was overlooked in this engraving.
(Photo: Musée Carnavalet, Photographie Bulloz)

visions of what the nation should become now that the Second Empire had fallen. Hostages taken by the communards to win release of some of their captured leaders were killed, among them the archbishop of Paris. On both sides prisoners were shot, and the bitter and bloody fighting lasted nearly two months before troops broke into the city in May. Even then the battle continued, barricade by barricade, into the working-class quarters, where the group commanded by Louise Michel—the most famous of hundreds of militant *citoyennes* who would later tell her captors, "I belong entirely to the Social Revolution"—was among the last to fall. Solid citizens shuddered at revolutionary excess (and especially the part played by women), but on the whole the victors were more brutal. Tens of thousands of Parisians died in the streets, and summary courts-martial ordered execution, imprisonment, or deportation for tens of thousands more.

The commune raised the red specter throughout Europe. From the first, Marxists hailed it as a proletarian rising, the dawning of a new era, though Marx was indignant with the communards' respect for property and legality and their lack of revolutionary daring. Former communards became the heroes of socialist gatherings for the next generation, and to this day the cemetery where many of them were executed remains a shrine honored by socialists and communists.[6]

Historians have been at great pains to show how little socialism, still less Marxism, there was in the Paris Commune (it respectfully left the Bank of Paris intact); yet myth has its historical importance too. This indisputably was class conflict, and the rage on both sides was more significant than mere differences of program. After 1871 a communist revolution became a credible possibility to radical and conservative alike, and working-class movements pointed to the martyrs of the Commune as evidence of the selfish cruelty of bourgeois rule.

The Founding of the Third Republic

Thiers' government quickly reestablished effective administration, thanks to a state apparatus stronger than any political group, and the loan needed to pay the indemnity to Germany was soon oversubscribed. As by-elections produced victories for moderate republicans, monarchists feared that their chance for a restoration might be slipping away. They rallied in 1873 to defeat Thiers in a close vote and united behind the Bourbon claimant, the childless count of Chambord, with the understanding that he would be succeeded by the claimant from the House of Orléans. His intransigent refusal to accept the tricolor, the flag of revolution, left the monarchists afraid to attempt a restoration yet. They borrowed time by electing Marshal Marie MacMahon as Thiers' replacement for a seven-year term. A monarchist who had fought under Napoleon III, he accepted from a sense of duty and brought to his post a dislike of politics that helped him act like the constitutional monarch for whom he was keeping the throne.

While the conservatives appointed by MacMahon risked defeats in the Assembly[7] and the monarchists grew more divided, the republicans gained in confidence. In 1875 a bill passed by one vote providing that the president of the republic should be elected by the votes of two legislative houses, and these in turn were established by laws stipulating that the Senate would be indirectly elected by local officials and the Chamber of Deputies by direct universal male suffrage.

The Third Republic was thus established without ringing phrases as the government

---

[6] A century later a Russian sputnik proudly carried not only a Soviet flag but a red flag from the Commune of 1871.

[7] MacMahon's ministers, led by the able Orléanist, the duke de Broglie, were so rich in noble names that the period has come to be called the Republic of the Dukes from a study published by Daniel Halévy in 1937.

that, in Thiers' epigram, divided Frenchmen least. A regime of compromise, for which republicans led by Gambetta had worked hard, it had earned acceptability by crushing the Commune and accepting a conservative Senate. Created by the most reluctant of founding fathers, it endured longer than any French regime since 1789.

In the elections of 1876, the republicans captured two-thirds of the seats in the Chamber and almost half those in the Senate. Although MacMahon chose a conservative republican, Jules Simon, as premier, tension between the president and the Chamber predictably grew. The republicans accused the Catholic Church of being the political agent of legitimists and criticized the military and the Orléanist prefects. MacMahon in turn reproved Simon for not combating such charges whereupon Simon resigned, denouncing presidential interference. This was the "crisis de seize mai" (May 16, 1877), which precipitated the final step in the establishment of the republic, for MacMahon, who had previously rejected every hint that he attempt a monarchical coup, now reacted strongly. He dissolved the Chamber, called new elections, and named a new ministry to manipulate their outcome. Although the republicans lost some seats, they preserved an overwhelming majority. Never again in the Third Republic did a French president use his power of dissolution; and the presidency, so strong under Thiers, declined further in authority.

When MacMahon resigned, in 1879, the two houses elected Jules Grévy, a republican who in 1848 had argued there should be no president at all. A good old man who frightened no one, Grévy exemplified the caution, the compromises, and the republican tradition on which the Third Republic rested. French public institutions preserved the remarkable continuity that characterized them after 1800 despite the changes of regime. Successive republican governments guaranteed political freedom and deferred to the middle class. Economic growth, less dramatic than in Great Britain or Germany, was also less disruptive. Like her European neighbors, France had painfully found an awkward balance, one peculiarly her own, between the demands for order and the need for change.

Great Britain 1854–1880

The moderation and flexibility of Great Britain's parliamentary system, like prosperity and empire, was a source of Victorian confidence. Many claimed that special qualities in the English character—respect for tradition, the emphasis on law and Parliament, habits of toleration and deference—accounted for the combination of industrial advance and political order.[8] Yet overwhelming social change as well as the reforms of the 1830s and 1840s required the state to become more active in a wider range of activities and more responsive to the public. Ultimately dependent on elections, the government nonetheless remained the province of the upper classes, who found it difficult and sometimes repugnant to reach the masses.

Even in matters of foreign policy, however, public opinion was increasingly important. The Crimean War evoked a patriotic enthusiasm astute politicians would seek to recapture, and the ineptitude with which it was conducted forced investigations into administration and the military that increased the cry for new reforms. During the American Civil War, many liberals favored the South, for resisting central government, as did most of the English upper classes, who viewed Southern culture with aristocratic sympathy. John Bright and many radical and working-class leaders on the other hand saw the cause of human dignity and democracy

---

[8] Walter Bagehot, one of the most noted political writers of the period, especially praised the Englishman's sense of deference to his social betters. Inequality and individual morality, he argued, allowed Britain to enjoy order without coercion and justice without anarchy.

represented by the North. The revival of British radicalism was closely connected with the willingness of the very textile workers who suffered from the scarcity of American cotton to cheer for President Abraham Lincoln's war.

Confronted by many pressures, the British political system maintained a remarkable capacity to generate limited but effective reforms. Lord John Russell built an effective coalition of liberal Tories and Whigs, and Lord Palmerston, prime minister from 1859 to his death in 1865, could at least arouse public affection—a quality that made him more popular in the nation than in Parliament. They presided over ministries of able men who soberly and sometimes imaginatively sought to lead a more efficient state to act more responsibly in behalf of social equity. Competitive examinations for entry into a restructured civil service marked an important departure achieved in 1855 after years of effort. Legal disabilities for Jews were removed, and the special taxes in behalf of the Church of England were dropped. British rule in India was thoroughly reorganized following a great mutiny in 1857 among native soldiers in the Indian army. In the same spirit the important act of 1867, which made Canada a dominion with her own representative institutions, was passed with little resistance.

The Parties of Gladstone and Disraeli

Such responsible accommodation was not sufficient, however, to meet the needs and aspirations of the lower-middle class and workers. More fundamental change followed a major political realignment that made possible the establishment of modern political parties, the extension of suffrage, and the emergence of two brilliant leaders who combined democratic appeal with masterly management of the established political system.

One of them was William Gladstone, who made his mark as chancellor of the exchequer under Palmerston. A skilled parliamentary tactician, a man of impeccable background, he was also a personal friend of some of the more doctrinaire liberal reformers and showed open sympathy for the left-wing liberals known as radicals. Gladstone was one of the former Tories who followed Sir Robert Peel in leaving the party upon their conversion to free trade in 1846, and he was instrumental in transforming the Whigs into the Liberal party. In liberal principles he found a moral cause around which to build a strong political movement.

Gladstone became an advocate of increased suffrage as that question, in the air since 1832, became compelling. Cautiously he and Russell sponsored a complicated bill, which was defeated. The issue was then snatched from them by the rising star of the Conservatives (as the Tories were now called), Benjamin Disraeli, who led his rather startled party to support a more generous measure, passed in 1867. The right to vote was extended to all men who were borough (town) residents and paid taxes either directly or indirectly through rent. An electorate that had risen to almost a million was now doubled, and two great parties were coming systematically to compete for popular favor in terms of national issues. As the parties became better organized and disciplined, they reached far deeper into society with greater awareness of the people's concerns, and the great parliamentary clashes of Gladstone and Disraeli became a dramatic part of British public life.

Despite Disraeli's remarkable role in promoting the Reform Bill of 1867, the elections of 1868 produced a great Liberal victory, and for six years Gladstone's first and perhaps most successful ministry did much to improve British society. Great Britain, well after most European nations, at last established the basis for a national educational system by providing state aid to both church schools and locally supported secular schools. Education was compulsory only by local option and was not yet free, but a giant step had been taken. It was accompanied by important reforms in the two great universities, Oxford and Cambridge, which encouraged new curricula and allowed men not Anglican to compete for fellowships and teaching posts. The Liberals also reformed the army, limiting traditional privileges, improving training, and establishing shorter terms of service on the Prussian model. Even the purchase of commissions was abolished despite great resistance from the House of Lords. Ireland too received their attention. Here the Liberal government disestablished the Church of England, restricted the abuses of absentee landlords, and provided guarantees that the peasant would receive some credit for improvements he made, some protection against eviction, and some help in purchasing land for himself.

Few doubted that Great Britain would become more democratic, and many suspected that the Conservative party was doomed. Yet the elections of 1874 returned it to power, for Disraeli more than Gladstone had inherited Palmerston's appeal to nationalism. Belief in the glory and wealth of empire and willingness to expand the authority of the state in matters of public welfare were to become the strong foundation for a modern Conservative party.

Under Disraeli colonial matters received greater and more public attention, and his purchase in 1875 of a large block of shares in the Suez Canal provided the basis for subsequent British domination in Egypt. When "Empress of India" was added to Victoria's title in 1876, it sounded foreign and flamboyant to many in the upper classes but caught the imagination of citizens proud of their national power and their queen. A public health act in 1875 took the important step of establishing a national code for housing and urban sanitation. Trade unions, their legality questioned by a court decision, had been recognized in a Liberal bill of 1871, but it was the Conservatives who removed restrictions that had prohibited picketing and kept strikes ineffectual.

An international flotilla marked the grand opening of the Suez Canal in 1869. As part of the elaborate ceremonies, for which both the Empress Eugenie and Emperor Franz Joseph came to Egypt, the Khedive commissioned Verdi to write an opera, *Aida*. The opera received its formal premiere in Cairo two years later.
(Photo: © BBC Hulton Picture Library)

This conception of Tory democracy was a British parallel to the policies of Bismarck and Napoleon III. Through the party system the sphere of politics was being extended and the role of the state increased beyond the intention of the upper-class men who made the system work. Its effectiveness, in addition to the wealth of industry and empire, made Britain the most powerful and most envied nation of the world.

Stabilizing International Relations 1870–1881

The unification of Italy and Germany and the defeat of France had fundamentally altered the relations of the European powers, and nationalist movements within the Austrian and Ottoman empires threatened new instability.

The Balkans remained the only area of Europe not fully controlled by a single government, and the strengthened European powers were quick to perceive the opportunities and dangers that fact implied. Russia, eager to undo her defeat in the Crimean War, snatched the occasion of the Franco-Prussian War to renounce the treaty clauses banning her navy from the Black Sea and looked hopefully for chances to extend her influence. The Hapsburg monarchy, hoping to compensate for its losses in Italy and Germany and aware of the threat nationalism posed to its rule, watched the Balkans with growing concern. Great Britain's interest also increased with the political popularity of empire and the opening of the Suez Canal in 1869. Built by French engineers, it offered a shorter route to India and made the eastern Mediterranean appear all the more vital.

Most of the Balkan peninsula was at least nominally under Ottoman rule (see Map 24.3), but throughout the area there was a ferment of nationalism, constitutionalism, and modernizing reform. Especially strong in the autonomous countries of Serbia and Rumania, it reached into the Ottoman Empire itself, where a proclamation of 1876 established at least in theory a constitution guaranteeing parliamentary government and individual liberties. The Bulgarian uprising against Ottoman rule in 1876 was thus not an isolated event, and it won immediate support from Serbia, which had long hoped for a Balkan federation against Ottoman power and for the acquisition of Bosnia and Herzegovina. After Ottoman forces put down the revolt with shocking brutality, Russia intervened, moved by traditional ambitions and pressure from her own pan-Slav movement, which had actively encouraged Balkan nationalists.

Russia's military campaigns were poorly conducted, but her gains were sufficient within the year to force the sultan to accept the treaty of San Stefano in 1878. Russia was to acquire territory across the Caucasus Mountains (from Batum to Kars), extending her centuries-long advance southward. Both Montenegro and Serbia were to be enlarged and granted full independence and, most important, the treaty provided for a large and autonomous Bulgaria. That new state, it was universally thought, would be a Russian puppet looming over the Balkan peninsula; and the European concert, which had exercised so little voice in the unification of Italy or Germany, the fall of the Papal States, or the cession of Alsace-Lorraine, was called into action.

The combined pressure of the great powers forced Russia to agree to an international conference to establish new terms of peace in the Balkans, and at the subsequent Congress of Berlin in 1878, as at the Congress of Paris in 1856, they administered a sharp rebuff to Russia. They granted autonomy to a greatly reduced Bulgaria, and lessened the gains given Serbia and Montenegro. Austria-Hungary was authorized to occupy Bosnia and Herzegovina, which also remained under Ottoman rule, and the British occupation of Cyprus, previously agreed to between the Ottoman Empire and Britain, was confirmed.

The balance thus established in the Balkans

MAP 24.3: THE DECLINE OF THE OTTOMAN EMPIRE 1683–1914

was precarious, achieved only by extending Russian, Austrian, and British interests at the expense of a weakening Ottoman Empire, while ignoring the nationalist ambitions of many Greeks, Bulgarians, Rumanians, and Serbians.[9] This was a pattern for preserving peace

[9] The southern part of Bulgaria, Rumelia, remained under Turkish rule as a separate province. Serbia, Montenegro, and Rumania received independence but less territory than they claimed. The Rumanian provinces of Wallachia and Moldavia had been joined in 1862 and received their own prince two years later. A Hohenzollern, he became King Carol in 1881. The tsar's nephew was elected to the Bulgarian throne.

in Europe that would become characteristic of imperialism.

The fact that the congress was held in Berlin reflected Germany's prestige and her new commitment to maintaining the balance of power. Germany and her chancellor had become preeminent in Continental relations. Russia, the offended power, had nowhere to turn for allies but Berlin, for France was too radical and Great Britain a consistent foe. Bismarck thus laid the groundwork for a system of alliances to isolate France and secure Germany's position. In 1879 Austria-Hungary and Germany signed a mutual defense pact that remained the foundation of German diplomacy, promising that the two countries would fight together in case either was attacked by Russia. Then Bismarck daringly turned to isolated Russia in 1881, reviving the Three Emperors' League he had attempted a decade earlier: Austria-Hungary, Germany, and Russia swore neutrality in the event of war between any of them and a fourth power.

More important than the precise provisions were the fear of international anarchy and the new relationship these alliances implied. Bismarck used Prussia's connections with both Eastern European empires, based upon an unstable balance in the Balkans, to re-create the conservative alliance of the three powers. At the same time he sought the friendship of Great Britain and Italy, leaving Germany supreme and France alone upon the Continent—an arrangement to be sealed by dangerously explicit treaties as if these could check domestic change or define the ambitions of national states.

By 1880 many of the aims of the revolutionaries defeated in 1848 had been accomplished. Italy and Germany were sovereign nations, and Hungary was autonomous. Serfdom had been abolished in Russia and religious disabilities largely removed in the United Kingdom. France and Germany enjoyed universal manhood suffrage. Representative government was firmly established in Britain, France, Italy, and Spain, and everywhere the state accepted a larger responsibility for social welfare. A dynamic middle-class culture flourished, and in a broad sense nationalism had triumphed outside Eastern Europe (few denied its potential importance there), though the policies of nationalists seemed to promote conflict, a strong army, and a vigorous state more than liberalism.

Political changes after 1850 were a response to ideas and to new economic and social conditions which radicals had been among the first to recognize, but these changes were brought about largely by the state, which radicals had failed to capture. Everywhere stronger and more specifically secular, the state increased its authority, its social role, its sovereign claims, and its expenditures. Bureaucracies expanded, their officials copying the Junkers in Germany, carrying the voice of Germanic Vienna through the Hapsburg Empire, following in France the rational style of the great state schools, and carrying an upright liberalism deeper into British life. If social tension only occasionally burst into the open violence of the Paris Commune, that stability depended upon an intricate balance of forces—different in each nation—maintained by the state.

In general, Europeans faced the last third of the nineteenth century with increased confidence, impressed with the evidence of economic and social progress and hopeful that institutional and moral improvement would naturally follow. They could point, and often did, to evidence that in all the ranges of human thought, they enjoyed one of history's greatest civilizations. But even as this optimism flourished, there were rumblings of discontent from intellectuals who found the fashionable faiths shallow and from groups lower in society who were only just beginning to make themselves heard. The combination of an emphasis on politics, rapid social change, and the expansion of the state could prove explosive if conflicting interests fought to see who would command the enormous power Western society had assembled.

RECOMMENDED READING

Studies

Barzun, Jacques. *Classic, Romantic, and Modern.* 1961. One of Barzun's many famous essays in defense of Romanticism.

Beales, Derek. *The Risorgimento and the Unification of Italy.* 1971. Concise, skeptical introduction to the history of Italian unification.

*Binkley, Robert C. *Realism and Nationalism: 1852–1871.* 1934. Interprets the history of this generation in terms of the victory in each country of centralizers over federalists.

*Craig, Gordon. *The Politics of the Prussian Army.* 1964. Establishes that much of Prussian history can be understood in terms of the influence and needs of the army.

Hamerow, Theodore S. *The Social Foundations of German Unification, 1858–1871.* 1972. The politics and ideas of unification placed in the context of a developing economy.

*Hauser, Arnold. *Social History of Art.* Vols. III and IV. 1958. Suggestive if sometimes mechanical effort to relate artistic trends to social change.

*Howard, Michael. *The Franco-Prussian War.* 1969. Exemplary study of how war reflects (and tests) an entire society.

*Jaszi, Oscar. *The Dissolution of the Habsburg Monarchy.* 1929. A work that has shaped most subsequent studies.

Kedourie, E. *Nationalism.* 1960. A valuable introduction to nationalism in Europe and elsewhere.

Kitson Clark, G. *The Making of Victorian England.* 1967. Graciously knowledgeable, stimulating, and wide-ranging essay.

Lukács, Georg. *The Historical Novel.* Hannah and Stanley Mitchell (trs.). 1962. Insightful and learned study of the nineteenth-century novel by one of Europe's leading Marxist scholars.

Mack Smith, Denis. *Garibaldi.* 1956. Ably summarizes the place recent scholarship gives Italy's popular hero.

Mosse, George L. *The Nationalization of the Masses: Political Symbolism and Mass Movements in Germany from the Napoleonic Wars Through the Third Reich.* 1975. One of the most recent and complete efforts to find the roots of Nazism in popular nationalism.

*Pflanze, Otto. *Bismarck and the Development of Germany.* 1963. A major revision of older views that has become a standard synthesis.

Stavrianos, L. S. *The Balkans, 1815–1914.* 1963. Places the international troubles of this region in the context of domestic developments.

*Taylor, A. J. P. *The Struggle for Mastery in Europe, 1848–1918.* 1971. A lively, controversial interpretation of the international relations of the period.

Thayer, William Roscoe. *The Life and Times of Cavour.* 2 vols. 1911. A solid and old-fashioned work that captures the liberal view of Cavour and the Risorgimento.

*Thompson, James M. *Louis Napoleon and the Second Empire.* 1967. A balanced assessment in the light of recent scholarship.

*Williams, Roger L. *The French Revolutions of 1870–1871.* 1969. An introduction to the recent findings and long-standing controversies about the Paris Commune.

*Woodham-Smith, Cecil. *The Reason Why.* 1971. A colorful account of the Crimean War.

Zeldin, T. *France: 1848–1945.* 2 vols. 1973 and 1977. Excellent on the society and the attitudes of the middle class.

*Available in paperback.

25

THE AGE OF PROGRESS 1860–1914

The half-century from the 1860s to 1914 saw the flowering of nineteenth-century civilization. In economic organization, technology, the arts and sciences, and politics, the revolutionary changes that had occurred before 1850 had now taken root, and in some respects the result was an almost incredible success story. European power, wealth, and prestige reached new heights and spread around the world; the benefits from increased knowledge, political freedom, and unfettered capitalism in most respects exceeded the early claims made for them. The pace of change seemed to increase in every domain of human activity, and the idea of historical progress became almost an obsession.

Paradoxically, an age that described itself in such tones of optimism and confidence also subjected itself to internal criticism of extraordinary severity. Literacy spread, but intellectuals denounced the mass culture it fostered. The arts flourished, but they expressed conflicting values and attitudes that made modern civilization seem lacking in coherence. The standard of living rose, but working people formed militant organizations to combat their employers, and socialists considered the very success of capitalism to be evidence of its imminent collapse. Conservatives assailed the threat to civilized values posed by excessive faith in reason, rampant avarice, and purposeless tolerance of every idea and faction. Christians continued to decry materialism and the exclusion of religion from its rightful role. The late nineteenth century is often described as the triumph of the middle class and the age of liberalism, but it was characteristic of that triumph and that age that many were moved to reject it.

These conflicts placed an added strain on political life at the very time that the state was expected to wield unequaled power. Each nation developed its own pattern for meeting this challenge, and remarkably every political system survived, though few escaped the threat of revolutionary upheaval. That fact, like the continuation of international peace and the spread of European empire, seemed evidence of the health of European civilization, but the period closed in the cataclysm of World War I. From the perspective of the troubled 1930s the late nineteenth century seemed an almost idyllic period remembered nostalgically as the "belle époque" of happy stability. Yet it was also the breeding ground of twentieth-century conflict and doubt.

I. ECONOMICS AND POPULATION

The Second Industrial Revolution

Economic growth in the second half of the nineteenth century resulted from a continuation of processes already under way, but with important differences that have led historians to call this the second industrial revolution. The rapid rate of growth now came from accelerated industrial change as new technology and large-scale production fed ever-expanding markets at home and abroad. While Europe's population grew more rapidly than ever before, the value of manufacturing went up three times as fast. Prosperity spread beyond the favored groups to affect all classes, and for the first time in history, a society expected economic growth to continue year after year.

The expansion of the German economy following unification was the most spectacular. Everything seemed to foster the new nation's industrialization. Already rich in natural resources, Germany acquired more raw materials as well as factories with the annexation of Alsace-Lorraine. Her system of railroads provided excellent communications; the famous educational system produced ample numbers of the administrators and engineers the commercial sector now required. The government, which had played an active role in every facet of industrialization, continued to cooperate with business interests. Military needs stimulated basic industry, and a growing population provided an eager domestic market. Being newer than those of Britain or France, German plants employed the latest and most efficient equipment, obtaining the necessary capital through a modern banking structure. By 1900 they were far bigger than anyone else's, and firms engaged in the various stages of production often combined in huge cartels dominating an entire field of enterprise as Germany became preeminent in new fields such as chemicals and electricity. Her salesmen appeared all over the world with catalogs in native languages and products suited to local conditions, selling with a drive and optimism British merchants resented as bad manners.

The older industrial economies of Great Britain, Belgium, and France continued to grow but more slowly; yet by 1900 France's industrial production, despite her loss of important textile and iron centers in Alsace, about equaled great Britain's a generation earlier, when Britain led the world. French iron production more than doubled in the first twenty-five years of the Third Republic, and new processes made the nation's ore output second only to that of the United States. In value of production per capita, a figure that suggests something of a nation's standard of living, France remained ahead of Germany, though behind the British Isles.

By the turn of the century, Great Britain, whose industrial superiority had seemed a fact of nature, was clearly being surpassed in some of the critical indexes of production by the United States and Germany. Although the economy did continue to expand, its state of health became a serious issue in English public life, and economic historians remain fascinated by the question of why its growth became sluggish.

There are almost too many explanations. British plants and equipment were old and owners hesitated to undertake the cost of modernizing or replacing them. Well-established firms often made it hard for new companies to get a start. British schooling was weak in technical subjects, and education provided less opportunity for social mobility than on the Continent. Indeed, social attitudes, always difficult to analyze precisely, may explain more than strictly economic factors. British industrialists, slow to appreciate the mere specialist and resistant to new ways, became less venturesome and perhaps a little complacent. Even so Lon-

ECONOMICALLY ACTIVE POPULATION CA. 1900

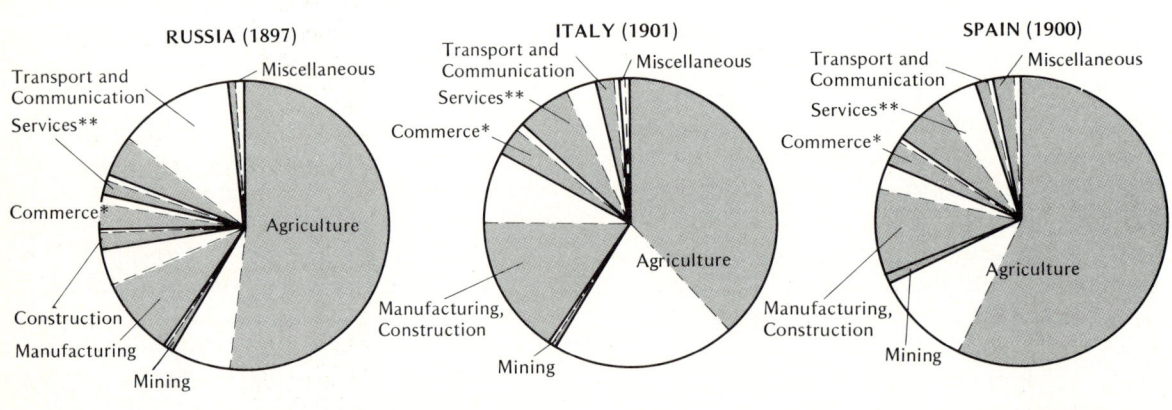

*Commerce includes banking, utilities, real estate, and insurance.
**Services includes armed forces and domestics.

(Source: Bairoch, P., et al., *The Working Population and Its Structure*, Brussels, 1968, p. 119.)

don remained the financial capital of the world—a world in which industrialization was rapidly spreading to Sweden and Italy, Russia and Japan.

Technological and Market Developments

Industrial expansion in this period was closely tied to new technology. By 1890 Europe was producing even more steel than iron, using the Bessemer converter developed in the 1860s, which permitted far higher temperatures in smelter furnaces; and subsequent discoveries made lower-grade ores profitable. British, German, and French maritime shipping, which doubled between 1870 and 1914, depended on faster and larger steamships. New chemical processes and synthetics led to improved products ranging from dyes, textiles, and paints to fertilizers and explosives. A whole new industry developed to produce and supply electricity.

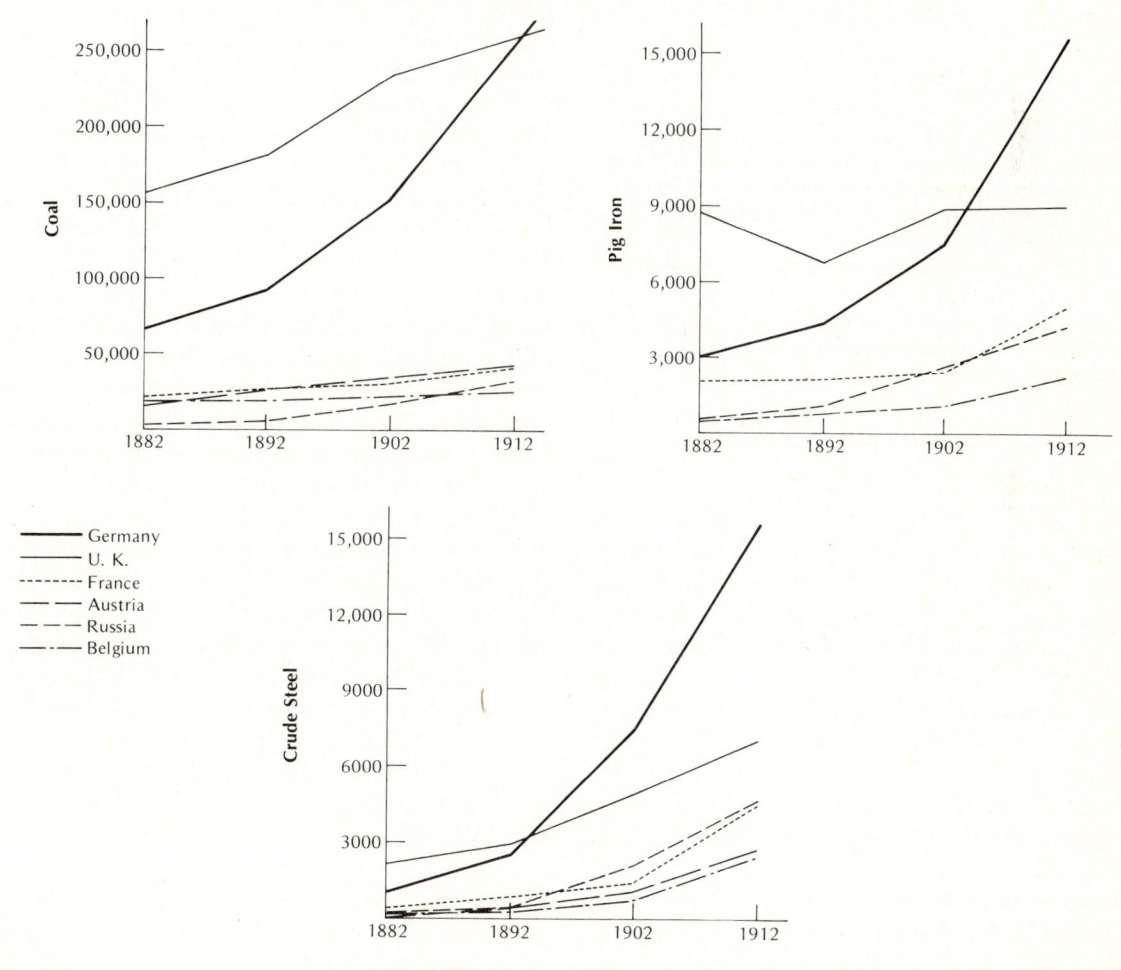

INDUSTRIAL PRODUCTION (THOUSANDS OF METRIC TONS)

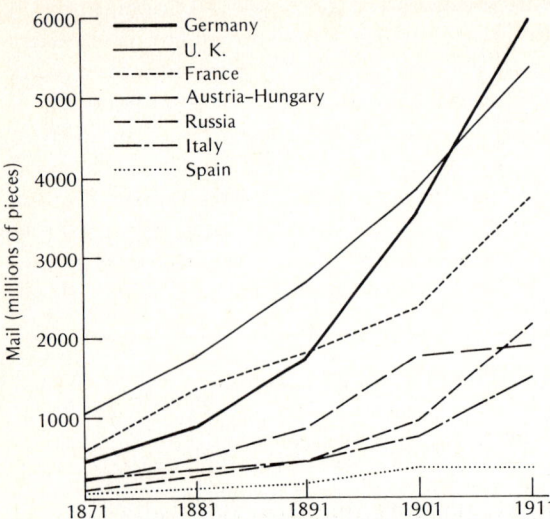

MAIL (MILLIONS OF PIECES)

The volume of mail has been used by some scholars as an indicator of modernization, reflecting increased literacy, internal communication, and commercial activity. In these terms, then, the relative position of the several nations on this chart is suggestive of more than gross population, as are the points at which Germany surpasses first France and then the United Kingdom or at which Russia surpasses Italy and then Austria-Hungary.

The incandescent lamp created a demand for large generating stations to distribute power over a wide area, and by 1900 the manufacture of generators, cables, and motors in turn allowed increased and cheaper production in scores of other fields.

As striking as the new technology itself was the speed with which it was adapted to commercial uses. The telephone, invented in 1879, became a business necessity and an established private convenience within a few decades. The steam turbine, shown in the 1880s to be more efficient than the reciprocating engine, was widely employed for a variety of tasks, and it could soon be fueled by oil as well as coal.

Home sewing machines and bicycles were created directly for the consumer market—in itself a significant reflection of the growing purchasing power of the masses. Inventions were now expected to change people's lives; the automobile in the 1890s, the airplane in the 1900s, and the radio a decade later were all greeted with enthusiasm even before their commercial possibilities were established.

Although greater prosperity and growing populations increased the demand for food, the percentage of the population that made its living in agriculture continued to decline, down to only 8 percent in Britain, 22 percent in Belgium, and 35 percent in Germany. In France, which maintained a more balanced economy, as did the Netherlands and Sweden, 43 percent of the population lived off the land. But everywhere the wider use of machinery and chemical fertilizers increased the capital investment required for farming, and improved transportation intensified international competition. These factors encouraged much greater specialization. The most famous example is Denmark, where agriculture began to center on a highly capitalized and profitable dairy industry. But in France too wheat and sheep production declined in favor of wine grapes and sugar beets, which farmers could raise more profitably. Britain now imported almost all her grain and Germany a great deal.

The influx of agricultural produce from the Americas and Eastern Europe, especially Russia, pushed prices down at the same time that farmers desperately needed cash for the improvements required to make farming profitable, and more young men were forced to leave the countryside. European agriculture was caught in recurrent crises, and landed interests pressed their governments for help. The most common response was protective tariffs, increased by France, Germany, Austria, Russia, Italy, and Spain. Initially applied primarily to agriculture, the new tariffs were soon extended to manufactured goods as well, reversing the

The Great Eastern, combining steam and sail in massive square lines, looms over all other vessels in this print of 1861.
(Photo: The Granger Collection)

earlier trend toward the liberal policy of free trade.

But the trade barriers did not stop the general decline in prices. Strangely, the second industrial revolution occurred in one of the longest and most severe periods of deflation in European history. From the 1870s to 1896, prices, interest rates, and profits fell, with far-reaching effects. Handicraft industries, which had survived side by side with mechanized manufacturing throughout Europe, were forced out of business. So were numerous smaller and less efficient industrial firms. As competition sharpened, many industrialists welcomed the support governments could give through tariffs, state spending, and colonial empire. The great boom in railroad building ended, and governments had to save socially useful lines deserted by bankrupt companies. Economic demands became a central theme of politics as more and more of economic life centered on great factories owned by large corporations (and closely tied to banks and government) that employed hundreds of workers who in turn increasingly organized into industrial unions.

The Demographic Transformation

The growing population that sustained the second industrial revolution evolved a quite different demographic profile from that of any previous period. Europe's population increased—from 295 million in 1870 to nearly

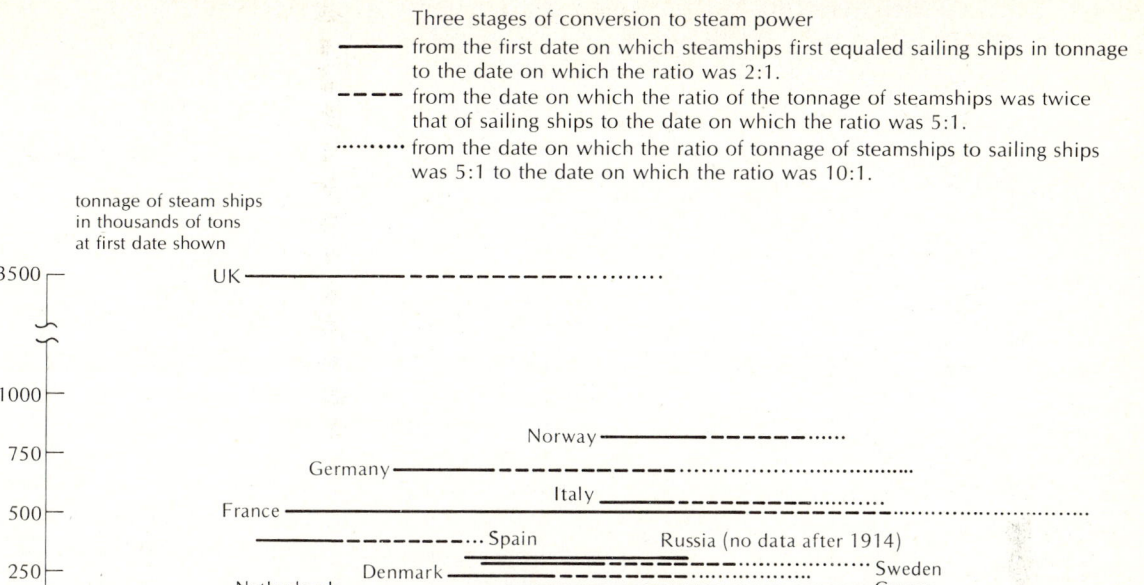

THE TRANSFORMATION FROM SAILING VESSELS TO STEAMBOATS

Three stages of conversion to steam power

―――― from the first date on which steamships first equaled sailing ships in tonnage to the date on which the ratio was 2:1.

– – – – from the date on which the ratio of the tonnage of steamships was twice that of sailing ships to the date on which the ratio was 5:1.

·········· from the date on which the ratio of tonnage of steamships to sailing ships was 5:1 to the date on which the ratio was 10:1.

This chart suggests several points about the conversion to steam from sail that are indicative of the process of industrialization in general: (1) most nations began the process at about the same time except for one or two early leaders, and (2) nations with a smaller investment in a preindustrial economy could convert to new technology more rapidly (Belgium and Spain, for example) so that even late-starters (such as Norway, Italy, and Greece) caught up with the others in the proportion of their ships driven by steam. Note the characteristic contrast between the United Kingdom and France. Britain, with a much larger fleet, converted to steam at a brisk pace, whereas France did so very slowly.

450 million by 1914—although in most of Europe birth rates had begun to decline. By the 1880s, however, mortality rates were falling still more steeply. This pattern of falling birth rates combined with a sharper decline in mortality rates has been named the demographic transition. Continuing in our own time, it has become one of the marks of modernity that has spread from Europe to the rest of the world.

Infant mortality in particular was reduced by improved sanitation, better diet, and the virtual elimination of diseases such as cholera and typhus. By the turn of the century, improvements in medical care were lowering mortality rates still further. This left a net population growth despite a declining birth rate.[1]

Launching an early version of a French airplane.
(Photo: J.-H. Lartigue from Rapho Guillumette)

[1] "Birth rate" is used here as the more familiar term, but "fertility rate"—the ratio of the number of children born to the number of women of child-bearing age—would be more precise.

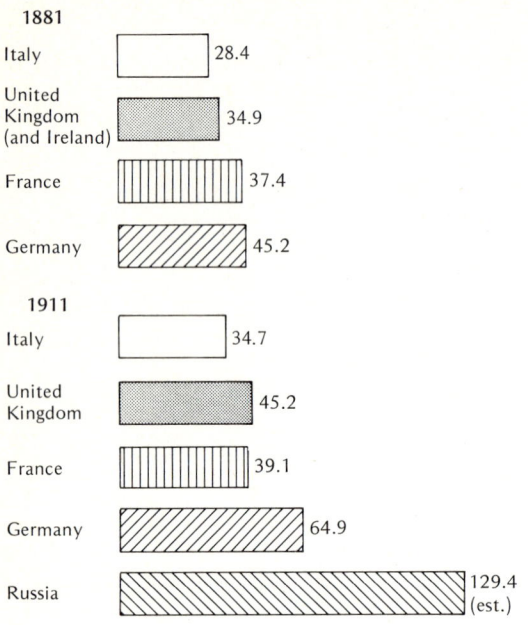

THE CHANGE IN NATIONAL POPULATIONS AT THE TURN OF THE CENTURY (POPULATION IN MILLIONS)

Declining death rates, then, reflect the benefits of industrial prosperity, but the declining birth rates indicate a subtler change. The number of children to have was becoming more a matter of choice aided by the spread of contraception, and where bourgeois values took root and child labor declined, workers followed the upper classes in the trend toward later marriage, fewer births, and smaller families. Although the issues are complicated and the statistics uncertain, the estimates of crude birth rates in about 1910 suggest the social significance of this changing pattern: they were highest in Rumania, Bulgaria, Portugal, Hungary, Italy, and Spain, and lowest in Switzerland, Belgium, and France. Parents who were confident their children would live, who wanted them to inherit property and receive some education, chose to have fewer of them. Before 1850 population growth had been higher in Western than in Central and Eastern Europe. That now was reversed, and the enormous increases in the populations to their east gave Frenchmen added reason to fear Germany's larger and younger population and Germans cause to worry about the Russian giant.

Migration

Another extraordinary demographic change resulted from the greatest movement of peoples in human history. Like the second industrial revolution, this wave of migration continued a century-old trend, but once again the scale of the change was unprecedented. Between 1875 and 1914 some 26 million Europeans emigrated overseas, more than half of them to the United States. The growth of population, an established pattern of internal migration to cities, unemployment in Europe and burgeoning opportunities in the New World, larger boats and cheaper fares, and visions of a better life spreading with literacy all pushed Europe's lower classes to crowd into the steerage of ship after ship. More people left the United Kingdom in total than any other country; in proportion to population the greatest exodus was from Ireland. Before 1890 the United Kingdom, the Scandinavian countries, and Germany sent migrants in the highest proportion to their population. After 1890 the leaders were the United Kingdom, Italy, Spain, and Portugal. But every nation except France (second to the United States as the new home of European emigrants) contributed significant numbers to the movement.

Perhaps a third of those who left their native land to go overseas eventually returned home, but for every one who took a ship, countless more moved from countryside to town and town to city (see Map A-27 in the Cartographic Essay). Mainly the young and the poor, they

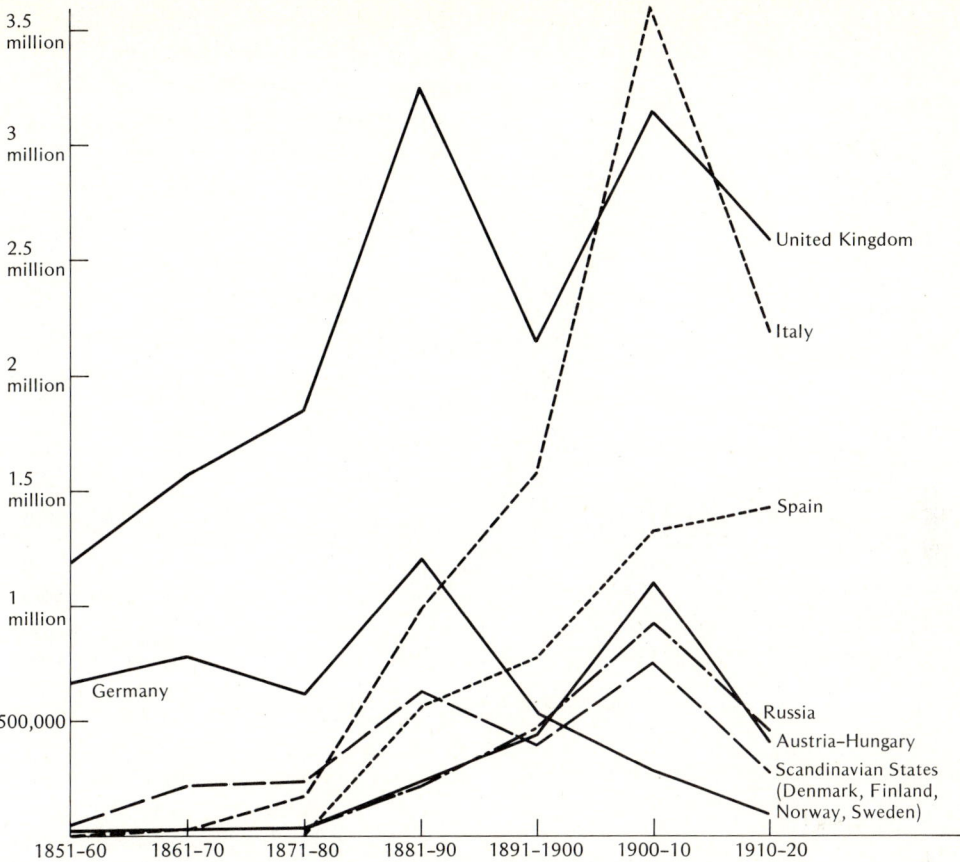

EMIGRATION FROM EUROPE

(Source: Mitchell, B. R., *European Historical Statistics, 1750–1970*, 1975, p. 135.)

were responding to new ambitions as well as perennial misery. In doing so they added to the restless change within Europe—in most cities a majority of residents had been born elsewhere—and carried European languages and cultures around the world. This economic and demographic growth reinforced the dynamism of late nineteenth-century society. New products, new businesses, new careers flourished everywhere, along with more freedom, education, and social mobility. Industrial civilization and progress reached into the peasant hut and the urban slum.

Even the lower classes benefited from the new prosperity. Meat and white bread became an expected although not daily part of the diet for most people in the industrialized countries. Commerce offered cheap products at fixed prices, and jobs in sales and distribution brought new opportunities to rise into the lower-middle class. City crowds in London, Paris, and Berlin in 1900 were strikingly different from those of 1850. They were larger—for cities were bigger (eight European cities had a population of half a million or more in 1880, twenty-nine by 1910) and even workers had

The new electric tram scoots above the ordinary bustle of the streets of Paris in the 1880s.
(Photo: The Granger Collection)

some free time—and they were healthier and cleaner. Their costumes told less about their trade or region; the worker could afford a dress suit, and the shopgirl could wear clothes that were not a mere uniform of her class. Fewer pickpockets and almost no beggars circulated in the streets. By 1900 nearly every city had its electric tramway, rapidly expanding the city beyond the circumferential boulevards that had replaced medieval walls, incorporating suburbs into a metropolitan area, and opening the prospect of better housing even for workers.

There was good reason then for belief in progress. Yet such rapid changes were unsettling, fatal for some occupations and hard on whole regions. In this turbulent society misery and insecurity were less tolerable and harder to excuse. Seen as the byproducts of the very social system that produced so much wealth, they stimulated renewed efforts to change society itself.

II. THE CULTURE OF INDUSTRIAL SOCIETY

By any standard the fifty years before World War I was one of the great periods in the history of music, painting, and writing. Yet much of the artistic expression most admired today was disturbing to contemporaries, different from what they expected and hard to understand.

DEMOGRAPHIC TRANSITION

(Source: Cipolla, Carlo, *The Economic History of World Population*, Pelican, 1962.)

Instead the public, though now more prosperous and literate, preferred commercial entertainments which offended intellectuals who found them wanting in either spontaneity or seriousness. But the expansion of knowledge, especially in the sciences, was such reassuring evidence of general progress that social theorists turned again, as the philosophes had done during the Enlightenment, to explaining it.

Theories of Progress: Comte, Darwin, and Spencer

The philosophy of Auguste Comte (1798–1857), enormously influential from midcentury on, was itself characteristic of much nineteenth-century thought. Clearly rooted in the ideas of the Enlightenment, it gave greater attention to the process of historical change. Like Hegel, Comte sought to erect a comprehensive philosophical system that would encompass all of human knowledge, and like him he believed that his own era had opened the final stage of historical development. Comte was especially impressed, as were most contemporary intellectuals, by the social role of religion, the conquests of natural science, and the possibilities of human progress. For many years private secretary to Saint-Simon, Comte retained the confidence of the early socialists that society would soon be reorganized on rational principles.

Note that everywhere both birth rates and death rates decline. The declining death rates reflect improved distribution of food and better hygiene and health care. The decline in birth rates reflects a change in social behavior. The space between them suggests the rate of population growth, very slight in the case of France, steady in England and Sweden, and sudden in Germany and Russia.

With self-conscious art, the photographer of old Charles Darwin suggests some timeless mystery.
(Photo: New York Public Library/Picture Collection)

terms. In the third, or positive, stage now dawning, human understanding was becoming scientific through objective and precise observation followed by generalization in the form of scientific laws. Every science, he argued, has already passed through the first two stages and into the third—astronomy first, then physics, chemistry, and biology. Now a new science, sociology (Comte coined the term), must crown the progression.

While thus honoring the role of established religion, Comte announced its demise, substituting a "religion of humanity" of his own invention. Some devoted followers accepted his complex scheme whole. But his importance rests rather in the wider agreement with his view that civilization progresses with increased knowledge discovered through scientific method and that the great contemporary need was for the scientific study of society and of man himself. This creed inspired and shaped much of the rapid development of the social sciences—economics, political science, anthropology, sociology, and psychology—achieved in the late nineteenth century.

A more concrete and more shocking theory of human progress emerged from Charles Darwin's *On the Origin of Species,* whose publication in 1859 was a milestone in the history of science.[2] With sober caution, Darwin (1809–1882) had worked much as Comte said a scientist should. Born into a well-known family of clergymen and doctors with ties to many of England's leading intellectuals, Darwin had difficulty in finding a suitable career. But his respect for facts led him to collect evidence in matters of natural history from every available source—his own observations from travel in the South Seas, the work of others, the lore of

He systematically elaborated his positive philosophy in ten volumes published between 1830 and 1845, and these with his other writings established positivism as an international movement even before his death, in 1857. The key to civilization, he argued, is man's understanding of the world, which has developed through three historical stages. In the first, the theological stage, mankind interpreted everything in terms of gods who lived in nature. In the second, or metaphysical, stage men learned through Christianity to think in more abstract

---

[2] The full original title of Darwin's work suggests its broad and provocative implications: *On the Origin of Species by Natural Selection, or the Preservation of Favoured Races in the Struggle for Life.* The first edition sold out on the day of publication.

farmers. He first formulated his concept of natural selection in 1838, but not until Alfred R. Wallace independently developed a very similar theory could he be persuaded to publish his findings. Although Darwin's presentation was the more fully and carefully developed, the parallel theories of the two men suggest how much both owed to ideas already current. Biologists had shown the relationship between biological form and function in impressive detail; geologists had begun to analyze the earth in terms of natural forces, without recourse to sudden cataclysms or divine intervention; classical economists, especially Malthus, had stressed the importance of the cruel conflict for food, which Darwin made the essential key to natural selection.

Darwin established that the variety of species is potentially infinite—rejecting the Classical and Christian idea of immutable forms in nature—and argued that there is an almost constant modification of species, each tested in the universal struggle for existence. He not only presented detailed evidence for evolution but described its mechanism: the fittest survived, a law of progress for all living things.

This scientific theory, expressed with caution and supported by massive evidence, almost instantly became the center of controversies that raged throughout Europe for a generation. Evolution, mutable species, survival determined by brute conflict rather than divine will—each of these challenged established assumptions in science and theology. Nor did Darwin hide his belief that the same laws apply to the development of man and beast. This seemed to many a scandalous disregard of divine providence and Christian teaching. Nowadays, except for fundamentalists, theologians and scientists generally agree that there is no necessary conflict between the concept of evolving species and Christian doctrine, but such tolerance required a distinction between the study of natural laws and religious tradition that in the nineteenth century few were willing to make. Nonetheless Darwinian ideas, often loosely understood, were enthusiastically extended to discussions of morality, politics, and society. "Social Darwinism" proved an invitingly tough-minded way to argue, in the name of human progress, for reform (a better environment makes for better people); but also for ruthless economic competition, racial differences, imperialism, and the necessity of war.

One of the grandest statements of the laws of progress was the *Synthetic Philosophy* of Herbert Spencer (1820–1903), published between 1860 and 1896. Spencer's ideas were closely tied to those of Comte and Darwin, and his contemporaries ranked him among the major philosophers of all time.

Spencer's central principle, which made progress "not an accident, but a necessity," was the evolution of all things from simplicity to complexity, from homogeneity to diversity. With heavy learning, he traced this process in physics and biology, sociology and psychology, economics and ethics. Such comprehensiveness was part of his appeal, and he applied his theses to physical matter, to human understanding, and to social institutions. He was admired for his claim to be hard-headed and practical; but while he refused to worry about the metaphysical abstractions of traditional philosophy, he maintained the assumptions of a narrow and rigid liberalism. He argued that the marketplace is the true test of the fittest, and that it must be uninhibited by state intervention even in behalf of welfare or public education.

When Spencer died, in 1903, much of his work was already outmoded by new developments in the several disciplines, strict laissez faire had been abandoned even by most liberals, and his sort of rationalism had come under heavy attack. His confidence that universal laws of development enshrined the values of middle-class English Protestants would soon seem quaint to most people.

The Natural Sciences

Discoveries in the natural sciences in this period supported the belief that a few universal principles underlie all existence. And in the nineteenth century these principles could still be understood, however imprecisely, by the educated public. The findings of science were expected to improve civilization through both their immediate application to technology and their contributions to general philosophy. Thermodynamics, the study of the relationship between heat and mechanical energy, provides an excellent example.

Building on theorems stated by Nicolas Sadi Carnot early in the century, thermodynamics became the core of nineteenth-century physics. It developed in many directions at once, treating practical problems of steam engines as well as fundamental properties of matter. By midcentury the combined work of scientists in many countries had established that formulas predicting the behavior of gases could be applied to the field of mechanics. This culminated in the mathematical formulation of the two fundamental laws of thermodynamics. One states the principle of the conservation of energy: energy can be transformed into heat or work and back again but can be neither created nor destroyed. The other declares that any closed physical system tends toward equilibrium, a state in which heat is uniformly distributed and therefore cannot be used to produce work.[3] In practical terms this means that heat can be made to do work only when connected through an engine to a cooler body. Philosophically it invites speculation about the universe as a giant machine in which the level of energy must inexorably decline.

The study of magnetism advanced in a similar way from the work of Michael Faraday. He had shown in the 1830s and 1840s that lines of magnetic force are analogous to gravity and that electricity can induce magnetism (and vice versa—the principle of the dynamo). In the 1860s James Clerk Maxwell's equations described the behavior of electricity, magnetism, and light in terms of a single, universal system. Thus gravity, magnetism, electricity, and light were all related. By the end of the century, physics had established mathematical laws of theoretical beauty and practical power extending from the universe to the atom, which was then conceived of as a miniature solar system.

The fundamental generalizations of chemistry are contained in the periodic law and periodic table published by Dmitri Mendeleev in 1869. Compounds and elements had been clearly distinguished for only half a century, and the difference between molecules and atoms came to be generally accepted only in 1860. Yet Mendeleev's table established a marvelous symmetry, so precise that the elements could all be charted by atomic weight, with similar elements occurring at regular intervals. This regularity even allowed for the prediction of unknown elements that would when discovered fill the gaps on the table.

Such achievements resulted from the efforts of hundreds of scientists, freely exchanging ideas across national boundaries, working with precise methods and the logic of mathematics. Experiments admired in the 1820s seemed crude by the 1870s, and science became the province of carefully trained professionals rather than inspired amateurs. Research demanded even more systematic organization and larger and more expensive laboratories. The success of science stimulated a general expansion of education, and most of the disciplines that constitute the modern university achieved their separate identity, establishing professional organizations and scholarly journals, in the late nineteenth century.

Much of the theoretical scientific knowledge opened the way to very practical benefits. Thermodynamics led to the development of

---

[3] The measure or amount of energy unavailable for work is called entropy, a term coined by the physicist Rudolf Clausius in 1865.

more efficient sources of power. The investigations of electricity led to the telegraph by midcentury and to electric lights and motors for hundreds of uses a generation later. Proof that germs were not spontaneously generated as was generally believed came from the Frenchman Louis Pasteur's studies in the 1860s of why wine spoiled, which led to techniques of pasteurization, of crucial importance in the wine, dairy, and silk industries. His work on immunology enabled him to find a preventive vaccine for rabies. In England Joseph Lister discovered that germs could be killed by carbolic acid, and the application of that knowledge made surgery a reasonable remedy rather than a desperate gamble. A decade later Robert Koch in Germany showed that different diseases were caused by distinct microbes, discovered the microorganism responsible for tuberculosis, and opened the way to new techniques in bacteriology and in the battle against communicable diseases. Advances such as these not only improved agriculture and medicine but stimulated the drive to make sanitation and public health into systematic sciences. Tangible evidence, as well as intellectual pride, supported the view that science progressed at an unprecedented pace for the benefit of all mankind.

Formal and Popular Culture

The creative arts continued to flourish, benefiting from high prestige and ever larger and more sophisticated audiences. Yet the forms and styles employed grew so diverse that the arts hardly seemed to speak for a single civilization. One reason, and the one that disturbed contemporaries least, was the trend toward national styles. The use of folk elements and distinct traditions gave an instantly recognizable national identity to English or Russian novels and French, German, or Russian music. Another reason for the variety of artistic styles was the tendency for artists to act as social critics, thereby bringing issues of politics and values that troubled society into the realm of aesthetics. Thus the tension between the individual and society, between the artist's personal perceptions and the unstable conventions of a world undergoing rapid change, remained a central theme of nineteenth-century art. These concerns and then the reaction against them in favor of a "purer" art led to the bewildering variety of competing movements. "Naturalism," the "Pre-Raphaelites," "Impressionism," the "Decadents," "Symbolism"—such self-conscious labels were frequently proclaimed with angry manifestoes against previous art and present culture.

Naturalists claimed that the artist, like a scientist, should present life in objective detail after careful research. This aim was particularly suited to the novel; and Emile Zola, with descriptions precise as acid of industrial and Parisian life, was a master of the school. Determinism, through blood inheritance or social class, was a favorite and related theme in this Darwinian age. It proved especially effective on the stage where the protagonists' destiny inexorably unfolded before the new audience slowly won over to realistic drama in the two decades before World War I.

For the realistic painters of midcentury or the Pre-Raphaelites of England (who took their name from the pious and simpler art of the early Renaissance), much of a painting's importance lay in its subject matter and message. Then a new generation of painters broke with this tradition to concentrate on capturing the effects of light and color almost as if the artist's brilliance in analyzing and recreating such effects was in itself the purpose of painting. Artists denied exhibition at the annual Paris Salon of 1867 established the Salon des Refusés, proudly contesting the validity of official taste. These are the painters we remember, for they included some of the leaders of Impressionism (see Plates 58–59), whose golden age was the 1870s and 1880s, among them Auguste Renoir and Claude Monet. They and the Post-Impressionist Paul Cézanne were recognized in their own lifetime as ranking among the great artists of Westen history, but painters only slightly younger, like Paul Gauguin and Vincent van Gogh, turned to still newer and more personal styles (see Plates 60–62).

Thus each of the arts tended to develop on its own terms, independent of established judgments. Art nouveau, turning its back on the practical and efficient industrial world of the turn of the century, delighted in applying ornamental arabesques to everything from wrought iron to poster lettering and printed cloth. Poetry, like painting, became an increasingly private expression indifferent to conventional morality, often obscure, and constructed in terms of complex aesthetic doctrines. The fashionable fascination with death, languid despair, and perfumed aestheticism was called decadent by its critics, a label willingly accepted until it gave way to Symbolism. A movement of French poets that spread throughout Europe, symbolism interpreted the things one sees and describes as symbolic of a deeper and more spiritual reality. Art, like life itself, was to be complexly understood on several levels of meaning at once, and individual style had become a personal conquest, a private bridge between the artist's identity and external society. Still more radical changes in the arts occurred in the decade preceding World War I, changes that further separated the artist from the broader public but would shape the art of the twentieth century.

In contrast, architecture, the most immediately social of all the arts, was the least innovative until the very end of the century. Only then were the structural and aesthetic possibilities hidden in railroad sheds, bridges, and exhibit halls developed into the skyscraper and a new architectural style. Perhaps the tension between individual and society so fruitful elsewhere was stultifying to so public and functional an art. Even when they achieved real beauty, the great buildings of the nineteenth century were eclectically dressed in the styles of other periods. Churches evoked the spiritual coherence of the High Middle Ages; banks and public buildings expressed in stone the civic virtues of Greece and Rome. Even apartment houses usually imitated some earlier epoch, as if to make new wealth feel more secure.

Popular Culture

European popular culture changed radically in the second half of the century. Traditional festivals and games, once tied to the local region, gradually gave way to public amusements reflecting an increasingly urban life and the greater leisure and wealth of the masses. With each change to a new popular medium, from operetta to music hall to vaudeville and—after the turn of the century—silent films, a larger part of the population shared in public entertainment. Popular culture thus tended to become more uniform within each nation and across Europe. It also became more formal (the Marquis of Queensberry rules for boxing, for instance, date from 1867) and increasingly commercial, both in the music hall and on the athletic field. Leading actors and actresses became stars whose offstage lives were part of their fascination as these forms of light entertainment, along with the circus and amusement parks, boomed, their clientele swelled by families from the lower-middle and working classes. Soccer, once the sport of the English public school, became professional (most of Europe's famous teams were formed around the turn of the century), attracting huge, noisy, Sunday crowds. While workers shared these urban entertainments, the middle classes began to crowd summer resorts and to play recently formalized games like golf and tennis. This profitable popular culture assumed and to some extent created an audience with common tastes and in doing so helped bridge the social gap between workers and the middle class, between

The bridge across the Firth of Forth stands as a monument to the age of iron and steel. This photograph was taken shortly after the bridge's completion in 1890.
(Photo: The Granger Collection)

town and city. Newspapers had similar effects as publishers learned to increase their circulation (several now approached daily sales of a million copies) through sensational articles and colorful features written in a direct and less literary style. Like the millions of popular novels (now more specialized into women's romances, adventure stories especially for children, and penny thrillers), such writing abandoned any pretense to cultivated taste, further separating formal from popular culture.

These changes were related to another of immeasurable importance: for the first time in Western history, in the major nations at least, a majority of the adult population could read and write. By the 1880s governments almost everywhere, recognizing the importance of literacy to politics and industry, had made education universal and compulsory; and school fees had been reduced or eliminated. In 1850 only in Prussia could most of the adult population read or write; by 1900 more than 90 percent of the adult population of Germany, France, and Great Britain was literate, and the proportion elsewhere was climbing rapidly. Mass schooling was usually limited to a few years of the most elementary subjects, and aside from special supplementary instructions in workers' classes, night schools, and special vocational institutes, few of the poor had any opportunity for further training. The amount and kind of education they received was one of the clearest distinctions between the middle class and those below it. Nevertheless the schooling available to everybody was steadily extended, and the barriers separating mass education from the sort of preparation that led to secondary school and university were gradually lowered.

For most contemporaries society's extraordinary commitment to education ranked with liberty, industrial prosperity, and scientific knowledge as proof of social progress. But there were some who saw in the quality of popular entertainment and mass journalism what they felt would prove to be an ominous new threat to Western culture.

III. ATTACKS ON LIBERAL CIVILIZATION

Much of liberalism's promise was being fulfilled in the last quarter of the nineteenth century. After 1870 new constitutions made governments more representative and civil rights more secure; expanding trade and production lifted the standard of living, and individuals enjoyed greater social opportunities; laws became more humane; peace, foreign and domestic, seemed more certain. Yet many intellectuals expressed contempt for middle-class society, radicals sought the end of the capitalist system, and conservatives and Christians mounted new attacks on liberal values. Moreover thinkers of many sorts strongly challenged optimistic liberal assumptions about the nature of progress and man's rationality.

Marxism

No criticism of contemporary society has proved more influential, no nineteenth-century theory more lasting than the work of Karl Marx. Marx was born in 1818 into a middle-class Rhineland Jewish family that had prospered with the emancipation from civil disabilities brought by the revolutionary armies from France. He was an able student and received an excellent education at the leading German universities. Too radical to be permitted an academic career, he turned to journalism and became editor of a famous liberal newspaper, the *Rheinische Zeitung*. But his attacks on censorship and his views on economics led the Prussian government to demand his removal, and in 1843 Marx left for Paris. There he met other exiles and leading French radicals, men to whom he would later give the enduring label of "utopian" socialists, and he established a friendship with Friedrich Engels that would become a lifetime's collaboration.

Trained in German philosophy, abreast of contemporary economics, and in touch with the currents of radicalism, Marx began in Paris the systematic development of his own ideas. He outlined his theory in a powerful, apocalyptic tone in the *Communist Manifesto,* written jointly with Engels, which was published just before the revolutions of 1848. Little noticed at first, it proved to be one of the great pieces of propaganda of all time, a specific program and a general call to action combined with a philosophy of history. Marx devoted the rest of his life—from 1849 to 1883, which he spent in poverty-stricken exile in London—to the painstaking elaboration of his ideas in essays, letters, and the first volume of *Das Kapital,* published in 1867. Engels, who shared Marx's exile in Britain, edited the second and third volumes, which appeared in 1885 and 1894.

Marx wrote with verve on contemporary affairs—his essays on the revolutions of 1848 and Louis Napoleon's coup d'état are classics—but fundamentally he wanted, like so many thinkers of his time, to build a comprehensive philosophical system. Later in the century his followers would compare him with Darwin as the "discoverer" of the "law" of history, dialectical materialism. The dialectic came from

THE IMAGE OF MAN

In Modern Art

The birth of the modern world is linked with two revolutions—the industrial revolution, symbolized by the invention of the steam engine, and the political revolution, which began in America and France under the banner of democracy. Both are still going on. Industrialization and democracy, as goals, are sought all over the world. Western science and political ideology (and in their wake all the other products of our civilization) are spreading to the remotest corners of the globe. Their impact has transformed every facet of our lives, at a rate so rapid and violent that many of us are said to be suffering from "future shock."

How have these twin revolutions affected artists? Their position in the modern world, when measured against the standards of the past, can only be called paradoxical. Industrialization has produced vast new wealth, but the share of our income, public or private, spent on art patronage is very much less than it was in earlier times. Yet the artist's public has grown tremendously in comparison with the past; museums, most of them founded within the past hundred years, attract millions of visitors today, and books on modern art are available in every bookshop. The artist's prestige, too, if not financial condition, is higher than ever before. In antiquity and the Middle Ages there had been no distinction between art and craft; the Renaissance invented the concept of artistic genius but reserved it for a very few such as Leonardo da Vinci and Michelangelo, and even they were dependent on the wishes of their patrons. From the early nineteenth century on, however, artists have been acclaimed as superior to any established authority, subservient to nothing but their own impulses. They assumed, in fact, a role as exalted and as independent from the rest of society as the prophets of the Old Testament. But, like prophets, artists now had to face the prospect of being without honor in their own country. Indeed, they were expected to be. The modern artist's ideal is the bohemian, the "glorious failure" who goes through life neglected and ridiculed, only to be hailed as a genius by posterity. Actually, few of them have had careers exemplifying this pattern—Vincent van Gogh is the most famous case—yet there can be no doubt that the modern artist's lot has been more troubled than that of artists in earlier periods. Freedom has had to be purchased at the expense of security. Even artists who were financially successful have often felt it incumbent upon them to live as if they were not, so as to avoid becoming dependent on the public's favor which to them seemed a betrayal of their calling.

In a world without the framework of traditional constraints, the artist's latitude of action is both more frightening and more exhilarating than anybody else's. One of the modern artist's risks—and at the same time an acknowledgment of importance—is suppression for ideological reasons. In Hitler's Germany any artist who did not work in the government-approved style was declared "degenerate" and forbidden to exhibit; a similar lack of freedom prevails in Russia today, where the dogma of "socialist realism" is enforced, even though in the early years after the Revolution of 1917 modern artists were welcomed as kindred spirits since they, too, were revolutionary. In the West too there have been times when artists working in unfamiliar idioms were denounced by conservative politicians as "subversive." Such experiences only tend to reinforce the modern artist's distrust of the Establishment. Nor can the creative person rely on public opinion, which is swayed all too often by the tides of taste and fashion. The modern artist thus seems to be forever cast in the role of the outsider, regardless of fame or prestige.

This basic change in the artist's condition may help to account for the fact that no coherent image of man has emerged in modern art. The shared values which enabled the artists of earlier ages to coin such an image have either disappeared or lost their reality; Jupiter (as Karl Marx once observed) could not survive against the lightning rod. Even portraiture, a continuous and vital tradition since the Early Renaissance, succumbed to the invention of photography in the mid-nineteenth century (see Plate 49). What, then, could take the place of traditional subject matter? The answer is summed up in such nineteenth-century slogans as "art for art's sake" or Walter Pater's claim that "all art aspires to the condition of music." Music, needless to say, is nonrepresentational; it arouses emotion through the harmonious and rhythmic manipulation of sound. Once it was acknowledged as the highest of the arts, painters began to think of their work as a kind of "visual music," governed by laws that could not be derived from observation of the outside world. At first they were content to give their works "musical" titles, with the subject mentioned only in second place as a sop to the public (the picture popularly known as "Whistler's Mother" was exhibited as "Arrangement in Black and Grey: The Artist's Mother" but by 1910 some painters had gone completely "nonobjective" by eliminating representation altogether, and their successors are still with us today.

Wherever we do encounter the human image in nineteenth-century art, man's condition is seen as shaped by the environment, physical or social, as in Daumier's "Third-Class Carriage" (Plate 55), Brown's "The Last of England" (Plate 56), Courbet's "Stone Breakers" (Plate 57), and Degas's "Glass of Absinthe" (Plate 58). The sympathy these pictures evoke has been consciously avoided by Seurat, whose "Bathers" (Plate 59) are so depersonalized that we perceive them only as a part of their setting rather than as individuals. A "musical" title would seem entirely appropriate to such a painting. It is only in what may be broadly termed the expressionist tradition of modern art that the human image retains a central importance; but its goal is to probe extreme states of the psyche, not to define the nature of man. The beginnings of this line of development go back to the great French Romantics of the early nineteenth century: Géricault's "Madman" (Plate 50) leads to Munch's "Scream" (Plate 61) seventy years later, and ultimately to Kienholz's "State Hospital" (Plate 64), just as Delacroix's "Chopin" (Plate 51) is prophetic of van Gogh's "Self-Portrait" (Plate 60), Rouault's "Christ" (Plate 62), and Picasso's "Weeping Woman" (Plate 63). Such images invite a twofold interpretation. They are surely signs of a general and continuing crisis due to the revolutionary changes we have been experiencing ever since the end of the eighteenth century. At the same time they afford an insight into the cause of these changes: Western man's heightened awareness of personal intellectual, moral, and emotional powers. Having so vastly expanded our range of thought, action, and feeling, we are faced with the task of redefining our own identity, to give meaning to our existence, outside the metaphysical framework that sheltered our ancestors. The modern artist senses, more sharply than the rest of us, that this is indeed a time to try men's souls.

Ingres, whose long career spans the first two-thirds of the nineteenth century, was the greatest disciple of David (see Plate 46). He is usually called a Neoclassicist and his opponents Romantics. Their quarrels recall the old debate between "Poussinists" and "Rubenists" (see Plates 43–45), with Ingres insisting that drawing is superior to color while the Romantics maintained the contrary. Actually, the views of both factions were far more doctrinaire than their pictures. In his portrait of *Louis Bertin,* Ingres's allegiance seems to be to observed reality pure and simple rather than to any theoretical convictions. There is so little "style" here that at first glance the picture looks like a superior kind of photograph. Had it been painted a decade later Ingres might well have been accused of working from a daguerreotype. In fact Ingres's realism and the development of photography sprang from the same impulse: a demand for the unvarnished scientific truth. Nothing less would do for the age of the industrial revolution. When the first practical photographic processes became available in the late 1830s, they were hailed as "the pencil of nature," and portraiture became their chief task. Thus Ingres was the last great professional in a field soon to be monopolized by the camera. His *Bertin,* however unvarnished it may seem, is a masterpiece of interpretation, endowing the sitter with a massive force of personality that is almost frightening. Individualistic, self-reliant, aggressive, Bertin seems the perfect image of the bourgeois entrepreneur, the hero of "free enterprise."

Plate 49. Dominique Ingres
LOUIS BERTIN
1832, canvas, height 46"
Louvre Museum, Paris

Plate 50. Théodore Géricault
THE MADMAN
1821–1824, canvas, height 24"
Museum of Fine Arts, Ghent

If Ingres's *Bertin* represents the class of men that shaped the character of post-Napoleonic Europe, the two portraits on these pages—one of a madman, the other of a great composer—seem more closely related to each other than to the forces and events of their time. Ingres shows his sitter as he wanted to be seen, squarely facing his public; Géricault's and Delacroix's subjects, in contrast, are so completely caught up in their private worlds that they remain unaware of the observer. They are indeed not portraits in the traditional sense but studies of extreme states of the human condition, and it is this that stamps them as Romantic.

Romanticism refers to an attitude of mind, rather than to a specific style, and is therefore harder to define. The word derives from the vogue for medieval tales of adventure, called "romances" because they were written in a Romance language, not in Latin. This interest in the long-neglected "dark ages," however, sprang from a revulsion against established values of any kind and had its roots in a craving for emotional experience. Almost any experience would do, real or imaginary, provided it was intense enough. The declared aim of the Romantics was to tear down the artifices barring the way to a "return to nature"—nature the unbounded, wild and ever-changing, nature the sublime and picturesque. Were man to act "naturally," giving his impulses free rein, evil would disappear. In the name of nature the Romantics worshiped liberty, power, love, violence, the Greeks, the Middle Ages, or anything that aroused their response, but actually they worshiped emotion as an end in itself. At its extreme this attitude could be expressed only through direct action, not through works of art, for the creation of a work of art demands some detachment and self-awareness. What Wordsworth, the great Romantic poet, said about poetry—that it is "emotion recollected in tranquillity"—applies also to painting. To cast his fleeting experience into permanent form, the Romantic artist needs a style. It is hardly surprising that painters such as Géricault and Delacroix preferred the vivid color, broad, open brushwork, and spontaneous emotion of Rubens, Hals, Velázquez, and Goya (see Plates 37–39, 48) to the meticulous draftsmanship and painstaking detail of Poussin, David, and Ingres (see Plate 43, 46, 49). Géricault, the older of the two, began his career as an admirer of Gros (see Plate 47), at a time when Napoleon was at the height of his glory. He died in 1824, at the age of 33. His interest in man's emotional life led him to befriend the director of the Paris insane asylum, for whom he painted a series of portraits of individual patients illustrating various types of derangement. Our picture belongs to this group. Géricault's sympathy toward the subject, his ability to see the victims of mental disease as fellow human beings rather than as accursed or bewitched outcasts, is one of the noblest fruits of the Romantic movement.

Delacroix had his first great public success in the year of Géricault's death. Until his own death almost forty years later, he remained the foremost Romantic painter of France and the acknowledged antagonist of Ingres. He rarely did portraits other than those of his personal friends and fellow victims of the "Romantic agony" such as the Polish composer Frédéric Chopin. Here we see the image of the Romantic hero at its purest: a blend of Gros's *Napoleon* and Géricault's *Madman,* he is consumed by the fire of his genius.

Plate 51. *Eugène Delacroix*
FRÉDÉRIC CHOPIN
1838, canvas, height 18"
Louvre Museum, Paris

Landscape had been part of the Western tradition of painting as early as Roman times (see Plate 6). In the seventeenth century it became an important subject in its own right. The Romantics, with their worship of nature, raised it to a new level of significance; landscape painting conveyed some of their most profoundly felt emotions. The *Monk at the Seashore* by the German painter Caspar David Friedrich, an early and memorable example, embodies an experience central to the Romantic imagination: that of the sublime. The tiny, lonesome figure contemplating the immensity of sea and sky becomes a moving symbol of man's insignificance when confronted with the cosmos. Turner's *Slave Ship* seeks to achieve the same effect in more dramatic fashion. First entitled *Slavers Throwing Overboard the Dead and Dying—Typhoon Coming On,* the painting is, on one level of meaning, a protest against the inhumanity of the slave trade: threatened by a storm, the captain casts his human cargo overboard. The typhoon appears to be nature's retribution for his greed and cruelty, but it is also

Plate 52. William Turner
THE SLAVE SHIP
1839, canvas, height 36"
Museum of Fine Arts, Boston

more than that, a catastrophe that engulfs everything, not merely the slaver and his victims but the sea itself with its crowds of fantastic and oddly harmless-looking fish. While we sense the force of Turner's vision, most of us today, perhaps with a twinge of guilt, tend to enjoy this explosion of color for its own sake rather than as a vehicle for the awesome emotions the artist meant to evoke. The English art critic John Ruskin, who owned *The Slave Ship,* saw in it "the true, the beautiful, and the intellectual"; to modern eyes it seems, rather, "an airy vision, painted with tinted steam" (to cite the uncharitable but acute characterization of Turner's work by John Constable, another important English landscape painter of the early nineteenth century). The very simplicity of Friedrich's *Monk at the Seashore,* painted three decades earlier, strikes us as more convincing than do the pyrotechnics of Turner.

Plate 53. Caspar David Friedrich
MONK AT THE SEASHORE
1808, canvas, height 43¼"
Schloss Charlottenburg
Berlin (West)

Plate 54. Camille Corot
SELF-PORTRAIT
ca. 1835, canvas, height 13½"
Uffizi Gallery, Florence

This self-portrait by the great French landscapist Camille Corot is so cool and straightforward that we can hardly think of it as Romantic. It contains no hint of the emotionalism we have come to associate with the movement. Yet in at least one important respect it mirrors a characteristically Romantic attitude—it is painted out-of-doors, in brilliant sunshine. Until the early nineteenth century, painting had been confined to the studio; artists would record their impressions of nature in drawings or watercolors, but to paint out-of-doors was regarded as undesirable, technically as well as aesthetically. The equipment it demanded was far too cumbersome to be carried about, and the process itself was too slow to record the ever-changing conditions of directly observed nature. The Romantics, sensitive to transitory moods, upset this centuries-old tradition; while some of them continued to paint landscapes indoors, others insisted on working under the open sky so as to capture all the subtle gradations of light and atmosphere they experienced at a particular moment. Soon industry came to their aid by producing ready-to-use oil paints in tubes, packed in convenient boxes, as well as portable easels and stools. The pictures produced on the spot with the aid of such equipment were small in size and lacked the precise detail of earlier landscapes, but they had a freshness and immediacy never achieved before. Corot was a pioneer in this novel kind of landscape painting; it is hardly a surprise, therefore, that he should have chosen to do his self-portrait in the same way. We see him in his working clothes, observing himself with the same directness and clarity that distinguish his views of the French and Italian countryside. The result is strangely timeless—it might have been painted yesterday rather than in the heyday of Romanticism.

Within a few decades after its beginnings in the last eighteenth century, the industrial revolution had profoundly disturbed and transformed every facet of man's existence in the Western world. It was not until the middle of the nineteenth, however, that artists began to reflect these changes in the themes they chose for their work. *The Third-Class Carriage,* by the French cartoonist and painter Honoré Daumier, is a powerful early example. It captures a peculiarly modern human condition, "the lonely crowd": these people have in common only that they are traveling together in the same railway car. They take no notice of one another—each is alone with his own thoughts. Daumier explores this state with an insight into character and a breadth of sympathy worthy of Rembrandt, whose work he revered. His feeling for the dignity of the poor also suggests Louis Le Nain (see Plate 42), whose work had recently been rediscovered by French critics. Ironically, Daumier found no public for his paintings, even though he was famous for his satirical cartoons. Only a few friends encouraged him and, a year before his death in 1879, arranged his first one-man show.

Plate 55. Honoré Daumier
THIRD-CLASS CARRIAGE
ca. 1862, canvas, height 26"
The Metropolitan Museum of Art, Bequest of Mrs. H. O. Havemeyer, 1929
The H. O. Havemeyer Collection, New York

Plate 56. Ford Madox Brown
THE LAST OF ENGLAND
1852–1853, wood panel, height 32½"
City Museum and Art Gallery
Birmingham, England

Although Daumier's *Third-Class Carriage* has a contemporary theme, its style is akin to that of the great Romantic, Delacroix (see Plate 51), whose sweeping brushwork and dramatic lighting derive from the Baroque. Other mid-nineteenth-century painters reacted against Romanticism not only in their choice of subject matter but by adopting a radically different style, as evidenced on these two pages. As early as 1846, the French poet and art critic Charles Baudelaire had called for paintings that would express "the heroism of modern life." His friend, the painter Gustave Courbet, made an artistic creed of this demand. A socialist in politics who was deeply affected by the revolutionary upheavals of 1848, Courbet came to believe that the Romantic stress on emotion and imagination was merely an escape from the realities of the time. The modern artist must rely on his own direct experience alone, he must be a realist ("I cannot paint an angel because I have never seen one," he said). Courbet's realism recalls the art of Caravaggio (see Plate 33); like Caravaggio, his work was denounced for its supposed vulgarity and lack of spiritual content. The storm broke when he exhibited *The Stone Breakers* (Plate 57), the first canvas fully embodying his goals. Courbet had seen two men working on a road and had asked them to pose for him in his studio. He has painted them solidly and matter-of-factly, without any pathos or sentiment; the young man's face is averted, the old one's half-hidden by a hat. Yet Courbet cannot have picked them casually; their contrast in age is significant—one is too old for such heavy work, the other too young. Endowed with the dignity of their symbolic status, they do not turn to us for sympathy. Another of Courbet's friends, the socialist Proudhon,

Plate 57. Gustave Courbet
THE STONE BREAKERS
1849, canvas, height 22½"
Collection Oskar Reinhart, Winterthur, Switzerland

likened them to a parable from the Gospels.

Meanwhile, a concern with the "heroism of modern life" asserted itself quite independently in England as well, although the movement lacked a leader of Courbet's stature and assertiveness. Its best known product is probably *The Last of England* (Plate 56) by Ford Madox Brown, which enjoyed vast popularity in the English-speaking world during the latter half of the century. The subject—a group of emigrants watching the coast of their homeland disappear as they set out on their long overseas journey—may no longer carry the same emotional charge it once did, yet there can be no question that Brown has treated an important modern theme and that he has done so with touching seriousness. If the pathos of the scene seems a bit theatrical to us, its documentary quality gains conviction from the impersonal precision of detail, which strikes us as almost photographic; no hint of subjective "handwriting" is permitted to intervene between us and the subject.

Plate 58. Edgar Degas
THE GLASS OF ABSINTHE
1876, canvas, height 36"
Louvre Museum, Paris

For realists such as Courbet or Ford Madox Brown, subject matter was a primary consideration; style was a means to an end, the end being to present significant aspects of modern life as concretely as possible. During the last third of the nineteenth century, this relationship came to be reversed: the "how" now overshadowed the "what." A group of painters in Paris, dubbed Impressionists by a hostile critic (because their work looked so sketchy and unfinished to him), painted "slices of life" that might or might not include human beings and that no longer claimed to be significant in themselves. What gave them importance was the way they were painted, their brilliance of light and color, their freshness and originality of vision. Often the scenes the Impressionists chose were studiedly casual, like *The Glass of Absinthe* (Plate 58) by Edgar Degas. The disenchanted pair at the café table is sharply observed but, as it were, out of the corner of the artist's eye. The design, at first glance, seems as accidental as a snapshot (Degas was an enthusiastic amateur photographer), yet the longer we look, the more we realize that everything has been made to dovetail precisely, that the zigzag of empty tables between us and the luckless couple reinforces their brooding loneliness. Degas had been trained in the tradition of Ingres (see Plate 49); this may account for his strong sense of human character, which sets him apart from his fellow Impressionists. Had he been born fifty years earlier, he might well have become the greatest professional portraitist of his time.

In one respect *The Glass of Absinthe* is uncharacteristic of Impressionism: its subdued color scheme. Seurat's *Bathers* (Plate 59), in contrast, shows the brightness and intensity which led one conservative critic to complain that such

Plate 59. Georges Seurat
BATHERS
1883–1884, canvas, height 79"
The National Gallery, London

pictures hurt his eyes. The choice of subject—people enjoying their leisure on a sunny midsummer day—is equally typical of Impressionist painting. So is its shimmering surface, which results from the way the paint has been applied in separate dots or flicks of pure color. Otherwise, however, Seurat's picture hardly conforms to what we would expect of a quick "impression"; the simplified, smooth contours and the deliberate spacing of these immobile figures give the scene a timeless stability such as we have not encountered since the time of Giotto and Masaccio (see Plates 14, 19). The triumph of Impressionism had indeed been short-lived. Within less than twenty years after its creation in the late 1860s, some of its chief exponents began to search for a style that would combine the virtues of Impressionism with the solidity and durability of the Old Masters. Seurat was the most consistent and methodical of these "Post-Impressionists" (as they have come to be called for lack of a more striking term). The very fact that *Bathers* is a very large canvas, carefully prepared by numerous preliminary studies, demonstrates his ambition to rival the great wall painters of the Renaissance.

Plate 60. Vincent van Gogh
SELF-PORTRAIT
1889, canvas, height 22½"
Collection Mr. and Mrs. John Hay Whitney
New York

While Seurat was reshaping Impressionism into a more severe, classical style, Vincent van Gogh pursued the opposite direction, for he believed that Impressionism did not give the artist enough freedom to express his emotions. His early interests were in literature and religion; profoundly dissatisfied with the values of industrial society and imbued with a strong sense of mission, he worked for a while as lay preacher among poor coal miners before he took up painting. Van Gogh's early work has the dark tonality of Daumier and Courbet (see Plates 55 and 57). In 1886, however, he went to Paris, where he met Seurat and other leading artists who opened his eyes to the vital importance of color. His Impressionist phase, although brief, was of key importance for van Gogh's further development; Paris had taught him to see the sensuous beauty of the visible world, yet painting continued to be a vessel for his personal emotions. In order to explore this inner reality with the new means at his command he went to Arles, in the south of France. It was there, between 1888 and 1890, that he produced his greatest pictures. The sectarian Christianity of his early years now gave way to a mystic faith in a creative force animating all forms of life—the missionary had become a prophet. We see him in that role in the *Self-Portrait* on this page, his emaciated, luminous head set off against a whirlpool of darkness. "I want to paint men and women with that something of the eternal which the halo used to symbolize," van Gogh had written, groping to define the human essence that was his aim in pictures such as this. Clearly, the methodical color dots of Seurat were inadequate for his purpose. Van Gogh's brushwork is inalienably personal, each stroke filled with so much movement that it becomes not merely a deposit of

Plate 61. Edvard Munch
THE SCREAM
1893, canvas, height 36"
National Museum, Oslo

color but an incisive graphic gesture. At the time of this *Self-Portrait* the artist had already begun to suffer fits of mental illness. Despairing of a cure, he committed suicide a year later, for he felt very deeply that art alone made his life worth living.

Van Gogh's discontent with the spiritual ills of Western civilization was widely shared toward the end of the nineteenth century. It pervades the early work of a gifted Norwegian, Edvard Munch, who came to Paris in 1889 and was influenced by van Gogh, among others. *The Scream* is an image of fear, the terrifying, unreasoned fear we feel in a nightmare. Its long wavy lines seem to carry the echo of the scream into every corner of the picture, making of earth and sky one great sounding board of fear.

Plate 62. Georges Rouault
HEAD OF CHRIST
*1905, oil on paper, mounted on canvas
height 54", Collection of the Chrysler Museum at Norfolk
Gift of Walter P. Chrysler, Jr.*

The twentieth century may be said to have begun several years late, so far as art is concerned. Between 1901 and 1906, several comprehensive exhibitions of the work of the great Post-Impressionists were held in Paris, making their achievements known to a broad public for the first time. The young painters who had grown up in the morbid mood of the 1890s were profoundly impressed, and several developed a radical new style full of violent color and bold distortions. They so shocked critical opinion that they were dubbed the Fauves (the wild beasts), a label they wore with pride. What brought them together was not a common program but a shared sense of liberation; their work was only loosely related, and the group dissolved after a few years. Nevertheless, its members exerted a lasting influence on that broad stream of modern art which we call expressionism. Among the Fauves, Georges Rouault was the only one for whom the image of man remained a central concern, the true heir of van Gogh. The savage expressiveness of his huge *Head of Christ* mirrors his anguish at the corrupt state of the world. But this expressiveness does not reside only in the "image quality" of the face; the slashing strokes of the brush speak with equal eloquence of the artist's rage and compassion. If we cover up the upper third of the picture, it ceases to be a recognizable image, yet its expressive power is hardly diminished.

Picasso's *Weeping Woman,* by comparison, strikes us as far more disciplined but at the same time more daringly distorted, as if the artist had first carved up this woman's head and hand and then reassembled the anatomical details in a new order, making them spiky and sharp-edged in the process. The inner logic of the method is attested by its success: Picasso has created an image of almost unbearable intensity, reflecting his horror and despair at the time of the Spanish Civil War, which he saw as the prelude of a still greater holocaust. The First World War had produced no such emotional involvement in Picasso; he spent those years perfecting a severely formal, semi-abstract style known as Cubism. It took the agony of his own country to turn him into an expressionist. In his *Weeping Woman* he found a way to put the austere precision of Cubism to new use, forging it into a tool for the creation of images that have lost none of their shattering force during the intervening decades. It was the finest moment in an artistic career without parallel in this century.

Plate 63. Pablo Picasso
WEEPING WOMAN
1937, canvas, height 23½"
Collection Mrs. Lee Miller Penrose, London

Plate 64. Edward Kienholz
THE STATE HOSPITAL
1966, mixed mediums, height 12'
Moderna Museet, Stockholm

Since the 1950s, we have been witnessing an artistic movement whose name, "Pop Art," derives from its use of popular imagery such as comic strips. To the Pop artist, our visual everyday world, shaped by the mass media and commercial culture and hitherto disdained as vulgar, is a fascinating source of raw material. The most radical results of this tendency to break down the barriers between art and reality are the so-called "environments," full-scale models of real-life situations that combine painting, sculpture, and stagecraft. Kienholz's *The State Hospital* is such an "environment": a cell in a ward for senile patients, with a naked old man strapped to the lower bunk. Neglect and mistreatment have reduced what little mental life he had almost to the vanishing point—his head is a glass bowl with live goldfish. But why the figure in the upper bunk? It duplicates the one below, but since it is enclosed within a comic-strip balloon it must be a mental image, the patient's awareness of himself. The balloon and the metaphoric goldfish bowl are alien to the horrifying realism of the scene, yet they play a vital part in it, for they make us think as well as feel. Kienholz's means may be Pop, but his aim is that of Greek tragedy.

Something of the power of his personality shows through this photograph of Karl Marx, the scholar (with reading glass) and bourgeois.
(Photo: The Granger Collection)

Hegel, the struggle between thesis and antithesis leading to a synthesis as the next stage in historical evolution. Marx, however, rejected Hegel's idealism—the view that the dialectic works through ideas that constitute the spirit of the age—insisting instead that any society rests fundamentally on the organization of its economy, the mode of production.

Political systems, Marx said, grow from these material underpinnings, and in each the dominant social class expresses the needs, the values, and the interests associated with that particular mode of production. The agricultural economy of the Middle Ages required the feudal system with its particular social values and laws, upheld by the land-owning aristocracy. That system produced its antithesis in the middle class, which is based on capitalism. But capitalist and industrial society dominated by the middle class was in turn producing a new antithesis through its own contradictions and embodied in the rising proletariat. Class conflict is the mechanism of historical progress, and the triumph of the proletariat will bring a new synthesis, a classless society. History would thus lead, by its own inevitable laws, to a world similar to the one envisioned by other socialists. In the classless society, men would no longer be forced into the inequality required for capitalist production. At present, compulsion is the primary purpose of the state, but in the new era the state would wither away, unneeded.

Revolutions, in this analysis, mark the arrival to power of a new class. They are, however, more than mere transfers of power. A new class brought changes in law, religion, and customs, which it then maintained in its own interest. The middle class, in Marxist terms, has represented a great, progressive force. But capitalism, despite all the ideologies and social institutions designed to shore it up, will fail through its own internal contradictions.

Marx's detailed analysis of capitalism took much from the classical economists (at a time when they were beginning to be outmoded). The value of a product, he insisted somewhat obscurely, comes from the value of all the labor required to produce it—to transform raw materials into manufactured goods. The capitalist makes a profit by keeping for himself part of the value added by other men's labor, by exploiting the working class. But capitalists must compete with each other, and to do so they are forced to lower prices, which in turn reduces profits. This has two effects. First, the capitalist must exploit his labor more harshly, cutting wages to the minimum required for subsistence. Second, the smaller producers will fail, which will lead to increased concentrations of capital and force more and more members of the middle class into the proletariat, composed of men with nothing but their labor to sell. Thus a shrinking capitalist class suffering from declining profits will face a growing proletariat. Capitalism therefore lays the basis for socialism by depriving all but a few of property. The contradictions will be resolved when the whole system fails.

Many of Marx's specific predictions now seem wrong. Although some of the rich have grown richer, the poor are not poorer. Marx simply did not see much that is central to the modern economy—ever-expanding technology, the spread of ownership through public sale of stocks, and mass consumption. He did not anticipate the social effects of literacy, popular democracy, and mass communication. Marxist psychology is inadequate, with little acknowledgment of the loyalties and the irrationality so important in human personality. He sought to combine in one system Hegel's most difficult ideas, the economic theories of liberalism, the "scientific" method of positivism, and the moral vision of socialism—a combination awkward at best. Such critical terms as "class" and "state" remained ambiguous, and the concept of class struggle, applied elastically to a petty event as well as centuries of history, lost its analytic force. The goal of history, according to Marx, is the classless society; yet he sketched that desired condition only vaguely and left unanswered fundamental questions about it and about the means of obtaining it.

The Appeal of Marxism

Despite such weaknesses, and the theory's every flaw has been widely broadcast, Marxism has deeply affected all modern thought, shaped the policies of all sorts of governments, and provided a core for some of the most powerful political movements of the last century. Such impact requires explanation, and perhaps four points can capture something of the answer.

First, Marxism not only sees society as a whole and explains historical change but demands systematic and detailed analyses of the interrelationship of social values, institutions, politics, and economic conditions. It also suggests methods for conducting such analyses, and these qualities account for its continuing importance in all the social sciences.

Second, Marxism accepts and indeed hails industrialization as inevitable and beneficial even while accepting most criticisms of industrial society. Many reformers dreamed of green gardens and simpler days; but Marx believed the machine can free man from brute labor and through greater productivity provide well-being for all. Industrialization could be made to provide solutions to the very problems it created. Thus Marxism has special appeal for societies eager to modernize.

Third, the theory is rich in moral judgments without having to defend any ethical system. Although social values are considered relative, and those of his opponents denounced as hypocritical, Marx's own rage at injustice rings out in a compelling call to generous sentiments that rejects sentimentality.

Finally, Marxism claims the prestige of science and offers the security of determinism. Knowing where destiny leads, its believers can accept the uneven flow of change, confident that any defeats are temporary. Opponents are to be recognized and fought less for what they say or do than for what they represent—for their "objective" role in the structure of capitalism. Accepting concessions does not compromise the fight, for tactics can be very flexible when the only requirement is that they assist the inevitable movement of history toward the victory of the proletariat. Marx believed that small social changes may lead to sudden qualitative ones, and Marxists thus can favor immediate reforms as well as revolution.

The variety inherent in Marx's system has been a source of bitter division as well as strength among socialists, but it has helped keep Marxism more vigorous and coherent than any other of the grand theories spawned in the nineteenth century.

The First International

Marx and Engels intended to be not merely authors of a theory but leaders of a political and social movement. When in 1864 a group of English labor leaders called a small international conference in London, Marx readily agreed to come as a representative of the German workers. The International Working Men's Association, usually called the First International, was founded at that meeting, and Marx dominated it from the start. He did his best to replace traditional radical rhetoric about truth and justice with the hard language of Marxism, and during the eight years of the First International's life, he gradually succeeded in expelling those who disagreed.

The French members were generally followers of Louis Auguste Blanqui and Pierre Joseph Proudhon, socialists for whom Marx had little use; he dismissed the Blanquists, with their fondness for violence and dreams of conspiracy, as romantic revolutionaries, and his first socialist writing had been a critique of Proudhon's plans for workers' cooperatives and his sympathy for anarchy. The International's English members did not accept Marx's emphasis on revolution or his claim that the Paris Commune was "the glorious harbinger of a new society."

The most important conflict, however, was with Mikhail Bakunin. A Russian anarchist, Bakunin had established himself as one of Europe's more flamboyant revolutionaries in 1848. Later sentenced to exile in Siberia, he escaped in 1861, eventually joining the International in 1867. Bakunin respected Marx and understood his materialist philosophy, while Marx seems to have felt some of the fascination of Bakunin's personality. But Bakunin supported nationalism and praised the revolutionary spirit of countries like Italy and Spain, whereas Marx insisted that the revolutionary cause was international and most promising in more industrial lands. The Russian's delight in conspiracies and plots seemed childish to the German expatriate; and Bakunin, who distrusted any state, found a dangerous authoritarianism in Marx and Marxism.

The 1872 meeting, at which Bakunin was expelled, was the First International's last, for Marx and Engels then let the association die. Its membership had never been large or even clearly defined. Yet it played a part in building a workers' movement by disseminating Marxism, by teaching others to view each strike or demonstration as part of a larger conflict, by stressing the international ties of workers in a period of nationalism, and by exemplifying the advantages of militant discipline. In these ways and in its intolerance of doctrinal error and its intemperate polemics, the First International helped set the tone of the growing socialist movement.

Socialism and Anarchism

Between 1876 and World War I, socialist parties became an important part of political life in nearly every European country. Except in Great Britain, most of them were at least formally Marxist. As they began to win elections, socialists disagreed over whether to follow a more moderate policy aimed at electoral success or adhere rigidly to the teachings of Marx. The most common compromise combined moderate policies with flaming rhetoric, and the Second International, formed in 1889 with representatives from parties and unions in every country, sought to maintain doctrinal rigor and socialist unity. Thus the Marxian critique of liberalism and capitalism was spread through

The leaders of the 1853 strike of Preston textile workers in England addressed friendly crowds but dressed differently from their men.
(Photo: The Granger Collection)

---

books, newspapers, and magazines, in parliamentary debate and every election.

Labor organizations outside of Germany were not often consistently Marxist, but their growth was another dramatic change of the period. Unions were everywhere class-conscious, frequently tempted by anarchism and suspicious of politics. Their membership soared, with millions of workers paying dues in the industrialized countries, and the strike became the common expression of social protest. Skilled artisans, threatened by new modes of production yet strengthened by their own traditions of cooperation, were often still the leaders in militant action; but the organization of labor spread especially in larger factories despite the forceful resistance of employers and of the state. In the last decades of the century European society faced the most extensive labor agitation it had ever known. Yet strikes were coming to be better organized and more orderly as well as larger, and they sometimes won important public sympathy.

Most people did not distinguish very clearly among the various radical movements and associated anarchist "propaganda of the deed" with socialists and labor organizers. Certainly anarchists were in the headlines; they assassinated the president of France in 1893, the prime minister of Spain in 1897, the empress of Austria in 1898, the king of Italy in 1900, and the president of the United States in 1901. In the 1880s and 1890s, bombs were thrown into parades, cafés, and theaters in cities all over Europe, and such incidents were followed by the arrest of radical suspects and spectacular trials.

But bomb throwers and assassins were only a tiny wing of the broad anarchist movement. Its intellectual tradition was continuous since the time of the French Revolution, and its most famous figure after Bakunin was Prince Pëter

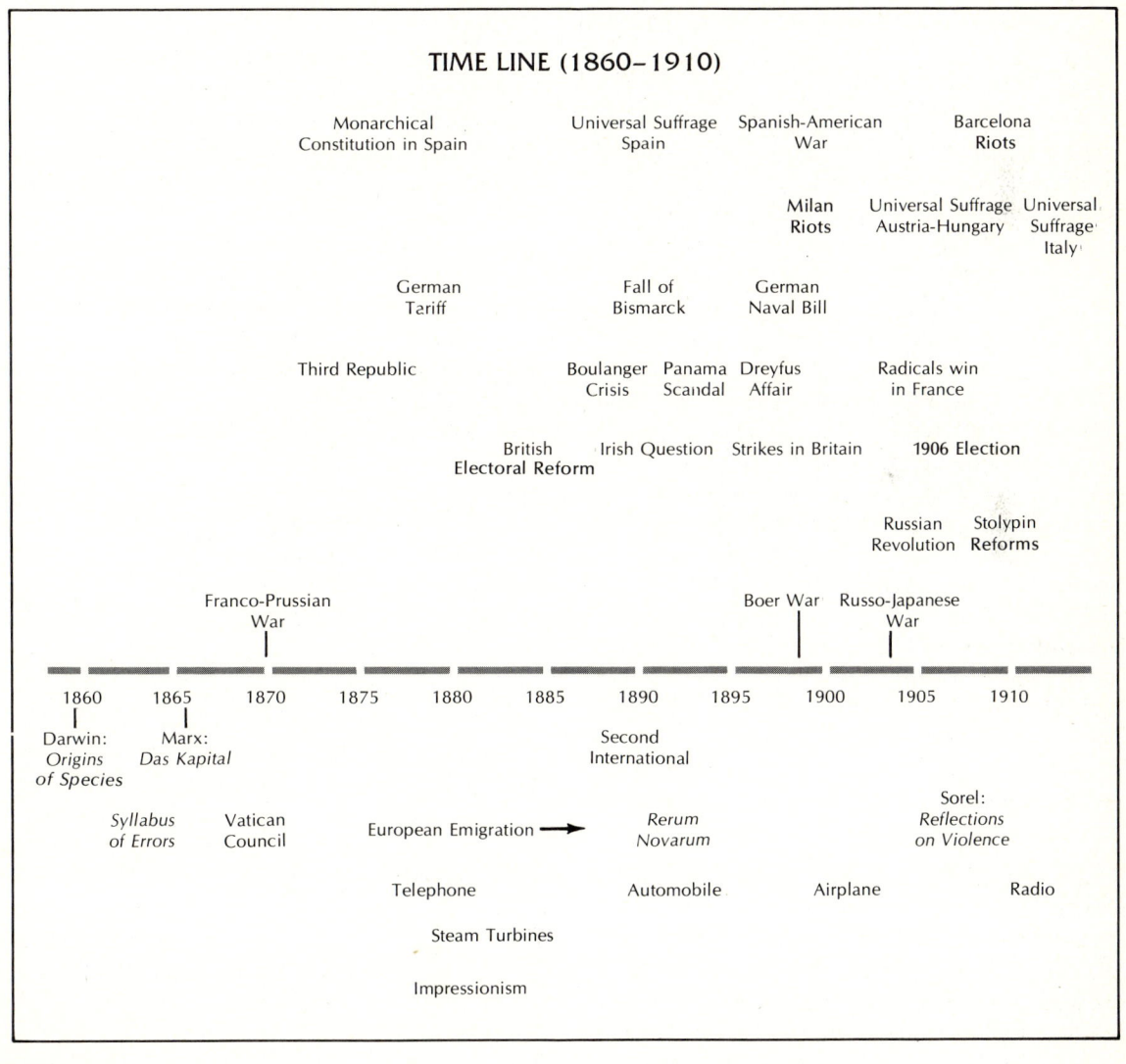

Kropotkin, an exiled Russian aristocrat. Kropotkin was a theorist whose gentleness and compassion made him a kind of spiritual leader, but his descriptions of anarcho-communism did not unify the movement. Some anarchists stressed individualism, some pacifism, and some the abolition of private property; all rejected imposed authority and sought instead a natural order in which men would cooperate as brothers. They won their largest following among the poor who felt themselves crushed by industrialization: immigrants to the United States, peasants in southern Spain, artisans and some workers in Italy and France. Anarchism was influential in the opposition to bureaucratic centralization and to militarism, and it appealed to artists and writers who shared the anarchists' contempt for bourgeois values; but its major contribution was the heroes and martyrs it gave to the growing mystique of the radical left.

The Christian Critique

The attack on liberalism came not only from the left but from the pulpits of every Christian denomination. Individualism, the charges ran, is often mere selfishness; religious tolerance masks indifference to moral issues; progress is another name for materialism. Churches tended to reject the growing claims of the state, especially in education and welfare, and many Christians denounced the injustices of capitalist society as forcefully as did the socialists.

The Roman Catholic Church was particularly hostile. In 1864 Pius IX issued an encyclical, *Quanta Cura*, with a syllabus of "the principal errors of our time" attached. Taken from earlier statements by the pope, its eighty items were written in the unbending tones of theological dispute. The syllabus listed false propositions, for example, declaring erroneous the opinion that ". . . it is no longer expedient that the Catholic religion should be held as the only religion of the State, to the exclusion of all other forms of worship." Catholics more politic than the pope were quick to point out that this denunciation of formal error was not the same as advocating religious intolerance, but such subtleties were easily lost. The syllabus denounced total faith in human reason, the exclusive authority of the state, and attacks on traditional rights of the Church; but its most noted proposition was the last, which declared it false to think that "The Roman Pontiff can, and ought to, reconcile himself, and come to terms with progress, liberalism and modern civilization."

The Vatican Council of 1869–1870, the first council of the Church in 300 years, confirmed the impression of intransigence. It was a splendid demonstration of the Church's continued power, and prelates came from around the world to proclaim the dogma of papal infallibility. It declared that the pope, when speaking *ex cathedra* (that is, formally from the chair of Peter and on matters of faith and morals), is incapable of error. This had long been a traditional belief, and its elevation to dogma confirmed the trend toward increased centralization within the Church and affirmed the solidarity of Catholics in the face of new dangers. Even as the council met, the outbreak of the Franco-Prussian War allowed the Italian government to take over Rome, and governments throughout Europe wondered if Catholics could now be reliable citizens of a secular state.

The expanding role of government, especially in matters of education and welfare, made conflicts between church and state a major theme of European life. While theories of evolution, positivism, and biblical criticism put defenders of traditional belief on the defensive, politicians worried about the influence of the churches, particularly in rural areas and among national minorities, as anonymous masses of people were increasingly called to the polls.

In the United Kingdom the Church of England had steadily been stripped of its special privileges in moves opposed at every step by the clergy, most peers, and conservatives; but religious differences continued to inflame the Irish question. Bismarck launched and then abandoned the Kulturkampf as the German government relied more and more on the Catholic Center party. In Russia the Orthodox Church became in effect a department of state, used to strengthen the dominance of Russians in the multinational empire, while the Austrian government in contrast broke its close ties (and its concordat) with the Roman Catholic Church in an effort to lessen opposition to Viennese rule. The conflict between church and state was most open and bitter, however, in Spain, Italy, and France, where it was the central political division of the 1880s and 1890s.

Generally these conflicts subsided somewhat after the turn of the century. Relatively secure states, having established the breadth of their authority, tended to become more tolerant; and anticlericalism came to seem outmoded as governments faced the rising challenge from the left. The Churches too responded more flexibly, in the style of Pope Leo XIII (1878–1903), who established an understanding with Bismarck and encouraged French Catholics to accept the Third Republic.

At the same time Christianity displayed renewed vigor. There was a general revival of biblical and theological studies, marked in the Roman Catholic Church by emphasis on the theology of St. Thomas Aquinas, whose arguments for the compatibility of faith and reason brought greater clarity and confidence to Catholic positions. Christian political and social movements learned to mobilize enormous support and became more active in social work (the Salvation Army, for example, was founded in 1865).

This engagement in charity, religious missions at home and overseas, education, labor unions, and hundreds of special projects not only strengthened Christian social influence but led to outspoken denunciations of immoral and unjust conditions. In his social encyclicals, especially *Rerum Novarum* issued in 1891, Leo XIII added a powerful voice to the rising cry for reform. He restated Catholic belief in private property, the sanctity of the family, and the social role of religion but went beyond these well-known views to speak to modern industrial conditions. The Catholic Church, he wrote, not only recognizes the right of workers to their own organizations and to "reasonable and frugal comfort" but warns the state against favoring any single class and society against viewing human beings as merely a means to profit.

The Churches recognized the altered circumstances that left neither public institutions nor private habit reliable supports of religion. Strongest in rural areas and with more women communicants than men, they strove to improve their position in the cities among workers and the middle class. The adjustments were neither easy nor smooth, but by 1910 Christianity was more respectable among intellectuals, more active in society, and more prominent in politics than it had been since the early nineteenth century. Whether of the political left or right, Christians found in their religion a whole arsenal of complaints against liberalism and industrial capitalism.

Theories of Irrationality

Until World War I European political thought remained predominantly liberal, but some of the optimism was fading. Liberals themselves made less of simple individualism and worried more about problems of community and social justice, and some writers even doubted that politics was much affected by the free exchange of ideas so dear to John Stuart Mill. Newer strains of thought questioned the power of human reason and argued for leadership by a small group of elite.

The Frenchman Georges Sorel shared the growing suspicion that public opinion owed more to prejudice than to reason. Like many intellectuals, he felt contempt for middle-class society but argued that its overthrow would not come in the way predicted by Marx. His most important book, *Reflections on Violence* (1908), postulated rather that historic changes like the rise of Christianity or the French Revolution come about when people are inspired by some great myth that stands beyond the test of reason. As a myth for his times, he proposed the general strike, a possibility then much discussed by European unions. Sorel thus contributed to the widespread syndicalist movement, which called on workers' groups, *syndicats*, to bring down bourgeois society; his larger significance was his rejection of bourgeois rationalism in favor of violence and the will. Like many contemporary writers in Italy and Germany, he found the energy for change in man's irrationality.[4]

Sorel's countryman Henri Bergson, the most eloquent and revered philosopher of his day, expounded a gentle, abstruse set of theories. In touch with contemporary movements in the arts, psychology, and religion, he too pictured much that is best in human understanding as arising not from reason but intuitively from subjective and unconscious feelings. Society therefore should encourage a spirit of energy and common endeavor, favoring the spontaneity that translates feeling into action.

The revolutionary challenge such ideas contained became clearer in the works of Friedrich Nietzsche. He too stressed the will in a philosophy that lashed contemporary civilization on every page. His disdain for ideas of equality and democracy was balanced by his hatred of nationalism and militarism; he rejected his society not only for what it was but for what it meant to be. The only hope for the future was the work of the few, of supermen who would drop the inhibitions of bourgeois society and the "slave morality" of Christianity.

Nietzsche's tone had the violence of a man trying to bring everything crashing down, but he was no mere nihilist. He wrote his passionate aphorisms as a man in terror for himself and his world. A deeply original thinker, he was a child of his times in his approach to culture and history but above all in his anger.

Anti-Semitism and the Right

Like Nietzsche's philosophy, anti-Semitism, which he detested, was part of the rising current of opposition to liberal society. Anti-Semitism in the 1890s was more than a continuation of centuries-old prejudices, and it was surprisingly universal. Venomous assertions of Jewish avarice and lack of patriotism were used to discredit the entire republic in France and opponents of imperial policy in Great Britain. Anti-Semitic parties elected sixteen deputies to the Reichstag in 1893, and the prestigious Conservative party in Germany added anti-Semitism to its program. The lord mayor of Vienna from 1895 to 1910 found anti-Semitism invaluable in winning his electoral victories, and it was an official policy of the Russian government from the terrible pogroms of 1881 on.

There is no simple explanation for a phenomenon seemingly so contrary to the major trends of the century. One reason relates to the perception of Jews as a ready symbol of liberal, capitalist society; they had received their civil rights at the hands of Napoleon and in liberal revolutions, lived primarily in urban environments, and found their opportunities for advancement in the expanding professions and businesses of the nineteenth century. They were prominent leaders in many of the most venturesome enterprises, most important scientific discoveries, and most striking social theories.

---

[4] Vilfredo Pareto and Sorel, both trained as engineers, are usually grouped together with Robert Michels as leading theorists of the new political "realism."

Nationalism, especially in Germany, had come to stress folk culture and race; by attacking Jews, conservatives could make the liberal, capitalist world itself seem alien to national traditions. Crude adaptations of Darwinism gave racial theories a pseudoscientific panache,[5] and indeed quack science generally flourished, for credulity was encouraged by the fact that much of academic science, especially physics, was no longer comprehensible to laymen. Theories of conspiracy gave concrete and simple explanations for the baffling pace of social change, offering the hope that by circumscribing specific groups—such as the Jews—society could resist change itself.

Neither irrationalism nor anti-Semitism belongs inherently to a single political persuasion, but both were used primarily by the political right in the decades preceding World War I. Rightist movements revived notably in these years, building on those social groups that felt most harmed by the changes of the century: aristocrats, rural people, and Christians. Often incongruously, they defended established constitutions—the House of Lords in Britain, the concordat with the Roman Catholic Church in France, three-class voting and government independent of the Reichstag in Germany, limited suffrage and an intrusive monarchy in Italy, the authority of the tsar in Russia. They added to this conservatism contemporary concerns about the shallowness of middle-class culture and the need for government intervention in behalf of a stable economy. They tried, frequently with success, to make patriotism and national strength their battle cry, learning to make an effective mass appeal. Denounced by Marxists as defenders of reactionary capitalism, they declared socialism the menace of the hour and the natural consequence of liberal error.

Thus critics from the right as well as the left gained vigor from attacking the very changes that most men still labeled progress. So many simultaneous assaults created grave political crises in many states, but for most a new equilibrium followed in which government accepted more responsibility for social justice, politics became more democratic, and society grew more tolerant. Neither before nor since have Europeans generally been so free to move about as they wished and say what they liked.

IV. DOMESTIC POLITICS

Growing populations and the second industrial revolution necessitated new policies, and every government had to meet that challenge. The Scandinavian nations became models of how to do so. When Norway voted for separation from Sweden in 1905, the decision was accepted peacefully; and the two nations lived thereafter in harmony, among the most democratic in the world.

In most countries political life from the 1880s to 1914 was marked by a continuity that appeared, on the surface at least, to be the working out of particular national traditions. Recent historical scholarship, however, tends to see the generation before World War I as a period of painful and uneven adjustment to social change, distinguished by rising tension and open conflict and by increased reliance on large, formal organizations—such as trade unions, parties, and especially the state. In general these conflicts centered on three different issues: first, the question of access to political life (who would be allowed to participate and to what extent); second, a question of national loyalty (were some groups—foreigners, Catholics, Jews—a threat to national life that should some-

---

[5] An important example is Houston Steward Chamberlain's *The Foundations of the Nineteenth Century,* published in Germany in 1899. A Germanophile Englishman and intense admirer of Wagner, Chamberlain traced all that was best in European civilization to its "Aryan" elements. The work was widely admired until the collapse of the Nazi regime.

how be excluded from it); third, essentially a question of social justice (what rights to organization and social welfare would workers be allowed). Each country in dealing with these issues in effect defined its social as well as its political structure. In each, international ambitions and dangers both increased domestic tensions and were ominously used to preserve domestic peace.

Russia 1881–1914: Liberal Revolution

Even in Russia political crises led to liberal concessions. To Europeans no evidence for the necessity of representative institutions was more impressive than their sudden introduction into Russia. Alexander III became tsar in 1881 on his father's assassination, an event he attributed to excessive talk about further reform following the abolition of serfdom. He used the Orthodox Church and the police to extend an official reactionary ideology through public life and gave nobles an increased role in regional zemstvos and rural administration. Local governors were authorized to use martial law, restrict or ban the religions and languages of non-Russian peoples, and persecute Jews.[6] This "Russification," meant to create a united nation, was continued with equal conviction but less energy by Tsar Nicholas II, who ascended the throne in 1894. Unrest increased, and many in the government welcomed war as a means of achieving the solidarity represssion had failed to create.

War came in 1904, when Japan suddenly attacked the Russians at Port Arthur, which they had leased from China in 1898 as part of their expansion into East Asia and Manchuria.

---

[6] One of history's famous forgeries, the *Protocols of the Elders of Zion,* was published (and written) by the Russian police in 1903. The protocols purported to be the secret minutes of a Zionist congress and to reveal a Jewish conspiracy to control the world.

For years these moves had troubled the Japanese, and Russia had neither kept promises to withdraw nor acknowledged Japan's proposals for spheres of influence. The war was a disaster for Russia. Surprise attack was followed by defeats in Manchuria, the fall of Port Arthur, and the annihilation of a large Russian fleet that had sailed around the world only to be sunk in Japanese waters. In the treaty, signed at Portsmouth, New Hampshire—the United States, like Japan, wished to demonstrate her status as a world power—Russia ceded most of her recent gains, including Port Arthur and the southern half of Sakhalin Island, and recognized Japanese interest in Korea.

So dramatic a defeat increased pressure for major reforms as had the Crimean War fifty years before, but the pressure came this time from deep within society. Peasant agitation had been on the rise since a terrible famine in 1891, secret organizations had arisen to defend subject nationalities, and industrialization had begun to fill St. Petersburg and Moscow with workers organizing to improve their miserable lot. The Social Revolutionaries, a party combining the traditions of populism and terrorism, grew more active; and the Marxist Social Democrats, hitherto composed of rather disparate groups, now organized in exile and strengthened their ties within Russia.

In this atmosphere liberal members of the zemstvos held a national congress in 1904, though forbidden to by the government, and demanded civil liberties. Then in January 1905 striking workers in St. Petersburg, demanding a national constitution as well as the recognition of labor unions, announced they would petition the tsar. They marched on the Winter Palace carrying icons and singing, "God save the tsar"; and when they had assembled, the troops opened fire, killing scores and wounding hundreds more.

"Bloody Sunday" led to agitation so widespread that in March the tsar promised to call an assembly of notables and announced immediate reforms: religious toleration, reduced restrictions on Jews and non-Russian nationals, and cancellation of part of the payments peasants owed for their land. Agitation for a constitution only grew stronger, expressed through urban strikes, peasant riots, and mutinies in both the army and navy. In August the tsar conceded more, declaring he would call a national assembly, the Imperial Duma, which was to be merely consultative and elected by limited suffrage. Many of those close to the court were shocked by so radical a step; few outside it were satisfied. The public's response was a wave of strikes beginning in Moscow and spreading from city to city and trade to trade. For the last ten days of October, Russia's economic life came to a halt, the most effective general strike Europe had ever seen. It won from the tsar the October Manifesto granting a constitution.

The manifesto provided for a Duma vested with legislative authority, elected by broad suffrage, and guaranteed freedom of speech and assembly. Crowds danced in the streets. For the first time the regime's opponents were divided: moderates willing to work with this constitution became known as Octobrists; lib-

On the morning of January 9, 1905, protesters petitioning the tsar marched to the Winter Palace and were fired upon by Russian soldiers. The event, known as "Bloody Sunday," triggered a series of strikes and mutinies among the military. (Photo: Soviet Life from Sovfoto)

erals who insisted on a constituent assembly and broader guarantees formed the Constitutional Democratic party, called Cadets for short; on the left socialists and revolutionaries rejected compromise, and the St. Petersburg Soviet, a committee of trade union leaders and socialists, called another general strike. It was only partially successful, however, for revolutionary fervor was dying down. Emboldened, the government arrested the leaders of the St. Petersburg Soviet in December, and when Moscow's workers rose in revolt, they were bloodily defeated.

Before the first Duma met in May 1906, Fundamental Laws announced more fully the form the constitution would be allowed to have. An upper house, half its members appointed by the tsar, would be added to the national legislature, thus making the Duma the lower house; the tsar would keep the power of veto, the right to name his ministers, and full command of the executive, the judiciary, and the armed forces. In elections boycotted by the left, the Cadets gained a large majority of the seats in the Duma, and they began the new era by demanding representative government. The Duma was dissolved after two months, but new elections, in which the left took part, produced a more radical assembly, also soon disbanded. The stalemate was broken by a new electoral law favoring the propertied classes that created a conservative majority in subsequent legislatures.

The Revolution of 1905 had nevertheless brought important changes. Russia now had parliamentary institutions and organized parties; the power of the aristocracy had been greatly reduced; and the nation was clearly set on a modern course. The prime minister from 1906 to 1911, Pëter Stolypin, reformed education and administration and strove to stimulate the economy with programs that abandoned the *mir* system in favor of full private ownership of land and that created land banks and social insurance. With the aid of foreign capital, the pace of industrialization rapidly increased. Radical movements were sternly repressed, and while discontent among workers and poorer peasants remained serious, Cadets were finding it possible to work with the new system. Liberals throughout Europe rejoiced that the giant of the East had at last begun to follow the path of Western progress.

Austria-Hungary 1879–1914: Political Stalemate

The Dual Monarchy did not experience the kinds of crises that set Russia on a new course and led to a more democratic equilibrium in France and Italy. Rather, social and national tensions no less grave resulted in political stalemate. Count Eduard von Taaffe was prime minister from 1879 to 1893, replacing German liberals who had sought reforms more generous than aristocracy or court could abide. His government was a coalition of German conservatives, Czechs, and Poles, but concessions to these nationalities antagonized the bureaucracy and the aristocracy, who were the pillars of the empire. The spread of education and its increased social importance made the language used in schools a divisive issue, one that exacerbated the conflicts among nationalities, eventually broke up Taaffe's coalition, and led to his downfall. Industrialization in Austria increased her economic conflicts with agrarian interests in Hungary and brought workers' agitation that Taaffe barely held in check by harshly repressing socialists while pushing through welfare measures that conservatives detested.

Subsequent governments tended to be even less venturesome, and after 1900 they relied increasingly on decree powers and the support of the crown rather than the Austrian parliament. Universal manhood suffrage, introduced without conviction in 1907, established the

Christian Socialists and the Social Democrats as the two largest parties, neither of them acceptable to the leadership of the empire. Thus they clashed to little purpose in a parliament largely ignored and with rising anger in the city of Vienna, where the Christian Socialists held sway by combining welfare programs with demagogic anti-Semitism.

Conflict with the autonomous regime of Hungary remained critical until the turn of the century. There Magyars maintained their dominance by requiring their language to be used in government and education, tightly controlling the electoral system, and maintaining administrative corruption. Their efforts to protect the interests of large landowners and to increase their independence of Vienna, however, led to contention that weakened the empire. When in 1903 they demanded greater autonomy for their own army and the adoption of Magyar as the language of command, they touched one issue about which Emperor Francis Joseph I cared too much to yield. He suspended the Hungarian constitution, ruled without parliament, and frightened the Magyars into submission by threatening to establish universal suffrage, which would leave them a political minority in their own country.

Magyars and the empire needed each other, and the new Hungarian government—led by István Tisza, son of Kálmán Tisza and a member of one of the leading Magyar families—sought to cooperate in strengthening the Dual Monarchy and lessening the open conflict of nationalities within Hungary. Magyar politics, which in the 1840s had won European admiration as a model of liberal nationalism, had turned by 1906 into the shrewd defensive strategy of a threatened aristocracy. Tisza became one of the most influential figures in imperial politics by recognizing that mutual survival depended on avoiding dangerous changes whenever possible and by using imperial foreign policy to strengthen from the outside a political system in danger at home.

Spain 1875–1914: The Problems of Modernization

As in Russia and Austria, Spain's pockets of urban industry (especially in Barcelona) existed in a larger society only partially affected by modern change. From the adoption of the constitution of 1875 until the Spanish-American War twenty-three years later, conservative and liberal parties held power alternately, tolerantly manipulating elections to assure each other's survival. Neither party, however, provided a consistent program for dealing with rising discontent at home or in the colonies. Unrest in Cuba was exacerbated by alternating policies of repression and laxity, and Cuban resistance had become guerrilla war by 1898, when the United States entered the conflict with an imperialist enthusiasm of her own. The brief war was a disaster for Spain that forced her to withdraw from Cuba and to cede Puerto Rico, Guam, and the Philippine Islands to the United States. That ferment brought to the fore a group of Spanish intellectuals known as the generation of 1898, and the question of what was wrong with the nation became the preoccupation of public life in Spain.

From 1899 to 1909 the Conservatives held power, but they grew increasingly intolerant, and they could not sustain the old political compromises. Then the liberals, already badly divided, launched a series of reforms; but these measures—restrictions on religious orders, taxation of the church's industrial properties, a progressive income tax, and toleration of strikes—hardly lessened conflict. Economic growth, particularly in the industrial centers of Bilbao and Barcelona, made old problems of rural poverty, poor communications, and regionalism more serious. Politics had become more unwieldy with the introduction of universal manhood suffrage in 1890, and while the church denounced liberals, the anarchists and socialists increased in strength. In Barcelona these conflicts burst forth in a week of violence in 1909 during which private citizens were murdered and churches were burned and looted. The revenge that followed reestablished Spain's reputation for brutality. A weak government caught between left and right and a king (Alfonso XIII had come of age in 1902) whose prestige declined with each ineffectual call for compromise could not resolve the problems tearing at Spanish society.

Italy 1878–1914: Stability and Crisis

The Kingdom of Italy developed her own pattern of political stability. The transition was smooth to the reign of Humbert I, in 1878, and to government by the anti-Cavourian "left," which soon repealed the hated grain taxes, established the principle of compulsory education (with a modest requirement for three years of schooling not always enforced), and extended suffrage to about one adult male in eight.

The prime minister maintained his majorities through an informal system called *trasformismo,* in which he built shifting alliances on successive issues and used patronage to bargain for votes. Coming to office in 1887, Francesco Crispi, a hero of the Risorgimento, sought popularity through outspoken anticlericalism, mild reforms, and above all concern for Italy's prestige. He drew her closer to Germany and met the general agricultural depression by repressing rural revolts and establishing high tariffs that led to a harmful trade war with France. As the economic crisis deepened and public order deteriorated, Crispi's ministry fell.

His successors, dedicated to balancing the budget, were weakened by a banking scandal that, like the collapse of the Panama Canal enterprise in France, sullied the entire parliamentary system. Returned to office in 1894, Crispi frankly relied on the army and martial law to maintain order while seeking an Italian protectorate in Ethiopia. At Aduwa in 1896, however, 25,000 Italian troops were nearly wiped out by well-prepared Ethiopian forces four times their number, the first notable defeat of a European army by African forces. Crispi fell again, and subsequent governments sought to salvage what they could, preserving Eritrea as an Italian colony and easing tensions with France.

Domestic unrest increased, and anarchist bomb throwing, socialist demonstrations, waves of strikes, and agrarian agitation culminated in riots that reached revolutionary scale in Milan in 1898. Order was restored at the cost of bloodshed, the suppression of scores of newspapers, and a ban on hundreds of socialist, republican, and Catholic organizations. A frightened Chamber of Deputies nevertheless refused to authorize continued restriction of civil liberties, and its stand was supported in the critical elections of 1900. In Italy as in France, parliament and public opinion defeated a revitalized right.

Prime minister almost continuously from 1903 to 1914, Giovanni Giolitti sought to give Italian politics a broader base. He prevented violence but not strikes, and socialists grew optimistic about parliamentarianism as the government nationalized railroads and life insurance, sponsored public health measures, and in 1911 accepted universal suffrage. Giolitti also encouraged Catholics to take part in national politics, which they had boycotted since 1870. In the decade before 1914, the Italian economy, less developed than that of the great industrial powers, experienced the fastest growth rate in Europe.

In an age of imperialism, Italian nationalists had yearned for an empire that would make Italy more nearly the equal of the other European powers. Their designs on Tunisia frustrated by the French in 1881, they had turned to the ill-fated venture in Ethiopia. After the clash of French and German interests in 1911 over dominance of Morocco (see Chapter 26), nationalist groups in Italy pressured the government to take Libya before someone else did.

Libya was formally part of the Ottoman Empire, but Italy had carefully staked her claim through years of cautious diplomacy, and in 1912 Giolitti found the excuse for war against the sultan. Italian troops landed at the port city of Tripoli and took Rhodes and the other major Dodecanese Islands, also Ottoman possessions. The sultan ceded Libya, and the year of war produced an enthusiasm Italian governments had rarely won, a moment of unity many would want to recapture.

Giolitti's accomplishments, however, rested on his skill at obscuring political issues, influencing elections, and using silent deputies. The economic problems of the south remained grave and the discontent of more and more organized and militant workers largely unappeased. A dull and sometimes corrupt government proved an easy target for increasingly vocal critics from the left and the right. In the elections of 1913, the first under the broadened suffrage, these critics achieved notable gains.

France 1878–1914: The Triumph of the Republicans

By the 1880s the Third Republic had established its political style: the executive was relatively weak, the presidency reduced to a ceremonial office; most cabinets lasted only about a year in office; and the many parties had little authority over deputies tied to local interests, who were proudly independent on national issues. Stability came from the frustrating fact that shifting majorities produced new governments not very different from their predecessors—most ministers served in several cabinets—and from an able civil service.

For twenty years, from 1879 to 1899, the leading politicians were moderate republicans who found in lack of daring the best guarantee of the republic's durability and in anticlericalism their most popular plank. Strong defenders of free speech and individualism, they recognized unions but initiated few projects of public works or social welfare. In the 1880s they made elementary education in state schools compulsory and established restrictions on the Catholic Church intended to weaken its political influence, a view of progress that carried national political divisions into the villages of France.

Moderate republicans had little gift for winning popular enthusiasm, however, and political crises occurred frequently. In 1889 General Georges Boulanger gained so much popularity by his appeal to patriotism and his sympathy for workers that there was danger of a coup d'état. Then in 1892, when companies planning a canal through Panama similar to their successful Suez venture went bankrupt, investigations uncovered political graft and provoked a stormy campaign against the corruption of Jewish financiers, liberal newspapers, and republican politicians. Only as the republic's opponents seemed close to toppling the regime did its defenders pull together.

The Third Republic's great trial came with the Dreyfus case. Captain Albert Dreyfus, a Jew and a member of the General Staff, was convicted by court-martial in 1894 of providing the German military attaché with secret French documents. Although the sensational press shouted Jewish treachery, the issue became the center of public attention only three years afterward, when evidence appeared pointing to the guilt of another officer. Generals, refusing to reopen the case, spoke darkly of honor and state secrets, and the right-wing press hailed their patriotism. The majority of Catholics, monarchists, and conservatives joined in patriotic indignation against Jews and socialists allegedly conspiring to sell out France and weaken a loyal army. The left—intellectuals, socialists, and republicans—came to view Dreyfus as the innocent victim of a plot against republican institutions. They won the battle for public opinion, though barely, and Dreyfus

A French newspaper headlined Émile Zola's now-famous "J'Accuse . . . !," a denunciation of the corrupt handling of the Dreyfus Affair. The case became the cause célèbre of the nineteenth century; opinion as to Dreyfus' guilt or innocence led to demonstrations, propaganda, street fighting, lawsuits, and political realignments.
(Photo: René Dazy)

was given a presidential pardon in 1899.[7] That victory set the tone of subsequent French politics, cementing traditions of republican unity on the left and greatly reducing the political influence of the church and monarchists. Years of polemics and street fights, however, left deep scars.

From 1900 until World War I, government was in the hands of republicans who called themselves radical. They set about purging the army of their opponents and launched new attacks on the church that subsided only with the passage of a law separating church and state in 1905. Yet they administered with restraint; solicitous of the "little man," of small businessmen and peasant farmers, they solidified support for the republic.

Indeed part of the Third Republic's achievement was its ability to draw radical politicians to moderate policies. A socialist even entered the cabinet in the aftermath of the Dreyfus affair (thereby earning the condemnation of the Second International for cooperating in a bourgeois state). The labor movement, more syndicalist than Marxist, doubled its membership in this period, but despite frequent strikes from the 1890s on, it never produced the more revolutionary general strike so much talked of. As prime minister from 1906 to 1909, Georges Clemenceau, once associated with the radical left, effectively combined policies of reform and conciliation. On the eve of world war, France, prosperous and stable, appeared to have surmounted her most dangerous divisions.

---

[7] Convicted again in 1897, Dreyfus had been court-martialed a third time in 1899 on the order of France's highest court. The verdict, guilty but "with extenuating circumstances," added new confusion and led to the presidential pardon. A few Dreyfusards continued collecting evidence and finally won acquittal in a civil trial in 1906. Dreyfus was then decorated and promoted to the rank of major.

Germany 1879–1914: Tensions Following Unification

German political life reflected a fragmented society in which the court, army, bureaucracy, and business were semi-independent centers of power and in which social classes were sharply demarcated. Yet Bismarck ran it until 1890 with an authority few modern figures have equaled, establishing a pattern his successors would strain to maintain.

The architect of so successful a system was understandably scornful of criticism, and a chancellor so overweening won many enemies; but Bismarck was untouchable until William II ascended the throne in 1888. Twenty-nine years old, bright but ill-prepared, William was infatuated with all things military, anxious to make himself loved, and eager to rule. He disagreed with parts of Bismarck's foreign policy and opposed the antisocialist laws, but theirs was primarily a conflict of wills. In 1890 the emperor, impatient with Bismarck's paternal arrogance, forced his resignation.

Succeeding chancellors (there were four between 1890 and 1917) served until the dissatisfaction of some powerful faction led to their replacement. In 1909 Theobald von Bethmann-Hollweg, the last peacetime chancellor of the Second Reich and the first of bourgeois origin, was chosen in part out of concern over a restive parliament, but that cautious bureaucrat was hardly the man to tame the forces of German politics.

The fundamental problems of the Second Reich were inherent in the system itself. A dynamic foreign policy whose successes could dazzle opponents at home proved impossible to sustain. Foreign policy and the political importance of the army required increases in armed strength that kept militarism at the center of politics. In 1887, when a seven-year renewal of the army bill had fallen due, Bismarck had asked for its enlargement. Resisted in parliament, he had made this an electoral issue and won a sizable victory, the last stable majority any chancellor enjoyed. Similarly in 1893, 1898, and 1911–1913, military appropriations were a source of intense conflict and propaganda; each time the army grew larger and the government's statements more nationalist.

Strident propaganda was also the mainstay of the political leagues—the Landlords', Peasants', Pan-German, Colonial, and Naval Leagues—organized in the 1890s. Well-financed by Junkers and some industrialists, they campaigned for the military, overseas empire, and high tariffs with attacks on socialists, Jews, and foreign enemies. As pressure groups they won significant victories—notably in the naval bill of 1898, which proposed to create a fleet that could compete with Britain's. Germany's conservative classes appealed to public opinion more effectively than their anti-Dreyfusard counterparts in France or the militant right in Italy.

Under Bismarck Germany had adopted comprehensive programs of health, old age, accident, and disability insurance that established a model of social welfare legislation unequaled elsewhere for a generation. William II was hailed as "the Labor Emperor" for supporting social security, labor arbitration, the regulation of workers' hours, and provisions for their safety. The workers, however, would not be wooed.

The Social Democrats, having been forced by harassment to rely on local organization, became powerful: they won more votes than any other party in every election from 1890 on, becoming in 1912 the largest party in the Reichstag despite the distortions of the electoral system (and the strongest socialist party in Europe). Socialists also dominated Germany's vigorous labor unions, which had 2.5 million members by 1912. A movement detested by the authorities, German socialism created its own subculture of newspapers and libraries and recreation centers.

In practice the Social Democrats were attentive to the concrete concerns of their constituents, but in principle and tone they remained firm revolutionaries. One of their leading theorists, Eduard Bernstein, proposed a modified doctrine in a daring book, *Evolutionary Socialism* (1897). He argued that many of Marx's predictions had proved wrong, that parts of his economic analysis were faulty, and that socialists should place less emphasis on economic determinism and revolution and seek instead to improve working conditions and strengthen democracy. Bernstein's revisionism became the focus of international debate and affected socialist movements everywhere, but it was formally rejected by the Social Democrats, who made Karl Kautsky's intransigent exposition of Marxism their official policy.

While organized factions glared and threatened, Bethmann-Hollweg presided over a bureaucracy rife with cabals and tried to hold in check a court where people spoke openly of using the army against radicals. Germany remained strong, prosperous, and apparently stable, but major political change proved impossible; even the attempt to make taxes more equitable was defeated. Thus Bethmann-Hollweg's mild program for modifying the political system came to nothing. When the Continent's most powerful nation entered into world war, the Reich was still dominated by Prussia, where voting continued by the three-class system, and ministers remained responsible to the crown and not the Reichstag.

Great Britain 1880–1914: Imperialism and Democracy

Gladstone returned to power in 1880 after a campaign that, in its effort to carry serious issues to the public, was a further step toward democracy; and in 1885 the Liberal majority led Parliament to adopt measures accepting the principle of universal manhood suffrage (it says much, however, that the requirement of an independent place of residence—which excluded domestic servants, sons living with fathers, and those without a permanent address—was enough to disqualify roughly one-third of all adult males). Gladstone's foreign policy, however, was decried as weak, and his popularity, which increased when Britain stumbled into the occupation of Egypt in 1882, was dissipated a few years later. As the Irish question became more heated, Gladstone responded with reforms that fixed fair rents and prevented the eviction of paying tenants; but Irish nationalists demanded home rule, an independent Irish parliament. When Gladstone acquiesced in 1886, his party split as badly as the Tories had a generation before over the corn laws. Joseph Chamberlain, a radical in social matters who had adopted the popular cause of imperialism, led an important group of Liberals into alliance with the Conservatives. Gladstone's perpetual compromises were beginning to seem old-fashioned in the face of these deeper divisions.

Conservative governments would hold office for sixteen of the next nineteen years, most of them under Lord Salisbury, successor to Disraeli, who had died in 1881. An able diplomat, Salisbury continued his party's emphasis on the importance of the empire and led the nation through a bitter conflict with the Dutch-speaking Boers of South Africa.

Many Boers had left Britain's Cape Colony in the 1830s, eventually establishing independent and frankly racist republics. Almost constantly at war with neighboring African peoples, they were also at odds with the expanding British interests in South Africa. In the 1850s the Boers had won recognition of the independence of their two major regimes, the Transvaal Republic (soon renamed the South African Republic) and the Orange Free State. In 1877, however, the British government had violated previous treaties by annexing the Transvaal. This produced a revolt in 1880 and Gladstone's concession of domestic autonomy in 1881. But the unstable situation had become explosive with the discovery of diamonds in the Boers' Orange Free State and gold in the South African Republic in the 1870s and 1880s. (See maps and the discussion of imperialism in Chapter 26.) New settlers poured in, and companies amassed enormous wealth; railroads were rushed to completion and natives driven away or forced to work for meager wages.

By 1890 the Boer republics were surrounded by British colonies and swarming with Britons, whom the Boers taxed heavily but disfranchised. Cecil Rhodes, an Englishman who had gained a near-monopoly over the world's diamond production before he was thirty, used his position as prime minister of the Cape Colony to further schemes for a South African federation, and the Boers found themselves resisting raids by whites as well as blacks. When Britain refused to withdraw her troops, the Boers declared war in 1899. The British rapidly occupied the major cities, but they subdued the Boers' expert guerrilla resistance only after two more years of destroying farms and herding the homeless Boers into concentration camps. This embarrassing war, with its heavy price in blood and prestige, stirred a fierce patriotism in England that increased the Conservatives' strength.

Despite public enthusiasm for their imperial policy, the Conservatives faced growing opposition at home which they attempted to meet by sponsoring major reforms. In 1888 and 1894 they restructured local government, a major source of the aristocracy's political power, making county councils elective. They made an expanding civil service more accessible to the middle class, and an act of 1902 established a far stronger national education system that for the first time included secondary schooling.

Yet these important changes did not satisfy the working class, whose rising dissatisfaction had spilled over in strikes by London match girls in 1888 and dock workers the next year. The strikes had won public sympathy and marked the beginning of a "new unionism" of unskilled workers organized on an industry-wide basis and prepared for political activism. The formation of the Labour Representation Committee in 1900 marked the beginning of what quickly became the Labour party. Its greatest strength came from the unions, but it included the Fabian Society, a group of prominent intellectuals whose propaganda in behalf of reformist, democratic socialism gained an influence far beyond their numbers. Twenty-nine Labour members of Parliament would be elected in 1906, and within a few years the ruling Liberals would come often to depend on Labour votes in the House of Commons. British labor was further pushed to political action by a court decision, upheld by the House of Lords in 1902, which made unions liable for losses caused by strikes. Overturning the verdict that crippled unions became a central issue of the 1906 election.

In that election the Liberals won the most one-sided victory since 1833. They immediately passed measures establishing workers' compensation, old age pensions, and urban planning. Since this legislation and the expanding arms race required new revenues, David Lloyd George, the chancellor of the Exchequer, proposed the "people's budget" in 1909. A skilled orator who delighted in the rhetoric of class conflict, he promised to place the burden of social welfare costs squarely on the rich.

In an unprecedented act an aroused House of Lords rejected the government's budget, forcing new elections and bringing on a constitutional crisis. Although the Liberals lost many seats, they retained office with Irish and Labour support, and King George V's threat to appoint hundreds of additional peers finally forced the upper house to accept not only the hated budget but a constitutional change forbidding the Lords to veto money bills and permitting any measure to become law when passed by the Commons in three sessions.

The peers' intemperate outburst, which cost them so much, was part of the general rise in social tension. From 1910 to 1914 strikes increased in frequency, size, and violence; a general strike became a real and much-talked-of threat. Women campaigning for the right to vote interrupted public meetings, invaded Parliament itself, smashed windows, and planted bombs. Arrested, they went on hunger strikes until baffled statesmen ordered their release. Such behavior from ladies was shocking in itself; but as the movement gained strength, recruiting women (and some men) from every social class, its outraged attack on smug male assumptions reinforced the rising challenge to a whole social order.

Nor was the threat of violence limited to the left. In 1914 the Commons passed a bill for Irish home rule for the third time, which made it immune to a veto in the House of Lords. The Protestants of northern Ireland, with support from many Englishmen, openly threatened civil war. Squads began drilling, and the British officer corps gave frightening indications that it might mutiny rather than fight to impose home rule on Protestant loyalists.

Only the outbreak of world war generated the national unity that neither imperialism nor social reform had been able to create. If the death of Queen Victoria in 1901 had symbolized the end of an age of British expansion, the ascent of George V to the throne (1910–1936) marked the opening of new conflicts. Edward VII's brief reign (1901–1910) would soon be remembered a little sadly as the Edwardian era, a happy time of relaxed confidence that prosperity and democracy were the natural products of progress and a guarantee of peace.

As the nineteenth century ended, Europeans seemed preoccupied with the future. A great many of the most optimistic predictions from the past were being fulfilled. In general, productivity and prosperity, while continuing to rise, were already at levels never achieved before. Science and technology promised still greater wonders. In most countries there was greater freedom of expression, political participation, and leisure, increased literacy and education, and better health care than in the past. Even in retrospect, the level of creativity in the arts and the expansion of professional expertise remains impressive. Yet the civilization that achieved all this was bitterly denounced not only for injustices, which by contrast seemed all the more blatant, but more fundamentally for its lack of coherent values, for its materialism, for the ugliness of industrial society, and for the privileged position of a middle class portrayed as self-serving and philistine.

The progress measured by general prosperity, knowledge, and freedom was shared in diminished portion by common people through rising standards of living, social mobility, universal education, and increased democracy. Yet millions of Europeans chose or were forced to leave their homelands, and that same progress also brought class conflict and clashing interests that threatened the social system. As each nation confronted these tensions, it fell to the state to balance repression and reform, social justice and special interests.

Often such compromises, usually sought through the political process, in fact made conflict and discontent more explicit.

For good or ill, the trend toward greater democracy (and large-scale organization) seemed irresistible. For a generation there had been no revolutions save in backward Russia and no European war, facts often cited as proof of progress. There was some reason to believe that the problems of the late nineteenth century might in their turn be resolved in the future. Then suddenly in 1914 the very compromises that had held society together and kept the peace exploded—not in revolution, but in total war.

RECOMMENDED READING

Studies

*Arendt, Hannah. *The Origins of Totalitarianism*. 1958. This original analysis is also a profoundly pessimistic application of hindsight to the late nineteenth century.

Avineri, S. *The Social and Political Thought of Karl Marx*. 1969. An important and fresh treatment.

*Dangerfield, George. *The Strange Death of Liberal England*. 1935. Skillfully and argumentatively written description of a society in crisis.

*Derfler, Leslie. *Socialism since Marx: A Century of the European Left*. 1973. Thoughtful discussion of the movements that stemmed from Marx.

*Eisley, Loren C. *Darwin's Century: Evolution and the Men Who Discovered It*. 1958. An attractive discussion of the history of evolutionary theory.

Fieldhouse, D. K. *Economics and Empire, 1830–1914*. 1973. Useful analysis using recent research to cast doubt on the primary importance of economic factors.

Hale, Oran J. *The Great Illusion, 1900–1914*. 1971. An able general survey in the same excellent series as the volume by Carlton Hayes.

*Hayes, Carlton J. H. *A Generation of Materialism, 1871–1900*. 1941. Though dated, still a stimulating indictment of the period.

*Hughes, H. Stuart. *Consciousness and Society: The Reorientation of European Social Thought, 1890–1930*. 1958. A gracefully written and indispensable analysis of the central currents of modern thought in a time of transition.

*Joll, James. *The Anarchists*. 1965. Discusses the ideas and motives of very disparate groups.

*Kindleberger, Charles P. *Economic Growth in France and Britain: 1851–1950*. 1969. An economist's careful assessment of the evidence for the major explanations of the differences in these two economies.

*Löwith, Karl. *From Hegel to Nietzsche: The Revolution in Nineteenth-Century Thought*. 1964. A sober essay on the transformations in modern thought.

*Masur, Gerhard. *Prophets of Yesterday*. 1961. Uses a broad selection of thinkers to provide a good survey of intellectual history.

*Pulzer, Peter. *The Rise of Political Anti-Semitism in Germany and Austria*. 1964. A clear and balanced survey of a difficult topic.

Schorske, Carl E. *Fin-de-Siècle Vienna: Politics and Culture*. 1980. Unusually sensitive and imaginative assessment of one of the important moments in European cultural history.

*Shattuck, Roger. *The Banquet Years*. 1968. A fascinating account of the artistic life in late nineteenth-century Paris.

Tannenbaum, Edward R. *1900: The Generation Before the Great War*. 1976. Interesting essays on the major facets of society.

Thayer, John A. *Italy and the Great War: Politics and Culture, 1870–1915*. 1964. Informed defense of Italian politics against its many critics.

Wagar, Warren W. *Good Tidings: The Belief in Progress from Darwin to Marcuse*. 1972. A wide-ranging account of the period's principal theme.

Weber, Eugen. *Peasants into Frenchmen: The Modernization of Rural France, 1880–1914*. 1976. Provocative treatment of the resistance of rural France to the pressures for change.

Wohl, Robert. *The Generation of 1914*. 1979. Theories of generations in conflict are related to the intellectual and political discontent preceding World War I in this important book.

* Available in paperback.

26

IMPERIALISM AND THE GREAT WAR 1870–1920

The political and economic changes transforming Europe since the eighteenth century had now been carried throughout the world, and all civilizations were forced in important ways to grow more alike. Imperialism carried Western power around the world, and initially the flow of culture and communication was primarily one-way: European technology, dress, etiquette, ways of doing business, wage payment, religion, and political ideas spread everywhere. Wherever they went and whether they came for gain or out of humanitarian concern, Europeans taught their Christianity and their ways of controlling power, the utility of their roads and railways and medicine, the lure of profit through international trade. Other cultures slowly developed their own ways of using European ideas of education, justice, and nationalism. In return Europeans enjoyed prestige, power, and wealth. Confident in their superiority, they were slow to borrow from non-Western cultures; but gradually, from strange foods, Eastern and African art, to Oriental religions and philosophy, European civilization came to be enriched by the cultures it had been so quick to overpower.

But imperialism also had deep roots within European society, and so did the arms race among Europe's most industrialized nations. This threatening competition had long been held in check by a complicated system of diplomacy. Then suddenly that system broke down, and in 1914 the nations of Europe willingly went to war. For the first time since the Napoleonic era, all the major powers engaged in battle on Continental soil, and during more than four years of unrelieved horror, the total energies of society were committed to the bloodiest conflict Europe had ever known. World War I strained the technological and organizing skills developed by the most industrialized and democratic states of the late nineteenth century. It ended with the collapse of the Russian, Austro-Hungarian, and German empires, defeated in war and torn by revolution. The new nations carved from them remade the map of Europe, and in Russia Communists established a government whose very existence altered political life throughout the West. On the winning side, the liberal Italian state never really recovered from the war, and victorious France and Great Britain emerged significantly changed.

Scholars have pondered the origins of World War I for half a century, and we can now see how a diplomatic system that seemed a triumph of flexible realism led to the disaster. Behind international relations lay domestic pressures within each country, and aggressive imperialism and nationalism were both used by conservative groups to preserve their power at home. In its causes as well as its conduct, the war was closely tied also to the economic and social changes of the preceding forty years. The machine guns, tanks, airplanes, and submarines that transformed military tactics were products of recent technology. The incredible quantities of armaments and ammunition consumed depended on modern methods of production and management. This war required the mobilization of the population to an extent possible only because of the levels of mass communication, literacy, popular participation, and efficient bureaucracy reached since the mid-nineteenth century.

The effects of the Great War were like those of a revolution. When it ended, fallen governments were replaced, buildings were rebuilt, and in the West, at least, groups previously dominant still held power; but the relations between town and country, peasant and landlord, worker and capitalist, citizen and government had been forever altered in most of Europe. The war thus had a significance beyond the immediate issue of victory and defeat. At the peace conference the desire to make sure so disastrous a conflict could never recur was strengthened by the suspicion that in 1914 a great civilization had come close to suicide.

I. EUROPEAN IMPERIALISM

The Meanings of Imperialism

Throughout European history the memory of ancient Rome stood as the great model of empire, and in modern times the term empire was employed in a related sense by both Napoleons, as it continued to be in Austria-Hungary and Russia up to 1918. To most Europeans in the late nineteenth century, however, those very examples suggested that empire as a form of government was distinctly on the wane. Imperialism came to be used primarily with regard to European rule overseas, and nowadays the term is commonly extended to economic and cultural domination that may or may not include direct political control. Thus current students of imperialism stress the spread of a world market, from the trade in luxuries and slaves of the seventeenth century to the multinational corporations of today.

European imperialism, understood in this sense, increased enormously throughout the nineteenth century but especially from the 1860s on. Trade expanded both in value and in geographical range. Wherever commerce took them, Europeans built docks and warehouses, established companies, and made new investments. Whether directed from Europe, by European settlers, or by local merchants, these commercial enterprises adopted European techniques of management, accounting, and technology. Businesses expanded by attracting European capital, and much of the profit they generated was returned to European banks and investors. Thus tied to foreign markets, such enterprises in turn transformed local economies through their labor policies and their purchases of local goods and services. This complex process was further stimulated by improved communication. Steamships required better ports, more reliable and expensive provisions, and larger cargoes. Telegraph lines connected India to Europe in 1865, and a cable ran from Vladivostok to Shanghai, Hong Kong, and Singapore by 1871. By the 1880s rail lines operated on every continent; and more were being built, all requiring European equipment, engineers, and investment. By the turn of the century the automobile began to generate a demand not only for highways and bridges but for a steady flow of petroleum, the basis for new international corporations.

Western influence was not limited to investments and trade. In the same period universities on the European model were established from Constantinople to India; and students from China, Japan, India, and the Middle East became familiar figures in European and American centers of learning. All these developments had fundamental social and political implications for daily life and for traditional elites in Latin America, Asia, and Africa. It is the cumulative effect of this process—a process that increases Western wealth and prestige while disrupting and transforming non-Western societies, that corrodes non-European traditions and cultures while feeding Western interests and power—that the term imperialism evokes today.

For the generation preceding World War I, the spread of empire was dramatic evidence of Europe's dynamism; and it was justified on grounds of progress—carrying higher civilization and Christianity to backward lands—as well as national interest. When they spoke of imperialism then (and they spoke and wrote about it a great deal), Europeans generally used the term somewhat more narrowly to mean direct intervention and domination by a European state outside Europe. (The British Empire was their great model.) This late nineteenth-century fascination with imperialism revealed a characteristic European emphasis upon politics and the state, and it reflected a striking new reality as well. In the past most liberals had considered overseas empire to be both impractical and undesirable, and they had cited the benefits of free trade and the obvious lesson of the American and Latin American revolutions. Then, rather suddenly, imperialism became an important issue in domestic politics and a stimulus to the international rivalries that would culminate in world war.

Explanations of Imperialism

In 1875, after centuries of close contact with Africa, European powers laid claim to no more than a tenth of Africa's land. Twenty years later, seven nations had through fierce competition established dominion over almost the entire continent. And they had carried their rivalry to most of Asia and the small islands of the Pacific Ocean. Won in open conquest, through protectorates, and by treaties granting special trading privileges, most of the newly acquired lands at first had few European settlers (the primary means of exploiting local wealth in the past) and most of them lay in tropical zones Europeans had heretofore found unappealing and unhealthy.

Such rapid and dramatic developments demand explanation, and by the turn of the century, the opponents of imperialism in particular sought to explain the pervasive imperial fever. In 1902 J. A. Hobson, a British economist, published *Imperialism: A Study*, a critical tract that has been heavily attacked by subsequent scholars but that remains the starting point of modern analysis. Writing during the Boer War, Hobson was eager to show that imperialism offered little to restless populations or to commerce. Emigrants, he noted, preferred to go to the Americas, and Britain's trade with the European continent and the Americas was far greater and growing faster than her trade with her colonies.

The economic explanation of imperialism Hobson found in financiers, small numbers of men controlling great wealth and looking for quick profits. They used their social and political connections to induce the government to protect their investments through political dominance over undeveloped lands. Similarly their social position enabled them to exploit the

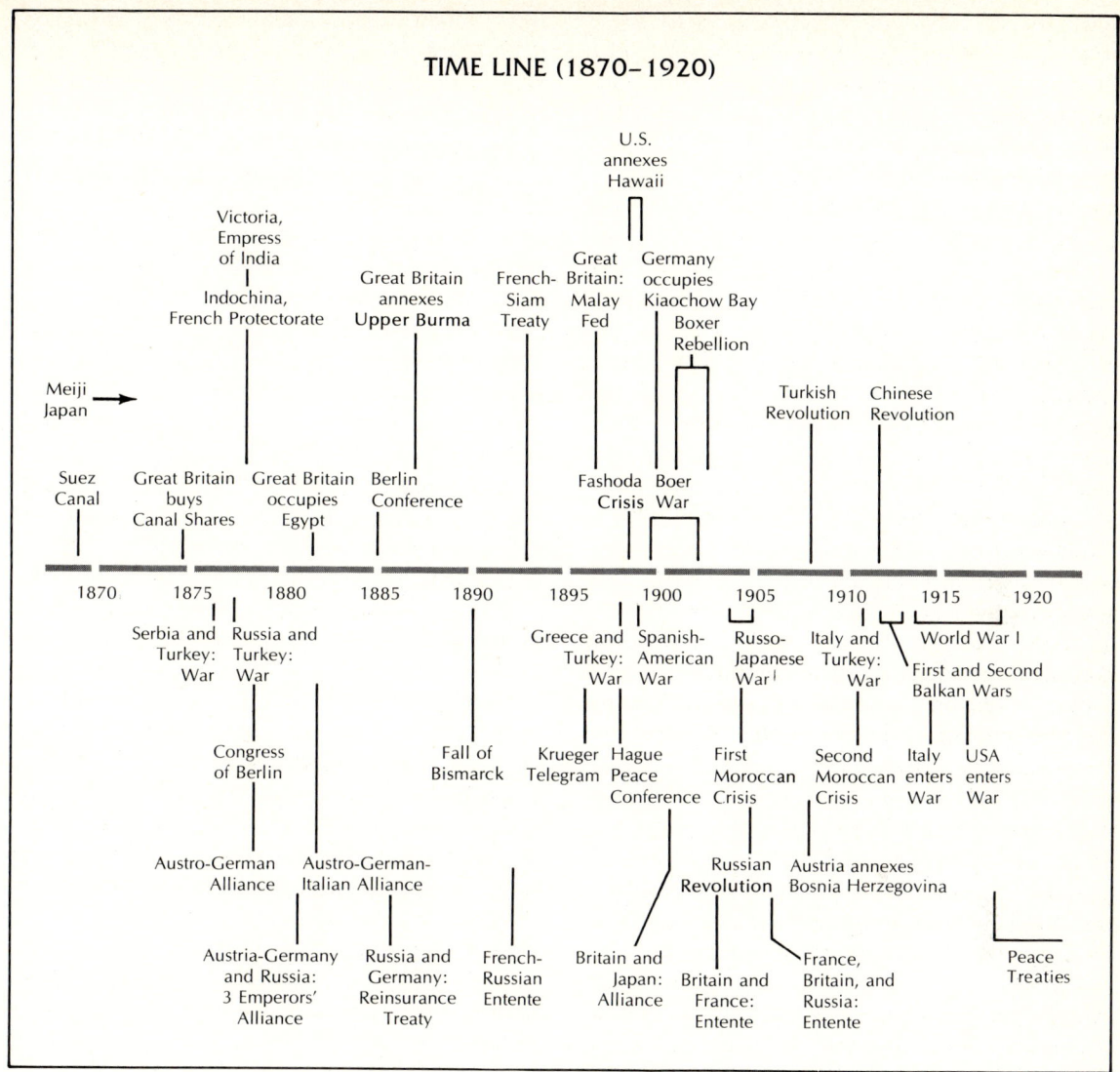

missionaries, soldiers, and patriotic dreamers who glorified empire. Imperialism thus stemmed from the manipulation of public opinion in the interests of certain capitalists.

Hobson's analysis inspired the still more influential theory of Lenin. The leader of Russia's Marxist revolutionaries, Lenin provided a Marxist interpretation of a subject on which Marx had written little. In *Imperialism: The Last Stage of Capitalism* (1916), Lenin agreed that the stimulus behind empire building was basically economic and that the essence of colonialism was exploitation. But for Lenin imperialist ventures grew from the very dynamics of capitalism itself. Competition produced both monopolies and lowered profits, and surplus capital was forced to seek overseas investments. The alternative, to enlarge the domestic market by raising wages, would increase competition, thus further reducing profit. Imperialism was therefore the last "stage" of capitalism, the product of its internal contradictions. Lenin would add in 1916 that imperial rivalries, involving whole nations, led to wars that further hastened the end of capitalism. "Imperialist" became an epithet for a system considered decadent as well as immoral.

Although influenced by these views, most historians have remained uncomfortable with them. They contribute little to an understanding of the actual process of imperial conquest, in which capitalists were often reluctant participants. They do not explain why imperialists called for political control beyond treaty rights or for the swift spread of European power into areas that offered small financial return; investment, like trade, remained heavier in more developed noncolonial countries. Nor do economic arguments tell us much about the role of the popular press, explorers, earnest missionaries, and ambitious soldiers in pressing hesitant politicians to imperial conquest.

Many factors help explain the sudden increase in the pace and importance of European imperialism, although all analysts today would agree that economic interests, at least in the long run, were among the most important. By the late nineteenth century, a society familiar with self-made men was readier to believe that new lands offered the chance to make a quick fortune. A general increase in trade and the growing demand for rubber, oil, and rare metals spurred the search for natural resources. Stiffening competition in international commerce and rising tariffs taught businessmen to seek the backing of their governments. Technology too played a part. Not only was regular trade with distant places made easier, but dynamite lessened the difficulty of building roads, while modern medicine reduced the dangers of the tropics. Coaling stations and telegraph posts acquired strategic as well as commercial importance, a fact that argued for military and political protection.

Beyond such rational calculations, however, imperialism was rooted in the values Europeans held and in their domestic society and politics. Mass-circulation newspapers gloried in imperialism, writing of adventure and wealth, Christianity and progress in the virile language of force. To the people of the late nineteenth century, exploration and conquest were high and noble adventure. Press reports made popular heroes of daring men like Henry M. Stanley, who followed the rivers of South Africa and penetrated the interior of the Congo, and Pierre de Brazza, who traveled up the Congo River, overcoming hardship and danger and dismantling a steamship so it could be carried around the rapids. Exploration seemed in itself an expression of progress, the brave adventurer the personification of individual initiative. If the explorer also gained wealth, that completed the parable.

The missionaries who risked their lives to build a chapel in the jungle and convert the heathen were as symbolically appealing as the explorer. For churches often at odds with the culture of their day and in conflict with the state, here was a dramatic outlet and a welcome reassurance of their importance in modern life. Hundreds of Social Darwinists preached the inevitable conflict of race with race and hailed the resultant spread of civilization, by which they meant of course their own. Geographical societies became prominent in every European country, proudly acclaiming yet another association of new knowledge with increased power.

Where class tensions were high and domestic conflict serious, colonial expansion offered all citizens a share in national glory and gain.

A German cartoon of 1896 lampoons African people and the Teutonic order brought to Africa by German imperialism.
(Photo: The Granger Collection)

Rudyard Kipling's poems of imperial derring-do in exotic lands hail the simple cockney soldier; whatever his lot at home, he was a ruler abroad. Thus in politics imperialism, like nationalism, cut across social divisions. It was an important part, especially in Great Britain and Germany, of the political resurgence of the right, allowing conservative groups strong in the army, the church, and the aristocracy to ally themselves with commercial interests in a program of popular appeal. Employment as well as glory was promised as the fruit of a policy of strength. Significantly imperialism never achieved comparable political effect in France, the nation with the second largest of the European empires, though hers too was built principally by soldiers and priests. The right fumbled its effort at mass appeal in the Dreyfus affair; patriots were preoccupied with avenging the loss of Alsace and Lorraine to Germany; and French nationalism retained ideas associated with the Revolution that often conflicted with those of imperialism. But everywhere empire offered the appeal of individual daring and dramatic action in a society becoming more organized into large institutions. It gave openings to groups such as the military and the clergy often disparaged at home, and it supplemented popular theories with concrete tales of risk, gain, glory, and conquest.

Patterns of Imperialism

Despite the general popularity of imperialist ideas, few wholehearted imperialists held high political office even in Great Britain. The history of colonial conquest in this period was less one of long-range schemes than of individual acts and decisions that appear almost accidental when viewed singly. Frequently individual explorers, traders, or officers established their claims in a given region through treaties with native leaders and then, usually later, obtained recognition from their home government. In the process of enforcing contracts and maintaining order, they tended to exceed their original authorization and to extend their territorial claims. Governments anxious not to appear weak before their public or other powers then supported such moves; trading concessions and protectorates became colonies. This pattern of expansion required little premeditation. Applying their own laws and practices to other cultures, Europeans were shocked when natives failed to honor Western rules, and they responded with increased force.

Even Europeans attracted by non-Western cultures or devoted to helping local populations, in the name of Western religion and medicine, undermined their host societies by introducing alien ideas, institutions, and technology as well as by sheer wealth and power. There is in fact a whole other history of imperialism just now being written from the perspective of the indigenous peoples that shows how native political, economic, and religious organization was disrupted by the arrival of outsiders. To the confident men of empire, such conditions left no alternative but further European control.

Africa

In the 1870s European involvement in Africa began a rapid spread inland from a few coastal posts that would end in the partition of the entire continent by 1895 (see Map 26.1). Early signs of the domination to come were the collapse of Egyptian finances, the energetic exploration of the Congo sponsored by King Leopold II of Belgium, and the increasing conflicts between the British and the Boers.

The Suez Canal was completed in 1869, the shares in its ownership held by French investors and the khedive of Egypt, who ruled as a monarch representing the nominal suzerainty of the Ottomans. When the debt-plagued khedive sold his shares in 1875, they were purchased by the British government in one of Disraeli's

MAP 26.1: AFRICA 1885

most dramatic coups. Determined to protect their investments, the British and French then established joint control over Egyptian finances. In 1882, however, a nationalist revolt by the Egyptian army against both the khedive and foreign influence threatened this arrangement. The British government decided to mount a show of strength (in which the French Parlement refused to allow France a part) and the Royal Navy bombarded Alexandria to teach Egyptians that contracts must be met. In the resulting chaos the British attempted to restore order, a process that quickly led to their occupying Egypt, and the country remained under their rule until after World War II. In Tunisia a similar pattern of increased foreign investments followed by a financial crisis and intricate diplomatic maneuverings brought about French occupation in 1881. Both events accelerated the competition for African empire.

Although reluctant to accept responsibility for all their countrymen did, European governments nevertheless found themselves drawn piecemeal into scores of treaties that prescribed for societies little understood and fixed boundaries in areas whose geography was barely known. The International Association for the Exploration and Civilization of Central Africa, founded in Brussels in 1876, quickly became a private operation of Leopold II. The association paid less attention to its lofty aims of furthering science and ending slavery than to the vast territorial claims it might make by sponsoring Stanley's explorations. From their outposts along the west coasts, the French, the English, Spaniards, and Portuguese hurried to push into the hinterlands of what are now Senegal and Nigeria.

French gains in West Africa were the most extensive of all, and in 1898 a group of soldiers

Cecil Rhodes as popular hero. In this engraving of 1897 Rhodes is shown leaving the Cape Town railway station, his carriage drawn by a private army (called the Matabili boys—after the Zulu warriors) through a crowd that is meant to depict the romance and color of empire.
(Photo: The Granger Collection)

MAP 26.2: AFRICA 1914

who had pushed two-thirds of the way across the continent at its widest point arrived at Fashoda, on the Nile, a few days before the British, who were moving into the Sudan. Both nations considered the encounter of their troops at Fashoda a matter of national honor, and imperialists plotted on maps how dominance over Africa was at stake. The French imagined holdings stretching from west to east across the continent, controlling the headwaters of the Nile. The British talked in terms of territory and maybe even a railway from the Cape of

Good Hope to Cairo, a north-south axis through the continent. Thus the obscure outpost at Fashoda sought by no general staff brought Great Britain and France close to war for weeks. The confrontation ended when the French, divided at home over the Dreyfus Affair, chose to give way.

In South Africa Cecil Rhodes typified the interconnection of local politics, private interest, and visions of empire. Confident of white and indeed Anglo-Saxon superiority, he schemed and propagandized relentlessly, stretching old claims and using trading companies and his own wealth to establish new ones. He died during the Boer War, but the British victory paved the way for the establishment of the Union of South Africa in 1910, a partial fulfillment of Rhodes' ambitions.

As the European states were drawn into the scramble, they sought through diplomacy to lessen the clear danger that clashes in Africa would lead to war in Europe. At Berlin in 1885 the powers established rules for each other. The most important was that coastal settlement by a European nation would give it claim to the hinterlands beyond. Straight lines drawn from haphazard coastal conquests cut across the little-known indigenous cultures, but they restrained the anarchy of European ambition. The powers also agreed at Berlin to prohibit slavery; and five years later they banned liquor and limited arms in the zone between the Sahara and the Cape Colony. Humanitarian considerations were not wholly forgotten, and by the turn of the century, the ruthless exploitation of the Belgian Congo was considered an international scandal. The men who bravely planted their flags and wrote out treaties for chieftains to sign did not doubt that theirs was a beneficial achievement to be measured by mission hospitals and schools, new roads and political order as well as profit. By 1912 only Liberia and Ethiopia were formally free of European domination (see Map 26.2). The social, cultural, religious, and political life of Africans was everywhere submerged under an imposed European order.

Asia

For more than a century the decline of the Ottoman Empire had been a major theme of international relations, one clearly demarked by the independence of Greece early in the century, the Crimean War at midcentury, and then by the growing turmoil in the Balkans and the British occupation of Egypt. As British, French, Russian, and German interests competed for political privileges and economic concessions (that the Germans won the right to build a railroad from the Bosporus to Baghdad was recognized as a major diplomatic triumph and a troubling challenge), it almost seemed as if those rivalries were what held the Ottoman Empire together.

In the East beyond the Ottoman Empire, Great Britain and Russia were again the main contenders for influence (see Map 26.3). Persia had felt their competition since the 1830s and by the 1870s had conceded control of the Imperial Bank of Persia to British interests. Russia competed by exerting military pressure along Persia's northern frontier and in the 1890s by offering a large loan and related concessions in an effort to reduce Britain's dominance. As part of a general entente reached in 1907 (see below), the two European powers agreed on spheres of influence: the British sphere would include the area of the Persian Gulf, in the south, and Russia's the north. Their competition, by limiting the intrusions of either power, had helped the Persian state preserve a nominal independence, but their presence increased its instability, and revolution erupted in 1905. The technique of playing off Russian and British ambitions was less successful in Afghanistan, however, where the emir's efforts to use the Russians as a counterweight to British influence could not match Britain's determination through her presence to guarantee the security of India on Afghanistan's southeast border.

MAP 26.3: IMPERIALISM IN ASIA

India remained the jewel of the British Empire, the envy of all imperial powers. As a British trading partner, India stood on a par with France (only the United States ranked higher). Her wealth and the prestige of her culture made India the very symbol of empire, a special status recognized in the proclamation of Queen Victoria as empress of India in 1877. Many of the leading figures of British political life made their reputations in the India service, and their techniques of administration through local lords and British courts were often proclaimed as models of enlightened rule. Yet the growth of trade and industry did not prevent devastating famines in the 1890s, and concessions to local government only stimulated increasingly organized and nationwide demands for a native voice in political life.

East of India and south of China only Siam (Thailand) preserved her independence of European control through a willingness to modernize—that is, to adopt European forms of political and economic organization—and thanks to the countervailing pressures of the three European powers present in neighboring realms, who in effect constrained each other. The British annexed upper Burma in 1886 and part of Malaya in 1896; the Dutch were on the island of Borneo; and French influence had steadily increased in Cambodia and Cochin-China (both parts of Indochina) during the 1860s, despite the indifference of the governments in Paris. Whenever Christians were attacked or a trader murdered, the local commander pressed native rulers for further political concessions without waiting for instructions from home. The French themselves seemed unable to constrain the extension of their authority. Even the modest goal of providing their enclave a secure frontier—a European conception that ignored social realities—usually led to war and expansion into another ancient realm. France in this way eventually found herself at war with China in 1883; and though Parlement voted down the government of Premier Jules Ferry, France's leading imperialist, the war nevertheless resulted in a French protectorate, reorganized in 1887 as French Indochina.

The weakness of China and the strengthening of Japan were the central realities of Southeast Asian history in the second half of the nineteenth century. Both proud nations had sought to keep intruding Europeans at a distance, and both failed, but with contrasting results. For the huge Chinese Empire, its administrative system threatened by inefficiency and provincial warlords, Western missionaries and traders were especially disruptive. When the Chinese attempted to restrict the importation of opium, which was as expensive and demoralizing for them as it was profitable for the British traders who brought the opium from India, the result was a brief war that led to the cession of Hong Kong to Britain (1841) and special foreign trading rights in a number of Chinese cities. The impact of missionaries contributed to the Taiping Rebellion (1850–1864), in which a Chinese-led millenarian movement incorporating elements of Christianity and social discontent produced revolts that threatened the empire. Battling for survival, the government was forced to grant new concessions to Britain, the United States, France, and Russia for trade, the protection of missionaries, and extraterritorial rights. In 1860 British and French forces occupied Peking and burned the summer palace in retaliation for the seizure of their envoys, and Russia took Vladivostok—a step recognized by China's Department of Foreign Affairs, a ministry not needed before.

Thus the French gains in Indochina, the extension of Russian interests in Manchuria, the arrival of more and more missionaries, and further trading concessions were all part of a continuing process. Again and again, a local riot, a missionary murdered, or a contract broken would lead to renewed demands and military pressure from Western powers. In 1898 inland waters were opened to foreign shipping (mainly British), and the Germans laid claim to Kiaochow Bay, as Germany and Japan now joined the competition for claims on China. Chinese efforts to raise revenues, reform administration, and stimulate railroads required in turn further loans from and concessions to Western nations. The Boxer Rebellion of 1900–1901, a complicated response by local militias outraged by foreigners and the weakness of their own government, brought another round of violence. Scores of Western missionaries, agents, and some diplomats were killed, prompting heavy military intervention, especially by Russia and Germany. When order was restored, China agreed to a large indemnity. The only defense against European imperialism even in a great and ancient nation appeared to be a westernization that deepened European influence. For China, that also meant the revolution of 1911, led by Sun Yat-sen, and the establishment of the Chinese Republic.

Japan, which for centuries had preserved its

isolation, was in 1853 successfully pressed by Commodore Matthew Perry of the United States to permit commerce with the West, an opening quickly followed by a series of treaties permitting trade and protecting the rights of foreigners. There followed the familiar pattern of misunderstandings, broken agreements, antiforeign feeling, and renewed Western demands; but domestic political transformation came quickly in Japan. A new generation of leaders joined with the emperor, after a brief civil war, in carrying out the Meiji Restoration (1868). The essentially feudal system that had lasted seven centuries was ended, and Japan embarked on a systematic policy of adapting Western industry, technology, education, laws, and governmental institutions, including a constitutional system (much influenced by Germany's) in 1889. The resultant economic growth, efficient administration, and modern army enabled Japan, like the nations of the West, to attack China and win easy victories in the war of 1894–1895. Japan's gains included Formosa and the control of Korea. As in her victory over Russia (1904–1905), Japan showed that successful imperialism, like the Western ambitions and power from which it stemmed, need not be limited to Europeans. With the United States in control of the Philippines, as a result of the Spanish-American War (1898), the Western system of power relations dominated Southeast Asia and encircled the globe.

II. THE COMING OF WORLD WAR

Realignments in the Bismarckian System

Despite many dangerous moments there was no war between major states for more than forty years after 1870. Remarkably, European governments appeared able to juggle competing worldwide interests abroad and complex social changes at home, including the altered bases of power created by industrialization and democracy. Between nations this flexibility was managed through a traditional diplomacy conducted by gentlemen, most of them aristocrats, in secrecy and according to elaborate rules. Only later did it become clear how limited the efficacy of that diplomacy was. Gradually the experience of imperialism and the greater importance of public opinion altered what could be negotiated and how negotiations were conducted, and foreign policy came to be more directly constrained both by military imperatives and domestic politics.

Bismarck had established the German Empire as the arbiter of Continental peace at the Congress of Berlin in 1878, and to preserve that position he relied first of all on Germany's alliance with Austria-Hungary. Central Europe was thus secure, and Austria-Hungary's ties to several of the Balkan states combined with the Three Emperors' Alliance (a treaty among Russia, Germany, and Austria-Hungary) to reduce any danger from the East. Italy was then added to this network when France occupied Tunisia and Bismarck took advantage of Italian resentment to form the Triple Alliance of Germany, Austria-Hungary, and Italy. Signed in 1882, the pact had a five-year term and could be renewed. Finally, in 1887 Italy and the United Kingdom made a vague mutual commitment to preserve the status quo in the Mediterranean.

At its height, therefore, the Bismarckian system achieved the diplomatic isolation of France, good Anglo-German relations, a formal understanding with Russia, an alliance with Italy and Austria-Hungary as well as additional ties extending into the Balkan and Iberian peninsulas. These accomplishments required great skill; Italy and Russia for example had more reasons for conflict with Austria-Hungary than with anyone else. Although their precise provisions were secret and defensive, the treaties were understood to imply far more than they specifically provided, and they placed Germany in a position of influence rare among sovereign states in peacetime.

Even before Bismarck fell from power, however, the system showed signs of weakness. The Three Emperors' Alliance, renewed in 1884, was allowed to lapse in 1887 because a flare-up of conflict among the Balkan States had reawakened suspicion between Austria-Hungary and Russia, a serious danger to Bismarckian diplomacy that could not be overcome. With characteristic flexibility Bismarck repaired the damage by immediately signing a separate Reinsurance Treaty with Russia, providing for the neutrality of either power if the other was at war. To preserve the Triple Alliance, which also came up for renewal in 1887, it was necessary to add recognition of Italian ambitions in the Balkans, Africa, and (in case of war with France) Corsica and Nice. Ironically, the weakest member of the Alliance could maneuver more freely than her powerful friends.

From the Germans' standpoint the keystone of the Bismarckian system was the alliance with Austria-Hungary. Beyond that their confidence rested on the assumption that enmities between France and Great Britain, Great Britain and Russia, and Italy and France would prevent any of them from aligning against the Second Reich. It was easy from Berlin to overlook one factor that might draw these powers together—common fear of Germany.

The Shifting Balance 1880–1905

An expression of German power, these treaties were supposed to provide security, but it required Bismarck's supple skill to offset the menace of sudden attack they advertised. With his fall the system he had constructed broke down. German diplomacy after 1890 was poorly coordinated, often inconsistent and disruptive.

Bismarck's successors did not renew the understanding with Russia; instead, a traditional dislike of Slavs reinforced by Junker objections to heavy imports of cheaper Russian grain led high German officials to prefer to keep the Triple Alliance uncluttered by a treaty with Russia.[1] France seized the opportunity to break out of diplomatic isolation and pressed the Russian government—hesitant but already turning to France for loans and arms purchases—for an alliance. The understanding the two nations reached in 1891 became a full alliance in less than three years, a major shift in European military commitments. Russia agreed to support France if she should be attacked by Germany or by Italy with German aid, and France agreed to support Russia if she was attacked by Germany or Austria-Hungary with German aid.

An accord between the Russian autocracy and the French republic had seemed politically impossible. But the tsar now greeted French delegates while a band played the "Marseillaise," previously prohibited as too revolutionary to be heard in Russia, and the Franco-Russian entente was to last as long as the Triple Alliance.

German diplomats in response sought to foster some understanding with the United Kingdom and to demonstrate their country's place in world affairs. Those aims conflicted. The "new course" of *Weltpolitik* ("world policy"), backed by imperial claims and navy building, appeared more threatening with each of the verbal explosions for which the emperor became famous.

In 1896 William II sent a telegram of congratulation to S. J. P. Kruger, president of the South African Republic, after the Boers had defeated a raid on the Transvaal by a small private army organized by Englishmen who

---

[1] Renewal of the Reinsurance Treaty was one of the issues that led to the break between Bismarck and William II in 1890. The charge that it was incompatible with the Triple Alliance was at least technically incorrect, for the promise of neutrality was not to apply if Russia attacked Austria.

hoped to stir a revolution there. The message, deeply resented in Great Britain, was meant to show the British how much they needed German friendship; instead it encouraged distrust of Germany. During the Boxer Rebellion the Kaiser's enthusiastic talk of the "yellow peril" and instructions for his soldiers to behave like the barbaric Huns of old did nothing to enhance his reputation for stability or lessen the atmosphere of menace. Germans proclaimed the "natural" alliance between the Teutonic and Anglo-Saxon races but also took soundings about a possible Continental coalition against the United Kingdom. The navy they were building, which looked like a direct challenge to Great Britain and a threat to her empire, became the central issue in all efforts at some rapprochement between the two powers. When the Germans demanded a formal alliance before they would limit their shipbuilding, the British were convinced that the German fleet was aimed at them.

During the difficult years of the Boer War, the United Kingdom had found her diplomatic independence no longer so splendid and was, as the Germans hoped, beginning to look for new international understandings. In 1902 she broke her long tradition of refusing peacetime alliances by signing a treaty with Japan. Her overall aim was of course to guard the empire through alliance; her immediate purpose was to prevent France from supporting Russia's expansion into East Asia.

The colonial clashes between Great Britain and France in the last decade of the century had seemed some of the gravest threats to European peace. When the French had withdrawn from the confrontation at Fashoda in 1898, Foreign Minister Théophile Delcassé had set about turning humiliation into gain by seeking a broader understanding with Great Britain. France had learned not to demand too much, and her delegation of extraordinarily able diplomats worked steadily for the reduction of conflicts. By the turn of the century, she had dropped her resistance to British domination in Egypt in return for recognition of French interests in North Africa, particularly Morocco.

Similarly France had won Italian acknowledgment of her interest in Morocco by recognizing Italian ambitions in Libya, and in 1902 the two nations pledged neutrality if either was attacked by a third power. Although the Triple Alliance was renewed in the same year, Italy in fact sat on the fence between the Franco-Russian and the Austro-German alliance. The culmination of France's policy was the Anglo-French Entente Cordiale of 1904. In one sweeping effort she and Great Britain sought to eliminate all the major issues of imperial conflict between them. From Siam to Newfoundland, the Niger River to North Africa, they agreed on their spheres of influence and dominant interests.

The Entente Cordiale was nothing more than an understanding, but France was right in seeing it as a major break in the diplomatic encirclement Bismarck had created around her. Without demanding very formal guarantees, she was achieving a great deal. Edward VII's visit to Paris in 1903 and the French president's to London that year and to Rome in 1905 testified to France's new place in European affairs. These understandings came in the nick of time, for they helped prevent the Russo-Japanese War of 1904–1905 from leading to conflict between France and Great Britain and effectively countered German efforts to break up the Franco-Russian alliance.

Hardening Alliances 1905–1912

Germany's diplomatic position remained strong—Britain and France were not allied; Russia's defeat at the hands of Japan and her subsequent revolution greatly reduced her influence; the chances of an Anglo-German understanding remained; and the Triple Alliance was intact. An assertive policy, German leaders reasoned, would enable them to capitalize on this situation. But the tenor of international relations was changing. Imperial ambitions, which had often threatened European relations in the preceding decades, were no longer so certain a source of antagonism as to prevent a coalition against Germany. The experience of imperialism and the politicians' increased concern for public opinion tended to transform international claims (and reactions to the Kaiser's bluster) into dangerous if vague issues of national honor. As armaments increased and treaties proliferated, each power became more obsessed with its own security. Thus within seven years three diplomatic crises—each of which at first seemed a victory for Germany—in fact brought her opponents closer together.

The first great crisis arose over Morocco. France had carefully won the acquiescence of each interested power, except Germany, in her designs on Morocco. The French planned to deal with Germany last; and the Germans, who had little direct interest there, intended to get the highest price possible for French annexation of the decaying sultanates. Wanting to test the loose understandings by which the French had improved their diplomatic position, the German chancellor Bernhard von Bülow demanded an international conference, for which there was solid basis in prior guarantees, and belligerently threatened France. Delcassé, the architect of French foreign policy, was forced from office, but the chancellor then sought more than this symbolic triumph. He reasoned that in a conference the other Triple Alliance nations would stand behind him, Russia and Great Britain would be won to the Germans' "correct" position, and a humiliated France would be left isolated once more.

The conference that met at Algeciras in 1906 did in fact produce a compromise, recognizing both international status for Morocco and the primacy of French interests, but it was a disaster for German diplomacy. Only Austria-Hungary loyally voted with her European neighbor. Italy, Russia, Great Britain, and the United States (now a regular participant in such international agreements) supported France. The German bludgeon led to military talks between French and British officials and a far stronger sense of mutual interest.

After Algeciras Anglo-German competition for supremacy on the seas grew more serious. Both sides increased their plans for naval construction despite two great conferences at The Hague in 1899 and 1907 on disarmament and compulsory arbitration. In fact no power was willing to sacrifice any of its strength, but it was the German delegates who bluntly accepted the onus for rejecting any limitation on the sovereign right to make war. Such actions, combined with her militarism and the threats of her diplomacy, made Germany increasingly appear the major danger to peace. When an interview in the London *Daily Telegraph* quoted Kaiser William complaining that England was ungrateful for his nation's neutrality in the Boer War, the reaction was sharp and angry. British statesmen and journalists indulged in public recriminations that heightened tension while the latest efforts to settle naval questions broke down.

Also in 1907 a series of agreements showed again that imperial issues, which the Germans expected would keep their antagonists apart, were not necessarily divisive. France and Russia each reached an accord with Japan, defining the areas of preeminent Japanese interest and agreeing to preserve the integrity of China. These understandings with Britain's Asian ally opened the way for an entente between Great Britain and Russia in which the two nations resolved points of contention from the straits controlling access to the Black Sea, to Persia, Afghanistan, and Tibet. An informal coalition of France, Russia, and Britain, the Triple Entente, now balanced the Triple Alliance. Its major beneficiary was France, which had long worked for this accommodation between her two European allies. The European powers were finding it surprisingly easy to mark out and limit their spheres of interest so long as they could ignore the internal politics of the places where they competed for influence.

Internal politics, however, could be neither ignored nor controlled in the Balkan States, and here the second crisis of the period arose. Serbia, led by a new king and a radical nationalist government, became Austria-Hungary's primary Balkan antagonist, and revolution in the Ottoman Empire in 1908—led by the Young Turks, whose movement sought to modernize the nation—foreshadowed a revival of Ottoman influence in the Balkans as well. Ever mindful of the dangers of nationalism, Austria-Hungary decided to strengthen her position there and at home by annexing Bosnia and Herzegovina, which she had occupied since the Congress of Berlin in 1878. She claimed she had Russia's agreement, but Russia, whose Slavophiles were infuriated by the annexation, demanded an international conference. Britain and France supported the call, even though they suspected the Russian foreign minister, Izvolsky, of some double dealing. Germany, angered by the precipitateness of Austria-Hungary's action, nevertheless stood by her ally. Diplomatic crises were becoming tests of alliances (and it was significant that Italy expressed resentment at not being consulted by Austria-Hungary rather than loyalty to the Triple Alliance).

The third major crisis once again involved Morocco. Both Germany and France were prepared to reach some definitive agreement, but the Germans thought to speed things up by sending the gunboat *Panther* to the Moroccan port of Agadir in 1911. They then asked for all of the French Congo in exchange for French annexation of Morocco. Both the proposal and the method seemed excessive, and in Great Britain Lloyd George publicly decried them. The powers concerned eventually reached a compromise: France would cede parts of her Congo lands and bits of her other African territories adjacent to German colonies. But the fact of the settlement counted for less than the rising tension in Europe and the growing distrust of the Germans. After a final effort at naval agreement failed, Britain decided in 1912 to withdraw her battleships from the Mediterranean, concentrating them in the North Sea, while France sent her fleet to replace them. With the crisis and the confrontation of 1908, the loose Triple Entente was becoming at least as binding as the Triple Alliance.

Two Wars in the Balkans

The Balkans became the focal point for the interplay of the forces of European imperialism, nationalism, and power politics. In Serbia, Bulgaria, Rumania, and Greece, social conflicts and the strains of modernization led to governments that won support by embracing nationalism. At the same time the Balkan policies of Austria-Hungary and Russia had become enmeshed in their own bitter domestic divisions, which further reduced their diplomatic flexibility. Moreover Germany, through railway concessions in Turkey, had also developed interests in the peninsula, as had Italy, whose victory over the Ottoman sultanate in 1912 (part of her conquest of Tripoli—see Chapter 25) encouraged Greece, Bulgaria, Serbia, and Montenegro to join forces against the empire. They succeeded in driving the Ottomans from all their remaining European holdings except Constantinople. Intervention by the great powers brought peace, but the tension between Austria-Hungary and Russian-backed Serbia sustained the ferment, as did their complex diplomatic maneuvers. Serbia also had territorial designs on weakly organized areas of Albania and Montenegro, and each Balkan state had boundary disputes with the others. These conflicting claims erupted in a second Balkan war within a few months when some Bulgarian troops launched an attack on Serbian and Greek forces. Bulgaria had gained more territory in the earlier war than the other Balkan states; and although the Bulgarian government quickly disavowed this latest move, Serbia, Greece, Rumania, and Turkey declared war and quickly defeated her. When the threats from Austria-Hungary forced Serbia to abandon some of her gains, Serbian nationalists replied by proclaiming their concern and sympathy for their fellow Slavs subject to Austrian rule in Bosnia and Herzegovina.

Thus tensions were high when on June 28, 1914, Archduke Francis Ferdinand, the heir to the Austrian and Hungarian thrones, paraded in Sarajevo, the capital of Bosnia. It was an act of some courage. One bomb just missed killing the archduke, and his car passed other conspirators who lost their courage and failed to fire. Then the car made a wrong turn; and as it backed up a young Bosnian revolutionary fired point-blank, killing both the archduke and his wife.

For the Austro-Hungarian government, convinced the Serbian government was involved in the assassination, here was a challenge that required strong action. It sent a special emissary to Berlin, where the German government, with a lack of reflection that remains remarkable, promised full support to Austria. On the other side the French president and prime minister went to Russia to declare their country's loyal backing of its ally. On July 23 the Austrians sent Serbia an ultimatum meant to be unacceptable: it gave Serbia forty-eight hours in which to apologize, ban all anti-Austrian propaganda, and agree to Austro-Hungarian participation in Serbia's investigation of the plot against Francis Ferdinand—in effect to a voice in her internal government.

Serbia replied with great tact, accepting all terms except those that diminished her sovereignty and offering to submit even these to arbitration. It seemed even to Berlin that another crisis would pass. Great Britain, wanting to reduce tensions further, proposed an international conference, to which France and Russia reluctantly agreed. The Germans then declared the controversy a matter for Austrians and Serbians alone, and on July 28 Austria-Hungary declared war on Serbia.

Austria-Hungary was in fact not yet ready to fight, and Germany and Great Britain still hoped she would limit herself to occupying Belgrade and then accept a conference. But Russia, explaining that she could not allow an occupation of Serbia, on July 29 ordered a partial mobilization, making clear that it was aimed only at Austria-Hungary; the following day the Russians discovered they were not pre-

This painting dramatizes the assassination of Archduke Ferdinand and his wife; the incident provided the immediate cause for World War I.
(Photo: Bildarchiv der österreichischen Nationalbibliothek, Vienna)

pared for a partial call-up and announced a general mobilization instead. On July 31 Germany declared herself in a state of readiness, sent Russia an ultimatum demanding demobilization within twelve hours, and asked France what course she would take in case of a Russo-German war. France answered that she would act in her own interests and then mobilized, but she held her troops ten kilometers (about six miles) from the frontier to prevent any incidents. The Germans, who had planned next to demand the surrender of France's border fortresses as a guarantee of neutrality, were unsatisfied with this response and planned their moves for the next several days accordingly.

Germany mobilized on August 1 and declared war on Russia; and convinced this meant fighting on the Western front as well, she invaded Luxembourg and sent an ultimatum to the Belgians demanding unobstructed passage for her troops. On August 3 she declared war on France and began invading Belgium. The following day the British declared war on the Germans, and within forty-eight hours each nation had 2 million soldiers under orders. World War I had begun.

The Origins of the War

The question of what caused the Great War—or more simply who was to blame—soon became a major issue in European politics. The Allies blamed Germany so insistently that they wrote her guilt into the treaty of peace, a view that most historians have considered one-sided at the very least and that German scholars rejected with special force, which explains the furor that first greeted the recent work of the German historian Fritz Fischer, who finds strong evidence that Germany's leaders had in fact looked forward to war and nurtured almost boundless ambitions for military dominance. But the question remains without a final answer, for the causes adduced depend very much on how long-range a look one takes.

The immediate cause, the assassination, almost did not happen. The tensions that made it so significant were more deeply rooted. The Balkan States, struggling to establish their strength, played on the competition among the major nations, who in turn treated Balkan affairs as matters of their own prestige. Serbia's policy, like her nationalism and her effort to modernize, challenged Austria-Hungary, apprehensive about her declining power and thus set on teaching the Serbians a lesson while there was still time. Individual statesmen can be blamed for Austria-Hungary's untoward haste, Germany's irresponsible support of Austria-Hungary, Russia's clumsy and confused diplomacy, France's eagerness to prove to the Russians that she was a good ally, Britain's unwillingness to admit she was tied to one side and her consequent inability to warn the Germans that an attack on France meant war with her as well.

Such an analysis may, however, make the statesmen seem to have been more autonomous and therefore more to blame than they were. The system of alliances with which each state sought security decreased the diplomats' freedom. The fact that every European power believed in the summer of 1914 that its very survival depended on its alliances meant in practice that each alliance would follow behind its least responsible member.

The fear that cemented these commitments was related to the foreign-policy goals of the major nations: Britain's conviction that empire required supremacy at sea; France's determination to revenge the defeat of 1870 and regain Alsace-Lorraine; Russia's 150 years of expansion toward the West, the Balkans, and East Asia; Italy's need to show herself a great power; Austria's dependence since Metternich on foreign policy to sustain a shaky regime; the desire of a powerful Germany fearful of encirclement for prestige abroad that might reduce conflict at home.

The arms race itself contributed to the outbreak of war. In 1889 Great Britain had adopted

Summer hats in the air, an August crowd in London's Trafalgar Square cheers the declaration of war on Austria. War on Germany had been declared a week earlier; similar scenes throughout that week of 1914 occurred in Paris and Berlin.
(Photo: The Bettmann Archives)

the principle that her navy must equal in size the two next-largest fleets combined, and in 1906 she had launched the *Dreadnought,* the first battleship armed entirely with big guns. By 1914 she had twenty-nine ships of this class afloat and thirteen under construction, and the German navy had eighteen, with nine being built. The French and German standing armies doubled between 1870 and 1914, and all ablebodied men had some military responsibilities from the age of twenty to the late fifties. Germany's victory over the French in 1871 had been understood in all Continental countries to prove the superiority of the Prussian system of universal conscription, large reserves, and detailed planning. Furthermore, it was believed that technology gave an attacker overwhelming advantages. But it required immense organization and took days to locate millions of reservists, get them to their proper units, equip them, and then effectively deploy them. Mobilization—in the eyes of some statesmen a cumbersome but effective show of seriousness—was considered by military men in each country to be an essential act of self-defense; but it had become by 1914 tantamount to war. Even slight disadvantages in numbers of men, quality of weapons, speed of deployment, or tactical foresight might prove fatal. Thus each increase in manpower and weapons was quickly matched, though in some cases only with enormous effort; France, for example, had but 60 percent of Germany's potential manpower and yet equaled her rival. The arms race, justified by the fear that it was meant to allay, fed on itself.

Such expenditures of money and resources, however, had to be justified to parliaments. Thus ultimately these enormous forces, like foreign policy, rested on domestic politics. In every country political parties now competing for broader popular support found nationalist programs to have effective appeal and to offer the chance of reaching across social, religious, and regional divisions. Special interests associated with the military and empire could thus join with all who feared a rising tide of socialism in dramatizing issues of national honor. This was especially the case in Germany where the very economic growth that made her powerful threatened the dominance of Prussia and of the Junker class in a still insecure new state. Throughout Europe then domestic conflict and the politics of nationalism had an important part in the statecraft that led to World War I.

Few Europeans really wanted war; yet its outbreak was hailed with joy everywhere. The strain of economic, demographic, and imperial competition prepared many to welcome with relief the open and total confrontation of armed conflict. Its excitement provided the unity and common purpose so long missed. In immediate terms world war could have been avoided; in a larger sense it was a product of the social structures it nearly annihilated.

III. THE COURSE OF THE WAR

The First Years of War

For decades European military staffs had prepared detailed plans for the eventuality they now faced. The French intended to drive into Alsace and Lorraine in carefully coordinated and dashing maneuvers that reflected their almost mystic belief in élan. The Germans' strategy rested on the Schlieffen "swinging door" plan, first adoped in 1905 to meet the awful challenge of fighting on two fronts simultaneously: using minimum forces against the Russians in the East and the expected French attack in Alsace, they would send their main armies wheeling through Belgium down on Paris and knock France out of the war before Russia could bring her massive armies into play or British aid could make a difference. That strategy, with its invasion of neutral Belgium, further labeled Germany as the aggressor and determined Britain's entry into the war.

All the belligerents in 1914 assumed that modern war would be swift, with the advantage to the offense. But the first few months of hostilities established that the war being fought was not the one planned, though commanders were slow to admit it. Increased fire power gave defensive forces unexpected strength, cavalry was ineffectual, and the common soldier proved able to absorb more punishment than anyone had thought possible. After slight gains the French offensive in Alsace was stopped, with heavy losses to both sides. The Germans were more nearly successful—the French command had underestimated by half the number of troops they would engage in immediate battle—and within a month they drove to within thirty miles of Paris (see Map 26.4).

But the German army was as battered as the defenders, its casualties were as high, and its lines of communication and supply were dangerously stretched. These factors, added to unanticipated Belgian resistance, infuriated and worried German commanders. And a small British force that had joined the French sooner than expected as well as Russian advances toward eastern Prussia altered the Schlieffen plan in practice. Extra German troops were sent to Alsace in hope of a breakthrough following earlier successes there, while the Russian move frightened the indecisive German chief of staff,

MAP 26.4: THE WESTERN FRONT

Helmuth von Moltke (nephew of the field marshal who had led Germany to victory in 1866 and 1870), into assigning to the East troops intended to be in the West. Overwhelming though they were, the forces that cut east of Paris, instead of running beyond it, were considerably fewer than German strategy called for.

After each bloody encounter the Allies had retreated, but they were not routed; and German officers were surprised to take so few prisoners. The French commander in chief, Joseph Joffre, kept his forces together even in defeat, imperturbably confident of the ultimate success of a great French drive. In September the French launched a counteroffensive along the Marne River that saved Paris and hurled the Germans back to the natural defenses of the Aisne River. There, despite repeated Allied attacks, the Germans held. In the next few months the armies tried to outflank each other but succeeded only in extending the front northward to the sea. With changes of only a few miles, the battle lines established by the end of 1914 would remain those of the Western front for the next four years. France had not been knocked out of the war, but Germany held a tenth of her territory and nearly all of Belgium (see Map 26.5).

On the Eastern front Russian armies scored important gains in early August, taking eastern Galicia from Austria-Hungary and beginning an invasion of eastern Prussia in the North. Moltke talked in panic of a general retreat until

MAP 26.5: WORLD WAR I

the victories of Generals Paul von Hindenburg and Erich von Ludendorff, who soon became Germany's greatest war heroes. At Tannenberg late in August, their forces surrounded and destroyed a Russian army; and German troops pushed on almost to Warsaw before being stopped. In the South Austria-Hungary halted the Russian advance with German aid; and despite the able fighting of the Serbian army, Austrian armies took Belgrade. By the end of 1914, the Central Powers had made impressive gains at every hand, and the Ottoman Empire's entry into the war on their side extended the threat to the Allies all the way to Suez.

War of Attrition

On the Western front especially, the great armies found themselves bogged down in a terrifying kind of siege warfare. Artillery became increasingly important, and shells were fired at rates unimaginable a few months before, devastating the pockmarked land and making any movement in it still more difficult. Dug into trenches and clinging to pillboxes, neither side could be uprooted. Military units worked out complex systems of communication by laying cables, building bridges, and maintaining roads and railways. For the first time poison gas was used, but the German troops could not follow up the momentary gains it permitted.

Again and gain the Allied armies attempted to mount a great offensive, only to be stopped after gaining two or three miles and losing hundreds of thousands of men. Battles were now numbered—the Second Battle of Ypres (April–May 1915), the Second Battle of Artois (May–June), the Second Battle of Champagne (September–November), the Third Battle of Artois (September–October); and after a year's bloodshed, the Western front remained essentially the same.

Italy's entry into the war had not broken the stalemate. She had declared her neutrality on the ground that Austria-Hungary's attack on Serbia was an offensive action and thus did not fall within the terms of the Triple Alliance, and this had kept her free to negotiate with both sides. Geography and Austria-Hungary's reluctance to give up territory the Italians sought had led them to favor the Allies. In April 1915 Italy had signed a secret agreement with Great Britain, France, and Russia, the Treaty of London, committing herself to the Allied side in return for the promise of lands along her border with Austria-Hungary (the southern Tyrol, Istria, Trieste, and Gorizia—see map, p. 949), important Dalmatian islands, and expansion of her colonial holdings. Italy had declared war on Austria-Hungary in May and soon advanced to a line along the Isonzo River. At that line eleven battles were fought in the next two years without significant gain.

The fighting in France in 1916 brought no decisive changes either. Early in the year the Germans launched an all-out offensive against the French fortifications at Verdun. Knowing the French would be determined to hold, their aim was more to bleed the enemy than to take territory. For days shells poured down, and then the Germans attacked in overwhelming numbers. From February to July the fighting continued at full pitch. German forces captured two outlying forts, but the French managed a brief counterattack. Verdun held; and though the French losses, more than 300,000 men, weakened the subsequent Allied offensive, German casualties were only slightly less. The Allied attack in the Battle of the Somme, from July to November, brought still heavier casualties and a maximum advance of seven miles.

For two years each side had believed its offensives about to succeed only to see them halted by some unexpected flaw. The doctrine of the offensive, like general morale, was sinking in gore. If the brilliant tactics of rapid maneuver planned at the war's outset could not guarantee victory, then attrition, systematically exhausting men and resources, seemed the only feasible alternative.

Casualties of the Battle of the Marne.
(Photo: René Dazy)

On the Eastern front (Map 26.5) Austro-German forces launched an offensive through Galicia in May 1915, pushing forward a hundred miles, and followed it with a general offensive in July. By late September the Russians had lost Poland and Lithuania; and as the Central Powers massed on a line from Riga in the north to the easternmost part of Hungary, their new ally, Bulgaria, pressed into Serbia. The following year, however, General Alexis Brusilov, in one of the few really well-conducted Russian campaigns, regained a large part of those losses. But the effort cost Russia a million men, and she lacked the organization, the supplies, and the leadership to do more. The Russian offensive brought Rumania into the war on the Allied side, but Austria-Hungary took Bucharest at the end of the year.

Naval strength did not in itself produce military success for either side during the war. The single large-scale attack by sea, the landing of Allied forces on the Gallipoli Peninsula in April 1915, was a failure. Having hoped to open the Dardanelles for shipping to Russia and to force the Ottoman Empire out of the war, the Allies were grateful to withdraw in December without serious loss.

Great Britain had nonetheless effectively maintained a blockade of Germany that was beginning to hurt. The Germans had tried to counter in 1915 by announcing a submarine blockade of Britain, but the angry reaction of neutrals led by the United States had forced them to abandon the tactic. The sinking of passenger ships—most sensationally, the *Lusitania*, killing more than a thousand civilians—gave way in 1916 to attacks on armed merchantmen and then, in the face of American warnings, to the renunciation of "unlimited" submarine warfare.

The one great naval battle of the war, at Jutland in May 1916, was indecisive. British and German fleets lost the same number of ships, though the British tonnage sunk was twice as great. Thereafter Admiral Alfred von Tirpitz's great fleet hid in its harbors and did not threaten Allied control of the sea.

The Home Front

By every measure this was war on an unprecedented scale, and adjustment to its demands strained the very fabric of society. At first the fighting produced not only enthusiasm but a euphoric spirit of national unity. In Great Britain the Liberal government gave way within a year to a coalition; the emergency left little room for party divisions. The French hailed their "sacred union," and the leading socialist militant took a post in the cabinet. The German parliament unanimously voted war credits, and though some Germans were shocked at the invasion of Belgium, the citizenry was convinced that the nation was fighting a just and defensive war. In Russia the government seemed almost popular.

War brought immediate dislocation. As factories closed, unemployment rose despite conscription; there then followed a labor shortage as war production became crucial to survival. Everywhere agricultural output dropped, contributing to the food shortages of subsequent years. Prices rose rapidly and consumer hoarding further strained faltering systems of distribution.

In response to domestic and military crises, the powers of governments to move men, censor the press, and control the railroads, the telegraph, and shipping, and even to direct the economy were extended as never before. Unprepared for their armies' requirements of ever more ammunition and supplies, governments quickly learned to use paper money, rationing, and central planning. In this and other ways, modern warfare involved the full participation of the civilian population. The refugees from Belgium pouring into France (and the German reprisals against Belgian civilians) were only the first and clearest symptom of this pervasive change. Just as unlimited submarine warfare, poison gas, and a blockade that treated consumer goods as contraband burst the rules of warfare among civilized nations, so the need to mobilize the home front overrode the restraints on which liberal society had depended.

In the United Kingdom the government, which was granted unparalleled power over the lives of civilians, requisitioned supplies and forced industry to new efficiency. Its professional army shattered, Britain had, despite voluntary enlistments that raised the largest army in her history, to adopt conscription in 1916, a step that Winston Churchill considered "the greatest revolution in our system since the institution of feudalism under William the Conqueror." Rebellion in Ireland that Easter was quickly put down; yet it was a serious diversion for British troops and a disturbing reminder of how cruelly war tested every weakness in the social structure.

Germany, deprived of critical raw materials, developed the most fully controlled economy of any of the combatants. Under the brilliant direction of Walther Rathenau, German resources were allocated and her industry deployed to the needs of war. Private firms were organized into sectors of production so that the most important could be favored, inefficient

After the siege that bled both armies the ruins of Verdun stand like a broken tombstone.
(Photo: Wide World Photos)

firms closed, and national planning enforced. The chemical industry developed ways of making rubber substitutes, manufactured fertilizers from nitrates in the air and textiles from wood pulp, and culled aluminum from local clays. Substitutes, which made "ersatz" an international word, included chestnut flour and clover meal used in the "war bread" that, like meatless days and conscription, soon made the civilian population feel the burden of all-out war.

In the first weeks of the fighting, half of France's iron ore and coal fields and more than half her heavy industry were captured or destroyed. Joffre exercised virtually dictatorial powers, and the French, too, began to develop techniques for mobilizing a whole society. Quotas and priorities were established by government and industrial committees, and supplies were allocated according to comprehensive plans. Production steadily increased. Although censorship was severe, the tradition of political dispute was in large part preserved; and if the custom of reshuffling cabinets was a source of some inefficiency, it also eased the task of recruiting men competent to undertake new administrative tasks. In France as in Great Britain civilian authority had begun to reassert itself in 1915.

These three were the states that adjusted most effectively to the revolutionary requirements of fielding huge armies while increasing industrial production and maintaining intricate networks of supply. They did it with governments that had the will and the capacity to organize their nations. Civilians were disciplined to all-out war through propaganda, compulsion, and systematic economic controls.

These were feats that the Austro-Hungarian and Russian empires could not match. Not only was their industry relatively sparse but its development was uneven, and even modern plants worked at less than capacity, hampered by lack of supplies and trained manpower. Neither government knew how or dared to squeeze from the economy the overwhelming quantities of food, ammunition, or clothes that war required. Russian armies increasingly showed the effects of fighting ill fed and ill shod, with inadequate weapons and ammunition, and without good communication. (Orders to Russian troops were broadcast uncoded, which contributed to Ludendorff's reputation as a great tactician.) Austria-Hungary could not rely in adversity on the continued loyalty of subject peoples, and soldiers were carefully dispatched to zones far from their homes so as not to be fighting against people who spoke their own tongue.

By the winter of 1916–1917, the grave strains were visible to all. Everywhere on the bloodied Continent, Europeans were thinner and more shabbily dressed, overworked, and grieved by the endless losses of husbands, sons, and homes. Poor crops and overloaded transportation systems reduced the diet further; this was the Germans' "turnip winter," when the best organized of the domestic war economies could barely keep its people healthy.

The strains of war were changing society. The queue became a kind of public rite as many of the subtler distinctions of social class disappeared. Each government awkwardly tried to restrict the consumption of alcohol and worried about rising rates of illegitimacy. Just as rationing had spread from nation to nation, becoming ever more restrictive, so did the need to employ women. British women were asked in 1915 to take any jobs they could, and by 1917 the government denied contracts to employers unwilling to hire women. The French government forbade hiring men for certain jobs that women could do; and the Krupp works, which had no women employees in 1914, counted 12,000 by 1917. In munitions industries in particular the number of women workers steadily rose to become one-third or more of the total; and women tilled the soil, served as bus conductors, fire fighters, and office workers in addition to more direct war work. Although labor agitation remained below prewar levels, signs of growing discontent had to be taken seriously. Trade unions were treated with new respect, and officials began to talk of the benefits to be granted after the war to those making such heavy sacrifices now. Even the Kaiser spoke of ending the three-class voting system and hinted at representative government, while the House of Commons in a notable reversal declared its support in principle for women's suffrage. Meanwhile, month upon month of bloodshed in muddy, disease-filled trenches took a psychological as well as physical toll. Morale was sinking.

Changes in Leadership

There were some hints in that terrible winter of the possibility of peace. In December 1916, after having gained the initiative on the Eastern front, the Central Powers indicated willingness to discuss a settlement; but the Allies' terms, stated a month later, were wholly unacceptable. Meanwhile both sides had been seeking to strengthen themselves by changes in leadership.

In the fall of 1916, Hindenburg had received overall command of German troops and with Ludendorff had taken charge of campaigns in the West. To destroy the shipping on which Britain's survival depended, the Germans returned to unlimited submarine warfare in January 1917. They were aware that this might bring the United States into the war, but they calculated that American power could not make itself felt before Britain would have to sue for peace. Britain and France also sought the formula for victory in new leadership. Joffre's intolerance of civilian leaders brought his downfall in December 1916; and General Robert Georges Nivelle, politically more tactful and personally more dashing, succeeded him as commander in chief of the French armies. He planned a massive offensive, and this one, he assured his government, would break through German defenses.

Changes in high political offices were more significant. Lloyd George, who was made minister of war in June 1916, became British prime minister in December. Eloquent and energetic, once a radical orator who had terrified the upper classes, he now seemed the kind of decisive leader who could galvanize the British into a well-organized effort to win. The French turned to the fiery Clemenceau, who became premier again in November 1917 after French morale hit a dangerous low. Change had come to Russia too—through revolution. In March 1917 the tsar had abdicated, and a new provisional government had proclaimed sweeping democratic reforms while promising to continue the war. Both sides knew that Russia was now more vulnerable than ever but that her immense resources had yet to be effectively tapped.

For the Allies these changes, especially in Russia, gave the war itself new meaning. Now democracies were fighting together against authoritarian governments dominated by the aristocracy and the military. A war that involved the people more fully than any before it took on an ideological meaning. In April the United States declared war on Germany, resentful of the sinking of her ships and of German overtures to Mexico promising the return of Mexican lands taken by the United States. American entry added to the Allies' sense of democratic purpose as well as their military strength.

The Great Trials of 1917–1918

In the fighting itself, however, neither new leaders nor shared ideals seemed to make much difference. On the Western front Nivelle launched his great offensive in April and May 1917 despite multiple handicaps. The Germans had strengthened their defenses along the Hindenburg line, near the French-Belgian border, and disagreements had arisen between the British and French commands. But most dangerous of all, there was grave disaffection among the French troops. Some refused to fight, and those who remained in the trenches were dispirited by two years of endless death on the same barren hills and slimy plains. Thus the offensive (the Second Battle of the Aisne and the Third Battle of Champagne) brought a toll as great as that of its predecessors and even slighter gains.

Nivelle was replaced by General Henri Philippe Pétain, the hero of Verdun, who began a concerted effort to raise their morale by recognizing many of the soldiers' grievances and by instituting regular leaves; and the government took severe measures against agitators who talked of peace. The results were encouraging, but it would be months before France dared another offensive.

The British went ahead with plans for an attack in the North, spurred by the desperate need to knock out at least some of the Germans' submarine bases, for the U-boats were sinking such enormous tonnages that the admiralty openly wondered how many months Great Britain could last. With only weak assistance from the French army, the British fared no better in the Third Battle of Ypres (July–November) than had the French in their spring offensive. The noise of battle could be heard in England, and hundreds of thousands of men fell, but there was no breakthrough. British morale too was shaken.

On the Eastern front Russian advances in July turned into almost constant retreat in the next few months. In November the Bolsheviks, a faction of the Social Democratic party, took over the government, invited all nations to join in peace without annexations or indemnities, and entered into independent negotiations with the Central Powers. The most populous of the Allies had been defeated. In October German troops had joined Austro-Hungarian troops in a concentrated attack on the Italian front that issued in an overwhelming victory at the Battle of Caporetto. Italy's armies collapsed as tens of thousands died, surrendered, or deserted. But the Italians regrouped along the Piave River while Britain and France rushed in reinforcements, and the Austro-German onslaught was slowed and then stopped.

German reserves of manpower and resources were nearing exhaustion. Submarine warfare had come close to its goal of defeating Britain, but though Allied losses remained serious, they had dropped to a tolerable level with the development of the convoy in mid-1917. The convoys, enlarged by American ships, brought tons of supplies and toward the end of the year even some fresh troops.

In February 1918 the Russians stopped fighting, a gesture of peace the Central Powers did not reciprocate; they continued their breathtaking eastward march. In the Treaty of Brest Litovsk, signed in March, Russia surrendered not only Russian Poland and the Baltic provinces but the Ukraine and Transcaucasia. When she needed them most, Germany had acquired the invaluable wheat and oil of the Ukraine and a respite on one front. But the gains were so immense that merely patrolling them took great numbers of badly needed troops, and the incredibly harsh terms of the treaty stiffened the resistance of the enemy elsewhere. Both Lloyd George and President Wilson, in his Fourteen Points, now stated formal war aims that expressed their confidence in victory and put revolutionary emphasis on the right to self-government.

In March also the Germans opened a great offensive on the West. With careful strategy, improved tactics, heavy artillery, and gas, they made the greatest advances seen on the Western front in four years. But the Allies held, and they sought to correct the weakness of divided command by naming General Ferdinand Foch supreme commander.

From March through June 1918 the Germans attacked British, French, and now American troops in sector after sector, scoring surprising successes; but the Allies were retaining their reserves while the Germans exhausted theirs. Enemy guns once more bombarded Paris as the Second Battle of the Marne and the Allied counteroffensive began in July. Slowly, then faster, the Germans were driven back over

British gas masks used by Indian soldiers in 1917 express the faceless horror of trench warfare.
(Photo: Gernschein Collection, Humanities Research Center, University of Texas at Austin)

the familiar and devastated landscape. By the end of August, German armies had retreated to the Hindenburg line; and the Allies continued their push in battles of the Argonne and Ypres in September and October, gaining less rapidly than hoped or expected but now inexorably.

Elsewhere the Central Powers collapsed

more dramatically. Meeting a large offensive begun in Palestine in September, Turkish and German troops were defeated by British and Arab forces led by T. E. Lawrence, whose exploits became part of the romantic lore in which this war was poorer than most. In October the sultan was deposed, and a new Ottoman government sued for peace. From Salonika combined Serbian, French, British, and Greek forces under French leadership drove up the Balkan Peninsula. Bulgaria surrendered at the end of the month, and the Allies moved toward Rumania.

The Austro-Hungarian Empire was disintegrating. Throughout 1918 Czech, Yugoslav, Rumanian, and (Austrian) Polish movements for independence had gained strength, encouraged by the Allies. On the Italian front Austria-Hungary attacked once more but withdrew after heavy losses. Defeated at the Battle of Vittorio Veneto at the end of October, her armies began simply to dissolve as the various nationalities left the battlefield for home and revolution. Czechoslovakia and the kingdom later called Yugoslavia both declared their independence, and in November Austria-Hungary would surrender unconditionally to the Italians.

Ludendorff had demanded that Germany seek an armistice at the end of September, and in October a new government under liberal Prince Maximilian of Baden, asked for peace on the terms of President Wilson's Fourteen Points. But Wilson now insisted on the evacuation of occupied territories and a democratic German government with which to negotiate. While German leaders hesitated, they faced the threat of revolution at home. Ludendorff resigned his command at the end of October; Kaiser William II abdicated on November 9 after a mutiny in the German fleet and revolution in Munich; and a German armistice commission met with Foch and agreed to terms on November 11. By then Allied troops were approaching the German borders in the West and had crossed the Danube in the East, taken Trieste on the Adriatic, and sailed through the Dardanelles. And revolution was sweeping Central Europe.

The Effects of World War I

The war itself had some of the effects of revolution. Its psychological impact is not easy to demonstrate, but there were endless examples among intellectuals of what one historian has called "minds scorched by war," and a cynical distrust of leaders and institutions seems to have spread after years of wartime promises. There was a cleavage too between those who had fought and those who stayed home, those whose lives were transformed and those who had more nearly maintained business as usual. And there was bitterness about the inequalities of sacrifice that surfaced in denunciations of war profiteers. Throughout society, there was after World War I a tendency to expect instability and change in social mores and structure. At the same time few forgot and some would yearn for the thrill of combat, the sense of common purpose, and the vision of national unity that war had brought.

Some of the psychological and social changes showed in public behavior and even in dress. Gentlemen had abandoned their top hats when forced to use public transportation, and women's clothes grew simpler and their skirts shorter. Women of the working class took to cosmetics, high-heeled shoes, and smoking and drinking in public, as did their middle-class sisters. These changes, even more than the increase in violent crime and juvenile delinquency, shocked moralists for whom they were related to casual encounters between the sexes, increased illegitimacy, and the popularity of dance halls. Such signs pointed to a more mobile and fluid society in which old customs and patterns of proper behavior had been so disrupted that they might never be recaptured. Millions of refugees represented a deep displacement, but millions more (especially peasants and women) would choose not to return to their old way of life.

Political life was directly affected and not just where revolution triumphed. In Germany ex-soldiers joined *Freikorps* ("free corps"), mercenary squads available for street fighting and marauding that preserved the camaraderie of arms. Throughout Central Europe political conflict adopted the techniques of force. Even in the West solid men of the older parties watched with apprehension the revival of the left. Clemenceau, Lloyd George, and Wilson, the spokesmen of victory, had all been vigorous reformers who understood and spoke to public opinion (even when the enthusiasm of patriotic unity came to seem a little hollow) as more traditional politicians did not. Even the most conservative governments had shown that the state could use its inflated bureaucracies and increased power to shape the economy, and no one could now deny that governments might improve the lot of the poor, recognition that resulted in a spate of postwar legislation on housing, education, and pensions.

The relative position of the various social classes was also altered. Inflation lessened the purchasing power of aristocrats and members of the middle class who lived on investments, especially in land. Taxes (particularly in England) and the relative decline in land values also weakened the aristocracy, whose power was further lessened even where there was no open revolution by the general democratization of political life. Members of the middle class, especially those on salary or fixed income, also suffered relatively more from inflation than those on workers' wages. Middle-class life became less lavish, with fewer servants (some 400,000 English women left domestic service in the course of the war) or occasions for ostentation. A middle class confident in 1914 found itself after the war exposed and vulnerable, its savings threatened, its possibilities limited, its values challenged. Workers, particularly the skilled, were on the whole relatively well off. Although rates of pay had usually run behind inflation, the years of full employment and more jobs for women had increased family income, and trade unions used their greater influence to maintain gains of shorter hours and higher pay. Peasants, though declining in numbers, were also often better off since inflation and the demand for food had helped them to pay off their debts and own more land free and clear.

The war affected economic life in other ways. The employment of new technologies was stimulated by their wartime use, as happened with automobiles and airplanes, radio, and some chemicals. World trade had not only been disrupted but Europe's place in it permanently altered. In 1914 Europe had been the world's greatest lender of money; in 1918 its states were debtors. The physical destruction of property, aside from the billions lost in war material, was greatest in Belgium and France. In France alone thousands of bridges, thousands of factories, and a million buildings were destroyed. Total European production in the 1920s would fall below the level in 1913.

All this required enormous adjustments. So did the war's simplest accomplishment: the killing of from 10 to 13 million people, perhaps one-third of them civilians. Moreover, for every soldier who died, two or three were wounded; millions were maimed for life. The casualty figures tell much about the history of the first third of the twentieth century (see accompanying table).

MILITARY FATALITIES IN WORLD WAR I (MAJOR POWERS)	
Germany	1,900,000
Russia	1,700,000
France	1,400,000
Austria-Hungary	1,200,000
British Empire	900,000
Ottoman Empire	700,000
Italy	600,000
United States	100,000

Among the armed forces, casualties ran about 50 percent for the major combatants except France, whose losses were higher. The weakness of Russian organization shows in the fact that a smaller percentage of the population was mobilized—about 7 percent, as compared with 16 percent of the German and 19 percent of the French—and that the fatalities can only be estimated. The high percentage of mobilization in France and Germany is a measure of the desperate efforts they made. Whole classes from the elite schools of each nation were virtually wiped out. For France, with her older population and low birth rate, the war was a demographic catastrophe in which a large part of an entire generation disappeared on the Western front. And throughout Europe the one-armed, the one-legged, and the blind would live on, supported by pensions and performing menial tasks, in silent testimony to the cost of total war. With all this before them, the leaders of exhausted nations sat down to make a lasting peace.

The gigantic effort victory required had been fueled by a vision, welded in the warring, of a better world in which governments would use their increased powers to insure greater justice and fuller democracy. With Wilson as its Presbyterian voice, democracy—meaning popular participation in public life and opportunity for all—seemed a guarantee of peace. Not only would states be forever prevented from making war for selfish reasons and autocratic governments doomed, but there would be an end, Wilson suggested, to the old secret diplomacy that juggled spheres of influence and national interests without regard for public opinion. To many, such vague promises seemed radical enough, but they paled beside the revolution rolling from the East.

IV. THE RUSSIAN REVOLUTION
The February Revolution

Nothing in their experience had prepared Western statesmen for the rapid triumph of communism in Europe's largest nation. With the outbreak of war in 1914, many Russians realized that to meet this challenge government would have to be more efficient and in closer touch with Russian society. The Duma, called into brief sessions in 1915, established a committee to help coordinate the war effort, and local zemstvos made valuable contributions. But when the Cadet party demanded liberal reforms sought since 1905, the Duma's session was suspended. Resentful that the war could be used for political ends—they still did not see the connection—the tsar and his officials became more isolated from the country. Nicholas II, no more skilled as a military strategist than as a head of state, grandly departed to command his army, leaving Tsarina Alexandra to oppose any program for reform. Her chief confidant was Grigori Rasputin, an ignorant and corrupt mystic, whose influence symbolized the decadence of the regime.

Throughout 1916 signs of failure accumulated. Production and transportation were undependable, refugees filled the roads, inflation soared, and food shortages became critical. The resulting discontent reached into the highest circles. In November in the reconvened Duma Pavel Milyukov, the Cadets' leader, courageously delivered a bitter attack on the government; one group of nobles murdered Rasputin in December, and others talked of the need to depose the tsar. Little seemed to change. Strikes spread; and, except for the Cossacks, the soldiers called out to quell them were increasingly inclined to join the workers.

In March 1917, when strikers again filled the streets of Petrograd (St. Petersburg's new name),[2] their economic demands quickly broadened to political issues, and troops could not be relied on to oppose them. Instead, much as in 1905, the Soviet of Workers' and Soldiers' Deputies became the voice of revolution. This

---

[2] "St. Petersburg" was a German name, and in 1914 Nicholas had changed it to the Russian "Petrograd." The capital until 1918, the city would become Leningrad in 1924.

The main street of Petrograd, July 1917, as the revolutionists open fire.
(Photo: Wide World Photos)

council of working-class leaders joined a Duma committee (the Duma itself was not then in session) in favoring a provisional government, and soviets organized the effective defense of Petrograd against tsarist forces that might be sent to put down the insurgents. Helpless, Nicholas II abdicated. The February Revolution, as it was dated by the Russian calendar,[3] seemed an almost easy transition in the chaos of war; and the news from Petrograd was hailed with joy and relief throughout the country.

The prime minister of the provisional government was the bland and moderate Prince Georgi Lvov, but its central figure was Milyukov. The only socialist included was Aleksandr Kerensky, a member of the Social Revolutionary party, who led the labor representatives in the Duma and was vice chairman of the Petrograd soviet, the most important center of political power in the capital.

On many matters the new government's policy was concrete and clear: it quickly established broad civil liberties, an amnesty for political prisoners, and the end of religious persecution; it favored a constitution for Finland and independence for Russian Poland, an eight-

---

[3] The Julian calendar, which the West had abandoned in favor of the Gregorian calendar, was still used in Russia (and today continues to be the calendar of the Orthodox Church). The revolutions that in the Gregorian system occurred on March 8–12 and November 7, 1917, each fell thirteen days earlier according to the Julian, and they continue to be called the February and October revolutions.

hour day for workers, and the abolition of class privileges. Beyond these points, however, the political terrain was less known, and the provisional government left most social issues for a constituent assembly, which it promised to call soon.

The revolutionary political parties were divided. The Cadets, who dominated the provisional government, came to accept the idea of a republic, political democracy, and distribution of land with compensation to former owners. To their left the Social Revolutionaries and the Social Democratic Mensheviks, especially strong in the soviets forming across the nation, demanded more. Some of these socialists wanted drastic reforms but were willing to postpone them until after the war, which, like the Cadets, they still meant to win. The more radical stressed an early end to the war, though they did not yet advocate an immediate armistice, and were contemptuous of merely political changes. The soviets were willing for the time being to allow the provisional government its chance, but they refused to be implicated in it, watching instead from the outside, ever ready to criticize. To the left of all these groups stood a small number of Bolsheviks.

The Bolsheviks

Russian Marxists had secretly formed the Social Democratic party in 1898, but its life centered mainly in the conspiratorial world of exile. At the party's second congress, held in Brussels and London in 1903, it had split into two groups, the Bolsheviks ("majority") and Mensheviks ("minority"). The points of debate between them were theoretical, organizational, and personal. Like socialists everywhere, they were divided over revisionism—the view that Marx's doctrines needed modification to fit new circumstances and to allow for the possibility of achieving socialist goals without violent revolution. The majority followed the two figures whose writings had already won them international reputations, Georgi Plekhanov and V. I. Lenin, in cleaving to an intransigent Marxist position.

The speeches and pamphlets of these debates from the outset combined theory and economics with harsh and intolerant name-calling, but the issues had and would continue to have practical implications. Given their position and the social development of Russia, Lenin and Plekhanov had agreed that theirs should be a disciplined elite rather than a mass party, its task to instruct and lead rather than merely represent the proletariat, which by itself was always likely to settle for immediate gains far short of real social transformation. But Lenin's concept of iron discipline had left no room for Plekhanov's independent efforts to heal the breach between the two camps, and he too had been quickly consigned to the Mensheviks.

Neither group had played a central part in the Revolution of 1905, and the socialism that had spread in Russia thereafter had been mainly that of the Mensheviks and the Social Revolutionaries, who were less consistently Marxist and closer to the peasants. The Social Democrats elected to the Duma had been mostly Mensheviks. Despite the bitter loneliness and doubts of exile, Lenin had continued from Switzerland to organize his selected followers, to denounce the heresies around him, and to develop a Marxist interpretation of contemporary affairs and of the Russian situation. As he had extended Marxism to explain that imperialism was a symptom of capitalist decay, so he had increasingly expanded on the role a militant party should play in a country like Russia that was just achieving modern capitalism. To do so required recognition of the revolutionary potential in the peasants' hunger for land—a topic most Marxists had found uncongenial.

Lenin's total rejection of World War I had suggested to the Germans that his agitation might be useful behind Russian lines, and in April 1917 they arranged for him to be sent by sealed train through Germany and Scandinavia to Russia. At this time the Bolsheviks were the smallest of the socialist groups, their differences from the left wing of the Mensheviks no longer very clear. Since all the socialists welcomed the revolution but considered it bourgeois, they were uncertain of their roles.

Lenin resolved this question too with the broader view that the Russian Revolution was part of a larger revolution about to sweep all of Europe. Free of local patriotism, he asserted that socialists had no interest in a capitalist war; and he argued that with the correct tactics they could push the revolution beyond its bourgeois phase to a "second stage." This he soon declared to be the surrender of power to the soviets as the true representatives of the revolutionary class. The Bolsheviks thus had to capture the soviets. Historians have emphasized Lenin's tactical flexibility, but in April his views seemed impossibly dogmatic even to radicals. It was the force of his personality and of his oratory that kept him leader of the Bolsheviks.

Summer Crisis

Issues of war policy and land reform and the many disagreements among those who had overthrown the tsarist regime were not the only problems the provisional government faced in 1917. Strikes continued as workers sought some immediate benefit from revolution; nationalist movements in Latvia, Georgia, and the Ukraine threatened a disintegration of the Russian state; and the bureaucracy, like the police, had largely disappeared. The soviets meanwhile were developing a national organization that claimed authority among the troops and over railroads and telegraph lines. The government was still pledged to pursue the war, but the soviets distrusted this policy and suspected the military of counterrevolutionary intentions. In March the Petrograd soviet issued its famous Order Number I: officers would be chosen by their men, and the military would be run by elected committees. The measure was adopted in most units, and the government, which merely watched as a good part of the army melted away, lost control over much of the rest.

Pressure for peace forced the provisional government to clarify its war aims. In May it declared that Russia had no intention of dominating other peoples; but even this vague formula was compromised by a secret addition promising that Russia would fulfill her commitments to the Allies. The split grew wider between the Cadets, convinced that honor required the country to continue the war, and the soviets, whose renewed demonstrations caused a change in the government. Milyukov resigned, four more socialists joined the cabinet, and Kerensky, as minister of war, became its leading figure, assuming the prime ministership in August. Although Social Revolutionaries and Mensheviks held a majority of the cabinet posts, the soviets still withheld their full support, demanding clear policies for ending the war and redistributing land. Kerensky, an energetic leader and effective orator, recognized that he had to seek broader backing, which meant support from outside the soviets.

The Bolsheviks too were feeling some frustration. At the first all-Russian Congress of Soviets in June they had succeeded in weakening the remaining support for Kerensky, but with just over 100 of the more than 800 delegates, they had not been able to gain full control. In July they had attempted a coup in Petrograd, but it had been decisively defeated; many Bolshevik leaders had been arrested, and Lenin had fled to Finland. The Bolshevist threat seemed over, and Kerensky tried to escape the dominance of the soviets by calling a great national congress of all other groups. He had little to offer it, however, and nothing that did not increase its grave divisions.

At the front, the July offensive, for which Kerensky had great hopes, failed after brief gains. The military situation, despite months of promising efforts at reorganization, became more desperate. In the countryside manor houses were burned and landlords murdered as the peasants rioted for land, and cities were torn by strikes and demonstrations. The social tensions of fifty years were exploding in an atmosphere of anarchy.

Convinced that a strong military hand was needed, the army's commander in chief General Lavr Kornilov decided in September to lead an attack on Petrograd; and Kerensky asked the soviets to defend the provisional government. The Bolsheviks were released from prison, and the defense of the capital was vigorously prepared. The threat passed quickly—most of Kornilov's men had refused to follow his orders—but the provisional government was more than ever dependent on the soviets. In six months in office, it had resolved few of the issues left pending in March, and Bolshevist propaganda was gaining ground with simple slogans about peace, land, and bread.

The Bolsheviks won control of the Moscow and Petrograd soviets, and Leon Trotsky was elected chairman of the latter. Trotsky had worked with Lenin in exile, but until recently he had stood somewhat aloof from both Bolsheviks and Mensheviks. Now he was firmly in Lenin's camp, and from his position in the soviet, he proceeded to organize the armed forces in Petrograd. When the Social Revolutionaries, fearful of losing their strong peasant following, supported peasant expropriation of land, the provisional government was left politically alone in a city it could not control trying to rule a nation in chaos and still at war.

The October Revolution

To the dismay of many in his party, Lenin boldly decided to seize power. The second all-Russian Congress of Soviets was scheduled to meet on November 7, and Lenin planned to greet it with a new government. A few days before Kerensky began to take countermeasures, but he was too late.

The revolution in November (October according to the Russian calendar) was not the amorphous, general rising of March but rather a carefully planned and executed coup. Red Guards (squads of armed workers), sailors, and soldiers of the Petrograd garrison captured the Winter Palace on November 6 while comrades efficiently seized strategic points and offices throughout the city. A simultaneous movement began in Moscow, and though fighting there lasted more than a week, the outcome was hardly in doubt. On the afternoon of November 7, Lenin announced to the Congress of Soviets that the Bolsheviks held power. A young officer was sent to take command of the armies, and at each stop the noisy acclaim of the troops dissuaded their commanders from resisting. Kerensky, who had escaped the capital, tried to muster armed support, but the one group of a few hundred Cossacks who moved on Petrograd was soundly defeated. Shaky though it was, the world's first communist government had taken office.

"All power to the Soviets!" had been one of the Bolsheviks' most effective slogans, and the Congress of Soviets readily approved the one-party cabinet Lenin presented it. The rudiments of a new form of government emerged: the Congress of Soviets, which replaced parliament; the Central Executive Committee, elected from the Congress to give advice when the larger body was not in session; and the Council of People's Commissars, the cabinet ministers. Bolshevik rule from the very first was not representative in the traditional sense, and the government did not in fact depend on any elected body. Elections for the promised constituent assembly, held at the end of November, provided the last open competition among parties in Russian history. The Bolsheviks won a quarter of the seats, other socialist parties more than 60 percent, and conservatives and liberals the rest. As the assembly met on its second day, the guards told it to adjourn, explaining that they were tired. A minority party had ruthlessly grasped the power of the state.

Photographed as a proletarian sitting on a bench in Gorky Park in 1923, Lenin still looks enigmatic and powerful. But in its deliberate contrast with most political portraits (and especially those of fascist leaders), the pose is a reminder of the appeal of the Soviet Revolution and of its leader.
(Photo: Keystone Press Agency, Inc.)

That ruthlessness was warranted in the Bolsheviks' thinking because of their historic role. Lenin had provided a basis for Bolshevist policy in his pamphlet "The State and Revolution," written in Finland in the summer of 1917. It kept the Marxist conception of the state as the coercive organ of the ruling class but argued that with the Bolsheviks in power, the proletariat would become the ruling class. Since backward Russia was barely ready for so advanced a revolution, only a dictatorship of the proletariat could provide the needed strength. By this reasoning Lenin accomplished three things: he justified the establishment of an authoritarian government free from the restraints of parliamentarianism; he gave theoretical sanction to dictatorship as a transition stage during which Russia's transformation would be directed by the Bolsheviks; and he preserved the Marxian vision of communism as a higher historical stage in which the state would no longer be necessary. During the dictatorship socialism would be achieved through the nationalization of land and factories. Communism would come once everyone had learned to work for the good of society and economic production could meet the needs of all.

In the interim the single party, the "vanguard of the proletariat," would have a special role. Model, teacher, and guide, it would prevent backsliding with its tight discipline; through it the masses would be heard. Lenin imagined that public criticism in party sessions would maintain efficiency and probity, combining the benefits of mass participation and dictatorship. Equality and justice remained explicit goals but sufficiently abstract to leave government unimpeded. Enthusiasm for a great cause would enable people to accept the hardships and sacrifices of the present for a glorious future.

The incongruous fusion of Marxist ideas and peasant demands that brought communism to power in the least industrial of the great nations surprised most Marxists. And ruling in such a country required an extension of socialist theory to deal with issues not foreseen in the writings of the previous fifty years. Thus Lenin, the principal architect of the first socialist state, ranks with Marx himself as a theoretician of modern communism.

The First Communist Government

The efficiency with which the Bolsheviks seized and wielded power went beyond theory. It rested rather on the fanatical self-confidence of able leaders hardened by years of revolutionary activity and determined now to snatch their historical moment, on the enthusiasm and dedication of hundreds of party members, and above all perhaps on the decisive energy of Lenin and Trotsky.

The day after taking the Winter Palace, the new government decreed that land, livestock, and all farm equipment belonged to the state but was to be held "temporarily" by peasant committees—this legitimized the rural revolution. No peasant was to work for hire, and committees of the poor would supervise the allocation of land and the distribution of agricultural produce.

In the next few months, railroads, banks, and shipping concerns were nationalized; foreign trade became a state monopoly (though there was precious little of it); and Russia's bonded debts were repudiated. Workers' committees were to share in the management of factories, and everyone was to be paid according to the work—the leading Bolsheviks assigned themselves laborers' salaries. All social titles and military ranks were abolished. "People's tribunals" replaced tsarist courts and workers' militias the police. Church and state were separated, and equality of the sexes was decreed, symbolized by the regulation that couples could obtain a divorce by mutual consent. The various nationalities of Russia were not only declared equal but granted the right of secession, and Finland severed herself from Russia in December 1917, though the Bolsheviks struggled to prevent the Ukraine and the Baltic regions from following suit. Even the alphabet was reformed and the Gregorian calendar adopted.

These revolutionary measures ratified the dissolution of traditional society. They made way too for a regime of terror. A new secret police, the Cheka, differed from the old in determination more than method. The citizens who sat on committees of the poor or the army or on the new tribunal often combined a useful revolutionary enthusiasm with personal ambition and vengeance against old enemies. Tens of thousands lost their property, their rights, and their lives for failing to perceive in a time of revolution the dangers of "mistaken" alliances, "false" ideas, or "suspicious" gestures.

Such radical policies won the Bolsheviks increased support and weakened potential opposition, but they also heightened the difficulties of operating any government at all. The old bureaucrats were gone, their replacements often ignorant and incompetent. Officials were dismissed and promoted with disrupting frequency as political suspects disappeared and talented men were transferred to meet some new crisis.

External dangers were even more pressing. Almost immediately on taking power, the Bolsheviks had asked all nations to accept peace without annexations. When rebuffed, they shocked the world by publishing secret Allied agreements. Forced to negotiate alone with the Central Powers, Russia, whose delegation was headed by Trotsky, proposed in February 1918 a policy of no peace, no war—Russia would stop fighting without a treaty. The Germans advanced to within 100 miles of Petrograd.

Desperate, the Russian government agreed to the Treaty of Brest Litovsk in March. Russia surrendered more than 1 million square miles of territory, including a third of her arable land, a third of her factories, and three-quarters of her deposits of iron and coal. She granted the independence of Finland, Georgia, and the Ukraine; left to Germany the disposition of Russian Poland, Lithuania, Latvia, and Estonia; and ceded parts of Transcaucasia to the Ottoman Empire.

The Bolsheviks had met the demand for peace, but they had done so at incredible cost. Although buoyed by confidence that revolution in Germany would nullify the Kaiser's gains, they could not be sure they would survive so serious an amputation.

Quickly the government set about legitimizing its position. In July a new constitution was promulgated. It met the problem of nationalities by declaring Russia a federation—the Russian Soviet Federated Socialist Republic (R.S.F.S.R.); Great Russia, extending through Siberia, was of course the largest member. Political power rested with the local soviets, organized by occupation, which elected delegates to the congress of soviets of their canton, the smallest administrative unit. Each canton's congress in turn sent delegates to a congress of soviets at the next administrative level, and the process continued by steps up to the all-Russia Congress. Suffrage in the local soviet was universal for men and women but excluded members of the clergy, former high officials, and bourgeois "nontoilers." Since the public elected higher congresses only indirectly, the possibilities for control were great.

Not mentioned in the constitution was the Russian Communist party, as it was now named, which soon became the real center of political authority. Its Central Committee elected the smaller Politburo, which with the governing Council of People's Commissars shared ruling power in Soviet Russia. In Politburo and council Lenin was the dominant figure.

The Bolsheviks, however, remained surrounded by enemies. To the Allies the Treaty of Brest Litovsk appeared an act of treachery, as did Russia's repudiation of her debts. In March Allied troops in small numbers had landed in Murmansk, Archangel, and Vladivostok to prevent supplies sent to Russia earlier from being taken by the Germans, but it was clear that those detachments might also be used to support a change of regime.

In addition the government had reluctantly permitted a Czech brigade of some 30,000 men to travel the Trans-Siberian Railroad from the Eastern front to Vladivostok so they might then sail around the world to continue fighting on the Western front. As the Czechs made the long train journey, they clashed with some Hungarian prisoners of war. The fighting spread, and the Czechs, aided by Russian anti-Bolsheviks, captured one station after another along the railway.

Struck by the ease of the Czech successes, Allied leaders decided not to let their opportunity pass and ordered the Czechs to move back along the railway toward the center of Russia. At the same time a number of tsarist generals, among them Kornilov and others who had escaped from prison, were preparing to lead a small but excellent army of Cossacks. It was the beginning of a civil war that would last for two terrible years.

While Trotsky undertook to organize a Red army, opponents of the new regime formed fighting units in the Ukraine, the Caucasus territory, the Baltic region, and Siberia, aided by reinforcements and supplies from the Allies. But the civil war was not just a battle of armies, for anti-Bolsheviks of every stripe—even the Social Revolutionaries, who had now gone underground—organized in hundreds of villages and towns. Food riots, battles over land, and skirmishes between workers and bourgeois added to the violence. The first communist government in modern history was facing its gravest threat.

V. THE PEACE

The Revolutionary Situation

Russia's was the most important revolution that resulted from World War I, but there were many others; and among the defeated nations, only Bulgaria's government survived. By default as well as victory, the Allies seemed free to set the terms they liked and to construct the Europe of peaceful democracies implied in so many wartime statements. Instead the diplomats assembled at the Paris Peace Conference found their task complicated by the very extent of victory and beset by more interests than they could satisfy. So grand an undertaking fed the extremes of hope and disillusionment, while far from Paris more direct means were being used to shape the postwar world.

From Ireland to Asia Minor, nationalist movements sought to capture power, and the peoples suddenly released from Hapsburg and Russian rule fought to define the boundaries of their new nations. In the Baltic lands, Lithuanian, Estonian, and Latvian republics marked their independence by war with Russia, but Lithuania was also at odds with the new republic of Poland. Poland in fact faced conflict on all her other borders as well—against Russians, Ukrainians, Czechs, Germans. The creation of Czechoslovakia and the new Kingdom of Yugoslavia led to renewed warfare as Czechoslovakia was attacked by Hungary, and in the Balkans the kind of hostility that had preceded World War I broke out again when Rumania attacked both Hungary and Yugoslavia.

Soviet Communists had good reason then to hope revolution would sweep from East to West, and Marxists throughout Europe looked in turn to the miraculous events in Russia as the beginning of the socialist future they had so long imagined. In March 1919 delegates from a score of countries met in Moscow to establish the Third International. Communists were active in the Baltic States, and Lenin's friend Béla Kun was to hold power as head of a Hungarian soviet in 1919 until Rumanian armies ended his brief reign. There was communist agitation in Vienna, where the provisional government of truncated Austria looked forward to union with the new German republic.

But Germany herself was the major communist goal. Marxists had long paid special attention to that highly industrialized nation with her class tensions and strong socialist movement. Defeat and a new government seemed the fulfillment of old portents. In January 1919 a communist revolt broke out in Berlin, and in the following spring another managed for a few weeks to make Bavaria a Soviet republic. Both uprisings were quickly defeated by remnants of the German army. So Russia remained the center of the communist world, but the chance remained that other revolutions would succeed.

The Conference Decisions

Peace had come so suddenly that there had been little time for discussion of specific terms. But through the pressure of public opinion, the German understanding of the armistice, and American influence, President Wilson's Fourteen Points had won acceptance as a basis for defining a new European order.

In many respects similar to the programs of other statesmen, Wilson's plan dealt mainly with territorial adjustments, but it raised such changes to the level of principle, associating them with the self-determination of peoples and a democratic peace. The remaining points cautiously yet courageously set forth a vision shared by the moderate left everywhere in the West. The removal of trade barriers and free navigation of the seas had long been part of the liberal canon. International attention to the welfare of colonial populations, the reduction of armaments, and open diplomacy were more radical suggestions; but by 1918 the belief was common that had steps been taken on these issues earlier, the world's most terrible war might have been averted. Wilson's final point, and the one closest to his heart, called for a League of Nations to guarantee the safety of all. In subsequent statements the American president had enlarged on the need for "impartial justice," "peace that will be permanent," and covenants that are "sacredly observed." His language and ideals caught the imagination of the world.

At the Paris Peace Conference, it was readily agreed that the mistakes of the Congress of Vienna must not be repeated. No defeated na-

When Woodrow Wilson paraded through the streets, Parisians cheered the representative of a new democratic era as well as an ally in victory. (Photo: The Granger Collection)

tions would take part in the early discussions—no German Talleyrand would divide the Allies. The atmosphere was one of sober business; the elegant aristocrats of 1815 had given way to commissions of expert advisers for every important issue, who were to provide the major negotiators with the detailed information they needed.

Thirty nations had joined the Allies at least formally,[4] but it was soon established that the momentous decisions would be taken by the five big powers—France, the United Kingdom, Italy, Japan, and the United States. In practice, since most questions did not directly concern Japan, primary authority resided in four men: Clemenceau, Lloyd George, Premier Vittorio Orlando, and Wilson.

Soon after the Congress opened, in January 1919, disagreements among the principal representatives of the Big Four powers became the center around which the negotiations turned. All were elected leaders, skilled in appealing to public opinion and sensitive to its demands. All

---

[4] Yugoslavia, Czechoslovakia, and Poland were treated as Allies; the new republics of Austria, Hungary, and Germany as the defeated Central Powers.

Orlando, Lloyd George, Clemenceau, and Wilson look the very epitome of their respective nations as they face the camera rather than each other in this photo, which contrasts interestingly with the picture of the Congress of Vienna in Chapter 22.
(Photo: The Granger Collection)

were faced with grave domestic problems and worried by the turmoil in Central and Eastern Europe. They had to hurry.

The Treaty with Germany

To settle by May the complicated terms for peace with Germany was a remarkable achievement. Haste itself probably made the treaty more severe than it might otherwise have been. Commissions, assuming their proposals would be subject to later bargaining, tended to begin with maximum terms, but these were often simply written into the treaty itself.

The territorial provisions were not extremely harsh; Germany lost Continental lands as well as colonies, but she was preserved as a great state. The new European boundaries, however, were the sort to give continuing difficulty (see Map 26.6). France got Alsace-Lorraine but not the left bank of the Rhine or the establishment of an autonomous Rhineland state, which she also wanted. Instead the Allies were to occupy the Rhineland for fifteen years

MAP 26.6: TERRITORIAL SETTLEMENTS 1919–1926

and the French to direct the coal-producing regions along the Saar River, but the latter were to remain under German sovereignty unless a later plebiscite determined differently. Plebiscites would also decide whether Germany would surrender part of Schleswig to Denmark or of upper Silesia to Poland.

The Polish provinces of eastern Prussia, where Germans formed about 40 percent of the population, were immediately ceded to Poland. Far more controversial, however, was the creation of a Polish corridor to the sea. Within the corridor a majority of the population was Polish, but its outlet was the port of Danzig, a German city, which was restored to its ancient status as a free city. Worse, the corridor awkwardly separated eastern Prussia from the rest of Germany, and Poland would always feel insecure with an arrangement Germans never accepted.

Naturally enough the Germans were required to disarm, and though the terms were stiff, this would not have seemed unreasonable if it had proved to be a first step toward general disarmament, as the treaty implied. Germany was to have no large artillery, submarines, or military air force, and her army was to be limited to 100,000 men on long-term enlistment. The lists of matériel Germany was to deliver to the Allies were more punitive: horses and railway carriages, quantities of coal, most of her present ships, and some new vessels to be specially built.

Most burdensome of all were the provisions for reparations. Despite fine talk of not requiring an indemnity, the Allies declared that Germany should pay for civilian damages. The claims of Belgium, a neutral attacked without warning, were easily justified; and Clemenceau could argue that the most destructive fighting had occurred in Belgium and France. But Lloyd George had campaigned on a platform of making Germany pay, and he insisted, over American objections, on including Allied military pensions as civilian costs. Pandora's box was opened. Germany was made liable for sums unspecified and without foreseeable end and forced to swear to accept "responsibility" for losses from a war "imposed . . . by the aggression of Germany and her allies." It was true that she had attacked first, and in the liberal view her militarism had been the great disruptive force in European politics for a generation. But it was false, as historians soon established, that she had deliberately planned and instigated World War I, a widespread conviction that these vague phrases echoed. The "war guilt clause" thus became a subject of controversy in every country and of bitter resentment, official and private, in every part of Germany.

Finally, in German eyes the terms of the treaty made it intolerable as a *Diktat,* a dictated settlement the country's delegates were not given a chance to dispute until it was already drafted; then only minor objections were met. Although in fact the Allies had made no clear commitment regarding terms, the German military had left the civilian government to make an armistice on the basis, they said, of Wilson's Fourteen Points. Faced with the terms set at Versailles, the German government resigned, and parliament at first rejected the stipulation of war guilt; but when the Allies held firm, parliament angrily accepted the *Diktat.* The treaty was signed on June 28, 1919, the fifth anniversary of the assassination at Sarajevo, in the Hall of Mirrors at Versailles, where Bismarck and William I had announced the German Empire forty-eight years before—the symbolism was complete.

Treaties with the Central and Eastern States

For the Big Four the most difficult question after the treatment of Germany was the Italian boundary. All agreed that Italy, for strategic reasons, should be given the Tyrol south of the Alpine Brenner Pass, a German-speaking area formerly held by Austria; but Wilson was determined to prevent those further violations of the principle of nationality incorporated in the

Treaty of London of 1915 (which promised Italy a great deal more, including much of the Slavic-speaking lands of the Dalmatian coast). By stubbornly demanding more than they expected to get, the Italians stimulated unkind references to their record in the war. Then too Wilson made a serious tactical error: in a Paris interview he in effect asked the Italian people to reject the position of their negotiators, and the Italian delegation withdrew in protest from the conference to a great outpouring of nationalist feeling at home. Eventually a compromise was reached, but from that time on Italy was another of the dissatisfied states resentfully seeking a revision of the treaties.

With the signing of the Treaty of Versailles, the Big Four dispersed to attend to their pressing domestic concerns, leaving the details of the remaining settlements (commonly named after the place where they were signed) to their foreign officers. The treaty with Austria signed at St.-Germain-en-Laye in September was closely modeled on the treaty with Germany. Provisions for reparations and demilitarization, including naval restrictions, hardly seemed appropriate for the shaky little landlocked Austrian republic. In addition to the southern Tyrol Italy was given the Istrian Peninsula and some islands but not Dalmatia, and boundaries with the other new states were settled on the basis of nationality in some cases and strategic needs in others. Treaties with Bulgaria (signed at Neuilly in November) and with Hungary (signed at the Trianon in June 1920) followed. Bohemia was given to Czechoslovakia on historical grounds, but Hungarian claims to a historical kingdom were largely ignored. Like Austria, Hungary lost almost three-quarters of the lands she had ruled in 1914. Although Bulgaria had surrendered relatively little territory, her resentment over her borders equaled that of the other defeated Central Powers.

Every state of Eastern Europe could claim injustice, usually with exaggerated statistics and with tales, too often true, of inhumane treatment. Railway lines and economic relationships, "natural" boundaries for defense, historical claims, and nationality simply did not coincide. At each point one consideration had to be sacrificed to another; and since the final dispositions were frequently influenced by favoritism, external political factors, or sheer ignorance, the inconsistencies were blatant. A major role in making these arrangements work would fall to the new League of Nations.

A number of oral agreements and the very creation of the Reparations Commission provided for by the Treaty of Versailles implied that the treaties might be modified, as logic and equity argued they should; the reparations required from Austria, for example, were divided among the defunct empire's former lands in a gesture of fairness that left some new states paying reparations to others. Many territories were to be assigned only after a plebiscite, and many others were ceded to the Allies to be dealt with later. Provisions promising minorities just treatment, an expression of the Allies' decent intent, struck sensitive states as an insulting infringement on their sovereignty. The issues for future conflict were without limit.

The final treaty was one with Turkey, not signed until August 1920 at Sèvres; much of it never went into effect. The Allies, who had encouraged Arab nationalism, were embarrassed when the Soviet regime released their secret plans for partitioning the Ottoman Empire. Now they faced indigenous movements as complex and uncontrollable as those in Eastern Europe. A Turkish revival under Mustafa Kemal assured the territorial integrity of Turkey itself despite the principle of autonomous states adopted at Sèvres. In addition Syria was to be under French influence, while a vaguely defined area—carved into Palestine, Trans-Jordan, and Iraq—was to be subject to British authority.

Aside from recognizing the presence of Britain and France, the quickly buried Treaty of Sèvres settled little, and more durable boundaries came only after the conflicts and the diplomacy of the next few years. There was confusion in particular about what the British intended by separating Palestine from Trans-Jordan. In 1917 the British foreign secretary, Arthur Balfour, had promised that a "national home" for Jews would be created in Palestine; but the Balfour Declaration, exemplifying the nationalistic propaganda and humanitarian concern of that difficult year, had also guaranteed the rights of the Arabs there. Subsequent British statements had been neither clear nor consistent. The independence of Arabia was recognized in the Sèvres agreement, but competition among native rulers left its status uncertain and the boundaries of the new state undefined. For Egypt the peace terms ratified her separation from Ottoman sovereignty and confirmed British authority—that too contested by local movements.

The Allied enthusiasm for dividing up the Ottoman Empire both abated and seemed more suspect now that neither the Russian nor the Austro-Hungarian Empire remained on the scene to demand a share. But the recognition of French and British interests in the region led to an important innovation. Colonial territories were declared "mandates" of the League of Nations and assigned to classes. The parts of the Ottoman Empire newly placed under British or French rule—Palestine, Trans-Jordan, Iraq, and Syria—were Class A mandates, states considered on the verge of self-government. Most of the reassigned African territories were Class B mandates, ones in which European rulers were to guarantee freedom of religion, prohibit trade in liquor and arms, refrain from subjecting natives to military training, and encourage commerce. Class C mandates were primarily Pacific islands, to be ruled essentially as colonies. In every case the mandate power had to submit annual reports to the League of Nations for review. Like much else in the treaties, the system of mandates can be seen as an expression of conscience and growing responsibility toward the rest of the world or as an effort to legitimize continued European dominance and wrap hypocrisy in legalism. In operation the system justified both interpretations.

Built-in Weaknesses

By 1920 it was clear that the war to make the world safe for democracy, as the Allied leaders had labeled it, had not quite accomplished that. Yet the terms of peace did concertedly promote democracy in their call for self-determination and plebiscites, provisions for the League of Nations (carefully written into each treaty at Wilson's shrewd insistence), and the development of the system of mandates. Allied victory had spurred the establishment of representative regimes throughout Central Europe, almost requisite for admission to Allied favor. Like the diplomats at Vienna a century before, the statesmen at Paris saw an integral relationship between the form of domestic government and international peace. The treaties showed the influence of democracy less happily in their responsiveness to Allied public opinion that expected a peace punitive enough to justify the war.

Not since 1848 had liberal spokesmen so thoroughly dominated European politics, but the revolutions of World War I quickly went beyond nineteenth-century liberalism. The men at Paris found it hard to cope with revolution. They never managed a place for Russia at the conference nor even agreed on a consistent response to communist governments. Believers in democracy, they were baffled and frightened by the turmoil unleashed by wars for democracy. Although they supported self-determination and therefore nationalism, they were more aware than their forefathers that nationalism is not necessarily democratic. They took little account, however, of the social complexities of Eastern Europe, where land division was more explosive an issue than political forms and nationality itself no more important than the antagonism between peasant and lord. Living in a revolution they helped make and largely welcomed, the statesmen who forged the peace were not revolutionaries. If they encouraged revolutionary changes, they wanted to limit their part to legal formulas; and slogans that sounded radical in November 1918 gave way to frightened insistence on order a few months later.

Much that was accomplished at Paris reflected a cold assertion of national interest and a realistic appraisal of power. Inevitably the treaties were compromises. But it was the Allies who had asserted that their handiwork should be measured by the standards of high principle and who had injected ideology into matters of power politics. Woodrow Wilson was the most dedicated and by his lights the most consistent spokesman of this new moral and democratic politics.[5] And critics blame him for many of the weaknesses of the treaties, charging that he was intransigent or yielding in the wrong places and that he sacrificed too much to gain his dream of the League of Nations in the belief that liberal procedures would produce liberal policies.

But Wilson is more responsible for arousing hopes than betraying them. If his doctrinaire approach often meshed unfortunately with Clemenceau's skepticism and Lloyd George's easy flexibility, there were far more fundamental difficulties. Perhaps the greatest was that none of the leaders yet fully understood how much had changed. Although they created a tiny and weak Austrian republic, they could not forget the wealth and power of the Austrian Empire and therefore forbade the union of Austria, now thoroughly German, with Germany. They did not see that the deep economic, social, and psychological dislocation following the war would continue to threaten democracy and peace no matter how many representative governments were established.

Contemporary Criticism

Some signs of weakness in the treaty settlements appeared very early among the drafters themselves. In March 1920 the Senate of the United States rejected the documents for the final time. The most powerful nation in the world, having claimed moral leadership, would not enter the League of Nations. The United States thus joined Italy in rejecting the terms of peace, and in the process she added France to the list of aggrieved states. The French had abandoned demands that Germany be further weakened in return for a joint guarantee from the United States and Great Britain against German aggression. When the United States refused to honor that agreement, France felt betrayed. Moreover France had also wanted the league to have a peacekeeping force of its own, but her allies had opposed this. Out of her dissatisfaction and alarm, she would seek to make the League of Nations not a flexible instrument for modifying the war settlements but rather an agency for rigidly maintaining the status quo.

China refused to sign the treaties because of terms that gave Japan, in addition to other gains, almost a protectorate over her. Japan was offended by the conference's refusal formally to declare all races equal. For Asian, Arab, and African peoples, it was hard to believe that European diplomacy was much more principled than in the past.

The reparations clauses were soon blamed for the economic difficulties of numerous countries—those forced to pay them and those granted much less than anticipated. But the very concept had many opponents. In a brilliant and influential pamphlet, the English economist John Maynard Keynes castigated the Cartha-

---

[5] Yet he returned to the Paris Peace Conference after a trip home insisting that the Monroe Doctrine be written into the Covenant of the League of Nations.

ginian peace the victors had exacted, attacking reparations in particular.[6] He argued that the Allies owed each other more money than Germany could pay and that reparations would merely slow the recovery of Europe's economy. His analysis helped undermine confidence in the terms of peace, but his prescriptions—cancellation of international war debts and recognition that the international economic system was essentially artificial—were heresies as utopian in their way as any of Woodrow Wilson's points.

Keynes was right that policies toward Russia, Germany, and the successor states were contradictory; but his criticisms, like those that for decades would ring from party platforms in every country, tended to exaggerate how much of the postwar world could be shaped by worried statesmen quarreling in Paris.

---

[6] John Maynard Keynes, *The Economic Consequences of the Peace* (1920); and the famous rebuttal, Etienne Mantoux, *The Carthaginian Peace: or the Economic Consequences of Mr. Keynes* (1946).

Although the European nations did not fight each other between 1871 and 1914, peace was precarious as imperialism abroad and tension at home encouraged militant posturing and an accelerating arms race. As foreign policy, economic competition, and domestic politics became more closely interrelated, any social or political conflict was likely to have international repercussions. One spark in the changing Balkans was sufficient to trigger the elaborate mechanisms of world war.

The war at first seemed to heal divisions in every nation, but the industrialization and democratization of the previous forty years had altered the nature of war. It required more in wealth, organization, manpower, and morale than any society could afford and more than the Austrian and Russian empires could provide. Defeat unleashed the divisions war had briefly masked between ideologies, classes, and neighboring nationalities; and social strain exploded into open, violent revolution in Central and Eastern Europe. Revolution in Russia, which began as an opening to democracy the West could welcome, quickly went beyond familiar concepts to bring the Bolsheviks to power. By war's end death and destruction, the changed relations of social groups, and weakened economies made even the victors appear more like the survivors of a revolution.

It fell primarily to Great Britain, France, and the United States to define international order and set the terms of peace for a torn and ravaged continent in which insecure new nations faced each other suspiciously and communism was now a reality. Led by the nonsocialist left, the great democracies approached the task bearing hopes resonant with the best in nineteenth-century optimism. Before the task was finished, disillusionment, confusion, and exhaustion measured how little freedom statesmen had to mold a new world. Like the great revolutions, World War I created a gulf between past and present that marks the beginning of a new era.

RECOMMENDED READING

Studies

Albertini, Luigi. *The Origins of the War of 1914.* 3 vols. 1952–1957. The most recent of the large-scale studies of the causes of the war.

*Bailey, Thomas A. *Woodrow Wilson and the Lost Peace.* 1963. Standard account, sympathetic to Wilson.

Carsten, F. L. *Revolution in Central Europe, 1918–1919.* 1972. An important treatment of these significant outbreaks following the war.

*Falls, Cyril B. *The Great War.* 1961. Skillful account by a noted military historian.

Fay, Sidney B. *The Origins of World War.* 2 vols. 1938. The still readable classic assessment from the interwar years.

Feldman, Gerald D. *Army, Industry and Labor in Germany, 1914–1918.* 1966. A fundamental analysis of the war's effects on institutions and power in Germany.

Ferro, Marc. *The Great War.* 1973. This stimulating, outspoken essay emphasizes economic and social factors.

Fieldhouse, D. K. *The Colonial Experience: A Comparative Study from the Eighteenth Century.* 1966. A valuable introduction to this complicated subject that combines older and newer approaches.

*Fischer, Fritz. *Germany's Aims in the First World War.* 1967. The reassessment that became the center of controversy among German historians.

*Gallegher, John, Ronald Robinson, and Alice Denny. *Africa and the Victorians: The Climax of Imperialism.* 1961. An important revision of older views of imperialism.

Haimson, Leopold. *The Russian Marxists and the Origins of Bolshevism.* 1955. Places the Bolsheviks in the context of Russian radicalism.

Hale, Orin J. *The Great Illusion, 1900–1914.* 1971. An able synthesis that captures the spirit of the period.

King, Jere C. *Generals and Politicians: Conflicts Between France's High Command, Parliament, and Government, 1914–1918.* 1951. Dissects the significance of the conflicts behind the lines that brought a reassertion of civilian dominance.

*Lafore, L. *The Long Fuse: An Interpretation of the Origins of World War I.* 1965. A useful, modern reinterpretation of this troublesome question.

Marwick, Arthur. *War and Social Change in the Twentieth Century: A Comparative Study of Britain, France, Germany, Russia and the United States.* 1975. Develops the case for the revolutionary effects of World Wars I and II on domestic society.

Mayer, Arno J. *Politics and Diplomacy of Peacemaking: Containment and Counterrevolution at Versailles, 1918–1919.* 1967. Argues that fear of Bolshevism shaped the peace.

*Nicolson, Harold G. *Peacemaking, 1919.* The analysis of a disappointed participant.

*Pipes, Richard. *The Formation of the Soviet Union.* 1964. A clear and comprehensive treatment.

*Tuchman, Barbara. *The Guns of August.* 1962. The strikingly written story of the war's outbreak.

*Ulam, Adam B. *Lenin and the Bolsheviks.* 1969. Combines the study of ideas and policy to explain Lenin's triumph.

Williams, John. *The Home Fronts: Britain, France, and Germany, 1914–1918.* 1972. Pulls together a variety of evidence of the war's domestic impact.

Williamson, Samuel R. *The Politics of Grand Strategy: Britain and France Prepare for War, 1904–1914.* 1969. The political background of the course that led to war.

---

* Available in paperback.

27

DEMOCRACY AND DEPRESSION 1920–1932

The great question was what kind of world the new postwar world would be. As war had disrupted society, so peace brought the possibility of further and more desirable change, an opportunity expressed in revolutions and civil wars in the lands that had known defeat and by expectations of fuller democracy and prosperity among the victors. States were more solidly identified with nationality and their citizens given greater voice in government than ever before in Europe's history. Where industrialization had been slight, social and political changes encouraged its development. The institutions of parliamentarianism had spread almost everywhere, and on the whole they seemed to work. Revolution more radical than that was defeated everywhere except in Russia.

International affairs centered at first on the economic problems left by the war and on the machinery of the League of Nations. Moderation prevailed in these matters too, and the principles represented by Woodrow Wilson came as close to realization as such peaceful dreams ever had. Great Britain and France dominated the postwar world not merely through their international power but through the influence of their political style as well.

In domestic and international politics a confident liberalism appeared triumphant, but European culture reflected—and stimulated—a growing malaise. New learning questioned old values and theories, while the arts rejected convention. Beneath the economic recovery of Western society, forces were at work undermining the stability of intricate financial structures. Much as the system of international relations had suddenly failed in 1914, the economic system collapsed with the crash of 1929.

The financial crisis added immeasurably to more localized ailments of the European states. The postwar spread of democracy had not preserved political freedom in Italy or stability in much of Eastern Europe or brought about disarmament, and representative governments had left critical issues, both international and domestic, unresolved. And then they failed to maintain prosperity. Efforts at international negotiation for economic cooperation as well as for disarmament broke down. The Great Depression, a disaster in the lives of millions, was also a disaster for the political and economic institutions of Western liberalism.

I. THE POSTWAR POLITICAL ORDER

Nothing appeared clearer at the end of the war than that European political life would henceforth be very different, for people everywhere seemed determined to effect changes. How fundamental these changes should be was the issue at stake as the left gained strength even in the West, as revolution and civil war spread across Europe east of the Rhine, and while in Russia the Bolsheviks struggled to keep power. By the early 1920s, a formal stability prevailed. Germany established the sort of democracy the Allies had hoped for; and between her borders and Russia's, thirteen nations, mostly new, established domestic institutions and international ties sufficient for survival. Despite all the political and economic complications, postwar Europe broadly resembled the world envisioned at the Paris Peace Conference. Uncertainty centered on Russia, the great exception—but the Soviet Union remained weak and isolated—and on Italy, whose turn to Fascism was the great surprise.

The Consolidation of Soviet Rule

The Bolsheviks had made peasants' demands their own, arranged a costly peace, and prevented anyone else from capturing power; but now they faced civil war and attack from experienced armies, foreign and domestic. In a land already devastated by war and defeat, in which communications were poor and the economy near collapse, the Bolsheviks adopted "War Communism," a desperate effort to gather the nation's remaining forces. They extended the nationalization of industry, requisitioned crops from the more affluent peasants, and ruthlessly used terror, police repression, and propaganda to extract from a country in chaos just enough men and supplies to fight a war. With the firm leadership of Lenin, the military talent of Trotsky, and above all the mistakes of their enemies, they were able to win.

The major threat remaining by mid-1919 was the armies gathered under former tsarist officers in Estonia, southern Russia, and the Urals. This latter army pushed toward Moscow early in the summer, but the assault from the East was stopped before troops under General Anton Denikin moved up from the basin of the River Don to take Kiev in August and reach within 300 miles of Moscow by October. At that time other "White" forces, as the "Red" Communists' internal enemies came to be called,[1] stood only thirty miles from Petrograd (see Map 26.5). Thereafter the tide turned, for the antigovernment armies could neither penetrate farther nor maintain a long siege against the Communists.

The White forces even at their peak were unable to coordinate their attacks effectively because of dissension and conflicting ambitions. Vague about the political solutions they sought, many of them behaved suspiciously like men intent on a tsarist restoration. Battlegrounds were often ill-defined, contested by units hardly more than marauding bands. And the areas under White control experienced a terror less efficient but possibly more brutal than in Red sectors. While the Communists appealed to peasants, workers, and the various nationalities, the Whites antagonized everybody, losing the popular support that was their only hope. With each defeat more of their troops

---

[1] The term "White Russian" is used in two completely unrelated senses. For centuries before the Bolshevik revolution, and still today, it has referred to one of three major divisions of the Russian people—Great Russians, Little Russians, and White or Byelo Russians. The "White Russians" inhabit the district around Minsk in western Russia and possess a language and a literature of their own, closely related to but still distinct from those of their Great Russian neighbors. This use of the term has no connection with "Whites" used to identify the opponents of the Bolsheviks during the civil war.

melted away, and their sympathizers (including the Allies) became more cautious.

By the end of 1919 the White armies were in general retreat. The most important group, under Denikin, withdrew to the Crimea early in 1920; there a new commander, General Pëter Wrangel, stubbornly fought on before finally heeding Allied advice and evacuating his remaining armies in November 1920.

The Communists were also successful against Poland. An Allied commission had proposed to place the Russo-Polish border along the Curzon Line, so named for the British statesman who advocated it, which assigned to Poland most areas in which ethnic Poles were clearly a majority. But cultural and historical arguments made Poland insist on a boundary that had existed in 1772, well to the east. Rejecting Russian proposals for compromise, she sent an army into the Ukraine in March 1920. Within a month it took Kiev, but Ukrainian nationalists who had fought against the Russians were unwilling to fight for the Poles. In August the Red army, by now a relatively efficient military machine, launched an assault that threatened Warsaw. An effective Polish counterattack led to terms set in 1921, establishing a frontier between Poland's demands and the Curzon Line.

Russia's western border was now fixed. In Transcaucasia an agreement in 1921 between Russia and Turkey that ignored local independence movements assigned Armenia and Georgia, where anti-Communists had been strong, to the Soviet federation and Kars and Ardahan to Turkey. The Bolsheviks' opponents were not entirely defeated in Asian Russia until 1922, after the Japanese agreed to withdraw from eastern Siberia. Russia was then firmly in Soviet hands.

The New Economic Policy

In some ways Russia's troubles aided the new government. Like the Bolsheviks' cessions of territory, their economic difficulties made them less frightening to other nations; and chaos itself made it easier for them to effect revolutionary changes in landholding, social structure, and political power. Now it was time to take stock.

Under War Communism regimentation and bloodshed were the means of survival, and by using them the Communist party had become an increasingly disciplined and powerful body. The militant arm of a new order, it paralleled the regular government in organization. Some saw in this a pattern for effective rule. Others argued that the loose terror had gone too far (most of the countryside was still subject to the whims of local party officials and roving bands of armed men) and that continuing crises required new policies. Cities were partially empty; a million Russians had gone into exile; tens of millions more had died; less than one-sixth as many manufactured goods had been produced in 1920 as in 1913, and the level had been far lower in some critical areas of heavy industry. Foreign trade had almost ceased. Poor harvests had left the nation faced with famine, and the continued requisitions of what food there was spurred unrest and even revolt. Black markets flourished, and bureaucratic bungling, political maneuvering, and perpetual suspicion retarded economic reconstruction in a country more lacking than ever in machinery and technicians. Thus the mutiny of sailors at the Kronstadt naval base in March 1921, though put down in a few weeks, was an ominous sign. These were just the sort of men who had made the October Revolution possible, but their demands—civil liberties, a secret ballot, and better treatment of peasants—were now rejected. Still Soviet leaders, especially Lenin, recognized the need not to depend on repression alone.

In the spring of 1921, he announced the New Economic Policy (NEP), a major turning point in the development of Communist Russia. Lenin's gift for clear and courageous analysis underlay this dramatic reversal of policy. To

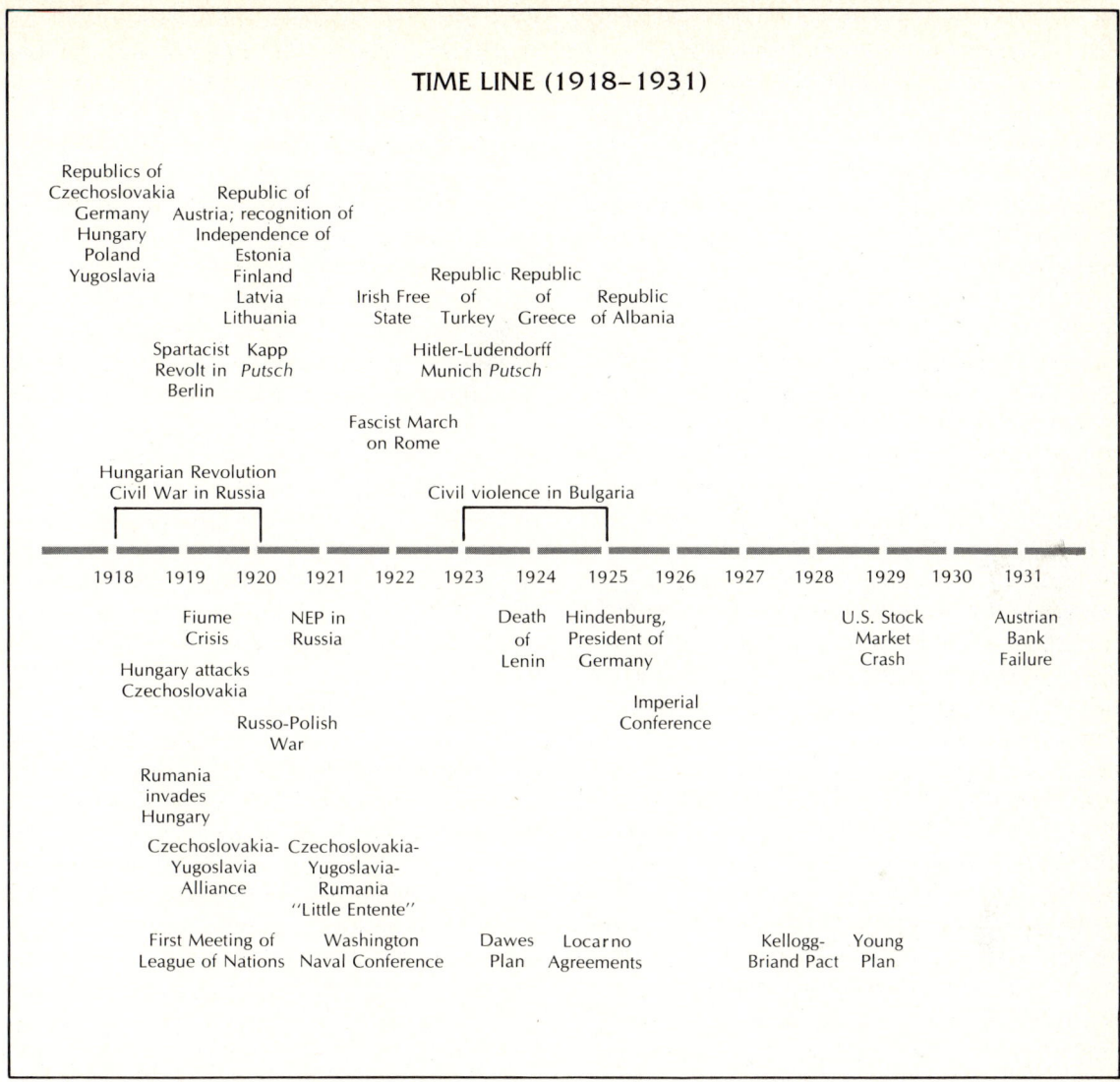

some Communists and many foreigners, the NEP seemed a departure from Marxism, but the failures Lenin recognized in propounding it were not failures of Marxist theory. Russia, he argued, was a special case, what today would be called an underdeveloped country; and the "citadel of capitalism"—a characteristic military metaphor—had been rushed too fast. Old habits and practices could not be uprooted overnight. Furthermore Russia lacked the cadres of technical specialists and managers a modern economy required. With noteworthy pragmatism Lenin proposed the sort of moderate course the Bolsheviks would earlier have opposed.

Under the NEP peasants were no longer subject to requisitions but rather to a tax in kind, and they could sell their surplus for profit on the open market. Retail concerns and manufacturers employing fewer than twenty workers could be run as private businesses. Even the larger industries, though they remained nationalized, could be leased to foreign entrepreneurs as a way of training Russians in efficient methods and new techniques. Fiscal reforms of the sort capitalist economists might have recommended guaranteed the stability of the currency while Russia's external trade emerged from the pattern of barter into which it had fallen.

Even with these new practices, economic recovery was slow. Millions died in the famine of 1920–1921 despite the extensive aid of the American Relief Administration, and not for another six years would production reach prewar levels. The NEP represented a surrender of the hope of creating communism all at once, but it was also a reaffirmation of Communist determination. Foreign trade, fiscal policy, large industry, wholesale commerce, and natural resources remained firmly in the hands of the state.

Creating a Communist Society

Meanwhile every social institution was recruited to help create a stable new society. The already numerous cooperatives for the sale of agricultural products and for consumer purchases were encouraged, as were trade unions. Both kinds of organization were used to strengthen allegiance to the government, teach efficiency, and instill a sense of class and national pride. Persecution of the church and organized campaigns against religion notwithstanding, by 1923 a certain relaxation permitted the Orthodox Church to function in a restricted fashion.

Russia's inadequate school system, which had nearly collapsed during the years of war and revolution, was improved and extended. Not until 1923 did enrollments pass prewar levels, but thereafter the rise was steady and impressive. The curriculum stressed official doctrines, and workers' children were favored for admission. Old practices of rote learning and ceremonial deference to teachers were to be abandoned. Higher education on the other hand developed more slowly, inhibited by the government's insistence that all subjects be taught in Marxist terms and by the emigration of many of Russia's best scholars.

The problems of ruling over multiple nationalities eased somewhat with the cession of so much territory; three-quarters of the remaining population could be called Russian. Still, non-Russian nationalities were in fact encouraged as never before. The four great Soviet republics—the Russian Soviet Federated Socialist Republic, the Ukrainian, White Russian, and (after 1922) Transcaucasian Soviet republics—were themselves divided into numerous regions for the various minorities. In theory at least each of these smaller constituent republics retained considerable autonomy under a new constitution that established the Union of Soviet Socialist Republics (U.S.S.R.).

Legally the authority of the government stemmed from the hierarchy of soviets described in Chapter 26. The largest, the all-union Congress of Soviets, consisted of some 2,000 representatives. The system of indirect universal suffrage that elected them heavily favored urban voters, though rural constituencies had five times the population. At infrequent and largely ceremonial meetings, the Congress elected the 750-member Central Executive Committee, which was more nearly the equivalent of a Western parliament, though it had only advisory powers. The Committee selected both the Council of People's Commissars and the Presidium, a directorate, whose chairman was the chief of state. Precise lines of authority among competing groups were left vague, and little distinction was made between legislative and executive functions.

In practice the Communist party, which remained a restricted elite, was the most important instrument of rule. Not all officials were

Trotsky sings the praises of the Red army at the 1922 meeting of the Third International, held in Moscow to celebrate the anniversary of the Bolshevik Revolution.
(Photo: Wide World Photos)

party members, but it dominated the upper reaches of government, and through a tightly organized hierarchy that paralleled the bureaucracy, it reached into every aspect of Soviet public life—factories, hundreds of new centers for adult education, and youth associations that soon had millions of members. These organizations stirred patriotic enthusiasm, explained the policies of the government, and prodded Russians in thousands of ways to create a modern industrial society.

At first Western artistic movements as well as technology had been welcomed and energetically adopted, but the challenge of creating a new society discouraged tolerance. In 1922 cultural activities were placed directly under the Ministry of Education. The books printed and art works exhibited were those that met the current definition of communist aesthetics: realistic in style, popular in appeal, and useful to the new order. The issues of how to translate ideology into practice, what technologies to use, and how bureaucracies should function were thrashed out within the government and the party. To be on the losing side in any of these disputes was politically and sometimes personally fatal. Experience thus led Communists to caution, and this in turn contributed to an atmosphere of apparent calm.

Even in foreign relations the Soviet Union, preoccupied with domestic problems, gave signs of accepting the world order despite the existence of the Third International. By 1924, the year of Lenin's death, every major power except the United States had recognized the new regime. And the bitter struggle for succession made it appear that even if communism remained firmly entrenched in the Soviet Union, that need not seriously disturb general European stability.

The New Regimes of Eastern Europe

From Finland to the Balkans, most of the postwar states of Eastern Europe were newly created by-products of the battle among the giants who had previously dominated these lands. Recognized as independent in the peace settlements, the new states represented the Allied commitment to self-determination, and most of them had new constitutions reflecting the latest fashions and the deepest hopes of democracy.

But in nearly every case statehood had brought war with neighboring regions; and independence, universal suffrage, and civil rights offered few solutions to the problems of conflicting nationalities and economic crisis. In most of the new states peasant revolution or military takeover threatened almost constantly, and most of the elected leaders depended on aroused national feeling for what consistent support they could muster. Peasant parties were dominant in most of these countries as they never had been in the West, and these parties often combined agrarian radicalism with distrust of urban values, modernizing changes, or parliaments.

These social conflicts in Eastern Europe intersected with ethnic and religious differences to increase centrifugal pressures. The German minorities in Poland, Czechoslovakia, Hungary, and Bulgaria were generally among the resented well-to-do. Anti-Semitism was especially virulent in Poland and Rumania, partly an expression of rural hostility toward urban finance. Town-country antagonism also often set rural Slovaks at odds with the Czechs of industrialized western Czechoslovakia. In Yugoslavia the claims of Greek Orthodox Serbians to be the "national" people angered the Roman Catholic Croats and Slovenes. Macedonians, divided among Yugoslavia, Greece, and Bulgaria, kept up an organized agitation that added to the instability in all three countries and produced chaotic insurrection in Bulgaria from 1923 to 1925.

Rising populations, widespread illiteracy, and lack of capital plagued economic development in the new states. Only Austria and Czechoslovakia had advanced industries of a size that could compete in European markets; elsewhere land remained the central economic issue. Independence brought the eviction of "foreign" landlords and the breakup of large estates in the Baltic countries; Bulgaria, Rumania, and Czechoslovakia also instituted significant land reforms. Everywhere, however, new policies were accompanied by resentment of any favored treatment given to certain nationalities and regions. Conservative peasants holding small plots generally proved the most resistant to agricultural modernization. In Poland and still more in Hungary (where 40 percent of the peasants were landless and the next 50 percent held less than three hectares), the great estate owners succeeded in protecting the interests of a native aristocracy.

Each state erected tariff barriers that interrupted the traditional flow of trade within the former empires. Furthermore, the successor countries began their existence burdened with a share of the debts of the Hapsburg Empire as well as complex schedules of payments due one another for lands gained or lost. Only intensive help from the League of Nations kept these claims from crippling them and enabled the financial system to function at all.

Yet gradually stable patterns emerged. The disappearance of the Russian, Austrian, and Ottoman empires had opened the way for systematic efforts at modernization. Schools were built by the thousands and functioned fairly effectively despite the issues of language and nationality to which they gave rise. On the whole the traditions of the Austrian bureaucracy served its heirs well, and Turkey, which became a republic under Mustafa Kemal in 1923, borrowed Western dress and institutions as avenues to national strength. The next year the Greeks, defeated by the Turks in the last of the Balkan conflicts that followed World War I, replaced their monarchy with a republic that achieved relative stability despite the continued danger of military intervention in domestic politics.

In general the socialists and agrarian radicals prominent in the first postwar years had given way to more conservative politicians. By 1920 the defeat of Béla Kun's brief communist regime in Hungary had led to authoritarian rule under Admiral Miklós Horthy, as regent for an empty throne, who abolished the secret ballot in rural areas as part of the reassertion of Magyar dominance. But most of the governments of Eastern Europe worked more or less within their constitutions; and Czechoslovakia, under President Tomáš Masaryk and Foreign Minister Eduard Beneš, became a model of the order, freedom, and prosperity democracy was supposed to bring.

The Weimar Republic of Germany

Pressures for a more democratic and responsible German government were powerful even before the armistice. Twice in 1917 Emperor William II had promised to make his cabinet subject to a majority in the Reichstag; and in October 1918, to begin this transformation from above, he appointed Prince Maximilian of Baden chancellor.

Prince Max symbolized a compromise that might have worked earlier, but he was not able to stem the uprisings sweeping through much of Germany in the name of peace, democracy, and socialism during the last weeks of war. Not only the political system but the very nation Bismarck had created threatened to break apart, and Prince Max pleaded with William to abdicate. When revolt had spread to Berlin, he announced the abdication without awaiting the Kaiser's approval. Then this liberal aristocrat who favored constitutional monarchy, this non-Prussian nobleman who opposed the dominance of Junkers and army, handed his office (quite unconstitutionally) to Friedrich Ebert, the leader of the Social Democrats. The provisional government, the first German government to include socialists, was established just in time to sign the armistice.

It talked proudly of the German "revolution," and it promulgated decrees in November promising democracy, freedom of speech, a return to the eight-hour workday, and measures to improve social security. Concerned first of all simply with survival, the provisional government avoided tackling the question of land reform lest disruption increase the real danger of starvation. Frightened of a Bolshevik revolution, it quickly reached an accommodation with the army—an army already recovering some of its confidence. Ludendorff, who had insisted that Germany had to sue for peace, later talked of holding out; and even before the terms of peace had been published, the legend began to spread of a valiant army stabbed in the back by radicals at home.

Although the German military had in fact been defeated, the nucleus of military strength remained intact. General Wilhelm Groener, who replaced Ludendorff in late October 1918 as Hindenburg's principal aide, promised to assist the new government provided it would not meddle in the army's affairs. Ebert accepted those terms, and when an uprising of left-wing Marxists called Spartacists brought most of Berlin under their control in January 1919, the army crushed the revolt and shot its leaders. The Spartacists had failed to win a large following, and Lenin's best hope for a communist revolution in Germany died with them.

Germany's new leaders remained committed democrats, and they held elections in January 1919 for a constituent assembly to meet in Weimar, a pleasant city associated with Goethe that recalled the culture of preindustrial Germany. Nearly three-quarters of the delegates elected were intent on installing a republic (Social Democrats held 40 percent of the seats), and with admirable dispatch they wrote a thoroughly democratic constitution that joined proportional representation to universal suffrage. The president, directly elected for a seven-year term, would nominate the chancellor, or prime minister, who would then have to be approved by the Reichstag. The Reichsrat, as the upper house was now called, would still represent the single states, but its authority was reduced. In the new Germany government would be responsible to parliament, minorities would be fairly represented, and the aristocracy would hold no political privilege. Both civil rights and private property were specifically guaranteed.

The government, however, continued to face grave threats from the left and an essentially independent army on the right. In addition Allied policies had effects quite contrary to those intended. The victors' insistence that a civilian government be established immediately allowed the generals to escape publicly acknowledging their defeat and left the founders of the new republic to bear the onus of the harsh treaty terms. The decision not to occupy Germany but to maintain the blockade made military collapse less visible than Allied severity. Thus resentment combined with social and economic distress and with the unfinished business of reparations and plebiscites to feed the strength of right-wing nationalists.

In March 1920 some of these tried a revolt of their own. Wolfgang Kapp, a lesser official and outspoken nationalist, led some *Freikorps* members and others in a march on Berlin. When the army, so ready to repress revolt from the left, declared its unwillingness to fire on "fellow soldiers" (that is, the men of the *Freikorps*), the government abandoned the capital. Its last-minute call for a general strike, however, produced the greatest demonstration of loyalty the Weimar regime would ever win. Workers across the nation left their jobs. In a matter of days the economy came to a halt, and the Kapp "government" gave up.

The Weimar Republic was making its way between the political extremes, but the Social Democrats lacked the strength to pursue the reforms their victory implied. The bureaucracy was not democratized. Nor was the army reformed, and its officer corps, though severely limited by the Treaty of Versailles, preserved its cohesion and reached another timely understanding with the politicians. The lack of reprisals following Kapp's fall contrasted strangely with the treatment of the Spartacists. Socialist talk of nationalizing some industries produced few concrete results, and the republic could not be certain of the workers' support in future crises.

New elections showed a shift to the right and brought in ministries resting primarily on the Catholic Center and the People's parties, the latter dominated by industrialists who had belonged to the right wing of the former National Liberals. Although the *Freikorps* were at last outlawed, many of their members merely

---

Poverty in Berlin, 1922; a family begging.
(Photo: UPI)

German firms in 1923 needed a handcart to carry the weekly payroll.
(Photo: Wide World Photos)

went into hiding; they remained prominent in the political violence that characterized the Weimar years. Scores of politicians were assassinated, including Matthias Erzberger, the Center party leader who had signed the armistice, and Walther Rathenau, a brilliant organizer of the German economy during the war and as foreign minister in 1922 a vigorous defender of German interests, shot primarily because he was a Jew. By 1924 the conservative National People's party was second in size to the Social Democrats.

The gravest problem of these years, however, was inflation. Early in 1923 French and Belgian forces occupied the Ruhr district because of Germany's failure to make coal deliveries required as reparations, and the local populace responded with passive resistance, a kind of general strike, that made the occupation fruitless. The resulting dislocation and scarcity also drastically accelerated the already serious inflation.

The German mark, once valued at 4 to the United States dollar, was rated at 8 to 1 in 1919 and 250 to 1 in 1921, and by August 1923 the exchange was more than 2,000 to 1. New money was run off the presses at top speed, and old notes with additional zeros printed on them were rushed to the banks before they too became valueless. Prices changed within hours, always upward; by November a newspaper could sell for nearly 100 billion marks. Recovery came slowly, following the imposition of stringent new financial measures (one source of inflation had been the government's reluctance to raise taxes), a general revival of the economy, and above all a moratorium on reparations and a subsequent new schedule of payments.

At the height of the Ruhr crisis, a nationalist *Putsch* was attempted in Munich. Led by a little-known man named Adolf Hitler, the revolt was more notable for Ludendorff's participation. It was quickly defeated, though the plotters' punishment was ludicrously light: Ludendorff was acquitted and Hitler given a five-year sentence in comfortable prison quarters, where he composed *Mein Kampf* ("My Struggle") in the thirteen months he actually served. It was reasonable to think in 1924 that Germany was on the road to stability. If democracy had not exactly taken root, the forms were operative; better relations with other powers now seemed possible, and the threat of internal revolution had faded.

The Fall of Liberal Italy

At the outbreak of the Great War, the Kingdom of Italy had lived by the rules of liberal politics and economics for more than half a century, a fact that had made it seem fitting for Italy to join the Allied side. The least industrialized of the major Western powers, she had but barely met the demands of total war, and peace brought inflation and unemployment that further weakened the economy. In many places peasants simply confiscated land long promised them; and when in 1920 industrialists began to meet growing waves of strikes with lockouts, workers answered by occupying factories. Italian institutions, strong enough to survive the war, were strong enough still to prevent revolution, but an atmosphere of bitterness, fear, and violence was undermining them.

For Italy the peace treaty was as disillusioning as modern war. Although granted considerable territory, she got less than she had expected, and her treatment at Paris was often humiliating. Disposition of the Dalmatian port of Fiume was still being argued when in 1919 a private expedition led by Gabriele d'Annunzio dramatically captured it for Italy. The nation's most famous living poet, d'Annunzio ruled Fiume for more than a year at the head of an "army" of the unemployed, whose nationalist frenzy and vulgar slogans were a welcome contrast to the wordy frustration of diplomacy. Eventually the Italian government evicted its filibustering poet (who had declared war on Italy), but the affair showed the appeal and the effectiveness of direct action.

The Fascist movement was born amid these crises. The term *fascio,* meaning "bundle," comes from an ancient Roman symbol of authority—a bundle of sticks, individually weak but strong in unity. Echoes of imperial Rome remained part of the Fascist party mystique. The movement centered around Benito Mussolini, whose polemical skills had earlier carried him to the top of Italy's Socialist party; he was editor of the party newspaper and led its intransigent wing until expelled in 1915 for favoring Italian intervention in the war. He had then become one of Italy's noisiest nationalists. After the war Mussolini continued to agitate, using the rhetoric of the left to denounce liberalism and parliamentary indecision while using the cries of nationalism to castigate Marxists and the Allies. Inconsistencies of doctrine and tactics hid beneath activism and symbols; the party militants in their black shirts seemed a small army.

At first the Fascists had little success—they did not win a single seat in the elections of 1919—but the hesitancy and confusion of others would soon give them an advantage. The two largest political groups, the Socialists and the Popular party, were well-organized mass parties opposed to the old politics and to each other but divided internally. Left-wing Socialists split off to form a Communist party, inspired by the Bolsheviks' success which increased the Socialists' reluctance to cooperate with bourgeois regimes; the Catholic Popular

Mussolini poses triumphantly with his chiefs after the Fascist march on Rome in 1922.
(Photo: Wide World Photos)

party demanded thoroughgoing reforms, but much of its real strength came from rural and conservative groups. The aging Giolitti, returning to the prime ministry in 1920, tried in the old ways to patch together a governing majority. In preparation for the elections of May 1921—the first held under a system of universal manhood suffrage—he brought the Fascists into a "national bloc" of candidates. The alliance, however, benefited only the Fascists, who won thirty-five seats in the new Chamber of Deputies; Giolitti's own Liberal supporters remained a poor third behind the Socialists and the Popularists. During the campaign Fascist squads had planted bombs, beaten up opponents, and disrupted meetings, enjoying violence and intimidating moderates while denouncing Marxists as a threat to order.

When left-wing unions called a general strike in 1922, which many believed would rapidly turn into revolution, Mussolini's Black Shirts increased their threats and open violence and began taking over town councils by force. The government of Luigi Facta—a caretaker prime minister who was holding office because no one could win a majority—resigned, and the Fascists staged their march on Rome in

October. Motley squads of party militants moved on the capital in a grand gesture of revolt while Mussolini cautiously waited in Milan. At the last minute Facta asked for martial law, but King Victor Emmanuel III refused—the gesture of revolt had been enough. Mussolini dashed to Rome, preserving his claims to both perfect legality and forceful conquest.

At thirty-nine Mussolini, invited by the king to form a cabinet, became prime minister of a coalition government; the violent man of order won from a desperate legislature the majority—and an overwhelming one—denied to parliamentary politicians. In the elections of 1924, Fascists won a massive victory. Intimidation and open violence contributed to this success, as did some fraud, but most Italians were willing to give the new party a chance.

In the following year, it became clearer what a Fascist regime would mean. Giacomo Matteotti, a Socialist who bravely enumerated Fascist crimes before the entire Chamber, was subsequently murdered in gangland style. As public condemnation mounted, Mussolini's government seemed about to topple, but the opponents of Fascism were no more able to unite now that they had become a parliamentary minority than when they had been stronger. On the contrary, the Fascists gradually isolated first the Socialist and then the Popular party. By 1925 all opponents had been expelled from the legislature, and newspapers either printed what they were told or risked suppression. The Fascist period had begun.

To most of the world outside Italy and to many Italian moderates, it seemed merely that the country had at last found a strong and antisocialist leader, one who could run it effectively and whose verbal excesses would undoubtedly be tempered by experience. Reasonable men found it hard to believe that a party whose program contained so many contradictions could be dangerous for long.

International Plans for Reparations and Peace

Gradually the remaining boundary disputes had been resolved one after another, sometimes by force, more often by complex negotiations, and occasionally with the aid of the plebiscites called for in the peace treaties. By the early 1920s, reparations rather than territory presented the most troublesome international problems. There was little agreement, for example, on how to evaluate payments in kind, which the Reparations Commission allowed Germany to offer as part of her total obligation; this was the issue that had led to the French and Belgian occupation of the Ruhr in 1923. That step, however, was disastrous for all, leaving France isolated and Germany the victim of runaway inflation.

As Germany fell behind in her payments, the Allies took the position that they in turn could not pay their war debts to the United States. Some compromise was essential, and in 1924 the nations involved accepted the proposals of an international commission of financial experts, headed by the American banker Charles G. Dawes. The Dawes Plan fixed Germany's payments on a regular scale, established an orderly mode of collection, and provided for loans to her equal to 80 percent of the sum due the first year of the plan—1 billion gold marks ($250 million; it would increase to 2.5 billion marks annually in the fifth year).[2] The plan did not, as many Europeans thought it should, admit any connection between Allied debts to the United States and German reparations to the European victors, but it did end the worst of the chaos. For the next six years, Germany, fed by loans largely from the United States, made her reparations payments on

---

[2] The United States having waived her claims, the apportionment of reparations among the Allies had been decided on in 1920: 52 percent to France, 22 percent to the British Empire, 10 percent to Italy, and 8 percent to Belgium.

schedule. The issue seemed forever resolved with the adoption of the Young Plan in 1929, which finally set a limit to Germany's obligations (fifty-nine years), reduced annual payments, and ended foreign occupation of the Rhineland.

From 1924 to 1930 the conduct of international affairs did really reflect some of the idealism of the Paris Peace Conference. The League of Nations, formally established in 1920, successfully resolved a number of disputes. Some of its procedures were impractically elaborate, and its authority was restricted by the absence of the United States, by Britain's greater concern for her empire than for the League, and by France's tendency to use it for her own security. The League thus dealt best with disputes in which no major power had a direct interest. Its special commissions made notable contributions, helping the disjointed economies of the new and contentious states of Eastern Europe, aiding refugees, and reporting on matters of public health and working conditions. This recognition that peace was related to social conditions was in itself an achievement, the liberal vision at its best. In the late 1920s at least, the decisions of the Permanent Court of International Justice, organized at The Hague under the League, were treated with

Germans returning to the city in 1923 after a potato raid into the countryside, where the poor could steal some precious food.
(Photo: Wide World Photos)

great seriousness; and men could imagine a world in which commonly accepted rules and evenhanded justice would greatly reduce the threat of war.

The Locarno Era

Both the League of Nations and the dominant Western democracies were inclined to make general principles a subject of international relations. Efforts to outlaw war foundered on definitions of aggression, but they led to a series of treaties known as the Locarno Pact in 1925. The major agreement, entered into by Germany, Belgium, France, Great Britain, and Italy, secured Germany's western frontier; she and her neighbors promised to arbitrate their disputes; and France made a mutual-defense alliance with Poland and Czechoslovakia. A Continental war caused by German aggression now seemed impossible; France and other nations could lay aside their fears.

The Locarno era, the name given to this brief period of international optimism, was capped by the Kellogg-Briand Pact of 1928. The French had suggested that the American entry into World War I be commemorated by a friendship pact, and the Americans proposed that the accord be extended to others as well. More than a score of nations immediately signed the pact, which renounced war "as an instrument of national policy." These ill-defined declarations, accompanied by no provisions for enforcement, soon proved empty, but they expressed the hope, the belief in law, and the confidence in public opinion that marked the Locarno era.

Disarmament provided another broad path to maintaining peace, and from 1921 on some League commission was always soberly studying the problem. Naval disarmament seemed especially promising. Britain no longer commanded sufficient resources to maintain a fleet twice the size of any other country's, given the enormous cost of capital ships; the expense of a sizable navy in fact made every nation hope to avoid unnecessary competition. At the Washington Conference of 1921–1922, called by President Warren G. Harding, Wilson's successor, the United States, Great Britain, Japan, France, and Italy had agreed after some difficulty to fix their relative strength in capital ships at current levels,[3] not to expand their naval bases, and even to scrap some of their larger vessels. About smaller ships there had been less agreement, but the Washington Conference had produced tangible results as well as statements of good will. Never again did disarmament discussions prove so fruitful. At Geneva in 1927 and London in 1930, Italy (citing the special needs of her geography) and France (arguing that all forms of disarmament should be discussed together) refused to accept a treaty. By 1935 Japan would reject even the Washington accord.

Attempts to limit land and air arms were even less successful. League commissions could not agree on which were offensive weapons, whether a professional army was comparable to a reserve force, and whether limitations should be expressed in terms of budgets, weapons, or men. Proposals from Germany and Russia that everyone else should disarm down to their level only aroused suspicion. When the conference on general disarmament that these commissions prepared was finally called in 1932, the dream of arms restrictions was more remote than ever. Discussions continued at length, but before agreements were reached, Hitler had come to power in Germany, and a new arms race ensued.

The Dominant Democracies

The international order characterized by the League of Nations, reparations, and the Locarno spirit rested on the policies and influence

---

[3] This was defined as parity between the United States and Great Britain at 525,000 tons apiece in capital ships, 315,000 tons for Japan, and 175,000 tons each for France and Italy.

of France and Great Britain and on the prosperity of the United States; and so, less directly, did the stability of German democracy, the maintenance of constitutional governments in Eastern Europe, and the effective isolation of the Soviet Union. The caution with which these democracies exercised their international role in turn reflected some unease within their own societies. Although much was changed after the war, few of the promised benefits had materialized. Society had not been radically reformed; indeed radicals had been as effectively defeated at the polls in Britain and France as by force in Germany and Italy. In every country the most militant Marxists felt strengthened by the presence of the Soviet Union as an international homeland for the proletariat. But that allegiance, and the founding of Communist parties that followed from it, split and weakened the left in domestic affairs.

The real social changes of this period were usually not the result of deliberate policy. Employment in services such as sales and office work increased more rapidly than in industry (and the proportion of those who were domestic servants declined). In most countries more women were gainfully employed than before the war at those jobs thought suitable for women, despite a sharp decline from the wartime peak and despite the strong tendency for women to leave work upon marriage. The number of (middle-class) youths enrolled in universities increased sharply, and the automobile, especially in Britain and France, began to alter middle-class life. Generally, the central government now spent a higher proportion of national wealth; and although most of that went to the military and to service debts and pay pensions left from war, some of it was used to lay the basis for broader measures of social security for all. Politically, both business interests and labor unions exercised a more direct influence, essentially supporting the effort to recapture economic stability. Yet despite periods of prosperity and a genuine boom in certain industries, the 1920s did not provide the steady growth of the prewar decade. Economic uncertainty, increased by inflation and unemployment, tended, like the disillusionment over reparations or the specter of Bolshevism, to stimulate a conservatism that was essentially defensive.

France

Life in France quickly returned to prewar patterns after 1918, including the political combination of a weak executive and moderate domestic policies. Raymond Poincaré, in office since 1913, was perhaps the strongest president the Third Republic had ever had, and his term expired in 1920. Clemenceau was a likely successor, but Parlement chose a safe and colorless man instead, a French version of the "normalcy" the United States sought in Harding. The Chamber of Deputies elected in 1919 at the height of patriotic pride in victory was the most conservative since the founding of the Third Republic.

For the next decade the leading figures of French politics were Aristide Briand and Poincaré, who alternated as premier, with Briand heading the ministry of foreign affairs in 1925–1932. Briand, who after a radical youth had become a moderate, led a number of short-lived compromise cabinets, reflecting in his skillful flexibility something of both the best and the worst in the French tradition of governing. Poincaré, the strong-willed man of integrity, made the decision to occupy the Ruhr in 1923 and was called back in 1926–1929 to head a state dedicated to saving the franc, which by then had slipped to one-fifth its former value.

France had become *par excellence* the land of the lower-middle class, the artisan, and the peasant proprietor fiercely attached to his tiny plot of land. Such people were loyal to their nation and proud of their heritage. Though the cornucopia of reparations they had expected never materialized, they accomplished miracles of reconstruction, carefully making their new buildings look as much as possible like those destroyed—but it took extraordinary courage to raise their taxes. Poor financing, beginning with inadequate taxes during the war, underlay the crisis of the franc, which had been one of the world's stablest currencies for a century before its postwar depreciation, and few things were as important to French citizens as their life savings. Demographically France had been hardest hit of all nations by World War I, and that fact as well affected her postwar psychology. She epitomized the tendency common throughout the West to live as if World War I and the revolutions following had made but a temporary difference.

Competent French leaders thus presided during a period of prosperity over governments whose policies allowed domestic stagnation and encouraged rigidity in foreign affairs. Poincaré's concern for national honor and a stable currency appealed to a cautious middle class much as Briand's complicated maneuvers did to parliamentarians, but neither encouraged Frenchmen to face more difficult long-term issues of working conditions, social inequality, or mass culture.

The United Kingdom

In the United Kingdom also, the 1919 elections—the first in which women (those over thirty) were allowed to vote—produced an overwhelming victory for the leaders who had promised to extract enough from Germany to make winning the war worthwhile. Lloyd George remained prime minister, but even in its modest social legislation—which included an increase in unemployment benefits—his government was essentially conservative, and his conflicts with other liberal leaders added to the Liberal party's decline. Dumped by the Conservative party in 1922, Lloyd George never returned to power. For most of that decade, Britain was led by Stanley Baldwin, who had the gift of making dullness seem statesmanship. In 1924 new elections brought the Labour party (which two years before had outpolled the Liberals) briefly to power. Except for recognizing the Soviet Union, it did little to recall its leftist origins.

Throughout the period the government met problems of unemployment, Irish nationalism, and empire by extending previous policies. Although the Conservatives expanded social welfare measures, a crisis in the coal industry led to a ten-day general strike in 1926. Frightened by the bitter class conflict the work stoppage vented, Britons were quick to praise the restraint used by both sides. Nevertheless the fervent interest of the well-to-do in maintaining essential services (and breaking the strike), like the antilabor legislation that followed, did much to deepen the resentment of the British working class.

Home rule, promised to Ireland before the war, had been suspended, and the Easter Rebellion of 1916 had been firmly suppressed. In 1919, however, the most militant Irish nationalists, led by the Sinn Fein (meaning "We Ourselves") party, refused to take their seats in the House of Commons and met instead at Dublin in a parliament of their own, the Dail Eireann, where they declared Ireland independent. To this defiance the London government responded slowly and ineptly, finally electing to suppress the Sinn Fein party and with it Irish independence. To support this action, the government sent reinforcements to the Royal Irish Constabulary in numbers sufficient to spread the fighting without ending it, and they soon became the most hated symbol of British repression. The Irish terrorists who resisted these British forces were by then named the Irish Republican Army. Against these civilian terrorists, the British could look only foolish or brutal; and by 1920 the two sides were fighting a bloody war.

Faced with mounting pressure at home and abroad to find a settlement, the British government in 1920 passed an Ireland act, which set up two Irish parliaments, one in the predominantly Catholic areas of the south and west,

The defeat of the Easter Rebellion, May 1916; British soldiers stand guard over the remains of a Dublin tramcar that had served as a barricade.
(Photo: BBC Hulton Picture Library)

and the other in the predominantly Protestant counties of the northeast (six of the nine counties of Ulster). A Council for Ireland was to coordinate policies between the two Irish governments. This concession of home rule did not, however, appease the leaders of the Sinn Fein, who opposed both the division of the island and the continuing ties with the British crown. Almost two more years of fighting and negotiating followed. In December 1922, the Irish parliament at Dublin proclaimed, with British acquiescence, the existence of the Irish Free State, which included all Ireland except the six counties of Ulster; Northern Ireland, as the six counties were called, maintained its traditional union with Great Britain. An uneasy peace was achieved, although the political division of Ireland would remain a source of tension and conflict.

Only in imperial affairs did habits of flexible compromise produce impressive success. Canadian complaints led the Imperial Conference of 1926 to a significant new definition of all dominions as "autonomous communities . . . equal in status . . . united by a common allegiance to the crown and freely associated as members of the British Commonwealth of Nations." The dominions, in other words, were recognized as completely autonomous in all domestic and foreign affairs; their ties to the British crown were entirely volitional, based on common traditions, loyalty, and friendship. Given legal sanction by the Statute of Westminster in 1931, this definition laid the foundation for a remarkable adaptation of empire to new conditions.

The Other Democracies

The second half of the 1920s was a period of notable prosperity in the Weimar Republic. But the divisions in German society, briefly obscured by defeat, had grown sharper. German workers felt that socialist governments and a republican regime had done little to benefit them. The middle class could not forgive the inflation, which had wiped out its savings. Prosperity brought moderate policies and relief from the assassinations and revolts of the earlier years, but it produced no significant group with primary loyalty to the existing regime.

The leading statesman was Gustav Stresemann, who sat in every cabinet, usually as foreign minister, from 1923 to his death, in 1929. Stresemann was closest to the businessmen of the center-right, who had few idealistic illusions and who saw the need for Germany to maintain good relations with her neighbors. If he acquiesced in the army's violations of the disarmament clauses of the Versailles treaty, its stringent limitations were at least partly to blame. Although Stresemann was a nationalist, a stance essential to his effectiveness, the right denounced him for his conciliatory tone toward former enemies and for bringing Germany into the League of Nations.

Throughout this period of relative calm, the political extremes were growing at the expense of the center. When President Ebert died, in 1925, a rightist coalition elected General von Hindenburg as his successor, defeating the candidate supported by both the Center and the Social Democratic parties; significantly the two million votes drawn to the Communist nominee would have been sufficient to defeat Hindenburg. Moreover the elections of 1930 brought Adolf Hitler's National Socialists to prominence; the Weimar Republic was far from secure.

Democracy fared rather better during the 1920s in some of the smaller Continental countries than it did in Italy and the Weimar Republic. Belgium, despite the war's destruction and conflicts over language and religion, recaptured her place among Europe's most prosperous and freest countries. The tensions between Czechs and Slovaks did not prevent Czechoslovakia from remaining a model of democratic stability and economic growth. Although the Netherlands faced nationalist unrest in her colonies, especially the East Indies, such problems hardly threatened democratic institutions at home; and the Scandinavian countries, while often at odds among themselves, continued to find in liberal institutions the means to imaginative foreign and domestic programs. There (Norway, 1907; Denmark, 1914; Sweden, 1919) and in Great Britain, women's suffrage had not destroyed the family; nor had it cleansed politics, but it seemed a natural expansion of democracy. For Europe as a whole, however, the flood tide of constitutional government that had followed the war had clearly begun to ebb. Nevertheless, constitutional democracy was the political norm, and many were convinced that even the Soviet Union and Italy would in due time become more like their neighbors. Economic recovery had proved slower than expected and more difficult, but by the mid-1920s a general prosperity contributed to the electoral victories of moderate and conservative parties.

II. THE CULTURE OF UNCERTAINTY

There were concrete reasons for satisfaction as middle-class Europeans bought their first car, or looked forward to a paid vacation while many millions bought their first radio and flocked to the motion pictures. Intellectuals, too, shared a sense of excitement as cultural institutions—from brash, commercial ones to the more staid and formal ones—flourished. Yet the most stimulating new ideas tended to be disquieting, building on trends apparent in the decade or so before World War I. The new directions of Western thought—the ones we identify as central to twentieth-century intellectual history—cannot therefore be said simply to result from the experience of total war; yet the currents most characteristic of the new era—the radical departures in psychology, physics, and philosophy as well as in art and literature—do fit with and reinforce attitudes that the war made almost commonplace: a nightmare sense of shock at what modern societies might do, skepticism toward accepted pieties, and reliance on personal feeling as a guide to conduct more than on the formal beliefs of reason or religion. The criticisms of liberal society developed in the previous generation were turned with increased animus against the bourgeois complacency and prosperity of the postwar era. Literature and the arts seemed more than ever at odds with society and traditional norms of behavior, and this tension was disseminated (sometimes in popularized form) in print, on the radio, and in art, theater, and motion pictures.

Freudian Psychology

No figure of the period just before and after World War I disturbed established thinking so deeply as did Sigmund Freud. A Viennese physician whose clinical studies had taken him gradually from neurology to psychiatry, he followed the method—close and detailed observation—of medical science, and his theoretical statements are as careful in their internal consistency as in their literary elegance.

Freud had done his most important work before 1914, and in many ways he was old-fashioned. For the most part, he accepted as socially necessary the norms of behavior of the nineteenth-century middle class. He was deeply influenced by ideas of evolution, and his metaphors and assumptions betray the liberal economist's conception of man.[4] His interest in the phenomenon of hysteria, his use of hypnosis, and his first ideas of the unconscious had grown from the work of French doctors with whom he had studied, but it was his genius to synthesize his particular observations into a general theory, a universal statement about the human mind, that could be tested in practical application.

In treating neurotics Freud found that they often experienced relief of their symptoms by recalling under hypnosis events they had otherwise forgotten. He deduced that it is the recollection and not the hypnosis that is crucial, later adding that though the events remembered may not actually have happened, they are the psychic reality with which the patient has been living. The center of psychic forces in the unconscious he labeled the id. Here the basic desires universal among human beings (very similar to what were called instincts) seek satisfaction, and increasingly he found the most troublesome and psychologically significant desires to be sexual. The ego tries to channel and control these desires as it is directed to do by the superego, which, rather like the conscience in more traditional conceptions, expresses a person's socially conditioned sense of what is acceptable behavior. Thus mental life is marked by perpetual tension between the id and the superego.

Most of this conflict, which is uncomfortably mediated by the ego, is unconscious. Indeed one of the mind's techniques for dealing with the id is repression from consciousness of the id's desires. Repression, however, is an enormous strain that often finds outlet in neurotic behavior. As the patient comes to face and understand what is being repressed, his neurosis is relieved.

From this conception of the human psyche, Freud developed an elaborate and subtle theory.

---

[4] This point is superbly developed in Philip Rieff, *Freud, the Mind of the Moralist* (1961).

Although Freud's theories were intended to be universally valid, his consultation room in Vienna is unmistakably an expression of the European upper-middle class of the late nineteenth century. (Photo: Edmund Engelman)

It was a shocking one which ascribed sexual lusts to every person at every age. The idea of infant sexuality was especially offensive, but so was the notion of the Oedipus or Electra complex, the child's angry competition with the parent of the same gender whom the child has a guilt-ridden desire to kill in order to possess the parent of the opposite sex. Victorian convention could not tolerate this supposition, asserting that decent people have no such base desires. Freudian theory proclaimed such people merely the most repressed, considered religion the satisfaction of infantile and obsessive needs, and explored the greatest achievements in the arts in terms of sublimation, the diversion of the demands of the id to other and higher purposes. Psychoanalysis, the name Freud gave his body of theory and his therapeutic technique, calls on the analyst to pass no judgments but rather to help the patient discover and say things about himself that proper society holds to be quite simply unmentionable.

Freud's ideas encouraged a shift in aesthetic and intellectual perceptions. He had replaced hypnosis in treatment by free association, which allows the mind to make the connections it wishes by its own mysterious processes without the intervention of objective logic. He considered psychic reality to be as important as any other, and he discovered that dreams or slips of the tongue furnish significant signs of psychic conflict. Here was a rationale for taking dreams and fantasies as seriously as external events and for understanding both literature and life on several levels at once in terms of symbols and expressed purposes, conscious and unconscious ends. And Freud himself provided the model in essays that are persuasively organized, stylistically sensitive, and philosophically suggestive.

Implications of Freudian Theory

In the 1920s the broad implications of Freud's discoveries were beginning to gain wide public recognition. They were cited again and again as evidence of how close man remains to the primitive. If repression leads to neuroses, one extrapolation went, then greater sexual freedom and above all greater candor will produce healthier people. This remains perhaps the most widespread popular notion drawn from Freudian teaching, though it does not properly follow. Related to this is the belief that guilt is evil, a kind of Christian perversion of human nature. Freudian insights encouraged literary and personal introspection and supported the view that childhood is the most important phase of life. Although his theories stimulated new visions of a freer and happier life, Freud's dark conclusion was that "the price of progress in civilization is paid in forfeiting happiness." For civilization is based upon the repression of man's primitive and still very powerful drives, which at any moment might lead him to revolt; Freud feared the revolt he foresaw, and he died in 1939, driven into exile by Nazi anti-Semitism.

Freud and to a lesser extent his disciples developed his ideas with a wealth of examples and terminology, but psychoanalysis won more outrage than respectability during its creator's lifetime. Moreover, its followers strove with Freud to maintain the doctrine whole, treating deviations as heresies. Among these were the ideas of the Swiss C. G. Jung, who broke with Freud and developed the theory of the collective unconscious, a psychic inheritance shared by human beings everywhere and reflected especially in the symbols and rituals of religion. Jung's somewhat looser and more mystical perspectives have fascinated and influenced philosophers, theologians, and artists.

Indeed the concepts of psychoanalysis have been applied, often loosely, to works of art, periods of time, and whole civilizations. It may even be that Freudian procedures and theories have so changed behavior that they are less apposite now than when he formulated them. Only today in fact are systematic modifications of Freudian theory beginning to find acceptance.

The Humanities

Some artists in the postwar period—the Surrealists with their dreamlike canvases are an example—applied Freudian ideas directly, and in his manifesto of Surrealism (1924), the writer André Breton proclaimed the liberation of the subconscious. Quite independent of Freud, explorations of the irrational within the human mind and in society fairly exploded in prose and poetry. The novels of Proust, Kafka, and Joyce most clearly mark the change in style and content. Marcel Proust died in 1922, soon to be hailed as one of the great stylists of the French language. His long novel, *Remembrance of Things Past,* built an introverted and delicately detailed picture of upper-class Parisian life into a monumental and sensitive study of one man's quiet suffering which became a model of interior monologue, of the novel in which the subject is not action seen from the outside but feelings observed from within. Franz Kafka, who wrote in German though born in Prague, died in 1924, leaving instructions for his manuscripts to be burned. Instead, his works have come to be accepted as quintessentially modern, with their realistic and reasonable descriptions of fantasies that convey the torture of anxiety. In *The Trial* the narrator tells of his arrest, conviction, and execution on charges he can never discover, an exploration of the psychology of guilt that also seems to foreshadow the totalitarian state. James Joyce's international fame came with the publication of his novel, *Ulysses* (1922), the presentation on a mythic scale of a single day in the life of a modest Dubliner written in an exuberant, endlessly inventive game of words in which puns, clichés, parody, and poetry swirl in a dizzying stream of consciousness.

Not all of the most important writers turned away from objective, chronologically precise narrative. But even those who made use of more familiar techniques tended, like Thomas Mann in Germany, André Gide in France, and D. H. Lawrence in England, to explore topics and attitudes offensive to convention. Shock and offense seemed at times to be a form of creative expression. A movement called Dada that had originated during World War I put on displays, part theater and part art exhibition, of noisy nonsense and absurd juxtapositions to infuriate the Parisian bourgeoisie. Italian Futurists, who promised to build a new art appropriate to a technological age—"The world has been enriched by a new beauty: the beauty of speed"—balanced such positive feelings with a call to "Burn the libraries . . . demolish the venerated cities" in their manifesto of 1909. The Fauves in France and the Expressionists in Germany and Scandinavia gloried in their reputation for wildness in style, content, and conduct. Where more sober traditions prevailed, as in the carefully constructed, cerebral poetry of William Butler Yeats, pessimism and obscurity were still the elements most readily noted. In every language serious poetry as much as serious art and music became more difficult for the lay person to appreciate. Cubist and Expressionist painters, like composers using the twelve-tone scale and dissonance, deliberately eschewed the merely decorative or pleasant. The approaches that excited artists wove a frightening violence and amorality into their contemptuous disregard for tradition. Today we confidently admire works from this period as part of a continuous development, but to contemporaries the frenzied new forms were both a source and a voice of serious malaise. They also measured the widening chasm between the "serious," creative art of "high culture" and the popular culture most intellectuals disdained.

The philosopher most widely read in the 1920s was Oswald Spengler, whose *Decline of the West* appeared in 1918. Spengler treated whole civilizations as biological organisms, each with a life cycle of its own, but his book won fame less for its interesting method than for its prediction of the West's deterioration, a prediction that labeled the world war the beginning of the final act and considered the very institutions liberals had hailed as progress to be symptoms of decay. José Ortega y Gasset's *The Revolt of the Masses,* published in 1930, was hardly more optimistic. The masses, he feared, were destined as they rose in power to destroy the highest achievements of Western civilization. Other philosophers, like contemporary artists, made much of man's irrationality, and scores of minor works that were vaguely Nietzschean, religious, or determinist rained scorn on a vapid, directionless culture.

The most striking innovation in philosophy came, however, from another tradition entirely. It found its first major expression in the *Principia Mathematica* (1910), by Bertrand Russell and Alfred North Whitehead, a cornerstone of what has come to be called Analytic Philosophy. On the Continent a group known as the Vienna Circle developed a related system, Logical Positivism; and the work of Ludwig Wittgenstein, especially his *Tractatus Logico-Philosophicus* (1921), became a major influence on both schools of thought. Wittgenstein attempted in a series of numbered propositions "to set a limit to thought." He sought to define, in other words, the areas of thought in which certainty could be achieved and those in which it could not. According to Wittgenstein and others of his school, logicians and philosophers should concern themselves only with what is precise and demonstrable, and their methods, based on symbolic logic, should be analogous to mathematical reasoning. The principles and techniques of symbolic logic have come to dominate philosophy in the universities of Great Britain and the United States.

Like the earlier positivists, analytic philosophers consciously set about to learn from the methodology of the natural sciences, but what they stress is the lean language of mathematics rather than observation or experiment. The philosopher's task is to analyze every statement, stripping away connotations and values that may appeal but do not convey precise meaning. "My propositions," Wittgenstein concludes in the *Tractatus,* "serve as elucidations in the following way: anyone who understands me eventually recognizes them as nonsensical. . . . What we cannot speak about we must consign to silence." At its most radical, such an approach rejects from consideration most of the issues theologians and moral philosophers have argued for centuries as too imprecise to merit debate. Philosophy, like the other disciplines, was turning from matters of general interest to its own specialized tasks.

The Sciences

Science also had moved beyond the lay person's comprehension long before the Great War. Discoveries in the life and physical sciences were communicated and put to use with increasing rapidity, and those in one discipline were applied in related fields, often giving birth to new hybrids such as biochemistry and biophysics. Progress in these studies represented a harmonious if accelerated continuation of the work of centuries past. But from the realm of the older natural sciences came mystifying reports of theoretical advances that would upset several venerable certainties.

Relativity and the Nature of Matter

One line of investigation stemmed from an experiment by two Americans, Albert A. Michelson and Edward W. Morley, in 1887. It had been assumed that the universe was filled with a motionless substance called "ether," because waves of light (or waves of any kind) could not pass through an empty space. This motionless ether presumably also provided a base from which motions of all sorts in the universe could be measured. But Michelson and Morley showed that the speed of light rays emanating from the earth was the same whether the rays traveled in the direction of the earth's movement or against it (the expected result had been that rays would travel faster in the direction of the earth's movement). The implications of this discovery had been explored in a variety of ways over the following decade and a half; then in 1905 Albert Einstein proposed an answer in his first, or special, theory of relativity (his second, or general, theory of relativity, expanding the insights of the first, was announced in 1915). His mathematical formulations led to striking conclusions of the highest philosophical interest: space and time are not absolute but must be measured in relation to the observer; and they also may be considered, on the most fundamental levels, as aspects of a single continuum.

As Einstein developed his theory of relativity, physicists were also achieving a new understanding of matter. Here, a principal stimulus came from Wilhelm Roentgen's discovery of x-rays in 1895, which gave the first important insight into the world of subatomic particles. Within two years the English physicist J. J. Thomson showed the existence of the electron, the subatomic particle carrying a negative electrical charge. The atom was clearly not the basic unit of matter. By the turn of the century Pierre and Marie Curie among others had found radium and other materials to be radioactive; that is, these materials emitted both particles and a form of electromagnetic radiation. Soon, largely through the work of Ernest

Einstein's face remains one of the best known of the twentieth century, a symbol both of universal genius and of Jewish exile.
(Photo: © Karsh, Ottawa/Woodfin Camp and Associates)

Rutherford, radioactivity was identified with the breakdown of heavy and unstable atoms. The discovery that the atom was composed principally of electrically charged particles made it possible to link the structure of atoms with Dmitri Mendeleev's periodic table of elements (see Chapter 25). Elements which possessed chemically similar properties were also similar in their atomic structures. These important discoveries promised for a time to simplify and clarify the understanding of matter.

But continuing research soon revealed phenomena inexplicable in terms of Newtonian physics. In 1902 the German physicist Max Planck startled the scientific world with the announcement of the "quantum theory" of energy. Energy in the subatomic world was released or absorbed not in a continuous stream but in discrete, measurable, and apparently irreducible units, which Planck called quanta. Energy, in effect, possessed many of the properties of matter, and the theory implied that matter and energy might be interchangeable. Einstein later incorporated this insight into his theory of relativity, proposing the famous equation, $E = mc^2$. Energy, he concluded, is equivalent to mass times the square of the speed of light; at least in theory, small quantities of matter could be turned into enormous amounts of energy.

In 1919 Rutherford established that bombarding nitrogen with subatomic particles produced changes in the structure of the nitrogen atom. The ancient dream of the alchemists—the transmutation of one material into another—was now possible, although not in the ways the alchemists had envisioned. With accelerating rapidity, other atomic changes were produced in the laboratory, while the study of cosmic radiation related the structure of terrestrial matter to that found in the universe beyond.

By the mid-1920s, however, scientists contemplating the expanded knowledge of matter had to face troubling anomalies. Planck's quantum theory, though apparently verified in numerous experiments, assumed among other things that particles behave in probabilistic rather than absolutely regular patterns—a concept Einstein himself could never wholly accept. Furthermore, electromagnetic radiation, of which visible light is one form, had to be treated for some purposes as a flow of particles and for other purposes as a wave, that is, a disturbance of particles in a medium which does not cause an advance of the particles themselves. The German physicist Werner Heisenberg argued that no fixed model of the atoms of a given element was possible; only its approximate and likely structure could be described, through complex equations. In a few years matter had been found to consist mostly of empty space and not to behave with absolute regularity. Moreover, it proved impossible to measure simultaneously both the energy and the mass of a subatomic particle, because the measurement of one altered the apparent values of the other—a disturbing effect which Heisenberg appropriately named "the uncertainty principle." In the subatomic world, as in the stellar universe, the position and the purposes of the observer fundamentally affected what he observed.

Physicists who chose to philosophize about such matters now spoke in humbler and more tentative tones, describing the implications of abstract ideas more than a fixed reality. But the new theories, especially perhaps the discovery of a constant relationship between energy and mass, proved powerful tools. Physics became one of the most prestigious and highly organized (and most expensive) of human activities. Research uncovered new and special particles in bewildering number, leaving the baffled lay person apprised of merely the most publicized technological results: x-ray technology, television, the electron microscope, and eventually the controlled fission of atomic energy.

The majority of physicists lived fairly comfortably with the contradictions and incompleteness of their theories. Newtonian principles, they often insisted, still obtained in most cases, as solid and predictable as ever. But the Western world had long looked to the sciences for support of its philosophy and even its theology, and it suffered a sense of loss in learning that physical laws were relative and that the very scientists who manipulated them were uncertain about what an atom looked like or what a particle was. In the twentieth century no Voltaire could build a view of society on a popularized version of the now wholly specialized disciplines. Coupled with developments in astronomy, which grappled with innumerable universes in a potentially infinite reach of space, the revolution in the understanding of matter left the world a little less certain. Some, occasionally even physicists, argued for a new mysticism or a turning to religion for the kinds of answers no longer available from science.

The Biological and Social Sciences

There was no comparable revolution in the biological and social sciences, but advances in these fields were rapidly unveiling the mysteries surrounding the human condition. Heredity had come to be better understood with the rediscovery around 1900 of the theory put forth by Gregor Mendel, the abbot of a Silesian monastery, in 1866, which distinguished between dominant and recessive characteristics and showed how they were passed on from parents to offspring. The isolation of viruses, first achieved in the 1890s, continued at a more rapid pace; and a range of important new drugs was synthesized, most notably penicillin, discovered by Sir Alexander Fleming and Sir Howard Florey in 1928. Just before the war, Sir Frederick Gowland Hopkins had identified organic substances in food that were later named vitamins A, B, C, and D. The others were discovered in the 1920s and their functions identified, findings that have made a major contribution to human health.

The other behavioral sciences were not so radically transformed during this period as psychology was by Freudian thought, but the work of the two giants of modern sociology, the Frenchman Emile Durkheim and the German Max Weber, had begun to change their own and related disciplines. Although very different sorts of scholars, they shared a concern for finding systematic and objective approaches to the study of society, and questions of methodology have remained central to the social sciences since. Durkheim, following the positivist tradition, explored the power of statistical tools, particularly in his investigation of suicides; and Weber's concept of the "ideal type" as a special form of generalization has led to the wide use of theoretical models. Both probed the social functions of apparently irrational custom and stressed the importance of religion. Weber's classic *The Protestant Ethic and the Spirit of Capitalism,* like Durkheim's concept of anomie—the disoriented condition of society when group norms have broken down—reflect the importance they also assigned to shared values as a cohesive factor in society, the very condition many feared the twentieth century had lost.

Similar themes emerged during the 1920s in anthropology (the discipline that had benefited most from imperialism) and history, though both fields remained primarily empiricist. And the idealism of the Italian philosopher-historian Benedetto Croce also contributed to the assumption that the values of any society are relative to its time and place as well as to a broadening of the range of human behavior studied by social scientists.

The creative ferment of the 1920s seemed less troubling when it went hand in hand with technology. The public began to accept the architecture and applied design of Walter Gropius' Bauhaus school in Germany, with its emphasis on relating form to function, and the still more daring endeavors of Le Corbusier in France to envision the modern city. In motion pictures, just now winning credentials as an art form, the distortions of time and perspective through flashbacks and close-ups were less disturbing than when conveyed through words or on canvas. Even the frothiest romance or adventure story of the silent screen could express (and perhaps mold) subtle subliminal themes of social or national concern—characteristically, themes of abandonment in France, betrayal in Germany.[5] Only in this decade did Berlin ever rival Paris as an artistic center—proof of the benefits of democracy, one might argue—but intellectuals generally expressed doubts about the future of Western civilization.

That the values of Western culture were changing few denied by the late 1920s. The recognition of man's irrationality, the new scientific knowledge, and the violence that could accompany popular participation in public life were all threatening; the arts and philosophy as well as science had not only moved beyond the average man's understanding but had in large measure rejected traditional assumptions and beliefs. In essays and sermons the public was warned of a crisis of values that neither art nor science could help, a crisis apparently related to the materialism of capitalism, the dull legalism of liberal forms, and the empty gentility of the middle class.

III. THE GREAT DEPRESSION

Europe's Economic Vulnerability

Disturbing though they were, the attacks on familiar conceptions in the realms of the creative arts and natural phenomena did not unduly alarm the average European. His daily life was secure from war and generally from want; a world of democratic nations at peace seemed to have achieved an impressive prosperity. The major nations reestablished prewar ratios between their currencies and gold, and productivity surpassed prewar levels. Then in October 1929 the American stock market crashed, inaugurating the most severe, widespread, and long-lasting of depressions in the modern history of the West. The gaps in postwar recovery were suddenly exposed, and waves of misery and instability challenged Western society and mocked liberal visions.

The dislocations of war—the destruction of plants, shifts of capital, and movements of men—had been accentuated by sudden demobilization and then by economic development itself. Not all wartime industries had been able to convert to peacetime enterprises nor all workers to regain their jobs; the prosperity of the 1920s rested heavily on new processes and on new products such as automobiles and synthetic fabrics, so that significant sectors of manufacturing declined. Italy and Great Britain, whose coal and textile industries had entered even before the war into a period of chronic depression, never fully shared in the postwar boom. Large industrial combines, closely tied to money markets, controlled concomitantly sizable shares of overall production and employment, restricting the diversification of businesses across the economic base. More people, men and women, worked in service activities such as sales and distribution that were susceptible to cutbacks.

This economic fragility was underscored by certain long-term trends. Old trade patterns had not revived. Goods traveled less freely within Europe, particularly the East, where debt-ridden and underdeveloped new countries—their industries often separated by national boundaries from traditional sources of capital—forced trade to find new routes. Germany's inflation as well as Russia's withdrawal from commerce had increased these difficulties, which had been only partly offset by industrialization in the new states and assistance from the League of Nations.

Moreover Europe did not regain its prewar percentage (about half) of world trade; its firms had lost many of their overseas markets to competitors, especially American, during the war. So also with foreign investments: Britain had lost a quarter of her $18 billion, France half of her nearly $9 billion (primarily in Russia),

---

[5] Paul Monaco develops this view in *Cinema & Society: France and Germany During the Twenties* (1976).

and Germany all of her $6 billion. American investments in Europe on the other hand had multiplied seven and a half times in seven years to reach $15 billion in 1920, and they continued to rise thereafter. Furthermore a dangerous part of Europe's apparent prosperity rested on the unproductive passing of paper from the United States to Germany as loans, from Germany to the Allies as reparations, and from the Allies to the United States as payment for war debts. The United States not only dominated world trade and demanded payment of war debts but raised tariffs in 1922 and again in 1930 to levels that made it nearly impossible for Europeans to earn dollars by selling goods to her.

The turmoil in Eastern Europe and Russia had led to increased imports of grain from Canada and the United States, where more land was turned to wheat and improved technology brought larger yields. By 1925 Europe's agricultural production had recovered, but only to face a glutted market and sluggish demand due to reduced population growth and the preference for meat over grains that accompanied rising standards of living. Agricultural surpluses became a problem throughout the West that drove down prices and pushed governments to increase subsidies and tariffs. Demographic patterns added other strains. Population expansion was considerable only in Eastern and Southern Europe, but new policies in the countries of immigration, especially the United States, discriminated against nationals from just those countries where overpopulation was critical. Overseas migration slowed to a trickle while pressures of numbers built up.

The war and the disruptions of the postwar years had made people as well as economies less resilient. The demographic deficit because of casualties and a low birth rate had left the population in Western Europe somewhat older and more dependent on pensions. The trauma of war had been followed by the shocks of instability, inflation, and unreliable currencies. Those whose social status depended on savings, pensions, or salaries, especially in Germany, faced poverty in the early 1920s while those who owned real property or industry went on to greater wealth. Debtors benefited while creditors were ruined, and the sense of insecurity was never wholly lost even in the good times of 1924–1929.

From Panic to Depression

Such dislocations did not slow the economy of the United States, now the world's wealthiest nation. Speculation in stocks and real estate had been running wild, driving purchase prices unreasonably high. Then suddenly, on October 24, 1929—the notorious "Black Tuesday" of American financial history—the price of stocks on the New York Exchange began to plummet. The crash was partially precipitated by the British decision to raise interest rates in order to bring back capital that had flowed to America, but it was more deeply rooted in the growing uneasiness among investors that the speculative inflation of stock prices had gone too far. Day after day tens of millions of dollars in paper assets disappeared. Such panics were not new to capitalism, and on several occasions in the previous century a collapse of the New York market had spread to Europe. But in the next few months the financial panic settled into full-scale depression. Banks had invested heavily in stocks and real estate, and some failed, causing runs on others. Businesses cut back, consumption declined, capital became more scarce, factories closed, and unemployment rose.

The crisis in the United States was soon felt abroad. European banks and exchanges were immediately shaken; more gradually world trade declined, and the American government and businessmen began to call in their investments and loans. At first, however, it seemed that the panic might be kept from affecting the entire European economy. Then in May 1931 the Austrian bank that held two-thirds of the nation's assets nearly went under, and this precipitated a run on Austrian and German banks that spread the now familiar cycle to other sectors of the economy and to other nations.

By 1932 the world's industrial production was two-thirds of what it had been three years before. Unemployment climbed to more than 13 million in the United States, 6 million in Germany, and nearly 3 million in Great Britain. Among leading industrial nations only France, with her balanced economy, demographic stability, and relative scarcity of labor, escaped unemployment of crisis proportions.

Statesmen hoped that tested techniques of international cooperation could prevent economic disaster. One major problem disturbing financial relationships was that of war debts and German reparations. France and England maintained that they could pay their debts to the United States only if they received reparations from Germany. Although successive conferences and the Dawes and Young plans had evolved a workable system for the payment of reparations, this system too broke down amid the world economic crisis. The United States had never admitted a connection between reparations and war debts, but President Hoover's proposal in 1931 that all intergovernment debts be suspended was quickly accepted (most European states were already making only token payments, and France had defaulted). Meeting at Lausanne in 1932 the European powers in effect agreed to abandon reparations altogether. Although the moratorium originally proposed by Hoover was supposed to be

The Dole—a government clerk, from behind the desks of officialdom, hands out checks to some of Britain's unemployed.
(Photo: The Bettmann Archive)

temporary, any hope that the debts or reparations would ever be paid had become an illusion.

When Austria's major bank teetered on the edge of bankruptcy in May 1931, threatening all Central European finances, it had been saved by British loans. Amid the deepening Depression, this and other financial burdens forced Great Britain to abandon the gold standard, no longer guaranteeing that pounds could be converted into gold at a fixed rate. The important bloc of countries trading in sterling quickly followed suit. This was tantamount to devaluation, as the value of the pound fell at once below the former, officially supported exchange rate with gold. Devaluation of this principal currency in turn threatened to throw international monetary exchanges, and the trade dependent upon them, into chaos.

But international understanding might once more prevent others from rushing to devaluate. To that end the League of Nations sponsored a World Economic Conference that met in London in 1933. Begun with visions of high statesmanship, it ended in failure. Debts to the United States were removed from the agenda at American insistence, and no agreements for reducing tariffs could be reached until international exchange rates were stabilized.

When the United States too went off the gold standard, an elaborate structure of credit and exchange that had been one of the signal achievements of liberal finance fell. France was the last major country to abandon gold. Less dependent on international trade, hit later and less suddenly by the Depression, and strongly attached to the traditions of stable finance, she resisted until 1936. A historic era in which nations, like so many bankers, supported international financial stability by honoring the laws of liberal economics had ended.[6]

---

[6] Karl Polanyi has elaborated the significance of the abandonment of the gold standard in a famous essay, "The Great Transformation: The Political and Economic Origins of Our Time."

National Policies

The interrelationship between politics and economics had come to be well understood in the nineteenth century; but whereas tariffs and taxes were acknowledged to be political issues, most governments had wished to leave large spheres of economic activity alone. During World War I, however, governments were forced to direct much of the economy, and in the following years issues of reconstruction, reparations, and currencies had drawn them more deeply into economic activity. Business increasingly turned to the state for assistance, and voters who had witnessed the miracles of wartime mobilization expected the state to lead them out of the Depression. By the early 1930s it was clear that each government had to act on its own to save its national economy.

On the whole, however, the measures taken had the effect of sinking the West deeper into the Depression. Austria and Germany in 1931 proposed a customs union, but French opposition led the World Court to forbid the step. Instead, nearly everywhere tariff barriers rose higher and import quotas were gradually extended to more and more items. The effect was a still further reduction in trade. Domestic programs varied, but the tendency was to protect interests that were politically strong, to shore up inefficient industries, and to support uncompetitive sectors of the economy—measures that slowed lasting recovery.

Such policies violated accepted economic precepts, but liberals were at a loss as to what else to do. Nor were socialists better prepared to solve the problems of declining commerce, insufficient capital, and unemployment, though they displayed a certain satisfaction at this new evidence of capitalism's weakness. They had a part in the governments of Germany, Austria, Sweden, Czechoslovakia, and Great Britain and were a leading force in most other countries; but their favorite nostrum, the nationalization of industry, was barely relevant. In practice socialists showed again the extent to which they had absorbed the orthodoxies of classical economics. They too usually thought governments had to reduce their budgets and ensure that exports exceeded imports. At the same time Socialist parties, closely tied to labor unions, supported whatever palliatives for unemployment could be suggested, though the dole, the most common one, strained the budgets they wanted to see balanced. As liberals and socialists tried one new measure after another, they were embarrassed by growing Communist parties, which let no one forget that while a whole system had been collapsing, Russian production had been advancing at a steady pace.

Gradually, conditions did improve. By 1937 production in Germany, Britain, and Sweden was well above the 1929 level of each, though it remained below that mark in the United States, Italy, Belgium, and France. Technological progress continued, and government intervention changed both economic and political life. But these changes were as socially divisive as the Depression itself, and the democracies that had dominated Europe faced the double threat of communism and fascism with a heavy burden of failure.

In 1919 much of Europe had been in the throes of revolution; yet the Western powers led the way to reasonable stability. New nations and a world order were created in their image, looking to democratic constitutions and the League of Nations as the means of organizing power. Despite the effects of war, social turmoil, and inflation, the new European order seemed by 1924 on its way to increased freedom and prosperity. Within a few years these achievements and the optimism that accompanied them were overshadowed by the calamity of the Depression. Liberal ideas and institutions appeared to be losing their capacity to deal with such problems as Europe was now facing, and the hopes of the 1920s quickly seemed foolish.

In retrospect the failures became clear. Britain, France, and Germany in their different ways had turned to cautious domestic policies that postponed rather than met the deepest social and economic issues. In less wealthy nations constitutions that did little to resolve conflicts of class and nationality were soon violated, while very different regimes in Russia and Italy moved with welcome dispatch. The League and the World Court showed themselves clearly most effective when the interests of no major power were at stake. Laborious negotiations for disarmament and monetary controls were often overrun by events, and the guardians of stability maintained their military forces while talking of reducing them and abandoned the gold standard while proclaiming its importance.

Individual liberty, democracy, and international law had seemed deeply rooted in Western culture when reaffirmed in the ruins of war; but those roots were not strengthened by the intellectual life of the 1920s, which turned inward to academic specialization or directly affronted the rationalism and genteel inhibitions on which bourgeois society was thought to rest. Those values, like capitalism itself, remained strong, but they would stand on the defensive throughout the next decade.

RECOMMENDED READING

Studies

★Carr, E. H. *The Twenty Years' Crisis, 1919–1939*. A balanced account that captures the sense of failure.

★Craig, Gordon A., and Felix Gilbert (eds.). *The Diplomats, 1919–1939*. 1965. Separate essays on major figures uncover the connection between international relations and domestic affairs.

★Galbraith, John K. *The Great Crash: 1929*. 1955. A pungent, dramatic account focused on the United States.

★Gamov, George. *Thirty Years That Shook Physics*. 1966. A leading physicist, Gamov is also an able popularizer.

Gay, Peter. *Weimar Culture: The Outsider as Insider*. 1968. Sensitively explores the insecurity within German culture even in a period of great creativity.

Gerschenkron, Alexander. *Bread and Democracy in Germany*. 1943. Emphasizes the ties between economics and politics in Germany.

★Graves, Robert, and Alan Hodge. *The Long Weekend: A Social History of Great Britain, 1918–1939*. 1963. A poet and a scholar recapture the feel of daily life among the middle classes.

★Greene, Nathaniel. *From Versailles to Vichy: The Third Republic, 1919–1940*. 1970. Balanced coverage of the interwar period.

★Hartnack, Justus. *Wittgenstein and Modern Philosophy*. Maurice Cranston (tr.). 1965. A good introduction to the topic.

★Jones, Ernest. *The Life and Work of Sigmund Freud*. Lionel Trilling and Steven Marcus (eds.). 1961. One of the best of many biographies, which studies the ideas of psychoanalysis as well as the movement that developed.

★Kahler, Erich. *The Tower and the Abyss*. 1967. Uses his learned understanding of the arts across Europe to discern the elements of decay in contemporary culture.

Kindleberger, Charles P. *The World in Depression*. 1973. A clear account of how the Depression spread and affected the world economy.

Lyttleton, Adrian. *The Seizure of Power: Fascism in Italy, 1919–1929*. 1973. The best study in English of the complicated process that brought Fascism to power.

Maier, Charles S. *Recasting Bourgeois Europe: Stabilization in France, Germany, and Italy in the Decade After World War I*. 1975. Uses the details of economic policy and political conflict to show the period as one of bourgeois defensiveness.

★Robbins, Lionel. *The Great Depression*. 1934. A distinguished British economist views the depression he has just experienced.

★Rogger, Hans, and Eugen Weber (eds.). *The European Right: A Historical Profile*. 1965. Separate chapters delineate the formation and political role in various European countries of the increasingly vigorous right.

★Rothschild, John. *East Central Europe Between the Two World Wars*. 1973. Now the best survey of the area in its critical era of independence.

Schuker, Stephen A. *The End of French Predominance in Europe*. 1976. Analyzes the diplomacy, domestic relations, and international finance that led to the Dawes Plan and efforts to deal with reparations.

★Sontag, Raymond J. *A Broken World, 1919–1939*. 1971. A senior historian's contribution to the best historical series on modern Europe.

★Stern, Fritz. *The Politics of Cultural Despair: A Study in the Use of the Germanic Ideology*. 1961. Focuses on three figures to assess the impact on politics of cultural attitudes.

★Taylor, A. J. P. *English History 1914–1945*. 1965. A wide-ranging survey by an able and provocative historian.

★Wolfers, Arnold. *Britain and France Between the Two Wars*. 1966. Traces in the relations between these two democracies the breakdown of the international system established at Versailles.

★ Available in paperback.

28

TOTALITARIANISM TRIUMPHANT AND WORLD WAR II 1924–1941

Democracy was in retreat within less than a decade after the Paris Peace Conference. By 1929 authoritarian regimes had violated or eliminated the liberal constitutions of Hungary, Spain, Albania, Portugal, Lithuania, Poland, and Yugoslavia as well as Italy. By 1936 political liberty had been suppressed in Rumania, Austria, Bulgaria, Estonia, Latvia, and Greece as well as Germany. Most of these countries were among the poorest in Europe, but their political difficulties illustrate the broader trend. Divided over issues of social reform, nationality, and religion, they suffered increased disruption with each economic crisis and foreign threat.

As the newer and poorer nations abandoned democratic forms of government, they were drawn to the political experiment unfolding in Italy, where fascism promised to mobilize all society and to combine mass politics and industrialization with stability and order. Fascist groups appeared throughout Europe, and in Germany the most radically violent of these movements took power. Fascism, which fed on all the tensions of postwar society, presented itself as the only alternative to communism and benefited from widespread fear of a radical left that was itself galvanized by admiration for the Soviet Union. In Russia, however, the effort to restructure a whole society rapidly led to comparable techniques of rule. Twentieth-century ideologies, the potentialities of industrial society, and the strains of social change had generated a new political form: totalitarianism.

Even in the prosperity of the 1920s, the great democracies of the West had had difficulty finding consistent policies to meet domestic demands for social justice or the threatening problems of international relations. The stock market crash of 1929 developed into the worst depression of modern history and created an economic disaster of a magnitude that free governments did not know how to repair. The social and ideological divisions within the Western democracies were only deepened by direct challenge from Germany and Italy and the more indirect challenge from the U.S.S.R. From 1935 to 1939 the fascist states maintained the initiative in a series of mounting diplomatic crises. By 1939 those crises produced a war that Britain and France had desperately tried to avoid and for which Germany was psychologically and militarily far better prepared. Germany and her allies marched from conquest to conquest until they controlled the Continent by the end of 1941, when Russia and the United States were forced to fight at Britain's side.

I. THE RETREAT FROM DEMOCRACY

The transition to an authoritarian regime usually won support from at least three groups. The army, concerned about external threats and domestic turmoil, favored a strong government. A second, more amorphous group of middle-class politicians and influential religious leaders, fearful of socialism, supported authoritarian rule to preserve established institutions. Often they formed Catholic parties that combined rural reform with traditionalism, distrusting democratic politics and the urban masses. Liberalism, they warned, had unleashed attacks on religion and opened the door to socialism. Nationalists were a third and overlapping element, who demanded a strong state to right old defeats, appealed to people in all social classes who felt themselves victimized by recent change, and yet (like the military) wanted industry to grow. Each of these groups thus sought selective modernization, controlled change along lines that would not threaten its own influence.

The sacrifice of parliamentary government was merely the first step. Authoritarian regimes also needed some popular support and soon found themselves at odds with various established interests, often the very conservatives who had brought them to power. Thus while some regimes adopted fascist techniques, others returned in the late 1930s to a limited constitutionalism. The political turmoil that accompanied both solutions was an important part of the crises leading to World War II.

Authoritarian Governments

Hungary had turned to authoritarian rule relatively early, preserving the façade of constitutional institutions and relying heavily on the support of traditionally conservative groups. The Magyar aristocracy used a rigged electoral system to maintain its political dominance, protect its privileges, and stifle land reform. Ardent opponents of the Paris treaties, Hungary's leaders had drawn closer to Italy. Admiral Horthy, who had become head of state in 1920, kept that office, but monarchists and fascists put successive cabinets under severe pressure. As the Depression reached Hungary, fascist trappings increased, and successive governments became more anti-Semitic, restricting the number of Jews permitted in business or the professions. Hungary would be quick to take what territory Hitler's policy in Eastern Europe permitted yet wary of German and Italian plans. Because the older aristocracy retained considerable influence, Hungary never became a full-fledged modern dictatorship and belatedly even dissolved some fascist parties in 1939.

In Poland domestic political divisions were complicated by the fact of powerful neighbors, and Poles disagreed on whether their national interest lay with Germany, Russia, or France. Socialists and Catholics, conservative landowners and radical peasants all had political strength, and the resulting instability had brought Marshal Józef Pilsudski to the fore. The marshal, a former Socialist, had taken power in 1926 with the aid of a military revolt. One of his followers had then been voted into the presidency while Pilsudski had served as premier; and though he had resigned after defeats at the polls in 1928, his supporters managed by persecuting the opposition to assure safer elections in the future.

From 1930 on Poland was ruled by men from the military. Constitutional changes in 1935 granted the president increased authority and gave the government a voice in the nomination of parliamentary candidates. Securely in power despite Pilsudski's death, in 1935, Poland's military men strove valiantly to strengthen a nation badly hurt by the Depression and threatened by both Russia and Germany. The noisy conflicts of fascists and socialists, however, measured the regime's failure to establish a firm popular base.

When the monarchs of Eastern Europe attempted authoritarianism, they often flirted with fascism, only to find the game so dangerous to the retention of their rule that they returned to more constitutional forms of government. In Yugoslavia Alexander I, who had ascended the throne of the new kingdom in 1921, had assumed dictatorial powers in 1929 in an effort to tame the divisive forces of Croatian, Slovenian, and Serbian nationalism. But as these conflicts continued, he tried a restricted parliamentarianism. After his death in 1934, the regent, Prince Paul, pursued a similar course: drawn at first to Germany and Italy, he decided by 1939 that Yugoslavia's international position and internal stability would best be served by a federal and democratic system. In Bulgaria a military coup ended parliament, parties, and free speech in 1934, and the regime moved closer to fascism as it sought both urban and rural support. But by 1936 the king was restricting the military, banning some fascist groups, and talking of constitutions.

Rumania's liberal government had begun to give way late in the 1920s before pressures from her ruling classes. Carol II, called to the throne in 1930, was an admirer of Mussolini's, and he secretly subsidized the Iron Guard, a fascist organization whose political violence and anti-Semitism imitated the worst of fascism elsewhere. In seeking popularity Carol's government became more extreme; the imposition of martial law and tight censorship was followed by an anti-Semitic campaign that stripped most Jews of land and citizenship. These policies, however, proved disruptive and brought protests from Britain and France, and by 1938 the king was leading the way in suppressing fascist activities and attempting to make a new constitution work.

The Trend to Fascism

The appeal of fascism was not limited to poor nations without parliamentary traditions. In Britain Sir Oswald Moseley, once considered a likely Labour prime minister, founded the British Union of Fascists. In Belgium fascism benefited from the antagonism between Catholics and anticlericals and between Walloons and Flemings. The Flemish speakers thought of themselves as a deprived group, dominated by the French-speaking Walloons in business, church, and government. Largely rural and conservative, the Flemings came to feel considerable sympathy for fascism and especially for the Nazis, whose language was close to their own. In the Netherlands also a National Socialist movement rose to prominence in the 1930s.

There were a number of fascist movements in France, of which the *Action Française* had the longest history and broadest influence. It reached prominence in the furor of the Dreyfus case, but remained primarily an intellectual movement aimed especially at monarchists and Catholics. Under the editorship of Charles Maurras, the *Action Française* maintained a biting critique of the bourgeois republic and developed doctrines useful to fascist parties everywhere. *Action Française* failed to achieve the common touch of the most successful fascist groups, and its conflicts with the papacy helped to restrict its effectiveness. But it served as an important bridge between disaffected rightists and the uniformed young militants who filled the streets of Europe in the 1930s.

The Greek and Austrian Republics

The republican government of Greece proved particularly vulnerable to fascism. Eleutherios Venizelos, the leader of the nation's liberals, dominated the republic's brief life, which lasted little more than a decade from its founding in 1924. Yet his party had been gradually losing ground to the monarchists even before the Depression deprived Greece of vital agricultural markets and forced Venizelos to resign in 1932. Republicans attempted a coup to ward off the restoration of the monarchy, but it was defeated, and a manipulated plebescite brought King George II back to the throne in 1935. When Liberals made gains in the 1936 elections, General Joannes Metaxas proclaimed himself dictator. He then clung to power in fascist style by balancing severe censorship and the abolition of political parties with extensive social welfare, public works, and armament.

In Austria the sharp division between a Catholic German countryside and a cosmopolitan imperial Vienna without an empire to administer undermined the republic. The Socialists, out of power since 1926, had little strength beyond the city, while the Christian Socialists, whose nineteenth-century programs of welfare, nationalism, and anti-Semitism had influenced the young Hitler, moved steadily toward fascism. In the 1920s each party had established its own paramilitary organization, and their violent clashes became a regular part of Austrian politics. Within the Christian Socialist party, older Catholic politicians vied for influence with German nationalists and the party army.

Prohibited by the Western powers from economic union with Germany as well as the Anschluss—the political "consolidation" desired by Nazis and others on both sides of the frontier—Austria survived financially after 1931 through foreign loans. Chancellor Engelbert Dollfuss drew Austria closer to Italy and ruled by decree, suspending parliament, outlawing communists, and banning party uniforms (a measure aimed at the Austrian Nazis). In 1934 all parties except those in the Fatherland Front, which supported Dollfuss, were abolished. The Socialists called a general strike, and the government responded as for war. When the army bombarded Karl Marx Hof, the public housing that Viennese Socialists had been so proud of, that act symbolized the end of Austrian democracy.

A new constitution, elaborately corporative and claiming direct inspiration from papal encyclicals, was announced in 1934 but never really put into operation, and a concordat gave the Roman Catholic Church control of Austrian education. Austria's Nazis, however, remained dissatisfied, and in July a group of them assassinated the chancellor. They expected the Anschluss to follow, but a quick movement of Italian and Yugoslav troops to the frontier prevented it. For the next few years, Austria depended on Italian support, and Kurt von Schuschnigg, Dollfuss's successor, maintained a relatively mild dictatorship as he attempted to dominate the sordid squabbles for leadership within the Fatherland Front. Having destroyed the left, Austria's authoritarian government had little basis from which to resist the growing Nazi pressure.

Dictatorship and the Spanish Republic

Alfonso XIII had kept Spain neutral in World War I, sparing her the direct ravages of war. But political and economic frictions were building toward a civil war that broke out in 1936.

Long before that date Spain's political system had begun to break down and her economy to suffer from the lack of capital investment and unresolved problems of land tenure. In Catalonia, the center of commercial and industrial activity, a vigorous regionalist movement flourished, drawing together various groups that opposed Madrid's policies. The army, overstaffed with ambitious officers, became increasingly active in politics; and discontented workers, divided among anarchists, socialists, and a faction soon to be called communist, staged frequent strikes that often ended in violence.

It was thus a strife-torn nation whose army in 1921 had been routed while attempting to subdue the Riffs, Berber tribes of Spanish Morocco. In the process Spain lost most of the territory she had acquired since 1909, and an embarrassed government had promised a full report, apprehensively awaited by the army. Just before it was due, in 1923, General Miguel Primo de Rivera issued a *pronunciamento* in

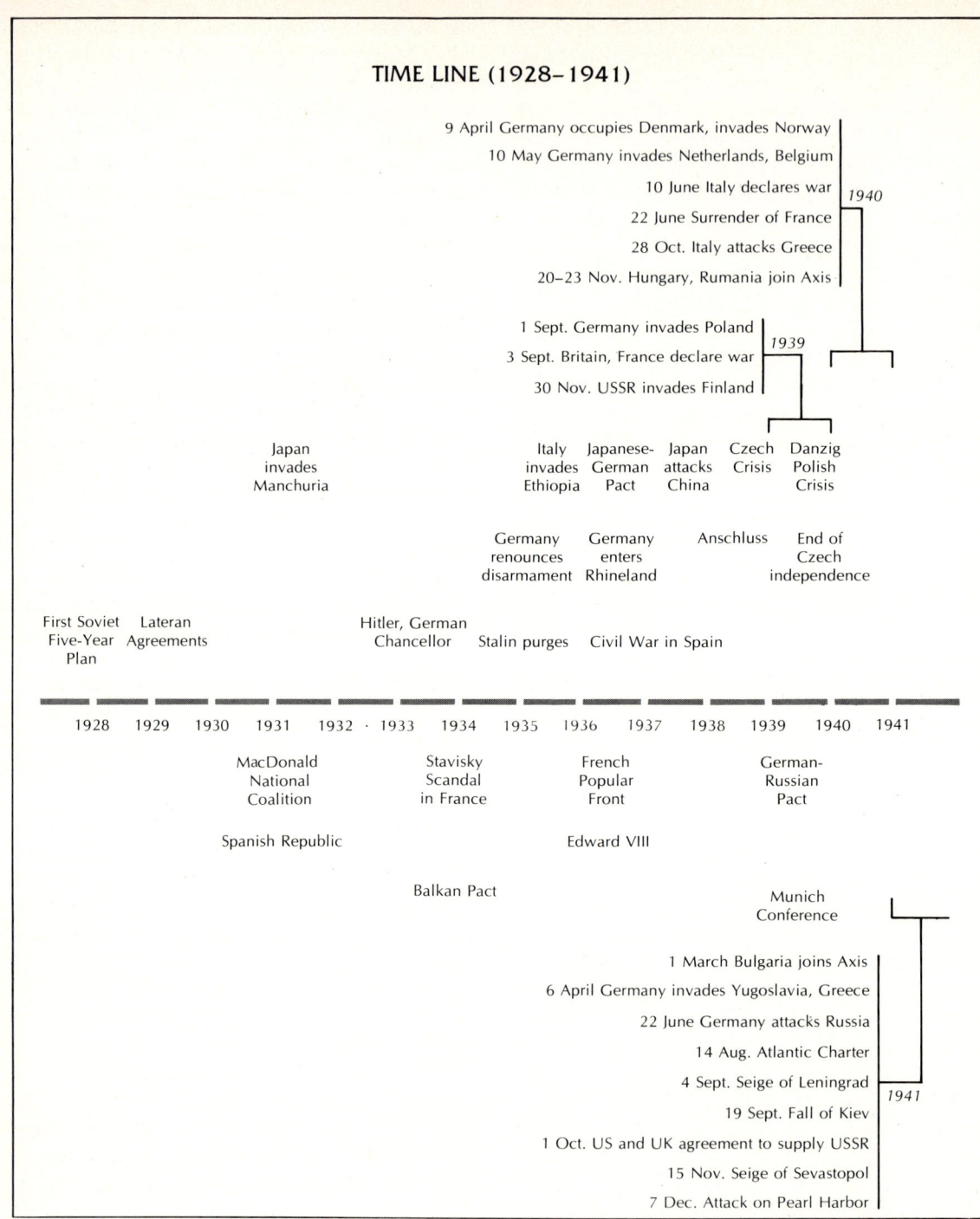

time-honored style and forced the king to appoint him prime minister—an office he assumed as de facto dictator.

Although he began without a clear program, Primo de Rivera used the themes of modern anti-liberalism to denounce soulless materialism and petty politics. With Mussolinian techniques he built his personal prestige, assuaged the complaints of socialists and further divided the left with extensive welfare programs, and established a political party of his own. By 1926 the regime was able to claim a number of accomplishments. It had defeated the Riffs, albeit with help from France, and it had made extensive use of expert engineers and economists and adopted a corporative code, giving its domestic program a progressive flavor.

Nevertheless the dictator's simplicity and candor had begun to lose their charm; his censorship antagonized intellectuals, threats of state ownership frightened business, and the government's propensity for meddling worried both church and army. When a constituent assembly proposed not merely a corporative legislature but a kind of fascist council of ministers that the king could not dissolve, Alfonso lost his taste for imitations of Mussolini. As the Depression began to be felt in Spain, Primo de Rivera's government faltered, and in 1930 he went into exile, where he died a few months later. The king now presented himself as the protector of traditional liberties and appointed as prime minister another general, this one old and cautious enough to alarm no one. Spain's government tried both martial law and the promise of constitutionalism, but all the old problems remained. When republicans and socialists scored impressive victories in the municipal elections of 1931, Alfonso also chose exile.

The second Spanish republic represented a democratic revival. Under the republican leader, Manuel Azaña, a government of the left tried to hold its divergent supporters together with progressive labor legislation and welfare programs, but these measures were ill-adapted to Spain's economic and social structure. Granting Catalonia autonomy, one of its most successful decisions, did not end regional conflicts, and land reform based more on general principles than on specific conditions proved difficult to administer. The separation of church and state and the secularization of education infuriated half of Spain without satisfying anticlericals, many of whom continued to practice independent harassment of religious institutions and activities. Elections in 1933 installed a more conservative government with more traditional policies, but the left drew together in the popular front which triumphed in the elections of 1936.

For the five years of the republic's struggle to survive, the left had grown more radical, and antirepublicans had been preparing action of their own. A movement called the Falange had been founded by José Antonio Primo de Rivera, the dictator's son, in direct imitation of Italian Fascism; and systematic street violence was commonplace by 1936, when a group of generals announced their revolt. The Spanish Civil War, which followed, was seen from the first as part of the European battle between the fascist right and the Marxist left. The insurgent officers counted on support from Italy, Germany, and Portugal, where Antonio de Oliveira Salazar had already established his dominance over a single-party, corporative, conservative, and Catholic state.

The Common Pattern

Whether they won power or not, Europe's fascist movements had much in common. They denounced liberalism and capitalism and coopted the socialist claim of representing a revolutionary movement. Fascists flexibly snatched every opportunity to discredit existing governments while combining a very modern mass appeal with important conservative backing. They spoke especially to elements of the populace that felt threatened by the current of change: men of religion threatened by a secular state, businessmen threatened by government intervention, a middle class threatened by socialism, rural society threatened by urbanization, the privileged threatened by democracy, workers threatened by unemployment, everyone threatened by the Depression.

They called on the spirit of nationalism, promising a state united in common purpose without petty politics or class conflict, and they played on a kind of nostalgia for the enthusiastic patriotism of World War I. Admirers of technology and organization, fascists presented themselves as the only alternative to Marxist revolution, and they sanctioned violence as the honest tool necessary for overcoming tradition and habit.

Corporatism as a theory had a long intellectual history. In its modern version it advocated the organization of political life in terms of occupations, grouping people by trade or industry. A society so structured, the argument went, would preserve natural hierarchies while avoiding the divisiveness characteristic of parliamentary systems, which amplified differences of class and ideology; this vision of social integration gained attractiveness during the Depression. Moreover in 1931, the fortieth anniversary of Leo XIII's *Rerum Novarum*, Pope Pius XI issued another influential social encyclical, *Quadragesimo Anno* ("In the Fortieth Year"). It went further in rejecting both the injustices of capitalism and the solutions of Marxism, calling instead for a harmonious society based on religion and cooperation through corporative organization. Many anxious people found in that papal pronouncement a sympathy for fascism that seemed to justify overlooking its deeply antireligious quality. Few European societies could wholly resist the multiple appeal and simple solutions of fascism.

II. TOTALITARIANISM

Dictatorship has been recognized since ancient times as one means of maintaining political order, but the effort to create totalitarian societies has been a twentieth-century phenomenon.[1] In Italy, Germany, and Russia, a single party, mass communications, economic control, and force were combined with an official revolutionary ideology in an overwhelming drive to create a new state, highly industrialized but monolithic. With the aim of unanimity, totalitarian governments set new standards of oppression, making terror a tool of power and crushing their "enemies," whom they labeled as such not merely for public acts, but simply for belonging to certain groups, which might be defined in terms of race, occupation, region, religion, or artistic taste.

In practice none of the totalitarian regimes fully realized its goals. Italian Fascism evolved relatively slowly and never achieved the social control or demonic power of Nazi Germany, and although German and Italian totalitarianism borrowed much from the communism they abhorred, they remained significantly different in values and policy from the Bolsheviks, who sought to transform an entire economy and all its social institutions. Fascist and Nazi rule tried instead to use existing structures, working with the business community, the bureaucracy, and the army. Beneath their radical claims lay a grudging respect for the established interests that helped them to power.

Fascist Italy

A series of special laws passed by 1926 assured Mussolini's control of power in Italy. The Duce

---

[1] Scholars agree that Hitler's Germany and Stalin's Russia were totalitarian, but some consider the differences between those regimes more important than their similarities. Many of those who find totalitarianism a useful term also include Fascist Italy while others object that it was too inefficient and mild. A few would extend the term to Franco's Spain and to other single-party dictatorial or fascist states.

("leader") of Fascism was declared head of state and granted the right to determine the Chamber's agenda and to govern by decree. For twenty years nearly all the laws of Italy would be issued in that way. Opposition parties were outlawed, scores of potential opponents arrested, and the civil service and judiciary purged of unreliable men.

Mussolini had a rare gift for propaganda, and Italy's newspapers were filled with unsmiling pictures of him, always in poses of command—awing visitors, captivating vast throngs, leaping hurdles on horseback, flying airplanes, harvesting grain. No story was too silly to be circulated for some effect: the Duce recited the cantos of Dante from memory; he worked all night (the light in his office was carefully left on); he inspired philosophers and instructed economists; American razor blades were inadequate to the toughness of his beard; his speed in race cars frightened experts; his stern but tender love for his subjects knew no bounds. Neither did the audacity or vulgarity of such propaganda. Disseminated day after day, it appeared to work, for Mussolini and Fascism were gradually placed beyond the range of normal criticism.

Slogans such as "the Duce is always right" or "Believe, Obey, Fight" soon covered walls from one end of Italy to the other, and medi-

Mussolini and his Black Shirt bodyguard give the Fascist salute.
(Photo: Wide World Photos)

ocre party officials were humorlessly labeled supermen and saviors. The victory of an Italian athlete or the birth of a child to a prolific mother became an occasion for hailing the new order. Through the cheap theatricality of parades and balcony speeches, Mussolini's machine pumped pride and confidence into a troubled nation. Most Italians probably maintained their distrust of any government, but the good news of the propaganda was nevertheless welcomed and some of the enthusiasm real. Even in its cynicism Mussolini's sensitivity to the masses brought to Italian government a popular touch that it had lacked. The nation responded to his energy, his skillful borrowing of ideas and programs, and his arrogant confidence.

The authoritarian single party, parallel to and even competing with the state, became a hallmark of totalitarian regimes; and the Fascist party, completely subordinate to the Duce, reached into every city and town. A warning presence to other authorities and to individual citizens, the party had its own militia, secret police, and tribunals. Recruited in its early years mainly from among the unemployed and alienated, it had soon won hundreds of thousands of new members eager for the advantages of influence with the regime. There were associations for Fascist teachers, workers, and university students. In youth organizations for every age group over four years old, the next generation wore black shirts, marched, and recited official slogans. But the party never became the elite it claimed to be, and the policy of encouraging wide membership was abandoned in the 1930s in favor of fewer, more disciplined militants. Even so, the party remained more an instrument of patronage than the disciplined hierarchy described in propaganda.

Fascist doctrine, used primarily as propaganda, was neither fully practiced nor wholly consistent; but official ideology, essential to the very nature of totalitarianism, colored every aspect of life. Fascism declared itself the antithesis of the principles of 1789 yet also truly the regime of the people. While ridiculing the idea of majority rule, Fascists were extremely concerned with public sentiment and found a façade of representative institutions indispensable. The conservative principle of authority was reduced to simple obedience to the Duce. Authority was deemed purer when arbitrary than when circumscribed by rules, more effective if kept visible rather than subtle, and traditional arguments for social responsibility justified the omnipresence of the state. Crude force, the secret police, and acts of official brutality were well advertised as fulfilling the slogan: "Nothing against the state, nothing outside the state." Citizens were to replace the handshake in favor of the extended right arm of the Fascist salute,[2] and regulations established the Fascist names to give one's children and the form of address to use with one's friends. There was a Fascist style in art and philosophy, sport and war; and the state provided academies, uniforms, medals, and pensions for those who adopted it while threatening the critical with unemployment, exile, or prison. A candid irrationalism suspicious of intellectuals and traditional culture stressed the virtues of intuitive "thinking with the blood." Revitalized by a new-found joy in war, Italians would reclaim the heritage of Imperial Rome. As the antithesis of the decadent materialism of Britain, France, and the United States, Italy would influence the world through the spread of Fascism, her millions of migrants in other lands, and her own might and empire.

Fascism promised a new society, and the government, like all totalitarian regimes, was loquacious about the new kind of person it was creating—obedient, tough, efficient. Fascists and Mussolini himself seemed embarrassed by

---

[2] The salute was a stylized form of the greeting used in ancient Rome and portrayed in the statue of Marcus Aurelius that now stands on the Capitoline Hill in Rome, where Michelangelo designed a piazza to frame it. The salute quickly became an international symbol.

"Sons of the Wolf," six to eight years old, parade past Roman ruins. They have begun their Fascist military training.
(Photo: Wide World Photos)

the stereotype of Italians as affectionate, volatile, inefficient, and artistic. Rome rather than the Renaissance, Machiavelli rather than Cavour, technology rather than opera were the traditions to be stressed.

Yet the new order in its twenty years did not remake Italy. Inconsistent policies and conflicts between party and bureaucracy added new inefficiencies, and neither government nor party overcame local customs of patronage or personal kindness. Despite the talk of discipline and sacrifice, Fascist rule produced the worst orgy of peculation Italy has ever known. The crude tyranny of Italian Fascism was not by twentieth-century standards outstandingly brutal, and the anti-Semitic policies borrowed from the Germans in the late 1930s never really took root. But freedom was crushed, the jails filled, hundreds of prominent figures exiled to dreary southern towns or desolate islands. The measure of the regime lies as much in the goals it sought as in its failure to achieve them.

Social, Religious, and Economic Policies

The government hoped to halt the rapid migration of peasants off the land into cities (a policy with clear appeal to rural employers), tried against all the best advice to increase the birth rate, and strove to make the Italian economy self-sufficient. But at the most it merely slowed the opposing trends. The regime did bring off some notable achievements, which it vigorously advertised. The Mafia was suppressed; the Pontine Marshes near Rome were drained and farmers moved into newly constructed houses there; new railroads were built and the service improved; some superhighways were started. An enormous amount of construction was sponsored by the state, usually in a monumental style, and archaeological excavations were favored as evocations of a glorious past. All these projects contributed to employment. In addition, an elaborate program to enrich workers' leisure-time activities provided recreation halls, meeting rooms, and libraries in most towns as well as vacations for workers at seaside or mountain resorts. Family bonuses gave the poor an increased sense of security, and reforms of the educational system put more people in school for longer periods.

But Fascism's most publicized accomplishment was its accommodation with the Vatican. Although Mussolini and most of his early followers were thoroughly anticlerical, they soon found it worthwhile to appease Catholic interests. Crucifixes reappeared in the classrooms, chaplains were appointed to the Fascist militia, and the budget for clerical salaries and church repairs was increased. Until 1929, however, the regime had garnered only intangible benefits—the good will of many prominent Catholics and the Church's failure to support anti-Fascist movements.

Then, after lengthy and difficult negotiations, the Lateran agreements of 1929 were announced to the world. A formal treaty ended sixty years of conflict over Rome by establishing the tiny area of Vatican City within the capital as an independent state under papal sovereignty. And a concordat established religious teaching in Italian public schools, guaranteed that marriage laws would conform to Catholic doctrine, promised to restrict Protestant activities, and fixed a sum of more than $87 million as an indemnity to be paid by the state for Church property confiscated during the unification of Italy.

Fascist prestige was at its height. The new agreements resolved a dispute that had seared the consciences of millions of Italians. Abroad the treaty seemed to suggest that fascism had won special favor from the papacy, and this impression was little dimmed by the sharp warning in an encyclical of 1931 against the paganism of worshiping the state or by subsequent conflicts over Catholic activities that competed with those of Fascist youth organizations. These conflicts were bitter, and relations between church and state never regained their former warmth. Still, Catholics and the Vatican were on the whole more generous in their attitude toward Mussolini's regime than they had been toward its liberal predecessors. The reduction of nineteenth-century hostilities between church and state remained one of Fascism's most important assets.

When Fascism came to power, two general principles seemed to govern its economic policy. The first was autarky, or national economic self-sufficiency, which emphasized industrialization and technological progress as the basis of military strength. The second, borrowed from socialism, favored national ownership while distrusting big business and a free market. Although this attitude was soon attenuated, the Fascist government remained more willing to intervene in the economy than its predecessors.

The government very early set the value of the lira to equal the French franc, a bid for prestige that hurt Italian exports. The accompanying import duties and credit restrictions then led to a painful deflation. In the interest of self-sufficiency and a more favorable balance of payments, the government launched its famous battle of grain in 1926. With enormous hoopla and a whole range of new incentives, Italy doubled her grain production by 1940—but only at the cost of more competitive agricultural production. Exports declined more than imports, and the official policy of autarky had a regressive effect. Output per capita declined in the Fascist era.

As for big business, Fascist government proved in practice a sympathetic ally. In 1925 the leaders of Italian industry agreed to recognize only Fascist-led unions and were assured their traditional monopolistic autonomy in return. Generally the industrial giants in steel, automobiles, rubber, and chemicals found it easy to deal with (and often to manipulate) Fascist bureaucracy. At the same time subsidies to weak industries, financed through the Institute for Industrial Reconstruction established in 1933, led to a significant extension of government ownership. The redistribution of land and tax reform were considered in high circles but not seriously attempted. By 1940, despite the early return to the nine-hour workday, real wages were down in both industry and agriculture, and the bureaucracy accepted a cut in salary though taxes remained high.

The Corporative State

Fascist theory and economic practice came together in the Corporative State, the most discussed aspect of fascism. By 1926 great confederations, or corporations, were established for major sectors of the economy (agriculture, commerce, industry, and so forth), each including a syndicate of employers and a syndicate of employees, a kind of official union. Both strikes and lockouts were prohibited, replaced by a grievance procedure through the corporations. The heads of syndicates were party members appointed by the government, and negotiations to establish industry-wide scales of wages were dominated by government and business. There was some basis for the Marxist charge that fascism was a device for protecting capitalists.

In 1928 the Fascist Grand Council—which included party chiefs, the heads of ministries, and leaders of parliament—became an organ of state whose duties included drawing up the list of candidates for election to the Chamber of Deputies, a list that the electorate (reduced to its wealthiest one-third) could only accept or reject as a whole. And in 1934 the number of corporations was fixed at twenty-two, each representing an entire sphere of production from extraction of raw material to manufacture and distribution.[3] For each corporation the Duce appointed a council consisting of delegates representing the syndicates and the separate phases of production (with Mussolini council president in every case), and all the councils together formed the National Council of Corporations. The importance of these institutions, however, was undercut by preparations for war and Mussolini's habit of legislating by decree. In principle this elaborate organization eliminated class conflict by unifying owners and workers behind the state; but the employers' syndicates maintained their traditional form and autonomy, and the workers' syndicates were not an extension of old unions but new organizations directed by the party. Both within the corporations and the Chamber the Fascist party was dominant, but Mussolini in turn was shrewdly alert to prevent the party from acquiring interests or policies of its own.

Resistance to Fascism

At first the new regime managed to associate some distinguished Italians with Fascism, men such as the poet Gabriele D'Annunzio, the sociologist Vilfredo Pareto, the composer Giacomo Puccini, and the playwright and novelist

---

[3] The comprehensive intent of this organization is shown by the breadth of the twenty-two corporations, which were divided into three groups: I—grains, fruits and vegetables, wines, edible oils, beets and sugar, livestock, forestry and lumber, and textiles; II—metals, chemicals, clothing, paper and printing, construction, utilities, mining, and glass and pottery; III—insurance and banking, fine arts and liberal professions, sea and air transportation, land transportation, public entertainment, and public lodging.

Luigi Pirandello. But relations with leaders in the arts and scholarly disciplines remained uneasy; many continued, as did Benedetto Croce, a quiet and safely intellectual opposition. Some, of whom the conductor Arturo Toscanini, the historian Gaetano Salvemini, and the physicist Enrico Fermi are best known to Americans, went into exile. In 1929 university rectors and deans had been required to join the party, and by 1931, when the government demanded that all professors sign a loyalty oath, only eleven refused. The government frightened most people into silence and broke up organized resistance; the remaining underground was centered in France and some secret Communist groups in Italy. Internal oppostion ceased to be a threat.

Within the country even the most skeptical were baffled by Mussolini's apparent successes and felt isolated and uncertain of what to believe. Indeed most Italians probably shared some pride in their nation's heightened prestige. Outside Italy important groups in all European and many South American nations sang the praises of fascism's "bold experiment" that ended petty squabbling, ran the trains on time, kept order, and eliminated the threat of communism.

Nazi Germany

The Nazi regime was the most complete and terrifying achievement of totalitarianism, the beneficiary of an advanced economy and a strong administrative tradition in a society that emphasized status, regional particularism, and reciprocal distrust among Junkers, bureaucrats, professional men and workers. Philosophies of the state were more fully developed and more widely accepted in Germany than elsewhere, as were theories that probed the weaknesses of liberalism, individualism, and rationalism. Racist ideas, current throughout Europe in the nineteenth century, won particular prominence and respectability there.

More immediately, Nazism profited from the unparalleled series of shocks German society had suffered since 1918. Defeat had brought charges of war guilt, a revolution, and a republic beloved by few. The drastic inflation of the 1920s had been followed by depression and the most extensive unemployment in Europe. German politics resounded with nationalist themes and cries of treachery, and the Weimar governments never managed to subordinate the army to civilian authority.

The Background of Nazism

Nazism itself differed from kindred movements elsewhere in its extraordinarily effective and daring leader, its simpler and more coherent ideology, and its well-organized party. As a young man, Adolf Hitler had gone to Vienna to become an artist. Rejected by the Academy, he had impressed those who knew him mainly by his bitterness and wild visions of vengeance. World War I had been a kind of salvation for him, providing comradeship, a sense of purpose, and some status—he had been promoted to the rank of corporal. After the war he found brief employment in Munich spying on the small German Worker's party, which the army considered dangerously radical. Hitler took to addressing party rallies and began molding in the beer halls of Munich the speaking style and the personal party that in 1933 would make him Führer. His oratory combined brutal accusations with a messianic tone and repeated simple themes over and over in a spiraling frenzy, each sentence delivered with utter conviction and the menace of controlled violence.

Hitler borrowed ideas from the left and from nationalists. With none of Mussolini's experience in the world of ideological battles, he did not pretend to sophistication or subtlety. At the core of his vision were his concepts of race and universal struggle. The German people were suffering from vast conspiracies mounted by foreign powers, businessmen, Marxists, and Freemasons, but above all Jews—the gutter anti-Semitism he had absorbed in Vienna was used to feed distrust of social change and provide simple explanations for any misfortune. The Jews were behind war profits, reparations, inflation, and depression; but Marxism was also Jewish, and communists were agents of the Jewish conspiracy. Internationalism and pacifism were Jewish ideas intended to destroy Germany as the bastion of Western (Aryan) civilization. Life was a desperate struggle won by the ruthless, and Germany must awake to her destiny. In Hitler's harangues Germany's defeat in World War I, the Versailles treaty, the weakness of the Weimar Republic, economic disasters, Red revolution, Jews, moral decay, and abstract art were somehow all connected in opposition to the German *Volk,* the people whose manly and primitive virtues must be welded into an irresistible force behind one leader. Admirers of an older culture, monarchists, and believers in order were invited to join the angry patriots and the unemployed in the new movement.

When in 1923 Hitler had led the party (now called the National Socialist German Workers' party) in the Munich *Putsch,* Germany was racked by many similar movements; yet the revolt had been an immediate failure. The book Hitler wrote in prison, *Mein Kampf,* became the party bible. More self-exposure than anything else, it is a turbulent and repetitious outpouring of his political views intermixed with naive but demoniac statements about how human beings are manipulated by fear, big lies, and simplistic explanations. Even in its cynicism, *Mein Kampf* touched on all the frustrations of modern German life while deemphasizing the party's earlier more leftist program. In prison and after his release in 1925 Hitler worked to reorganize and strengthen the party. He added the SS, an elite corps in black uniforms serving as his bodyguard and as a special police force, to the SA, the brown-shirted storm troopers who were one of the more fearsome of the street armies. Some ideas and useful phrases were contributed to Nazi thought by Moeller van den Bruck, a literary figure respected in conservative circles, whose *The Third Reich* advocated revolution in behalf of a new, corporative and nationalist regime. The party established its own newspaper, edited by Alfred Rosenberg, which propagandized vigorously; and in 1930 Rosenberg would expand the canon of Nazi doctrine with his *The Myth of the Twentieth Century,* a wordy, turgid exposition of Hitler's racist ideas.

Nazism thus developed an ideology and the organizations to express it; yet until 1933 its crude appeal enjoyed only modest success. In 1928 the party's 60,000 members were still not enough to have much weight in German politics. It had some notable assets, however, and was establishing more. General von Ludendorff had joined Hitler in the 1923 *Putsch,* and there remained the possibility that other officers would cooperate, despite their contempt for the rabble to whom the Nazis appealed. Some circles of Bavarian conservatives and Rhineland industrialists showed interest in the movement, and in 1929 the Nazis gained national prominence by loudly promoting the petition against the Young Plan. Four million Germans declared it high treason not to renounce the "war guilt clause" of the Versailles treaty or to agree to any further reparations.

Hitler's intensity, fits of temper, and frequent bad manners offended many, but others felt the fascination of a personality that radiated power and could at times be charming. Early in the movement's history he gathered that small group of absolutely loyal men who would rule the Nazi state until its defeat: Hermann Göring, an air ace; Joseph Goebbels, journalist and party propagandist; and Heinrich Himmler. Dedicated fanatics, they worked ceaselessly to enlarge the party, orchestrate the impressive rallies inspired by Hitler's fertile sense of tactical possibilities, and spread Nazi doctrine.

The Nazis were gaining. In 1930 they became the second largest party in the Reichstag, and the following year Hitler reached an un-

A sea of fascist salutes from the floor of the Reichstag greets the announcement by Chancellor Adolf Hitler on September 1, 1939 that German troops have begun the invasion of Poland in response to Polish fire. At the same time, Hitler named Hermann Göring (standing at the podium as Reichstag president) as his eventual successor.
(Photo: UPI)

derstanding with a group of Rhineland industrialists who promised to pay the party's election deficits and to provide funds for its growing armies. (Leading Nazis critical of capitalism were shunted aside.) Like Mussolini, whom he greatly admired, Hitler combined the attractions of revolution and social order, appealed to the lower classes, and reassured the respectable. To a society broken by the Depression, the party promised recovery, with higher agricultural prices for the peasants and more employment for workers (tens of thousands of whom found jobs in the SS and SA). Hitler guaranteed as well to rebuild the army and save society from the Reds. Scholars have given a great deal of attention to the question of what groups were first drawn to the Nazis. By the 1930s, the party was broadly based. Workers were probably the biggest single group among its members, but they constituted a much larger proportion of society as a whole. Most workers continued to support socialists and communists. Disproportionately large numbers of Nazi supporters were small businessmen and tradesmen, civil service employees, and (to a lesser extent) farmers.

In 1931 right-wing nationalists, some industrialists, and an important group of militarists joined the Nazis in a manifesto denouncing the "cultural Bolshevism" of the Weimar Republic and the threat of Marxism, hinting that when the Nazis seized power, they would protect only those who joined them now. They had learned to speak simultaneously like a government already in office and an underworld gang. Their propaganda and their menace increased, and they expressed their seriousness of purpose by beating up Jews and socialists.

Collapse of the Weimar Republic

The Social Democrats, who had gained in the elections of 1928, led the government that faced the Great Depression. Without great imagination, they did the best they could, but their majority in the Reichstag was shaky, and President von Hindenburg refused to authorize decree powers. In 1930 the government resigned, to be replaced by the Center party's Heinrich

Brüning, a cautious, sober man with little popular appeal whom Hindenburg allowed to rule by decree for most of his years as chancellor. The elections of 1930 increased by over a hundred the number of Nazi deputies contemptuously ready to disrupt the Reichstag, and Hitler was so impressed with these successes that he became a presidential candidate when Hindenburg's term expired in 1932. Worried politicians persuaded the field marshal to run for reelection, and he won handily, but Hitler had over 13 million votes on the second ballot against the senile, eighty-four-year-old Hindenburg, now pathetically cast as the defender of the constitution. When Brüning proposed the expropriation of some East Prussian estates as part of a program of financial reform, the president dismissed him. Brüning, who proved to have been the Weimar Republic's last chance, had lost the confidence of nearly every segment of the Reichstag.

The subsequent period of palace intrigue led to Hitler. Hindenburg turned to Franz von Papen, a self-confident friend of important army officers and Junkers. Hoping to establish a conservative coalition of industrialists, Junkers, and the military, von Papen lifted Brüning's ban on the SA and SS, named four barons and a count to his cabinet, and declared martial law in Prussia, a step that was in effect a coup d'état to unseat the socialist government there.

Hindenburg then called new elections, which produced a Nazi landslide. With 230 seats they constituted some 40 percent of the Reichstag's membership and thus by far its largest party. He could find no chancellor but Hitler, who insisted on full decree powers. The field marshal refused and sent the nation to the polls again, but while the Nazis lost some seats, they remained the largest party. Hindenburg next appointed as chancellor General Kurt von Schleicher, a conventional army man who made an easy target for the abuse of Nazis, communists, and the disgruntled von Papen. Hoping to use Hitler's popularity, von Papen then led the men of Hindenburg's coterie in urging Hitler to serve as chancellor in a coalition government. The unsuccessful leader of a Munich *Putsch* ten years before took the oath of office late in January 1933.

Although he came to office legally, Hitler's arrival marked a further breakdown in the German political system. The Nazis increasingly won the votes of the right, and while the ballots cast for Marxist parties remained nearly constant, the communist share increased. Yet no party now seemed capable of establishing a reliable majority in the Reichstag. Of the twelve men in Hitler's cabinet, only two others were Nazis, and the men around Hindenburg imagined they could use the demagogue and then discard him. Instead the Nazis established their dictatorship within two months.

Seeking to increase the party's strength, Hitler called for another election almost immediately on assuming the chancellorship. The campaign that followed was one of systematic terror, especially in Prussia, where Hermann Göring was now minister-president and the police were used as principal electoral agents. The climax came with the burning of the Reichstag, a fire that the Nazis probably set but that they loudly blamed on the communists. Hindenburg agreed to issue special laws, Ordinances for the Protection of the German State and Nation, that ended most civil liberties, including freedom of the press and assembly. The voters gave the Nazis 44 percent of the seats, which, when combined with those of nationalist allies in other parties, assured them a bare majority.

Hitler pressed on. Communists were expelled from the Reichstag, conservatives wooed with calls to nationalism, and Center party members won over with promises to respect the privileges of the Catholic Church. In March Hitler dared to demand a special enabling act giving him as chancellor the right for four years to enact all laws and treaties independent of constitutional restraints. Of the 566 deputies left in the Reichstag, only 94 Social Democrats (out of 121) voted no. Blandishment and terror had done their work, but the tragedy went deeper: German politics offered no clear alternative to Hitler.

The Nazi regime moved quickly. It established concentration camps, first on private estates and then in larger and more permanent institutions. By July all parties except the National Socialist had been outlawed, and soon all other political organizations disappeared. In the elections of November 1933, the Nazis won more than 90 percent of the vote. They proceeded to restructure the administration of government, purge the civil service and judiciary, outlaw strikes, and clamp stricter controls on the press. In a few months Hitler had won fuller power than Mussolini had managed in years.

At this point the chancellor's most serious potential opposition was within his own party. Hitler's solution was barbarically simple. On a long weekend in June 1934, Ernst Röhm and Gregor Strasser, leaders of the Nazi left wing who took seriously the socialist aims of a Nazi revolution, were shot or stabbed. So, among hundreds of others, were General von Schleicher and his wife, some Catholic leaders, some socialists, and some taken by mistake. The Night of the Long Knives, directed primarily by the SS, meant the destruction of any serious leftist element within the party. Hitler admitted to some 74 deaths; subsequent estimates raise the figure to as many as a thousand. That summer weekend proved that any horror was possible, and the purge, like the noisy accusations of homosexuality that accompanied it, established the tone of Germany's new totalitarianism. When Hindenburg died in August, Germans voted overwhelmingly in a referendum to unite the presidency and the chancellorship in the person of Hitler, who took the occasion to assume officially the title of Führer ("Leader").

Administrative and Economic Policies

The government undertook a systematic administrative reorganization. Called *Gleichschaltung* ("coordination"), the plan extended to all national functions and could be used against any institution or individual considered likely to inhibit the Führer's will. The federal states lost their autonomy, and the Nazi party extended its function, establishing administrative *Gaue* ("regions"). The party Gauleiter, or regional director, might or might not be the appointed governor. This duplication of state organizations was carried further in Germany than in Italy; the party even formed its own office of foreign affairs as well as a secret police, the Gestapo, which infiltrated both the bureaucracy and the army. A law of March 1933, which had expelled Jews from public service and universities, had made all government employees appointees of the Führer. New people's courts heard secret trials of cases of treason, now very broadly defined, and rewritten statutes allowed prosecution for intent as well as for overt acts. Arrest and detention without charge or trial became a regular practice.

In its economic policies the Nazi regime scored impressive successes, especially at first. Unemployment, the crying problem of German life, dropped steadily as the result of great public works projects—the construction of highways, public housing, and government offices, the reclamation of swamps and reforestation—many using special labor battalions, in which one year's service was soon made compulsory. Later the burgeoning armaments industry and a growing military establishment eliminated the problem of joblessness entirely. By spending money while more traditional governments thought it essential to balance their budgets, the Nazis reduced unemployment more effectively than any Western nation. But such programs were expensive, and they were paid for in several ways.

The government restricted internal move-

NUMBER OF WORKERS OFFICIALLY LISTED AS UNEMPLOYED AS A PERCENTAGE OF WORKING AGE (15–64) POPULATION

There were variations in the definition of unemployment, but the curves can be taken as one indicator of social distress. Because most women did not seek jobs, those actually out of work were a much higher proportion of the normal work force than shown here.

ments of workers and goods and controlled foreign trade, directing that payments be made with special marks whose value altered according to the goods and the nations involved. This currency scheme was largely the work of Hjalmar Schacht, a financial wizard who though never a Nazi contributed his skills to the new Germany. Imports were reduced, which lowered the living standard in some sectors and raised costs in many others, as part of a policy intended to make Germany as economically self-sufficient as possible. Trade thus became an explicit weapon in international relations; Germany bought produce and raw materials from the Balkan countries, for example, at prices well above the world market but with marks redeemable only through the purchase of German manufactured products. Tantamount to barter, this system increased Germany's influence in countries dependent on her for trade.

The Nazis gained additional revenues out of property confiscated from Jews, high taxes, forced loans, and carefully staged campaigns urging patriotic Germans to contribute their personal jewelry to the state. A four-year plan launched in 1936 was directed toward economic self-sufficiency rather than domestic wealth, for by then the German state was organizing for war. Ultimately the government would cover these growing costs by printing paper currency, the effects of which would long be hidden by a war economy and the exploitation of conquered lands. By 1945 the mark fell to about 1 percent of its 1933 value.

Labor policies also produced visible gains while increasing government control. Outlawing strikes reassured business without gravely damaging wage levels that unemployment would have kept from rising. The National Labor Front, which included all workers and management, froze wages and directed personnel in the interests of business and government, but it was accompanied by an extensive array of benefits. All welfare programs, including plans previously regional or private, were taken over by the state, which claimed full credit for the funds and services provided from them. A Strength Through Joy program sent German workers to summer camps or on special cruises, furnishing pleasures once available only to the well-to-do. The workers' share in an expanding economy may have declined, but workers were grateful for jobs and vacations and perhaps for the sense of their own importance all the propaganda conveyed.

The professional military had reasons of its own for gratitude to the Nazi regime: disregarding the disarmament clauses of the Treaty of Versailles (he would repudiate them formally in 1935), Hitler had set about openly and rapidly rearming Germany on becoming chancellor. While regular officers remained resentful of Nazi paramilitary organizations and disdainful of their social inferiors who now directed the state, they nevertheless appreciated the emphasis on fighting strength, and they accepted the oath of personal loyalty Hitler required of them after he had won the presidency. With the return of universal compulsory service in 1935 and the creation of an air force, Germany was soon spending several times as much on arms as Britain and France combined.

In 1938, strengthened by his diplomatic successes, Hitler asserted control more directly, removing the minister of war, the chief of staff, and more than a dozen generals. They were not merely fired but disgraced amid public tales of private vice. Baron Konstantin von Neurath, a nationalist of the old school in office as foreign minister since 1933, was replaced by Joachim von Ribbentrop, a good Nazi and no aristocrat at all. The Nazi hold on both the foreign service and the army, traditional strongholds of conservatives and aristocrats, now seemed secure.

Religious and Racial Policies

The churches presented a less tractable problem. A concordat with the Vatican in July 1933 gave the state some voice in the appointment of bishops while guaranteeing that Catholic orders and schools would be unmolested. The Protestant denominations agreed to form a new body, the Evangelical Church, under a national bishop; but when the man Hitler chose as bishop tried to "Aryanize" it, dissidents formed the separate Confessional Church. In 1935 the minister for Church Affairs was given the power to confiscate ecclesiastical property, withhold funds, and have pastors arrested. Thereafter the state fought the churches primarily through steady harassment of individual ministers by local authorities.

Some priests and ministers cooperated with the regime, enthusiastically supporting war, race, and Reich. But most resisted at least the more outrageous demands made of them, and individual voices spoke out against Nazism clearly and courageously. In 1937 Martin Niemoeller, the leader of the Confessional Church, was arrested for his opposition to Nazism; and Pope Pius XI condemned both the deification of the state and Nazi racial doctrine. In the following years some Catholic churches were burned, members of religious orders were frequently brought to trial on morals charges, and the claims of the Hitler Youth—the Nazi or-

Nazi propaganda against the Jews, Catholics, and wealthy reactionaries who would subvert the Führer was disseminated by earnest young party members.
(Photo: Keystone)

ganization for adolescents—challenged religious education. The churches, although not centers of organized resistance, still permitted individuals some escape from the incessant pressures of totalitarianism.

The relentless logic and dynamism of totalitarianism showed most clearly in the government's racial policy. Nazism had always made much of its anti-Semitism, and the Nuremberg laws of 1935 not only removed Jews from the public service (anyone with one or more Jewish grandparents was considered a Jew) but declared Jews no longer citizens and prohibited marriage or sexual intercourse between Jews and Aryans. Subsequently Jews were expelled from one activity after another, required to register with the state and to give their children identifiably Jewish names. The murder of a German diplomat by a young Jewish boy in 1938 touched off a new round of terror. Many Jews were arrested, and the SS led an orgy of violence in which Jews were beaten and murdered, their synagogues burned, their homes and businesses smashed. A fine of 1 billion marks was levied on the Jews of Germany, and this was followed by still further measures to humiliate and isolate them; they were barred from the theater and concerts, forbidden to buy jewelry, forced to sell their businesses or property, denied access to certain streets, and made to wear a yellow star. Worse would come, for totalitarianism could never fulfill its vision of unanimity and total security any more than it could forgo violence.

From the beginning the Nazis' publicity had been flamboyant, their posters striking, and their rallies well staged; after the movement came to power, propaganda became a way of

As part of its anti-Semitic policy the German government forced Jews to wear yellow stars on their clothing for immediate identification. It was the mildest of the government's discriminatory tactics.
(Photo: The Bettmann Archive)

Chamber of Culture saw to it that cinema, theater, literature, art, and music all became instruments for promoting Nazism. Things primitive and brutal were praised as Aryan; one who opposed or even doubted the Führer ceased to be German. Warfare was for the new regime its natural state.

Communist Russia

Fascists insisted that only they could prevent the triumph of communism, but they learned much from the Soviet example of a revolutionary movement using dictatorial powers to direct an entire society. For communists, on the other hand, dictatorship was incidental and supposedly temporary; and to many in Russia and in the West the Soviet Union remained the antithesis of fascism and its only consistent opponent, despite resemblances to fascism in its enforcement of ideology through a single party, its use of compulsion and terror, and its deification of the party leader. Lenin's death in January 1924 proved a turning point. For as issues of policy and leadership were slowly resolved, Joseph Stalin emerged as one of history's most effective dictators.

For more than a year, Lenin had been nearly incapacitated, but his prestige had precluded any public scramble for power, and many expected a more relaxed government by committee to follow. In a famous letter Lenin had assessed two likely successors: Trotsky, whom he called the best man in the Politburo, though overconfident; and Stalin, whom Lenin found "too rude" though an able organizer (Stalin already held enormous power as general secretary of the party's Central Committee).

Over the next three years, Russia's leaders publicly debated the complex issues of Communist theory and practical policy. Trotsky led those who clung to the traditional vision of revolution spreading across Europe, and he thus favored an uncompromising radical pro-

life. Torchlight parades, chorused shouts of *"Sieg Heil!"* ("Hail to victory!"), book burnings, the evocation of Norse gods, schoolyard calisthenics, the return to Gothic script: a thousand such events sought to give each citizen a feeling of participating, of being swept up—and implicated—in some great historical transformation. Joseph Goebbels at the Reich gram at home and abroad. Stalin's stand was that the Soviet Revolution could and must survive alone through "revolution in one country." No theoretician and little informed about the world outside Russia, Stalin was not wholly at ease in these debates with more intellectual and experienced opponents. But they in turn underestimated his single-minded determination. His argument was formally adopted by the Politburo in December 1925.

Stalin used his position with skill. He was the link between the Politburo and the party organization below it, and he could count on the loyalty of party officials, many of whom he had appointed. He played effectively on personal antagonisms and on the bad feelings created by Trotsky's tactless arrogance. When the Politburo elected three new members at that December meeting, all were Stalin's associates.

Leading opponents of Stalin on the left began to cooperate with Trotsky in public agitation, but Stalin made each such move seem a threat to party solidarity and communist rule itself. Although Grigori Zinoviev had supported Stalin, his position as head of the Comintern—the Third International—gave him independent power. He and Trotsky were expelled from the Politburo in 1926 and from the party itself in 1927. The left was broken, and Zinoviev recanted his "mistake" the following year. So did Nikolai Bukharin, perhaps the party's subtlest theoretician and a leader of the right, who believed Russia's social transformation must necessarily be slow. Trotsky, who tenaciously refused to change his mind, was exiled and then deported, continuing from abroad his criticism of Stalin's growing dictatorship.

It may seem odd that these men, all veterans of the October Revolution, did not attempt to oust Stalin; even Trotsky, who had built the Red army, never tried to use it against him. But these old Bolsheviks fervently accepted the need for party loyalty and revolutionary unity. Stalin, who favored the younger and less intellectual party members, made the most of this mystique to assure that the open debates of those years were not allowed again.

The First Five-Year Plan: Agriculture

The First Five-Year Plan, launched in 1928, was a daring program that reflected some of the qualities that had brought Stalin to the top. It shamelessly incorporated ideas and suggestions Stalin had denounced when his opponents had put them forth just months before, but it was thoroughly his in its bold assumption that Russia could transform herself into an industrial power by mobilizing her every resource.

By 1928 Russian production had regained prewar levels in most sectors, but the recovery had come through serious concessions to free enterprise. Lenin's New Economic Policy had depended heavily on private entrepreneurs in commerce, the so-called NEP men, and on peasant owners in agriculture. The task now was to change the very nature of the economy itself by socializing it on both fronts.

As a first step the plan inaugurated the collectivization of agriculture, a measure with multiple aims: to bring socialism to the countryside; to increase production by spreading the improved techniques and the mechanization that peasants had on the whole resisted; and to give the state control over agricultural output, enabling it to feed industrial workers and to sell produce abroad so it could pay for the imported machinery industrialization required.

Although Russian peasants had many traditions of common effort, they bitterly resisted collectivization despite inducements of equipment and credit. Poor by international standards, perhaps 4 or 5 percent of them nonetheless had the means to hire labor and lend money within their villages, which gave them a hold over the entire economy. Significantly these farmer-employers would come to be called kulaks, the old, pejorative term for grasping merchants and usurers.

As agricultural prices fell—though others soared—peasants withheld their goods from the market. Famine threatened, and the government, blaming the kulaks, mounted a sweeping campaign of propaganda and police action against them. It seized their grain (informers were given a quarter of any hoard uncovered), killed hundreds of thousands of kulaks, and deported untold numbers of them to till the unbroken soil of Siberia. Meanwhile peasants destroyed crops and animals rather than let the government have them. The antagonisms of rural society were thus proving unexpectedly explosive, and Stalin had to intervene in 1930 to halt what had escalated to virtual civil war. By then more than half the peasants had joined collective farms, but the losses in animal power and able farmers had hurt production severely. Serious famine in 1932–1933 showed how badly the First Five-Year Plan had failed to reach its goals in agriculture.

The pattern of collectivization that then emerged proved to be a durable compromise. Even on collective farms peasants were permitted individual plots and privately owned tools. Larger machinery was concentrated at Machine Tractor Stations, which became the rural base for agricultural agents and party officials—modernization and political supervision went hand in hand. By 1933 output was sufficiently controlled to permit the government to concentrate on the central aim of the plan: the most massive and rapid industrialization in history.

The First Five-Year Plan: Industry

According to the five-year forecast, industrial production was to double in less than five years and in some critical areas, such as electrical power, to increase sixfold. More than 1,500 new factories were to be put into operation, including large automobile and tractor plants; and there were projects on a still grander scale, among them a Dnieper River power station and a great coal and iron complex in a whole new city, Magnitogorsk. These goals would be met somewhat ahead of schedule, and there would be only slight exaggeration in the government's proud claim to have made Russia an industrial nation almost overnight.

All this had to be financed internally, and it was paid for primarily by the dead, displaced, and collectivized peasants. Indirect tolls were levied on the rest of the populace as well. Workers' wages were increased only slightly, and the plan postponed improvements in even such basic facilities as housing and rail service. Food and then most consumer items were rationed, with allotments varying according to one's contribution to the plan.

Russia's First Five-Year Plan was responsible for the look of anticipation on the faces of these villagers; they are about to switch on the first electric light bulb ever to appear in Bryansk Province (1928).
(Photo: Novosti Press Agency)

Most Russian laborers, unskilled or poorly trained, were unaccustomed to the pace now required; thus their rate of turnover was high, the quality of their work poor, and their output per man-hour low. The state resorted to a continuous workweek—multiple shifts kept the precious machines going—and moved special "shock brigades" of abler workers from plant to plant as a stimulus to higher production. Women and young people were urged into industrial jobs. "Socialist competition" pitted groups of workers and whole factories against each other for bonuses and prizes, and piecework payment, once a hated symbol of capitalist avarice, became increasingly common. Violators of shop rules were fined; indolence, malingering, pilfering, and sabotage, often loosely defined, became crimes against the state. Punishment frequently included time in a corrective labor camp, so that what had initially been a mode of prison reform became another means of getting more work done.

Many of the essential managers and engineers were foreigners, but the government was eager for Russia to supply her own talent. Special courses were established in factories, and the numbers enrolled in the higher technical schools trebled. This training, like the quality of goods produced, was often inferior, but it laid a base for the future.

The plan's sober goals required a stability and discipline that led to the sacrifice of some earlier enthusiasms. In schools the formal examinations, homework, and academic degrees, once abolished, began to return; and classroom democracy gave way before the strengthened authority of the teacher. By the 1930s the virtue of marriage was being emphasized, divorce and abortion discouraged, and prolific families specially rewarded.

The five-year programs, which had taken years to devise, had to be constantly amended, requiring the development of new skills, detailed reports on every sector of the economy, and above all increased authority for the planners themselves.

The great venture mobilized every aspect of society. Associations of writers, musicians, and artists worked with party help to establish the themes and styles of propaganda useful to the plan. Mass organizations of youth and workers met for indoctrination, and kulaks and church were subject to renewed attacks. Within the party itself criticism or even skepticism about any aspect of the plan was akin to treason; hundreds of thousands of party members were expelled, and new recruits were carefully screened for absolute reliability. The state used propaganda, mass organizations, and secret police to create unanimity. "Overfulfillment" was announced in 1932, but the miracle of industrialization also marked the creation of a Russian totalitarianism holding together a society rent by rapid change. The very purpose of society seemed to lie in the statistics of production quotas met.

Growth in the Prewar Decade

The Second (1933–1937) and Third (1938–1942) Five-Year plans were continuations of the First at somewhat lower pressure. Although the emphasis on industrialization continued, the rate of capital investment was reduced, consumer goods became more available, and rationing was eliminated by 1936. Standards of quality rose, and there were new undertakings as well. Dramatic improvement in transportation, especially domestic aviation, made previously remote territories accessible and led to the serious exploitation of Arctic regions. Partly for reasons of military security, industrialization east of the Ural Mountains was stressed.

By 1939 Soviet Russia ranked third among the world's industrial producers, behind only the United States and Germany. That year she produced twenty-four times more electrical power and five times more coal and steel than in 1913. Housing and clothes were improving, though the Russian standard of living remained low compared to the West. Seven years of compulsory schooling for all remained a goal yet to be met, but the literate population had grown from less than 50 percent of those over school age in 1926 to more than 80 percent in 1939; enrollment in higher schools had trebled and the number and size of libraries and hospitals more than doubled. In these years one-seventh of the population moved to the cities, where a higher proportion lived than ever before, and over 90 percent of peasant households were on collective farms serviced by the Machine Tractor Stations.

Russia, the government proudly announced, had reached the stage of socialism, and this justified a new constitution in 1936. The changes it made were mainly formal. Direct voting by secret ballot replaced the cumbersome indirect elections, the government explained, now that the reactionary classes had ceased to exist. The body thus elected was the Soviet of the Union, one of two houses of the Supreme Soviet; the other, the Soviet of the Nationalities, represented the republics. The Supreme Soviet elected the Presidium, which legislated most of the time and whose chairman was head of state, and the Council of Ministers, the executive arm (the revolutionary term Commissars thus passed away). The constitution divided some of the larger federal republics, making eleven in all, and on paper at least left them considerable autonomy. It provided social and political guarantees that communists hailed as the most democratic in the world, and it officially noted the special position of the Communist party as "the vanguard of the working people." When new elections were held, 96 percent of the population voted, 98 percent of it for the single list the party presented in most constituencies.

Stalinism

With the new constitution many expected an easing of political controls. Amnesty had been granted some political prisoners in 1935, and the sinister secret police in operation since 1922 had been replaced by a somewhat more controlled political police, the NKVD. The campaign against religion was abating, and the white-collar classes and leaders generally were being honored—the military had officers again, and foremen were returning to factories. Opportunities for advancement in this modernizing society were great, and special awards recognized those who excelled. But tyranny remained, justified by the dangers of "capitalist encirclement."

Soviet art and literature became timid; writers, Stalin commented ominously, were "engineers of human souls." Music perhaps fared better, notably in the sophisticated and dynamic works of Dmitri Shostakovich and of Sergei Prokofiev. If intellectuals were harassed less in the later 1930s than during the First Five-Year Plan, they had long since learned the necessity of caution. The Russian Academy of Science, as lavish in its support of some kinds of research as it was arbitrarily unfriendly to others, was never far from politics.

At the center of Soviet society stood Stalin, increasingly adulated. He was honored as leader and expert in every activity; works of art were dedicated to him, factories named after him, his picture everywhere. His authority was virtually absolute, even though until 1941 he held no official position other than party secretary. Patriotism overshadowed the socialist internationalism of an earlier generation, and Soviet achievement was presented as the culmination of a long Russian development. Stalin was taking his place with Ivan the Terrible and Peter the Great among the molders of Russia.

That his power exceeded theirs showed in the great purges of the late 1930s, directed against very disparate people—engineers, Ukrainian separatists, former Mensheviks, party members—accused of being counterrevolutionaries. They were touched off by the assassination in 1934 of Sergei Kirov, who had been close to Stalin, and a member of the Politburo, an event treated as part of a large con-

The ubiquitous Stalin: his picture was encountered everywhere, even afloat at this Russian beach resort.
(Photo: Sovfoto)

spiracy but probably the act of young communists who admired some of Stalin's old opponents, especially Zinoviev. Zinoviev and members of the "left opposition" were tried for treason and imprisoned in 1935, tried again, and executed in 1937. Their trials were followed by others, always public: party leaders and army officers in 1937 and members of the "right opposition," Nikolai Bukharin and other old Bolsheviks, in 1939.

To the outside world the indictments seemed vague and the evidence unconvincing; yet the accused consistently confessed—and disappeared. Perhaps their admissions of guilt were merely the result of torture, but they also seemed a final act of faith by men who had always believed that anyone resisting the inevitable course of history was "objectively" a traitor.

Russia was profoundly shaken by the purges and the reign of terror, which, like the earlier campaign against the kulaks, swept the country until in 1939 Stalin once again called a halt. The dead were countless; jails and labor camps were bursting with prisoners—perhaps 10 million. More than twice that many had gone into exile. Russia's leaders, except for Stalin, were primarily from a new generation of men who had made their whole careers under communism. And the institutions and techniques of Soviet totalitarianism had grown ominously like those of Germany and Italy, even though their raison d'être was a much more fundamental transformation of society. Only in the values she professed did Russia remain closer to the humane traditions of European civilization, and it was not clear in 1939 what part the isolated and untested nation would play as Western democracy faced its greatest challenge.

III. THE DEMOCRACIES' RESPONSE

Where democracy survived the Depression, the results were unimpressive. Parties of the right center pursued sound finance and embittered the unemployed; liberals reluctantly jettisoned old principles to support higher tariffs and subsidies for business and agriculture; socialists resentfully compromised welfare projects for better-balanced budgets. Even where strong at the polls, the left was politically weakened by the fratricidal conflict between Communists and socialists. If voters turned toward the militant left or the radical right, the political system became unworkable, and governments resorted to decree powers and bans on extreme parties. By the mid-1930s, when there were some promising signs of new ideas, policies, and political coalitions, international dangers brought further divisions and worse crises. As England's Lord Tweedsmuir dryly noted, "But for the bold experiment of Fascism the decade has not been fruitful in constructive statesmenship."

Social Change and Political Uncertainty

Slow economic recovery underscored important social changes. Agriculture was becoming more productive as it became more mechanized and scientific. Better transportation, mechanical refrigeration, cheaper clothes, and more leisure were clearly raising standards of living as well as changing life styles. Throughout Europe the middle classes recouped much of the status and security threatened by inflation and depression. University enrollment, still a privilege of class, rose higher than ever before—highest in France, it rose to almost 2 percent of college-age youth in Scandinavia, Britain, Italy, and Germany (where it dropped sharply after the Nazis came to power). But small business and craft industry had suffered much more than the larger corporations, the first to benefit from the economic upturn. Economic life was clearly dominated by large-scale production and large organizations, including more effective trade unions. Women, though usually paid less than men, were now an accepted part of the industrial work force, constituting from one-quarter to one-third of such workers in the more industrialized countries; their incomes contributed to their chances for independence as well as to their families' well-being. If workers generally enjoyed a forty-hour week with more leisure time and more ways of spending it, work itself was more subject to "American" efficiency; supervisors maintained relentless discipline to keep production moving at a pace set by machines.

Technology now seemed a mixed blessing even as talking motion pictures and radio did much to bridge the gap between urban and rural life and to build a popular culture common to all classes. The very form of prosperity thus stimulated discontent among intellectuals disdainful of mass culture, small-business owners frightened at their precarious position, and workers who disliked the conditions under which they worked and resented their limited share of national wealth. The transformation of Russian society or even the symbolic gains of better-lit factories and vacation resorts for workers glorified through propaganda in Germany and Italy, as well as the elimination of

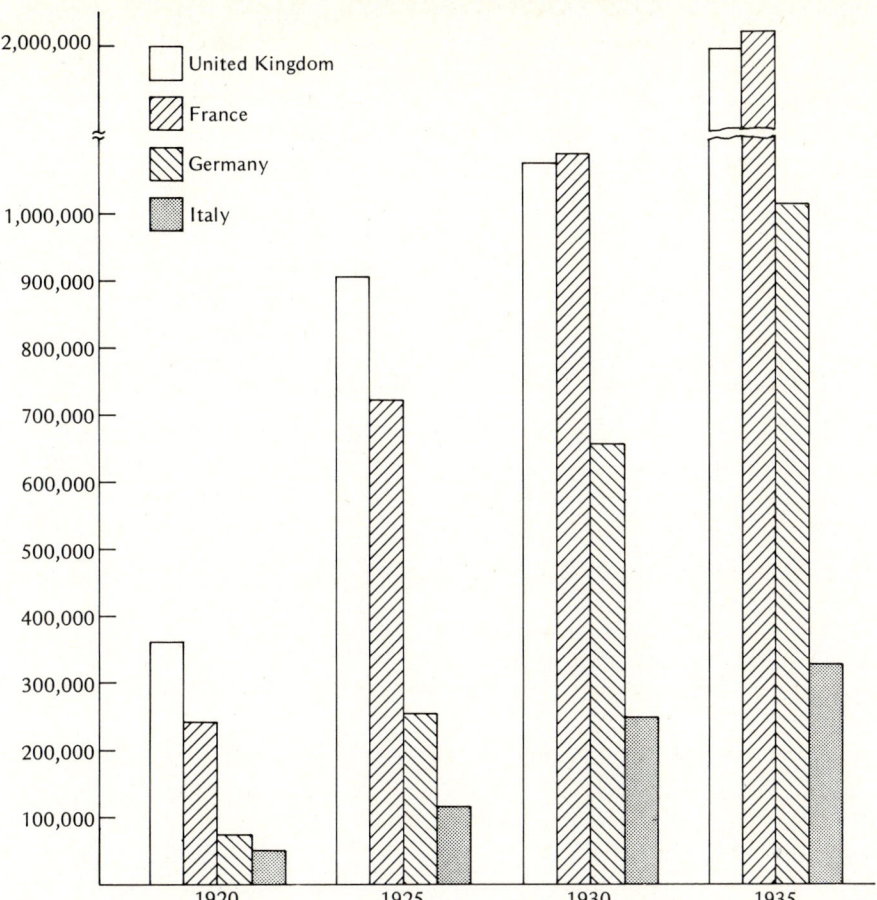

strikes there, thus seemed purposeful in contrast to what many criticized as aimless dislocation in the democracies. Wherever freedom permitted, political conflict both reflected and contributed to social division.

Among the smaller democracies, Switzerland, socially the most conservative, and Sweden, which combined social welfare programs and a mixed economy, fared the best. Finland and Czechoslovakia, whose economic growth and political freedom had made them models of the new postwar nations, suffered from divisions almost as grave as those that would drive Spain to civil war. At the same time,

The number of automobiles in a society reflects its general wealth, adaptation to a consumer economy, and changing patterns of communication. (Note that the United Kingdom, France, and Italy each had about 40 million people; Germany had 65 million.) This graph gives evidence of impressive prosperity and change; by 1935 France and the United Kingdom had one vehicle for every twenty people.

Britain and France were beset by fumbling governments that made an embarrassing contrast with the dynamic totalitarian regimes.

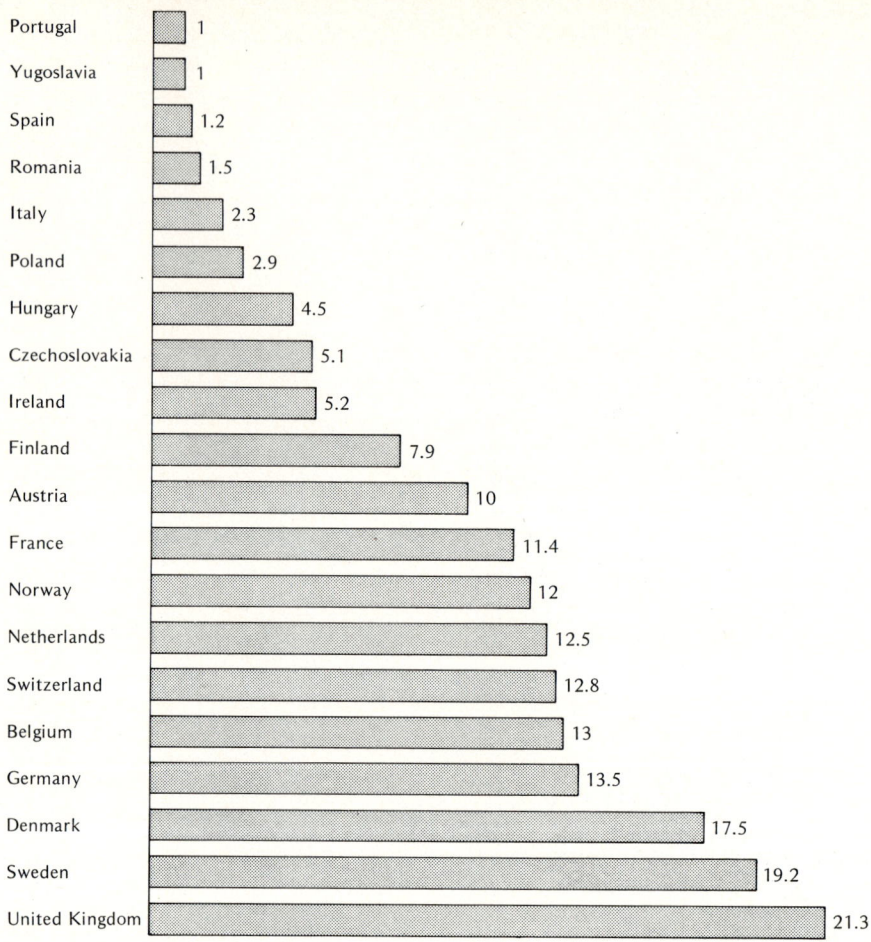

APPROXIMATE NUMBER OF RADIOS LICENSED FOR EVERY 100 PEOPLE IN TWENTY SELECTED COUNTRIES (1938)

Radio was an important new instrument of communication and propaganda. These statistics suggest that most families in the United Kingdom had a radio, that nearly everyone could sometimes listen to the radio in Finland and Austria, and that from Italy to Portugal, millions of people only heard the radio on special occasions when speakers blared in public places.

Great Britain

The British political system in the 1930s was able to resist the drift to extremes, but domestic moderation resulted as much from a breakdown in party structures as from political skill. The elections of 1929 had made Ramsay MacDonald prime minister again in a Labour cabinet, but neither Labour nor its Liberal allies could find acceptable remedies for the Depression. A special commission in 1931 recommended drastic economies, as financial experts in the 1930s usually did, but these required cuts in welfare and unemployment payments intolerable to most of Labour. The cabinet itself divided, and then MacDonald announced to his stunned followers the formation of a national government, including members of all three parties. MacDonald and his followers were expelled from the Labour party, his "treachery" a source of recriminations that nearly destroyed it.

Helped by ineffectual opposition, the national government won overwhelmingly in the subsequent elections; but the coalition had become a disguise for conservative rule. MacDonald nonetheless remained prime minister, weathering riots and a mutiny that greeted reduced budgets and battling the economic crisis with controls on foreign exchange and increased tariffs that split the Liberal party. When MacDonald resigned in 1935, tired and unloved, his government had overseen a slow recovery of the British economy, redefined imperial relations, and initiated some cautious steps toward government planning. It had done so by pursuing others' policies and in the process struck a devastating blow to the proletarian movement to which MacDonald had devoted his life.

MacDonald was followed by the Conservative Stanley Baldwin, who returned for his third prime ministership armored in the complacent virtues of the middle class. His considerable political gifts masked a habit of indecision, but he easily won the elections of 1935 thanks to a divided opposition and to strong statements in favor of the League of Nations, in which he actually had little deep interest. The Parliament elected the same year would continue through 1945, the longest-lived in modern history, and the impressive talent it would prove to contain testified to the continued vitality of British political life.

But the lack of imaginative leadership in the 1930s was remarkable. As international affairs grew more ominous, the uncertainty of British policy further weakened democratic governments in Europe. One issue, however, was resolved with vigor. King Edward VIII, who acceded to the throne in 1936, was determined to marry an American divorcee; and when he abdicated, as Baldwin and the archbishop of Canterbury insisted he must, the transition to George VI went smoothly, an assertion of tradition that averted the crises widely predicted. When Baldwin retired in 1937, his successor was his earnest Chancellor of the Exchequer, Neville Chamberlain, who was convinced that from his high office he could preserve peace in Europe.

France

The Depression hit France later and less severely than other highly industrialized countries, but when the decline came, it lasted. Politically France faced not so much a single crisis as a myriad of smaller problems that exhausted the old answers and undermined confidence. By the mid-1930s the French seemed more bitterly divided than at any time since the Dreyfus affair.

The left won the legislative elections of 1932 as the economic slump began to be felt, but the socialist members refused to participate in bourgeois governments. The Radical Socialists (who were really moderate republicans) remained therefore the dominant party and sought allies toward the center and the right. Ironically the left's electoral victory thus produced unstable governments committed to reducing expenditures and protecting established interests. Outside the Chambers rightist factions, including the fascist Croix de Feu ("Cross of Fire"), grew increasingly noisy. Demonstrations led by their uniformed militants before the Chamber of Deputies building on February 6, 1934, produced more bloodshed than Paris had seen since the Commune; many believe that the Third Republic nearly died that day.

The crisis arose suddenly over the revelation of a gigantic investment swindle perpetrated by one Serge Stavisky, whose scheme, it became clear, had relied on important political connections and a strange reluctance to prosecute him. His suicide encouraged scurrilous charges that became the basis of a campaign against bourgeois government, in which protofascist groups used all the familiar devices, including uniforms, anti-Semitism, demonstrations, and propaganda. To meet the emergency Gaston Doumergue, a former president of the republic, was recalled from retirement to take the premiership and was given full power to govern by decree. The sober old man was supported by every party except the royalists and Marxists, and held office for nine calming months before losing his majority. But when he proposed that presidential power be permanently enlarged, many deputies were indignant. The republic still rejected strong presidents.

The left knew that in order to capture political power, it would have to heal its divisions and generate the cooperation that trade unions and others had long sought. When the Comintern, which had ruled that Communist parties must operate independently of other political organizations, declared that they could now join antifascist coalitions, the French left was able to organize a Popular Front in time for national elections in 1936. Radical Socialists, Socialists, and Communists agreed not to run against each other on the second or run-off ballot. Such rare solidarity won them a resounding victory, with the Socialists for the first time gaining more seats than the Radical Socialists and the Communists sending a sizable delegation to the Chamber. France had her first Socialist premier, Léon Blum, a learned, humane intellectual and a Jew—qualities that made conservatives distrust him all the more.

The Popular Front and the political campaign that produced its victory was in part a great rallying to the Republic and to French radical traditions, but the hopes it aroused were soon disillusioned. Even as the new government took office, it was faced with a wave of strikes by workers intent on collecting the fruits of their victory. They occupied factories, which to many of the French smacked of dreaded revolution. With difficulty the government negotiated an accord, passing legislation that provided for a general 12 percent increase in wages, two-week paid vacations, a forty-hour workweek, and compulsory arbitration. Other reforms were soon added; public works were launched; the Bank of France (long the object of the left's suspicion) was restructured to give public representatives a controlling vote; and the arms industry was nationalized. The government increased pensions for veterans and subsidies for small businessmen and farmers both to stimulate the economy and to win still wider support.

But each of these measures, like the devaluation of the franc, which in 1937 could no longer be avoided, frightened the business classes. New programs proved easier to institute than to finance and the economy more accessible to regulation than stimulation. Blum's government—one of the Third Republic's most admired and most hated—had hardly begun the tax reforms needed to underwrite its plans when, after a year in office, it was defeated in the conservative Senate. The Popular Front itself soon broke up.

Subsequent governments rested on the Radical Socialists and the parties of the center, with Édouard Daladier prime minister from 1938 to 1940. French politics, while sensitive to popular sentiment and capable of innovative progress, had failed to give effective direction to a society rent by multiple factions and bitter slander. Meanwhile France's carefully constructed international position was collapsing.

The Ideological Struggle

The inability of the established democracies to cope with social and political strains coupled with the vitality of the totalitarian nations put old and tested values on the defensive. All of Europe seemed divided in a great ideological battle. Intellectual positions and newspaper articles alike took on apocalyptic tones in which the bland decencies of bourgeois democracy were easily lost. If the strident claims of radicals and fascists dominated the debate, it is all the more important to note that there was at the same time an important revival of the commitment to freedom, expressed by four major groups.

The most prominent was Marxist. The Russian Revolution had enthralled millions of Europeans with visions of economic progress in a backward nation and of social equality and high culture in a mass society. This appeal grew as capitalist economies staggered, and it reached a peak with the Russian constitution of 1936. At the same time socialists and even communists belatedly learned from fascism that all bourgeois governments were not the same. Many of the left renewed their dedication to the principles of liberty while asserting that dictatorship in Russia was a special case.

In Christian thought traditional arguments against the idolatry of the state gained new meaning. The Protestant Karl Barth and the Catholic Jacques Maritain built on firm theological orthodoxy—Barth's Pauline, Maritain's Thomist—to stress the importance of individual freedom and social justice. Similar concerns emerged in the writings of Nikolai Berdyaev, Russian Orthodox, and Martin Buber, Jewish.

Artists and writers tended in the 1930s to espouse themes of social responsibility. Poets and novelists like W. H. Auden, Thomas Mann, or André Malraux stressed the dignity of the human being, social justice, the dangers of power, and the evils of war. Much that was written was narrowly ideological, closer to political tracts than lasting art; but where they were free to do so, most European intellectuals clearly identified with the humane tradition now threatened.

Nor were liberals silent. Most vigorous in the politics and universities of Britain and France, they were heard even in Italy. In his important *History of European Liberalism,* Guido de Ruggiero probed the liberal tradition of England, France, Germany, and Italy, arguing even as he explained the decline of liberal traditions that—amended yet again—they could offer much to modern man. A decade later Benedetto Croce's historical and philosophical writings highlighted the theme of liberty as the meaning of progress, a brave perspective in 1938.

Liberal economic theory, still dominant in the academic and business worlds, was given a major restatement by John Maynard Keynes, whose *The General Theory of Employment, Interest and Money* appeared in 1936. Keynes rejected the classical view of economic man and the self-regulating economy. Few people, he argued, consistently act in their own financial interest, for no one is free of ideas, values, and tastes that shape his actions. Nor do iron economic laws inexorably dictate a pattern of booms and busts. The kind of unemployment facing Britain, which Keynes called simply intolerable, demonstrated that a free economy is not necessarily efficient and may stabilize in unproductive and unacceptable ways. At the same time he dismissed Marxism as outmoded, a vision from a time already past.

In lucid prose Keynes presented a sophisticated theory that correct governmental policies can smooth out the economic cycle. When the economy lags the government should lower the interest rates charged to borrowers, especially businesses, to encourage production, while spending money on public works and social welfare to put more money in circulation and thus stimulate consumption. As the economy expands the opposite policies should be followed to check inflation and excessive speculation. Thus he formulated the theoretical foundation for practices already partially adopted under Swedish socialism, the French Popular Front, and the American New Deal, President Franklin D. Roosevelt's program of social and economic reform inaugurated in 1933. More important, Keynes made the case for a free economy while rejecting social evils traditional thinkers had accepted. Both socialists and liberals would apply his principles when next they had the chance to direct an economy in peacetime.

Neither malaise nor conflict seemed to inhibit cultural creativity, as the new directions of the 1920s became less shocking a decade later. But two trends characteristic of the 1930s stand out. Science, social science, and the arts where not restricted by the state became more international. This was the result in part of better communication and easier mobility. But much of it was also tragically involuntary, as exiles brought the achievements of Russian ballet, Bauhaus architecture, science and scholarship from Russia, Germany, and Italy to Paris, London, and most of all the United States. And culture generally became more politicized, more ideologically divided. In Paris the Spanish painter Pablo Picasso became the dominant figure of twentieth-century art, restlessly experimenting with one new style after another. But his most famous work, *Guernica* (see also his *Weeping Woman* of the same year—Color Plate 63), was a searing comment on war prepared for the Spanish pavilion at the Paris world's fair of 1937. Social scientists, poets, and novelists not only probed the themes of alienation and faceless mass society but actively organized to do battle in the political conflicts of the period, believing that art and social engineering could change the world. Some defended the "experiments" of Hitler and Mussolini; far more joined Marxist groups to combat the injustices of capitalist society and aid the cause of workers, minorities, or the Spanish republic. Their poetic visions tended to the apocalyptic:

> Financier, leaving your little room
> Where the money is made but not spent,
> You'll need your typist and your boy no
>   more;
> The game is up for you and for the others.
>   . . .[4]

But the socialist anger of W. H. Auden, the British poet who chose to live in America, was balanced by the Christian outrage of T. S. Eliot, the American poet who chose to live in Britain, "The term 'democracy' . . . does not contain enough positive content to stand alone. . . . If you will not have God (and He is a jealous God) you should pay your respects to Hitler or Stalin."[5]

International Tensions

In retrospect the diplomacy of the 1930s was a contest between those seeking radical changes in the international balance, led by Italy and Germany, and those attempting to maintain the postwar international order, led by Britain and France. To contemporaries, however, the lines did not seem so clear. The isolation of two great powers—Russia, effectively ostracized, and the United States, absorbed in her domestic affairs—made European diplomacy somewhat unreal, and the divergent policies of Britain and France often obscured their common interest. Hitler played skillfully on a certain bad conscience among the World War I victors about the Versailles treaty, and Western diplomats were ill-prepared for the shrill propaganda and shifting demands of dictatorships. Foreign policy in the democracies was further weakened by reversals in domestic political platforms: the left, previously committed to disarmament and supporting the League of Nations, favored strong measures against fascist aggression, whereas the right, heretofore readier to defend national interest with a show of force, was more inclined to advocate patient compromise with fascist powers.

Even before the advent of Hitler, Wilsonian internationalism had clearly begun to fail. The complicated claims for reparations and war debts had simply been abandoned rather than resolved by negotiation, and international con-

---

[4] W. H. Auden, "Consider This and In Our Time." In *A Little Treasury of Great Poetry,* edited by Oscar Williams, Charles Scribner's Sons, 1947, p. 689.

[5] T. S. Eliot, *The Idea of a Christian Society,* Harcourt, Brace, 1960.

ferences on disarmament had proved no more successful. A Far Eastern clash weakened the League of Nations still further. In 1931 Japanese troops in Manchuria occupied the major cities of the south, and China's protests led a league committee to investigate. Painfully deliberate, it recommended in 1933 that Japan be ordered to withdraw, but Japan withdrew from the League instead. The next year she renounced international limitations on her naval strength, undoing the laboriously wrought understanding of the 1920s. A four-power pact of 1933 signed by Germany, France, Italy, and Britain, reaffirming their Locarno agreements, was so obviously empty as to be wishful thinking. Later in the same year, Germany withdrew from the disarmament conference that had opened in 1932 and from the League of Nations as well.

Efforts to restrain the growing German threat through a more tightly drawn balance of power were only slightly more effective. The Eastern European nations, as frightened of Russia as of Germany, were disinclined to take unnecessary risks. The Little Entente—an alliance of Czechoslovakia, Yugoslavia, and Rumania, each also allied with France—had established a permanent council to provide fuller diplomatic and military cooperation, and Greece and Turkey were added to this French sphere by the Balkan Pact of 1934. But Hungary and Bulgaria remained outside it, authoritarian states attracted to Italy, impressed by German resurgence, and vulnerable to the economic pressures of German trade.

Austria's Nazis abandoned their attempt at a coup in 1934 when Yugoslav and Italian troops were rushed to the border to prevent the Anschluss, and for a year Italy seemed the key to the European balance of power, a position Mussolini enjoyed immensely. He encouraged the so-called Stresa Front, formed by Italy, France, and Great Britain after Germany renounced the disarmament clauses of the Versailles treaty in 1935; but the fragility of the tripower alignment showed in their separate moves thereafter. France signed a mutual assistance pact with Russia, which worried Britain, frightened Poland, and bothered so many of the French that it was never given real strength. Britain reached a naval agreement with Germany, establishing that the German navy, excluding submarines, was not to exceed 35 percent of the British fleet; such dealings with Germany outraged France. And Italy was preparing all the while for an invasion of Ethiopia.

The Western powers had protested and the League of Nations condemned Germany's formal negation of the disarmament clauses, but everyone knew she had long since been rebuilding her fighting forces, and so after all had everyone else. In 1936 German troops marched into the Rhineland, demilitarized by the Versailles treaty, and this time Italy did nothing. France, unwilling to act alone as she had in 1923, consulted the British who urged acquiescence. The German troops were widely cheered. Only the year before, France had returned the Saar to German control after a plebiscite had shown an overwhelming preference for German rule. The initiative belonged to the fascist powers.

The Ethiopian Crisis

In October 1935 Italy began an invasion of Ethiopia, seemingly an old-fashioned imperialistic venture that followed careful understandings with Britain and France. But the style of the operation, marked by enthusiastic bombings of defenseless populations and racist propaganda, signaled something new. Europeans were shocked, and the League, declaring Italy an aggressor, promptly banned the sale of essential war materials to her.

Only a few countries[6] refused to impose

---

[6] They were Austria, Hungary, and Albania. Switzerland was exempt from having to impose sanctions, a recognition of her formal and permanent neutrality.

these sanctions, but even Germany and the United States, though not members of the League, prohibited increased shipments of restricted items. Most of Europe seemed united in this crucial test of the League's peacekeeping powers. But while the embargoes angered Italy and caused some hardship, they did not stop the war, partly because oil, the most important commodity of all, was not included on the list.

The French foreign minister, Pierre Laval, determined on a hidden course divergent from France's public position. In his successful political career, he had drifted steadily to the right, earning along the way the respectful distrust of all parties. He now sought to keep Italy a useful friend against Germany, and in secret meetings with Sir Samuel Hoare, his British counterpart, he arranged for a settlement of the Ethiopian crisis that would in effect give most of the country to Italy. When the plan was leaked to the press, public outrage swamped it and its sponsors; Hoare was dismissed, and Laval soon fell from power. The plan, however, not only delayed a decision on the crucial question of adding oil to the list of sanctions but undermined confidence in the two democracies. By May 1936 Ethiopia had capitulated, and a few months later Italians celebrated the League's formal lifting of the bans. The League of Nations could no longer be taken seriously as a force for peace.

The Spanish Civil War

Shortly after the conquest of Ethiopia, a nationalist revolt broke out in Spain led by the military. Both Italy and Germany quickly proffered their support to the insurgents, and before the end of the year, the two fascist powers signed an agreement creating the Rome-Berlin Axis, which Germany followed with the Anti-Comintern Pact between herself and Japan. The Spanish Civil War immediately deepened Europe's international and ideological division into competing camps.

Many times previously the Spanish army had claimed to represent the national will, but this civil war seemed to one side the defense of democracy against fascist aggression and a battle for social justice against reactionaries, while to the other the war was a crusade of traditional society and religion against the ravages of anarchists and communists. Throughout the West the public was sharply divided; and idealistic young men, most of them Marxists, went to Spain by the thousands to fight as volunteers in national units like the Lincoln or the Garibaldi Brigade (whose greatest moment was the defeat of regular Italian troops sent by Mussolini).

Spain's government had the support of republicans, socialists, communists, anarchists, labor groups, and Catalan and Basque nationalists organized in a loose coalition and calling themselves Loyalists. They were never fully controlled by the government, and local groups often went far beyond official policy in launching the radical changes the republic had promised. As the war progressed the Loyalists became increasingly dependent on Russia for supplies; by 1938 this and the Communists' greater efficiency made them prominent in a government dangerously divided.

The Nationalists were dominated by the army, which held somewhat aloof from the monarchists, fascistic Falangists, and clericals who flocked to the insurgents' standard. The accidental death of the general who had led the uprising left General Francisco Franco their leader. He had commanded the units stationed in Morocco—the revolt had in fact begun there—that were the Nationalists' best troops; and though little interested in doctrines or ideologies, he recognized the utility of a modern mass appeal in building a disciplined movement.

Most of the Spanish navy remained loyal to the republic, and one of the insurgents' first problems was getting their armies from Morocco to the mainland, where many garrisons

Photographs helped make the Spanish Civil War a divisive reality for all Western civilization. Robert Capa, who took this shot of a Loyalist soldier carrying a wounded comrade, became famous for his pictures of the war.
(Photo: © Robert Capa/Magnum)

had risen in their favor. By July Italian and German planes were providing the needed transport. The help of the fascist powers—Italian troops in significant numbers and military advisers, planes, tanks, and ammunition from both states—remained essential to the strength of Franco's cause. Mussolini welcomed the chance to enhance Italian prestige, and Hitler used the opportunity to test new military technology.

Only Russia gave reliable if limited aid to the Loyalists—until 1938, when Stalin decided to cut his losses. Blum's government in France favored the Loyalists but feared the domestic and international consequences of openly aiding them; Britain's Conservative government shared France's caution, but with a deeper distaste for the radicals of Madrid and a greater hope for good relations with Italy. The democracies thus chose neutrality and thought thereby to lead Germany and Italy to the same position. An international commission formed to prevent foreign intervention merely upheld the ponderous legalism that starved the republic while helping to hide the active role of the fascist powers.

Foreign aid, trained troops, better military organization, and modern weapons made the victory of Franco's forces almost inevitable. They nearly won Madrid and the war itself in the summer of 1936, but the Loyalists held on and in a last-minute counterattack broke the Nationalists' assault. For more than two years, despite poor equipment and internal conflict,

With the fall of the Spanish republic, a French gendarme leads members of the International Brigade to safety across the French border.
(Photo: © Robert Capa/Magnum)

the republicans would show occasional spurts of skill and élan.

Franco's troops spread slowly from their capital, Burgos, in the north, and also up from the south against the Loyalist strongholds of Madrid, Valencia, and Barcelona; but to the disgust of his Axis supporters, the general conducted a war of attrition. Not until the spring of 1939, when Russian supplies had ceased to come and Britain had signed special treaties of friendship with Italy, did the Spanish republic finally fall. Thousands of refugees wearily crossed into France while Franco filled Spain's capacious prisons with potential enemies, undid radical measures, and restored the power of the church over education. Franco then joined the Anti-Comintern Pact and took Spain out of the League of Nations.

The civil war had cost more than a million Spaniards their lives, many of them at the hands of firing squads and mobs. The bombing of Guernica by German aircraft in 1937 made men shudder before the vision of what war now meant for civilians, and the conflict between the democracies and the Axis was established as fundamental. But the democracies, fearful and divided, accepted defeat while the Axis acted.

The Anschluss and the Czech Partition

During the course of the Spanish Civil War, attention shifted to the center of Europe. In February 1938 Hitler summoned Austria's chancellor Kurt von Schuschnigg to Berchtesgaden, the Führer's fortified mountain retreat, and after a long, humiliating harangue won his promise to include Austrian Nazis in his cabinet. Feeling braver after he returned home, Schuschnigg called for a plebiscite. He hoped it would rally the people to save Austria's independence, though he could hardly hope for Socialists to forgive the suppression of their party; moreover, Italy warned that she would no longer offer military backing. Hitler was furious at Schuschnigg's action, and while Austrian Nazis rioted, Germany massed military units on the border and sent an ultimatum demanding that the plebiscite be postponed and that Schuschnigg resign.

Friendless, the Austrian chancellor had no choice; he was replaced by Artur von Seyss-Inquart, a Nazi, who invited German troops to restore order. They did so on March 13, and within a month Austria's annexation to Germany was almost unanimously approved in a plebiscite run by the Nazis. The dream of Anschluss had been fulfilled (see Map 28.1). Hitler's popularity at home rose still higher, and German influence spread more deeply into the Balkans. The lesson was clear: Germany was Europe's greatest power; alliances with the Little Entente were of small value; and when Hitler moved, Britain and France merely protested.

Two weeks after the plebiscite in Austria, Hitler demanded autonomy for the Sudetenland, an overwhelmingly German-speaking section of Czechoslovakia. The parallel with Austria was lost on no one, though the challenge to the Czech republic was far more daring, for Czechoslovakia was a prosperous industrial state protected by a respectable army, well-fortified frontiers, and mutual-aid treaties with both France and Russia. Supported by her allies, Czechoslovakia mobilized, and Hitler ordered Konrad Henlein, the Sudeten Nazi leader, to quiet down.

Internal divisions as well as geography made Czechoslovakia vulnerable. She was barely able to maintain the loyalty of the Slovaks, and she had met the threat of a pro-Nazi party—which in the elections held in 1935 had won more votes than any other—only by restricting political parties. Nor were the great powers united in their reactions to Hitler. Determined to prevent war, Chamberlain wanted to parlay directly with Germany, believing that no nonnegotiable British interest was at stake in the Sudetenland, and he rejected suggestions from the United States and Russia for a meeting to consider means of restraining the Nazi dictator. Many in France and England, deeply alarmed at how close to war they were, wondered whether Czech sovereignty over a German population was worth such a risk.

Throughout the summer Sudeten Nazi leaders negotiated with the Czech state while demonstrations there and in Germany heated the atmosphere. In August Chamberlain, with French concurrence, sent his own emissary to mediate while German troops held maneuvers on the Czech border and Hitler pointedly toured Germany's fortifications in the west.

In September the pressure increased. Hitler's speeches became more bellicose, and war seemed imminent. Chamberlain decided, once again with French support, to visit Berchtesgaden. When he met with Hitler there on September 15, the Führer raised his demand—to annexation of the Sudetenland. After a few days Britain and France advised Czechoslovakia to submit. Desperately the Czechs sought some escape, but only Russia was ready to support resistance. On September 22 Chamberlain flew back to Germany with the good news that Czechoslovakia had agreed to Hitler's terms only to find them changed again: German troops must occupy the ceded territory immediately, leaving the Czechs no time to provide for citizens who wished to escape Nazi rule or to move factories and military supplies. A shocked Chamberlain said no, and for five days the world listened for war.

Then, persuaded by Mussolini, Hitler agreed to a meeting with Britain, France, and Italy. The brief conference took place on September 29 in Munich, where just fifteen years earlier Hitler had failed to capture the town hall. Now he dealt with nations. Hitler, von Ribbentrop, Mussolini, Chamberlain, and Daladier talked for an afternoon and evening; and Hitler was granted all he asked. Neither Russia

MAP 28.1: EUROPE 1935–1939

nor Czechoslovakia was consulted. The next day Czechoslovakia submitted to the terms of the Munich Pact and to the demands added by Poland and Hungary, for the Teschen region and a piece of Slovakia respectively. At a single stroke Czechoslovakia surrendered one-third of her population, her best military defenses, and much of her economic strength.

Thus Central Europe's strongest democracy was reduced to a German dependency and a keystone of France's continental security shattered. As Daladier's plane circled the Paris airport, he watched the crowd below with dread. But it cheered him, and in Britain Chamberlain became a hero. Peace, the papers echoed, had been preserved.

The Path to War

Europe was shaken by the Munich Pact and by the brutality and anti-Semitism goose-stepping troops carried with them into expropriated territory. Inspired by the democracies' ready capitulation, Italy began a noisy campaign to get Nice and Corsica from France.

German might, Hitler's speeches, the news of life in lands annexed or in Germany itself—all gave Jews, non-Aryans, peoples along the German borders, and whole nations reason for terror. To hold such fear in check there stood the sane temptation to believe that even the Nazis, even Hitler, could not want another world war. Then early in 1939, following the now-familiar pattern of agitation, Germany occupied all of Czechoslovakia (except for part of the Carpatho-Ukraine, taken by the Hungarians) and in the same month annexed the seaport of Memel from a terrified Lithuania. The pretext of absorbing only German peoples had now been abandoned. Chamberlain, still ready to risk personal and national honor in the hope of winning Germany to a responsible place in European councils, led those who believed that concessions could appease Hitler. But by this time most of the English and the French had resigned themselves to the necessity of stopping the Nazis with force.

The summer of 1939 brought more alarms. Italy invaded and annexed Albania, and the Italo-German Axis was formally tightened into the "Pact of Steel." Germany kept chancelleries quaking with demands for nonaggression agreements. Late in August the leader of the Nazi party in Danzig declared that his city must be returned to the fatherland. Everyone now knew what to expect; denunciations of the Versailles boundaries and of the persecution of Germans within the Polish corridor—cries that would once have won a sympathetic hearing—clearly meant that Poland was next. As they had all summer, Britain and France renewed their pledges to assist her.

The summer's most important contest, however, was for the allegiance of Russia, and Hitler won that too: a Russo-German nonaggression pact was suddenly announced at the height of the Polish crisis. Russia had made overtures to Britain and France for some time, suggesting that they join her in guaranteeing the territorial integrity of all the states between the Baltic and Black seas. But the Western powers had not been ready to grant the communist nation so extensive a zone of influence and had responded weakly to Russian approaches, sending lesser officials rather than their foreign ministers, who had been invited to meetings in Moscow during the summer. Despite Russian policy—which since 1935 had advocated disarmament, supported the League of Nations (Russia had entered it just as Germany had left), supplied the republican government of Spain, and offered support to Czechoslovakia—Chamberlain, like most Western statesmen, remained more willing to talk with Hitler than with Stalin.

In May 1939 Maxim Litvinov, the eloquent spokesman for this pro-Western policy, had been replaced by Stalin's tougher and less cosmopolitan friend and Russia's premier, Vyacheslav Molotov, as minister of foreign affairs. Stalin suspected the democracies would welcome a war between Germany and the Soviet Union, whereas Hitler had offered just what Russia asked: an understanding that if Germany sought any changes in her eastern border, Russia was to have a free hand in Finland, Estonia, Latvia, eastern Poland up to approximately the old Curzon Line, and the Bessarabian portion of Rumania. The Russo-German agreement was a masterpiece of cynical accommodation between the sponsors of antifascist fronts and the authors of the Anti-Comintern Pact that shocked a world still unaccustomed to totalitarian flexibility.

The last days of August resounded with formal warnings and clarifications between the Western powers and Germany, but to no avail. Hitler invaded Poland on September 1, and Britain and France mobilized and sent him an ultimatum, determined in this world conflict to make their intentions clear. On September 3, 1939, they declared war, offering battle to defend an authoritarian Poland just one year after surrendering Czechoslovakia.

IV. WORLD WAR II: 1939–1941

Hitler's Quick Victories

Appeasement had failed, not simply because it was a policy of weakness—the appeasers insisted that theirs was a serious effort to resolve differences—but because Hitler wanted war, preferably in the short bursts he was likely to win. Although Britain and France had gained some time with conciliatory policies, they had not always used it well. Memories of World War I and internal divisions made it harder to prepare for the one activity above all others to which fascism was now dedicated: the conquest of Europe. For two years the Axis would score one victory after another (see Map 28.2).

The Germans had prepared carefully for the invasion of Poland, and they attacked her with overwhelming force. Even so the speed of their victory was surprising. Poland fell in less than a month under the impact of Europe's first blitzkrieg, and Russia hastily marched in to claim her share. More nervous than ever about the trustworthiness of her fascist partner, Russia pressed Finland for territory that would move the Russian frontier a safer distance than the twenty miles from Leningrad where it then lay. The Finns, willing to negotiate, refused to cede all the Russians demanded, and in November the Red army marched. Finnish resistance against such odds won worldwide admiration and a brief respite during the winter but could not prevent defeat the following spring. Russia, having regained boundaries close to those the last tsars had enjoyed, could afford to wait.

The Western powers had been waiting too. Hitler suggested that with Poland gone there was no longer reason to fight, but few were tempted by his hints of peace. On the other hand, the British and French commanders were resolved not to risk their precious planes too soon or to launch the pointless assaults of World War I. Since Hitler refrained from attacking along the French border, the Allies followed suit. This was the so-called phony war, during which arms production and mobilization speeded up, the world waited, and little happened. The strain was bad for morale. French Communists now thought the war a mistake and said so loudly, even though their party had been suppressed, but the democracies searched, as they had in the previous war, for more effective leaders. Paul Reynaud, energetic and determined, replaced Daladier as premier. Chamberlain resigned in May after a wide-ranging debate on his whole conduct of the war (Norway had just fallen). Britain's new government included all parties under the firm hand of Winston Churchill, a Conservative who believed in empire and old-fashioned sonorous sentences, a political maverick who had been both a reformer and a defender of national interest through forty years of political life. An opponent of appeasement now given his chance by disaster, Churchill would prove one of England's greatest leaders.

The war had again become terribly real. The Allies were beginning to prepare the de-

MAP 28.2: THE HEIGHT OF AXIS POWER 1942

fense of Norway when Germany attacked, taking Denmark in a day, April 9, 1940. Norway's most strategically important points were captured in short order, giving Germany a dangerous base for assaults on numerous British ships and cities.

In Warsaw, German tanks, fresh from their lightning destruction of the Polish army, pass in review before Adolf Hitler on October 5, 1939.
(Photo: Wide World Photos)

The Fall of France

On May 10 and without warning, German troops flooded the Netherlands and Belgium. The Dutch, who had expected to escape war—as they had since Napoleon I—surrendered in five days; the better-prepared and larger Belgian army held out for eighteen. On May 14 a skillfully executed German offensive broke through the Ardennes forest, thought to be impervious to panzer tactics, reached Sedan, and drove to the Channel, trapping the Belgian and British forces fighting there and much of the French army. The Luftwaffe controlled the air, and only Hitler's greater interest in taking Paris and their own fortitude permitted the Allies' proudest achievement in the battle for France: between May 26 and June 4, most of their 340,000 troops pinned against the sea were evacuated from the port town of Dunkirk and bravely carried across to the British Isles in a motley flotilla of naval vessels, commercial ferries, and private sailboats.

Hitler seemed invincible and the blitzkrieg some terrible new Teutonic force, a totalitarian achievement other societies could not hope to equal. In fact, however, many of the tactical ideas on which it rested were first put forward by British and French experts, including General Charles de Gaulle, an advocate of military mechanization and especially tank warfare; but German officers had the experience of defeat, which makes armies more open to new ideas, and they trained their forces well. The blitzkrieg was the result not so much of new technology as of new strategy. It combined air attacks with rapid movements of motorized columns to overcome the advantages defensive positions had previously enjoyed.

In a blitzkrieg tanks roared through and behind enemy lines, a maneuver nearly forbidden in older theories and requiring great speed and careful drill. In the flat terrain of Poland, the panzer divisions were able to encircle the enemy; in France they often assaulted troops so far in the rear that the defense was unprepared for battle. The aim was less to capture ground than to break up communications, a task furthered by the air force, which was used to disorient and terrify the retreating army. Even the machine-gunning of French roads clogged with refugees and the bombing of Rotterdam thus had their place in the campaign to demoralize.

Clearly the German tactics worked. It does not follow, however, that France's military inferiority was so great as her defeat. French commanders were able but a little too rigid and, like their nation perhaps, too inclined to think in defensive terms. They preferred larger tanks—not necessarily an unsound attitude—but they lacked the time to deploy them for maximum effect. French strategists were too slow perhaps to recognize the full importance of air power, and their air force was temporar-

Norwegians silently observe the arrival of German army reinforcements at Oslo station in 1940.
(Photo: Wide World Photos)

ily weakened by being in the midst of changing models. More fundamentally, Britain and France had allowed Germany years of massive arming, but their own planning was incomplete.

Excessive reliance on the Maginot Line, France's system of fortifications extending from the Swiss to the Belgian border, was a fatal temptation in a country of unstable governments, a tax-conscious electorate, demographic decline, and pained memories of World War I. That supposedly impregnable line, which gave a false sense of security, stopped at the Belgian border. The French had not wanted to wall out Belgium and Holland, whose reassertion of neutrality made joint planning impossible. As a result, too much was staked on Germany's maintaining a similar sensitivity to the rights of neutrals. When Germany invaded the Low Countries in May, the defending armies were poorly coordinated. Defensive strategies lost their meaning when Panzer divisions crashed through forests expected to stop them, leaving defenders no time to regroup or restore communications.

And morale in France was not high, though the phony war and the rout of what many thought to be Europe's best army have perhaps made it seem worse than it was. Suspicions of the British, of the army, of the politicians, of the left—like the miscalculations of her officers and the inexperience of her troops—might have been rectified with time, but that above all France was not granted.

The Allied defense of France was broken after Dunkirk, and Germans renewed their attack on June 5. They took Paris in a week. Mussolini attacked France on the tenth, anxious lest he miss the war entirely; and he had in fact but barely demonstrated the inferiority of his forces before France surrendered, on June 16. The armistice was signed in the railway car used for Germany's surrender in 1918. More ironic still, the man who chose to sign for his people was the World War I hero of Verdun and marshal of France, Henri Philippe Pétain.

Pétain, who had replaced Reynaud as premier following the fall of Paris, believed France must now make her way in Hitler's Europe. He accepted terms that put the northern and eastern three-fifths of the country under Nazi occupation and allowed French prisoners of war to be kept in Germany. For a moment the nation turned to the octogenarian marshal with stunned unanimity. The headquarters of unoccupied France were established the following month at Vichy, and a reconvened parliament maneuvered by Pierre Laval named Pétain chief of state.

The new regime, a confused coalition of militant fascists and the traditional right, was never to be really independent of Germany. After adopting bits of corporatism and some fascist trappings, it settled into a lethargy of its own, ruling a truncated state as rife with intrigue, personal ambition, and shifting alliances as the Third Republic it so heartily denounced. The abler politicians of the Third Republic drifted away from Vichy, while the few convinced totalitarians preferred the more efficient atmosphere of Nazi-occupied Paris.

The Battle of Britain

Great Britain stood alone. While German officers—themselves unprepared for such victories on the Continent so soon—planned an invasion, their bombers roared over England in air attacks that many believed would in themselves force Britain to sue for peace. Instead in September the projected invasion was postponed, and by the following spring the air raids were letting up. For Britain merely to survive from June 1940 to June 1941 was a kind of victory, which Churchill proudly called her "finest hour."

There had been signs that such resilience was possible. During the Norwegian campaign, which had otherwise cost Germany so little, her navy had suffered enough damage in encounters with the British to reduce its effectiveness and make it more cautious. The Dunkirk evacuation had testified to the resourcefulness of the thousands of civilians who lent the military eager assistance. And in the man-to-man air battles, British fighters, particularly their newer designs, proved at least the equal of the German.

Thus the waves of the German planes flying over the island kingdom sustained losses far greater than those of the Royal Air Force, losses increased by new techniques of antiaircraft defense, including radar, an English development that was the most critical addition to military technology displayed in these years. German attacks concentrated at first on ports and shipping, then on airfields, and finally on cities, leaving great burning holes in London and destroying Coventry. But shifting targets dissipated the economic and military effects of the bombing, and the citizens of London reacted very differently from refugees on a crowded highway to terror from the skies. Britain's morale rose as, ever better organized, she fiercely carried on.

War in the East

The Battle of Britain was Hitler's first serious check, but Germans could be reassured by fascist victories elsewhere. They did not come easily. Italian forces, launching an offensive into Egypt from Libya in September 1940, were driven back in a successful British counterattack until the British themselves had to withdraw into Egypt because of the Axis challenge in the Balkans. When Italian forces invaded Greece from Albania in October, the Greeks pushed them back, and Hitler had to bail out Mussolini.

The Balkan States were rapidly losing their independence. Russia stretched previous agreements to annex Bessarabia in June 1940, and Germany promised to defend what remained of Rumania (after Hungary and Bulgaria each took a bit). Rumania, Hungary, and Bulgaria, all implicated in Hitler's map-making, were closely tied to the Nazi Reich. It was no great step for them to welcome German troops in March 1941 and to join Hitler in attacking Yugoslavia, which had hesitated too long, and Greece, which had fought Mussolini too well.

The attack was launched in April and swept through both countries within the month. Some Greek and British forces pulled back to Crete, only to be forced out almost immediately by history's first large glider and paratroop attack. The Allies retreated to Egypt, herself now seriously endangered by the Axis domination of the Mediterranean. Hitler still appeared invincible in the summer of 1941.

Germany's expansion into the Balkans disturbed the Russians, but a confident Hitler suggested they interest themselves in Iran and India instead. Both sides anticipated conflict, and Stalin assumed the premiership in May as part of the preparation for war. Yet when the Germans attacked the Soviet Union on June 22, 1941, the Russians appeared genuinely surprised—at least by the timing and the size of the attack. The assault, in three broad sectors, was the largest concentration of military power that had ever been assembled.

Once more the blitzkrieg worked its magic, though everyone now understood how it operated. German armored divisions ripped through Russian lines and encircled astonishing numbers of troops. Quickly they crossed the vast lands Russia had acquired since 1939, taking Riga and Smolensk in July, reaching the Dnieper in August, claiming Kiev and the whole Ukraine in September. Then the pace slowed; but while one German force lay siege to Leningrad in the north, a second hit Sevastopol in the south and moved into the Crimea, and by December still another penetrated to the suburbs of Moscow.

There the German advance stopped temporarily, halted by an early and severe winter, by strained supply lines, and at last by sharp Russian counterattacks. Germany now held territory that had accounted for nearly two-thirds of Russia's production of coal, iron, steel, and aluminum; 40 percent of her grain and hogs. The December snows, however, raised the specter of a continuing two-front war, which Hitler had sworn to avoid. For all its losses of men and territory, the Red army was intact, and the Germans had little to live on in the wasteland the Russians systematically created as they retreated. The battle for Russia was not over as Hitler's timetable predicted it would be.

Strains on the Axis

By mid-December 1941 the Axis faced great threats from Russia, from within the vast lands they ruled, from the British Empire, and from the United States, the world's most powerful nation.

Despite her deep partisanship for France and Britain, the United States remained technically at peace in 1940. With the intention of keeping the country out of European conflicts, Congress had passed the second Neutrality Act in 1937. The law, which had helped withhold armaments from republican Spain, had been amended in 1939 to permit governments to buy war materials from American suppliers if the purchasers paid in cash and carried the goods

American servicemen survey the ruins on an airfield at Pearl Harbor; the United States had entered the war.
(Photo: Navy Department/National Archives)

on their own ships. That, everyone knew, could benefit only one side of the European conflict. In 1940 the American government sold weapons to private corporations for transfer to Great Britain and traded fifty old American destroyers for the lease of British bases in the western Atlantic, thus reducing the areas Britain needed to patrol.

A year later the United States formally accepted the role of "the arsenal of democracy," and she began extending loans, first to Britain and then the Soviet Union, to help them pay for desperately needed supplies. In August Winston Churchill and Franklin Roosevelt met at sea to draft the Atlantic Charter, which looked forward in very Wilsonian terms to a world "after the destruction of the Nazi tyranny" in which there would be collective security and self-determination for all nations so that "all the men of all the lands may live out their lives in freedom from fear and want."

Even so firm an ideological commitment, however, did not bring the United States into the war. Japanese airplanes did that. Tension between the two nations had reached a new high when Japan absorbed French Indochina in 1941. Then on December 7, confident that Russia was so occupied as to be no threat and that the United States could be rendered nearly harmless in one blow, Japan attacked the Hawaiian port of Pearl Harbor, a key U.S. naval base. The effects of the attack were devastating and three days later Germany and Italy declared war on the United States. American entry into the war would prove fatal to the Axis, but Hitler had fallen into the habit of underestimating his opponents.

In late 1941 he ruled virtually the entire Continent from the Atlantic to the Ukraine in the name of a new order, and he had found sympathizers and allies in every country, from Vidkun Quisling in Norway to Francisco Franco in Spain.[7] But the Nazis alienated those they conquered by their labor conscription, their racial policies, and their oppressive brutality. A high percentage of Ukrainians, for example, had been inclined to welcome liberation from Russian rule, but brief acquaintance with how Nazis treated "inferior" Slavs ended any enthusiasm for cooperation with the Germans and cost them an invaluable asset.

By the end of 1941, organized resistance movements in most countries were harassing the Nazi order. Mussolini, perhaps the one man Hitler truly admired, had weakened the Axis with his misjudgments of his own strength. Although no contemporary could yet know it, the Axis had begun to lose the war.

---

[7] Only Sweden, Spain, Portugal, Switzerland, and Eire remained even technically neutral by grace of geography.

The democracy so optimistically extended after World War I fared badly in the following twenty years. Not only did it fail in poor and strife-torn new nations, but in the most advanced it fumbled before the social crises of the Depression and mass politics. Totalitarianism offered alternatives that fed on disenchantment with bourgeois culture and liberalism. Its fascist forms appealed to all those who had been the "losers" in the growth of the liberal, secular state, all who had been hurt or alienated by rapid change. The fear of Russian communism strengthened the view that the future lay with those who could ruthlessly mobilize masses. Ideologically and in terms of force, fascism challenged the traditional institutions and values of European culture.

Western leaders faced the challenge only slowly. By the time they had abandoned the illusion that they could buy peace, they had lost the initiative (and much of Europe), and uncertain nations faced another world war. Within two years the Axis had conquered the European Continent. Japanese airplanes then brought the United States into World War II as German submarines had done in World War I. In this most global of wars, the Allies once again stood for democracy—a democracy more socially aware and less confident than thirty years before. If Russia was as embarrassing an ally in 1941 as in 1914, the humane traditions of Western civilization clearly rested with the Europeanized societies—Russia, the Americas, and the British Empire—that set out to reconquer Europe.

RECOMMENDED READING

Studies

Branson, N., and M. Heinemann. *Britain in the 1930s.* 1971. Ably relates the interconnections of political life with the social and economic stress of the period.

*Bullock, Alan. *Hitler: A Study in Tyranny.* 1971. The best biography of Hitler and one that gives an effective picture of Nazi society.

*Carr, E. H. *The Soviet Impact on the Western World.* 1947. Although much recent scholarship adds to our understanding, this remains a valuable overall view with a participant's feeling for the importance of Soviet influence.

*Carsten, F. L. *The Rise of Fascism.* 1967. The careful synthesis of a distinguished scholar.

*Churchill, Winston. *The Second World War.* 6 vols. (also available in a one-volume condensation). 1948–1953. This powerful history is also an important document that conveys much of Churchill's greatness and prejudices.

*Fromm, Erich. *Escape from Freedom.* 1941. A psychoanalytic argument about Western man's historic reluctance to bear the burdens of freedom.

*Jackson, Gabriel. *The Spanish Republic and the Civil War, 1937–1939.* 1965. An informed, insightful treatment of a still controversial and complex period.

*Kirkpatrick, Sir Ivone. *Mussolini: Study of a Demagogue.* 1964. By a former British diplomat, this is the fullest study available in English.

Mack Smith, Denis. *Mussolini's Roman Empire.* 1976. A lucid account with much new information by the leading English scholar of modern Italy.

Nettl, J. P. *The Soviet Achievement.* 1967. Effectively tackles the difficult task of assessing both the economic development of the U.S.S.R. and its social cost.

*Nolte, Ernst. *The Three Faces of Fascism.* A learned effort to trace the intellectual history of fascism in France, Germany, and Italy.

*Schoenbaum, David. *Hitler's Social Revolution: Class and Status in Nazi Germany, 1933–1939.* 1966. An important study of the social policies, in theory and practice, of the Third Reich.

*Shirer, William L. *Rise and Fall of the Third Reich.* 1960. The somewhat tendentious and widely read account of a noted and knowledgeable journalist.

*Sontag, Raymond J. *A Broken World, 1919–1939.* 1971. A senior scholar's assessment that emphasizes international relations.

Tannenbaum, Edward R. *The Fascist Experience: Italian Society and Culture, 1922–1945.* 1972. A wide-ranging effort to recapture the meaning in practice of Fascist rule.

Weinberg, Gerhard L. *The Foreign Policy of Hitler's Germany.* 1970. A major study by a leading American diplomatic historian.

*Wright, Gordon. *The Ordeal of Total War, 1939–1945.* 1968. A thoughtful and stimulating assessment of the psychological, scientific, and economic aspects of the war as well as a balanced account of its course.

---

* Available in paperback.

29

WORLD WAR II AND THE SURVIVAL OF EUROPE 1941–1958

World War II challenged the very survival of European society, and not simply in the primitive sense that any war seems to menace civilization. The killing and destruction attacked the civilian heart of society, and the conqueror of the Continent made rapine and genocide his policy. Controlling the Continent and wide sweeps of Pacific and Asian territories, the Axis amassed a concentration of power so great that most of the remaining industrialized world had to mobilize to dislodge it. Thus the liberation of Europe began in the depths of Russia, on the sea lanes, and in North Africa, requiring enormous feats of organization and terrible sacrifice. The occupied Continental nations could contribute little more than the old-fashioned heroic work of small, secret bands.

The immediate aftermath of the war was a kind of social collapse that reduced political, economic, and social organization to a skeleton. In terms of international power, Europe appeared to have been all but conquered by the Russians and the Americans. Their conflicts, practical and ideological, were the extension of the European experience that now shaped the conditions of postwar reorganization. The Eastern European countries freed by the Soviet Union could not prevent the Russians from dominating their internal affairs; the Western states, heavily reliant on economic aid from the United States, cautiously fell back on old institutions and parliamentary forms as the basis from which to rebuild. It was doubtful whether such structures could be adequate to postwar needs.

Yet Europe accomplished a remarkable recovery. Politically an enforced moderation gave some stability to the rapidly changing world. In the West prosperity eased the accommodation to altered conditions, and the Eastern states gradually achieved an equilibrium between the relaxation of tyranny and the preservation of dictatorship, between communist alliances and national autonomy. Unprecedented increases in productivity, new techniques for directing the economies, and new policies for broadening social welfare suggested that European societies might move in directions distinctly their own. It was not clear, however, how they could achieve such autonomy.

I. THE END OF WORLD WAR II

The Shifting Balance

At the beginning of 1942, Nazi power was at its height. Germany ruled most of the people and controlled most of the wealth of the Continent (see Map 29.1). Her military power that spring consisted of between 7 and 10 million men in ground forces, a superb air force, and a significant navy, including more than 150 submarines, which in the four summer months would cost the Allies nearly 400 ships. Italy added sizable forces to the Axis that were especially important in Africa. Yet Axis dominance was short-lived.

From the 1930s on, the fascist powers had held the initiative in politics, international relations, and war. The two years of staggering military defeat (1939–1941) that left England alone in Europe followed a long string of political, economic, and diplomatic failures for the liberal democracies. In retrospect, however, it is possible to see that in 1942 the tide was beginning to turn. Britain was becoming stronger; Russia remained a formidable foe, most of its military might still intact. Unless the Allies were driven from the seas, the industrial and military power of the United States would be able to tip the scales. Despite the advantage of shorter lines of communication, Germany had little time to consolidate its vast gains, and the system that took so naturally to ruthless conquest was less well adapted to the mobilization of the enormous resources under its control. The brutal realities of war made propaganda less effective, and Germany was losing the advantage of superior preparation and surprise. The Germans were unaware, of course, that in London the secret codes they believed to be unbreakable had been cracked as early as 1940 by a project code-named Ultra, one of the earliest triumphs of the computer. Confidently, German officials (and especially those of the Luftwaffe) continued to transmit orders and plans that left the Allies increasingly well informed, an advantage that would be more important as the war progressed.[1] Germany was racing against time. If she was to secure her massive victories, Russia must be knocked out of the war.

The Eastern Front

Neither the lengthening siege of Leningrad nor the attack on Moscow had achieved that. In the summer of 1942, the Germans drove farther into southern Russia, taking Sevastopol and depriving the nation of ever more desperately needed grain. But the crucial battle of the Eastern front took place from August to October at Stalingrad (now Volgograd), a major communications center, where a breakthrough would open to Hitler the oilfields of southern Russia.

By September the Germans had penetrated the city, where they fought the Russians at such close quarters that sometimes the antagonists battled from within the same building. But the German offensive weakened as supplies dwindled, and Russia's heroic defense had allowed time to amass troops for a counterattack, which broke through and encircled the German army. Hitler frantically ordered his army to stand its ground; and when it surrendered, in February 1943, less than one-third of its 300,000 men were left. The giant Russian pincers pushed on until March, costing the Germans more than half a million casualties. Stalingrad was the turning point of the European war.

The War in the West

The dominant Axis position in the West was deteriorating as well. By early 1943 the worst

---

[1] The secret of Ultra has been revealed only in the last few years, and historians are busily assessing its impact. The information the Allies gained through Ultra appears to have been especially important in the Battle of Britain, the protection of Atlantic shipping, and above all in the Normandy landing.

MAP 29.1: THE ALLIED VICTORY IN WORLD WAR II

threats from U-boats had been overcome, and the air supremacy Great Britain had won over her own islands extended to the Continent by the time the Germans invaded Russia. Thousands of tons of explosives fell on Germany each month in 1942, and five times as much was dropped in 1943. The Americans favored pinpoint bombing of strategic targets; the British preferred nighttime area bombing, with a city itself as the target. The fire bombing of Hamburg in 1943 created a holocaust, but its horror would be exceeded two years later with a yet more massive raid that leveled Dresden, a city of miserable civilians and refugees and without significant industry. Indifference to the suffering of noncombatants had become a common quality of modern war.

For the Allies the major strategical dispute of the war was becoming critical: how to attack Hitler's "fortress Europe." The Russians repeatedly urged the opening of a second front on the Continent, and most of the American military favored an immediate invasion, whereas the British warned against the dangerously high cost of such an operation. With Roosevelt's support Churchill prevailed, and it was decided to invade Morocco and Algeria, the lightly defended western regions of North Africa then under the control of Vichy France. Success would end the Axis threat to Egypt and open southern Europe—the "soft underbelly" of the Continent, as Churchill called it—to Allied assault.

North Africa and Asia

Until 1942 the battle lines in North Africa had ebbed and flowed, as two skilled commanders—Erwin Rommel, the German "desert fox" and the British general, Bernard Montgomery—parried each other's thrusts in the deserts between Libya and Egypt. Then in October 1942 the British defeated the German *Afrikakorps* at El Alamein in Egypt, barely seventy miles from the Nile delta. As at Stalingrad so too at El Alamein, the Nazi tide reached a high point and then began to recede. In November 1942, in the largest amphibious action yet attempted, British and American forces landed in Morocco and Algeria and attacked the *Afrikakorps* from the west. The campaign was an important test for the still green American troops; it was also a test of Allied strength and coordination, ably directed by an American commander, General Dwight D. Eisenhower. By May 1943 and after heavy losses, the Axis powers had been pushed out of Africa.

In July another mammoth amphibious assault carried Anglo-American forces into Sicily. As they advanced across the island, the Fascist Grand Council voted Mussolini out of office; and in September Allied forces landed in southern Italy. In the year since Stalingrad and the North African invasion, the course of the war had changed. Hitler still controlled most of Europe and much of the heaviest fighting lay ahead, but the eventual outcome no longer seemed in doubt.

Japan meanwhile had made sweeping gains in East Asia and the Pacific (see Map 29.2). Shortly after Pearl Harbor Roosevelt and Churchill had agreed to give their battle against Germany priority over the war in Asia. The decision acknowledged the bonds of Western culture, the importance of European industrial power, and the danger that Russia might not long survive without massive help. In effect the policy required the United States to postpone revenge for her defeats in the Pacific. She had lost the Philippine Islands after dramatic and costly defensive stands at Bataan and Corregidor early in 1942. Later in May a naval engagement in the Coral Sea, just north of Australia, ended with no clear-cut victory but reduced the immediate threat of further Japanese gains. In June the Japanese landed in the Aleutian Islands, but American air power drove off their attempt to invade Midway Island. By the end of the year, U.S. forces had taken the first steps in their slow progress back through the Pacific territories.

The Demands of Total War

In this total war, which required the coordination of entire national economies, long-range planning, and the cooperation of every sector of society, Germany, the state in theory most devoted to militarism, managed in practice less well than its enemies.

MAP 29.2: WORLD WAR II IN THE PACIFIC

The Allies

The Soviet Union suffered the heaviest losses of any combatant whether measured in terms of people killed by war and starvation or the capacity for agricultural and industrial production that was lost. Accustomed to central planning, the Soviets quickly mobilized every resource, subjecting civilians to severe rationing and factory workers to military discipline and to increased hours of labor. Even before 1939 Stalin had adopted the policy of industrializing the more backward and safely distant regions east of the Urals, and in the months before Hitler's attack in 1941 hundreds of factories had been dismantled and moved piece by piece, and some 3500 new industrial enterprises were established there. From this base the Soviet Union was able throughout the war to produce most of the military supplies it needed, aided by the established practice of employing women (who were over half the industrial work force by war's end). The prodigies performed despite hardship and defeats testify to sustained morale. Patriotism of a rather old-fashioned and bourgeois sort became the dominant theme of Soviet public life.

Great Britain responded more slowly; not until the fall of France did the grim meaning of the war make itself felt at home. The bombing of Britain, however, seemed to stiffen civilian morale; and gradually the government developed a capacity to coordinate and command national resources with an efficiency any dictator could have admired. Although the number of workdays lost to strikes increased in the course of the war, so did production; and, as in World War I, the end of unemployment (a million workers remained without work in the first year of the war), better wages, the employment of more women, and higher taxes somewhat narrowed class differences. The United States also mobilized its full economic resources for this war, producing by the end of 1942 more war matériel than all its enemies combined. Ships, planes, arms, and munitions poured from American factories and, with food from American farms, flowed across the oceans to Britain and the Soviet Union. In this war of total economies, where organization was more important than brilliant strategy or even technological discoveries, the Allies were clearly superior.

Nazi Rule

Until 1943 German civilians experienced few real hardships and nothing comparable to the sacrifices by which the Soviets or the lowered standard of living by which the British squeezed the maximum war production from their economies. Nor was German output much greater than at the war's outset. This changed when Albert Speer was given increased powers to direct the economy, as he had been demanding. In mid-July 1943 German production was twice what it had been in 1939 despite Allied bombing, and a year later it was three times the prewar level. By then, however, advancing Allied armies were rapidly reducing the resources available to the country.

The delayed and incomplete social and economic mobilization of Nazi Germany stemmed from the very nature of the regime. The illusion, supported by breathtaking successes and official propaganda, that the war would soon be over encouraged interim measures rather than long-range planning. Disdainful of intellectuals and distrustful of established interests, the Nazis failed to achieve the effective cooperation with science and industry that marked the British and American war effort. In their incessant battles for power the party, the army, and local officials often pursued conflicting or self-defeating policies. Europe's Nazi rulers had an unparalleled opportunity to bend the Continent to their purposes. Yet the much-advertised New Order remained curiously ill defined, while policies of terror and destruction reduced efficiency and undermined even its clearest goal, the exploitation of conquered territory.

Truly totalitarian control in subject lands proved beyond the German reach. Content with ruthless terror and intermittent demonstrations of their power, Nazi administrators tended in practice to leave day-to-day affairs to established institutions and local officials. Despite the fear they induced, the conquerors never felt secure. Their rule was most severe and most destructive in Eastern Europe. Unoccupied France, governed from Vichy, was taken over in November 1942; and the French, although relatively better treated than Eastern Europeans, suffered severe deprivations in the remaining years of the war, including food rations that provided about half the minimum needed for decent health. Having stockpiled critical supplies and gained access to more through conquest, Germany's most crucial need was for workers. Slave labor was the answer chosen in accordance with Nazi racial theory. The "Aryan" populations of Nordic lands and the "mixed races" of the industrial West were generally better treated and encouraged to maintain production (although a million French, including 220,000 Jews, were taken to

German soldiers prepare to execute a Jew near Lodz, Poland. The doomed man has had to dig his own grave. This was one of many photographs found in German headquarters after the Allies invaded Poland.
(Photo: UPI)

Germany). Slavs were rated much lower on the Nazi racial scale, and they were driven from the German borders in "population transfers" that vacated land for German settlers; eventually some 5 million were shipped like cattle to labor in Germany. By 1944 the 7 million foreign workers in Germany constituted one-fifth the work force.

But the hysteria of racial hatred dominated rational planning. Brutalized and starved workers could hardly be efficient; transporting and guarding them became an enormous, corrupting, and expensive enterprise. Hounding Jews and Gypsies or cramming Jews into ghettos was not enough; in 1942 a meeting of the regime's high officials adopted, in a phrase the century will never forget, "the final solution of the Jewish question." That solution was extermination. By 1945, nearly 6 million Jews and probably as many others—Poles, Gypsies, and Magyars especially—had died in places like Auschwitz, Buchenwald, and Dachau. These camps were also supposed to be centers of production. A Krupp arms factory, an I. G. Farben chemical plant, and a coal mine were part of the Auschwitz complex. But its chief product was corpses, at a rate that reached 12,000 a day.

Resistance Movements

Such horror on such a scale challenges every concept of civilization and raises almost unbearable doubts about Western society and human nature. For contemporaries who did not know the full extent of Nazi policies, there was nevertheless plenty in public practice to stimulate opposition to Nazi rule; that opposition gradually and against great odds evolved some organization, its every act a declaration of heroic confidence that the Nazis must someday fail. Small cells of resisters formed loose networks that spread through each nation and assumed an importance far beyond their power or steadily growing numbers. Always based on a small minority, the partisan movements achieved particular strength in Denmark and Norway, the Netherlands, France, and Yugoslavia. A number of them received material help and direction from their formal or unofficial governments in exile operating from London, which also commanded whatever fighting men had been able to escape the occupied homelands, the most notable of which was the Free French national committee, headed by General Charles de Gaulle.

Millions of Europeans came to rely on the BBC for encouragement and reliable news, for the Germans were losing the propaganda war as well. Some of the most active resistance fighters were simply individual members of neighborhood groups, but most were attached to parties with developed ideologies describing a better postwar world. The resistance movements thus revived faith in democracy and social justice even as they echoed prewar politics; in France for example moderates, Christian Democrats, Socialists, and Communists each had their organization. Generally the Christian Democrats and especially the Marxists developed the largest and most effective groups, thus laying the basis for powerful postwar parties.

The Nazis levied the harshest of reprisals for acts of resistance. When Czechs assassinated the new "Reich protector of Bohemia and Moravia" in June 1942, the Germans retaliated by wiping out the village of Lidice, which they suspected of hiding the murderers—every man was killed, every woman and child deported; and on a single day in 1943, the Germans put 1,400 men to death in a Greek village.

Yet the underground movements continued to grow, and their maneuvers became a barometer of the course of the war. In France partisan activities expanded from single exploits—smuggling Allied airmen out of the country, dynamiting a bridge, or attacking individual German officers—to large-scale operations closely coordinated from London. Norway's resistance helped force the Germans to keep 300,000 troops there and away from the more active fronts. In Yugoslavia the partisans, divided between two political groups, maintained an active guerrilla war; and the British decision to support the group led by Tito as the more effective all but assured his control of the country at the end of the war. After the Allied invasion of Italy, partisan groups there maintained an unnerving harassment of Fascist and Nazi forces. Even in Germany herself some members of the army and the old aristocracy began to plot against Hitler, and in July 1944 a group of conspirators planted a bomb under the table at which the Führer stood to conduct a conference with his staff. Hitler escaped serious injury, but the sense of his doom had spread to the heart of Germany.

The Politics of Coalition

Almost until the end, however, Hitler remained firmly in command, and Nazi strategy was wholly committed to holding off Germany's enemies. Mussolini, a victim of his own propaganda who had consistently overestimated Italian strength and yet was reluctant to demand that Italians make the sacrifices of total war, had little influence on German plans. With his fall, the Italian Peninsula, too, came under the direct control of the German army. There was no such unanimity among the Allies. Although the nature of Nazism and its fearful power provided one simple common purpose, the Allies said less about their long-range goals than they had in World War I. And their mutual distrust complicated the conduct of the war itself.

War Aims

When Anglo-American successes in North Africa were not followed by invasion of the Continent, the Russians suspected that they and the Germans were being left to annihilate each other. The Americans continued to favor a direct attack on the mainland, but the British still argued in terms of tightening the blockade in the west and of encircling Germany by means of more limited assaults from the eastern Mediterranean. Churchill, it became clear, would like to have his troops so placed as to give the Western powers a voice in the disposition of Eastern Europe.

Stalin insisted that Russia should regain the Polish territory taken in 1939; Poland could be compensated to the west at the expense of a defeated Germany. The British rightly warned that the Americans would find this unacceptable; and in fact the Anglo-American powers never forgot that Communists had encouraged revolution from Moscow to the Rhine after World War I or that Russian imperialism had sought to expand into Eastern Europe since the eighteenth century. In London the exiled leaders of the Eastern European nations agitated for their various nationalist aims while Stalin's ominous references to the need for "friendly" governments along Russia's borders made everyone shudder.

With such issues before them, Roosevelt and Churchill met at Casablanca in January 1943. There they agreed to invade Sicily (to the Russians' disgust) and to demand the unconditional surrender of Italy and Germany, an expression of moral outrage against facism that has been heavily criticized since for strengthening the Axis powers' determination to resist. Its main purpose, however, may well have been to reassure the suspicious Allies that none would seek a self-serving, separate peace.

Sponsored Regimes

Spokesmen for the powerless governments in exile viewed what they could learn about the meeting with some misgivings, for in practice the Anglo-Americans were not above dealing with regimes that bore a fascist taint. At the time of the North African invasion, for example, Admiral Jean François Darlan, a former vice premier of Vichy and then commander of its armed forces, had happened to be in Algiers. Eisenhower's staff had quickly negotiated an agreement with him so that his forces would not resist the invasion, in return for which Darlan had been named governor-general of French Africa. De Gaulle was outraged. Since his call for continued resistance in 1940 and his organization from London of the French forces fighting with the Allies, the general had pressed his claim to represent the voice of France. His hauteur, his persistent demand for a French part in Allied policy, and his considerable success in winning support in French colonies had made his relations with Britain and the United States cool at best. Darlan's assassination in December 1942 reduced tension a bit, though the British and Americans continued to deal with Vichy and authorities in French North Africa even after the Germans occupied all of France.

The issue of what governments to foster soon extended to Italy. In July 1943, two weeks after the landing in Sicily, Italy's Fascist Grand Council met in a hasty session, voted Mussolini out of office, and had him arrested, naming Marshal Pietro Badoglio prime minister. A new coalition of monarchists and more moderate Fascists then sought an armistice. The Committees of National Liberation, composed of anti-Fascists from liberals through Communists, were now prominent throughout Italy, however, and they wanted nothing to do with the marshal, a Fascist hero who had led the campaign in Ethiopia, or with the king, who had bowed to Mussolini for twenty years.

Again the Allies were divided. Britain favored the monarchy and feared leftist influence in the Committees of Liberation; the Americans leaned toward the Committees but shared the British concern about communist influence and so joined in excluding the Russians from active participation in the Allied military government installed in Italy. Stalin accepted this, recognized the new Italian regime, and encouraged Italy's Communists to pursue a policy more flexible and accommodating than even the Socialists could swallow. But arguments about spheres of influence and the need for military control which were used against the Russians in Italy would soon be used by them elsewhere.

All this bargaining had occurred without an actual encounter among the Big Three. Finally, in December 1943, Roosevelt, Churchill, and Stalin met for the first time, at Teheran. Whereas the British had earlier served as mediators between the United States and the Soviet Union, it was the Americans who now appeared closer to a middle position. The conversations were not easy, but they provided a basis for continued cooperation. Churchill proposed an invasion of the Dardanelles, but this move was rejected and an invasion of France agreed to for the following year. There was

Stalin, Roosevelt, and Churchill, meeting for the first time at Teheran, reached an understanding that laid the groundwork for Allied cooperation in pursuing the war.
(Photo: UPI)

tentative understanding that Russia would accept a boundary with Poland along the old Curzon Line, and the nature of the postwar Polish government was left open. Stalin also promised to declare war on Japan as soon as Germany surrendered. The Big Three maintained their unity largely by postponing action on difficult and divisive issues; but that at least assured the continued, vigorous prosecution of the war.

The Road to Victory

By late September 1943 the Allies were well entrenched in Italy and rapidly amassing still greater power. Germany could not hope to win but might prevent cataclysmic defeat by taking advantage of her shortening lines of communication and defensive strength. Meanwhile the Allied air assault subjected Germany to constant pounding, and the war in Russia was exhausting the German capacity to fight.

The Italian and Eastern Fronts

Although the Allies captured Naples in October, their campaign in Italy was bogged down in difficult terrain and faced fierce German resistance with an insufficient number of troops, for their main forces were assigned to the forthcoming invasion of France. It took the Allies five months to fight their way past a costly new beachhead at Anzio; not until May 1944 did they finally seize the old Benedictine abbey of Monte Cassino, less than seventy-five miles inland, and then only after a destructive bombardment. Rome, the first European capital to be liberated, fell in June.

Mussolini, who had been rescued from prison the previous September in a daring maneuver by German troops, had proclaimed a Fascist republic in the north and was now frankly a German puppet. For Italians, with their country a battleground for foreign armies, the war also became a civil war against Fascism. In December 1943 King Victor Emmanuel III announced his intention to abdicate in favor of his son (though he did not actually do so until 1946), and Badoglio gave way to a cabinet drawn from members of the Committees of National Liberation. The new government joined the Allied cause, and the slow push northward was aided by partisan risings against Nazi occupation. German resistance now converged on the so-called Gothic Line, running from Pisa to Rimini. Not until this line was pierced, in September 1944, could further drives lead to the capture of Ravenna (in December), Bologna, Verona, and Genoa (in April 1945). At that point German resistance ceased.

Russia's successes were more spectacular. In the spring of 1943, the Germans still had vitality enough to launch an offensive of their own, but it slowed within weeks. In July the Russian army began a relentless advance that continued with few setbacks for almost two years. Its armies now outnumbered the Germans, and it enjoyed a growing edge in matériel as well. Soviet forces reached the Dnieper and Kiev by November. In February 1944 they were at the Polish border; they retook the Crimea in the spring; in August Rumania surrendered; Finland and Bulgaria fell a few weeks later. When the Allied leaders met next, at Yalta in February 1945, Russian troops held part of Czechoslovakia and stood on the German frontier of Poland.

The Western Front

The opening of the final act of the war in Europe was the Allied invasion of France across the English Channel. The Germans knew that such an attack must come, but they believed that it would concentrate on the area around Calais, the shore closest to England. The Allies encouraged this belief through various feints and then actually landed in Normandy to the west of Caen on June 6, 1944. The operation was enormous: it called for putting 150,000 men ashore within two days, supported by 5,000 ships and 1,500 tanks. But the Anglo-Americans were now expert in amphibious assaults, they held overwhelming control of the air, and the Germans failed to coordinate their defenses.

In a complex series of costly landings, Eisenhower's Allied force poured onto the French beaches, the first of more than a million men to disembark within a few months. In July they broke through the German defense and began a series of rapid drives through France. A second amphibious attack, in southern France in mid-August, led to swift advances inland greatly aided by well-organized French resistance groups. On August 24 the Parisian underground rose against the Germans, and French forces under Charles de Gaulle quickly entered the cheering city. Brussels fell a week later, and ten days after that American troops crossed the German frontier.

Hitler's desperate replies to the Allied blows included the launching in June of a new "miracle" weapon, the relatively ineffective V-1 pilotless plane, followed in September by the far more dangerous V-2 rocket. Had the Nazis earlier recognized the potential of this new weapon and pushed its development, its effects might have been devastating. The V-2 flew faster than

Charles de Gaulle, the symbol of French resistance, greeted by Parisians on the day of the city's liberation in 1944.
(Photo: © Robert Capa/Magnum)

the speed of sound and was almost impossible to intercept; but these rockets were hard to aim, too few, and utilized too late to be decisive. More threatening was a counterstroke in December through the Ardennes on either side of Bastogne that rocked the Allied line back. The Battle of the Bulge, which cost about 70,000 men on each side before the Allies regained the initiative in January, was the last offensive the Germans would mount.

Competing Allies

As Allied troops drove farther into the Continent, the Big Three met again, this time at Yalta, for their last wartime conference; and the decisions they made that February, though widely hailed at the time, have become the most controversial of World War II. The hurried meeting dealt with four broad issues:

1. The creation of a United Nations Organization. The U.S.S.R.'s request for 16 votes to counterbalance the votes of the British Commonwealth and of U.S.-dominated Latin America was reduced to 3, and the veto she also demanded was restricted slightly.

2. Russian entry into the war against Japan. Russia agreed to declare war against Japan within ninety days after the defeat of Germany; she was to receive in compensation the territories she had surrendered to Japan in 1905 and was guaranteed a sphere of influence in Man-

churia. The agreement clearly strengthened her position in Asia.

3. The treatment of Germany. The assignment of zones of occupation to each of the Big Three presented little problem, and Russia reluctantly accepted the proposal that France also be given a zone to occupy. But the reparations and "labor services" the Russians demanded were enormous, and the agreements on specific terms had to be postponed.

4. The establishment of new governments in the liberated nations. This, the most difficult issue of all, could not be postponed much longer; and yet every effort at accord merely exposed the distrust between Russia and the Western powers.

By this time the form of Italy's government had been largely set, and de Gaulle was reasserting the independence of France; but the degree of Soviet dominance in Eastern Europe was an open question. There were indications that Soviet leaders might show restraint. In most of the Eastern nations they occupied, the Russians were tolerating all the old antifascist parties and seemed to support fairly broad coalitions, but Soviet officials rejected participation by the Western powers in the affairs of the new governments and restricted Allied observers. Four months earlier, when Churchill visited Moscow, he boldly proposed that Russia should have overwhelming predominance in Rumania and the largest influence in Bulgaria, that the British be given a free hand in Greece, and that Russia and Britain have an equal interest in Yugoslavia and Hungary. And Stalin in fact did nothing when Churchill strongly intervened in the civil war raging in Greece, routing the leftists.

Such crude understandings, however, offered little protection against the cold self-interest Russia had shown on other occasions. As Soviet troops had approached Warsaw in August 1944, the Polish underground arose against the Germans. But these partisans were closely tied to the anti-communist Polish government in London, and the Russians had simply halted their advance until the Germans wiped out the Polish resistance fighters.

At Yalta no real agreement could be found about the borders of Poland or the independence of her government. The general formula adopted, with its references to democratic governments and assurances of free elections for all liberated nations, would prove subject to many interpretations. An adamant Stalin, a pugnacious Churchill, and a weary and ill Roosevelt turned back to the wars they still faced in Germany and against Japan.

The End of the War

As the Allies pushed into Germany from all sides, it became clear that Berlin would be the final battle. Eisenhower feared that Hitler intended to make a last desperate stand in his famed mountain redoubt at Berchtesgaden in the south German mountains (in fact, German resistance was everywhere collapsing); he therefore halted the eastward advance of American and British armies at the Elbe River in preparation for the battle in the south, which was never joined. The Russians took Berlin. Hitler had characteristically ordered the German garrison to defend the capital to the death, which assured the maximum destruction of the city. Hitler himself committed suicide on April 30, 1945; his aides burned the body, and the remains have never been found. Four days later a group of German officers signed the final, unconditional surrender. The war in Europe was over.

But in Asia the world conflict continued. Despite massive bombing and repeated naval victories, progress toward Japan had been agonizingly slow the past three years. Hundreds of islands in the Pacific and thousands of miles of jungle had to be laboriously reconquered in the face of the fierce resistance.

As the American forces, commanded by Douglas MacArthur, closed in on Japan, they

Hiroshima: The Japanese were victims of one of science's great achievements and the beginning of the atomic age. They suffered both human and environmental destruction.
(Photo: Wide World Photos; UPI)

unleashed an air bombardment of unprecedented intensity. During the three months after Germany's surrender, the raids obliterated Japan's navy, industrial plants, and large parts of her cities—nearly 200,000 people were killed in Tokyo in just one week. But still the Japanese would not surrender.

On August 6 the new president of the United States, Harry Truman (Roosevelt had died in April), authorized the use of a new weapon, developed after years of secret research, the atomic bomb. In one blow half of the city of Hiroshima was wiped off the face of the earth and a quarter of its 320,000 inhabitants killed. Two days later Russia declared war on Japan, and on August 9 the Americans dropped an even more powerful atomic bomb on the city of Nagasaki.

Faced by total annihilation, the Japanese surrendered unconditionally on September 2. Remarkable accomplishments in science and technology, sustained by great wealth and reinforced by scores of European scientists driven to sanctuary in the United States, had permitted a great democracy to end World War II by unleashing a new order of terror upon humanity. Later, some would question the decision to use so terrible an instrument; but even in the jubilation of victory, leaders busily reordering a shattered world had to recognize that another war could mean the end of civilization.

II. THE CIRCUMSTANCES OF PEACE

The Europe That Survived

Wartime conditions did not disappear for years. It took the better part of a decade for the millions of refugees and displaced persons to find settled lives; the rationing of food and clothes continued in many countries into the 1950s; some of the most severely bombed cities, such as London and Dresden, were still engaged in reconstruction in the 1960s. Moreover, troops from the two world powers, the United States and Russia, swarmed over the Continent, symbols as well as instruments of a new era of foreign domination.

The Devastation

In contrast to World War I, a majority of the fatalities in World War II were civilians, killed by bombs, conquerors, or concentration camp officials. Russia alone lost about 20 million people, and the Germans murdered more than 12 million in concentration camps, half of them Jews who had never seen combat. Elsewhere the casualties were not on this scale—perhaps 5 million Western Europeans and a similar number in all other theaters of war (the number of noncombatants who died in China is unknown). For every person killed, two were either wounded or taken captive. But civilian deaths are harder to categorize than those of soldiers, and often there was no one who could or cared to do the counting. So the total casualties of World War II—dead, wounded, or crippled by inhumane treatment—remain an estimate, a number hard to comprehend: some 55 million people.

The physical destruction was likewise unprecedented. In 1945 Europe's industrial capability, crippled by the obliteration of factories, communications facilities, and large segments of cities, was perhaps half of what it had been in 1939. In France alone some 2 million buildings needed reconstruction, and only one-tenth of the country's vehicles were usable. Less than half of such major cities as Frankfurt, Dresden, Brest, and Toulon were still standing. The Continent's most important ports, bridges, and rail lines had been destroyed by Allied bombs. Ironically, Germany's industry was in better shape than any on the Continent west of Russia, its fixed assets higher in 1945 than in 1939 despite Allied bombing.

Agriculture was also hard hit: France's cattle population had been reduced by half, and large areas of farmland in France, Italy, and Germany could not be cultivated. The need for food was so urgent during the first months of peace that supplies were sometimes dropped by parachute to speed distribution; in the winter of 1945–

1946, starvation stalked the Continent, and in some places, such as Vienna, thousands died—many of them children—before sufficient food arrived. Disease was also an ever-present danger, although a newly developed drug, penicillin, did help limit the epidemics that erupted as a result of inadequate sanitation and medical facilities.

Some experts estimated that it would take twenty years for the Continent to regain its prewar prosperity. The very necessities of life were in desperately short supply, and Europeans had few means of producing goods themselves, and often only an illicit black market made essential supplies available to the few who could afford them. Impoverished and ravaged nations thus looked to the United States and Russia for relief.

The Disruption

Normally, the killing and destruction of war leaves great holes in societies that themselves remain intact—families survive despite missing members, local institutions remain despite major changes. World War II brought with it not only more deaths than in any previous war but, especially in Eastern Europe, unprecedented disruption of social ties. Nazi rule evicted 100,000 French from Alsace-Lorraine and 1,500,000 Poles from "German" areas, and forced 8 million foreigners to work in Germany by war's end. In the Balkans and Hungary hundreds of thousands of people were expelled or fled under the Germans. On a similar scale Stalin had driven Germans from occupied Poland in 1939, a large proportion of whom returned when the Germans took Poland, only to flee again when Russia recaptured the country. Thus the millions of refugees who fled bombings and conquering armies toward the end of the war were added to those already displaced. The ethnic conflicts and the problems of "minorities" that had plagued Eastern Europe after World War I culminated, by the end of World War II, in the greatest dislocation of populations in European history. In 1945, some 12 million Europeans were officially recognized as displaced persons, separated from home, kin, and possessions and facing disease and starvation before they could know how or where to reconstruct their lives.

Millions more, not officially called displaced, found themselves without property or employment in societies that were barely functioning. Whether the Germans had ruled directly or through local authorities, their reign had brought extensive purges and fundamental changes in social and political institutions. When those rulers disappeared (often followed by more purges and massacres), a vacuum was left, to be filled by armies of occupation—the Soviet army in Eastern Europe, the other Allied armies in Germany and Italy. Military rule, a reminder of war, was thus a peacetime necessity while political groups and social institutions vied for a role in shaping a new society.

The Settlement

Unlike the treaties prepared at the Paris Peace Conference after World War I, the settlements of 1945 were limited, relatively informal, and indeterminate arrangements. Although the leaders of Russia, Britain, and the United States met at Potsdam for two weeks in July 1945, they hardly hammered out broad new policies. Indeed they barely knew each other, for of the Big Three only Stalin was also present at the Yalta Conference five months before. President Truman had been in office only three months, and in the midst of the meeting, Winston Churchill was defeated in the British elections and replaced by Clement Attlee.

Nevertheless the Allies did agree on basic regulations for the future of Germany: the dissolution of all Nazi institutions, the restoration of free speech and democratic politics, the abolition of all armaments production, and the control of heavy industry. For a while the Americans had leaned toward a plan that would have banned industrial activity, but in the end the Potsdam conferees took no such radical measures.

The Peace Terms

The resolution of most political issues was left to unspecified future meetings. Ostensibly Allied forces were merely occupiers and were not to influence local politics except to repress Nazism. In fact, the distrust between Russia and the Western powers led unintentionally to a peculiarly harsh retribution—Germany was not only occupied but effectively divided into two states. But the absence of definitive decisions at Potsdam long continued to bedevil the Allies, particularly in regard to Berlin; divided into four occupation zones and originally administered by an Interallied Control Council, the city was isolated in the midst of the eastern (Russian) sector to be the focus of contention for more than twenty years.

The major political penalty imposed on Germany at the conference was the relocation of her eastern border to the west, at the rivers Oder and Neisse, which thus enlarged Poland. This shift produced huge new flows of refugees, which increased when Czechoslovakia, independent again, expelled all her Germans.

It was agreed that a Council of Foreign Ministers of the four principal Allies (France was now included) would continue to meet after Potsdam; and though the council soon became a forum for quarrels between the Russians and the others, it did draft a series of peace treaties in 1946. The nations that had fought the Axis in Europe gathered in Paris early in 1947 to sign treaties with Germany's cobelligerents: Italy, Rumania, Hungary, Bulgaria, and Finland, each of which ceded minor territories to her neighbors. Austria, however, like Germany, obtained no formal treaty and remained divided in four occupied zones, with the difference that the Austrians held their own capital, Vienna, from which to establish a unified government that could prepare the way for eventual independence.

The Potsdam conference also laid down the terms of the peace with Japan. The Soviet Union would get some territory and the European nations would regain their colonies in Asia. But the prime beneficiaries were China and above all the United States, whose troops occupied Japan and most of the other strategic islands in the Pacific. Little account of Europe needed to be taken in these arrangements.

Within Europe the first concern was to root out fascism. In the lands the Germans had occupied, this took the form of summary executions of ordinary collaborators and, notably in France, emotional prosecutions against leading figures like Pierre Laval and Marshal Pétain. In Germany herself, however, the vastness of the problem made enforcement of anti-Nazi regulations difficult against all but the highest leaders. Millions of forms were filled out and hundreds of trials held. But the energy needed to sustain the drive against former Nazis soon waned, and only those prosecuted early received significant punishments.

To signify that their massacres and genocide had gone beyond the limits that a civilized world could endure, even in wartime, the Allies created an international tribunal to try Hitler's closest associates for war crimes. Held in Nuremberg in 1945 and 1946, the trials were also intended to inform the German people of the full horror of Nazi rule and to establish some acceptable standards of warfare. Yet to many, trials not conducted by some neutral body seemed a veneer for vengeance and without juridical basis. The appalling revelations of those solemn hearings were nonetheless followed by restrained judgments—only twelve of the twenty-two prime defendants were condemned to death, and three were acquitted.

An American lieutenant colonel talks to some two hundred German civilians forced to observe a scene inside Landsberg concentration camp.
(Photo: Wide World Photos)

The United Nations

Although the League of Nations had failed, the creation of some organization for effective international cooperation had become an official Allied aim; the Atlantic Charter, issued in 1941 by Great Britain and the United States, led gradually to the creation of the United Nations Organization.

Its first agency, the United Nations Relief and Rehabilitation Administration (UNRRA), established late in 1943 to aid countries reconquered from the Axis, came to play a major role in the reconstruction of postwar Europe. The following year Italy, though a former enemy, was allocated $50 million, mainly in medical supplies. A related effort concentrated on economic rehabilitation. To avoid the devastating inflation that had followed World War I, the United Nations Conference at Bretton Woods, New Hampshire, in 1944 created an International Monetary Fund and an International Bank for Reconstruction and Development. Those institutions, with nearly $20 billion in assets, proved important in maintaining the stability of currencies and international exchange after the war.

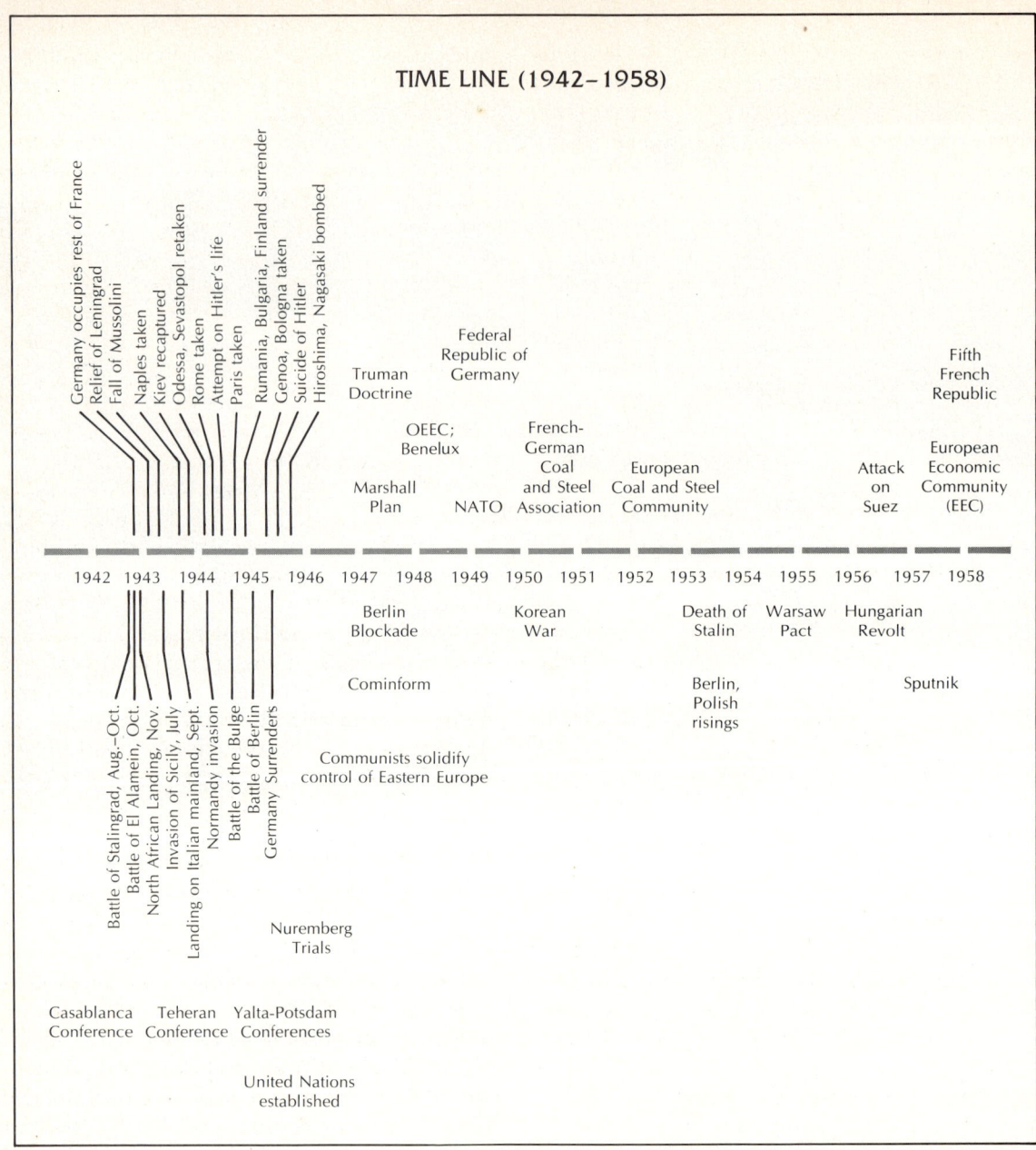

But the main aim of the United Nations was much grander. At a meeting at Dumbarton Oaks in Washington, D.C., in 1944, representatives of the United States, the Soviet Union, and the British Commonwealth agreed to create an international organization to preserve peace throughout the world. A few months after the discussions in 1945 at Yalta, fifty-one countries approved the United Nations Charter at a special conference held in San Francisco.

The charter established a General Assembly of all members to determine policy; a decision-making Security Council of eleven members to supervise "the maintenance of international peace"; and various economic, social, and legal agencies. Permanent Security Council seats were reserved for the great powers—the United States, the Soviet Union, China, Great Britain, and France—with the remainder rotating by election from among the other member states. But the Big Five were given, at Russia's insistence, the right to veto any council action, and Soviet opposition to much that was proposed eventually shifted some of the initiative to the General Assembly, where a two-thirds majority could overrule a veto. In this maneuvering both Russia and the United States needed the support of the so-called Third World, the nations of Asia, Africa, and Latin America that were not formally tied to one of the two major blocs.

Despite the position of Britain and France on the Security Council, therefore, and the election of Scandinavians as the UN's secretary general (chief executive officer) until 1961, most of the organization's attention was focused on Asia and Africa after 1945, and many major decisions depended entirely on the United States or Russia. Even the UN's relief work after 1945 was primarily an American undertaking. Thus the United Nations, though structurally similar to the League of Nations, in fact represented a redistribution of international power that left Europe no longer dominant.

Europe Divided Between East and West

Liberation resulted in a battle for domestic power throughout Europe. Nearly everywhere, communists had played a leading part in the resistance movements, frequently as their very core. They emerged at war's end with their prestige high to take the lead in denouncing fascists and profiteers. Although socialist and centrist resistance movements joined the communists in demanding a new era of democracy and equality, these groups came to distrust each other and to seek the support of foreign powers, a practice that often determined what liberation would mean. Europe, whose political and ideological divisions in the 1930s had led to world war, became in the postwar world more sharply divided than ever.

Eastern Europe: The Politics of Puppets

Nowhere was the direct influence of foreign domination more visible than in Eastern Europe. In 1945 Soviet troops held the entire area from the Adriatic to the Baltic just short of a line stretching between Trieste and Hamburg. In the Soviet Union, whose economic future would largely determine the recovery of all of Eastern Europe, industrial production was less than two-thirds of its prewar level, and the Five-Year Plan announced in 1946, which was designed to increase Russia's industrial output by more than 50 percent over her 1940 level, depended openly on her ransacking East Germany and the other occupied areas for materials. Three formerly independent states, Estonia, Latvia, and Lithuania, became Soviet republics, and Russia further extended her western border with annexations of territories once belonging to East Prussia, Poland, Hungary, and Rumania. Elsewhere the subordination of local institutions to Communist orthodoxy soon became no less blatant.

The Russians restrained the forces of revolution in Eastern Europe, more explosive in 1945 than in 1918, that were fed by long-ignored issues of land distribution and industrial development. But they used these issues, skillful political maneuvers, and the crudest coercion to establish Communist governments subservient to Russia. The exclusion of leading anti-Communists from a ruling coalition was usually the first step in the common procedure, followed by propaganda campaigns, electoral pressures, and sudden arrests that eliminated non-Communists from positions of power. Finally a heavy-handed dictatorship set about creating a Soviet satellite with purge trials and secret police.

Rumania was first to feel the full weight of these techniques, and late in 1947 King Michael was forced into exile by the Communists. Poland, where the Communists were weakest, had explicitly been promised free elections; but when these were held in 1947 a series of repressive measures against the minority National Peasant party left the dominant Independent Socialists with an overwhelming majority. The United States and Britain complained but to no avail. A few months later the leader of the National Peasant party fled to London, and his followers were purged. The Catholic Church was persecuted, the Independent Socialist party subordinated to the Workers' party (Communist), and a Russian placed in command of the army. In short order Poland was firmly tied to the Soviet Union economically and politically.

A similar pattern developed elsewhere. Hungary's coalition government at first had an anti-Communist majority, but another dubious election, in 1949, gave the Communists complete control, and close links with Russia were quickly established.

With one exception, even where popular support gave Communist dominance considerable legitimacy, results were much the same. Albania and Bulgaria became solid members of the Communist bloc by 1950. Czechoslovakia, with a notable democratic tradition, did not succumb so easily. The Communists constituted the largest postwar party but not a majority, and the president and foreign minister, Eduard Beneš and Jan Masaryk, were heirs to the liberal politics of prewar Czechoslovakia. But in 1948, when peaceful means had proved unsuccessful, the Communists threatened with Russian support to take over the country by force. Bowing to this pressure, Beneš placed the government under Communist control; a month later Masaryk died in a mysterious fall from a window; and late in the year a one-party election gave the Communists complete ascendancy, and Beneš resigned.

Yugoslavia, however, did not meekly follow the Russian lead, though Communists dominated her government after Marshal Tito easily won the 1945 national election. Tito had had close contacts with the West throughout the war, and he resisted the Soviet Union's repeated efforts to control his foreign policy and interfere in domestic affairs. An open break came in 1948. Yugoslavia had joined with Russia and other Eastern European states the previous year to create the Cominform, an agency designed to coordinate international Communist political activity, but she was now expelled from the organization and denounced by her neighbors, who also severed economic relations. While remaining Communist in politics and ideology, Yugoslavia established ties with the West that gave her an independence not enjoyed by Soviet allies. Tito's insubordination seemed recklessly daring, but he demonstrated how a small state could use the tense balance between the superpowers to survive without total reliance on either of them.

In the eastern zone of Germany the Russians followed the same procedures as in the states of Eastern Europe. Early in 1946 they forced the major political group, the Social Democratic party, to merge with the Communist party, which put the Russians in complete control thereafter. Interpreting the economic restrictions imposed at Potsdam as severely as possible, they dismantled scores of factories, appropriated the Germans' postwar production, and forbade trade with the West—the latter two actions in violation of the Potsdam agreements. As West Germany began to revive economically in 1947, however, the Russians gradually allowed the eastern zone to increase its industrial activity, and in 1949 gave it independent status as the German Democratic Republic. The first elections, in 1950, confirmed the Communists' dominance.

Western Europe: The Politics of the Past

In circumstances that seemed unprecedented, each Western country was nevertheless drawn toward its prewar pattern of parliamentary life. The reestablishment of functioning institutions and reconstruction of a viable economy took precedence over vaguer visions of reform. Before such needs, old ways were the natural recourse however much such conservatism belied the broader hopes of resistance movements and wartime rhetoric.

In West Germany elections held in 1946 produced a victory for the Christian Democrats over their somewhat less conservative opponents, the Social Democrats, both parties being firmly rooted in Germany's pre-Nazi political traditions. To speed the process of recovery, the Americans and British then combined their zones into a single economic unit and soon relaxed restrictions on economic activity. Early in 1949 the area occupied by the Western powers was granted its independence, the ad hoc division of Germany thereby acknowledged with the proclamation of the Federal Republic of Germany.

West Germany's federal structure, reinforced during the occupation period, allowed considerable autonomy to local states. But the truncated new state was more centralized and its political system (dominated by the two large parties) more stable than the old Weimar Republic which it otherwise strongly resembled. The chancellor for the next fourteen years was the Christian Democratic leader Konrad Adenauer, who was seventy-three years old in 1949 and who had been mayor of Cologne from 1917 to 1933. Under his firm and conservative leadership, West Germany, closely allied with the United States, rapidly prospered in an atmosphere of efficient calm.

In France the new Fourth Republic looked much like the Third. Political life was shaped by three large parties—the Communists, the Socialists, and a new Catholic party of the left, the MRP (Popular Republican Movement), which soon forced De Gaulle out of office as provisional president despite economic policies that included the nationalization of many important industries. And whereas De Gaulle favored a strong president directly elected, the left wrote a constitution providing for a single representative chamber intended to dominate the executive—a position traditional to the left—only to have it rejected in a national referendum. The constitution narrowly adopted in 1946 then returned to the familiar bicameral system with most executive authority in the hands of a prime minister responsible to parliament (its only major innovation the granting of a larger voice to colonial representatives). Governments were once again dependent on unstable coalitions, an instability increased by the fact that the Communists, the largest party, were the least tempted by compromise. The political balance thus shifted toward the shaky center as cabinets confronted strikers and agitation on the left and a dramatic revival of De Gaulle's popularity on the right.

In Italy more than 54 percent of the electorate voted in 1946 to replace the monarchy with a republic; and subsequent governments were dominated by the Christian Democrats, a sprawling Catholic party that combined much conservative sentiment with a more radical core inherited from the pre-Fascist Popular party. From 1945 to 1953 the leader of the Christian Democrats and the central figure of Italian politics was Alcide De Gasperi. Prime minister during most of this time, he ostracized the Communists and took advantage of divisions among Socialists to bring Italy into close alliance with the United States. In the crucial elections of 1948, the Christian Democrats, aided by extensive American pressure, won an absolute majority, and the threat that the largest Communist party in the West might obtain power began to fade. With a program of moderate reform, including efforts to revitalize the economy of southern Italy and stimulate industry in the north, and a strong parliamentary leader manipulating a diffuse coalition of interests, Italy returned to the unheroic political traditions subverted by Fascists in the 1920s.

Among the smaller nations of Western Europe, the resumption of old ways was equally evident. Spain and Portugal, ostracized for their links with the Nazis, remained defiant dictatorships. In the democracies the traditional parties reemerged, though they were often faced by active Communist minorities and forced to promote domestic welfare through interventionist social and economic policies. Belgium for example retained her monarchy and returned to a government of shifting alliances as the old Socialist and Catholic parties jockeyed for power. Although the antagonism between the Walloons and Flemings persisted, the Belgians were nonetheless able to begin a rapid economic recovery and to provide broadened welfare services. The Netherlands and the Scandinavian countries, where the Communists were generally not strong, underwent a similar growth of prosperity and social programs guided by often fragile coalition governments, most often led by Socialists.

In many respects postwar politics brought greater change in Great Britain than in Continental countries where the regimes themselves were new. Winston Churchill's defeat in the elections of 1945 was a turning away from wartime unity and sacrifice, for the Labour party won its enormous majority by promising to launch domestic reforms long postponed. Under Clement Attlee, who had led the party since 1935, it nationalized the Bank of England and a wide range of major industries and services, including the coal-mining, transportation, electrical, and—after great controversy—iron and steel industries. It also instituted extensive welfare programs and established public housing, national insurance, and free medical care for all Britons. At the same time, the government began to withdraw from the overseas empire to which men like Churchill had been so attached, granting India independence in 1947.

The International Context

In the postwar atmosphere of dislocation, domestic instability, and colonial revolt, the world dominance of one or the other of these superpowers seemed at stake in nearly every political conflict. Each of these dominant powers professed a comprehensive ideology held to be universally valid and deeply rooted in the European experience. The struggle between Russian Communism and American democratic capitalism reached the intensity of war without open battle.

The Cold War

President Truman increasingly agreed with his advisers (and with Churchill) that only the strongest measures could stop Soviet expansion, and he determined to devote the full weight of American manpower and money to containing Russian influence. When, therefore, the Western powers began to encourage the economic recovery of Germany, the Russians countered in July 1947 by closing off overland access to Berlin. War seemed imminent, and for nearly a year all supplies to West Berlin were ferried to the city in a remarkable airlift. By the time the crisis had been resolved, West and East Germany had beocme autonomous republics bearing the political trappings of the alliance to which they belonged.

In 1947 the American president also announced the Truman Doctrine, promising military and economic aid to nations threatened by Communist takeovers. Money and supplies at once poured into Greece, rent for more than a year by a recurrence of civil war in which the

In a little less than a year, 277,264 flights were completed in the Berlin airlift.
(Photo: Fenno Jacobs/Black Star)

Communists were being helped by neighboring Yugoslavia. The American response, combined with Yugoslavia's break with Russia, enabled the Greek government to crush the opposition by 1949. Turkey, slowly moving toward the establishment of democratic institutions, received similar assistance.

A few months after the announcement of the doctrine, U.S. Secretary of State George Marshall unveiled a more far-reaching plan. To stimulate European recovery—and eliminate the economic conditions in which Communism prospered—he offered massive economic aid to all nations still struggling to recover from the effects of the war. But Russia forbade the Eastern European states to participate in the American-sponsored program and established her own Council of Mutual Economic Assistance (Comecon) instead.

These antagonisms became major domestic issues as Communist parties throughout the West opposed the Marshall Plan despite its obvious benefits. In the East the last vestiges of non-Communist political activity were removed, and in the West Communists were excluded from coalition governments in France and Italy in 1947 and from all government positions in Switzerland in 1950; West Germany banned the party itself in 1956.

Local issues were thus tinged by international implications. Every trade agreement was a litmus test of a country's intentions; strikes were denounced as Communist-inspired attempts at subversion; spy scandals made sensational headlines; and travel between East and West became almost impossible. The relatively limited question of whether the city of Trieste belonged to Italy or Yugoslavia became the subject of intense great-power maneuvers. Unmistakably Europe had become a battleground in the Cold War.

And the two halves of Europe followed the lead of their powerful patrons. When the news arrived that the Soviet Union had tested her own atomic bomb in 1949, it was seen as a direct challenge to the United States, and Truman met it by announcing that American scientists were working on an even more devastating explosive, the hydrogen bomb. But the loss of the U.S. monopoly over atomic weapons made ground forces seem essential to deter further Soviet aggression without resort to the total annihilation of atomic war. Consequently in 1949 the North Atlantic Treaty Organization (NATO) was created to coordinate the military planning of the United States, Canada, and ten Western European states,[1] which in effect now received U.S. military aid. The Russians replied with the Warsaw Pact in 1955, which performed the same function for the Eastern Europeans. And when the Communist North Koreans invaded South Korea in 1950, the United States at once felt duty-bound to seek the approval of the Western-controlled UN Assembly and to send troops to repel the incursion. Europe was but the most important zone of a Cold War now world-wide. (see Map 29.3.)

The Loss of Empire

The most dramatic evidence of the decline in European power was the rapid dwindling of colonies and influence overseas. World War II had severely shaken the colonial empires, which no longer had the material means to suppress the increasingly powerful demands for independence in their overseas possessions. For a few months after the war ended, Great Britain and France enjoyed the luxury of their old rivalries in the Middle East. But in 1946 both withdrew from the new states of Lebanon and Syria, Trans-Jordan became independent, foreign troops left Iraq and Iran, and negotiations began for British forces to depart from Egypt and the Sudan.

At the same time, despite Arab hostility, Great Britain undertook concrete planning for the establishment of separate Jewish and Arab states in Palestine. Mounting terror campaigns from both sides notwithstanding, the British decided to remove all their troops in May 1948, and the United Nations, eager to give Jews a refuge following Hitler's persecutions, endorsed the creation of the state of Israel. The Arabs invaded the day the British left but were driven back despite a huge numerical superiority, and UN mediators were able to bring about a shaky truce that confirmed Israel's existence.

Colonialism weakened in Asia as well. The French recognized Vietnam as a free state in 1945; Ceylon and Burma gained their independence from Great Britain in 1948; and Indonesia won her freedom from the Dutch after a long struggle in 1949. Where they failed to grant true autonomy, however, as in Indonesia and Vietnam, Europeans found themselves fighting wars they could not win. In Vietnam, for instance, a French-educated Communist leader, Ho Chi Minh, organized a brilliant guerrilla

---

[1] Great Britain, France, Belgium, the Netherlands, Luxembourg, Italy, Portugal, Denmark, Norway, and Iceland were the European members. Greece and Turkey would be added in 1952 and West Germany in 1955.

World War II and the Survival of Europe 1941–1958

MAP 29.3: THE COLD WAR OF THE 1950s

campaign that became a serious and costly war, culminating in the capture of a major French base at Dien Bien Phu in 1954 and the expulsion of the French.

Throughout Asia the end of European domination left a heritage of ties to international capitalism, of bureaucracy and parties organized on Western models, and of nationalist and socialist ideas increasingly tempered by local traditions and such indigenous forms as passive resistance, developed to a fine political art by India's religious leader and social reformer Mohandas K. Gandhi. Local cultures often remained decisively important, however, and the prospect of Indian independence produced serious conflict only gradually reduced by dividing the subcontinent, with most Muslims giving allegiance to the newly created state of Pakistan and most Hindus loyal to India.

The resolution of all these struggles was outside European control. The creation of Israel, for example, depended primarily on UN intervention and above all on the diplomatic recognition of the new nation by the United States and the Soviet Union. Similarly the critical conflict in Iran was between the Russians, whose influence rapidly waned, and the Americans, whose economic aid rose with equal speed. Although Africa was less directly affected by the Cold War, the competition between the great powers encouraged formal independence there as well.

As the Europeans withdrew from these lands long under their hegemony, the U.S.-Soviet conflict remained. Pakistan committed herself to the West; India tried to steer a middle course; and a major communist revolt broke out in Burma immediately after independence. In Vietnam the French were encouraged by the United States, while Ho Chi Minh was strongly supported by Russia and by the most formidable of the newly communist states, China, where, after long civil conflict, the Communists under Mao Zedong consolidated power in 1949.

As a counterweight to these advances in Asia, the United States promoted the economic revival of a now democratic Japan and gave strong economic and military support to Taiwan (a large island off China still held by the Chinese nationalists). The American government also founded the Southeast Asia Treaty Organization (SEATO), a Pacific equivalent to NATO, in which Britain, Pakistan, Australia, New Zealand, and various Asian states joined with the United States in common defense. The creation of SEATO marked the further institutionalization of the Cold War on a worldwide scale.

In all these developments Europeans could be little more than spectators. Great Britain did attempt to use the Commonwealth of Nations, binding together all her former colonies under technical allegiance to the royal family, as a means of continuing her influence. But it was little more than a grand international club, incapable even of restraining conflicts among its members (between India and Pakistan for example) and rejected by the fiercely anti-British republic of Eire, which the British formally recognized in 1949. The main accomplishment of a similar French organization, the *Union Française*, was the survival of France's language and culture in her former colonies. Although right-wing elements within Europe resented these many losses, most Europeans were reconciled to the disappearance of world-wide possessions by a political and economic revival at home that could hardly have been foreseen during the late 1940s.

III. EUROPEAN RECOVERY

The Basis of Economic Revival

In economic affairs, in contrast to domestic and international politics, renewed vitality led to innovations that eventually transformed society. Initially, however, in economic matters, too, Europe's debt-ridden and disrupted nations appeared dependent on the superpowers. But Europe still had extraordinary resources, and the decade between 1947 and 1957 was one of amazing economic growth as well as sharply defined limits on political change. The homeland of the Industrial Revolution, its populations possessed high levels of experience and skill. World War II, for all its destructive impact, had in many respects promoted the efficient use of these resources, taking up the considerable slack left by a decade of depression.

Full production and employment in wartime were related to one notable social phenomenon: the number of births remained steady and in some countries even increased. During World War I the birth rate had plummeted, reducing the size of the generation that followed. Western Europe, at least, had a nearly opposite experience in World War II. The birth rate in France, for example, had declined by 45 percent in 1914–1918, and through the 1930s deaths had outnumbered births so persistently that many observers thought the country was embarked on a path of "national suicide." But during World War II the birth rate increased 11 percent over the preceding decade. Similarly, England's birth rate had fallen by 25 percent in the First World War but showed a relative increase of 18 percent during the Second. The figures rose as well in almost all the neutral countries (Ireland, Spain, Sweden, Switzerland), whose economies had benefited from sales to the belligerents. In Germany herself the birth rate had dropped by 50 percent in World War I but by only 22 percent in World War II, despite the mobilization of millions of men and the death of more than a million. The Italian patterns were similar.

In sum, in the midst of the fighting, Western Europe witnessed the beginnings of a "baby boom," comparable to though never so large as that which occurred in the United States during the same period. Relatively high birth rates were maintained until 1963, when a slow decline ensued. Given the war losses and Europe's sustained industrial potential, the increase in births undoubtedly helped stimulate and sustain economic recovery.

In 1945 Europe like the United States also had access to a large backlog of unexploited technology, much of which derived from military research. Atomic power, the jet engine, the rocket engine, television, computers, antibiotics, and frozen and dehydrated foods are only the best known of technical advances destined to have major economic impact. And the increased economic importance of advanced technology benefited a Europe richer in technology, experience, and organization than in natural resources.

Finally, even the destruction and dislocations caused by the war contributed to recovery in that rebuilt factories could utilize the best available machinery and methods. The millions of refugees, some highly skilled, formed a large and usually cheap increment to the labor force; and the need to construct thousands of factories, offices, housing units, and other buildings was a powerful stimulus to economic growth. Defeated Germany also enjoyed the negative benefit of having no large military expenditures. Thus, in the depths of distress during the early years of peace, the Europeans, who never lost their resilience, established the basis of subsequent prosperity.

The Role of the Soviet Union and the United States

The recovery of Eastern Europe depended heavily on the Soviet Union, which through strenuous efforts was able to reach and surpass its prewar industrial output by 1953, and leaders such as Politburo member Nikita Khrushchev confidently predicted that the U.S.S.R. would exceed America in industrial production by 1970.

Impressive as these achievements were, the very size of Russia's economy raised unexpected problems that have persistently slowed the relative rate of growth. As Soviet production and wealth expanded, the costs of administration increased disproportionately, and the inefficiencies of the nation's centralized management became more pronounced. The absence of a free market deprived planners of an effective means of judging costs, profits, and performance. In several critical areas the "command economy" of the U.S.S.R. proved less successful than the West's mixed economy, combining national planning and private enterprises. Russian agriculture in particular has been a major disappointment. In 1953 the cereal harvest was only slightly larger than in 1913, when the population had been smaller by a quarter.

Nevertheless, the growth of Russian industry and its developed technology provided an important market for and stimulus to production in the countries of the Communist bloc. After 1945 these states attempted to organize their economies on the Russian model. All but Poland collectivized farmlands, and all instituted five-year plans to achieve rapid industrialization. In varying degrees these governments adopted elements of a mixed economic system—"goulash socialism," as Hungary's compromise has been called: the state retains ownership of most means of production, but managers operate within the structure of a largely free market. The formula first proved most successful in the already advanced economies of Czechoslovakia and East Germany. Even under the new conditions a prewar heritage of economic and social modernization proved an invaluable asset; and Eastern Europe, though dramatically less prosperous than the West, had the highest rate of economic growth in its history by the 1950s.

The Western European nations, looking across the Atlantic for help, found the United States slow to appreciate the depths of their plight in 1945. In 1946 the United States extended to Great Britain a long-term credit of $4.4 billion and subsequently provided a credit of $1.2 billion to France. Following these steps, several developments—aside from the escalating competition for international power with the Soviet Union—persuaded the American government to adopt the systematic policy of aid embodied in the Marshall Plan. The economies of the European countries continued to founder; currency reserves were nearing depletion, which would have halted imports, removed all limits to inflation, and dealt a final blow to hopes of steady recovery.

Dramatically announced in 1947, the Marshall Plan, unprecedented in scope and breadth of vision, was initiated with the massive sum of more than $5 billion appropriated by Congress in 1948. The distribution of the aid reflected not the alliances of World War II but the alignments of the Cold War—in 1948, for example, Italy received more than $600 million to finance a broad program of industrial reconstruction. Over the next four years, the Marshall Plan channeled into Europe more than $15 billion under the direction of the Organization for European Economic Cooperation (OEEC), which eighteen Western states established for this purpose. Subsequently the European Payments Union (1950–1958) was created to regulate currency exchanges; and imports from the United States, made possible by credits under the Marshall Plan, benefited America while helping the OEEC countries to rebuild their industries and to lay the foundations for rapid recovery.

In 1948, 1949, and 1950, the combined gross national product of the OEEC participants spurted at an annual rate of 25 percent and by 1952 was approximately half again as large as it had been in 1938. In spite of a bigger population, per capita income increased by more than a third. Western Europe had never been wealthier, and this was only the basis for further advances. In the decade of the 1950s, Europe achieved the highest rate of growth it had ever recorded. The Marshall Plan was a spectacular economic success that demonstrated the value of the experience and renewed enthusiasm of the Western European peoples.

Government Policies in Western Europe

In stimulating and sustaining their nations' recovery, the policies of the OEEC governments were of major importance. Nearly everywhere in Europe the state was expanding the public sector of the economy and assuming leadership in planning for economic growth. The United Kingdom's Labour government began its program of systematic nationalization of industry, starting with the coal mines, in 1947. The French government in 1945 and 1946 took over the Bank of France and other major banks, large insurance companies, ultilities, coal mines, and the Renault automotive works (made vulnerable by its owner's collaboration with the Germans). Italy, through a legacy from the Fascist regime, already controlled the biggest publicly held complex of industries anywhere in Western Europe. Two huge, state-owned aggregates—the Institute for Industrial Reconstruction, which consisted of more than 100 companies, and the National Hydro-carbon Corporation, which directed the production of gas, oil, and other energy sources—dominated the economy. West Germany alone made no effort to expand the number of publicly owned industries, but there, too, the government had an important role (as it had during the war, under Speer) in coordinating economic growth that would come to be known in the late 1950s as the German miracle.

In one sense nationalization proved a disappointment, as state ownership gave no assurance of efficient management, good labor relations, or a high return on capital. But it helped governments develop all-encompassing economic plans that would guide both public and private enterprises to function in the general interest. Through the Monnet Plan (1946–1950) and subsequent designs for balanced economic growth, France set the model of loose but effective control. Utilizing refined methods of national income accounting, economists and other "technocrats" were able to turn the flow of investments in directions favored by the government. In doing so, they successfully built on institutions and policies many of which had developed under the Vichy regime. Britain created a National Economic Development Council in 1961 and adopted a five-year plan in 1962 for similar purposes. Comparable plans overseeing the operations of a mixed economy were devised and followed in almost all European and Mediterranean countries from Sweden to the new state of Israel. In West Germany a private trade association with close government ties, the Federation of German Industries, as well as a number of the largest banks exercised effective influence over the economy.

The policies of European governments were closely comparable in another respect: all undertook to promote the welfare of their citizens and in particular to protect workers and their families against sickness, impoverished old age, and unemployment. Great Britain provided the earliest and (Sweden excepted) probably the most complete example of what has come to be called the welfare state. Its cornerstone was the National Health Service, inaugurated in 1948, which assumed nearly the total cost of medical, dental, and hospital care for all residents of the United Kingdom. The Continental governments instituted similar programs, including such benefits as family allowances—payments for the support of minor children—which in turn may have helped sustain the birth rate.

Welfare programs had considerable economic impact. They relieved people of the need to save in anticipation of sickness and old age. At the same time, to meet welfare costs, the state developed more efficient methods for collecting taxes. The government thus accumulated large monetary reserves, which it could invest according to its economic plans, further enlarging its role in leading the nation to recovery.

The First Steps Toward Integration

From 1948 on the OEEC sought to coordinate the policies of participating governments, recognizing that the free international movement of the factors of production—capital and labor—as well as of finished products was critical to high domestic growth rates. But efforts to change this organization into a tariff union failed, except for a small "common market" established in 1948: Benelux, a customs union embracing Belgium, the Netherlands, and Luxembourg. At the same time, an important group of Western leaders urged that the European states take steps toward political integration. A meeting at The Hague in 1948, chaired by Winston Churchill, to discuss the formation of a Council of Europe, led to the creation of a Council of Ministers and a Consultative Assembly, with headquarters at Strasbourg. The new organization's powers, however, were very limited; and it became clear that few governments, least of all Great Britain's, were willing to surrender any sovereignty or significant decision-making power to a supranational authority.

Two leading French integrationists, the economist Jean Monnet and Foreign Minister Robert Schuman, then decided to proceed by working for fuller integration in one limited sector at a time. Their efforts led to the creation of the French-German Coal and Steel Authority in 1950 as an imaginative solution to problems that had plagued relations between the two countries. In 1952, propelled by the euphoria of recovery, these two nations joined with Italy and the three Benelux states to establish the European Coal and Steel Community (ECSC), the real kernel of a common market. Each member appointed a representative to the ECSC's executive body, which was then left significantly autonomous in planning and coordinating the production and distribution of the coal and steel critical to industrial growth. As the union proved its economic value and steadily increased its authority, it excited renewed visions of a close economic and political federation.

The Limits of Political Change

By the early 1950s, recovering from the war was no longer the focus of European life, and that in itself was a striking achievement. Instead, economic growth and the consumer goods it brought were giving European society a new look of health and stability. Not surprisingly in such an atmosphere the political balance shifted toward the center and center right. Of course, a move toward the political center or simply more relaxed rule meant something quite different in Franco's Spain, Great Britain, or Soviet Russia. But everywhere the business of daily life in peacetime seemed to take precedence as prosperity, based on sophisticated technology and expanding trade, became again a common European goal.

Having adopted extensive welfare measures and accepted a large governmental role in economic planning (often including the nationalization of major industries), European society seemed resistant to further or more fundamental change. And this resistance was strengthened by the pressures of the Cold War which even in domestic affairs divided and isolated much of the left. In the Soviet Union, too, a somewhat comparable shift occurred. East and West, moderate governments in stable societies were tempted to assert themselves; but the effect of such assertiveness in the years 1956–1958 was to establish once again Europe's secondary position on the world stage.

Western Europe

In Britain the Conservatives regained power in 1951 and held it for the next thirteen years

PERCENT OF ANNUAL INCREASE IN GNP 1950–1960 AT CONSTANT PRICES IN SELECTED COUNTRIES

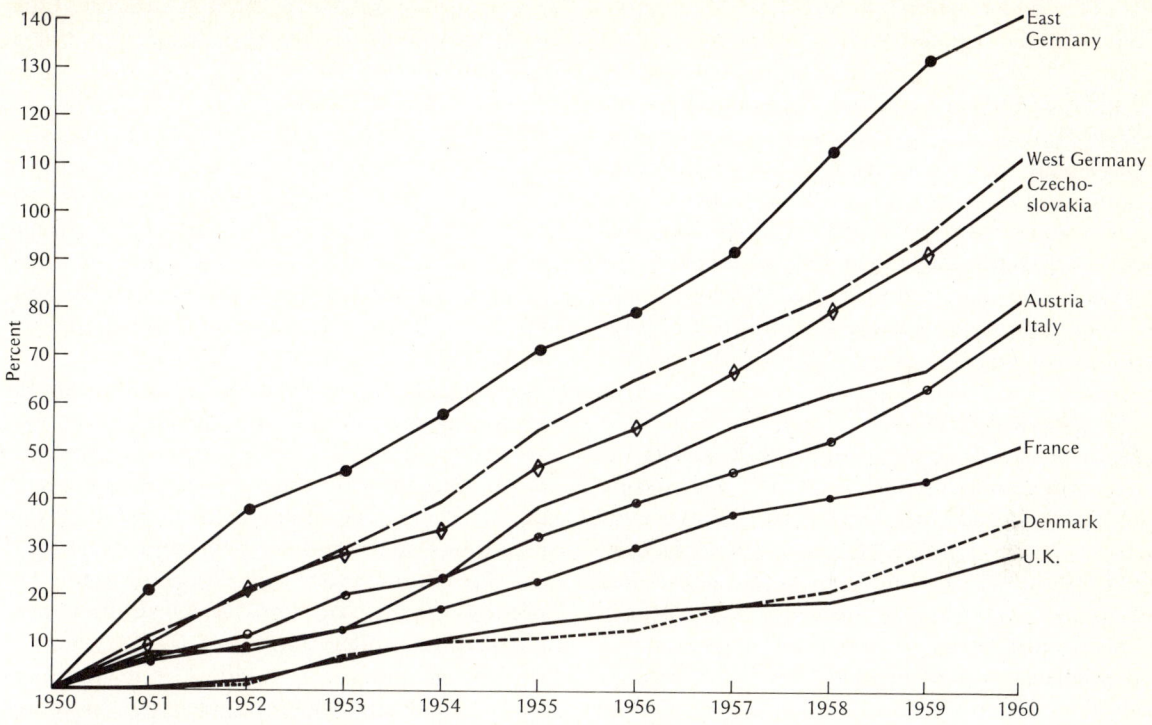

Note that even for the United Kingdom, the growth rate averaged about 3 percent a year, about the same as in the period of industrial "takeoff" in the nineteenth century. Growth rates tend to be higher, of course, where the starting point is lower.

despite Churchill's retirement in 1955. Although rationing ended and taxes were lowered, the new measures introduced by the Labour government were not undone, the Conservatives promising rather to accomplish similar ends with an administration that would be more efficient and less intrusive. In 1953 the coronation of Queen Elizabeth II seemed to mark the beginning of a new and more pleasant era.

West Germany under Adenauer vied with Britain as America's primary European ally, joining NATO in 1955 and winning diplomatic recognition even from the Soviet Union. In a notable easing of international tension a peace treaty with Austria was signed by all the former Allies in the same year and quickly led to the withdrawal of occupation forces and to the full recognition of Austria's sovereignty. In Italy, although the formation of political coalitions became more complex after the fall of De Gasperi in 1953 and despite the Communists' continued importance as the nation's second largest party, the Christian Democrats dominated every government. Within that party the factions of the center and the right increased their strength, and programs of social reform and public welfare tended to be subordinated to the party's ties to business, the Catholic Church, and the United States.

The dictatorships of Spain and Portugal, bolstered by good relations with the United States, faced minimal domestic oppositions. Only in Europe's smaller democracies—the Scandinavian and Benelux countries and Austria—were Socialist parties (firmly anti-communist) able to remain in office in the 1950s. The stability bravely hoped for in the Marshall Plan was achieved with unexpected speed; the threat of chaos and despair had clearly passed, taking with it the likelihod of political revolutions.

The Soviet Union

Equally remarkable, a comparable relaxation occurred in the Soviet Union after the passing of Stalin, whose dictatorship had grown even more intense and repressive in the years following World War II. Intellectuals and artists had been required to follow more closely the official view, whether socialist realism in the arts or the fallacious genetic theories of Trofim Lysenko. Clearly the regime had been anxious to counteract the effects of wartime appeals to regional sentiment and of postwar contacts with the West. But the tough intolerance, like the ugly touches of anti-Semitism, also reflected the personality of Joseph Stalin. There were signs suggesting a new wave of purges when he died of a stroke in 1953.

After thirty years of dictatorship, such a loss was necessarily traumatic in itself; and the problem of succession, always difficult in an absolutist system, was one the Soviet Union had faced but once before. There were other issues too. Shortly before his death Stalin himself had hinted that the pace of industrialization might be slowed in favor of other needs, since Russia was meeting the high goals of the current Five-Year Plan, and had implied the possibility of less contentious relations with the West.

The succession went surprisingly smoothly. Party and state officials performed their duties, and at the very top a form of collective leadership emerged even while its members engaged in intense competition for power. Only in 1956–1957 did it become clear that Nikita Khrushchev was emerging victorious.

Khrushchev's triumph showed again that control of the Communist party was central to political power in Russia, but it had to do with policies as well. Some of his competitors, initially more powerful, had favored a sharper break with old policies than officialdom could accept (emphasizing the needs of consumers, for example, or the advantages of more decentralized decision making). Khrushchev took a more conservative position. And though the infighting was ruthless and included executions as well as sudden dismissals, his preeminence was marked not by the purge of his opponents but by their assignment to minor and distant positions—steps approved by majority votes in the Presidium and Central Committee. The political forms of the Soviet Union now worked for moderation.

Khrushchev's rise within the government was most dramatically signaled by his speech at the Twentieth Party Congress in 1956. He launched a full attack on the "cult of personality" that had been devoted to his predecessor, presenting a kind of bill of particulars of Stalin's excesses, his paranoid distrust, his interference in the conduct of war, his responsibility for the purge trials of the 1930s. Nothing like this had occurred before in the Soviet Union; myths that for a generation had been central to a great nation's enormous sacrifices were being attacked by its own leader. Khrushchev's charges circulated widely in secret and then more openly, with effects in the Soviet Union and Eastern Europe and among Communist movements everywhere still to be measured. Suddenly streets and squares were renamed; statues and pictures disappeared. The thaw[2] following

---

[2] The metaphor of the thaw, which has come to be generally applied to these changes, is derived from a novel of that title by the noted Russian fiction writer and journalist Ilya Ehrenburg.

Stalin's death reached its peak, and a freer, more open society appeared in prospect.

Built-in counterpressures quickly made themselves felt. The needs of the party, the problems of administering a vast socialist state, rumblings of excitement from other peoples of the Soviet bloc who believed a real thaw might mean autonomy for them—all this led Khrushchev to clamp controls on criticism once more. But the restraints were never again so rigid or so arbitrary as under Stalin. When in 1957 the Soviet Union celebrated the fortieth anniversary of the Russian Revolution by launching the world's first space satellite, Russia's status as one of the most powerful and stable nations was dramatically confirmed.

Forays at Independence

On the Continent prosperity and peace raised the prospect that European nations might pursue policies quite independent of American or Soviet influence. The effort, led by the United States, to strengthen European defenses clearly pointed to the rearming of Germany, a measure the French could hardly welcome and Russia was determined to prevent. As a safeguard the French proposed in 1952 the creation of a European Defense Community, in effect a common European army that would benefit from German strength without the risks of a separate German military force.

The proposal was accepted by most of the European members of NATO and pushed hard by the United States; but its implication of permanent Continental engagement was distasteful to the British, and growing doubts, increased by resentment of extraordinary pressure from the United States, led the French Parlement to reject the EDC in 1954. There was in short a limit to how far European governments could be pushed, and American intransigence in the face of Khrushchev's professed desires to improve relations (John Foster Dulles, secretary of state under President Dwight D. Eisenhower, Truman's successor, considered even Churchill a bit weak in his opposition to the Communist menace) only strengthened that view.

The Suez Crisis

With a kind of stalemate in Europe, the more immediate confrontations of the Cold War shifted to other parts of the world, particularly those in which European dominance had recently been overcome. Great Britain, her economy beginning to lag badly behind those of other European countries and fearful of losing her special role as America's primary ally, attempted one dramatic foreign venture. In Egypt, once a crucial part of the British Empire, Gamal Abdel Nasser's government raised growing distrust in the West by its domestic policies and its turning to the Communist bloc for help in industrialization. When the Western powers, following the United States, refused aid for the construction of a high dam across the Nile at Aswan, Nasser announced the nationalization of the Suez Canal, still owned by a British-controlled company. Britain led in demanding strong measures and after international efforts at compromise broke down, conspired with Israel and France to take military action. Israel's attack on Egypt in October 1956 was followed by an Anglo-French bombardment and occupation of the canal banks. Within a week, however, the protests of the Soviet Union and the opposition of the United States enabled the United Nations to force a cease-fire. Shortly afterward foreign troops withdrew.

Nothing had been gained by this sudden outburst of an outdated imperialist mentality, and much was lost in prestige and in good relations with Arab states and the whole Third World. Although Britain soon became the third nation to possess a hydrogen bomb, she was increasingly dependent even for her own defense on American policy.

The Nations of the Soviet Sphere

Until 1953 the Communist governments of Eastern Europe outdid themselves in mimicry of the Soviet fatherland, including the idolization of Stalin and the ruthless use of secret police and internment camps. But Russia's open exploitation of her neighbors' resources to aid her own industrial growth was inevitably resented, and Stalin's death allowed that resentment to show.

Within three months the workers of East Berlin were in the streets proclaiming a general strike in protest against increased production quotas that they believed to be primarily for the benefit of the Soviet Union. Russian tanks rushed in to put down the revolt, but it had long-lasting effects. Walter Ulbricht became the new leader of East Germany; and while strengthening the party's dictatorship, he offered a reform program of higher wages and better living conditions. He also won from the Russians recognition of East German sovereignty and the end of occupation. Still tightly tied to the Soviet Union and limited in her autonomy, East Germany developed a voice of her own in the councils of Communist countries and expanded her trade with West Germany and other states outside the Soviet orbit.

A far more serious outburst erupted in Poland following Khrushchev's speech attacking Stalin in 1956. This too began as a workers' protest, but it quickly gathered support from the growing faction of the national Communist party critical of Russian policies in Poland. Again Soviet forces intervened, to be jeered and sometimes attacked, and the Polish party elected Wladyslaw Gomulka party secretary in preference to the pro-Russian candidate. Gomulka, who remained the dominant figure in the government until 1970, was a firm Communist who insisted, however, that socialist states must follow somewhat different paths from Russia's in accordance with their national traditions. He convinced Soviet leaders of his loyalty to the Russian alliance, a loyalty he subsequently proved on many occasions, and he thereby won their acquiescence to his more independent course. Russia and Poland began to deal with each other more nearly as sovereign equals. The presence of Russian troops was limited; Poland demanded and got a share of the reparations Germany paid; and she negotiated economic aid from the United States. Gomulka also mitigated the repression of the Catholic Church, and by the 1960s he conceded greater independence to Polish intellectuals and allowed increased contacts with the West.

Another revolt in 1956 ended more tragically. Rioting broke out in Hungary in October following a series of conflicts within her Communist party. From the outset the uprising was even more markedly anti-Russian than Poland's, and at first the Russians withdrew, seemingly disposed in this case too to accept increased national autonomy. But then Imre Nagy, who had been arrested the year before for "right-wing deviationism," was recalled as premier. Bowing to popular pressure, he showed that he was willing to break the alliance with Russia and favor neutrality. The Russian attitude hardened, and then the Soviet army attacked in force to crush the revolution in ten days of bitter fighting.

Many in Hungary expected Western aid, for which rebel radio stations pleaded, but none came. Indeed Washington, hurling denunciations of Russian imperialism, was embarrassed by the fact that while Russian tanks were crunching across Hungary, the troops of three American allies were invading Egypt. Russia had made it clear that the satellite states would not be permitted to break their alliance to her, and the West had confessed that a Russian sphere did indeed exist. A wave of refugees left the country, and Nagy himself was kidnapped by the Russians and executed in 1958. Hungary was punished with harsh repression, a heavy-handed Soviet presence, and a general worsening of working conditions, but her new premier, Janos Kadar, who had supported the more moderate phase of the rising, slowly led her on a more national course.

Soviet tanks occupy the streets of Budapest after the revolt had been crushed.
(Photo: UPI)

Czechoslovakia fared no better. The most industrialized of the states in the Russian orbit, she had not taken easily to communism. Although the regime was secure after trials and purges in the 1950s, the economy prospered but without the technological transformation or growth in consumer goods so apparent in the West. The divisions between the dominant Czechs and the Slovaks hardened.

Greater geographic isolation aided some of the other Communist nations to achieve greater autonomy. Albania, the most backward country on the Continent, increasingly allied herself to mainland China in diplomatic and dogmatic opposition to Russia. Rumania, which with Bulgaria had been among the most Stalinist of the satellite regimes, found the adjustments to Soviet policy after 1953 more difficult to make. While maintaining a strict domestic dictatorship her insistence on an independent foreign policy made her the most venturesome of the Russian-dominated regimes in establishing good relations with Western powers.

Yugoslavia had never been a satellite state. After her expulsion from the Cominform in 1948, she improved her relations with her non-Communist neighbors and benefited from American aid. Reconciliations with Khrushchev in 1954 and 1957 did not reduce her independence or her trade with the West nor diminish Tito's prestige as a leader capable of dealing with both the Soviet Union and the United States. Partly of necessity, Yugoslavia developed a Communism of her own that by the 1960s was relaxing central economic controls and encouraging local participation in decision making. No other communist nation was able to move so far from the common model.

Two New Starts in the West

The launching of Sputnik in 1957, remarkable enough in itself, had also signaled the continued advance of the superpowers. The suppression of revolt in Eastern Europe had, like the debacle at Suez, further defined the limits constraining single European states. And almost simultaneously, two events reflected distinctly different responses to this situation: the fall of the Fourth Republic in France and the founding of the European Common Market.

Under the Fourth Republic the French government had in many respects performed very well—how well would become clear only in the prosperity of the 1960s. But coalition governments also shared the best-known weaknesses of the Third Republic. With the Communist party ostracized since 1947 but still sizable, the other three large parties—the Socialists and more often the Radical Socialists and the MRP (Popular Republicans)—had to seek alliances to capture a parliamentary majority. It appeared briefly in 1954 as if the able Radical Socialist Pierre Mendès-France could continue to make the system work, as so often happened (in the nick of time) in the past. He extricated France from Vietnam, sought ways to grant Algeria independence, and tried to win his party to a program of economic planning that would bring it closer to the Socialists. But too many issues divided his own supporters, and the extremes of left and right were gaining strength at the expense of the center. The MRP was challenged by the rising Gaullist party and by conservatives; and in the elections of 1956 the Communists gained and the Socialists declined while on the right a movement of resentful small shopkeepers and farmers—people bypassed by the benefits of modernization—briefly won political importance.

One ministry after another proved unable to cope with the divisive issues before it, the most demanding of which was the growing revolt against French rule in Algeria. Beset by colonial uprisings in Africa and Asia since 1945, the French army had expended itself in repressive measures only to have "the politicians" concede autonomy or independence.[3] In the spirit of the Cold War, many officers saw themselves fighting alone against communist conspiracy around the world, and they were determined not to permit their efforts to be scuttled in Algeria, a French colony since 1830, in which a sizable French population had lived for generations. At the same time leftists and intellectuals expressed outrage at the atrocities committed by a furious army and at the kind of democracy that waged war against Algerians seeking to govern themselves.

Algerian nationalists had taken to open revolt in 1954, and for the next four years, the Algerian question brought down more French governments than any other issue. Then in 1958 a group of French army officers turned from fighting Algerians to seize political control of Algeria from which they threatened to move against the indecisive government of metropolitan France. Uncertain that any ordinary ministry could effectively resist and preferring De Gaulle to the military insurgents, a majority in the National Assembly welcomed his announcement that he would serve and invested him with extraordinary powers for six years. He led France for the next ten.

Long convinced that France needed a stronger political system, De Gaulle had been shrewdly ambiguous in his pronouncements on Algeria. The army, the center, and the right all

---

[3] In 1958 in Africa alone, eight new states chose to be autonomous within the French Union: Senegal, Mali, the Ivory Coast, Mauritania, Niger, Upper Volta, Cameroun, and Gabon. French Somaliland (Afars and Issas Territory) preferred to remain a territory; and Guinea, Togo, the (Brazzaville) Congo, and the Central African Republic chose full independence.

found him acceptable, and he used his strength to consolidate support and win France to a new constitution. Overwhelmingly approved by popular referendum in September 1958, it established the Fifth Republic as a presidential regime whose chief executive would be indirectly elected for a seven-year term. De Gaulle was chosen president two months later and Gaullists became by far the largest party in the Parlement, where the Communists were reduced to a handful.

The president moved cautiously on the Algerian question, quietly weakening and dispersing the leaders of the military revolt. Only gradually did it become clear that De Gaulle accepted Algerian self-determination, a proposal approved by three-quarters of the voters in a referendum held in January 1961. Effectively isolated, the most intransigent of the officers formed the Secret Army Organization (OAS) and for eighteen months indulged in terrorism in France and Algeria. But the French president, having arranged peace with the Algerian rebels, declared war on the army rebels. By the end of 1962, they had disbanded, Algeria was independent, and France's presidential regime could turn to other questions.

None of these were to have greater long-range importance than the establishment of the European Economic community, known as the Common Market, in itself a kind of practical compromise between grand visions of a united Europe such as lay behind the formation of the Council of Europe in 1948 and the concrete achievements of the Coal and Steel Community founded four years later. The six nations belonging to the latter—Belgium, the Netherlands, Luxembourg, France, Germany, and Italy—in 1957 signed the Treaty of Rome (Britain among others declined to do so) which created the new Community to go into effect January 1, 1958. Formally it was a limited agreement, an addition to the Coal and Steel Community establishing an agency to coordinate the development of atomic energy and binding the six nations to a careful series of steps leading to the elimination of tariffs between the member states and to a common tariff toward all other nations. The France of the Fourth Republic, which long favored the creation of international European agencies with independent authority, had played a leading part along with the three smaller states in pressing for the new agreement. "Europe," the French government said at the time, "will not be made all at once, or according to a single, general plan. It will be built through concrete achievements." That larger hope was still far from realization, and it would take some time to tell whether the opening words of the new treaty would ever have more than rhetorical weight in declaring its signatories "Determined to establish the foundations of an ever closer union among the European peoples."

The European nations regained a place among the economic, social, and cultural leaders of the world even in an age in which rapid development was no longer a Western monopoly. They recovered from war with astonishing speed and on the whole adjusted to the loss of empire and international dominance realistically. Indeed the achievement was so great that visions of a still more prosperous and egalitarian united Europe no longer seemed merely utopian. But there was disillusionment, too. Neither the Communists nor the democratic opponents of fascism managed in victory to create the societies they promised, and prosperity did not itself resolve old conflicts. Political leaders operating in a prewar style attempted domestic compromise and the assertion of national autonomy in international affairs, but that led to a test of power no European state save the Soviet Union could meet. The contrived stability of de Gaulle's Fifth Republic and the optimism of the founders of the European Economic Community, uncertain as the prospects were for either, at least implied the possibility of trying other approaches.

RECOMMENDED READING

Studies

Allsop, Kenneth. *The Angry Decade: A Survey of the Cultural Revolt of the 1950s.* 1969. Captures very well postwar disillusionment.

*Aron, Raymond. *The Imperial Republic: The United States and the World, 1945–1973.* 1974. A leading French thinker analyzes the period of American dominance.

Beer, Samuel H. *British Politics in the Collectivist Age.* 1965. A comprehensive treatment of the new political life of Great Britain.

*Crossman, Richard H. (ed.). *The God That Failed.* 1950. The moving testimony of former Marxists about their lost faith in the era of Stalin and the Cold War.

*Crouzet, Maurice. *The European Renaissance Since 1945.* 1971. An optimistic essay on the politics, society, and culture of postwar Europe.

*Dahrendorf, Ralf. *Society and Democracy in Germany.* 1969. A German sociologist assesses the special qualities of German society.

Dawidowicz, Lucy S. *The War Against the Jews, 1933–1945.* 1976. A full and balanced assessment of the twentieth century's greatest horror.

*Deakin, F. W. *The Brutal Friendship.* 1966. A detailed account of the Axis primarily in terms of Hitler's relations with Mussolini.

Feis, Herbert. *Churchill, Roosevelt, Stalin: The War They Waged and the Peace They Sought.* 1957. A balanced and insightful account of Allied relations.

Fejto, François. *A History of the People's Democracies: Eastern Europe Since Stalin.* 1971. A careful study of the conflicts and variety among Eastern European states under Soviet dominance.

Halle, Louis J. *The Cold War as History.* 1967. Sets the historical context of the great ideological and military division of the modern world.

*Hoffmann, Stanley, et al. *In Search of France.* 1965. A group of distinguished scholars attempt to define the unique patterns of French political and social life.

*Laqueur, Walter. *Europe Since Hitler.* 1972. One of the ablest of the surveys of contemporary Europe.

Michel, Henri. *The Shadow War: The European Resistance, 1939–1945.* 1972. Combines recent scholarship in a solid study of the most attractive (and romanticized) aspect of World War II.

*Paxton, Robert. *Vichy France: Old Guard and New Order, 1940–1944.* 1972. Stresses the continuity and lasting significance for French society and institutions of this twilight period.

Postan, Michael M. *An Economic History of Western Europe, 1945–1964.* 1967. A noted economic historian analyzes the roots of European recovery.

Sherwin, M. J. *A World Destroyed: The Atomic Bomb and the Grand Alliance.* 1975. A scholarly and balanced account of this controversial and complicated subject.

*Snell, John L. *Illusion and Necessity: The Diplomacy of Global War, 1939–1945.* 1963. A clear assessment of the interrelationship of the great issues among warring powers.

*Ulam, Adam B. *The Rivals: American and Russia Since World War II.* 1972. Surveys the wide-ranging effects of the Cold War in geopolitical, ideological, and social context.

Wilkinson, James D. *The Intellectual Resistance in Europe.* 1981. A wide-ranging and sensitive assessment of the content and legacy of the resistance and its place in contemporary thought.

---

*Available in paperback.

30

THE PRESENT IN HISTORICAL PERSPECTIVE

Since 1945 Europe has enjoyed an unusually long period without war or any major territorial changes. And in the generation since 1957 Europe has embraced the social organization and high technology said to mark "advanced industrial societies" like those of the United States, Canada, and Japan and that distinguish Europe as a privileged zone compared to most of the rest of the world. In the first decade of this period economic growth was the overwhelming reality, and in important respects the nations of Europe became more alike. Understood as a self-sustaining process of modernization, European development offered to less fortunate countries an example in two models: the democratic capitalism of the West and the state socialism of the East. Then in 1968 and for the next several years a wave of revolutionary discontent brought to the fore complex social and cultural problems that also appeared to be characteristic of advanced societies. Responses to these problems varied, however—most sharply between Eastern and Western Europe but also within each country, according to its political realities, social traditions, and economic potential, so that older regional and national differences once again showed their importance. Few of these problems have been solved, but the varied attempts to deal with them provide important examples and perhaps even instructive lessons. Since 1973, social and economic change has apparently slowed, and by the end of the 1970s Europe, like the United States, was suffering a serious recession. Nevertheless, the striking fact about Europe today is its wealth, and the great surprise (some would say disappointment) is its relative stability.

Europe's place in the contemporary world is still being defined. Individually more prosperous and influential than all but a few of the nations of the world, only collectively can European countries match the power and influence of the superpowers. With the relaxation of tensions between the United States and the Soviet Union in the 1960s and 1970s, European states pursued more independent policies and developed important ties to the developing and underdeveloped nations. The growing bonds of the European Community raised the possibility of a truly independent Europe; yet by choice, pressure, and force the two halves of Europe remained closely tied to the United States and the Soviet Union.

Attitudes toward the present thus remain ambivalent, prospects for the future uncertain. One reason for studying the past is to better understand the present, and the tendency for Westerners to see themselves in terms of their place on some scale of historical evolution has grown stronger in the last two centuries. The French Revolution, industrialization, theories of liberalism and progress, World War I, the Russian Revolution, totalitarianism, and World War II not only have made social change a central preoccupation of modern life but have opened a continuing debate about the direction in which it leads. Predictions that society is steadily, even inevitably, marching toward greater individualism, democracy, and wealth have been countered by equally confident predictions of dehumanization, cultural and moral decline, and loss of freedom. In every case predictions rest on the assessment of social organization, technological development, and human rationality that the commentators draw from history; for the present is always understood as a period of transition to a different future.

I. THE NATURE OF ADVANCED SOCIETIES

Social Effects

Europe's economic growth since the mid-1950s has probably been greater than at any other time in history. Often the triumph of a mixed economy, of that combination of private enterprise and state planning practiced in most European states, this growth has produced far-reaching changes. In advanced societies, adults are literate and families small. Because people live longer, the population tends to become older. Leisure time increases for everyone, and more women work for wages. Steadily increasing productivity requires high rates of investment and frequent changes in production and marketing, which reduce costs while adding new products, releasing workers to the service sector of society which becomes steadily larger. Standards of consumption rise throughout society, and the cycle of growth continues. In all this, European traditions of technical skill, high levels of education, ease of communication, effective government, and social flexibility have been important advantages. Such rapid growth, however, threatens to transform society in disagreeable ways through pollution, urban crowding, and the weakening of old social ties. It also raises fundamental questions about how the benefits of prosperity should be distributed.

Urbanization

While the inner core of older cities may lose population (exacerbating problems of urban decay), the agglomeration grows, and in effect the larger cities continue to spread. In France one person in five and in Great Britain nearly that proportion lives within an hour's drive of the capital city. Volgograd stretches for forty-five miles along the river after which it was named, and some fourteen cities in Russia have a population of over a million. In general, the new highways, extended subways, and bus lines that push the city outward rarely keep pace with the congestion of traffic at its core. As similar skyscrapers rise in the centers (along with criticism of them), similar residential districts sprawl across the outskirts. In the 1950s new housing tended, East and West, to look like dreary concrete barracks and often provided few of the services necessary to create a sense of community. In nearly every country efforts at better planning led to the creation of whole new cities, often bleak and artificial, surrounding the metropolis; five towns of 24,000 people each were planned around Paris, twenty-four such towns now surround Moscow.

The more recent trend has been toward new centers on a smaller scale, carefully planned to have shopping, recreational, and cultural centers of their own as well as some light industry so that most of the working population need

ACTIVE WORK FORCE

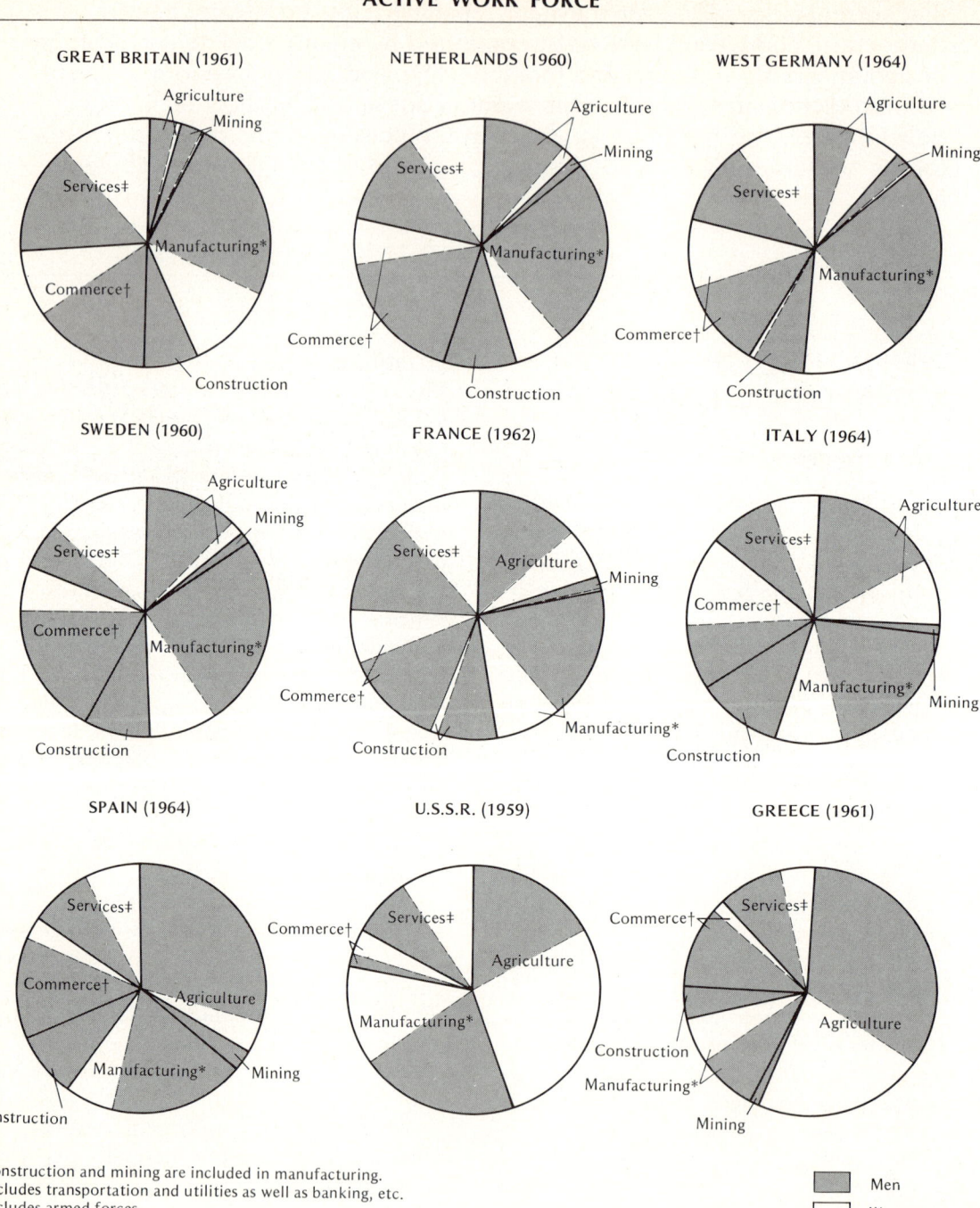

*Construction and mining are included in manufacturing.
†Includes transportation and utilities as well as banking, etc.
‡Includes armed forces.

SOME OF EUROPE'S LARGEST CITIES
(1971–1979 estimates)

	City	Metropolitan Area
Moscow	7,831,000	10,001,000
London	6,970,000	
Paris	2,317,227	8,612,531
Leningrad	4,073,000	4,588,000
Madrid		3,200,067
Rome	2,897,505	
Kiev	2,144,000	
Budapest	2,091,360	
Bucharest	1,858,418	1,934,000
Berlin	1,909,706	
Milan	1,706,268	
Hamburg	1,663,305	
Warsaw	1,542,500	
Munich	1,296,970	
Athens	867,023	2,101,103
Cracow	1,444,000	
Gorky	1,344,000	
Naples	1,225,227	
Barcelona		1,742,355
Glasgow	832,097	1,727,625
Lisbon	829,900	1,611,887
Stockholm	653,929	1,380,426

The results of the rush to meet the demand for new housing in these Parisian suburbs range from crowded new houses meant to evoke Norman cottages to high-rise apartments on a bleak hilltop. The remaining trees mark the forests displaced, and the smog hints at the great city beyond.
(Photo: Viva/Woodfin Camp and Associates)

not commute. Many of these, especially perhaps in Scandinavia (Tapiola, outside Helsinki, being one of the most successful), have proved very attractive, mixing large and small modern buildings, pleasant streets, and restful green spaces.

Thus, despite the uneven results and the absence of wholly satisfactory solutions, Europe contains the world's most interesting experiments in urban planning. Cities like Rome and Vienna have found that banning traffic from the narrow, medieval streets of the old centers of the city can lead to a renewal that makes those sections among the most attractive (and most expensive) for shops and housing. Although loud laments accompanied the closing of Les Halles in Paris, the great sheds built in the Second Empire for the provisioning of the capital, the efficiency and improved traffic that resulted were (like the controversial but exciting new cultural center and apartments that replaced them in the 1970s) undeniable benefits. In London Covent Garden, too, became a cultural center; and Billingsgate, the fishmarket that gave the language another word for verbal abuse, closed in 1981. In Communist Europe good housing remains scarce, and there are long waiting lists for cramped apartments; in capitalist Europe the renovation of city centers continues the process that pushes all but the well-to-do to distant and often faceless suburbs. Although the price paid in terms of social cohesion and convenience is still disputed, in the narrow terms of living space and hygiene far more Europeans are far more comfortably housed than ever before.

Communication and the Environment

In many parts of Western Europe canals continue to carry significant quantities of cargo, and air travel is especially important across the distances of the Soviet Union; but ground transportation remains the heart of commerce. In the 1960s every nation launched new road-building projects, and by 1980 the most important of these were completed nearly everywhere in the West (except Great Britain and the Iberian peninsula). Superhighways run from Stockholm to south of Valencia and from Naples to Hamburg; already many of the older highways have become overcrowded and in need of repair. In Europe railroads are valued for passenger travel as well as for transport, although nowhere are they expected to turn a profit. In 1981 French trains, which hold world speed records, began to carry passengers from Paris to Lyon at 165 miles per hour.

Western European nations have also become technological leaders in electronic communication, experimenting with interactive uses of computers that permit home subscribers to pay bills, consult encyclopedias, or record their opinions by means of their television sets. Although the international broadcasts of the Western European television network have had far greater success with sporting events than with drama or politics, politicians and governments worry about the internationalization of information and culture. In the West private stations have in effect ended the state's monopoly, and even in much of the East it is impossible to prevent audiences from turning to foreign stations. In some senses Europeans now know each other better and have been drawn closer together than ever before. Yet in matters of communication the differences between East and West remain great; and despite increased travel and information, ethnic and regional differences have not lost their hold.

The most obvious by-product of industrial growth is the pollution that contaminates air, waterways, and countryside, pouring from factories and automobiles and littering the landscape. Especially shocking in Europe, where monuments and scenic places revered for centuries have become seriously threatened, the problem calls for coordinated planning and severe restrictions that governments intent upon encouraging growth have been reluctant to take. The Rhine is now one of the most pol-

TELEVISION LICENSES PER 100 INHABITANTS, EUROPE, 1975

Finland	36.3
Sweden	36.3
Denmark	32.3
United Kingdom	31.7
West Germany	31.1
East Germany	30.9
Luxembourg	29.3
Switzerland	28.5
France	27.4
Netherlands	27.4
Norway	27.0
Belgium	26.8
Czechoslovakia	25.4
Austria	23.6
Hungary	23.6
Italy	22.0
USSR	21.7
Ireland	20.7
Poland	19.8
Spain	18.5
Bulgaria	17.6
Yugoslavia	16.1
Rumania	13.8
Greece	12.7
Portugal	7.6

luted of international waterways, and high concentrations of mercury have been recorded in Geneva's Lac Leman. It is dangerous to bathe in or eat fish from much of the Baltic and Mediterranean seas. Escaped industrial gases have caused illness and death in the outskirts of Milan, and the magnificent palaces of Venice were discovered to be slowly sinking, apparently because the earth beneath their pilings gives way as underground water is pumped up on the mainland for industrial use. The remaining monuments of ancient Greece and Rome and the ornate façades of Gothic churches show signs in city after city of crumbling and cracking from the vibrations and fumes of modern traffic.

There are, of course, signs that mankind and modern technology can clean up as well as pollute. Through stern regulations Great Britain has eliminated the smog that plagued London since the sixteenth century and killed thousands of people as recently as 1952. The Thames has become a clean river for the first time in centuries. Nearly every building in Paris was cleaned in the 1960s and 1970s, stripping away the somber, dark patina of soot accumulated through one hundred and fifty years of industrialization. Huge demonstrations against nuclear power, like the ecological movements (especially in Germany, the Low Countries, and France), testify to a growing concern; and several international agencies are pledged to press for enforceable European standards for protecting the environment. But it remains too early to say whether enough can or will be done to prevent the disasters pessimists predict.

The Distribution of Benefits

As advanced nations increase their wealth, they by no means distribute it equally; but by any measure—real wages, per capita income, or consumer expenditures—the standard of living of the working classes has risen impressively in the past two decades. The gap between the very rich and wage earners has narrowed only slightly, however, in the West (in Sweden and the Netherlands the poorest third of the nation receives a larger proportion of the country's wealth than does the bottom third in other Western societies; in France, the distribution of wealth has tended to be slightly more uneven than elsewhere in Europe). In Communist Europe professional people and officials live at a much higher standard and with far greater freedom of choice than workers or peasants. The full impact of these inequalities has been softened throughout Europe by complex provisions for social security, free education, subsidized or free medical care, and a wide variety of family benefits and services; and social differences are generally more acceptable in periods of rapid economic growth when nearly everyone's lot is improving.

In the 1970s, however, unemployment began steadily to rise in the West, exposing the weak position of those in declining industries and crafts and small-scale agriculture. Women, the young, and, above all, foreign immigrants have been hardest hit. As unemployment virtually disappeared in the industrial zones in the 1960s, large numbers of people from the less developed periphery had moved to the more prosperous regions—southern Italians to northern Italy, Switzerland, and Germany; Spaniards, Portuguese, and North Africans to France; Yugoslavs and Turks to Germany; Caribbean and African blacks from former colonies to England. In general they found employment as domestic servants, street sweepers, and the least skilled industrial workers—by the 1970s contributing 17 percent of the work force in Switzerland, some 8 percent in Germany (approximately 2.5 million people) and France. Often different in physical appearance, language, and culture, these migrants were drawn together and forced by poverty to live in crowded slums that quickly became ghetto sub-

APPROXIMATE STANDARDS OF LIVING GNP/PER CAPITA, 1978 (US Dollars)

European Nations		Selected Other Nations	
Switzerland	12,100	Kuwait	14,890
Luxembourg	10,410	United Arab Emirates	14,230
Sweden	10,210	Qatar	12,740
Denmark	9,920	Brunei	10,640
West Germany	9,600	United States	9,700
Norway	9,510	Canada	9,170
Belgium	9,070	Saudi Arabia	8,040
Netherlands	8,390	Australia	7,920
Iceland	8,320	Japan	7,330
France	8,270	Brazil	1,570
Austria	7,030	Mexico	1,290
Finland	6,820	China	460
East Germany	5,660	India	180
United Kingdom	5,030		
Czechoslovakia	4,720		
Italy	3,840		
USSR	3,700		
Poland	3,660		
Spain	3,520		
Ireland	3,470		
Hungary	3,450		
Greece	3,270		
Bulgaria	3,200		
Yugoslavia	2,390		
Portugal	2,020		
Rumania	1,750		
Turkey	1,210		
Albania	740		

These figures, based on estimates of varying reliability and distorted by exchange rates, do not take into account the actual distribution of national income, the cost of living, or the style of life in each country.

cultures, resistant to and misunderstood by the larger society. Without the full protection of citizenship, resented by native workers competing for jobs and higher pay, despised as sources of crime and heavy welfare costs, these migrants recreated some of the gravest social problems of the early nineteenth century, now exacerbated by prejudices of race and color.

There are, of course, other groups that have not fully shared in the general prosperity. In every country whole regions labeled as backward have been made the target of special subsidies and tax incentives intended to encourage their industrialization, often with disappointing results. Neither, in general, do women receive equal pay or equal opportunity for advancement, despite the fact that 36 percent of the work force are women in Britain, France, and Germany, with the proportion higher in Sweden and Finland, lower elsewhere. On the average, women workers earn between two-thirds (in Britain) and three-fourths (in France)

WESTERN EUROPE, 1970s: Proportion of Medical Expenses Paid Through State Plans

	Percent		Percent
United Kingdom	95	Spain	42
Ireland	76	Sweden	35
Finland	70	Greece	30
West Germany	69	Norway	26
Austria	67	France	24
Denmark	67	Italy	21
Luxembourg	59	Belgium	16
Switzerland	50	Netherlands	6
Portugal	42		

as much as men. Although in Sweden, France, and Britain women have leading roles in many occupations of high prestige, nowhere are they more than a small minority in such positions except for the medical profession in the Soviet Union, which they dominate.

Education

Access to the professions and important managerial positions is restricted even more by education than by sex. Traditionally in Europe secondary education has been the great dividing point, at which a small fraction of young people were admitted to schools that prided themselves on the demanding and usually classical curriculum required for admission to a university. Many more students attended a somewhat more vocational secondary school whose graduates did not normally go on to universities, and half or more of all students beyond the ages of twelve or fourteen went directly to work. Throughout Europe the elites shared a high formal culture, access to which was with few exceptions first a matter of social class and only second a matter of academic inclination. After World War II, the Communist regimes of Eastern Europe gave preference to the children of workers and party members but only slowly enlarged the number allowed entrance into college-preparatory programs. In the West the proportion of school-age youths undertaking the more prestigious education has steadily increased. And that change has been accompanied by a move toward "comprehensive" schools, more like the American high school, which less sharply segregate the college-bound.

In each country such reforms in the late 1960s and early 1970s were the subject of controversy, often even riots and demonstrations. Education in advanced societies stood as the institutional bridge between social changes that prolonged the period of youth and occupational changes that made formal education the key to social mobility. Reform at the secondary level has been paralleled by major reforms of universities. Despite the creation of hundreds of new institutions, often with American-style campuses, enrollments in many places have swollen beyond their capacity. The particular pattern in each nation reflects its own traditions of culture and class distinction, but the emerging tendency is clear. Those European nations with the highest proportion of twenty to twenty-four years old enrolled in universities (roughly 15 to 20 percent) are the Netherlands, Sweden, Denmark, France, Italy, and Norway, where traditions of democratic access if not equality are stronger. Those with the lowest proportion (less than 10 percent in Yugoslavia, Spain, and Portugal) are the least developed. And nearly all the rest of Europe, both East and West, falls in between. The present balance, however, is everywhere only a temporary and much-criticized compromise, subject to pressures for further change and expansion.

Social Welfare

In most of Europe, universities charge no tuition, and the state subsidizes other forms of culture. But as the battles over education made clear, the citizens of Europe's advanced societies also look to the state as a major instrument of social justice. In practice this has meant less the elaboration of utopian programs for social change, even in Eastern Europe, than efforts to guarantee a minimum standard of living. In the Communist nations, for example, housing and transport are relatively cheap, and in the West governments extensively subsidize both (about one-third of new housing in Germany is government sponsored, one-half in Great Britain, two-thirds in Sweden and France). Social welfare payments of wide-ranging variety are an important part of the family economy for nearly everyone, not just the poor. Similarly, a high proportion of private medical expenses are paid through the state in most countries, and governments have encouraged a steady increase in the number of physicians and hospital beds available. Not surprisingly, rates of infant mortality have declined and rates of longevity have improved so that among Europe's most advanced nations they are the highest in the world. The variations among countries and among regions and classes within the same country reflect, on the other hand, important and troublesome disparities. These government expenditures in addition to those for other services and for defense mean that taxes are relatively high (between 21 and 24 percent of the GNP in the wealthiest nations of Europe and 33 percent in the United Kingdom). Insofar as these taxes are levied with the same social concerns so as to fall most heavily on the rich (and in fact they often do not), that can, as liberal economists have argued, discourage investment, thereby creating yet another incentive for government planning and the nationalization of critical industries.

The Economic Base

Although the coal fields of Britain, West Germany, and Eastern Europe, the iron ore fields of France and Sweden, and the newly discovered North Sea oilfields are tremendously important, Europe's industrial economy rests primarily upon the efficient transformation of raw materials, much of which have to be imported. Wealth comes from productivity, which requires heavy investment, advanced technology, able managers, skilled and willing workers, efficient marketing, and high consumption. Governments from one end of Europe to the other have sought to stimulate these components of productivity through general policies and by exercising direct control, enacting specific measures (such as taxes or tariffs), and providing the infrastructure on which they rest (communication and education, for example). These policies worked to some extent in the boom years of the 1960s, as growth everywhere but in Great Britain was impressive. Sweden, with the most socialist economic system, and Switzerland, with the most thoroughly free market one, achieved the highest per capita income in the industrial world. The most consistently high growth rates, however, belonged to the six states of the original European Economic Community as per capita productivity increased at an amazing rate of over 4 percent a year (compared to 2.5 percent in the United States).

In Eastern Europe, although various countries could point to impressive increases in single sectors, there were no such examples of consistent, overall growth. The exuberant consumerism that filled the shops of Western cities with material goods was not a communist goal; but even the sober quotas for increased consumer consumption announced in most plans, following Khrushchev's of 1958, were usually not quite met. The contrasts between East and West were even greater in agricultural production. In the West, the number of people who worked the land continued to decline (in Ireland, one of the West's least developed nations, 60 percent of the work force was employed in agriculture in 1960, only 20 percent in 1980), but production increased. Nearly one-half the tractors in use in the world are in Europe. With only about 3 percent of the world's farmland, Western Europe produces 15 percent of the world's eggs, potatoes, and wheat (of which France alone is the fifth largest producer, after the U.S.S.R., the United States, China, and India) and nearly one-third of the world's dairy products and sugar beets. In the Soviet Union, by contrast, agricultural production has tended to stagnate and the crucial wheat crop in particular has been disappointing nearly every year. Agricultural production has generally been less disappointing in Yugoslavia and Poland, which may be related to the fact that large proportions of their farmlands remain in private hands.

II. EUROPE'S PLACE IN THE WORLD

Wealth and Power

One of the world's superpowers, the Soviet Union, can be considered a European state with much of its power and influence manifested in its hegemony over Eastern Europe. Western Europe, the second wealthiest region of the world, has been gaining on the first, North America; and in 1979 for the first time the GNP of the nine members of the European Community exceeded that of the United States. Europe's population grows less rapidly than do populations in most other parts of the world, but Europe's international importance is assured both by its great wealth and by the fact that this wealth depends very heavily on trade. It is not surprising, then, that nearly one-half of the world's largest banks are Western European or that Europeans play so great a role in international economic organizations such as the International Monetary Fund, the Organization for Economic Cooperation and Development, or the Trilateral Commission, a pri-

THE WORLD ECONOMY
Gross National Product, Leading Countries, 1978 (Billions of US Dollars)

United States	2,118
USSR	966
Japan	836
West Germany	588
France	440
China	425
United Kingdom	281
Italy	218
Canada	216
Brazil	187
Spain	129
Poland	128
Netherlands	117
Australia	114
India	113
East Germany	96
Sweden	85
Mexico	84

GNP should be taken only as a rough estimate of the relative size of national economies.

THE WORLD ECONOMY
World Trade, 1981 (Leading Free Market Countries Only) (Billions of US Dollars)

World	1243.7
West Germany	124.5
United States	119.8
France	88.3
United Kingdom	79.9
Netherlands	63.7
Italy	59.3
Belgium	58.5
Canada	44.1
Switzerland	39.4
Japan	39.2
Sweden	24.4
Saudi Arabia	23.1
Austria	18.6
Spain	16.6
Denmark	15.6

These figures are one standard measure of the overall weight of national economies in the open world market.

WORLD INDUSTRIAL LEADERS

Electrical Energy, 1978 (Billions of Kilowatt Hours)

United States	2,328,300
USSR	1,190,552
Japan	565,135
West Germany	352,100
Canada	327,080
United Kingdom	288,900
China	225,000
France	218,200
Italy	173,400
Poland	114,832

Steel Production, 1979 (Millions of Metric Tons)

USSR	164
United States	136
Japan	123
West Germany	51
China	38
Italy	27
France	26
United Kingdom	24
Poland	21
Canada	18

Coal Mining, 1979 (Millions of Metric Tons)

USSR	803
United States	781
China	700
East Germany	281
Poland	262
West Germany	247
Australia	139
Czechoslovakia	136
United Kingdom	136
India	120

Automobile Manufacturing, 1979 (Millions of Passenger Cars)

United States	8.4
Japan	6.2
West Germany	3.9
France	3.2
Italy	1.5
USSR	1.3
United Kingdom	1.1
Canada	0.99
Spain	0.97
Brazil	0.5

vately based group of business and political leaders from Europe, the United States, and Japan.

At the end of World War II, the European powers had generally recognized the independence of their former colonies and protectorates in the Middle East and Asia, but the comparable process in Africa took longer. There, most of today's states won their independence between 1960 and 1965.[1] Often that change was less abrupt than it might appear, some self-government having been followed by autonomy within the British Commonwealth or the French Community before actual independence. The long African struggle and the European resistance to it left much bitterness and suspicion, but not all ties were broken. Bureaucracies, courts, churches, and educational

---

[1] Morocco and Togo gained independence from France in 1956; Tunisia in 1957; Guinea in 1958; Cameroun, the Central African Republic, Chad, Congo, Dahomey, Gabon, the Ivory Coast, Malagasy, Mali, Mauritania, Niger, Senegal, and Upper Volta in 1960. Zaire gained independence from Belgium in 1960. Ghana, Nigeria, and Somalia gained independence from Great Britain in 1960; Sierra Leone, South Africa, and Tanzania in 1961; Uganda in 1962; Kenya in 1963; Malawi, Rhodesia, and Zambia in 1964; and Gambia in 1965.

WORLD POPULATION, 1982, ESTIMATED

		Annual Growth Rate in Percent
World	4,596,000,000	1.88
Asia	2,674,000,000	2.10
Europe	491,000,000	0.59
USSR	272,000,000	0.96
Africa	442,000,000	2.75
Latin America	388,000,000	2.69
North America	254,000,000	0.95
Oceania	24,000,000	1.82

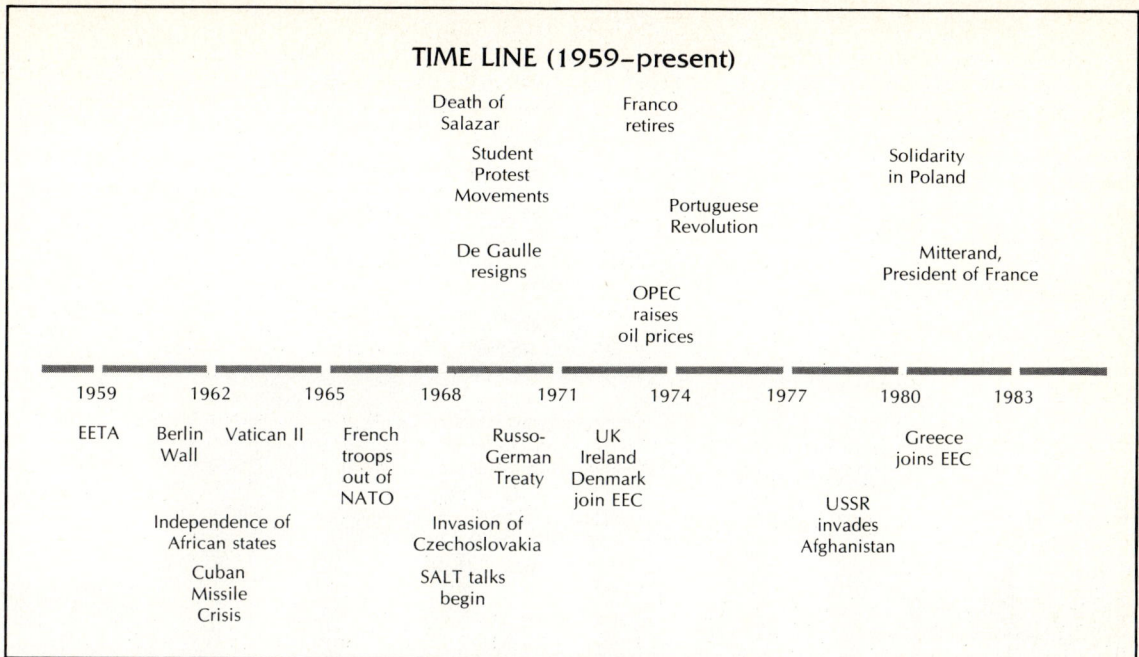

systems; patterns of trade and investment; and political interests and sentiment all guaranteed continuing connections. Britain played a major role in the transformation of white-ruled Rhodesia into black-ruled Zimbabwe, in 1979; and France intervened during civil strife in Chad and the Central African Republic. But colonial issues are no longer the major preoccupation of European foreign ministers.

European Foreign Policies

The foreign policies of European nations exist within a framework largely set by the superpowers. That is, the Communist governments of Eastern Europe depend upon the Soviet Union for economic assistance and, perhaps, for their stability; most Western European governments recognize the power of the United States as the primary deterrent to possible Soviet aggression in Europe. The Warsaw Pact and the NATO alliance have continued to be important, but within that framework there has been room for some independence and even disagreement. In 1961 the Cold War seemed a permanent fact of life as the government of East Germany closed the border between East and West Berlin, building a wall across the center of the city to keep its citizens from leaving for the West—the culmination of a long crisis over division of Germany and the terms of a formal peace treaty. Another crisis arose over Cuba; in 1961 the United States had sponsored an invasion aimed at the overthrow of Fidel Castro, who allied himself more and more closely with the Soviets; in the following year the Russians began to base some missiles on Cuba. They were soon withdrawn under severe pressure from the United States, but for a moment war had seemed quite possible. Both crises, however, underscored the mutual interest in not disturbing the balance of power.

The sharp rift between the Soviet Union and China (supported only by Albania among European Communist governments) also became more public and threatening after 1960,

The Brandenburg gate in Berlin had been erected as a monument to Prussia's past military achievements. Blocked by barbed wire in 1961, it is the dividing line between East and West.
(Photo: Wide World Photos)

and encouraged the view that much could be gained by diplomatic talks. Since then, European governments have favored East-West negotiations at summit conferences or on specific matters and have promoted agreements on space exploration in 1967, the beginning of the Strategic Arms Limitation Talks in 1969, and their extension to human rights issues at the Helsinki Conference in 1975. Through trade, loans, and technical agreements, the governments of Western Europe have encouraged those of Eastern Europe toward whatever autonomy they were willing to attempt. Each of the Western nations has also tended to emphasize its own traditional policies and interests. Great Britain has generally been most supportive of United States policy (and been most favorably treated by it); France has stressed her ties to Eastern Europe and the Third World; more recently, Germany has asserted a more independent policy toward the East, and the

Scandinavian countries have been especially active in the United Nations.

The most flamboyant search for an independent policy was de Gaulle's. Resentful of American policy toward France and determined that the loss of empire need not result in loss of influence, he set upon an independent course that by 1966 led to the withdrawal of French forces from NATO command (and of NATO forces from French soil) although France remained a member of the alliance. He persisted in building from scratch a French nuclear force, and began an exchange of visits with Eastern European leaders that contributed to increasing cultural and economic ties between the two parts of Europe. De Gaulle also emphasized the importance of aid to developing nations, making France second only to the United States as a grantor of foreign aid and bringing Europe into the worldwide competition for the sale of arms to less industrial nations. Although much of the rhetoric that accompanied these policies soon seemed dated, the policies themselves continue as an important part of the French and European diplomatic arsenal.

Germany, too, gradually came to assert some of the political weight her wealth implied. Through his close allegiance to the United States and then his close cooperation and friendship with de Gaulle, Adenauer had made his pariah nation respectable and even trusted. Thus, when the Social Democrats came to power, Willy Brandt, who was more willing in principle to deal with Communist nations, was able to use his negotiating skill in a new opening to the East. By then East Berlin had been absorbed into an East German state that had established itself as a loyal and relatively prosperous member of the Soviet bloc. The resulting treaty between West Germany and the Soviet Union, signed in 1970, was a milestone, for which Brandt was awarded the Nobel peace prize. While leaving open the possibility of a peaceful reunification of Germany, the treaty ratified the Oder-Neisse Line as Germany's eastern boundary, pointed to a normalization of Berlin's status, and paved the way for extensive relations between the governments of Eastern Europe and the Continent's second most powerful nation, after the Soviet Union. Germany's *Ostpolitik* not only stimulated trade (culminating in the 1981–1982 agreements for a natural gas pipeline from Russia to Germany, Italy, and France) and strengthened permissible diversity among Eastern European governments but encouraged some of the European left, especially in the Low Countries and Germany, in their call to have Europe declared a nuclear-free zone—that is, exempt from the nuclear weapons of either side.

The European Community

But it is among themselves that the Western European nations[2] have achieved the most, beginning with the founding of the Council of Europe in 1949. Its Ministerial Committee and Assembly can pass no binding legislation, but they can provide important forums. The Council's statutes require its members to uphold individual and political freedom and the rule of law—provisions that have effectively excluded the Eastern European states as well as Spain, Portugal, and Greece when ruled by dictators; and its Human Rights Commission hears petitions from individuals as well as nations. When in 1977 the attorney general of Great Britain admitted Irish charges that torture had been used against members of the Irish Repub-

---

[2] Geographers list eighteen nations as belonging to Western Europe: Austria, Belgium, Denmark, Finland, France, Greece, Iceland, Ireland, Italy, Luxembourg, Netherlands, Norway, Portugal, Spain, Sweden, Switzerland, the United Kingdom, and West Germany. All of these save Portugal, Spain (which can expect to be admitted soon), and Finland belong to the Council of Europe, which also includes Cyprus, Malta, and Turkey.

Belgium, Denmark, Iceland, West Germany, Italy, Luxembourg, Netherlands, Norway, Portugal, Turkey, the United Kingdom, Canada, and the United States belong to NATO, as do France and Greece, although their armed forces no longer are under NATO command.

lican Army and promised to punish the guilty, it seemed as if some of the bright dreams symbolized by the Council's adoption of the "Ode to Joy" from Beethoven's Ninth Symphony as its anthem might someday be realized.

By far the most important development in Europe's international and economic affairs has been the success of the Common Market. The product of painfully negotiated compromises at every stage, its accomplishments have come so slowly that they can easily be underestimated. When the Common Market was first established, Great Britain refused to join. Reluctant to accept permanent involvement in the political affairs of the Continent or to loosen her Commonwealth ties, she led in the creation of a counterpoise to the European Economic Community (EEC), joining with Sweden, Norway, Denmark, Austria, Switzerland, and Portugal in the European Free Trade Association (EFTA), which had more limited goals (free trade but not a common tariff among its members), a looser structure, and less success than the EEC. In the decade of the 1960s, the "inner six" enjoyed nearly unprecedented growth and prosperity, while the United Kingdom remained at the bottom of the list of major European countries in the rate of economic expansion. In 1961–1963, 1967, and 1971 successive British governments sought to join the EEC, but the first two times Britain's desire for special terms with regard to the Commonwealth nations, differences over agricultural policies, and De Gaulle's opposition prevented agreement. Following the French president's resignation and concessions from both parties, Great Britain, accompanied by Ireland and Denmark, formally joined in 1972. In a surprising referendum Norwegians voted not to follow suit, but in a referendum held in 1975 to quiet opposition within Great Britain two-thirds of the voters supported the decision to enter the Common Market. The Communist nations of Eastern Europe countered with their own agency for economic coordination, Comecon, but by the 1970s they were vying with

GROWTH RATES—in Annual Percentage, 1960—1970, in Western Europe

GDP Per Capita		Productivity/ Man/Hour	
6.9	Greece	Spain	8.6
6.3	Spain	Sweden	7.4
5.2	Portugal	Netherlands	7.2
4.8	Italy	Greece	6.9
4.8	Finland	Portugal	6.8
4.6	France	West Germany	6.5
4.3	Belgium	France	6.2
4.2	Austria	Italy	6.0
4.1	Norway	Austria	5.9
4.0	Denmark	Belgium	5.5
4.0	Netherlands	Norway	5.3
3.6	West Germany	Finland	4.9
3.5	Sweden	Switzerland	4.9
3.4	Ireland	Denmark	4.8
2.3	Switzerland	Ireland	4.0
2.1	United Kingdom	United Kingdom	3.1

each other for increased trade and loans from the EEC. (See Map 30.1.)

The Community's progress has often been slow and disappointing. Although the elimination of trade barriers evolved more rapidly than planned, the goals of further integration were not met on schedule. Agricultural prices and subsidies have been the greatest difficulty, resulting in huge and costly stockpiles of produce as each nation presses for the protection of its own farmers. For Britain, which imports most of her food from outside the EEC and has fewer farmers at home to protect, the Community's agricultural policies were costly. Britain's share of EEC farm subsidies was far greater than EEC expenditures in Britain until 1981 when the vigorous protests of the British government forced adjustments that may actually lead to reform of the Community's entire agricultural program, destined to experience further strain as additional nations join the EEC. Expansion to nine members made agreement more difficult to obtain, as did the addition of Greece in January 1981, for unanimity is required on new issues despite the consider-

MAP 30.1: EUROPE SINCE WORLD WAR II

able autonomy granted the EEC's executive to carry out policies previously agreed to.

The process of integration continues nevertheless. At the suggestion of the French president, in 1972 the heads of government of the EEC countries began the practice of meeting four times a year. Increasingly, EEC officials have acted as an executive independent of single nations, and in 1979 for the first time citizens of the member nations voted directly for delegates to the Community's parliament, where the representatives sit according to party rather than nationality.[3] That step, one of its negotiators declared, "marks the birth of the European citizen." Decisions of the Community's Court of Justice lead toward regulations and legal protections that are increasingly uniform as do provisions covering the rights of migrant workers. And special programs, including significant expenditures intended to bring poorer regions, such as the northwestern part of the British Isles and southern Italy, closer to the Community's general level of prosperity, are giving it a voice in matters long considered the exclusive concern of national governments.

By far the world's greatest trader, the European Economic Community is an important element in world affairs and one that exercised considerable influence on the democratization of Greece, Portugal, and Spain, especially as they looked forward to joining the EEC. In fact, most trade barriers between the Community and other Western European nations have been eliminated, and formal ties to individual Eastern European states, beginning with Yugoslavia, have grown each year. From the first, members of the Community recognized both a desire and an obligation to sustain something of the older trade patterns with their former colonies, and this led to preferential trade agreements and the creation of associate status for such countries, arrangements subsequently extended under various terms to more than fifty states. When in 1972 the EEC offered preferential tariffs to all Mediterranean nations, every country but Libya responded favorably. Agreements with most of the nations of sub-Sahara Africa and with present and former colonies in the Caribbean and Pacific grant them access to the markets of the Community, often with guarantees to stabilize their export income while protecting their domestic industries. In addition, the Community provides sizable aid to developing countries. Thus in relations between North and South—that is, between developed and developing nations—as well as between East and West, the European Economic Community is likely to play a major role in the future.

III. THE POLITICS OF PROSPERITY

Representative Democracy

The kind of political system advocated by liberal democrats in the nineteenth century and all but imposed at the Versailles Peace Conference has become universal in Western Europe. Since World War II parliamentary government, multiple parties, and universal suffrage have lasted in countries like Germany and Italy that loudly eschewed them earlier in the century and have been more recently adopted in every nation that could exercise the choice. In the 1960s, most governments lowered the voting age to 18 and in other ways encouraged increased political participation.

Alternating Parties: Great Britain and Germany

Formally, at least, the British and West German political systems have been models of stability,

---

[3] France, Great Britain, Italy, and West Germany each has eighty-one representatives (the large number being necessary to assure Scotland and Wales more representatives than Denmark or Ireland); the Netherlands has twenty-five but Belgium twenty-four (having surrendered one so that the Flemings and Walloons would have equal representation); Denmark has sixteen (after the gift of a representative from Belgium), Ireland fifteen, and Luxembourg six.

in which two dominant parties have smoothly alternated in power and pursued policies of an underlying continuity. In Britain the Conservatives (in office from 1951 to 1964, 1970 to 1974, and since 1979) placed greater emphasis on the role of the private sector in economic matters—they returned iron and steel to private hands and stopped further nationalization—but largely accepted the extensive welfare programs and mixed economy they inherited. Conversely, the Labour governments (in office from 1964 to 1970 and, by a thin majority, 1974 to 1979) were severely constrained by the plight of the British economy, pressuring their trade-union constituents to accept wage limits and cutting public expenditures in an effort to balance the budget sufficiently to halt the fall of the value of the pound and to reassure such creditors as the International Monetary Fund whose loans have become essential to prevent collapse.

All these governments shared in the efforts to improve public services, especially transportation, and to make education more democratic by encouraging comprehensive high schools and an impressive expansion of higher education. Each party, however, divided internally on the newer issues of joining the Common Market, protecting black immigrants from discrimination, and allowing Scotland and Wales to have local representative assemblies. Britain's overwhelming problem, however, remained economic. Plants were not modernized nor productivity improved at the pace required to compete with the leading industrial nations, while inflation threatened to reduce further the rate of investment. Analysts have found it easier to lay the blame—on the enormous cost to Britain of World War II, unimaginative and weak managers, an inadequate educational system, the selfish conservatism of labor unions, the high costs of welfare and defense—than prescribe the solution. Even membership in the European Economic Community and the development of the rich oilfields of the North Sea provided no automatic solution.

In economic terms the contrast with West Germany could hardly have been greater, and within the Federal Republic (which recently surpassed even the United States in world trade) political issues tended to be overshadowed by the satisfying fact of prosperity. Even the significant change in government from the Christian Democrats to the Social Democrats did not lessen the commitment to encouraging investment, expanding trade, and preventing inflation. Often surprisingly conservative in their economic policies, the Social Democrats nevertheless pursued democratization in other ways, carrying through educational reforms and expanding social services (steps that have incidentally brought greater centralization and given the bureaucracy more power). Their most venturesome measure required all firms with more than 2,000 employees to have a central board of directors half of whose members are elected representatives of labor. Yet even as Germany won a more central place in European affairs, dissension was growing within both major parties; and the discovery that one of Willy Brandt's aides was a Soviet spy forced Brandt's resignation in 1974 in favor of the firmly centrist Social Democrat, Helmut Schmidt.

Including the Opposition: Italy and France

The Italian Republic, whose economic miracle was perhaps even more remarkable than Germany's, has always had a national government dominated by the Christian Democrats, a party far more heterogeneous than its German counterpart. In fact, elements of Italy's Christian Democratic party were closely tied to most of the nation's other major political currents, so that the process of coalition building always began within the semisecret confusion of the dominant party. While the Christian Democrats sought allies from among smaller parties in the center, the Communists—Italy's second

An expanding market for consumer products was an important part of the economic boom in Europe in the '60s and early '70s. These washing machines are being tested at a factory in Italy, one of the world's largest exporters of home appliances.
(Photo: Tony Howarth/Woodfin Camp and Associates)

largest party—and a smaller group of monarchists and neo-Fascists on the right maintained loud and often effective opposition.

Room for maneuver was thus limited, and until 1958 the center coalitions supported governments that postponed most major reforms and left the most important economic initiatives to the state-owned holding companies. While the economy boomed, politics often sank into immobility beneath labyrinthine deals.

From 1958 on, however, there was growing talk of an "opening to the left," an understanding that would woo Socialists from their Communist allies and permit a left-center coalition. Italy's rapid modernization, the need for administrative reform, and the change in Catholic attitudes associated with Pope John XXIII, all pointed to this course.

Finally achieved in 1963, the new coalition lasted until 1972, and it accomplished some of the promised changes. But the Socialists were more divided than ever, and the Christian Democratic factions lost none of their autonomy; the process of compromise remained infinitely complex; and few ministries survived a whole year. Unprestigious governments and a sprawling, inefficient bureaucracy nevertheless maintained a tension-filled nation in reasonable peace and freedom during a period of rapid social transformation.

The growing influence of the left in France was a somewhat more surprising outcome of the years of Gaullist supremacy, for by 1962, when his followers won a firm majority in the Chamber of Deputies, Charles de Gaulle seemed to have established the stability and even the popularity of the Fifth Republic. France had become the fourth nation in the world to have nuclear weapons and exercised an independent position in world affairs. At home too the regime had a style all its own centered in the powerful personality of de Gaulle. Economic and social policy was firmly in the hands of able, even brilliant, technocrats; not only was parliament docile but the bickering and factionalism of traditional political life seemed dead as de Gaulle relied instead on plebiscites and public relations to maintain presidential government's tie to public opinion. That France prospered in such stability was tangibly apparent on every side. Nevertheless, the presidential election of 1965 (the first since 1848 conducted by direct universal suffrage) required

A French missile-firing nuclear submarine is launched at Cherbourg. More than other European nations, France sought to maintain an independent, technologically advanced military force. (Photo: Wide World Photos)

a run-off ballot between François Mitterand, the rising leader of the left, and de Gaulle before the general could win a majority. The opposition was strengthened by discontent among workers convinced they were not receiving their share of France's prosperity, by a broader dissatisfaction with many of the effects of rapid economic growth, including urban problems, inadequate housing, and the neglect of underdeveloped regions, and by criticisms especially from intellectuals of an often arbitrary bureaucracy and of de Gaulle's sometimes pompous paternalism.

In May 1968 the regime was nearly toppled by the surprisingly effective revolt of students in the Parisian universities, a revolt that began with specific objections to an overcrowded, excessively centralized, and outmoded educational system but quickly became a broader attack on the society of consumption and the technocratic policies Gaullists represented. As the students occupied buildings and battled with police, millions of workers went on strike. With firmness and skill, the storm was weathered; most workers, ambivalent at best toward the students, who appeared rich and privileged to them, were interested rather in higher wages. And the Communists somewhat uncomfortably kept their distance from the student radicals, whose rising so frightened much of French society that Gaullists were able to gain impressively in the elections held that June. But the Fifth Republic was never the same. The government promised and carried out extensive reforms of education, increasing options and access and giving students and parents a larger voice at every level; it reformed much in its own administration, and turned to broader programs of welfare and social improvement, including somewhat vague plans to give workers a role in factory management. A few months later, de Gaulle put forth a complex set of proposals for administrative reforms leading to some regional decentralization. Characteristically, the proposals were both vague and far-reaching, and the electorate was asked to approve them in a referendum, while leaving all the details to the president. This time the voters refused, and in April 1969 de Gaulle resigned.

His successor, Georges Pompidou, was a firm Gaullist whose new government was both more open and more willing to reconsider established policies. The election of Valéry Giscard d'Estaing as president in 1974 marked a further evolution. A member of the government's majority but not of the Gaullist party, he had campaigned with a direct informality that seemed to promise a more accessible, democratic, and relaxed administration, one that might even lead to a new coalition of the center reaching from reform-minded Gaullists to the Socialists. Instead, the Socialists stayed closer to the Communists with whom they had contracted a common electoral program in 1972 that included nationalization of many industries, more even distribution of income, and better housing. Significantly, in addition to these more common Marxist goals, it also called for more decentralized political authority and steps to assure greater opportunities for leisure, a more vigorous cultural life, and pleasanter cities. French political life, despite the fact that most voters appear closest to the center, remained organized in terms of a Marxist left and a technocratic right of about equal strength.

The Chances of Revolution

For a few weeks in May 1968 it had seemed as if the students of Paris might recapture the revolutionary spirit of 1848, as their barricades of paving stones and trees, their imaginative posters and endless slogans paid homage to a revolutionary tradition. In France, Germany, Italy, Great Britain, and the United States students in 1968–1969 behaved as an independent political force, mounting attacks on university regulations that became denunciations of a middle-class and capitalist society, which they portrayed as hypocritical and repressive. Inspired by the values and successes of national liberation movements in the Third World and appalled by the war in Vietnam, the students voiced criticisms of national foreign policy and of the military that became an indictment of continuing imperialism. They proclaimed that history was at a turning point, but once again history failed to turn. In general these protests led to reforms of education and amended government policies in other spheres, but in the short term at least they strengthened the old order. Labor unions and parties of the left were suspicious of youthful anarchy while reformers and liberals were as offended as conservatives by the violence and indifference to legal procedure. As revolutions, these movements thus failed in a cloud of angry rhetoric disproportionate to their strength, but in the long term they influenced a style of protest that others would take up and publicized criticisms that remain in the modern consciousness about the society of consumption, the value of work and competition, the trustworthiness of elites, and the injustices of hierarchy. These concerns are now at least acknowledged in the programs of the left in nearly every Western country, while fear of disorder and of a declining belief in traditional values has increased among conservatives.

Students were active as well in the movement that briefly transformed Czechoslovakia in 1968, where Alexander Dubček, as first secretary of the Communist party, led the adoption of a program calling for freedom of speech, assembly, and religion and the granting of greater autonomy to Slovakia. These liberal and nationalist goals, very much like those expounded in the revolutions of 1848 but now called "communism with a human face," were seen in Moscow as an intolerable danger, and Czech resistance to Soviet pressure was overcome in August by the armed invasion of troops from the Soviet Union, East Germany, Hungary, and Poland. It was the largest military operation in Europe since World War II; and within a few months all the liberal reforms save a grant of Slovakian autonomy had been reversed, the Soviet troops invited to remain, and Dubček ousted from office.

Greece, Portugal, and Spain

Despite the enormous concentration of power in the hands of the modern state, revolutions nevertheless remain a possibility. In Greece they have come primarily as military coups, first in 1967, when a group of army officers overthrew the unstable parliamentary system and eventually the monarchy itself and then in 1973 when the military in turn gave way to civilian leaders who arrested the officers and restored democracy. Despite harsh, even brutal, repression, Greece's military rulers had found it necessary gradually to restore freedoms that further exposed their unpopularity. Having to strengthen a fragile but modernizing economy, weakened by conflict with Turkey over control of Cyprus, they had to draw closer to Western Europe where there was little disposition to treat with Greek dictators.

The restoration of political freedom in Portugal and Spain was even more remarkable. Less dictatorial than the Salazar regime which it succeeded on his death in 1968, the government of Marcello Caetano continued along essentially the same lines. But although opposition at home was effectively stymied, that proved impossible in Portugal's African colonies. The last of Europe's colonial powers to hang on to its empire, Portugal used force and cruel repression in Portuguese Guinea, Angola, and Mozambique only to see liberation movements there grow stronger. Portugal was subject to increasing condemnation in the United Nations, among African states and other European nations while the government's political and economic strength at home was sapped despite censorship and further restrictions on the right of assembly. Suddenly in April 1974 a group of Portuguese army officers seized control, ousting the old regime, promising full freedom and civil rights at home and self-determination for the colonies. Crowds filled the streets to dance and cheer before smiling soldiers whose rifles were decorated with flowers.

The euphoria could not last as Portugal came to grips with a series of staggering problems. A poor and backward country hoping to modernize, Portugal faced raging inflation and declining production with its agriculture in disarray as peasants claimed the land they had long coveted, socialist and communist unions competed to capture a following in critical industries, many of the nation's skilled managers sought employment in Switzerland and Brazil, and rural and business groups battled to make their interests heard. The army leaders themselves were divided ideologically (among Communists, socialists, Christians, and conservatives) and over policy, both domestic and colonial. Seven governments in little over two years tried to cope with these problems. Extensive nationalizations of banks and industry were followed by free elections in 1975 and 1976. A series of attempted revolts of the left and the right, usually led by military factions, have all been defeated; and since 1976 with the election of the moderate General António Ramalho Eanes as president, there has been reasonable stability. The Socialists are the largest party, though not a majority, and their minority government and then more centrist coalitions have succeeded in drawing Portugal closer to the other governments of Western Europe than ever before.

The political transformation in Spain has been less dramatic, but it follows on the most rapid industrial growth in Europe. Not until the 1950s did Spanish production exceed the level of 1935, so slow was the nation's recovery from the years of civil war. By the 1960s, however, the money attracted through tourism, the encouragement of efficient large-scale agriculture at the expense of the small producer, and systematic government programs of industrialization on the familiar European model all began to have effect. The gross national product of 1960 had increased fivefold fifteen years later; and a new generation of leaders in business, the professions, and the Church kept some distance from the old pieties of the Franco regime while sporadic strikes and demonstrations (in which Basque nationalists and priests were prominent) expressed a growing discontent with the government's corruption, suppression of freedom, and social conservatism. Still the aging Franco skillfully kept his hand on power even after his retirement from the conduct of daily affairs in 1973 and the formal naming of Don Juan Carlos, the son of the Bourbon claimant to the throne, as his successor. When Franco died in 1975, the revolution many feared did not take place; and the new king proved both more flexible and adept than most anticipated. Political repression and censorship were steadily relaxed, and successive prime ministers edged toward genuinely representative government. The army remains powerful, the police highly political, and some censorship in force; but while Communists and Socialists compete for popular support, the parties of the center and the right jockey for influence, and Catalonian and Basque nationalists agitate, the Spanish nation, suddenly quite modern and more prosperous than ever before, seems nevertheless to be moving toward a democracy healthier than the one expunged forty years earlier.

The Varieties of Communism

Communism remained much the most powerful European movement that claimed to believe in revolution—highly organized in parties and trade unions in the West and in the complex organs of the state in the East. The communist movement, however, was no longer united. Its second major division (after Yugoslavia's break with the Cominform in 1948) was the antagonism between the Soviet Union and China that became public and seemingly permanent in the 1960s, to be echoed by small groups of Maoists in Western Europe who from the extreme left criticized and harried the large Communist parties in the name of the principles represented by Chairman Mao Zedong. As its fatherland, the Soviet Union remained the model and dominant force of European communism; but domestic developments within Russia and across the Continent combined with the relaxation of the Cold War to introduce considerable national variety in a movement once considered monolithic.

The Soviet Union gained immense prestige as the first nation to launch a space vehicle in 1957, initiating a peaceful, but frenzied, race for preeminence in space between the superpowers. By the '70s, however, the tone was more one of cooperation, reflected here in this exhibit held in Los Angeles in 1977.
(Photo: Wide World Photos)

The Soviet Union's most impressive achievement, one admired throughout the world, was her industrial growth. By the 1960s her economy was second in overall production and wealth only to that of the United States.

In 1961 she sent the first man into orbit around the earth; and as the world's largest producer of steel, iron, and, more recently, oil, the U.S.S.R. was apparently gaining on the West. With this basis for confidence, Khrushchev, brash and outspoken, became an international personality who did much to humanize the image of the Soviet government. His foreign policy suggested that the Soviet regime had no desire to risk its achievements and its empire in a world conflagration. At home, the very success of heavy industry led to increased demand for consumer products, higher standards of quality, and adequate housing.

These pressures, like the logic of de-Stalinization, opened the possibility of a new evolution in Soviet rule, but it was not to be. Khrushchev's plans to increase agricultural production through the application of the latest technology and by the cultivation of millions of acres of land in Asian Russia did not achieve the desired result. Soviet agriculture remained a perennial disappointment, and the question of whether to invest in consumer goods or heavy industry revived long-standing conflicts within the highest circles. Many Kremlin leaders worried, as well, about the restiveness in Eastern Europe and the growing rift with China. When, in the process of solidifying his authority, Khrushchev antagonized the military, they and his opponents in the Politburo and the Central Committee felt strong enough to speak against him. He was voted out of office in 1964 and sent into quiet retirement. The Soviet Union was developing practices that, though preserving dictatorship and a tradition of internal battles for power, permitted orderly transitions.

Khrushchev's successors were cool and tough party technicians, Aleksei Kosygin and Leonid Brezhnev. The firm grip on power, strengthened as Brezhnev emerged as the dominant figure, provided no simple resolution of the problems that had weakened Khrushchev.

The cold-blooded invasion of Czechoslovakia established the limits to freedom or autonomy to be allowed in Eastern Europe, but significantly greater diversity could not be prevented. The relatively low yield of Russian agriculture continued to produce crises in bad years and had to be met in 1972 and 1975 by huge purchases of grain from the United States (made possible by better relations with the administration of President Richard M. Nixon). The emphasis on consumer production was partially reversed as the Soviet Union turned for the latest technology to Western firms, particularly in Italy and France, to build huge new plants in Russia.

The issue of civil rights for at least some forms of dissent proved impossible to squelch either in world opinion or at home. When Boris Pasternak was awarded the Nobel prize for literature in 1958, he was forbidden permission to go to Stockholm to receive it. But his work, especially the novel *Doctor Zhivago*, had, like Khrushchev's denunciation of Stalin, done much to disseminate a view of the seamy and repressive aspects of Soviet life. The case of Alexander Solzhenitsyn caused still more international furor. His *Gulag Archipelago* was a haunting account of the terrors of the Soviet concentration camps, and he too was prevented from receiving the Nobel prize awarded him in 1970. Four years later he was arrested and then deported, to become an outspoken critic of the Soviet regime, thereby joining his voice to a score of Russian writers and scientists whose denunciations, widely published outside the U.S.S.R., came to be increasingly known in their own country. To this was added the plight of Soviet Jews, subject to discrimination and attack, then intermittently permitted to emigrate. Although international conventions (and American policy under President Jimmy Carter) underscored the demands for greater liberty, they neither shook the Soviet regime nor undermined its place in world affairs.

The Soviet Sphere

The Soviet presence remained the central fact of politics in Eastern Europe, with ties to the U.S.S.R. the keystone of each nation's foreign policy and Soviet approval the measure of domestic orthodoxy. Yet differences once submerged came to seem increasingly important, and each country enlarged its particular ties to Western Europe through cultural exchanges, communication, and trade. Bulgaria sought better relations with other Balkan States, and Rumania formed economic ties with Yugoslavia and attempted to establish herself as a nonaligned state, while East Germany, the second industrial power among communist states (the seventh in Europe and the eleventh in the world), oscillated between friendlier relations and renewed tensions with West Germany and between repression and concessions at home to meet the sort of discontent expressed in bloody riots in the early 1970s.

Although the invasion of Czechoslovakia was followed by efforts to strengthen Comecon and by the enunciation of the "Brezhnev doctrine," which declared a "threat to socialism" in one country to be a threat to all, that policy was rejected by Rumania as well as by Yugoslavia and by the Italian Communists. Not content to be a Russian granary, Rumania launched its own course of industrialization; and private ownership continued to have an important role in the economies of Poland and of Hungary, which developed one of the strongest and most consumer-oriented of the Eastern European economies. The Catholic Church, influential in Hungary, Czechoslovakia, and Poland, became especially outspoken in the latter, where opinion could be more openly expressed. Protests, demonstrations, and even riots against the police or over the price of food served as a constant reminder to the Communist leaders of Eastern Europe of the need to maintain a balance of cooperation with the Soviet Union and a firm grasp of domestic power, on the one hand, with concern for public opinion, on the other.

Each country thus cautiously evolved foreign ties and domestic policies that reflected something of her history and traditional culture. Yugoslavia, the maverick among communist states, cautiously established better relations with her more orthodox neighbors while firmly maintaining her independence. Domestically, too, she stood between East and West, combining something of a market economy and decentralized factory management (in which workers were given a large voice) with state ownership, elections allowing more than one candidate for each office within a single party, and greater freedom for dissent—despite crackdowns on figures like Milovan Djilas, a life-long Communist whose systematic and Marxian critique of Soviet society and of party officials as a new ruling class led to years of imprisonment, or like the professors associated with the theoretical journal *Praxis,* the only officially tolerated voice of criticism, who all were suspended from their positions in 1975.

Eurocommunism

Europe as a whole thus offers an extraordinary variety of experiments in social systems ranging from the capitalism of Switzerland and West Germany to the mixed economies of Western Europe, the market Communism of Yugoslavia, and the other varieties of Communism in Eastern Europe and the Soviet Union, with Europe's least developed nation, Communist Albania, completing the spectrum as China's best ally outside Asia. This variety of experiments aimed at combining a directed economy with social justice and political freedom stimulated the development within Western European Communist parties known as Eurocommunism, with Italy's Communist party, the largest in the world in a non-Communist country, its model and major proponent. In Antonio Gramsci, who died in a Fascist prison, the party had one of the ablest of modern Marxist theoreticians; his emphasis on the importance of local history and culture in determining the path to Communism gave the party's flexibility a justification beyond mere tactical pragmatism. And through the years of opposition and close ties to the Italian Socialist party, the Communists developed, under the leadership of Enrico Berlinguer, a suave and attractive politician, a detailed program for the reform of Italian society, which accepts the principles of formal democracy—including civil rights, multiple parties, and free elections.

The successes of the Italian party increased its influence at home and abroad and led the French Communist party, once among Europe's most Stalinist, toward a similar stance. Both parties denounced the invasion of Czechoslovakia in 1968. The Italian party even accepted NATO, and the French one not only ceased to oppose France's nuclear weapons but, determined to prove its respect for free elections, in 1976 officially rejected the dictatorship of the proletariat as an item of party dogma. With the liberalization in Spain after the death of Franco, the Spanish Communist party, under Santiago Carrillo (whose years of exile were spent in the United States rather than the Soviet Union), adopted similar views and moved even closer toward democratic socialism.

This form of communism, ready to cooperate with other parties on single points and insistent on its own democratic convictions, appeared to have been accepted by most Western European Communist parties (with the notable exceptions of Portugal's and Finland's).[4] Despite heavy Soviet pressure and public denunciations of these Western Communists as "bourgeois ideologists," the Russians have been unable to restore the unity of European Communism. On the sixtieth anniversary of the Russian Revolution in 1977, Eurocommunism thus marked a third schism in the communist ranks; and part of its Western appeal was its claim to seek Europe's independence from both Soviet and American influence. Many voters even on the left remained skeptical, of course, of the Communists' dedication to liberal freedoms, noting that the parties themselves remain highly centralized, intolerant, suspicious of the Common Market, and in foreign affairs closely tied to Soviet and anti-American positions. But Eurocommunism opened the possibility that Communists might again share power in Italy and France for the first time since 1947 and that this Western form of communism might begin to exert a significant attraction in Eastern Europe (Dubček, ostracized in his own country, has published his critiques of the Czechoslovakian regime in Italian Communist journals). The sharp distinctions between Communists and non-Communists, and between Eastern and Western Europe, were coming to seem less fundamental.

The Shadow of Recession

Predictions of the future, however, tended to be more confident early in the 1970s than in the 1980s. To be sure, reforms continued to be made, particularly in education as the French university system was decentralized and German students were given an official voice in university affairs. Catalans seemed pleased with the increased autonomy granted them in 1977, and agitation in the Basque provinces declined after the concessions granted there two years later. Ecological movements occasionally had some effect at the polls, and there was even an echo of the 1960s in the demonstrations against placing nuclear warheads in Western Europe that in 1981 saw nearly half a million young

---

[4] Communist parties traditionally attract nearly a third of the electorate in Italy, one-fifth in France and Finland, one-eighth in Spain, and much less elsewhere: about 5 percent in Sweden, 4 percent in Denmark, 3 percent in Belgium, 2 percent in Greece and the Netherlands, and less than 1 percent in West Germany and Great Britain.

people marching in Bonn and perhaps another million in other capitals. Except for a rising regionalism, however, public life was largely dominated by more conventional concerns and duller issues. Although often willing to admit that the traditional programs of left and right were losing relevance, established parties remained uncomfortable with these new issues. Instead, governments were forced to grapple with problems that appeared to be deeply rooted in their social and economic systems and complicated by broad international connections. And they had to do so without dramatic solutions or impressive successes.

Energy and Inflation

The clearest challenge came in October 1973, when the oil-exporting nations (mainly in the Middle East) first banded together to raise international prices, for Europe imported nearly two-thirds of its energy in the form of petroleum. Only the Soviet Union could meet its own energy needs through domestic production. Subsequent development of North Sea oilfields has made Norway self-sufficient and Britain nearly so, but the talk in other European countries of achieving independence of foreign oil by 1985 has proved illusory. Self-sufficiency depended heavily on nuclear power (in 1976 over half of the world's nuclear power plants in operation and of those under construction were in Europe), which has proved more costly than anticipated and raised questions of pollution and safety that have challenged its practicality. Continued prosperity in the advanced industrial nations will require answers not yet clear to the rapacious demand for energy.

A second and more complicated but related problem has been inflation, rising to an annual rate of increase in 1975–1976 (more than 20 percent in Britain and Italy, 30 percent in Portugal) that undermined planning, savings, and trade while squeezing salaried employees and many workers between rising costs and lagging incomes, thus increasing agitation and discontent. Only West Germany among major capitalist nations has consistently managed to hold the rate of inflation below 5 percent. The general causes of the inflation are well known—governments spending more than their income, more money in circulation, the higher prices of imports, the tendency of businesses to maintain or increase profits by raising prices rather than increasing efficiency, the assumption on all sides that prices are bound to go up—but the solution is difficult. Government expenditures reflect social policies and political pressures not easily reversed, and organized workers are not inclined to absorb the losses that would follow from not seeking higher wages. In fact the debate as to what interests should be sacrificed can easily become an exercise in social conflict, as it has tended to do in Britain and Italy.

By the 1980s the advanced economies of Western Europe were facing other difficulties, too. Increased competition from the Japanese and from new plants in other parts of the world (often ones built with European capital) gave dangerous competition to the now-aging industries of Europe. From Denmark to California, tax revolts threatened many long-established governmental programs, while a significant proportion of the work force (its size could only be guessed) worked for barter or for cash that went unreported, to avoid both taxes and regulations intended to improve the standard of living. Only in Italy was the proportion of this "underground economy" thought to approach the size it reached in the United States (where estimates of its value ranged from 7 to 25 percent of GNP), but the underground economy was believed to account for nearly 10 percent of GNP in a number of European countries. Above all, it was clear that, like the threat of new competition, the problems of energy, inflation, and monetary policy were international in scope.

Then a new word, stagflation—the paradoxical combination of economic stagnation

and rising prices—gave way in economic discussions to an ominous older one, recession. Everywhere unemployment was rising. The classic tight-money policies insisted upon by Britain's Prime Minister Margaret Thatcher had slowed inflation—although it remained high—but at the price by 1982 of having 12 percent of the work force without jobs. In France and Italy, too, unemployment rose to about 8 percent, levels not experienced since World War II; even in Germany, the rate climbed to 6 percent. Foreign workers were hardest hit, which meant that the recession rapidly extended to poorer countries. And within Europe unemployment was second highest among the young, a fact of frightening political and social implications.

Terrorism

Some small, radical groups, rather than abandon the fading hope for revolution, had turned to terrorism. Modern society in its very complexity and urban anonymity seemed especially vulnerable to such tactics. In the demimonde of international crime and espionage, the necessary skills and equipment were not hard to come by; and if governments could be provoked into repressive responses, they might alienate their own citizens. Until they were largely defeated by the severe but efficient measures of police and government, German terrorists made business leaders as well as politicians their targets. The more extensive activities of Basque terrorists, which brought death to numbers of officials and lesser-known victims, shook several Spanish governments and led many, especially in the military, to decry the weakness of a democratic state. In Italy Marxist and neo-Fascist underground bands accompanied shooting, kidnapping, and bombings with proclamations of revolutionary rhetoric. Groups such as the Red Brigades heightened tension and insecurity; and when in 1978 they followed a series of dramatic actions by the kidnapping of Aldo Moro, the whole nation held its breath. The police were unable to locate Moro, one of the most respected Christian Democratic politicians (he had been prime minister five times); finally, his bullet-ridden body was left in a car in central Rome. Yet the public responded with remarkable firmness and unanimity, and the state neither turned to repression nor collapsed. Thus terrorism was on the wane when the Red Brigades captured an American NATO commander in 1982. This time the police, armed with information garnered from years of trials and investigations, were able to free the American and to capture a sufficient number of terrorists to deal a serious blow to their movement. Such incidents, like the shooting of Pope John Paul II by a Turkish terrorist in 1981, provoked outcries about modern society—for the alienation that produces terrorists, the values that condone violence, and the technology that makes such acts easy—but changed society very little.

Terrorism was most effective when it fed regional or religious animosities, as when supporters of the Palestine Liberation Organization killed Israeli athletes at the Munich Olympic Games in 1972, or in Northern Ireland, where terrorism rose to the level of a continuous war. There the Irish Republican Army, an underground organization repudiated by the Irish Republic, and extremist Protestant groups have killed hundreds of innocent people and pushed the British government to abandon its program for local rule by both Protestants and Catholics. Centuries of religious and national conflict, dis-

Traffic jams have become an almost universal symptom of prosperity. This one shows vacationers returning to Rome from the resorts and beaches to the south of the city.
(Photo: Wide World Photos)

A crowd gathers at the spot in Rome where the body of Aldo Moro was found, and two women in an ancient gesture reach out to touch the picture of Moro on posters put up by the Christian Democratic party, declaring "his faith in liberty lives in our hearts."
(Photo: Wide World Photos)

crimination, and repression have enabled the most fanatic on both sides to win support against the political policies and military efforts of the British government as the number of martyrs mounts.

The Stability of Frustration

The political stability of Europe was no less significant for being precarious, yet no party's solutions worked well enough to win it a very solid position. In Spain and Portugal moderate groups held a thin majority, but it took decisive action by King Juan Carlos to foil an attempted coup d'état by right-wing officers of the Spanish army in 1981. In Scandinavia socialist parties lost their dominance (losing office in Sweden in 1976 for the first time since 1932), then showed signs of a modest comeback. And the cautious international and domestic policies of Germany's Social Democratic government led to increasing criticism from within its own ranks. Nor did Italy's Communist party achieve the "historic compromise" that would have given it a share in power. In coalition with the Socialists, the Communists had gained control of most of Italy's major cities and, after regional governments were finally established

Children taunt ill-at-ease British soldiers in Belfast; hatreds centuries old have been passed on to the new generation.
(Photo: Jim Anderson/Woodfin Camp and Associates)

in the 1970s, of the regions. Their reputation for probity, organizational efficiency, and moderate policies led to steady gains; but they lost ground in the elections of 1979, and the Christian Democrats remained the party of government even though the prime minister chosen in 1981 was the first from outside their party in the history of the Republic.

In Britain, where there were serious urban riots in the summer of 1981, the deflationary policies of the Conservatives became increasingly unpopular while internal divisions weakened the Labour party and made its left-wing dominant over the moderates, many of whom bolted from the party in 1981 to form a new Social Democratic party that in coalition with the Liberals showed signs of equaling the two major parties in strength—a remarkable transformation in British politics. Giscard d'Estaing's government in France had also followed an orthodox policy of deflation and austerity that fell especially heavily on the workers, and that contributed to the victory of Mitterand in the presidential elections of 1981 and the even more stunning victory of the Socialists in subsequent parliamentary elections (elections in which their Communist allies, who had returned to a more pro-Soviet program, lost nearly half their normal support). Pledged to extensive nationalization of French industry and heavy government expenditure for social programs, the new government (which gave some minor posts to the Communists) broke from the common approach to the economic crisis and added new strains within the European Community. It was challenged, too, by its newest member; for socialists won power in Greece in 1981 with talk of leaving NATO and maybe even the Common Market. Yet from the first, all such new directions faced severe economic and international constraints.

Even in Eastern Europe a kind of stability triumphed. The death of Marshall Tito in 1980 did not lead to the chaos in Yugoslavia many had predicted, and in Poland the military squashed the changes many had hoped for. There, protests over the scarcities and high prices that had followed an inept program of rapid industrialization based on borrowing from the West produced an unprecedented popular movement. Led by a rising workers' organization, Solidarity, the movement in 1980–1981 won an exciting array of concessions from a shaky government, including freedom of assembly and the right to strike. Lech Walesa, the leader of Solidarity, became a national and then an international hero; and the movement, increasingly supported by the Church, grew steadily stronger, criticizing the government and the Communist party and eventually demanding free elections. But rumblings from

In a scene that, except for the television camera, is reminiscent of the long history of industrial labor movements, Lech Walesa addresses Polish workers outside a factory in Zyrardow, not far from Warsaw, in October 1981.
(Photo: Giansanti/Sygma)

Moscow were a warning of things to come, and in December 1981 General Wojciech Jaruzelski took charge, with Russia's strong support. Under martial law, with thousands arrested and troops in the streets, Poland at least for the moment again grew silent, its economy in shambles. There was a hardening within the Soviet Union also; for the government that could boast full employment—in contrast to the West—continued to suffer low productivity for an industrial nation, marked by stifling inefficiencies, absenteeism, and alcoholism. An aging leadership, determined to maintain heavy military expenditures, was turning away from the cultural and economic ties to the West that had proved stimulating to other Eastern European nations—a tendency expressed with surprising stridency in the Kremlin's attacks on the Italian Communists in 1982.

In international affairs, too, Europe slipped back to familiar uncertainties. The steady growth of Soviet military power, Russia's invasion of Afghanistan in 1979 (because the pro-Soviet regime there had become too unreliable), and the crackdown on dissidents at home and the chill in relations with the United States which increased with the election of President Reagan, raised memories of the Cold War. Not only were the superpowers engaged in an arms race, but European nations competed around the world for the sale of arms. Strains in the NATO alliance surfaced again, and recession brought pressure in each Western nation for independent economic policies and—to internationalists—raised the specter of a new round of protectionism. The drive for European unity clearly slowed, and negotiations stalled for the entry of Spain and Portugal into the European Community, which would add enormously to the still-unsolved problems of agricultural surpluses. Yet the Community's agencies continued gradually to expand their authority, and all sides admitted that European monetary policy had done much to ease the disruptions that had begun with the oil crisis.

To many politicians, journalists, and ordinary citizens, it was frightening and frustrating to find that after so many years of breathtaking change, so much remained disappointingly familiar. In principle, though, students of history need not share that feeling.

IV. A NEW ERA

The Sense of Change

A concern, almost an obsession, with where we stand in historical evolution is part of the self-awareness of modern man. In every country politicians are fond of forecasting what "history will say" about their even quite minor decisions; change seems so central a trait of current life that the word "revolution" becomes a commonplace, and we speak easily of contemporary "revolutions" in everything from world politics to the roles of the sexes and food processing. At least in part this expresses a fear for the future and an effort to predict it or even control it by extending a surveyor's line from some point in the past through the present and on to the decades ahead. In part it follows from the hopes and the habits of thought of the past two centuries.

Analyses of how the world today differs from the past emphasize different aspects of society, but most commentators write of a present that is as distinct from the past as the periods of nineteenth-century industrialization, the Enlightenment, the Renaissance, and the Middle Ages were from each other. Some analyses begin with politics as the organization of power within and between nations. Some focus on economic distribution and the modes of production. Others concentrate on social structures and institutions. Finally, some stress changes in social values, attitudes, and ideas. Yet all these approaches tend to concur that a major historical change has occurred in the last few years.

If one dates the new era from the 1940s, the

Axis domination of Europe then marks the tragic end of one epoch, Russian and American influence and European recovery the beginning of another. To put the date in the late 1950s places more emphasis on social change and prosperity but points to the same evidence of European societies that no longer directly dominate the world. The watershed, some would argue, lies in the 1960s, with the increasing strength of the Common Market and the autonomy of Europe after a long period of European self-doubt and floundering extending back to the eve of World War I. Or the year 1968 can stand as the symbol of worldwide changes, led by North America and Europe, in values, outlook, and life style. Seen in any of these ways, our own era becomes the one in which a new age is clearly taking shape.

The varied role of European nations in world affairs is one obvious indication of change. In 1940 France dropped from the ranks of the world's most powerful states; Germany did so five years later; and in the 1950s even victorious Great Britain could no longer sustain a position comparable with that of the United States or the Soviet Union. Russia alone among the European states attained the position of a superpower. The economic crises of the postwar period and the loss of colonial empires confirmed a process of relative decline in Western Europe's strength. And many shared the Spenglerian gloom of Arnold Toynbee in his multivolume *Study of History* in placing this decline on a world-historical scale as the end of the European millennium.

The Locus of Power

Subsequent recovery has not restored Europe's former international dominance. The Common Market countries roughly equal the United States or Russia in population and productive capacity, but they are not one nation. Rather the European states have come to exercise their diplomatic influence in the interstices of Cold War competition. The Soviet Union has found a limit to the effectiveness of her power even in Eastern Europe, and the United States could not prohibit communism in Cuba or defeat it in Vietnam; and both superpowers, faced with economic problems at home and concerned over the rising strength of China and Japan, have had to seek good relations with European nations less dependent on them than in the past.

Political and economic relations between the Communist states of Eastern Europe and the capitalist ones of the West, continue to be a central issue. Economic expansion in both groups as well as the strength of the left in Western Europe foreshadow growing ties that will pull European governments closer together. Another long-range question regards the changing relationship of these countries to the Third World. Already the major European powers play a somewhat more independent role in the Middle East, show a deepening interest in South America, and have established stronger economic and political connections with the independent nations of Africa. Developing nations may have reason to prefer an association with industrial countries less overwhelming and ideologically committed than Russia or the United States.

At the same time the increasing importance of Japan, China, and eventually perhaps India and Brazil, will open new diplomatic opportunities. It is not hard to imagine on a global scale international understandings among half a dozen major powers and scores of lesser ones much like those among European nations in the eighteenth and nineteenth centuries. In such a world the wealth and the diplomatic skill of Europe will count for much.

Two favorite descriptions of the contemporary era, have been the "Atomic Age" and the "Space Age," chosen to express the critical role technology now plays. In both fields the Soviet Union and the United States achieved rough parity in the 1960s. Although European scientists contributed much to the progress these two giants have made, no other nation can match their capacity to sustain the immense organization and expend the massive funds large atomic arsenals and space flights require. On the other hand Britain and France produce nuclear weapons; and Western Europe is a leader in peaceful applications of nuclear energy and the use of satellites for communications and other purposes.

In most branches of technology, Western Europe surpasses Russia, and it lags behind the United States and Japan only in specific sectors, notably the application of computer technology. Its automated assembly lines, refineries, and switchyards are in fact often models for similar facilities in Eastern Europe and the United States. On the whole then Europe has essentially regained the position it held on the eve of World War II but not that of the nineteenth century. Such a rapid adaptation in a period of headlong technological advance has precipitated Europe into the postindustrial age.

Postindustrial Society

The somewhat misleading term "postindustrial society" was coined to indicate that the conditions and problems characteristic of the most advanced societies constitute a new historical stage. No longer is industrial production the dominant, absorbing activity in such countries; rather the white-collar occupations constitute some of the largest job categories, and service activities such as sales and distribution employ as many workers as production (a fact related to the changes in "proletarian" parties).

Postindustrial society then tends to take its lead from the professional groups. Expert managers, staff specialists, and technicians, usually highly specialized in their functions and often in their training, form a very large part of society—about the same proportion as the entire middle class in the nineteenth century. Even the very wealthy tend to exercise their influence through their connections with these groups. This in itself represents a crucial change in social structure. Furthermore, the majority of people—members of the lower-middle class, industrial workers, and most farmers—have become more similar in standard of living and even life style. Most European families now spend less than half their income on food and could easily reduce that proportion if they chose to. At the bottom of this society and often sadly separated from the rest of it are the rural poor and urban slum dwellers. Although a far smaller proportion of the population than the "deserving poor" of the nineteenth century, they are often cruelly distinguished by lack of education and by language or race.

Both the white-collar, and working classes tend to be highly mobile, ready to shift jobs and location as new opportunities arise; and this is essential for the flexible adjustment to new demands on which advanced countries depend. But increased mobility and related changes affect the very fabric of society, most clearly perhaps with regard to the family. More than ever likely to be living at some distance from grandparents or cousins, the members of a family are rarely able to work together even in fields or factories, mines or small shops. Rather, increased leisure allows them to take their recreation together.

As domestic servants become scarce, household appliances become an essential benefit of the consumer society. Combined with smaller families, this means that women can approach salaried labor not merely as an interim measure to occupy their time until marriage or temporarily to supplement family income but as a lifelong occupation. The women's liberation movement, generally more prominent in the United States than in Europe, thus results from the recognition of social opportunities as well as ideas of equality, on both counts opening the possibility of a redefinition of traditional social roles. Specialization on the other hand extends the period of training and therefore depen-

The supermarket, once the key symbol of American affluence, was rapidly adapted to differing national tastes. This one is in France.
(Photo: Viva/Woodfin Camp and Associates)

dency; the teen-ager of today would have been considered a young adult, already working, through most of history. And society has come to recognize that increased longevity requires special provisions for the needs of the retired and the elderly.

In theory a mobile society would identify the talents of each citizen (of either sex) and provide the training to allow those talents to be used to the full. Education would thus become the critical social filter, selecting the talent and providing the training society needs. In practice this has proved difficult even in Communist countries, nor have European societies settled the question of what sort of education is in fact most beneficial to the individual and to society.

An assumption underlying the concept of postindustrial societies is that everywhere they become more alike. To Europeans this change has seemed to come in the form of influences from the United States, and reactions to that challenge have reflected judgments about American society viewed as fluid, democratic, and open but also violent, crass, and culturally shallow. European economies, which in 1939 were barely familiar with installment buying, now enthusiastically employ easy purchase terms and credit cards to stimulate consumption. In the 1950s Coca-Cola was attacked as lamentable Americanization, but now supermarkets, discount stores, and packaged products are common. Television has not only become a focal point in most homes and altered the style of politics, but Eurovision allows national networks to share Europe-wide transmissions. Cities continue to expand and to grow more similar in appearance. Paid vacations, often both winter and summer, and the ubiquitous automobile carry commercial blight and common behavior to the seashores and mountains, whose isolation poets praised a few generations ago. Regional and class differences are no longer so readily and publicly identified by the clothes people wear, the places they go, or the diversions they enjoy.

As this happens, new problems arise requiring concerted social action, and matters once largely resolved by custom—such as diet, dress, popular culture, or the appearance of the countryside—become the object of deliberation. More people have more choices to make about their way of life, their occupations, their housing, and their leisure; but as such choice is extended—for example in the recent spread of legislation making divorce and abortion easier—it can also be burdensome to the individual and a challenge to traditional social values. These concerns and the tensions to which they give rise stand as another mark of modern society.

The Role of the State

Not only do postindustrial societies require that the state play a very active economic and social role but that role also seems to become more similar from nation to nation. As always the government is a final source of social stability, but this control extends far beyond mere police power to a legal and political part in labor disputes and corporate mergers, a responsibility for general welfare and the distribution of resources, and a major part in general planning for social change as well as economic growth.

In principle the welfare state as accepted throughout Europe implies the constant reallocation of wealth from the well-to-do in favor of the poor. In practice the middle of society probably benefits as much as the less fortunate, and the accompanying tax burden is too great to fall on the rich alone. But for most Europeans the fear of going hungry, of facing illness without medical care, or of being destitute in old age has been greatly reduced. Public welfare appears almost as essential a part of state activity as the building of superhighways.

The state is also expected to assure the fiscal policies, at least some of the investments, the trade arrangements, the educational system, detailed information on economic and social matters, and the means of communication that postindustrial societies require. Such tasks tend to make the government bureaucracy a model of postindustrial society itself: efficiently organized for special functions, open to people of talent and technical training who can expect promotion on merit (as well as seniority), approaching specific problems with rational objectivity. In practice, of course, no government agency is so removed from special interests and political prejudices, and this makes the bureaucracy itself a central issue of modern politics. Such tasks also lead the state into extensive long-range planning. In the French system a planning office with a large staff of experts and a consultative assembly representing affected interests both creates long-range programs and drafts legislation for parliamentary action.

Most other Western countries are beginning to adopt similarly comprehensive arrangements and have discovered how to manage the economy indirectly through tax and fiscal policies as well as through nationalized industries and direct subsidies much as they indirectly shape society through policies on housing, welfare, and education. In communist nations on the other hand, the advantages of indirect controls and more decentralized decision making are coming to be appreciated. Despite fundamental differences in the two systems, there is thus reason to see them drawing closer even in the roles assigned to the central governments. And the institutions with which governments deal—political parties, businesses, unions, education systems, hospitals—tend to manifest a similarly bureaucratic organization. That organization can itself become a force inhibiting change.

When the economy falters, whole groups believe themselves the victim of injustice; when social customs break down, protest focuses on the state. Not surprisingly the wave of changes since World War II and the picture of the future that can follow from them have produced resistance and serious criticism. Just as contemporary change continues a process centuries old, so the criticisms of those changes build on a long tradition of disenchantment with claims of progress. For many the new era threatens much that was fundamental to Western civilization and that made European culture so vital. In that view society since World War II offers disturbing indications that ours is an age of crisis.

The Crisis of Society

Applied to society, the metaphor of a crisis suggests some breakdown or spasm (the term was once primarily medical) that challenges survival itself and after which nothing is likely ever to be quite the same. The idea of crisis is usually accompanied by other terms loosely used—"breakdown," "revolution," "depression," "failure"; but the imprecision of "crisis" makes it useful to describe a feeling that things cannot go on as they are and makes it appropriate to a time that seems on the eve of something drastically new. One of the favorite terms in current commentary and central to Marxist analysis, it is most often applied to the functioning of society, the state of contemporary culture, and the issue of what values people hold.

The dominant style of Western social analyses is to write as if society is a patient whose illness needs diagnosis. Such a view, common in novelists and congenial to modern psychology and sociology as well, is assumed in most contemporary assessments of our age; thus any private act, any social behavior, any publication is likely to be taken as a symptom of some larger tendency or need. Combined with an intense historical consciousness, including a fear that Western civilization may be in decline and a nostalgia for other eras, this orientation easily leads to a kind of cultural hypochondria.

Clearly there is much that does not function well. The totalitarian regimes of the 1930s and 1940s were terrifying evidence of that; worse, part of their justification was a disgust with the civilization from which they sprang—a civilization many denounced as materialistic, torn by ideological and class conflicts, lacking in universally accepted values either aesthetic or moral. If totalitarianism has subsided, it is not certain that such criticism is now less valid. Even in democracies the political process often seems far removed from the people, a sort of private game based on the manipulation of public opinion. And save for self-interest the great parties have largely lost the refreshing clarity of purpose with which they emerged from the resistance movements. The Christian Democrats, who dreamed of a Christian social vision above politics and were among the first to see the promise of European unity, have become but another coalition mediating among established influences, weak in France, stronger but hardly more creative in Germany and Italy. The socialists, once sure their hour had come, remain torn between allies on the left and in the center; no longer confident of many of their old panaceas, they are neither the incisive critics nor the innovative leaders they once showed promise of being.

On the Continent generally issues of civil liberties and charges of corruption still challenge the political system. In the Scandinavian countries and Britain, where such questions are less troubling, governments have hardly done better in consistently meeting the needs of a new era. Disillusionment in the Communist regimes is only a little more effectively disguised, and everywhere policies that were supposed to have furthered freedom or equality can be shown merely to have left the poor and unfortunate more subordinate to the rich and powerful. Thus critics are sure of a despairing answer when they ask what Western nation is now moved by a great purpose or what government is truly free, honest, efficient, and farsighted.

Meritocracy and Bureaucracy

Indeed the state itself is an object of suspicion, not so much in the classic Marxist sense as the captive agent of the ruling class nor in the traditional liberal view as a threat to individual liberty, but simply in itself as a concentration of power dedicated to its own interests. And the criticism is applied with equal vigor to other large organizations, business corporations, political parties, and universities.

Max Weber saw bureaucracy, with its functional organization, uniform application of rules, and awards of status according to ability, as central to modern society. And its growth has been a result of efforts to make society more equitable as well as of the need to assemble great amounts of information and to act with rational efficiency. The undeniable achievements of such an approach encouraged a view of society itself as a meritocracy in which in every generation and in all fields new leaders would be selected by essentially objective criteria. Since the 1960s, however, this extension of a liberal vision has been subject to severe attack.

Elites that confidently claim to have earned their position may be as self-interested as and sometimes more offensive than an aristocracy born to privilege. The process of selection has remained relatively restrictive after all, and even formal criteria—examinations and superiors' recommendations—are often narrow and warped by political favoritism and social prejudice. If the virtue of bureaucracy is the evenhanded application of general rules (and many deny that it accomplishes that in practice), its weakness is faceless impersonality. Citizens often find themselves helpless before regulations that defeat the purpose intended, unable to locate the source of decisions that seriously affect their lives and treated in the dehumanized terms of multiple forms to be filled and filed. Even in societies committed to justice and freedom, the individual often cannot find any authority willing to consider his whole person and his real, human needs.

The reaction against the world of meritocracy and bureaucracy, though strong, has been marked by a certain hopelessness. Political movements throughout the West have denounced the trend toward more and more social regulation; but without solutions to offer, they have appealed in the rhetoric of nostalgia primarily to groups whose importance has been waning. From Russia to the United States, politicians' promises to make government (and society) less officious have produced few clear results. Intellectuals, artists, and students have spoken out more effectively. In England the playwright John Osborne was typical of a whole group of "angry young men" who shook the complacency of the late 1950s with their attacks on the establishment. Soviet dissidents unmasked rule in the name of the proletariat as just another autocracy. The disturbances and riots in East Germany, Poland, Hungary, and Czechoslovakia underscored that complaint; and student revolts from Berkeley to Harvard to the Sorbonne, in Britain, Germany, and Italy directly attacked all the central assumptions of meritocracy. Yet so far at least, all this outrage has produced more alienation than change.

Alienation

To Marx one of the great evils of industrial capitalism was the separation of workers from the product of their labor so that they were deprived of a craftsman's pride in what they did. On the cleaner, well-lit, and partially automated assembly lines of the postindustrial era, there is evidence that a similar alienation continues. It underlies much of the agitation even among prosperous workers; and the frequent strikes, especially common in Great Britain and Italy, have to do as much with issues of the workers' privileges and dignity as with their wages. Many lament the cultural loss in the disappearance of artisanship generally. Perhaps, the argument runs, a society is poorer if it has more things but almost none individually carved or blown or tailored with great care to be treasured by fabricator and owner.

Craftsmanship is not the only victim of technological unemployment, for in many fields people find themselves threatened by new methods and by younger specialists with more recent training. Perhaps new efforts to provide additional training on the job, to make factory work more interesting (in which the Swedish have pioneered), and to give workers a voice in management (something the Germans have tried extensively, the French, Italians, and Americans have experimented with, and the British Labour party is now beginning to demand) can make a real difference. The question remains whether the modern cult of efficiency leaves room for such human and aesthetic considerations, whether the rewards of leisure and wealth can compensate for a sense of alienation from one's own labor.

More troubling still are the deeper signs of a general alienation: the attraction to crime, the escapism of commercial pornography, alcoholism, and drug abuse. The very freedom prosperity provides brings a heavy burden of self-direction. Yet in large, highly organized societies individuals today often feel powerless even though they are confronted with a more bewildering array of personal choices than most of humanity ever faced. It is significant that social control—perceived to operate through advertising, religion, and custom as well as institutions—has become a favorite subject for social research.

The Cultural Crisis

The end of World War II and the fall of the Axis brought the sudden stimulus of ideas and artistic styles long banned, as works produced in secret could be brought into the open. In all the arts but especially painting, a flood of exciting works came from the United States, whose culture had been enriched by European émigrés, free there to continue their creativity. Artists already famous in the 1930s, like the painter Pablo Picasso (see Color Plate 63) and the poet T. S. Eliot, could simultaneously be honored as grand old figures and savored with a freshness usually reserved for the young. There was great continuity between the cultural outburst that followed liberation and the prewar world even though the new European works focused on the intervening experience of dictatorship and war.

Neo-realism flourished, especially in Italy, where the novels of Ignazio Silone and Alberto Moravia gave incisive, detailed accounts of the daily lives of little people buffeted by movements and events beyond their control, and where the films of Roberto Rossellini and Vittorio de Sica combined the harsh eye of the candid camera with sympathy for the minor characters who are society's victims and its strength. French films and the plays of the German Bertolt Brecht, who moved to East Berlin in 1949, pursued similar themes with more formal ideological purpose. The arts had never been more international, and works produced in one country were quickly appreciated throughout the West.

The New Wave

The *nouvelle vague* of the 1960s in literature and film was primarily a French phenomenon, but the term can fairly be extended to describe a major and continuing shift in the arts. The novels of Alain Robbe-Grillet and the films of Jean François Truffaut, Ingmar Bergman, and Federico Fellini are more like personal essays, held together by the sensitivity and imagination of a single creator that the audience is permitted to share in whatever way it can. In painting abstract expressionism, which dominated earlier, gave way to a great variety of styles often deliberately garish and disturbing—Pop Art, Op Art, and the satirically representational. And composers shifted their explorations from the twelve-tone scale and dissonance, avant-garde interests for more than a generation, to the new sounds of *musique concrète* (using everyday noises as well as musical sounds carefully arranged on spliced tapes) and of electronic music in the manner of the American John Cage and the German Karlheinz Stockhausen. Sculpture, generally a more conservative art, experimented with the use of common objects, new materials of every sort, strange forms, and work on a gigantic scale. The Englishman Henry Moore's huge reclining figures, with their combination of clean lines, solid masses, and empty spaces (influenced by African art), are perhaps the most admired; "environmental" sculptures, tracing lines across deserts or wrapping whole buildings in various materials, have been the most controversial.

The arts insisted on being radical, questing for new modes of expression, deliberately shocking and yet highly personal, sometimes almost private (see Color Plate 64). But few artistic conventions remained to be burst (the inhibitions on displays of sex in motion pictures eroded rapidly in the 1960s), and to do something new becomes more difficult although, in the tradition of the avant-garde, still required. One trend is to absorb and distort technology. Thus some artists have made use of electric lights, random noise, plastics, or mechanical motion, giving them aesthetic meanings much as artists had long done with nature. Another is to break the barriers between "serious" and commercial art, for each uses the other; much that begins as formal art quickly reaches the populace in articles of mass production and slick packages of advertising. In the process commercial art and popular movies have become more sophisticated, and some popular music, originally associated with the Beatles, has become artistically more serious and complex. This intersection of "high" and "popular" culture, lessening a division within Western civilization that has lasted for centuries, may foretell a new explosion of creativity; the more common comment is to note the decay both of folk culture and of the traditional canons of high art. Yet in the 1970s there was also some turning back, with a "new" taste among serious artists for ornamentation in architecture, representation in art, and lyricism in music.

Classical and Modern

During the Enlightenment, when the comparison of ancient and modern culture became a popular theme, writers were tempted to feel that the moderns had the better of it, combining ancient wisdom with new knowledge. Contemporary commentators are less confident.

The high-bourgeois culture of the nineteenth century remains strong. Symphony orchestras are numerous and of superb quality, their concerts well attended. Paintings old and new sell for ever higher prices. The great literary works of all ages are taught in schools and universities and still read with pleasure. Yet the tendency for such interests to be made academic, a matter of special study by experts, may suggest some decline in their power to attract. The very forms of that culture—long novels and epic poems, symphonies, operas, enormous museums—have by current standards become terribly expensive in time and money. Ironically their place appears least threatened in the Soviet Union, where the state

In the central produce market in downtown Madrid, striking architecture and bright lights provide a modern setting for a rich variety of fruits and vegetables while maintaining the tradition of small specialty shops.
(Photo: EPA, Inc.)

is committed to excluding the competition offered by much of contemporary Western culture. Nowhere is ballet more honored or more old-fashioned. But critics wonder whether people elsewhere will continue to receive the long preparation, maintain the patience, or preserve the values necessary to appreciate the West's traditional culture.

Paperback books, records, and reproductions of paintings have carried the arts more broadly into society, but the fear remains that they are not an integral part of it. To many the signs are disturbing: the tendency for the creative life itself to become institutionalized in universities; the frenetic search for new techniques that bespeaks some deep dissatisfaction; the danger that serious culture will be eroded by the commercial, the shocking, the fashionable aspects of mass culture. The arts have expanded to encompass almost all forms of communication and fabrication. This, like the increased interest in good design and attractive cities, may mark the hope of the new era, or it may indicate a fatal loss of focus and of that common core of values and tradition on which great cultures in the past have rested.

The Crisis of Values

On no other issue are contemporary moralists so agreed as that the lack of universally respected values is the source of serious discontent and a symptom of fatal decay. But both historical self-consciousness and the social sciences teach that values change with time and place. Once value systems are seen as relative, however, it becomes difficult to insist on imposing any particular set. The symptom of social disintegration becomes one of its causes.

Existentialism

Existentialism, one of the most influential movements of the postwar period, offered a radical solution. Jean Paul Sartre, French philosopher and writer, was existentialism's most important figure, but his ideas were based in turn on the prewar work of German philosophers, especially Karl Jaspers and Martin Heidegger. Once again the intellectual continuity across the war is striking.

Sartre extended relativism to its ultimate implication: life is absurd, without purpose or meaning. But from this point he slowly built: people become what they are through the things they do in a lifetime; individual actions follow from decisions; and each decision to act is a moral choice. Thus Sartre constructed a radical individualism but one that keeps people morally responsible (and in the highest sense free) whatever their fate. There is in existentialism a sense of the heroic that had special meaning perhaps to those formed in the resistance movement and that was expressed with great power in the writings of Albert Camus, most encouragingly perhaps in his early novel *The Plague*.

As a statement of the human condition, existentialism blends remarkably with the mainstream of modern thought; there were Christian existentialists and existentialist Marxists; positivists, liberals, and Freudians have also incorporated its insights. But its very breadth of appeal is also a weakness. The values an existentialist chooses rest, after all, on blind experience or some other philosophy. Like neorealism, existentialism belonged to the early postwar period and spoke more clearly to the abnormal years of terror and rebuilding than to a time of routine and prosperity.

Older Doctrines

In the public anguish over values that has marked this period, Christian voices, individually strong, have collectively had a rather uncertain effect. After the war the leading theologians—once again, mainly men of an older generation who were already well known two decades earlier, like Jaspers, Karl Barth, and Jacques Maritain—were studied with new interest. The Protestant Paul Tillich and the Catholic Pierre Teilhard de Chardin achieved a large following with their systematic efforts to establish the relevance of Christianity to every fact of modern life and to accommodate contemporary modes of thought. Pope John

XXIII was beloved as few popes have ever been by non-Catholics as well as Catholics for his gentleness, his tolerance, and his receptivity to change. All this combined with the postwar vigor of Christian political parties and a rise in church attendance in the 1950s suggested a major revival of Christianity.

Yet by the 1960s society seemed to have been little affected. Although some theologians hailed the benefits of the greater openness about sex in literature, dress, and practice, most found it anathema. While churches became socially more aware and sometimes even radical, Marxist parties and the modern state accomplished more. Civil marriages (and divorces) increased, and religious vocations declined. When Christians evoked rigid, traditional standards of morality, they could be dismissed as reactionaries; when they embraced modern psychology or worked for social change, they were accused of opportunism. But when they charged that society was in a moral crisis, they were widely heard. The election of John Paul II as pope in 1978 (significantly, a Pole and the first non-Italian pope in 455 years) clearly marked the continuing changes in the Roman Catholic Church. He, too, proved immensely popular, but on theological and moral matters involving the family, sex, and the priesthood remained resolutely conservative.

If Christians have been outspoken about the crisis of values in this generation, philosophers have on the whole been silent. In Britain and the United States, the dominance of logical positivism and analytic philosophy is all but complete, so that philosophy has become a highly specialized, quasi-mathematical discipline inclined to view the ethical questions troubling most thoughtful people as too loosely defined to merit comment. But elsewhere there are few signs of philosophical creativity. We still seem to take our intellectual problems very largely as formulated in the nineteenth century, by Kierkegaard, Marx, Nietzsche, and Freud. (Significantly the nineteenth-century schools of thought less critical of Western society or more optimistic about human nature are largely ignored.) Ours may be an era dominated by science, but social philosophy today—despite some interesting efforts to extend new findings in biology to theories of human society—is less affected by the theories of natural science than at any time since Voltaire applied Newton to society or Hobbes sought to analyze the mechanics of politics.

There have in fact been few efforts at constructing grand philosophical systems in the nineteenth-century style, although the widespread revival of interest in Hegel, especially through the work of the German philosopher Edmund Husserl, has given a common vocabulary to much of the discourse among existentialists and Marxists eager to reconcile an emphasis on human consciousness with respect for reason, on the meaning of history with assertions of human liberty.

Some have suggested that the absence of systematic philosophies is in itself a historic change: the end of ideologies following from the end of class conflict in postindustrial society. But dissatisfaction has certainly not disappeared nor conflict either. And theories of conflict tended in the 1970s to supplant the emphasis on consensus so common in the 1950s. Above all, Marxism remains impressively alive. Freed somewhat by the new variety within communism, it dominates European intellectual life, spreading into much of academic history, sociology, and anthropology and stimulating a variety of literary movements and a range of new insights in literary criticism. Many of the century's most influential intellectuals, like Antonio Gramsci in Italy and Georg Lukacs in Hungary, have been theoreticians of Marxism. Part of its appeal remains its humane concerns; yet the record of its rule as well as its historical determinism and ethical relativism makes it unreassuring as a source of social values.

But there are few alternatives. The death of

liberalism has been so confidently announced for so long that one may conclude it survives; but as a systematic doctrine, rather than tolerant practice, it is in disarray, although the "new philosophers" who in France have launched an assault on Marxism suggest a revival is possible. Conservative social theories which contributed richly to Western thought now appear primarily by implication in ideas of biological determinism or theology. The most influential aspect of conservative thought was its critique of "mass" culture and technological progress, but those concerns too have largely been absorbed by the left much as the social theorists of the Frankfurt school combined a distaste for modern society which was common among German intellectuals with a heavy debt to Marxism in their influential writings on psychology, sociology, and philosophy. Herbert Marcuse, who like most of the Frankfurt group spent World War II in the United States—Hitler as well as Marx helped to make Western intellectual life more international—found himself a hero to leaders of the student revolts of 1968, although few of the new generation shared his admiration of Freud as well as Marx.

The Social Sciences

In the West the social sciences have enjoyed an enormous increase in prestige and analytic power, primarily through the application of behavioral methods of model building and of quantitative research, first in economics, then in sociology, political science, and history. But these methods all begin by seeking to be "value-free." Another of the important movements in social science is structuralism, and its roots too lie in the early part of the twentieth century, in the work of the Swiss linguist Ferdinand de Saussure, who coined the term "semiology" to describe the study of the signs by which people communicate. For the French anthropologist Claude Lévi-Strauss, a leading structuralist, every aspect of supposedly primitive society—its kinship systems, customs, rituals, and myths—can be analyzed as the extension of complex, integrated structures of thought. Not consciously held, these structures nevertheless reflect the nature of the human mind. This radical subjectivism, which can lead Lévi-Strauss to an admiration of premodern societies comparable to that of many modern artists, speaks only indirectly to questions of values. In contemporary matters Lévi-Strauss, like Sartre, whose historical relativism he opposed, considers himself a Marxist.

Linguistics in the social sciences and biology in the natural sciences are currently the fields of most rapid development and the ones that energetically invade and synthesize their neighboring disciplines. But the excitement of such abstract and mathematical discussions remains largely confined to specialists who inevitably disparage the few attempts to carry their new findings into the analysis of social issues. Never has any previous civilization supported so much scholarship, so many centers of learning, or so many artists. But there is no test to tell whether that achievement should be a source of comfort or is itself a sign of some dangerous dispersion. Scholars barely able to keep abreast of their own disciplines speak ominously of a knowledge explosion, and professors of humanities defensively decry the dearth of interest in the things they study. Doubt about human rationality and disdain for elites have made anti-intellectualism respectable even among intellectuals, and alienation or some eternal human quest has led to a remarkable revival of interest in the occult. Computers, after all, can also be used to plot astrological charts.

The Consolation of History

Beyond doubt there is cause for concern. The question is whether these signs mark a fatal crisis or even a fundamental transformation. Seen in historical perspective, they may not be quite so terrible nor this era so drastically different as our heightened sense of change leads us to believe. One should at least consider how many great crises Western civilization has survived and how strongly traditional values and institutions still intricately attach the present to the past.

Since every era tends narcissistically to believe its own problems the most important and therefore the gravest, the assumption needs to be carefully probed. Although Europe is a lesser force in the world than it was in the nineteenth century, it is surely not so seriously threatened as were the Greeks by Xerxes, the Romans by the barbarians, or medieval Christendom by Islam. European countries are more comparable in wealth and power to the United States than the struggling medieval principalities were to Constantinople. No twentieth-century war has been more devastating than the Black Death. It is doubtful that the ideological conflict and spiritual crisis of the present are so severe as those that followed the Reformation. Nor is it clear why centuries of peasant revolts, the alcoholism of Hogarth's London, or the highway robbery, cock fighting, prostitution, and public hangings of the eighteenth century were any less signs of alienation than the manifestations that trouble us today. If social change now is rapid, we have learned to expect and even anticipate it; the changes that followed the fifteenth century or those in the hundred years after 1760 may well have been more shocking and harder to absorb.

We should not assume that earlier ages enjoyed a comforting unanimity cruelly denied to us. At few moments in Western history has a single philosophy or set of values enjoyed undisputed hegemony. The view that other eras were informed by a single spirit is largely the product of distance which makes outlines clearer and fissures more obscure. The rights of throne and altar or the forms of transubstantiation were once questions as socially shattering as those of public and private ownership or the right to an abortion. Neither is it certain that village life was less cruel than the impersonal city or that peasants were less materialist than the modern middle class. The crises of the past that strained and altered Western civilization ultimately left it with new vitality.

Modern Expectations

The tendency to assume that the quality of social life has deteriorated may also reflect a rise in expectations. We have learned to smile at the simple optimism of nineteenth-century visions of progress, but we expect "autonomy" and "spontaneity" and "self-fulfillment" for every individual. Society is asked to reinforce in all people qualities Western thinkers traditionally believed to be beyond most of mankind. Today's intellectuals are not demonstrably more at odds with the mass of society than the elites of other times, but they resent it more. There is greater concern today, however badly practice lags, for racial equality, good education, and humane treatment of society's misfits than at any time in the past.

Contemporary anxiety over the family as a social institution is a good example of how higher expectations as well as changing behavior affect the perception of the present. That the family may be about to disappear or is at least threatened now as never before is a cliché rarely challenged. But it has been a cliché for centuries, hurled from thousands of pulpits; and serfdom, slavery, poverty, and maybe human nature have also endangered the family. But since the eighteenth century, the demands placed on it have steadily increased. Paradoxically this began at the very time that industrialization separated household members for nearly all their waking hours, moved millions of people to new places, and deprived the family of the traditional social support of relatives and village custom. Yet the institution survived, and the Victorians tried hard to make the family function according to the highest Christian norms while adding still other requirements.

At La Grande Motts on the French Mediterranean, thirty-two concrete pyramids and 12,000 campsites provide space for 35,000 vacationers who crowd the beaches. With vacations available to nearly everyone, tourism has become an industry. (Photo: Henri Cartier-Bresson/Magnum)

Marriage is now expected to be a matter of mutual choice and to be more a delightful partnership than a mere division of labor; the rearing of children lasts longer and is intended to be far more intensive. Protected by the state and honored by religion, the family is supposed to provide a secure place for happiness and mutual growth, and its joys of sex and solidity are propagandized in the mass media in utopian terms that risk making reality drab at best. That contraceptives allow more couples to postpone marriage and that laws make it easier to abandon the commitment to wedlock need not mean that the institution is crumbling. It is more likely that the family itself, its social functions, and the social roles within it are simply being yet again redefined.

The Western Tradition

The painful questioning of values in modern society is in large part a continuation of a Western tradition. Ambivalence toward the past and toward change, for example, is an ancient one, especially pronounced since the French Revolution and the Romantic era. Similarly the conflict between individual and society so explosive today was a theme of Sophocles and central to early Christianity, neatly dissected by Hobbes, restated in quite different terms by Rousseau, and a major preoccupation throughout the nineteenth century. Contemporary experiments in communal living and a return to nature draw on the anarchists and utopian socialists of the nineteenth century as well as a Christian practice continuous from medieval monasteries through Anabaptists to the present. The threat of the overbearing state has been a subject of endless discussion since Machiavelli.

The distrust of rationalism as a force that can inhibit creativity and the obverse, a fear of mankind's dark irrationality, twist through the novels and plays of the nineteenth century, are floodlit in the writings of Freud, and have concerned theologians since Augustine. The arguments about free will and determination continue between Catholics and Protestants, existentialists and Marxists. When modern Westerners approach the most important issues of the day, they necessarily bring with them some part of a cultural heritage long concerned with similar problems. In this way the past is constantly reinvoked in the present, and current conflicts are given some shape and limit by the past.

Continuity in Modernization

The impressive pattern of social change in the last two hundred years has come to be called modernization—a typical Western conception that sees history moving in a single direction and tends to assume that the changes which have transformed the West will be repeated elsewhere until "developing" countries become more like their European models. Clearly all societies are feeling the effects of expanding technology, the trend toward secularization, the increased role of the state, and the growth of bureaucracy. But Western history also continues to demonstrate, as it always has, that the specific effects of such trends will be fundamentally affected by local conditions and customs, by social systems and economic organization, by politics, and by deliberate choice. The West has both retained its unity and preserved its diversity through these centuries of change. National and regional differences in manners and taste alter even the most similar institutions and continue to find expression in the most modernized societies. Despite greater travel and better communication, a universal technology, comparable standards of living, and an international style in dress and architecture, London, Paris, New York, Rome, or Berlin each remains unique.

Since the establishment of the national monarchies, European governments have used sumptuary laws, mercantilist measures, and social legislation to alter the effect of economic forces. Handicrafts, for example, have often been favored by political measures and public taste although industrial competition threatened their survival; and individual farms are in most countries sustained through the social choice of subsidies as well as by rural tenacity. A sociologist has noted that the different forms and scale of organization in contemporary industries, and even the way they use technology, reflect whether those industries were founded before the industrial revolution as were the building trades, during the nineteenth century as was the textile industry, or in the twentieth century as were the smaller and more decentralized electronics firms.[5] As concern now rises for the protection of the environment, public policy once more limits private interest. But then some of Europe's most famous parks can be traced back to the common lands and hunting preserves of the Middle Ages. Technological imperatives alone do not shape society.

Secularization describes the historical development whereby religion shifts from the center to the periphery of social concern and functions once performed by the church are given over to other, secular agencies. This is primarily an institutional change and one that need not denote a decline of belief. In fact the nineteenth and twentieth centuries have probably been

---

[5] A. L. Stinchcombe, "Social Structure and the Invention of Organization Forms," in Tom Burns (ed.), *Industrial Man* (1969), 153–194.

more "religious" than the eighteenth. As the practice of faith has ceased to be a matter of universal custom, it has become a matter of conscious, personal choice.

Even the growth of the state, in power and in social penetration, has brought with it new restrictions on the exercise of government influence. The use of representative forms and legal codes has been one way of restraining the state, and more recently the Scandinavian device of the ombudsman paid to respond to individual complaints has come to be widely adopted. Local resistance to central control has been revived, from Ireland, Scotland, and Wales to Brittany and Languedoc, Catalonia, and the Basque country; from regions of Italy to the Croatian portions of Yugoslavia and the Slovak provinces of Czechoslovakia; from Sweden to the Soviet Union. The dialects and customs that the state once strove to suppress were, it was believed just a few years ago, doomed to be eliminated through force of example, by radio, television, and easy travel. Instead, once isolated regions have used familiarity with dominant cultures to assert their equality. Now the fashionable question is whether the national state is by nature a machine for war-making that has begun to lose its function.

But the most effective defense against the intrusive power of the state may be a subtle change in the boundary between the affairs considered to be properly public and those protected as private. The nuclear family and the individual dwelling have steadily widened the zone for formally sanctioned privacy. In the nineteenth century religious tolerance, security of the postal service, and the secret ballot were steps in a gradual enlargement of privacy to include one's personal convictions (steps which often required a revolution). That recognition of individualism in the twentieth century extends even from our styles of dress and sexual practices to conscientious objection to military service.

The growth of bureaucracy, another of the themes of modernization, has strengthened institutions independent of state control as well as the state itself; and these institutions have proved a major source of continuity, carrying within them old values and attitudes to be applied to new situations. The West's courts of justice, parliaments, churches, universities, and banks are powerful establishments with independent but continuous traditions that extend back often to the Middle Ages and beyond. And the tendency now is to seek ways to make all social institutions, from welfare agencies to factories, more responsive to the individual and more accessible. Many French and a few American firms now allow their employees to set their own hours, and the German system of worker representation on management councils has parallels in France, Italy, and Yugoslavia as well as in some countries within the Soviet sphere. These schemes may or may not work, but any artisan of the early nineteenth century would have understood the need to try them.

The Vatican Council that opened in 1962 under the inspiration of Pope John XXIII was perhaps the most noted of all these efforts at institutional reform. Dedicated to *aggiornamento* ("renewal"), the council sought to bring the Catholic Church up to date not only in its organization but in its social policy, expressing concern for developing nations, respect for Jews, and belief in religious liberty. The church's leadership was made more international, and the decision to say masses in the vernacular instead of Latin put the understanding of the individual believer above institutional uniformity. Yet efforts to go much further, to give national or regional church councils autonomous authority, for example, or to abandon the celibacy of priesthood, have been firmly resisted. Even while showing impressive adaptability, Western institutions tend to slow the process of change, carefully weaving the new into the old social fabric.

Predictions of the future that take several

Prelates from around the world, in Rome for the Vatican Council, stand as Pope Paul VI is carried on his throne into St. Peters, a sixteenth-century church in the city that dominated Europe two thousand years earlier. The splendid ceremonies of one of the world's oldest religions maintained its fascination to the modern world as the Church itself undertook a wide-ranging aggiornamento.
(Photo: Wide World Photos)

centuries of history into account can still be wrong, but knowledge of the past should at least leave the present more comprehensible. In the light of historical experience we have little reason to feel sorry for ourselves or to feel confident of our superiority. Every age has been a time of transition, and all have given wise prophets cause to predict an apocalypse. In our era the possibility of atomic warfare forces everyone to bear the burden of such wisdom. Over the last century Western society has dealt with many of its social needs on the assumption of ever-expanding prosperity and received reassurance from its dominance in the world. Now many believe that continued economic growth and unchallenged dominance must end. If that should happen, such fundamental change would make the future in important respects more like the distant past, with the significant difference that non-Western societies are likely to be more similar to the West in ideologies, social organization, and technology than ever before, adding new perspectives and possibilities to a rich and varied tradition.

In terms of well-being, creativity, or general decency, Europe as a whole and Western Europe in particular compares well with any society past or present. Yet the limits on the autonomy of its sovereign states seem to weigh more heavily than their worldwide influence. Where free expression is allowed, the inadequacies and inequities of Europe's societies produce criticism more resounding than the praise their prosperity and freedom can win, and the ideas of their extraordinary intellectual tradition and the continued creativity of their culture come to focus on defining the nature of the current crisis.

Western civilization is often said to be entering a new era troubled by many signs of crisis; yet that description could fit most of the past two thousand years. It has since Roman times been a diverse civilization, built of Greek philosophy and Roman institutions and an Eastern religion, a mixture of many races and cultures and political systems, all borrowing from and competing against each other. Such qualities have helped make the West particularly adaptable and ready to learn from the outside world. It still is. Its long history has been filled with wars and revolutions that have bred a flexible toughness in its institutions, and its future is probably no more doubtful than futures normally are. As for the present a troubled civilization still finds nourishment and individuals still seek guidance in the Western experience.

RECOMMENDED READING

Studies

*Barraclough, Geoffrey. *An Introduction to Contemporary History*. 1967. A historian's assessment of the main currents of world history, making Europe no longer its dominant center.

Blackmer, Donald L. M., and Sidney Tarrow (eds.). *Communism in Italy and France*. 1975. American social scientists study the nature and meaning of communist strength in two Western democracies.

Boulding, Kenneth E. *The Meaning of the Twentieth Century*. An economist's stimulating look at the present and the future.

Brown, B. E. *Protest in Paris: Anatomy of a Revolt*. 1974. The student revolt subject to scholarly study.

Carré, Jean-Jacques, et al. *French Economic Growth*. 1975. Several experts analyze Europe's leading example of capitalist planning.

Ehrmann, Henry W. *Politics in France*. 1976. Social and institutional change are incorporated into this survey.

*Ellul, Jacques. *The Technological Society*. 1964. One of the most striking and influential of contemporary attacks on the effects of technology.

Grosser, Alfred. *Germany in Our Time*. 1971. A thoughtful study of the place of Germany in modern Europe.

Heidenheimer, Arnold J., Hugh Heclo, and Carolyn Teich Adams. *Comparative Public Policy: The Politics of Social Choice in Europe and America*. 1975. Studies the background and implications of the varied approaches to social policy.

Heilbronner, Robert G. *An Inquiry into the Human Prospect*. 1974. A hopeful discussion of the prospects for old Western values in a new society.

Hoffmann, Stanley, and Paschalis Kitromilides. *Culture and Society in Contemporary Europe*. 1981. An anthology of essays by leading intellectuals.

Hughes, H. Stuart. *The Sea Change: The Migration of Social Thought, 1930–1965*. A study by a leading intellectual historian of the implications for contemporary understanding of the spread of European social thought to America.

Kindleberger, Charles P. *Europe's Postwar Growth*. 1967. The comparative study of Europe's advanced economies and the policies of growth.

Mowat, R. C. *Creating the European Community*. 1973. A diplomatic historian turns to Europe's most striking international achievement.

Parker, Geoffrey. *The Logic of Unity*. 1975. The very useful analysis of the force of European unity by a geographer.

Payne, Stanley G. *Politics and Society in Twentieth-Century Spain*. 1976. A series of essays putting Spain's rapid development in historical perspective.

*Poster, Mark. *Existential Marxism in Postwar France*. 1975. The close investigation of this central theme provides a framework for understanding much of contemporary European thought.

Rostow, Walt W. *The World Economy: History and Prospect*. 1977. A leading student of economic development assays the directions of the future.

Shils, Edward. *Tradition*. 1982. An outstanding sociologist speculates on the beneficial role of tradition in shaping society in an era of change.

*Stromberg, Ronald N. *After Everything: Western Intellectual History Since 1945*. 1975. A disenchanted and provocative essay on contemporary intellectual fashions.

---

* Available in paperback.

INDEX

Absolute monarchies (absolutism), 563–580, 621; in eighteenth century, 609–615; German, 651–655
Abstract expressionism, 1125
Academies of art: British, 651; French, 588
Academies of science: at Berlin, 576; British, 535, 588, 594; French, 535, 633–634; at St. Petersburg, 580, 1018
Academy of Inscriptions and Literature (French), 588
Action Française, 996
Act of Toleration, 583
Addison, Joseph, 643
Adenauer, Konrad, 1065, 1075, 1097
Afghanistan, 914, 1117
Africa: slave trade and, 621–624; Anglo-French rivalry in, 629; European imperialism in, 910–914; United Nations and, 1063; uprisings in, 1080n; in contemporary era, 1094n
Africa, North: in World War II, 1047, 1051–1052; in contemporary era, 1094n
Agriculture: Industrial Revolution and, 663, 673–676; population growth and, 786; nineteenth century, 786, 792–794; specialization in, 866; post-World War I productivity and surpluses, 987; under first Soviet five-year plan, 1015–1016; World War II damages and, 1058–1059; in Soviet Union, 1072, 1108; in contemporary era, 1092–1093
Airplanes, 866
Albania, 1109; annexed by Fascist Italy, 1033; Soviet control of, 1064; China and, 1079, 1095
Alchemy, 521, 984
Alembert, Jean Le Rond d', 636, 641–642
Aleutian Islands, 1047
Alexander I, King of Yugoslavia, 996
Alexander I, Tsar, 733, 737, 747, 750
Alexander II, Tsar, 831–832, 848
Alexander III, Tsar, 848, 890
Alexandra, Tsarina, 938
Alexis I, Tsar, 514–515
Alfonso XII, King of Spain, 850
Alfonso XIII, King of Spain, 894, 997
Algeria, 1052; revolt against French role in, 1080–1081; in World War II, 1047

Alienation: in nineteenth century, 804; as theme of inquiry in 1930s, 1026; in contemporary era, 1123–1124, 1127, 1129–1130
Alsace-Lorraine, 843–844, 863
Alva, Duke of, 481
Amadeus I, King of Spain, 850
American colonies, *see* New World colonies
American Philosophical Society, 636
American Relief Administration, 962
American Revolution, 687–688
Analytic Philosophy, 981–982, 1128
Anarchism, 883–886
Anglican Church, *see* Church of England
Angola, 1105
Anne of Austria (widow of Louis XIII), 503
Anne, Queen of Great Britain, 584
Anomie, 985. *See also* Alienation
Anthropology, 985
Anti-Comintern Pact (1936), 1028, 1030, 1034
Anti-Corn Law League, 762–763
Anti-Semitism, 890n; in Russia, 888–891; in France, 888–889, 895; in Great Britain, 888–889, 895; used by Rightist movements, 889; in Austria, 888, 893, 997, 1007; in Italy, 895, 1003; Dreyfus case and, 895–896; in postwar Poland and Rumania, 964, 966; in Hungary, 995; of Nazis, 980, 1007, 1010, 1049–1050, 1058. *See also* Jews
Antwerp, port of, 685
Apprenticeship system, 794
Aquinas, St. Thomas, 887
Arabs, 952
Archimedes, 522
Architecture, 648n, 785; in St. Petersburg, 580; pre-World War I era, 878; of the 1920s, 985
Aristocracy: seventeenth century, 511, 556, 558; Louis XIV and, 563, 565; Holy Roman Empire under Leopold I and, 572–574; seventeenth and eighteenth century rise of, 572–598; English (gentry), 581–584; in the United Provinces, Sweden, and Poland, 586–587; French, 615–617; English, 617–619; eighteenth century resurgence of, 684–685; French Revolution and, 688–700, 704; restoration in Italy and, 755–756; nine-

teenth century British reforms and, 760–761; British Anti-Corn Law League and, 762; agricultural societies the work of, 786; nineteenth century social change and, 790–792, 799. *See also* Social class

Aristotle, 521, 525, 527

Arkwright, Richard, 679

Arms race: before World War I, 923–925; in contemporary era, 1096. *See also* Disarmament

Art: Baroque, 540–545; sixteenth and seventeenth century, 508, 537–548; classical, 540, 545–548; eighteenth century, 589–592, 649–651; nineteenth century, 821–823, 825, 829; pre-World War I, 872–873, 877–878; in Soviet Union, 963; during and after World War I, 978, 980–981; popular culture less separated from, 981, 985–986; in Nazi Germany, 1014; in Soviet Union, 1018; in the 1930s, 1025–1026; in the contemporary era, 1124–1125. *See also* Architecture; Literature; Music

Art nouveau, 878

Asia: European imperialism in, 914–917; World War II and, 1047; United Nations and, 1063; in contemporary era, 1094

Astrology, 521, 1129; scientific revolution and, 524–525

Astronomy: scientific revolution and, 521–524, 527–528; Newton and, 594–595

Atlantic Charter, 1041, 1061

Atomic bomb, 1057–1058, 1068. *See also* Nuclear weapons

Atomic energy, *see* Nuclear energy

Atomism, 521

Attlee, Clement, 1059, 1066

Auden, W. H., 1025–1026

Augustine, St., 534

Auschwitz, 1050

Austen, Jane, 802

Austerlitz, Battle of, 730, 732

Australia, 760

Austria, in Holy Roman Empire, 572–574

Austria (republic): after World War I, 946, 951, 953, 964–965; Great Depression and, 988–990; fascist movement in, 996–997; anti-Semitism in, 888, 893, 997; Nazis in, 1027, 1030–1031; annexed to Nazi Germany, 1030–1031; after World War II, 1075–1076

Austrian Empire (Austria-Hungary): 1657–1718, 573; War of the Austrian Succession, 613–614; Seven Years' War, 624–626; Netherlands and, 613, 684; French Revolution and, 698, 718; Napoleon and, 724, 730, 732, 737–739; Congress of Vienna and, 743–745, 747; in German Confederation, 747; revolutions of 1848 and, 767, 770–771, 773; nineteenth century reforms in, 828; international relations and, 830; Crimean conflict and, 831; Piedmont invaded by (1859), 836; unification of Germany and, 839–846, 849; in Three Emperors' League, 859; Catholic Church and, 887; political stalemate in (1879–1914), 892–893; alliances before World War I, 917–925; in World War I, 925–936; after World War I. *See also* Austria (republic)

Automobiles, 866, 974, 1021

Azaña, Manuel, 999

Babeuf, Gracchus, 722

Bach, Johann Sebastian, 651n

Bacon, Francis, 494, 522, 530, 532, 536, 633

Badoglio, Marshal Pietro, 1052, 1054

Bakunin, Mikhail, 848, 883, 885

Baldwin, Stanley, 975, 1023

Balfour, Arthur, 952

Balfour Declaration, 952

Balkan states, 921–923

Balzac Honoré de, 822–824

Banking: Dutch, 508, 516; preconditions of industrialization and, 670; international ties and, 782; role of government in, 782–783; American stock market crash and, 987; Great Depression and, 987–990

Bank of Amsterdam, 508

Bank of England, 585, 670, 782; nationalization of, 1066

Bank of France, 779, 782, 1024, 1073

Baroque art, 540–545

Barth, Karl, 1127

Batavian Republic, 723; Napoleon and, 725, 731, 733

Battle of Britain, 1038–1039

Battle of the Books, 593

Battle of the Bulge, 1055

Baudelaire, Charles, 825

Bauhaus architecture, 985, 1026

Bayle, Pierre, 635

BBC, 1050

Beatles, the, 1125

Beauharnais, Eugène de, 733

Beauharnais, Joséphine de, 733

Beccaria, Cesare Bonesana, Marquis de, 636

Beethoven, Ludwig van, 650–651, 821, 823

Belgium: independence of, 757–758; liberal constitutionalism in, 761n, 764–765; industrial growth in, 780–785; imperialism and, 910, 914; in World War I, 923, 925–936; effects of World War I in, 936–937; Locarno Pact and, 973; in the 1920s, 977; fascist movement in, 996; in World War II, 1038; after World War II, 1066; Benelux and, 1074

Bell, Sir Thomas, 679

Benelux, 1074, 1076

Benes, Eduard, 965, 1064

Bentham, Jeremy, 808, 810, 817

Berdyaev, Nikolai, 1025

Berg, grand duchy of, 732

Bergman, Ingmar, 1125
Bergson, Henri, 888
Berlin: as developed by Frederick III, 575–577; revolution of 1848 in, 769–770; Spartacist revolt in, 966; divided after World War II, 1060; airlift to, 1066–1067; as divided city, 1095–1097
Berlinguer, Enrico, 1110
Bernini, Giovanni Lorenzo, 543
Bernstein, Eduard, 898
Berry, Charles Ferdinand de Bourbon, Duke of, 757, 763
Berry, Duchess of, 763
Bessarabia, 1034, 1039
Bethmann-Hollweg, Theobald von, 897–898
Bill of Rights (English), 597
Biological sciences, 985–986, 1129
Birth rate: social class and, 787–788; after World War II, 1071. *See also* Population
Bismark, Otto von, 820, 840–846, 859,887, 897, 918, 950, 965
Black Death, 1130
Blanc, Louis, 768, 771
Blanqui, Jérôme Adolphe, 852
Blanqui, Louis Auguste, 883
Bloody Sunday, 890–892
Blum, Léon, 1024, 1029
Bodin, Jean, 483–484
Boer War, 898–899, 906, 914, 918–920
Bohemia, 572, 613–614, 827; Thirty Years' War and, 484–485
Boileau, Nicolas, 589
Bolívar, Simon, 755
Bolsheviks, 719*n*, 940–941
Bonald, Louis de, 749
Bonaparte, Jérôme, 732–733, 834
Bonaparte, Joseph, 735–736
Bonaparte, Louis, 733, 735
Bonaparte, Louis Napoleon, *see* Napoleon, French Emperor
Boris Godunov, Tsar, 514
Bossuet, Bishop, 563
Boulanger, Gen. Georges, 895
Boulton, Matthew, 680
Bourbon dynasty, 482–483, 604–605, 624, 736, 739; restored in France, 745–747; restored in Spain, 755–756
Bowdler, Thomas, 802
Boxer Rebellion, 916, 918
Boyle, Robert, 535
Brahe, Tycho, 524–525
Brandenburg, Diet of, 574–575
Brandenburg-Prussia, 574, 610–613
Brandt, Willy, 1097, 1101
Brazil, 549, 1118
Brazza, Pierre de, 908

Brecht, Bertolt, 1124
Breton, André, 980
Brezhnev, Leonid, 1108
Briand, Aristide, 974
Bright, John, 762, 854
Brissot, Jacques, 705
Britain, *see* England; Great Britain
British Museum, 822
British Order of Merit, 802
British Union of Fascists, 996
Brontë sisters, 802
Bruck, Moeller van den, 1007
Brueghel, Pieter, 480–481
Braumaire Coup, 725–726
Brüning, Heinrich, 1008–1009
Brunswick, Karl Wilhelm Ferdinand, Duke of, 698
Buber, Martin, 1025
Buchenwald, 1050
Buffon, Georges Louis Leclerc de, 634
Bukharin, Nikolai, 1015, 1018
Bulgaria, 857–858, 921, 945; in World War I, 930, 933; after World War I, 951, 964–965; before World War II, 1027; in World War II, 1039, 1054; after World War II, 1060; Soviet control of, 1064; in contemporary era, 1109
Bülow, Bernhard von, 920
Bunyan, John, 590–591
Buonarroti, Filippo, 722
Bureaucracy, 1123
Burke, Edmund, 659, 748–749
Burma, 1068
Bute, John Stuart, Earl of, 625
Byelo-(White) Russians, 959*n*

Caetano, Marcello, 1105
Cage, John, 1125
Calendars, 939*n*; Julian, 524; Gregorian, 524; French Revolutionary, 713–714, 728
Calonne, Charles Alexandre de, 692
Calvinists, 496, 667; in religious wars, 482, 485; Anglican prayer book rejected by, 494; French, 501. *See also* Huguenots
Cambridge University, 856
Camus, Albert, 1127
Canada, 549, 629, 855, 976, 987
Canning, George, 760
Capa, Robert, 1029
Capitalism, 804, 1026; early socialist indictment of, 814; Marxist critique of, 881–883; Christian critique of, 886–887; Italian fascism and, 1005; Nazi movement and, 1008

Carbonari, 756, 766, 773
Carlism, 765–766, 838, 850
Carlos, Don (Carlos de Borbón), 765–766, 1106
Carlsbad Decrees (1819), 752
Carnot, Nicolas Sadi, 876
Carol II, King of Rumania, 996
Caroline, Queen of Great Britain, 760
Carrillo, Santiago, 1110
Cartels, German, 845
Carter, Jimmy, 1108
Cartwright, Edmund, 679
Castlereagh, Robert Stewart, Viscount, 744, 747, 760
Castro, Fidel, 1095
Catherine II (the Great), Empress of Russia, 652, 654
Catherine de Médicis, Queen of France, 482–483
Catholic and Royalist Army, 706
Catholic Church, 997; sixteenth century Spanish crusades and, 478–482; French civil war and, 482–484; Thirty Years' War and, 484–490; in sixteenth and seventeenth century Poland, 895–896; appeased in Fascist Italy, 1004; Nazism and, 1012–1014; in Soviet-controlled Poland, 1078, 1109; in Spain, 1106; in contemporary era, 1109, 1128, 1133–1135. *See also* Papacy
Catholic League, 483
Catholic Reformation (Counter Reformation), 540–541, 543, 571
Cavaignac, Gen. Louis Eugène, 771–772
Cavour, Count Camillo, 833–837
Cecil, Robert, Earl of Salisbury, 491
Central African Republic, 1095
Cervantes Saavedra, Miguel de, 538–539
Cesi, Prince Federigo, 536
Ceylon, 1068
Cézanne, Paul, 878
Chad, 1095
Chamberlain, Joseph, 898
Chamberlain, Neville, 1023, 1031, 1033–1034
Chambord, Count Henri Charles de, 851, 853
Charity organizations, 806, 887
Charles I, King of England, 494–497
Charles II, King of England, 497–499, 535, 581–582, 584–585
Charles II, King of Spain, 568, 574
Charles IV, King of Spain, 735
Charles VI, Holy Roman Emperor, 613–614
Charles X, King of France, 757–758, 768
Charles X Gustavus, King of Sweden, 512
Charles XI, King of France, 586–587
Charles XII, King of France, 586–587
Charles, Duke of Lorraine, 572
Charles Albert, Duke of Bavaria, 613–614
Charles Albert, King of Sardenia, 756, 773
Chartism, 761–763, 768, 796

Cherbourg Academy, 642
Child labor, 795, 800–801, 870; restrictions on, 761, 808
China, 920, 1027, 1058; Western imperialism and, 916–917; Boxer Rebellion, 916, 918; Japan and, 917; World War I treaty terms rejected by, 953, after World War II, 1060; in United Nations, 1063
China, People's Republic of, 1070; Albania and, 1079, 1095; Soviet Union and, 1095, 1107; in contemporary era, 1118
Christianity, 1025, 1131–1132; nineteenth century fascination with, 749; early socialist views of, 815; liberalism and, 886–887; in the contemporary era, 1127–1128. *See also* Catholic Church, Church of England; Eastern Orthodox Church; Protestantism
Christina, Queen of Sweden, 512, 586
Churchill, Winston, 931, 1034, 1038, 1041, 1047, 1051–1052, 1059, 1066, 1074–1075, 1077; Big Three meetings, 1052, 1055–1056
Church of England, 493, 496, 808; in seventeenth and eighteenth centuries, 581–583; attacked as bastion of privilege, 760; removal of taxes beneficial to, 855; disestablished in Ireland, 856; stripped of privileges, 886–887
Cisalpine Republic, 724
Cities: before 1700, *see* Urban Societies; in 1700, 552; in nineteenth century, 783–784, 788–790, 856; in pre-World War I era, 871–872; destroyed in World War II, 1057–1058; in contemporary era, 1085, 1087–1088
Class, *see* Social class
Classicism, 540, 545, 548
Clemenceau, Georges, 896, 933, 937, 947–948, 950, 953, 974
Coal and Steel Community, 1074, 1081
Coal industry, 676–678, 681
Cobden, Richard, 762
Coke, Thomas William, 674
Colbert, Jean Baptiste, 565, 567, 570, 668, 681
Cold War, 1066–1070, 1072, 1074, 1080, 1095, 1117–1118; Suez crisis and, 1077; relaxation of, 1107
Colonization, *see* Imperialism; New World colonies
Combination Acts (Great Britain), 760
Cominform, 1064, 1079, 1107
Commerce, *see* Trade
Common Market (European Economic Community), 1074, 1080–1081, 1092, 1097–1101, 1116–1118
Communes, utopian, 813–814
Communism: in eighteenth century France, 722; Russian revolution, 938, 943–946 (*see also* Soviet Union); in Italy, 969–971; fascism and, 1006, 1025; Nazism and, 1009; in Resistance movements, 1063; in post-Depression years, 1020; Marshall Plan and, 1067–1068; in China, 1070; in contemporary era, 1106–1110; Eurocommunism, 1109–1110

Companies, *see* Trade
Comte, Auguste, 811, 873–874
Concentration camps, 1010, 1050, 1058
Concert of Europe, 754–755, 759
Concordat of 1801, 728, 756
Condé, Louis II de Bourbon, Prince de, 501, 504
Condorcet, Marie Jean de Caritat, Marquis de, 636, 641
Confederation of the Rhine, 733, 737
Confessional Church, 1012
Congress of Vienna, 743–745, 747, 751, 754, 946, 948
Constant, Benjamin, 758
Constituent Assembly (French), 692–697
Continental system, 733–735
Contraception, 870, 1131
Convention of Westminster, 625
Copernicus, Nicolaus, 522–525, 529, 594
Corneille, Pierre, 547–548
Corn Laws (British), 760, 762–763
Corporation and Test acts, 655
Cort, Henry, 678
Cossacks, 513
Council of Constance, 488
Council of Europe, 1097–1098
Council of Mutual Economic Assistance (COMECON), 1067
Counter Reformation (Catholic Reformation), 540–541, 543, 571
Crédit Mobilier, 783, 829
Crimean War, 802, 829, 831–834, 854
Crispi, Francesco, 894
Croce Benedetto, 985, 1006, 1025
Crompton, Samuel, 679
Cromwell, Oliver, 495–499
Cromwell, Richard, 499
Cuba, 1118; Spanish-American War and, 893; missile crisis and, 1095
Cubism, 981
Culture: eighteenth century, 588–597, 640–648; nineteenth century institutions of, 821–826; in the post-World War I era, 977–986; in the 1930s, 1025–1026; classical and modern, 1125, 1127. *See also* Architecture; Art; Culture, popular; Literature; Music
Culture, popular: seventeenth century, 553–555; eighteenth century, 645–648; in industrial society, 872–880; in Soviet Union, 963–964; technology and, 1020; contemporary, 1124–1125, 1127. *See also* Leisure activities
Curie, Pierre and Marie, 982
Czechoslovakia, 936, 1021, 1072; after World War I, 946, 947n, 951, 964; in mutual-defense alliance with France and Poland, 973; stability and economic growth in, 977; in Little Entente, 1027, 1031; partitioned and occupied by Nazi Germany, 1031–1033; in World War II, 1051, 1054; after World War II, 1060; postwar Soviet control of, 1064, 1079; Soviet invasion of, 1105, 1108–1110; in contemporary era, 1123

Dachau, 1050
Dada movement, 981
Daladier, Edouard, 1024, 1031, 1033–1034
d'Annunzio, Gabriele, 969, 1005
Danton, Georges Jacques, 690, 706, 709, 718
Darby, Alexander, 678
Darlan, Adm. Jean François, 1052
Darwin, Charles, 874–875
Daumier, Honoré, 822
Dautsky, Karl, 898
David, Jacques Louis, 651, 684
Dawes, Charles G., 971
Dawes Plan, 971, 988
Déak, Ferencz, 849
Decembrist coup, 750, 754
Declaration of Independence (American), 597
Declaration of the Rights of Man (French), 694
Defoe, Daniel, 608
De Gasperi, Alcide, 1065, 1075
De Gaulle, Gen. Charles: in World War II, 1036, 1050, 1052, 1054–1056; in French government, 1065, 1080–1081, 1097–1098, 1103–1104
Delacroix, Ferdinand Victor Eugène, 825
Delcassé, Théophile, 919
Demography, *see* Population
Denikin, Gen. Anton, 960
Denmark, 510, 512n; Prussia and Russia at war with (1864), 841; agricultural specialization in, 866; women's suffrage in, 977; resistance movement in, 1050; contemporary, 1098
Depressions, of 1846 and 1857, 803. *See also* Great Depression
Descartes, René, 530–533, 536, 594, 596, 633, 635
de Sica, Vittorio, 1124
Determinism, 877
Dickens, Charles, 823–824
Diderot, Denis, 636–641, 652, 658
Dien Bien Phu, 1070
Diggers, 498
Directory (French), 720–722, 724–725, 728–729
Disarmament, 1026–1027, 1033; Washington Conference on (1921–1922), 973; as contemporary issue, 1096
Disraeli, Benjamin, 763, 855–857, 898, 910–911
Djilas, Milovan, 1109
Dollfuss, Engelbert, 997
Dominican Order, 528
Doré, Gustave, 789, 804–805
Doumergue, Gaston, 1024

Dresden, 1047, 1058
Dreyfus, Capt. Albert, case of, 895–896, 914, 996, 1023
Dryden, John, 589
Dubcek, Alexander, 1105, 1110
Dulles, John Foster, 1077
Dumas, Alexandre, 822–823
Dumbarton Oaks Conference, 1062
Dumouriez, Gen. Charles François, 706
Durkheim, Emile, 985

Eanes, Gen. António Ramalho, 1106
Eastern Orthodox Church, 513; seventeenth century dissension within, 515; Peter the Great and, 577; nineteenth century Russian conservatism and, 750; Crimean War and, 831–833; in effect a department of state, 887, 890; in communist Russia after 1923, 962
Easter Rebellion of 1916 (Ireland), 975
East India Company, 615–616, 667
Ebert, Friedrich, 965–966, 977
Economics: Adam Smith and the physiocrats, 636, 638, 809; Ricardo's theory, 809, 813; Keynesian, 953–954, 1025; classical, 990
Edict of Nantes (1598), 483, 502; revoked by Louis XIV, 569, 635
Edict of Restitution (1629), 485, 487
Education: seventh century, 549; in nineteenth century, 808, 830, 848n, 855–856; in pre-World War I era, 879–880, 899; in Soviet Union, 962, 1017–1018; in Fascist Italy, 1004; in contemporary era, 1091, 1110, 1120. *See also* Literacy; Universities
Edward VII, King of Great Britain, 900, 919
Edward VIII, King of Great Britain (duke of Windsor), 1028
Egalitarianism, 655
Egypt (modern): Napoleon in, 725, 728; British domination of, 856–857, 898; Suez Canal and British occupation of, 910–912, 914, 1077; World War I treaty terms and, 952; in World War II, 1039, 1047; independent from Britain, 1068
Einstein, Albert, 982–984
Eire, republic of, 1070
Eisenhower, Dwight D., 1047, 1054, 1056, 1077
Electron microscope, 984
El Greco, 538
Eliot, George (Mary Ann Evans), 802
Eliot, T. S., 1026, 1124
Elizabeth, Empress of Russia, 625
Elizabeth I, Queen of England, 478–479, 490–493, 761
Elizabeth II, Queen of Great Britain, 1075
Enclosure movement, 674–675
Energy issues, 1111–1113

Engels, Friedrich, 880, 883
England: Philip II of Spain and, 478–480; in sixteenth and seventeenth centuries, 490–499; Elizabeth I, 490–492; colonization by, 493; civil war in, 495–497; Charles I, 494–497; under Cromwell, 497–499; gentry in, 581–584; succession in, from Stuarts to Hanoverians, 583; emergence of party system in, 584–585; colonization by, 585; at war with Spain, 606; enclosure in, 674–675. *See also* Church of England; Parliament (English); after 1707, *see* Great Britain
Enlightenment, 632–640, 651–659, 749, 873
Epidemics, 806–807. *See also* Black Death
Erzberger, Matthias, 968
Espartero, Gen. Baldomero, 766
Essex, Robert Devereux, Earl of, 490
Estates General (France), 684–685; summoned by Marie de Medici, 501; Revolution and, 692–697
Estonia, 946, 1063
Ethiopia, 894, 914; Italian invasion of, 1027–1028
Eugène, Prince of Savoy, 568, 572–573
Eugénie, Empress of France, 827, 856
Eurocommunism, 1109–1110
Europe, Eastern: in seventeenth century, 512–515; in eighteenth century, 606; nineteenth century conservative order in, 750–751, 794; Treaty of Versailles and, 950–952; postwar regimes of, 964–965; in World War II, 1063–1065; in contemporary era, 1087–1088, 1092, 1096–1098; Soviet hegemony over, 1093, 1095, 1109; EEC and, 1100. *See also individual countries*
Europe, Western: war and revolt in (1560–1660), 475–516; wars of religion in, 478–490; scientific revolution in, 521–537; late seventeenth century culture in, 537–555; social patterns in, 548–558; demographic patterns in seventeenth century, 550–553; population by regions (1600–1700), 551; witch hunts in, 555; village life in, 556, 558; in seventeenth and eighteenth centuries, 563–598; absolute monarchies in, 563–580; eighteenth century cultural life in, 588–597, 640–651; in eighteenth century, 603–629, 632–659; state system in, 603–609; absolutism in, 609–615; maritime powers in, 615–624; Seven Years' War, 624–626; Great War for Empire, 628–629; the Enlightenment in, 632–640, 651–659; absolutism modified in, 651–659; Industrial Revolution and, 663–682; price movements in eighteenth century, 671; population of, 672–673; constitutional conflicts in, 682–688; popular movements in, 685–686; French Revolution, *see* French Revolution; revolutionary republics in, 722–724; Napoleon's rise, rule, and conquests, 722–739; restructured by Congress of Vienna, 743–749; restoration regimes in, 747–759; conservatism in, 748–749; nineteenth century liberal movements in, 757–779; revolutions of 1848, 767–779; progress of industrialization in,

779–784; social structure in (1800–1860), 786–809; population growth, 786–788; social classes, 790–798; social conditions, 798–809; social theories current in nineteenth century, 809–818; health and public welfare in, 804–809; middle class culture in, 821–826; politics of nationalism in (1850–1880), 826–846; established states reshaped, 846–859; second industrial revolution in, 863–872; migration patterns (1875–1914), 870–872; culture of industrial society, 872–880; criticisms of contemporary society, 889–900; imperialism, 905–917; World War I, 917–954; postwar political order, 959–977; disarmament talks, 973; culture of pre and postwar era in, 977–986; economic vulnerability in, 986–987; Great Depression in, 986–990; authoritarian governments in, 995–1000; totalitarianism in, 1000–1020; democracies in, 1020–1027; internal tensions and crises in, 1027–1034; in World War II, 1034–1041, 1045–1058; after World War II, 1058–1066; international relations in, 1066–1070; economic recovery in, 1070–1081; effects of economic growth in, 1085–1093; nations of, 1097n; world power structure and, 1093–1100; political systems in, 1100–1117; contemporary, 1117–1135

European Coal and Steel Community (ECSC), 1074, 1081
European Defense Community, 1077
European Economic Community (EEC), see Common Market (European Economic Community)
European Free Trade Association (EFTA), 1098–1099
European Payments Union, 1072
Eurovision, 1121
Evangelical Church, 1012
Exchange rates: Great Depression and, 989; after World War II, 1061; European Payments Union and, 1072
Exclusion Crisis, 582, 584
Existentialism, 1127
Expedition of the Thousand, 836
Expressionists, 981

Facta, Luigi, 970–971
Factory Act (Great Britain), 761
Factory workers, see Labor (working class)
Falange, 999
Families: seventeenth century, 550–552, 568, 571; eighteenth century, 568, 571, 648n; nineteenth century, 788, 798–803; early twentieth century, 870; World War II displacements and, 1059; in Soviet Union, 1017; contemporary, 1119, 1130–1131
Famines: French Revolution and, 693; in Ireland (1846–1849), 768; in Soviet Union (1920–1921 and 1932–1933), 962, 1016; following World War II destruction, 1058–1059

Faraday, Michael, 876
Fascism, 1000n; in Italy, 969–971, 1000–1006; appeal and growth of, 995–1000; common pattern of takeover by, 995, 999–1000; resistance to, 1005–1006; in Spain, 1028–1030; after World War II, 1060. See also Nazism
Fauves, 981
Federation of German Industries, 1073
Fellini, Federico, 1125
Feminism, 643. See also Women's movement
Feodor I, Tsar, 514
Ferdinand II, Holy Roman Emperor, 485, 487
Ferdinand II (Bomba), King of Naples and Sicily, 771, 773
Ferdinand VII, King of Spain, 735–736, 755, 765
Fermi, Enrico, 1006
Ferry, Jules, 916
Fichte, Johann Gottlieb, 826
Fielding, Henry, 648–649
Fifth Monarchists, 498
Films, see Motion pictures
Finland, 1021; in seventeenth century, 511; nationalism in, 827; declared independent of Russia (1918), 944; in World War II, 1034–1035, 1054; after World War II, 1060
First International, 852, 883
Fischer, Fritz, 923
Flaubert, Gustave, 824
Fleming, Sir Alexander, 985
Fleury, André Hercule de, Cardinal, 616
Flood, Henry, 687
Florey, Sir Howard, 985
Foch, Gen. Ferdinand, 934, 936
Fontenelle, Bernard de, 633
Football, 647
Formosa, 917
Fouché, Joseph, 728
Fourier, François Marie Charles, 812–813, 815, 852
France: civil war in, 482–484; in Thirty Years' War, 485–490; in sixteenth and seventeenth centuries, 499–504; under Henry IV, 499–501; the Fronde in, 503–504, 507; under Louis XIV, 563–571; eighteenth century culture in, 588–593; after Louis XIV, 615–617; overseas possessions of (1713), 620–624; in Seven Years' War, 624–626; New World colonies of, 626–629; Great War for Empire and, 628–629; French and Indian War and, 628–629; eighteenth century liberal thought in, 655–659; preconditions for industrialization in, 668–669; Industrial Revolution in, 681; revolutionary origins in, 688–690; Revolution in, see French Revolution; the Directory in, 720–722; Napoleon's rise and rule, 722–739; Congress of Vienna and, 743–745; Napoleon's Hundred Days, 745–746; Bourbon restoration in, 756–757; Metternich's Concert of Europe and, 754–755, 759; restoration regimes in Spain

and Italy, 755–756; Bourbon restoration in, 756–757; renewed uprising in, 757–758; suffrage in (1830), 761n; under Louis Philippe, 758, 761, 763–764; 1840s in, 764; Second Republic declared in, 768; June Days, 771–772, 795; industrial growth in, 780–785; public services in, 784; urbanization in, 788–790; aristocracy in, 792; peasantry in nineteenth century, 793–794; working class in, 795–797; education in, 808; under Napoleon III, 763, 820, 827–836, 841–842, 853; in Crimean War, 831–833; Franco-Prussian War, 838, 843; reshaped (1870–1878), 850–854; Paris Commune, 852–853; founding of Third Republic, 853–854; international balance of power and, 859; agricultural specialization in, 866; church-state conflicts in (1880–1900), 887; anti-Semitism in, 808–889, 895; before World War I, 895–896; Dreyfus case, 895–896; imperialism of, 910–917; alliances before World War I, 917–925; in World War I, 925–936; effects of World War I on, 936–937; Locarno Pact and, 973; in mutual-defense alliance with Poland and Czechoslovakia, 973; postwar years in, 974–975; Great Depression and, 988–990; fascist movement in, 996, 1023; in the 1930s, 1021, 1023–1024; pre-World War II pacts signed by, 1027–1028; Nazi aggression and, 1031–1034; in World War II, 1034–1041, 1045–1058; resistance movement in, 1050; after World War II, 1060; United Nations and, 1063; postwar policies in, 1065, 1073; Vietnam and, 1068, 1070, 1080; Suez crisis and, 1077; American aid to, 1172; fall of Fourth Republic in, 1080; under de Gaulle, 1080–1081, 1097; GNP of (1978), 1093; current alliances of, 1096; political achievements and changes, 1103–1104; Communist party in, 1110, 1115; in contemporary era, 1118–1119

Francis II, Holy Roman Emperor (Francis I of Austria), 698, 732–733, 738–739, 751, 773
Francis Ferdinand, Archduke of Austria, 921
Francis Joseph I, Emperor of Austria, 773, 848–849, 893
Franco, Gen. Francisco, 1028–1030, 1041, 1106
Franco-Prussian War of 1870, 838, 843, 857
Franklin, Benjamin, 636, 642
Franz Joseph, Emperor of Austria, 856
Frederick I, King of Prussia (Frederick III, Elector of Brandenburg), 575–577, 610
Frederick II, Elector of the Palatinate, 485
Frederick II (the Great), King of Prussia, 586, 606, 610–613, 625, 641, 652, 654
Frederick William, Elector of Brandenburg, 574–577
Frederick William I, King of Prussia, 610–612
Frederick William III, King of Prussia, 738, 752
Frederick William IV, King of Prussia, 754, 830, 839n; in revolution of 1848, 770–771, 773
Freemasonry, 642

Freikorps, 966, 968
French Academy, 588
French and Indian War, 628–629
French Revolution, 553, 658, 766, 792–794, 812, 826; Austrian Netherlands and, 685; ideals of, 688; origins of, 688–690; French fiscal crisis and, 690–692; Estates General and Constituent Assembly, 692–694; restructuring of France, 694–696; counterrevolution, 697–700; National Convention, 704–708; Jacobin dictatorship, 708–710; Reign of Terror, 710–711; sans culottes, 708–715; turning points in, 712; participatory democracy, 713–715; foreign policy, 715–716; armies, 716–718; Thermidorian reaction, 718–720; conservative ideology consolidated against, 748; honored by liberals, 758
Freud, Sigmund, 978–980, 1128
Freudian psychology, 978–980
Fronde, the, 503–504, 507
Futurists, 981

Galen, 521–522
Galileo Galilei, 520, 522, 525–526, 529–530, 532, 594
Gambetta, Léon, 850–851
Gandhi, Mohandas K., 1070
Garibaldi, Giuseppi, 836–838, 850
Garibaldi Brigade, 1028
Gaskell, Elizabeth, 802
Gauguin, Paul, 878
Geneva, 685–686
Genoa, 755n
George I, King of Great Britain, 584, 605, 617
George II, King of Great Britain, 617
George II, King of Greece, 997
George III, King of Great Britain, 651, 686–687
George IV, King of Great Britain, 760
George V, King of Great Britain, 899–900
George VI, King of Great Britain, 1023
German Confederation, 747, 751–754, 841
German National Society, 839
Germany, 793, 917; in Holy Roman Empire, 844n (see also Holy Roman Empire); in Thirty Years' War, 484–490; in seventeenth century, 574; in eighteenth century, 606; in Napoleonic wars, 738–739; nineteenth century conservative order in, 750–751; 1848 revolution in, 768–771; industrial growth in, 780–785; education in, 808; unification of, 839–846; North German Confederation, 842–843; Second Reich, 843–846, 897–898; in Three Emperors' League, 859; economic expansion in, 863; anti-Semitism in the 1890s in, 888–889, 895; before World War I, 897–898; imperialism and resur-

gence of the right in, 910, 916; alliances before World War I, 917–925; in World War I, 925–936; after World War I, 946, treaty terms, 948–950, 953–954; Weimar Republic, 965–969, 977, 1008–1010; right-wing nationalists in, 966, 968; inflation in, 968–969, 971, 986; reparations and, 968–969, 971–973, 987–988; Locarno Pact and, 973; Nazi regime in, 1006–1014; collapse of Weimar Republic, 1008–1010; Rome-Berlin Axis, 1028, 1030; Anti-Comintern Pact with Japan, 1028; Spanish Civil War and, 1028–1030; Anschluss, 997, 1027, 1030–1031; Czechoslovakia partitioned, 1031–1033; in World War II, 1033–1041, 1045–1058; after World War II, 1059–1066; current alliances of, 1096–1097; student revolts in, 1104–1105

Germany, East (German Democratic Republic), 1066–1067, 1072, 1078, 1095, 1109, 1123

Germany, West (Federal Republic of Germany), 1065; government role in, 1073; GNP of (1978), 1093; treaty with Soviet Union (1970), 1097; political system in, 1101; world power balance and, 1118–1119

Gibbon, Edward, 636
Gide, André, 981
Giolitti, Giovanni, 894, 970
Girondists, 705–706, 708, 710, 719
Giscard d'Estaing, Valéry, 1104, 1115
Gladstone, William, 855–857, 898
Glorious Revolution of 1688, 655
Godoy, Manuel de, 735
Goebbels, Joseph, 1007, 1014
Goethe, Johann Wolfgang von, 648, 966
Goldsmith, Oliver, 644
Gold standard abandoned, 989
Gomulka, Wladyslaw, 1078
Göring, Hermann, 1007, 1009
Goya y Lucientes, Francisco, 736, 738
Gracchus, Tiberius, 713
Gramsci, Antonio, 1109, 1128
Grand Alliance, 568
Grand Remonstrance, 495
Grattan, Henry, 687

Great Britain: before 1707 *see* England; eighteenth century aristocratic dominance in, 617–618; New World colonies of, 619–629, 672; eighteenth century naval powers of, 620–622; newspapers in, 643–645, 686; guilds abolished in, 666–667; preconditions for industrialization in, 667–668; enclosure movement in, 674–675; Industrial Revolution in, 670, 676–681; late eighteenth century popular movements in, 686–687; Napoleon and, 725, 730–735; Congress of Vienna and, 743–745; Metternich's Concert of Europe and, 754–755, 759; continental popular movements and, 754–755; and independence for southern Netherlands, 758; nineteenth century liberal politics in, 759–763; Peterloo Massacre, 759–760; Reform Bill of 1832, 760–761; 1840s in, 761–763; industrial growth in, 780–785; public services in, 784; international industrial exhibition in (1851), 784; urbanization in, 788–790; aristocracy and influence in, 792; peasantry in nineteenth century, 793–794; standard of living in, 803–804; Irish potato famine and, 808; Poor Law (1834), 808; as model of liberalism, 809–812; nationalism in, 831; in Crimean War, 831–833; reshaped (1854–1880), 854–859; parties of Gladstone and Disraeli in, 855–857; Egypt and, 856–857, 910–912, 914; international balance of power and, 859; lag in economic growth of, 863–864; anti-Semitism in, 888–889, 895; voting rights (1885–1914), 898, 900; Boer War, 898–899; labor interests in, 899; resurgence of the right in, 910; imperialism of, 910–917; alliances before World War I, 917–925; in World War I, 925–936; conscription adopted (1916), 931; effects of World War I in, 936–937; after World War I, 953, 975–977; Locarno Pact and, 973; ten-day national strike in (1926), 975; Ireland and, 975–976; dominions recognized as autonomous by, 976; women's suffrage in, 975, 977; Great Depression and, 988–990; gold standard abandoned by, 989; fascist movement in, 996; in the 1930s, 1021–1023; Spanish Civil War and, 1029; Nazi aggression and, 1031–1034; in World War II, 1034–1041, 1045–1058; settlements and peace terms after World War II, 1059–1060; United Nations and, 1061–1063; industries and services nationalized in, 1066; American aid to, 1072; postwar politics in, 1074–1075; Suez crisis and, 910–912, 914, 1077; current alliances of, 1096; Ireland and, 1097–1098; political system in, 1100–1101; student revolts in, 1104–1105; in contemporary era, 1113–1115, 1118–1119. *See also* Church of England; Parliament (English)

Great Depression: European economic vulnerability and, 986–987; panic preceding, 987; spread and effects of, 987–990, 995, 999, 1022–1023; national policies during, 989–990

Great Fear (France), 693
Great Northern War, 587
Great War for Empire, 628–629

Greece (modern), 1089, 1116; independent from Ottoman Empire (1829), 755; in pre-World War I period, 921; post-World War I conditions in, 964–965; republic established in, 965; fascist movement in, 996–997; in Balkin Pact of 1934, 1027; in World War II, 1051; leftists routed by Churchill in, 1056; American aid to, 1060–1067; Common Market and, 1098, 1100; military corps in, 1105

Greek Orthodox Church, *see* Eastern Orthodox Church

Gregorian calendar, 524, 713–714, 728
Gregory XIII, Pope, 524
Greuze, Jean Baptiste, 651
Groener, Gen. Wilhelm, 965
Gropius, Walter, 985
Gross national product (1978), 1093
Guam, 893
Guatemala, 506
Guericke, Otto von, 680
Guernica bombing, 1030; painted by Picasso, 1026
Guilds: preconditions of industrialization and, 666–667, 669, 679; development of organizations to replace, 794–795
Guinea, 1105
Guise family, 482–483
Guizot, François, 764, 766, 768, 772, 790
Gunpowder, 475–476
Gustavus III, King of Sweden, 683
Gustavus Adolphus (Gustavus II), King of Sweden, 476–477, 485, 510–512, 586–587
Gypsies, 1050

Hals, Frans, 531
Hancock family, 621
Hanover, principality of, 605
Hanssmann, Georges, 829
Hapsburg dynasty, 501, 512–513, 540–541, 543, 568, 604–605, 624, 841–842; Thirty Years' War and, 474, 485, 487; in Vienna and Madrid, 572–574; 1721–1772, 612–615; absolutism and reform in, 653–655; under Joseph II, 685; French Revolution and, 698; Napoleon and, 731, 733; German Confederation and, 751–754; reshaped (1859–1875), 848–849; postwar debts of, 964
Harding, Warren G., 973–974
Hargreaves, James, 679
Harvey, William, 529
Haydn, Franz Joseph, 649, 651
Health, public, see Public health and welfare
Hébert, Jacques René, 709, 718
Hegel, Georg Wilhelm Friedrich, 815, 817, 873, 881–882, 1128
Heidegger, Martin, 1127
Heine, Heinrich, 754
Heinsius, Antonius, 586
Heisenberg, Werner, 984
Helsinki Conference (1975), 1096
Helvetic republic, 723, 725, 731
Helvétius, Claude Adrien, 636
Henlein, Konrad, 1031
Henry II, King of France, 482
Henry III, King of France, 482
Henry IV, King of France (Henry of Navarre), 478, 482–483, 499–501

Herder, Johann Gottfried von, 826
Hermeticism, 521
Hero of Alexander, 679
Herzen, Alexander, 848
Himmler, Heinrich, 1007
Hindenburg, Gen. Paul von, 928, 933, 966, 977, 1008–1010
Hiroshima, 1057–1058
History, 985; contemporary era in historical perspective, 1129–1135
Hitler, Adolf, 977, 995, 1026; in Munich *Putsch*, 969, 1007, 1009; as Nazi dictator, 1010–1014, 1029–1041, 1045–1058; suicide of, 1056
Hobbes, Thomas, 533–534, 536, 597, 1131
Hobson, J. A., 906
Hoche, Lazare, 717
Ho Chi Minh, 1068, 1070
Hogarth, William, 648, 651
Hohenzollern family, 606, 610–611, 754, 839, 842–843; at Berlin, 574–577
Hohenzollern-Sigmaringen, Leopold von, 843
Holbach, Paul Henri Dietrich, Baron d', 636–637
Holland, Kingdom of, 733, 735
Holland (province), 509–510. See also Netherlands; United Provinces
Holy Alliance, 747
Holy Roman Empire: in Thirty Years' War, 484–490; Louis XIV and, 565, 567–568; in eighteenth century, 606; end of, 732, 747; called First German Reich, 844n
Hong Kong, 916
Hooke, Robert, 594
Hoover, Herbert, 988
Hopkins, Sir Frederick Gowland, 985
Horthy, Adm. Miklós, 995
Housing, 648n; for nineteenth century industrial workers, 789, 803–804; British national code for (1875), 856; pre-World War I era, 872; contemporary, 1085, 1087–1088
Hugo, Victor, 823–825
Huguenots, 500–502; first national synod of, 482; Edict of Nantes and, 483; in seventeenth century, 569
Humanism, philosophes' beliefs contrasted with, 637
Humanities, 980–982
Humbert I, King of Italy, 894
Hume, David, 636–637
Hundred Days (Napoleon), 745–747, 756
Hungary, 572; kingdom of, 613; in nineteenth century, 751; 1848 uprising in, 768, 773; constitutional regime established in, 770–771; autocracy in nineteenth century, 791–792; nationalism in, 827. See also Austrian Empire (Austria-Hungary)
Hungary (republic), 849; World War I treaty terms and, 951; postwar years in, 965; authoritarian rule restored

in, 995; before World War II, 1027, 1032; in World War II, 1039; after World War II, 1060, 1063; post-war Soviet control of, 1064; "goulash socialism" in, 1072; revolution crushed by Soviets in, 1078; contemporary, 1123

Huskisson, William, 760
Husserl, Edmund, 1128
Hydrogen bomb, 1068

Imperialism, 905–917, 985; Spanish, 620, 627, 912; Portuguese, 620, 912; diplomacy of Empire similar to, 755; Lenin's theory of, 907–908; justified as progress, 906, 908; in Africa, 910–914; in Asia, 914–917; international politics and, 920; in Suez crisis, 1077; student indictment of, 1105
Impressionism, 877
India, 639, 916, 1039, 1070; reorganization of British rule in, 855; as a symbol of empire, 914–915; contemporary, 1118
Indochina, 917
Indonesia, 1068
Industrial economy, characteristics of, 663–669
Industrialization, 784–785; preconditions of, 667–669, 779; patterns of, 779–782; government role in, 782–784; living conditions and, 803–804; second revolution in, 863–872; conversion from sail to steam, 867, 869; culture and, 872–880; anarchism and, 886; in Russia, 890, 892, 1015–1018, 1048. See also Industrial Revolution; Industry
Industrial Revolution, 637, 663–667, 681–682; preconditions for, 667–669; economics and demography of, 669–673; agriculture and, 663, 673–676; coal and iron production, 676–678; textile production, 678–679; use of steam, 679–681. See also Industrialization
Industry: in France under Louis XIV, 570–580; technology and (Industrial Revolution), 663–682; nineteenth century, 752; during World War I, 931–932; Great Depression and, 988–990; in Fascist Italy, 1005; in Nazi Germany, 1008, 1010–1011, 1058; under first Soviet Five Year Plan, 1016–1017; after World War II, 1071–1073; in contemporary era, 1092, 1094, 1107–1108. See also Industrialization; Industrial Revolution
Inflation, 977, 987; in Germany (post-World War I period), 968–969, 971, 986; in contemporary era, 1111–1113
Innocent X, Pope, 490
Inquisition, 480; Galileo before, 528
Institute for Industrial Reconstruction, 1073
International Association for the Exploration and Civilization of Central Africa, 912
International Bank for Reconstruction and Development, 1061

International Monetary Fund, 1093, 1101; creation of, 1061
Invisible College, 535
Iran, 1039, 1068
Iraq, 951–952, 1068
Ireland: 1649 rebellion in, 497; population of (1712–1777), 673; revolutionary agitation in, 687–688, 760; potato famine in, 768, 808; typhus in, 806; nationalism in, 827; mid-nineteenth century British reforms in, 856; home rule issue (1886–1914), 898–900; 1916 rebellion in, 931; at war with British forces, 975–976; Irish Republican Army, 975, 1097–1098, 1113–1114; political division of, 976; in contemporary era, 1097–1098, 1113–1114
Ireland, Northern, 976, 1113
Irish Republican Army, 975, 1097–1098, 1113–1114
Iron, Industrial Revolution and, 676–678, 681
Isabella II, Queen of Spain, 765–766, 843, 849–850
Isabey, J. B., 743
Islam, *see* Muslims
Israel (modern): creation of, 1068; Suez crisis and, 1077; Palestine Liberation Army and, 1113
Italian National Society, 834, 836, 839
Italy: as music center, 650; Napoleon and, 723–725, 728, 730, 733; Congress of Vienna and, 745; nineteenth century conservative order in, 750–751; post-Napoleon revolts in, 758; Giuseppe Mazzini and, 766–767; 1848 revolution in, 770–771; industrial growth in, 780–785; nationalism in, 827; unification of, 833–839; Expedition of the Thousand, 837–838; political and economic problems in (1860–1876), 838–839; church-state conflicts in (1880–1900), 887; in pre-World War I period, 894–895; alliances before World War I, 917–925; in World War I, 928–936; treaty terms, 950; League of Nations membership refused by, 953; postwar conditions in, 969; Fascist movement in, 967–971, 1000–1006; Locarno Pact and, 973; Fascist dictatorship of Mussolini, 1000–1006, 1027–1028, 1031; the corporative state, 1005; resistance to fascism in, 1005–1006; Ethiopia invaded by, 1027–1028; Spanish Civil War and, 1028–1030; Nazi rise and, 1027, 1031; in "Pact of Steel," 1033; in World War II, 1038, 1045–1058; Allied military government installed in, 1052; after World War II, 1060, 1065–1066, 1075; American aid to, 1072; state-owned industries in, 1073; political shifts in, 1101–1102; student revolts in, 1104–1105; Communist party in, 1109–1110; in contemporary era, 1111, 1113
Ivan IV (the Terrible), Tsar, 513–514, 1018

Jackson, Andrew, 782
Jacobins (Jacobin Club), 697, 705–706, 708–710, 713,

715, 719, 725, 727, 758
Jacobites, 584
James I, King of England (James VI of Scotland), 491, 493
James II, King of England, 582–584
Jansen, Cornelis, 534
Jansenism, 534, 569–570
Japan, 920, 1027; Russo-Japanese War, 890, 919; European imperialism in, 916–917; imperialism of, 917; in Paris Peace Conference, 947; World War I treaty terms and, 954; Anti-Comintern Pact with Nazi Germany, 1028; French Indochina absorbed by, 1041; Pearl Harbor attacked by, 1040–1041; in World War II, 1047–1048, 1053, 1055–1058; after World War II, 1060; American aid to, 1070; GNP of (1978), 1093; Trilateral Commission and, 1093–1094; in contemporary era, 1111, 1118–1119
Jaspers, Karl, 1127
Jefferson, Thomas, 636
Jellachich, Gen. Joseph, 772
Jerusalem, Crimean War and, 831–833
Jesuits (Society or Company of Jesus), 483, 528, 534; Philip II of Spain and, 480; in Poland, 513
Jesus Christ, *see* Christianity
Jews, 1068, 1133; in seventeenth century Amsterdam, 508; emancipated by Joseph II, 653; legal disabilities for, removed in England, 855; Napoleon and, 888; under Nazism, 980, 1007, 1010–1014, 1049–1050, 1058; Soviet, 1108. *See also* Anti-Semitism
Joffre, Gen. Joseph, 926, 932
John III Sobieski, King of Poland, 587
John XXIII, Pope, 1102, 1127–1128
John Paul II, Pope, 1128
Johnson, Samuel, 641, 644
Joseph II, Holy Roman Emperor, 614, 653–655, 685, 750
Journalism, 728, 886
Joyce, James, 980–981
Juan Carlos, King of Spain, 1114
Julian calendar, 524, 939*n*
Jung, C. G., 980
Junkers, 575, 827–828, 918, 925, 1009; Prussian public life as influenced by, 792; military dominated by, 840; German political leagues financed by, 897

Kadar, Janos, 1078
Kafka, Franz, 980–981
Kant, Immanuel, 636–637
Kapp, Wolfgang, 966
Kaunitz, Count Wenzel Anton von, 606, 625
Kay, John, 678, 681
Keats, John, 825
Kellogg-Briand Pact (1928), 973

Kemal, Mustafa (Atatürk), 951, 965
Kepler, Johannes, 524–527, 594–595
Kerensky, Aleksandr, 939, 941
Keynes, John Maynard, 953–954, 1025
Khrushchev, Nikita, 1071, 1076–1078, 1092, 1108
Kierkegaard, Sören, 1128
Kipling, Rudyard, 910
Kirov, Sergei, 1018
Koch, Robert, 806, 877
Kolowarat, Count, 751
Korea, 890, 917, 1068
Kornilov, Gen. Lavr, 942, 945
Kossuth, Lajos, 751, 768–770
Kosygin, Aleksei, 1108
Kropotkin, Prince Pëter, 885–886
Kruger, S. J. P., 918
Kulturkampf, 845, 887
Kun, Béla, 946, 965

Labor (working class): French Revolution and, 711–715; Napoleon's regulation of, 729–730; protests and deportations in England (1830), 760; in Chartist movement, 761–762, 796; British legislative reform, 761; in revolutions of 1848, 767–771; housing conditions for, 789; nineteenth century urbanization and, 788–790; child labor, 761, 795, 800–801, 808, 870; British Combination Acts, 760; nineteenth century work and living conditions, 794–797; women as workers, 800, 802–803, 932–933, 1048–1049; Utopian experiments, 813–815; distribution of occupations (ca. 1900), 864; worker migrations, 870–872; industrialization process and, 872–880; Marxist view of, 880–883; in pre-World War I era, 883–886; Bloody Sunday in Russia, 890–892; in World War I, 931–933; Great Depression and, 988–990; in Soviet Union, 1016–1018; in postindustrial society, 1119–1122; alienation and, 804, 1026, 1123–1124, 1127, 1129–1130. *See also* Labor movement; Social class
Labor movement, 830, 856; eighteenth century secret societies, 646; prohibited in Napoleonic France, 729; mid-nineteenth century secret workers' societies, 795–796; class consciousness and, 884; anarchism and, 885; growth and intellectual tradition of, 884–886; in Russia, 890–892; in France, 896; in Germany, 897–898; in England, 899; during World War I, 932–933; in postwar England, 975; in contemporary era, 1124. *See also* Guilds; Labor (working class)
Lafayette, Marquis de, 758
Laissez faire, 637, 695, 708
Lamartine, Alphonse de, 768, 773
Lamennais, Félicité Robert, Abbé de, 826

Landsberg concentration camp, 1061
Language, nationalism and, 827
Latin America, 506, 829–830, 933; Portuguese imperialism in, 620; nineteenth century revolts in, 755; Garibaldi in, 836
Latvia, 1063
Laval, Pierre, 1028, 1060
Lavoisier, Antoine Laurent, 633
Law, John, 615, 618
Law codes: English Common Law, 494; Napoleonic Code, 729, 736, 779
Lawrence, D. H., 981
Lawrence, T. E., 936
League of Augsburg, 568
League of Nations, 946, 951–953, 1023, 1026, 1061; Eastern European states assisted by, 965, 972; Permanent Court of International Justice organized by, 972–973; Germany brought into, 977; World Economic Conference (1933) sponsored by, 989; withdrawal of Germany from, 1027; weakness of, 1027; Ethiopian crisis and, 1027–1028; Franco's Spain withdrawn from, 1030; supported by Russia, 1033
Lebanon, 1068
Le Corbusier, 985
Ledru-Rollin, Alexandre, 768, 773
Leibniz, Gottfried Wilhelm von, 577
Leisure activities, 1021; in eighteenth century, 646–648; in pre-World War I era, 871–872, 878–879; sponsored in Fascist Italy, 1004; sponsored in Nazi Germany, 1012
Lely, Sir Peter, 589
Lenin Vladimir Illyich, 722, 907–908, 942–944, 959–960, 966, 1014–1015
Leo XIII, Pope, 845, 887
Leopold I, Holy Roman Emperor, 568, 572–575
Leopold I, King of Belgium, 765
Leopold II, Holy Roman Emperor, 685
Leopold II, King of Belgium, 910, 912
Lessing, Gottfried Ephraim, 636, 641
Levellers, 497–498
Lévi-Strauss, Claude, 1129
Liberalism, 764, 888–889; nineteenth century development of, 758–759; as an international movement, 809–812; Christian critique of, 886–887; pre-World War II ideological debate and, 1025
Liberia, 914
Libya, 895, 919
Liebniz, Baron Gottfried von, 594
Life expectancy: in seventeenth century, 550–551, 553; in eighteenth century, 672–673; in nineteenth century, 786
Lincean Academy, 535
Lincoln, Abraham, 855
Lincoln Brigade, 1028

Lind, Jenny, 823
Linguistics, 1129
List, Friedrich, 827
Lister, Joseph, 877
Liszt, Franz, 823
Literacy: in eighteenth century, 643–645; in nineteenth century, 804, 806; mail volume as a reflection of, 866; in pre-World War I era, 879; in Soviet Union, 1018. *See also* Education
Literature: sixteenth century, 537–548; seventeenth century, 537–548; Classical style in, 547; popular eighteenth century, 645–646; eighteenth century, 645–649; nineteenth century, 822–825; pre-World War I, 872–873, 877–878; in postwar era, 978, 980–981; in Nazi Germany, 1014; in Soviet Union, 1018; in the 1930s, 1025–1026; in the contemporary era, 1124–1125
Lithuania, 946, 1033, 1063
Little Entente, 1027, 1031
Litvinov, Maxim, 1033
Lloyd George, David, 921, 933–934, 937, 947–948, 950, 953, 975
Locarno Pact (1925), 973, 1027
Locke, John, 595–597, 633, 636, 655, 758
Logical positivism, 981–982, 1128
Loménie de Brienne, Étienne Charles, 692
London: seventeenth century conditions in, 585; in eighteenth century, 788–789; as world financial capital, 863, 865; resistance groups based in, 1050; World War II damage to, 1058; in contemporary era, 1087, 1089
Louis XIII, King of France, 501
Louis XIV (Sun King), King of France, 504, 535, 603, 607, 619, 635, 642, 668; army of, 476; reign of, 563–572, 575, 584, 586, 590, 592; centralism of, 655
Louis XV, King of France, 616, 642, 669, 690, 692–695
Louis XVI, King of France, 617, 656, 688, 691–692, 717, 743, 758; execution of, 704–705
Louis XVIII, King of France, 743–745, 756–757
Louis Napoleon, *see* Napoleon III (Louis Napoleon)
Louis Philippe, King of France, 758, 761, 763–765, 768
Louvois, Marquis de, 565, 567
Low Countries, 504–505. *See also* Netherlands
Ludendorff, Gen. Erich von, 928, 933, 936, 965–966, 969, 1007
Lukacs, Georg, 1128
Lunar Society, 642
Luther, Martin, 752
Luxembourg, 923, 1074
Lvov, Prince Georgi, 939
Lyons Academy, 643

Mably, Gabriel Bonnet de, 638
MacArthur, Gen. Douglas, 1056

MacDonald, Ramsay, 1022–1023
MacMahon, Marshal Marie, 853–854
Mafia, the, 1004
Magazines, 822–823; for women, 643, 802
Magical practices, 521–522, 525, 555, 1129
Magyars, 792; political strategies of, 893; post-World War I reassertion of, 965; conservative influence of, 995; murdered by Nazis, 1050
Maistre, Joseph de, 749
Malraux, André, 1025
Malthus, Thomas R., 788
Manin, Daniele, 834
Mann, Thomas, 981, 1025
Mannerism, 537–538
Manzoni, Alessandro, 824
Mao Zedong, 1070, 1107
Marat, Jean Paul, 706
Marcus Aurelius, Roman Emperor, 1002n
Marcuse, Herbert, 1129
Maria II, Queen of Portugal, 766
Maria Louisa, Queen of Spain, 735
Maria Theresa, Archduchess of Austria, 613–615, 750
Marie Antoinette, Queen of France, 688, 691
Marie de Médicis, Queen of France, 501, 503
Marie Louise (daughter of Frances I, wife of Napoleon), 733, 745
Maritain, Jacques, 1127
Marlborough, John Churchill, Duke of, 568
Marriage, 1128, 1131; in Soviet Union, 1017
Marseillaise, 698–699
Marshall, George C., 1067
Marshall Plan, 1067, 1072–1073
Martin, Albert, 768
Marx, Karl, 688, 722, 771, 800, 815, 817, 880–883, 888, 898, 1123, 1128
Marxism, 880–883, 974; in Paris Commune, 852–853; Lenin and, 907–908; in Russian revolution, 940–941; in post-World War I period, 946; Lenin's New Economic Policy and, 961; in postwar Germany (Spartacists), 966; denounced by Nazis, 1008; pre-World War II ideological debate and, 1025; in Spanish Civil War, 1028; in World War II resistance movements, 1051; in contemporary era, 1128–1129
Mary Queen of Scots, 491
Mary II, Queen of England (wife of William III), 582
Masaryk, Jan, 1064
Masaryk, Tomás, 965
Mathematics: scientific revolution and, 522, 525; Newtonian, 594–595
Matteotti, Giacomo, 971
Maupeou, René Nicholas de, 616, 690
Maurice of Nassau, 476, 482, 509–510
Maurras, Charles, 996
Maximilian, Archduke of Austria, Emperor of Mexico, 830
Maximilian I, Elector of Bavaria, 485
Maximilian, Prince of Baden, 936, 965
Maxwell, James Clark, 876
Mazarin, Giulio, Cardinal, 503–504
Mazzini, Giuseppe, 766–767, 773, 787n, 814, 827, 833–834, 848
Mechanics' Institute, 804
Medicine, 985; scientific revolution and, 521–522, 529; nineteenth century, 806–807; in pre-World War I era, 869, 873, 877
Meiji Restoration, 917
Mendel, Gregor, 985
Mendeleev, Dmitri, 876, 983
Mèndes-France, Pierre, 1080
Mercantilism: in sixteenth and seventeenth centuries, 500–501; in reign of Louis XIV, 565, 567; in eighteenth century, 621–624; attacked by Adam Smith, 638
Mersenne, Marin, 535
Mesmerism, 633–634
Metaxes, Gen. Joannes, 997
Metternich, Prince Klemens von, 738, 744, 747, 749–752, 754–755, 759, 770, 773
Mexico, 506, 829–830, 933
Michael, King of Rumania, 1064
Michel, Louise, 853
Michelangelo Buonarroti, 537–538, 543, 1002n
Michelet, Jules, 800
Michelson, Albert A., 982
Mickiewicz, Adam, 827
Middle class: eighteenth century publications aimed at, 643–645; French Revolution and, 706, 711–715; in French Directory, 720–722; in Napoleonic France, 729; in nineteenth century, 797–798, 800, 802, 821–826; cultural institutions of, 821–826; nationalism in, 833. *See also* Social class
Mikhail Feodorovich, Tsar, 514
Milan, revolution of 1848 in, 769–771
Military tactics: in sixteenth and seventeenth centuries, 475–478; in eighteenth century, 608–609; in World War I, 928–930, 933, 935, 1057–1058; in World War II, 1036–1039, 1046, 1054–1055
Mill, John Stuart, 798, 803, 810–812, 887
Milton, John, 498
Milyukov, Pavel, 938–939, 941
Mitterand, François, 1104, 1115
Modernization: technology and, 865–866; mail volume as an indicator of, 866; culture and, 872–880; in Spain, 893–894; in Japan, 917; pre-World War I political strains and, 921; political structure and, 1100–1117; continuity in, 1132–1135. *See also* Industrialization
Molière (Jean Baptiste Poquelin), 591–593

Molotov, Vyacheslau, 1033
Moltke, Marshal Helmuth von, 843
Moltke, Gen. Helmuth von, 926
Monck, Gen. George, 499
Monet, Claude, 878
Monnet, Jean, 1074
Monnet Plan, 1073
Monroe Doctrine, 755
Montaigne, Michel Eyquem de, 467n, 538
Montcalm, Gen. Louis Joseph, 629
Montesquieu, Charles de Secondat, Baron de, 636, 641, 649, 651, 655–657, 684
Monteverde, Claudio, 545
Montgomery, Gen. Bernard, 1047
Moore, Henry, 1125
Moors, *see* Muslims
Moravia, Alberto, 1124
More, Sir Thomas, 530
Morley, Edward, 982
Moro, Aldo, 1113
Morocco, 919–921; in World War II, 1047
Moscow: Napoleon in, 737; in World War II, 1039, 1045
Moseley, Sir Oswald, 996
Motion pictures, 985–986, 1014, 1020, 1124–1125
Mozambique, 1105
Mozart, Wolfgang Amadeus, 649
Munich Pact, 1032–1033
Murat, Joachim, 732
Museums, 1126
Music: centers of (1500–1800), 546; patronage of Leopold I and, 572; in seventeenth and eighteenth centuries, 545, 591, 649–651; nineteenth century, 821, 823, 825; pre-World War I, 872–873, 877–878; in post-war era, 981; in Soviet Union, 1018; contemporary, 1125
Muslims, persecuted by Philip II of Spain, 478
Mussolini, Benito, 969–971, 996, 1008, 1010, 1026, 1028–1029; dictatorship of, 1000–1006; rise of Nazis and, 1027; Hitler and, 1031; in World War II, 1038, 1041; voted out of office, 1047, 1052; a German puppet, 1054
Mysticism, 521–522; science and, 985

Nagasaki, 1058
Nagy, Imre, 1078
Naples, kingdom of, 791
Napoleon, French Emperor, 695, 744–745, 756, 791–792, 888; rise of, 722–726; Brumaire Coup and, 725–726; empire of, 726–740; Catholic Church and, 728; social policies imposed by, 728–730; Napoleonic Code, 729, 736, 779; resistance to, 735–739; "Spanish ulcer," 736; Russian campaign of, 736–737; the Hundred Days of, 745–747

Napoleon III (Louis Napoleon), 763, 783, 795, 820, 838, 841–843, 853; reign of, 827–830; Crimean War and, 831–833; Cavour and, 834, 836
Napoleonic Code, 729, 736, 779
Narváez, Gen. Ramón María, 766, 849
Nasser, Gamal Abdel, 1077
National Economic Development Council, 1073
National Health Service (British), 1073
National Hydro-Carbon Corporation, 1073
Nationalism: nineteenth century politics of, 826–846; language and, 827; middle class, 833; Italian, 833–839, 884–885; German, 839–846, 889, 1007–1008; reflected in artistic styles, 877; racial theories and, 889
Natural sciences, 876–877
Nazism, 980, 997, 1008–1010, 1030–1034; background of, 1006–1008; administrative and economic policies of, 1010–1012; anti-Semitism of, 980, 1007, 1010, 1049–1050, 1058; churches and, 1012–1014; in Austria, 1027, 1030–1031; in World War II, 1034–1041, 1045–1058; war crimes tribunals and, 1060
Necker, Jacques, 692–693
Negre, Charles, 807
Nelson, Adm. Horatio, 725, 732
Neoclassicism, 648–649, 651
Neoplatonic philosophy, 521, 523
Neo-realism, 1124
Netherlands, 509–510, 733, 735; revolt against Spain by, 478, 480–482; and creation of Belgium, 758; industrial growth in, 780–785; democratic stability in, 977; fascist movement in, 996; in World War II, 1038; resistance movement in, 1050; after World War II, 1066; Benelux and, 1074. *See also* United Provinces
Netherlands, Austrian, 613; resurgence of aristocracy in, 684; independent of Kingdom of Netherlands, 745
New Christianity cult, 812
Newcomen, Thomas, 680
New Harmony community, 813
Newspapers: eighteenth century, 643–645, 686; suppressed by Napoleon, 728; prosecution of, lifted in England by Peel, 760; revolutions of 1848 and, 770; nineteenth century growth and importance of, 821–823; Crimean War popularized by, 832; popular culture and, 879
Newton, Sir Isaac, 525–526, 594–595, 633, 636
New Wave art, 1124–1125
New World colonies, 619–620; Spanish, 506, 755; flow of treasure from, 506; social order in, 549–550; English, 585, 672; European diplomatic relationships and, 606; Anglo-French rivalry in, 621–629; French and Indian War, 628–629; revolutionary agitation in, 687–688; expansion of French interests in, 731
Nicholas I, Tsar, 750
Nicholas II, Tsar, 890, 938–939

Niemoller, Martin, 1012
Nietzsche, Friedrich, 888, 1128
Nigeria, 912
Nightingale, Florence, 802, 832
Nile, Battle of the, 725
Nivelle, Gen. Robert Georges, 933–934
Nixon, Richard M., 1108
Nobel Prizes, 1097, 1108
Nobility, see Aristocracy
North, Lord, 687
North American colonies, see New World colonies
North Atlantic Treaty Organization (NATO), 1070, 1075, 1077, 1095, 1097, 1110, 1116–1117; creation of, 1068
Norway, 1111; separation from Sweden (1905), 889; women's suffrage in, 977; in World War II, 1034–1035, 1037, 1050; resistance movement in, 1050–1051; after World War II, 1066
Nouvelle vague, 1124–1125
Nuclear energy, 984, 1089, 1111, 1119
Nuclear weapons, 1068, 1097, 1110–1111, 1119

Occult, the, 1129. See also Astrology; Magical practices
O'Connell, Daniel, 827
O'Dónnell, Gen. Leopoldo, 849
Ohio Company of Virginia, 628
Oldenbarneveldt, Jan van, 510
Olivares, Count de, 506
Op Art, 1125
Opera, 649–650, 1126; nineteenth century, 825
Orange, House of, 509–510
Orange Free State, 898–899
Order of the Black Eagle, 576
Order of the Legion of Honor, 729
Organization for Economic Cooperation and Development (OECD), 1093
Organization for European Economic Cooperation (OEEC), 1072, 1074
Orléans, House of, 758, 763, 853
Orléans, Philippe II, Duke of, 615
Orry, Philibert, 669
Ortega y Gasset, José, 981
Osborn, John, 1123
Ottoman Empire, 831; in sixteenth and seventeenth centuries, 512–513; Greek revolt against (1821), 755; treaty of San Stefano (1878) and, 857; decline of (1683–1914), 858; Italian moves against (1912), 895; Western imperialism and, 914–917; 1908 revolution in, 921; in pre-World War I period, 921; in World War I, 928, 936; secret Allied plans for partition of, 951–952
Ottoman Turks, see also Ottoman Empire
Owen, Robert, 812–815

Oxenstierna, Axel, 511
Oxford University, 535, 856

Pacifico, Don, 831
Paganini, Niccolò, 823
Pakistan, 1070
Palacky, Francis, 827
Palestine: Balfour Declaration on, 952; partitioning of, 951–952, 1068
Palestine Liberation Organization, 1113
Palmerston, Henry John Temple, Viscount, 831, 855–856
Panama, 895
Papacy: Vatican Council of 1869–1870 and, 886; Italian fascist rule and, 1004. See also Catholic Church; and individual popes by name
Papen, Franz von, 1009
Paracelsus, 521
Pareto, Vilfredo, 1005
Paris: in nineteenth century, 788, 829, 872; rebuilt in 1850s, 829; contemporary, 1089
Paris Commune, 852–853
Paris Peace Conference, 945–954, 972, 1059
Parlement of Paris: Mazarin and, 504; Louis XIV and, 570; dissolved by Maupeou, 690–691
Parliament (English): in sixteenth and seventeenth centuries, 492–499; under Cromwell, 495–499; gentry control and, 581–584; in eighteenth century, 617; nineteenth century reforms of, 760–763; agitation for reform of, 867; in the 1930s, 1023
Parma, 745
Parmigianino, 538
Pascal, Blaise, 534–535, 679
Passive resistance, 1070
Pasternak, Boris, 1108
Pasteur, Louis, 829, 877
Paul, Prince, regent of Yugoslavia, 996
Paul II, Pope, 1113
Paul VI, Pope, 1135
Peace of Amiens (1801), 731
Peace of Hubertusburg (1763), 625–626
Peace of Utrecht, 602–604, 617, 620
Peace of Westphalia (1648), 482, 487–490, 510
Pearl Harbor attack, 1040–1041, 1047
Peasants: in sixteenth century France, 500, 553; in seventeenth century France, 500, 503, 553; under Louis XIV, 517; in pre-Revolutionary France, 676; in French Revolution, 688–700, 706; in revolutions of 1848, 770, 774; nineteenth century reforms and, 786–788, 792–794, 800; effects of World War I on, 936; in Russian revolution, 938–945; under postwar Soviet rule, 959–960, 1015–1016; in postwar Eastern Europe, 964–965
Peel, Sir Robert, 760, 762–764, 790, 855

Peninsular War, 736
Peoples Charter (British), 761*n*
Pepys, Samuel, 585, 591
Permanent Court of International Justice, 972–973
Perry, Matthew, 917
Persia, 917. *See also* Iran
Pétain, Gen. Henri Philippe, 934, 1038
Pétain, Marshal, 1060
Peter I (the Great), Tsar, 515, 1018; at St. Petersburg, 577–580, 587
Peter III, Tsar, 625
Peterloo Massacre, 759–760
Petition of Right, 494
Philip II, King of Spain, 474, 478, 504–506, 652
Philip III, King of Spain, 506
Philip IV, King of Spain, 506, 568–569
Philippine Islands, 893, 917, 1047
Philology, 827
Philosophes, 637, 641, 652, 655, 659, 873
Philosophy: in sixteenth and seventeenth centuries, 521–537; in seventeenth and eighteenth centuries, 595–597; in the Enlightenment, 636–640; in post–World War I era, 981–982; contemporary, 1127–1129
Physics, 984
Physiocrats, 631–638, 809; Turgot and, 691
Picasso, Pablo, 1026, 1124
Piedmont, 756, 767; French Revolution and, 718; 1848 revolutions and, 771, 773–774; Crimean War and, 832–833; Italian unification and, 833–839
Pilsudski, Marshal József, 995
Pirandello, Luigi, 1006
Pitt, William, the Elder, 606, 618–619, 625, 628–629
Pius VII, Pope, 728
Pius IX, Pope, 767, 771–773
Pius XI, Pope, 1012
Plagues, *see* Black Death
Planck, Max, 984
Platonic Academy, 588
Poincaré, Raymond, 974–975
Poland, 848, 1032, 1072; in sixteenth and seventeenth centuries, 513, 587; aristocracy in, 587, 791; eighteenth century partition of, 605, 608; preconditions for industrialization and, 676; under Napoleon, 732–733; Congress of Vienna and, 744–745; revolution in (1830), 758; crushed by Russia, 758; in World War I, 934; after World War I, 946, 947*n*, 950, 964, 973; authoritarian rule established in, 995; in World War II, 1034–1037; World War II peace terms and, 1060, 1063; postwar Soviet control of, 1064; in contemporary era, 1093, 1109, 1116–1117, 1123
Pollution: in nineteenth century, 803; in contemporary era, 1088–1089
Polytechnic Association of France, 804
Pompidou, Georges, 1104
Pomponne, Simon de, 568
Poor Law (British), 655, 808
Pop Art, 1125
Pope, Alexander, 595
Popes, *see* Papacy; *and individual popes by name*
Popular culture, *see* Culture, popular
Population: in nineteenth century, 786–788; second industrial revolution and, 864, 867, 869–870, 873; in post–World War I period, 987; World War II and, 1071; in contemporary era, 1094
Pornography, 645
Portugal, 549; in seventeenth century, 507; overseas expansion by, 620, 912; Napoleon and, 735; minor revolts in (1830), 758; under Maria II, 766; World War II and, 1066, 1076; EEC and, 1100; in contemporary era, 1105–1106, 1114, 1117
Post-Impressionists, 878
Postindustrial society, 1119–1122
Potato famine (Ireland), 768, 808
Potsdam conference, 1060
Poussin, Nicolas, 545, 547
Pragmatic Sanction, 613
Pre-Raphaelites, 877
Presbyterians, 496
Price, Richard, 686
Priestley, Joseph, 633, 686
Prim, Gen. Juan, 850
Primogeniture, 799
Prokofiev, Sergei, 1018
Propaganda: used by Napoleon, 728; in Fascist Italy, 1001–1002, 1020; in Nazi Germany, 1007, 1013–1014, 1020, 1045, 1049–1050; in Soviet Union, 1016–1017
Protestantism: persecuted by Philip II of Spain, 478–482; civil war in France and, 482–484; in religious wars, 482–487; Edict of Nantes and, 483, 502, 569, 635; reforms of Joseph II and, 653
Proudhon, Pierre Joseph, 852, 883
Proust, Marcel, 980
Prussia: rise of, 610–613; Seven Years' War and, 624–626; absolutism and reform in, 651–653; population of (eighteenth century), 672; French Revolution and, 718; Napoleon and, 737–739; Congress of Vienna and, 743–745, 747; German Confederation and, 747, 751–754; Metternich's Concert of Europe and, 754–755, 759; revolutions of 1848 and, 770–771, 773; influence of Junkers in, 792 (*see also* Junkers); aristocratic dominance in nineteenth century, 792; education in, 808, 879; constitution of 1850 retained in, 827–828; unification of Germany and, 839–846; Franco-Prussian War, 838, 843, 857; international relations (1870–1881), 857–859; Second Reich dominated by, 898; rise of Nazis and, 1009

Psychology, Freudian, 978–980
Ptolemy, 521, 523
Public health and welfare, 877; in nineteenth century, 804–809, 856; British legislation for, 856; church and state conflicts over, 886–887; Great Depression and, 990; in post-World War I decades, 1066, 1073–1074; nationalization of services for (Britain), 1066; in contemporary era, 1089, 1091–1092, 1121–1122
Publishing, 643–645. *See also* Magazines; Newspapers
Puccini, Giacomo, 1005
Puerto Rico, 893
Pugin, Augustus, 817
Purcell, Henry, 590
Puritans, 494–496
Pushkin, Alexander, 824
Pym, John, 495

Quakers, 667
Quantum theory of energy, 984
Quisling, Vidkin, 1041

Racine, Jean, 547–548, 590–592
Radetzky, Count Joseph, 772
Radio, 866, 1020, 1022; in World War II, 1050
Radioactivity, 982–984
Railroads, 780–782, 867; in nineteenth century, 752; in contemporary era, 1088
Rasputin, Grigori, 938
Rathenau, Walter, 931, 968
Razin, Stenka, 515
Reagan, Ronald, 1117
Recession, 1110–1113, 1117
Recreation, *see* Leisure activities
Red Brigades, 1113
Reformations: Catholic (Counter Reformation), 540–541, 543, 571; social impact of, 1130
Reformed Church (Dutch), 508, 545
Reinsurance Treaty, 918
Relativity, theory of, 982–984
Religion: sixteenth and seventeenth century wars of, 478–490; seventeenth century life conditions and, 553; in France under Louis XIV, 569–570; the Enlightenment and, 634–636, 640, 655; eighteenth century reforms of Joseph II and, 653; preconditions for industrialization and, 667; in nineteenth century Russia, 750; nineteenth century living conditions and, 806; nineteenth century culture and, 825–826; in post-World War I Eastern Europe, 964; science and, 985; transition to authoritarian regimes and, 995–1000; Nazism and, 1012–1014; in the contemporary era, 1127–1128, 1132–1133. *See also* Catholic Church; Christianity; Eastern Orthodox Church; Protestantism
Rembrandt van Rijn, 536, 545, 547
Renault automobile works, 1073
Renoir, Auguste, 877–878
Resistance movements (World War II), 1050–1051, 1056, 1063
Reynaud, Paul, 1034, 1038
Reynolds, Sir Joshua, 651
Rhodes, Cecil, 899
Ribbentrop, Joachim von, 1031
Ricardo, David, 809, 813
Richardson, Samuel, 648
Richelieu, Armand du Plessis, Cardinal de, 501–502, 547, 588
Riffs, the, 997, 999
Rightist movements, 888 889; imperialism and, 910; in post-World War I Germany, 966, 968. *See also* Fascism; Nazism; Totalitarianism
Rivera, Gen. Miguel Primo de, 997, 999
Robbe-Grillet, Alain, 1125
Robespierre, Maximilien, 690, 706, 709, 714, 716, 718–719
Roentgen, Wilhelm, 982
Rohm, Ernst, 1010
Roman Catholicism, *see* Catholic Church
Romanov dynasty, 514
Roman Republic, 1089
Romanticism, 649–651, 749, 758; nineteenth century culture and, 824–826
Rome (city): in revolution of 1848 (Roman Republic), 772–773; in World War II, 1054; contemporary, 1087
Rommel, Gen. Erwin, 1047
Roosevelt, Franklin D., 1025, 1047, 1051; Atlantic Charter drafted with Churchill, 1041; Big Three meetings, 1052–1053, 1055–1056
Rosenberg, Alfred, 1007
Rossellini, Roberto, 1124
Rossi, Count Pellegrino, 772
Rouget de Lisle, Claude Joseph, 698
Rousseau, Jean Jacques, 651, 657–659, 686
Royal Academy of Architecture (French), 588
Royal Academy of Arts (British), 651
Royal Academy of Painting and Sculpture (French), 588
Royal Academy of Sciences (French), 535
Royal Society of London for Improving Natural Knowledge, 535, 588, 594
Rubens, Peter Paul, 541, 543, 545, 547
Rudolf II, Holy Roman Emperor, 485, 524–525
Ruggiero, Guido de, 1025
Rumania: before World War I, 921; in World War I, 930;

authoritarian rule and anti-Semitism in, 996; in Little Entente, 1027; in World War II, 1039, 1054; after World War II, 1060, 1063, 1079; contemporary, 1109

Rurik dynasty, 514

Russell, Bertrand, 981

Russell, Lord John, 763–764, 855

Russia: in sixteenth and seventeenth centuries, 513–515; under Peter the Great, 577–580; in the Great Northern War, 587; eighteenth century expansion of, 605; Seven Years' War and, 624–626; under Catherine II, 652; population of (eighteenth century), 672; preconditions for industrialization and, 676; Napoleon and, 732–733, 736–737, Congress of Vienna and, 743–745; Decembrist coup (1825) and conservatism in, 749–750; Metternich's Concert of Europe and, 754–755, 759; in aid to Austria in 1848 revolutions, 773–774; power of aristocracy in nineteenth century in, 791; reshaped (1855–1881), 846–848; serfdom abolished in, 846–847; international relations (1870–1881), 857–859; in Three Emperors' League, 859; Orthodox Church in effect a department of state, 887, 890; official anti-Semitism in, 888–891, 895; Revolution of 1905, 890–892; Russo-Japanese War, 890, 919; Bloody Sunday, 890–892; imperialism of, 914–917; alliances before World War I, 917–925; in World War I, 925–936, 944–945; Bolshevik takeover in, 934; World War I military fatalities of, 937–938; Revolution of 1917, 938–945; Bolsheviks, 719n, 940–941; civil war in, 945; after 1917 see Soviet Union

Russian Orthodox Church, see Eastern Orthodox Church

Russian Soviet Federated Socialist Republic, 962

Russo-Japanese War, 890, 919

Rutherford, Ernest, 982–984

Saint-Simon, Claude Henri de Rouvroy, Comte de, 812, 814–815, 852, 873

Saint-Simon, Louis de Rouvroy, Duke de, 571

Salazar, Antonio de Oliveira, 1105

Salisbury, Lord, 898

Salvation Army, 887

Salvemini, Gaetano, 1006

Sand, George, 802

San Marino, 755n

San Martin, José de, 755

Sans-culottes, 708–715, 719

Sartre, Jean Paul, 1127, 1129

Saussure, Ferdinand de, 1129

Savery, Thomas, 680

Scarlatti, Alessandro, 649

Schacht, Hjalmar, 1011

Schiller, Friedrich von, 649

Schleicher, Gen. Kurt von, 1009–1010

Schmidt, Helmut, 1101

Schönbrunn, 572, 577

Schuman, Robert, 1074

Schuschnigg, Kurt von, 997, 1030–1031

Schwarzenberg, Prince Felix von, 773, 830

Science: scientific revolution, 521–537; scientific method, 529–530; institutionalization of, 535–537; in seventeenth and eighteenth centuries, 593–598; broadening impact of, 633–634; in pre-World War I era, 829, 873–877; in postwar period, 982–986; in the 1930s, 1026

Scotland, 1101; in sixteenth and seventeenth centuries, 474–475; Charles II and, 497

Scott, Sir Walter, 823–824

Second International, 883

Secret Army Organization (OAS), 1081

Secret societies: of eighteenth century journeymen artisans, 646; of eighteenth century aristocrats, 685; nineteenth century Italian (Carbonari), 756, 766, 773; nineteenth century workers', 795–796; to defend subject nationalities in Russia, 890

Secularization, 634–636, 1132

Serbia, 921–922; in World War I, 928–930

Serfs: Junkers and, 575; Russian, 578, 750, 794, 846–847

Seven Years' War, 604, 624–626

Seyss-Inquart, Artur von, 1031

Shakespeare, William, 539–540, 591

Shelley, Percy Bysshe, 825

Shostakovich, Dmitri, 1018

Siam (Thailand), 915

Sieyès, Emmanuel Joseph, 682, 725

Sigismund III, King of Poland, 513

Silesia, 613–614, 624, 626

Silone, Ignazio, 1124

Silver, 505–506

Simon, Jules, 854

Slaves, 912; as foundation of eighteenth century empires, 621–624; abolished in British colonies (1833), 761; under Nazis, 1049–1050

Smith, Adam, 636, 638, 809

Soboul, Albert, 689

Social class: growth of military and, 476, 478–479; seventeenth century life conditions and, 515, 548–550, 553; in seventeenth and eighteenth century, 571, 585; in Russia under Peter the Great, 577–580; Enlightenment and, 640–643, 645–648; enlightened absolution and, 654–655; eighteenth century French liberal thought and, 655–659; Industrial Revolution and, 667–673, 675; French Revolution and, 688–690, 704–715; revolutions of 1848 and, 768–770, 773–774; birth rate and (differential fertility), 787–788; in nineteenth century, 790–798, 803–804; Paris Commune and, 852–853; late nineteenth century mobility and, 870–872; popular culture and, 878–879, 1020; Marxist view of, 880–883; in pre-World War I Germany, 897; imperialism and, 908, 910; effects of World War I on, 936–937; effects of World War II on, 1049; in contemporary era, 1089–1090, 1119, 1121. *See also* Aristocracy; Labor (working class); Middle class; Peasants

Social Darwinism, 875, 908

Socialism, 771, 969; in European political life (1876–1914), 883–886; Marxism and, 882–884; repressed by Bismarck, 845–846; spread of, 848; in Russia, 940–941; in post-World War I Germany, 965–966; Great Depression and, 989–990; fascist movement and, 999, 1025; Nazi movement and, 1010; in post-Depression years, 1020

Social Sciences, 985–986, 1026; contemporary, 1129

Social welfare, *see* Public health and welfare

Society for the Diffusion of Useful Knowledge, 804

Society of Friends, 498

Society of Jesus, *see* Jesuits

Society of St. Vincent de Paul, 806

Sociology, 874, 985

Solidarity movement, 1116–1117

Solzhenitsyn, Alexander, 1108

Sons of the Wolf, 1003

Sophocles, 1131

Sorel, Georges, 888

South African Republic, 898–899, 918

South America, *see* Latin America

Southeast Asia Treaty Organization (SEATO), 1070

South Seas Trading Company, 618

Soviet Union, 1014–1015, 1091; postwar consolidation in, 959–964; Lenin's New Economic Policy (NEP) in, 960–962; constituent republics in, 962; governmental and party structure in, 962–964; withdrawal from commerce of, 986; Great Depression in Europe and, 990; first Five Year Plan in, 1014–1017; prewar decade in, 1017–1018; Stalinism in, 1018–1020; purges in (1930s), 1018–1019; Spanish Civil War and, 1028–1029; Nazi aggression and, 1031–1034; prewar overtures to Western powers by, 1033; in nonaggression pact with Germany, 1033–1034; in World War II, 1039–1040, 1045–1058; war losses of, 1048, 1058; settlements and peace terms after World War II, 1059–1060; United Nations and, 1061–1063; postwar Eastern Europe and, 1063–1065; Cold War and, 1066–1070, 1072, 1074, 1080, 1095, 1117–1118; postwar European economic recovery and, 1071–1073; end of Stalin dictatorship in, 1076; Khrushchev years in, 1076–1077; and Communist bloc nations, 1078–1080, 1093, 1095, 1109; Hungarian revolt against, 1078–1079; GNP of (1978), 1093; Cuba and, 1095; China and, 1095–1096, 1107; in 1970 treaty with West Germany, 1097; Czechoslovakia invaded by, 1105, 1108; political stability in, 1108; in contemporary era, 1093, 1095, 1108, 1117–1119, 1125

Space exploration, 1077, 1080, 1096, 1118–1119

Spain: military powers of, 476; sixteenth century Catholic crusades and, 478–482; in sixteenth and seventeenth centuries, 504–508, 544; New World treasure brought to, 505–506; Union of Arms pressed in, 507; succession in (1700), 568–569; at war with England, 606; eighteenth century overseas possessions of, 620, 627; population of, 672; French Revolution and, 718; Napoleon and (Spanish Ulcer), 735–736, 739; post-Napoleon uprisings in, 749; constitutional regime in, 755; restoration regimes in, 755–756; minor revolts in (1830), 758; nineteenth century liberal reforms in, 765–766; aristocracy in nineteenth century, 791; reshaped (1854–1876), 849–850; church-state conflicts in (1880–1900), 887; problems of modernization in (1875–1914), 893–894; Spanish-American War, 893, 917; imperialism of, 912; neutral in World War I, 997; dictatorship in, 997–999; Spanish Civil War, 999, 1028–1030, 1040; after World War II, 1066, 1076; EEC and, 1100; in contemporary era, 1105–1106, 1110, 1114, 1117

Spanish-American War, 893, 917

Spartacists, 966

Speer, Albert, 1073

Spencer, Herbert, 875

Spengler, Oswald, 981

Spinola, Ambrogio di, 506

Spinoza, Baruch, 633

Sports, 646–648, 878–879

Stagflation, 1111, 1113

Stalin, Joseph, 1029, 1033, 1048, 1076; dictatorship of, 719n, 1014–1020; absolute authority of, 1018–1020; in World War II, 1039, 1051–1052; Big Three meetings, 1052–1053, 1055–1056; "cult of personality" rejected after death of, 1076–1077

Stalingrad (Volgograd), 1045, 1047, 1085

Standard of living: in 1700 (England), 667; Industrial Revolution and, 673; nineteenth century, 803–804; preference for meat over grains with rise in, 987; in Soviet Union, 1017; in the 1930s, 1020–1022; contemporary, 1089, 1092

Stanley, Henry M., 908, 912

Star Chamber court, 494–495, 581

Statute of Westminster (1931), 976

Stavisky, Serge, 1023

Steele, Richard, 643

Stein, Baron Heinrich von, 737–738

Sterne, Laurence, 604, 648

Stockhausen, Karlheinz, 1125

Stolypin, Peter, 892

Strasser, Gregor, 1010

Strategic Arms Limitation Talks (SALT), 1096

Stresemann, Gustav, 977

Structuralism, 1129
Stuart kings, 491, 496, 498
Student revolts: suppressed by Metternich (nineteenth century), 752; in contemporary era, 1104–1105, 1123
Suburbs, 872
Sudan, 1068
Sudetenland, 1031
Suez Canal, 856–857, 910–911, 1077
Suffrage, *see* Voting rights
Suleiman II (the Magnificent), Sultan, 512
Sully, Duke of, 501
Sun Yat-sen, 916
Surgery, *see also* Medicine
Surrealism, 980
Sweden, 1021; in Thirty Years' War, 485, 489–490; under Gustavus Adolphus, 510–512; aristocracy in, 586; monarchial reform in, 683; Norway separate from (1905), 889; women's suffrage in, 977; contemporary, 1092
Swift, Jonathan, 593, 648
Switzerland (Swiss Confederation), 733, 1021; industrial growth in, 681; development of representative government in, 722–723; nineteenth century reforms in, 765; neutral status of, 1027n; contemporary, 1092
Symbolic logic, 982
Symbolism, 878
Syria: after World War II, 951–952; Britain and France withdraw from (1946), 1068

Taaffe, Count Eduard von, 892
Taiping Rebellion, 916
Taiwan, 1070
Tallyrand, Prince de, 744
Tariffs, 866–867; Zollverein and, 752; Corn Laws, 760, 762–763; Great Depression and, 989
Teilhard de Chardin, Pierre, 1127
Television, 984, 1088, 1120–1121
Teresa, St., 543
Terrorism, 975–976, 1068, 1113–1114
Thatcher, Margaret, 1113
Thermidorian reaction, 718–720, 729
Thiers, Adolphe, 764, 851, 853–855
Third International, 946, 963, 1015
Third World, 1096, 1105, 1118; United Nations and, 1063
Thirty Years' War, 475, 484–490, 506, 511; effects of, 551–552, 572, 574
Thomas Aquinas, *see* Aquinas, St. Thomas
Thomson, J. J., 982
Three Emperors' League, 859
Tillich, Paul, 1127
Tirpitz, Adm. Alfred von, 930
Tisza, István, 893

Tisza, Kálmán, 849, 893
Titian, 538
Tito, Marshal, 1064, 1079, 1116
Tocqueville, Alexis de, 690
Tolstoy, Leo, 580
Toscanini, Arturo, 1006
Totalitarianism, 1000–1029; Fascist Italy, 1000–1006; Nazi Germany, 1006–1014; Communist Russia, 1015–1020. *See also* Fascism; Nazism
Townshed, Charles "Turnip," 674
Toynbee, Arnold, 1118
Trade: in sixteenth century, 500; Dutch, 508–510; Louis XIV and, 571; seventeenth century, 500, 585–586; eighteenth century, 621–624; preconditions of industrialization and, 667–669; Zollverein and, 752; British Corn Laws disputes, 760, 762–763; industrialization and, 779–784, 866–867; imperialism and, 905–908, 916–917; post-World War I, 986–987; Great Depression and, 987–988; by Nazi Germany, 1011; Cold War politics and, 1068; Common Market and, 1074, 1098–1100; in contemporary era, 1093, 1098–1100
Trade unions, *see* Labor movement
Trafalgar, Battle of, 732, 735
Transcaucasian Soviet republic, 962
Trans-Jordan, 951–952, 1068
Transvaal, 918
Transvaal Republic, 898–899
Treaty of Aix-la-Chapelle (1748), 614, 676
Treaty of Brest Litovsk (1918), 944–945
Treaty of Campo Formio (1797), 724
Treaty of Copenhagen (1660), 489
Treaty of Kardis (1661), 489
Treaty of London (1915), 928
Treaty of Lunéville (1801), 730
Treaty of Paris, (1763), 686; (1814), 743
Treaty of Prague (1635), 487
Treaty of Pressburg (1805), 732
Treaty of Pyrenees (1659), 489
Treaty of Rome (1957), 1081
Treaty of Sèvres (1920), 951
Treaty of Tilsit (1807), 733
Treaty of Versailles (1919), 950–951, 966, 1007, 1012, 1026
Trilateral Commission, 1093–1094
Triple Alliance, 917–921, 928
Triple Entente, 920–921
Tristan, Flora, 802
Trotsky, Leon, 942–944, 959, 963, 1014–1015
Truffaut, Jean François, 1125
Truman, Harry, 1058–1059, 1066
Truman Doctrine, 1066
Tull, Jethro, 674
Tunisia, 912
Turenne, Henri, Vicomte de, Marshal, 504, 569

Turgenev, Ivan, 848
Turgot, Jacques, 636, 656
Turkey: post-World War I treaty terms and, 951; under Mustafa Kemal, 951, 965; in Balkan Pact of 1934, 1027; American aid to, 1067
Tweedsmuir, Lord, 1020

Ukraine, 1041; in World War I, 934; as republic, 962
Ulbricht, Walter, 1078
Ultra project, 1045*n*
Unemployment: in nineteenth century, 803; Great Depression and, 988–990; 1929–1939, 1011; in contemporary era, 1089, 1113
Uniate churches, 513
Union Française, 1070
Union of South Africa, 914
Union of Soviet Socialist Republics (U.S.S.R.), *see* Soviet Union
Unions, *see* Labor movement
United Nations, 1061–1063, 1097; Big Three agreement to, 1055; charter of, 1062–1063; creation of Israel endorsed by, 1068; Korean crisis and, 1068; Suez crisis and, 1077; Portugal condemned in, 1105
United Nations Relief and Rehabilitation Administration (UNRRA), 1061
United Provinces: structure of, 508–509; domestic tensions in, 509–510; seventeenth century art in, 545; Louis XIV and, 565, 567–568; aristocracy in, 586; decline of, 619; role of, in eighteenth century colonial struggles, 619; development of representative government in, 722–723
United States, 744, 784, 890; constitution of, 656, 719*n*; Monroe Doctrine of, 755; Jackson's banking policies in, 782; world effects of Civil War in, 803, 841, 854–855; European migration to (1875–1914), 870; Spanish-American War, 893, 917; political involvement before World War I, 920; in World War I, 930, 933–936; League of Nations membership refused by, 953, 972; World War I reparations and, 971–972, 987; postwar disarmament talks and, 973; stock market crash in, 986–987; Great Depression in, 986–990; immigration policies in, 987; Nazi aggression and, 1031–1034; Neutrality Act passed in 1937, 1040; in World War II, 1040–1041, 1045–1058; settlements and peace terms after World War II, 1059–1060; United Nations and, 1061–1063; alliances after World War II, 1065; Cold War and, 1066–1070, 1074, 1077, 1080, 1095, 1117–1118; postwar European economic recovery and, 1071–1073; Suez crisis and, 1077; GNP of (1978), 1093; Trilateral Commission and, 1093–1094; European foreign policies and, 1095–1097; student revolts in, 1104–1105; in contemporary era, 1111, 1118–1121
Universities, 906, 1020; nineteenth century, 752; German, 845; English reforms in, 855–856; in post-World War I period, 974; contemporary, 1091
University of Glasgow, 680
University of Vienna, 653
Urban VIII, Pope, 543
Urban planning, 1085, 1087
Urban societies: in seventeenth century, 575–576; after 1700, *see* Cities
Utilitarianism, 810
Utopian socialists, 803

Values, crisis of, 1127–1134
van Gogh, Vincent, 878
Vatican Council, Vatican I (1869–1870), 886; Vatican II (1962), 1133, 1135
Vauban, Sébastien Le Prestre, Marquis de, 571
Velásquez, Diego Rodriguez de Silva, 542–543, 545
Venezia, 838, 841
Venice, 755*n*, 1089; in revolution of 1848, 769–771, 774
Venizelos, Eleutherios, 996
Verdi, Giuseppe, 683, 825
Versailles, 692; in French Revolution, 693–694; in reign of Louis XIV, 563–571, 577, 591; William I crowned at, 844
Versailles Peace Conference, 1100. *See also* Treaty of Versailles (1919)
Versalius, Andreas, 522, 528
Victor Emmanuel II, King of Sardinia, King of Italy, 834, 836–837, 850
Victor Emmanuel III, King of Italy, 971, 1054
Victoria, Queen of Great Britain, 761, 765*n*, 900; as Empress of India, 856, 915
Vienna: reforms of Joseph II and, 653; revolution of 1848 in, 769–770; anti-Semitism in, 888, 893; post-World War II famine in, 1059; peace terms and, 1060; contemporary, 1087
Vienna Circle, 981–982
Vietnam: French in, 1068, 1070; United States in, 1118
Villages in sixteenth and seventeenth centuries, 556, 558
Volgograd (Stalingrad), 1045, 1047, 1085
Voltaire, François Marie Arouet, 611, 633, 635–638, 641, 645–646, 649, 651–652, 655, 657–659
Voting rights: British Reform Bill of 1832 and, 761; in France (1830) and Belgium (1840–1848), 761*n*; in Switzerland (1848), 765; in France (nineteenth century), 828; in unified Italy, 838; in England (1885–1914), 898, 900, 933; in contemporary era, 1100
V-2 rocket, 1054–1055

Wagner, Richard, 825, 845
Wales, 617, 1101

Walesa, Lech, 1116
Wallenstein, Albrecht von, 485, 487, 511
Walpole, Sir Robert, 584, 617–619
War of the Austrian Succession, 604, 626
War of the Spanish Succession, 574–575, 671
Warsaw, duchy of, 732–733
Warsaw Pact (1955), 1095
Wars of religion, 478–490
Wartburg Festival, 752
Washington, George, 628, 812
Washington Conference (1921–1922), 973
Watt, James, 680
Watteau, Antoine, 589–590
Weber, Max, 985, 1123
Weimar Republic, 965–969, 977; collapse of, 1008–1010
Welfare programs, 1073–1074, 1089, 1091–1092. *See also* Public health and welfare
Wellington, Arthur Wellesley, Duke of, 736, 760
West Indies, 620–622, 626; Anglo-French rivalry in, 627, 629
Whitehead, Alfred North, 981
White Russians (Byelorussians), 959n, 962
Whitney, Eli, 679
Wilkes, John, 686–687
Wilkinson, John, 678
William I, King of Prussia, German Emperor, 839–840, 843; crowned at Versailles, 844
William II, German Emperor, 897, 918, 920, 936, 965
William II of Orange, Stadholder (William the Silent), 481–482, 509–510
William III, King of England (Stadholder of Netherlands), 510, 568, 583–584, 586
Wilson, Woodrow, 934, 936–938, 946–948, 950–954
Windischgrätz, Prince Alfred zu, 772
Witchcraft, 555
Witt, Jan De, 510, 586
Wittgenstein, Ludwig, 981–982
Wolfe, Gen. James, 629
Women, 887, 1020; in seventeenth century, 550–551, 553; uprisings led by, 553, 729; eighteenth century culture and, 642–643; Napoleonic Code and, 729; nineteenth century role of, 798, 800; employment of, 800; socialist championship of, 802–803, 814–815; relief work by, 806; in the Communards of Paris, 853; suffrage movement in England and, 900, 933; employed during World War I, 932–933; effects of World War I on, 936–937, 974; given vote in 1919 United Kingdom elections, 975; in Soviet Union, 1017, 1048; employed during World War II, 1048–1049; in contemporary era, 1089–1091, 1119
Women's movement: utopian socialists' support of, 802–803;
suffrage movement in England, 900, 933; in contemporary era, 1119. *See also* Women
Wordsworth, William, 649
Working class, *see* Labor (working class)
Workingman's Association for Benefiting Politically, Socially, and Morally the Useful Classes, 796
World Court, 972–973
World Economic Conference (1933), 987
World War I, 917–954; domestic politics in generation preceding, 889–900; imperialism preceding, 905–917; alliances before, 917–923; origins of, 923–925; first years of, 925–928; poison gas and trench warfare, 928, 933, 935; as war of attrition, 928–930; submarine and naval warfare in, 930, 933; homefront during, 930–933; military fatalities in, 937; social and economic effects of, 931–938; political effects of, 937; peace and settlement terms following, 945–954; political order following, 959–977
World War II, 1034–1041, 1045–1058; initial Nazi victories, 1034–1035; fall of France, 1036–1038; Battle of Britain, 1038–1039; Eastern front, 1039–1041, 1045, 1053–1054; Western front, 1045–1047, 1054–1055; North Africa and Asia, 1047; devastation of, 1047–1051, 1058–1059; end of, 1051–1058; resistance movements during, 1050–1051; atomic bomb used in, 1057–1058; settlements and peace terms after, 1059–1060
Wrangel, Gen. Peter, 960
Wren, Sir Christopher, 535, 585

Xerxes, 479, 1130
X-ray technology, 982, 984

Yeats, William Butler, 981
Young Ireland, 827
Young Italy, 766, 787n
Young Plan, 972, 988, 1007
Young Turks, 921
Yugoslavia, 936, 1079–1080; after World War I, 947n, 964–966; in Little Entente, 1027; in World War II, 1039, 1050–1051; resistance movement in, 1050–1051; after World War II, 1064; break with Russia, 1067; EEC and, 1100; in contemporary era, 1093, 1109

Zeeland, 509
Zimbabwe, 1095
Zinoviev, Grigori, 1015, 1018
Zola, Émile, 877, 896
Zollverein, 752, 784, 839

Color Illustration Sources

33–35/ Scala New York/Florence 36/ Eberhard Zwicker, Würzberg 37/ Verlag Joachim Blauel, München 38/ Scala New York/Florence 39/ Rijks-museum, Amsterdam 40/ Giraudon 41/ National Gallery of Art, Washington, D.C. 42/ Service de Documentation Photographie de la Réunion des Musées Nationaux 43/ Giraudon 44–45/ Service de Documentation Photographie de la Réunion des Musées Nationaux 46/ Scala New York/Florence 47/ Giraudon 48/ MAS 49/ Service de Documentation Photographie de la Réunion des Musées Nationaux 50/ Museum voor Schone Kunsten, Gent 51/ Service de Documentation Photographie de la Réunion des Musées Nationaux 52/ Boston Museum of Fine Arts 53/ Walter Steinkopf, Berlin 54/ Scala New York/Florence 55/ The Metropolitan Museum of Art 56/ Reilly & Constantine, Birmingham, England 57/ Oskar Reinhart Collection, "Am Römerholz," Winterthur 58/ Service de Documentation Photographie de la Réunion des Musées Nationaux 59/ National Gallery, London 60/ Mr. & Mrs. John Hay Whitney 61/ O. Vaering, Oslo 62/ Chrysler Museum at Norfolk 63/ The Tate Gallery, London 64/ Moderna Museet, Stockholm

CONTEMPORARY EUROPE

0 100 200 300 400 Miles

About the Authors

Mortimer Chambers is Professor of History at the University of California at Los Angeles. He was a Rhodes scholar from 1949–1952 and received an M.A. from Wadham College, Oxford, in 1955 after obtaining his doctorate from Harvard University in 1954. He has taught at Harvard University (1954–1955) and the University of Chicago (1955–1958). He was Visiting Professor at the University of British Columbia in 1958 and the State University of New York at Buffalo in 1971. A specialist in Greek and Roman history, he is coauthor of *Aristotle's History of Athenian Democracy* (1962) and editor of a series of essays entitled *The Fall of Rome* (1963). He has contributed articles to the *American Historical Review* and *Classical Philology* as well as other journals.

Raymond Grew is Professor of History at the University of Michigan. He earned both his M.A. (1952) and Ph.D. (1957) from Harvard University in the field of modern European history. He was a Fulbright Fellow to Italy (1954–1955), Guggenheim Fellow (1968–1969), Director of Studies at the Ecoles des Hautes Etudes en Sciences Sociales in Paris (1976), and a Fellow of the National Endowment for the Humanities (1979). In 1962 he received the Chester Higby Prize from the American Historical Association, and in 1963 the Italian government awarded him the Unita d'Italia Prize. He is an active member of the A.H.A., the Society for Italian Historical Studies, and the Society for French Historical Studies. He is the author of *A Sterner Plan for Italian Unity* (1963), edited *Crises of Development in Europe and the United States* (1978), and is presently the editor of *Comparative Studies in Society and History*. His articles and reviews have appeared in a number of European and American journals.

David Herlihy, Professor of History at Harvard University, is the author of several books on the economic and social history of the Middle Ages: *Pisa in the Early Renaissance, A Study of Urban Growth* (1958), *Medieval and Renaissance Pistoia, The Social History of an Italian Town* (1968), and *Medieval Culture and Society* (1968). He received his M.A. from the Catholic University of America in 1953 and his Ph.D. from Yale University in 1956. He is former president of both the American Catholic Historical Association and the Midwest Medieval Conference. He was a fellow of the Guggenheim Foundation (1962–1963), the American Council of Learned Societies (1966–1967), and the Center for Advanced Study in the Behavioral Sciences (1972–1973). His articles have appeared in *Speculum, Economic History Review,* and *Annales-Economies-Sociétiés-Civilisations.*

Theodore K. Rabb is Professor of History at Princeton University. A specialist in early modern European history, he received his B.A. degree from Oxford University (1958) and his Ph.D. from Princeton University (1961). He was a Guggenheim Fellow in 1970. He has taught at Harvard University, Stanford University, Northwestern University, Johns Hopkins University, and the State University of New York at Binghamton. He is co-founder and coeditor of the *Journal of Interdisciplinary History,* a member of the National Research Council, and a fellow of the Royal Historical Society. He is the author of *The Thirty Years' War* (1964) and *Enterprise and Empire* (1967), and coeditor of *Action and Conviction in Early Modern Europe* (1969). He has contributed articles to the *American Historical Review, Journal of Modern History, Commentary, Past & Present,* the *Economic History Review,* and other journals.

Isser Woloch is Professor of History at Columbia University. He received his Ph.D. (1965) from Princeton University in the field of eighteenth-and nineteenth-century European history. He has taught at Indiana University and at the University of California at Los Angeles where, in 1967, he received a Distinguished Teaching Citation. He has been a fellow of the A.C.L.S., the National Endowment for the Humanities, the Guggenheim Foundation, and the Institute for Advanced Study at Princeton. His publications include *Jacobin Legacy: The Democratic Movement Under the Directory* (1970), *The Peasantry in the Old Regime: Conditions and Protests* (1970), *The French Veteran from the Revolution to the Restoration* (1979), and *Eighteenth-Century Europe: Tradition and Progress, 1715–1789* (1982).

A Note on the Type

The text of this book has been set via computer-driven cathode-ray tube in a typeface named Bembo. The roman is a copy of a letter cut for the celebrated Venetian printer Aldus Manutius by Francesco Griffo, and first used in Cardinal Bembo's *De Aetna* of 1495—hence the name of the revival. Griffo's type is now generally recognized, thanks to the researches of Mr. Stanley Morison, to be the first of the old face group of types. The companion italic is an adaptation of the chancery script type designed by the Roman calligrapher and printer Lodovico degli Arrighi, called Vincentino, and used by him during the 1520s.

Composed by
Ruttle, Shaw & Wetherill, Inc.
Philadelphia, Pennsylvania

Printed and bound by
Von Hoffmann Press, Inc.
St. Louis, Missouri

Inserts printed by
Universal Printing Co., Inc.
St. Louis, Missouri

Text design by Leon Bolognese